XML FAMILY OF SPECIFICATIONS

XML FAMILY OF SPECIFICATIONS

A PRACTICAL GUIDE

Kenneth B. Sall

Addison-Wesley

Boston • San Francisco • New York • Toronto • Montreal
London • Munich • Paris • Madrid
Capetown • Sydney • Tokyo • Singapore • Mexico City

The publisher offers discounts on this book when ordered in quantity for special sales. For more information, please contact:

Pearson Education Corporate Sales Division
201 W. 103rd Street
Indianapolis, IN 46290
(800) 428-5331 corpsales@pearsoned.com
Visit AW on the Web: *www.awprofessional.com*

Library of Congress Cataloging-in-Publication Data

Sall, Kenneth B.
XML family of specifications : a practical guide / Kenneth B. Sall.
p. cm.
Includes bibliographical references and index.
ISBN 0-201-70359-9 (alk. paper)
1. XML (Document markup language) 2. Web sites—Design. 3. Internet programming.
I. Title
QA76.76.H94 S22 2002
005.7'2--dc21 2002022640

ISBN 0-201-70359-9
Text printed on recycled paper

1 2 3 4 5 6 7 8 9 10–CRS–0605040302
First Printing, May 2002

To all of the bright minds who have contributed to the numerous XML Working Groups. Without your creative ideas and considerable efforts, this book would not have been possible, quite literally.

Contents

List of Figures

List of Tables

Preface

> XML: It's a cheese spread. No, it's a floor wax. No, it's two—two—two products in one! Or maybe it's everything but the kitchen sink? Say, have you heard the one about the XML Kitchen Sink Language?—see *http://blogspace.com/xkitchensink/*.

XML: What It's All About

It has been said that XML, the Extensible Markup Language, will become the ASCII of the twenty-first century because it is rapidly becoming ubiquitous. XML is expected to have an impact on both the Web and application development comparable to that of Java and JavaScript because it has opened up a wide variety of new capabilities and has been embraced by so many sectors of human endeavor.

XML is a *metalanguage*—a syntax for describing other languages. These languages span diverse vertical industries including accounting, advertising, aerospace, agriculture, astronomy, automotive products, biology, chemistry, database management, e-commerce/EDI, education, financial institutions, health care, human resources, mathematics, publishing, real estate, software programs, supply chain management, and many more (for the many more, see *http://www.xml.org/xml/industry_industrysectors.jsp*). In one sense, XML is really a very trivial thing—just a markup syntax for describing structured text using angle brackets. But in another sense, XML is a basic building block—an enabling technology that makes it possible to develop more complex, more interesting, and more powerful tools.

In the Web arena, XML is facilitating exciting improvements such as user-controllable views and filtering of information, highly focused searching based on element hierarchies, creation of truly device-independent content that can be re-purposed for vastly different devices, and more sophisticated and flexible linking mechanisms. In the business and application arena, XML makes it easier to deliver filtered content from databases, to more readily share data between applications and between companies, and to exchange EDI messages that describe complex transactions. In the scientific arena, XML is a natural fit for describing complex datasets, models, control of instruments, images, chemical compounds, and much more.

Just as Java made data processing platform-independent, XML has done the same for data, making the exchange of information much easier than ever before. But, no, XML is not the kitchen sink; it is not the solution to all of the world's problems in one tidy package; nor is it the solution to all your computer needs either, at least not alone. Rather, XML is a tool, or more accurately, a set of tools from the same toolbox. That toolbox is the XML *family of specifications*. This book will help you see what XML can and cannot do by describing how to use each tool.

Although XML shares a number of concepts with its ancestor, SGML (Standard Generalized Markup Language), XML is said to yield 80 percent of the benefits of SGML, but with only 20 percent of the complexity. It is precisely this 80/20 rule that has excited countless companies and developers, encouraging them to support the efforts of the World Wide Web Consortium (W3C) in the development of XML. A few of the more than 500 companies and organizations that actively support XML development as members of the W3C include IBM, Sun Microsystems, Microsoft, Oracle, Commerce One, and NASA.

Audience: Who Should Read This Book?

The book is intended for Web developers, which includes programmers, content writers, and designers. Depending on your background and interests, some chapters may be more relevant to you than others. It's intended for those who may be familiar with particular aspects of XML but who have not been formally exposed to all of the major W3C specifications, as well as those who have never dealt with XML before. Later in this preface, I provide a roadmap to help orient you.

I've assumed that most readers are familiar with HTML elements and syntax, although the XML and DTD syntax discussions in Chapters 3 and 4 pretty much cover the concepts of elements, attributes, types, entities, and content that carry over from HTML to XML. In other words, you can get by without knowing HTML, except the XHTML chapter, which will make much more sense to you if you do. For those who would like to brush up on HTML, see "For Further Exploration: HTML and Java" at the end of this preface.

Some examples require programming knowledge, but for most examples, anyone with general Web development skills will find them beneficial. Generally, scope and breadth of treatment is favored over depth. On the other hand, some readers will find that the depth is more than they expected, but they should still be able to "tread the water." My intent in writing this book was to cover a number of XML-related technologies in varying degrees of detail. I'd like to make it clear that although there are three chapters containing Java examples, this is not a book about Java and XML. You don't need a Java background for the vast majority of what's in this book.

Although I do assume the Windows operating system, this is not a statement of preference. My formative years were spent on UNIX (I still use UNIX utilities to maintain a ski club site) at the office and on a Mac at home. Rather, since Windows tends to be somewhat ubiquitous, it seems appropriate to show Windows command lines and mention some Windows-only tools. UNIX and Mac users are encouraged to share their experiences with fellow readers via the book's Web site. Personally, I have found cygwin—a UNIX environment for Windows developed by Red Hat—to be very handy (see *http://cygwin.com/*).

What's Special About This Book?

There are several features that contribute to making this book an invaluable resource for anyone beginning to plunge into the somewhat turbulent "seas" of XML.

- *XML Family of Specifications Big Picture*—Since early 1998, I've periodically updated a diagram I call "The Big Picture of the XML Family of Specifications." This unique diagram (front inside cover) depicts virtually all of the key W3C efforts related to XML, with colors to indicate each specification's status (maturity); it includes related non-W3C efforts as well. Physical positioning denotes a relationship among neighboring specifications, as explained in Chapter 2. Best of all, the Big Picture diagram appears as an imagemap on the CD-ROM and on this book's Web site, possibly as a more up-to-date version. The Big Picture imagemap on the Web site expands acronyms as your mouse hovers over a term. Clicking on the acronym or name connects you instantly to the actual specification or, in some cases, a collection of documents relating to that specification.
- *History Timeline*—A detailed "History of the Web and XML" in timeline form—the product of a considerable amount of research—is broken down into three time periods in Chapter 1, which should be interesting to many readers. Historical perspectives are also presented for particular specifications in their own chapters. A rather unique pullout at the back of the book shows, in bar chart format, the gestation periods of all of the XML specifications in this book, giving you a visual picture of what developments occurred in sequence and/or in tandem.
- *Coverage*—I've selected what are generally considered to be the most significant XML-related specifications from the W3C: XML/DTDs, XML Namespaces, XML Schema, the DOM, CSS, XSLT, XPath, XSLFO, XLink, XPointer, XHTML, and RDF. Several of the less frequently discussed specifications, such as XML Information Set, Canonical XML, XML Base, and XML Inclusions, are also covered. In addition, I've included four topics that are not under the purview of the W3C: RDDL, SAX, JDOM, and JAXP. The focus is on breadth rather than

depth of coverage because if you have a general understanding of a lot of XML topics, you can better appreciate which are most relevant to your needs and you can "drill down" to the details by following the links I provide. The hope is that as you become more familiar with each of the topics I present, you'll know which areas you'll want to explore by buying more specialized Addison-Wesley or Prentice Hall books (e.g., about XSLT, XML with Java, or XHTML). I've tried hard to make the information current and have spent a good bit of time in the final months polishing and updating details here and there. All topics are as up-to-date as possible, except where noted otherwise.

- *For Further Exploration*—Each chapter ends with a section called "For Further Exploration," which presents quite a few links that serve not only as my bibliography but point to resources that contain more details than what can be provided here without killing way more than my fair share of trees. Links are provided to the specifications themselves, to articles that explain the specs in more everyday language than the precision required for formal specifications, and to articles describing subtleties or nuances of the specs. Links to tutorials, books, software, special references, and so on are also supplied. My intention is that readers will use the links, so they all appear in HTML form on the book's CD-ROM. Professors may wish to consider some of these links for students' research assignments.
- *Tables*—I'm a big fan of the use of tables. When I read a technical book, I seldom read it word for word, cover to cover. Often I want to locate some particular detail pretty quickly, so I look it up in the table of contents or index—I don't want to have to skim through paragraph after paragraph to find the little tidbit I need. Therefore, I feel that tables will help you do the same thing, maximizing the use of your time. The List of Tables that follows the Contents is something with which you might want to familiarize yourself; let a table be your friend.
- *CD-ROM*—The CD that accompanies the book contains all the sample code presented in the text, as well as most of the software I used while writing this book, including the following:
  - Code Examples—every example that appears as a code listing plus a number of variations
  - XML Environment—batch files to simplify using XML with Java on Windows operating systems
  - For Further Exploration—all links from the end of each chapter
  - Big Picture XML Family of Specifications Imagemap—links to more than 60 specifications, including many not covered in this book (see Chapter 2)
  - W3C XML Specifications in PDF Form—every W3C specification discussed in this book is available (unedited) for offline reading (hours and hours of fun for the whole family)

- Glossary of terms, provided by TIBCO Extensibility.
- Chapter 12, "Practical Formatting Using XSLFO" by G. Ken Holman, in HTML format with two useful appendices—A, XSLFO object summary; B, XSLFO property summary—that aren't included in the printed book. This HTML version benefits from links between the prose and the appendices, which also link to relevant sections in the Extensible Stylesheet Language (XSL) Version 1.0 of the W3C Recommendation of October 15, 2001. (*Note:* The HTML version on the CD contains references to chapters 1 through 10; these identify the chapters of Holman's training materials rather than chapters in this book.)
- Freeware and evaluation copies of commercial software (XML/DTD/XML Schema editors, validators, parsers, XSLT processors, and more)

- *Web Site*—The book's main Web site is hosted by Web Developer's Virtual Library, an Internet.com site. I maintain the extensive XML section of WDVL.com. The book's URL there is *http://WDVL.Internet.com/Authoring/Languages/XML/XML-Family*. There you'll find all the links from the "For Further Exploration" sections organized by chapter, as well as the online version of the Big Picture imagemap, and of course the inevitable corrections to the text. While this material appears on the CD-ROM, the Web site versions may be more up-to-date. The Web site will be kept current; you can register to receive e-mail when the site is updated, if you wish.

Organization and Roadmap: How You Should Read This Book

This book is divided into five conceptual parts. With the exception of a few chapters in Part I, it is not absolutely necessary to read this book chapter by chapter (and I'll tell you right up front: "the butler did it"). Chapter 1, "History of the Web and XML," provides an interesting historical perspective about the development of XML; but some readers may prefer to skip it entirely or at least defer reading it until they've completed other chapters, or find themselves on a long, boring plane flight with neither good movies nor readable magazines. Readers without a Java background may wish to gloss over the three chapters that contain Java examples, instead focusing on the concepts that are discussed in these chapters. The following describes the book's organization and suggested reading emphasis.

- *Introduction: History of the Web and XML*—As mentioned, Chapter 1 provides an historical perspective. It's divided into three eras: Ancient History (1945 to 1985), Medieval History (1986 to 1994), Premodern History (1994 to 1998), and Ultramodern History (1998 to 2001).

- *Part I: Fundamental XML Concepts and Syntax*—This part introduces XML Syntax, DTD Syntax, the XML Information Set, Canonical XML, Namespaces, RDDL (Resource Directory Description Language), and XML Schema, corresponding to Chapters 2 through 6, intended to be read in sequence. All readers should read these chapters, although if you won't be developing your own vocabularies, you might be able to skim the DTD and XML Schema chapters (4 and 6, respectively).

Even though XML Schema is expected to replace the use of DTDs in many applications, your project's needs may dictate sticking with DTDs in which case you could skip the XML Schema chapter, although I still recommend that you read the sections in Chapters 4 and 6 that highlight DTD limitations and XML Schema advantages.

If you are tempted to skip the chapter on Infoset, Canonical XML, Namespaces and RDDL (Chapter 5), be sure to at least read the Namespaces section because this concept is central to many XML specifications. All chapters following Chapter 5 assume that you are familiar with XML Namespaces. Although RDDL is a recent grassroots effort as I write this, it's bound to have gathered a lot of momentum by the time you read this.

- *Part II: Parsing and Programming APIs*—This part presents SAX (Simple API for XML), DOM (Document Object Model), JAXP (Java API for XML Processing) and JDOM (see Chapters 7 through 9). All of these are application programming interfaces (APIs) to parsing and manipulating XML documents. This is the part of the book with the most Java examples. While all readers are encouraged to read the initial sections of the SAX and DOM chapters, non-Java developers can completely skip Chapter 9, which covers JAXP and JDOM, as well as the code examples in the SAX and DOM chapters. However, be sure to read the section and explanation of parsing at the beginning of Chapter 7 and study the comparison section and table at the end of Chapter 9, "SAX vs. DOM vs. JDOM vs. JAXP—Who Wins?"

- *Part III: Transforming and Displaying XML*—This part covers CSS (Cascading Style Sheets), XSLT (Extensible Stylesheet Language Transformations), XPath (XML Path Language), and XSLFO (Extensible Stylesheet Language Formatting Objects), presented in Chapters 10 to 12. Of these, the lengthy Chapter 11 on XSLT and XPath is essential reading for anyone who wishes to display or transform XML into other formats (including HTML, XHTML, text, or other kinds of XML, particularly in e-commerce applications). Chapter 10 on CSS is more important if your XML display needs are more modest and your transformation needs are nill. The chapter can be skimmed for XML hooks if you are already familiar with CSS.

  Chapter 12 concerns XSL Formatting Objects, sort of the next-generation CSS for desktop publishing quality layout, PDF, and targeting your output for different devices. The XSLFO chapter was contributed by noted XSL expert and instructor, G. Ken Holman, chair of the OASIS XSLT/XPath Conformance Technical Committee. See his home page at *http://www.CraneSoftwrights.com/* for more thorough coverage of XSLFO and also XSLT/XPath; his comprehensive tutorial on XSLFO is available in PDF formats there.

- *Part IV: Related Core XML Specifications*—This part focuses on XLink (XML Linking Language) and XPointer (XML Pointer Language)—Chapters 13 and 14. Most developers will benefit from reading about XLink and XPointer in these chapters, because the languages greatly extend the notion of linking and fragment access beyond what is possible in HTML 4.01, including one-to-many links, multidirectional links, links stored external to the documents, and linking to specific elements without hooks being provided by the original author.
- *Part V: Specialized XML Vocabularies*—This part presents two unrelated XML-based languages: XHTML (Extensible HyperText Markup Language) in Chapter 15 and RDF (Resource Description Framework) in Chapter 16. Please consider Chapter 15 on XHTML as essential reading for all developers. As you'll see, XHTML is its own nuclear family of specifications that is currently replacing HTML, especially in the increasingly popular world of handheld devices, voice browsers, and other alternative Web interfaces. RDF should be of particular interest to developers and scientists with an interest in metadata (data about data), site descriptions, catalogs, intelligent software agents, and so on. RDF attempts to add semantics to the Web; related concepts are the recent XML Topic Maps (XTM) effort and the older Dublin Core work.

  The RDF chapter was contributed by Ora Lassila, coauthor of the Resource Description Framework Model and Syntax Specification for the W3C and contributor to the RDF Core Working Group and Web-Ontology (WebOnt) Working Group. For more information, see his home page at *http://www.lassila.org/*.

This book does not cover XQuery, an XML Query language, or Scalable Vector Graphics (SVG), except in passing. XQuery was still very much in flux at the time of this writing. As for SVG, with a more than 500-page specification, I felt I could not do the topic justice in the time I had left after writing the rest of this book. Well, there's always the Second Edition, I guess.

What You Need to Get the Most Out of This Book

All code examples have been developed on a Dell Dimension XPS R450 PC (a paltry 450 MHz) running Windows 98. DOS .bat files are provided to help you configure your environment so that you can run the examples on your own. UNIX developers should be able to study the .bat files and set environment variables accordingly, such as CLASSPATH for Java and variables that point to the location of XML parsers and XSLT processors. I can't say much to Mac developers at this point (sadly, my own ancient PowerMac 7100/80 hasn't been used for the better part of three years), but if you contact me via the Web site and want me to share your experiences with others, I will gladly do so. I'll give you credit and a free copy of this book—it makes a great gift and keeps its flavor longer than fruitcake.

XML and DTD examples are plain text, so they are viewable in their raw form on all platforms using any text editor. To process XML in a browser, however, you'll need the most current generation of browsers, such as Netscape 6.x, Internet Explorer 5.5 or 6.x, Amaya 5.x, or Opera 5.x or higher. If you're not the type of reader who has to try out every example in his or her own browser, then perhaps the many screenshots in this book will be sufficient. Evaluation copies of commercial XML, DTD, and XML Schema editors appear on the CD that accompanies this book; XML parsers and XSLT processors also appear there. The CD-ROM also contains a page of links to the current versions of all provided software.

The Java code examples should compile and run fine with either JDK 1.2.x or 1.3.x, also known by other confusing names and numbers such as Java 2 SDK, J2EE, and J2SE—or their equivalent as provided with your favorite Java IDE (Integrated Development Environment). This book does not attempt to teach Java; on the other hand, you really don't need to know Java to follow most of the discussions. Interested readers who desire a better Java background should refer to the key Java resources listed in "For Further Exploration: HTML and Java" that follows.

I truly hope you enjoy this book and find the XML family of specifications as fascinating as I do.

Conventions Used in This Book

The typographic conventions used in this book are as follows:

- Glossary terms look like this where they are defined: **node-set**
- Code excerpts, code listings, command lines, filenames, element names, and attribute names look like this: `<xsl:template match="/CD">` or `collection8.xml`.
- Quotations (material excerpted from another source) are indented both left and right and set in a smaller type size.
- Notes, important information and/or things to watch out for, are called out by an arrow in the left margin and rules above and below their text.

For Further Exploration: HTML and Java

Cafe au Lait Java FAQs, News, and Resources
http://www.ibiblio.org/javafaq/

Getting Started with HTML, Dave Raggett
http://www.w3.org/MarkUp/Guide/

Google's HTML Tutorials Category
http://directory.google.com/Top/Computers/Data_Formats/Markup_Languages/HTML/Tutorials/

Google Web Directory: Java [includes a Books category]
http://directory.google.com/Top/Computers/Programming/Languages/Java/

Google Web Directory: Java IDEs
http://directory.google.com/Top/Computers/Programming/Languages/Java/Development_Tools/Integrated_Development_Environments/

Java Technology Products and APIs
http://java.sun.com/products/

The Java Tutorial
http://java.sun.com/docs/books/tutorial/

Web Design Group's HTML 4.0 Reference
http://www.htmlhelp.com/reference/html40/

Acknowledgments

There are many people whose support has been invaluable to me either directly or indirectly during the development of this book.

First, I would like to especially thank Troy Ames of NASA Goddard Space Flight Center for his willingness to try out this new-fangled XML technology on the Instrument Remote Control project in early 1998 when XML was more than a little risky. Thanks to Carl Hostetter and Rick Shafer (NASA), Craig Warsaw, Lisa Koons, David Fout, Steve Clark, Randy Wilke, Melissa Hess, Ken Wootton, Lynne Case, and the rest of the Century Computing/AppNet/Commerce One/Aquilent team who helped make the Instrument Markup Language a reality. Thanks also to Jim Sombke for help with `xmlsetup.bat` and to Karl Wolf for his continued interest and encouragement. Thanks to Mark Allen and Mike McEwen for giving me some time to follow my writing whim.

I'd like to express my deepest gratitude to Julie Breed of NASA/GSFC for giving me the opportunity to research the XML family of specifications and prepare many presentations for NASA. Thanks also to Lisa Kane, Emma Kolstad Antunes, Tracy Lundien, and Pam Mullay for coordinating logistics for these presentations.

Lynne Pusanik, Bob McCune, and Doug Trimble, thank you for your help in testing the CD-ROM and for providing a screenshot in a crunch. Thanks to my many Columbia Ski Club friends who listened to far too many updates on my progress, especially Donna Carollo, Diane Corwin, Tom Delaney, Ted Dietz, Georgia Glashauser, Benita Koller, Rich Krell, Kathy MacGillivray, Steve Martin, Sue Muller, Steve and Sherry Panzer, Bill Parlock, Kathy Pohlmeyer, Melinda Press, Kevin Smith, Doug Trimble, Ki and Carol von der Linden, Grant Wagner, and Joyce Wronka—to name just a few whose ears I bent the most.

I am very appreciative of the contributions of G. Ken Holman and Ora Lassila. Thank you for making the time in your busy schedules to participate. A big thanks to the entire Addison-Wesley team that worked so hard on this project: Mary O'Brien, Alicia Carey, Chanda Leary-Coutu, Curt Johnson, Katie Noyes, and Marilyn Rash and her team of book production specialists—Hartley Ferguson, Joan Flaherty, Ted Laux, Connie and Doug Leavitt, and Angela Stone.

Thanks to my sister-in-law Julie and brother Eric Sall for their continued interest in my (very) long-term project. Abby Hechtman, Mark Leonardo, and Erik Walters—thank you all for your very helpful legal advice.

Special thanks to author/editor Simon St. Laurent for some helpful writing tips and words of encouragement about the writing process. Thanks very much to Linda Cole for her support during the creation of this book's Web site on WDVL. Internet.com, including the production of the sample chapter in HTML format.

A warm thank you to author Priscilla Walmsley who did a very thorough review of my manuscript, particularly the XML Schema chapter (her specialty). Her comments greatly improved the chapter; any errors that remain are, of course, mine alone to claim. The XML Development Timeline pullout poster at the back of this book is based on a suggestion from Pamela after she read Chapter 1. Thanks also to my other reviewers, especially Leigh Dodds, for some very helpful feedback.

Last but not least, this book would not have made its way into your hands without the ongoing encouragement and support from my very dear friend, Diane Mastroianni. During the entire writing, editing, and production of this hefty volume, Diane asked me on a weekly (and often daily) basis how things were going. Although the Web is far from her passion, she listened politely to hundreds of my "book reports." She offered advice that I often found invaluable. She provided good cheer when I was discouraged. She helped me to remember that the goal was always within my reach. Thank you from the bottom of my heart, SLC, SLCPA, SL sister. You are a wonderful inspiration and a true godsend to your friends!

Oh—one more. I'd like to thank my nontechie mother for repeatedly asking me "So, Ken, what is your book about again?" Well, Mom, now you can read it and find out for yourself! You might find it to be a handy sleeping aid ;-).

I'd like to say thank you on behalf of the group and ourselves, and I hope we passed the audition.

Introduction

Chapter 1

History of the Web and XML

In this chapter, we'll examine the significant events that led to the development of the Internet, the Web, HTML, and eventually XML. First, we discuss the beginnings of SGML, the Internet, the creation of HTML and the Web, and the early efforts of the World Wide Web Consortium (W3C). This chronology is presented in four parts: "Ancient History," covering SGML and the birth of the Internet; "Medieval History," covering the early development of HTML and the birth of the Web; "Premodern History," tracing the early efforts of the W3C that led to XML; and "Ultramodern History," discussing the emergence of XML and the related family of specifications.

Ancient History (1945 to 1985)

Stop me if you've heard this one. (Or better yet, go on to chapter 2 or 3.)

Believe it or not, there was a time in the early days of the Internet when documents and data were not easily accessible. Scientists, software engineers, and students knew a bunch of arcane network communication software such as ftp, telnet, and eventually something called gopher, but the Internet was largely a place you could visit only if you knew exactly where you wanted to go and often exactly what you were going to find. And, if you weren't an egghead, there was no easy on-ramp to the Internet. There were certainly no students researching papers, moms hunting for recipes, or real estate agents downloading housing updates, mainly because the kind of information on the 'Net was simply not for everyone.

So, how did our society go from an Internet accessible primarily to research scientists to the World Wide Web, the phenomenon that has become the pervasive communication medium it is today? For that matter, how did the Internet, on which the Web is based, get its start? And how did we progress from a clunky, text-based command interface to a flashy video-, graphics-, and sound-oriented, point-and-click interface? Before we can truly appreciate the beauty, simplicity, and power of the Extensible Markup Language (XML), it will be enlightening to explore the pioneering efforts that led to the creation of HyperText Markup

Language (HTML) and Standard Generalized Markup Language (SGML), the precursors of XML.

Hypertext and Early User Interfaces

Our story begins near the end of World War II, in July of 1945 when Vannevar Bush, the earliest pioneer of what would become known as hypertext, published his futuristic and influential article, "As We May Think" in *Atlantic Monthly.* Among other things, this insightful article describing the theoretical memex system predicted hypertext and the Internet.

In October 1957, the (then) Soviet Union launched *Sputnik I,* the world's first artificial satellite. This technological triumph had a profound impact on the U.S.' scientific and military communities, as well as the average citizen, by creating a crisis of confidence. How could the Soviets achieve such a technological triumph before the United States? Would the Soviet Union gain mastery of space, the new frontier? The most immediate response to the Sputnik was the launch of *Explorer 1* in January 1958 by the US military.[1]

The so-called Sputnik Crisis prompted President Eisenhower to call for the creation of two agencies, which are still very influential in science and technology. The first of these was the Defense Advanced Research Projects Agency (DARPA, *http://www.darpa.mil*), established in February 1958. DARPA, originally named simply ARPA[2], was tasked with research and application of state-of-the-art technology for military purposes, especially to prevent surprise attacks. As we'll soon see, DARPA was ultimately responsible for the creation of the Internet.

The second agency, created in October 1958, was the National Aeronautics and Space Administration (NASA, *http://www.nasa.gov*). After a half year of debate about how to administer nonmilitary space exploration efforts, the President's Science Advisory Committee (PSAC) decided to greatly expand the charter of the National Advisory Committee for Aeronautics (NACA) that was formed in 1915 to encourage progress in aviation. The new space flight organization, renamed NASA, was to focus on defining and conducting aeronautical and space activities with active involvement of the scientific community. NASA was also charged with disseminating information about its activities to the public, especially to stimulate public interest in space exploration and to spin-off scientific and technological advances to the public and private sectors for commercial application. NASA's earliest, high-profile program was Project Mercury, initiated in 1958 with manned flights from 1961 to 1963. Project Mercury was an effort to learn if humans could

1. For details concerning *Sputnik* and its impact on the United States, see *http://www.hq.nasa.gov/office/pao/History/sputnik/sputorig.html* and *http://www.sputnikbook.com/intro.php.*

2. ARPA was renamed DARPA in 1972, reverted back to ARPA in 1993, and then back to DARPA in 1996. Both *darpa.mil* and *arpa.mil* URLs resolve to the agency's site.

survive the rigors of space flight. In April 1961, Yuri Gagarin became the first human to orbit Earth in a Soviet spacecraft, *Vostok 1.* And so began the Space Race. NASA, a member of the World Wide Web Consortium, created many of the earliest Web sites along the Information Superhighway.

In 1963 just as the Beatles were becoming a major phenomenon in the United Kingdom, Douglas Engelbart and his colleagues developed the On-Line System (NLS), the world's first implementation of what would eventually be called *hypertext.* This user interface work included many innovations: the first mouse, display editing, windows, cross-file editing, outline processing, hypermedia, groupware, and more. Engelbart's work influenced researchers at Xerox Palo Alto Research Center (PARC) where the idea of graphical user interface with windows materialized in the 1970s, which in turn influenced both Apple's user-friendly Mac and Microsoft's derivative Windows operating system.

In 1965 Ted Nelson coined the term *hypertext.* Not until 1987, however, did a serious hypertext application appear, when HyperCard was released by Bill Atkinson of Apple. This early hypertext system had features still not available in Web browsers. Soon Apple revolutionized the human-machine interface by bundling HyperCard with the Mac. In the mid-1980s, Microsoft succeeded in recycling many of these ideas in Windows, making such interfaces available to home and office PC users worldwide.

GML and SGML: Content vs. Presentation

Meanwhile, in 1969 IBM needed a way to share legal documents across diverse hardware platforms and types of displays. Numerous documents needed to be represented so that their contents could be accessible by lawyers and other users regardless of their computer choice. IBM needed to enable the sharing of documents across text editing, formatting, and information-retrieval subsystems. In addition, it needed a way to verify whether a particular legal document adhered to various conventions; that is, did it contain all the required component pieces?

To solve this problem, Charles Goldfarb, Ed Mosher, and Ray Lorie developed a language they eventually called *Generalized Markup Language* (*GML;* the acronym also stands for Goldfarb, Mosher, and Lorie, which is not a coincidence). GML was an important breakthrough primarily because it separated content and display, a distinction that would also become a major characteristic of XML. GML, originally called Text Description Language, was an alternative to the more prevalent *procedural markup languages,* in which the markup of a document drives a script that renders the result (e.g., PostScript). Procedural languages may be efficient with their one-pass processing, but they tie the document to a particular output format, making it difficult to repurpose the information content for other devices or uses.

In contrast, GML was an early example of *descriptive markup,* in which document sections were identified with names that logically defined the pieces of a document and then were translated into device-dependent formatting in a two-pass process. The beauty of this solution is that the same descriptive markup can be reused with a different mapping of tags to render information when the content needs to be targeted for different output media.

The idea of separating content and presentation that Goldfarb and colleagues promoted with GML actually dates back to at least 1967, when William Tunnicliffe of the Graphic Communications Association (GCA) proposed GenCode (generic coding), which used descriptive tags such as "heading," instead of more specific (and therefore less flexible) tags such as "TimesRoman-24-Bold." Similarly, Stanley Rice, a book designer, was proposing a common catalog of "editorial structure" tags in the late 1960s. GML went beyond simply tagging the content by adding the notion of a *Document Type Definition (DTD)*, which, among other things, made explicit the nesting relationship of document elements. For example, the DTD might specify that Subsection elements may optionally appear within a Section element, and Section elements nest inside a Chapter element, which nests within a Book element. The DTD also stipulated the rules by which an individual document's compliance could be judged with respect to the standard for that type of document.

It was soon obvious that GML applied to a far wider domain of documents than the legal material for which it was developed. IBM and early adopters of GML recognized its true potential. The American National Standards Institute (ANSI) formed a committee in 1978 with participation from Goldfarb and the GCA GenCode group. The first *Standard Generalized Markup Language (SGML)* working draft was published in 1980. After five more working drafts, it was proposed as a GCA standard in 1983, but it took several more drafts and three more years before SGML was accepted in 1986 by the International Organization for Standardization (ISO) as ISO 8879:1986. SGML defined a syntax for creating application-specific markup languages in which the grammar was expressed by a custom DTD. In fact, a DTD is a requirement of an SGML application, in contrast to XML, for which a DTD is optional.

Two early applications of SGML were the Electronic Manuscript Project of the Association of American Publishers (AAP) and the Computer-aided Acquisition and Logistic Support (CALS) initiative of the US Department of Defense (DoD). In fact, in addition to the DoD, the US Internal Revenue Service was an early adopter of SGML technology. The CALS model for representing tabular data eventually influenced the HTML table model, as well as the XML table model developed by the Organization for the Advancement of Structured Information Standards (OASIS) in 2000.

Several years after SGML's emergence as an ISO standard, beginning in 1989, Tim Berners-Lee conceived of HyperText Markup Language (HTML) originally as a simple descriptive markup language (containing tags such as "head", "body", "p", etc.). However, HTML soon evolved (or devolved, depending on your viewpoint) into a blend of procedural and descriptive markup (for example, "h1" and "h2", "font", etc.). HTML became an extremely successful application of SGML, which is a **metalanguage**—a language used to create other languages. (We'll later see that this relationship is analogous to that of XHTML and XML; the former is an application of the latter.)

Before we see how the Web was created and how SGML played an important role in its development, we'll learn how the Internet, upon which the Web is layered, got its start.

ARPANET and the Internet: Infrastructure

Depending on your definition of the term, the *Internet* began either in the early 1960s (as architectural diagrams), in 1969 (when it connected four universities), in 1973 (when it went international), or in 1982 (when the term the *Internet* was first used). The general consensus, however, seems to be 1969.

The Internet was begun in the 1960s by the US Department of Defense Advanced Research Projects Agency (ARPA) to facilitate the exchange of information among researchers and the military, with particular concern given to the development of continued connectivity for a command-and-control infrastructure in the aftermath of a nuclear war. The solution proposed by the think-tank people was a loosely connected network with no one point of failure—no single central machine—and for which connectivity between any two points was always assumed to be subject to failure. In retrospect, it is precisely this decentralization that has contributed so significantly to the success of the Internet.

Initially an architecture only on paper in 1962, the idea developed into a paper presented at an Association for Computing Machinery (ACM) meeting in 1967. This soon resulted in an (at first) exclusive network called ARPANET when the first four universities were connected in 1969. Stanford Research Institute, UCLA, UC-Santa Barbara, and the University of Utah hold the distinction of being the four original hosts.

The 1970s saw a promulgation of special-purpose networks, such as those used by the Department of Energy (MFENet), NASA (SPAN), computer scientists (CSNET), UNIX users (USENET, which used UUCP, or UNIX-to-UNIX Copy Protocol, invented in 1976), and BITNET, as well as several commercial networks like XNS from Xerox, DECNet from DEC, and SNA from IBM. The early seventies also saw the rise of e-mail as the most used software on the Internet. In 1979 the first USENET newsgroup was formed by three students. It is interesting to note that these two applications—e-mail and newsgroups (reinvented as chat rooms)—emerged again as the "killer apps" of a whole new generation of users in the late 1990s when the Web made them ubiquitous.

By 1971, twenty-three universities and research centers were connected via ARPANET. In October 1972, at a conference in Washington, D.C., a public demonstration of the ARPANET was given by setting up an actual node with forty machines. The same year, the InterNetworking Working Group (INWG) became the first standards body dedicated to the fledgling network. Vinton Cerf, who would later be called the "Father of the Internet," was elected as the INWG's first chairperson. In 1973 the network became international with the addition of the University College in London, England, and the Royal Radar Establishment in Norway.

Beginning in 1974, ARPANET started to evolve from its research-and-military orientation when a commercial version of the network, Telnet, was created. Just as the late seventies saw the ever-growing use of e-mail and then newsgroups, the mid 1980s witnessed a huge market for personal computers that could tap into the power and services of remote hosts, thanks to the Internet's connectivity. At the same time, corporations began to do business with each other via the Internet, although on a far smaller scale than they do today using the Web.

From 1969 to 1982 ARPANET used something called Network Control Protocol (NCP) as its transmission protocol, after which time the Transmission Control Protocol/Internet Protocol (TCP/IP) took its place. In the next few years, TCP/IP became the language spoken by all networked computers, regardless of manufacturer. The term *Internet* was first used in 1982 to describe the vast and ever-growing connection of hosts (there were 213 by 1981), although DARPA had used the term "Internetting project" for connecting packet networks in the early 1970s.

This early network called ARPANET eventually split into MILNET for defense and ARPANET for research in 1983. The Domain Name System (DNS) began in 1984, with few, if any, guessing that generic domain names such as software.com, beer.com, and shoes.com would become worth a fortune in just fifteen years.

The Internet Activities Board (IAB) was formed in 1983 to guide the new Internet. This group eventually split into the now familiar Internet Engineering Task Force (IETF) and the Internet Research Task Force (IRTF) in 1986. The IETF is still concerned mostly with protocols (such as the Web's HTTP—HyperText Transfer Protocol), while IRTF is interested more in exploring advanced networking concepts.

There were 1,000 hosts on the Internet by 1984. In 1985 the six top-level domains were established: *gov, mil, edu, com, org,* and *net.* In 1986, the US National Science Foundation (NSF) established the NSFNET, which was opened up to all universities and research organizations within a few years. By 1987 there were 28,000 hosts on the Internet. The Computer Emergency Response Team (CERT) was formed by DARPA in response to an early Internet worm attack in late 1988 that disabled one out of every ten Internet hosts; thus the term *hacker* entered our collective vocabulary.

By 1989 there were 100,000 hosts on the Internet. The ARPANET became the Network Formerly Known as ARPANET in 1990; it was decommissioned when it grew to 300,000 hosts. In 1991 the menu-driven information system called *gopher* was released by the University of Minnesota (named after its mascot). The year 1991 also saw the creation of the Internet Society, under the sponsorship of the Corporation for National Research Initiatives (CNRI) and the leadership of Vinton

Cerf. The number of hosts topped 1,000,000 by 1992, the year that the phrase "surfing the Internet" was first used by Jean Armour Polly. The NSF created InterNIC in 1993 to provide domain name registration and database services.

Meanwhile, in a research facility in Geneva, Switzerland, the World Wide Web was going through growing pains.

Medieval History (1986 to 1994)

In this section, we trace the beginnings of the WWW, HTML, and the W3C.

Berners-Lee, the Web, and HyperText Markup Language

The story of how Tim Berners-Lee, a British software engineer, conceived of the World Wide Web has been often told, but it wasn't until 1999 that "TB-L" himself told the tale in detail. His first book (1999), *Weaving the Web: The Original Design and Ultimate Destiny of the World Wide Web by Its Inventor,* is a detailed and highly enjoyable look at the birthing process, beginning with his role at CERN in the early 1980s and including his notion of "the Semantic Web," which he first described publicly in the mid 1990s.

CERN is the French acronym for Conseil Européen pour le Recherche Nucléaire, the European Particle Physics Laboratory in Geneva, Switzerland. This huge facility was staffed by scientists and engineers from all over Europe, each with his or her hardware and software preferences, working on DEC, UNIX, Control Data, or the new rage, PC and Macintosh computers. Berners-Lee worked at CERN for most of the 1980s and was eventually tasked with making information easily available, regardless of the document's original format or the user's hardware. Sounds a little bit like the IBM and GML situation, doesn't it?

Berners-Lee wanted to create a system that would accommodate technical papers, meeting notes, software documentation, and so on. His goal was to provide an interface that anyone could use on any computer to access any document without knowing where it was physically stored. Furthermore, he believed that no predetermined sequential ordering of documents was viable. Instead, he wanted a way to link documents so that a user could traverse the links in any order desired.

Although the Internet did not yet enjoy widespread popularity in Europe at this time, e-mail was an application that held great appeal, if only the messages could be permanently accessible. But the Internet used a pervasive protocol called TCP/IP, which we learned was created in 1982 and perfected several years later. Berners-Lee thought this would be ideal for the transport layer of information transmitted among diverse computers. And he was aware of Nelson's notion of hypertext, which he had seen used in Apple's HyperCard. He thought that hypertext was the ideal way to link documents in a universal yet simple way.

His original proposal that begot the Web (initially called "[Information] Mesh"), was entitled "Information Management: A Proposal" and was dated March 1989. The manager who reviewed the proposal scribbled a comment on page one: "Vague but exciting." Little did he know how truly exciting it would become! In his book, Berners-Lee recounts how he struggled to come up with just the right name; somehow names like Mine of Information (MOI, French for "me") and The Information Mine (TIM) sounded a bit too egocentric. He eventually hit upon *World Wide Web* in 1990.

What was missing? In addition to the infrastructure provided by the Internet and its TCP/IP protocol, three concepts needed to be developed to make the Web possible, according to Berners-Lee. The three missing pieces were: HTTP, Uniform Resource Identifier (URI), and HTML. He therefore defined HTTP as a simple protocol that fit well with existing Internet protocols such as ftp, telnet, news (NNTP), gopher, and wais (Wide Area Information Servers), as well as supported its own type of quick, single-access connection. HTTP is a stateless connection that essentially makes a request for a URI, a server receives and processes the request, and replies to the request with a status or error code, and, if possible, returns the requested resource. A URI identifies the resource that is requested, typically a Web page, an image or other multimedia file, a script, or whatever.

And what about HTML? Berners-Lee was familiar with SGML because it was in use on the IBM computers at CERN. He thought it would be advantageous to use a markup language similar to something that was familiar to a number of the CERN staff. Since it is a metalanguage, however, SGML itself was far too complicated for the average person to contend with. What was needed instead was a basic SGML application—a simple way to describe the basic structure of documents: titles, section headings, lists, and so forth. Wherever possible, he created HTML by selecting similar markup elements from other SGML application languages. In his original view, authors would use an HTML editor that would function like a word processor; there would be no need to type the actual markup characters. (As it turned out, however, the early Web browsers and authoring tools were completely separate applications, for the most part.)

He called his initial browser/editor simply *WorldWideWeb.* He wrote it in Objective C, an object-oriented language that was part of the development environment of his NeXT computer, the computer that would soon support the world's very first Web server—*nxoc01.cern.ch* (no longer supported). On Christmas Day, 1990, Berners-Lee succeeded in establishing a client-server connection between his computer and that of his colleague in the adjacent room, with HTTP-based file transfer over the Internet. This server was soon replaced by the hostname of *info.cern.ch.*

During the first half of 1991, he distributed the server and browser software exclusively to others at CERN. However, in August 1991, he announced his work on the `alt.hypertext` newsgroup and made the basic, platform-independent server, the WorldWideWeb browser for NeXT users, and a line-mode browser for those using other operating systems freely available from CERN's ftp site. The Web, although hardly worldwide, was born.

This new technology caught on fairly quickly among the proponents of hypertext and NeXT developers. Soon a newsgroup dedicated to the topic, `comp.infosystems.www`, was necessary, and shortly thereafter Berners-Lee created a CERN mailing called `www-talk@info.cern.ch` to answer questions. In 1992 the IEFT decided on the name URL (Uniform Resource Locator) as the basic addressing mechanism of the new Web. The year 1992 also saw the proliferation of a number of platform-specific browsers such as Erwise, Viola, Midas, and Samba. The Berners-Lee book (1999) provides interesting anecdotes about these early browsers.

It was in 1993 and 1994, however, that this new World Wide Web started expanding in all directions. By the end of 1993, the Web accounted for 2.5 percent of Internet traffic, according to the NSF. In 1993 Dave Raggett from Hewlett-Packard created the Arena browser/editor, which would eventually become an offering (renamed Amaya) of the W3C. Raggett went on to become a key architect of subsequent versions of HTML, as well as the creator of a handy validator tool called HTML Tidy, discussed in detail in chapter 15.

In February 1993 a team of developers from the National Center for Supercomputing Applications (NCSA) at the University of Illinois released the first version of a browser called Mosaic for the X Window System (a graphical interface to UNIX). I fondly remember downloading Mosaic version 0.9 and marveling at its ease of installation and advanced features that eventually made it the world's most popular browser (until the second versions of Netscape and Internet Explorer a few years later). The team, led by Marc Andreessen and Eric Bina, along with Jim Clark (previously with Silicon Graphics), went on to form Mosaic Communications in April 1994, which was soon renamed Netscape Communication Corporation for legal reasons (and is now part of AOL).

In March 1993 Lou Montulli at the University of Kansas modifed a hypertext browser named Lynx (*lynx.browser.org*) to work over the Web. This was the first text-based, screen-mode browser. (Lynx still exists and is a useful tool for testing the navigation and compatability of your Web site since it is the lowest common denominator of browsers.) Later that year, Tom Bruce's Cello became the first browser for Microsoft Windows.

Ed Kroll's *Whole Earth Internet Catalog,* published by O'Reilly and Associates in early 1994, was probably the first book to cover the World Wide Web in any detail, although its thrust was mainly older Internet protocols and client applications. Later that year, Mosaic from NCSA was available on all three major platforms, UNIX, Windows, and Mac—another factor in its rapid rise in dominating the browser "market" (all browsers were free at that time).

Due to Berners-Lee's publishing his server and browser source code, the number of Web servers grew to at least 200 in 1994. Early Internet Service Providers

(ISPs) such as AOL, Compuserve, and Prodigy made Internet access very easy for businesses and individuals. In May 1994 the first World Wide Web International Conference (WWW1) was held at CERN and drew 350 people. Some of the discussions there would ultimately drive the direction of HTML for a long time, not the least of which was the germ of the idea to form the World Wide Web Consortium.

Historic Timelines

The three tables in this chapter trace in detail the birth of the Internet, the Web, HTML, and the XML family of specifications. The dates are culled from many sources listed in the "For Further Explorarion" section. Specification status such as Working Draft, Candidate Recommendation, and Recommendation are described in chapter 2; see "W3C Recommendation Process." Although the tables are very detailed, they are not all-inclusive. Many W3C specifications that are either peripheral or unrelated to XML have been omitted, most notably the admirable Web Accessibility Initiative (WAI) of the W3C.

Table 1-1 presents a timeline of these historical events from 1945 to 1994. In the remainder of this chapter, we will explore the work of the W3C from 1994 until the present; since 1998 it has become very much focused on XML and the family of XML specifications. (The actual specifications are summarized in Appendix A.)

TABLE 1-1 Ancient and Medieval History Timeline

Ancient History	
July 1945	Vannevar Bush, the earliest pioneer of what became known as hypertext, publishes his futuristic and influential article, "As We May Think" in *Atlantic Monthly;* predicts hypertext and the Internet
1957	USSR launches the first artifical satellite, *Sputnik I.*
1958	United States forms DARPA to promote science and technology with military purpose. NASA is created to apply science and technology to space exploration.
1960	Extended Backus-Naur Form (EBNF) is invented by John Backus and Peter Naur as a formal expression of the ALGOL60 computer language. EBNF eventually becomes the syntax used to express most modern computer languages, as well as for describing syntax for various XML specifications from the W3C.
1962	The Internet is first conceived by the Department of Defense's Advanced Research Project Agency (ARPA); initially an architecture on paper only, the idea develops into a by-invitation-only network called ARPANET for collaboration among researchers and the US military.
1963	Douglas Engelbart and colleagues develop the On-Line System (NLS), the world's first implementation of what was eventually to be called hypertext; this user interface work included many innovations: the first mouse, display editing, windows, cross-file editing, outline processing, hypermedia, and groupware.

TABLE 1-1 *(continued)*

1965	DoD's ARPA begins research into a cooperative network of computers that can share resources. Ted Nelson coins the term *hypertext;* influenced by work of Douglas Engelbart.
1969	The Internet (then named APRANET) comes into physical being with the initial four ARPANET hosts: Stanford Research Institute, UCLA, UC-Santa Barbara, and the University of Utah. GML developed by Goldfarb, Mosher, and Lorie of IBM to share legal documents among various processes.
1970s	Xerox PARC originates idea of graphical user interface with windows; popularized by Apple Macintosh in the 1980s and later by Microsoft Windows.
1972	InterNetworking Working Group (INWG) is formed to oversee the new Internet consisting of 40 hosts.
1975	Bill Gates, a Harvard dropout, forms Microsoft Corporation at age 19.
1977	The Internet has 100 hosts.
1980	IBM selects Microsoft's MS-DOS as the standard operating system for its new personal computers.
1983	TCP/IP becomes the common Internet communication language.
1984	Domain Name System starts for registering new hosts; Internet reaches 1,000 hosts. William Gibson coins "cyberspace" in science fiction novel, *Neuromancer.* Term not applied to the Internet until 1991.
1985	E-mail and newsgroups become widespread in universities. Six top-level domain names established—*gov, mil, edu, com, org,* and *net.*
Medieval History	
1986	ISO approves SGML, which has an impact on publishing industry by separating content from presentation. Internet consists of 5,000 hosts.
August 1987	HyperCard released by Bill Atkinson; this early hypertext system had features still not available in Web browsers; Apple revolutionized the human-machine interface by bundling HyperCard with its computers. There are 28,000 hosts.
1989	Internet reaches 100,000 hosts.
March 1989	Tim Berners-Lee writes "Information Management: A Proposal," which outlines an information "mesh"; the proposal is initially ignored at CERN.
1989–1991	Tim Berners-Lee developed HTML as a major simplification of SGML for his new World Wide Web concept; later referred to as HTML 1.
early 1990s	Document Style Semantics and Specification Language (DSSSL, ISO/IEC 10179:1996) is created to transform and format SGML, much like XSLT and XSL will eventually be used to transform and format XML.
1990	ARPANET is decommissioned with 300,000 hosts on the Internet.

continued

TABLE 1-1 Ancient and Medieval History Timeline (*continued*)

May 1990	"Information Management: A Proposal" revised and distributed at CERN.
Christmas 1990	The term *World Wide Web* is coined by Tim Berners-Lee, its inventor; he demonstrates WorldWideWeb browser/editor and establishes the first server (in CERN).
1991	An application called *gopher* is created; it is the first easy-to-use, menu driven interface for the Internet.
August 1991	Tim Berners-Lee announces his new free software called WorldWideWeb [*sic*] on the *alt.hypertext* newsgroup. The Web is born.
late 1991	Stanford Linear Accelerator Center (SLAC) becomes the first U.S. Web server.
1992	The infant WWW has 50 Web servers, whereas the Internet has reached one million hosts.
	NSF grants Network Solutions (then InterNIC) exclusive rights to assign domain names. Some consider this the birth of the consumer Internet. Network Solutions' unique status changed in 1999; there are now numerous accredited registrar sites.
(revised 1997)	Hypermedia/Time-based Structuring Language (HyTime, ISO/IEC 10744) released by ISO and IEC. HyTime defines location specifier types for all kinds of data, which is relevant to XPointer. HyTime also defines inline and out-of-line link structures and some semantic features, including traversal control and presentation of objects, which is a basis for XLink.
December 1992	Marc Andreessen of the Mosaic development team from NCSA appeared on the `WWW-talk` newsgroup and proposed the IMG element to reference images—and the Web was never the same.
1993	The Web starts spreading rapidly to 600 servers, foreshadowing even greater popularity in the near future. Internet has two million hosts.
	Forms are introduced into HTML. Forms eventually become an integral part of the Web, especially for e-commerce and e-business.
March 1993	Lou Montulli releases Lynx, a text-based browser.
November 1993	Mosaic 1.0 is released by NCSA for Sun workstations with support for images, nested lists, and forms. (Beta releases appeared throughout 1993.)
1994	On its twenty-fifth anniversary, the Internet has grown to three million hosts. Meanwhile, the WWW grows fast to 10,000 servers.
May 1994	The first World Wide Web Conference (Geneva) draws 350 attendees, mostly from academia.
	Text Encoding Initiative (TEI) first published in nondraft form. TEI provides a formal syntax for location specifiers for structured data, graphics, and other data relevant to XPointer. The XPointer language is based on TEI extended pointers. TEI P3 (Guidelines) also provides structures for creating links, aggregate objects, and link collections, all of which are relevant to XLink.
July 1994	HTML 2.0 specification is released on the Internet by Dan Connolly and colleagues (after soliciting comments from newsgroups).

Premodern History (1994 to 1998)

Toward the end of the summer of 1994, Tim Berners-Lee made the fateful decision to move from scenic Geneva to MIT's Laboratory of Computer Science (LCS) in Cambridge, Massachusetts. This move was motivated by his desire to lead the formation and direction of what was initially called the World Wide Web Organization, but it was quickly renamed the World Wide Web Consortium (W3C—see *http://www.w3.org*) in the fall of 1994. Berners-Lee discusses the details surrounding the creation of the W3C quite enjoyably in his book *Weaving the Web.*

After the success of the first World Wide Web Conference in Geneva in May 1994, followed in July by the release of HTML 2.0 specification, and then the second World Wide Web Conference in Chicago just one-half year after the first, the newly formed W3C held its first meeting in Boston and began its benevolent attempts to guide the course of this already important new form of communication.

The year 1995 was particularly significant, with the birth of Java by Sun Microsystems and RealAudio by RealNetworks, with Internet access provided by Compuserve, America Online, Prodigy, and with a new enormously successful IPO from Netscape Communications Corporation, the makers of a wonderful new Web browser, originally called Netscape Navigator (later Netscape Communicator).

As Mosaic/Netscape was forming, Bill Gates decided in 1994 that Microsoft's Windows 95 should support Internet access. In January 1995 he announced the Microsoft Network (MSN). The new Netscape Communications Corporation released its Netscape Navigator 1.0 in December 1994. By August 1995 version 1.0 of the Microsoft Internet Explorer was shipped with the Windows 95 PLUS pack. Internet Explorer 1.0 was not at all impressive, but by the end of 1995, Microsoft's 2.0 browser started to give Netscape a run for its money. Netscape countered with its version 2.0 browser in March 1996, adding support for Java applets, which had just been introduced by Sun Microsystems in May 1995. By August 1996 versions 3.0 of both Netscape and Internet Explorer hit the Web. The browser war was in full heat.

Most people think of XML as coming into existence in early 1998, but actually its beginnings were in May 1996 when the still young W3C initiated an effort called "SGML for the Web," aimed at creating a data-focused application of SGML; it soon became called the Extensible Markup Language. Actually, the origin of XML can be traced back even further to November 1994, when, at the second WWW Conference, C. M. Sperberg-McQueen and Robert F. Goldstein presented a paper entitled "HTML to the Max: A Manifesto for Adding SGML Intelligence to the World-Wide Web." However, it was mid 1996 when the XML groundwork began, especially with the creation of what became known as Phase 1 of the XML Activity Area of W3C in June 1996. Phase 1 concentrated on three specifications: XML (syntax), XLink (linking), and XSL (stylesheet language) to parallel the ISO/IEC standards SGML, HyTime (and TEI), and DSSSL, respectively.

The W3C was also incredibly busy in 1996 trying to nail down HTML 3.0, a task fraught with charged political battles since both Netscape and Microsoft had implemented a number of nonstandard features in their version 3.0 browsers. Trying to reach agreement about what was legal HTML was very difficult. In fact, HTML 3.0 never materialized as a formal spec at all. Instead, the HTML 3.2 Recommendation appeared in January 1997. By this time, the specification was largely documenting what had become de facto standards, such as tables, applets, flowing text around images, and so on.

By early 1997 in typical Internet grass-roots fashion, the `XML-DEV` mailing list had formed for developers seriously interested in XML technical discussions; this list is still very active (see *http://www.xml.org/*).

In April 1997 the first Working Draft of what was initially called "Extensible Markup Language: Part 2: Linking" was posted. This eventually split into XLink and XPointer. A few months later, "A Proposal for XSL" was submitted by Microsoft Corporation, Inso Corporation, ArborText, University of Edinburgh, and James Clark. At that time, *XSL* stood for "Extensible Style Language." This influential W3C Note eventually split into three specifications: XSL, XSLT, and XPath.

Shortly before Christmas 1997, HTML 4.0 became a W3C Recommendation, less than a year after 3.2. Few people outside the W3C realized at the time that this would be the last major version of this *lingua franca* of the Web, to eventually be replaced by XHTML and XML. In fact, the HTML Working Group disbanded in January 1998, only to be reborn later to work on XHTML.

Also in January 1998 several great minds from Microsoft, DataChannel, ArborText, Inso, and the University of Edinburgh submitted a W3C Note entitled simply "XML-Data." This insightful paper was the inspiration behind what eventually morphed into XML Schema in 2001. The same month David Megginson announced the creation of SAX (Simple API for XML) 1.0, a grass-roots effort to provide a common interface to XML parsers, an effort only one month in the making with many contributors from the `XML-DEV` mailing list. And yet, XML was not even a W3C Recommendation!

Table 1.2 lists the events discussed in this section, as well as some other notable events.

TABLE 1-2 Premodern History Timeline

September 1994	IETF establishes HTML Working Group.
November 1994	C. M. Sperberg-McQueen and Robert F. Goldstein present "HTML to the Max: A Manifesto for Adding SGML Intelligence to the World-Wide Web" at the second World Wide Web Conference in Chicago.
Fall 1994	W3C founded with headquarters at MIT in Cambridge, Mass., and eventually at INRIA in France and Keio in Japan.

TABLE 1-2 *(continued)*

November 1994	Netscape Communications Corp. (called Mosaic Communications until NCSA protested) is formed by Marc Andreessen and Jim Clark.
December 1994	Netscape Navigator 1.0 is released (preceded by Mozilla beta in October 1994 and followed by version 1.1 in April 1995). First W3C meeting with about 25 members meets in Boston with Tim Berners-Lee.
June 1995	RealAudio by RealNetworks makes its debut.
1995	W3C has problems defining HTML 3.0 (originally called HTML+) due to browser extensions. Birth of Java by Sun Microsystems, RealAudio by RealNetworks; Internet access provided by Compuserve, America Online, Prodigy; and Netscape's IPO.
January 1995	Bill Gates announces one-click access to the Internet and Microsoft Network (MSN) to be built into Windows 95.
May 1995	Sun Microsystems introduces Java; major impact on the programming world and the Web soon follows.
1995	The young WWW experiences a tenfold increase in one year to 100,000 servers. The Internet consists of 6.5 million hosts.
August 1995	Microsoft includes a rudimentary Internet Explorer 1.0 in its Windows 95 PLUS pack (when Windows 95 is released).
Fall 1995	HTML Working Groups formed as vendors come together under W3C's encouragement.
November 1995	HTML 2.0 becomes RFC 1866, submitted by W3C leaders Tim Berners-Lee and Dan Connolly, and developed by the IETF's HTMLWorking Group. Microsoft releases Internet Explorer 2.0, the first significant release of its Web browser, as a direct challenge to Netscape Navigator's lead in browser market share. Mosaic 2.0 is released by NCSA; followed by 2.1 in January 1996.
December 1995	JavaScript introduced by Netscape. Bill Gates outlines Microsoft's commitment to supporting and enhancing the Internet by integrating the PC platform with the public network.
1996	The Internet doubles to 12.8 million hosts, but the WWW increases fivefold to 500,000 servers.
March 1996	Netscape 2.0 appears; includes support for Java.
August 1996	Browser war heats up as both Netscape Navigator 3.0 and Internet Explorer 3.0 are released.
May 1996	W3C charters effort to create "SGML for the Web," a simplification that soon became known as XML. Initial plans called for only three specifications: XML (syntax), XLink (linking), and XSL (stylesheet language) to parallel the ISO/IEC standards SGML, HyTime (and TEI), and DSSSL, respectively.
June 1996	XML committee formed as XML Activity area, Phase 1.

continued

TABLE 1-2 Premodern History Timeline (*continued*)

November 1996	First public XML specification draft presented at SGML 96 Conference in Boston; Tim Bray and C. M. Sperberg-McQueen, editors. W3C's unique browser/editor, Amaya 0.9, premieres. In the years to come Amaya serves as a testbed for the latest HTML, CSS, and XML technology.
December 1996	Cascading Style Sheets (CSS) Level 1 Recommendation released. New browser called Opera 2.1 makes the scene with emphasis on CSS support.
1997	The Web grows to 1.2 million servers while the Internet supports 19.5 million hosts.
January 1997	Final version (3.0) of Mosaic is released. HTML 3.2 Recommendation issued by the W3C; adds widely deployed features such as tables, applets, text flow around images, superscripts, and subscripts (there was no formal HTML 3.0 specification).
February 1997	`XML-DEV` mailing list formed by Peter Murray-Rust and Henry Rzepa.
March 1997	*XML, Java, and the Future of the Web* published; seminal article by Sun Microsystems' Jon Bosak, XML Working Group Chair for several years. Jon Bosak and Tim Bray are often called the "fathers of XML." Microsoft announces XML support, which generates considerable excitement. First XML Conference held in San Diego by Graphic Communications Association (GCA).
April 1997	Extensible Markup Language, Part 2: Linking becomes the first Working Draft of what will eventually split into XLink and XPointer.
June 1997	Netscape Communicator 4.0 is released.
August 1997	"A Proposal for XSL" submitted to the W3C by Microsoft, Inso, ArborText, University of Edinburgh, and James Clark. At that time, *XSL* stood for "Extensible Style Language." This influential W3C Note eventually grows into XSL, XSLT, and XPath.
October 1997	Internet Explorer 4.0 is released and soon makes a significant dent in Netscape's browser market share. Bill Gates demos XML at Seybold Conference. *XML Principles, Tools and Techniques,* Fall '97 issue of *WWW Journal;* first all-XML publication (now out-of-print).
December 1997	HTML 4.0 becomes a W3C Recommendation (revised April 1998). Opera 3.0 released.
1997 to 1998	Common Business Library (CBL) 1.0 was a "pure XML" R&D effort beginning in 1997, partly funded by an Advanced Technology Program award from the US Department of Commerce (NIST) to Veo Systems. The goal was to push the envelope in using XML for an e-commerce architecture. Limitations of DTDs resulted in a very complex architecture. This experience led to the invention of Schema for Object-oriented XML (SOX), the first XML schema language with object-oriented properties, which greatly simplified the structure of CBL by providing a library of relatively simple base components that could be extended.
1998	The WWW has 4.2 million serves while the Internet has 36.7 million hosts, meaning that more than one of every ten hosts is now a Web server.

TABLE 1-2 *(continued)*

January 1998	HTML Working Group disbands (later reforms to work on XHTML). Authors from Microsoft, DataChannel, ArborText, Inso, and University of Edinburgh submit XML-Data Note to W3C. This becomes very influential in most schema attempts that follow. Microsoft releases a technology preview that supports XML and a very early draft of XSL. SAX 1.0 is announced just one month after discussions began on `XML-DEV` about the need for a common API to XML parser, spearheaded by Peter Murray-Rust and coordinated and implemented by David Megginson.

Ultramodern History (1998 to 2001)

On February 10, 1998, XML became a W3C Recommendation. From that moment on, the vast majority of W3C specifications, roughly 80 percent, have been XML-related in one way or another. Like SGML, XML is a metalanguage, a syntax for describing other languages. It took only two months for the first XML application to emerge with the release of the Mathematical Markup Language (MathML) Recommendation in April.[3] By July XML media types were submitted to the IETF.

In August 1998 XML Activity Phase 2 began with six XML Working Groups plus one each for XSL and the Document Object Model (DOM). Development began that month on XSL, now renamed "Extensible Stylesheet Language." Also that month "XML-QL: A Query Language for XML" was submitted to W3C by AT&T, INRIA, and several universities. DOM Level 1 became a Recommendation in October. In December a Query Language workshop was held in Boston; more than 60 proposals were submitted by fewer than 100 attendees.

January 1999 saw the publication of Namespaces in XML. This relatively brief Recommendation ultimately raised more questions than it answered. It is still the source of considerable confusion; the Namespaces specification has implementation impacts on many subsequent specifications.

The first mainstream browser to support XML was Internet Explorer 5.0, released in March 1999. Although XML by definition does not specify a style for display (in fact, it separates data from display), Microsoft thought users would be happier to see their XML displayed using a built-in Cascading Style Sheet, which renders XML as a hierarchical tree with collapsing and expanding nodes. This tree view has proved popular and is implemented in one way or another in most XML editors, for better or worse.

3. Many regard Chemical Markup Language (CML) as the first XML application because it appeared in 1997. However, since CML predated the final XML recommendation, this point is debatable.

In April 1999 the third draft of XSL split out the Transformations (XSLT) portion into its own document. The XSL spec itself is sometimes called XSL Formatting Objects.

Industry interest in XML had been smoldering from about mid 1998, but the creation of BizTalk.org by Microsoft and XML.org by OASIS (an organization that had its roots in SGML) in May 1999 certainly stoked the fires a good bit. A few months later in September, UN/CEFACT and OASIS announced that they had banded together to form an Electronic Business XML Working Group (*http://ebXML.org*). By now XML had become a widely accepted alternative, or at least supplement to, Electronic Data Interchange (EDI) for e-commerce.

In the summer of 1999 browser vendors and Web designers were given an easy way to associate style sheets with XML documents. XLink and XPointer Working Drafts appeared. In September Phase 3 of the XML Activity began, focusing on XML Schema, Linking, Query, and XSL. This is the current phase, although an XML Protocol Working Group was added in September 2000. Phase 4 is also planned, with the goal of cleaning up existing specifications primarily so that they are consistent with one another, rather than adding significant new functionality.

November 1999 saw the finalization of two very important specifications, Extensible Stylesheet Language-Transformations (XSLT) Version 1.0 and XML Path Language (XPath) Version 1.0, both from the earlier XSL efforts. The Apache XML Project was also begun that month. The Apache press release mentioned goals that included promoting an open source approach to XML and XSL tools. In 2000 Apache released a significant array of both desktop and server-side XML tools, including Xerces, Xalan, Cocoon, FOP, Xang, and Batik.

At the end of 1999 the HTML Working Group published a roadmap that outlined its plans for the creation of XHTML (Extensible HTML). In January 2000 it delivered "XHTML 1.0: The Extensible Hypertext Markup Language: A Reformulation of HTML 4 in XML 1.0," soon followed by related specifications that promoted a modular approach to XHTML to make it feasible to implement Web content delivery on devices with limited memory.

Thoroughout the year 2000, there was considerable interest in Voice Markup Language (VoiceXML) and in development of related specifications for speech and natural language. Interest in an alternative to XML Schema called RELAX (REgular LAnguage description for XML) grew steadily. Beta versions of Netscape 6.0 appeared in 2000 with support for XML technology. At the same time, Microsoft improved its MSXML3 parser for use with Internet Explorer and as a standalone tool.

In May 2000 Simple Object Access Protocol (SOAP) 1.1 was issued as a W3C Note by representatives from DevelopMentor, IBM, Lotus Development Corporation, Microsoft, and UserLand Software. SOAP was quickly embraced by the business community and was eventually adopted by the newly formed XML Protocol Working Group in September, tasked with defining mechanisms for application-to-application communication via XML-based messaging and remote procedure call

(RPC) systems, layered on standard transport mechanisms such as HTTP and SMTP.

Microsoft released its Internet Explorer 5.5 in July 2000 with improved XML, XSLT, CSS, and DOM support. Not until November of that year did the production version of Netscape Communicator 6.0 appear with somewhat similar areas of support: XML, RDF, DOM, CSS1, and HTML 4.0. Netscape did not choose to implement Microsoft's built-in stylesheet approach to rendering XML.

A second edition of the XML 1.0 Recommendation, published in October 2000, addressed errata from the February 1998 first edition. At the end of 2000 the HTML Working Group revised its roadmap, detailing a long list of deliverables in the growing XHTML family. In December XHTML Basic became a W3C Recommendation, paving the way for lightweight, modular implementations of HTML for devices with limited memory and needs. This was followed by Modularization of XHTML and XHTML 1.1 in mid 2001.

January 2001 saw an IETF proposal for additional XML media types. In related developments, a Last Call Working Draft of XPointer was issued. XPointer (which is based on XPath) describes addressing internal fragments of XML documents. Unfortunately, this is a backward step, since XPointer achieved Candidate Recommendation status in June 2000. Complications included a namespace issue and a possible patent conflict concerning related technology. XPointer was restored to its Candidate Recommendation status in September 2001.

Interest in XML Query Language grew throughout 2001 amidst a flurry of working drafts from the W3C in the summer. At the risk of a major oversimplification, XQuery attempts to combine the power of XPath and SQL to provide flexible query facilities to extract data from Web documents, regardless of the type of data source.

In addition to XHTML efforts, many other significant specifications reached maturity in 2001, including MathML 2.0 in February, XML Schema in May, XLink in June, Synchronized Multimedia Integration Language (SMIL) 2.0 in August, Scalable Vector Graphics (SVG) in September, and Extensible Stylesheet Language (XSL) in October. The year 2001 was certainly a busy one for the W3C and one in which the XML family of specifications grew considerably.

Meanwhile, OASIS took an increasingly active leadership and coordination role in 2001 in forming technical committees (TC), some tasked with developing conformance test suites, while others focused on a schema effort called RELAX NG (Next Generation). Still other TCs concentrated on e-commerce technology, such as maintaining and enhancing ebXML and defining a new Universal Business Language (UBL), positioned to become a synthesis of existing XML business document libraries, starting with Commerce One's xCBL (XML Common Business Library) 3.0.

Table 1-3 highlights the events described in this section, as well as listing some not presented in the prose.

TABLE 1-3 Ultramodern History Timeline

February 1998	XML 1.0 Recommendation issued by W3C.
April 1998	Mathematical Markup Language 1.0 (MathML, revised July 1999) becomes the first XML-based language from W3C.
	Adobe and others submit Precision Graphics Markup Language (PGML) Note to W3C; some ideas were later used in SVG.
May 1998	Cascading Style Sheets (CSS) Level 2 Recommendation is published.
	W3C's "Future of HTML" workshop results in a new HTML working group and leads eventually to XHTML.
June 1998	Windows 98 is released by Microsoft; Internet Explorer is an integral part of the operating system, adding fuel to US Justice Department allegations from 1997 that Microsoft is forcing computer manufacturers to feature its browser.
	Synchronized Multimedia Integration Language (SMIL) 1.0 Recommendation.
July 1998	XML media types `text/xml` and `application/xml` proposed in IETF RFC 2376.
	XML Data Reduced (XDR) is published as Charles Frankston and Henry S. Thompson refined and subsetted the Microsoft XML-Data Note; used in BizTalk.
August 1998	XML Activity, Phase 2 begins: 6 XML Working Groups, XSL, DOM.
	XSL becomes a W3C Working Draft (renamed "Extensible Stylesheet Language"), with a second draft in December 1998 that becomes the basis for Microsoft's support for XSL in IE 5.
September 1998	Schema for Object-oriented XML (version 1.0) submitted as W3C Note by Veo Systems (later Commerce One). SOX adds extensible datatypes, inheritance, namespaces, polymorphic content, and more to the developing notion of schema. SOX, like Microsoft's XDR proved very influential in the XML Schema effort.
October 1998	Document Object Model (DOM) Level 1 Recommendation.
	Netscape 4.5 released.
November 1998	AOL announces plans to acquire Netscape Communications for $10 billion.
	XML '98 and Markup '98 held in Chicago, by GCA; major XML conferences.
	Opera 3.5 released.
December 1998	QL '98: Query Language Workshop held in Boston (for W3C members only); more than 60 submissions.
	Premiere of Google.com search site.
1999	Numerous milestone releases of what will become Netscape 6.0 are released by the mozilla.org project. Many of these releases include support for XML, RDF, DOM, CSS, and other key specifications.
January 1999	Namespaces in XML Recommendation published.
February 1999	Resource Description Framework (RDF) Model and Syntax Specification becomes a Recommendation.
	The first of ten Scalable Vector Graphics Working Drafts is issued by the W3C. It ultimately takes 2.5 years to finalize SVG.

TABLE 1-3 *(continued)*

March 1999	Resource Description Framework (RDF) Schemas becomes a Proposed Recommendation, a status it retains for a long time. Internet Explorer 5.0 is released by Microsoft; first mainstream browser to support XML. Uses a complex built-in stylesheet to render XML as a color-coded tree with collapsible nodes. Also supports the Dec. 1998 XSL Working Draft. Includes MSXML2 parser.
April 1999	In the third draft of XSL, the XSL Transformations (XSLT) portion is moved to a separate document. The main XSL spec is sometimes called XSL Formatting Objects.
May 1999	The eighth InternationalWorld Wide Web Conference held in Toronto, marking the tenth anniversary of the World Wide Web, as measured from the original proposal in 1989. WWW8 was largely XML-focused. BizTalk.org formed by Microsoft. (Announcements began in March.) XML.org formed by OASIS. "XML and the Second-Generation Web" by Jon Bosak and Tim Bray, published in *Scientific American.* Initial Working Drafts for the two main parts of XML Schema appear: XML Schema Part 1: Structures, and XML Schema Part 2: Datatypes. Part 0: Primer followed in early 2000.
June 1999	Associating Style Sheets with XML documents is released to placate browser vendors who need some way to render XML. Two new Working Drafts, XLink and XPointer, are published from what had previously been the single Extensible Markup Language, Part 2: Linking spec. XLink was influenced by HyTime and XPointer by TEI, two technologies from the SGML community. XPath becomes a separate document, extracted from the XSLT Working Draft (which itself was extracted from the XSL spec). Schema for Object-Oriented XML (SOX) 2.0 submitted as W3C Note by Commerce One. Common Business Library 2.0 is released by Commerce One to facilitate mass business-to-business Web-based commerce. CBL is based on SOX.
August 1999	HTML 4.01 Recommendation (revised December 1999) supersedes HTML 4.0.
September 1999	XML Activity, Phase 3 begins: XML Schema, Linking, Query, and XSL Working Groups formed or extended. (XML Protocol Working Group added in September 2000.) A landmark book is published: *Weaving the Web: The Original Design and Ultimate Destiny of the World Wide Web by Its Inventor* by Tim Berners-Lee with Mark Fischetti (Contributor). ebXML is born. The United Nations body for Trade Facilitation and Electronic Business (UN/CEFACT) and the Organization for the Advancement of Structured Information Standards (OASIS) initiates a worldwide project to standardize XML business specifications; the Electronic Business XML Working Group is formed. Netscape 4.7 released, still without XML support.

continued

TABLE 1-3 Ultramodern History Timeline (*continued*)

November 1999	Extensible Stylesheet Language-Transformations (XSLT) Version 1.0 and XML Path Language (XPath) Version 1.0 become Recommendations. HTML Working Group Roadmap published, defining W3C's goals, schedule, and deliverables for HTML as XML. Creation of the Apache XML Project. The press release discusses the goals of the project, which include promoting an open source approach to XML and XSL tools. In 2000 Apache released a significant array of XML tools, including Xerces, Xalan, Cocoon, FOP, Xang, and Batik.
December 1999	A number of VoiceXML requirements documents are released as Working Drafts: Model Architecture for Voice Browser Systems, Speech Synthesis Markup Requirements for Voice Markup Languages, Natural Language Processing Requirements for Voice Markup Languages, Grammar Representation Requirements for Voice Markup Languages, and Dialog Requirements for Voice Markup Languages. HTML 4.01 Specification becomes a Recommendation that supersedes both the 1997 and 1998 versions of HTML 4.0.
2000	The new millennium sees a heavy barrage of XML specifications, some of which are new kids in the family, while other more senior members reach or near maturity.
January 2000	XHTML 1.0: The Extensible HyperText Markup Language—A Reformulation of HTML 4 in XML 1.0 becomes a Recommendation. XHTML 1.1-Module-Based XHTML and Building XHTML Modules are considered Last Call Working Drafts. MSXML2 (really version 2.6) released by Microsoft.
February 2000	XML Schema Part 0: Primer first appears to help explain the complex Parts 1 and 2.
March 2000	Resource Description Framework (RDF) Schema Specification 1.0 becomes a Candidate Recommendation. However, this is a revision of the Proposed Recommendation of March 1999, which incorporates editorial suggestions received in review comments. (*Note:* A CR is less advanced than a PR.) First ebXML Initiative Technical Specifications released for public comment. RELAX, a specification for describing XML-based language, is published as a JIS (Japanese Industrial Standards) Technical Resolution. Microsoft releases beta version of Microsoft XML Parser Technology Preview Release version 3 (MSXML3 beta) which, in addition to parsing, supports both the outdated Dec. 1998 XSL Working Draft and the current XSLT Recommendation, based on which namespace is specified.
April 2000	US District Judge rules Microsoft guilty of breaking antitrust laws; Microsoft found guilty of hurting competition.
April to October 2000	Three beta versions of Netscape 6.0 appear with XML support.
May 2000	XML Query Data Model is published as an initial Working Draft.

TABLE 1-3 *(continued)*

May 2000 *(continued)*	SOAP 1.1 is issued as a W3C Note by representatives from DevelopMentor, IBM, Lotus Development, Microsoft, and UserLand Software. VoiceXML version 1.0 is issued as an initial Working Draft. VoiceXML 2.0 is eventually proposed before 1.0 becomes a W3C Recommendation.
June 2000	XPointer version 1.0 becomes a Candidate Recommendation but later becomes embroiled in a patent claim by Sun Microsystems. Opera 4.0 is released.
Summer 2000	Working Drafts of Speech Synthesis Markup Language Specification for the Speech Interface Framework and Speech Recognition Grammar Specification for the W3C Speech Interface Framework are published. Voice Browser Activity is very active in 2000 and 2001.
July 2000	Microsoft releases Internet Explorer 5.5 with improved XML, XSLT, CSS, and DOM support.
September 2000	XML Protocol Working Group created to define mechanisms for application-to-application communication via XML-based messaging and remote procedure call (RPC) systems, layered on standard Web transports such as HTTP and SMTP. SOAP, XML-RPC, and WebBroker are a few of the technologies the so-called XP WG is examining. Renamed Web Services WG in early 2002. DOM Level 1 Specification (Second Edition) issued as a Working Draft to incorporate editorial changes to the Oct. 1998 DOM Level 1 Recommendation. Initial Working Drafts of DOM Level 3 Core Specification Version 1.0 and DOM Level 3 Events Specification Version 1.0 are posted.
October 2000	XML 1.0 (Second Edition) is published. Rather than being a second version of XML, it simply integrates the changes resulting from the first-edition errata. MSXML Parser 3.0 (non-beta) is released by Microsoft with server-safe HTTP access, complete implementation of XSLT and XPath, and changes to the Simple API for XML (SAX2) implementation.
November 2000	Five DOM Specifications become W3 Recommendations: Level 2 Core, Level 2 Views, Level 2 Events, Level 2 Style, and Level 2 Traversal and Range. (However, the sixth part, DOM Level 2 HTML Specification, is demoted from Proposed Recommendation to a Working Draft.) Netscape 6.0 is released with support for XML, RDF, DOM, CSS1, and HTML 4.0. Compare to IE 5.x. Commerce One XML Common Business Library (xCBL) 3.0 is released.
November to December 2000	The HTML Working Group Roadmap is revised and defines deliverables for a long list of XHTML efforts: XHTML 1.0-Extensible HTML, HTML 4 , XHTML Modularization, XHTML 1.1, XHTML Basic, XHTML Profile Requirements, XHTML Profile Vocabulary, Extended Events Module, Applying XML Schema to XHTML, and XHTML 2.0. Several releases of W3C's Amaya 4.x appear in rapid succession. Amaya supports HTML, XHTML, SVG, CSS, MathML, and more.

continued

TABLE 1-3 Ultramodern History Timeline (*continued*)

December 2000	Completion of the XML Topic Maps (XTM) 1.0 specification is announced at XML 2000 conference. This non-W3C spec was completed as an ISO/IEC effort in roughly six months. XHTML Basic becomes a W3C Recommendation, paving the way for lightweight, modular implementations of HTML for devices with limited memory and needs.
2001	Query Working Group produces a number of XML Query specifications throughout the year (XML Query Language, XQuery 1.0, XPath 2.0 Data Model, XML Query Use Cases, etc.).
January 2001	XML Linking Working Group released a Last Call Working Draft of XPointer Version 1.0. Together with the IETF Internet-Draft "XML Media Types," XPointer (which is based on XPath) describes addressing internal fragments of XML documents. This is a backward step; XPointer had achieved Candidate Recommendation status in June 2000. Complications include a namespace issue and a possible Sun patent conflict concerning related technology from August 1997 called "Method and System for Implementing Hypertext Scroll Attributes."
February 2001	MathML version 2.0 becomes a Recommendation. Canonical XML version 1.0 becomes a Recommendation. This spec establishes a method for determining whether two documents are identical, or whether changes are transformations permitted by the XML 1.0 and Namespaces in XML Recommendations.
April 2001	Modularization of XHTML becomes a Recommendation. This proves to be a boon for Web-enabled handheld devices.
May 2001	XML Schema Part 1: Structures and XML Schema Part 2: Datatypes (and XML Schema Part 0: Primer) become Recommendations. XHTML 1.1: Module-based XHTML becomes a Recommendation. ebXML approved: "UN/CEFACT and OASIS Deliver on 18-Month Initiative for Electronic Business Framework."
June 2001	XLink Version 1.0 finally becomes a Recommendation; so does XML Base. OASIS forms several ebXML Technical Committees (TC) to continue ebXML maintenance and enhancements: the ebXML Messaging TC, the ebXML Collaboration Protocol Profile and Agreement TC and the ebXML Implementation, Interoperability and Conformance TC; work continues on Registry/Repository. OASIS TC formed to define RELAX NG, a combination of TREX (Tree Regular Expressions for XML) and RELAX, each of which takes a simpler approach to schema creation than W3C's XML Schema.
August 2001	SMIL 2.0 becomes a Recommendation; SMIL Animation follows in October.
September 2001	SVG 1.0 finally becomes a Recommendation. OASIS TC formed to create Universal Business Language (UBL), to become a synthesis of existing XML business document libraries, starting with Commerce One's xCBL 3.0 and developing the standard UBL library based on industry experience with other XML business libraries and with similar technologies such as Electronic Data Interchange (EDI).

TABLE 1-3 *(continued)*

October 2001	XSL Version 1.0 finally becomes a Recommendation. The Formatting Objects portion is finalized nearly two years after the Transformation part (XSLT). XML Information Set becomes a Recommendation. VoiceXML 2.0 Working Draft appears, but 1.0 is not yet a Recommendation. OASIS Web Services Component Model (WSCM) TC formed to create an XML and Web services-centric component model for interactiveWeb applications. Microsoft XML Core Services 4.0 RTM (formerly MSXML parser) debuts, with support for XML Schema Recommendation, faster SAX parser and XSLT processing, and removal of some nonstandard features (i.e., Dec. 1998 XSLT Working Draft).
December 2001	Working drafts of XSLT 2.0, XPath 2.0, XQuery, SOAP 1.2, and RDF/XML Syntax are published. Controversial XML 1.1 working draft appears addressing the so-called XML Blueberry Requirements. The Netcraft Survey reports 36.3 million Web servers. Netsizer indicates 157 million Internet hosts. The ratio of Web servers to hosts is now nearly one to four.
January 2002	Netsizer indicates there are 617 million Internet users worldwide, 123 million in the United States alone. Working drafts of XForms 1.0, DOM Level 3, Mobile SVG Profiles, and SVG 1.1 appear.

Summary

This chapter provides a detailed examination of the events that shaped the development of the Internet, the World Wide Web, the W3C, and the XML family of specifications. The focus, like that of the rest of this book, is largely on technology developed by the W3C; grassroots efforts such as SAX, non-W3C specifications such as RELAX, and business-related developments such as SOAP and ebXML are mentioned where appropriate to provide a wider context.

All links in the "For Further Exploration" sections appear on this book's Web site organized by chapter: *http://wdvl.Internet.com/Authoring/Languages/XML/XMLFamily.*

For Further Exploration

Articles

As We May Think, Vannevar Bush (July 1945, *Atlantic Monthly*)
http://www.theatlantic.com/unbound/flashbks/computer/bushf.htm

XML, Java, and the Future of the Web
http://metalab.unc.edu/pub/sun-info/standards/xml/why/xmlapps.htm

XML and the Second-Generation Web, Jon Bosak and Tim Bray (May 1999, *Scientific American*)
http://www.sciam.com/1999/0599issue/0599bosak.html

Books

Where Wizards Stay Up Late: The Origins of the Internet, Katie Hafner, Matthew Lyon (1998, Touchstone Books; ISBN: 0684832674)
http://www.amazon.com/exec/obidos/ASIN/0684832674/

Weaving the Web: The Original Design and Ultimate Destiny of the World Wide Web by Its Inventor, Tim Berners-Lee with Mark Fischetti (1999, Harper, San Francisco; ISBN: 0062515861)
http://www.w3.org/People/Berners-Lee/Weaving/Overview.html

Historical

The Electronic Labyrinth Time Line
http://jefferson.village.virginia.edu/elab/hfl0267.html

Douglas Engelbart—Bootstrap Institute Publications
http://bootstrap.org/library.htm

Robin Cover's History of Generalized Markup and SGML
http://www.oasis-open.org/cover/general.html#hist

Charles F. Goldfarb's The SGML History Niche
http://www.sgmlsource.com/history/index.htm

SGML: The Reason Why and the First Published Hint (*Journal of the American Society for Information Science,* 48(7), July 1997)
http://www.sgmlsource.com/history/jasis.htm

The World Wide Web History Project
http://www.webhistory.org/home.html

All About the Internet: History of the Internet [links to several timelines]
http://www.isoc.org/internet/history/index.shtml

A Brief History of the Internet and Related Networks
http://www.isoc.org/internet/history/cerf.shtml

A Brief History of the Internet
http://www.isoc.org/internet-history/brief.html

WDVL's History of the Internet and the World Wide Web
http://wdvl.Internet.com/Internet/History/

Hobbes' Internet Timeline
http://www.isoc.org/zakon/Internet/History/HIT.html

The History of the Net
http://www.ocean.ic.net/ftp/doc/nethist.html

PBS Life on the Internet
http://www.pbs.org/internet/timeline/timeline-txt.html

History of the Internet and WWW: The Roads and Crossroads of Internet History, Gregory R. Gromov
http://www.netvalley.com/intval.html

History of the Internet and WWW: Growth of the Internet: Statistics
http://www.netvalley.com/intvalstat.html

Internet Growth, Dave Marsh (circa August 1997)
http://www.netvalley.com/archives/mirrors/davemarsh-stats-1.htm

History of the Internet, Dave Marsh (1997)
http://www.netvalley.com/archives/mirrors/davemarsh-timeline-1.htm

Internet Pioneers
http://www.ibiblio.org/pioneers/

Building the Information Superhighway (speech by Vice President Al Gore on September 19, 1994)
http://www.robson.org/gary/captioning/gorespeech.html

A Little History of the WWW [Historical archives of the W3C]
http://www.w3.org/History.html

Information Management: A Proposal (March 1989, May 1990; Tim Berners-Lee, CERN) [original proposal of the WWW, HTMLized]
http://www.w3.org/History/1989/proposal.html

WorldWideWeb: Proposal for a HyperText Project (November 12, 1990; T. Berners-Lee/CN, R. Cailliau/ECP)
http://www.w3.org/Proposal

Bruce Sterling's Short History of the Internet (*The Magazine of Fantasy and Science Fiction*, February 1993)
http://www.forthnet.gr/forthnet/isoc/short.history.of.internet

Sputnik and the Origins of the Space Age
http://www.hq.nasa.gov/office/pao/History/sputnik/sputorig.html

Sputnik: The Shock of the Century
http://www.sputnikbook.com/intro.php

The Original Surfing the Internet
http://www.netmom.com/about/surfing_main.htm

Next Generation HTML XML Timeline
http://www.cen.com/ng-html/xml/xml-timeline.html

Bill Gates and the Internet
http://www.interesting-people.org/archive/1883.html

Microsoft Outlines Internet Commitment
http://www.microsoft.com/billgates/bio/1995.htm

W3C's XML Events/Publications Timeline
http://www.w3.org/XML/#events

Raggett on HTML 4, Dave Raggett et al.—Chapter 2: History of HTML [covers 1989–1997]
http://www.w3.org/People/Raggett/book4/ch02.html

Index DOT HTML [HTML and browser history]
http://www.blooberry.com/indexdot/html

Historical Style Sheet Proposals
http://www.w3.org/Style/History/

HTML to the Max: A Manifesto for Adding SGML Intelligence to the World-Wide Web
http://www.ncsa.uiuc.edu/SDG/IT94/Proceedings/Autools/sperberg-mcqueen/sperberg.html

W3C Standards Support in IE and the Netscape Gecko Browser Engine
http://home.netscape.com/browsers/future/standards.html

Shaping the Future of HTML (W3C Workshop)
http://www.w3.org/MarkUp/future/

The XML Revolution
http://helix.nature.com/webmatters/xml/xml.html

The Semantic Web
http://www.w3.org/Talks/1999/05/www8-tbl/slide1-0.html

Resources

ArborText's Getting Started with SGML
http://www.arbortext.com/Think_Tank/SGML_Resources/Getting_Started_with_SGML/getting_started_with_sgml.html

Nua Internet Surveys: How Many Online? [worldwide statistics]
http://www.nua.ie/surveys/how_many_online/

Defense Advanced Research Projects Agency (DARPA)
http://www.darpa.mil

National Aeronautics and Space Administration (NASA)
http://www.nasa.gov

Computer Emergency Response Team (CERT)
http://www.cert.org/

InterNIC
http://www.internic.net/

Network Solutions
http://www.networksolutions.com

IETF (Internet Engineering Task Force) Home Page
http://www.ietf.cnri.reston.va.us/home.html

Next Generation HTML, Ken Sall
http://www.cen.com/ng-html

Raggett on HTML 4, Dave Raggett, Jenny Lam, Ian Alexander, and Michael Kmiec (Addison-Wesley, 1998, ISBN 0-201-17805-2)
http://www.w3.org/People/Raggett/book4/ch01.html

Microsoft XML Parser Technology Preview Release
http://msdn.microsoft.com/downloads/webtechnology/xml/msxml.asp

Mailing List: XML-DEV
http://www.xml.org/xml/xmldev.shtml

W3C Specifications and Information

HTML Home Page (W3C)
http://www.w3.org/MarkUp

HTML 1.0
http://www.w3.org/History/19921103-hypertext/hypertext/WWW/MarkUp/MarkUp.html

HTML 2.0 (RFC 1866)
http://www.w3.org/MarkUp/html-spec/

HTML 3.0 Specification
http://www.w3.org/MarkUp/html3/CoverPage

HTML 3.2 Specification
http://www.w3.org/TR/REC-html32

HTML 4.0 specification
http://www.w3.org/TR/REC-html4

Tim Berners-Lee's home page at W3C
http://www.w3.org/People/Berners-Lee/

First XML Working Draft (November 1996)
http://www.w3.org/TR/WD-xml-961114.html

Notes

All addresses and phone numbers used in this book are fictitious.

Nick Danger, Betty Jo Bialowsky, Rocky Rococo, George Tirebiter, Ralph Spoilsports Motors, and Shoes For Industry are fictional characters or concepts appearing in Firesign Theatre comedy routines. Firesign Threatre, an original comedy group, has been performing and recording since the late 1960s; the group consists of Phil Austin, Peter Bergman, David Ossman, and Phil Proctor. Visit *http://www.firesigntheatre.com/* for audio and video samples of Firesign Theatre. Many of their recordings are available at *https://www.lodestone-media.com/firesign.html*.

All screen captures were created using Jasc Paint Shop Pro. Please note the following with regard to vendors' copyrights:

- Netscape browser window views © 2000–2002 Netscape Communications Corporation.
- Internet Explorer browser window views © 2000–2002 Microsoft Corporation.
- Opera browser window views © 2001–2002 Opera Software.
- Amaya browser window views © 2001–2002 World Wide Web Consortium (W3C).
- XML Spy editor views © 2001–2002 Altova GmbH, Altova, Inc.
- TurboXML editor views © 2001–2002 TIBCO Extensibility.
- IML and AIML code used with permission from NASA (for more information contact: Troy.J.Ames.1@gsfc.nasa.gov).

Part I

Fundamental XML Concepts, Syntax, and Modeling

Chapter 2

Overview of the XML Family of Specifications

The chapter is intended for newcomers to XML who are looking for a gentle, broad, but not overly technical introduction. In this chapter, we discuss what XML is, what it looks like, and how it meets a wide variety of needs. We also preview the family of XML specifications from a very high level and from several viewpoints. Most of the specifications mentioned in this chapter are covered in greater detail later in the book. Many of the terms and concepts presented in this chapter are formally presented in subsequent chapters. Appendix A summarizes the specifications and will help you feel more comfortable with the inevitable forward references, especially if you start drowning in acronym soup. The Big Picture diagram (see inside front cover) is useful for capturing all the acronyms in one place and showing how certain specifications are related.

Fixing the Web

If it ain't broke, don't fix it. That's what some people might say with respect to the World Wide Web. After all, millions of people surf the Web every day—homemakers searching for a recipe, investors seeking the latest stock quotes, students researching the assassination of Abraham Lincoln, readers purchasing the latest novel from an online e-commerce site. The Web seems to work well for them.

Or does it? Let's kick the tires a bit to see if the Web can take it. The sections that follow discuss a few of the problems that hindered the pre-XML Web and beg for solutions using the XML family of specifications, which collectively are the next generation (or "now" generation, if you prefer) of Internet technologies.

HTML Standards Change Too Slowly

During most of the Web's history, there have been essentially only three major versions of the HTML specification: HTML 2.0, HTML 3.2, and HTML 4.0. (HTML 1.0

predates almost all Web sites. At the time of this writing, the current version is HTML 4.01.) When HTML 3.2 was finally approved in January 1997, it was more of a rubber stamp of then-current practices than an innovation because nearly all of the elements it defined had been in use unofficially for as long as a year. It simply took too long for the World Wide Web Consortium (W3C) to agree on the specification (presumably due largely to the browser-specific extensions discussed next).

Browser-Specific Extensions Are Problematic

In 1996, prior to HTML 3.2, Netscape and Microsoft began the unfortunate practice of introducing their own "extensions" to the HTML language. This was partially a result of the competition that existed between these two major browser vendors and partially a result of the unacceptable amount of time it took for the W3C members to agree on the introduction of new tags, more properly called *elements,* such as `CENTER`, `EMBED`, `IFRAME`, and so on. This was (and still is) an endless cause of headaches for content developers who struggled to make their pages accessible to all users while needing to use the latest features introduced by the browser vendors. Less ambitious authors succumbed to the "This site best viewed with {Netscape/Microsoft}" virus which has contributed to some truly horrible sites. These authors forgot that the Web isn't truly "World Wide" if Web developers entrench themselves in different camps and embrace extensions that aren't universally supported.

No Meaningful Markup of Data

HTML was originally intended to provide a simple way to mark up any type of document to reflect its structure (title, major headings, minor headings, lists, etc.) as well as some stylistic aspects (bold, italics, etc.). Add to this the hypertext linking capability HTML offered, as well as browser support for a long list of MIME types, and it isn't hard to understand the phenomenal rate at which the Web developed, especially since Web authoring fell within the capabilities of grade school students. HTML was (and still is) great for marking up documents. However, in today's Web-oriented world, businesses and scientists also need the Web to exchange *data.* A new language was needed to express the hierarchical relationship of data, such as that which is represented by e-commerce transactions (messages) database records and object hierarchies. HTML reflects presentation, but conveys little about the *structure* of the marked-up document.

In particular, exchange of data between organizations and within divisions of a single organization requires a language that is capable of expressing the structure of data, as well as datatypes of each element. This is important to enterprise integration, for data validation, and so on. Data interchange may require filtering data as it's passed between applications, supplying default values, integrating data from multiple sources, and verifying that the data values are of the appropriate type or within a certain value range.

Presentation Is Often Fixed for Monitors

By nature HTML is focused primarily on the presentation of information, not on data structure. As we will see, if we are interested in conveying data in a way that is independent of the device on which it will be displayed, HTML is very limiting. In fact, as many Web developers know only too well, when HTML is displayed on screens of different resolutions, the rigidity of HTML makes it difficult to accommodate even the standard monitor sizes. In today's Web environment, in which the Internet reaches not only desktop computers, but also to laptops, handheld devices, Web TV, and more, it is crucial to be able to repurpose the same information for devices with widely different layout constraints. For example, if we want to display a table with a wide navigation bar on the right side, this might be fine for a large display, but an alternative presentation is necessary for a Palm Pilot. Perhaps the navigation graphics need to be replaced by a horizontal row of menus across the top. Creating completely different layouts of every page for an assortment of devices is extremely time intensive, as well as a major maintenance headache. What is needed is a way to separate the information (content) from the way that it is displayed.

Content Changes Cause Problems

What happens when the content changes? Someone has to update a set of pages for every change, which is clearly not efficient. Consider a complex, data-intensive Web site such as that of Dell Computers (*www.dell.com*). In 1999 Dell realized that it had a major content management problem. Prices and computer configurations changed quite frequently. This information was embedded in many Web pages because the same content (software, accessories, etc.) could be presented in different computer configurations. Whenever the prices or part numbers changed, numerous pages had to be updated. (Dell switched to XML, as discussed in detail in *Mastering XML* by Navarro, White, and Burman, 2000.)

Browser Paradigm Is Too Constraining

With the advent of Java and JavaScript, the Web browser quickly became far more than merely a tool for surfing the Web; it became the launcher of applications. However, often the browser gets in the way of the application. Customers want applications that look and feel more like their familiar desktop tools, such as word processors and spreadsheets. While MIME-type content handling helps in this regard, there are times when the browser paradigm just doesn't make sense. Even if you can "lose the chrome" (i.e., remove the browser menus and controls), sometimes there is a need to pass information between two or more cooperating applications. What we really need is Web-enabled applications—programs that understand common Internet protocols such as HTTP—so we can access Web resources without using a browser. This is not science fiction; more and more companies are creating such applications, especially since languages like Java simplify the use of Internet protocols, as well as make reading and writing HTML easy.

Search Engines Need Better Focusing

Unless you become a master of your favorite search engines by learning their similar yet annoyingly different query syntax, you'll undoubtedly receive hundreds or even thousands more hits than you have time or patience to examine. If you're incredibly lucky (or skillful), the reference you're looking for may be in the first page or two of results—but don't count on it. The problem is that most search engines can only index frequency of words, document titles, filenames, and, in some cases, meta tags that describe the contents of a page. What is needed, however, is a way to mark up the significant portions of a document and to convey the semantics of the information so search engines can ignore the noise and focus on the signal. Sometimes searches require a finer granularity of control than most search engines permit. For example, how would you search for books *written by* Paul McCartney, rather than books that refer to him, or to the Beatles, or Wings? If the words "Paul McCartney" could be tagged as `<Author>Paul McCartney</Author>` to indicate a specific meaning, such finely tuned searches would eventually become possible, as soon as search engines consider the tags as well as the content, that is. An example of such an XML-friendly search engine is GoXML at *http://www.xmlglobal.com*.

Can't Specify Collections of Related Pages

Often you encounter a Web page that is obviously part of a larger collection. You may be lucky enough to find a link to a table of contents, a home page, or some other means of listing or navigating the collection. But how do you print the collection? Current answer: very slowly, one HTML file at a time. There has to be a better way to express the interrelationship of a set of pages so they can be processed as a group. We need to be able to attach metadata ("information about information" or "machine-understandable information") to Web pages to express the relationships among pages of the same document, as well as among different documents. Resource Description Framework (RDF) is helpful in this regard.

One-Way Linking Is Too Limited

Although the Web's current one-way hypertext link capability has proved extremely useful, did you know that far more flexible schemes have existed for many years in the publishing industry? Since 1992 Hypermedia/Time-based Structuring Language (HyTime) and the Text Encoding Initiative (TEI) have enabled publishers to express complex link relationships, such as links with multiple targets, multidirectional links, and automatically updated link databases. We need a richer linking language for the Web.

In summary, HTML together with CGI scripts, Java applets, JavaScript (and its derivatives), and plugins such as Shockwave, Flash, RealPlayer, and Quicktime provide Web authors and commercial sites with a rich array of techniques for displaying *content* that is visually compelling and possibly even informative. However, these techniques do little if anything for the representation of structured data unless proprietary middleware solutions such as ColdFusion or WebObjects are introduced. Although such solutions may suffice in some situations, there are ever-increasing needs to share data across a wide variety of applications from different vendors and often located across corporate boundaries and firewalls. A vendor-neutral, platform-independent solution is needed.

Enter XML and Its Many Benefits

What is the solution to all of these limitations of the first-generation Web? The Extensible Markup Language. XML is a non-mutually exclusive alternative to HTML and the pre-XML technologies. XML provides a basic syntax for creating markup languages that describe data. In contrast to HTML which describes document structure and visual presentation, XML describes data in a human readable format with no indication of how the data is to be displayed. It is therefore device independent, a perfect solution to the problem of repurposing data for different screen sizes and different devices. XML may look like HTML, but it is in fact much closer to Standard Generalized Markup Language (SGML) discussed in chapter 1. Like SGML, XML is a metalanguage, but it's less complex than SGML. It has been said that XML provides 80 percent of the benefit of SGML with 20 percent of the effort.

But more important than being human readable, is the fact that XML is *machine understandable,* meaning that its self-describing structure makes it possible for it to be parsed easily by any one of a number of (typically free) XML parsers. Parsers and XML APIs exist in every major computer progamming language—Java, C++, C, perl, Python, and so on. In fact, the number of tools that support XML is quite impressive. All the major software companies that previously concentrated on SGML tools now have stripped-down (and usually cheaper) XML versions of their flagship products. In addition, major software companies including Sun, Microsoft, Oracle, and IBM have a wide variety of software that supports XML.

How is this self-description possible? Well, XML is a metalanguage used to define other domain- or industry-specific languages. To construct your own XML language (also called a "vocabulary" or an "application" of XML), you supply a specific *Document Type Definition (DTD),* which is essentially a context-free grammar like the Extended BNF (Backus Naur Form) used to describe computer languages. In other words, a DTD provides the rules that define the elements and structure of your new language. We will consider a specific example in the next section.

The fact that XML supports the creation of languages that are highly structured and well-formed contributes to another of the major benefits; that is, XML is *easily verifiable.* An XML message or document must follow an internally consistent structure to be *well-formed* XML. If it does not follow the XML syntax rules (presented in the next chapter), it cannot be considered an XML document. Furthermore, if it includes a reference to a DTD or XML Schema, the content can also be *validated* for correctness and integrity, according to the model described in the DTD or XML Schema. Furthermore, XML is a database-neutral and device-neutral format; data marked up in XML can be targeted to different devices using *Extensible Stylesheet Language (XSL).*

The advent of Extensible HyperText Markup Language (XHTML), an XML application language, is a carefully planned progression of a set of specifications that is already weening bleeding-edge Web developers, especially those interested in handheld devices, away from HTML and toward XML.

It is crucial to understand that XML is fundamentally a *data representation format and syntax.* It is not a programming language like Java nor a scripting language like perl. However, by leveraging these programming and scripting languages XML becomes truly useful since processing XML requires the use of software that can interface with parsers. Sun Microsystems and others have justifiably touted the catch phrase "portable code, portable data" to emphasize the powerful combination of Java for platform-independent processing and XML for platform-independent data representation.

In the remainder of this chapter, we discuss the various members of the ever-expanding XML family of specifications. For a convenient alphabetical summary of the major XML specifications, see Appendix A. I also recommend *The Pros and Cons of XML,* a free report from ZapThink Research, available from *http://www.zapthink.com/reports/proscons.html.* This excellent report presents roughly eighteen advantages of XML, as well as nine arguments that challenge XML.

What Does XML Look Like?

XML looks like HTML in that it consists of start and end tags (that mark up elements) with content (character data or other elements) between them. The best way to understand how it differs from HTML is to consider an example of information that could be marked up in either HTML or XML.

Presentation vs. Structure

Suppose we wish to create a table that reflects employee contact information, such as name, sex, job title, projects, e-mail, multiple phone numbers, and home address. One approach would be to represent this information using HTML 4.01, as shown in Listing 2-1 (see filename `employee-directory.html` on the CD-ROM that accompanies this book; see also Notes on page 32).

Listing 2-1 HTML Employee Information (employee-directory.html)

```
<!DOCTYPE html PUBLIC "-//W3C//DTD HTML 4.01 Transitional//EN"
          "http://www.w3.org/TR/html4/loose.dtd">
<html>
  <head>
    <title>Employee Directory</title>
  </head>
  <body>
    <h1 align="center">Employee Directory</h1>
    <table align="center" cellspacing="2" cellpadding="2" border="1">
      <tr>
        <th>Name<br>
        (sex)</th>
        <th>Title</th>
        <th>Projects</th>
        <th>Email</th>
        <th>Office Phone/<br>
         Home Phone/<br>
         Cell Phone</th>
        <th>Address</th>
      </tr>
      <tr>
        <td><b>Ken Sall</b><br>
        (male)</td>
        <td>Sr. Software Engineer</td>
        <td>Writing book, developing XML training course,
        SmallProject</td>
        <td><i>Ken.Sall@home.com</i></td>
        <td>555-abc-1234<br>
         555-xyz-1234<br>
         443-abc-0987</td>
        <td>123 Milky Way<br>
         Columbia, MD 20777</td>
      </tr>
      <tr>
        <td><b>Betty Jo Bialowsky</b><br>
        (female)</td>
        <!-- aka: Melanie Haber, Audrey Farber, Susan Underhill, Nancy -->
        <td>Project Leader</td>
        <td>MegaProject, SmallProject, others</td>
        <td><i>BettyJo.Bialowsky@home.com</i></td>
        <td>555-abc-1235<br>
         555-xyz-4321<br>
         555-pqr-1267</td>
        <td>321 Carmel Court<br>
         Columbia, MD 20777</td>
```

```
      </tr>
      <tr>
        <td><b>Nick Danger</b><br>
        (male)</td>
        <td>Technical Lead</td>
        <td>ThirdEye Project</td>
        <td><i>Nick.Danger@home.com</i></td>
        <td>555-abc-1236<br>
         555-xyz-2222<br>
         555-pqr-1268</td>
        <td>456 Pickup Sticks Lane<br>
         Columbia, MD 20777</td>
      </tr>
    </table>
  </body>
</html>
```

This HTML can be rendered in any browser (such as Netscape 6), as shown in Figure 2-1. This table looks fine and might meet certain basic needs. But what if our requirements include some flexibility in the processing and displaying of the employee information? Suppose we need to be able to display employee information based sometimes on projects and sometimes by job title? Perhaps some day we'll need to sort the employee records by sex. Maybe we want to leave open the possibility of adding a column, such as number of years with the company, which could also become the basis for sorting.

HTML would no longer be a good choice for our markup language because it does not permit this flexibility. That is, HTML is all about presentation (display) of information, and has very little to do with the structure of the data. For example, although our table shows a column entitled "Name," there is nothing inherent in the markup that tells the browser that it is rendering a name. The HTML fragment

```
<td><b>Ken Sall</b><br>(male)</td>
```

informs the browser: "Here is a cell of the table. Render the string 'Ken Sall' in bold font, break a line, and output the string '(male)'." There no notion that a person's name is the content of this HTML example; nor is there a distinction between first and last names. Nor is the string that indicates sex identified in any special way, other than appearing at the beginning of a line. In fact, the browser is merely rendering text with no knowledge of the data that the text represents. As humans, we recognize that this example represents information about an employee: name, phone, address, and so on. However, the elements used to mark up this snippet do not in fact reveal any such interpretation! The markup merely describes how the lines should be displayed. When the HTML is processed by the browser, no semantics can be inferred; your poor computer has no understanding of the kind of information being rendered.

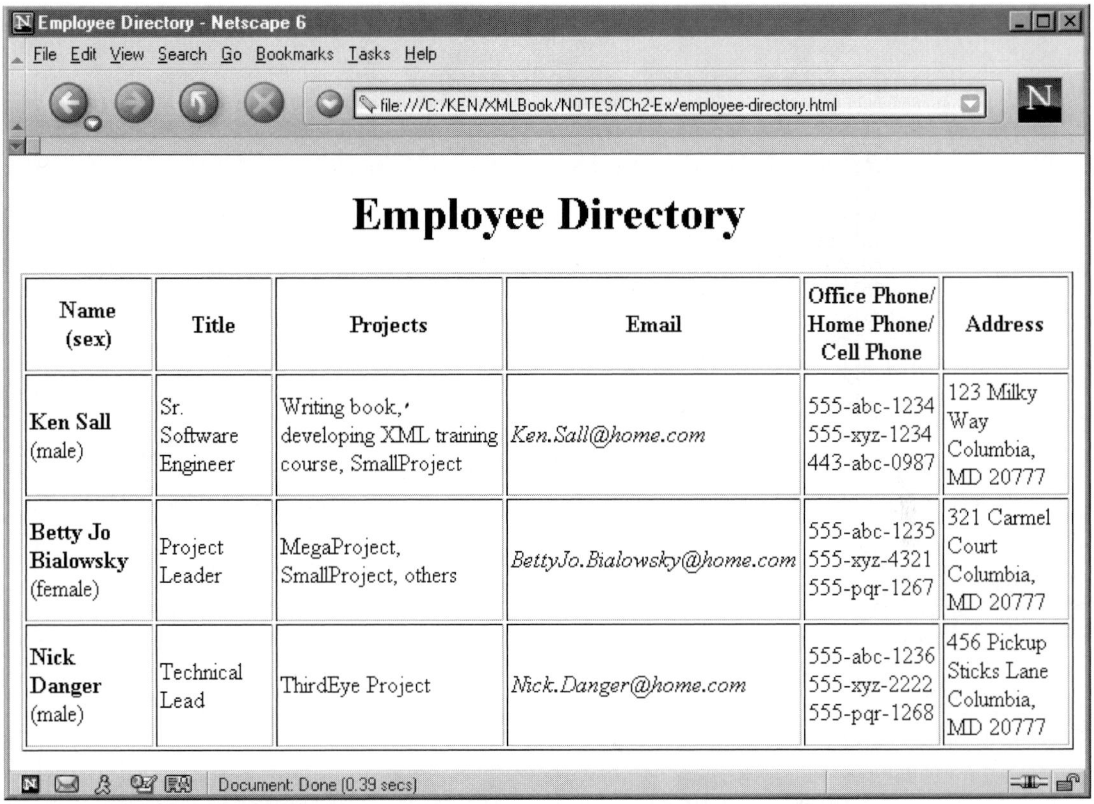

Employee Directory - Netscape 6

File Edit View Search Go Bookmarks Tasks Help

file:///C:/KEN/XMLBook/NOTES/Ch2-Ex/employee-directory.html

Employee Directory

Name (sex)	Title	Projects	Email	Office Phone/ Home Phone/ Cell Phone	Address
Ken Sall (male)	Sr. Software Engineer	Writing book,' developing XML training course, SmallProject	*Ken.Sall@home.com*	555-abc-1234 555-xyz-1234 443-abc-0987	123 Milky Way Columbia, MD 20777
Betty Jo Bialowsky (female)	Project Leader	MegaProject, SmallProject, others	*BettyJo.Bialowsky@home.com*	555-abc-1235 555-xyz-4321 555-pqr-1267	321 Carmel Court Columbia, MD 20777
Nick Danger (male)	Technical Lead	ThirdEye Project	*Nick.Danger@home.com*	555-abc-1236 555-xyz-2222 555-pqr-1268	456 Pickup Sticks Lane Columbia, MD 20777

Document: Done (0.39 secs)

FIGURE 2-1 HTML representation of employee information

Notes: All addresses and phone numbers used in this book are fictitious. For information on names used in this book, see Notes on page 32.

In the XML world, we have essentially the reverse situation. We want to model data in terms of its structure, while initially ignoring specific considerations of how it will be rendered (other than maximizing the flexibility).

XML Representation with a DTD

Let's consider a possible XML representation of the same information that conveys the relationships of various data objects. How should we model this information in XML? One approach is to implement a basic hierachical structure for our data, as shown in Figure 2-2 (screenshot produced using the XML Authority component of TurboXML suite by TIBCO Extensibility). Listing 2-2 shows an XML representation of this hierarchy filled in with the data from the HTML.

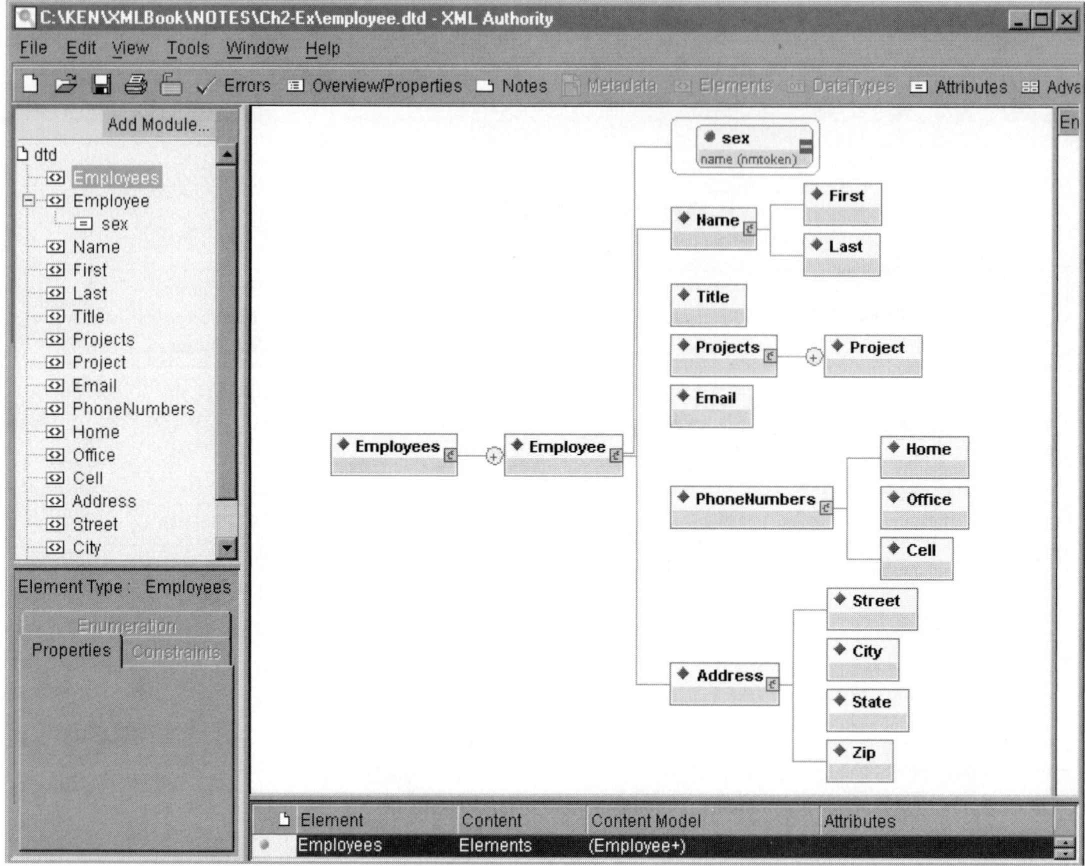

FIGURE 2-2 Graphical view of employee DTD in TurboXML

Listing 2-2 Employee Information, XML Version (employee-directory.xml)

```
<?xml version='1.0' standalone='no'?>
<!DOCTYPE Employees SYSTEM "employee.dtd" >
<Employees>
  <Employee sex="male">
    <Name>
      <First>Ken</First>
      <Last>Sall</Last>
    </Name>
    <Title>Sr. Software Engineer</Title>
    <Projects>
      <Project>Writing book</Project>
      <Project>developing XML training course</Project>
      <Project>SmallProject</Project>
    </Projects>
    <Email>Ken.Sall@home.com</Email>
```

```
    <PhoneNumbers>
      <Home>555-abc-1234</Home>
      <Office>555-xyz-1234</Office>
      <Cell>n/a</Cell>
    </PhoneNumbers>
    <Address>
      <Street>123 Milky Way</Street>
      <City>Columbia</City>
      <State>MD</State>
      <Zip>20777</Zip>
    </Address>
  </Employee>
  <Employee sex="female">
    <Name>
      <First>Betty Jo</First>
      <Last>Bialowsky</Last>
      <!-- aka: Melanie Haber, Audrey Farber, Susan Underhill, Nancy -->
    </Name>
    <Title>Project Leader</Title>
    <Projects>
      <Project>MegaProject</Project>
      <Project>SmallProject</Project>
      <Project>others</Project>
    </Projects>
    <Email>BettyJo.Bialowsky@home.com</Email>
    <PhoneNumbers>
      <Home>555-abc-1235</Home>
      <Office>555-xyz-4321</Office>
      <Cell>555-pqr-1267</Cell>
    </PhoneNumbers>
    <Address>
      <Street>321 Carmel Court</Street>
      <City>Columbia</City>
      <State>MD</State>
      <Zip>20777</Zip>
    </Address>
  </Employee>
  <Employee sex="male">
    <Name>
      <First>Nick</First>
      <Last>Danger</Last>
    </Name>
    <Title>Technical Lead</Title>
    <Projects>
      <Project>ThirdEye Project</Project>
    </Projects>
    <Email>Nick.Danger@home.com</Email>
    <PhoneNumbers>
      <Home>555-abc-1236</Home>
      <Office>555-xyz-2222</Office>
      <Cell>555-pqr-1268</Cell>
    </PhoneNumbers>
    <Address>
      <Street>456 Pickup Sticks Lane</Street>
      <City>Columbia</City>
```

```
      <State>MD</State>
      <Zip>20777</Zip>
    </Address>
  </Employee>
</Employees>
```

We won't concern ourselves at this point with the details of the syntax of XML, except to make a few significant observations:

- Each conceptual piece of information is represented by its own element, represented by an angle-bracketed name, similar to HTML tags.
- Related data items are grouped under container elements. For example, `<Name>` contains `<First>` and `<Last>`, and `<Address>` contains `<Street>`, `<City>`, `<State>` and `<Zip>`.
- The second line contains a reference to a DTD.
- None of the elements (tags) are part of HTML. In fact, they are part of the custom language defined by the DTD, `employee.dtd` (Listing 2-3).

Note that in the XML representation, there is no description of how to display the content. While this might at first appear to be undesirable, the separation of content from visual representation makes possible several of the benefits described later in this chapter.

The advantage of XML in this example is that it preserves the structure of the data. We can think of this information as hierarchical data. The parallels to database records should be obvious.

So, what does the DTD that describes our employee data hierarchy look like? See Listing 2-3.

Listing 2-3 DTD for Employee Information (employee.dtd)

```
<!ELEMENT Employees ( Employee+ ) >
<!ELEMENT Employee ( Name, Title, Projects, Email, PhoneNumbers, Address ) >
<!ATTLIST Employee sex NMTOKEN #REQUIRED >
<!ELEMENT Name ( First, Last ) >
<!ELEMENT First ( #PCDATA ) >
<!ELEMENT Last ( #PCDATA ) >
<!ELEMENT Title ( #PCDATA ) >
<!ELEMENT Projects ( Project+ ) >
<!ELEMENT Project ( #PCDATA ) >
<!ELEMENT Email ( #PCDATA ) >
<!ELEMENT PhoneNumbers ( Home, Office, Cell ) >
<!ELEMENT Home ( #PCDATA ) >
<!ELEMENT Office ( #PCDATA ) >
<!ELEMENT Cell ( #PCDATA ) >
<!ELEMENT Address ( Street, City, State, Zip ) >
<!ELEMENT Street ( #PCDATA ) >
<!ELEMENT City ( #PCDATA ) >
<!ELEMENT State ( #PCDATA ) >
<!ELEMENT Zip ( #PCDATA ) >
```

Well, that certainly doesn't look like HTML! However, it does convey the structure quite nicely, once you get used to the weird syntax, that is. Again deferring the many details until next chapter, we note that an `Employee` consists of the elements `Name`, `Title`, `Projects`, `Email`, `PhoneNumbers`, and `Address`, and also that a `Name` has both a `First` and `Last` component, and so forth. The DTD also defines the order of elements, so the first name must appear before last name, based on the rule:

```
<!ELEMENT Name ( First, Last ) >
```

As we will see, DTD rules can also indicate whether any of the nested elements is optional, whether it can be repeated, and if it has a default value.

It is important to understand that any browser (or XML-aware application) that uses an XML parser *could* interpret our employee document instance by "learning" the rules defined by the DTD. The new elements of this Employee Markup Language did not require browser extensions or a committee with representatives from different companies to decide on what they should be. XML gives you the freedom and power to create your own application-specific, company-specific, or domain-specific structured language.

Strictly speaking, a DTD is not absolutely necessary. XML parsers can process documents without a DTD because all XML documents are well-formed; they follow a handful of basic syntax rules, enabling parsers to split XML data into elements, attributes, and content. However, in a more complex XML vocabulary, the presence of a DTD (or something called an XML Schema) is very likely.

We can visualize the data hierarchy better by viewing our DTD in a tool such as the XML Authority component of TurboXML by TIBCO Extensibility, as shown in Figure 2-2.

Our XML example can be displayed (although perhaps not exactly as you might think!) in any XML-aware browser such as Internet Explorer 5.5, Opera 6, and Netscape 6 (or later). The default views in Netscape 6 and IE 5.5 are shown in Figures 2-3 and 2-4, respectively. Opera displays XML the same way that Netscape

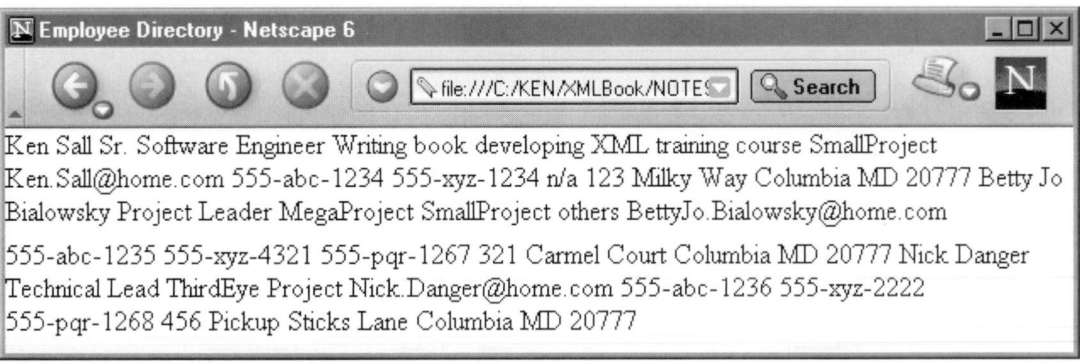

FIGURE 2-3 Default view of employee XML in Netscape 6.2

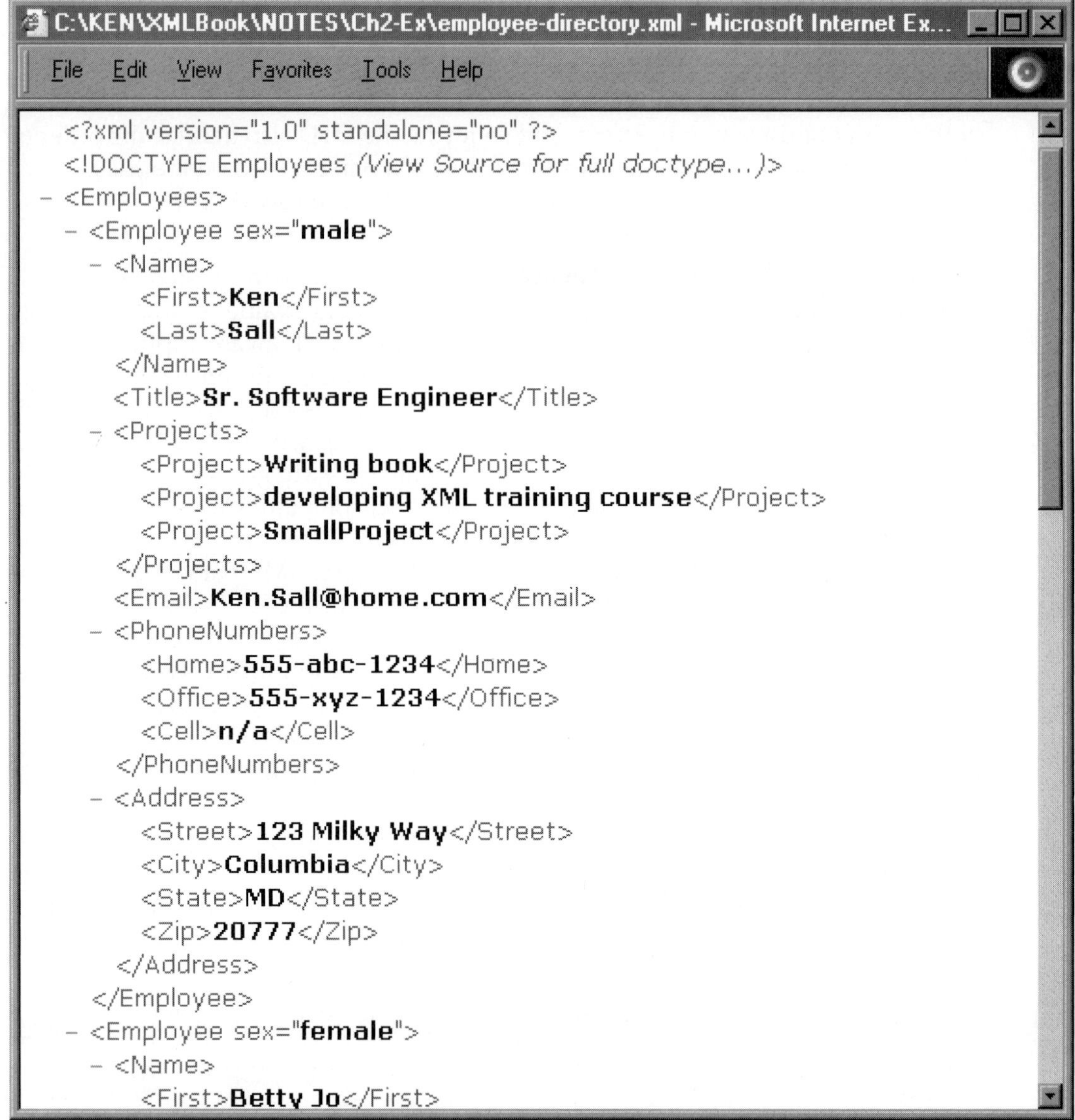

FIGURE 2-4 Default view of employee XML in Internet Explorer 5.5

does, which is simply to display the text content without the tags and without line breaks, indentation, or styling. Internet Explorer, in contrast, applies a built-in stylesheet that renders XML in a collapsible tree view. While the IE representation of XML "looks pretty" and is certainly useful for humans who want to see what the XML looks like structurally, actually the Netscape and Opera representations are more "correct" in the pure sense that there is no style information whatsoever contained in our XML document. In particular, there is no reference to an external Cascading Style Sheet or XSLT stylesheet, and no CSS or XSLT internal to the XML instance, so simply displaying the text content (PCDATA, as we'll soon learn) is the only reasonable action. XML is displayed as a tree by Internet Explorer because Microsoft applies a built-in stylesheet to render the document, unless the content provider overrides this default by supplying a customized stylesheet.

Document-Centric vs. Data-Centric

XML documents can be either document-centric or data-centric. **Document-centric** instances have lots of text (PCDATA, as we'll learn) mixed with "markup" (angle-bracketed elements). This is called a **mixed content model** because child elements can be mixed with content. For example, consider this possible XML representation of a simple purchase order.

```
<Purchase-Order>
   Please ship <Quantity>12</Quantity>
   crates of sku#<SKU>34521</SKU> to customer
   <Customer>George Tirebiter</Customer>
   by <Ship-Date>April 30, 2001</Ship-Date> at
   <Price>17.95</Price> each.
</Purchase-Order>
```

Although it contains the essential information (Quantity, SKU, Customer, Ship-Date, and Price), there is no hierarchy except that everything is contained within the Purchase-Order element. This outer element also contains text strings such as "Please ship" and "crates of sku#".

Is this a good representation of a purchase order? Certainly not! A mixed content model is more appropriate for documents, in which text is intermixed with formatting information such as Bold, Emphasis, Italics, and Paragraph. A document-centric approach is therefore useful for manuals, books, magazines, and other desktop publishing situations.

This approach, however, is inadequate when modeling hierarchical data, which typically requires a **data-centric** paradigm in which documents have an even more well-defined structure. Consider this alternative purchase order hierarchy:

```
<Purchase-Order>
   <SKU>34521</SKU>
   <Price>17.95</Price>
   <Quantity>12</Quantity>
   <Ship-Date>
      <Year>2001</Year>
      <Month>4</Month>
      <Day>30</Day>
```

```
    </Ship-Date>
    <Customer>
        <Last>Tirebiter</Last>
        <First>George</First>
    </Customer>
</Purchase-Order>
```

Note that there is no extraneous text. All informational content is nestled within elements (that is, their start and end tags). Although we can't be certain without a DTD, it's highly likely that the sequence shown is invariant: first comes `SKU`, then `Price`, then `Quantity`, then `Ship-Date`, and finally `Customer`. Within `Ship-Date`, we've added `Year`, `Month`, and `Day`, also with an implied order. The `Customer` element also encloses children now, namely `Last` and `First`. This hierarchy means we can more readily extract the individual data items that we need, such as the month or last name, by specifying the path to the element. (We'll see this a bit more concretely in the section "XPath Language" later in this chapter.) Data-centric models are easier for a computer to process because the information is well structured and predictable, making this a better representation choice for business and scientific applications.

Processing XML with XSLT

The beauty of representing employee information in XML rather than in HTML is that we can subsequently filter or sort the data or repurpose it for different devices using *Extensible Stylesheet Language Transformations (XSLT)*. First, we'll extract only the value of the elements `Last`, `First`, `Email`, and `Cell` (but not other `Phone-Numbers`), sorted alphabetically by last name. The XSLT stylesheet needed to accomplish this is shown in Listing 2-4 and the result of viewing our input XML document to which this stylesheet has been applied appears in Figure 2-5. Again, we'll defer the discussion of exactly how to apply the stylesheet until chapter 11.

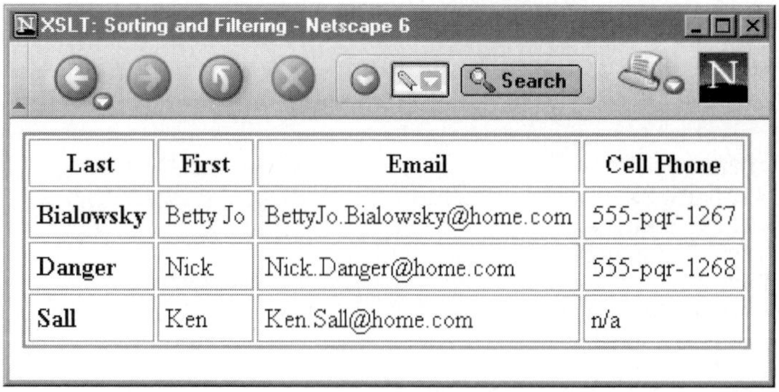

XSLT: Sorting and Filtering - Netscape 6

Last	First	Email	Cell Phone
Bialowsky	Betty Jo	BettyJo.Bialowsky@home.com	555-pqr-1267
Danger	Nick	Nick.Danger@home.com	555-pqr-1268
Sall	Ken	Ken.Sall@home.com	n/a

FIGURE 2-5 Sorted and filtered data using XSL Transformations

Suffice it to say at this point that we are using XSLT to transform XML into HTML, which then can be displayed by your garden-variety browser.

Listing 2-4 XSLT Stylesheet (employee-sort1.xsl)

```
<?xml version="1.0"?>
<xsl:stylesheet   version="1.0"
  xmlns:xsl="http://www.w3.org/1999/XSL/Transform">
<xsl:output method="html"/>

<xsl:variable name="label">XSLT: Sorting and Filtering</xsl:variable>

<xsl:template match="/">
   <html>
     <head>
       <title><xsl:value-of select="$label" /></title>
     </head>
     <body>
        <table border="2" bgcolor="white" cellpadding="4" cellspacing="2" >
          <tr>
            <th>Last</th>
            <th>First</th>
            <th>Email</th>
            <th>Cell Phone</th>
          </tr>
          <xsl:for-each select="Employees/Employee" >
          <xsl:sort order="ascending" select="Name/Last" />
          <tr>
            <td><b><xsl:value-of select="Name/Last"/></b></td>
            <td><xsl:value-of select="Name/First"/></td>
            <td><xsl:value-of select="Email"/></td>
            <xsl:choose>
            <xsl:when test="PhoneNumbers/Cell[. != '']">
              <td><xsl:value-of select="PhoneNumbers/Cell" /></td>
            </xsl:when>
            <xsl:otherwise>
              <td align="center">none</td>
            </xsl:otherwise>
            </xsl:choose>
          </tr>
        </xsl:for-each>
      </table>
     </body>
   </html>
</xsl:template>
</xsl:stylesheet>
```

Alternatively, we can extract `Projects`, `Last`, `First`, `Home` phone, and `Cell` phone, and sort in reverse alphabetical order by the first project listed for each employee, given by first `Project` element of the `Projects` parent element, referenced as `Projects/Project[1]`. We need to change only a few lines of the XSLT to accomplish this (ignoring changes for column headings).

```
<xsl:for-each select="Employees/Employee" >
 <xsl:sort order="descending" select="Projects/Project[1]" />
 <tr>
   <td><b><xsl:value-of select="Projects/Project[1]"/></b></td>
   <td><b><xsl:value-of select="Name/Last"/></b></td>
   <td><xsl:value-of select="Name/First"/></td>
   <td><xsl:value-of select="PhoneNumbers/Home"/></td>
   <!-- etc. -->
 </tr>
</xsl:for-each>
```

The result of applying the modified stylesheet to the original XML input file, `employee-directory.xml`, appears in Figure 2-6.

Now suppose we need to list *all* of the `Projects` instead of just the first project. We need to change only the XSLT line that references the first `Project`

```
<td><b><xsl:value-of select="Projects/Project[1]"/></b></td>
```

to a `<xsl:for-each>` loop that iterates over all of the `Project` elements:

```
<xsl:for-each select="Employees/Employee" >
<xsl:sort order="descending" select="Projects/Project[1]" />
<tr>
  <td>
    <xsl:for-each select="Projects/Project" >
      <b><xsl:value-of select="."/></b><br />
    </xsl:for-each>
  </td>
<!-- etc. -->
```

The result is shown in Figure 2-7.

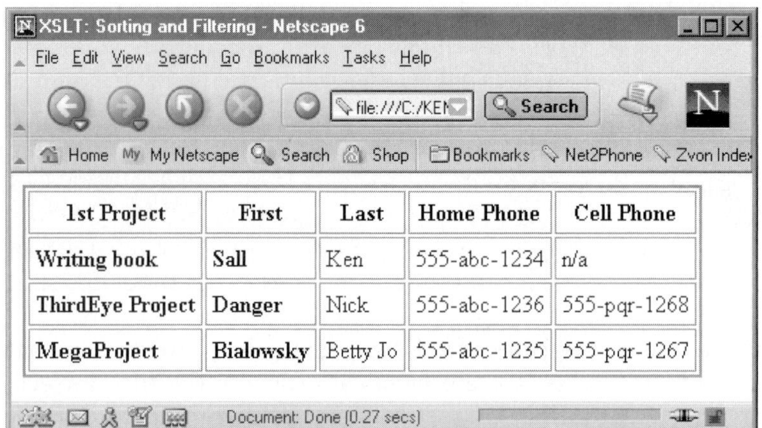

1st Project	First	Last	Home Phone	Cell Phone
Writing book	Sall	Ken	555-abc-1234	n/a
ThirdEye Project	Danger	Nick	555-abc-1236	555-pqr-1268
MegaProject	Bialowsky	Betty Jo	555-abc-1235	555-pqr-1267

FIGURE 2-6 Reverse sort by first project

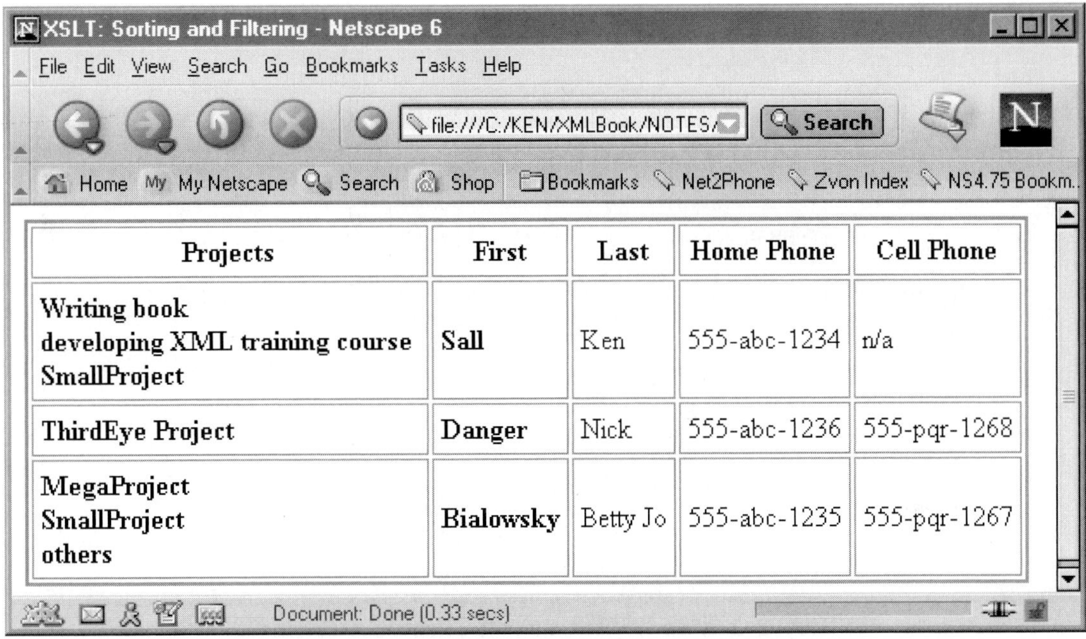

FIGURE 2-7 Project sort with multiple projects listed

Another possible ordering of this data is to sort by the `sex` attribute of the element `Employee`, as indicated in the start tag:

```
<Employee sex="male">
```

Again, this is easily accomplished just by changing a few lines of XSLT:

```
<xsl:for-each select="Employees/Employee" >
  <xsl:sort order="ascending" select="@sex" />
  <tr>
    <td><b><xsl:value-of select="@sex"/></b></td>
    <td>
      <xsl:for-each select="Projects/Project" >
        <b><xsl:value-of select="."/></b><br />
      </xsl:for-each>
    </td>
<!-- etc. -->
```

The output is shown in Figure 2-8. Notice that in this case we are keying off the attribute, illustrating that XML processing by XSLT can be fine grained.

Please don't think the point of this section is to give you a crash course in XSLT. We've got a huge chapter planned for that purpose much later. Instead, the aim is just to give you a good feeling about how flexible an XML format can be, in terms of changing needs in processing structured information. Don't get bogged down on any of the details (i.e., XSLT syntax) for now.

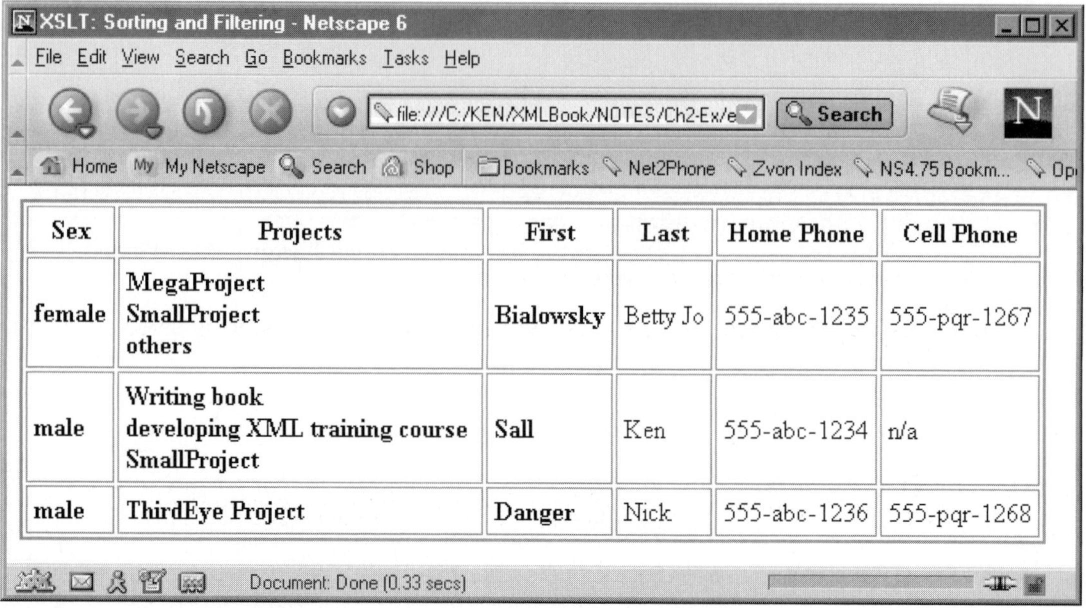

Sex	Projects	First	Last	Home Phone	Cell Phone
female	MegaProject SmallProject others	Bialowsky	Betty Jo	555-abc-1235	555-pqr-1267
male	Writing book developing XML training course SmallProject	Sall	Ken	555-abc-1234	n/a
male	ThirdEye Project	Danger	Nick	555-abc-1236	555-pqr-1268

FIGURE 2-8 Sort by sex attribute of employee element

XPath Language

There is also what is called a *Document Object Model (DOM),* an interface that can be implemented in Java, C++, Python, JavaScript, or ECMAScript, that accommodates our employees hierarchy. For example, we can reference the value of the last name of the second employee ("Bialowsky") like this:

```
doc.Employees.Employee[1].Name[0].Last[0].value
```

An expression language called *XML Path Language (XPath)* was developed in 1999 for use with both XSLT and XPointer, and eventually with XQuery. XPath uses UNIX-like pathnames and a few special characters to reference specific nested elements or attributes of elements. We already saw this notation in the slash-separated element names in the previous XSLT examples. The XPath expression[1] needed to extract the last name of second employee (Bialowsky) is:

```
/Employees/Employee[2]/Name/Last
```

The following XPath expression references the `sex` attribute of the `Employee` element using the XPath predicate `[@sex]`. More specifically, the expression selects the second *male* employee (as opposed to the second employee, in general), namely Nick Danger.

1. Note that indices in XPath begin with one, not zero.

```
/Employees/Employee[@sex = 'male'][2]
```

Two additional XPath examples, shown in Figure 2-9, use a handy little utility called XPathTester (see *http://www.fivesight.com/downloads/xpathtester.asp*) by FiveSight Technologies to apply an XPath expression to a particular XML document instance. The highlighted elements or attributes are those selected (that is, specified) by the expression. The `Last` name element of the first Employee (Sall) is selected by the XPath expression

```
/Employees/Employee[1]/Name/Last
```

whereas the `sex` attribute of the second employee (Bialowsky) is selected by the expression

```
/Employees/Employee[2]/@sex
```

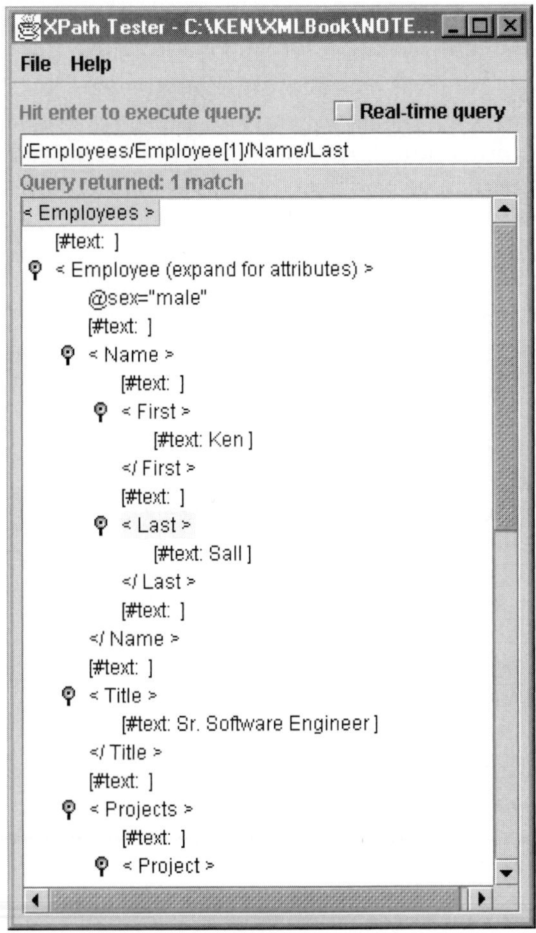

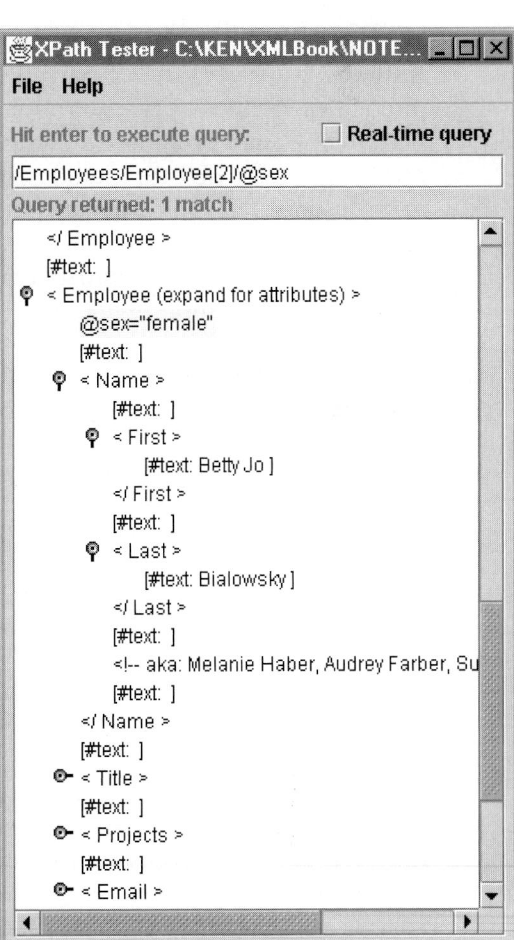

FIGURE 2-9 XPath expressions displayed by XPath Tester

The point of this section is that, in addition to powerful transformation of XML data by XSLT, we can use XPath to select specific elements from a hierarchical XML structure.

Benefits and Applications

Not only is XML good for transmission of data from server to browser, it is also ideal for passing data from application to application and from machine to machine (including between companies). Since XML is database-neutral, it has played a major role in connecting heterogeneous databases. In this section we examine a number of ways that XML can extend our Web solution set. For a summary of the relevant XML specifications, refer to Appendix A.

Domain-Specific Vocabularies

XML can be used to define new tags that all browsers with XML parsers can decipher (e.g., mathematical, astronomical, and graphics markup languages). XML vocabularies can provide a standard way for doctors to transmit prescriptions to pharmacists, for EDI transactions to be transmitted, for astronomical instruments to be described, and so on. Such languages can be horizontal-industry vocabularies (i.e., software distribution and e-commerce) or vertical-industry vocabularies (i.e., telecommunications and aerospace).

Less than two months after the XML specification became a W3C Recommendation, on April 7, 1998, the Mathematical Markup Language Specification (MathML) was approved as the first major XML vocabulary, a domain-specific language based on the XML metalanguage. According to the MathML Recommendation,

> MathML is an XML application for describing mathematical notation and capturing both its structure and content. The goal of MathML is to enable mathematics to be served, received, and processed on the World Wide Web. (*http://www.w3.org/TR/MathML2/*, accessed February 21, 2001)

The language supports rich mathematical notation with more than 100 domain-specific markup elements; it is intended to provide a basis for mathematical authoring tools to be used by scientists. In February 2000, the MathML 2.0 Working Draft was announced by the W3C. MathML Version 2.0 became a W3C Recommendation in February 2001. Amaya, the W3C browser, has native support for MathML, as illustrated in Figures 2-10 and Figure 2-11.

Netscape and Internet Explorer can render MathML with the help of the IBM Techexplorer Hypermedia Browser and plugin (see *http://www-4.ibm.com/software/network/techexplorer/*), which enables the display of MathML, TeX, and LaTeX, and therefore supports the publishing of interactive mathematical and

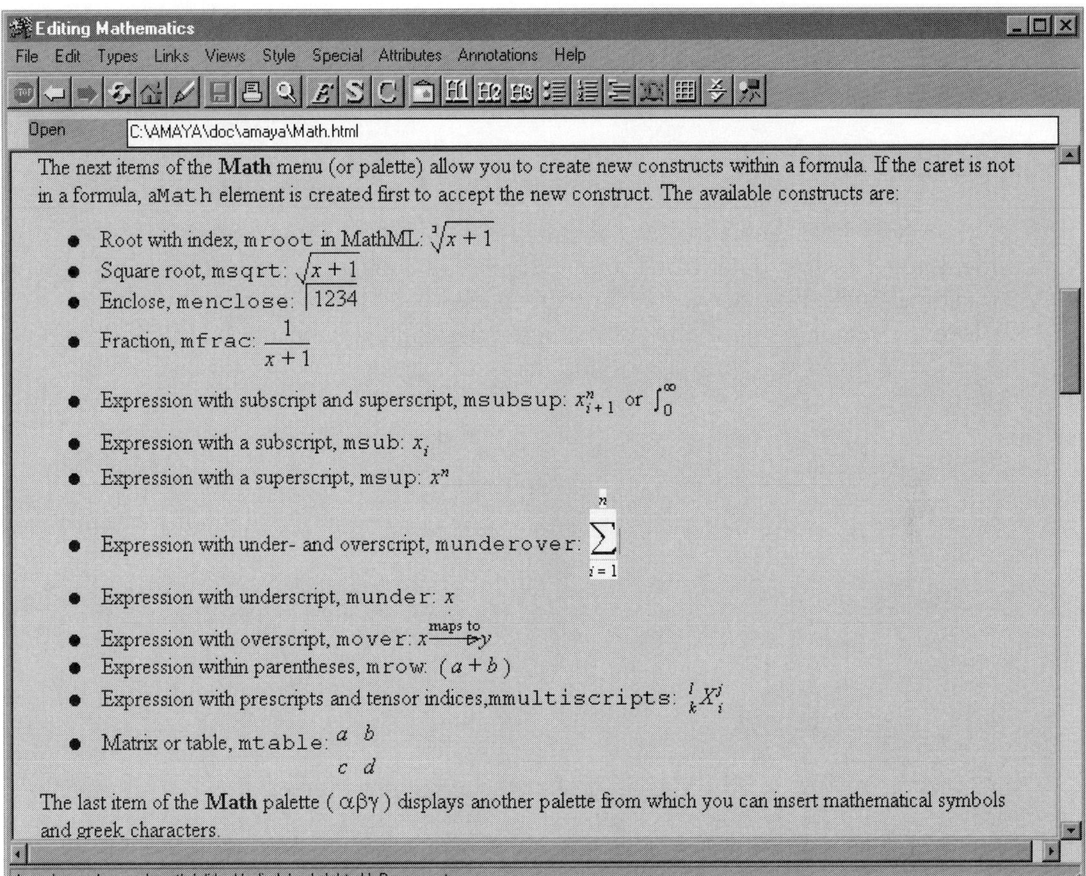

FIGURE 2-10 MathML displayed natively in W3C's Amaya 5.0 browser

scientific material on the Web, as well as in Microsoft Office documents by means of an ActiveX control.

The Synchronized Multimedia Integration Language (SMIL) 1.0 Specification became a W3C Recommendation in June 1998. SMIL (pronounced "smile"), another XML vocabulary, is intended for "integrating a set of independent multimedia objects into a synchronized multimedia presentation." In other words, SMIL enables content developers to coordinate the timing of different multimedia events by means of a common timeline. SMIL supports hyperlinking to media objects. The specification is the work of representatives from more than a dozen companies, including Lucent/Bell Labs, DEC, Philips, Apple, Microsoft, Netscape, and RealNetworks. SMIL version 2.0, formerly called SMIL Boston, became a W3C Recommendation in June 2001. Web designers are excited because SMIL can be used to add timing of visual and auditory events to their Web pages. For example, see the

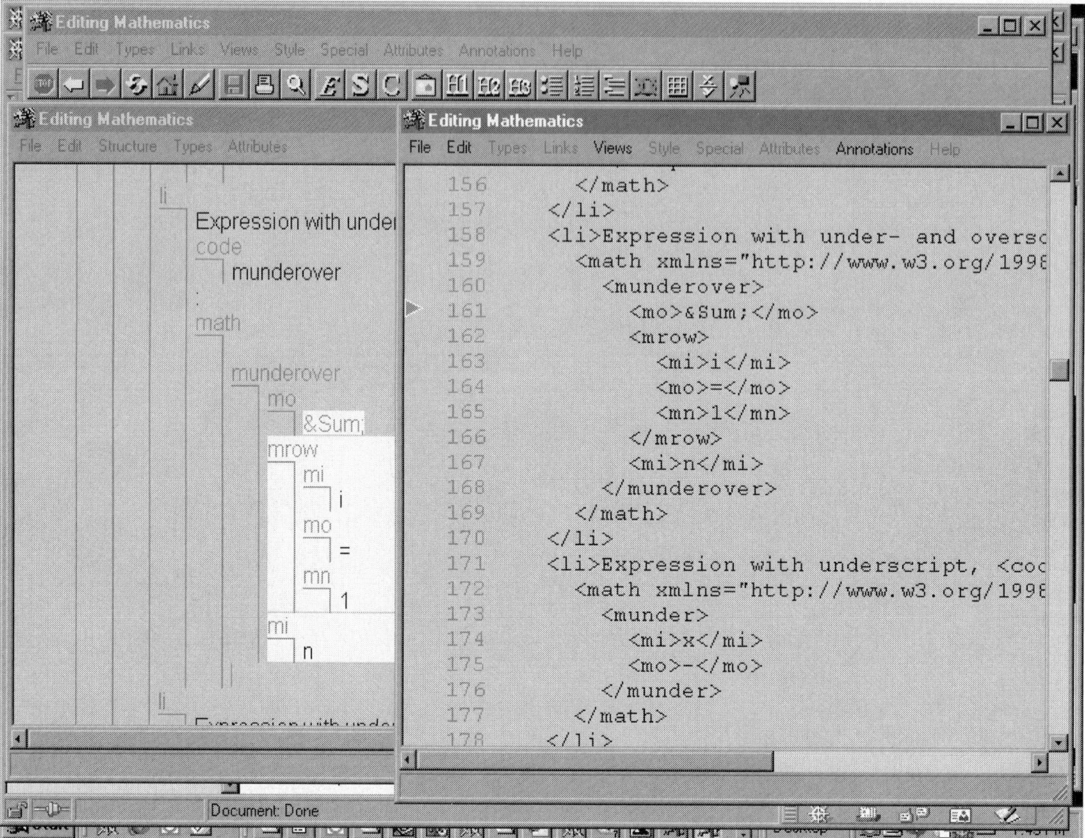

FIGURE 2-11 Structure view and source view of MathML in W3C's Amaya browser

tutorials on HTML+TIME with SMIL at *http://smw.internet.com/smil/tutor/* that are available from Just SMIL portion of the Streaming Media World Web Site, shown in Figure 2-12.

Wireless Application Protocol (WAP) is an evolving architecture for wireless information and telephony services, coordinated by the WAP Forum. Wireless Markup Language (WML) is the HTML of WAP expressed in XML. WAP has been endorsed by a large list of vendors including Nokia, Motorola, Nortel, Lucent, Novell, Mitsubishi, IBM, Microsoft, Sprint, and Sun Microsystems. For example, Nokia has a WAP Client that interprets WML.

In 2000 and 2001, there has been considerable interest in Voice Extensible Markup Language (VoiceXML), the goal of which is to make Internet content accessible via voice and phone. VoiceXML is actively promoted by the VoiceXML Forum, founded by industry leaders AT&T, IBM, Lucent and Motorola. An initial W3C Note was submitted in May 2000 to describe VoiceXML 1.0. This early document was aligned with the dialog requirements identified by the W3C Voice

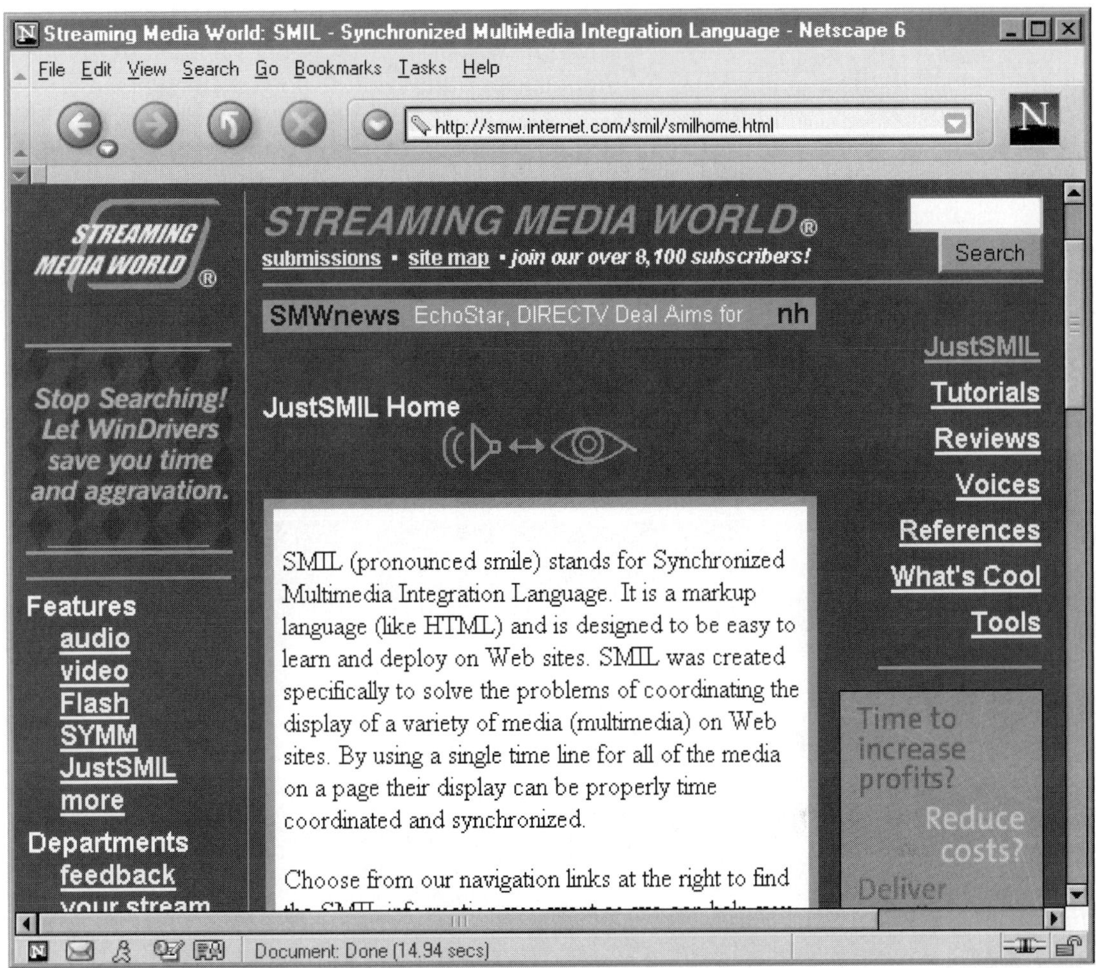

FIGURE 2-12 JustSMIL home page

Source: Reprinted with permission from *http://www.internet.com*.

Browser working group at the time. More recently, VoiceXML 2.0 appeared as a first Working Draft. According to the VoiceXML 2.0 W3C Working Draft of October 23, 2001:

> VoiceXML is designed for creating audio dialogs that feature synthesized speech, digitized audio, recognition of spoken and DTMF key input, recording of spoken input, telephony, and mixed-initiative conversations. Its major goal is to bring the advantages of Web-based development and content delivery to interactive voice response applications. (*http://www.w3.org/TR/2001/WD-voicexml20-20011023*)

Although never submitted to the W3C, Music Markup Language by Recordare is an interesting application of XML in which Java is used to render the parsed MusicML document representing musical notation as a non-GIF image (see *http://www.recordare.com/*).

The Chemical Markup Language (CML) was the earliest of all XML vocabularies, even prior to MathML, although it too has not been subjected to the W3C specification development process (see *http://www.xml-cml. org/*).

Sports Markup Language (SportsML) is yet another example of a specialized vocabulary based on XML, in this case, for the exchange of sports scores, schedules, standings, and statistics for a wide variety of competitions. The SportsML home page (see *http://www.SportsML.com/*) is shown in Figure 2-13.

In April 1998, two months after XML 1.0 became a W3C Recommendation, I had the opportunity to propose that NASA Goddard Space Flight Center develop an XML vocabulary for the command and control of astronomical instruments. As

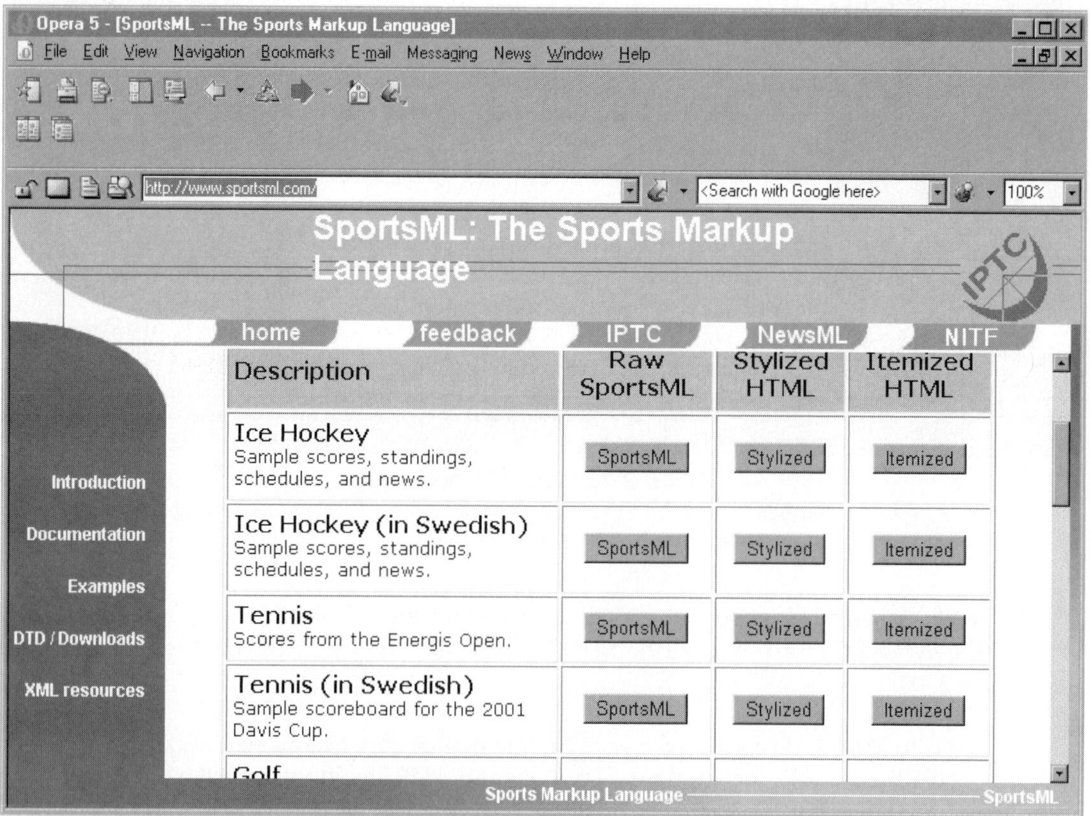

FIGURE 2-13 SportsML home page

Source: Screen capture used with kind permission from IPTC (*www.itpc.org*).

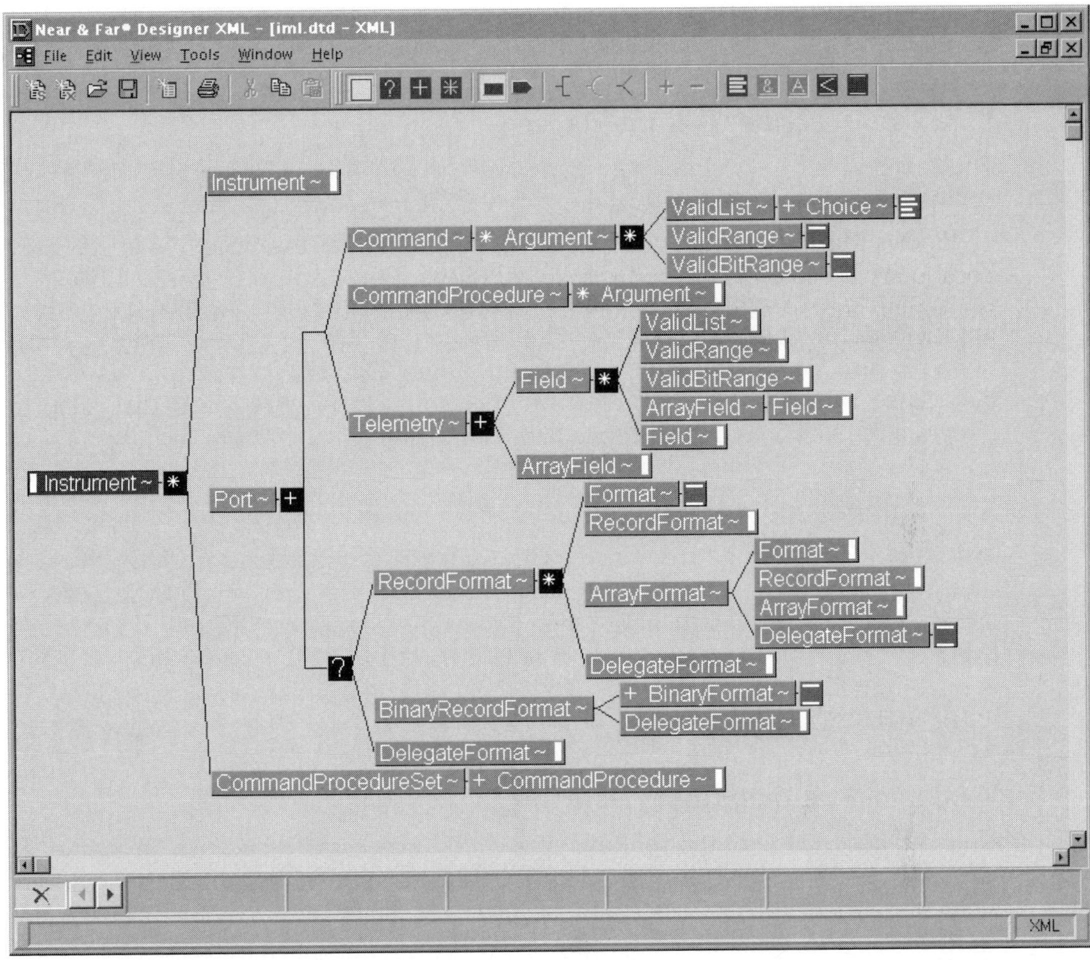

FIGURE 2-14 Astronomical Instrument Markup Language (NASA and Aquilent)

Source: IML and AIML code used with permission from NASA (contact: Troy.J.Ames@gsfc.nasa.gov).

a member of a team of developers from NASA/GSFC and Century Computing,[2] we developed what was initially called Astronomical Instrument Markup Language (AIML). The core DTD hierachy for AIML applies to more than just astronomical instruments, so a parallel effort is under way to define the more generic Instrument Markup Language (IML). Both AIML and IML are discussed in some detail in Simon St. Laurent's book *Inside XML DTDs: Scientific and Technical* (1999). Figure 2-14 shows the DTD from early 1999; current efforts include rewriting and

2. Century Computing was later acquired by AppNet, which in turn was acquired by Commerce One. The eGovernment division divested and is currently a separate entity known as Aquilent (*http://www.aquilent.com*).

expanding this considerably as a more general and extensible XML Schema (see *http://pioneer.gsfc.nasa.gov/public/iml/*).

XML Can Describe User Interfaces

The eXtensible User Interface Language (XUL)—see *http://www.mozilla.org/xpfe/xulref*—is a vocabulary based on XML syntax used to describe cross-platform graphical user interfaces (GUI). The original motivation behind XUL was to provide a mechanism for dynamically instantiating the user interface for Netscape 6. For example, the complete look and feel of Netscape 6 can be changed by modifying themes (customizable browser skins) written in XUL. However, entire applications can also be constructed by combining XUL, CSS, and JavaScript. A separate but related effort is the jXUL project, an open source project begun in early 2001 to integrate the XUL language into the Java Platform (see *http://www.jxul.org/*).

XML Complements HTML

XML and HTML can be combined, with each performing the portion of the task that it does best. For example, XML data can be used to populate HTML forms or tables. We will also learn about the Extensible HyperText Markup Language (XHTML), which is the reformulation of HTML 4.01 in XML syntax. Since XHTML is well-formed XML, integration with other XML vocabularies such as MathML, SMIL, and SVG is possible.

Validated, Self-Describing Data

No prior knowledge of the sending application is necessary because the syntax of an XML message or document describes the relationships among the various elements, either explicitly via a DTD or XML Schema or implicitly by means of element context. At least, this is true at the structural level; semantics is of course a more difficult issue.

The majority of today's XML parsers are *validating* parsers; they optionally parse the external DTD or XML Schema and construct rules before they continue to parse the XML document. As a result, many types of errors are automatically detected and reported to the application that invoked the parser. (In Java applications, this report may be sent to other classes that belong to the same application.) For example, Figure 2-15 illustrates what you might expect in an XML editor if the end `Title` tag appears as `<Title>` rather than `</Title>`. The document is not *well-formed* and, even without a DTD, this type of error can be detected because elements can't overlap. XML editors typically have built-in parsers so they can report precisely where the error is detected. (This screenshot is from a flexible XML editor called XML Instance, another part of the TurboXML suite from TIBCO Extensibility.)

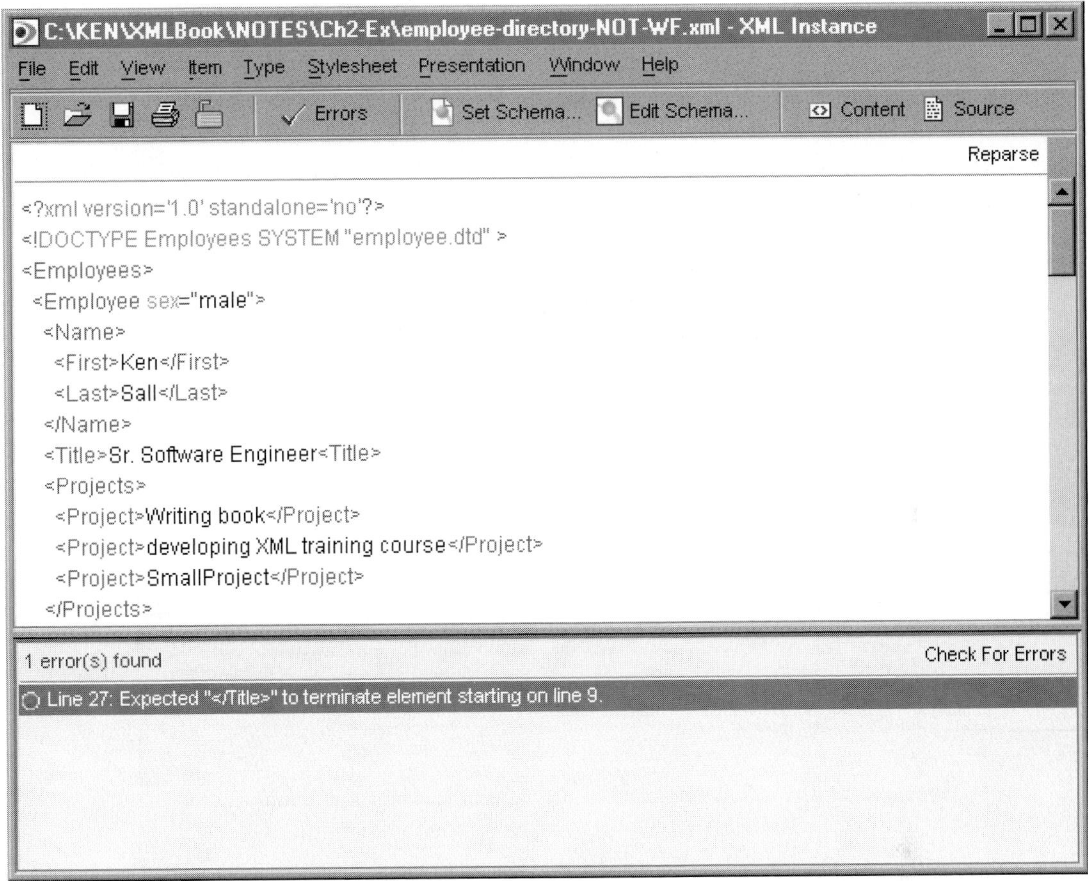

FIGURE 2-15 Detection of well-formedness error due to missing end tag

Although the examples in this section depict validation by XML, DTD, and XML Schema editors, the same principles and similar error messages apply to interapplication transmission of XML. XML parsers are the common thread in all cases as the validation engines.

Another type of problem that validating parsers detect is extraneous (unknown) elements, not declared in the DTD, as is the case with the element `<Sell>` in Figure 2-16. In this case, the document is well formed with no syntax errors, but the author mistakenly wrote `<Sell>` rather than `<Cell>` for the first employee. The screenshot, also made using the XML Instance editor, illustrates explicit messages. We are told `PhoneNumbers` element must have a `Cell` child and that an element called `Sell` is unexpected.

If an XML editor had been used to create the file and if the document referenced a DTD, such a typo would not be possible; editors are context sensitive

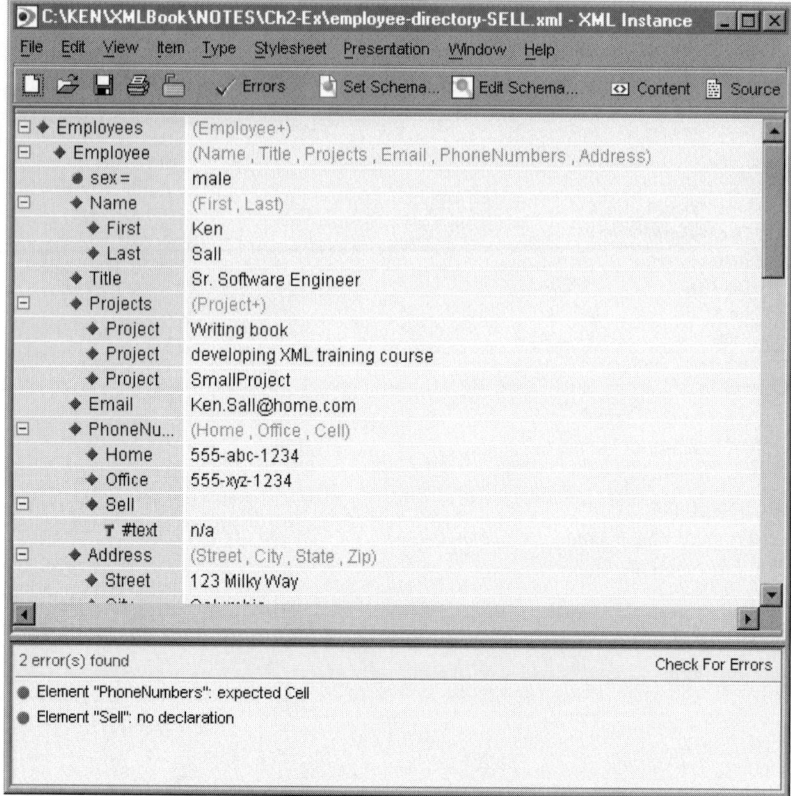

FIGURE 2-16 Detection of an undeclared element

and usually present only the valid child choices. For example, when editing the `PhoneNumbers` element, only the valid choices `Home`, `Office`, and `Cell` would be presented.

In contrast to the previous examples, it is also entirely possible that the errors are in the DTD itself, rather than in the XML instance. Consider the case where we've inadvertently introduced a misspelling of an element name, such as misspelling `Cell` as `Sell`:

```
<!ELEMENT PhoneNumbers ( Home, Office, Cell ) >
<!ELEMENT Home ( #PCDATA ) >
<!ELEMENT Office ( #PCDATA ) >
<!ELEMENT Sell ( #PCDATA ) >
```

DTD editors will indicate that something is wrong. In XML Spy by Altova, for example, the element `Cell` is flagged as undefined because although it is referenced by `PhoneNumbers`, it is `Sell` that is defined but never referenced (see Figure 2-17). XML Spy does allow for the possibility that the definition of `Cell`

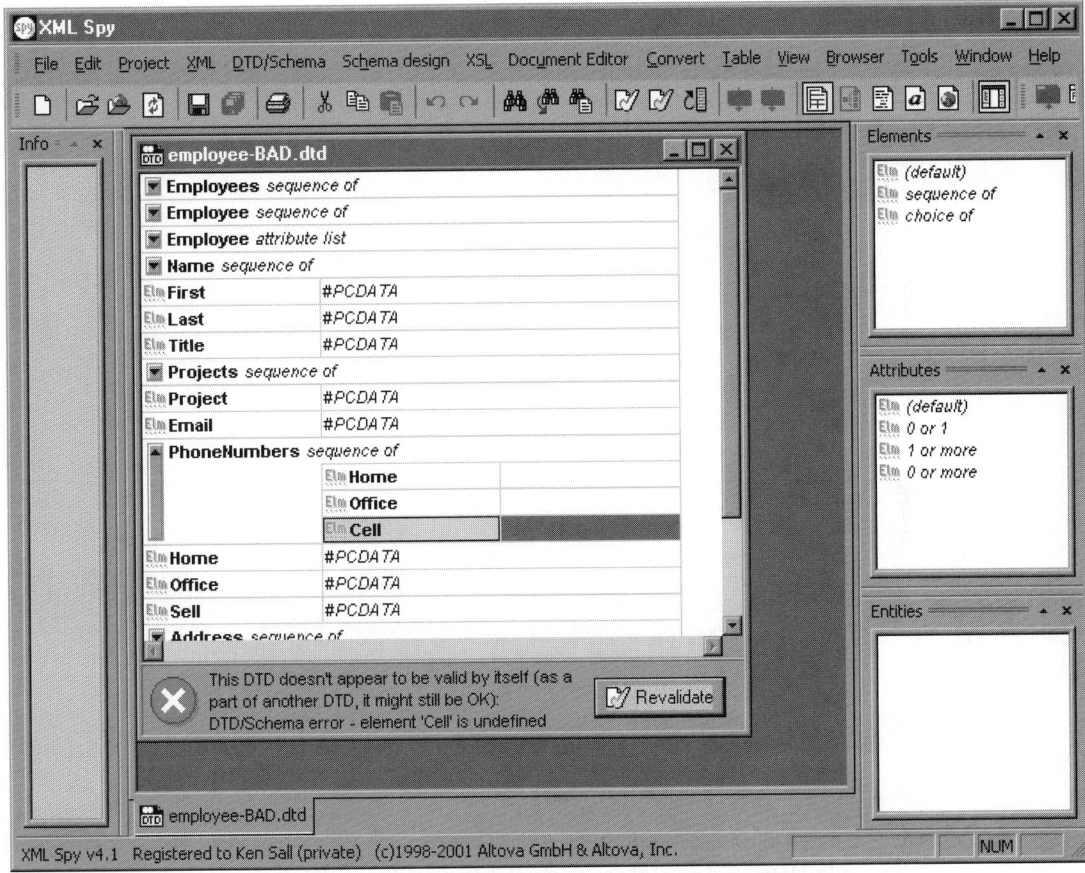

FIGURE 2-17 Erroneous DTD in XML Spy

might be in another DTD that is to be combined with this one. (In this case, we are using the DTD editor to modify a DTD that was created initially using a text editor.)

If an XML document references the invalid DTD and uses the `Cell` element, the parser will report that the element is undeclared. In Figure 2-18, opening the XML document in XML Spy, for example, triggers the automatic display of the DTD and points to the error.

Metadata

Metadata, or information about data, can be used to describe Web sites, to describe a collection of related pages, or to "push" structured content channels (e.g., news items or stock quotes) to the desktops or other Web-enabled devices of interested subscribers.

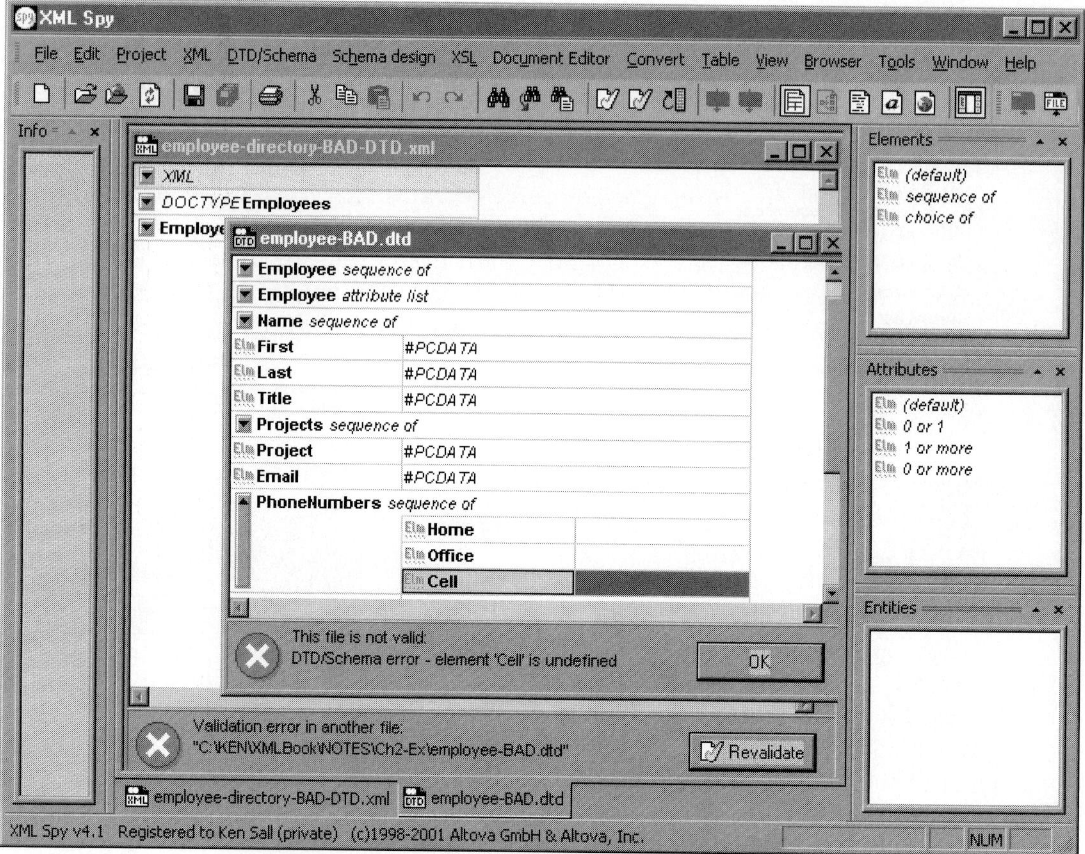

FIGURE 2-18 XML document referencing invalid DTD

The Resource Description Framework (RDF), enables applications to exchange machine-*understandable,* as opposed to merely machine-readable, metadata in an interoperable manner. There are primarily two specifications that address this capability: the RDF Model and Syntax Specification (a W3C Recommendation approved February 1999) and RDF Schemas (from March 1999, which became a Candidate Recommendation in March 2000). The Model and Syntax document suggests a number of categories of potential RDF applications:

- Resource discovery to aid search engines
- Cataloging Web sites and digital libraries
- Supporting intelligent software agents
- Defining content ratings (as in PICS)
- Describing page collections
- Defining intellectual property rights

- Stating user privacy preference and site privacy policies
- Enabling digital signatures for e-commerce

The RDF Model and Syntax Recommendation states that "[t]he definition of the mechanism should be domain neutral, yet the mechanism should be suitable for describing information about any domain." RDF is covered in chapter 16.

The Platform for Internet Content Selection (PICS) provides a mechanism for associating metadata (called PICS "labels") with Web content. The PICS Recommendation was an earlier W3C publication from 1996 and therefore is not XML-based. However, recent efforts have been made to express PICS in RDF syntax, published in a W3C Note entitled "PICS Rating Vocabularies in XML/RDF."

Search Engines

With XML content markup, queries are more likely to retrieve relevant files as a result of contextual information. Instead of ignoring most tags as search engines previously did, XML-aware engines can leverage the markup to constrain the search, as indicated by our earlier `<Author>Paul McCartney</Author>` example. Furthermore, using XPath and XQuery, search engines can retrieve a specific portion of a file, rather than the entire document. With increased relevance and better targeted document passages, user satisfaction in the search process should increase dramatically. Of course, this can only happen as more and more content is marked up as XML. The GoXML search engine is one of the first to begin to tap this potential. GoXML DB from XML Global Technologies stores XML documents directly and features a complementary context-based search engine for fast retrieval of data. Their other product, GoXML Transform, connects to 120 kinds of databases and supports XQuery.

Distributed Applications

In a pipeline of interconnected XML applications, each application can extract data elements it needs and either pass the entire dataset downstream or pass filtered content to participating applications. For example, we can imagine our Employee Directory residing in a database with a Java Database Connectivity (JDBC) application that extracts the data, and passes it to Java code that outputs XML elements according to our Employee Markup Language DTD. This XML output is then acted upon by an XSLT processor that produces the HTML output for the browser as we've seen. Perhaps another application grabs just the employee names and project information and passes it to an accounting program.

Granular Updates

In the XML portion of their MSDN Web site, Microsoft explains how with XML data islands embedded in HTML pages, only the changed elements need to be downloaded from a server; the client updates without refreshing the entire page (in some cases); data can be cached in the client. This is accomplished by binding data in HTML pages using a XML Data Source Object (XML DSO), which is part of Internet Explorer 5. Although it is not part of any W3C standard, this is not radically different from the W3C DOM capabilities that permit dynamic access to any part of an HTML or XML document via a language-independent interface (i.e., implemented in Java, JavaScript, etc.).

User-Selected and User-Specific View of Data

XML also enables client-side data manipulation. Once the data is sent from the server to the browser or other XML-based application, it can be manipulated by the client application, often without the need to burden the server with additional requests. The user selects one, several, or all records, sorts by attributes, switches from a tabular to a graphical view, and so on—manipulations made possible by the DOM or Microsoft Data Source Objects. A good example of user-selectable views is the XML/XSL Viewer demo from the Microsoft MSDN site. The demo illustrates how the same XML data can be displayed differently using different XSLT stylesheets. (Regrettably, I can no longer find this demo on the Microsoft site. Maybe you'll be luckier ;-).)

Two additional examples of user-selectable view are included as demo applications from the menus of the Mozilla browser "Milestone" releases since early 2000. The screenshots in Figures 2-19 through 2-23, however, were created using Netscape 6.2, a browser based on the Mozilla Milestones. Netscape/Mozilla support for XML is described completely on the Mozilla.org site, *http://www.mozilla.org/newlayout/xml/*, which demonstrates XML, associating stylesheets with XML, displaying XML with CSS, Namespaces in XML, XHTML, simple XLinks, and manipulation of XML with scripts via DOM.

The first demo (*http://www.mozilla.org/newlayout/xml/books/books.xml*) illustrates Amazon book listings in random order, with one button to toggle a graphic display of the books' covers and other buttons to control the sorting order of the book data. Figure 2-19 shows the initial, unsorted view without graphics. Figure 2-20 shows the effect of toggling a style that switches from a text-only view to one that includes images of the book covers. Figure 2-21 on page 71 illustrates the view when the same XML data is sorted alphabetically by author's last name. Figure 2-22 on page 72 shows the initial view of the second Mozilla XML demo. It resembles a regular garden-variety HTML page. At the click of a button, however, the user can change the view to include a hierarchical table of contents on the left, as in Figure 2-23 on page 73.

In addition to enabling user-selectable views of data, XML representations support *user-specific* views. The same data can be presented differently, perhaps as a subset, depending on the viewer's role with respect to the data. For example, imagine a scenario in which a CPA in an accounting department needs to see more

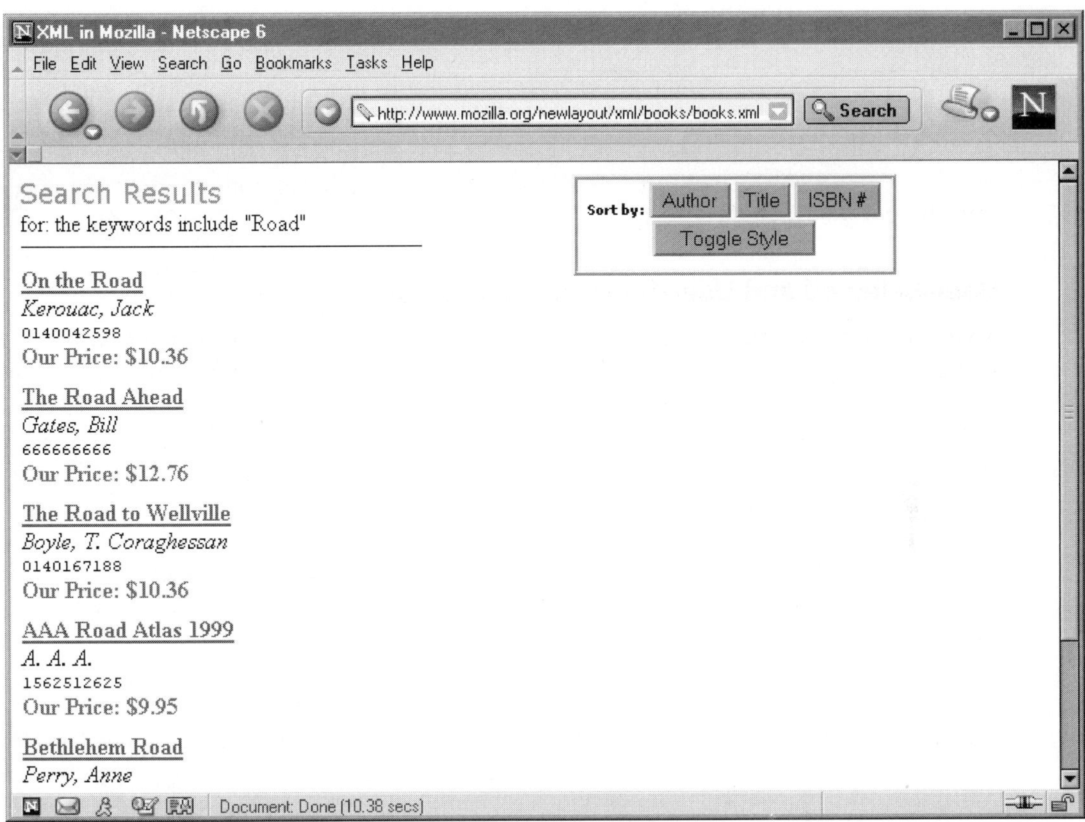

FIGURE 2-19 Mozilla XML sorting demo: initial unsorted, text-only view

details by default than the purchaser, whereas a manager sees only a summary of the data by default, with the option to view more details.

Device-Dependent Display of Data

We have already seen the power of XSLT to produce a variety of HTML outputs from the same XML data with only minor changes to the styleseheet. Similarly, XSLT can be used in conjunction with a Web server to produce different versions of the same data tailored for specific display devices. Carefully written stylesheets can be targeted for the particular flexibilities and limitations of desktop monitors, printers, handheld devices, WebTV, and so forth. This targeting will become increasingly important as more and more people access the Web by means of devices other than a desktop PC, which typically have smaller screens, more limited fonts and graphics, and memory constraints. Modularization of XHTML is a major step toward enabling device-dependent targeting of content.

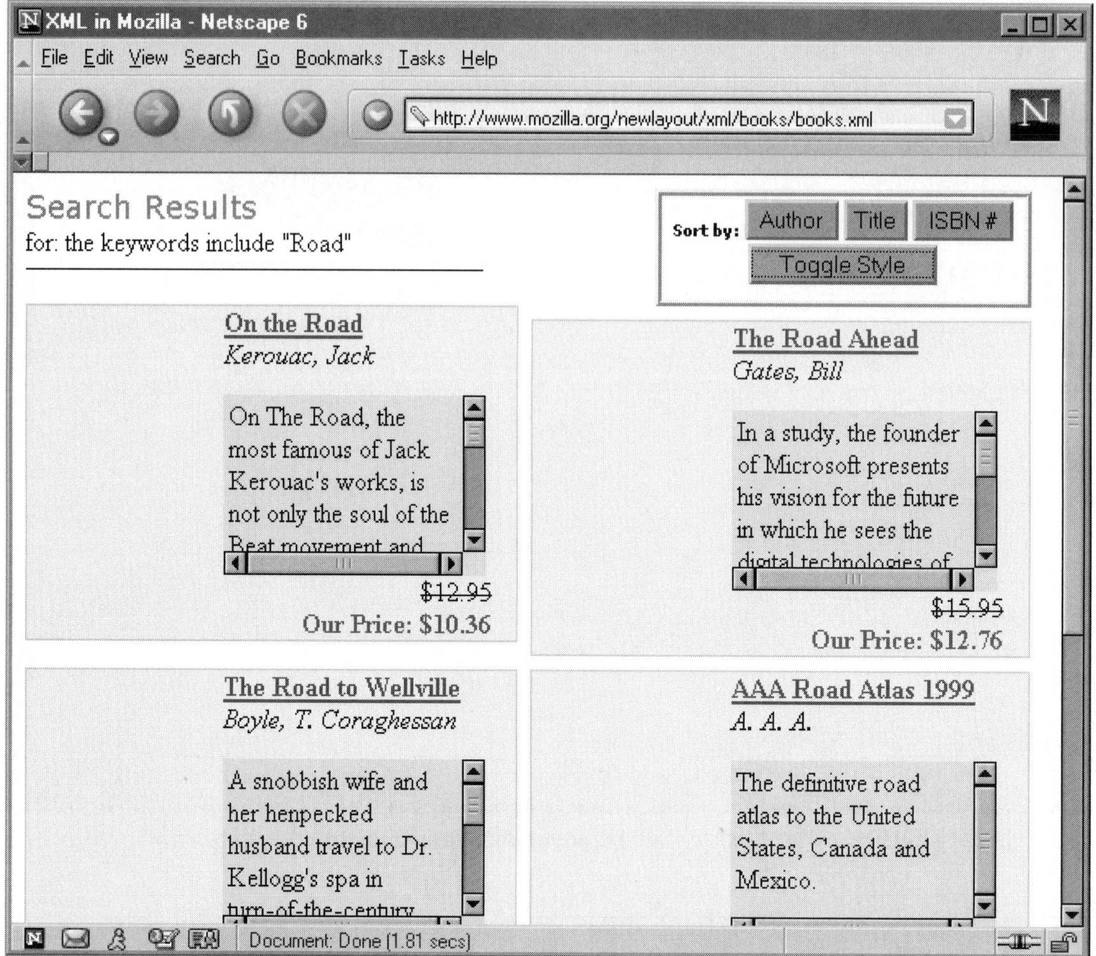

FIGURE 2-20 Mozilla XML sorting demo: unsorted, graphical view

One server-side XML/XSLT effort is Cocoon from the Apache XML Project. Cocoon is aimed at reducing content duplication efforts and site management costs by generating different presentations targeted to particular requesting clients. Apache defines a three-stage document-generation process that lends itself well to a division of labor:

- *XML creation*—content providers use DTD- and XML-aware tools and text editors but need not be concerned with the presentation of the content.
- *XML processing*—an external "logicsheet" is applied to the content, resulting in an intermediate XML document; logic is separated from the content.
- *XSL rendering*—the created document is rendered by applying a target-specific XSL stylesheet (HTML, PDF, XML, WML, XHTML, etc.).

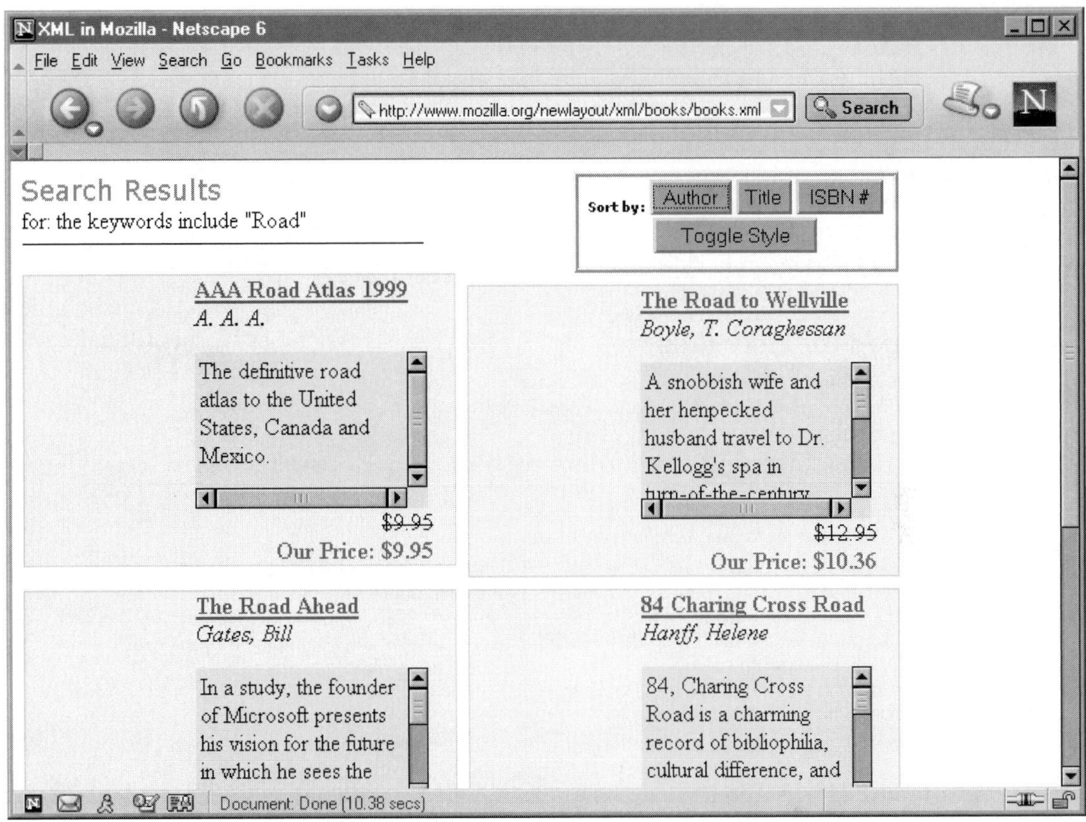

FIGURE 2-21 Mozilla XML sorting demo: sorted by author

According to the Cocoon home page,

> Even if the most common use of Cocoon is the automatic creation of HTML through the processing of statically or dynamically generated XML files, Cocoon is also able to perform more sophisticated formatting, such as XSL:FO rendering to PDF files, client-dependent transformations such as WML formatting for WAP-enabled devices, or direct XML serving to XML and XSL aware clients. (*http://xml.apache.org/cocoon/index.html*, accessed January 2002)

Resolution-Independent Graphics in a Text Format

Scalable Vector Graphics (SVG), a language for defining two-dimensional vector graphics in a compact text format, is a fascinating example of the benefits of leveraging a number of the XML specifications. SVG defines three types of graphic objects: vector graphic shapes, images, and text. Graphical objects can be grouped, styled, transformed, animated, and combined. SVG will probably be widespread

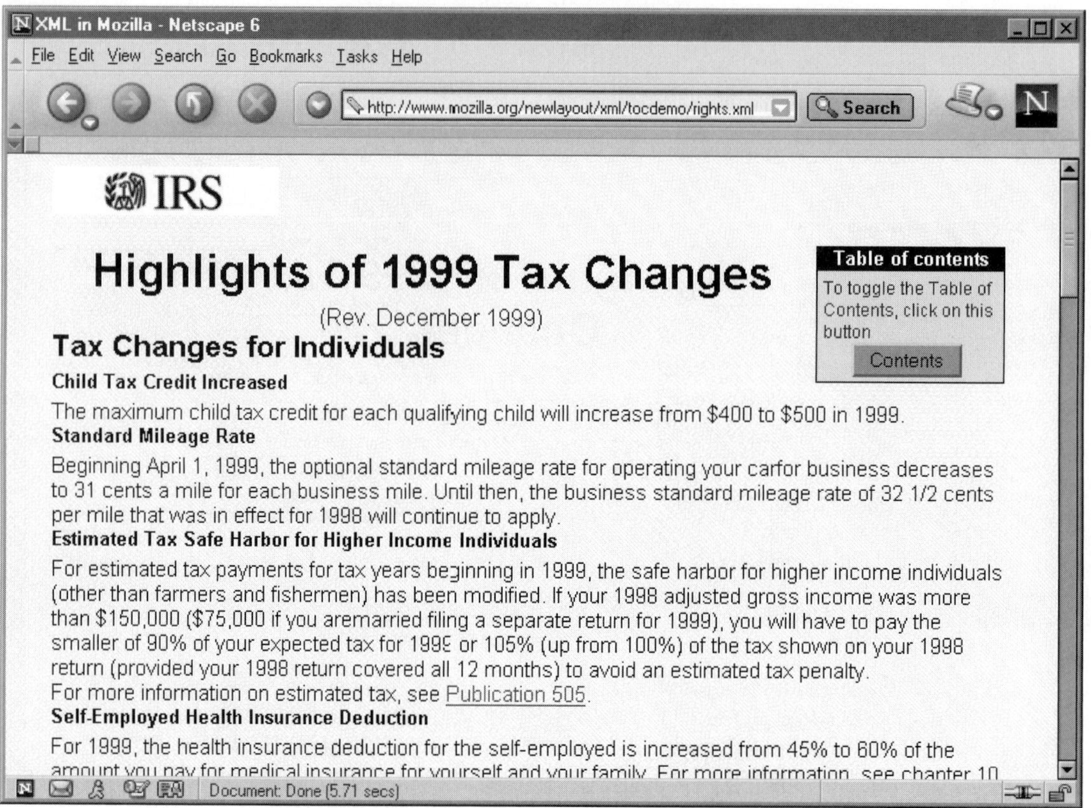

FIGURE 2-22 Mozilla XML IRS demo: initial view

by the time you read these words. The example in Figure 2-24 on page 74 demonstrates rotated text, styling, opacity, and a Gaussian blur filter effect. The SVG file I created for this example is less than 2 KB and is about 40 lines of markup and declarations. It is rendered in Figure 2-24 using Java 2D by Adobe's SVG browser plugin to Netscape 4.7x; the plugin also supports IE 5.x and above and Netscape 6.x. (See the Adobe SVG Zone; *http://www.adobe.com/svg/main.html*, to download the SVG Viewer plugin, to see a large number of impressive demos, and to try a great tutorial.)

Another SVG example I created combines JPEG and GIF images with SVG. In Figure 2-25 on page 75, the JPEG of the Beatles has been made semitransparent (actually, the image's opacity changes over time) and the Beatles logo is a static GIF.[3] Various SVG objects are input-sensitive, some triggering links and some executing JavaScript code.

3. If you're a Beatles fan, you will love Harald Gernhardt's sites: *http://gernhardt.com/beatles/index.html* and *http://gernhardt.com/macca/index.shtml*.

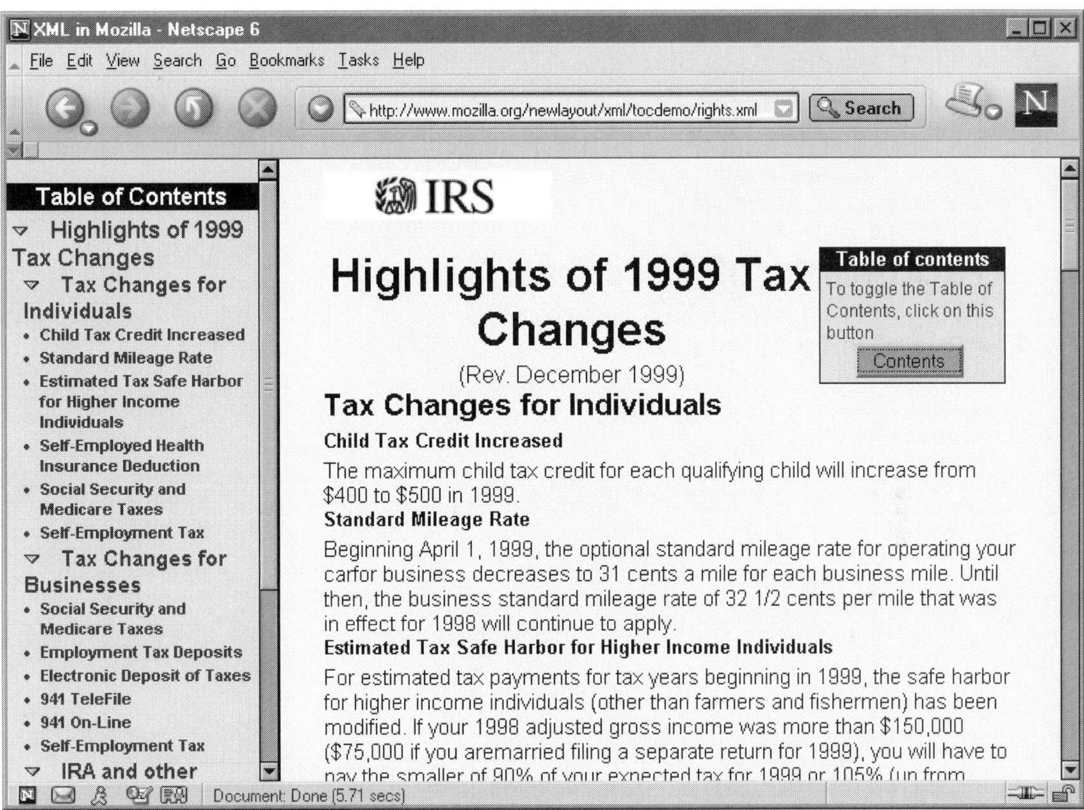

FIGURE 2-23 Mozilla XML IRS demo: table of contents view

The advantages of SVG over bitmapped graphics like GIF and JPEG are many. SVG

- Is resolution and device independent (can be scaled to match different devices).
- Requires smaller files so download times are faster compared to bitmapped graphics.
- Is better suited for devices with low bandwidth and limited memory.
- Has better printing capabilities.
- Permits panning around images.
- Allows incorporation of JPEG, GIF, and PNG image files as part of the graphic foreground, as semitransparent background, as a pulse or other animation.
- Supports zooming in on details not visible when an image is initially displayed.
- Is fully compatible with XHTML so SVG can be well integrated into Web pages.
- Defines interactivity through scriptable events based on the DOM (e.g., JavaScript event handlers).

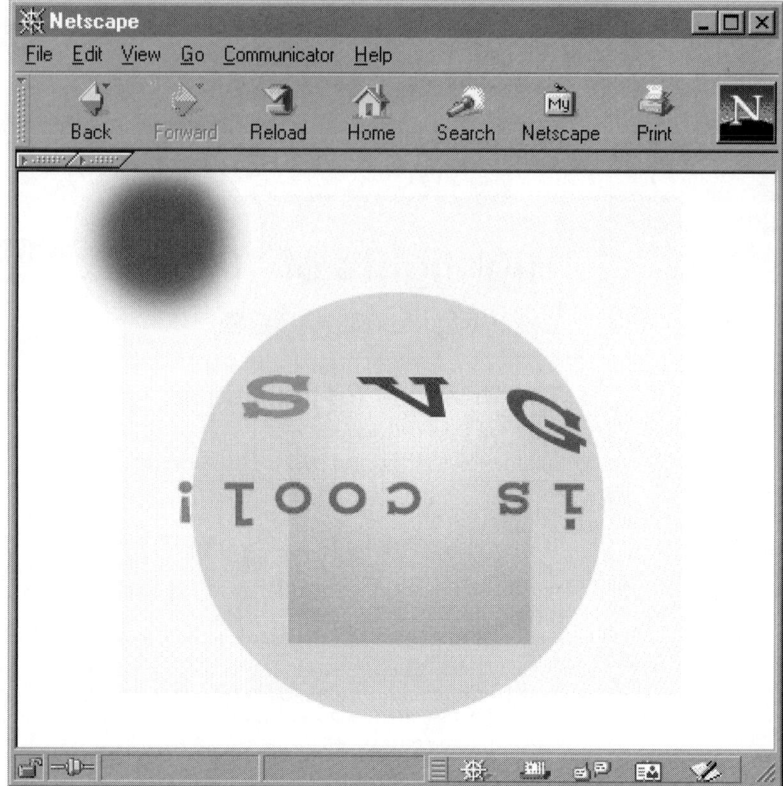

FIGURE 2-24 Rotated text, opacity, and Gaussian blur in compact SVG file

- Has text labels and descriptions that are directly searchable (can be indexed by search engines).
- Permits linking from any portion of a complex object based on XLink.
- Supports complex animations and transformations.
- Is not limited to fonts available on the target device.
- Need not come from a static file; it can be generated from a database on the fly.
- Uses CSS-style information to share rendering styles among portions of the graphic.
- Supports conditionals based on the SMIL 1.0 Recommendation (e.g., for device checking).

Roughly the second half of this set of advantages also distinguishes SVG from earlier vector graphics formats, such as Flash and QuickTime. Products by major

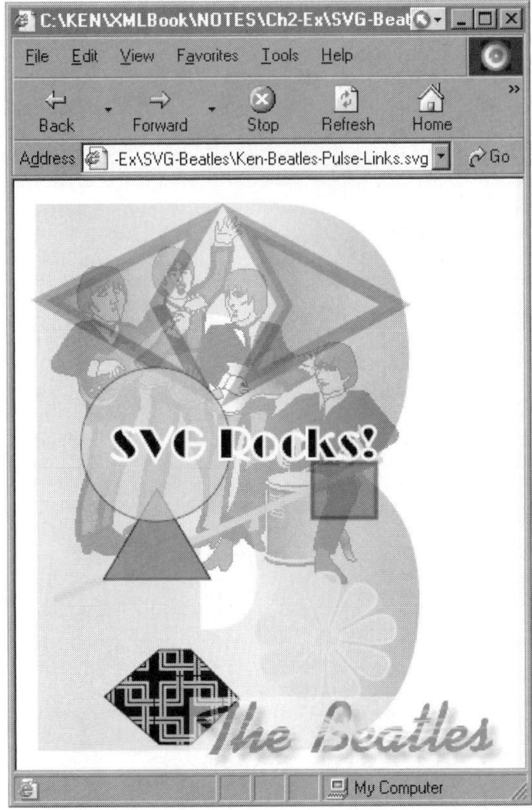

FIGURE 2-25 The Beatles: SVG Rocks!

graphics vendors such as Adobe, Corel, and Jasc already support SVG as an output or export format. Some of these advantages are quite apparent from the demos at Adobe's SVG site, as illustrated in the next several figures.

Figures 2-26 through 2-28 depict an earlier SVG demo of maps of Moscow, no longer available on the Adobe site (see pages 76, 77 and 78). Please check out their current demos once you have installed the SVG Viewer plugin. The demo allows us to add more graphics to the map, thereby increasing the amount of detail conveyed, as in Figure 2-27. We can also access a popup menu from the plugin to zoom in to see far more detailed information, as in Figure 2-28.

Rendering with Formatting Objects

Extensible Stylesheet Language (XSL) consists of two parts: the transformation part, which we've already seen in action, and the formatting objects portion, which

FIGURE 2-26 Adobe SVG Moscow demo: initial view

Source: Screenshots in Figures 2-26 through 2-28 used with permission from Adobe (*http://www.adobe.com*).

specifies how the XSL transformation result is to be rendered when targeted for a particular device. The formatting objects in XSL are very sophisticated, allowing content providers far more control in layout and rendering than is possible with HTML and CSS (Cascading Style Sheets).

Chess Viewer is a compelling example of XSLFO (as it is cometimes called) that appears on the RenderX.com site (*http://www.renderx.com/chess.html*). A chess game is described in move-by-move notation in XML. A chess-oriented XSLT stylesheet is applied to the specific game instance to produce a gameboard view corresponding to each move (Figure 2-29, on page 79). Another XSL formatting objects stylesheet is applied to the intermediate stylesheet to render the boards as a PDF (Adobe's Portable Document Format (see *http://www.adobe.com/products/acrobat/adobepdf.html*)) document, as shown in Figure 2-30 on page 80.

FIGURE 2-27 Adobe SVG Moscow demo: additional details

As another example of XSL Formatting Objects, let's look at the barcode generator also from RenderX (*http://www.renderx.com/barcodes.html*). This demo takes a Universal Product Code/European Article Numbering (UPC/EAN) barcode and converts it to XSLFO, and then to PDF and SVG. As explained on the RenderX site, barcodes are black vertical bars of varyious widths, separated by white space. XSLFO and SVG representations of these patterns are relatively easy to create. The challenge is in creating an XSL stylesheet that calculates the bar widths, given any string of numbers that represents a valid barcode, needed to produce the graphical XSLFO or SVG output. For example, given the numeric string that represents the barcode for the "Beatles 1" CD, which is `7 2435 29325 2`, the RenderX barcode generator applies the specialized, several-hundred-line stylesheet on its server to produce the PDF shown in Figure 2-31 (page 81), as well as the SVG shown in Figure 2-32

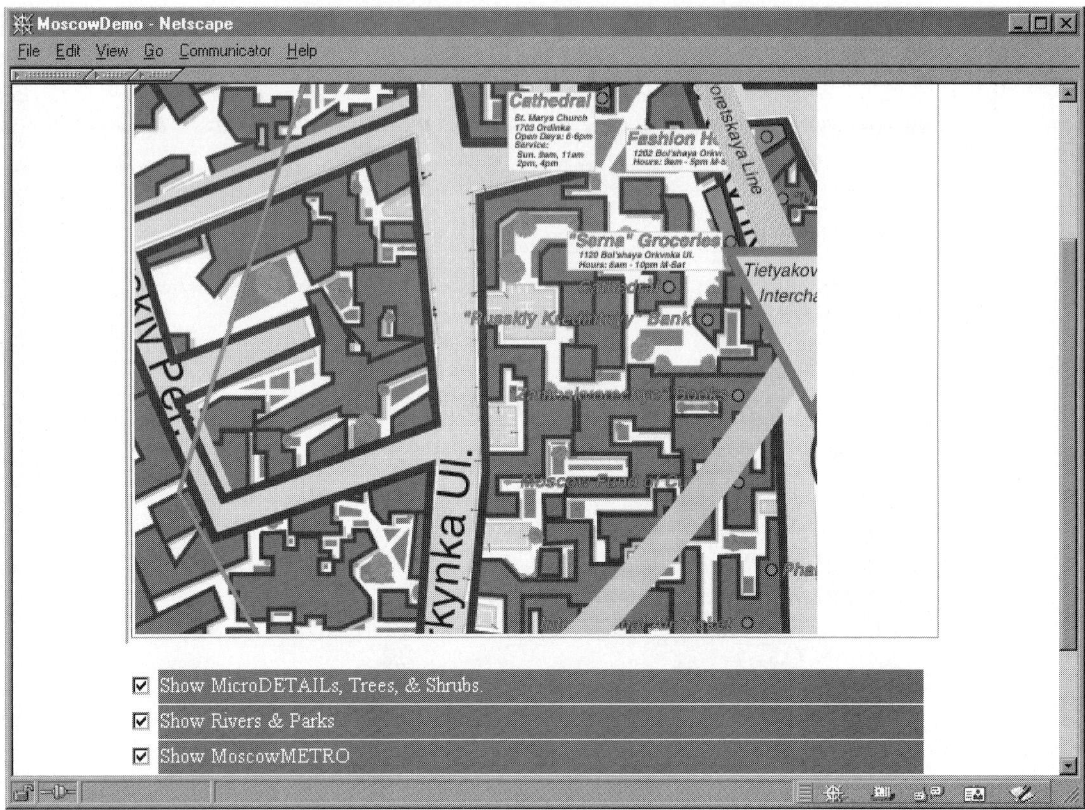

FIGURE 2-28 Adobe SVG Moscow demo: zoomed-in view

(page 81). If you dig through your CD collection and compare these results to the UPC barcode on the back of "Beatles 1," you'll discover they are identical.

Unicode and Alternate Character Set Support

One other advantage of XML is that the language supports most common character sets, as well as Unicode.[4] This is important to enable XML to represent content from any language on any platform. According to this excerpt from the Unicode Consortium,

> Unicode assigns a unique, platform-independent and language-independent number to every character. In addition to being accepted by most major IT companies, Unicode is a requirement of many industry standards, such as XML, Java,

4. You can learn about Unicode from the Unicode Consortium at *http://www.unicode.org* and from the Addison-Wesley book, *Unicode Standard Version 3.0*, 2000 (ISBN 0-201-61633-5); see also *http://www.unicode.org/unicode/uni2book/u2.html*.

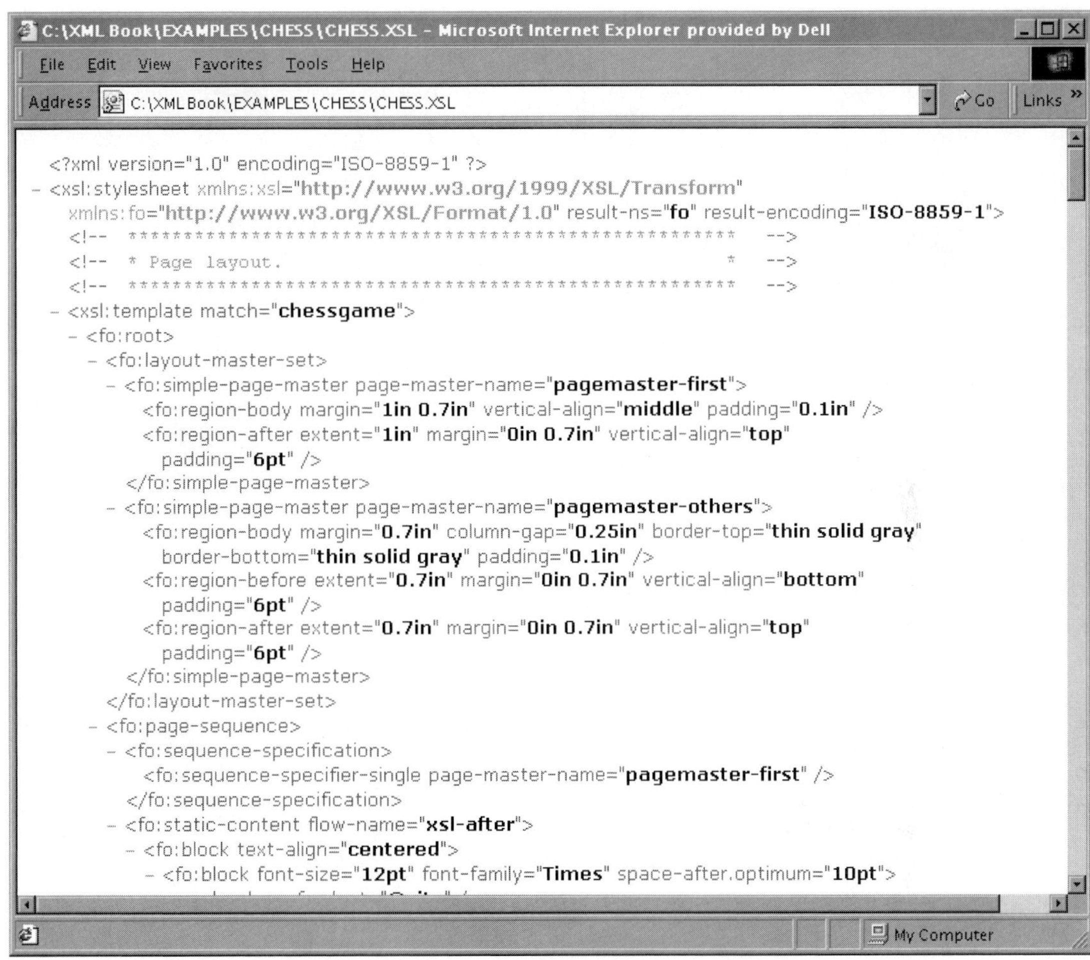

```
C:\XML Book\EXAMPLES\CHESS\CHESS.XSL - Microsoft Internet Explorer provided by Dell
File  Edit  View  Favorites  Tools  Help
Address  C:\XML Book\EXAMPLES\CHESS\CHESS.XSL                    Go  Links

  <?xml version="1.0" encoding="ISO-8859-1" ?>
- <xsl:stylesheet xmlns:xsl="http://www.w3.org/1999/XSL/Transform"
    xmlns:fo="http://www.w3.org/XSL/Format/1.0" result-ns="fo" result-encoding="ISO-8859-1">
    <!-- ******************************************************* -->
    <!-- * Page layout.                                        * -->
    <!-- ******************************************************* -->
  - <xsl:template match="chessgame">
    - <fo:root>
      - <fo:layout-master-set>
        - <fo:simple-page-master page-master-name="pagemaster-first">
            <fo:region-body margin="1in 0.7in" vertical-align="middle" padding="0.1in" />
            <fo:region-after extent="1in" margin="0in 0.7in" vertical-align="top"
              padding="6pt" />
          </fo:simple-page-master>
        - <fo:simple-page-master page-master-name="pagemaster-others">
            <fo:region-body margin="0.7in" column-gap="0.25in" border-top="thin solid gray"
              border-bottom="thin solid gray" padding="0.1in" />
            <fo:region-before extent="0.7in" margin="0in 0.7in" vertical-align="bottom"
              padding="6pt" />
            <fo:region-after extent="0.7in" margin="0in 0.7in" vertical-align="top"
              padding="6pt" />
          </fo:simple-page-master>
        </fo:layout-master-set>
      - <fo:page-sequence>
        - <fo:sequence-specification>
            <fo:sequence-specifier-single page-master-name="pagemaster-first" />
          </fo:sequence-specification>
        - <fo:static-content flow-name="xsl-after">
          - <fo:block text-align="centered">
            - <fo:block font-size="12pt" font-family="Times" space-after.optimum="10pt">

My Computer
```

FIGURE 2-29 RenderX Chess Viewer demo: XSLT and XSLFO stylesheet

Source: Figures 2-29 through 2-32 used with permission of RenderX (*http://www.renderx.com*).

CORBA, ECMAScript, and so on (see *http://www.unicode.org/unicode/standard/WhatIsUnicode.html*)

By default, XML processors assume that documents use the UTF-8 (compressed Unicode) encoding, which includes the ASCII character set. A nondefault Unicode character set, such as UTF-16 (compressed UCS) or ISO-10646-UCS-2 (raw Unicode) can also be specified.[5] However, you can also tell XML tools that your

5. UCS stands for Universal Character Set, which is specified by International Standard ISO/IEC 10646.

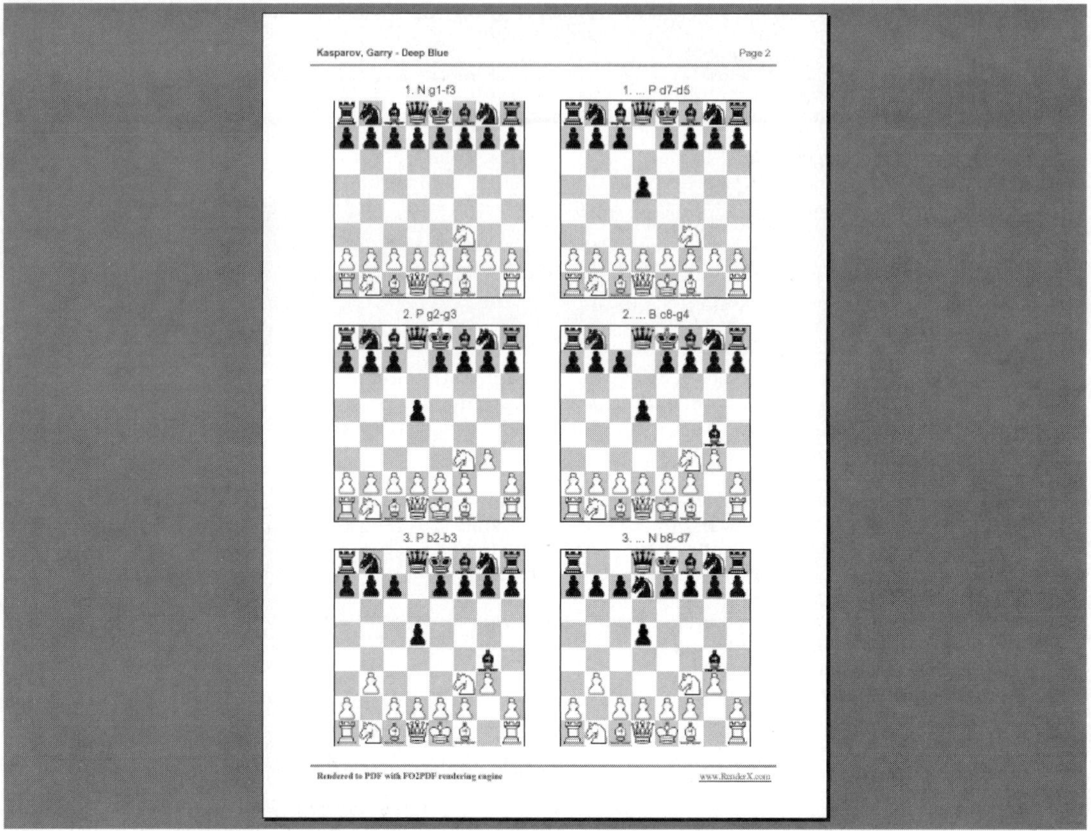

FIGURE 2-30 RenderX Chess Viewer demo: XSLFO generation of PDF

document contains a different *non-Unicode* encoding. For example, Japanese on a UNIX platform is specified by the encoding

```
<?xml version="1.0" encoding="euc-jp"?>
```

Figure 2-33 illustrates Japanese for both content and element names. Notice how Internet Explorer (left) uses its built-in stylesheet to render the Japanese XML; Netscape (right) simply displays the Japanese content, analogous to what we saw in Figures 2-3 and 2-4.

As another example,

```
<?xml version="1.0" encoding="ISO-8859-1"?>
```

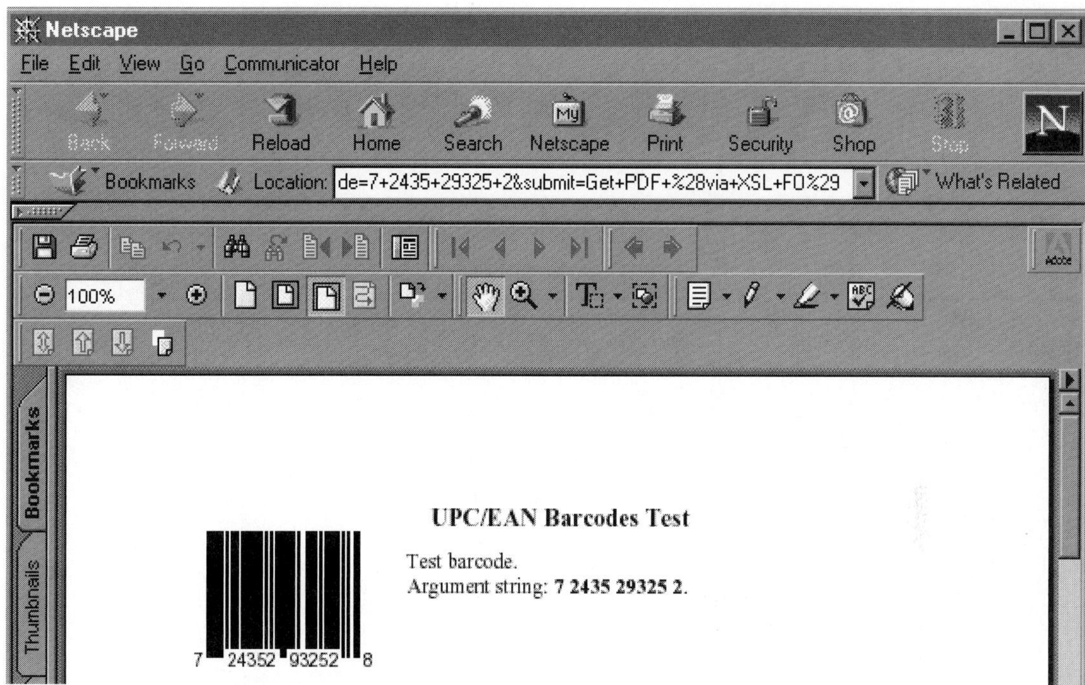

FIGURE 2-31 PDF generated from numeric barcode using XSLT (RenderX)

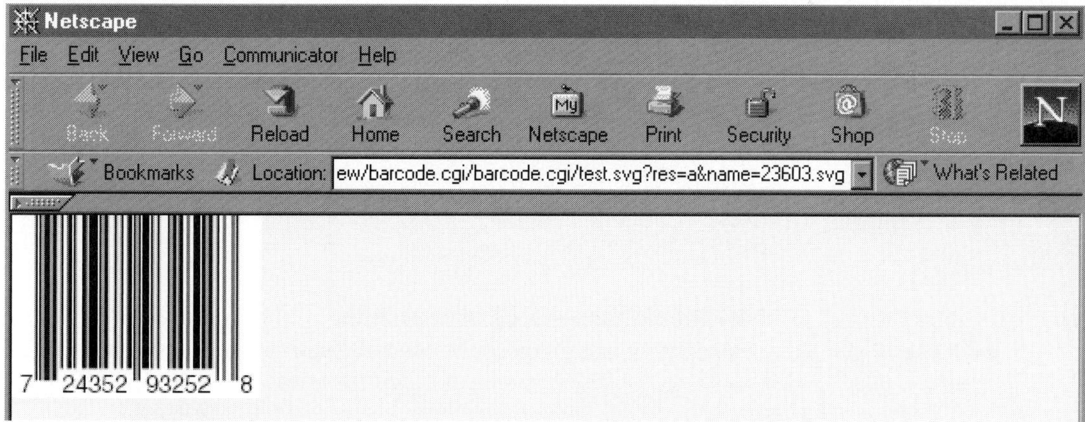

FIGURE 2-32 SVG generated from numeric barcode using XSLT (RenderX)

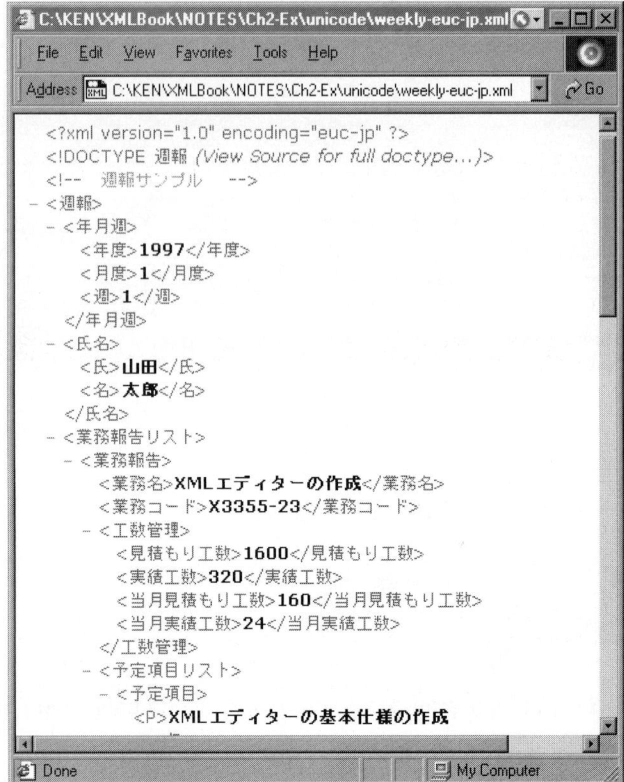

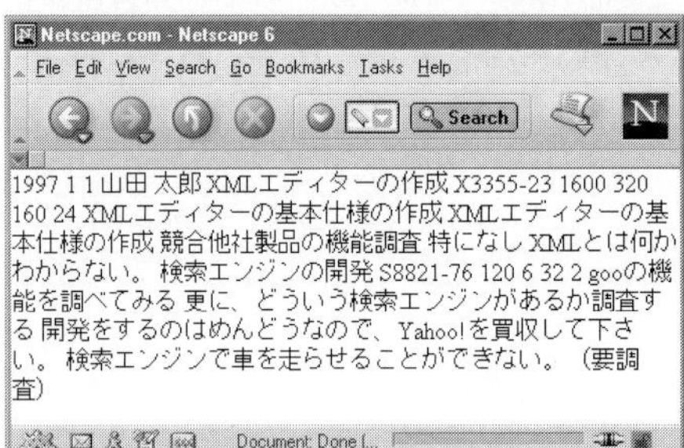

FIGURE 2-33 Japanese content and elements in Internet Explorer and Netscape

Source: Screen captures used with permission—copyright © 1999–2002 The Apache Software Foundation. All rights reserved. The Apache software consists of voluntary contributions made by many individuals on behalf of the Apache Software Foundation and was originally based on software copyright © 1999, International Business Machines, Inc. (*http://www.ibm.com*). For more information on the Apache Software Foundation, please see <*http://www.apache.org/*>.

indicates the Latin-1 encoding. Russian (or more precisely, ASCII plus Cyrillic) is identified similarly:

```
<?xml version="1.0" encoding="ISO-8859-5"?>
```

See Figure 2-34 for an example of Russian encoding of content, as displayed by Internet Explorer.

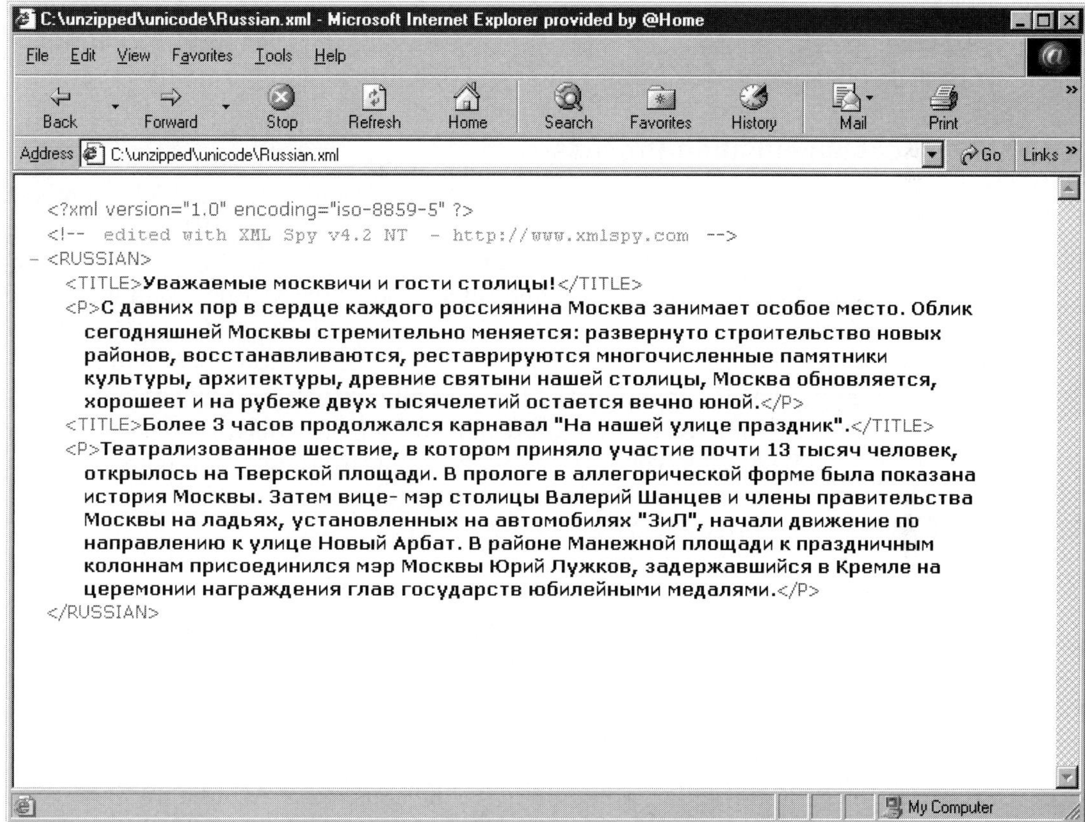

FIGURE 2-34 Russian content in Internet Explorer

Source: The figure was originally created with XML Spy 2.0, as delivered with XML Spy 4.2. Used with permission of Altova GmbH, The XML Spy Company (*http://www.xmlspy.com*).

The Big Picture and the Role of the W3C

In the preceding sections, we've introduced many members of the large family of XML specifications without showing their family tree. Now is the time to get the Big Picture straight.

The members of the World Wide Web Consortium approved the XML 1.0 Specification as a W3C Recommendation on February 10, 1998. However, the W3C XML efforts began in July 1996 when the SGML Editorial Review Board became the XML Working Group, eventually producing the first XML draft in November 1996. (These and other events are detailed in the timeline presented in chapter 1.)

Before we examine that complicated family tree, we'll take a brief detour to cover the process the W3C follows when considering new technical specifications and to understand the W3C activity areas.

W3C Recommendation Process

The W3C[6] consists of a relatively small full-time staff and more than 500 members (corporations, government agencies, universities, etc.). Unlike IETF, OASIS, and other standards groups, the W3C creates recommendations that explain how certain Web technology should be used and integrated with existing technology. The W3C has no official jurisdiction to enforce its recommendations, although the hope is that once a consensus is reached on a particular specification, there will be sufficient vendor and developer support so that compliance results from something like peer pressure and a desire to be a good player. Unfortunately, this hope has not always been realized; some vendors choose to depart from the recommendations in ways that sometimes result in significant incompatibilities.

It's important to understand that W3C specifications go through several discrete (and often lengthy) stages before they become standards (see *http://www.w3.org/TR/#About*—see Figure 2-35). For example, the difference in maturity between the XSLT Version 1.0 *Recommendation* and the XSLT Version 2.0 *Working Draft* is significant. The former term denotes a solid, mature, well-tested specification, and the latter is an early version of a work in progress, certain to change, perhaps in major, backward-incompatible ways. When you base your development on a Working Draft, you must be prepared to make considerable code changes in later stages, or to release something that might not be consistent with the ultimate W3C Recommendation, which is the closest W3C comes to a "standard."

Initially, an idea for new Web technology comes from a member, from the industry, or from the W3C team itself. If it is from a member, a **Submission** is

6. There are three W3C host institutions: in North America, the Massachusetts Institute of Technology Laboratory for Computer Science (MIT/LCS); in Europe, Institut National de Recherche en Informatique et en Automatique (INRIA); and in Asia, Keio University (KEIO).

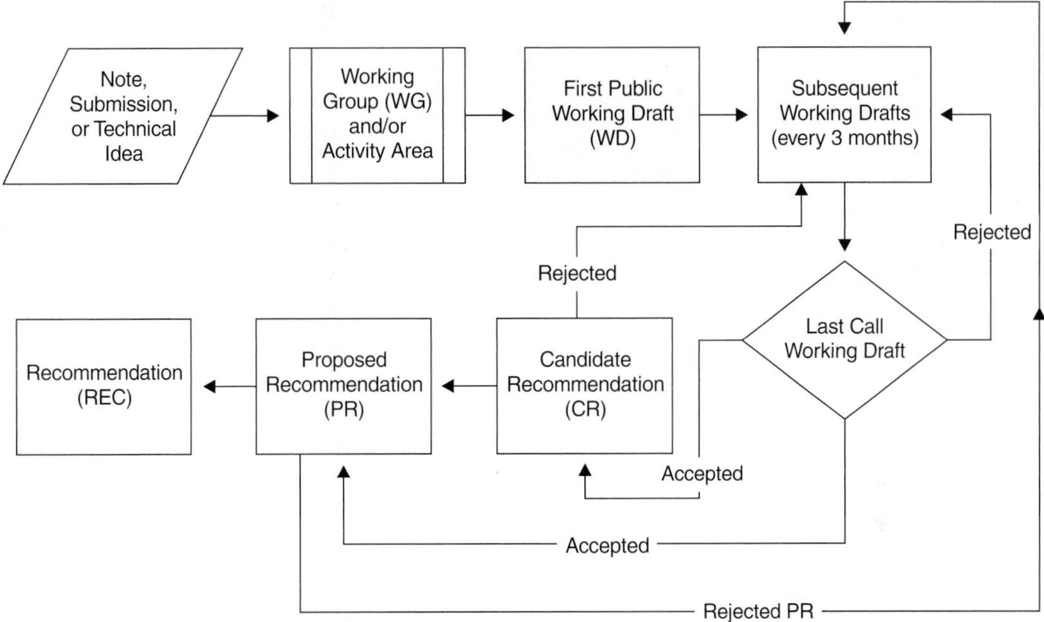

FIGURE 2-35 W3C recommendation process

logged. This may result in an Activity Proposal to membership which, in turn, may add to the scope of an existing Activity Area or, if none is appropriate, may result in the creation of a new Activity Area. The proposal is assigned to one of the many Working Groups (WG), a special Interest Group, or a Coordination Group.

A proposal from a member company or from nonmembers in the technical community may also be published on the W3C site as a **Note**. The Consortium clearly explains that a Note carries no endorsement or guarantee that the proposal will ever become a recommendation; developers should not base plans on a W3C Note, although if the idea appears promising, it is useful to monitor its progress as it goes through the W3C process, if it does at all.

If sufficient interest is generated by a proposal (either a Submission or a Note), a Working Group refines the concepts until eventually a first public **Working Draft (WD)** is produced. At that point, the W3C announces the Working Draft and actively solicits feedback from its members, the technical industry, and the developer community, as well as from official standards groups, where appropriate. From that point, subsequent revisions of the Working Draft are published approximately every three months. Although Working Drafts are typically defined well enough for companies to begin developing plans, the W3C emphasizes that a WD is a "work in progress" and it reserves the right to make incompatible changes in subsequent drafts. Furthermore, publication of a Working Draft does not imply commitment on the part of W3C to evolve the proposal into a Recommendation (although in practice, this almost always is the case).

When the Working Group believes the refinements are complete, the W3C publishes the **Last Call Working Draft**, again requesting feedback from all interested parties (including nonmembers). Occasionally, the Working Draft is rejected at that point (sending it back for more revisions), but it is more likely that issues are raised, recorded, and eventually addressed by the Working Group. This typically results in a **Proposed Recommendation (PR)**, which lasts from one to three months, providing the membership one final chance to suggest changes. A Proposed Recommendation must contain a statement indicating how the current proposal relates to existing documents and standards.

Members vote on whether to accept the proposal as is or with changes, to return it to the Working Draft state, or to reject it (drop it from the W3C activities); members submit questions that must be addressed. After incorporating the latest comments and revisions, if the W3C members reach a consensus, the document becomes a W3C **Recommendation (REC)**, the highest possible status of such specifications. Although the W3C does not use the word *standard,* a Recommendation is essentially a standard since all major browser and tools vendors will tend to adhere (more or less) to its descriptions and proscriptions.

In 1999 a new category called **Candidate Recommendation (CR)** was added to this process. A CR has already had significant technical review by those involved in the Working Group and in the development community, so a Candidate Recommendation is "an explicit call to those outside of the related Working Groups or the W3C itself for implementation and technical feedback." Direct experience of developers and the industry helps the W3C finalize the Candidate Recommendation into a Proposed Recommendation (or send it back to the Working Draft phase). Although every specification nominally goes through the CR stage, it is quite possible that this might take zero time if implementations already exist (i.e., are developed by companies as the Working Drafts are revised). Therefore, it's possible for a specification to progress from Last Call Working Draft to Proposed Recommendation, although in the year 2000, quite a few specifications lingered in the Candidate Recommendation state. The W3C Process documentation (*http://www.w3.org/Consortium/ Process/Process-19991111/*) indicates that the CR stage may last from zero delay to a maximum of one year.

W3C Domains, Activities, and Working Groups

The resources of the W3C are spread across five domains and defined by roughly thirty activities, as described on *http://www.w3.org/Consortium/* and *http://www.w3.org/Consortium/Activities*.

- *Architecture Domain:* to develop the underlying technologies of the Web; includes DOM, Jigsaw (W3C's Java-based Web server), URI, XML, and XML Protocol (also included HTTP until that activity met its goals in mid 2000).
- *Document Formats Domain:* to perfect formats and languages that Web content developers and users use to effectively perceive and express information; includes Amaya browser/editor, graphics (SVG, PNG, etc.), HTML (which includes XHTML), internationalization, MathML, and style (CSS and XSL).
- *Interaction Domain:* to improve user interaction with the Web, and to facilitate universal systems for distributing and accessing information (benefiting both users and content providers); includes device independence (mobile access, etc.), synchronized multimedia (SMIL), and voice browser (including speech recognition).
- *Technology and Society Domain:* to develop Web infrastructure to address social, legal, and public policy concerns; includes Platform for Privacy Preferences Project (P3P), Semantic Web (RDF), XML Encryption, and XML (Digital) Signature.
- *Web Accessibility Initiative (WAI):* to promote a high degree of usability for people with disabilities, as well as for people not so challenged, in the areas of specific technology, guidelines, tools, education and outreach, and research and development; includes producing Web content guidelines to increase accessibility of Web sites, as well as guidelines for designers of user agents (browsers, multimedia players, etc.) and authoring tools (HTML and stylesheet editors, site management tools, etc.).

Activity proposals from members that generate enough consensus become official Activities, which are then organized into Groups. Most activities are Working Groups, but some are Interest or Coordination Groups. The majority of these Activities have their own Working Group, although some share a Working Group, and in the case of XML, some require multiple Working Groups.

The Extensible Markup Language Activity Statement is located at *http://www.w3.org/XML/Activity*. In addition to describing the four phases of XML development mentioned in chapter 1, this page describes the WGs that apply to XML.

There are presently five XML Working Groups and three related WGs:

- *XML Core Working Group:* working on XML Information Set (Infoset), XML Fragment Interchange, and XInclude (XML Inclusions), a corrected version of XML 1.0, and version 1.1 of Namespaces in XML.
- *XML Schema Working Group:* defining a schema language for datatyping, subclassing, and more flexible content models to replace DTDs.
- *XML Linking Working Group:* finalizing XPointer (an extension of XPath used by XSLT) and XLink (complex link arcs and behavior), as well as XML Base (base URI for interpreting relative URIs).

- *XML Query Working Group:* developing a query data model followed by the development of query algebra and eventually the query language itself.
- *XML Coordination Group:* coordinating all XML activities, coordinating workflow, monitoring dependencies, maintaining a public roadmap, and so on.
- *XSL Working Group:* defining XML transformation and display languages; completed XSLT Recommendation and XSL Formatting Objects (which significantly extend the capabilities of Cascading Style Sheets). See *http://www.w3.org/Style/Activity* and *http://www.w3.org/Style/XSL/*.
- *Document Object Model Working Group:* defining models for creating, deleting, and manipulating content, style, and behavior of documents; Level 2 is complete and Level 3 is under way. See *http://www.w3.org/DOM/Activity* and *http://www.w3.org/DOM/*.
- *Web Services Working Group:* newest WG, formed in January 2002; charter calls for defining mechanisms for XML-based message parsing for application-to-application communication; actively exploring existing mechanisms, such as SOAP, XML-RPC, XMI, Jabber, ebXML, WDDX, BizTalk, ICE, P3P, BXXP, and so on. Currently developing SOAP 1.2. See *http://www.w3.org/2002/ws/*. Formerly known as XML Protocols WG, formed in September 2000.

In July 2001, the *Technical Architecture Group (TAG)* was formed to oversee the ever-growing group of specifications. According to the TAG charter (*http://www.w3.org/2001/07/19-tag*), the group's threefold mission is:

1. To document and build consensus around principles of Web architecture and to interpret and clarify these principles when necessary;
2. To resolve issues involving general Web architecture brought to the TAG;
3. To help coordinate cross-technology architecture developments inside and outside W3C.

Formal meetings of TAG began in January 2002.

The Big Picture

Now that we have an understanding of the various stages that a specification moves through during the W3C Recommendation process, as well as of the W3C Working Groups chartered with developing the specifications, we can better appreciate the color-coded "Big Picture" that represents the XML family tree (see inside front cover). This is a diagram of my own design that was first created in early 1998 (when the family was considerably more sparsely populated), and it is not implicitly or explicitly endorsed by the W3C.

An updated version of this diagram is available from the book's Web site, *http://wdvl.Internet.com/Authoring/Languages/XML/XMLFamily*. The online version of the Big Picture is an imagemap. Clicking on the name or acronym of any specification links you to either the document or a collection of related documents. Acronyms are expanded as you "mouse over" each rectangle.

When the W3C chartered the original "SGML for the Web" effort in May 1996, initial plans called for only three specifications: XML (syntax), XLink (linking), and XSL (stylesheet language) to parallel the ISO/IEC standards SGML, HyTime (and TEI), and DSSSL, respectively. In 1998 the XML family was essentially just XML itself, plus early versions of XML Linking Language (XLink) and XSL. However, XML Pointer Language (XPointer) was separated out from XLink and XSL split into XSLT and XSLFO (in April 1999) and eventually XML Path Language (XPath, July 1999). However, since mid 1999 and especially in 2000, the family members have been fruitful and multiplying. In 2001 a large number of Working Drafts matured into Recommendations.

It seems useful to construct our family tree with several interest criteria in mind. A color key at the bottom of the Big Picture diagram indicates the maturity of the various specifications. We will let physical proximity generally denote some relationship between specifications, the exact nature of which depends on the specs in question. We can also group the specifications into one or more of several broad functional categories, such as markup languages, scripting, stylesheets, linking and pointing, support and infrastructure, schemas, e-commerce, and graphics.

Markup Languages

Markup languages are the core of a considerable portion of the W3C efforts, and so they are central to our diagram; they appear in the center left. We've seen that XML is a syntax for a metalanguage upon which we can build domain- and application-specific vocabularies. The Markup section is the heart of our diagram because it is the most fundamental part. This includes HTML, XHTML, XML, and SGML. HTML is a relatively simple application of the SGML metalanguage. SGML was also the basis for other more complex document-centric languages prior to the Web, for example, to describe comprehensive multivolume flight manuals.

XHTML 1.0 is an application of the XML metalanguage (much as HTML is an application of SGML). In this case, the element names happen to be the same as those of HTML 4.01, but the syntax adheres to the rules of XML (which we'll cover in chapter 3). That's why XHTML 1.0 is also known as a "reformulation of HTML in XML syntax". XHTML 1.0 became a Recommendation in January 2000, followed by a number of related efforts in 2000 and 2001 to define lightweight, modular implementations of HTML for devices with limited memory and needs. All future HTML development will be defined in terms of XHTML, as indicated in the HTML

Working Group Roadmap (see *http://www.w3.org/MarkUp/xhtml-roadmap/* and also *http://www.w3.org/MarkUp/Activity*). Other XML applications closely related to XHTML appear in the lower left corner: Modularization of XHTML (very important to portable devices with limited memory), XHTML Basic, XHTML 1.1, and so on.

The color code tells us that HTML 4.01, XHTML 1.1, XHTML 1.0, and XML are all full-fledged W3C Recommendations because they appear in red. In contrast, SGML is not a specification controlled by the W3C and is therefore shown in black text.

We've read a little about some of the specialized markup languages (e.g., MathML, SMIL, WML, SVG, and VoiceXML), all of which are built on XML syntax rules; these are all applications of XML. Again, the color code tells us MathML, SMIL, and SVG are Recommendations, Voice Browser efforts are still Working Drafts, and WML is not under the purview of the W3C. Most of these XML application languages take into account XML Namespaces, a recommendation from January 1999, nearly a year after XML 1.0.

Schema and Metadata

You might wonder why the acronym DTD doesn't appear in our Big Picture—it's because there is no separate DTD specification. Instead, the explanation of DTD syntax and processing is part of the XML 1.0 Recommendation. As powerful as DTDs are, their ability to meet the demands of the data-centric worlds of e-commerce and the sciences is limited. Two major shortcomings of DTDs are the inability to constrain values to datatypes commonly found in database applications and programming languages (e.g., integer, float, and a range of values), and the lack of a mechanism for subclassing existing types by either restricting or extending their definitions. Fortunately, all of the schema efforts shown in the picture—XML Schema, RELAX Next Generation (RELAX NG), XML Data Reduced (XDR), Schema for Object-oriented XML (SOX), etc.—do overcome these DTD limitations, to various degrees. In chapter 6, we'll touch on of these approaches, but the primary focus is on XML Schema, W3C's Recommendation that was two years in the making, having benefited from the ideas of earlier approaches such as XDR and SOX. On the other hand, RELAX NG is a newer and somewhat simpler approach, one that can leverage the numerous datatypes defined by XML Schema; it is certainly an effort worthy of your attention, especially if you find XML Schema too involved.

XML Schema, sometimes informally known as XSD or XSDL (XML Schema Definition Language), is a way to describe the content and data model of a particular XML vocabulary with strong datatyping, subclassing, and constraints expression, far surpassing anything possible with DTDs. The specification is divided into three parts: XML Schema Part 1: Structures (which specifies the language constructs) and XML Schema Part 2: Datatypes (which describes facilities for defining datatypes or using any of the 40+ built-in datatypes), as well as a detailed tutorial-like introduction, XML Schema Part 0: Primer. (By convention, XML Schema files typically have a `.xsd` extension.)

Resource Description Framework (RDF) and the Platform for Internet Content Selection (PICS) were discussed in the section on metadata. Platform for Privacy Preferences (P3P) 1.0 "enables Web sites to express their privacy practices in a standard format that can be retrieved automatically and interpreted easily by user agents. P3P user agents will allow users to be informed of site practices (in both machine- and human-readable formats) and to automate decision making based on these practices when appropriate." P3P can be expressed in terms of RDF and its interaction with user agents is a good fit with the goals of RDF.

Scripting, Object Models, and Parsing

Once we have defined a document structure by means of a markup language and have created an instance of that type of document, we may need to access or modify elements or attributes, possibly from a client-side application. JavaScript and the DOM provide these capabilities.

Netscape first introduced scripting of Web pages with JavaScript 1.0 in Netscape Navigator 2.0 beta (autumn 1995). Actually, JavaScript was called "LiveScript" until someone at Netscape decided it would be beneficial to capitalize on the early crests of the Java wave. At the time, Java and JavaScript were completely unrelated. Now, however, well-defined interfaces exist between the two languages. Microsoft introduced a derivative of JavaScript, called JScript, soon thereafter in Internet Explorer 3.0 beta (spring 1996). To make matters even more confusing, Internet Explorer also supports JavaScript—with some exceptions. Underlying both JavaScript and JScript is the notion of an *object model*, with an object hierarchy rooted by a `window` object, with children named `document`, `location`, `history`, and `frame`. (The JScript model details differ.) Each object has properties, the values of which can be accessed with the general syntax:

```
ancestorObjectName.objectName.propertyName
```

ECMAScript[7] (Standard ECMA-262) is the evolving effort to create a general-purpose, cross-platform programming language. ECMAScript is technology based largely on Netscape's JavaScript and Microsoft's JScript.

The W3C's Document Object Model (DOM) is conceptually a tree view of the hierarchy defined by a specific XML or HTML document instance. The DOM tree is the basis of one of the XML parsing models. Once an XML document has been parsed into its corresponding DOM tree, nodes can be accessed to extract or alter

7. Founded in 1961, ECMA is an international industry association dedicated to the standardization of information and communication systems.

information, or to insert or delete nodes, and possibly output a modified XML document. According to the W3C, the DOM provides a "platform- and language-neutral interface that allows programs and scripts to dynamically access and update the content, structure, and style of documents." In general, any element or attribute of an HTML or XML document can be accessed, changed, deleted, or added using the DOM. Levels 1 and 2 have been completely defined, and Level 3 is in progress. Each level defines a superset of the capabilities of the earlier level.

Dynamic HTML is a term introduced by Netscape and Microsoft, but not used by W3C. The consortium's position is that DHTML is nothing more than "the combination of HTML, stylesheets and scripts that allows documents to be animated." ECMAScript and DOM are efforts to arrive at vendor-neutral scripting solutions.

Although not related to scripting or object models, the Simple API for XML (SAX), a grassroots effort from the XML development community, is another parsing paradigm that is often used as an alternative to, or in conjunction with, the DOM. Both SAX and DOM are covered in detail in later chapters.

XForms, promoted as the next generation of Web forms, is targeted for diverse platforms, such as desktop computers, handhelds, information appliances, and even paper. The key goals of XForms is to decouple data, logic, and presentation; to support sophisticated forms logic; and to enable multiple-page forms. The XForms User Interface provides a standard set of visual controls that will eventually replace HTML (and XHTML) form controls. As the successor to HTML forms, XForms can function as XHTML modules, or they can be integrated with other XML languages. XForms consist of the data model (composite datatypes and constraints), the user interface widgets, and XML data transmitted with the form. Datatypes used in XForms are based on XML Schema: Part 2, although in some cases, they differ. The flexible XForms model also supports integration of independently developed user interface controls, such as for voice browsers. Originally an effort of the HTML Working Group, XForms is presently under the purview of its own XForms Working Group.

Stylesheets for Processing and Displaying XML

Since an XML document carries no explicit visual representation, in applications where the information needs to be displayed (as opposed to being passed as a message between two XML-aware applications), stylesheets are necessary. The least complex type of stylesheet is Cascading Style Sheets (CSS) Level 1. CSS 2 is also a Recommendation and Level 3 is emerging.

We've already seen examples of the more powerful XSL/XSLT stylesheets. As we can tell from the black text in the Big Picture diagram, the powerful but complex Document Style Semantics and Specification Language (DSSSL) standard is not controlled by the W3C.

CSS Level 1 can be used when the display requirements do not depend on attributes and when there is no need to transform or reorder the elements. CSS Level 2 supports processing of attributes. On the other hand, when it is necessary to filter, sort, or otherwise transform XML data before it is rendered, the much more powerful XSLT, either with or without XSL Formatting Objects (XSLFO), is necessary. We will cover the advantages and disadvantages of CSS, XSLT, and XSL in later chapters.

Extensible Stylesheet Language (XSL) is a far more sophisticated style language than is CSS. XSL draws on earlier specifications including CSS and DSSSL. XSL is a language for expressing stylesheets; it consists of two parts:

- A language for transforming XML documents, namely XSLT, and
- An XML vocabulary for specifying formatting semantics called XSL, but sometimes called XSLFO

An XSLT stylesheet tells a processor how to convert logical structures (the source XML document represented as a tree) into a presentational structure (the result tree). Note that an XSLT stylesheet is actually an XML document! XSLFO is focused on presentational structure such as page layout in PDF or SVG graphics.

XPath, while no longer part of the XSL specification, is a syntax for addressing parts of a document. The XPath Recommendation is also significant in XPointer and to the emerging XML Query Language.

Linking, Pointing, and Querying

The XML Linking Language (XLink) provides a way to associate powerful linking capabilities to XML elements with arbitrary names. In addition to describing simple unidirectional links (like the <a> element in HTML), XLink provides for multidirectional links, links with multiple destinations, linking two documents without write access to either, sophisticated behavior like automatically inserting content inline from a linked document, as well as something called *linkbases,* which are databases for organizing link locations, external from the linked documents themselves. XLinks may optionally include attributes that fine-control their behavior.

XPointer specifies a mechanism for pointing to arbitrary chunks (fragments) of a target document, even when the original author of the target document did not provide fragment identifiers. XPointer uses XPath, originally developed as a spinoff specification from XSLT, for its pathlike syntax. For example, this XPointer expression

```
doc.xml#xpointer(//myList/item[position() = 7])
```

points to the seventh `item` element whose immediate parent is a `myList` element (at any level in the document hierarchy). Expressions can be based on element types, attribute values, character content, relative position, ranges, or even a series of noncontiguous strings.

XLink and XPointer are based in part on two mature standards for the desktop publishing world, Text Encoding Initiative (TEI) and Hypermedia/Time-based Structuring Language (HyTime), neither of which falls under the jurisdiction of the W3C.

At the time of this writing, there is no official XML Query Language Recommendation endorsed by the W3C, although there is a very large and active XML Query Working Group. The language under development is called XQuery (*an*, as opposed to *the*, XML Query language). Proposals date way back to 1998, including XML-QL by AT&T Labs, INRIA, and others (August 1998) which is SQL-like in syntax. Another proposal was XML Query Language (XQL), a submission by Texel, webMethods, and Microsoft, described as a natural extension to the XSL pattern syntax (which eventually became XPath). W3C's Query language requirements dictate that the XML Query Language must be declarative, more than one syntax binding must be supported, some syntax must be convenient for humans to read and write, that it must be protocol independent, and so forth.

According to the home page (*http://www.w3.org/XML/Query*, accessed January 2002) of the XML Query Working Group:

> The mission of the XML Query working group is to provide flexible query facilities to extract data from real and virtual documents on the Web, therefore finally providing the needed interaction between the Web world and the database world. Ultimately, collections of XML files will be accessed like databases.

The ever-growing list of specs from the Query Working Group includes XML Query Requirements, XML Query Use Cases, XQuery 1.0 and XPath 2.0 Data Model, XQuery 1.0 Formal Semantics, XQuery 1.0: An XML Query Language, XML Syntax for XQuery 1.0 (XQueryX), and XQuery 1.0 and XPath 2.0 Functions and Operators Version 1.0, all of which are available from *http://www.w3.org/XML/Query*.

Support and Infrastructure

A number of the XML family members don't fit so neatly into the categories I've identified. Arguably, they provide some sort of infrastructure upon which other specifications can be defined, or they provide support at a core level. The specifications in this admittedly miscellaneous category are Namespaces in XML, P3P, Canonical XML, XML Base, XML Infosets, XML Inclusions, and XML-Signature Syntax and Processing. Note that most of these specs fall within the scope of the XML Core Working Group and the XML Schema Working Group.

The Namespaces in XML Recommendation (often called "XML Namespaces" or simply "namespaces") introduces the notion of qualified names to prevent conflicts between identically named XML elements by associating a prefix that identifies an intended namespace with a URI. The namespaces concept has become fundamental to most XML specifications since 1999, each of which declares its own namespace.[8] We've already seen the use of namespaces in our XSLT examples, although we did not call attention to it. For example, in the following XSLT and XSLFO fragment, two namespaces are declared (in bold): the conventional `xsl` prefix (for XSLT transformations) which maps to the URI to `http://www.w3.org/1999/XSL/Transform` and `fo`, the formatting objects prefix, which maps to `http://www.w3.org/1999/XSL/Format`. The element `xsl:template` is now qualified to distinguish it from, for example, `fo:template` (if there were such an element). We say that these qualified element names belong to different namespaces.

```
<?xml version='1.0'?>
<xsl:stylesheet
     xmlns:xsl="http://www.w3.org/1999/XSL/Transform"
     xmlns:fo="http://www.w3.org/1999/XSL/Format"
     version='1.0'>
  <xsl:template match="figure">
    <fo:block>
      <xsl:apply-templates/>
    <fo:block>
  </xsl:template>
  <xsl:template match="photo">
    <fo:block text-align="center">
      </fo:external-graphic src="{@image}"/>
    </fo:block>
  </xsl:template><!-- etc -->
</xsl:stylesheet>
```

The Canonical XML Recommendation describes the subset of a XML document that defines its logical structure. Two XML documents with identical Canonical XML representations are considered logically equivalent for the purposes of many applications. Converting a document to canonical form often will result in some information loss, however. For example, comments are optional for inclusion in the canonical form.

The XML Information Set (Infoset) Recommendation describes an abstract data set containing the information available from a well-formed XML document that follows the Namespaces spec. The information set consists of two or more information items (document, element, attribute, character, processing instruction, and so on).

The XML Base Recommendation provides a mechanism analogous to the <base> element in HTML to resolve a relative URI. XML Base defines `xml:base` attributes that can be used by any XML language, especially XLink.

8. Unfortunately, exactly what type of file, if any, needs to be at the URI pointed to by the Namespace is a hotly debated issue, as of this writing. It originally was just an identifying string, but many people want documentation, XML Schema, or other validation aids to be indicated by the Namespace.

XML Inclusions (XInclude) "specifies a processing model and syntax for general-purpose inclusion. Inclusion is accomplished by merging a number of XML Infosets into a single composite Infoset." There is no relationship to DTD validation defined by XInclude; and XInclude syntax is based on the element `xi:include`, and URI references of XML. In contrast to the XLink attribute `show="embed"` type of graphical inclusion, XInclude specifies a media-type specific transformation (see *http://www.w3.org/TR/xinclude*, accessed January 2002).

XML-Signature Syntax and Processing is a joint effort of the IETF and the W3C to specify XML syntax and processing rules for creating and representing digital signatures. "XML Signatures provide integrity, message authentication, and/or signer authentication services for data of any type, whether located within the XML that includes the signature or elsewhere" (*http://www.w3.org/TR/xmldsig-core/*, accessed January 2002).

Graphics Standards

Earlier in this chapter, we covered SVG and extolled its many virtues as a resolution-independent way of delivering non-bitmapped graphics with low bandwidth requirements and with optimal flexibility in terms of its integration with other XML specifications, such as DOM, CSS, XSLT, XLink, and XHTML. However, SVG wasn't the first approach to this problem proposed by members of the W3C. Actually, it is the culmination of and improvement upon several earlier efforts. In 1998 there were several graphics submissions to W3C based on XML: DrawML, Adobe's Precision Graphics Markup Language (PGML), Hyper Graphics Markup Language (HGML), and Vector Markup Language from Microsoft (VML). Although based on XML, these earlier approaches were all missing something, especially in terms of complete integration with the rest of the XML family of specifications (which, in all fairness, were changing rapidly in 1998 and most of 1999). SVG is an attempt to take the best ideas from PGML and VML and make something that is a truly flexible, open standard. With the debut of SVG, the others become defunct, except VML in certain Microsoft camps. SVG became a full W3C Recommendation in September 2001.

Other W3C graphics efforts include Portable Network Graphics (PNG), which is essentially a replacement for JPEG, and WebCGM Profile, a Web-based version of the 1987 Computer Graphics Metafile standard. WebCGM Profile became a W3C Recommendation in January 1999. It is used by aerospace, defense, automotive, and electronics industries because it is especially good for technical graphics and is integrated with HTML. Inclusion of graphics in HTML and XML is discussed on the W3C Graphics Activity page (*http://www.w3.org/Graphics*).

XML Family of Specifications in a Nutshell

Appendix A provides a concise summary of the major XML specifications (listed in alphabetical order), most of which are covered in some detail in later chapters of this book. This list is constantly growing. The entries we've selected have emphasized W3C heritage, so numerous industry-specific languages are not listed here, although many appear on the right side of the Big Picture diagram.[9]

E-Commerce

While e-commerce is not otherwise within the scope of this book, it is worth pointing out in passing some of the major organizations and initiatives in this area, listed alphabetically in Appendix B. For those who wish to learn more, both the appendix and the section "For Further Exploration" contain links to all organizations and efforts.

Summary

It has been said that if HTML makes easy things easy, XML will make hard things possible. When the XML 1.0 specification was announced in February 1998, the press release was accompanied by glowing testimonials from Adobe, IBM, Lotus, Microsoft, Netscape, SoftQuad, and many others. XML has been heralded as the enabling technology for a Brave New Web, a whole new generation of Web applications. However, to fully appreciate the true power of XML, we must free ourselves from the all-too-familiar browser paradigm. We must think in terms of Web-enabled applications, often not involving a traditional Web browser, that are capable of accessing data in ways previously not possible. When we think of representing structured data on the Web, we should think in terms of using XML because XML is to data as HTML is to display.

As Web developers, you might prefer to think in terms of Web pages, form data, and application objects. You'd like to be able to think in terms of higher-level abstractions that model your data. At first blush, it might seem like XML is all about angle brackets, elements, attributes, and characters that aren't limited to ISO-Latin. However, once an XML parser digests the XML chunks, it breaks your document or message into abstract morsels called **information items** (from the XML Information Set specification). The abstractions represented by the so-called **infoset** are at a minimum well-formed or perhaps may be valid with respect to a DTD or XML Schema associated with the XML instance. Precise datatype information can be associated with individual attributes by an XML Schema processor. XSLT can then be used to transform your original infoset into another that represents a different XML structure, or to transform the input XML into a non-XML format, such as HTML or flat files. XLink and XPointer technology can add to the usefulness of your data representation. Finally, if your intent is to pass messages among processes or companies, the emerging XML Protocol from the W3C, based on SOAP, will be of interest.

9. For long lists of other XML vocabularies, see *http://xml.org/xmlorg_registry/index.shtml*, *http://xml.org/registry/*, or *http://www.biztalk.org/library/library.asp*.

The Gartner Group, the premier source of business and technology intelligence, predicts big developments in the XML world by the end of 2002. They predict that 80 percent of the XML family of specifications defined by the end of 2000 will be merged, shelved, or discarded by the end of 2002.

In February 2001, in an article for the excellent e-zine, XML.com, noted XML author Simon St. Laurent lamented on the ever-growing XML family:

> The learning curve for XML is growing rapidly, and even XML "experts" can no longer keep track of every specification. Monitoring XML's growth is a full-time job. 1200 pages is no longer enough to describe the XML family of specifications in any kind of depth, even without getting into best practices. ("XML Ain't What It Used To Be," *http://www.xml.com/pub/a/2001/02/28/eightytwenty.html*)

For this reason, the links included with each chapter of this book supplement the material and should help you keep current with new developments in areas that most interest you. These links, organized by chapters and sorted alphabetically, are all available on the book's Web site.

For Further Exploration

Articles

ZapThink Research: The Pros and Cons of XML [free 50+-page report]
http://www.zapthink.com/reports/proscons.html

XML.com: XML-related Activities at the W3C, by C.M. Sperberg-McQueen
http://www.xml.com/pub/a/2001/01/03/w3c.html

Books

Inside XML DTDs: Scientific and Technical, Simon St. Laurent, Robert J. Biggar (1999, Osborne McGraw-Hill, ISBN 007134621X)
http://www.amazon.com/exec/obidos/ASIN/007134621X/

Mastering XML, Ann Navarro, Chuck White, Linda Burman (2000, SYBEX, ISBN 0782122663)
http://www.amazon.com/exec/obidos/ASIN/0782122663

Historical

Standard Generalized Markup Language (SGML): General Introductions and Overviews—Robin Cover's page
http://xml.coverpages.org/general.html

Text Encoding Initiative (TEI)—Robin Cover's page
http://xml.coverpages.org/tei.html

Hypermedia/Time-based Structuring Language (HyTime)—Robin Cover's page
http://xml.coverpages.org/hytime.html

Document Style Semantics and Specification Language (DSSSL)—Robin Cover's page
http://xml.coverpages.org/dsssl.html

Resources

XML FAQ (Peter Flynn, editor)
http://www.ucc.ie/xml/

VoiceXML Forum
http://www.voicexml.org

Wireless Markup Language (WML)
http://www1.wapforum.org/tech/terms.asp?doc=WAP-238-WML-20010626-p.pdf

Wireless Application Protocol (WAP) Forum
http://www.wapforum.org/

Nokia WAP Client and Related Products
http://www.nokia.com/wap/products.html

Netscape and Mozilla XML Support
http://www.mozilla.org/newlayout/xml/

Mozilla XML Sorting Demo
http://www.mozilla.org/newlayout/xml/books/books.xml

Mozilla XML IRS Demo
http://www.mozilla.org/newlayout/xml/tocdemo/rights.xml

Astronomical Instrument Markup Language (AIML)
http://pioneer.gsfc.nasa.gov/public/aiml/

Instrument Markup Language (IML) [more general and more current than AIML]
http://pioneer.gsfc.nasa.gov/public/iml/

Chemistry Markup Language (CML)
http://www.xml-cml.org/

ECMAScript (European Computer Manufacturers Association) Language Specification
http://www.ecma.ch/ecma1/STAND/ECMA-262.HTM

MusicML: Complete MusicXML Example
http://www.musicxml.org/xml/mut.html

Simple API to XML (SAX) [SAX1, SAX2, and extensions]
http://www.saxproject.org/

Adobe's Scalable Vector Graphics site
http://www.adobe.com/svg/main.html

Adobe's Portable Document Format (PDF)
http://www.adobe.com/products/acrobat/adobepdf.html

Just SMIL Home
http://smw.internet.com/smil/smilhome.html

Annotated XML Specification, Tim Bray
http://www.xml.com/xml/pub/axml/axmlintro.html

XML Data Reduced (XDR)
http://www.ltg.ed.ac.uk/~ht/XMLData-Reduced.htm

ANSI ASC X12/XML and DISA
http://xml.coverpages.org/ascX12-disa.html

BizTalk.org
http://www.biztalk.org/

CommerceNet
http://www.commercenet.com/

eCo Framework Project (CommerceNet)
http://eco.commerce.net/

cXML (Commerce XML)
http://www.cxml.org/home/

ebXML (Electronic Business XML)
http://www.ebxml.org/

ECML (Electronic Commerce Modeling Language)
http://www.ecml.org/

IDEAlliance
http://www.idealliance.org/

Open Applications Group [numerous OAGIS business DTDs and XML Schema]
http://www.openapplications.org/

RosettaNet
http://www.rosettanet.org/

UBL (Universal Business Language)
http://www.oasis-open.org/committees/ubl/

UCC (Uniform Code Council, Inc.)
http://www.uccnet.org/

UCC's XML Strategy
http://www.uc-council.org/e_commerce/ec_xml_strategy.html

xCBL (XML Common Business Library—from Commerce One)
http://www.xcbl.org/

XML.org
http://xml.org/

XML.org Vertical Industry Directory [older DTD Repository with hundreds of DTDs]
http://www.xml.org/xml/industry_industrysectors.jsp

XML.org Search Schema Registry [newer Schema Repository]
http://www.xml.org/xml/registry.jsp

XML/EDI Group
http://www.xmledi.org/

UDDI: Universal Discovery Description and Integration
http://www.uddi.org

WSDL: Web Services Description Language
http://www-4.ibm.com/software/developer/library/w-wsdl.html

XML and Databases, Ronald Bourret [major source of database-related aspects of XML]
http://www.rpbourret.com/xml/XMLAndDatabases.htm

XUL Programmer's Reference Manual
http://www.mozilla.org/xpfe/xulref/

jXUL Project
http://jxul.sourceforge.net/

Software

TurboXML, XML Authority and XML Instance from TIBCO Extensibility
http://www.tibco.com/products/extensibility/solutions/turbo_xml.html

Amaya [W3C browser/editor]
http://www.w3.org/Amaya/

IBM's techexplorer [browser plugin for MathML]
http://www-4.ibm.com/software/network/techexplorer/

Apache XML Project [Xerces parser, Xalan XSLT processor, Cocoon publishing framework, etc.]
http://xml.apache.org/

GoXML Search Engine
http://www.xmlglobal.com/

RenderX Barcode Generator
http://www.renderx.com/barcodes.html

RenderX Chess Viewer
http://www.renderx.com/chess.html

Java Technology and XML (Sun Microsystems)
http://java.sun.com/xml/index.html

Microsoft XML home page [frequent site changes make direct links difficult]
http://msdn.microsoft.com/xml

Mozilla Milestones [Netscape browser snapshots]
http://www.mozilla.org/

W3C Specifications and Information

Technical Reports and Publications [all W3C specifications]
http://www.w3.org/TR/

Process [Recommendations, Working Drafts, Notes, etc.]
http://www.w3.org/TR/#About

Process Document, Technical Reports section [details the W3C Recommendation Track]
http://www.w3.org/Consortium/Process/tr

About W3C
http://www.w3.org/Consortium/

Members List
http://www.w3.org/Consortium/Member/List

Activities master list
http://www.w3.org/Consortium/Activities

XML Home Page
http://www.w3.org/XML/

XML: Extensible Markup Language Activity Statement
http://www.w3.org/XML/Activity

HTML: Hypertext MarkUp Language Activity Statement
http://www.w3.org/MarkUp/Activity

HTML Working Group Roadmap
http://www.w3.org/MarkUp/xhtml-roadmap/

DOM: Document Object Model Activity Statement
http://www.w3.org/DOM/Activity

Metadata Activity Statement
http://www.w3.org/Metadata/Activity

Style Activity Statement
http://www.w3.org/Style/Activity

Graphics Activity Statement
http://www.w3.org/Graphics/Activity

Synchronized Multimedia Activity Statement
http://www.w3.org/AudioVideo/Activity

XML Working Groups [W3C member-only link]
http://www.w3.org/XML/Group

XML Query Working Group [W3C member-only link]
http://www.w3.org/XML/Group/Query

Technical Architecture Group (TAG)
http://www.w3.org/2001/tag/

Architecture Domain
http://www.w3.org/Architecture/

User Interface Domain
http://www.w3.org/UI/

Technology and Society Domain
http://www.w3.org/TandS/

Web Accessibility Initiative (WAI)
http://www.w3.org/WAI/

Voice Browser Working Group [VoiceXML, Speech Recognition, etc.]
http://www.w3.org/Voice/

Cascading Style Sheets, Level 2 (CSS2) Specification
http://www.w3.org/TR/REC-CSS2

Cascading Style Sheets (CSS1) Level 1 Specification
http://www.w3.org/TR/REC-CSS1

Document Object Model (DOM) Technical Reports [Level 1, Level 2, and Level 3 Specifications and status]
http://www.w3.org/DOM/DOMTR

HTML 4.01 Specification
http://www.w3.org/TR/html401

Mathematical Markup Language (MathML) 1.01 Recommendation
http://www.w3.org/TR/REC-MathML

Mathematical Markup Language (MathML) 2.0 Recommendation
http://www.w3.org/TR/MathML2/

PICS Rating Vocabularies in XML/RDF
http://www.w3.org/TR/rdf-pics

Platform for Privacy Preferences (P3P)
http://www.w3.org/TR/P3P

Resource Description Framework (RDF) Model and Syntax Specification
http://www.w3.org/TR/REC-rdf-syntax

Resource Description Framework (RDF) Schemas
http://www.w3.org/TR/rdf-schema

Scalable Vector Graphics (SVG)
http://www.w3.org/TR/SVG/

Synchronized Multimedia Integration Language (SMIL) 1.0 Specification
http://www.w3.org/TR/REC-smil

Synchronized Multimedia Integration Language (SMIL) 2.0 Specification
http://www.w3.org/TR/smil20/

XForms [the next generation of Web forms]
http://www.w3.org/MarkUp/Forms/

XHTML 1.0: The Extensible HyperText Markup Language—A Reformulation of HTML 4 in XML 1.0
http://www.w3.org/TR/xhtml1

XHTML Basic
http://www.w3.org/TR/xhtml-basic

XHTML 1.1—Module-based XHTML
http://www.w3.org/TR/xhtml11

Modularization of XHTML
http://www.w3.org/TR/xhtml-modularization

XML: Extensible Markup Language 1.0 Specification
http://www.w3.org/TR/REC-xml

XML Base (XBase)
http://www.w3.org/TR/xmlbase

XML Inclusion (XInclude)
http://www.w3.org/TR/xinclude

XML Information Set (XML Infoset)
http://www.w3.org/TR/xml-infoset

XML Linking Language (XLink)
http://www.w3.org/TR/xlink

XML Path Language (XPath), Version 1.0
http://www.w3.org/TR/xpath

XML Pointer Language (XPointer)
http://www.w3.org/TR/xptr

XML Query Home Page [links to all XQuery specifications]
http://www.w3.org/XML/Query

XML Schema Part 0: Primer
http://www.w3.org/TR/xmlschema-0

XML Schema Part 1: Structures
http://www.w3.org/TR/xmlschema-1

XML Schema Part 2: Datatypes
http://www.w3.org/TR/xmlschema-2

XML-Signature Syntax and Processing
http://www.w3.org/TR/xmldsig-core

XSL: Extensible Stylesheet Language, Version 1.0
http://www.w3.org/TR/xsl/

XSL Transformations (XSLT), Version 1.0
http://www.w3.org/TR/xslt

Chapter 3

XML Syntax and Parsing Concepts

In this chapter, we cover the rules of XML syntax that are stated or implied in the XML 1.0 Recommendation from the W3C. A considerable amount of XML terminology is introduced, including discussions of parsing, well-formedness, and validation. XML document structure, legal XML Names, and CDATA are also among the topics. The XML 1.0 specification also discusses rules for Document Type Definitions (DTDs), which we present in chapter 4. The material in chapters 3 and 4 is very interrelated.

Elements, Tags, Attributes, and Content

To understand XML syntax, we must first be familiar with several basic terms from HTML (and SGML) terminology. XML syntax, however, differs in some important ways from both HTML and SGML, as we'll see.

Elements are the essence of document structure. They represent pieces of information and may or may not contain nested elements that represent even more specific information, attributes, and/or textual content. In our employee directory example from chapter 2 (Listing 2-2), some of the elements were `Employees`, `Employee`, `Name`, `First`, `Last`, `Project`, and `PhoneNumbers`.

Tags are the way elements are indicated or marked up in a document. For each element,[1] there is typically a **start tag** that begins with < (less than) and ends with > (greater than), and an **end tag** that begins with </ and ends with >. Some of the start tags in our example were `<Employees>`, `<Employee>`, `<Name>`, and so forth. The corresponding end tags for these elements were `</Employees>`, `</Employee>`, and `</Name>`.

If an element has one or more attributes, they must appear between the < and > delimiters of the start tag. **Attributes** are qualifying pieces of information that add detail and further define an instance of an element. They are typically details that the language designer feels do not need to be nested elements themselves; the

1. With the exception of something called an **empty element**, as we will soon discuss.

assumption is that the attributes will generally be accessed less often than the elements that contain them, but this tends to be application dependent.[2] In our employee example, the only element that had an attribute was `Employee`, and the attribute was `sex`, with two kinds of instances:

```
<Employee sex="male">
```

or

```
<Employee sex="female">.
```

Each attribute has a **value**, the quoted text to the right of the equal sign. In the preceding examples, the values of the two instances of the sex attribute are "male" and "female". Although in this case the value is a single word, values can be any amount of text, enclosed in single or double quotes. HTML permits attributes that do not require values (e.g., the `selected` attribute to denote a default choice in a form, as in `<OPTION selected>`), but this so-called **attribute minimization** is expressly not permitted in XML.

Content is whatever an element contains. Sometimes element content is simply text. In other cases, elements contain nested elements; the inner (child) elements are called the content of the outer (parent) element. Content is the data that the element contains. For example, in this fragment:

```
<Address>
  <Street>123 Milky Way</Street>
  <City>Columbia</City>
  <State>MD</State>
  <Zip>20777</Zip>
</Address>
```

"123 Milky Way" is the text content of the `Street` element, "Columbia" is the text content of the `City` element, and `Street`, `City`, `State`, and `Zip` are all nested element content of the parent `Address` element, in other words, "123 Milky Way Columbia MD 20777". (The space preceding the last three words is due to newlines, as we'll see.)

Notice that the content of `Zip` is the text string "20777". Why do we not say that this is a number or, better yet, an example of some zip code datatype (constrained to either the valid five-digit or five-plus-four-digit ddddd-dddd values for zip codes)? Because there is nothing about the `Zip` element that conveys its content is numeric! We could, however, denote the element's datatype explicitly by means of an attribute.

```
<Zip type="integer">20777</Zip>
```

2. This is a tremendous oversimplification. For more about this, see "Elements vs. Attributes: Guidelines," in chapter 4.

We'll eventually see how an alternative to DTDs called XML Schema makes data typing easier and far more flexible.

Another possibility, called *mixed content*, was illustrated in chapter 2 in the section "Document-Centric vs. Data-Centric," in which both text and element content may appear as the content of a parent element. We'll see how to handle this in chapter 4.

XML Document Structure

The XML Recommendation states that an XML document has both logical and physical structure. Physically, it is comprised of storage units called **entities**, each of which may refer to other entities, similar to the way that `include` works in the C language. Logically, an XML document consists of declarations, elements, comments, character references, and processing instructions, collectively known as the **markup**.

Although throughout this book we refer to an "XML document," it is crucial to understand that XML may not exist as a physical file on disk. XML is sometimes used to convey messages between applications, such as from a Web server to a client. The XML content may be generated on the fly, for example by a Java application that accesses a database. It may be formed by combining pieces of several files, possibly mixed with output from a program. However, in all cases, the basic structure and syntax of XML is invariant.

An XML document consists of three parts, in the order given:

1. An XML declaration (which is technically optional, but recommended in most normal cases)
2. A document type declaration that refers to a DTD (which is optional, but required if you want validation)
3. A body or document instance (which is required)

Collectively, the XML declaration and the document type declaration are called the **XML prolog**.

XML Declaration

The **XML declaration** is a piece of markup (which may span multiple lines of a file) that identifies this as an XML document. The declaration also indicates whether the document can be validated by referring to an external Document Type Definition (DTD). DTDs are the subject of chapter 4; for now, just think of a DTD as a set of rules that describes the structure of an XML document.

The minimal XML declaration is:

```
<?xml version="1.0" ?>
```

XML is case-sensitive (more about this in the next subsection), so it's important that you use lowercase for `xml` and `version`. The quotes around the value of the `version` attribute are required, as are the ? characters. At the time of this writing, `"1.0"` is the only acceptable value for the `version` attribute, but this is certain to change when a subsequent version of the XML specification appears.

Do not include a space before the string `xml` or between the question mark and the angle brackets. The strings `<?xml` and `?>` must appear exactly as indicated. The space before the `?>` is optional. No blank lines or space may precede the XML declaration; adding white space here can produce strange error messages.

In most cases, this XML declaration is present. If so, it must be the *very first line* of the document and must not have leading white space. This declaration is technically optional; cases where it may be omitted include when combining XML storage units to create a larger, composite document.

Actually, the formal definition of an XML declaration, according to the XML 1.0 specification is as follows:

```
XMLDecl ::= '<?xml' VersionInfo EncodingDecl? SDDecl? S? '?>'
```

This Extended Backus-Naur Form (EBNF) notation, characteristic of many W3C specifications, means that an XML declaration consists of the literal sequence `'<?xml'`, followed by the required version information, followed by optional encoding and standalone declarations, followed by an optional amount of white space, and terminating with the literal sequence `'?>'`. In this notation, a question mark not contained in quotes means that the term that precedes it is optional.

The following declaration means that there is an external DTD on which this document depends. See the next subsection for the DTD that this negative standalone value implies.

```
<?xml version="1.0" standalone="no" ?>
```

On the other hand, if your XML document has no associated DTD, the correct XML declaration is:

```
<?xml version="1.0" standalone="yes" ?>
```

The XML 1.0 Recommendation states: "If there are external markup declarations but there is no standalone document declaration, the value 'no' is assumed."

The optional encoding part of the declaration tells the XML processor (parser) how to interpret the bytes based on a particular character set. The default encoding is UTF-8, which is one of seven character-encoding schemes used by the Unicode standard, also used as the default for Java. In UTF-8, one byte is used to represent the most common characters and three bytes are used for the less common special characters. UTF-8 is an efficient form of Unicode for ASCII-based documents. In fact, UTF-8 is a superset of ASCII.[3]

```
<?xml version="1.0" encoding="UTF-8" ?>
```

For Asian languages, however, an encoding of UTF-16 is more appropriate because two bytes are required for each character. It is also possible to specify an ISO character encoding, such as in the following example, which refers to ASCII plus Greek characters. Note, however, that some XML processors may not handle ISO character sets correctly since the specification *requires* only that they handle UTF-8 and UTF-16.

```
<?xml version="1.0" encoding="ISO-8859-7" ?>
```

Both the standalone and encoding information may be supplied:

```
<?xml version="1.0" standalone="no" encoding="UTF-8" ?>
```

Is the next example valid?

```
<?xml version="1.0" encoding='UTF-8' standalone='no'?>
```

Yes, it is. The order of attributes does not matter. Single and double quotes can be used interchangeably, provided they are of matching kind around any particular attribute value. (Although there is no good reason in *this* example to use double quotes for version and single quotes for the other, you may need to do so if the attribute value already contains the kind of quotes you prefer.) Finally, the lack of a blank space between `'no'` and ?> is not a problem.

Neither of the following XML declarations is valid.

```
<?XML VERSION="1.0" STANDALONE="no"?>
<?xml version="1.0" standalone="No"?>
```

The first is invalid because these particular attribute names must be lowercase, as must "xml". The problem with the second declaration is that the value of the standalone attribute must be literally `"yes"` or `"no"`, not `"No"`. (Do I dare call this a "no No"?)

3. UTF stands for Unicode (or UCS) Transformation Format. UCS is Universal Character Set. Complete information about Unicode is available from *http://www.unicode.org/*.

Document Type Declaration

The **document type declaration** follows the XML declaration. The purpose of this declaration is to announce the root element (sometimes called the *document element*) and to provide the location of the DTD.[4] The general syntax is:

```
<!DOCTYPE RootElement (SYSTEM | PUBLIC)
        ExternalDeclarations?  [InternalDeclarations]? >
```

where `<!DOCTYPE` is a literal string, `RootElement` is whatever you name the outermost element of your hierarchy, followed by either the literal keyword `SYSTEM` or `PUBLIC`. The optional `ExternalDeclarations` portion is typically the relative path or URL to the DTD that describes your document type. (It is really only optional if the entire DTD appears as an `InternalDeclaration`, which is neither likely nor desirable.) If there are `InternalDeclarations`, they must be enclosed in square brackets. In general, you'll encounter far more cases with `ExternalDeclarations` than `InternalDeclarations`, so let's ignore the latter for now. They constitute the *internal subset,* which is described in chapter 4.

Let's start with a simple but common case. In this example, we are indicating that the DTD and the XML document reside in the same directory (i.e., the `ExternalDeclarations` are contained in the file `employees.dtd`) and that the root element is `Employees`:

```
<!DOCTYPE Employees SYSTEM "employees.dtd">
```

Similarly,

```
<!DOCTYPE PriceList SYSTEM "prices.dtd">
```

indicates a root element `PriceList` and the DTD is in the local file: `prices.dtd`.

In the next example, we use normal directory path syntax to indicate a different location for the DTD.

```
<!DOCTYPE Employees SYSTEM "../dtds/employees.dtd">
```

As is often the case, we might want to specify a URL for the DTD since the XML file may not even be on the same host as the DTD. This case also applies when you are using an XML document for message passing or data transmission across servers and still want the validation by referencing a common DTD.

```
<!DOCTYPE Employees SYSTEM
    "http://somewhere.com/dtds/employees.dtd">
```

4. A *Document Type Definition* is a set of rules that describe the hierarchical structure of any XML document instance based on that particular DTD. These rules are used to determine whether the document is valid. DTDs are discussed in detail in chapter 4.

Next, we have the case of the PUBLIC identifier. This is used in formal environments to declare that a given DTD is available to the public for shared use. Recall that XML's true power as a syntax relates to developing languages that permit exchange of structured data between applications and across company boundaries. The syntax is a little different:

```
<!DOCTYPE RootElement PUBLIC PublicID URI>
```

The new aspect here is the notion of a PublicID, which is a slightly involved formatted string that identifies the source of the DTD whose path follows as the URI. This is sometimes known as the **Formal Public Identifier (FPI)**.

For example, I was part of a team that developed (Astronomical) Instrument Markup Language (AIML, IML) for NASA Goddard Space Flight Center.[5] We wanted our DTD to be available to other astronomers. Our document type declaration (with a root element named Instrument) was:

```
<!DOCTYPE Instrument PUBLIC
    "-//NASA//Instrument Markup Language 0.2//EN"
    "http://pioneer.gsfc.nasa.gov/public/iml/iml.dtd">
```

In this case the PublicID is:

```
    "-//NASA//Instrument Markup Language 0.2//EN"
```

The URI that locates the DTD is:

```
    http://pioneer.gsfc.nasa.gov/public/iml/iml.dtd
```

Let's decompose the PublicID. The leading hyphen indicates that NASA is not a standards body. If it were, a plus sign would replace the hyphen, except if the standards body were ISO, in which case the string "ISO" would appear. Next we have the name of the organization responsible for the DTD (NASA, in this case), surrounded with double slashes, then a short free-text description of the DTD ("Instrument Markup Language 0.2"), double slashes, and a two-character language identifier ("EN" for English, in this case).

Since the XML prolog is the combination of the XML declaration and the document type declaration, for our NASA example the complete prolog is:

```
<?xml version="1.0" encoding="UTF-8" standalone="no"?>
<!DOCTYPE Instrument PUBLIC
    "-//NASA//Instrument Markup Language 0.2//EN"
    "http://pioneer.gsfc.nasa.gov/public/iml/iml.dtd">
```

5. Thanks to NASA and Commerce One project participants, Julie Breed, Troy Ames, Carl Hostetter, Rick Shafer, Dave Fout, Lisa Koons, Craig Warsaw, Melissa Hess, Ken Wootton, Steve Clark, Randy Wilke, and Lynne Case, among others.

As another example, let's consider a common case involving DTDs from the W3C, such as those for XHTML 1.0.

```
<?xml version="1.0" encoding="utf-8"?>
<!DOCTYPE html PUBLIC "-//W3C//DTD XHTML 1.0 Transitional//EN"
    "http://www.w3.org/TR/xhtml1/DTD/xhtml1-transitional.dtd">
```

W3C is identified as the organization, "DTD XHTML 1.0 Transitional" is the name of the DTD; it is in English; and the actual DTD is located by the URI *http://www.w3.org/TR/xhtml1/DTD/xhtml1-transitional.dtd*. Similarly, the prolog for XHTML Basic 1.0 is:

```
<?xml version="1.0" encoding="utf-8"?>
<!DOCTYPE html PUBLIC "-//W3C//DTD XHTML Basic 1.0//EN"
    "http://www.w3.org/TR/xhtml-basic/xhtml-basic10.dtd">
```

The XHTML Basic 1.0 `PublicID` is similar but not identical to the XHTML 1.0 case and of course the DTD is different since it's a different language.

If you noticed that the NASA example uses uppercase for the `encoding` value UTF-8 and the W3C examples use lowercase, you may have been bothered because that is inconsistent with what we learned about the case-sensitive value for the `standalone` attribute. The only explanation I can offer is that although element and attribute *names* are always case-sensitive, attributes *values* may or may not be. A reasonable guess is that if the possible attribute values are easily enumerated (i.e., "yes" or "no", or other relatively short lists of choices), then case probably matters.

DTD-related keywords such as `DOCTYPE`, `PUBLIC`, and `SYSTEM` must be uppercase. XML-related attribute names such as `version`, `encoding`, and `standalone` must be lowercase.

Document Body

The **document body**, or instance, is the bulk of the information content of the document. Whereas across multiple instances of a document of a given type (as identified by the `DOCTYPE`) the XML prolog will remain constant, the document body changes with each document instance (in general). This is because the prolog defines (either directly or indirectly) the overall structure while the body contains the real instance-specific data. Comparing this to data structures in computer languages, the DTD referenced in the prolog is analogous to a `struct` in the C language or a `class` definition in Java, and the document body is analogous to a runtime instance of the `struct` or `class`.

Because the document type declaration specifies the root element, this *must* be the first element the parser encounters. If any other element but the one identified by the DOCTYPE line appears first, the document is immediately invalid.

Listing 3-1 shows a very simple XHTML 1.0 document. The DOCTYPE is "html" (not "xhtml"), so the document body begins with <html ....> and ends with </html>.

Listing 3-1 Simple XHTML 1.0 Document with XML Prolog and Document Body

```
<?xml version="1.0" encoding="UTF-8"?>
<!DOCTYPE html
    PUBLIC "-//W3C//DTD XHTML 1.0 Transitional//EN"
    "http://www.w3.org/TR/xhtml1/DTD/xhtml1-transitional.dtd">
<html xmlns="http://www.w3.org/1999/xhtml" xml:lang="en" lang="en">
  <head>
    <title>XHTML 1.0</title>
  </head>
  <body>
    <h1>Simple XHTML 1.0 Example</h1>
    <p>See the <a href=
"http://www.w3.org/TR/xhtml1/DTD/xhtml1-transitional.dtd">DTD</a>.</p>
  </body>
</html>
```

Markup, Character Data, and Parsing

An XML document contains text characters that fall into two categories: either they are part of the document markup or part of the data content, usually called **character data**, which simply means all text that is not part of the markup. In other words, XML text consists of intermingled character data and markup. Let's revisit an earlier fragment.

```
<Address>
  <Street>123 Milky Way</Street>
  <City>Columbia</City>
  <State>MD</State>
  <Zip>20777</Zip>
</Address>
```

The character data comprises the four strings "123 Milky Way", "Columbia", "MD", and "20777"; the markup comprises the start and end tags for the five elements Address, Street, City, State, and Zip. Note that this is similar but not identical, to what we previously called content. For example, although each chunk of character data is the content of a particular element, the content of the Address element is *all of the child elements.* We can think of all the character data belonging to both the element that directly contains it and indirectly to Address. (In fact, in some

XML applications such as XSLT, if we ask for the text content of `Address`, we'll get the concatenation of all the individual strings.)

The **markup** itself can be divided into a number of categories, as per section 2.4 of the XML 1.0 specification.

- start tags and end tags (e.g., `<Address>` and `</Address>`)
- empty-element tags (e.g., `<Divider/>`)
- entity references (e.g., `&footer;` or `%otherDTD;`)
- character references (e.g., `<` or `>`)
- comments (e.g., `<!-- whatever -->`)
- CDATA section delimiters (e.g., `<![CDATA[ insert code here ]]>`)
- document type declarations (e.g., `<!DOCTYPE ....>`)
- processing instructions (e.g., `<?myJavaApp numEmployees="25" location="Columbia" .... ?>`)
- XML declarations (e.g., `<?xml version=.... ?>`)
- text declarations (e.g., `<?xml encoding=.... ?>`)
- any white space at the top level (before or after the root element)

We will discuss each of these markup aspects in either this chapter or the next. Note that for all types of markup, there are some delimiters, most but not all of which involve angle brackets.

The specification states that all text that is not markup constitutes the character data of the document. In other words, if you stripped all markup from the document, the remaining content would be the character data. Consider this example:

```
<?xml version="1.0" standalone="no" ?>
<!DOCTYPE Message SYSTEM "message.dtd">
<Message mime-type="text/plain">
<!-- This is a trivial example. -->
  <From>The Kenster</From>
  <To>Silly Little Cowgirl</To>
  <Body>
  Hi, there. How is your gardening going?
  </Body>
</Message>
```

The character data when the markup is removed would be:

```
The Kenster Silly Little Cowgirl Hi, there. How is your gardening going?
```

In general this is essentially the text between the start and end tags, which we previously called the content of the element, but there is a subtlety related to parsing. Depending on parser details, the newlines after `</From>` and `</To>` might be replaced by single spaces, as shown. Alternatively, the newlines might be preserved.

Parsing is the process of splitting up a stream of information into its constituent pieces (often called tokens). In the context of XML, parsing refers to scanning an

XML document (which need not be a physical file—it can be a data stream) in order to split it into its various markup and character data, and more specifically, into elements and their attributes. XML parsing reveals the structure of the information since the nesting of elements implies a hierarchy. It is possible for an XML document to fail to parse completely if it does not follow the *well-formedness rules* described in the XML 1.0 Recommendation. A successfully parsed XML document may be either well-formed (at a minimum) or valid, as discussed in detail later in this chapter and the next.

There is a subtlety about processing character data. During the parsing process, if there is markup that contains entity references, the markup will be converted into character data. A typical example from XHTML would be:

```
<p>&quot;AT&amp;T is a winning company,&quot; he said.</p>
```

After the parser substitutes for the entities, the resultant character data is:

```
"AT&T is a winning company," he said.
```

After parsing and substituting for special characters, the character data that remains after the substitution is **parsed character data**, which is referred to as `#PCDATA` in DTDs and always refers to textual content of elements. Character data that is not parsed is called `CDATA` in DTDs; this relates exclusively to attribute values.

XML Syntax Rules

In this section, we explain the various syntactical rules of XML. Documents that follow these rules are called *well-formed,* but not necessarily *valid,* as we'll see. If your document breaks any of these rules, it will be rejected by most, if not all, XML parsers.

Well-Formedness

The *minimal* requirement for an XML document is that it be **well-formed**, meaning that it adheres to a small number of syntax rules,[6] which are summarized in Table 3-1 and explained in the following sections. However, a document can abide by all these rules and still be invalid. To be **valid**, a document must both be well-formed and adhere to the constraints imposed by a DTD or XML Schema.

6. See the well-formedness discussion in the XML 1.0 Recommendation, *http://www.w3.org/TR/REC-xml#sec-well-formed*.

TABLE 3-1 XML Syntax Rules (Well-Formedness Constraints)

- The document must have a consistent, well-defined structure.
- All attribute values must be quoted (single or double quotes).
- White space in content, including line breaks, is significant by default.
- All start tags must have corresponding end tags (exception: empty elements).
- The root element must contain all others, which must nest properly by start/end tag pairing.
- Elements must not overlap; they may be nested, however. (This is also technically true for HTML. Browsers ignore overlapping in HTML, but not in XML.)
- Each element except the root element must have exactly one parent element that contains it.
- Element and attribute names are case-sensitive: `Price` and `PRICE` are different elements.
- Keywords such as `DOCTYPE` and `ENTITY` must always appear in uppercase; similarly for other DTD keywords such as `ELEMENT` and `ATTLIST`.
- Tags without content are called empty elements and must end in "/>".

Legal XML Name Characters

An **XML Name** (sometimes called simply a **Name**) is a token that

- begins with a letter, underscore, or colon (but not other punctuation)
- continues with letters, digits, hyphens, underscores, colons, or full stops [periods], known as **name characters**.

Names beginning with the string "`xml`", or any string which would match `(('X'|'x')('M'|'m')('L'|'l'))`, are reserved.

Element and attribute *names* must be valid XML Names. (Attribute *values* need not be.) An **NMTOKEN** (name token) is any mixture of name characters (letters, digits, hyphens, underscores, colons, and periods).

The Namespaces in XML Recommendation assigns a meaning to names that contain colon characters. Therefore, authors should not use the colon in XML names except for namespace purposes (e.g., `xsl:template`).

Listing 3-2 illustrates a number of legal XML Names, followed by three that should be avoided but may or may not be identified as illegal, depending on the XML parser you use, and four that are definitely illegal. (This is file `name-tests.xml` on the CD; you can try this with your favorite parser, or with one of the ones provided on the CD.)

Listing 3-2 Legal, Illegal, and Questionable XML Names

```
<?xml version = "1.0" standalone = "yes" encoding = "UTF-8"?>
<Test>
<!-- legal -->
    <price />
    <Price />
    <pRice />
    <_price />
    <subtotal07 />
    <discounted-price />
    <discounted_price />
    <discounted.price />
    <discountedPrice />
    <DiscountedPrice />
    <DISCOUNTEDprice />
    <kbs:DiscountedPrice />
    <xlink:role />
    <xsl:apply-templates />
<!-- discouraged -->
    <xml-price />
    <xml:price />
    <discounted:price />
<!-- illegal -->
    <7price />
    <-price />
    <.price />
    <discounted price />
</Test>
```

From the legal examples, we see that any mixture of uppercase and lowercase is fine, as are numbers, and the punctuation characters that were in the definition.

Since the last three examples in the first group use a colon, they are assumed to be elements in the namespaces identified by the prefixes "kbs", "xlink", and "xsl". Of these, the last two refer to W3C-specified namespaces; `xlink:role` is an attribute defined by the XLink specification and `xsl:apply-templates` is an element defined by the XSLT specification. The "kbs" prefix refers to a hypothetical namespace, which I could have declared (but didn't), since namespaces do not come only from the W3C. (See chapter 5 for a thorough discussion of namespaces.)

The three debatable examples are `xml-price`, `xml:price`, and `discounted:price`. The first two use the reserved letters "xml"; you shouldn't use them, but most parsers won't reject them. The `discounted:price` example uses a colon, which is frowned upon if "discounted" is not meant to be a prefix associated with a declared namespace.

The four illegal cases are much more clear. The first three, `7price`, `-price`, and `.price`, are illegal because the initial character is not a letter, underscore, or colon. The fourth example is illegal because a space character cannot occur in an XML Name. Most parsers will think this is supposed to be the element named `discounted` and the *attribute* named `price`, minus a required equal sign and value.

XML Names and NMTOKENS apply to elements, attributes, processing instructions, and many other constructs where an identifier is required, so it's important to understand what is and what is not legal.

Elements and Attributes Are Case-Sensitive

Unlike HTML, which is case *insensitive* (as is the SGML metalanguage of which HTML is an appplication), *XML is strictly case-sensitive*, and so therefore is every application of XML (e.g., XSLT, MathML, SVG and so forth, plus any languages you create). Therefore, the following elements are all unique and are in no way related to one another in XML:

```
price
Price
PRICE
```

The case sensitivity nature of XML often confuses novices. Be sure to remember this when doing string comparisons in code.

The W3C's Extensible HyperText Markup Language (XHTML) recasts HTML in XML syntax. In XHTML, all elements and attributes have *lowercase* names, such as:

```
body
h1
img
href
```

Notice that this is not merely a convention; it is an absolute requirement. An XHTML document that contains capital letters in element or attribute names is simply invalid, even though uppercase or mixed-case names such as `BODY`, `Body`, or even `bOdY` would be perfectly acceptable in HTML.

Uppercase Keywords

Since XML is case-sensitive, it should not be surprising that certain special words must appear in a particular case. In general, the keywords that relate to DTDs (e.g., `DOCTYPE`, `ENTITY`, `CDATA`, `ELEMENT`, `ATTLIST`, `PCDATA`, `IMPLIED`, `REQUIRED`, and `FIXED`) *must* be all uppercase. On the other hand, the various strings used in the XML declaration (e.g., `xml`, `version`, `standalone`, and `encoding`) *must* appear in all lowercase.

Case Conventions or Guidelines

When creating your own XML vocabulary, it would be desirable if there were conventions to explain the use of uppercase, lowercase, mixed case, underscores, and hyphens. Unfortunately, no such conventions exist in XML 1.0. It is a good idea to adopt your own conventions and to apply them consistently, at least across your project, but ideally throughout your entire organization.

For example, for element names I prefer using what is often called *CamelCase* because the initial letter of each word in a multiword name is uppercase and all others are lowercase, creating humps like a camel's back. (It's also sometimes called *TitleCase* because it resembles the title of a book.) For example:

```
<DiscountPrice rate="20%" countryCode="US" />
```

Note that for attributes, I also use CamelCase, except the first word is always begun with a *lowercase* letter, as in "countryCode". In fact, the terms *UpperCamelCase* (as I use for elements) and *lowerCamelCase* (as I use for attributes) are often used to make this distinction more clear. One reason that I favor this convention is that in any context (including documentation), it's easy to distinguish elements from attributes.

It would be just as reasonable, however, to use all uppercase letters for elements, all lowercase for attributes, and a hyphen to separate multipart terms as in the following examples, or even to use all uppercase for elements and attributes.

```
<DISCOUNT-PRICE rate="20%" country-code="US" />
```

As stated earlier, for XHTML, the W3C elected to use all lowercase letters. The most important thing is to pick a convention for your project (or your company) and to be consistent across developers and applications.

We've seen UpperCamelCase for elements and lowerCamelCase for attributes in the employee example: Employee with its sex attribute, Address, PhoneNumbers, and so on. The following fragment from the W3C's SOAP 1.2 Part 2 Adjuncts Working Draft (*http://www.w3.org/TR/2001/WD-soap12-part2-20011002/#N4008D*) illustrates its use of UpperCamelCase for element names and lowerCamelCase for attributes, as well as for namespace prefixes.

```
<env:Body >
  <m:GetLastTradePrice
      env:encodingStyle="http://www.w3.org/2001/09/soap-encoding"
      xmlns:m="http://example.org/2001/06/quotes" >
    <m:Symbol>DEF</m:Symbol>
  </m:GetLastTradePrice>
</env:Body>
```

Root Element Contains All Others

There must be one **root element**, also known as the **document element**, which is the parent of all other elements. That is, all elements are nested within the root element. All descendants of the root, whether immediate children or not, represent the content of the root. Recall that the name of the root element is given in the

DOCTYPE line if a DTD is referenced (either an external or internal one). We also noted that this document element must be the first element the parser encounters (after the XML prolog, which does not contain elements).

A somewhat surprising aspect, at least to this author, is that the XML Recommendation does not preclude a recursive root! In other words, it is possible for a root element to be defined in a DTD as containing itself. Although this is not common, it is worth noting. For example, in NASA's IML DTD, we allowed that the root element Instrument could contain other Instrument children. (The DTD syntax shown here is formally described in chapter 4.)

```
<!ELEMENT Instrument (Instrument | Port | CommandProcedureSet)* >
```

Start and End Tags Must Match

Every start tag must have a corresponding end tag to properly delimit the content of the element the tags represent. The start and end tags are indicated exactly as they are in HTML, with < denoting the beginning of a start tag and </ indicating the beginning of the end tag. The end delimiter of each tag is >.

```
<ElementName>content</ElementName>
```

Empty Elements

An exception to the rule about start and end tags is the case in which an element has no content. Such **empty elements** convey information simply by their presence or possibly by their attributes, if any. Examples from XHTML 1.0 include:

```
<br />
<hr />
<img src="someImage.gif" width="100" height="200" alt="Some Image" />
```

An empty element begins like a start tag but *terminates* with the sequence />. Optional white space may be used before the two terminating characters. This author prefers to include a space to emphasize empty elements. The space before /> is necessary for XHTML 1.0 to be handled correctly by older browser versions. Of course, it's also possible to specify an empty element by using regular start and end tags, and this is syntactically identical (from the parser's viewpoint) to the use of empty-element notation.

```
<img src="someImage.gif" width="100" height="200" alt="Some Image"></img>
```

Note that just like in HTML (or more appropriately, XHTML), an empty element is often used as a separator, such as <br /> and <hr />, or to indicate by its presence a particular piece of data, or to convey metadata by its attributes. If the term *empty element* seems strange to you when attributes are involved, just think in terms of the content of the element. There is no content, even when there are attributes, which is why it's called empty.

Proper Nesting of Start and End Tags

No overlapping of start and end tags from different elements is permitted. Although this might seem like an obvious requirement, HTML as implemented by major browsers is considerably more forgiving and recovers from improper tag overlap. Correct nesting looks like this:

```
<OuterElement>
  <InnerElement>inner content</InnerElement>
</OuterElement>
```

An example of improper nesting is:

```
<OuterElement>
  <InnerElement>inner content</OuterElement>
</InnerElement>
```

Believe it or not, most browsers recover from this type of error in HTML, but they cannot and will not in XML or any language based on XML syntax. The improper nesting example results in either one or two fatal errors, with a message similar to this (depending on the parser):

```
Fatal error: end tag '</OuterElement>' does not match start tag.  Expected
    '</InnerElement>'
Fatal error: end tag '</InnerElement>' does not match start tag.  Expected
    '</OuterElement>'
```

Parent, Child, Ancestor, Descendant

The notion of the root element and the proper nesting rules leads us to some conclusions and terminology about the hierarchy of elements that are invariant across all XML documents. The terms *ancestor* and *descendant* are not used in the XML 1.0 Recommendation, but they certainly are in the DOM, XSLT, XPath, and so on, which is why they are introduced here:

- An element is a *child* of exactly one *parent*, which is the element that contains it.
- A parent may have more than one child.
- Immediate children and also children of a child are *descendants* of the parent.
- An element is an *ancestor* of all its descendants.
- The root is the ancestor of all elements.
- Every element is a descendant of the root.
- Every element has exactly one parent, except the root, which has no parent.

Attribute Values Must Be Quoted

In HTML (but not in XHTML), we are permitted to be inconsistent in the use of quotation marks to delimit the values of attributes. Generally, single-word values do not require quotes in HTML. For example, both of these are acceptable and equivalent in HTML:

```
<IMG SRC=someImage.gif>

<IMG SRC="someImage.gif">
```

In XML (and in XHTML), however, we are not allowed to be so cavalier about quotes. *All attribute values must be quoted,* even if there are no embedded spaces.

```
<img src="someImage.gif" />
<img src='someImage.gif' />
<img src="someImage.gif" width="34" height="17"/>
```

Notice that either single or double quotes may be used to delimit the attribute values. Of course, if the attribute value contains double quotes, then you must use single quotes as the delimiter, and vice versa.

```
<Book title="Tudor's Guide to Paris" />
<Object width='5.3"' height='7.1"' />
```

White Space Is Significant

White space consists of one or more *space characters, tabs, carriage returns, line feeds* (denoted as `#x20`, `#x9`, `#xD`, and `#xA`, respectively). In the XML 1.0 Recommendation, white space is symbolized in production rules by a capital "S", with the following definition (See *http://www.w3.org/TR/REC-xml#sec-common-syn* and *http://www.w3.org/TR/REC-xml#sec-white-space*):

```
S ::= (#x20 | #x9 | #xD | #xA)+
```

In contrast to HTML, in which a sequence of white space characters is collapsed into a single white space and in which newlines are ignored, in XML all white space is taken literally. This means that the following two examples are not equivalent:

```
<Publication>
  <Published>1992</Published>
  <Publisher>Harmony Books</Publisher>
</Publication>

<Publication>
  <Published>1992</Published>
  <Publisher>Harmony
Books</Publisher>
</Publication>
```

By default, XML parsers handle the `Publisher` element differently since in the second example, the string "Harmony Books" contains a newline between the two words. The application that invokes the parser can either consider the white space important, ignore it (i.e., strip it), or inform the parser that it wants white space normalized (collapsed like in HTML).

Comments

Comments in XML are just like they are in HTML. They begin with the character sequence `<!--` and end with the sequence `-->`. The parser ignores what appears between them, except to verify that the comment is well-formed.

```
<Publication>
  <Published>1992</Published>
  <!-- This appears to be the second edition. -->
  <Publisher>Harmony Books</Publisher>
</Publication>
```

In XML, however; there are several restrictions regarding comments:

- Comments cannot contain the double hyphen combination "--" anywhere except as part of the comment's start and end tags. Thus, this comment is illegal: `<!-- illegal comment --->`
- Comments cannot be nested. This means you need to take care when commenting out a section that already contains comments.
- Comments cannot precede the XML declaration because that part of the prolog must be the very first line in the document.
- Comments are not permitted in a start or end tag. They can appear only between tags (as if they were content) or surrounding tags.
- Comments may be used to cause the parser to ignore blocks of elements, provided that the result, once the commented-out block is effectively removed by the parser, is still well-formed XML.
- Parsers are not required to make comments available to the application, so don't use them to pass data to an application; use Processing Instructions, discussed next.
- Comments are also permitted in the DTD, as discussed in chapter 4.

Processing Instructions

Processing instructions (often abbreviated as PI) are directives intended for an application other than the XML parser. Unlike comments, parsers are required to pass processing instructions on to the application. The general syntax for a PI is:

```
<?targetApplication applicationData ?>
```

Where `targetApplication` is the name (any XML Name) of the application that should receive the instruction, and `applicationData` is any arbitrary string that doesn't contain the end delimiter. Often `applicationData` consists of name/value pairs that resemble attributes with values, but there is no requirement concerning the format. Aside from the delimiters "<?" and "?>", which must appear exactly as shown, the only restriction is that there can be no space between the initial question mark and the target. Some examples follow.

```
<?xml-stylesheet type="text/xsl" href="foo.xsl" ?>
<?MortgageRateHandler rate="7%" period="30 years" ?>
<?javaApp class="MortgageRateHandler" ?>
<?javaApp This is the data for the MortgageRateHandler, folks! ?>
<?acroread file="mortgageRates.pdf" ?>
```

Processing instructions are not part of the actual structure of the document, so they may appear almost anywhere, except before the XML declaration or in a CDATA section. The parser's responsibility is merely to pass the PI and its data on to the application. Since the same XML document could be processed by multiple applications, it is entirely possible that some applications will ignore a given PI and just pass it down the chain. In that case, the processing instruction will be acted upon only by the application for which it is intended (has meaning).

Although an XML declaration looks like a processing instruction because it is wrapped in the delimiters `"<?"` and `"?>"`, it is not considered a PI. It is simply an XML declaration, the one-of-a-kind markup that may or may not be the first line of the document.

The target portion of the processing instruction can be a *notation* (defined in chapter 4). For example:

```
<!NOTATION AcrobatReader SYSTEM "/usr/local/bin/acroread">
```

The corresponding PI would be:

```
<?AcrobatReader file="Readme.pdf" size="75%" ?>
```

Entity References

Entity references are markup that the parser replaces with character data. In HTML, there are hundreds of predefined character entities, including the Greek alphabet, math symbols, and the copyright symbol. There are only five predefined entity references in XML, however, as shown inTable 3-2.

TABLE 3-2 Predefined Entity References

Character	*Entity Reference*	*Decimal Representation*	*Hexidecimal Representation*
`<`	`<`	`<`	`<`
`>`	`>`	`>`	`>`
`&`	`&`	**`&`**	**`&`**
`"`	`"`	`"`	`"`
`'`	`'`	`'`	`'`

We've already seen how entity references can be used as content. They can also appear within attribute values. According to Table 3-2,

```
<CD title="Brooks &amp; Dunn&apos;s Greatest Hits" />
```

is equivalent to the decimal representation:

```
<CD title="Brooks &#38; Dunn&#39;s Greatest Hits" />
```

and to the hexidecimal representation:

```
<CD title="Brooks &#x26; Dunn&#x27;s Greatest Hits" />
```

However, the next line is *illegal* because ampersand ("&") must be escaped by using either the entity reference or one of its numeric representations:

```
<CD title="Brooks & Dunn&apos;s Greatest Hits" />
```

This is because ampersand and less-than are special cases.

You are *required* to use the predefined entities < and & to escape the characters < and & in all cases other than when these characters are used as markup delimiters, or in a comment, a processing instruction, or a CDATA section. In other words, the literal < and & characters can appear only as markup delimiters, or within a comment, a processing instruction, or a CDATA section.

Listing 3-3 illustrates the use of all five predefined character entities, several decimal representations of Greek letters, and the three legal variations of the Brooks & Dunn example. If we run this through an XML parser, we can verify that it is well-formed; we did not use the literal ampersand or the literal less-than

Listing 3-3 Examples of Predefined Entities and Greek Letters (predefined-entities.xml)

```
<?xml version="1.0" standalone="yes"?>
<Predefined>
  <Test>The hot tip from today&apos;s &lt;StockWatch&gt; column is:
&quot;AT&amp;T stock is doing better than
Ralph Spoilsports Motors&apos; stock.&quot;
  </Test>
  <PS>Now, wasn&apos;t that as easy as &#928;?
Or &#945;, &#946;, &#947;?</PS>
  <CD title="Brooks &amp; Dunn&apos;s Greatest Hits" />
  <CD title="Brooks &#38; Dunn&#39;s Greatest Hits" />
  <CD title="Brooks &#x26; Dunn&#x27;s Greatest Hits" />
</Predefined>
```

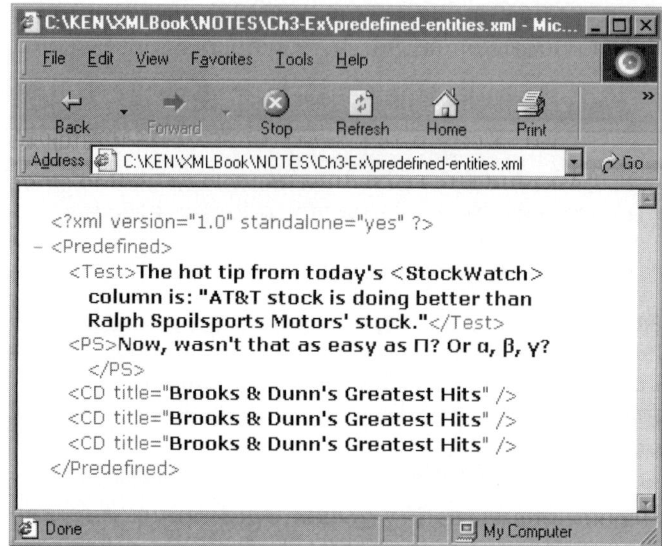

FIGURE 3-1 Predefined entities displayed in Internet Explorer

before the word `StockWatch`. Figure 3-1 shows how this example looks in Internet Explorer, which renders the characters that are represented by the entities. It also confirms that the three Brooks & Dunn variations are equivalent.

HTML (and therefore XHTML) includes three large sets of predefined entities: Latin1, Special, and Symbols. You can pull these definitions into your XML document using *external entities,* covered in chapter 4. The files containing the entities are:

```
http://www.w3.org/TR/xhtml1/DTD/xhtml-lat1.ent
http://www.w3.org/TR/xhtml1/DTD/xhtml-special.ent
http://www.w3.org/TR/xhtml1/DTD/xhtml-symbol.ent
```

CDATA Sections

Sometimes it is necessary to indicate that a particular block of text should *not* be interpreted by the parser. One example is a large number of occurrences of the five predefined entities in a block of text that contains no markup, such as a section of code that needs to test for the numeric less-than or Boolean &&. In this case, we want text that would normally be considered markup to be treated simply as literal character data. **CDATA sections** are designated portions of an XML document in which all markup is ignored by the parser and all text is treated as character data instead. The main uses of `CDATA` sections are:

- To delimit blocks of source code (JavaScript, Java, etc.) embedded in XML
- To embed XML, XHTML, or even HTML examples in an XML document

The general syntax for a CDATA section is:

```
<![CDATA[
multi-line text block to be treated as character data
]]>
```

No spaces are permitted within the two delimiters "<![CDATA[" and "]]>".

Here's a CDATA section used to escape a block of code:

```
<![CDATA[
function doIt()
{
    var foo = 3;
    var bar = 13;
    if (foo < 8 && bar > 8)
        alert("Help!");
    else
        alert("I'm Down");
}
]]>
```

An example of embedded XML in XML follows.

```
<Example>
  <Number>2.4</Number>
  <XMLCode>
<![CDATA[
<?xml version="1.0" standalone="no" ?>
<!DOCTYPE Message SYSTEM "message.dtd">
<Message mime-type="text/plain">
<!-- This is a trivial example. -->
  <From>The Kenster</From>
  <To>Silly Little Cowgirl</To>
  <Body>
  Hi, there. How is your gardening going?
  </Body>
</Message>
]]>
  </XMLCode>
</Example>
```

In contrast to our earlier use of the Message example, the character data is not simply the three lines of content of the From, To, and Body elements. When this example is embedded within a CDATA section, the *entire block* is character data, which in this case means from the XML declaration to and including the </Message> end tag. In other words, the XML prolog, the comment, the start and end tags, and so on, are no longer markup; in this context, they constitute the character data contained by the CDATA section.

Well-Formed vs. Valid Documents

We learned that if a document follows the XML syntax rules discussed in the previous section, the document is said to be well-formed, the minimal requirement to be an XML document. That is, if a document isn't well-formed, it can't even be called XML (excepting XML fragments).

Validity

Even if a document is well-formed, however, it may not be **valid**. According to the XML specification (see *http://www.w3.org/TR/REC-xml#sec-documents* and *http://www.w3.org/TR/REC-xml#dt-valid*),

> A data object is an XML document if it is well-formed, as defined in this specification. A well-formed XML document may in addition be valid if it meets certain further constraints. . . . An XML document is valid if it has an associated document type declaration and if the document complies with the constraints expressed in it.

In other words, since a document type declaration (and therefore a DTD) is optional, *only* documents that refer to a DTD can be checked for validity. This makes sense because following the well-formedness rules *only* indicates adherence to basic syntactical constraints; it says nothing about meeting the more stringent requirements of a specific structural model.

To reinforce the difference, let's take another look at the Employees example from chapter 2. The DTD is repeated here in Listing 3-4 for convenience.

Listing 3-4 Employees DTD (employee.dtd)

```
<!ELEMENT Employees ( Employee+ ) >
<!ELEMENT Employee ( Name, Title, Projects, Email, PhoneNumbers, Address ) >
<!ATTLIST Employee sex NMTOKEN #REQUIRED >
<!ELEMENT Name ( First, Last ) >
<!ELEMENT First ( #PCDATA ) >
<!ELEMENT Last ( #PCDATA ) >
<!ELEMENT Title ( #PCDATA ) >
<!ELEMENT Projects ( Project+ ) >
<!ELEMENT Project ( #PCDATA ) >
<!ELEMENT Email ( #PCDATA ) >
<!ELEMENT PhoneNumbers ( Home, Office, Cell ) >
<!ELEMENT Home ( #PCDATA ) >
<!ELEMENT Office ( #PCDATA ) >
<!ELEMENT Cell ( #PCDATA ) >
<!ELEMENT Address ( Street, City, State, Zip ) >
<!ELEMENT Street ( #PCDATA ) >
<!ELEMENT City ( #PCDATA ) >
<!ELEMENT State ( #PCDATA ) >
<!ELEMENT Zip ( #PCDATA ) >
```

Now consider the document in Listing 3-5. Is it valid?

Listing 3-5 Employee Example 1 (employee-WF.xml)

```
<?xml version='1.0' standalone='yes'?>
<Employees>
  <Employee sex="female">
    <Name>
      <First>Betty Jo</First>
      <Last>Bialowsky</Last>
      <!-- aka: Melanie Haber, Audrey Farber, Susan Underhill, Nancy -->
    </Name>
    <Title>Project Leader</Title>
    <Projects>
      <Project>MegaProject</Project>
      <Project>SmallProject</Project>
      <Project>others</Project>
    </Projects>
    <Email>BettyJo.Bialowsky@home.com</Email>
    <PhoneNumbers>
      <Home>555-abc-1235</Home>
      <Office>555-xyz-4321</Office>
      <Cell>555-pqr-1267</Cell>
    </PhoneNumbers>
    <Address>
      <Street>321 Carmel Court</Street>
      <City>Columbia</City>
      <State>MD</State>
      <Zip>20777</Zip>
    </Address>
  </Employee>
</Employees>
```

At first glance, it *appears* to be valid because it follows the structural rules of the DTD. However, because it does not contain a document type declaration, the parser has no DTD to compare the document instance against in order to determine validity. Therefore, it is *well-formed, but not valid,* or at least its validity cannot be determined. What about the document in Listing 3-6?

Listing 3-6 Employee Example 2 (employee-Miss-Elt.xml)

```
<?xml version='1.0' standalone='no'?>
<!DOCTYPE Employees SYSTEM "employee.dtd" >
<Employees>
  <Employee sex="female">
    <Name>
      <First>Betty Jo</First>
      <Last>Bialowsky</Last>
      <!-- aka: Melanie Haber, Audrey Farber, Susan Underhill, Nancy -->
    </Name>
    <Projects>
      <Project>MegaProject</Project>
```

```
      <Project>SmallProject</Project>
      <Project>others</Project>
    </Projects>
    <Email>BettyJo.Bialowsky@home.com</Email>
    <PhoneNumbers>
      <Home>555-abc-1235</Home>
      <Office>555-xyz-4321</Office>
    </PhoneNumbers>
    <Address>
      <Street>321 Carmel Court</Street>
      <City>Columbia</City>
      <State>MD</State>
      <Zip>20777</Zip>
    </Address>
  </Employee>
</Employees>
```

With the inclusion of a reference to a DTD, a validating parser can check this instance. It will conclude, however, that there are two missing elements, namely `Title` and `Cell`, so this document is *well-formed but invalid.* In fact, most parsers diagnose the problem quite clearly. For example, the free parser `XML Validator` from ElCel Technology (*http://www.elcel.com/products/xmlvalid.html*) reports:

```
employee-Miss-Elts.xml [10:15] : Error: element content invalid. Element
'Projects' is not expected here, expecting 'Title'
employee-Miss-Elts.xml [19:20] : Error: premature end to content of element
'PhoneNumbers'. Expecting child element 'Cell'
```

This indicates, among other things, that the errors are detected on lines 10 and 19. And what about this one in Listing 3-7?

Listing 3-7 Employee Example 3 (employee-BJB.xml)

```
<?xml version='1.0' standalone='no'?>
<!DOCTYPE Employees SYSTEM "employee.dtd" >
<Employees>
  <Employee sex="female">
    <Name>
      <First>Betty Jo</First>
      <Last>Bialowsky</Last>
      <!-- aka: Melanie Haber, Audrey Farber, Susan Underhill, Nancy -->
    </Name>
    <Title>Project Leader</Title>
    <Projects>
      <Project>MegaProject</Project>
      <Project>SmallProject</Project>
      <Project>others</Project>
    </Projects>
    <Email>BettyJo.Bialowsky@home.com</Email>
    <PhoneNumbers>
      <Home>555-abc-1235</Home>
      <Office>555-xyz-4321</Office>
      <Cell>555-pqr-1267</Cell>
```

```
    </PhoneNumbers>
    <Address>
      <Street>321 Carmel Court</Street>
      <City>Columbia</City>
      <State>MD</State>
      <Zip>20777</Zip>
    </Address>
  </Employee>
</Employees>
```

This document is *well-formed and valid* because it matches the structure defined by the DTD, which is referenced in the document type declaration.

Well-Formed or Toast?

Ignoring for a moment the potential importance of validity to data-oriented applications, you might wonder why even when an XML document does not require a DTD (i.e., is standalone), it still must be well-formed. In fact, if a document is not well-formed, it cannot even be called an XML document.

The reason for insisting on well-formedness is to counteract the "browser bloat" syndrome that occurred when the major browser vendors decided they wanted their browser to be able to render the horribly inaccurate HTML developed by graduates (or perhaps flunkies) of the Learn HTML in 2 Days or Less school. Many Web pages contain completely invalid HTML, with improperly nested elements, missing end tags, misspelled element names, missing delimiters, and other aberrations. Browsers such as Netscape Communicator and Internet Explorer do an admirable job of recovering from these errors, but only at the expense of a considerable amount of built-in recovery code.

Fortunately, with XML (and XHTML), parsers do not need to implement recovery code and can therefore stay trim and lightweight. If the parser encounters a well-formedness problem, it should only report the problem to the calling application. It explicitly must not attempt to correct what might be missing, overlapping, or misspelled. Violations of well-formedness constraints are considered *fatal* errors, according to the XML 1.0 Recommendation. The bottom line here is: *either a document is well-formed XML, or it's toast*; that is, it's not XML.

The extra code necessary to do the HTML-like corrections might not be a significant problem for a desktop PC with lots of memory. It's more of an issue as XML is fed to handheld PCs and other devices with limited memory and/or processing power.

Validating and Nonvalidating Parsers

The differences between validating and nonvalidating parsers are not quite as clear as you might think. According to the XML 1.0 specification (*http://www.w3.org/TR/REC-xml#proc-types*),

> Validating processors must, at user option, report violations of the constraints expressed by the declarations in the DTD, and failures to fulfill the validity constraints given in this specification. To accomplish this, validating XML processors must read and process the entire DTD and all external parsed entities referenced in the document. Non-validating processors are required to check only the document entity, including the entire internal DTD subset, for well-formedness.

In other words, validating parsers *must* read the entire DTD and check the document against the structural constraints it describes. You might conclude, therefore, that nonvalidating parsers do not need to consult the DTD, but that turns out to be incorrect. Even nonvalidating parsers need to supply default values for attributes and to replace text based on internal entities (discussed in chapter 4).

Although there used to be a class of strictly nonvalidating parsers, they tend to be much less popular of late. Most modern parsers (2000 and beyond) can be run in either validating or nonvalidating mode. Why run in nonvalidating mode when a parser is capable of validation? Because validation can significantly impact performance, especially when long and complex DTDs are involved. Some developers find that while enabling validation during development and test phases is crucial, it's sometimes beneficial to surpress validation in production systems where document throughput is most valued and the reliability of the data is already known. Consult the documentation of prospective parsers to determine how to toggle this switch, and which is the default mode. For example, the Apache Xerces parser is nonvalidating by default.

Some of the more highly regarded XML parsers include:

- Apache XML Project's Xerces
- IBM's XML Parser for Java (xml4j)
- JavaSoft's XML Parser
- MSXML 4.0 Release: Microsoft XML Core Services component (aka MSXML Parser) and SDK
- Oracle's XML Parser
- ElCel Technology's XML Validator

URLs for these parsers and many more can be found on the XML Parsers/Processors list at XMLSoftware.com, *http://www.xmlsoftware.com/parsers/*.

Event-Based vs. Tree-Based Parsing

We will cover tree-based and event-based parsing in some depth when we cover SAX and DOM in chapters 7 and 8, respectively. For now, an overview should be sufficient.

Event-Based Parsing

Event-based parsers (SAX) provide a data-centric view of XML. When an element is encountered, the idea is to process it and then forget about it. The event-based parser returns the element, its list of attributes, and the content. This is more efficient for many types of applications, especially searches. It requires less code and less memory since there is no need to build a large tree in memory as you are scanning for a particular element, attribute, and/or content sequence in an XML document.

Tree-Based Parsing

On the other hand, tree-based parsers (DOM) provide a document-centric view of XML. In tree-based parsing, an in-memory tree is created for the entire document, which is extremely memory-intensive for large documents. All elements and attributes are available at once, but not until the entire document has been parsed. This technique is useful if you need to navigate around the document and perhaps change various document chunks, which is precisely why it is useful for the Document Object Model (DOM), the aim of which is to manipulate documents via scripting languages or Java.

David Megginson, the main force behind Simple API for XML (SAX), contrasts these two approaches in "Events vs. Trees" on the SAX site (*http://www.saxproject.org/?selected=event*). The W3C presents its viewpoint in an item from the DOM FAQ, "What is the relationship between the DOM and SAX?" (*http://www.w3.org/DOM/faq#SAXandDOM*).

Summary

This chapter covered XML syntax rules and basic parsing concepts.

- We were introduced to fundamental XML terminology, such as element, attribute, tag, and content.
- XML document structure was discussed, including the XML prolog, consisting of the XML declaration and the document type declaration, both of which are optional but desirable.
- Names of elements, attributes, and many other XML identifiers are required to conform to the definition of an XML Name.
- An XML Name consists of a leading letter, underscore, or colon, followed by name characters (letters, digits, hyphens, underscores, colons, or periods).
- XML is case-sensitive. Although there is no universal convention concerning use of uppercase or lowercase when developing your own language, one recommendation is to use UpperCamelCase for elements and lowerCamelCase for attributes, a convention used in SOAP.

- We learned the difference between markup and character data; all text that isn't markup is character data.
- We covered most of the types of markup, including start and end tags, empty element tags, entity references, character references, comments, CDATA sections, document type declarations, processing instructions, and XML declarations.
- The minimal requirement for an XML document is that it be *well-formed*, meaning that it adheres to a number of XML syntax rules.
- Although well-formedness is a prerequisite for validity, a document can be valid only if it also conforms to the constraints imposed by a DTD or XML Schema.
- More modern parsers can be toggled between two states: validating and non-validating. Validation mode is crucial during development. In a production environment, however, it may be desirable (under certain circumstances) to disable validation for efficiency.
- Event-based (e.g., SAX) and tree-based (e.g., DOM) parsing were briefly contrasted.

For Further Exploration

Articles

XML Conformance Update (validation), David Brownell
http://www.xml.com/pub/2000/05/10/conformance/conformance.html

XML.com: Being Too Generous, Leigh Dodds [discusses XML conformance in Internet Explorer 6]
http://www.xml.com/pub/a/2001/09/19/being-too-generous.html

To Validate or Not to Validate: Controversy
http://WDVL.Internet.com/Authoring/Languages/XML/DoingIt/ValidationControversy.html

Resources

XML Checkers and Validation Services
http://WDVL.Internet.com/Software/XML/parsers.html#checking

XML.com: Search for Conformance
http://www.xml.com/search/index.ncsp?sp-q=Conformance&search=search

Software

XML Parsers at XMLSoftware
http://www.xmlsoftware.com/parsers/

XML Editors at XMLSoftware
http://www.xmlsoftware.com/editors/

W3C Specifications

Extensible Markup Language (XML) 1.0 [W3C XML Recommendation, Second Edition]
http://www.w3.org/TR/REC-xml

Well-Formed XML Documents
http://www.w3.org/TR/REC-xml#sec-well-formed

Validating and Non-Validating Processors
http://www.w3.org/TR/REC-xml#proc-types

XHTML 1.0: The Extensible HyperText Markup Language—A Reformulation of HTML 4 in XML 1.0
http://www.w3.org/TR/xhtml1/

Chapter 4
DTD Syntax

In this chapter, we continue from chapter 3 with details presented in the W3C XML 1.0 Recommendation. Our focus here, however, is on the syntax of Document Type Definitions. We discuss element declarations, content models, attribute list declarations, attribute types and default values, occurrence indicators, sequences and choices, general entities, parameter entities, and more. Guidelines for when to use an element rather than an attribute are suggested. Most original examples appear on the CD-ROM. Some examples draw from the DTDs used in the W3C specifications themselves. The chapter concludes with ways to generate a DTD from your XML instances (and vice versa). The concept of validating and nonvalidating parsers is presented in chapter 3, as is terminology necessary to understand this chapter.

What Is a DTD and When Is It Needed?

A **Document Type Definition (DTD)** is set of rules that describe the hierarchical structure of any XML document instance that is based on that particular DTD. These rules are used by the XML parser to determine whether a given instance conforms to the particular vocabulary, and to thereby determine whether the document is valid. In other words, a DTD describes the structure of a class of possible documents, each of which is a valid instance of that DTD.

DTDs have been used for many years in the SGML community.[1] The description of XML DTDs can be found only in the W3C Recommendation, Extensible Markup Language (XML) 1.0 (Second Edition); there is no separate DTD specification from the W3C. XML DTDs are a simplification of those DTDs possible in SGML. For example, XML DTDs require deterministic expressions and

1. One explanation of SGML DTDs appears in the TEI specification, Guidelines for Electronic Text Encoding and Interchange (TEI P3); see *http://www-tei.uic.edu/orgs/tei/sgml/teip3sg/index.html.* SGML DTDs are also described in the HTML 4.01 Recommendation, *http://www.w3.org/TR/html401/intro/sgmltut.html.*

don't permit attribute minimization (discussed in chapter 15), whereas SGML DTDs are more flexible. There are other simplifications where necessary to make it possible to construct lightweight XML parsers that can be downloaded in a Java applet or embedded in devices with limited memory.

What exactly can you specify in your DTD? You can specify:

- Elements and their attributes (if any)
- Nesting of elements (which elements can contain which children elements)
- Order of elements (sequence)
- Whether elements can contain character data (non-markup)
- Whether elements can contain a mixture of child elements and character data (mixed content)
- Whether an element contains neither children nor character data (and is therefore empty)
- Whether certain elements are optional or required (choices)
- Whether certain elements can be repeated (occurrence indicators)
- Whether attributes are required, optional, or fixed in value
- Default values for attributes
- Fixed values for attributes
- Datatype of attributes (to a *very* limited degree; XML Schema is much better in this regard)
- Reusable sections of text called *entities* and also *notations* (described later in this chapter), if any
- Dependence on other DTDs, if any

In this chapter, we'll see how each of these things is accomplished. It follows that if a DTD is referenced, validating XML Parsers, in addition to supplying default values not in the XML document, can detect:

- Missing elements or attributes
- Misspelled elements or attributes
- Extra, unexpected elements or attributes (not defined in the DTD)
- Improper nesting of elements
- Character data in an element that permits only children elements, or vice versa
- Incorrect sequencing of elements
- Too many or too few occurrences of an element
- Incorrect attribute values from enumerated sets

However, there are also major shortcomings of DTDs, originally developed for document-centric applications, that prevent them from being the complete answer for data-centric applications.

What can't you do with DTDs? You can't:

- Constrain attribute values or character content of elements to even basic datatypes like integer, float, or boolean

- Constrain attributes to a range of values without enumerating every possible value
- Define your own datatypes that inherit from primitives such as integer and constrain values to a particular pattern, such as a phone number
- Define an element and then subclass it to define elements that inherit certain aspects and also add others, or perhaps constrain some aspect of the base class

Fortunately, these DTD limitations are addressed by XML Schema, the subject of chapter 6.

If DTDs are limited, then when are they useful? You need a DTD when you require:

- Automatic validation of your own XML data or data from external sources
- Sharing your document structure rules within your company or across organizational boundaries as a common format for data exchange
- Exchanging data between heterogeneous databases
- XML parsers to supply default values or fixed values for attributes that aren't explicit in each document instance

On the other hand, if your intention is merely to transmit well-formed XML messages without validation requirements, a DTD is not required. For many applications, this is unlikely; validation is usually necessary. However, as noted previously, in a production system where rapid transmission and processing of XML messages is of primary importance, performance improvements will be realized by removing validation requirements (e.g., by disabling validation in your XML parser, not by deleting the DTD reference). This is most feasible when validation is enabled during development and testing phases, to ensure that all parts of the system are creating or processing the XML structure defined by the DTD.

DTDs are typically defined in files external to the XML document to encourage reuse, but they may also be embedded directly in XML instances if necessary, or used to extend external DTDs. Large, complex DTDs are often constructed from multiple pieces called *modules* or *entities*. In this chapter, our short examples include revisiting the employee directory, introducing a new basic invoice DTD, and introducing a record and book collection DTD. After we cover entities, we'll examine some of the techniques used by the W3C in development of the SVG 1.0 and MathML 2.0 DTDs. Much later, in chapter 15 on XHTML, we encounter additional examples of complex DTD integration.

Elements and Content Models

The elements in a DTD collectively define the structure of the set of XML documents that reference the DTD. Elements can be listed in any order in the DTD, although it is wise to define some order that is meaningful. Some developers prefer alphabetical order based on the name of the element, either with attributes defined after the element that contains them or alphabetized separately. I prefer listing element declarations in an order that resembles the hierarchy, with the root (document) element first, followed by declarations for its immediate children, then their children, and so on. I declare attributes immediately after the element to which they belong.

An element is defined in a DTD in terms of its **content model**, a description of the kinds of elements and/or character data it may contain. In other words, a parent element defines which children it supports and anything else that may appear between its start and end tags. (An element is also defined in terms of the attributes its supports, as discussed later in this chapter.) The content model describes the order of the children, which children are optional, which may be repeated, whether there is a choice among several children, and whether non-markup character data can appear.

The general syntax for declaring an element, more formally called an **element type declaration**, in a DTD is:

```
<!ELEMENT ElementName ContentModel >
```

The `ElementName` is any legal XML Name[2] and `ContentModel` is any of the following:

1. an expression (or *grouping*) involving one or more child elements
2. the keyword `#PCDATA` (indicating textual content)
3. a mixed-content model involving both `#PCDATA` and child elements
4. the keyword `EMPTY`
5. the keyword `ANY`

The first case is called the **element content model** because the element can contain children elements. The second and third cases are both called **mixed content model**, indicating that the element may contain either character data (text) by itself or character data interspersed with children elements. The fourth and fifth cases are simply called the EMPTY and ANY content models, respectively. All five cases are illustrated and explained in this section.

Along the way, we'll also cover sequencing, grouping, choices, and occurrence indicators. Just to give you a quick idea what element type declarations look like, here are a few unrelated examples (without explanation).

```
<!ELEMENT D      (A, B, C) >
<!ELEMENT E      (A?, B*, C) >
<!ELEMENT poem   (title, poet, stanza+) >
<!ELEMENT APPLET (PARAM | %flow;)* >
<!ELEMENT para   (#PCDATA) >
```

2. XML Names consist of a leading letter, underscore, or colon, followed by name characters (letters, digits, hyphens, underscores, colons, or periods)—see "Legal XML Name Characters" in chapter 3.

```
<!ELEMENT pz      (#PCDATA | qt)* >
<!ELEMENT p       (#PCDATA | %font; | %phrase; | %special; | %form;)* >
<!ELEMENT hr      EMPTY >
<!ELEMENT block   ANY >
```

Element Content Model

An element content model specifies the legitimate children of the element that is being declared. Examples of declarations of element content models follow.

```
<!ELEMENT Employees ( Employee+ ) >
<!ELEMENT Employee (Name, Title, Projects, Email, PhoneNumbers, Address)>
<!ELEMENT Name ( First, Last ) >
```

Each of these is an example of an element type declaration involving an element content model. That is, each declaration indicates that the content of the element consists of one or more child elements. For example, the element type declaration of `Employee` states that its content consists of the children `Name`, `Title`, `Projects`, `Email`, `PhoneNumbers`, and `Address`. We'll cover the meaning of the plus and comma notation next before we discuss the remaining content models.

Sequencing and Choosing Elements

Element order is very significant in XML; a parser must be able to determine which elements are properly contained in which others, as per the DTD's element type declarations. It's also important to be able to declare an element that contains a choice of multiple child elements.

In Table 4-1, `A`, `B`, and `C` represent any arbitrary elements or expressions involving groups of elements. An element group is surrounded by parentheses. Technically, the comma is a "then" **connector** and the vertical bar is an "or" connector. For readers familiar with the SGML "and" connector ("&"), the SGML model of (`A` & `B` & `C`), meaning all three but in any order, is *not* acceptable in XML. This is another of the many simplifications made from SGML to XML so that parsers could be lightweight. (XML Schema does provide this additional possibility, however.)

An example of a simple sequence of elements is:

```
<!ELEMENT Name (First, Middle, Last) >
```

TABLE 4-1 Element Sequences and Choices

Sequence or Choice	*Meaning*
`( )`	An expression or grouping of elements; groups can be nested to any level
`(A, B, C)`	First `A`, followed by `B`, and then `C`; *all three are required* and must appear in the indicated sequential order
`(A | B | C )`	Either `A` or `B` or `C`, but only one; choices with vertical bars are *mutually exclusive*

An XML fragment that follows this model is:

```
<Name>
  <First>Kenneth</First>
  <Middle>Brian</Middle>
  <Last>Sall</Last>
</Name>
```

In the absence of occurrence indicators (Table 4-2), a **sequence** declares that *all elements are required*. This declaration means that not only must the children appear in the order listed, they must also all be present. This precludes the possibility of accepting an instance without a middle name, for example.

A **choice** of *mutually exclusive* elements is indicated using vertical bars. In the following declaration, the content model of `ShipTo` is a sequence of child elements, but the second child is an expression indicating a choice between `CustomerID` or `SocSecNo`.

```
<!ELEMENT ShipTo   (Name, (CustomerID | SocSecNo), Address?,
                    City?, State?, Zip?)>
```

One possible XML fragment that is valid with respect to this model[3] is:

```
<ShipTo>
  <Name>
    <First>Rocky</First>
    <Last>Rococo</Last>
  </Name>
  <CustomerID sex="male">1312363</CustomerID>
  <Address>456 Kuttemoffatta Pass</Address>
  <City>Columbia</City>
  <State>MD</State>
  <Zip>20707</Zip>
</ShipTo>
```

Another possibility is to use the other choice:

```
<ShipTo>
  <Name>
    <First>Rocky</First>
    <Last>Rococo</Last>
  </Name>
  <SocSecNo>098-20-5555</SocSecNo>
  <Address>456 Kuttemoffatta Pass</Address>
  <City>Columbia</City>
  <State>MD</State>
  <Zip>20707</Zip>
</ShipTo>
```

3. At this point, we haven't shown the declarations for the child elements, nor have we declared the `sex` attribute, so just focus on the element hierarchy for now. The complete `invoice.dtd` is shown in Listing 4-1.

Occurrence Indicators

The XML specification defines several **occurrence indicators** that are used in DTDs to declare whether an element is optional and whether it is repeatable. In Table 4-2, let E be any arbitrary element or element expression.

In the sequencing discussion we've already seen that the presence of an element name in a declaration normally implies that the element is required. We can also follow the element name (or an element grouping) with an occurrence indicator to clarify whether it is truly required and/or repeatable.

For example, an alternative definition of the Name element is:

```
<!ELEMENT Name (First, Middle?, Last) >
```

In this case the middle name is now *optional.* However, if the element Middle is present, there can be *only one* per Name and it must appear between the First and Last elements. This declaration would support both of these instances:

```
<Name>
  <First>Kenneth</First>
  <Middle>Brian</Middle>
  <Last>Sall</Last>
</Name>

<Name>
  <First>Nick</First>
  <Last>Danger</Last>
</Name>
```

Alternatively, we might want to permit *one or more* middle names with this declaration:

```
<!ELEMENT Name (First, Middle+, Last) >
```

TABLE 4-2 Occurrence Indicators

Indicator	*Meaning*
E	No indicator symbol means *exactly one* E; this indicates a required element or expression
E+	One or more E; *required* and may repeat any number of times
E?	Zero or one E; *optional* element or expression
E*	Zero or more E; *optional* but also *repeatable* any number of times

The preceding declaration supports these instances:

```
<Name>
  <First>Kenneth</First>
  <Middle>Brian</Middle>
  <Last>Sall</Last>
</Name>

<Name>
  <First>George</First>
  <Middle>Leroy</Middle>
  <Middle>Porgy</Middle>
  <Last>Tirebiter</Last>
</Name>
```

Note that the declaration with `Middle+` does *not* apply to the earlier Nick Danger instance because the + occurrence indicator requires that the element be present (and may optionally repeat).

Finally, we can achieve the greatest flexibility (but unfortunately the smallest degree of automatic validation, in effect) with a declaration that allows *zero, one, or more than one* middle names by using the * occurrence indicator.

```
<!ELEMENT Name (First, Middle*, Last) >
```

All of the preceding instances (Ken, Nick, and George) are valid based on this declaration. While the asterisk occurrence indicator certainly covers the most cases, in general it is preferable to use a more constraining indicator (none, +, or ?) if that more accurately reflects the data you are modelling. You may find it useful, however, to initially use the liberal * and tighten the constraints as you refine your data requirements.

Let's consider another example that illustrates grouping, choice, sequence, and occurrence indicators all in one compact element type declaration:

```
<!ELEMENT Collection ( (Book | CD)*, Owner?) >
```

This declares `Collection` to consist of a sequence of `Book` or `CD` children in any number of repetitions, followed by at most one `Owner` element. Ignoring the content of these children for now, valid instances include:

```
<Collection>
 <Book /><CD /><Book /><CD /><CD /><CD /><Owner />
</Collection>

<Collection>
 <Book /><Book /><Book /><CD /><CD /><Owner />
</Collection>
```

```
<Collection>
 <CD /><CD /><CD /><CD />
</Collection>

<Collection>
 <Owner />
</Collection>
```

and even simply

```
<Collection />
```

which represents an empty Collection.

Mixed Content Model

By far, the most common form of the **mixed content model** declares the element to contain *only text (character data) but no children elements*. This involves the keyword #PCDATA surrounded by parentheses. For example:

```
<!ELEMENT First ( #PCDATA ) >
```

A valid instance of the `First` element is:

```
<First>Ken</First>
```

It's worth noting that since character data is completely unconstrained, the following examples of the `First` element are also valid according to the element type declaration, although they are certainly meaningless if `First` is meant to represent a first (given) name.

```
<First>Ken Sall</First>
<First>98.6</First>
<First>Every Good Boy Deserves Favor</First>
```

Character data content of elements cannot be type checked. There is no notion of string, integer, float, boolean, dateTime, and so on. This is a major limitation of DTDs that XML Schema addresses.

Because mixed content model also refers to declarations in which character data may be mixed with element children, let's look at an example of this case from the XHTML 1.0 DTD,[4] simplified somewhat for our purposes.

```
<!ELEMENT pre (#PCDATA | a | br | span | bdo | map | tt | i | b )*>
```

4. XHTML 1.0: The Extensible HyperText Markup Language: A Reformulation of HTML 4 in XML 1.0; W3C Recommendation dated 26 January 2000, *http://www.w3.org/TR/xhtml1/#dtds*.

Given this declaration, the following are all valid instances of the `pre` (preformatted text) element.

```
<pre>some text</pre>

<pre>some <i>italicized text</i></pre>

<pre>some text<br/>and more text</pre>

<pre>
  some text<br/>
  and some <b>bold text</b>
  and some <i>italicized text</i>
  and so on....
</pre>
```

There are several subtle points regarding this element type declaration, all of which are characteristic of mixed content model declarations.

- The `#PCDATA` reference must always be listed first (prior to all child elements).
- The vertical bars (the "or" connectors) must be present to separate all possible child elements.
- The asterisk must be included after the closing parenthesis to indicate the entire expression may repeat. In other words, any of the children may repeat any number of times in any order, mixed with character data at any point.
- You cannot attach occurrence indicators to any of the child elements in this expression, nor can you impose any kind of order on the elements, nor can you state which are optional.

The point here is that although the mixed content model affords you greater flexibility, it is at the expense of being able to impose constraints that might otherwise be useful. It is therefore advisable to minimize the use of mixed content models (other than ones that declare only `#PCDATA` as their content). You can always convert a mixed content model to an element content model simply by introducing another element to handle the `#PCDATA` case, thereby removing some of the restrictions. For example:

```
<!ELEMENT Parent (#PCDATA | ChildA | ChildB | ChildC)* >
```

can be replaced by:

```
<!ELEMENT Parent      (ChildPCData | ChildA | ChildB | ChildC)* >
<!ELEMENT ChildPCData (#PCDATA) >
```

This permits you to further constrain the children, if necessary, such as by replacing the `Parent` declaration with one that imposes constraints on child element order and optionality, such as

```
<!ELEMENT Parent      (ChildPCData, ChildB+, ChildA, ChildC? )+ >
```

EMPTY Content Model

The EMPTY content model corresponds to the empty element discussed in chapter 3, an element that contains no content whatsoever. Two examples of empty elements are:

```
<Divider />
<Image href="picture1.gif" width="120" height="70" />
```

Their corresponding element type declarations are:

```
<!ELEMENT Divider  EMPTY >
<!ELEMENT Image    EMPTY >
```

The keyword EMPTY is not surrounded by parentheses, as was the case with previous content models. In fact, if you add parentheses, the declaration will be invalid because a parser will think you are referring to an *element* named EMPTY. (In contrast, content models using #PCDATA must include parentheses.)

An EMPTY content model simply means that the element may not contain children of any kind (neither text nor other elements). It does not mean that the element is prohibited from having *attributes*, however. (We'll see the attribute definition for this example soon.) Typically, empty elements are used either to mark a boundary or to convey certain details about the element instance via their attributes. For example, the href attribute of the Image element indicates the location of the image file.

In an XML document, empty elements can also be written in a long form as start and end tags with nothing between them.

```
<Divider></Divider>
<Image href="picture1.gif" width="120" height="70"></Image>
```

The long form is identical to the so-called minimized (abbreviated) form shown earlier. In fact, as we'll see in chapter 5, the Canonical XML Recommendation indicates that empty elements be converted to start end tag pairs to produce the canonical form. However, it is more common to see the minimized form and there is no disadvantage to it. In fact, in chapter 15, when we discuss XHTML, we'll see that some browsers have difficulty with the long form, so it's best to use the minimized form *and* to include a space before the slash:

```
<hr />
<img src="picture1.gif" width="120" height="70" />
```

Most of the examples of empty elements in this book include the optional space.

ANY Content Model

The ANY content model, on the other hand, is a kind of "anything goes" model, which should be used sparingly, if at all. Elements designated as ANY may contain text, other elements, or a combination of text and other elements, or may even be empty. In other words, there is no restriction on what such an element may contain, except that its content must adhere to the well-formedness rules for all XML.

An example of the ANY content model is:

```
<!ELEMENT AppSpecifics ANY >
```

Note that the keyword ANY must not be enclosed in parentheses, as was the case with the EMPTY keyword.

The following XML fragments all match this model:

```
<AppSpecifics />

<AppSpecifics>X=23</AppSpecifics>

<AppSpecifics>
  <X>23</X>
  <Y>76.8</Y>
  <Description>Something here.</Description>
</AppSpecifics>

<AppSpecifics>
  The value of X is <X>23</X> and the value of Y is <Y>76.8</Y>.
</AppSpecifics>
```

Since this model is open-ended, under what circumstances would you want to use it? Certainly if you have in mind a more constrained notion of the element being defined, the ANY model is usually not appropriate. However, in the early stages of developing your DTD, you may find it useful to start with an unconstrained structure for a particular element, then refine it over time to be more restrictive with respect to the content it may contain.[5] This flexibility of content may also be useful if you are adding an element that needs to be extensible because its use isn't completely known at the time it is introduced.

Expressions: The Good, the Bad, and the Ugly

By grouping elements with parentheses and using sequence, choice, and occurrence indicators, we've seen that content models can become fairly elaborate and far more interesting than some of our earlier examples. Consider this example from the AIML DTD (see *http://pioneer.gsfc.nasa.gov/public/aiml/*), which describes the arguments (parameters) to a command for an instrument. In AIML, an Argument

5. There are other cases where the opposite approach may be useful—to begin with a very restrictive content model that is refined to be more relaxed over time.

element may contain a list of valid choices, a range of values, or a bit range. It may also contain a combination of these constraints because of the asterisk (*).

```
<!ELEMENT Argument (ValidList | ValidRange | ValidBitRange)* >
```

For example, all of the following instances[6] match the above declaration:

```
<Argument />

<Argument><ValidList /></Argument>

<Argument><ValidRange /></Argument>

<Argument><ValidBitRange /></Argument>

<Argument><ValidList /><ValidList /></Argument>

<Argument><ValidList /><ValidBitRange /></Argument>

<Argument>
  <ValidRange />
  <ValidList />
  <ValidBitRange/>
  <ValidList />
</Argument>
```

The definition for a `Port` (below) is more complex and the parentheses are important to understand the structure. At the most basic level, a `Port` consists of ordered pairs of commands (the first set of three choices)[7] and their formats (the second set). However, the format is optional due to the ? following the second expression. The + tells us that the ordered pairs (the whole content model, in this case) may repeat and there must be at least one command with (optional) format pair associated with a `Port`.

```
<!ELEMENT Port
( (Command | CommandProcedure | Telemetry),
  (RecordFormat | BinaryRecordFormat | DelegateFormat)?)+ >
```

Another interesting example is from the DTDs that accompany the W3C XHTML 1.0 specification which defines a `table` element (attributes omitted for simplicity) and its children as follows:

```
<!ELEMENT table
     (caption?, (col*|colgroup*), thead?, tfoot?, (tbody+|tr+))>
<!ELEMENT caption  %Inline;>
<!ELEMENT thead    (tr)+>
<!ELEMENT tfoot    (tr)+>
```

6. For simplicity, the attributes are not shown, nor is the actual content of the valids (the choices and range limits). We are focusing on the structure here.

7. Actually the `Telemetry` element indicates data rather than a command.

```
<!ELEMENT tbody    (tr)+>
<!ELEMENT colgroup (col)*>
<!ELEMENT col      EMPTY>
<!ELEMENT tr       (th|td)+>
<!ELEMENT th       %Flow;>
<!ELEMENT td       %Flow;>
```

These element type declarations tell us that `caption`, `thead`, and `tfoot` are optional children of a `table`. Elements `col` and `colgroup` are also optional, but also repeatable; however, you can't specify both a `col` and a `colgroup`. The only required child of a `table` is either a `tbody` or `tr`, both of which are also repeatable but mutually exclusive (although a `tbody` is nothing more than a set of one or more `tr` elements. We also see that a `tr` consists of a series of at least one `th` and/or `td` children. In other words, we can have one or more `th` mixed with one or more `td` children. The declaration does not insist that a `th` appear before `td`. (Entity references such as `%Inline;` and `%Flow;` are discussed in the section "Entities and Notations" later in this chapter.)

Clever use of parentheses and occurrence indicators can be extremely powerful in expressing very specific content models. For example, consider this slightly altered content model from the SVG 1.0 specification[8] from the W3C:

```
<!ELEMENT descTitleMetadata
      (((desc,((title,metadata?)|(metadata,title?))?)|
      (title,((desc,metadata?)|(metadata,desc?))?)|
      (metadata,((desc,title?)|(title,desc?))?))?) >
```

This declaration says that `descTitleMetadata` contains at most one of `desc`, `title`, and `metadata` in any order. It may be clever, but the expression is also ungainly and a little hard for mere humans to parse. XML Schema makes such constraints much easier to express.

A related point is that it's hard to use DTD occurrence indicators to express bounded numbers of occurrences of an element. For example, as David Mertz illustrates in his IBM developerWorks article, "Comparing W3C XML Schemas and Document Type Definitions" (*http://www-106.ibm.com/developerworks/xml/library/x-matters7.html*), if we need to express the constraint that an `Invoice` contains from 3 to 15 `Item` elements in a DTD, we'd need a declaration like this:

```
<!ELEMENT Item     (#PCDATA)>
<!ELEMENT Invoice  (Item, Item, Item,
                    Item?, Item?, Item?, Item?, Item?, Item?,
                    Item?, Item?, Item?, Item?, Item?, Item?)
```

8. Scalable Vector Graphics (SVG) 1.0 Specification, W3C Recommendation dated 04 September 2001; see *http://www.w3.org/TR/SVG/svgdtd.html*. The SVG spec actually defines the `descTitleMetadata` *entity*, which I've changed to an element type declaration since entities have yet to be explained.

It's easy to see that this quickly becomes unweildy as the bounds increase; consider what it would look like if the minimum were 35 and the maximum were 999. Fortunately, XML Schema lets us express bounds much more naturally, such as:

```
<xsd:element name="Item" type="xsd:string"
           minOccurs="35" maxOccurs="999" />
```

Deterministic Content Models

For reasons of simplicity compared with SGML, all expressions that involve content models must be **deterministic**. XML parsers do not have look-ahead capability, so it must always be unambiguous which element is being processed at any given time. Consider the content model:

```
( (A, B) | (A, C) )
```

This is a nondeterministic expression because the reference to `A` is ambiguous; which one is being matched? In this case, the expression can be converted into an unambiguous equivalent expression, which is therefore deterministic and acceptable:

```
( (A, (B | C) )
```

Comments

DTD syntax accepts exactly the same style of comments that we've seen in XML documents. The liberal use of comments to elaborate on content models, assumptions, and limitations of your DTD is highly recommended. For example:

```
<!--
     This invoice DTD is strictly illustrative.
     It is not intended for actual use in an eCommerce system.
     As if you couldn't guess.
-->
<!ELEMENT Invoice  (ShipTo, Date, ItemInfo+, Summary*)>
<!ELEMENT Date     (#PCDATA)>  <!-- in CCYY-MM-DD format -->
```

Attributes, Attribute Types, and Default Values

Attributes qualify and further define the details of an element. An element may have any number of attributes, including zero. In a DTD, the attributes of a given element need not be declared in the same place that the element type declaration appears; however, doing so greatly adds to readability. Attribute names are case-sensitive (unlike HTML) and are comprised of any of the characters in an XML Name, just like the element names. As mentioned earlier, I prefer to use *lowerCamelCase* (e.g., `unitOfMeasure`) for attributes, but *UpperCamelCase* (e.g., `ShipTo`) for elements. This is not a standard convention, however, and the examples used in this book vary depending on their source. For example, the W3C tends to use all *lowerCamelCase* for elements and attributes alike.

Here's an overview of attributes:

- Attributes are always associated with an element.
- Same attribute name can be used with different elements, perhaps with a different type or default value, but not necessarily. For example, a `name` attribute is fairly common.
- Attributes may be required or optional, or they may have a default value or a fixed value.
- An attribute declaration may specify an enumerated set of possible values, with or without a default.
- The value may be slightly constrained to one of several string-like types.
- An attribute value is always (single or double) quoted in XML.

Attribute-List Declaration

The general syntax for an **attribute-list declaration** is:

```
<!ATTLIST ElementName AttrDef+ >
```

`ATTLIST` is a literal keyword in uppercase, `ElementName` is the XML Name that associates the attributes that follow with the element they qualify, and `AttrDef` is the repeatable triplet:

```
AttrName AttrType AttrDefaultDecl
```

Here `AttrName` is the name of the attribute (also an XML Name), `AttrType` is the type of the attribute, and `AttrDefaultDecl` is a description of the so-called attribute default value. Table 4-3 on page 154 explains the legal values for `AttrType` and Table 4-4 on page 157 describes the values for `AttrDefaultDecl`.

Another way of describing an attribute-list declaration is to combine the two parts:

```
<!ATTLIST ElementName AttrName AttrType AttrDefaultDecl >
```

This is a bit deceptive, however, because the last three terms can repeat. In other words, multiple attributes can be declared in one attribute-list declaration associated with a single element.

Let's consider a few examples. First, we'll look at the `Invoice` element declaration and its attribute from Listing 4-1 later in this chapter.

```
<!ELEMENT Invoice  (ShipTo, Date, ItemInfo+, Summary*)>
<!ATTLIST Invoice  version CDATA  #IMPLIED>
```

The ATTLIST line means that version is the name of an attribute contained within the start tag of the Invoice element. The attribute type is the generic CDATA (unconstrained character data; see Table 4-3). The attribute default declaration is the keyword #IMPLIED. As we see from Table 4-4, #IMPLIED means that the attribute is completely optional. An XML fragment that matches the two declarations is:

```
<Invoice version="2.7" >
  <ShipTo>
  <!-- etc. -->
</Invoice>
```

Now let's consider a simple case from the AIML DTD in which two attributes are declared in one attribute-list declaration.

```
<!ELEMENT ValidRange  EMPTY>
<!ATTLIST ValidRange
          low   CDATA #REQUIRED
          high  CDATA #REQUIRED >
```

Extra white space, including new lines, is not significant in DTDs, so the preceding ATTLIST declaration is equivalent to

```
<!ATTLIST ValidRange low CDATA #REQUIRED high CDATA #REQUIRED>
```

A ValidRange element contains no content, so it is identified by the EMPTY keyword. It is completely defined by its two attributes, low and high. These attributes are both of type CDATA, and the DefaultDecl states that they are both required. If an instance of the ValidRange element is missing either attribute, it will be flagged as invalid by a validating parser. A valid instance of this element and its attributes is:

```
<ValidRange low="-25.6" high="76.8" />
```

Values of an attribute are only loosely typed to one of the ten cases in XML, each of which is a slightly constrained string derivative. Therefore, the values shown here may look like floating point numbers, but they are merely unconstrained CDATA.

Attribute Types

The ten attribute types defined in XML 1.0 are given in Table 4-3. Examples of several of these types follow. An example of NOTATION is presented later in the chapter.

If you are looking for common computer datatypes like integer, float, and boolean, you won't find them here. Unfortunately, you'll need XML Schema for that. Specifically, this means that although the low and high attributes from the previous

TABLE 4-3 Attribute Types Allowed in XML 1.0 DTDs

Attribute Type	*Meaning*
CDATA	Character data; no markup allowed; completely unconstrained text string
NMTOKEN	Consists of Name characters; a sequence of letters, digits, hyphens, underscores, colons, and periods; no white space permitted but may begin with any Name character
NMTOKENS	White-space separated list of things of type NMTOKEN
ID	XML Name that must be unique in a given XML document; only one attribute per element can be of type ID
IDREF	Value of another element's ID; points to that element whose attribute of type ID has the same value as this attribute of type IDREF
IDREFS	White-space separated list of IDREFs
ENTITY	External unparsed entity, described later in this chapter
ENTITIES	White-space separated list of things of type ENTITY
enumeration	Vertical-bar separated list of mutually exclusive choices (literal values); each choice must be a NMTOKEN, so no spaces are permitted; (value1 | value2 | value3 ...)
NOTATION	This keyword is followed by an enumerated list of NOTATIONS declared in the same document; (notation1 | notation2 | ...)

example look like floating point values, they are really only CDATA (unconstrained strings) as far as XML is concerned. One way around this that we used effectively in pre-XML Schema AIML was that every Argument (the parent of ValidRange) contained a datatype attribute called type expressed as a Java class name (e.g., java.lang.Float). Our application performed the conversion from string to the designated type at runtime using Java's ClassForName. Another approach involves entities; as we'll see later, entity references such as %Float; can serve as placeholders to document the datatypes we expect for a particular attribute.

CDATA

When there are multiple attributes of an element, each may be written as a separate attribute-list declaration, if desired.

```
<!ELEMENT ValidRange  EMPTY>
<!ATTLIST ValidRange  low   CDATA #REQUIRED >
<!ATTLIST ValidRange  high  CDATA #REQUIRED >
```

Use of CDATA attribute type is common since character text can represent any string. This declaration has exactly the same meaning as the earlier declaration of ValidRange, so use of combined or separate declarations is really a matter of personal preference. I definitely prefer the combined approach, which is also the norm for W3C DTDs. It saves typing and greatly reduces the number of bytes in the file. Note also that the element declaration need not always precede the attribute-list declaration, but this is the typical case.

Enumerated Values

Another useful attribute type is the enumerated set of legal literal values. In the following EDI example, the value of the attribute named code is constrained to be one of three strings, namely, CTN25, BAG79, or MIX71.

```
<!ELEMENT ShipmentPackagingCode   EMPTY >
<!ATTLIST ShipmentPackagingCode
          code ( CTN25 | BAG79 | MIX71 ) #REQUIRED >
```

The enumerated list of strings tells the parser the acceptable values. The keyword #REQUIRED indicates that a value must be specified in the XML document. Specifying any other value for this attribute or omitting the attribute will be flagged by the parser as invalid. A legitimate instance of this element and its attribute is:

```
<ShipmentPackagingCode code="BAG79" />
```

An illegal instance is:

```
<ShipmentPackagingCode code="secret" />
```

NMTOKEN

An attribute of type NMTOKEN is similar to an XML Name, except that the initial character is not as restricted. An attribute value of this type consists of a sequence of letters, digits, hyphens, underscores, colons, and periods. Given the element and attribute-list declarations:

```
<!ELEMENT MyNMTOKEN   EMPTY >
<!ATTLIST MyNMTOKEN   value NMTOKEN #REQUIRED >
```

these are all valid instances of MyNMTOKEN:

```
<MyNMTOKEN value="123" />
<MyNMTOKEN value="xyz" />
<MyNMTOKEN value="xyz123" />
<MyNMTOKEN value="some_xyz-123.98" />
```

However, the next instance is invalid since the + symbol is not a legal name character.

```
<MyNMTOKEN value="+xyz123" />
```

ID and IDREF

Let's see how to take advantage of the ID and IDREF attribute types to associate related elements. We need an element that has an attribute of *type* ID, regardless of the actual attribute *name*, and a different element with an attribute of type `IDREF` with any arbitrary attribute name. The declarations below declare `MyObject` with the attribute `id` of type `ID` and the element `MyPointer` with an attribute named `ref` of type `IDREF`. (Remember, the choice of the attribute names `id` and `ref` is purely for clarity. They could have been named `target` and `pointer`, for example.)

```
<!ELEMENT MyObject  (#PCDATA) >
<!ATTLIST MyObject
          id ID #REQUIRED >

<!ELEMENT MyPointer (#PCDATA) >
<!ATTLIST MyPointer
          ref IDREF #REQUIRED >
```

The value of an attribute of type `ID` is constrained to be an XML Name, so the leading characters are more limited than in the `NMTOKEN` case. More importantly perhaps, *the values of type* `ID` *must be unique throughout a document.* No two instances can have the same `ID` value. Also, no element can have more than one attribute of type `ID`. Following are five valid instances of `MyObject`, each with a different `id` attribute. Then there are three valid instances of `MyPointer`.

```
<MyObject  id="n123" >hello</MyObject>
<MyObject  id="n124" >hello again</MyObject>
<MyObject  id="n125" >hello goodbye</MyObject>
<MyObject  id="_n125" >hello goodbye</MyObject>
<MyObject  id="some_xyz-123.98" >hello goodbye</MyObject>
<MyPointer ref="n124" >hello there</MyPointer>
<MyPointer ref="n124" >hello where</MyPointer>
<MyPointer ref="_n125" >hello where</MyPointer>
```

Effectively, the `ref` attribute is a pointer to the `MyObject` element whose `id` attribute has a matching value. For example:

```
<MyPointer ref="_n125" >hello where</MyPointer>
```

associates this specific instance of `MyPointer` with the `MyObject` element whose `id="_n125"`:

```
<MyObject  id="_n125" >hello goodbye</MyObject>
```

Of particular note is the fact that although `ID`s must be unique within a document, `IDREF`s need not be; two instances of `MyPointer` have the same value (`"n124"`) for the `ref` attribute.

The next example is illegal because an `ID` cannot begin with a digit.

```
<MyObject  id="555" >hello goodbye</MyObject>
```

This linkage concept of elements with `IDREF` attributes to elements with `ID` attributes is important to the XPointer specification which we will discuss in chapter 14.

All `ID`, `IDREF`, and `NMTOKEN` examples can be found in the files `attrs.xml` and `attrs.dtd` on the CD-ROM.

Attribute Default Values

In contrast to element type declarations, attribute-list declarations must have **attribute default values**, as explained in detail in Table 4-4. The uppercase keywords `#IMPLIED` and `#REQUIRED` indicate whether a particular attribute is optional or mandatory, respectively, similar to the role of occurrence indicators for elements. However, the same attribute can never be repeated within one element's start tag, so the repeatability concept doesn't apply. As the table shows, you can also specify a default value for an attribute in the DTD that XML instances are free to override, or supply a fixed value that can't be overriden.

#IMPLIED and #REQUIRED

Every attribute-list declaration must contain at least one of the attribute default values shown in Table 4-4. That does not mean that every attribute must *have* a default value since `#IMPLIED` and `#REQUIRED` don't include default values. Therefore, this declaration is illegal since it contains no attribute default value:

```
<!ELEMENT Imp EMPTY >
<!ATTLIST Imp val CDATA >
```

TABLE 4-4 Attribute Default Values in XML 1.0 DTDs

Attribute Default	*Meaning and Use*
`#IMPLIED`	Optional attribute; if no value is provided in the XML document, no default will be supplied by the parser; most useful for attributes that merely provide nonessential details
`#REQUIRED`	Mandatory attribute; each instance of the element must specify a value for this attribute; there is no default value; most useful for attributes that are crucial in defining an element instance (e.g., the `src` attribute for the `img` element)
`"defaultValue"`	If *no* value is explicitly provided in the XML document, this default value will be supplied by the parser; however, if the XML instance provides a *different* value, the default value is overriden; most useful when a typical value is known but not necessarily the only possible value
`#FIXED "fixedValue"`	Value is supplied by the parser and cannot be changed (although it can be explicitly stated in the XML instance if the value is identical); any other value is invalid

To turn this into a valid declaration that describes an *optional* attribute, we need the keyword #IMPLIED:

```
<!ELEMENT Imp EMPTY >
<!ATTLIST Imp val CDATA #IMPLIED >
```

Two valid instances of the Imp element with a val attribute are:

```
<Imp val="specified" />
<Imp />    <!-- no default, attr is optional -->
```

Suppose we want to declare a *mandatory* attribute with an unconstrained value. The keyword #REQUIRED does the trick:

```
<!ELEMENT Req EMPTY >
<!ATTLIST Req val CDATA #REQUIRED >
```

A valid example of its use is:

```
<Req  val="whatever" />
```

In this case, however, if we omit the attribute, it's illegal as we intended:

```
<Req />
```

Previously, we learned about enumerating the set of valid values of an attribute, which is often used with #REQUIRED to indicate a multiple choice:

```
<!ELEMENT Req2 EMPTY >
<!ATTLIST Req2 val (alpha | beta | gamma)  #REQUIRED >
```

An example of this declaration is:

```
<Req2 val="beta" />
```

Of course, since an element can have more than one attribute, and since there is also attribute *type* to consider, we could have both an optional attribute of type CDATA and a required attribute of type NMTOKEN:

```
<!ELEMENT ImpReq EMPTY >
<!ATTLIST ImpReq ival CDATA   #IMPLIED
                 rval NMTOKEN #REQUIRED >
```

Two valid instances follow. In the first, both attributes are supplied, but in the second, the #IMPLIED attribute is omitted.

```
<ImpReq rval="_some_xyz-123.98" ival="optional attr" />
<ImpReq rval="_some_xyz-123.98" />
```

As this example illustrates, order of attributes in the DTD places no constraint on the order of attributes in the instance. In XML, attribute order is undefined. Applications should never rely on attribute order.

Default Value and Fixed Value

Suppose we need to specify a *default value* that will be supplied by the parser if an instance omits the attribute. This is accomplished without a keyword by supplying the default as a *quoted string* (in either single or double quotes):

```
<!ELEMENT Def EMPTY >
<!ATTLIST Def val CDATA 'default value' >
```

Quotes are mandatory around a default value even if the value is a single word or number. This declaration results in two possible cases:

```
<Def val="override" />
<Def />              <!-- should default to 'default value' -->
```

In the first, the instance supplies a value different from the default, which is perfectly fine. The value "override" simply overrides the default value. In the second case, since no value is supplied, the parser supplies the default, which is exactly equivalent to the instance:

```
<Def val="default value" />
```

In fact, if you display the file `attrs.xml` in Internet Explorer, you'll see the default substituted, rather than the `<Def />` that appears in the source file.

Sometimes an attribute is assigned a *fixed value* in the DTD. This case applies when you don't want creators of XML documents to override this immutable value. A fixed value is declared using the `#FIXED` keyword followed by the quoted constant value.

```
<!ELEMENT Fix EMPTY >
<!ATTLIST Fix val CDATA #FIXED 'constant' >
```

Similar to the default value case, if a fixed attribute is omitted in the instance, the fixed value is supplied by the parser. However, in contrast to the default value case, if any other value is supplied, it is an error. Therefore, in the following example the first and second instances are equivalent; the parser will supply the fixed value `"constant"` in the first case, and there's no harm in supplying the correct value in the XML document. The third case is illegal, however, because no value except `"constant"` is acceptable.

```
<Fix />
<Fix val="constant" />
<Fix val="wrong" />
```

A subtle point is what type to declare a fixed attribute. I used CDATA here. However, the W3C prefers to use the fixed value itself for the type, as follows:

```
<!ELEMENT Fix2 EMPTY >
<!ATTLIST Fix2 val (constant) #FIXED 'constant' >  <!-- W3C way -->
```

This makes sense and is more precise in a way; if the value is truly fixed, then it's the only possible value and it's like a very, very narrowly defined type. (Discuss among yourself ;-).)

We can combine enumeration with default values, so rather than requiring an instance to select among alternatives, we can provide a default.

```
<!ELEMENT Enum EMPTY >
<!ATTLIST Enum val (this | that | other) 'this' >
```

In this case, the quoted default value appears in place of #REQUIRED. Valid instances are:

```
<Enum val="other" />
<Enum />              <!-- should default to 'this' -->
```

One small wrinkle with the members of an enumeration: They must all be of NMTOKEN type, which means (among other things) that no spaces can appear and therefore no multiple word choices are permitted. So this illegal declaration:

```
<!ELEMENT Enum2 EMPTY >
<!ATTLIST Enum2 val (this | that | "the other thing") "this" >
```

must be replaced by one like this, using hyphens or underscores to separate the words:

```
<!ELEMENT Enum2 EMPTY >
<!ATTLIST Enum2 val (this | that | the-other-thing) "this" >
```

A few more examples will help bring the attribute concepts together. Looking back at our earlier ValidRange example, recall that both the low and high attributes are required. This is especially important because this empty element is completely defined by these two attributes. Any instance of the element ValidRange that fails to explicitly specify both of these attributes is flagged as invalid by the parser. On the other hand, it is often the case that some or all of an element's attributes are *not* so crucial to its definition. Instead, they are *optional* qualifiers that may or may not be needed in every instance. Consider this (simplified) example, again from AIML:

```
<!ATTLIST Argument
          name     CDATA #REQUIRED
          type     CDATA #REQUIRED
          default  CDATA #IMPLIED
          unit     CDATA #IMPLIED >
```

We require that an Argument always include a name and type (datatype), but we specify via the #IMPLIED keyword that the argument's attributes named default and unit are optional attributes. (Don't be confused by the Argument attribute names type and default in this example. Like all other attributes, they have their own attribute type and default declaration; there is nothing special about the names of these attributes.) Given this declaration, the following are all valid instances. The first case supplies both optional attributes, the second supplies only unit, and the third omits both.

```
<Argument name="Delay"
          type="java.lang.Integer"
          default="100" unit="ms" >
  <ValidRange low="1" high="1000000" />
</Argument>

<Argument name="amplitude"
          type="java.lang.Float"
          unit="V_pp" >
  <ValidRange low="0.05" high="10.0" />
</Argument>

<Argument name="Resolution"
          type="java.lang.String">
  <ValidList  name="Resolution">
    <Choice name="Default">DEF</Choice>
    <Choice name="Highest">MIN</Choice>
    <Choice name="Lowest">MAX</Choice>
  </ValidList>
</Argument>
```

We've seen that attribute declarations may also optionally specify a default value (in quotes following the attribute type) that will be supplied by a parser if the attribute is not explicitly included in the XML document.

```
<!ELEMENT Command  (Argument)* >
<!ATTLIST Command
          name     CDATA     #REQUIRED
          timeout  NMTOKEN   '0' >
```

In this example, the timeout attribute (of type NMTOKEN) has a default value of zero. If it is omitted, the parser will supply zero. Therefore, these two instances are effectively identical after parsing:

```
<Command name="move" timeout="0">
  <Argument name="x" /><Argument name="y" />
</Command>

<Command name="move">
  <Argument name="x" /><Argument name="y" />
</Command>
```

However, if a value is supplied in an XML instance, it will take precedence; the default value will be ignored. This example illustrates overriding the timeout default:

```
<Command name="moveSlow" timeout="100000">
  <Argument name="x" /><Argument name="y" />
</Command>
```

It's often useful to constrain values to an enumerated list of choices and also to specify which of these is the default value. For example, we could alter our earlier EDI example to illustrate this point:

```
<!ELEMENT ShipmentPackagingCode   EMPTY >
<!ATTLIST ShipmentPackagingCode
          code ( CTN25 | BAG79 | MIX71 ) "CTN25" >
```

The `code` attribute is constrained to three possible values, but if none is supplied, the default value of `CTN25` will be provided by the parser. We've removed the `#REQUIRED` keyword from the earlier example since explicitly stating the value of `code` is no longer mandatory.

Next, we present a set of guidelines to help you determine when to model data as an element and when to model as an attribute.

Elements vs. Attributes: Guidelines

One of the most frequently asked questions in XML is, when is it appropriate to model a particular piece of data as an element as opposed to as an attribute? Is it best to make almost everything elements, with attributes used only for details? Or is it better to create fewer elements and use attributes liberally? This question goes back to the days of SGML (at least to 1992) and, perhaps surprisingly, there is no specific rule of thumb that applies in all cases. You must carefully evaluate your specific needs.

However, Robin Cover's XML site collects discussions of this topic with guidelines suggested by several SGML and XML experts (*http://xml.coverpages.org/elementsAndAttrs.html*). The gist of the debate focuses on how elements and attributes differ.

- Attributes are more like metadata and details that people (or processes) at the end of the transmission chain need not know about, rather than the content. Examples include coordinates and dimensions of SVG objects, which are attributes, as opposed to the kind of shape, represented as elements.
- Attributes are often used for details that aren't necessarily visible. For example, link-related information such as `src` or `href` attributes in XHTML and attributes of type `ID` and `IDREF` in XML are typically invisible information.

- The order in which attributes are returned by the parser is not defined and cannot be controlled. If your application needs to depend on the order of attributes, change the attributes to elements so you can enforce order via their content model (sequencing).
- Similarly, a given attribute cannot be repeated in a particular element instance. If you require repeatability, you need elements with occurrence indicators.
- If you need to access the information directly or frequently, elements are generally more efficient.
- Whereas elements are typically for data objects or components of data objects, attributes are essentially for properties.
- Attributes represent unstructured details and cannot be hierarchical, so if you need nesting, you must use elements.
- If your model is evolving, reliance on more elements and fewer attributes is often desirable because you can always add child elements to the model. Elements are extensible but attributes are difficult to convert to elements later without extensive editing.
- Attributes are useful for specifying enumerated values. Therefore, if you want to constrain values to a set of choices, you cannot do this with elements (except with XML Schema), so attributes would be more appropriate.
- If you need to supply a default value, you must use attributes (except with XML Schema).

Example DTD and XML Instance

In this section, we'll see a short DTD that describes the structure of a very simplistic kind of invoice. This DTD illustrates the various kinds of content models and attribute-list declarations, rather than indicates a practical invoice DTD to be used for e-commerce. We'll also see an example of an XML instance that is valid according to this DTD. Snippets of both the DTD and the XML were discussed earlier in the chapter. This is a chance to see a complete DTD about one page long and a corresponding instance of similar size. Both files (`invoice.dtd` and `invoice.xml`) are on the CD for your experimentation.

Invoice DTD

The simple invoice DTD in Listing 4-1 illustrates the five content models we discussed and several of the attribute cases. Many of the content models have occurrence indicators (?, *, and +). An `Invoice` consists of `ShipTo` information, a `Date`, one or more `ItemInfo` elements, and zero or more `Summary` elements. `ShipTo` begins with a `Name`. Element choice is exemplified by the grouping `(CustomerID | SocSecNo)` in the `ShipTo` content model. `Address`, `City`, `State`, and `Zip` are optional components of ShipTo (even though the package won't travel very far without this info). Invoice has an optional version attribute of unconstrained character data.

The declarations

```
<!ELEMENT CustomerID (#PCDATA)>
<!ATTLIST CustomerID sex  (male | female | unknown )  #REQUIRED>
```

indicate that CustomerID is unconstrained parsed character data with a mandatory sex attribute that must be one of three enumerated values. ItemInfo always has SKU, Quantity, and Weight, one or more Price elements, and optionally an ItemName, Note, and Divider. The declaration

```
<!ELEMENT Note      (#PCDATA | Link | Emph )* >
```

defines Note as having a mixed content model that permits intermixing character data with any number of Link and Emph elements in any order. Divider and Summary exemplify EMPTY and ANY content models. Therefore Divider has no content and serves as a marker, while Summary can have any content whatsoever. The declarations

```
<!ELEMENT Weight    (#PCDATA)>
<!ATTLIST Weight    unitOfMeasure    (lb | oz)     "oz"
                    measurementType CDATA  #FIXED "US" >
```

defines the Weight element as having two optional attributes. Attribute unitOfMeasure is an enumerated list of two choices, with a default value of "oz". The measurementType attribute, on the other hand, has a fixed value of "US".

Listing 4-1 Simple Invoice DTD (invoice.dtd)

```
<?xml version='1.0' encoding='UTF-8' ?>
<!--
     This invoice DTD is strictly illustrative.
     It is not intended for actual use in an eCommerce system.
     As if you couldn't guess.
-->
<!ELEMENT Invoice  (ShipTo, Date, ItemInfo+, Summary*)>
<!-- #IMPLIED means attribute is completely optional. -->
<!ATTLIST Invoice version CDATA  #IMPLIED>

<!ELEMENT ShipTo   (Name, (CustomerID | SocSecNo),
                    Address?, City?, State?, Zip?)>
<!ELEMENT Name     (First, Last)>
<!ELEMENT First    (#PCDATA)>
<!ELEMENT Last     (#PCDATA)>

<!ELEMENT CustomerID (#PCDATA)>
<!-- #REQUIRED means attribute cannot be omitted & has no default. -->
<!ATTLIST CustomerID sex  (male | female | unknown )  #REQUIRED>
<!ELEMENT SocSecNo   (#PCDATA)>
```

```
<!ELEMENT Address  (#PCDATA)>
<!ELEMENT City     (#PCDATA)>
<!ELEMENT State    (#PCDATA)>
<!ELEMENT Zip      (#PCDATA)>

<!ELEMENT Date     (#PCDATA)>  <!-- in CCYY-MM-DD format -->

<!ELEMENT ItemInfo (ItemName?, SKU, Quantity, Weight, Price+,
                    Note?, Divider?)>
<!ELEMENT ItemName (#PCDATA)>
<!ELEMENT SKU      (#PCDATA)>
<!ELEMENT Quantity (#PCDATA)>

<!ELEMENT Weight   (#PCDATA)>
<!-- #FIXED means attribute has constant (immutable) value-->
<!ATTLIST Weight   unitOfMeasure   (lb | oz)     "oz"
                   measurementType CDATA  #FIXED "US" >

<!ELEMENT Price    (#PCDATA)>
<!ELEMENT Note     (#PCDATA | Link | Emph )* >
<!ELEMENT Emph     (#PCDATA)>
<!ELEMENT Link     (#PCDATA)>

<!ELEMENT Divider  EMPTY >
<!ELEMENT Summary  ANY >
```

Invoice XML Instance

Listing 4-2 illustrates an instance of an XML document that is valid according to the invoice DTD. In this case, Rocky Rococo will be the lucky recipient of a copy of the Beatles Anthology and a Firesign Theatre DVD, the two `ItemInfo` components of this `Invoice`. The content models are shown in comments to more easily map the document structure to the DTD (or vice versa). In a real application, it is unlikely that you would include such comments.

The first item has a `Note`, which shows us another example of mixed content:

```
<Note>Price reflects <Emph>20% savings</Emph> from Amazon:
     <Link>http://www.amazon.com/exec/obidos/ASIN/0811826848/</Link>
</Note>
```

The `Summary` element, defined to permit *any* content model, happens to also use a mixed content model in this instance.

Listing 4-2 XML Instance Matching Invoice DTD (invoice.xml)

```
<?xml version = "1.0" encoding = "UTF-8"?>
<!DOCTYPE Invoice SYSTEM "invoice.dtd">
<Invoice version = "2.7">
  <!--(ShipTo, Date, ItemInfo+, Summary*)-->
  <ShipTo>
    <!--(Name, (CustomerID | SocSecNo), Address?, City?, State?, Zip?)-->
```

```
    <Name>
      <!--(First, Last)-->
      <First>Rocky</First>
      <Last>Rococo</Last>
    </Name>
    <CustomerID sex="male">1312363</CustomerID>
    <Address>456 Kuttemoffatta Pass</Address>
    <City>Columbia</City>
    <State>MD</State>
    <Zip>20707</Zip>
  </ShipTo>
  <Date>2002-04-19</Date>
  <ItemInfo>
    <!--(ItemName?, SKU, Quantity, Weight, Price+, Note?, Divider?)-->
    <ItemName>Beatles Anthology</ItemName>
    <SKU>0811826848</SKU>
    <Quantity>1</Quantity>
    <Weight unitOfMeasure="lb" measurementType="US">6</Weight>
    <Price>48.00</Price>
    <Note>Price reflects <Emph>20% savings</Emph> from Amazon:
         <Link>http://www.amazon.com/exec/obidos/ASIN/0811826848/</Link>
    </Note>
    <Divider />
  </ItemInfo>
  <ItemInfo>
    <!--(ItemName?, SKU, Quantity, Weight, Price+, Note?, Divider?)-->
    <ItemName>The Firesign Theatre: All-Day Matinee</ItemName>
    <SKU>B00005Q65U</SKU>
    <Quantity>1</Quantity>
    <Weight unitOfMeasure="oz" measurementType="US">12.3</Weight>
    <Price>22.46</Price>
  </ItemInfo>
  <Summary>2 items to be <Emph>shipped together</Emph> from
Amazon.</Summary>
</Invoice>
```

External and Internal DTD Subsets

External Subsets

In chapter 3, we learned that the *document type declaration* (the part of the XML prolog that begins with the delimiter "<!" and the keyword DOCTYPE) specifies whether a DTD is needed. So far, we have discussed the cases where there is no DTD (standalone="yes") and when there is a DTD external from the XML document (standalone="no").[9] We refer to the external DTD as the **external subset**, in that it effectively is a subset of the XML document that references it, namely the subset that defines the document structure, defines attributes and default values,

9. Technically, standalone="no" means that parsing *is* effected by the external DTD subset, whereas standalone="yes" means parsing is *not* effected by the external subset.

and so forth. In the section entitled "Document Type Declaration" in chapter 3, we saw that the general syntax for the document type declaration is:

```
<!DOCTYPE RootElement (SYSTEM | PUBLIC)
        ExternalDeclarations?  [InternalDeclarations]? >
```

However, so far, we've ignored `InternalDeclarations`, so the effective document type declaration has been (and usually is in practice):

```
<!DOCTYPE RootElement (SYSTEM | PUBLIC) ExternalDeclarations >
```

For example:

```
<!DOCTYPE PriceList SYSTEM "prices.dtd" >

<!DOCTYPE PriceList SYSTEM "http://Ex.com/prices.dtd" >

<!DOCTYPE HTML PUBLIC
  "-//W3C//DTD HTML 4.0//EN"
  "http://www.w3.org/TR/REC-html40/strict.dtd">

<!DOCTYPE InstrumentControl PUBLIC
   "-//Code588//DTD Instrument Control//EN"
   "http://Ex.nasa.gov/xml-vocabs/aiml.dtd" >
```

If we consult the XML 1.0 Recommendation, Second Edition (*http://www.w3.org/TR/REC-XM/#sec-prolog-dtd*) we see that the formal definition of "DTD" is the *external subset* or the *internal subset* or *both*, if present.

> The XML **document type declaration** contains or points to markup declarations that provide a grammar for a class of documents. This grammar is known as a **document type definition**, or **DTD**. The document type declaration can point to an external subset (a special kind of external entity) containing markup declarations, or can contain the markup declarations directly in an internal subset, or can do both. The DTD for a document consists of both subsets taken together.

Internal Subsets

We can define an **internal subset**, which is physically contained in the XML document. To do so, we embed the element and attribute declarations that would have otherwise appeared in an external DTD directly in the document type declaration after `RootElement`.

```
<!DOCTYPE RootElement [ InternalDeclarations ]>
```

Note the use of square brackets (`[ and ]`) to delimit the internal subset, followed by the closing angle bracket (>) that always terminates the document type declaration. Also note the absence of the `SYSTEM` and `PUBLIC` keywords. Listing 4-3 is a complete example of an XML document with an internal subset. The example shows an internal subset consisting of five element type declarations and one attribute-list declaration. Such an XML instance can be tested for validity exactly as you would if an external DTD were referenced.

Listing 4-3 Internal Subset Example (internal-subset.xml)

```
<?xml version="1.0" standalone="yes" ?>
<!DOCTYPE PriceList [
  <!ELEMENT PriceList     (TodaysSpecial+)>
  <!ELEMENT TodaysSpecial (Item, Price, Discount)>
  <!ATTLIST TodaysSpecial
            department CDATA #IMPLIED
            profit     CDATA #REQUIRED >
  <!ELEMENT Item     (#PCDATA) >
  <!ELEMENT Price    (#PCDATA) >
  <!ELEMENT Discount (#PCDATA)>
]>
<PriceList>            <!-- begin document instance -->
  <TodaysSpecial department="Records" profit=".27" >
    <Item>Listen to What the Man Said</Item>
    <Price>18.98</Price>
    <Discount>.30</Discount>
  </TodaysSpecial>
</PriceList>           <!-- end document instance -->
```

This XML document is considered standalone because no external file is referenced (or more precisely, because no external subset affects the parsing), even though there is an embedded DTD. (This expands the simplification of the meaning of *standalone* presented in chapter 3.) As you might expect, this approach does not provide the reusability that we get with an external DTD, and in practice you will probably not see it in use often. You may encounter it in tutorial examples intended to keep the DTD and instance in a single file.

External Subset with Internal Subset

So, what's the point of an internal subset? When is this technique useful? Well, it turns out that *both an external and internal DTD may be combined*, with the internal subset extending the external subset. This is advantageous when a content author wishes to leverage a common DTD but needs to add element or attribute declarations of his own. For example, let's revisit the previous example and define a small DTD called `prices.dtd` as follows:

```
<!ELEMENT Prices   (ItemInfo+)>
<!ELEMENT ItemInfo (Item, Price)>
<!ELEMENT Item     (#PCDATA) >
<!ELEMENT Price    (#PCDATA) >
```

Suppose all we care about reusing from this DTD is the element declarations for `Item` and `Price`; we'll ignore the other two elements. We keep the XML instance from Listing 4-3 the same, but we add a reference to the *external subset* in the usual manner of the keyword `SYSTEM` followed by the URI. Note that the document is no longer standalone, however, since we're referencing an external subset. Then we modify the previous *internal subset*, removing the declarations for `Item` and `Price`, but retaining those for `PriceList`, `TodaysSpecial`, and `Discount`. This effectively extends `prices.dtd` by introducing additional elements and attributes. Duplicate element declarations (i.e., one for `Item` in the external subset and one for `Item` in the internal subset) are not allowed. Given the minimal DTD in the file `prices.dtd`, Listing 4-4 shows how the DTD can be extended with an internal subset. The examples in this section are on the CD-ROM.

Listing 4-4 Instance with Both External and Internal Subset (internal-external-subset.xml)

```
<?xml version="1.0" standalone="no" ?>
<!DOCTYPE PriceList SYSTEM
          "prices.dtd" [
  <!ELEMENT PriceList     (TodaysSpecial+)>
  <!ELEMENT TodaysSpecial (Item, Price, Discount)>
  <!ATTLIST TodaysSpecial
          department CDATA #IMPLIED
          profit     CDATA #REQUIRED >
  <!ELEMENT Discount (#PCDATA)>
]>
<PriceList>           <!-- begin document instance -->
  <TodaysSpecial department="Records" profit=".27" >
    <Item>Listen to What the Man Said</Item>
    <Price>18.98</Price>
    <Discount>.30</Discount>
  </TodaysSpecial>
</PriceList>          <!-- end document instance -->
```

Entities and Notations

The term *entity* has many meanings in XML and DTD terminology, which can be the cause for considerable confusion. In general, entities are a convenient way to represent information that either occurs repeatedly or is expected to change, either in XML instances or DTDs. While the term **entity** generally means a basic storage unit for the parts of an XML document, it can be used to represent a number of things:

- A block of repeated text
- A special character
- A constant (fixed) string
- An entire XML document

TABLE 4-5 Entity Overview and Categories

- *Document entity*—XML declaration, optional document type declaration, root element and all its children
- *General entity*—content merged into an XML document; several subtypes:
  - *Internal parsed general entity*—predefined character entities and replacement text in XML
  - *External parsed general entity*—included XML content from an external file
  - *External unparsed general entity*—non-XML data, typically binary data
- *Parameter entity*—defined and used strictly in the DTD
  - *Internal parameter entity*—DTD replacement text, typically for content model or attribute sets
  - *External parameter entity*—complete element and attribute declarations included from an external file

- A portion of a larger XML document
- A portion of a larger DTD
- A content model or set of attributes in a DTD
- A binary image

It is the task of a validating parser to combine the various entities to form the complete (and logically single) XML document. Table 4-5 provides an overview of the various meanings of *entity*, which are described in considerable detail in the following sections.

Document Entity

The **document entity** serves as the root of the entity tree and a starting point for an XML processor. The XML Recommendation does not specify how the document entity is to be located by an XML processor. Unlike other entities, the document entity has no name and might well appear on a processor input stream without identification. It consists of:

- the XML declaration
- the optional document type declaration
- the root element and all its children

General Entities

There are three kinds of general entities:

- Internal parsed general entities
- External parsed general entities
- External unparsed general entities

General entities are strictly for use in the XML document content, although they are declared in the DTD, either the internal or external subset. This implies that even if you do not care about validation, to use general entities, you must at a minimum have an internal subset in which the entities are declared.

General entities divide into *parsed* and *unparsed;* parsed entities divide into two more categories. While general entities vary in their purpose, their content is always merged into the XML instance. A **parsed entity** contains well-formed XML or other replacement text. Parsed entities, which are far more common than unparsed entities, are either internal or external with respect to the document instance into which they are merged.

An **internal parsed entity** is defined in either the internal or external DTD subset, but is strictly for merging content into the *XML document*. This is sometimes called an *internal parsed general entity,* but more typically it's known simply as an **internal entity**. In contrast, an **external parsed entity**, or simply **external entity**, is a chunk of XML elements stored in a *separate file* that is referenced from the document instance with which it is merged. External entities are especially useful for sharing content that needs to appear in multiple XML documents, such as a copyright notice, a list of references, and an author's biography. Like internal entities, external entities are defined in either the internal or external DTD subset.

An **unparsed entity**, on the other hand, contains non-XML data, such as binary content (GIF, JPEG, etc.) or simply unstructured text that is not well-formed. It is sometimes called an **external unparsed entity** because the non-XML data is stored external to the instance. We won't cover them until after we discuss both parsed entities and parameter entities because they are fundamentally different from the other kinds of entities is most respects.

When the term *entity* is not qualified, it typically means a parsed entity. Let's next focus on internal and external entities in more detail.

Internal Entities

Internal (parsed general) entities are replacement text defined *within* an XML document and referenced from one or more locations in the same document. The general syntax for an internal entity declaration is:

```
<!ENTITY EntityName "QuotedReplacementText" >
```

Here `ENTITY` is a literal keyword, `EntityName` is an XML Name, and `QuotedReplacementText` is a single- or double-quoted string of replacement text that may be a single line, may span multiple lines, and may contain markup. In the case of internal general entities, the replacement text must be well-formed, so you can't include a start tag without also including the end tag, for example.

The purpose of such an entity is to serve as shorthand for a fixed string or block of text that is expected to be used repeatedly in the XML document, especially text that may someday need to change. For readers old enough to remember the C programming language, an internal general entity is similar to a C `#define`. The text that it is replaced must be static (there is no mechanism for passing in variables to alter the text). For example, here are three internal entity declarations, each of which happens to consist of text without markup:

```
<!ENTITY ProductName "eCommerce Enabler" >
<!ENTITY ProductId
"Version 2.01; Build Date: 04/19/2002. Copyright 2002." >
<!ENTITY CompanyName "ShoesForIndustry, Inc." >
```

To refer to an entity, we use this general syntax of wrapping its name inside an *ampersand* and *semicolon*:

```
&EntityName;
```

where `EntityName` is declared as an `ENTITY` in either an internal or external DTD subset. Forward references are allowed, so an earlier line can reference an entity before its declaration appears. Listing 4-5 shows the three entity declarations in an internal subset and then referenced in the document instance.

Listing 4-5 Internal Entity Declaration in Internal Subset (internal-entity.xml)

```
<?xml version="1.0" standalone="yes"?>
<!DOCTYPE ProductDescription [
  <!ENTITY ProductName "eCommerce Enabler" >
  <!ENTITY ProductId
  "Version 2.01; Build Date: 04/19/2002. Copyright 2002." >
  <!ENTITY CompanyName "ShoesForIndustry, Inc." >
  <!ELEMENT ProductDescription (#PCDATA)>
]>
<ProductDescription>
This product is &ProductName; by &CompanyName;
Details: &ProductId;
</ProductDescription>
```

As you might hope, one internal entity may reference another, providing this does not lead to recursion. Therefore, we could redefine `ProductId` in terms of three pieces of data and combine them, as illustrated in Listing 4-6.

Listing 4-6 Internal Entities Referencing Other Internal Entities

```
<?xml version="1.0" standalone="yes"?>
<!DOCTYPE ProductDescription [
  <!ENTITY ProductName       "eCommerce Enabler" >
  <!ENTITY ProductVersion    "Version 2.01" >
  <!ENTITY ProductDate       "04/19/2002" >
  <!ENTITY ProductCopyright  "2002" >
  <!ENTITY CompanyName       "ShoesForIndustry, Inc." >
  <!ENTITY ProductId         "&ProductVersion;; Build Date: &ProductDate;.
```

```
Copyright &ProductCopyright;." >
  <!ELEMENT ProductDescription (#PCDATA)>
]>
<ProductDescription>
This product is &ProductName; by &CompanyName;
Details: &ProductId;
</ProductDescription>
```

As we can see from Figure 4-1, Internet Explorer 5.x displays both XML instances exactly the same. All internal entity references are replaced by their replacement text. Although you might *think* the order of these internal entity declarations matters, it doesn't. You can actually reference internal entities before they are declared! The following order achieves the same result as Listing 4-6, although it seems more logical to declare them in the previous order.

```
  <!ENTITY ProductName        "eCommerce Enabler" >
  <!ENTITY ProductId          "&ProductVersion;; Build Date: &ProductDate;.
Copyright &ProductCopyright;." >
  <!ENTITY ProductVersion     "Version 2.01" >
  <!ENTITY ProductDate        "04/19/2002" >
  <!ENTITY ProductCopyright   "2002" >
  <!ENTITY CompanyName        "ShoesForIndustry, Inc." >
```

An internal (or external) general entity may span multiple lines and may include markup, as long as the special characters ampersand, percent, and quote (&, %, and ") aren't used directly (without escaping them by means of character references, that is). Listing 4-7 illustrates this case in which the entity reference

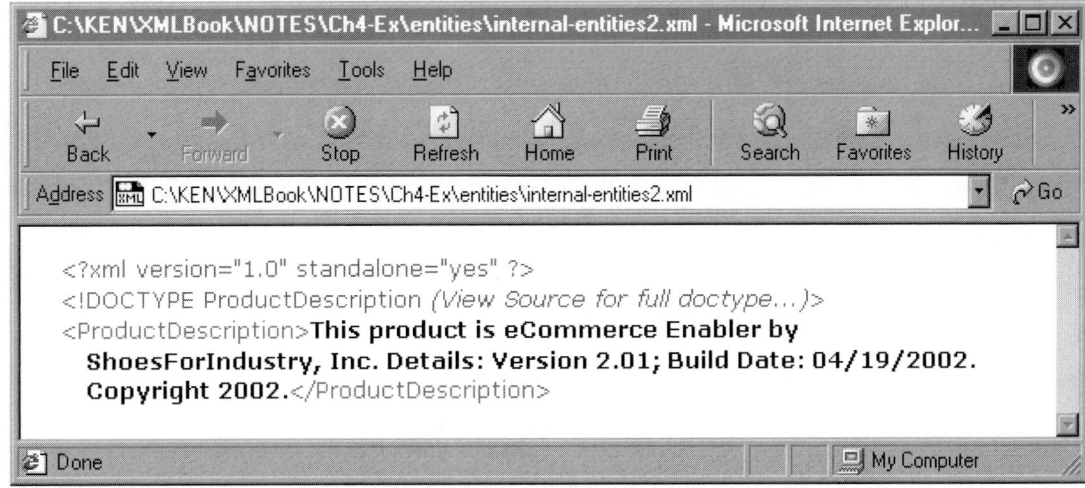

FIGURE 4-1 XML Instance with internal entity references replaced by text in IE 5.x

`&ProductInfo;` is replaced by three elements, `ProductName`, `ProductId`, and `CompanyName`, along with their content. Note that it's necessary to adjust the internal DTD subset to accommodate the new elements.

Listing 4-7 Internal Entity Containing Multiline Markup (internal-entity3.xml)

```
<?xml version="1.0" standalone="yes"?>
<!DOCTYPE ProductDescription [
  <!ENTITY ProductInfo
    "<ProductName>eCommerce enabler</ProductName>
    <ProductId>Version 2.01; Build Date: 04/19/2002.
Copyright 2002.</ProductId>
    <CompanyName>ShoesForIndustry, Inc.</CompanyName>"
  >
  <!ELEMENT ProductDescription (ProductName,ProductId,CompanyName)>
  <!ELEMENT ProductName        (#PCDATA)>
  <!ELEMENT ProductId          (#PCDATA)>
  <!ELEMENT CompanyName        (#PCDATA)>
]>
<ProductDescription>
&ProductInfo;
</ProductDescription>
```

The expansion of the replacement text in this case is shown in Figure 4-2. Note that while the content is essentially the same, each piece is now the content of a child element.

FIGURE 4-2 Expansion of multiline internal entity declaration in IE 5.x

Special Character Entities Revisited

We've previously encountered the five predefined general entities in XML (in chapter 3). Here are their XHTML 1.0 declarations again:

```
<!ENTITY quot  "&#34;" >
<!ENTITY amp   "&#38;#38;" >
<!ENTITY lt    "&#38;&#60;" >
<!ENTITY gt    "&#62;" >
<!ENTITY apos  "&#39;" >
```

They are (parsed general) entity declarations too, so they can be referenced like any other external entity with an ampersand and semicolon. For example:

```
&lt;Here Comes The Sun&gt;
```

results in:

```
<Here Comes The Sun>
```

In addition, there are hundreds of other special characters at your disposal. Appendix A of the XHTML 1.0 Recommendation (*http://www.w3.org/TR/xhtml1/#dtds*) links to the DTD and three ".ent" (entity set) files—`xhtml-special.ent`, `xhtml-lat1.ent`, and `xhtml-symbol.ent`—which define the special character, Latin 1, and symbol entities, respectively, in XHTML 1.0. An example from each of these follows:

```
<!ENTITY dagger  "&#8224;">
<!ENTITY copy    "&#169;">   <!-- copyright -->
<!ENTITY beta    "&#946;">
```

The URLs that locate the entity sets that contain these entities are:

http://www.w3.org/TR/xhtml1/DTD/xhtml-lat1.ent
http://www.w3.org/TR/xhtml1/DTD/xhtml-special.ent
http://www.w3.org/TR/xhtml1/DTD/xhtml-symbol.ent

This means that you can explicitly declare particular special characters that you need, provided you determine the correct entity reference from the XHTML entity set files, or you can declare an entire entity set, as we'll cover when we discuss *parameter entities* later in this chapter.

Listing 4-8 illustrates a DTD (`prodInfo.dtd`) that both explicitly declares two special entities (`dagger` and `copy`) and pulls in one of the XHTML entity sets as well (details deferred for now). An XML instance (`internal-entity4.xml`, shown in Listing 4-9) accesses the external DTD subset by means of a document type declaration, as usual.

Listing 4-8 Declaring Special Entities and External Entity Set in a DTD (prodInfo.dtd)

```
<!-- Include complete symbol entity set from XHTML 1.0 -->
<!ENTITY % HTMLsymbol PUBLIC
      "-//W3C//ENTITIES Symbols for XHTML//EN"
      "http://www.w3.org/TR/xhtml1/DTD/xhtml-symbol.ent">
%HTMLsymbol;

<!-- Define 2 others from the other 2 XHTML 1.0 entity sets -->
<!ENTITY dagger  "&#8224;">
<!ENTITY copy    "&#169;">   <!-- copyright -->

<!ENTITY ProductName "eCommerce Enabler&dagger;" >
<!ENTITY ProductId
"Version 2.01; Build Date: 04/19/2002. &copy; Copyright 2002." >
<!ENTITY CompanyName "ShoesForIndustry, Inc." >

<!ELEMENT ProductDescription (ProductName,ProductId,CompanyName)>
<!ELEMENT ProductName        (#PCDATA)>
<!ELEMENT ProductId          (#PCDATA)>
<!ELEMENT CompanyName        (#PCDATA)>
```

Notice that we can use entity references in the DTD (`†` and `©`) or in the instance (`β`). The instance also takes advantages of two predefined entities (`<` and `>`).

Listing 4-9 Referencing General Entities Declared in a DTD (internal-entity4.xml)

```
<?xml version="1.0" standalone="no"?>
<!DOCTYPE ProductDescription SYSTEM "prodInfo.dtd" >
<ProductDescription>
  <ProductName>&ProductName;</ProductName>
  <ProductId>&ProductId; &lt;&beta; version&gt;</ProductId>
  <CompanyName>&CompanyName;</CompanyName>
</ProductDescription>
```

Figure 4-3 shows how this instance looks in IE 5.x. All entities are replaced by their correct symbols, including those that are part of other entity references. For example, `†` is embedded in the `ProductName` entity in the DTD, but the expansion of the `&ProductName;` entity reference in the `<ProductName>` element in the XML instance works just fine; we see a dagger after the product name.

Three subtle points worth noting are:

1. Using the same name for an element and an entity is not a problem since a (parsed general) entity reference can always be distinguished by ampersand and semicolon.
2. Although not shown in this example, we could have declared the `dagger` and `copy` entities after the `ProductName` and `ProductId` references to them in the DTD, if we wished.

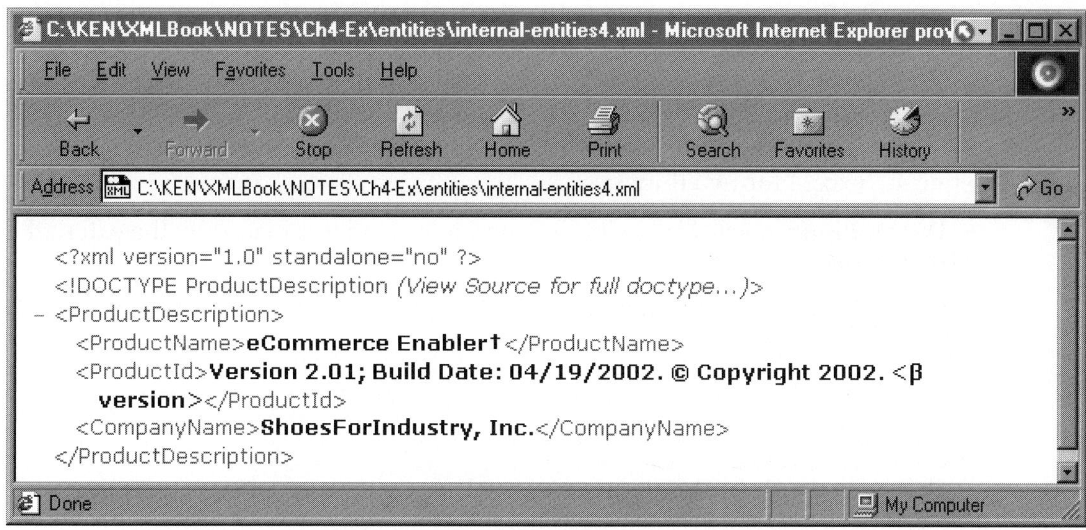

FIGURE 4-3 Displaying XML instance with various internal entities in IE 5.x

3. With the exception of the predefined `<` and `>` entity references, if we had not declared the other entities in the DTD, the instance would have been invalid.

External Entities and Document Reuse

Just as internal general entities are like the C `#define`, **external (parsed general) entities** function much like a C `#include` statement. They are used to include other XML chunks (usually, but not necessarily, well-formed) from an external file into the current XML document entity being parsed. This is a useful technique for constructing large XML documents from a set of smaller files, a modular approach that is often beneficial for large-scale projects and Web sites. External entities are also typically used to share repeated content in multiple XML documents. They are not permitted to contain either internal or external DTD subsets. Therefore, validation of the external XML fragments cannot be attempted until the pieces are incorporated into a particular `DOCTYPE`. The general syntax for an external entity declaration is:

```
<!ENTITY EntityName SYSTEM "URIofExternalXML" >
```

where `ENTITY` and `SYSTEM` are literal,[10] `EntityName` is an XML Name, and `URIofExternalXML` is a single- or double-quoted URI that points to the XML document to

10. Actually, you can also use the keyword `PUBLIC` and a Formal Public Identifier in place of `SYSTEM`, as discussed in the section "Document Type Declaration" in chapter 3.

be included. It may be given as a URL or a pathname, either absolute or relative with respect to the XML document from which the reference is made.

Consider the file `external-entity.xml`, shown in Listing 4-10, which declares the external entity `ProductInfo`, associated with a URI of `prodInfo.xml` in the same directory as the XML instance. This document is very similar to the one in Listing 4-7 except for two things:

- The multiline internal entity of the previous figure is replaced by the external entity declaration.
- The document is no longer considered standalone since an external file must be processed.

Listing 4-10 External Entity ProductInfo Declaration and Reference (external-entity.xml)

```
<?xml version="1.0" standalone="no"?>
<!DOCTYPE ProductDescription [
  <!ENTITY ProductInfo SYSTEM "prodInfo.xml" >
  <!ELEMENT ProductDescription (ProductName,ProductId,CompanyName)>
  <!ELEMENT ProductName        (#PCDATA)>
  <!ELEMENT ProductId          (#PCDATA)>
  <!ELEMENT CompanyName        (#PCDATA)>
]>
<ProductDescription>
&ProductInfo;
</ProductDescription>
```

What about the contents of the external file `productInfo.xml`? If you'd expect it looks pretty much like the replacement text of a multiline internal entity declaration, you'd be reasonably correct. See Listing 4-11.

Listing 4-11 Text Declaration Referenced by External Entity Declaration (prodInfo.xml)

```
<?xml encoding="UTF-8"?>
<!-- This is a Text Declaration, not an XML Declaration. -->
<ProductName>eCommerce Enabler</ProductName>
<ProductId>Version 2.01; Build Date: 04/19/2002.
Copyright 2002.</ProductId>
<CompanyName>ShoesForIndustry, Inc.</CompanyName>
```

The three elements that previously constituted the replacement text of the internal entity in Listing 4-7 are present. However, the first line of the file looks a little strange. Is it an XML declaration? No, because it's missing the required `version` attribute. Instead this is called a **text declaration**, which differs from an XML declaration in two important respects:

- The `encoding` attribute is *required*, but the `version` attribute is not.
- The markup that follows a text declaration need not be well-formed.

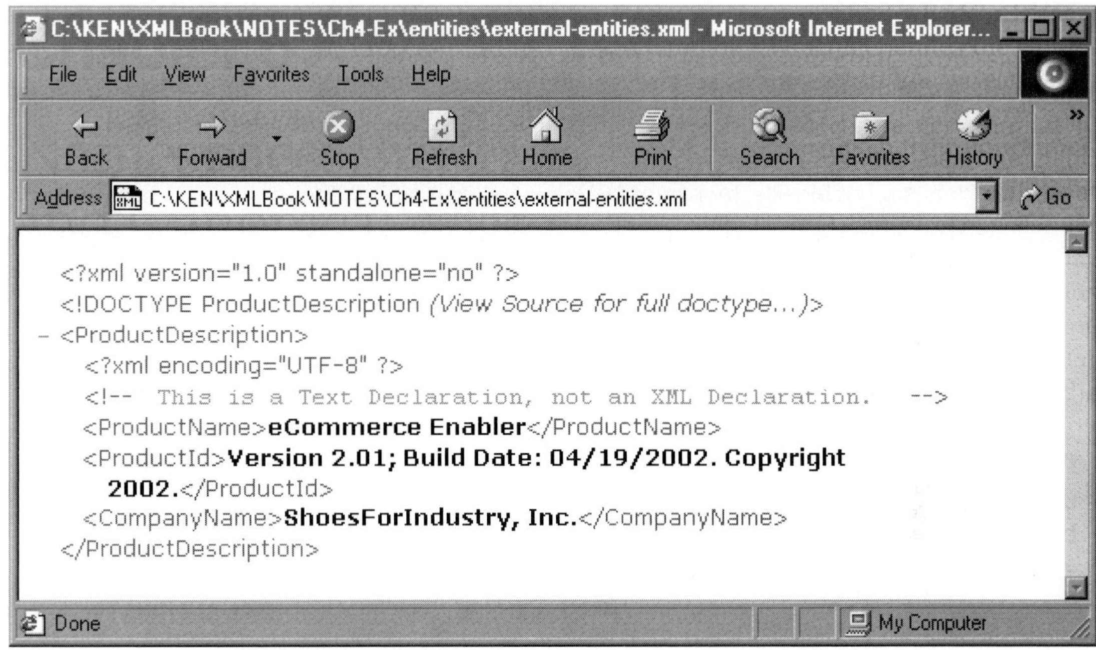

FIGURE 4-4 Display of XML instance referencing an external entity with text declaration

The file `prodInfo.xml` is *not well-formed* XML because there is no single element that contains all others; by definition, it isn't an XML document, just an XML fragment. In other words, it can't be considered well-formed because there is no root element that encloses all others. However, this is exactly what we want in order to construct a document from pieces.[11]

Figure 4-4 shows how IE 5.x displays `external-entity.xml` with its reference to `prodInfo.xml`. If you compare it to Figure 4-3, the only difference (other than the standalone declaration) is the text declaration that appears in the new case. This in no way impacts the document content, however. Although external entities are permitted to begin with a text declaration, they aren't required to have them. The chief reason for including them is to identify the encoding of the entity in the event that it is combined with documents of a different encoding.

Because one of the main reasons for using external parsed general entities is to share the same content in multiple documents (especially content that may change), let's see how we can reuse `prodInfo.xml` in a different document, `external-`

11. At the time of this writing, a W3C specification called XML Inclusions (XInclude) Version 1.0 is still in development. XInclude proposes more flexible mechanisms for combining XML documents but its support in parsers and other tools is understandably very limited. This will certainly change after XInclude becomes a W3C Recommendation.

Nonvalidating parsers are not *required* to resolve external entity references, although they are required to handle *internal* entities. (Nor are they required to handle unparsed entities, discussed later.) This does not mean that nonvalidating parsers always ignore external entities, just that it is implementation dependent. Browsers in particular handle this differently; these examples do not work in Netscape or Mozilla, for example. Validating parsers, on the other hand, are required to resolve both internal and external entities.

entity2.xml. The structure of this new instance is shown in Listing 4-12; compare it to Listing 4-10.

Listing 4-12 Second XML Instance that Shares External Entity (external-entity2.xml)

```
<?xml version="1.0" standalone="no"?>
<!DOCTYPE Catalog [
  <!ENTITY ProductInfo SYSTEM "prodInfo.xml" >

  <!ENTITY ProductAbbrev  "e-Enabler" >
  <!ELEMENT Catalog             (Product+) >
  <!ELEMENT Product             (ProductIdent, ProductDesc) >
  <!ELEMENT ProductDesc         (#PCDATA)>

  <!-- Note that ProductIdent is called ProductDescription in other ex. -->
  <!ELEMENT ProductIdent        (ProductName, ProductId, CompanyName)>
  <!ELEMENT ProductName         (#PCDATA)>
  <!ELEMENT ProductId           (#PCDATA)>
  <!ELEMENT CompanyName         (#PCDATA)>
]>
<Catalog>
  <Product>
    <ProductIdent>&ProductInfo;</ProductIdent>
    <ProductDesc>The new &ProductAbbrev; is the greatest thing since sliced
bread. Speaking of which, besides enabling eCommerce, it does slice bread!
    </ProductDesc>
  </Product>
</Catalog>
```

This instance is a different DOCTYPE (Catalog, as compared to the previous ProductDescription). In fact, the entire hierarchy is different, with the exception of the three elements from the external entity, ProductName, ProductId, and CompanyName. Even the name of the parent element that contains the three common elements is different. There's also an internal entity (ProductAbbrev) declared in the internal subset of this document. The point is that although the instances shown in Listing 4-10 and Listing 4-12 are fairly different, they both can reuse the XML fragment that they have in common.

Combining XML Documents Using External Entities

External entities can also be used to combine XML documents. Listing 4-13 shows two external entity declarations; one refers to `collection7.xml` and the other to `collection8.xml`, neither of which happens to have entity references (although they certainly could have). By using entity references, we effectively create a document that is a concatenation of the two smaller documents. The result as displayed in IE 5.x is shown in Figure 4-5.

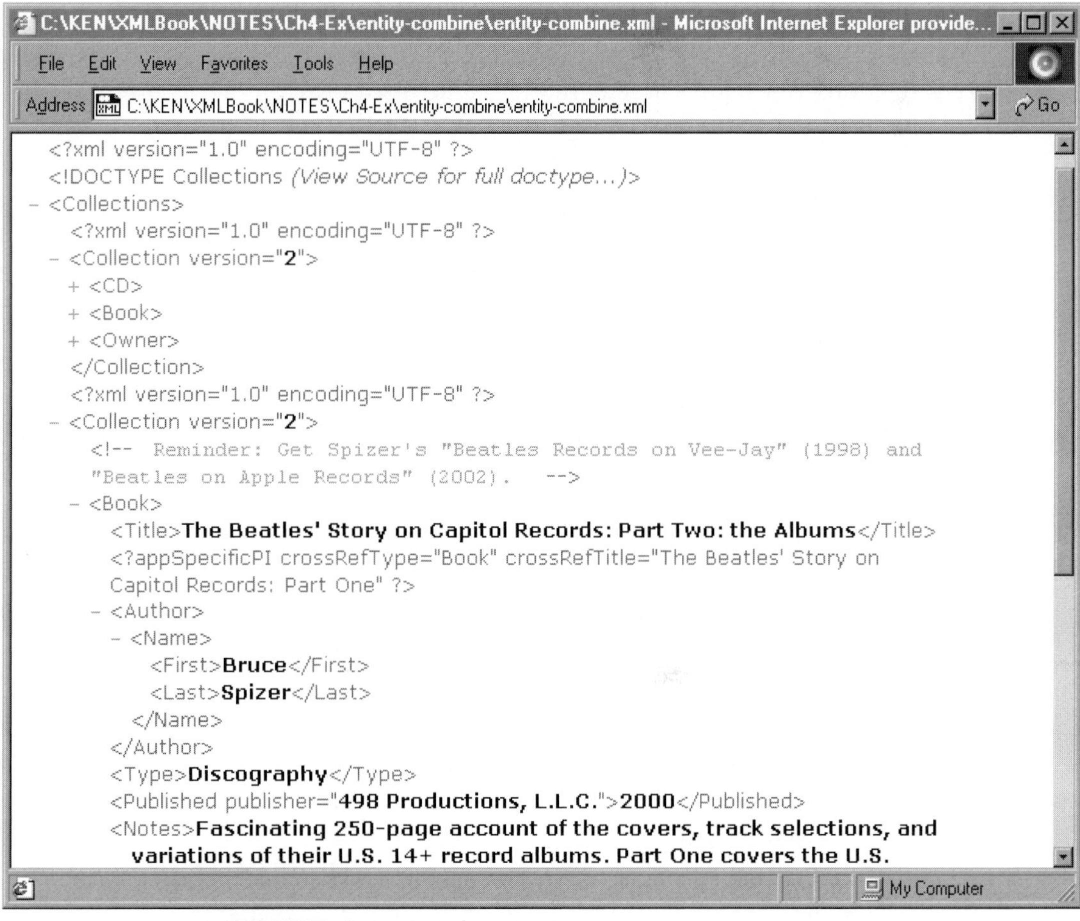

FIGURE 4-5 Display of document using external entities to combine two others in IE 5.x

Listing 4-13 XML Document Combines Two Other Documents (entity-combine.xml)

```
<?xml version="1.0" encoding = "UTF-8"?>
<!DOCTYPE Collections [
  <!ENTITY Col7 SYSTEM "collection7.xml" >
  <!ENTITY Col8 SYSTEM "collection8.xml" >
]>

<Collections>
  &Col7;
  &Col8;
</Collections>
```

This particular example happens to be *invalid* because the internal DTD subset is incomplete. It has no declaration for the Collections element, nor are there declarations for any of the many elements that are in the external entities. We can easily remedy this by augmenting the internal subset with an external DTD that describes the content models and attributes of the external entities (collection7.xml and collection8.xml), and adding a declaration for the container element, Collections, to the internal subset. (All referenced files appear on the CD-ROM.)

```
<?xml version="1.0" encoding = "UTF-8"?>
<!DOCTYPE Collections SYSTEM "collection6.dtd" [
  <!ENTITY Col7 SYSTEM "collection7.xml" >
  <!ENTITY Col8 SYSTEM "collection8.xml" >
  <!ELEMENT Collections (Collection+) >
]>
<Collections>
  &Col7;
  &Col8;
</Collections>
```

Parameter Entities

Whereas both internal and external parsed general entities are part of the content that is merged into the XML document, **parameter entities** are defined in the DTD and *used only in the DTD*. (As we've seen, parsed general entities are *declared* in the DTD, but their replacement text always becomes part of the XML document.) Parameter entities are declared in the *external* DTD subset, where they may contain fragments (e.g., reusable element content models or attribute sets). They should not be used in the internal subset.

Internal Parameter Entities

Like the parsed general entities, parameter entities come in both internal and external flavors. In addition to their DTD-only aspect, they differ slightly in syntax from parsed general entities. An internal parameter entity is declared like this:

```
<!ENTITY % EntityName "QuotedReplacementText" >
```

It is referenced like this:

```
%EntityName;
```

The only syntactical difference between parameter entity and general entity declarations is the use of a percent (%) sign for the former and no special character for the latter. A parameter entity *reference* requires percent (%), as compared to an ampersand (&) for a general entity reference.

Internal parameter entities are used extensively in many W3C DTDs, primarily for one of three purposes:

1. To serve as documentation of an intended specific datatype for an attribute that is actually defined simply in terms of CDATA, NMTOKEN, and so on.
2. To specify a *content model* that is common in the DTD.
3. To collect a group of *related attribute declarations* that are used repeatedly in various content models in the DTD.

We'll consider each of these cases in turn.

The first case is a very common and simple way to clearly identify the datatypes you have in mind, if it were possible to define real datatypes (like those we *are* able to define using XML Schema). For example, the following excerpts from the SVG 1.0 Recommendation (dated 5 September 2001, *http://www.w3.org/TR/SVG/*) typify this use of internal parameter entities as pseudo-datatypes:

```
<!ENTITY % Coordinate "CDATA">      <!-- a <coordinate> -->
<!ENTITY % Color "CDATA">           <!-- a <color> value -->
<!ENTITY % Integer "CDATA">         <!-- a <integer> -->
<!ENTITY % Length "CDATA">          <!-- a <length> -->
<!ENTITY % Script "CDATA">          <!-- script expression -->
<!ENTITY % Number "CDATA">          <!-- a <number> -->
<!ENTITY % StyleSheet "CDATA">      <!-- style sheet data -->
<!ENTITY % URI "CDATA">  <!-- a Uniform Resource Identifier, see [URI] -->
<!ENTITY % LanguageCode "NMTOKEN">
                         <!-- a language code, as per [RFC3066] -->
```

All of these internal parameter entities are essentially aliases that indicate an *intended* datatype for an attribute value. Most often, the *actual* attribute type is our familiar CDATA, that is unconstrained. However, any attribute type can be used, such as NMTOKEN for LanguageCode which cannot contain white space. As far as the parser is concerned, they are merely strings. So why bother? The point is that when these entities are used in declarations, their very names connote the specific type that the DTD authors had in mind.

The next excerpt, with many attributes omitted for (relative) simplicity, is the attribute-list declaration for the svg element itself, which illustrates how these pseudo-datatypes are referenced (wrapped inside % and ;) and how they are helpful in clarifying a declaration:

```
<!ATTLIST svg
  xmlns CDATA #FIXED "http://www.w3.org/2000/svg"
  %stdAttrs;
  %testAttrs;
  %langSpaceAttrs;
  ....
  style %StyleSheet; #IMPLIED
  version %Number; #FIXED "1.0"
  x %Coordinate; #IMPLIED
  y %Coordinate; #IMPLIED
  width %Length; #IMPLIED
  height %Length; #IMPLIED
  .... >
```

Another common technique used in DTDs for which internal parameter entities is used is to group attributes that have related functionality and/or are likely to occur together as a set in more than one attribute declaration. For example, again from the SVG 1.0 DTD:

```
<!ENTITY % stdAttrs "id ID #IMPLIED
                     xml:base %URI; #IMPLIED">
```

This declares that the parameter entity `stdAttrs` represents two optional attributes, `id` of type `ID` and `xml:base` of the pseudo-type `URI` (really `CDATA`). Similarly, the next declaration identifies `animationEvents` as the internal parameter entity that represents three optional scripting events, `onbegin`, `onend`, and `onrepeat`.

```
<!ENTITY % animationEvents
      "onbegin %Script; #IMPLIED
       onend %Script; #IMPLIED
       onrepeat %Script; #IMPLIED" >
```

Then, in the attribute list declaration for the `animate` element, both parameter entities are referenced, along with many others (*http://www.w3.org/TR/SVG/svgdtd.html#DefinitionsAnimate*).

```
<!ELEMENT animate (%descTitleMetadata;%animateExt;) >
<!ATTLIST animate
  %stdAttrs;
  %testAttrs;
  externalResourcesRequired %Boolean; #IMPLIED
  %animationEvents;
  %animElementAttrs;
  %animAttributeAttrs;
  %animTimingAttrs;
  %animValueAttrs;
  %animAdditionAttrs; >
```

These entities are reused in the attribute-list declaration of `animateEvents`.

```
<!ELEMENT animateTransform (%descTitleMetadata;%animateTransformExt;) >
<!ATTLIST animateTransform
  %stdAttrs;
  %testAttrs;
  externalResourcesRequired %Boolean; #IMPLIED
  %animationEvents;
  %animElementAttrs;
  %animAttributeAttrs;
  %animTimingAttrs;
  %animValueAttrs;
  %animAdditionAttrs;
  type (translate | scale | rotate | skewX | skewY) "translate" >
```

The advantage is clear; if the DTD authors ever find the need to alter the set of attributes, attribute types, or whether attributes are optional or required, the change is localized. In the SVG 1.0 DTD, `animationEvents` is used in 5 declarations, and `stdAttrs` is used for all 81 elements!

As another example, consider this declaration of the `focus` entity, a collection of attributes that control input focus, defined in XHTML 1.0:

```
<!ENTITY % focus
 "accesskey   %Character;     #IMPLIED
  tabindex    %Number;        #IMPLIED
  onfocus     %Script;        #IMPLIED
  onblur      %Script;        #IMPLIED"  >
```

Considering the pseudo-types in this declaration, we have a reasonable idea that any element that uses the `focus` parameter entity as part of its attribute list should look something like this, at least with respect to the first four attributes shown:

```
<button
  accesskey="b"   tabindex="7"
  onfocus="handleButtonFocus()"   onblur="handleButtonBlur()"
  name="submitMe" type="submit" value="Press to Submit" />
```

Note, however, that the actual parameter entities are restricted to use in the DTD, even though they help us to understand what needs to be in the XML instance. We cannot refer to `%Number;` in an XML document, for example.

The third application of internal parameter entities is in defining content models that are expected to be repeated or potentially altered in the DTD. Several examples from XHTML 1.0 (strict) DTD follow:

```
<!ENTITY % special      "br | span | bdo | object | img | map">

<!ENTITY % fontstyle    "tt | i | b | big | small">
```

```
<!ENTITY % phrase        "em | strong | dfn | code |
  q | sub | sup | samp | kbd | var | cite | abbr | acronym">

<!ENTITY % inline.forms  "input | select | textarea | label | button">

<!ENTITY % inline
  "a | %special; | %fontstyle; | %phrase; | %inline.forms;">
```

This declaration of the `inline` entity illustrates that parameter entities can reference *other* internal parameter entities, *provided that the embedded referenced entities have been defined earlier in the DTD.*

This is another difference between parameter entities and general entities. Order of declarations *matters* for parameter entities; it does not for general entities.

The content models may be of any arbitrary complexity. For example, also from the XHTML 1.0 Recommendation, here is the declaration of an internal parameter entity representing a mixed content model for the `pre` element (preformatted text) with embedded internal parameter entity references:

```
<!ENTITY % pre.content
  "(#PCDATA | a | br | span | bdo | map | tt | i | b |
  %phrase; | %inline.forms;)*">
```

The reference later in the DTD is:

```
<!ELEMENT pre %pre.content;>
```

This reference expands after replacement to:

```
<!ELEMENT pre (#PCDATA | a | br | span | bdo | map | tt | i | b
  | %phrase; | %inline.forms;)*>
```

It further expands after resolving `%phrase;` and `%inline.forms` to:

```
<!ELEMENT pre (#PCDATA | a | br | span | bdo | map | tt | i | b
  | em | strong | dfn | code |
  q | sub | sup | samp | kbd | var | cite | abbr | acronym
  |input | select | textarea | label | button)*>
```

Since entities are XML Names, they may contain punctuation, namely period, hyphen, and underscore, as in `pre.content`.

Listing 4-14 presents a simple DTD (`internal-param.dtd`) that illustrates all three uses of internal parameter entities. Notice that `alphaNumeric` must be declared before it can be used in the `deptAttr` declaration.

Listing 4-14 DTD Illustrating Three Uses of Internal Parameter Entites (internal-param.dtd)

```
<!-- internal parameter entity as fake datatype -->
<!ENTITY % float        "CDATA" >
<!ENTITY % alphaNumeric "CDATA" >

<!-- internal parameter entity as attribute declaration -->
<!ENTITY % deptAttr
          "department %alphaNumeric; #IMPLIED" >

<!-- internal parameter entity as content model -->
<!ENTITY % todaysSpecial "(Item, Price, Discount)" >

<!ELEMENT PriceList     (TodaysSpecial+, OtherSpecial?)>

<!ELEMENT TodaysSpecial %todaysSpecial; >
<!ATTLIST TodaysSpecial
          %deptAttr;
          profit     %float;        #REQUIRED >

<!ELEMENT OtherSpecial ( %todaysSpecial;, Wholesale) >
<!ATTLIST OtherSpecial
          %deptAttr; >

<!ELEMENT Item     (#PCDATA) >
<!ELEMENT Price    (#PCDATA) >
<!ELEMENT Discount (#PCDATA)>
<!ELEMENT Wholesale     (#PCDATA)>
```

An example of an instance that uses this DTD is shown in Listing 4-15. There is nothing remarkable about this XML document. In fact, since parameter entities appear only in the DTD, there's no way to conclude that this instance has anything to do with parameter entities. (Okay, okay, I guess the name of the external DTD subset would be a big clue ;-) There's no point in showing the browser view of this document because it looks just like the code listing (in IE 5.x, that is).

Listing 4-15 XML Instance with External DTD That Contains Internal Parameter Entities (internal-param.xml)

```
<?xml version="1.0" standalone="no" ?>
<!DOCTYPE PriceList SYSTEM "internal-param.dtd" >
<PriceList>
  <TodaysSpecial department="Records" profit=".27" >
    <Item>Listen to What the Man Said</Item>
    <Price>18.98</Price>
    <Discount>.30</Discount>
  </TodaysSpecial>
  <OtherSpecial department="Records" >
    <Item>Best of George Harrison</Item>
    <Price>18.98</Price>
    <Discount>.30</Discount>
    <Wholesale>11.98</Wholesale>
  </OtherSpecial>
</PriceList>
```

External Parameter Entities

External parameter entities are also exclusively for use in a DTD just like their internal cousins; their replacement text is limited to DTDs. In contrast to internal parameter entities, however, **external parameter entities** refer to an *external file* that contains DTD content (declarations of elements, attribute lists, other entities, etc.). The main uses of external parameter entities are:

- to combine small, reusable modules of a DTD into a larger DTD, which may entail sharing modules among several DTDs[12]
- to include sets of special characters, Latin 1 characters, and symbols (e.g., `dagger`, `copy` and the Greek letter `Epsilon`, respectively)

One form of the declaration syntax is:

```
<!ENTITY % EntityName SYSTEM IncludedURI >
```

Here `ENTITY` and `SYSTEM` are literal, `EntityName` is an XML Name, and `IncludedURI` is a quoted URI or path that specifies the absolute or relative location of the file that contains the DTD declarations of elements, attribute lists, or other entities to be included.

To reference the external parameter entity, we again use the percent notation:

```
%EntityName;
```

which, like a C language `#include`, effectively includes the contents of the other file at the point of reference. In fact, it's most common to see the declaration immediately followed by the reference, as the following examples illustrate.

Let's revisit our earlier `TodaysSpecial` example and split the DTD (from Listing 4-14) into two files, `external-param.ent`, which will contain only the entity declarations for `float`, `alphaNumeric`, `deptAttr`, and `todaysSpecial`, and `external-param.dtd`, which will contain the content models and attribute declarations. See Listing 4-16 and Listing 4-17, respectively.

Listing 4-16 DTD Module: Internal Parameter Entities (external-param.ent)

```
<!-- internal parameter entity as fake datatype -->
<!ENTITY % float        "CDATA" >
<!ENTITY % alphaNumeric "CDATA" >

<!-- internal parameter entity as attribute declaration -->
<!ENTITY % deptAttr
          "department %alphaNumeric; #IMPLIED" >

<!-- internal parameter entity as content model -->
<!ENTITY % todaysSpecial "(Item, Price, Discount)" >
```

12. A good real-world example of this is W3C's Modularization of XHTML, which is discussed in chapter 15.

Don't let the fact that Listing 4-16 contains internal parameter entities throw you. No matter what it contains (even simply additional element and attribute declarations), it's the *way* in which we refer to it in Listing 4-17 that makes this an *external* parameter entity. The file `external-param.dtd` includes `external-param.ent` by means of an external parameter entity declaration followed immediately by the entity reference that results in the inclusion of the contents of Listing 4-17 in place of the reference:

```
<!ENTITY % paramEnts  SYSTEM  "external-param.ent" >
%paramEnts;
```

The net effect is that the entire external DTD subset consists of both files and is identical to the version we started with in Listing 4-14. You can imagine how this could be extended to include many separate modules in a larger, real-world DTD.

Listing 4-17 Main DTD with External Parameter Entity Reference to Include Other DTD (external-param.dtd)

```
<!ENTITY % paramEnts  SYSTEM  "external-param.ent" >
<!-- now instantiate the entities from the other file -->
%paramEnts;

<!ELEMENT PriceList     (TodaysSpecial+, OtherSpecial?)>

<!ELEMENT TodaysSpecial %todaysSpecial; >
<!ATTLIST TodaysSpecial
          %deptAttr;
          profit     %float;        #REQUIRED >

<!ELEMENT OtherSpecial ( %todaysSpecial;, Wholesale) >
<!ATTLIST OtherSpecial
          %deptAttr; >

<!ELEMENT Item     (#PCDATA) >
<!ELEMENT Price    (#PCDATA) >
<!ELEMENT Discount (#PCDATA)>
<!ELEMENT Wholesale     (#PCDATA)>
```

And if you'd rather not imagine but instead see this firsthand in black and white, study the W3C DTDs listed in "For Further Exploration." The W3C DTDs use the keyword `PUBLIC` and Formal Public Identifiers (discussed in the section "Document Type Declaration" in chapter 3). The general syntax for this type of entity declaration is:

```
<!ENTITY % EntityName PUBLIC FormalPublicID IncludedURI >
```

Here `ENTITY` and `PUBLIC` are literal, `EntityName` is an XML Name, `FormalPublicID` is a Formal Public Identifier (FPI), and `IncludedURI` is a quoted URI or path that specifies the absolute or relative location of the file that contains the DTD module to be included. The entity reference is the same as other parameter entity references:

```
%EntityName;
```

Now we finally see how the entities were incorporated in an earlier example (Listing 4-8).

```
<!ENTITY % HTMLsymbol PUBLIC
      "-//W3C//ENTITIES Symbols for XHTML//EN"
      "http://www.w3.org/TR/xhtml1/DTD/xhtml-symbol.ent">
%HTMLsymbol;
```

The second line of the entity declaration gives the FPI for symbol entities in XHTML, and the third line states the URI at which these entities are located (type the URI into your browser to see them). The fourth line causes the entities to be included into the DTD which contains the entity declaration (`prodInfo.dtd` from Listing 4-8, in our case).

This brings us back to XHTML 1.0, which defines six modules identified by the following six FPIs and the associated relative URIs.

```
PUBLIC  "-//W3C//DTD XHTML 1.0 Strict//EN"          "xhtml1-strict.dtd"
PUBLIC  "-//W3C//DTD XHTML 1.0 Transitional//EN"    "xhtml1-transitional.dtd"
PUBLIC  "-//W3C//DTD XHTML 1.0 Frameset//EN"        "xhtml1-frameset.dtd"
PUBLIC  "-//W3C//ENTITIES Latin 1 for XHTML//EN"    "xhtml-lat1.ent"
PUBLIC  "-//W3C//ENTITIES Symbols for XHTML//EN"    "xhtml-symbol.ent"
PUBLIC  "-//W3C//ENTITIES Special for XHTML//EN"    "xhtml-special.ent"
```

The first three are the mutually exclusive slices of XHTML 1.0 (analogous to the similarly named DTDs in HTML 4.01). The other three are for the entity sets. All URIs are relative to:

http://www.w3.org/TR/xhtml1/DTD/

The entity sets reside in the same directory on the W3C server as the XHTML 1.0 DTDs. The declarations appear as follows in the W3C DTDs (for example, in *http://www.w3.org/TR/xhtml1/DTD/xhtml1-strict.dtd*):

```
<!ENTITY % HTMLlat1 PUBLIC
   "-//W3C//ENTITIES Latin 1 for XHTML//EN"
   "xhtml-lat1.ent">
%HTMLlat1;

<!ENTITY % HTMLsymbol PUBLIC
   "-//W3C//ENTITIES Symbols for XHTML//EN"
   "xhtml-symbol.ent">
%HTMLsymbol;
```

```
<!ENTITY % HTMLspecial PUBLIC
   "-//W3C//ENTITIES Special for XHTML//EN"
   "xhtml-special.ent">
%HTMLspecial;
```

To refer to them from our *own* DTDs, however, we need the complete URI, as we've already seen:

```
<!ENTITY % HTMLlat1 PUBLIC
   "-//W3C//ENTITIES Symbols for XHTML//EN"
   "http://www.w3.org/TR/xhtml1/DTD/xhtml-symbol.ent">
%HTMLlat1;
```

This modular approach of keeping the actual definitions of the various character and symbol entities in files separate from the main DTD allows for a division of labor. W3C DTD authors could modify one of the smaller referenced DTDs without impacting the main DTD (assuming no entities named in the external file are changed), and vice versa. In addition, this separation into modular chunks allows other developers (W3C or non-W3C) to reuse just the modules they need, rather than the whole DTD.

Similary, the MathML 2.0 Recommendation uses the Modularization of XHTML to extend XHTML for mathematics. Studying the twenty-four DTD modules that comprise MathML 2.0 is informative (although a bit daunting). The MathML modules are:

- mathml2.dtd—main driver module that includes mathml2-qname-1.mod via an external parameter entity reference and also defines attributes and content models
- mathml2-qname-1.mod—defines the qualified names of all elements (with possible namespace prefix)
- xhtml-math11-f.dtd—prototype extension of XHTML 1.1 incorporating MathML 2.0; result of combining all of the pieces
- Numerous entity sets—isoamsa.ent, isoamso.ent, isocyr2.ent, isolat2.ent, isonum.ent, isoamsb.ent, isoamsr.ent, isodia.ent, isomfrk.ent, isopub.ent, isoamsc.ent, isobox.ent, isogrk3.ent, isomopf.ent, isotech.ent, isoamsn.ent, isocyr1.ent, isolat1.ent, isomscr.ent, mmlalias.ent, and mmlextra.ent.

For example, to include the Greek alphabet, mathml2.dtd contains the external parameter entity declaration and reference:

```
<!ENTITY % ent-isogrk3
      PUBLIC "-//W3C//ENTITIES Greek Symbols for MathML 2.0//EN"
             "isogrk3.ent" >
%ent-isogrk3;
```

Here the file `isogrk3.ent` contains entity declarations such as:

```
<!ENTITY alpha          "&#x003B1;" ><!--/alpha small alpha, Greek -->
<!ENTITY beta           "&#x003B2;" ><!--/beta small beta, Greek -->
<!ENTITY gamma          "&#x003B3;" ><!--/gamma small gamma, Greek -->
```

Some of the techniques in the MathML DTD modules such as their heavy use of entities will look familiar to you now, and other aspects are covered in chapter 15 on XHTML. However, a thorough tutorial in DTD modularization is beyond the scope of this book. Interested readers should see the article, "XHTML Modules and Markup Languages: How to create XHTML Family modules and markup languages for fun and profit," Shane McCarron (editor), at *http://www.w3.org/MarkUp/Guide/xhtml-m12n-tutorial/*.

Notations

In order to explain unparsed entities, we must first learn about XML notations. We encountered the keywords `NOTATION` and `NOTATIONS` as attribute types in Table 4-3.

A **notation** is another type of DTD declaration, one that makes an association between a name and some special type of content that will be referenced from the XML document. Usually, the notation is a reference to an external standard such as MIME types. Notations are intended to let the application know that some special non-XML data is available, if the application is capable of dealing with it and so chooses. The general syntax is:

```
<!NOTATION NotationName SYSTEM Identifier >
```

Here `NOTATION` and `SYSTEM` are literals, `NotationName` is an XML Name, and `Identifier` is the external reference. Actually, `SYSTEM` can be replaced by `PUBLIC`, when appropriate, as we've seen in document type declarations and entity declarations.

The most straightforward examples involve any of the binary datatypes that browsers handle using MIME types. GIF, JPEG, PNG, TIFF, and AVI files are examples, although notations are not restricted to image formats, nor even to binary data. Suppose we want to declare in our DTD that we will permit JPEG data to be referenced from our documents. Our notation might look like this:

```
<!NOTATION Jpeg SYSTEM "image/jpg" >
```

Here `Jpeg` is our arbitrary name (emphasized here by the atypical capitalization) and `image/jpg` is the MIME type. The idea is that when we refer to the notation `Jpeg` elsewhere in the DTD, we are identifying the content as the MIME type `image/jpg`. If the processing application, such as a cell phone, cannot render this non-XML data, it may simply choose to ignore it.

Notations are not widely implemented by XML processors as of this writing. When they are used, however, they are often in conjunction with unparsed entities.

Unparsed Entities

We finally come to the third type of general entity, called *external unparsed entity,* or *unparsed entity* for short. Although the declaration for unparsed entities resembles that of external parsed (general) entities, they are unrelated in purpose, other than to include external content.

An **unparsed entity** is used to incorporate (typically binary) non-XML data unmodified by the parser into the application and is used in conjunction with a notation, whereas an external parsed entity refers to XML data and does not require a notation. The general syntax for an unparsed entity is:

```
<!ENTITY EntityName SYSTEM URI NDATA NotationName >
```

Here `ENTITY`, `SYSTEM` and `NDATA` (standing for *non-XML data*) are literals, `EntityName` and `NotationName` are XML Names, and `URI` is the quoted path to the binary content. Additionally, `NotationName` must also be defined in the DTD, as discussed in the previous section. For example, consider this notation declaration and an unparsed entity declaration that uses the notation:

```
<!NOTATION Jpeg SYSTEM "image/jpg" >
<!ENTITY USFlag SYSTEM "USflag.jpg" NDATA Jpeg >
```

These two DTD declarations establish the `Jpeg` notation and the unparsed entity (`NDATA`) called `USFlag` that is this particular type of non-XML data.

Another difference between unparsed entities and the parsed entities we've encountered is that the unparsed entity reference occurs in the context of an *attribute*, not via an `&EntityName;` reference. The element that has this attribute is often an empty element, although this is not a requirement. For example, if the DTD contained:

```
<!ELEMENT Country EMPTY >
<!ATTLIST Country
          name CDATA  #REQUIRED
          flag ENTITY #REQUIRED >
```

then an example of an XML document that referenced the unparsed entity would be:

```
<Country name="USA" flag="USFlag" >
```

where `USFlag` is the entity associated with the `USflag.jpg` data. Similarly, if we added other unparsed entities declared as:

```
<!ENTITY UKFlag SYSTEM "UKflag.jpg" NDATA Jpeg >
<!ENTITY FRFlag SYSTEM "FRflag.jpg" NDATA Jpeg >
```

then using the same attribute list declaration, other valid `Country` element instances would be:

```
<Country name="United Kingdom" flag="UKFlag" >
<Country name="France" flag="FRFlag" >
```

Since notations are not widely implemented, XML processors are *not required* to handle unparsed entities. Therefore, if you need to use this feature, be sure to check your processor's documentation for support.

Generating DTDs and XML Instances

This section covers techniques that are useful in bootstrapping your DTD development and in supplementing your testing environment once DTDs have been finalized. Some readers may wish to skip this section, since it does not cover new concepts. Instead, it focuses on how a few tools (two free and two commerical) can assist you in your development and testing. The commercial tools are also quite useful throughout the design and development cycle, and serve as validating parsers as well.

Generating a DTD from an XML Instance

Since a DTD describes the content of a *class* of documents, it is difficult to imagine how a single instance of an XML document could be used to generate the more general DTD (except for the most trivial DTDs). However, there are at least two ways to generate a DTD from XML.

The oldest of the two techniques is to use a free application called **DTDGenerator**, which was originally part of **SAXON**, Michael Kay's XSLT processor. DTDGenerator is a tool to generate an XML DTD from a single instance document as input. In late 2001, SAXON became a SourceForge project, as did DTDGenerator. Both are Java applications that can be downloaded from SourceForge (*http://saxon.sourceforge.net/dtdgen.html*).

However, you don't even need to download SAXON to try DTDGenerator! There is an online service provided by Paul Tchistopolskii called **DTDGenerator FrontEnd** that generates a DTD from your local XML instance via a file upload browser form (*http://www.pault.com/pault/dtdgenerator/*). Visit the Web site and press the form's `Browse...` button, and locate your local copy of the XML file that is representative of your structured data. Press the `Generate DTD!` button. The generated DTD will appear in a new browser window. Either copy all of the generated text from your browser's window and paste it into a new file, or use your browser's "save as" capabilities to create a .dtd file.

For example, one of the recurring examples in this book uses XML documents that describe a fraction of my collection of books about and music by the Beatles: I used the earliest version of an XML instance, shown in Listing 4-18, as input to DTDGenerator FrontEnd.

Listing 4-18 Input XML Instance of Book and CD Collection (collection1.xml)

```
<?xml version="1.0" standalone="yes" ?>
<!-- A Collection consists of Book and CD elements in no particular order. -->
<Collection owner="Ken Sall" location="nevermind">
  <Owner>Ken Sall</Owner>
  <Book>
    <Title>Complete Beatles Chronicle, The</Title>
    <Author>Lewisohn, Mark</Author>
    <Type>Chronology</Type>
    <Published publisher="Harmony Books">1992</Published>
    <Rating>5 stars</Rating>
    <Notes>Covers the years 1957 through 1970. No solo info.
  Great appendices with chart info, discography, composer index,
  radio, tv, and live performances, and much more.
    </Notes>
  </Book>
  <CD>
    <Title>Band on the Run</Title>
    <Artist>McCartney, Paul and Wings</Artist>
    <Chart>
      <Peak weeks="4">1</Peak>
      <Peak country="UK">1</Peak> <!-- guess -->
    </Chart>
    <Type>Rock</Type>
    <Label>Capitol</Label>
    <Label country="UK">EMI</Label>
    <AlbumReleased>1973</AlbumReleased>
    <Remastered format="gold CD">1993</Remastered>
    <Remastered format="2 disc box set with booklet">1999</Remastered>
  </CD>
  <CD>
    <Title>Venus and Mars</Title>
    <Artist>McCartney, Paul and Wings</Artist>
    <Chart>
      <Peak weeks="1">1</Peak>
      <Peak country="UK">2</Peak> <!-- guess -->
    </Chart>
    <Type>Rock</Type>
    <Label>Capitol</Label>
    <Label country="UK">EMI</Label>
    <AlbumReleased>1975</AlbumReleased>
    <Remastered format="gold CD with 3 bonus tracks">1994</Remastered>
  </CD>
  <Book>
    <Title>Many Years From Now</Title>
    <Author>McCartney, Paul</Author>
    <Type>Autobiographical</Type>
    <Published publisher="Henry Holt and Company">1997</Published>
```

```
  <!-- Notice the absence of Notes and Rating elements.
  I haven't read this book yet. This illustrates some optional
  elements that are children of Book element.
  -->
  </Book>
</Collection>
```

Given this input XML document, DTDGenerator FrontEnd produced the DTD shown in Listing 4-19.

Listing 4-19 DTD Generated by DTDGenerator FrontEnd (collection1-dtdgen-web.dtd)

```
<!-- Generated by http://www.pault.com/pault/dtdgenerator
     using SAXON 5.5.1 interface.
-->
<!ELEMENT AlbumReleased ( #PCDATA ) >
<!ELEMENT Artist ( #PCDATA ) >
<!ELEMENT Author ( #PCDATA ) >
<!ELEMENT Book ( Title, Author, Type, Published, Rating?, Notes? ) >
<!ELEMENT CD ( Title, Artist, Chart, Type, Label+, AlbumReleased, Remastered+ ) >
<!ELEMENT Chart ( Peak+ ) >
<!ELEMENT Collection ( Book | CD | Owner )* >
<!ATTLIST Collection location NMTOKEN #REQUIRED >
<!ATTLIST Collection owner CDATA #REQUIRED >
<!ELEMENT Label ( #PCDATA ) >
<!ATTLIST Label country NMTOKEN #IMPLIED >
<!ELEMENT Notes ( #PCDATA ) >
<!ELEMENT Owner ( #PCDATA ) >
<!ELEMENT Peak ( #PCDATA ) >
<!ATTLIST Peak country NMTOKEN #IMPLIED >
<!ATTLIST Peak weeks NMTOKEN #IMPLIED >
<!ELEMENT Published ( #PCDATA ) >
<!ATTLIST Published publisher CDATA #REQUIRED >
<!ELEMENT Rating ( #PCDATA ) >
<!ELEMENT Remastered ( #PCDATA ) >
<!ATTLIST Remastered format CDATA #REQUIRED >
<!ELEMENT Title ( #PCDATA ) >
<!ELEMENT Type ( #PCDATA ) >
```

This example was purposely constructed to show that `Rating` and `Note` elements for `Book` elements were optional, that the `country` attribute of the `Peak` element is optional, and that there can be more than one `Remastered` element for a `CD` (since CDs are often remastered more than once so avid collectors like me will buy multiple copies). Examine the generated DTD to verify these details were detected by DTDGenerator.

As we have learned, the `?` after `Rating` and `Notes` confirms that these are optional elements; question mark means zero or one occurrence. The keyword `#IMPLIED` for the `country` attribute of the `Peak` element means that the attribute is optional.[13] The + after `Remastered` means one or more instances of this element are allowed (the same is true for `Label` and `Peak`).

DTDGenerator is a great jumpstart if you've spent lots of time considering how your XML data should be structured but were reluctant to create a DTD by hand from scratch. DTDGenerator produces an initial DTD that you can tailor to your needs, as long as you understand a few limitations:

- It requires a local file as input, no URLs.
- The XML input cannot contain external references such as a DTD module, entities, and so on.
- The result is only as complete as your instance is representative of the cases you will be modeling.
- The attributes are likely to be incomplete, especially with regard to default values.
- You'll almost certainly need to edit the results to make the DTD conform more closely to the model you have in mind.
- DTDGenerator FrontEnd may be using a previous version of DTDGenerator, so results are likely to differ somewhat from what you'd get using the downloadable zip from SourceForge.

Still, if you are new to DTDs, this is a great way to get started (no cost, no installation, quick bootstrap).

XML Spy, a commercial product by Altova, also permits DTD generation from an XML document (*http://www.xmlspy.com/*). Click on the `DTD/Schema` menu and the select the `Generate DTD/Schema choice`. Given the same input, Listing 4-20 shows the DTD generated by XML Spy. If you compare this result to that of DTDGenerator FrontEnd, you'll see that both generate element declarations in alphabetical order, with attribute declarations immediately following the associated element. However, with XML Spy multiple attributes for a given element share one declaration (e.g., `Collection` and `Peak`) and there are some different assumptions about occurrence indicators and when to generate `NMTOKEN` vs. `CDATA` for an attribute type.

Listing 4-20 DTD Generated by XML Spy (collection1-spy.dtd)

```
<?xml version="1.0" encoding="UTF-8"?>
<!-- edited with XML Spy v4.1 (http://www.xmlspy.com) by Ken Sall (private) -->
<!--DTD generated by XML Spy v4.1 (http://www.xmlspy.com)-->
<!ELEMENT AlbumReleased (#PCDATA)>
<!ELEMENT Artist (#PCDATA)>
<!ELEMENT Author (#PCDATA)>
<!ELEMENT Book (Title, Author, Type, Published, Rating?, Notes?)>
<!ELEMENT CD (Title, Artist, Chart, Type, Label+, AlbumReleased, Remastered+)>
```

13. Actually, my intention was that if country is not specified, the default value should be "US". This is an example of something that would need to be added to the generated DTD.

```
<!ELEMENT Chart (Peak+)>
<!ELEMENT Collection (Owner | Book | CD)+>
<!ATTLIST Collection
        owner CDATA #REQUIRED
        location CDATA #REQUIRED
>
<!ELEMENT Label (#PCDATA)>
<!ATTLIST Label
        country CDATA #IMPLIED
>
<!ELEMENT Notes (#PCDATA)>
<!ELEMENT Owner (#PCDATA)>
<!ELEMENT Peak (#PCDATA)>
<!ATTLIST Peak
        weeks (1 | 4) #IMPLIED
        country CDATA #IMPLIED
>
<!ELEMENT Published (#PCDATA)>
<!ATTLIST Published
        publisher CDATA #REQUIRED
>
<!ELEMENT Rating (#PCDATA)>
<!ELEMENT Remastered (#PCDATA)>
<!ATTLIST Remastered
        format CDATA #REQUIRED
>
<!ELEMENT Title (#PCDATA)>
<!ELEMENT Type (#PCDATA)>
```

Another way to generate a DTD from an XML instance is to use another commerical product, TurboXML from TIBCO Extensibility (*http://www.tibco.com/products/extensibility/solutions/turbo_xml.html*). Select `New Schema`, then pick `File | Import | XML Document`, browse to your input file, and then select `Save As...` and pick `DTD`. Given the same input XML, the result is shown in Listing 4-21. The most obvious difference is that elements are generated in the order they are encountered in the instance (called *document order*). I'll leave it as an exercise to the reader to determine the other differences; compare to the XML Spy results in Listing 4-20.

Listing 4-21 DTD Generated by TurboXML (collection1-turbo.dtd)

```
<?xml version='1.0' encoding='UTF-8' ?>
<!--Generated by XML Authority [version 2.2]-->
<!ELEMENT Collection (Owner , Book , CD+ , Book)>
<!ATTLIST Collection  owner    CDATA  #REQUIRED
                      location CDATA  #REQUIRED >
<!ELEMENT Owner (#PCDATA)*>
<!ELEMENT Book (Title , Author , Type , Published , Rating , Notes)>
<!ELEMENT Title (#PCDATA)*>
<!ELEMENT Author (#PCDATA)*>
<!ELEMENT Type (#PCDATA)*>
<!ELEMENT Published (#PCDATA)*>
```

```
<!ATTLIST Published  publisher CDATA  #REQUIRED >
<!ELEMENT Rating (#PCDATA)*>
<!ELEMENT Notes (#PCDATA)*>
<!ELEMENT CD (Title , Artist , Chart , Type , Label+ , AlbumReleased ,
Remastered+)>
<!ELEMENT Artist (#PCDATA)*>
<!ELEMENT Chart (Peak+)>
<!ELEMENT Peak (#PCDATA)*>
<!ATTLIST Peak  weeks   CDATA  #IMPLIED
                country  (UK )  #IMPLIED >
<!ELEMENT Label (#PCDATA)*>
<!ATTLIST Label  country  (UK )  #IMPLIED >
<!ELEMENT AlbumReleased (#PCDATA)*>
<!ELEMENT Remastered (#PCDATA)*>
<!ATTLIST Remastered  format CDATA  #REQUIRED >
```

The point in showing you three ways to generate a DTD is that although the three generated DTDs are different, the input XML instance does conform to each one. (I'll leave this as another quick exercise for the reader to verify this.) How well each of the three DTDs will also apply to *other* instances depends both on how representative the initial sample was and how well the tools were able to generalize from a single data point. In all cases, the bootstrapping is quite helpful.

Note: Evaluation copies of XML Spy and TurboXML appear on the CD-ROM.

Generating XML Instances from a DTD

Once you've invested considerable time (and sweat!) in developing your DTDs, it's important to have a set of test cases that you can validate against the DTD, both to be sure that all members of your team agree that model and data match, and for your Quality Assurance team to have instances they can use in a test plan. Although you certainly can create instances by hand, for all but the most trivial DTDs, this can become quite laborious. Therefore, having the ability to easily generate sample instances, especially with some variability, is quite useful. The two commercial products mentioned earlier, TurboXML and XML Spy, and freeware from IBM called XML Generator are three ways to accomplish this.

To generate XML using TurboXML from the startup panel, select `File...`, browse to the DTD of your choice, and select `File | Export | Example XML Document`. It stands to reason if we use the DTD that we previously created by providing an XML instance to TurboXML we might obtain something reasonably similar to our original input. You can try that on your own, if you wish.

For the examples in this section, we'll start with a different DTD: `invoice.dtd` from Listing 4-1. TurboXML lets us control the `#PCDATA`, such as the phrase "only text," each time we generate an instance. The result when taking all defaults for #PCDATA is shown in Listing 4-22. The tool conveniently inserts content models as comments, which is useful when visually inspecting the result.

Listing 4-22 Instance Generated by TurboXML from Invoice DTD (invoice-turbo.xml)

```
<?xml version = "1.0"?>
<!--Generated by XML Authority.-->
<Invoice version = "string">
  <!--(ShipTo , Date , ItemInfo+ , Summary*)-->
  <ShipTo>
    <!--(Name , (CustomerID | SocSecNo) , Address? , City? , State? , Zip?)-->
    <Name>
      <!--(First , Last)-->
      <First>only text</First>
      <Last>only text</Last>
    </Name>
    <CustomerID sex = "required">only text</CustomerID>
    <Address>only text</Address>
    <City>only text</City>
    <State>only text</State>
    <Zip>only text</Zip>
  </ShipTo>
  <Date>only text</Date>
  <ItemInfo>
    <!--(ItemName? , SKU , Quantity , Weight , Price+ , Note? , Divider?)-->
    <ItemName>only text</ItemName>
    <SKU>only text</SKU>
    <Quantity>only text</Quantity>
    <Weight unitOfMeasure = "oz" measurementType = "string">only text</Weight>
    <Price>only text</Price>
    <Note>any mixture of text and the following elements
      <!--(Link | Emph)*-->
      <Link>only text</Link>
      <Emph>only text</Emph>
    </Note>
    <Divider/>
  </ItemInfo>
  <Summary>any combination of text and elements</Summary>
</Invoice>
```

To generate XML from a DTD using XML Spy, we again use the `DTD/Schema` menu, but this time we select `Generate Sample XML File`. XML Spy gives us a bit more control, as shown in the screenshot in Figure 4-6. We can decide whether to generate nonmandatory attributes and elements, which alternatives to use, what number of occurrences to generate for repeatable elements, and whether to fill attributes and elements with canned data. The result of taking all defaults, except for setting the number of repeatable occurrences to two, is shown in Listing 4-23.

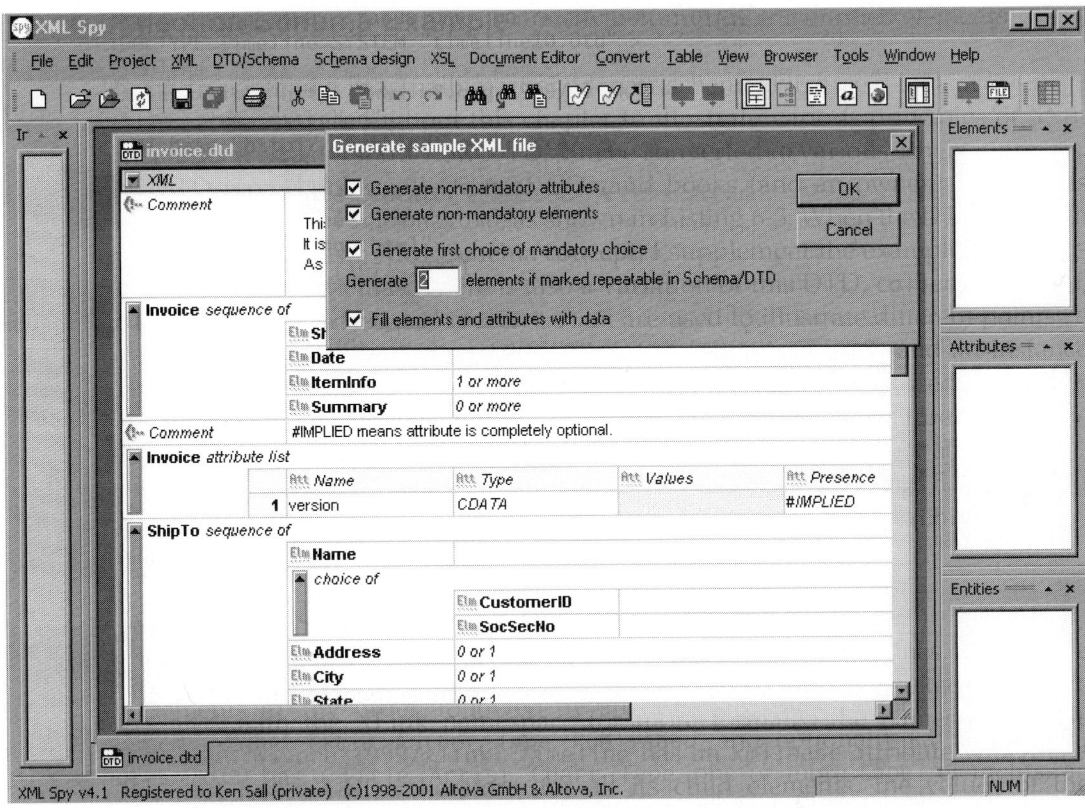

FIGURE 4-6 XML generation options provided by XML Spy

Listing 4-23 Instance Generated by XML Spy from Invoice DTD (invoice-spy.dtd)

```
<?xml version="1.0" encoding="UTF-8"?>
<!-- edited with XML Spy v4.1 (http://www.xmlspy.com) by Ken Sall (private) -->
<!--Sample XML file generated by XML Spy v4.1 (http://www.xmlspy.com)-->
<!DOCTYPE Invoice SYSTEM "C:\KEN\XMLBook\NOTES\Ch4-Ex\generating\invoice.dtd">
<Invoice version="Text">
  <ShipTo>
    <Name>
      <First>Text</First>
      <Last>Text</Last>
    </Name>
    <CustomerID sex="male">Text</CustomerID>
    <Address>Text</Address>
    <City>Text</City>
    <State>Text</State>
    <Zip>Text</Zip>
  </ShipTo>
  <Date>Text</Date>
  <ItemInfo>
```

```
    <ItemName>Text</ItemName>
    <SKU>Text</SKU>
    <Quantity>Text</Quantity>
    <Weight unitOfMeasure="oz" measurementType="US">Text</Weight>
    <Price>Text</Price>
    <Price>Text</Price>
    <Note>Text</Note>
    <Divider/>
  </ItemInfo>
  <ItemInfo>
    <ItemName>Text</ItemName>
    <SKU>Text</SKU>
    <Quantity>Text</Quantity>
    <Weight unitOfMeasure="oz" measurementType="US">Text</Weight>
    <Price>Text</Price>
    <Price>Text</Price>
    <Note>Text</Note>
    <Divider/>
  </ItemInfo>
  <Summary>Text</Summary>
  <Summary>Text</Summary>
</Invoice>
```

The third option for generating XML from a DTD is a freeware Java application from the IBM alphaWorks site (*http://www.alphaWorks.ibm.com/tech/xmlgenerator*) called **XML Generator**. As you can see from the screenshot in Figure 4-7, this tool provides a number of useful options, including how deep to permit element nesting, the number of repetitions, setting probabilities for fixed, implied, and default attributes. These options can also be stored in a configuration file, which is especially useful for regression testing.

From the interface, select `Load DTD`, set the desired options (or load a configuration file), then pick `Generate XML`, and then `Save Result XML`. The results of two runs using the same options are shown in Listings 4-24 and 4-25. Since generation is partially randomized, results even with the same DTD and same options are different. However, this is quite useful in constructing a set of instances that exercise different possibilities inherent in the model described by the DTD.

Listing 4-24 XML Document Generated from a DTD by IBM's XML Generator (invoice-XMLGen1.xml)

```
<?xml version='1.0'?>
<!DOCTYPE Invoice SYSTEM "invoice.dtd" >
<!-- Created by IBM XML Generator
numberLevels=7, maxRepeats=3, Random seed=1006903785570
fixedOdds=4, impliedOdds=4, defaultOdds=4
maxIdRefs=3, maxEntities=3, maxNMTokens=3
isExplicitRoot=true, root element name is 'Invoice'
entOdds=1 Entity list:[]
doctype declaration?true
 -->
```

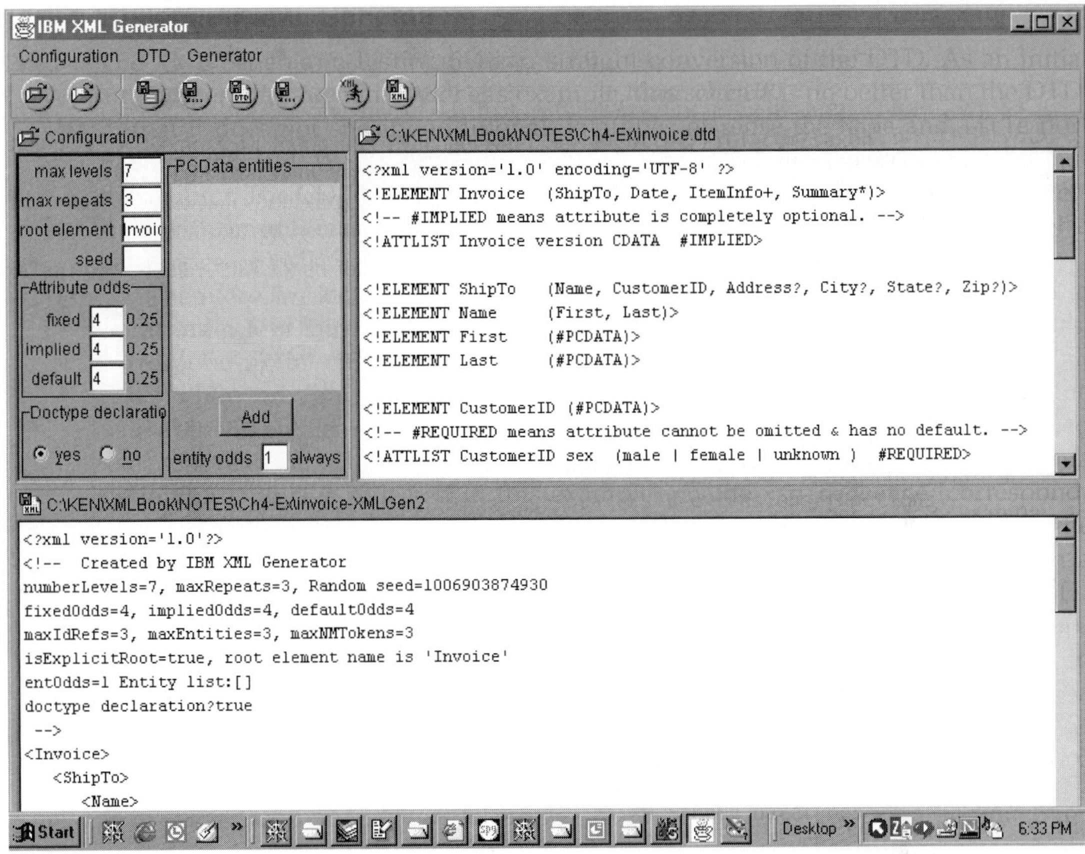

FIGURE 4-7 IBM XML Generator

```
<Invoice>
   <ShipTo>
      <Name>
         <First>level 3</First>
         <Last>level 3</Last>
      </Name>
      <CustomerID sex="unknown">level 2</CustomerID>
      <Address>level 2</Address>
   </ShipTo>
   <Date>level 1</Date>
   <ItemInfo>
      <ItemName>level 2</ItemName>
      <SKU>level 2</SKU>
      <Quantity>level 2</Quantity>
      <Weight measurementType="US" unitOfMeasure="lb">level 2</Weight>
      <Price>level 2</Price>
      <Price>level 2</Price>
      <Price>level 2</Price>
```

```
    </ItemInfo>
    <ItemInfo>
       <ItemName>level 2</ItemName>
       <SKU>level 2</SKU>
       <Quantity>level 2</Quantity>
       <Weight>level 2</Weight>
       <Price>level 2</Price>
       <Divider/>
    </ItemInfo>
    <ItemInfo>
       <ItemName>level 2</ItemName>
       <SKU>level 2</SKU>
       <Quantity>level 2</Quantity>
       <Weight unitOfMeasure="oz">level 2</Weight>
       <Price>level 2</Price>
       <Price>level 2</Price>
       <Note>
          <Emph>level 3</Emph>
          level 2<Link>level 3</Link>
       </Note>
       <Divider/>
    </ItemInfo>
</Invoice>
```

Listing 4-25 Alternative XML Document Generated from a DTD by IBM's XML Generator (invoice-XMLGen3.xml)

```
<?xml version='1.0'?>
<!DOCTYPE Invoice SYSTEM "invoice.dtd" >
<!--  Created by IBM XML Generator
numberLevels=7, maxRepeats=3, Random seed=1006923909770
fixedOdds=4, impliedOdds=4, defaultOdds=4
maxIdRefs=3, maxEntities=3, maxNMTokens=3
isExplicitRoot=true, root element name is 'Invoice'
entOdds=1 Entity list:[]
doctype declaration?true
 -->
<Invoice>
   <ShipTo>
      <Name>
         <First>level 3</First>
         <Last>level 3</Last>
      </Name>
      <SocSecNo>level 2</SocSecNo>
      <Address>level 2</Address>
   </ShipTo>
   <Date>level 1</Date>
   <ItemInfo>
      <SKU>level 2</SKU>
      <Quantity>level 2</Quantity>
      <Weight unitOfMeasure="lb">level 2</Weight>
      <Price>level 2</Price>
      <Price>level 2</Price>
      <Price>level 2</Price>
```

```
    </ItemInfo>
    <ItemInfo>
       <SKU>level 2</SKU>
       <Quantity>level 2</Quantity>
       <Weight unitOfMeasure="lb">level 2</Weight>
       <Price>level 2</Price>
       <Price>level 2</Price>
       <Price>level 2</Price>
       <Note/>
    </ItemInfo>
    <ItemInfo>
       <ItemName>level 2</ItemName>
       <SKU>level 2</SKU>
       <Quantity>level 2</Quantity>
       <Weight measurementType="US" unitOfMeasure="oz">level 2</Weight>
       <Price>level 2</Price>
       <Price>level 2</Price>
       <Price>level 2</Price>
       <Note/>
    </ItemInfo>
    <Summary/>
    <Summary/>
</Invoice>
```

Overall DTD Structure

Although there is no agreed-on standard for the order of the sections of a DTD, we can infer a common and useful structure from the DTDs that accompany the various XML and HTML specifications. The URLs for these DTDs among others appear in the section "For Further Exploration."

```
Descriptive comment identifying author and/or organization,
    often with URL and/or namespace
Entity definitions, if any:
    Parameter entities
    Character mnemonic entities and/or included character entities in
        external file
    Entities for attribute groups
    Entities for enumerated lists of choices
Generic (general) attributes
Included modules
Document structure and grouping (content models):
    Root element definition
    Root element attributes
    Child element definitions
    Child element attributes
    Grandchild element definitions
    Grandchild element attributes
```

Keep in mind that most of these DTD sections are optional, especially the various entities, and few DTDs need all sections. Even fewer use this order of sections.

Instead, take this outline as a general structure with which you can take considerable latitude. Also, refer to the HTML 4.01, XHTML 1.0, XHTML 1.1, MathML 2.0, and SVG 1.0 DTDs for specific examples. URLs for all of these appear in "For Further Exploration."

Summary

This chapter begins with the very basics about DTDs but also covers many details, especially about entities and their roles in XML and DTDs.

- DTDs describe the structure of a class of possible documents by defining content models and other constraints against which XML documents can be checked for validity.
- It lists things you can and cannot do in DTDs. A number of reasons for needing DTDs are highlighted.
- Five element content models are described: child elements only, text-only content, mixed content model involving both `#PCDATA` and child elements, `EMPTY` and `ANY` models.
- Sequence and choice of elements in a parenthesized group is covered. A comma is the "then" connector (sequence) and a vertical bar is the "or" connector (choice).
- Occurrence indicators for element repeatability are discussed: ? means optional, * means optional and repeatable, and + means required and repeatable. No occurrence indicator means required and not repeatable.
- Character data content of elements cannot be type checked. There is no notion of string, integer, float, boolean, dateTime, and so on. This is a major limitation of DTDs, which XML Schema addresses.
- Elements and attributes are declared in a DTD using the keywords `ELEMENT` and `ATTLIST`, respectively.
- Attributes are always associated with an element. An attribute value is always (single or double) quoted in XML.
- Attributes may be required (`#REQUIRED`) or optional (`#IMPLIED`), or they may have a default value or a fixed value (`#FIXED`).
- An attribute declaration may specify an enumerated set of possible values, with or without a default.
- Attribute values may be slightly constrained to one of several stringlike types (`CDATA`, `NMTOKEN`, `ID`, etc.), but this capability is minimal compared to XML Schema datatyping.
- Guidelines for when to use an element and when to use an attribute are presented.

- Internal and external DTD subsets are compared along with more details about the `DOCTYPE` declaration. An example that combines both subsets is discussed.
- A basic but complete invoice DTD and sample XML instance are presented.
- The overloaded term *entity* is covered in detail. The two most broad categories are general entity and parameter entity.
- Many examples of entities are introduced, culminating with examples from complex W3C DTDs (XHTML 1.0, SVG 1.0, and MathML 2.0).
- Entities are declared in a DTD with the keyword `ENTITY`.
- General entity is content merged into an XML document, but defined in a DTD (either in the internal or external subset).
- All parsed general entities are referenced with an ampersand (&) and a semi-colon (`;`).
- Internal parsed general entities, or simply internal entities, are predefined character entities and replacement text in XML.
- External parsed general entities, or simply external entities, are included XML content that comes from an external file.
- External unparsed general entities, or simply unparsed entities, are non-XML data, typically binary data defined using the attribute type called `NOTATION`.
- Parameter entities are defined and used strictly in the DTD.
- The only syntactical difference between parameter entity and general entity declarations is the use of a percent (%) sign for the former and no special character for the latter. A parameter entity reference requires percent (%), as compared to an ampersand (&) for a general entity reference.
- Internal parameter entities are DTD replacement text, typically used for content model, attribute sets, or faking attribute datatypes.
- External parameter entities are complete element and attribute declarations included from an external file.
- Nonvalidating parsers are not required to resolve external entity references, although they are required to handle internal entities.
- Validating parsers, on the other hand, are required to resolve both internal and external entities.
- DTDs can be generated from an XML instance using tools such as TurboXML, XML Spy, and DTDGenerator.
- XML instances can be generated from DTDs using tools such asTurboXML, XML Spy, and IBM's XMLGenerator.

For Further Exploration

Articles

Attributes Versus Elements: The Never-ending Choice, Sean McGrath
http://www.itworld.com/nl/xml_prac/12132001/

XML.com: Mapping DTDs to Databases, Ronald Bourret
http://www.xml.com/pub/a/2001/05/09/dtdtodbs.html

Books

Structuring XML Documents, David Megginson [discusses five industrial-strength XML DTDs]
http://www.amazon.com/exec/obidos/ASIN/0136422993

Developing SGML DTDs: From Text to Model to Markup, Eve Maler with Jeanne El Andaloussi (contributor) [pre-XML but very useful]
http://www.amazon.com/exec/obidos/ASIN/0133098818/

XML: The Annotated Specification, Bob DuCharme [easy-to-read, concise interpretations of the XML 1.0 Recommendation, First Edition]
http://www.snee.com/bob/xmlann/

Historical

Guidelines for Electronic Text Encoding and Interchange (TEI P3) [includes SGML DTD explanation]
http://www-tei.uic.edu/orgs/tei/sgml/teip3sg/index.html

Resources

Annotated XML Specification [useful interpretations by Tim Bray, co-author of XML 1.0; based on the XML Recommendation, First Edition from 10 February 1998]
http://www.xml.com/axml/testaxml.htm

Astronomical Instrument Markup Language (AIML) [shorter, less complex example than W3C DTDs]
http://pioneer.gsfc.nasa.gov/public/iml/

Using Elements and Attributes, Robin Cover
http://xml.coverpages.org/elementsAndAttrs.html

Element and Attribute Guidelines, G. Ken Holman
http://xml.coverpages.org/holmanElementsAttrs.html

The Attribute/Text Conundrum. "Document-Centric" vs. "Data-Centric"
http://www.xmleverywhere.com/newsletters/20000525.htm

The XML Guide [useful summary of and reference for the XML 1.0 Recommendation by Wattle Software]
http://www.xmlwriter.com/xml_guide/xml_guide.shtml

Software

SAXON [XSLT Processor by Michael Kay]
http://saxon.sourceforge.net/

DTDGenerator [generates DTD from XML sample; originally included with SAXON]
http://saxon.sourceforge.net/dtdgen.html

DTDGenerator FrontEnd, Paul Tchistopolskii [online interface]
http://www.pault.com/pault/dtdgenerator/

IBM's XML Generator [generating random instances of valid XML from a DTD; useful for testing]
http://www.alphaWorks.ibm.com/tech/xmlgenerator

IBM's Visual XML Tools including Visual DTD
http://www.alphaWorks.ibm.com/tech/visualxmltools

TurboXML including XML Authority from TIBCO Extensibility
http://www.tibco.com/products/extensibility/solutions/turbo_xml.html

XML Pro bundle with Near and Far Designer from Vervet [DTD and XML editor]
http://www.vervet.com/

XML Spy [XML Schema, DTD and XML editor]
http://www.xmlspy.com/

W3C Specifications and Information

Extensible Markup Language (XML) 1.0 [W3C XML Recommendation, Second Edition]
http://www.w3.org/TR/REC-xml

XML Inclusions (XInclude) Version 1.0
http://www.w3.org/TR/xinclude/

XML Core Working Group [tasked with elaborating on the XML 1.0 Recommendation]
http://www.w3.org/XML/Activity.html#core-wg

On SGML and HTML [from HTML 4.01 Recommendation]
http://www.w3.org/TR/html401/intro/sgmltut.html

Comparison of SGML and XML, James Clark [W3C Note from 1997]
http://www.w3.org/TR/NOTE-sgml-xml-971215

HTML 4.01 DTDs [discusses XML DTD concepts]
http://www.w3.org/TR/html401/sgml/dtd.html

XHTML 1.0 DTDs [3 DTDs and 3 entity sets]
http://www.w3.org/TR/xhtml1/#dtds

Modularization of XHTML [DTD modularization for subsetting and extending XHTML]
http://www.w3.org/TR/xhtml-modularization/

An Overview of XHTML Modularization [informative, not normative explanation]
http://www.w3.org/MarkUp/modularization

XHTML Modules and Markup Languages: How to create XHTML Family modules and markup languages for fun and profit, edited by Shane McCarron
http://www.w3.org/MarkUp/Guide/xhtml-m12n-tutorial/

Mathematical Markup Language (MathML) 2.0 DTD [complex and useful DTD example]
http://www.w3.org/TR/MathML2/appendixa.html#parsing_dtd

Scalable Vector Graphics (SVG) 1.0 DTD [complex and useful DTD example]
http://www.w3.org/TR/SVG/svgdtd.html

Chapter 5

Namespaces, XML Infoset, and Canonical XML

In this chapter, we'll examine three W3C recommendations that don't exactly capture the fancy of the trade magazines and technology-focused Web sites. We'll cover *Namespaces in XML*, for resolving element and attribute name conflicts when multiple DTDs or XML Schema are referenced from a single XML instance; *XML Information Set*, for describing the common set of items that are relevant across many XML specifications; and *Canonical XML*, for determining whether two documents are logically equivalent. Of these three specifications, definitely the most controversial is Namespaces in XML, which we'll discuss in the most detail. I recommend that you read about XML namespaces *now* because later chapters assume an understanding of this topic. Also most W3C XML specifications since 1999 have something to say about the relevance of namespaces. The other two topics in this chapter may be skipped if you're in a hurry, although if you're interested in digital signatures in XML, you'll want to read about Canonical XML. Another approach is to return here to read about XML Information Set and Canonical XML after you've read the rest of the book.

Namespaces

Briefly stated, the primary purpose of XML namespaces is to define a mechanism for uniquely naming elements and attributes so that different vocabularies can be mixed in an XML document without name conflicts. For example, if you want to refer to both the `price` element defined in the `SuperDuperCatalog.dtd` and also the `price` element from the `DiscountHouseCatalog.dtd`, you need a way to unambiguously identify which type of `price` you are referring to at any point in an XML instance that references both DTDs. This name collision is a potential problem when you consider that the content models and/or attribute lists for these elements may differ. Consider for example these fragments:

```
<!-- from SuperDuperCatalog.dtd -->
<!ELEMENT price (#PCDATA) >
<!ATTLIST price currency CDATA "US" >

<!-- from DiscountHouseCatalog.dtd -->
<!ELEMENT price (#PCDATA) >
<!ATTLIST price type (wholesale | retail) #REQUIRED >
```

Although these two have the same content model, their attributes differ, so what is valid for one is invalid for the other, not to mention the fact that the two `price` elements may be based on completely different factors. (In fact, if we were using XML Schema, the two elements could even be different datatypes.) So we clearly need a way to differentiate which `price` element we mean at all times.

The Namespaces in XML Recommendation (*http://www.w3.org/TR/REC-xml-names/*) wasn't published until January 1999, nearly a full year after the XML 1.0 Recommendation. Therefore, although the concept of namespaces is now considered part of the core XML technology, you won't see them mentioned in the original XML 1.0 Recommendation or in any of the W3C specifications that appeared in 1998. You will, however, find a few references to namespaces in the XML 1.0 Recommendation, *Second* Edition, from October 2000 (*http://www.w3.org/TR/1998/REC-xml-19980210* and *http://www.w3.org/TR/REC-xml*, respectively). Virtually every major W3C specification from 1999 onwards contains some mention of the role played by namespaces, or at least states the namespaces that apply to that spec. Namespaces aren't fully supported by some tools (especially those that handle DTDs but not XML Schema), but they are very important to XSLT, XML Schema, XLink, and most of the more recent XML family of specifications.

Even if you don't plan to create documents that use mixed vocabularies, you need to understand what XML namespaces are and how they are used because you will encounter them in XSLT, XML Schema, and XLink, as well as in programming APIs such as DOM Level 2 and SAX2.

Although the Namespaces in XML specification itself is only fourteen pages, it has managed to generate far more pages of controversy since its publication. For example, Ronald Bourret's excellent XML Namespace FAQ (*http://www.rpbourret.com/xml/NamespacesFAQ.htm*) is forty-six pages, more than three times the length of the W3C recommendation on which it is based. How can this be possible? In his XML.com article, "Namespace Myths Exploded" (*http://www.xml.com/pub/a/2000/03/08/namespaces/*), Bourret points out that the actual Namespace in XML Recommendation omits many details about issues that programmers have raised, although the specification does achieve its stated purpose of defining a two-part naming scheme for elements and attributes. In his FAQ, Bourret also contends that namespaces do not themselves provide a technology for merging documents that reference different DTDs, although they are useful in developing this capability. Furthermore, the URIs[1] used as XML namespace names need not point to anything at all since they are merely intended to be unique identifiers, a distinction that often confuses newcomers. Another point of confusion and controversy is the problem namespaces pose for validation based on DTDs, which are to some degree incompatible with the Namespace in XML Recommendation.

Why is there so much controversy? And what are namespaces anyway? Why do we need them, and how do we use them? This chapter addresses these questions. Readers interested in many more subtle issues concerning namespaces should refer to Bourret's two previously cited resources.

Why Namespaces Are Needed: Resolving Name Conflicts

The element name `title` appears in many vocabularies: XHTML, SVG, XLink (as both an element and an attribute), XSLFO, Schematron, RSS, and Dublin Core (as `Title`). The familiar `table` element from XHTML also appears in XSLFO (and as `mtable` in MathML[2]). Both SVG and MathML define a `set` element. Both SVG and XSLT have a `text` element. (You can check for element names, attribute names, function names, keywords, and much more using the Smart Reference Search of XML specifications on ZVON.org at *http://zvon.org/php/Search/codes.php*.)

What happens when we need to refer to identically named elements from different XML languages from within the same XML document? This need can arise when we are combining W3C languages or, as in the example at the beginning of this chapter, referencing multiple custom languages that include common element names like `price` and `item`. It is also necessary if you wish to convert between two versions of the *same* language, such as when translating an XSLT stylesheet originally written for the early MSXML parser from Microsoft to a stylesheet compatible with the XSLT 1.0 Recommendation, or eventually when converting from a XSLT 1.0 stylesheet to a 2.0 stylesheet. We need a way to unambiguously differentiate "the element named `title` from the XLink namespace" from "the element `title` from the SVG namespace" from "the element `title` from the XSLFO namespace" from "the element `title` from the XHTML namespace."

1. Recall that URI is *Uniform Resource Identifier,* which is the more general case of a handle to a resource than URL (Uniform Resource Locator). URIs identify a resource but not necessarily in a Web-accessible manner. For example, a book's ISBN can be used to construct a URI. URLs are a subset of the possible URIs that can be constructed.

2. MathML tends to add the letter "m" before common element names, such as `mtable`, `msub`, `msup`, `mstyle`, `mtext`. Presumably, this was needed prior to the acceptance of namespaces.

One way to achieve unique naming is to leverage the uniqueness provided by URIs. Since the Domain Name System guarantees unique names, identifiers based on unique addresses are also unique. That is, if we combine an element name with a URI in some manner, an element with that same name but combined with a *different* URI will not be considered identical by parsers. For example, we could consider four references to a unique `title` element, each from a separate namespace, as indicated by a URI for each language (thinking of each language as defining a separate namespace):

```
{http://www.w3.org/1999/xlink}title
{http://www.w3.org/2000/svg}title
{http://www.w3.org/1999/XSL/Format}title
{http://www.w3.org/1999/xhtml}title
```

If the languages are created and maintained by different organizations, this scheme still works fine:

```
{http://www.EverythingUNeed.com/2002/SuperDuperCatalog}price
{http://www.HouseOfDiscounts.com/namespaces/Discounts}price
```

While this URI-based naming approach solves the problem of possible name collision, it certainly makes for ungainly element names. As it turns out, the syntax shown here is conceptual, rather than literal, since slash and curly braces are not legal characters in XML Names.[3] So, how do we really declare and use these unique names?

Qualified Names, Prefixes, Local Names, and Other Terminology

Rather than use the curly braces notation, we can achieve the same uniqueness of naming with a simpler notation, given a few important conventions. We learned earlier that the colon character (:), although a legal character in an XML Name, is reserved for use in namespaces.

Before we see how to declare namespaces, it will be helpful to cover some of the terminology used by W3C in the Namespaces in XML Recommendation. First, let's see how W3C defines **XML namespace**.

> XML namespaces provide a simple method for qualifying element and attribute names used in Extensible Markup Language documents by associating them with namespaces identified by URI references. . . . An **XML namespace** is a collection of names, identified by a URI reference [RFC 2396], which are used in XML docu-

3. Recall that an XML Name is a token beginning with a letter or an underscore (or a colon) and continuing with letters, digits, hyphens, underscores, colons, or periods, known as name characters.

> ments as element types and attribute names. XML namespaces differ from the "namespaces" conventionally used in computing disciplines in that the XML version has internal structure and is not, mathematically speaking, a set.[4]

Element types are really nothing more than an element identified by its name, so the element type of the element whose start tag is `<price>` is simply `price`.

The Namespaces in XML specification briefly refers to **universal names**, the uniquely named elements (or attributes) associated with a particular namespace. However, the more frequently used term is **qualified name** (sometimes shown as `QName`), which is an XML Name consisting of a prefix, a single colon as a separator, and the **local part** (sometimes called the **local name**):

```
QName::= (Prefix ':')? LocalPart
```

Both `Prefix` and `LocalPart` consist of any characters that are valid in an XML Name except colon. Examples of qualified names follow:

```
xsl:apply-templates
xlink:href
xhtml:title
xlink:title
svg:title
fo:title
SuperDuperCatalog:price
Discount:price
price
```

So we speak of the prefix `xsl` and the local part `apply-templates` (an element), the prefix `xlink` and the local part `href` (which happens to be an *attribute*), four prefixes (`xhtml`, `xlink`, `svg`, and `fo`) with the same local part `title`, and so on.

Although the prefix may be any length, it is typically short to reduce typing, so `SuperDuperCatalog` is not a likely prefix. On the other hand, it's a good idea to keep them to at least three characters to reduce the chance of ever needing to refer to another prefix that happens to be the same. (The W3C has made some of its namespace prefixes only two or three characters, such as `xsl`, `fo`, `xf`, however.) It's also probably wise not to just use your company's acronym (e.g., abc for ABC.com) because other developers at your company might be tempted to use the same prefix for a different language.

Note that technically a `QName` does not have to include a prefix and colon (e.g., the last `price` example in the preceding list). If the qualified name *does* contain a prefix, however, it must map to a specific URI reference.

4. *Namespaces in XML Recommendation,* 14 January 1999, Tim Bray, Dave Hollander, Andrew Layman; *http://www.w3.org/TR/REC-xml-names/.*

It is the *URI*, not the prefix, that is the actual namespace name. The prefix is merely a proxy for the URI reference because URIs may contain characters such as slash and curly braces that are not permitted in an XML Name. This means that the prefix is just a convenience; the particular prefix chosen for W3C languages (such as `xsl` for XSLT or `xsd` for XML Schema) is really only a *convention*. It is the URI that really matters. The actual namespace names (URIs) for common XML namespaces are shown in Table 5-1 on page 234.

Another way to conceptualize an XML namespace is that it merely encompasses the set of all local parts of universal names that happen to have the same namespace URI.[5]

Declaring Namespaces in XML Documents

In an XML document, a namespace is always declared in the start tag of an element. Which element you choose to attach the namespace to determines the scope of the declaration. A **namespace declaration** involves a special attribute called `xmlns`, followed by a colon, a somewhat arbitrary prefix, and the associated URI. This special `xmlns` attribute can be attached to any element (and is not itself something you declare). The syntax is:

```
xmlns:somePrefix="someURI"
```

Like all attributes, it must appear in the start tag of its associated element. (Technically, `xmlns` is a *namespace declaration* that looks like an attribute with a URI as its value.) For example, here's how to declare the XLink namespace for an element called `Timeline`:

```
<Timeline
  xmlns:xlink="http://www.w3.org/1999/xlink"
  ...>
```

Similarly, this namespace declaration pertains to the catalog example earlier in this chapter:

```
<Disc:DiscountCatalog
  xmlns:Disc="http://www.HouseOfDiscounts.com/namespaces/Discounts"
  ...>
```

The main difference between these two namespace declarations is that for the `Timeline` element, we're declaring that it will be using attributes from the XLink

5. Although the Namespaces in XML Recommendation does not forbid relative URIs, after much controversy, a W3C plenary ballot in July 2000 determined that the use of relative URIs for namespace names is to be deprecated, so specifications subsequent to Namespaces in XML should state that the use of relative (as opposed to absolute) URIs is out of scope or undefined. See *http://www.w3.org/2000/09/xppa*.

namespace, although `Timeline` itself is not defined in XLink. In the case of `DiscountCatalog`, we are declaring a namespace whose prefix is `Disc` and `DiscountCatalog` *is* an element from the language. That's why the `DiscountCatalog` element itself needs a prefix. Now, if it strikes you as slightly strange that in this second example we're *using* the prefix a nanosecond before we've actually declared it, then that gives you an idea of one of the headaches that parser developers have to consider (you didn't *really* want to write your own parser, did you?). This is the correct way to declare the namespace in this case, however.

The *scope* of a namespace declaration is the element in which it is declared, plus all descendants of that element, unless a descendant explicitly overrides the namespace it inherits from its ancestors by declaring another namespace. Therefore, we can use XLink attributes with any descendant of `Timeline`, or on the `Timeline` element itself:

```
<Timeline
  xmlns:xlink="http://www.w3.org/1999/xlink"
  xlink:type="extended" >
  <Band   xlink:type="locator"
    xlink:label="index"
    xlink:href="wings.html">
    Wings Timeline (1971-1981)
  </Band>
  <Recording    xlink:type="locator"
    xlink:label="wwl"
    xlink:href="a/wwl.html"
    year="1971">Wings Wild Life
  </Recording>
<!-- etc. -->
</Timeline>
```

If we had declared the XLink namespace in the start tag of the `Band` element rather than on `Timeline`, we could not use it with `Recording` (or with `Timeline`) without an additional namespace declaration.

Similarly, we can use elements from the namespace named `http://www.HouseOfDiscounts.com/namespaces/Discounts` by using the `Disc` prefix:

```
<Disc:DiscountCatalog
  xmlns:Disc="http://www.HouseOfDiscounts.com/namespaces/Discounts">
  <Disc:category name="Wild Animals">
    <Disc:item name="Lion">
      <Disc:price type="wholesale">999.99</Disc:price>
    </Disc:item>
    <Disc:item name="Tiger">
      <Disc:price type="wholesale">879.99</Disc:price>
    </Disc:item>
    <Disc:item name="Bear">
      <Disc:price type="wholesale">1199.99</Disc:price>
    </Disc:item>
  </Disc:category>
</Disc:DiscountCatalog>
```

Notice that the *attributes* of our `DiscountCatalog` language (e.g., `name`) do not require prefixes. That's because attributes are associated with the element whose start tag contains them. Although the prefix could be used, it is unnecessary.

For this reason, attributes are not considered to be in any particular namespace unless an explicit prefix is used. We already saw one situation where a prefix *is* definitely necessary—XLink, which makes attributes available to any element of any language. In this case, the prefix is needed partly to avoid potential name collision with other attributes of the elements, and also to signal an XLink processor that these elements have special linking capabilities. For example, XLink defines a `type` attribute whose qualified name is `xlink:type`, so if I require another attribute named `type` for my `Timeline` element, the name `type` is distinguishable from `xlink:type`.

If for some reason we needed to override an ancestor's namespace, we could declare another namespace at any point in the hierarchy. For example, we could also declare the `SuperDuperCatalog` namespace for the item whose name is "Tiger":

```
<Disc:DiscountCatalog
  xmlns:Disc="http://www.HouseOfDiscounts.com/namespaces/Discounts">
  <Disc:category name="Wild Animals">
    <Disc:item name="Lion">
      <Disc:price type="wholesale">999.99</Disc:price>
    </Disc:item>
    <Disc:item name="Tiger"
          xmlns:Super="http://www.EverythingUNeed.com/2002/SuperDuperCatalog">
      <Disc:price type="wholesale">879.99</Disc:price>
      <Super:price currency="US">859.85</Super:price>
    </Disc:item>
    <Disc:item name="Bear">
      <Disc:price type="wholesale">1199.99</Disc:price>
    </Disc:item>
  </Disc:category>
</Disc:DiscountCatalog>
```

However, since the namespace declaration associated with the `Super` prefix appears at this nested level, its scope is strictly limited to the `Disc:item` element that declares it and to its `Disc:price` child, but not to any other `Disc:item` or `Disc:price` in the catalog. The `Disc` prefix is still in scope, so we can mix `Disc:price` and `Super:price` elements as children of `Disc:item`. (We have not said anything about validation yet and we can only verify that this example is well-formed. The content model of `Disc:item` would need to be defined as `ANY` to permit this element from another namespace, or else we would need to explicitly name the foreign elements that are allowed as content.)

Although you may declare namespaces at any point in your hierarchy, it is generally better to declare them on the root (document) element so that they can be applied to every child of the root. While some developers prefer to push namespace declarations down to the lowest level where they occur (e.g., attached to an SVG element nested deep inside an XHTML table), declaring them at a high level allows you to change or add to your hierarchy with the least namespace impact. The tradeoff is that you must use prefixes to specify fully qualified names.

Therefore, the example would be more likely to have both namespaces declared in the root element so that elements of the namespace with the Super prefix can be used anywhere (assuming the DTD or schema supported this model, or when validation is not an issue):

```
<Disc:DiscountCatalog
  xmlns:Disc="http://www.HouseOfDiscounts.com/namespaces/Discounts"
  xmlns:Super="http://www.EverythingUNeed.com/2002/SuperDuperCatalog">
  <Disc:category name="Wild Animals">
    <Disc:item name="Lion">
      <Disc:price type="wholesale">999.99</Disc:price>
    </Disc:item>
    <Disc:item name="Tiger" >
      <Disc:price type="wholesale">879.99</Disc:price>
      <Super:price currency="US">859.85</Super:price>
    </Disc:item>
    <Disc:item name="Bear">
      <Disc:price type="wholesale">1199.99</Disc:price>
    </Disc:item>
  </Disc:category>
</Disc:DiscountCatalog>
```

Namespace declarations at the document element level generally applies if we are mixing W3C vocabularies in an XML document, as we'll see in the next section.

Default Namespace

What if you have existing documents that haven't used namespaces and then you find you need to reference another vocabulary, but perhaps only within a limited scope of elements? In others words, suppose 90 percent of your elements are from one language and 10 percent are from another. It certainly would be tedious to add prefixes for every element. It would be much more convenient to specify only namespace prefixes for the elements from the additional vocabulary. This is one way in which a **default namespace** can be helpful. You declare a default namespace with the xmlns attribute as before, but you omit the colon and the prefix:

```
xmlns="someURI"
```

For example, this fragment declares XHTML to be the default namespace from an element named `html` and all its descendants:

```
<html xmlns="http://www.w3.org/1999/xhtml">
```

When a default namespace is used, all elements in its scope are considered to be in that namespace without adding a prefix, except for those elements that include a qualified name containing a prefix associated with a different namespace. Consider Listing 5-1, which combines XHTML, XLink, MathML, and SVG (example file `amaya-xhtml-svg-mml-xlink.html`). The example was initially created using W3C's Amaya 5.0, an editor/browser that supports these four XML vocabularies (to various degrees).[6] One way to combine these languages is to use a default namespace for each vocabulary "island." There are four namespace declarations, three of which establish the current default namespace:

```
<html xmlns="http://www.w3.org/1999/xhtml">
....
<math xmlns="http://www.w3.org/1998/Math/MathML">
....
<span xmlns:xlink="http://www.w3.org/1999/xlink"
      xlink:type="simple"
      xlink:href="http://www.w3.org/Graphics/SVG/">SVG</span>
<svg xmlns="http://www.w3.org/2000/svg">
```

The scope of the XHTML default namespace is the entire document, except where that default is overriden by subsequent default namespace (re)declarations. That is, within the `<math>` element's start tag and within its descendants, the default namespace becomes `http://www.w3.org/1998/Math/MathML`. After the end tag `</math>`, XHTML is again the default namespace. The `<span>` element declares the XLink namespace, which goes out of scope as soon as the end tag `</span>` is encountered. The `<svg>` element redefines the default namespace to be SVG, again until it comes to its end tag, and then XHTML regains the default namespace distinction.

Amaya 5.0 handles each XML vocabulary, as you can see in Figure 5-1. (The rectangle appears around the summation symbol [sigma] because I selected the symbol in Amaya before taking the screenshot to illustrate that the math portion wasn't merely a GIF image; the highlighted portion corresponds to the entity reference `∑` defined in MathML.)

Alternatively, we could attach *all* of the namespace declarations to the root element, `html` in this case, so that they are all within scope for the entire document. Of

6. You can download this free W3C browser from *http://www.w3.org/Amaya/*.

Listing 5-1 Mixed XHTML, XLink, MathML and SVG with 3 Default Namespaces (amaya-xhtml-svg-mml-xlink.html)

```
<?xml version="1.0" encoding="iso-8859-1"?>
<html xmlns="http://www.w3.org/1999/xhtml">
<head>
  <meta http-equiv="Content-Type" content="text/html; charset=iso-8859-1" />
  <title>Mixed XHTML, XLink, MathML and SVG</title>
  <meta name="GENERATOR" content="amaya V5.0" />
</head>

<body style="background-color:white">
<h1 style="text-align:center">Mixed XHTML, XLink, MathML and SVG</h1>

<h4>List</h4>
<ul>
  <li>one</li>
  <li>two</li>
  <li>three</li>
</ul>

<h4>Switching to MathML</h4>

<p>Expression with under- and overscript, <code>munderover</code>:
<math xmlns="http://www.w3.org/1998/Math/MathML">
  <munderover>
    <mo>&Sum;</mo>
    <mrow>
      <mi>i</mi>
      <mo>=</mo>
      <mn>1</mn>
    </mrow>
    <mi>n</mi>
  </munderover>
</math>
</p>

<h4>Back to XHTML</h4>

<h4>Switching to
<span xmlns:xlink="http://www.w3.org/1999/xlink"
      xlink:type="simple"
      xlink:href="http://www.w3.org/Graphics/SVG/">SVG</span></h4>

<svg xmlns="http://www.w3.org/2000/svg">
  <rect stroke="black" fill="red" x="40px" y="15px" width="300px"
        height="45px" stroke-width="4"/>
  <circle stroke="black" fill="blue" cx="180px" cy="40px" r="40px"
          stroke-width="2" />
</svg>

<h4>Back to XHTML</h4>
</body>
</html>
```

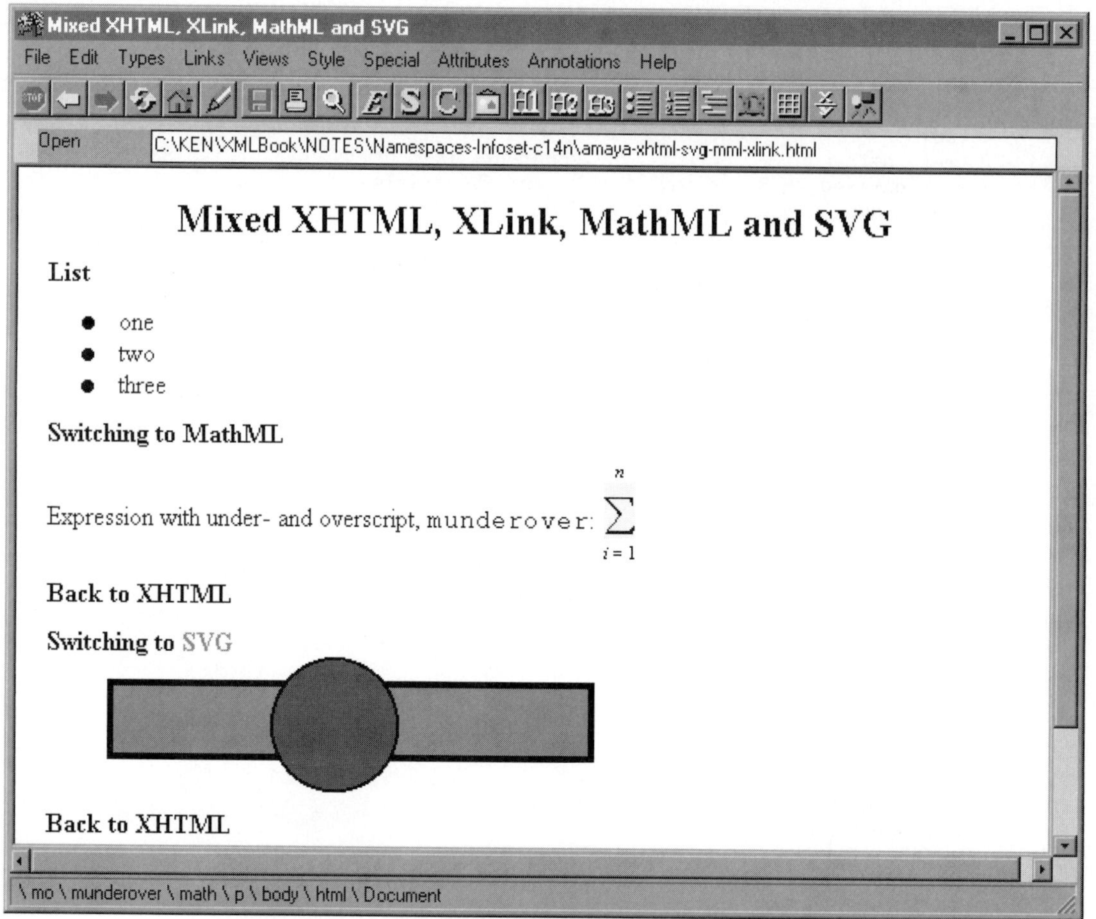

FIGURE 5-1 Display of mixed vocabularies in Amaya 5.0

course, then there can be only one default namespace declaration. Since the XHTML elements are the most prevalent and the document consists of embedded MathML and SVG islands, let's give XHTML that distinction. This means that MathML and SVG now require a prefix both in their declaration and in their use (`m:math`, `m:mo`, `svg:svg`, `svg:rect`, etc.). See Listing 5-2 (file `ns-amaya-xhtml-svg-mml-xlink.html`). This change in the way that namespaces are specified has no impact whatsoever on the way Amaya renders the example, nor the link behavior (of the word "SVG" in the phrase "Switching to SVG"). Personally, I prefer this approach to the one in Listing 5-1 because it's less prone to mixing up which default namespace is in effect, and because it is considerably more clear which elements come from which vocabulary. This reasoning becomes much more compelling in a longer, more complex document.

Listing 5-2 Mixed XHTML, XLink, MathML, and SVG with 1 Default Namespace (ns-amaya-xhtml-svg-mml-xlink.html)

```
<?xml version="1.0" encoding="iso-8859-1"?>
<html xmlns="http://www.w3.org/1999/xhtml"
      xmlns:m="http://www.w3.org/1998/Math/MathML"
      xmlns:svg="http://www.w3.org/2000/svg"
      xmlns:xlink="http://www.w3.org/1999/xlink" >
<head>
  <meta http-equiv="Content-Type" content="text/html; charset=iso-8859-1" />
  <title>Mixed XHTML, XLink, MathML and SVG</title>
  <meta name="GENERATOR" content="amaya V5.0" />
</head>

<body style="background-color:white">
<h1 style="text-align:center">Mixed XHTML, XLink, MathML and SVG</h1>

<h4>List</h4>
<ul>
  <li>one</li>
  <li>two</li>
  <li>three</li>
</ul>

<h4>Switching to MathML</h4>

<p>Expression with under- and overscript, <code>munderover</code>:
<m:math>
  <m:munderover>
    <m:mo>&Sum;</m:mo>
    <m:mrow>
      <m:mi>i</m:mi>
      <m:mo>=</m:mo>
      <m:mn>1</m:mn>
    </m:mrow>
    <m:mi>n</m:mi>
  </m:munderover>
</m:math>
</p>

<h4>Back to XHTML</h4>

<h4>Switching to
<span xlink:type="simple"
      xlink:href="http://www.w3.org/Graphics/SVG/">SVG</span></h4>

<svg:svg>
  <svg:rect stroke="black" fill="red" x="40px" y="15px" width="300px"
        height="45px" stroke-width="4"/>
  <svg:circle stroke="black" fill="blue" cx="180px" cy="40px" r="40px"
          stroke-width="2" />
</svg:svg>

<h4>Back to XHTML</h4>
</body>
</html>
```

Handling Namespaces in a DTD or XML Schema

Remember how I emphasized that it's the URI, not the prefix, that matters? Well, I told a *little* lie. When it comes to DTDs, the reverse is true: the *prefix* matters. Why? Because DTDs declare element names, content models, and attributes, all of which require fully qualified names that must reflect the same prefix used by all instance documents. That implies that if we decide to change the prefix in the XML documents for any reason, we must also change the prefix in the DTD.

Since XML DTD syntax predates XML namespaces, qualified names such as `Disc:price` and `xlink:href` are really nothing special; they are simply cases of legal XML Names that happen to contain colons. From the perspective of the DTD, *there is no such thing as a namespace declaration or namespace use.* In fact, a "prefix" isn't meaningful either; the letters and semicolon that follow are just part of the element or attribute name. This is not just a matter of semantics, as we'll see when we discuss validity with respect to namespaces in the next section.

That doesn't mean that prefixes can be used in DTDs without some definition. They need to be declared in an attribute-list declaration for the elements with which they are to be associated. The general syntax for this attribute-list declaration is:

```
<!ATTLIST prefix:ElementName
          xmlns:prefix CDATA #FIXED "URI">
```

The variable portions are in italics. For example, the attribute-list declaration for the earlier discount namespace attached to the root element `DiscountCatalog` is:

```
<!ATTLIST Disc:DiscountCatalog
          xmlns:Disc CDATA #FIXED
          "http://www.HouseOfDiscounts.com/namespaces/Discounts">
```

Notice that this is just an *attribute* declaration involving the `xmlns` *attribute,* rather than a namespace declaration. DTDs have no syntax for expressing a "namespace declaration" because they were developed long before XML namespaces. This implies that although `Disc:DiscountCatalog` *looks* exactly like the universal name in our XML document namespace example, in the DTD, it is merely an element name. It has nothing at all to do with namespaces! And even though I referred to the part before the colon as a "prefix," from the perspective of DTD syntax, `Disc:DiscountCatalog` just happens to be an element name that contains a colon. As far as the DTD is concerned, there is no separate notion of a prefix!

We'll defer a detailed discussion of how namespaces are handled in XML Schema until chapter 6. For now, we'll simply observe that since XML Schemas are written in XML syntax, designation of namespaces is similar to the way they are specified in an XML *instance*. Namespaces typically are declared on the root element, which in this case is xsd:schema. For example, one possibility is:

```
<?xml version="1.0"?>
<xsd:schema
   xmlns:xsd="http://www.w3.org/2001/XMLSchema"
   targetNamespace="http://www.YOUR.com"
   xmlns="http://www.YOUR.com"
   elementFormDefault="qualified">
  <xsd:element name="YourElement" />
</xsd:schema>
```

In contrast to DTDs, XML Schema *redefines* validity for universal names because, as we'll see, a local name in an element or attribute declaration can be associated with an XML namespace.

Validating Documents with Namespaces

So then, how do we produce a valid document when namespaces are involved? Since namespace-enhanced XML is syntactically Good Old Fashioned XML that happens to have elements (and possibly attributes) with colons in their names, at least *well-formedness* is not at all affected.

As Ron Bourett points out, validity is a concept that is independent of the proper use of XML namespaces. He provides examples that are invalid (although you might think they should be valid), that are valid but incorrectly use namespaces, and that are invalid even though namespaces are handled properly (*http://www.rpbourret.com/xml/NamespacesFAQ.htm#q7*).

To ensure that your documents both are valid XML 1.0 *and* comply with the Namespaces in XML Recommendation:

- In the DTD, you must declare all xmlns attributes corresponding to namespaces in the XML document;
- Match qualified names in the DTD to universal names in the XML document (by using the same prefix and declaring the exact namespace names given as fixed values in xmlns attributes);
- Limit yourself to one default XML namespace (at most); and
- Ensure that prefixes are unique among document collections you will be processing.

For example, regarding the attribute-list described in the previous section, we would declare and use the Disc prefix in the XML instance like this:

```
<Disc:DiscountCatalog
    xmlns:Disc="http://www.HouseOfDiscounts.com/namespaces/Discounts">
```

Consider the following document (`invalid-internal.xml`), which uses an internal subset for a DTD and correctly declares the `xmlns` attribute. It is not valid, however, because the instance document uses universal names only for the `kbs:myRoot` element, but not for `child1` or `child2`. That conflicts with the DTD, which indicates that the content of `kbs:myRoot` is `kbs:child1` followed by one or more `kbs:child2` elements, not `child1` and `child2`.

```
<?xml version="1.0" ?>
<!DOCTYPE kbs:myRoot [
  <!ELEMENT kbs:myRoot (kbs:child1, kbs:child2+) >
  <!ATTLIST kbs:myRoot
       xmlns:kbs CDATA #FIXED "http://www.example.com/">
  <!ELEMENT kbs:child1 (#PCDATA) >
  <!ELEMENT kbs:child2 (#PCDATA) >
]>
<kbs:myRoot>
  <child1>invalid</child1>
  <child2>doc</child2>
</kbs:myRoot>
```

We can make this document valid simply by attaching the appropriate prefix to each of the children (`valid-internal.xml`).

```
<?xml version="1.0" ?>
<!DOCTYPE kbs:myRoot [
  <!ELEMENT kbs:myRoot (kbs:child1, kbs:child2+) >
  <!ATTLIST kbs:myRoot
       xmlns:kbs CDATA #FIXED "http://www.example.com/">
  <!ELEMENT kbs:child1 (#PCDATA) >
  <!ELEMENT kbs:child2 (#PCDATA) >
]>
<kbs:myRoot>
  <kbs:child1>valid</kbs:child1>
  <kbs:child2>doc</kbs:child2>
</kbs:myRoot>
```

As long as we can guarantee that we'll be using a validating parser, which is required to process any external subset, we can move the DTD into an external subset. Suppose we store the DTD in the file `valid-external.dtd`.

```
<!ELEMENT kbs:myRoot (kbs:child1, kbs:child2+) >
<!ATTLIST kbs:myRoot
          xmlns:kbs CDATA #FIXED "http://www.example.com/">
<!ELEMENT kbs:child1 (#PCDATA) >
<!ELEMENT kbs:child2 (#PCDATA) >
```

We then alter the document type declaration of the document instance to reference the DTD, as usual:

```
<?xml version="1.0" standalone="no" ?>
<!DOCTYPE kbs:myRoot SYSTEM "valid-external.dtd" >
```

```
<kbs:myRoot>
  <kbs:child1>valid</kbs:child1>
  <kbs:child2>doc</kbs:child2>
</kbs:myRoot>
```

However, this XML example, although valid, doesn't use *namespaces* at all; it merely uses element names that contain a colon. In the external DTD subset, once again we have an `xmlns` attribute declared, but in the XML instance, there is no matching namespace declaration, so these elements aren't in *any* namespace, even though they have what appears to be a prefix, and it is in fact just part of their element name. (Is your head hurting yet?)

Thus, to satisfy both the constraints of the Namespaces in XML Recommendation and the XML 1.0 Recommendation for validity, you have to *specifically declare the namespace using the same prefix given in the* `xmlns` *attribute declaration in the DTD* ("kbs" in this case). So the DTD is the same as shown previously:

```
<!ELEMENT kbs:myRoot (kbs:child1, kbs:child2+) >
<!ATTLIST kbs:myRoot
          xmlns:kbs CDATA #FIXED "http://www.example.com/">
<!ELEMENT kbs:child1 (#PCDATA) >
<!ELEMENT kbs:child2 (#PCDATA) >
```

But we need to modify the root element in the XML instance (`ns-valid-explicitNS.xml`):

```
<?xml version="1.0" standalone="no" ?>
<!DOCTYPE kbs:myRoot SYSTEM "ns-valid-explicitNS.dtd" >
<kbs:myRoot
     xmlns:kbs="http://www.example.com/">
  <kbs:child1>valid</kbs:child1>
  <kbs:child2>doc</kbs:child2>
</kbs:myRoot>
```

This poses a bit of an editing headache because not only must the DTD and XML instances use the same prefix (and namespace URI), but this method also requires *all* elements in the instance to use universal names. In this trivial example, that's no problem, but imagine having to add the prefix to every element name in a several-thousand-line XML document! One solution, when dealing with a *single* namespace, is to declare a default namespace in the instance, attached to the root element. In this case, we remove the prefixes from all elements in the DTD and use `xmlns` without the colon or prefix, as we saw earlier:

```
<!ELEMENT myRoot (child1, child2+) >
<!-- Declaration for what is the default namespace in instances. -->
<!ATTLIST myRoot
          xmlns CDATA #FIXED "http://www.example.com/">
<!ELEMENT child1 (#PCDATA) >
<!ELEMENT child2 (#PCDATA) >
```

Then make the corresponding change to the instance:

```
<?xml version="1.0" standalone="no" ?>
<!DOCTYPE myRoot SYSTEM "ns-valid-defaultNS.dtd" >
<myRoot
    xmlns="http://www.example.com/">
  <child1>valid</child1>
  <child2>doc</child2>
</myRoot>
```

Now the only line that changes from a non-namespace, nonprefix version of the XML document is the document element itself, certainly a much more manageable editing task.

However, if we are dealing with *multiple* namespaces, we need a prefix for each namespace declared in the DTD and used in the document, in general. We can declare multiple `xmlns` attributes for a single element, for example with URIs corresponding to the XLink and XHTML namespaces for a `Recording` element. In the fragment shown below, the `Recording` element does not need a prefix because it is not part of either language; it just uses elements from XHTML and attributes from XLink. (This fragment appears in a complete example in chapter 13 about XLink.) The attribute-list declaration

```
<!ATTLIST Recording
    xmlns:xlink     CDATA        #FIXED  "http://www.w3.org/1999/xlink"
    xmlns:xhtml     CDATA        #FIXED  "http://www.w3.org/1999/xhtml"
    xlink:type      (extended)   #FIXED   "extended"
    xlink:title     CDATA        #IMPLIED >
```

corresponds to an instance that begins:

```
<?xml version="1.0" standalone="no"?>
<!DOCTYPE Recording SYSTEM "recording9.dtd" >

<Recording
   xmlns:xlink="http://www.w3.org/1999/xlink"
   xmlns:xhtml="http://www.w3.org/1999/xhtml"
   xlink:type="extended"
   xlink:title="Various versions of a recording by Wings" >
```

We could also declare one of the namespaces as the default and use explicit prefixes for the others. That is precisely what we saw in Listing 5-2. In that example, the default namespace was XHTML and prefixes were used to represent MathML, SVG, and XLink namespaces. (We did not concern ourselves with validity.)

As you can see, using namespaces in valid documents can be a little tricky. You have to keep switching your point of orientation. When you consider validity, the normal rules apply and the focus is on the DTD and `xmlns` attributes; ignore that the fixed values of these attributes are namespace names (URIs). However, when you consider the document instances, namespace declarations must be added;

prefixes must be attached to every element that has an `xmlns` attribute in the DTD, and the prefix must match the `xmlns` attribute. For a more detailed discussion of issues concerning namespace-aware validation, see the XML Namespaces FAQ by Bourret.

What Does a Namespace Point To?

The fact that a namespace name is identified by a URI makes many people think that a namespace points to some specific Web resource. Well, it may or it may not, so don't count on it! Furthermore, even if it does resolve to a filename, don't expect it to be a DTD or XML Schema on the other end. In fact, if you type into your browser the common namespace names listed in Table 5-1 on page 234, you'll find a wide variety of results, even among those from the W3C. In the early days of namespaces, the W3C namespace names did not resolve to pages at all and there is no reason you should expect them to do so. More recently, the W3C namespace URIs do result in a page, but they are not required to do so.

Why? Because *there is absolutely no convention expressed or implied by a namespace name other than the fact that it is a unique identifier.* That's all it is, even though you'll often wish it pointed to something a bit more useful, especially something that could be processed programmatically.

On the other hand, there are lots of good reasons for developers to want namespace URIs to point to something. Resource Directory Description Language (RDDL) is a clever grassroots (not W3C) solution to the problem of what a namespace should point to: a DTD, an XML Schema, an RDF schema, or simply an HTML page? (See *http://www.rddl.org/*. The site is also an example of the *use* of RDDL.) A resource directory includes a textual description of a particular class of resources, as well as resources related to that class, together with a directory of links to these related resources. This description is both human-readable and machine-processible.

As we'll see in detail in chapter 15, RDDL is an extension of XHTML Basic that adds the element `rddl:resource`, which is defined in terms of a simple XLink, with `xlink:role` indicating the nature of the resource being linked to and `xlink:arcrole` describing the purpose of the link.

Namespace Support and Use

Due largely to the fact that XML namespaces post-date work on many XML specifications, they are treated differently by various XML technologies. Namespaces are treated simply as *attributes* by older technology like DTDs, DOM Level 1, and SAX1; they're treated as *namespace declarations* by XSLT, XPath, and XML Schema. However, with both DOM Level 2 and SAX2, they can be treated as either `xmlns` attributes or namespace declarations, depending on the context. XML Information Set, discussed later in this chapter, considers them Namespace Declaration Items.

The implication here is that tool support also varies and it is often necessary to enable namespace processing, especially with parsers. For example, when we cover SAX2, we'll see that by default namespaces are ignored, unless we enable them with something like this Java snippet:

```
saxParser.setFeature("http://xml.org/sax/features/namespaces",
                      true);
```

We'll also see that although DOM Level 1 is completely (and some might say, blissfully) ignorant of namespaces, DOM Level 2 is not. In addition to the older `getAttribute`, `setAttribute`, and `getElementsByTagName` methods, DOM Level 2 provides namespace-aware versions of these (and many others), all with names that end in "NS": `getAttributeNS`, `setAttributeNS`, and `getElementsByTagNameNS`.

Namespaces are an integral part of XSLT. In fact, you can't write an XSLT stylesheet without them because every element in XSLT requires a prefix so it can be easily differentiated from the elements of the language the stylesheet is processing or using in some other way. For example, in the following example, the `xsl:` prefix, which is associated with the namespace name `http://www.w3.org/1999/XSL/Transform`, identifies the stylesheet's instructions (elements such as `xsl:output`, `xsl:template`, `xsl:value-of`, etc.) whereas the unprefixed elements are from HTML (`html`, `head`, `title`, `body`, `h1`, etc.).

```
<?xml version="1.0"?>
<xsl:stylesheet   version="1.0"
  xmlns:xsl="http://www.w3.org/1999/XSL/Transform">
<xsl:output method="html"/>

<xsl:template match="/">
   <html>
     <head>
       <title>XSLT Example</title>
     </head>
     <body>
       <h1>XSLT Example</h1>
       <xsl:apply-templates select="//Book"/>
     </body>
   </html>
</xsl:template>

<xsl:template match="Book">
   <br /><xsl:text>Book title: </xsl:text>
   <i><xsl:value-of select="Title" /></i>
</xsl:template>

</xsl:stylesheet>
```

Namespace support can be found in some of the better XML editors that let you map a prefix to a URI, set default namespaces, and so on. Most of the more recent XML parsers also have methods for enabling namespace awareness. Therefore, in addition to nonvalidating and validating parsers, we now have *namespace-aware validating parsers*.

Special Attributes: xmlns, xml:space, xml:lang, and xml:base

This section briefly discusses several unrelated, special-case attributes that are namespace related.

xmlns

Originally, `xmlns` was created exclusively as a syntactic mechanism for declaring either a specific namespace (`xmlns:foo="URI"`) or the default namespace (`xmlns="URI"`) and therefore it did not itself belong to any namespace. However, some application contexts (e.g., the DOM) require all XML attributes to be represented as pairs (namespace name and local name). In those contexts, the namespace name `http://www.w3.org/2000/xmlns/` is assigned. Note, however, that only `xmlns` can be used to declare namespaces; no other prefix will work.

xml:space

The second edition of the XML 1.0 Recommendation describes `xml:space` and `xml:lang`, two attributes that can be used with any element. They are discussed here simply because they are related to namespaces.

The prefix `xml` is by definition bound to the special namespace URI `http://www.w3.org/XML/1998/namespace`. Other than `xmlns` itself (which is used strictly to bind a prefix to a URI and isn't actually associated with any namespace except in the context just mentioned), `xml` is the only namespace prefix that does not need to be declared.

The special attribute named `xml:space` may be associated with an element to indicate whether white space should be preserved by applications. For validation purposes, this attribute (like all others) must be declared. It can either be fixed as "preserve" or "default," an enumeration of both choices. For example:

```
<!ATTLIST SourceCode xml:space (default|preserve) 'preserve'>
```

This attribute-list declaration indicates that the `SourceCode` element has an attribute named `xml:space` limited to the values "default" and "preserve," with the latter as the default.

xml:lang

Another special attribute named `xml:lang` of type `NMTOKEN` may be used to specify the natural (human) language used in the contents and attribute values of any element in an XML document. Examples of valid `NMTOKEN` values of this attribute are: "en", "fr", "de", "da", "es", "he", "it", "zh", and "ja", indicating English, French, German, Danish, Spanish, Hebrew, Italian, Chinese, and Japanese, respectively.[7] (Sorry, no Klingon yet.) Some languages have country codes or dialects, such as English with "en-GB" for Great Britain and "en-US" for the United States. Suppose we had the DTD declarations:

```
<!ELEMENT ToDo (ShoppingList+, OtherTask*) >
<!ELEMENT ShoppingList (Item+) >
<!ATTLIST ShoppingList xml:lang NMTOKEN #IMPLIED >
<!ELEMENT Item (#PCDATA) >
```

Now, using `xml:lang` we can create a shopping list that is intelligible (although not particularly nutritious) on both sides of the Atlantic:

```
<ToDo>
  <ShoppingList xml:lang="en-GB">
    <Item>crisps</Item>
    <Item>bangers</Item>
    <Item>biscuits</Item>
    <Item>maize</Item>
    <Item>tin of mince</Item>
  </ShoppingList>
  <ShoppingList xml:lang="en-US">
    <Item>potato chips</Item>
    <Item>sausages</Item>
    <Item>cookies</Item>
    <Item>corn</Item>
    <Item>can of chopped beef</Item>
  </ShoppingList>
</ToDo>
```

Of course, it's also possible to make `xml:lang` a fixed value:

```
<!ATTLIST ShoppingList xml:lang NMTOKEN "en-US" >
```

xml:base

The final special attribute, `xml:base`, may be inserted in XML documents to specify a base URI other than the base URI of the document or external entity. The value of this attribute is interpreted as a URI Reference as defined in RFC 2396 [IETF RFC 2396]. XLink uses XML Base to interpret relative URI references in `xlink:href` attributes. Consider this excerpt from an example we'll later encounter in more detail in the XLink chapter.

7. Language codes are defined in IETF (Internet Engineering Task Force) RFC 1766: Tags for the Identification of Languages, *http://www.ietf.org/rfc/rfc1766.txt*. See also *http://www.ics.uci.edu/pub/ietf/http/related/iso639.txt*.

```
<?xml version="1.0" standalone="no"?>
<!DOCTYPE Timeline SYSTEM "timeline10.dtd" >
<Timeline
  xmlns:xlink="http://www.w3.org/1999/xlink"
  xlink:type="extended"
  xml:base="http://gernhardt.com/macca/" >

  <Band   xlink:type="locator"
    xlink:label="index"
    xlink:href="wings.html">
    Wings Timeline (1971-1981)
  </Band>
  <Recording    xlink:type="locator"
    xlink:label="wwl"
    xlink:href="a/wwl.html"
    year="1971">Wings Wild Life
  </Recording>
  <Recording    xlink:type="locator"
    xlink:label="rrs"
    xlink:href="a/rrs.html"
    year="1973">Red Rose Speedway
  </Recording>
<!-- etc. -->
</Timeline>
```

If we ignore all details about XLink and focus only on the bold lines, we can see that the `Timeline` element and all of its children such as `Band` and `Recording` are associated with the XLink namespace (or more formally, the namespace name `http://www.w3.org/1999/xlink`). `Timeline` has an `xml:base` attribute which is a URL, (not just a URI). Therefore, for all its child elements, the values of the `xlink:href` attributes are relative to the base URL. For example, the `xlink:href` for `Band` will be interpreted as *http://gernhardt.com/macca/wings.html* by an XLink processor.

Common Namespaces

Before we turn to XML Information Set and Canonicalization of XML, there's one more Namespace topic to cover.

Table 5-1 presents an illustrative but not exhaustive list of namespaces with which you should become familiar.[8] Although I've included mostly W3C namespaces, you'll note a few namespaces from other organizations as well. A more extensive list of namespaces can be found on ZVON.org in their Namespace Reference (*http://www.zvon.org/index.php?nav_id=172*). Note that the prefix given is strictly by convention; you will most likely encounter the prefixes shown, but

8. Thanks to Priscilla Walmsley of Vitria Technology for the suggestion to include a table of namespaces.

TABLE 5-1 Common Namspaces

Prefix Convention	*Purpose and/or Specification*	*Namespace URI*
Core Namespaces		
`xml:`	Limited namespace for the `xml: prefix`, as used in `xml:lang`, `xml:space`, `xml:base`, etc. See *http://www.w3.org/TR/REC-xml-names/*.	`http://www.w3.org/XML/1998/namespace`
`xmlns:`	Limited namespace containing *only* the `xmlns:` attribute, used only in specialized contexts such as the DOM. See *http://www.w3.org/TR/REC-xml-names/* and the resource that just happens to be located by the namespace URI, `http://www.w3.org/2000/xmlns/`.	`http://www.w3.org/2000/xmlns/`
`xhtml:`	Extensible HyperText Markup Language (XHTML) namespace. See *http://www.w3.org/TR/xhtml1* and chapter 15.	`http://www.w3.org/1999/xhtml`
`xlink:`	XML Linking Language (XLink) namespace, often used in conjunction with *attributes* attached to arbitrary elements from other namespaces, such as `xlink:simple`, `xlink:href`, `xlink:show`, `xlink:actuate`, etc. See *http:// www.w3.org/TR/xlink/* and chapter 13.	`http://www.w3.org/1999/xlink`
`xi:`	XML Inclusions (XInclude) namespace. See *http://www.w3.org/TR/xinclude/*.	`http://www.w3.org/2001/XInclude`
XSL/XSLT Namespaces		
`fo:`	XSL Formatting Objects namespace from the XSL 1.0 Recommendation. See *http://www.w3.org/TR/xsl/* and chapter 12.	`http://www.w3.org/1999/XSL/Format`
`xsl:` or `transform:`	XSL Transformations namespace from the XSLT 1.0 Recommendation. See *http://www.w3.org/TR/xslt* and chapter 11.	`http://www.w3.org/1999/XSL/Transform`
`xsl:`	[Obsolete] XSL Transformations namespace from the April 1999 XSLT Working Draft.	`http://www.w3.org/XSL/Transform/1.0`
`xsl:`	[Obsolete] XSL Transformations namespace from the December 1998 XSL Working Draft supported by early versions of Microsoft's MSXML3 (and in early version of Internet Explorer 5.x).	`http://www.w3.org/TR/WD-xsl`

TABLE 5-1 *(continued)*

Prefix Convention	*Purpose and/or Specification*	*Namespace URI*
`saxon:`	Saxon XSLT Extensions [Michael Kay]. See *http://saxon.sourceforge.net/saxon6.5/extensions.html* or generally *http://saxon.sourceforge.net/* and chapter 11.	`http://icl.com/saxon`
`xalan:` or `lxslt:`	Xalan XSLT Extensions and Extension Library. See *http://xml.apache.org/xalan-j/extension.html* and also *http://xml.apache.org/xalan-j/extensionslib.html* and chapter 11.	`http://xml.apache.org/xslt`
`exsl`	Extensions to XSLT 1.0 (EXSLT 1.0)—Common [Jeni Tennison]. See chapter 11 and *http://www.jenitennison.com/xslt/exslt/common/*, *http://www.jenitennison.com/xslt/exslt/functions/*, *http://www.jenitennison.com/xslt/exslt/math/*, and *http://www.jenitennison.com/xslt/exslt/sets/*.	`http://xmlns.opentechnology.org/xslt-extensions/common` `http://xmlns.opentechnology.org/xslt-extensions/functions` `http://xmlns.opentechnology.org/xslt-extensions/math` `http://xmlns.opentechnology.org/xslt-extensions/sets`
Schema Namespaces		
`xsd:`	XML Schema Part 1: Structures namespace. See *http://www.w3.org/TR/xmlschema-1/* and chapter 6.	`http://www.w3.org/2001/XMLSchema`
`dt:`	XML Schema Part 2: Datatypes namespace. See *http://www.w3.org/TR/xmlschema-2/* and chapter 6.	`http://www.w3.org/2001/XMLSchema-datatypes`
`xsi:`	Namespace for XML Schema attributes used in XML *instances* (documents), such as `xsi:type`, `xsi:schemaLocation`, and `xsi:nil`. See chapter 6 and *http://www.w3.org/TR/xmlschema-1/#Instance_Document_Constructions*.	`http://www.w3.org/2001/XMLSchema-instance`
`rdfs:`	Resource Description Framework (RDF) Schema Specification 1.0. See *http://www.w3.org/TR/2000/CR-rdf-schema-20000327/* and chapter 16.	`http://www.w3.org/2000/01/rdf-schema#`
`rdf:`	Resource Description Framework (RDF) Model and Syntax Specification. See *http://www.w3.org/TR/REC-rdf-syntax/* and chapter 16.	`http://www.w3.org/1999/02/22-rdf-syntax-ns#`
[none]	XML Topic Maps (XTM) 1.0	`http://www.topicmaps.org/xtm/1.0/`

continued

TABLE 5-1 Common Namespaces (*continued*)

Prefix Convention	*Purpose and/or Specification*	*Namespace URI*
Specialized Namespaces		
`xf:`	XQuery 1.0 and XPath 2.0 Functions and Operators Version 1.0 namespace. See *http://www.w3.org/TR/xquery-operators/*.	`http://www.w3.org/2001/08/xquery-operators` *Note:* Since this applies to a working draft, the URI is likely to change.
`svg:`	Scalable Vector Graphics namespace. See *http://www.w3.org/TR/SVG/*.	`http://www.w3.org/2000/svg`
`smil:`	Synchronized Multimedia Integration Language (SMIL) 2.0. See *http://www.w3.org/TR/smil20/*.	`http://www.w3.org/2001/SMIL20/`
`smil:`	[Obsolete] Synchronized Multimedia Integration Language (SMIL) 1.0. See *http://www.w3.org/TR/REC-smil/*.	`http://www.w3.org/TR/REC-smil`
`m:` or `mml:`	Mathematical Markup Language (MathML) Version 2.0. See *http://www.w3.org/TR/MathML2/*.	`http://www.w3.org/1998/Math/MathML`

you may actually use any prefix *as long as it is associated with the correct URI*. Several key aspects of namespaces are illustrated in this table and are worth emphasizing:

- The same prefix appears in several rows (e.g., `xsl:`), but each is associated with a different URI. Once again, it's the actual URI that really matters, not the prefix. Therefore, each of the `xsl:` prefixes refers to a different namespace.
- The namespace URI given in the rightmost column need not resolve to an actual Web page or document. In other words, don't expect that following the link will have a useful result.
- There is no convention about the format of the URI itself. As the table entries illustrate, the URI may end in a slash, it may be a HTML page or a fragment within a page, it may be XML, or it may be simply a URI that is nothing more than an identifier, with no physical manifestation. It is crucial that you use *exactly* the URIs shown in the table, character for character, uppercase or lowercase as shown. If not, results will vary across tools. XSLT processors, for example, produce cryptic errors if you use anything but the `http://www.w3.org/1999/XSL/Transform` URI for the XSLT namespace. (A lowercase "t" or an ending slash can cause havoc.)

- The year portion of a W3C namespace URI is not the year of the specification; it's the year the namespace was *assigned*. For example, the MathML URI contains the year 1998, even though MathML 2.0 is a 2001 recommendation. Note that most, but not all, W3C assigned namespaces contain a year-of-assignment designation. Those that do not, however, are of particularly old vintage and generally should not be used.

XML Information Set

XML Information Set, often called simply **Infoset**, is an attempt to define a set of terms that other W3C specifications (and presumably specs from other organizations) can use to refer to the information chunks in a well-formed (but not necessarily valid) XML document. The Infoset is partly defined by what it *isn't* as well; it does not attempt to define a complete set of information, nor does it represent the minimal information that an XML processor should return to an application. The initial working draft was published in May 1999; XML Information Set became a W3C Recommendation in October 2001, located at *http://www.w3.org/TR/xml-infoset/*.

An **information set** is the collection of *information items* of a particular XML document. An **information item** is an abstract model of a portion of an XML document that is characterized by certain **properties**, denoted in bold, square brackets in the spec (e.g., **[children]**). Some properties are characteristic of more than one kind of information item (e.g., **[local name]** applies to element and attribute information items), while others are unique to a specific information item type (e.g., **[document element]** applies only to the document information item). There are eleven kinds of information items, described in the next subsection "What's In the Infoset?"

While valid documents also may have an information set, any document that is well-formed and meets XML namespace constraints described in the Infoset specification has an information set. *Documents that do not conform to the Namespaces in XML Recommendation cannot have meaningful information sets, even though they may be well-formed.* In cases where an XML processor, especially a validating parser, expands entity references, there are information items that contain the replacement text. Since a nonvalidating parser is not required[9] to do this expansion, there is a special information item called an unexpanded entity reference information item.

9. The October 2001 Appendix B: XML 1.0 Reporting Requirements of the XML Information Set W3C Recommendation is an informative and useful collection of all the XML 1.0 requirements for document information reporting that XML processors should honor.

Conformance with the XML Information Set specification is really a matter of concern for the *other* specifications that use Infoset definitions. Specifications that reference the Infoset must:

- Indicate which information items and properties they support.
- Specify whether information items and properties are passed through unchanged to the application or how they are modified.
- Specify additional information they consider significant that is not defined by the Infoset.
- Designate any departure from Infoset terminology (which is discouraged).

What's in the Infoset?

The eleven information items described by the Infoset are shown in Table 5-2. For each, a representative sample of properties is listed. Refer to the specification for details and a complete list of properties and more detailed descriptions.

TABLE 5-2 Information Items and Selected Properties

Name	*Description and Selected Properties in [ ]*
Document Information Item	There is *always exactly one* document information item, which is the single root from which all other information items are accessible (directly or indirectly) via properties. *Note:* This is *not* the item corresponding to the document element, although that element is one of the properties of this item. Properties mainly pertain to the XML prolog, including [children], [document element], [base URI], [character encoding scheme], [version] and [standalone]. The [document element] property identifies the unique document element, which is the root of all elements in the document. The [children] property is an ordered list of information items containing one element (the document element), plus one information item for each processing instruction or comment that appears outside the document element. If there is a document type declaration, then one child is the document type declaration information item described later in this table.
Element Information Items	There is one element information item for each element in the document, including one for the unique *document element*, through whose [children] property all other elements are reachable. Properties include [namespace name], a URI or possibly no value,[a] [local name], [prefix], [children], an ordered list in document order of element, processing instruction, unexpanded entity reference, character, and comment information items that are immediate children, [attributes], an unordered possibly empty set, [namespace attributes], [in-scope namespaces], [base URI], and [parent].
Attribute Information Items	There is one attribute information item for each attribute of each element, including any attributes from the DTD with default values that are not explicit in the XML document. Properties include [namespace name], [local name], [prefix], [normalized value], [specified], a flag designating

TABLE 5-2 *(continued)*

Name	*Description and Selected Properties in [ ]*
Attribute Information Items (*continued*)	whether the attribute was explicit in the owner element's start tag, [attribute type], one of the 10 values such as `ID`, `IDREF`, `CDATA`, `NMTOKEN`, `ENUMERATION`, [references], meaningful only for certain attribute types such as `IDREF` or `ENTITY`, and [owner element], the element whose start tag contains the attribute.
Processing Instruction Information Items	There is one of these for each PI. The XML declaration is not considered a processing instruction. Properties include [target], the application to receive the data, [content], the PI's data such as name/value pairs, and [parent], the item that contains this item in its [children] property.
Unexpanded Entity Reference Information Items	Items of this type serve as placeholders for XML processors (primarily nonvalidating parsers) to indicate which external parsed entities have not been expanded. Properties include [name], the entity referenced, [system identifier], and [public identifier].
Character Information Items	There is a character information item *for each character* in the document, although applications are free to combine contiguous characters. This applies to `#PCDATA` content of elements, `CDATA` sections, and character entity references. Properties include [character code], [element content whitespace], a flag indicating true if the character is white space within element content, and [parent], which is always an element information item.
Comment Information Items	There is one of these for each comment in the instance document, but not for comments in the DTD. Properties are [content] and [parent].
Document Type Declaration Information Item	There is *at most one* document type declaration information item, if and only if the document has a document type declaration. Properties are [system identifier] of the external subset (if any), [public identifier] of the external subset (if any), [children], which in this context is the ordered list of processing instructions from the DTD, and [parent], the document information item that contains this item.
Unparsed Entity Information Items	This information item pertains to unparsed general entities declared in the DTD, which relate to notations. Properties include [name], [system identifier], [public identifier], [notation name], and [notation].
Notation Information Items	This information item applies to notations declared in the DTD, used to represent binary data (e.g., images) or other non-XML data. Properties include [name], [system identifier], and [public identifier].
Namespace Information Items	Each element has a namespace information item f*or every in-scope namespace*, identified by the [in-scope namespaces] property of the element information item. Properties are [prefix], the portion that follows `xmlns:` prefix (or no value if the attribute name is `xmlns` denoting the default namespace) and [namespace name], the URI to which the prefix is bound. Namespace information items are what we have called *xmlns attributes* earlier in this chapter.

a. The Infoset terms *no value* and *unknown* for property values are not to be confused with the empty string or the empty set, nor with the term *null*, which is similar but may have particular connotations and is therefore not used by the Infoset.

What's Not in the Infoset?

Appendix D of the XML Information Set Recommendation presents a nonexhaustive list of about twenty items not within scope (*http://www.w3.org/TR/xml-infoset/#omitted*). A sampling of the list is illustrative of what the Infoset does not attempt to define.

- DTD content models
- DTD attribute order and grouping
- DTD comments
- Whether characters are represented by character references or not (e.g., <)
- White space in specific contexts
- White space with end tags and start tags (excepting significant white space contained within attribute values)
- End-of-line character
- Single vs. double quotes around attribute values
- Default values of attributes declared in the DTD
- Whether declarations are from the internal or external subset
- Empty element format (e.g., <empty/> vs. <empty></empty>)

Keep this list in mind as we discuss Canonical XML shortly. Although the XML Information Set specification does not refer to Canonical XML, there is mention of Infoset in the Canonical XML specification.

Canonical XML

Since XML syntax permits a number of options (e.g., which form of empty elements to use, whether to use single or double quotes for attribute values, the order of attributes in a start tag, places where white space is considered insignificant, etc.), it is quite easy to create documents that are physically different and yet *logically equivalent*. The purpose of Canonical XML is to define an algorithm by which a particular physical representation of an XML document can be reliably and repeatedly reduced to its canonical (simplest) form. When the same algorithm is applied to physically different representations to produce their canonical forms, documents can be compared at this logical level.

Although it is true that two documents with the same canonical form are logically equivalent, it is not *necessarily* true that two documents that differ in canonical form must be logically different. This apparent contradiction makes sense when you consider that there are application-specific equivalences that might apply, such as when an RGB value is substituted for a color word, or an IP address is substituted for its fully qualified domain name, or even when a later version of a DTD employs different element or attribute names that are logically equivalent to their earlier counterparts. It's not possible for a general algorithm to account for such application-specifics, and therefore they are not within the scope of Canonical XML.

The Canonical XML Recommendation (*http://www.w3.org/TR/xml-c14n*) was published in March 2001. The initial Working Draft appeared in November 1999. Although you might think there would be a close correspondence with the XML Information Set, this is not the case. While the January 2000 Working Draft (*http://www.w3.org/TR/2000/WD-xml-c14n-20000119.html*) was explicitly based on the Working Draft of the Infoset at that time, it was ultimately decided to base canonicalization (sometimes abbreviated "c14n") on the XPath data model instead. See the "Resolutions" section of Canonical XML for details and rationale (*http://www.w3.org/TR/xml-c14n#Resolutions*).

Why Is Canonical XML Needed?

It is possible to produce multiple physical variations of the same logical document due to a number of aspects considered insignificant in terms of XML syntax and Namespaces in XML. Therefore, applications may change an XML document in ways that are logically insignificant yet still (in my opinion) annoying and inconvenient.

A common example is XML editors that insist on reformatting XML by adding or removing white space, changing indentation, changing quotation marks, and perhaps even changing the order of DTD declarations. Although Canonical XML does not address these annoying differences, it can be used to verify whether an application that processes XML has changed the *information* by comparing the canonical form of the original input to the canonical form of the processed document. In other words, these editors may muck quite freely with the optional aspects of XML, but they certainly must not change the information items; this can be verified with a Canonical XML processor.

Perhaps the most important application of Canonical XML is in terms of digital signatures to ensure that the information content has not changed since the document was digitally signed. The signature is initially generated using a digest calculation based on the canonical form of the document. After its transmission, the receiving application applies the same algorithm to the document, producing another digest of the canonical form, and the two digests are compared. If they differ, it means the canonical forms differ, so the document must have been altered since signature.

In fact, Canonical XML was originally under the purview of the XML Core Working Group (*http://www.w3.org/XML/Activity#core-wg*), which also developed the Infoset, XML Inclusions, and XML Fragment Interchange specifications. Work was transferred midstream to the joint IETF/W3C XML Signature Working Group (*http://www.w3.org/Signature/*) in early 2000.

Canonical XML Terminology

The specification defines the **canonical form** of an XML document as the physical representation that results when a certain algorithm is applied, changing the document in a number of ways:

The document is encoded in UTF-8

- Line breaks normalized to #xA on input, before parsing
- Attribute values are normalized, as if by a validating processor
- Character and parsed entity references are replaced
- CDATA sections are replaced with their character content
- The XML declaration and document type declaration (DTD) are removed
- Empty elements are converted to start-end tag pairs
- Whitespace outside of the document element and within start and end tags is normalized
- All whitespace in character content is retained (excluding characters removed during line feed normalization)
- Attribute value delimiters are set to quotation marks (double quotes)
- Special characters in attribute values and character content are replaced by character references
- Superfluous namespace declarations are removed from each element
- Default attributes are added to each element
- Lexicographic order is imposed on the namespace declarations and attributes of each element[10]

The term **canonical XML** refers to XML reduced to its simplest, canonical form. The **XML canonicalization method** is the algorithm defined by the specification that produces this canonical form. The process of applying this algorithm is called **XML canonicalization**. Since the specification borrows from the XPath data model that defines node types (root, element, attribute, text, comment, processing instruction, and namespace), it also borrows the term *node-set*. However, in contrast to XPath, which selects or rejects nodes based on expression evaluation (as we will see in chapter 11), in this context, **node-set** directly determines whether particular nodes should be output in the canonical form, independent of the determination for its parent or descendant nodes.

Canonical XML Example: Different but Equal

In this section, we'll examine two XML instances that are physically different and determine whether they are logically equivalent based on a comparision of their

10. *Canonical XML Version 1.0*, 19 March 2001 (John Boyer)—available at *http://www.w3.org/TR/xml-c14n*.

canonical forms. To accomplish this, we'll use a handy utility called `xmlcanon`, the Canonical XML Processor, from ElCel Technology, which generates the canonical form of a document; `xmlcanon` is freely available (see *http://www.elcel.com/products/xmlcanonman.html*). See this book's CD-ROM.

Listings 5-3 and 5-4 show the two original XML documents in their noncanonical form.

Listing 5-3 Input Variation 1 (catalog1.xml)

```
<?xml version="1.0" encoding="ISO-8859-1"?>

<!DOCTYPE Disc:DiscountCatalog [
<!ELEMENT Disc:DiscountCatalog (Disc:category) >
<!ATTLIST Disc:DiscountCatalog
          xmlns:Disc CDATA #FIXED
          "http://www.HouseOfDiscounts.com/namespaces/Discounts" >
<!ELEMENT Disc:category (Disc:item+) >
<!ATTLIST Disc:category name CDATA #REQUIRED >
<!ELEMENT Disc:item     (Disc:price, Disc:extra*) >
<!ATTLIST Disc:item name CDATA #REQUIRED >
<!ELEMENT Disc:price (#PCDATA) >
<!ATTLIST Disc:price type (wholesale|retail) "wholesale">
<!ATTLIST Disc:price currency CDATA '$US' >
<!ELEMENT Disc:extra (#PCDATA) >
<!ENTITY  internalEnt   "Internal Entity Replacement Text" >
<!ENTITY  externalEnt   SYSTEM    "oz.txt">
]>

<!-- Comment outside doc root may or may not be discarded. -->
<Disc:DiscountCatalog>
<!-- Note quotes around 'Wild Animals' and 'Lion' on input. -->
  <Disc:category name='Wild Animals'>
    <Disc:item            name = '      Lion'>
      <Disc:price      type="wholesale">999.99</Disc:price>
    </Disc:item>

<?somePI        target1="foo"       target2="bar"    ?>
<!-- Comment with entity ref &internalEnt; which won't expand. -->

    <Disc:item name="Tiger">
      <Disc:price type="wholesale">879.99</Disc:price>
      <Disc:extra>&#169;</Disc:extra>
      <Disc:extra>&internalEnt;</Disc:extra>
      <Disc:extra/>   <!-- empty element -->
    </Disc:item>

    <Disc:item name="Bear"><Disc:price type="wholesale">1199.99</Disc:price>
<Disc:extra>External entity replacement: &externalEnt;</Disc:extra>
<Disc:extra>
<![CDATA[
   sale > "500.00" && sale < "2000.00" ? 'munchkin' : 'monkey'
]]>
```

```
</Disc:extra></Disc:item>
  </Disc:category>
</Disc:DiscountCatalog>
```

Listing 5-4 Input Variation 2 (catalog2.xml)

```
<?xml version="1.0" encoding="ISO-8859-1"?>
<!DOCTYPE Disc:DiscountCatalog [
<!-- Different order of declarations in DTD -->
<!ENTITY  externalEnt   SYSTEM   "oz.txt">
<!ELEMENT Disc:DiscountCatalog (Disc:category) >
<!ATTLIST Disc:DiscountCatalog
          xmlns:Disc CDATA #FIXED
          "http://www.HouseOfDiscounts.com/namespaces/Discounts" >
<!ELEMENT Disc:item     (Disc:price, Disc:extra*) >
<!ATTLIST Disc:item name CDATA #REQUIRED >
<!ELEMENT Disc:price (#PCDATA) >
<!ATTLIST Disc:price type (wholesale|retail) "wholesale">
<!-- Inline in this version: ATTLIST Disc:price currency CDATA '$US' -->
<!ELEMENT Disc:extra (#PCDATA) >
<!ELEMENT Disc:category (Disc:item+) >
<!ATTLIST Disc:category name CDATA #REQUIRED >
]>

<!-- Comment outside doc root may or may not be discarded. -->
<Disc:DiscountCatalog>
<!-- Note quotes around 'Wild Animals' and 'Lion' on input. -->
  <Disc:category name="Wild Animals">
    <Disc:item  name="      Lion">
      <Disc:price type="wholesale" currency="$US" >999.99</Disc:price>
    </Disc:item>

<?somePI target1="foo"       target2="bar"    ?>
<!-- Comment with entity ref &internalEnt; which won't expand. -->

    <Disc:item               name="Tiger">
      <Disc:price     currency  =  "$US"      type="wholesale"     >879.99</
Disc:price>
      <Disc:extra>&#169;</Disc:extra>
      <Disc:extra>Internal Entity Replacement Text</Disc:extra>
      <Disc:extra></Disc:extra>   <!-- empty element -->
    </Disc:item>

    <Disc:item name="Bear"><Disc:price currency="$US"
type="wholesale">1199.99</Disc:price>
<Disc:extra>External entity replacement: &externalEnt;</Disc:extra>
<Disc:extra>
<![CDATA[
   sale > "500.00" && sale < "2000.00" ? 'munchkin' : 'monkey'
]]>
</Disc:extra></Disc:item>
  </Disc:category>
</Disc:DiscountCatalog>
```

Some of the differences are fairly obvious, but others are subtle, so I've used the UNIX `diff` command to compare the two input documents.[11] The comparison appears in Listing 5-5, in which < marks lines from variation 1 and > denotes lines from variation 2. The major differences between the two XML documents include:

- The DTDs (internal subset) differ in order of declarations.
- The DTD portion of variation 1 contains a default attribute declaration for `currency`, but variation 2 explicitly provides the values in the XML instance.
- Variation 1 declares the internal entity `internalEnt` as the string "Internal Entity Replacement Text" but variation 2 explicity provides this string as CDATA.
- The words `Wild Animals` and `Lions` appear with single quotes in variation 1 but double quotes in variation 2.
- In variation 1, the empty element is shown as `<Disc:extra/>`, whereas it is expanded in variation 2.
- There are many differences concerning the use of white space between the two versions.
- Variation 1 is 1,735 bytes, whereas variation 2 is 1,834 bytes, as determined by the UNIX wc (word count) command.

Listing 5-5 UNIX-Style Differences between Variations 1 and 2 (diff-input.txt)

```
2d1
<
3a3,4
> <!-- Different order of declarations in DTD -->
> <!ENTITY  externalEnt   SYSTEM   "oz.txt">
8,9d8
< <!ELEMENT Disc:category (Disc:item+) >
< <!ATTLIST Disc:category name CDATA #REQUIRED >
14c13
< <!ATTLIST Disc:price currency CDATA '$US' >
---
> <!-- Inline in this version: ATTLIST Disc:price currency CDATA '$US' -->
16,17c15,16
< <!ENTITY  internalEnt   "Internal Entity Replacement Text" >
< <!ENTITY  externalEnt   SYSTEM   "oz.txt">
---
> <!ELEMENT Disc:category (Disc:item+) >
> <!ATTLIST Disc:category name CDATA #REQUIRED >
23,25c22,24
<   <Disc:category name='Wild Animals'>
<     <Disc:item           name = '      Lion'>
<       <Disc:price      type="wholesale">999.99</Disc:price>
---
```

11. Cygwin is a UNIX environment for Windows that includes most standard utilities such as `diff`. This freeware is available from *http://cygwin.com/*.

```
>   <Disc:category name="Wild Animals">
>     <Disc:item  name="      Lion">
>       <Disc:price type="wholesale" currency="$US" >999.99</Disc:price>
28c27
< <?somePI        target1="foo"       target2="bar"    ?>
---
> <?somePI target1="foo"       target2="bar"    ?>
31,32c30,31
<     <Disc:item name="Tiger">
<       <Disc:price type="wholesale">879.99</Disc:price>
---
>     <Disc:item              name="Tiger">
>       <Disc:price     currency  =  "$US"      type="wholesale"
>879.99</Disc:price>
34,35c33,34
<       <Disc:extra>&internalEnt;</Disc:extra>
<       <Disc:extra/>   <!-- empty element -->
---
>       <Disc:extra>Internal Entity Replacement Text</Disc:extra>
>       <Disc:extra></Disc:extra>   <!-- empty element -->
38c37
<     <Disc:item name="Bear"><Disc:price type="wholesale">1199.99</Disc:price>
---
>     <Disc:item name="Bear"><Disc:price currency="$US"
type="wholesale">1199.99</Disc:price>
```

So, now that we have a good idea of how the two files differ, our next step is to generate the canonical form of each variation and compare the results. Although `xmlcanon` supports a number of useful options, for our purposes, we can use the default behavior.

```
C:\>xmlcanon catalog1.xml > canon1.xml
C:\>xmlcanon catalog2.xml > canon2.xml
```

Listing 5-6 shows the canonical form of the first file (`canon1.xml`). There are several noteworthy aspects of the canonical form when compared to the input file `catalog1.xml` (Listing 5-3).

- The entire DTD (an internal subset) has been stripped, along with the XML declaration.
- All single quotes surrounding attribute values that have been replaced by double quotes, although single quotes appearing in comments have remained intact.
- White space in start tags has been reduced (normalized), except where it occurred within attribute values, such as "   `Lion`".
- The default value for the `currency` attribute of the `Disc:price` element has been substituted.
- White space after the target of the PI has been removed, but white space has been preserved in the content of the PI.

- The entity reference `&internalEnt;` was not expanded within a comment, but was expanded in the `Disc:extra` element.
- The character code `©` has been replaced with the copyright symbol.
- The external entity `&internalEnt;` has been replaced by the content of the file `oz.txt`, which is just the string `Oh, my!` plus a newline.
- The CDATA section has been replaced by characters and entity references.
- The canonical form is only 1,107 bytes, due largely to the removal of the DTD and partially due to stripping unnecessary white space.

Listing 5-6 Canonical Form of InputVariation 1 (canon1.xml)

```
<!-- Comment outside doc root may or may not be discarded. -->
<Disc:DiscountCatalog xmlns:Disc="http://www.HouseOfDiscounts.com/
namespaces/Discounts">
<!-- Note quotes around 'Wild Animals' and 'Lion' on input. -->
  <Disc:category name="Wild Animals">
    <Disc:item name="      Lion">
      <Disc:price currency="$US" type="wholesale">999.99</Disc:price>
    </Disc:item>

<?somePI target1="foo"       target2="bar"    ?>
<!-- Comment with entity ref &internalEnt; which won't expand. -->

    <Disc:item name="Tiger">
      <Disc:price currency="$US" type="wholesale">879.99</Disc:price>
      <Disc:extra>Â©</Disc:extra>
      <Disc:extra>Internal Entity Replacement Text</Disc:extra>
      <Disc:extra></Disc:extra>   <!-- empty element -->
    </Disc:item>

    <Disc:item name="Bear"><Disc:price currency="$US"
type="wholesale">1199.99</Disc:price>
<Disc:extra>External entity replacement: Oh, my!
</Disc:extra>
<Disc:extra>

   sale &gt; "500.00" &amp;&amp; sale &lt; "2000.00" ? 'munchkin' : 'monkey'

</Disc:extra></Disc:item>
  </Disc:category>
</Disc:DiscountCatalog>
```

From a cygwin UNIX shell window, I used the `diff` command to verify that the two canonical forms were in fact identical:

```
$ diff canon1.xml canon2.xml
```

The `diff` command produced no output, which indicates that the inputs were identical.

ElCel's `xmlcanon` gives you the option of trying the original XML canonicalization method proposed by XML expert James Clark (*http://www.jclark.com/xml/canonxml.html*) in one of the working drafts of Canonical XML. While the canonical form that Clark's method produces is very different from that produced by the final W3C Recommendation, I verified that it too produced equivalent canonical forms for the two sample input files, using the command lines:

```
C:\>xmlcanon --method="JClark" catalog1.xml > clark1.xml
C:\>xmlcanon --method="JClark" catalog2.xml > clark2.xml
$ diff clark1.xml clark2.xml
```

Listing 5-7 shows `clark1.xml`, the canonical form first proposed by James Clark. The output that appears without line breaks has been wrapped to make it at least semireadable. It contains only 990 bytes.

Listing 5-7 James Clark's Canonical Form (clark1.xml)

```
<Disc:DiscountCatalog
xmlns:Disc="http://www.HouseOfDiscounts.com/namespaces/Discounts">&#10;
&#10; <Disc:category name="Wild Animals">&#10; <Disc:item name="
Lion">&#10; <Disc:price currency="$US"
type="wholesale">999.99</Disc:price>&#10; </Disc:item>&#10;&#10;<?somePI
target1="foo" target2="bar" ?>&#10;&#10;&#10; <Disc:item
name="Tiger">&#10; <Disc:price currency="$US"
type="wholesale">879.99</Disc:price>&#10;
<Disc:extra>Â©</Disc:extra>&#10; <Disc:extra>Internal Entity Replacement
Text</Disc:extra>&#10; <Disc:extra></Disc:extra> &#10;
</Disc:item>&#10;&#10; <Disc:item name="Bear"><Disc:price currency="$US"
type="wholesale">1199.99</Disc:price>&#10;<Disc:extra>External entity
replacement: Oh, my!&#10;</Disc:extra>&#10;<Disc:extra>&#10;&#10; sale
&gt; &quot;500.00&quot; &amp;&amp; sale &lt; &quot;2000.00&quot; ?
'munchkin' : 'monkey'&#10;&#10;</Disc:extra></Disc:item>&#10;
</Disc:category>&#10;</Disc:DiscountCatalog>
```

When we again use the UNIX `diff` command to compare `clark1.xml` and `clark2.xml`, we find no difference. Therefore, although the canonicalization method that produced these files in not the same as the one the W3C ultimately implemented, Clark's method also proves that our original two input files, `catalog1.xml` and `catalog2.xml`, have the same canonical form (i.e., they are logically equivalent despite many physical differences).

Summary

In this chapter, we learned about Namespaces in XML, XML Information Set, and Canonical XML, three specifications that at least at one time were the the work of the W3C XML Core Working Group. All three of these specifications followed the

XML 1.0 Recommendation, attempting to address particular areas that are fundamental. The main points covered are:

- XML namespaces are necessary to resolve element (or attribute) name conflict when a document refers to multiple vocabularies (DTDs or XML Schema).
- Namespaces are useful to understand because many specifications depend on them for one reason or another, such as XSLT, XML Schema, and XLink.
- A universal name (or qualified name) consists of a prefix and a local name, separated by a colon.
- A prefix is just shorthand for the actual namespace name, which is represented by a URI.
- A namespace declaration appears in an XML document, rather than the DTD. This declaration associates the prefix with the namespace name (URI).
- Prefixes are added to elements or attributes in the XML document, except if a default namespace is used.
- Namespace scope applies to the element that declares the namespace and all its descendants.
- Although *namespaces* cannot be declared in DTDs, you do need to declare the URI as a fixed value for an `xmlns` attribute.
- Validation and XML namespaces are two different concepts. Creating valid documents that correctly use XML namespaces can be tricky.
- A namespace need not point to any physical resource at all, although many do. What the namespace URI maps to is completely undefined. RDDL is a possible way to provide a flexible solution to this ill-defined endpoint.
- Special attributes `xmlns`, `xml:space`, `xml:lang`, and `xml:base` are discussed.
- A table of common namespace names, their conventional prefixes, and the specifications with which they are associated is presented.
- XML Information Set (Infoset) is an attempt to define a set of terms that other W3C specifications can use to refer to information in a well-formed (but not necessarily valid) XML document that conforms to Namespaces in XML.
- Infoset defines eleven kinds of information items, such as element information item and attribute information item, and a different set of properties for each information item type.
- It is helpful to understand what is not in the Infoset too, including many details from the DTD.
- Due to XML syntax details, it is quite easy to create documents that are physically different and yet *logically equivalent*.
- The purpose of Canonical XML is to define an algorithm by which a particular physical representation of an XML document can be reliably and repeatedly reduced to its canonical (simplest) form.
- Perhaps the most important application of Canonical XML is in terms of digital signatures to ensure that the information content has not changed since the document was digitally signed.

- When a document is converted to its canonical form, single quoted values become double quoted, abbreviated form of empty element is expanded to paired empty tags, attribute default values from the DTD are substituted in the instance if no value is provided, extraneous white space is stripped, and so on.
- A handy free tool for use with Canonical XML is `xmlcanon`, the Canonical XML Processor, by ElCel Technology.

For Further Exploration

Articles

XML.com: Namespace Nuances (July 2001)
http://www.xml.com/pub/a/2001/07/05/namespaces.html

19 Short Questions about Namespaces (with Answers), David Megginson
http://www.megginson.com/docs/namespaces/namespace-questions.html

RDDL Me This: What Does a Namespace Locate?
http://xml.oreilly.com/news/xmlnut2_0201.html

Namespace Myths Exploded, Ronald Bourret [highly recommended]
http://www.xml.com/pub/a/2000/03/08/namespaces/index.html

Clean XML Namespacing Pattern
http://www.tbradford.org/clean-namespaces.txt

Namespaces in XML: Best Practices, Risky Business, Simon St. Laurent
http://www.simonstl.com/articles/namespaces/index.html

Resources

Resource Directory Description Language (RDDL)
http://www.rddl.org/

ZVON: Namespaces Tutorial
http://www.zvon.org/xxl/NamespaceTutorial/Output/index.html

XML Namespace FAQ, Ronald Bourret [highly recommended especially for fine points]
http://www.rpbourret.com/xml/NamespacesFAQ.htm

Robin Cover: Namespaces in XML
http://xml.coverpages.org/namespaces.html

ZVON: List of Namespaces
http://zvon.org/index.php?nav_id=172

xmlhack: Namespace Category of Articles
http://xmlhack.com/list.php?cat=7

xmlhack: XML Information Set: Search of Articles
http://xmlhack.com/search.php?q=infoset&s=Search+site

xmlhack: Canonical XML: Category of Articles
http://xmlhack.com/search.php?q=canonical&s=Search+site

ElCel Technology: xmlvalid and xmlcanon [very useful standalone validator and canonical XML processors with namespace support]
http://www.elcel.com/products/

W3C Specifications and Information

XML Core Working Group
http://www.w3.org/XML/Activity.html#core-wg

Namespaces in XML [Recommendation, January 1999]
http://www.w3.org/TR/REC-xml-names/

XML Information Set (Infoset) [Recommendation, October 2001]
http://www.w3.org/TR/xml-infoset/

Canonical XML [Recommendation, March 2001]
http://www.w3.org/TR/xml-c14n

XML Signature Working Group
http://www.w3.org/Signature/

XML-Signature Syntax and Processing [Proposed Recommendation, August 2001]
http://www.w3.org/TR/xmldsig-core/

XML Fragment Interchange [Candidate Recommendation, February 2001]
http://www.w3.org/TR/xml-fragment

XML Base [Recommendation, June 2001]
http://www.w3.org/TR/xmlbase/

XML Inclusions (XInclude) Version 1.0 [Working Draft, May 2001]
http://www.w3.org/TR/xinclude/

Chapter 6

XML Schema: DTDs on Steroids

In this chapter, we'll examine XML Schema, the W3C-developed alternative to DTDs, and stress the advantages of the former, as well as how to convert from one to the other. Emphasis is on the powerful datatyping and subclassing capabilities provided by XML Schema, which are completely lacking in DTD syntax. We'll also take a brief look at some predecessors of XML Schema, as well as a few alternatives. This chapter provides only an introduction to the rich *XML Schema definition language* (also called "W3C XML Schema"), since the two relevant W3C specifications plus the primer total more than 400 pages. The "For Further Exploration" section contains links to tutorials, reference guides, and articles that provide additional details.

The Need for Schemas: Why DTDs Aren't Always Enough

In the chapter on DTDs, we highlighted the limitations of DTDs, which are not always adequate in the world of data processing. These limitations by no means imply that DTDs aren't useful for certain kinds of applications and content models, but it's important to understand exactly what they can't do because these shortcomings are precisely the needs that the W3C XML Schema effort addresses.

- DTDs were developed for SGML and are therefore document-centric.
- Metadata about the content model is not available to the application.
- You can't constrain element content or attribute values to even the most common datatypes such as integer, float, and boolean.
- You can't constrain attributes to a range of values without enumerating all possible values.
- DTD syntax provides no mechanism for defining datatypes that inherit from primitives, such as integer, and constrain values to a particular pattern, such as a phone number, a credit card number, and a part number.
- You can't define an element and then subclass it to declare elements that inherit certain aspects and either add or remove other characteristics.

- DTDs don't accommodate XML Namespaces used to avoid name collisions when multiple vocabularies are referenced from the same XML instance document.
- DTDs require a particular syntax that does not resemble XML 1.0 syntax.

Let's examine each of these limitations more closely to appreciate better what XML Schema is intended to address.

Document-centric

XML DTDs are a simplification of Standard Generalized Markup Language (SGML) DTDs. SGML is entirely document focused; it provides a metalanguage for defining vocabularies that describe the content of documents such as articles, books, flight manuals, and multivolume sets. For example, an SGML content model can describe a book that consists of frontmatter, a body, and backmatter; indicate that frontmatter may contain a title page, a copyright page, acknowledgments, a preface, a table of contents, and a list of figures; and so on. An SGML DTD is perfectly fine for expressing which frontmatter elements is optional, which is mandatory, which may occur more than once, and in what order the components must appear. But XML isn't just for documents; it's a metalanguage for developing vocabularies that express data relationships.

No Metadata Access

DTDs don't convey metadata[1] (data about data) that is accessible to the application. Once the parser reads the DTD, the application cannot access the DTD via the Document Object Model (DOM). In particular, if the DTD designer went to great lengths to group related attributes into entities to be reused in multiple places in the DTD, the application cannot discover the grouping or easily determine which elements share attributes. (More recently, however, some DOM implementations provide nonstandard hooks for application access to the specific DTD model.)

Limited Datatypes

In chapters 3 and 4, we learned that elements in XML may be empty (have no content), may contain children elements, may contain `#PCDATA`, or may have a mixture of parsed character data and children. In terms of datatypes, this is extremely limited since `#PCDATA` is nothing more than unconstrained text. For example, if we declare a `Street` element in a DTD to contain `#PCDATA`, an instance might be:

```
<Street>Maryland 20707</Street>
```

1. A discussion of metadata and its importance appears in chapter 16 concerning Resource Description Framework (RDF).

This is valid, even though it is obviously not a street. Furthermore, if we declare another element, `State`, and expect a two-letter abbreviation, there is simply no way to enumerate the possible legal values (unless we make it an attribute). Similarly, there's no way to enforce that `ZipCode` is a 5-digit number. In other words, it's impossible to automatically check validity with `#PCDATA`. Only the application can verify such a loose datatype.

We also saw that for *attributes*, only a small set of ten XML DTD datatypes are available (`CDATA`, `NMTOKEN`, `ID`, `IDREF`, `ENTITY`, etc.) All of these types are essentially only slightly different variants of a string datatype, woefully inadequate for constraining numeric information such as prices, quantities, and part numbers. The data community needs a much richer set of datatypes, which can be found in database systems and in languages such as Java.

In addition to common datatypes, such as integer, float, and boolean, that are available in every modern computer language, developers need specialized types to express date and time, URIs, binary values, plus many variations of integers (long, short, unsignedInt, positiveInteger, and so on). Furthermore, they need the ability to define complex types, such as zip code, address, employee, and so forth, as well as patterns against which a data value could be compared, such as a certain number of digits in a credit card number, optionally with space or hyphen separators between groups of digits. This is all very doable with XML Schema.

Hard-to-Define Ranges or Sets

DTD syntax enables you to specify an enumeration of legal values for *attributes*, but not for element content. This is fine if the number of possible attribute values is small, or even if it's the fifty two-letter abbreviations for each of the United States. However, it is nearly useless if your legal values are every integer between 1 and 9,999, and simply impossible if your attribute defines a range of floating point values (with an infinite number of intermediate values). Since DTD enumeration is limited to attributes, you might be forced to use attributes simply to be able to enumerate a set of values when elements would be more appropriate for your content model. Again, this is easy to do with XML Schema using constaints called `minInclusive` and `maxInclusive`, for example.

No Subclassing

The lack of inheritance and subclassing capabilities of DTDs is an extremely serious limitation for object-oriented (OO) developers, such as the millions of Java programmers, many of whom have otherwise embraced XML. Object-oriented programming holds reuse as a central tenent. I can tell you from personal experience that reuse of portions of a DTD can be very dissatisfying when compared to the reuse that subclassing affords. For example, on an e-commerce project, we were developing DTDs to represent EDI messages, with one DTD per EDI message type. Certain elements, such as `LineItem`, appeared in multiple EDI transactions with small differences in the content of the element depending on the type of transaction. All EDI messages had a `UPCCode` for the `LineItem`, some had a `MerchantSKUNumber`, some had a `WebSiteSKUNumber`, and some had both a `MerchantSKUNumber` and a `WebSiteSKUNumber`. Any object-oriented programmer would naturally want to define a `LineItem` class that embodied all of the commonalities and then define subclasses to handle the special cases. With DTDs, this was impossible; with XML Schema, this is relatively straightforward using something called *derivation by extension*.

Order of Children Is Too Rigid

With DTDs, we must always list the children elements, including optional child elements, if any, in the order in which they occur. When we declare a content model for element `P` such as:

```
<!ELEMENT  P  (A, B+, C?) >
```

we're stating that `A` is always first, followed by one or more `B` elements, and optionally followed by a `C`. To list the possible children of `P`, we must decide on a fixed order.

With XML Schema, however, we have the opportunity to consider child elements as a set (or "model group") in which the members do not always need to occur in *any* particular order. That is, we can say that `A`, `B`, and `C` are all possible children of `P` and we do not care about their order. (This was possible in SGML but was deliberately omitted in the design of XML 1.0 to make parsing more deterministic and therefore easier to create lightweight parsers.)

Limited Way to Express Number of Repetitions

In the sample `P` element declaration, suppose that rather than one or more `B`, we needed to specify 14 `B` elements? We'd be forced into something like this:

```
<!ELEMENT  P  (A, B,B,B,B,B,B,B,B,B,B,B,B,B,B, C?) >
```

Not very pretty, is it? And if the number of repetitions were large, you can imagine how unwieldy this would be. Furthermore, the declaration requires *exactly* 14 occurrences of `B`. What if we needed to specify that there could be as few as 3 or as many as 14, or any number in between? There is no reasonable way to do this in a DTD (except for a very small range). However, we'll soon see that this is a piece of cake in XML Schema using `minOccurs` and `maxOccurs` attributes.

Lacks Namespace Support

As we saw in chapter 5, DTDs and XML namespaces aren't a perfect fit. If you want to use namespaces and still ensure validity, you must keep the prefixes in document instances in synch with the DTD. If you change one, you must change the other. XML Schema, which is itself XML, has direct support for namespaces intended to make it easier to reference multiple schema.

Enter XML Schema

Fortunately, efforts to overcome these shortcomings by developing various schema approaches have been under way since January 1998. Central to these approaches is the assumption that DTD syntax had to be replaced by some form of XML syntax; nearly everyone agreed that the awkward and unique syntax, although still useful in the SGML community, was inappropriate for XML. Virtually every XML-based specification used XML syntax so it seemed unnecessary to rely on DTDs that required developers to learn their unique syntax and to require tools to implement special parsing of DTDs. Using XML syntax seemed like a more natural solution, since the true flexibility of a language is often demonstrated by its ability to define itself in terms of itself (e.g., a Java compiler written in the Java programming language).

The result is **XML Schema**, also known as XML Schema definition language (XSD).[2] XML Schema provides 44 built-in datatypes, including about 20 variants of numeric types, plus several time-oriented types, boolean, URI, and binary types, as well as support for the original 10 types defined in XML DTDs.

In addition to predefined datatypes, XSD gives developers the ability to derive application-specific or industry-specific datatypes by combining or constraining the values of built-in types. We'll examine powerful constraint mechanisms (or *facets*, as they are called) such as `enumeration`, `pattern`, `minInclusive` and `maxInclusive` (to limit a range of values), and so forth. We'll also see how we can define complex types, such as an address, that consist of several elements, each of which is constrained, and how to subclass the address type to create variants, such as an international address.

However, XML Schema is not the only approach to a replacement for DTDs. We'll briefly cover a few alternatives near the end of the chapter. In addition, there are situations where DTDs are still needed or may be preferable to XML Schema. In fact, much of the discussion in this chapter relates XML Schema concepts and syntax to DTDs. If you skipped the DTD chapter, I encourage you to go back and read

2. Technically, the W3C prefers the term *W3C XML Schema* and does not officially use the acronym XSD. The term *XML Schema definition language* appears in XML Schema Part 0: Primer, XML Schema Part 1: Structures, and XML Schema Part 2: Datatypes, so I have taken some liberty in abbreviating this as XSD. The acronym is in common use however.

it now. DTDs may not be the latest technology, but they are not dead. It's likely that DTDs will be in use for several years to come (and even longer for document-centric applications). Since it's also possible to reference both an XML Schema and a DTD from the same XML instance, knowledge of DTDs is crucial to a thorough understanding of the XML family of specifications.

Historical Perspective: Forerunners of XML Schema

In this section, we briefly survey the major schema-related efforts that ultimately influenced XSD. These early efforts include XML-Data Reduced (XDR), Document Content Description (DCD) for XML, Schema for Object-oriented XML (SOX), and Document Definition Markup Language (DDML). The purpose of presenting these precursors of XML Schema is not to teach you these languages; it is to make you aware of the ideas that shaped XML Schema. Links to these specifications appear in the section "For Further Exploration." Most of these specifications provide a rich set of datatypes and use XML instance syntax. Nearly all provide a superset of the functionality provided by DTDs.

Readers not interested in these forerunners of W3C XML Schema may skip this section. However, you should be aware of the terms XDR by Microsoft et al. and SOX by Commerce One because they are still relevant to BizTalk and ebXML and are supported to various degrees by schema design tools such as TurboXML and XML Spy.

The book's CD contains this chapter's running example, `collection2.dtd`, as both XDR and SOX schema, in addition to W3C XML Schema versions. It also contains `collection3.dtd`, `collection3dtd.xsd`, and other variations used in examples.

XML-Data and XML-Data Reduced

Microsoft and others recognized the need for some type of schema support while the XML 1.0 specification was still being discussed by the W3C working group in late 1997. XML-Data (*http://www.w3.org/TR/1998/NOTE-XML-data-0105/*) was the first schema-related effort, submitted as a W3C Note by Microsoft, ArborText, University of Edinburgh, DataChannel, and Inso Corporation (authored by Andrew Layman, Edward Jung, Eve Maler, Henry S. Thompson, Jean Paoli, John Tigue, Norbert H. Mikula, and Steve De Rose—names that you'll encounter often in XML technology) way back in January 1998, one month *before* the XML 1.0 specification became a W3C Recommendation. XML-Data called for the use of XML syntax (rather than DTD syntax) to define the rules of the schema. Its primary emphasis was datatyping, along with providing hooks for databases.

Appendix A of the XML-Data Note reveals an early use of XML Namespaces, user-defined element types and datatypes, ranges constrained by minimum and maximum values, reference to a superclass of a datatype, whether an element is optional, and database key and foreign key designations. Many of these notions have made their way into XSD, although with some important differences. We will therefore not dwell on understanding the specifics of XML-Data, but rather remember its proper place in stimulating the search for a solid schema language for XML.

Moreover, the complete XML-Data specification was never fully realized. Instead, a subset called **XML-Data Reduced (XDR)** was implemented by Charles Frankston (Microsoft) and Henry S. Thompson (University of Edinburgh)[3] and others in July 1998. Compared to the XML-Data specification, the XDR document provided a more readily implementable subset and, at the same time, incorporated changes suggested in response to the note.

XDR was incorporated into the XML parsing module (sometimes referred to as MSXML) of Internet Explorer 5.0 and also became available as a standalone component. XDR also is the basis for the initial BizTalk.org schema repository, as once described by Microsoft's Andrew Layman in the BizTalk white paper entitled "XML-Data Schemas Guide," at one time available on the BizTalk.org Web site.

Document Content Description

Very close on the heels of the XDR effort was Document Content Description for XML, published in August 1998. DCD was another W3C Note by Tim Bray (Textuality), Charles Frankston (Microsoft), and Ashok Malhotra (IBM). Like XDR, DCD subsetted XML-Data. However, unlike XDR, DCD's data model and syntax were based on the W3C **Resource Description Framework (RDF)**. DCD also provided a rich set of datatypes nearly identical to those specified by the XDR document. Subclassing, inheritance, and database interface were identified as future work in the DCD Note, which presents an example of an airline booking schema.

Schema for Object-oriented XML

Schema for Object-oriented XML, or SOX (*http://www.w3.org/TR/NOTE-SOX*) presented a decidedly different approach. The original SOX 1.0 Note from September 1998 was by Matthew Fuchs (then with Veo Systems, presently with Commerce One), Murray Maloney (Muzmo Communication), Alex Milowski (then with Veo Systems).[4] SOX was subsequently revised in July 1999 as SOX 2.0, submitted as a W3C Note by Commerce One, again coauthored by Matt Fuchs and Murray

3. Thompson is a coauthor of the eventual recommendation XML Schema Part 1: Structures, as well as the person responsible for XSV, the XML Schema Validator, which we'll learn about in this chapter.

4. Fuchs, Maloney, and Milowski went on to become active participants in the W3C XML Schema Working Group. Fuchs coauthored XML Schema: Formal Description. Maloney is a coauthor of the eventual XML Schema Part 1: Structures recommendation. See "Relevant Specifications."

Maloney, along with several others from Commerce One (Andrew Davidson, Mette Hedin, Mudita Jain, Jari Koistinen, Chris Lloyd, and Kelly Schwarzhof).

Like XDR and DCD, SOX provides strong datatyping. SOX is also expressed in XML syntax. The main difference, as its name implies, is that SOX focuses on an object-oriented approach (and especially inheritance), something that was admittedly missing from the earlier schema efforts. Furthermore, SOX derives some of its requirements from the needs of the distributed computing world and the Java language. According to the SOX FAQ (*http://www.xcbl.org/sox/faq.html*), SOX extends XML DTDs by providing:

- An extensive and extensible set of datatypes
- Object-oriented features such as inheritance of attributes and content models across element types
- Namespace enhancements
- Modularization mechanisms designed for decentralized schema evolution around the Internet
- Embedded documentation support
- An extended notion of validity covering all these features
- Polymorphic content to allow instances to use element types from multiple schemas.

The benefits of SOX are enumerated in the same SOX FAQ:

> For the application developer, SOX enables developers to use XML/SOX processors to transform SOX documents to programming language code, XML DTDs, and documentation. SOX also adds data type, enumeration, and bounds condition support for document validation. For the document designer, SOX adds object-oriented programming principles to XML, defines document modularization and reuse through inheritance, makes document definitions more readable, allows any XML editor to define SOX documents, and easily incorporates definitions from other schemas.

Examples of complete SOX 2.0 schema and document instances that adhere to the schema can be found in the SOX Tutorial by Commerce One (*http://www.xcbl.org/sox/downloads/soxtutorial10r1.pdf*). SOX is the basis for XML Common Business Library (xCBL), an influence on ebXML (*http://ebXML.org*).

Document Definition Markup Language

Another different approach was taken in the grassroots specification called Document Definition Markup Language (DDML; previously known as "XSchema"). DDML was submitted as a W3C Note in January 1999 by Ronald Bourret, John Cowan, Ingo Macherius, and Simon St. Laurent, and included contributions from numerous developers from the xml-dev mailing list. DDML attempts to define the logicial (rather than the physical) content of a schema. In a concerted effort to reduce complexity, the specification considers datatyping and schema reuse as future extensions (*http://www.w3.org/TR/NOTE-ddml*).

Relevant Specifications

Now that we've been introduced to the forerunners of the official W3C schema effort, the XML Schema definition language, we're able to appreciate what the W3C Schema Working Group accomplished over a period of a little more than two years, by taking the best ideas of datatyping from XDR and the object-oriented ideas from SOX and combining them to create XML Schema. (This is of course a major oversimplification.)

XSD is described by a requirements document, two W3C specifications, a primer, and a formal mathematical description, together totaling well over 400 pages (see Table 6-1).

TABLE 6-1 XML Schema Specifications (W3C Only)

Specification and URL	*Description*
XML Schema Part 0: Primer [W3C Recommendation, May 2001]—*http://www.w3.org/TR/xmlschema-0/*	Part 0 is a readable 60–70 page introduction to Part 1 and Part 2, intended to serve as a tutorial. The excellent running example is a purchase order in various stages of modeling.
XML Schema Part 1: Structures [W3C Recommendation, May 2001]—*http://www.w3.org/TR/xmlschema-1/*	Part 1 describes the basis and syntax of XML Schema definition language, used to describe and constrain the content of XML 1.0 documents. XSD provides a superset of XML 1.0 DTD functionality, including support for XML namespaces. Part 1 depends upon Part 2 for datatypes.
XML Schema Part 2: Datatypes [W3C Recommendation, May 2001]—*http://www.w3.org/TR/xmlschema-2/*	Part 2 describes a mechanism for defining datatypes that can be used to constrain attribute values or element content. This mechanism is used by XML Schema Part 1, as well as by other W3C specifications. Part 2 also describes 44 predefined, built-in datatypes, most of which are not available in XML 1.0 DTDs.
XML Schema: Formal Description [W3C Working Draft, September 2001]—*http://www.w3.org/TR/xmlschema-formal/*	This specification provides a formal (mathematical) description of XML types and validity as specified by XML Schema Part 1. It also defines a way to address each component of an XML Schema by a URI, expected to be useful for XML Query, RDF, XML Topic Maps, etc.
XML Schema Requirements [W3C Note, February 1999]—*http://www.w3.org/TR/NOTE-xmlschema-req*	This requirements document describes the purpose, basic usage scenarios, design principles, and base requirements for an XML schema language. It may not reflect all requirements that the Schema Working Group later derived.

Basic Example

XML Schema is fairly complex. Before we jump into all the details, we'll look at a small example to introduce several concepts that we'll develop in the rest of the chapter.

Since XML Schema is an alternative to DTDs, it's worth starting with a tiny DTD fragment to see what this might look like as an XML Schema. Throughout the chapter, we'll revisit this small example, as well as a larger schema that includes this piece. As usual, all examples are on the book's CD.

Address DTD and Instance

Consider the simplest way to define a snail mail address in XML—an `Address` element containing `Street`, `City`, `State`, and `Zip` children.

```
<?xml version="1.0" standalone="no" ?>
<!DOCTYPE Address SYSTEM "address.dtd" >
<Address>
  <Street>123 Milky Way Dr.</Street>
  <City>Columbia</City>
  <State>MD</State>
  <Zip>20777</Zip>
</Address>
```

It's easy to see that this format leaves a great deal to be desired: it's limited to US addresses and doesn't allow 9-digit zip codes. However, this version will be sufficient initially.

The DTD fragment for the sample XML instance is straightforward:

```
<!ELEMENT Address (Street, City, State, Zip)>
<!ELEMENT Street  (#PCDATA)>
<!ELEMENT City    (#PCDATA)>
<!ELEMENT State   (#PCDATA)>
<!ELEMENT Zip     (#PCDATA)>
```

Address Schema and Instance

Various tools can help you convert a DTD to XML Schema (covered in "Converting DTDs to XML Schema" later in this chapter). One possible representation is shown in Listing 6-1. (Later we'll see another representation that is a bit longer.)

Listing 6-1 Basic XML Schema Example (address1.xsd)

```
<?xml version="1.0" encoding="UTF-8"?>
<xsd:schema
     xmlns:xsd="http://www.w3.org/2001/XMLSchema">
  <xsd:element name="Address">
    <xsd:complexType>
      <xsd:sequence>
        <xsd:element name="Street" type="xsd:string"/>
        <xsd:element name="City"   type="xsd:string"/>
        <xsd:element name="State"  type="xsd:string"/>
        <xsd:element name="Zip"    type="xsd:string"/>
      </xsd:sequence>
    </xsd:complexType>
  </xsd:element>
</xsd:schema>
```

We can see that an XML Schema is an XML document with the usual optional XML declaration. The document element is `xsd:schema`, where `xsd` is the most common convention for the prefix associated with the invariant namespace name `http://www.w3.org/2001/XMLSchema`.[5]

This particular schema contains only one element that is the direct child of `xsd:schema`, namely the `xsd:element` that has a `name` attribute with the value of `Address`. This declares that an `Address` element can appear in instance documents that use this XML Schema. It may seem a little confusing at first that there is an element called `xsd:element` and we'll soon see another called `xsd:attribute`. However, these are among the many elements defined in XSD and are analogous to `<!ELEMENT>` and `<!ATTLIST>` in DTD syntax.

The only direct child is an `xsd:complexType` element (more about that shortly). Nested in that is an `xsd:sequence` element that contains four elements with `name` attributes identifying them as `Street`, `City`, `State`, and `Zip`. The fact that they are enclosed in an `xsd:sequence` element means that they must appear in the order that they appear in the XML Schema, first `Street`, then `City`, and so on. Each of these innermost elements has a `type` attribute that identifies it as `xsd:string`, which is the typical string datatype found in most programming languages. It's no accident that the `xsd` prefix is used here; it indicates that this type is built in to the XML Schema language. Any conformant XML Schema processor (such as the most current XML parsers) understands that type and forty-three others, and knows how to validate content and attribute values against them.

5. Another common prefix is `xs`. We use these interchangeably in this chapter, mainly because some tools as well as some W3C examples use `xs` rather than `xsd`. As usual, it's the URI, not the prefix, that really matters. Older books and examples may use a namespace name that refers to 1999. However, those examples are generally no longer valid due to changes in the final XML Schema recommendation.

If we take the instance introduced at the beginning of this section and rewrite it as an instance that uses the XML Schema just shown, rather than a DTD, we get the result shown in Listing 6-2.

Listing 6-2 Basic XML Schema Instance (address1.xml)

```
<?xml version="1.0" ?>
<Address
  xsi:noNamespaceSchemaLocation="address1.xsd"
  xmlns:xsi="http://www.w3.org/2001/XMLSchema-instance">
  <Street>123 Milky Way Dr.</Street>
  <City>Columbia</City>
  <State>MD</State>
  <Zip>20777</Zip>
</Address>
```

Notice that the only differences between this and the earlier DTD-based instance is that the XML Schema version does not have a `<!DOCTYPE>` declaration nor a `standalone` attribute in the XML declaration; instead there are attributes attached to the root `Address` element.

The `xsi:noNamespaceSchemaLocation` attribute tells us where to find the schema, given as a relative or an absolute URI. The `xmlns:xsi` attribute declares another namespace, associated with the namespace name `http://www.w3.org/2001/XMLSchema-instance`; this is the invariant namespace for all of the instance documents that use XML Schema. By convention, the namespace prefix for instances is `xsi`.

What Have We Gained?

Perhaps you aren't so impressed? We've replaced a 5-line DTD with a 14-line XML Schema, which in itself does not appear to gain us anything. As for the instance documents, they are almost the same, except that one references a DTD and the other references an XML Schema (and the XML Schema namespace). Has this conversion bought us anything? Not initially. The DTD and XML Schema are functionally equivalent, as are the instances. Exactly the same `Address` structure is required in both cases. Exactly the same kind of content (`PCDATA`, or string) is valid for each subelement. So, why bother?

What we *have* gained is a solid foundation upon which to build a better schema, one that incorporates more stringent datatyping than merely string, or reuses the `Address` structure to define more general addresses that are valid in other countries, or both. It is precisely this datatyping and subclassing that make XML Schema so attractive. As we introduce other concepts throughout this chapter, we'll revisit this example and note ways we could improve the minimalistic schema in Listing 6-1.

Collection Schema Example

The address schema is actually part of a larger schema. First we'll look at a simple DTD[6] that is used throughout this chapter to illustrate various principles of XML Schema, as well as to show how DTDs can be converted to various schema formats. The DTD represents a collection of CDs and books (and an owner: me), and is therefore called `collection2.dtd`, as shown in Listing 6-3. When the DTD isn't rich enough to illustrate an XML Schema concept, I supplement the example with fragment from other schemas. There is also a variation of this DTD, `collection3.dtd`, on the book's CD; fragments of this variant are used to illustrate different points.

Then I present the corresponding XML Schema (Listing 6-4) and an instance that adheres to the schema (Listing 6-5). Although the DTD is discussed in this section, a detailed discussion of the schema and instance appears throughout the chapter, together with possible improvements. So please don't worry about understanding the schema now. Just skim it and as you read the rest of the chapter, and if you want to see the fragments in their context within the whole schema, return to Listing 6-4.

Collection DTD

In the DTD in Listing 6-3, a `Collection` consists of an arbitrary number of `Book` and `CD` elements in any order, followed by an optional `Owner`. A `Book` has children elements called `Title`, `Author`, `Type`, `Published`, and optionally `Rating` and/or `Notes`. A `CD` has a `Title`, `Artist`, `Chart`, `Type`, one or more `Label` elements, an `AlbumReleased` date, and one or more `Remastered` dates.

Note that the element `Name` (and its children, `First` and `Last`) is used both for a book `Author` and for the collection `Owner`. Similarly, `Title` applies to both `Book` and `CD`. The only elements with attributes are `Collection`, `Published`, `Name`, `Peak`, `Label`, and `Remastered`. Finally, note that all attributes except `Remastered` have default values specified. The fact that `publisher` is an attribute of the `Published` element may not be the best design; it could have been an element at the same level as `Published`; or it could have been reversed, with the date of publication an attribute of the publisher. However, the DTD as written is sufficient for our examples.

You might want to convince yourself that an empty `<Collection/>` element with the proper `<!DOCTYPE>` declaration satisfies the constraints of this DTD, although it would certainly make an exceptionally boring collection!

6. The initial version of this DTD was published in an article the author wrote long, long ago for a Web site not far away, called *Web Developer's Virtual Library* (WDVL). The article, written in April 1999, is "Doing It With XML,"—*http://wdvl.Internet.com/Authoring/Languages/XML/Tutorials/DoingIt/*.

Listing 6-3 CD Collection DTD (collection2.dtd)

```
<?xml encoding='UTF-8' ?>
<!-- Collection DTD, Version 2 -->
<!ELEMENT Collection  ( (Book | CD)*, Owner?)>
<!ATTLIST Collection  version CDATA '2' >

<!ELEMENT Owner  (Name, Address?)>
<!ELEMENT Address  (Street, City, State, Zip)>
<!ELEMENT Street  (#PCDATA)>
<!ELEMENT City  (#PCDATA)>
<!ELEMENT State  (#PCDATA)>
<!ELEMENT Zip  (#PCDATA)>

<!ELEMENT Book  (Title, Author, Type, Published, Rating?, Notes?)>

<!ELEMENT Title  (#PCDATA)>

<!-- Title defined under CD; applies to Book also. -->
<!-- Name defined under Owner; applies to Book also. -->
<!ELEMENT Author  (Name)>

<!ELEMENT Name  (First, Last)>
<!ATTLIST Name  sex  (male | female )  'male' >
<!ELEMENT First  (#PCDATA)>

<!ELEMENT Last  (#PCDATA)>

<!ELEMENT Type  (#PCDATA)>

<!ELEMENT Published  (#PCDATA)>
<!ATTLIST Published  publisher CDATA  #REQUIRED >
<!ELEMENT Rating  (#PCDATA)>

<!ELEMENT Notes  (#PCDATA)>

<!ELEMENT CD  (Title, Artist, Chart, Type, Label+, AlbumReleased, Remastered+)>

<!ELEMENT Artist  (#PCDATA)>

<!ELEMENT Chart  (Peak+)>

<!ELEMENT Peak  (#PCDATA)>
<!ATTLIST Peak  country NMTOKEN  'US'
                weeks   NMTOKEN  #IMPLIED >
<!ELEMENT Label  (#PCDATA)>
<!ATTLIST Label  country NMTOKEN  'US' >
<!ELEMENT AlbumReleased  (#PCDATA)>

<!ELEMENT Remastered  (#PCDATA)>
<!ATTLIST Remastered  format CDATA  #REQUIRED >
```

Collection XML Schema

The XML Schema in Listing 6-4 is a straight conversion of the DTD. As an initial attempt, as we saw in the `Address` example, this schema is no better than the DTD, in that it does not specify additional datatypes or reuse the `Name` and `Title` portions, as it could. We'll consider various improvements to this version throughout the chapter. The CD-ROM contains this version (`collection2.xsd`) as well as a version with improvements (`collection3-mods.xsd`). Just skim this listing to get a better idea of XML Schema than was possible with the `Address` example.

Therefore, we defer a detailed discussion of this initial schema, other than to point out a few things. All `xsd:element` declarations (those with `name` attributes, corresponding to `<!ELEMENT ...>` in the DTD) appear in bold. Notice that in all cases, they are immediate children of the `xsd:schema` element. Use of the `xsd:element` element with the `ref` attribute occurs nested inside elements called `xsd:complexType`. More about this shortly. Other elements of the XML Schema definition language reflected in this example include `xsd:sequence` (corresponding to a comma-separated list in the DTD), an `xsd:choice` (corresponding to the DTD's vertical bar), and `xsd:attribute` (corresponding to `<!ATTLIST ...>` in a DTD). In addition, there are several elements that do not conjure up DTD comparisons, such as `xsd:complexType`, `xsd:simpleType`, `xsd:simpleContent`, `xsd:restriction`, and `xsd:extension`. All of these elements are discussed in detail, as are others not shown in this example. A complete list of XML Schema elements and attributes appears in Tables 6-2 and 6-3, respectively.

If you've concluded that XSD is considerably more verbose than DTD syntax, you're right! In this case, the XML Schema version is roughly four times as long as the DTD version. Just like XML itself, compactness has never been one of the claims to fame of XML Schema.

Listing 6-4 Generated XML Schema for CD Collection (collection2.xsd)

```
<?xml version="1.0" encoding="UTF-8"?>
<!-- Generated by XML Authority. White space edits: kbs.
     Conforms to w3c http://www.w3.org/2001/XMLSchema -->
<xsd:schema xmlns:xsd="http://www.w3.org/2001/XMLSchema">
<!-- Collection DTD, Version 2 -->
  <xsd:element name="Collection">
    <xsd:complexType>
      <xsd:sequence>
        <xsd:choice minOccurs="0" maxOccurs="unbounded">
          <xsd:element ref="Book"/>
          <xsd:element ref="CD"/>
        </xsd:choice>
        <xsd:element ref="Owner" minOccurs="0"/>
      </xsd:sequence>
      <xsd:attribute name="version" default="2" type="xsd:string"/>
    </xsd:complexType>
  </xsd:element>
```

```
<xsd:element name="Owner">
  <xsd:complexType>
    <xsd:sequence>
      <xsd:element ref="Name"/>
      <xsd:element ref="Address" minOccurs="0"/>
    </xsd:sequence>
  </xsd:complexType>
</xsd:element>
<xsd:element name="Address">
  <xsd:complexType>
    <xsd:sequence>
      <xsd:element ref="Street"/>
      <xsd:element ref="City"/>
      <xsd:element ref="State"/>
      <xsd:element ref="Zip"/>
    </xsd:sequence>
  </xsd:complexType>
</xsd:element>
<xsd:element name="Street" type="xsd:string"/>
<xsd:element name="City" type="xsd:string"/>
<xsd:element name="State" type="xsd:string"/>
<xsd:element name="Zip" type="xsd:string"/>
<xsd:element name="Book">
  <xsd:complexType>
    <xsd:sequence>
      <xsd:element ref="Title"/>
      <xsd:element ref="Author"/>
      <xsd:element ref="Type"/>
      <xsd:element ref="Published"/>
      <xsd:element ref="Rating" minOccurs="0"/>
      <xsd:element ref="Notes" minOccurs="0"/>
    </xsd:sequence>
  </xsd:complexType>
</xsd:element>
<xsd:element name="Title" type="xsd:string"/>
<xsd:element name="Author">
  <!-- Title defined under CD; applies to Book also. -->
  <!-- Name defined under Owner; applies to Book also. -->
  <xsd:complexType>
    <xsd:sequence>
      <xsd:element ref="Name"/>
    </xsd:sequence>
  </xsd:complexType>
</xsd:element>
<xsd:element name="Name">
  <xsd:complexType>
    <xsd:sequence>
      <xsd:element ref="First"/>
      <xsd:element ref="Last"/>
    </xsd:sequence>
    <xsd:attribute name="sex" default="male">
      <xsd:simpleType>
        <xsd:restriction base="xsd:NMTOKEN">
          <xsd:enumeration value="male"/>
          <xsd:enumeration value="female"/>
```

```
          </xsd:restriction>
        </xsd:simpleType>
      </xsd:attribute>
    </xsd:complexType>
  </xsd:element>
  <xsd:element name="First" type="xsd:string"/>
  <xsd:element name="Last" type="xsd:string"/>
  <xsd:element name="Type" type="xsd:string"/>
  <xsd:element name="Published">
    <xsd:complexType>
      <xsd:simpleContent>
        <xsd:extension base="xsd:string">
          <xsd:attribute name="publisher" use="required" type="xsd:string"/>
        </xsd:extension>
      </xsd:simpleContent>
    </xsd:complexType>
  </xsd:element>
  <xsd:element name="Rating" type="xsd:string"/>
  <xsd:element name="Notes" type="xsd:string"/>
  <xsd:element name="CD">
    <xsd:complexType>
      <xsd:sequence>
        <xsd:element ref="Title"/>
        <xsd:element ref="Artist"/>
        <xsd:element ref="Chart"/>
        <xsd:element ref="Type"/>
        <xsd:element ref="Label" maxOccurs="unbounded"/>
        <xsd:element ref="AlbumReleased"/>
        <xsd:element ref="Remastered" maxOccurs="unbounded"/>
      </xsd:sequence>
    </xsd:complexType>
  </xsd:element>
  <xsd:element name="Artist" type="xsd:string"/>
  <xsd:element name="Chart">
    <xsd:complexType>
      <xsd:sequence>
        <xsd:element ref="Peak" maxOccurs="unbounded"/>
      </xsd:sequence>
    </xsd:complexType>
  </xsd:element>
  <xsd:element name="Peak">
    <xsd:complexType>
      <xsd:simpleContent>
        <xsd:extension base="xsd:string">
          <xsd:attribute name="country" default="US" type="xsd:NMTOKEN"/>
          <xsd:attribute name="weeks" use="optional" type="xsd:NMTOKEN"/>
        </xsd:extension>
      </xsd:simpleContent>
    </xsd:complexType>
  </xsd:element>
  <xsd:element name="Label">
    <xsd:complexType>
      <xsd:simpleContent>
        <xsd:extension base="xsd:string">
          <xsd:attribute name="country" default="US" type="xsd:NMTOKEN"/>
```

```
        </xsd:extension>
      </xsd:simpleContent>
    </xsd:complexType>
  </xsd:element>
  <xsd:element name="AlbumReleased" type="xsd:string"/>
  <xsd:element name="Remastered">
    <xsd:complexType>
      <xsd:simpleContent>
        <xsd:extension base="xsd:string">
          <xsd:attribute name="format" use="required" type="xsd:string"/>
        </xsd:extension>
      </xsd:simpleContent>
    </xsd:complexType>
  </xsd:element>
</xsd:schema>
```

Collection Schema Instance

Listing 6-5 shows a particular instance, `collection2-xsi.xml`, that references the initial XML Schema in Listing 6-4. Once again, the instance namespace name is `http://www.w3.org/2001/XMLSchema-instance` and the attribute/value pair

```
xsi:noNamespaceSchemaLocation="collection2.xsd"
```

tells the schema processor where to locate the schema relative to the instance document. As we saw with the address example, we could easily drop these two attributes from the `Collection` element and add a `<!DOCTYPE>` declaration to check this instance against the DTD in Listing 6-3. However, as we improve the XML Schema by adding datatypes and so on, schema-based instances and DTD-based instances quickly diverge. The later section "Schema Validation" shows how to validate a schema to be sure it's a valid application of the XML Schema definition language, and also how to validate instances against our own schema.

Listing 6-5 XML Instance Based on Initial XML Schema (collection2-xsi.xml)

```
<?xml version="1.0"?>
<Collection   version="2"
  xsi:noNamespaceSchemaLocation="collection2.xsd"
  xmlns:xsi="http://www.w3.org/2001/XMLSchema-instance">
  <Book>
    <Title>Complete Beatles Chronicle, The</Title>
    <?javaPI foo="One darn good book" bar="You bet!" ?>
    <Author>
      <Name>
        <First>Mark</First>
        <Last>Lewisohn</Last>
      </Name>
     </Author>
    <Type>Chronology</Type>
    <Published publisher="Harmony Books">1992</Published>
```

```
  <Rating>5 stars</Rating>
  <Notes>
Covers the years 1957 through 1970. No solo info.
Great appendices with chart info, discography, composer index,
radio, tv, and live performances, and much more.
</Notes>
</Book>
<CD>
  <Title>Band on the Run</Title>
  <Artist>McCartney, Paul and Wings</Artist>
  <Chart>
    <Peak weeks="4">1</Peak>
    <Peak country="UK">1</Peak>
    <!-- guess -->
  </Chart>
  <Type>Rock</Type>
  <Label>Capitol</Label>
  <Label country="UK">EMI</Label>
  <AlbumReleased>1973</AlbumReleased>
  <Remastered format="gold CD">1993</Remastered>
  <Remastered format="2 disc box set with booklet">1999</Remastered>
</CD>
<CD>
  <Title>Venus and Mars</Title>
  <Artist>McCartney, Paul and Wings</Artist>
  <Chart>
    <Peak weeks="1">1</Peak>
    <Peak country="UK">2</Peak>
    <!-- guess -->
  </Chart>
  <Type>Rock</Type>
  <Label>Capitol</Label>
  <Label country="UK">EMI</Label>
  <AlbumReleased>1975</AlbumReleased>
  <Remastered format="gold CD with 3 bonus tracks">1994</Remastered>
</CD>
<Book>
  <Title>Many Years From Now</Title>
  <Author>
  <Name>
    <First>Paul</First>
    <Last>McCartney</Last>
  </Name>
  </Author>
  <Type>Autobiographical</Type>
  <Published publisher="Henry Holt and Company">1997</Published>
<!-- Notice the absence of Notes and Rating elements.
I haven't read this book yet. This illustrates some optional
elements that are children of Book element.
-->
</Book>
  <Owner>
  <Name sex = "male">
    <First>Ken</First>
    <Last>Sall</Last>
```

```
    </Name>
    <Address>
      <Street>123 Milky Way Dr.</Street>
      <City>Columbia</City>
      <State>MD</State>
      <Zip>20794</Zip>
    </Address>
  </Owner>
</Collection>
```

Key Concepts and Terminology

As we've seen, the XML Schema definition language is itself represented using XML 1.0 syntax. A particular XML Schema that uses XSD is an XML document that is both well-formed and valid in terms of the "schema for schemas," which is an XML Schema itself[7] that effectively bootstraps the process so that all schemas based on XML Schema can use the elements, attributes, and datatypes it declares and defines. The schema that you write describes, defines, and documents a specific *class* of XML documents in terms of the valid elements, attributes, default values, datatypes, constraints, and content models of the vocabularly you're developing. Documents that conform to a particular XML Schema (and usually explicitly refer to the schema) are said to be **instances** of that schema.

Strictly speaking, a DTD is a **schema** in the generic sense of the term since it does describe content models and vocabulary rules for a class of documents. However, due to the inadequacies of DTDs, when the term *schema* is unqualified, most XML developers are referring to the various XML-syntax-based attempts such as XML Schema or one of its forerunners or alternatives such as XDR, SOX, and RELAX NG (covered later). In this chapter, it should be clear from the context whether lowercase *schema* refers to an XML Schema or whether it refers more generically to any schema language.

Schema Components

In the XML Schema specification, **schema components** is the generic term for the building blocks that describe the abstract data model of the schema. There are thirteen schema components, divided into three categories: primary components, secondary components, and helpers. **Primary components** are simple and complex type definitions, as well as element and attribute declarations; each is covered in detail in this chapter. The specification describes **secondary components** as attribute group definitions, identity-constraint definitions, model group definitions, and notation declarations, only some of which are covered in this chapter.

7. *http://www.w3.org/TR/xmlschema-1/#normative-schemaSchema* is the normative version. A non-normative version is available as a separate file at *http://www.w3.org/2001/XMLSchema.xsd*.

Helper components are annotations, model groups, particles, and wildcards, few of which are presented here. Rather, our goal is to understand the basic principles at play in XML Schema to learn how we can take advantage of them in constraining our XML data.[8] Additional tutorials providing further detail are listed in the section "For Further Exploration." Of the thirteen schema components, we'll focus primarily on the following:

- Simple type definitions (e.g., a constrained range of integers)
- Complex type definitions (e.g., an address type that contains a sequence of elements)
- Attribute declarations
- Element declarations
- Attribute group definitions (e.g., similar to parameter entities used to group related attributes in a DTD)
- Model groups (e.g., sequence or choice of elements)
- Model group definitions (named model groups for reuse)
- Annotations (for documentation and application-specific purposes)

The schema component `xsd:schema` itself, which is the document element of all XML Schemas, may consist of sets of:

- Named simple and complex type definitions
- Named (top-level) attribute declarations
- Named (top-level) element declarations
- Named attribute group definitions
- Named model group definitions
- Notation declarations
- Annotations

Some of these sets may not be present in a given XML Schema. For example, there might not be any attribute group definitions or notation declarations.

Next, we'll explore the main concepts of XML Schema and introduce a considerable amount of terminolgy.

Keywords: DTD vs. XML Schema

Just by way of comparsion, recall that the entire DTD syntax at our disposal was limited to:

- `ELEMENT`
- `ATTLIST`

8. At the time of this writing, there is considerable controversy about the complexity of XML Schema. Readers are advised to learn about alternatives; see "XML Schema Alternatives" later in this chapter.

- #PCDATA
- EMPTY
- ANY
- IGNORE and INCLUDE
- #FIXED, #REQUIRED, #IMPLIED, and default values
- CDATA, ID, IDREF, IDREFS, NMTOKEN, NMTOKENS, ENTITY, ENTITIES, and NOTATION
- Enumerations (pipe-separated alternatives)
- Grouping (parentheses)
- Occurrence indicators (*, +, ?)
- Sequence (comma)
- Choice (pipe)

In XML Schema, the complete list of elements and attributes is considerably more vast, as shown in Tables 6-2 and 6-3, respectively. In these tables, the xsd prefix has been omitted since it applies to all elements but the xsi prefix has been preserved because it occurs infrequently. Similarly, throughout this chapter, the xsd prefix is omitted in the prose when it seems redundant, but is preserved when it adds clarity, such as when talking about the xsd:attribute element.

We saw the elements attribute, choice, complexType, element, enumeration, extension, restriction, schema, sequence, simpleContent, and simpleType briefly in Listing 6-4. Some of these elements and attributes have fairly obvious parallels to their DTD counterparts, but the majority are unique to XML Schema, contributing to the greater expressiveness of the language. We'll cover perhaps half of these in this book. For an index with links to formal descriptions of each element and attribute, as well as examples, see Appendix E of the XML Schema Part 0: Primer at *http://www.w3.org/TR/xmlschema-0/#index*.

TABLE 6-2 Elements Defined in XML Schema

all	annotation	any	anyAttribute
appInfo	attribute	attributeGroup	choice
complexContent	complexType	documentation	element
enumeration	extension	field	fractionDigits
group	import	include	key
keyref	length	list	maxExclusive
maxInclusive	maxLength	minExclusive	minInclusive
minLength	notation	pattern	redefine
restriction	schema	selector	sequence
simpleContent	simpleType	totalDigits	union
unique	whiteSpace		

TABLE 6-3 Attributes Defined in XML Schema

abstract	attributeFormDefault	base
block	blockDefault	default
elementFormDefault	final	finalDefault
fixed	form	itemType
memberTypes	maxOccurs	minOccurs
mixed	name	namespace
xsi:nil	nillable	xsi:noNamespaceSchemaLocation
processContents	public	ref
refer	schemaLocation	xsi:schemaLocation
source	substitutionGroup	system
targetNamespace	type	xsi:type
use	value	version
xpath		

Elements, Declarations, and Definitions

The XML Schema recommendation makes a distinction between definitions and declarations. A **definition** covers aspects of a schema that pertain *only to the schema itself*, such as simple and complex type definitions, content model definitions, and attribute group definitions. Such definitions are not directly reflected in the XML instance. Their purpose is to create new types, either simple or complex. Definitions are internal schema components. On the other hand, **declarations** are the parts used in an XML *instance* document that references the schema, such as element and attribute declarations. The purpose of declarations is to state which elements and attributes may appear in an instance that adheres to the schema. In other words, declarations pertain to instance validation. A simple or complex type definition may or may not be named, whereas an element or attribute declaration always has a name. Both definitions and declarations may be either local or global in scope.

In XML Schema, an element is declared with the `xsd:element` element. An element declaration associates a name with a datatype. The name, given by the `name` attribute, is the handle by which the element may be referenced via a `ref` attribute. It is also the name that will appear in an instance between angle brackets. The datatype, given by the `type` attribute, is either a built-in type or a user-defined type. These types are either simple or complex. Consider the following fragment.

```
<xsd:element name="Street" type="xsd:string"/>
<xsd:element name="Zip"    type="xsd:positiveInteger"/>
```

It declares two elements, one named `Street` of type `xsd:string` and the other named `Zip` of type `xsd:positiveInteger`. Both refer to simple built-in types, typically identified by a prefix associated with the XML Schema namespaces (usually `xsd` or `xs`). Here's an example with a user-defined complex type that doesn't use the XSD namespace:

```
<xsd:element name="Address"  type="AddressType"/>
```

Element declarations may contain default values for the content of the element.

```
<xsd:element name="Zip" type="xsd:positiveInteger"  default="20707" />
```

This example declares a `Zip` element that defaults to the integer 20707 if and only if the element appears without a value in an instance document (i.e., is an empty element).

A more thorough example is a variation of the `Address` declaration we saw earlier. `Address` is a sequence of elements. Although two of these, `City` and `State`, are declared locally (via the `name` and `type` attributes), the other two refer to global elements identified by the `ref` attribute, `Street` and `Zip`, declared as we saw earlier. In other words, `ref="Street"` points to the `name="Street"` declaration. As you may have guessed, `name` and `ref` are mutually exclusive; only one can appear in any given `xsd:element` occurrence.

```
<xsd:element name="Address">
  <xsd:complexType>
    <xsd:sequence>
      <xsd:element ref="Street"/> <!-- refers to global -->
      <xsd:element name="City" type="xsd:string"/>
      <xsd:element name="State" type="xsd:string"/>
      <xsd:element ref="Zip"/> <!-- refers to global -->
    </xsd:sequence>
    <xsd:attribute name="home-or-office" type="xsd:string" />
  </xsd:complexType>
</xsd:element>
```

Note the `xsd:attribute` declaration that appears in the `xsd:complexType` element, after the `xsd:sequence`. We cover attributes in the section "Attribute Declarations and Occurrence," but for now, just consider that the preceding element declaration (essentially) corresponds to a pair of DTD declarations:

```
<!ELEMENT Address (Street, City, State, Zip) >
<!ATTLIST Address home-or-office CDATA #IMPLIED>
```

In our XML Schema, the datatype of `Address` is defined by the unnamed `xsd:complexType` element, which consists of a sequence of four elements. In general, however, if `type` is omitted in an element declaration, the **default datatype**, known as `anyType`, is implied. This type is so generic it does not constrain its content in any way. In other words, these two declarations are equivalent:

```
<xsd:element name="Address"  type="xsd:anyType" />
<xsd:element name="Address" />
```

Consider the example in Listing 6-6, which shows an alternative version of the tiny schema presented in Listing 6-1. In the new version, we have a single `xsd:complexType` *definition* and five element *declarations*, one for each `xsd:element` outside the type definition. The definition is identified by the `name` attribute, `AddressType` in this case. This definition tells us that the elements `Street`, `City`, `State`, and `Zip`, will appear in the XML instance, within an `Address` element. They must appear in the order shown in the `AddressType` definition due to the `xsd:sequence` element that contains them in the schema. Conceptually, these four elements in sequence are known to the schema as the `AddressType` type, which could be referenced from multiple places in a more elaborate version of the schema. That is, multiple element declarations can refer to the same `complexType` by means of their `type` attribute; it is resuable.

Listing 6-6 Address Schema with an AddressType Definition (addressType.xsd)

```
<?xml version="1.0" encoding="UTF-8"?>
<xsd:schema
    xmlns:xsd="http://www.w3.org/2001/XMLSchema"
    elementFormDefault="qualified">
  <xsd:complexType name="AddressType">
    <xsd:sequence>
      <xsd:element ref="Street" maxOccurs="2" />
      <xsd:element ref="City"/>
      <xsd:element ref="State"/>
      <xsd:element ref="Zip"/>
    </xsd:sequence>
  </xsd:complexType>

  <xsd:element name="Address" type="AddressType" />
  <xsd:element name="City" type="xsd:string"/>
  <xsd:element name="State" type="xsd:string"/>
  <xsd:element name="Street" type="xsd:string" />
  <xsd:element name="Zip" type="xsd:string"/>
</xsd:schema>
```

You probably noticed that within the `xsd:complexType` definition, there are four element *references*, each denoted by the `ref` attribute of the `xsd:element`. This signifies that the actual element declarations appear elsewhere in the schema. In this case, they appear after the definition, but they could just as well appear before it; it makes no difference to a schema processor. You may have also noticed that the order of the element declarations is not the same as the order of the references in the type definition. That's perfectly fine, too, because it's the definition (or rather the `xsd:sequence` element) that determines the order that really matters, which is how they'll appear in the instance document.

Similarly, the DTD declaration of the `Owner` element from Listing 6-3

```
<!ELEMENT Owner  (Name, Address?)>
```

can be represented in an XML Schema as follows:

```
<xsd:complexType name="OwnerType">
  <xsd:sequence>
    <xsd:element name="Name" type="NameType"/>
    <xsd:element name="Address" type="AddressType" minOccurs="0"/>
  </xsd:sequence>
</xsd:complexType>
```

Here we are declaring an `Address` element of type `AddressType` that follows the `Name` element in the sequence that defines the `OwnerType` content model. In this case, the optional nature of the `Address` element is indicated in the schema by the use of the attribute `minOccurs`. Let's take a brief detour to cover `minOccurs` and `maxOccurs`.

Element Repeatability: minOccurs and maxOccurs

The special attributes `minOccurs` and `maxOccurs` define the repeatability of an element or a content model. Their relationship to the DTD syntax you've come to know and love is illustrated in Table 6-4. If your first thought is that DTD occurrence notation is much more compact, that's true, but the XML Schema approach solves the DTD limitation of bounds other than 0, 1, or unbounded (asterisk). Now you can specify any arbitrary number of occurrences, such as a minimum of 5 and a maximum of 999. You can also indicate that an exact number of occurrences is required by assigning the desired number to both `minOccurs` and `maxOccurs`. This is a major improvement over DTDs in specifying occurrences.

It should be noted that the `minOccurs` and `maxOccurs` attributes are themselves optional. Each of these attributes has a default of 1, so if both are absent, the

TABLE 6-4 XSD Occurrence Indicators (Element Repeatability)

DTD Syntax	*XML Schema Syntax and Description (repeatability attributes of* `xsd:element` *element)*
elementName [exactly one]	`minOccurs="1" maxOccurs="1"`. The default is *exactly one* occurrence of the element, so these attributes may be omitted, and usually are in this case.
? [optional]	`minOccurs="0" maxOccurs="1"` Since 1 is the default, we can simply say `minOccurs="0"`
* [zero or more]	`minOccurs="0" maxOccurs="unbounded"`
+ [one or more]	`minOccurs="1" maxOccurs="unbounded"` Since 1 is the default, we can simply say `maxOccurs="unbounded"`
[very hard to specify in DTDs for large `m` and `n` values]	`minOccurs="m" maxOccurs="n"` where `m` and `n` are any integers >= `0` and `m` <= `n` To specify an *exact* number of occurrences, set `minOccurs=maxOccurs`.

element is required and must appear exactly once. If an element declaration omits minOccurs, since the default is 1, the element is required and maxOccurs determines whether it is repeatable. If maxOccurs is not specified, then minOccurs must be either 0 or 1, since minOccurs must always be less than or equal to maxOccurs.

For example, if we modify the content model of the Owner element to include Occupation and Phone as in the DTD element declaration:

```
<!ELEMENT Owner (Name, Occupation+, Address?, Phone*)>
```

the corresponding XML Schema declaration is:

```
<xsd:element name="Owner">
  <xsd:complexType>
    <xsd:sequence>
      <xsd:element ref="Name"/>
      <xsd:element ref="Occupation" maxOccurs="unbounded"/>
      <xsd:element ref="Address" minOccurs="0"/>
      <xsd:element ref="Phone" minOccurs="0" maxOccurs="unbounded"/>
    </xsd:sequence>
  </xsd:complexType>
</xsd:element>
```

This indicates that the content model for an Owner element consists of exactly one Name element, followed by an unlimited number of Occupation elements (with a minimum of one), from zero to one (i.e., optional) Address elements, and any number of Phone elements (with a minimum of zero).

These occurrence attributes can also be applied to a content model, or any part of one. Consider the declaration of the Collection element:

```
<!ELEMENT Collection  ((Book | CD)*, Owner?)>
```

Consider also its XML Schema equivalent:

```
<xsd:element name="Collection">
  <xsd:complexType>
    <xsd:sequence>
      <xsd:choice minOccurs="0" maxOccurs="unbounded">
        <xsd:element ref="Book"/>
        <xsd:element ref="CD"/>
      </xsd:choice>
      <xsd:element ref="Owner" minOccurs="0"/>
    </xsd:sequence>
  <!-- etc -->
  </xsd:complexType>
</xsd:element>
```

The optional nature of the Owner element is reflected by the line:

```
<xsd:element ref="Owner" minOccurs="0"/>
```

The fact that a `Collection` contains zero or more `Book` or `CD` elements is captured by:

```
<xsd:choice minOccurs="0" maxOccurs="unbounded">
  <xsd:element ref="Book"/>
  <xsd:element ref="CD"/>
</xsd:choice>
```

You've probably guessed that specifying a minimum of 5 and a maximum of 999 is trivial in XML Schema; we simply need to be explicit about both bounds:

```
<xsd:element name="Widget" minOccurs="5" maxOccurs="999" />
```

If there are only four `Widgets` in say, a purchase order, or if there are 1,000 or more, a schema processor will flag this as an error. Similarly, if we require 17 `Gadgets` in an order, set `minOccurs` and `maxOccurs` accordingly:

```
<xsd:element name="Gadget" minOccurs="17" maxOccurs="17" />
```

One less than obvious restriction concerning the use of `minOccurs` and `maxOccurs` is that they cannot be used with global element declarations. That's why in Listing 6-6 `maxOccurs="2"` is attached to the reference to the `Street` element rather than to its declaration.

XML Representation Summary of xsd:element

We've only scratched the surface of the possible attributes and content of the `xsd:element` element. The full syntax for all XML Schema elements is given in what the W3C specification refers to as XML Representation Summary form. For example, the XML Representation Summary for `xsd:element` is:

```
<element
       abstract = boolean : false
       block = (#all | List of (extension | restriction | substitution))
       default = string
       final = (#all | List of (extension | restriction))
       fixed = string
       form = (qualified | unqualified)
       id = ID
       maxOccurs = (nonNegativeInteger | unbounded) : 1
       minOccurs = nonNegativeInteger : 1
       name = NCName
       nillable = boolean : false
       ref = QName
       substitutionGroup = QName
       type = QName
       {any attributes with non-schema namespace . .  .}>
       Content: (annotation?, ((simpleType | complexType)?,
                (unique | key | keyref)*))
</element>
```

This summary (from XML Schema, Part 1: Structures; W3C Recommendation 2 May 2001, *http://www.w3.org/TR/xmlschema-1/#declare-element*) lists all the possible attributes, their datatype or enumerated values and, where appropriate, default values after the colon. The `xsd:element` summary tells us, among other things, that the `maxOccurs` attribute defaults to 1, and its value is limited to any `nonNegativeInteger` or the actual value "unbounded." Attributes that are required are shown in bold, although there are none in this particular summary. An element's content model appears last in these summaries in DTD-like syntax, complete with the occurrence indicators ?, +, and *.

XML Representation Summaries appear for each element of the language in Part 1 of XML Schema. Rather than repeat them all here, I've included direct links to the summaries for the key elements `schema`, `element`, `attribute`, `simpleType`, `complexType`, `simpleContent`, `complexContent`, `attributeGroup` in the section "For Further Exploration."

Local vs. Global Scope

If you peeked back at the long example in Listing 6-4, you might have been bothered by the fact that, in contrast to what appears in the earlier section, `xsd:elements` named `Owner` and `Address` contain *unnamed* `xsd:complexTypes` in Listing 6-7, excerpted from Listing 6-4.

Listing 6-7 Global Elements with Anonymous Types (from collection2.xsd)

```
<xsd:schema xmlns:xsd="http://www.w3.org/2001/XMLSchema">
  <!-- etc -->
  <xsd:element name="Owner">
    <xsd:complexType>
      <xsd:sequence>
        <xsd:element ref="Name"/>
        <xsd:element ref="Address" minOccurs="0"/>
      </xsd:sequence>
    </xsd:complexType>
  </xsd:element>
  <xsd:element name="Address">
    <xsd:complexType>
      <xsd:sequence>
        <xsd:element ref="Street"/>
        <xsd:element ref="City"/>
        <xsd:element ref="State"/>
        <xsd:element ref="Zip"/>
      </xsd:sequence>
    </xsd:complexType>
  </xsd:element>
  <xsd:element name="Street" type="xsd:string"/>
  <xsd:element name="City" type="xsd:string"/>
  <xsd:element name="State" type="xsd:string"/>
  <xsd:element name="Zip" type="xsd:string"/>
  <!-- etc -->
</xsd:schema>
```

As far as instance documents go, this makes absolutely no difference. However, as far as the schema itself goes, Listing 6-6 defines the *reusable type* AddressType (as well as OwnerType in the fragment following Listing 6-6). The similar fragment in Listing 6-7 does not define types that can be used anywhere except within the elements that contain them. In fact, since both of the complexType definitions in Listing 6-7 do not use the name attribute, they are called **anonymous types**, which aren't reusable.

By the way, don't get the incorrect impression that all type names must end in "Type." That's merely a (useful) convention used by a tool called XML Spy. It's also a good idea when you're creating your own types. However, the built-in types (string, integer, dateTime, etc.) in XML Schema do not follow this convention. A type name can be any valid XML Name.

In XSD terminology, types defined as *immediate* children of the xsd:schema element are considered *global* in scope; they can be referenced from anywhere within the schema, such as the OwnerType and AddressType. By way of contrast, the unnamed complexTypes that appear as children of the xsd:elements named Owner and Address are *local* type definitions, relevant only to the elements that contain them; they cannot be referenced outside these elements because their scope is local.

Elements and attributes may also be declared locally or globally. For example, in the Collection schema, Address is only used as part of the content of the Owner element. We could nest Address and all its children within the Owner definition, as in Listing 6-8.

Listing 6-8 Local Elements (scollection2-ElementLocal.xsd)

```
<xsd:schema xmlns:xsd="http://www.w3.org/2001/XMLSchema">
  <!-- etc -->
       <xsd:element name="Owner" minOccurs="0">
          <xsd:complexType>
            <xsd:sequence>
              <xsd:element ref="Name"/>
              <xsd:element name="Address" minOccurs="0">
                <xsd:complexType>
                  <xsd:sequence>
                    <xsd:element name="Street" type="xsd:string"/>
                    <xsd:element name="City" type="xsd:string"/>
                    <xsd:element name="State" type="xsd:string"/>
                    <xsd:element name="Zip" type="xsd:string"/>
                  </xsd:sequence>
                </xsd:complexType>
              </xsd:element>
            </xsd:sequence>
          </xsd:complexType>
        </xsd:element>
  <!-- etc -->
</xsd:schema>
```

Of course, it's easy to see that if you have a schema with even a few levels of children, local declarations and definitions can become quite nested very quickly. Therefore I tend to prefer global declarations and definitions, except when I'm positive there are portions that I will never want to reuse. Still, there are a few limitations you must consider when using global elements and attributes.

- Global element declarations cannot use the `ref` attribute; instead they must directly state their type via a `type` attribute. (Alternatively, they can use an anonymous type definition, as we saw.)
- The `minOccurs` and `maxOccurs` attributes can't be used with global element declarations.
- The `use` attribute (such as `use="required"` or `use="optional"` in Listing 6-4 and discussed later) can't be used with global attribute declarations.

You will find the complete versions of `collection2.xsd` and four variations, `scollection-ElementGlobal.xsd`, `scollection-ElementLocal.xsd`, `scollection-ComplexGlobal.xsd`, and `scollection-ComplexLocal.xsd` on this book's CD.

Attribute Declarations and Occurrence

We've seen that an element either has a name or a reference to a name via the `ref` attribute. An `xsd:element` declaration can either refer to a datatype using the `type` attribute, or it can nest either an `xsd:complexType` or an `xsd:simpleType` definition within itself.

The `xsd:attribute` element is used to declare an attribute that will appear in the instance document. Much like `xsd:element`, `xsd:attribute` supports `name`, `ref`, and `type` attributes, with the same purpose as in the element case. As with element declarations, an attribute declaration associates the name with a type, occurrence information (optional, required, etc.), and perhaps a default value.

The type associated with an attribute is always an `xsd:simpleType`, however, because attributes cannot contain other elements or other attributes. Furthermore, all `xsd:attribute` declarations must appear *after* the child `xsd:element` declarations.

Attribute declarations pertain to the parent element in which they are nested, rather than to the element declaration that they immediately follow at the same level. For example, in the following fragment from Listing 6-4, `version` is an attribute of `Collection`, not of `Owner`. Note also that the children elements of `Collection` (`Book`, `CD`, and `Owner`) are declared before the attribute.

```
<xsd:element name="Collection">
  <xsd:complexType>
    <xsd:sequence>
      <xsd:choice minOccurs="0" maxOccurs="unbounded">
        <xsd:element ref="Book"/>
        <xsd:element ref="CD"/>
      </xsd:choice>
      <xsd:element ref="Owner" minOccurs="0"/>
    </xsd:sequence>
    <xsd:attribute name="version" default="2" type="xsd:string"/>
  </xsd:complexType>
</xsd:element>
```

This corresponds to the DTD fragment

```
<!ELEMENT Collection  ( (Book | CD)*, Owner?)>
<!ATTLIST Collection  version CDATA '2' >
```

In both cases, we're declaring an attribute named `version` of string type with a default value of `"2"`.

When declaring an `xsd:attribute`, the datatype may be indicated either by a `type` attribute or by a nested `xsd:simpleType` child. Attributes cannot contain an `xsd:complexType`, although they can be contained *by* an `xsd:complexType`. Again, if no type is specified, the default type is the generic anything-goes `xsd:anyType`.

For example, the following declaration of the `Name` element contains an anonymous `xsd:complexType` definition containing the elements `First` and `Last`. `Name` has a `sex` attribute that isn't just any old string. Instead, its value is constrained to be an `xsd:NMTOKEN` with only two possible values, "male" or "female". (I could argue that there should be a third choice for androgynous "Pat" from *SNL*, but that would really show my age!) Notice that in this example, rather than a `type` attribute, we have an `xsd:simpleType` definition contained *within* the `xsd:attribute`, which is itself contained within an `xsd:complexType` definition.

```
<xsd:element name="Name">
  <xsd:complexType>
    <xsd:sequence>
      <xsd:element ref="First"/>
      <xsd:element ref="Last"/>
    </xsd:sequence>
    <xsd:attribute name="sex" default="male">
      <xsd:simpleType>
        <xsd:restriction base="xsd:NMTOKEN">
          <xsd:enumeration value="male"/>
          <xsd:enumeration value="female"/>
        </xsd:restriction>
      </xsd:simpleType>
    </xsd:attribute>
  </xsd:complexType>
</xsd:element>
```

This is the same as the attribute-list declaration

```
<!ELEMENT Name  (First, Last)>
<!ATTLIST Name  sex  (male | female )  'male' >
```

Attribute declarations also support `fixed`, `use`, and `default` attributes, shown in Table 6-5 with their DTD counterparts. Specify `fixed` to supply a constant value for an attribute that will be invariant across all instance documents. Use `default` to provide a default value if none is supplied in the instance document. The default value can be overridden, however, by an explicit value provided in the XML instance.[9] The `use` attribute has three possible values; it controls whether the attribute is "required," "optional," or "prohibited." The meaning of "required" and "optional" is fairly obvious. The value "prohibited" means that the named attribute is explicitly disallowed as an attribute of the current element. If no `use` attribute is present in the attribute declaration, "optional" is implied. In other words, attributes are optional by default.

We've seen an example of the default value case:

```
<xsd:attribute name="version" default="2" type="xsd:string"/>
```

TABLE 6-5 XSD Attribute Occurrence and Default Values

DTD Syntax	*XML Schema Syntax and Description (attributes of* `xsd:attribute` *element)*
`#FIXED` *`fixedValue`*	`fixed="`*`fixedValue`*`"` Indicates a fixed value for the attribute.
`#REQUIRED`	`use="required"` Indicates the attribute is mandatory in an instance document. The instance is invalid if an attribute of this designation is omitted.
`#IMPLIED`	`use="optional"` Signifies the attribute is optional, but *attributes are optional by default,* unless otherwise indicated, so you may omit this.
[not applicable]	`use="prohibited"` This attribute is *not permitted* to appear for the current element.
`"`*`defaultValue`*`"`	`default="`*`defaultValue`*`"` Establishes a default value for the attribute, which instances can override. A default value can be specified in an XML Schema only for optional attributes (i.e., when `use="optional"` or `use` is omitted).

9. Elements can also have default values. However, if an element is *missing* in an instance document, the default is not supplied. Only when the element appears as an *empty* element do element defaults apply.

An example of specifying a fixed value is:

```
<xsd:attribute name="version" fixed="2" type="xsd:string"/>
```

which is like a DTD attribute-list

```
<!ATTLIST someElementName  version CDATA #FIXED '2' >
```

Here's an example illustrating a "required" attribute:

```
<xsd:element name="Published">
  <xsd:complexType>
    <xsd:simpleContent>
      <xsd:extension base="xsd:string">
        <xsd:attribute name="publisher" use="required" type="xsd:string"/>
      </xsd:extension>
    </xsd:simpleContent>
  </xsd:complexType>
</xsd:element>
```

This corresponds to the DTD declarations

```
<!ELEMENT Published  (#PCDATA)>
<!ATTLIST Published  publisher CDATA  #REQUIRED >
```

Finally, here's an example of an "optional" attribute (weeks), as well as one with a default value (country).

```
<xsd:element name="Peak">
  <xsd:complexType>
    <xsd:simpleContent>
      <xsd:extension base="xsd:string">
        <xsd:attribute name="country" default="US" type="xsd:NMTOKEN"/>
        <xsd:attribute name="weeks" use="optional" type="xsd:NMTOKEN"/>
      </xsd:extension>
    </xsd:simpleContent>
  </xsd:complexType>
</xsd:element>
```

The corresponding element and attribute-list declarations are:

```
<!ELEMENT Peak  (#PCDATA)>
<!ATTLIST Peak  country NMTOKEN  'US'
                weeks   NMTOKEN  #IMPLIED >
```

Since attributes are optional by default, however, we can omit the use attribute from the weeks declaration:

```
<xsd:attribute name="weeks" type="xsd:NMTOKEN"/>
```

Remember when we noted that global element declarations cannot use the `maxOccurs` or `minOccurs` attributes? The Schema for Schema make this explicit for a so-called `topLevelElement` using "prohibited":

```
<xs:attribute name="minOccurs" use="prohibited"/>
<xs:attribute name="maxOccurs" use="prohibited"/>
```

Content Model and Model Groups: Introduction

A **model group** is a way of constraining a series of elements in a content model; it consists of a list of particles used to control the content of an `xsd:complexType` definition. A **particle** is a piece of element content: an element declaration, a wildcard (`xsd:any` or `xsd:anyAttribute` elements) or a model group, plus occurrence constraints (`minOccurs` and/or `maxOccurs`). When a particle is used in a complex type definition to constrain the valid children of an element, this is called a **content model**. As with XML 1.0 DTDs, content models can be used to specify a sequence or a choice of child elements. However, XML Schema content models have two major expressive capabilities not found in DTDs:

- It's possible to constrain the model to a set of elements *in any order*.
- They can be used to constrain the order of elements in mixed content (more about this later in the chapter).

In XML Schema, there are three kinds of model groups, that is, three ways to combine elements, `xsd:sequence`, `xsd:choice`, and `xsd:all`, as shown in Table 6-6. Collectively, these three are known as **compositors**. Each supports the `minOccurs` and `maxOccurs` attribute that apply to the whole group. As usual, individual elements in a group may independently specify values for `minOccurs` and `maxOccurs` as well.

TABLE 6-6 Element Model Groups (Compositors): Sequence, Choice, and All

XML Schema Compositor Element	*Description*
`sequence`	Elements must occur exactly in the order indicated and *all* must occur (unless `minOccurs` of individual elements indicates otherwise); `minOccurs` is 0 or more for the sequence group, and `maxOccurs` may be any integer.
`choice`	*Exactly one* of the grouped elements may occur; the elements in the group are mutually exclusive.
`all`	All of the grouped elements may appear, but *in any order*; `minOccurs` is either 0 or 1, and `maxOccurs` must be 1, meaning each element in an `all` group may occur no more than once, or may be omitted; can contain local and top-level element declarations only; cannot contain a `sequence` or `choice` child.

In some earlier examples, we've seen `xsd:sequence` and `xsd:choice`. The element, `xsd:sequence`, corresponds to the comma that separates terms in a DTD content model expression, while the `xsd:choice` equates to the pipe (the vertical bar) symbol in DTDs. We can nest these elements to create more involved content models, analogous to the way we used parenthesized expressions in DTDs. For example:

```
<xsd:element name="Address">
  <xsd:complexType>
    <xsd:sequence>
      <xsd:element ref="Street"/>
      <xsd:element ref="City"/>
      <xsd:choice>
        <xsd:element ref="State"/>
        <xsd:element ref="Province"/>
      </xsd:choice>
      <xsd:element ref="Zip"/>
    </xsd:sequence>
  </xsd:complexType>
</xsd:element>
<xsd:element name="Street" type="xsd:string"/>
<xsd:element name="City" type="xsd:string"/>
```

This corresponds to the DTD element declaration:

```
<!ELEMENT Address (Street, City, (State | Province), Zip)>
```

Both forms portray a choice nested within a sequence. Any number of levels of nesting of choice and sequence are possible, again like nested expressions in DTDs.

The `xsd:all` element is somewhat like the SGML & connector (e.g., `A & B & C` means A, B, and C in any order). Note that the ability to indicate that elements may occur *in any order* is a powerful feature not provided by XML DTDs (although it is with SGML DTDs). This would have helped me on an e-commerce project where we needed to express name/value pairs of elements that could occur in any order, as long as each value element was preceded by a name element.

For an example of `xsd:all`, first consider the content model of the `Book` element from Listing 6-4:

```
<xsd:element name="Book">
  <xsd:complexType>
    <xsd:sequence>
      <xsd:element ref="Title"/>
      <xsd:element ref="Author"/>
      <xsd:element ref="Type"/>
      <xsd:element ref="Published"/>
      <xsd:element ref="Rating" minOccurs="0"/>
      <xsd:element ref="Notes" minOccurs="0"/>
    </xsd:sequence>
  </xsd:complexType>
</xsd:element>
```

This corresponds to the rigid sequential content model

```
<!ELEMENT Book  (Title, Author, Type, Published, Rating?, Notes?) >
```

However, some applications might be unconcerned with the actual order of the data as long as all the required elements are present. If we really didn't care about the order of these elements, we could instead declare the Book with the xsd:all model group:

```
<xsd:element name="Book">
  <xsd:complexType>
    <xsd:all>
      <xsd:element ref="Title"/>
      <xsd:element ref="Author"/>
      <xsd:element ref="Type"/>
      <xsd:element ref="Published"/>
      <xsd:element ref="Rating" minOccurs="0"/>
      <xsd:element ref="Notes" minOccurs="0"/>
    </xsd:all>
  </xsd:complexType>
</xsd:element>
```

This seemingly minor change in the schema has a significant impact on instances since now documents can contain *any* sequence of these child elements, just as if the DTD read (in part):

```
<!ELEMENT Book (
          (Title, Author, Type, Published, Rating?, Notes?) |
          (Author, Type, Published, Rating?, Notes?, Title) |
          (Type, Published, Rating?, Notes?, Title, Author) |
          (Rating?, Notes?, Title, Author, Type, Published) |
          (Rating?, Title, Author, Type, Published, Notes?) |
          (Title, Rating?, Author, Notes?, Type, Published) |
          .... )>
```

Although the name "all" might make you think that every element in the model needs to appear, element occurrence is controlled as usual by minOccurs and maxOccurs, which still both default to 1 in this context. So a valid Book element need not necessarily contain a Rating or Notes element. However, only 0 or 1 occurrences of each element is permissible.

Several restrictions apply to the element xsd:all:

- It must occur as the only immediate child at the *beginning* of a content model.
- The xsd:all model either appears or doesn't in an instance.
- Each part of the xsd:all model must be an *element*, not a nested group (can't have an xsd:sequence or xsd:choice as a child of xsd:all).
- Each xsd:element child can either occur or not occur; no element can occur more than once. In other words, for each child, minOccurs must be 0 or 1; maxOccurs must be 1.

Therefore, if we wanted to allow the possibility of multiple authors and we wanted them to appear before the other Book children, we could *not* use xsd:all in the manner shown in this invalid example (since xsd:all is not the top of the content model):

```
<xsd:element name="Book">
  <xsd:complexType>
   <xsd:sequence>
    <xsd:element ref="Author" maxOccurs="20" />
    <xsd:all>          <!-- invalid -->
      <xsd:element ref="Title"/>
      <xsd:element ref="Type"/>
      <xsd:element ref="Published"/>
      <xsd:element ref="Rating" minOccurs="0"/>
      <xsd:element ref="Notes" minOccurs="0"/>
    </xsd:all>
   </xsd:sequence>
  </xsd:complexType>
</xsd:element>
```

Later in the chapter, we'll cover xsd:group, xsd:attributeGroup, xsd:any, and mixed content models.

Creating and Using Datatypes

Just as element and attribute declarations are primary schema components, so too are simple and complex type definitions, the two type definition schema components. The fact that W3C devotes a whole separate document to datatypes gives you a good idea of their importance to XML Schema. Understanding datatypes is therefore key to appreciating XML Schema and using this technology effectively.

Two of the most important features of XML Schema are the large number of built-in datatypes (44 to be precise) and the ability to easily create new types based on those provided by the W3C. Built-in types include all of the numeric datatypes provided by popular computer languages (integer, float, double, boolean, byte, long, short, etc.), plus many variations of the string datatype (including the types such as ID and NMTOKEN from XML DTDs), as well as a wide variety of date/time types perhaps more familiar to database developers and scientific programmers. Creating a datatype based on those provided can take as little as a half dozen lines of code (i.e., a simpleType definition). Additional types can also be derived from the ones you define, either by further restricting the values that are legal or by creating complexType definitions that include elements and attributes that use the new types. It's also possible to limit the ways in which a user of your schema can extend it, if you wish. Furthermore, datatypes are analogous to object classes in object-oriented languages in that they can be exchanged as structured description between applications, whether they are simpleType or complexType (e.g., dateTime or Address, respectively).

In this long section, a considerable amount of terminology is introduced. Examples follow later in the chapter, where many of the terms are elaborated. A running example describes a dozen alternatives for defining a temperature datatype (`temperature.xsd`). This example is not intended to be a complete schema, but rather a number of different ways to devise a datatype, given the needs of your application. Additional examples not related to the running example are introduced as necessary. Many of these are based on the running collection example.

Definition of Datatype

Let's briefly cover a few terms that are used in the formal definition of the term *datatype*. In the XML Schema Part 2: Datatypes specification, a **datatype** is formally defined as a 3-tuple, consisting of

- A set of distinct values, called its **value space**; values can be primitive (built-in), enumerated, derived by restricting the values of an existing type, or the result of a `list` or `union` of values (e.g., the value space of a datatype called `positiveInteger` is the set of integers greater than zero)
- A set of lexical representations, called its **lexical space**; different literals can represent the same numeric or character values (e.g., 6333 and 6.333E3 are the same value; ` ` and ` ` are both the same value, namely the space character)
- A set of **facets** that characterize or constrain properties of the datatype (e.g., `pattern`, `enumeration`, `minInclusive`, `maxLength`, etc.)

Of the terms discussed in this section, the one we'll encounter most frequently is *facets*. The specification distinguishes between fundamental facets and constraining facets (also called nonfundamental facets). A **fundamental facet** is an abstract property of a datatype that helps to describe its legal values; these facets are equal, ordered, bounded, cardinality, and numeric. In contrast, a **constraining facet** is an *optional* constraint that can be applied to a datatype to restrict its values, such as to a range or set of values, to match a particular pattern, to be of a certain length, and so on. Facets can be used to restrict the acceptable content of an element or to constrain the legal values of an attribute. We'll cover the twelve constraining facets in detail later in this section.

Object-Oriented Analogy: A Brief Detour

If you are familiar with object-oriented programming, think of an XML Schema datatype as an abstraction—a class definition of an element or an attribute, or an element containing attributes. The abstract class is referenced by the datatype name, which is the handle by which you refer to elements or attributes, just like a class name is the handle for referencing an object. For example, when we want to reference the built-in type `xsd:date`, we specify the name in the `type` attribute of a declaration such as:

```
<xsd:element name="OrderDate" type="xsd:date" />
```

The `xsd:date` handle maps to the built-in type definition defined in *http://www.w3.org/TR/xmlschema-2/#date* and in the Schema for Schemas as the `simpleType name="date"`. This class (datatype) is characterized by a particular set of facets (`pattern`, `enumeration`, `totalDigits`, `maxInclusive`, `maxExclusive`, `minInclusive`, `minExclusive`, etc.) and has certain properties (it is partially ordered, is unbounded, is countably infinite in cardinality, and is not fundamentally numeric, even though it consists of numeric pieces). It's defined as a restriction of the generic base type `xsd:anySimpleType`; that is, `xsd:date` is a subclass of the base class `xsd:anySimpleType`. An instance of the `xsd:date` class is 2001-10-20, representing October 20, 2001:

```
<OrderDate>2001-10-20</OrderDate>
```

Similarly, we can use the same `xsd:date` class in an *attribute* declaration

```
<xsd:attribute name="manufactured" type="xsd:date" />
```

An instance of this declaration might be

```
<AVComponent make="Panasonic" model="DVDRP91K"
             manufactured="2002-03-22" />
```

Just as we can reuse `simpleType` classes, we can create `complexType` definitions that can be referenced by name and therefore reused without change, or extended, or restricted. For example, consider the definition

```
<xsd:complexType name="CDType">
  <xsd:sequence>
    <xsd:element ref="Title"/>
    <xsd:element ref="Artist"/>
    <xsd:element ref="Chart"/>
    <xsd:element ref="Type"/>
    <xsd:element ref="Label" maxOccurs="unbounded"/>
    <xsd:element ref="AlbumReleased"/>
    <xsd:element ref="Remastered" maxOccurs="unbounded"/>
  </xsd:sequence>
</xsd:complexType>
```

Ignoring the actual definitions of the elements such as `Title` and `Artist` which aren't shown, we can see that the `complexType` named `CDType` has a particular structural description (a sequence of seven elements). This class definition is readily reusable, as was the `simpleType`. We need only declare an element and use the type name as the handle:

```
<xsd:element  name="CD"  type="CDType" />
```

Types represent class information and the element declarations use the types. We'll see later in the chapter how to create new types from this base type that are either extensions or restrictions of the base. These derivation techniques are fundamental to reuse in XML Schema.

Simple Types, Complex Types, Simple Content, Complex Content, and Derivation

In this section, we introduce the key concepts of the type hierachy and derivation mechanisms of XML Schema. The examples that follow in later sections expand on these concepts.

The root of the datatype hierachy is `xsd:anyType`, which is generic. It doesn't constrain content in any way, so an element of `type="xsd:anyType"` can be numeric or string, can contain child elements, can be a list of values, can consist of anything at all. When you declare an element and do not specify a datatype via the `type` attribute, `xsd:anyType` is implied since it is the default type.

When you develop an XML Schema, you will undoubtedly use many of the built-in simple types that are referenced by their type name (e.g., `type="xsd:dateTime"`—see the section on "Built-in Datatypes.") You'll often need to create your own datatypes by restricting built-in ones using `xsd:simpleType` and using facets (e.g., `xsd:pattern` or `xsd:maxInclusive`) to constrain the set of legal values (see the section "Derivation by Constraining a Simple Type with Facets"). You will also frequently create complex types, none of which are defined in XML Schema. The key difference is that **simple types** can *only contain character data* (numbers, strings, dates, etc.); they cannot have either element children or attributes. If you need a type that contains subelements (children) and/or attributes, you must create a **complex type** using the `xsd:complexType` element. We've seen these in use in earlier examples, but we'll introduce more complete examples shortly.

Another way of looking at types is to consider them as forming a hierarchy with the most fundamental types at the top and the more specialized (constrained) types lower in the hierarchy. A **restriction** is a subset that narrows the value range or limits the choices. An **extension** allows extra elements or attribute content in addition to those in the type on which the extension is based. The type definition on which a restriction or extension is based is called the **base type**. Any instance of a type that is a member of a restriction is also a member of the base type. For example, the built-in type `xsd:unsignedLong` is a restriction of a `xsd:nonNegativeInteger`, which in turn is a restriction of an `xsd:integer`. The number 123456789 is a valid example of `xsd:unsignedLong`, and is therefore also acceptable as a value of the datatypes `xsd:nonNegativeInteger` or `xsd:integer`. In other words, the base type of `xsd:unsignedLong` is `xsd:nonNegativeInteger`, while the base type of `xsd:nonNegativeInteger` is `xsd:integer`. In terms of a hierarchy, `xsd:integer` can be considered as the parent of `xsd:nonNegativeInteger`, which is the parent of `xsd:unsignedLong`.

A **derived** datatype is defined in terms of other datatypes whereas **primitive** datatype are not; they're based directly on the generic `xsd:anySimpleType`. All of the types in the previous paragraph are derived directly (in the case of `xsd:integer`) or indirectly from `xsd:decimal`, which is a primitive. **Derivation** is the process of creating a new type from a base type, regardless of whether the base is itself derived or primitive; the base may even be a complex type (with children and/or attributes). There are four kinds of derivation defined in XML Schema, as described in Table 6-7. Most of the examples in this chapter are of restriction and extension; they are the most common derivation methods.

In addition to `xsd:simpleType` and `xsd:complexType`, the `xsd:simpleContent` and `xsd:complexContent` elements are fundamental to type derivation. The four terms are described in Table 6-8. Examples are provided throughout the chapter.

From Tables 6-7 and 6-8, we can draw several very important conclusions, shown in Table 6-9. Let's call these *Rules for Type Derivation*, which we'll refer to by number later. Donald Smith's excellent article for XML.com, "Understanding W3C Schema Complex Types," provides additional insight into these distinctions, as well as a useful "Schema Type Syntax Decision Tree." His article should be considered required reading for anyone interested in XML Schema (see *http://www.xml.com/pub/a/2001/08/22/easyschema.html*).

TABLE 6-7 Kinds of Derivation

Derivation Method	*Description*
`restriction`	New type is a subset of the original; the restricted type has either a more narrow range of acceptable values or a more limited set of choices. Restriction is the basis for 41 of the 44 built-in types. Facets are usually involved in restriction of `simpleType` and `simpleContent` elements. New datatypes are created by restricting the facets of a base type. For example, the `maxLength` facet can be used to limit the number of characters of a type derived by restriction from `xsd:string`.
`extension`	New type has additional elements and/or attribute content (which may or may not be constrained by restriction) beyond what is accepted by the base type. The additional elements must follow the elements of the base type in an instance. (Appending is the only form of extension permitted by XML Schema at this time.)
`list`	New type is a white space–separated list of tokens (each of which should not contain spaces); applies only to `simpleType`.
`union`	New type is the combined set of all legal values of each of the types that comprise the union; applies only to `simpleType`.

TABLE 6-8 simpleType, complexType, simpleContent, complexContent

Term	*Description*
`simpleType`	Defines element type that contains *only character data; no children and no attributes* are permitted; analogous to `#PCDATA`. Also used to define the datatype of an *attribute*, analogous to `CDATA`; used within `xsd:attribute` to constrain the value of a built-in type and thereby restrict the value of the attribute. Derived by `restriction`, `list`, or `union`. Typically contains facets since derivation by restriction is most common.
`complexType`	Defines element type that contains *child elements and/or attributes*. A `complexType` definition often consists of element declarations, element references, and/or attribute declarations. Extending a `complexType` is accomplished by adding content model particles at the end of the base type's content model, or by adding attribute declarations, or both. A mixed content model can be defined by setting the optional `mixed` attribute to true. Derived by `extension` or `restriction`.
`simpleContent`	Defines a content model that contains *only character data*, optionally attributes, but *no element children*. Derived by `extension` or `restriction`.
`complexContent`	Defines a content model that may contain *character data, element children*, and optionally attributes. Derived by `extension` or `restriction`. *Note:* `complexContent` is the default case for `complexType`, so this element is often omitted. Also restriction is the default derivation method in this case, so the `restriction` element may be omitted. When these defaults are omitted, it is called the *abbreviated* (or *shorthand* or *compact*) *form* of the type definition.

TABLE 6-9 Rules for Type Derivation

Rule 1	If you're creating a type that simply constrains the *value of an attribute*, `simpleType` will suffice.
Rule 2	If you need to constrain the *character content of an element that has no attributes*, you can also use `simpleType`.
Rule 3	If your new type *adds attributes* to the base type, you must use `complexType` (because `simpleType`s are not permitted to have attributes).
Rule 4	If the content model requires only character data and attributes (but no children), use `complexType` with `simpleContent`.
Rule 5	If, however, the content model of the new type requires *children elements* (and optionally attributes), you must use `complexType` with `complexContent`.
Rule 6	Derivation of a `simpleType` by `restriction` involves *facets*.
Rule 7	Derivation by `list` or `union` can be used only if the base type is `simpleType`, so elements that comprise these types cannot contain children or attributes.
Rule 8	Of the four derivation methods, only `restriction`, `list`, and `union` apply to `simpleType` definitions.
Rule 9	In contrast, `extension` as well as `restriction` apply to `complexType`, `complexContent`, and `simpleContent`. However, `list` and `union` do not.

Built-in Datatypes

The forty-four datatypes built in to XML Schema are shown in Table 6-10 and are presented formally in the W3C XML Schema Part 2: Datatypes specification. They're listed here grouped into four categories: XML DTD types, other string types, numeric types, and date/time types. You can quickly access the complete details about each built-in datatype (including the facets that apply) by using the type name exactly as it appears in the table as a fragment identifier that is appended to the URL of Part 2 of the specification. For example, to see the formal description of the `short` datatype, use the URL: *http://www.w3.org/TR/xmlschema-2/#short*. To access details about the `dateTime` datatype, use *http://www.w3.org/TR/xmlschema-2/#dateTime*.

Note: Datatypes with XML DTD type names (`ID`, `NMTOKEN`, etc.) should be used only as types for *attribute* declarations (to be compatible with XML 1.0).

TABLE 6-10 Built-in Datatypes

Datatype[a]	*Description and/or Examples*
XML DTD Types[b]	
`ID`	Must be unique within document; used only with attributes; for example, `section27`
`IDREF`	Matches a unique `ID` attribute; used only with attributes; for example, `section27`
`IDREFS`	Space-separated list of `IDREF`s; used only with attributes
`ENTITY`	Unparsed entity as per XML 1.0 Recommendation, with an associated `NOTATION`; used only with attributes; scope is only a specific instance document
`ENTITIES`	Space-separated list of `ENTITY` objects; used only with attributes; derived by `list`
`NMTOKEN`	Any combination of XML Name character (letters, digits, hyphens, underscores, colons, or full stops [periods]); used only with attributes; for example `table.cell`, `book-title`, `ChapterName`, `MySchema:BookTitle`
`NMTOKENS`	Space-separated list of `NMTOKEN`s; used only with attributes; derived by `list`
`NOTATION`	Corresponds to a notation attribute, declared in the DTD with associated system and/or public identifiers, used in interpreting the element to which the attribute is attached, usually for binary data such as an image; used only with attributes

TABLE 6-10 *(continued)*

Datatype[a]	*Description and/or Examples*
Other String Types	
`string`	Comparable to `CDATA` in DTDs, except *not* restricted to use only with attributes; "XML Family of Specifications: A Practical Guide", "Beatles", "John, Paul, George and Ringo"; may optionally contain any amount of white space (tabs, space, multiple spaces, carriage return, linefeed); defined with facet `<xsd:whiteSpace value="preserve"/>`
`normalizedString`	Specialization of `string` that collapses white space sequences; strings that don't contain the carriage return (`#xD`), linefeed (`#xA`), or tab (`#x9`) characters; defined with facet `<xsd:whiteSpace value="replace"/>`
`token`	Another specialization of `string`; does not contain linefeed (`#xA`) or tab (`#x9`) characters, has no leading or trailing spaces (`#x20`), and has no sequences of multiple spaces; defined with facet `<xsd:whiteSpace value="collapse"/>`.
`Name`	An XML 1.0 `Name`[c]; base type for `NCName` from the XML 1.0 Recommendation; may optionally contain a colon; for example, `BookTitle`, `MySchema:BookTitle`, `Author`, `price`, `xlink:actuate`, `xsd:complexType`
`NCName`	"Non-colonized" name from the XML Namespace Recommendation; element name *without* namespace prefix; also called "local name"; for example, `BookTitle`, `Author`, `price`
`QName`	Element name usually *with* namespace prefix, unless a default namespace declaration is in scope as per XML Namespace Recommendation; also called "qualified name"; for example, `MySchema:BookTitle`, `xlink:actuate`, `xsd:complexType`
`language`	Natural language identifiers as discussed in the XML 1.0 Second Edition recommendation and defined by RFC 1766 (*http://www.ietf.org/rfc/rfc1766.txt*); for example, `en`, `en-US`, `en-GB`, `fr`, `de`, `da`, `el`, `it`
`anyURI`	An absolute or relative URI, often a URL, possibly with a fragment identifier, such as *http://www.awlonline.com/*, *http://www.awl.com/cseng/*, *http://www.w3.org/TR/xmlschema-2/#built-in-datatypes*, or . . . */Schemas/default.asp*; defined with facet `<xsd:whiteSpace value="collapse"/>`
Numeric Datatypes	
`boolean`	True, false, 1, 0 (true is equivalent to 1)
`float`	IEEE single-precision 32-bit floating point number; for example, 98.6, –17E5, 45.67E2, 1.8e-3, 107, 1267.43233E12, INF, NaN; defined with facet `<xsd:whiteSpace value="collapse"/>`
`double`	IEEE double-precision 64-bit floating point number; for example, 1.5E-85, –17E5, 45.67E2, 1.8e-3, 107, INF, NaN
`decimal`	Base type for all integer types; arbitrary precision decimal number; minimally conforming processors must support at least 18 digits; scientific notation (`E` for exponent) not allowed; for example, –1.17, 67.233, +99.00, 99, 12678967.543233

continued

TABLE 6-10 Built-in Datatypes (*continued*)

Datatype[a]	*Description and/or Examples*
`integer`	Normal notion of an integer; the set of numbers {..., –2, –1, 0, 1, 2, ...}; derived from `decimal` datatype by fixing the value of the `fractionDigits` facet to be 0; for example, 47; 123456789
`nonNegativeInteger`	Includes 0 and all integers greater than 0; {0, 1, 2, ...}
`positiveInteger`	Integer greater than 0; {1, 2, ...}
`negativeInteger`	Integer less than 0; {..., –2, –1}
`nonPositiveInteger`	Includes 0 and all integers less than 0; {..., –2, –1, 0}
`byte`	One-byte integer in the range –128 to 127
`short`	Two-byte integer in the range –32768 to 32767
`int`	Four-byte integer in the range –2147483648 to 2147483647
`long`	Eight-byte integer in the range –9223372036854775808 to 9223372036854775807
`unsignedByte`	One-byte unsigned integer in the range 0 to 255
`unsignedShort`	Two-byte unsigned integer in the range 0 to 65535
`unsignedInt`	Four-byte unsigned integer in the range 0 to 4294967295
`unsignedLong`	Eight-byte unsigned integer in the range 0 to 18446744073709551615
`base64Binary`	Encodes every 3 bytes as 4 bytes, selecting from 64 possible ASCII characters (plus "=" for a special processing function); used by XML Digital Signatures specification; see RFC 2045 (*http://www.ietf.org/rfc/rfc2045.txt*); for example, GpM7
`hexBinary`	Each byte is encoded as 0–9 or A–F (or a–f); each binary octet is represented by two hexidecimal characters; for example, `0FB7` (= 16-bit integer 4023 = 111110110111 binary)
Date/Time Datatypes	
`duration`	Duration of time of arbitrary length, given in the order: Gregorian year, month, day, hour, minute, and second, using the ISO 8601 Date and Time Formats[d] of `PnYnMnDTnHnMnS`, with mandatory leading `P` and date/time separator `T`, and an optional minus sign before the `P` to indicate a negative duration; seconds may have any decimal fraction (for example, 75.126S); `T` may be omitted if there is no time component; for example, `P2Y4M7DT10H30M17.5S` = 2 years, 4 months, 7 days, 10 hours, 30 minutes, 17.5 seconds; -P8D = negative 8 days
`date`	Specific date in a given year, using the format `CCYY-MM-DD`, where `CC` is century (00–99), `YY` is year (00–99), `MM` is month (01–12) and `DD` is day (01–31, the upper limit dependent on the value of `MM`); note that the order of components is *year/month/date* for all related datatypes; for example, `2000-07-15` = July 15th, 2000

TABLE 6-10 *(continued)*

Datatype[a]	*Description and/or Examples*
`time`	Specific time of day that recurs every day, using the format `hh:mm:ss.sss`, where `hh` is hour (00–23), `mm` is minute (00–59), and `ss` is second (00–59, with optional fractional part); an optional time zone indicator in the format `-hh:00` may follow the seconds, to indicate number of hours from Coordinated Universal Time (UTC); for example, `15:07:00` = 3:07 pm; `06:41:14.25-08:00` = 14.25 seconds past 6:41 am, Pacific Standard Time, 8 hours behind UTC
`dateTime`	Specific nonrecurring instant in time, in ISO 8601 format `CCYY-MM-DDThh:mm:ss.sss`, where `T` is a date/time separator, `CC` is century, `YY` is year, `MM` is month and `DD` is day, `hh` is hour, `mm` is minute, and `ss` is second; optionally with a leading minus sign to indicate a negative number; for example, `2001-09-22T15:07:00-05:00` = 3:07 pm on September 22, 2001, Eastern Standard Time which is 5 hours behind Coordinated Universal Time
`gYear`	Particular year in `CCYY` format; for example, 1964
`gMonth`	Gregorian month that recurs every year, using the format `--MM`; for example, `--02` = February
`gYearMonth`	Specific Gregorian month in a specific Gregorian year, using the format `CCYY-MM`; for example, `1951-02` = February 1951 (*Note:* must include year)
`gDay`	Specific recurring day of the month (wildcards such as * are not permitted), in the format `---DD`; for example, `---01`=1st of the month; `---15`=15th of the month
`gMonthDay`	Recurring day of the year, in the format `--MM-DD`; for example, `--02-27` = February 27th of each year

a. All datatypes are listed here without the conventional `xsd:` prefix (e.g., `xsd:string` is shown as simply `string`).

b. Enumeration is accomplished using the `enumeration` facet, rather than being an explicit datatype.

c. Recall that an XML Name begins with a letter or underscore or colon and continues with letters, digits, hyphens, underscores, colons, or full stops (periods), known as **name characters**.

d. See *http://www.w3.org/TR/xmlschema-2/#isoformats* or *http://www.iso.ch/iso/pages/CatalogueDetailPage.CatalogueDetail?CSNUMBER=26780*

There's a very useful diagram (*http://www.w3.org/TR/xmlschema-2/#built-in-datatypes*) in Part 2 of the spec that illustrates the built-in type hierarchy, showing which types are derived from which base types. The root of the class hierarchy is `anyType`, which is also the default type if an element is declared without an explicit `type` attribute. As mentioned earlier, `anyType` is completely generic; it doesn't constrain data in any way. All `complexType`s and all `simpleType`s (that is, all possible types that are either built-in or created by developers) are derived indirectly from `anyType`. All forty-four of the built-in types are derived from `anySimpleType`. All but three of the forty-four are derived by restriction. (The three exceptions are derived by `list`: `NMTOKENS`, `ENTITIES`, and `IDREFS`. Each is the plural form of the obvious base type.) In the Datatypes specification, the built-in datatypes are divided into these two groups: *primitive* and *derived*. Nineteen of the built-ins are primitive types, meaning they are derived directly from `anySimpleType`. Examples of primitives are `dateTime`, `float`, `decimal`, and `string`. The remaining built-in types, called derived, are based on either the primitive `string` (i.e., all XML DTD types and a few more) or `decimal` (i.e., all integer types).

One simple way to benefit from these built-in datatypes is to reexamine our `AddressType` definition, which defined `Zip` as a `string`. We can modify this slightly to use the much more relevant `positiveInteger` datatype.

```
<xsd:element name="Zip" type="xsd:positiveInteger"/>
```

We'll soon see how to constrain the value much further using facets.

Similarly, we can take advantage of types to constrain the character data of an element that contains attributes. In our definition of `Published` element (Listing 6-4), any string was acceptable because of the definition:

```
<xsd:element name="Published">
  <xsd:complexType>
    <xsd:simpleContent>
      <xsd:extension base="xsd:string">
        <xsd:attribute name="publisher" use="required" type="xsd:string"/>
      </xsd:extension>
    </xsd:simpleContent>
  </xsd:complexType>
</xsd:element>
```

This supported instances such as:

```
<Published publisher="Harmony Books">1992</Published>
```

It unfortunately also supports instances such as:

```
<Published publisher="Harmony Books">Not a very good year, eh?</Published>
```

Obviously, what we really had in mind was a *year*, so let's use the built-in type called `gYear` (Gregorian year), which we see from Table 6-10 is in the 4-digit format `CCYY`. (We could specify `date` with a format of `CCYY-MM-DD`, but perhaps we don't know the exact date of publication.) We need change only the base type:

```
      <xsd:extension base="xsd:gYear">
```

The acceptable content for a `Published` element is now a 4-digit number (e.g., 2002). This is an example of Rule 4: *If the content model requires only character data and attributes (but no children), use complexType with simpleContent.*

Although directly using one of the many built-in types is sufficient for some element definitions, you'll often find the need to refine a datatype using facets.

Derivation by Constraining a Simple Type with Facets

For example, suppose we wanted to restrict `Published` to a year between 1900 and 2010. We would need facets to derive a restricted dataype. XSD defines twelve **constraining facets**—properties that can be used to constrain the legal values that can be used for an element's character data content or for an attribute value. The complete list of constraining facets is shown in Table 6-11 along with a brief description

TABLE 6-11 Constraining Facets and Representative Datatypes

Facet	*Description*	*Built-in Datatypes That Support This Facet (illustrative, not all inclusive)*
`length`	Exact number of units required in element content or attribute value; units are typically characters, but is datatype dependent	`string`, `normalizedString`, `anyURI`, `hexBinary`, `NMTOKEN`, `ID`, `ENTITY`, `QName`
`minLength`	Minimum number of units (typically characters)	`string`, `normalizedString`, `anyURI`, `hexBinary`, `NMTOKEN`, `ID`, `ENTITY`, `QName`
`maxLength`	Maximum number of units (typically characters)	`string`, `normalizedString`, `anyURI`, `hexBinary`, `NMTOKEN`, `ID`, `ENTITY`, `QName`
`pattern`	A regular expression defines what kind of content matches (i.e., is valid); multiple `pattern` facets can be used for one `simpleType` definition	`string`, `normalizedString`, `anyURI`, `hexBinary`, `NMTOKEN`, `ID`, `ENTITY`, `QName`, `byte`, `integer`, `float`, `double`, `long`, `unsignedLong`, `dateTime`, `duration`, `date`, `time`, `gYearMonth`
`enumeration`	Multiple `enumeration` facets are used for one `simpleType` definition; each enumeration element defines a single possible legal value; order of these elements does not impose additional constraints	`string`, `normalizedString`, `anyURI`, `hexBinary`, `NMTOKEN`, `ID`, `ENTITY`, `QName`, `byte`, `integer`, `float`, `double`, `long`, `unsignedLong`, `dateTime`, `duration`, `date`, `time`, `gYearMonth`
`whiteSpace`	Constrains how white space is handled; three options: `preserve`—no normalization (value is unchanged); `replace`—tab, linefeed, and return and replaced by a single space; `collapse`—in addition to replacing tab, linefeed, and return by a single space, leading and trailing spaces are stripped and contiguous sequences of spaces collapse to a single space	`string`, `normalizedString`, `anyURI`, `hexBinary`, `NMTOKEN`, `ID`, `ENTITY`, `QName`, `byte`, `integer`, `float`, `double`, `long`, `unsignedLong`, `dateTime`, `duration`, `date`, `time`, `gYearMonth`
`minInclusive`	Lower bound of a range of numeric or date/time values, including the endpoint	`byte`, `short`, `integer`, `float`, `double`, `long`, `unsignedLong`, `dateTime`, `duration`, `date`, `time`, `gYearMonth`

continued

TABLE 6-11 Constraining Facets and Representative Datatypes (*continued*)

Facet	*Description*	*Built-in Datatypes That Support This Facet (illustrative, not all inclusive)*
`maxInclusive`	Upper bound of a range of numeric or date/time values, including the endpoint	`byte`, `short`, `integer`, `float`, `double`, `long`, `unsignedLong`, `dateTime`, `duration`, `date`, `time`, `gYearMonth`
`minExclusive`	Lower bound of a range of numeric or date/time values, excluding the endpoint	`byte`, `short`, `integer`, `float`, `double`, `long`, `unsignedLong`, `dateTime`, `duration`, `date`, `time`, `gYearMonth`
`maxExclusive`	Upper bound of a range of numeric or date/time values, excluding the endpoint	`byte`, `short`, `integer`, `float`, `double`, `long`, `unsignedLong`, `dateTime`, `duration`, `date`, `time`, `gYearMonth`
`totalDigits`	Maximum number of digits of a value derived from `decimal` type	`byte`, `short`, `integer`, `long`, `unsignedLong`, `float`
`fractionDigits`	Maximum number of digits in the fractional part of a value derived from `decimal` type	`byte`, `short`, `integer`, `long`, `unsignedLong`, `float`

and representative datatypes that support each facet. (For a complete list of datatypes and their corresponding facets, see the tables that are in Appendix B of the W3C XML Schema Primer, *http://www.w3.org/TR/xmlschema-0/#SimpleType-Facets*.) These facets are described in Part 2 of the spec—see *http://www.w3.org/TR/xmlschema-2/#rf-facets*. To locate the explanation of a particular facet, append the fragment identifer `rf-FacetName` to the spec. For example, to learn more about `totalDigits`, use the URL *http://www.w3.org/TR/xmlschema-2/#rf-totalDigits*.

A facet is a name/value pair; you identify the facet you're using and assign its value via the `value` attribute. The general syntax for using facets to constrain values is to list them as (unordered) children in a `simpleType` definition, which uses the restriction method of derivation and specifies the base type:

```
<xsd:simpleType name="yourNewTypeName" >
  <xsd:restriction base="builtinTypeName_or_userDefinedSimpleType">
    <facet1 value="Value1" />
    <facet2 value="Value2" />
    <facet3 value="Value3" />
    <!-- etc. -->
  </xsd:restriction>
</xsd:simpleType>
```

Derivation of a simple type by restriction always involves this hierarchy: `xsd:simpleType` contains one `xsd:restriction`, and one or more facet children are contained within `xsd:restriction`. The examples in this section illustrate Rule 6: *Derivation of a simpleType by restriction involves facets.*

For example, by using the minLength and maxLength facets, we can define a type called string5to10 that limits a string to from 5 to 10 characters using the element declaration and type definition:[10]

```
<xsd:element name="String5to10" type="string5to10" />
<xsd:simpleType name="string5to10" >
  <xsd:restriction base="xsd:string" >
    <xsd:minLength value="5" />
    <xsd:maxLength value="10" />
  </xsd:restriction>
</xsd:simpleType>
```

A valid instance of this type is:

```
<String5to10>123456789</String5to10>
```

Similarly, we can constrain a price to the range of $0.01 to $9999.99 by means of the minInclusive and maxInclusive facets with the type definition:

```
<xsd:element name="Price1" type="PriceType1" />
<xsd:simpleType name="PriceType1" >
  <xsd:restriction base="xsd:float" >
    <xsd:minInclusive value="0.01" />
    <xsd:maxInclusive value="9999.99" />
  </xsd:restriction>
</xsd:simpleType>
```

A valid instance of this type is:

```
<Price1>123.33</Price1>
```

Another valid instance is:

```
<Price1>123.33333</Price1>
```

If we need to ensure that the fractional part of the price is at most two digits, we can either add a third facet called fractionDigits to the PriceType1 definition *or* we can create yet another type based on PriceType1 (rather than xsd:float) to enforce this constraint:

```
<xsd:element name="Price2" type="PriceType2" />
<xsd:simpleType name="PriceType2" >
  <xsd:restriction base="PriceType1" >
    <xsd:fractionDigits value="2" />
    </xsd:restriction>
</xsd:simpleType>
```

Notice that if the base type is not one of the built-in XSD types, we do not include the xsd: prefix. For example, we have base="PriceType1".

10. Most of the facets examples are contained in the file facets.xsd and facets.xml on the CD.

The next type definition uses the `length` facet to constrain strings to be exactly twenty characters:

```
<xsd:simpleType name="string20" >
  <xsd:restriction base="xsd:string" >
    <xsd:length value="20" />
  </xsd:restriction>
</xsd:simpleType>
```

We've seen the `enumeration` facet in earlier examples. Here's another example that constrains the content of the element `Enum1` to one of five broadcasting companies:

```
<xsd:element name="Enum1" type="enum1" />
<xsd:simpleType name="enum1" >
  <xsd:restriction base="xsd:string" >
    <xsd:enumeration value="UPN" />
    <xsd:enumeration value="FOX" />
    <xsd:enumeration value="ABC" />
    <xsd:enumeration value="NBC" />
    <xsd:enumeration value="CBS" />
   </xsd:restriction>
</xsd:simpleType>
```

Although `minInclusive` and `maxInclusive` include the endpoints of a range, `minExclusive` and `maxExclusive` do not, so this definition permits values from 2 to 998:

```
<xsd:simpleType name="exclusives1" >
  <xsd:restriction base="xsd:integer" >
    <xsd:minExclusive value="1" />
    <xsd:maxExclusive value="999" />
  </xsd:restriction>
</xsd:simpleType>
```

In addition to specifying the number of fractional digits, we can constrain the maximum total digits with the `totalDigits` facet.

```
<xsd:element name="Digits1" type="digits1" />
<xsd:simpleType name="digits1" >
  <xsd:restriction base="xsd:float" >
    <xsd:totalDigits value="8" />
    <xsd:fractionDigits value="3" />
  </xsd:restriction>
</xsd:simpleType>
```

Both of these facets define maximums, so the first two instances are valid but the third is not:

```
<Digits1>12345.007</Digits1>
<Digits1>3.14</Digits1>
<Digits1>44444412345.007</Digits1>  <!-- invalid -->
```

Of the twelve facets, six apply only to ordered types, such as the numeric and date/time-oriented types. These more specialized facets are `maxInclusive`, `maxExclusive`, `minInclusive`, `minExclusive`, `totalDigits`, and `fractionDigits`.

The only facets that may appear more than once in a particular `simpleType` definition are `pattern` and `enumeration`. All others are strictly one occurrence at most. However, each `simpleType` may contain several different facets, as we've seen. For example, one definition might use `minLength`, `maxLength`, and `pattern`. Expression syntax for the `pattern` facet is covered in the next subsection, but for now, here's a brief example:

```
<xsd:element name="Pattern1" type="pattern1" />
<xsd:simpleType name="pattern1" >
  <xsd:restriction base="xsd:string" >
    <xsd:pattern value="[A-Z]+" />
    <xsd:pattern value="[a-z]+" />
  </xsd:restriction>
</xsd:simpleType>
```

This definition constrains strings to *either* of two patterns. The first pattern describes a string of one or more uppercase letters, and the second applies to a run of lowercase letters. However, the instance

```
<Pattern1>QWERTYasdfg</Pattern1>
```

is not valid because the two patterns are ORed together; the string must be either uppercase or lowercase, *not* a mixture.

The one facet that really has nothing to do with validation is `whiteSpace`. Its value is limited to `preserve`, `replace`, or `collapse`, as described in Table 6-11. This facet simply informs the application how to treat white space in element content. An example of the `whiteSpace` facet is:

```
<xsd:simpleType name="whitespace1" >
  <xsd:restriction base="xsd:string" >
    <xsd:whiteSpace value="collapse" />
  </xsd:restriction>
</xsd:simpleType>
```

As you can imagine, specifying facets, or more generally derivation of simple types by restriction, is an *extremely* powerful capability, especially compared to the limited expressiveness of DTDs using `#PCDATA` for elements or `CDATA` , `NMTOKEN`, and so on for attributes. With XML Schema, it's very easy to constrain any type of number to a range (for example), and thereby guarantee automatic validation of instances of the element content or attribute value with no need for application-specific code.

Before we examine the pattern facet in more detail, let's introduce the temperature example (`temperature.xsd` and `temperature.xml`), which we'll keep coming back to in later sections. The idea behind this example is to consider a variety of ways to define a datatype with or without attributes, sometimes constraining the element content, sometimes restricting attribute values, sometimes constraining both element content and attribute value, and sometimes including child elements. At this point, we'll consider only the basics. The initial case is just to use an unconstrained built-in type to define the element. We do this simply in one line:

```
<!-- Case 0: Unconstrained character content -->
<xsd:element name="Temperature0" type="xsd:string" />
```

This supports instances such as:

```
<Temperature0>98.6</Temperature0>
```

It also supports slightly less precise data:

```
<Temperature0>How hot is it? We're having a heat wave.</Temperature0>
```

We have learned that we can improve on this considerably just by using a simple type with restriction and facets, perhaps to constrain the value to be a float between 50.0 and 110.0. This is an example of Rule 2: *If you need to constrain the character content of an element that has no attributes, you can also use simpleType.*

```
<!-- Case 1: Constrained float content (valid range) -->
<xsd:element name="Temperature1" type="TemperatureType1" />

<xsd:simpleType name="TemperatureType1">
  <xsd:restriction base="xsd:float">
    <xsd:minInclusive value="50.0" />
    <xsd:maxInclusive value="110.0" />
  </xsd:restriction>
</xsd:simpleType>
```

What we *haven't* learned is where to factor in attributes here; it would be very useful to designate the temperature scale as an attribute. Of course, once we can specify attributes, we'll want to know how to constrain them also. Stay tuned.

Here's the actual definition of the `short` datatype from the W3C datatypes spec (see Appendix A: Schema for Datatype Definitions (normative) at *http://www.w3.org/TR/xmlschema-2/#schema*). It indicates that `short` is derived from `int` (a subclass of `integer`) and is constrained to the values –32768 to 32767, inclusive. (This example uses `xs:` rather than `xsd:` for the namespace prefix.)

```
<xs:simpleType name="short" id="short">
  <xs:annotation>
    <xs:documentation
      source="http://www.w3.org/TR/xmlschema-2/#short"/>
  </xs:annotation>
  <xs:restriction base="xs:int">
    <xs:minInclusive value="-32768" id="short.minInclusive"/>
    <xs:maxInclusive value="32767" id="short.maxInclusive"/>
  </xs:restriction>
</xs:simpleType>
```

Regular Expressions for Pattern Facet

The value of the pattern facet is set by specifying a regular expression that describes the intended content that matches the pattern. Table 6-12 lists the major regular expressions defined in XML Schema, most of which are very similar to those found in perl. However, the perl meaning of ^ and $ to match beginning and end of a string, respectively, does not apply here. See the W3C specification at *http://www.w3.org/TR/xmlschema-2/#regexs* for details. You can also experiment with regular expressions using Daniel Potter's interface located at *http://www.xfront.org/xml-schema/*. This Web form interface contains a Java applet that permits you to enter a pattern and then test a string against the pattern to determine whether it matches. This is very handy when you want to be sure the regular expression you've added for the value of the pattern facet actually matches the kinds of strings you intend it to. Roger Costello also offers a free regular expression generator for numbers (see *http://www.xfront.org/#regex-Gen*).

TABLE 6-12 Regular Expressions Used with Pattern Facet

Expression	*Description and/or Example*
*	0 or more; for example, a*x matches x, ax, aax, aaax, etc.
+	1 or more
?	0 or 1
.	Any single character; equivalent to the expression [^\n\r]
(a|b)	Either a or b
(abc)	*All* of the characters a, b, c, in that order
[abc]	Any *single* member character in the set {a, b, c}; for example, [abc]x matches only ax, bx, and cx
[a-e]	Any *single* letter in the range ASCII range a to e
[a-zA-Z]	Any single letter in lowercase or uppercase form
[0-9]	Any single digit in the numeric range 0 to 9; for example, [0-1][0-9] matches 00, 01, 02, ... 09, 10, 11, ... 19
[^0-9]	Any *non*digit (^ denotes set negation)
\d	Any single digit; for example, \d\d matches any two-digit number
\D	Any *non*digit (capital letter denotes set negation)
\s	Any white space character (space, tab, newline, return); equivalent to [#x20\t\n\r]; for example, Volume\s\d+ matches Volume 1, Volume 2, ... Volume 99, Volume 999, ...
\w	Any *word* character (XML 1.0 letter or digit character class; all characters except the set of "punctuation", "separator" and "control" characters); equivalent to the less compact expression [#x0000-#x10FFFF]-[\p{P}\p{Z}\p{C}]

continued

TABLE 6-12 Regular Expressions used with Pattern Facet (*continued*)

Expression	*Description and/or Example*
`\W`	Any *non*word character
`\c`	`Name` character, as per XML 1.0 Recommendation; letters, digits, hyphens, underscores, colons, or full stops (periods); for example, `over:under-sideways_down` matches the expression `\c+`
`\i`	Initial `Name` character, as per XML 1.0 Recommendation; namely, a letter or underscore or colon
`(expr){n}`	Exactly `n` repetitions of the expression `expr`; for example, `(Jingle Bell,\s){2} Jingle Bell Rock` matches `"Jingle Bell, Jingle Bell, Jingle Bell Rock"`
`(expr){m,n}`	Anywhere from `m` to `n` repetitions of the expression `expr`; `m` may = `0`; `m < n`; for example, `(01){2,4}` matches `0101`, `010101`, or `01010101`
`(expr){n,}`	`n` *or more* repetitions of the expression `expr`; for example, `(Yesterday ){2,}` matches `"Yesterday Yesterday "`, `"Yesterday Yesterday Yesterday "`, `"Yesterday Yesterday Yesterday Yesterday "` (etc.)
`.*substring.*`	Matches any string containing the substring "substring"; for example, `.*Help.*` matches `"Help"`, `"Help Me"`, `"Please Help Me"`, etc.
`\n`	Matches the newline character (`#xA`)
`\r`	Matches the return character (`#xD`)
`\t`	Matches the tab character (`#x9`)
`\\`	Matches the slash character (see note about metacharacter matching)
`\p{X}`	Matches one character from Unicode *character class* `X`; based on Unicode Character Database [*http://www.unicode.org/Public/3.1-Update/UnicodeCharacterDatabase-3.1.0.html*]. *Note:* Representative examples follow in this table
`\P{X}`	Capital `P` negates the set; any character *not* in the character class `X`
`\p{Lu}`	Matches any uppercase letter in Unicode
`\p{L}`	Matches any letter in Unicode
`\p{IsBasicLatin}`	Matches any ASCII character (using what is called a *block escape*)
`\p{IsGreek}`	Matches any Greek character; the `Is` form may be applied to any block name (e.g., `Greek`) as defined by Unicode—see *http://www.w3.org/TR/xmlschema-2/#regexs*
`\p{M}`	Matches any mark
`\p{N}`	Matches any number (integers, fractions, Roman numerals, etc.)
`\p{Nd}`	Matches any decimal digit; equivalent to `\d`
`\p{P}`	Matches any punctuation
`\p{Z}`	Matches any separator (e.g., various types of spaces and line separators)
`\p{S}`	Matches any symbol
`\p{Sm}`	Matches any mathematical symbol
`\p{Sc}`	Matches any currency symbol
`\p{Cc}`	Matches any control character

Note that the metacharacters ., \, ?, *, +, {, }, (,), [, and] can be escaped (using a slash, "\") to obtain their literal meaning. For example, to match a literal question mark, you would use the regular expression "\?" (without the quotes), so to match the string "why?", the needed regular expression is "why\?".

Earlier, we saw an example in which two pattern facets were ORed to constrain element content to either uppercase or lowercase letters. From Table 6-12, we see that the expression [a-zA-Z] represents all uppercase or lowercase letters, so we need only one pattern facet. Let's throw in a maxLength facet to stipulate that the type is restricted to 15 characters.

```
<xsd:element name="Pattern2" type="pattern2" />

<xsd:simpleType name="pattern2" >
  <xsd:restriction base="xsd:string" >
    <xsd:pattern value="[A-Za-z]+" />
    <xsd:maxLength value="15" />
  </xsd:restriction>
</xsd:simpleType>
```

Now this type definition will validate instances such as these:

```
<Pattern2>QWasdfgERTYaX</Pattern2>
<Pattern2>Rubber Soul</Pattern2>
```

Suppose we want to define a datatype for phone numbers that includes the 3-digit area code surrounded by parentheses, followed by a space, the 3-digit exchange, a hyphen, and the 4-digit number. We start with the base type xsd:string and use the following pattern facet:

```
<xsd:element name="PhoneNumber" type="PhoneNumberType" />

<xsd:simpleType name="PhoneNumberType" >
  <xsd:restriction base="xsd:string">
    <xsd:pattern value="\(\d{3}\)\s\d{3}-\d{4}"/>
  </xsd:restriction>
</xsd:simpleType>
```

The following instance matches this pattern:

```
<PhoneNumber>(301) 555-1212</PhoneNumber>
```

Note that our expression requires us to escape the left and right parentheses with the slash character so that the literal value prevails over the XSD metacharacter meaning of parentheses to delimit an expression. The expression takes advantage of \d to match any digit (equivalent to [0-9]) and {n} notation to repeat the previous expression n times. We also use \s to match the space and include a literal "-" for the hyphen.

We can make the area code and surrounding parentheses optional by wrapping that portion in unescaped parentheses and following it with a "?" like this:

```
<xsd:pattern value="(\(\d{3}\)\s)?\d{3}-\d{4}"/>
```

As we've seen, it is also possible to indicate multiple pattern values, in which case an instance need match only one of the patterns to be valid according to the schema. Suppose we wanted to introduce patterns to allow for phone numbers in the United Kingdom, or a country code, or maybe a 2-digit area code as in Israel.

```
<PhoneNumber3>0870 55 512 12</PhoneNumber3>
<PhoneNumber3>+44 141 555 1212</PhoneNumber3>
<PhoneNumber3>(03) 555-1212</PhoneNumber3>
```

One possible type definition using multiple `pattern` facets would be:

```
<xsd:element name="PhoneNumber3" type="PhoneNumberType3" />
<xsd:simpleType name="PhoneNumberType3" >
  <xsd:restriction base="xsd:string">
    <xsd:pattern value="\(\d{3}\)\s\d{3}-\d{4}"/>
    <xsd:pattern value="\d{4}\s\d{2}\s\d{3}\s\d{2}"/>
    <xsd:pattern value="\+\d{2}\s\d{3}\s\d{3}\s\d{4}"/>
    <xsd:pattern value="\(\d{2}\)\s\d{3}-\d{4}"/>
  </xsd:restriction>
</xsd:simpleType>
```

You may have noticed that we can combine the first and last pattern quite easily using the `{n,m}` type of regular expression syntax.

```
<xsd:element name="PhoneNumber3" type="PhoneNumberType3" />
<xsd:simpleType name="PhoneNumberType3" >
  <xsd:restriction base="xsd:string">
    <xsd:pattern value="\(\d{2,3}\)\s\d{3}-\d{4}"/>
    <xsd:pattern value="\d{4}\s\d{2}\s\d{3}\s\d{2}"/>
    <xsd:pattern value="\+\d{2}\s\d{3}\s\d{3}\s\d{4}"/>
  </xsd:restriction>
</xsd:simpleType>
```

We could of course devise more complicated regular expressions and reduce this example to one pattern:

```
  <xsd:pattern value="\(\d{2,3}\)\s\d{3}-
\d{4}|\d{4}\s\d{2}\s\d{3}\s\d{2}|\+\d{2}\s\d{3}\s\d{3}\s\d{4}"/>
```

But to what advantage? The present form nicely distinguishes among the three (or four) cases we want to consider. It better documents the data we're trying to model. The schema processor will OR together the patterns, so we haven't really impacted performance.

We can also define a type that corresponds to a SKU number that consists of exactly 9 letters (uppercase or lowercase) and spaces, followed by a literal hyphen, followed by exactly 20 digits.

```
<xsd:element name="SKU" type="SKUType" />
<xsd:simpleType name="SKUType" >
  <xsd:restriction base="xsd:string" >
    <xsd:pattern value="[A-Za-z\s]{9}-\d{20}" />
  </xsd:restriction>
</xsd:simpleType>
```

An instance that adheres to this datatype definition is:

```
<SKU>DTDs R Us-12345678901234567890</SKU>
```

Pattern facets can also be used instead of `xsd:float` to describe valid strings that represent prices with a Unicode currency symbol, which Table 6-12 tells us is denoted by `\p{Sc}`. Suppose we want an optional currency symbol, followed by an optional space, from 1 to 4 digits, a decimal point, and exactly 2 digits in the fractional part. This will do the trick:

```
<xsd:element name="PriceString" type="PriceStringType" />
<xsd:simpleType name="PriceStringType" >
  <xsd:restriction base="xsd:string" >
    <xsd:pattern value="\p{Sc}?\s?\d{1,4}\.\d{2}" />
  </xsd:restriction>
</xsd:simpleType>
```

Sample instances are:

```
<PriceString>123.33</PriceString>
<PriceString>$123.33</PriceString>
<PriceString>$ 7890.25</PriceString>
```

Derivation by List

We briefly mentioned that three of the built-in types (`NMTOKENS`, `IDREFS`, and `ENTITIES`) are defined by means of derivation by list, rather than by restriction. A list type is a white space–separated list of tokens, each of which meets the validation check indicated by the base type from which the list is derived. One catch—the base type must be a simple type, which means no attributes and no children elements. Examples in this section and the next illustrate Rule 7: *Derivation by list or union can be used only if the base type is simpleType, so elements that comprise these types cannot contain children or attributes.*

Let's return to the temperature example. Recall that `TemperatureType1` was defined as a float type constrained to the range 50.0 to 110.0. To define a list type, we use `xsd:list` within an `xsd:simpleType` element. We supply the required `itemType` attribute (rather than `base`) to denote the type of each item in the list.

```
<xsd:element name="TemperatureList" type="TemperatureListType" />
<xsd:simpleType name="TemperatureListType">
  <xsd:list itemType="TemperatureType1" />
</xsd:simpleType>
```

A valid example of this list type is:

```
<TemperatureList>98.6 57.0 104.5 100 101.4</TemperatureList>
```

Although this may look like a string, a schema processor will validate each item (token) in the list against the constraints imposed by `itemType`. Furthermore, we can use the facets `length`, `minLength`, `maxLength`, and `enumeration` to refine the list type, that is, to subclass it. For example, this definition ensures that the subclassed list contains no more than three items.

```
<xsd:element name="ShortTemperatureList"
             type="ShortTemperatureListType" />
<xsd:simpleType name="ShortTemperatureListType" >
  <xsd:restriction base="TemperatureListType" >
    <xsd:maxLength value="3" />
  </xsd:restriction>
</xsd:simpleType>
```

Similarly, if I wanted to define a `StateType` consisting of two-letter abbreviations and then create a list type to represent the three US states I've lived in, a simple solution is:

```
<xsd:simpleType name="StateType">
    <xsd:restriction base="xsd:NMTOKEN">
    <!-- Enumeration of all 50 two-letter values would be better. -->
      <xsd:pattern value="[A-Z]{2}" />
    </xsd:restriction>
</xsd:simpleType>

<xsd:simpleType name="StateList">
  <xsd:list itemType="StateType" />
</xsd:simpleType>

<xsd:element name="StatesWhereLived" type="KensStateList" />
<xsd:simpleType name="KensStateList">
  <xsd:restriction base="StateList">
    <xsd:length value="3" />
  </xsd:restriction>
</xsd:simpleType>
```

And for the curious, a (truly) valid instance is:

```
<StatesWhereLived>NY PA MD</StatesWhereLived>
```

Furthermore, these three state abbreviations could have been added to the restriction as enumeration facets for even tighter validation.

Derivation by Union

Derivation by union also applies only to simple types (Rule 7). It provides a way to indicate that the content of an element can be valid values according to any of the member types of the union. A union type is defined using `xsd:union` in an `xsd:simpleType`, with the `memberTypes` attribute set to a space-separated list of the types in the union.

Suppose in addition to `TemperatureType1`, we defined `TemperatureType1A` to represent a narrow range of negative temperatures.

```
<xsd:simpleType name="TemperatureType1A">
  <xsd:restriction base="xsd:float">
    <xsd:maxInclusive value="-50.0" />
    <xsd:minInclusive value="-110.0" />
  </xsd:restriction>
</xsd:simpleType>
```

We can define `TemperatureUnionType` as the union of `TemperatureType1` and `TemperatureType1A`, representing restricted ranges of both positive and negative temperatures:

```
<xsd:element name="TemperatureUnion" type="TemperatureUnionType" />
<xsd:simpleType name="TemperatureUnionType">
  <xsd:union memberTypes="TemperatureType1 TemperatureType1A" />
</xsd:simpleType>
```

Instances of the union are not lists; they have single-valued contents, so valid examples are:

```
<TemperatureUnion>104.5</TemperatureUnion>
<TemperatureUnion>98.6</TemperatureUnion>
<TemperatureUnion>-57.0</TemperatureUnion>
<TemperatureUnion>-100</TemperatureUnion>
```

However, this next instance is not valid because it doesn't fall within either of the ranges `-110.0` to `-50.0` nor `50.0` to `110.0`.

```
<TemperatureUnion>17.5</TemperatureUnion>
```

As another example, suppose we want to model both 5-digit and 9-digit zip-codes (of the form `ddddd-dddd`). One approach is:

```
<xsd:simpleType name="Zip5Type">
  <xsd:restriction base="xsd:positiveInteger">
    <xsd:pattern value="\d{5}" />
  </xsd:restriction>
</xsd:simpleType>
```

```
<xsd:simpleType name="Zip9Type">
  <xsd:restriction base="xsd:string">
    <xsd:pattern value="\d{5}-\d{4}" />
  </xsd:restriction>
</xsd:simpleType>

<!-- format: ddddd or ddddd-dddd -->
<xsd:simpleType name="ZipUnion">
  <xsd:union memberTypes="Zip5Type Zip9Type" />
</xsd:simpleType>
```

However, we can implement the same constraints much more succinctly without a union, simply by defining an optional part of a `pattern` facet:

```
<xsd:simpleType name="ZipType">
  <xsd:restriction base="xsd:string">
    <xsd:pattern value="\d{5}(-\d{4})?" />
  </xsd:restriction>
</xsd:simpleType>
```

More about Complex Types

Most of the examples so far have focused on simple types. We now turn our attention to complex types, defined with the `xsd:complexType` element.

All `xsd:complexType` definitions have one of two content models:

- `xsd:simpleContent`—permits character data content and attributes
- `xsd:complexContent`—permits children elements, as well as attributes

An `xsd:complexType` definition includes a content type and a set of zero or more attribute declarations. The content type describes the allowable content as:

- Empty (no subelements or character data, but possibly attributes)
- Character data of some particular simple type
- Element model group (`xsd:sequence`, `xsd:choice`, `xsd:all`, or combination)
- A mixture of elements and character data (mixed content)

An `xsd:complexType` can be derived in four ways:

- Extension of an `xsd:simpleType`
- Extension of another `xsd:complexType`
- Restriction of another `xsd:complexType`
- Restriction of the generic `xsd:anyType`

In the next section, we'll see how `xsd:simpleContent` is used.

Adding and Constraining Attribute Values

So far, nearly all of the examples in this section involved elements with character content. We've ignored cases concerning either attributes or nested children elements. Let's first turn to attributes and reconsider our temperature example. Our original, unconstrained definition of temperature was:

```
<xsd:element name="Temperature0" type="xsd:string" />
```

Now we want a new definition that supports instances with attributes such as:

```
<Temperature2 scale="Fahrenheit or whatever">98.6</Temperature2>
```

How do we simply add an attribute to a type definition? Rule 3: *If your new type adds attributes to the base type, you must use complexType (because simpleTypes are not permitted to have attributes).* It may seem counterintuitive at first that simply adding an unconstrained attribute requires a `complexType` definition, whereas the `TemperatureType1` case that defined a range of acceptable floating point values only required a `simpleType`. However, by definition, `simpleTypes` cannot contain attributes. This process is sometimes called "deriving a complex type from a simple type" because adding an attribute (or element children) effectively promotes the simple type to complex.

Now we have a second decision to make: Should the `complexType` use `simpleContent` or `complexContent`? The answer is `simpleContent`. Rule 4: *If the content model requires only character data and attributes (but no children), use complexType with simpleContent.*

Next, we have to decide whether to derive by restriction or extension. Well, extension by definition means adding elements or attributes, so that's what we need. Putting all this together, and assuming we want a mandatory `scale` attribute of type `xsd:string`, we have:

```
<!-- Case 2: Float content; unconstrained attribute -->
<xsd:element name="Temperature2" type="TemperatureType2" />

<xsd:complexType name="TemperatureType2">
  <xsd:simpleContent>
    <xsd:extension base="xsd:float">
      <xsd:attribute name="scale" type="xsd:string" use="required"/>
    </xsd:extension>
  </xsd:simpleContent>
</xsd:complexType>
```

Notice that the base type for the extension is `xsd:float`, but this has nothing to do with the datatype of the attribute `scale`. What takes some getting used to is that the attribute declaration is nested in the `xsd:extension` element. Also note that although our element content is constrained to be an `xsd:float`, the attribute is an unconstrained `xsd:string`. Clearly, we can do better than that.

Suppose we now wish to create a type that supports floating point element content and constrains the `scale` attribute to one of three values: `"C"`, `"F"`, or `"K"` (for Celsius, Kelvin, or Fahrenheit temperature scales). The outer hierarchy remains the same, but we must drop the type attribute from the scale attribute declaration and instead nest a simpleType definition inside. Rule 1: *If you're creating a type that simply constrains the value of an attribute, simpleType will suffice.* Since we're constraining the string type, we use restriction and, in this case, enumeration facets, one for each of the three valid values.

```
<!-- Case 3: Float content; constrained attribute (enumeration) -->
<xsd:element name="Temperature3" type="TemperatureType3" />

<xsd:complexType name="TemperatureType3">
  <xsd:simpleContent>
    <xsd:extension base="xsd:float">
      <xsd:attribute name="scale" use="required">
        <xsd:simpleType>
          <xsd:restriction base="xsd:string">
            <xsd:enumeration value="C" />
            <xsd:enumeration value="F" />
            <xsd:enumeration value="K" />
          </xsd:restriction>
        </xsd:simpleType>
      </xsd:attribute>
    </xsd:extension>
  </xsd:simpleContent>
</xsd:complexType>
```

Note that the xsd:simpleType child of the scale attribute has no name attribute. This is called an **anonymous type definition**; its scope is limited to the scale attribute within which it is defined; since it is local, it cannot be reused. But for this example, that's exactly what we want. An instance of this type is:

```
<Temperature3 scale="F">12348.6</Temperature3>
```

Now suppose we wish to constrain the element content to the float range 50.0 to 110.0 *and also* limit the attribute value as before. We still want complexType with simpleContent, but we replace the xsd:extension with xsd:restriction because we are limiting the value of the float and use minInclusive and maxInclusive facets to specify the range (as we did earlier in the chapter). Again, the scale attribute is nested within another xsd:restriction element.

```
<!-- Case 4: Constrained float content (range); constrained attr. -->
<xsd:element name="Temperature4" type="TemperatureType4" />

<xsd:complexType name="TemperatureType4">
  <xsd:simpleContent>
    <xsd:restriction base="xsd:float"> <!-- for element content -->
      <xsd:minInclusive value="50.0" />
      <xsd:maxInclusive value="110.0" />
      <xsd:attribute name="scale" use="required">
        <xsd:simpleType>
```

```
          <xsd:restriction base="xsd:string"> <!-- for attribute -->
            <xsd:enumeration value="C" />
            <xsd:enumeration value="F" />
            <xsd:enumeration value="K" />
          </xsd:restriction>
        </xsd:simpleType>
      </xsd:attribute>
    </xsd:restriction>
  </xsd:simpleContent>
</xsd:complexType>
```

A valid instance is:

```
<Temperature4 scale="F">98.6</Temperature4>
```

Finally, what if we wanted constrained float content (range), but an *unconstrained* attribute? As you probably guessed, our definition shrinks considerably. We remove the `xsd:simpleType` child of the `scale` attribute and all its contents.

```
<!-- Case 4A: Constrained float content (range); unconstrained attr.-->
<xsd:element name="Temperature4A" type="TemperatureType4A" />

<xsd:complexType name="TemperatureType4A">
  <xsd:simpleContent>
    <xsd:restriction base="xsd:float"> <!-- for element content -->
      <xsd:minInclusive value="50.0" />
      <xsd:maxInclusive value="110.0" />
      <xsd:attribute name="scale" use="required" type="xsd:string" />
    </xsd:restriction>
  </xsd:simpleContent>
</xsd:complexType>
```

If you compare this to the earlier `TemperatureType2` case, which permitted *any float* and any string value for `scale`, the only difference is that here we need `xsd:restriction` and facets for the narrowed float range, whereas in Case 2 at the beginning of this section, we used:

```
<xsd:extension base="xsd:float">
```

I hope all these temperature examples don't leave you cold. We'll put them on the back burner for a while, but we'll come back to thaw them out when we discuss `complexTypes` with `complexContent` and also empty elements.

Let's briefly revisit the Collection example to underscore the difference between extension and restriction with regard to element character content and attribute values. When we add an attribute, we use extension:

```
<xsd:element name="Remastered">
  <xsd:complexType>
    <xsd:simpleContent>
      <xsd:extension base="xsd:string">
        <xsd:attribute name="format" use="required" type="xsd:string"/>
```

```
      </xsd:extension>
    </xsd:simpleContent>
  </xsd:complexType>
</xsd:element>
```

This corresponds to the DTD fragment

```
<!ELEMENT Remastered  (#PCDATA)>
<!ATTLIST Remastered  format CDATA  #REQUIRED >
```

However, when we constrain the element's character content and have an attribute, we use restriction for the element and nest the attribute declaration(s) inside. For example, this definition of the Peak chart position limits it to an integer between 1 and 100 and contains two attributes.

```
<xsd:element name="Peak" type="PeakType" />
<xsd:complexType name="PeakType">
  <xsd:simpleContent>
    <xsd:restriction base="xsd:positiveInteger">
      <xsd:minInclusive value="1" />
      <xsd:maxInclusive value="100" />
      <xsd:attribute name="country" default="US" type="xsd:NMTOKEN"/>
      <xsd:attribute name="weeks" use="optional" type="xsd:NMTOKEN"/>
    </xsd:restriction>
  </xsd:simpleContent>
</xsd:complexType>
```

Here's a valid instance of this complex type:

```
<Peak country="UK" weeks="5">2</Peak>
```

Restricting a User-Defined Type

Suppose you want to limit the values of a simple type that is *not* one of the built-in types? Recall `TemperatureType3`, which allowed any float element content but restricted the `scale` attribute to the three one-letter abbreviations. If we want to derive a new type that is based on `TemperatureType3` but constrain the element content to float values between 50.0 and 110.0, we can restrict `TemperatureType3`, rather than `xsd:float`, and supply facets as usual.

```
<!-- Case 8: Restriction of Case 3 by constraining float range -->
<xsd:element name="Temperature8" type="TemperatureType8" />

<xsd:complexType name="TemperatureType8">
  <xsd:simpleContent>
    <xsd:restriction base="TemperatureType3"> <!-- note -->
      <xsd:minInclusive value="50.0" />
      <xsd:maxInclusive value="110.0" />
    </xsd:restriction>
  </xsd:simpleContent>
</xsd:complexType>
```

A valid instance is:

```
<Temperature8 scale="F">98.6</Temperature8>
```

Does this look familiar to you? If you compare this to the previously illustrated `TemperatureType4`, which also constrained both the element content and attribute value, you will be able to see that although the two definitions look quite different (`TemperatureType4` specifies a base type of `xsd:float`), they are functionally equivalent. The key difference is that `TemperatureType8` demonstrates *reuse of an existing user-defined type,* whereas `TemperatureType4` defines a whole new type from scratch. We've merely restricted the permissible values, so `TemperatureType8` represents a subset of the values defined by `TemperatureType4`.

Adding Element Children

So far we've been dealing with a pretty flat hierarchy. Suppose we'd like to define a temperature element with the usual `scale` attribute, but instead of character data as content, we want two element children named `Value`, which contains the actual temperature (as element content), and `Recorded`, which indicates the date and time at which the measurement was taken. The instance should look like this:

```
<Temperature6B scale="F">
  <Value>-12345.6</Value>
  <Recorded>2001-11-22T15:07:00</Recorded>
</Temperature6B>
```

We know we'll need `xsd:complexType` because we have an attribute. But this time we can't use `xsd:simpleContent` because by definition it applies to a content model that contains *only character data,* optionally attributes, but no element children. Finally, we get the opportunity to see `xsd:complexContent` in action! Rule 5: *If, however, the content model of the new type requires children elements (and optionally attributes), you must use complexType with complexContent.*

Within the `xsd:complexContent` element, we can use `xsd:extension` if our new type adds elements to an existing user-defined type. However, in this case, our `TemperatureType6B` is a brand new type, so we must use `xsd:restriction` of the completely generic `xsd:anyType`. We'll also use the `xsd:sequence` compositor element to contain the declarations for `Value`, an `xsd:float`, and `Recorded`, using the built-in `xsd:dateTime` datatype. As we've seen before, the definition of the `scale` attribute is next, contained within the `xsd:restriction`.

```
<!-- Case 6B does not constrain Value element beyond xsd:float. -->
<xsd:element name="Temperature6B" type="TemperatureType6B" />

<xsd:complexType name="TemperatureType6B" >
 <xsd:complexContent>                   <!-- implied -->
 <xsd:restriction base="xsd:anyType">  <!-- implied -->
```

```
    <xsd:sequence>
      <xsd:element name="Value" type="xsd:float" />
      <xsd:element name="Recorded" type="xsd:dateTime" />
    </xsd:sequence>
      <xsd:attribute name="scale" use="required">
        <xsd:simpleType>
          <xsd:restriction base="xsd:string">
            <xsd:enumeration value="C" />
            <xsd:enumeration value="F" />
            <xsd:enumeration value="K" />
          </xsd:restriction>
        </xsd:simpleType>
      </xsd:attribute>
   </xsd:restriction>                   <!-- implied -->
   </xsd:complexContent>                <!-- implied -->
  </xsd:complexType>
```

You've probably guessed where we're going next. We'd like to constrain the element content of `Value`. This is essentially the same as what we did when we limited the float range of `TemperatureType4`, except now the restriction of an anonymous simple type is placed within the `Value` element.

```
<xsd:element name="Temperature6A" type="TemperatureType6A" />

 <xsd:complexType name="TemperatureType6A" >
  <xsd:complexContent>                  <!-- implied -->
  <xsd:restriction base="xsd:anyType">  <!-- implied -->
   <xsd:sequence>
     <xsd:element name="Value" >
       <xsd:simpleType>
         <xsd:restriction base="xsd:float"> <!-- for element content -->
           <xsd:minInclusive value="50.0" />
           <xsd:maxInclusive value="110.0" />
         </xsd:restriction>
       </xsd:simpleType>
     </xsd:element>
     <xsd:element name="Recorded" type="xsd:dateTime" />
   </xsd:sequence>
     <xsd:attribute name="scale" use="required">
       <xsd:simpleType>
         <xsd:restriction base="xsd:string"> <!-- for attribute -->
           <xsd:enumeration value="C" />
           <xsd:enumeration value="F" />
           <xsd:enumeration value="K" />
         </xsd:restriction>
       </xsd:simpleType>
     </xsd:attribute>
  </xsd:restriction>                    <!-- implied -->
  </xsd:complexContent>                 <!-- implied -->
 </xsd:complexType>
```

Now a valid instance must have a `Value` of 50.0 to 110.0, as well as a `Recorded` element:

```
<Temperature6A scale="F">
  <Value>98.6</Value>
  <Recorded>2001-11-22T15:07:00</Recorded>
</Temperature6A>
```

Have you wondered why I have the comment `<!-- implied -->` after the comment `xsd:complexContent` and the outermost `xsd:restriction` elements? The W3C Schema Working Group figured that when defining complex types, a common need would be to add element children to the content model of the type being defined, without having a user-defined type from which to derive by extension. Therefore, they decided the default case for `xsd:complexType` is a nested `xsd:complexContent` child container with `xsd:restriction` specifically of the generic `xsd:anyType` base. Since these are the defaults, you may omit them from the definition (and probably will typically see them omitted, especially by tools that generate XML Schema). When the defaults are omitted, the compositor (`xsd:sequence`, in this case) comes immediately after `xsd:complexType`. In other words, `Temperature6A` reduces to:

```
<xsd:element name="Temperature6" type="TemperatureType6" />

 <xsd:complexType name="TemperatureType6" >
   <xsd:sequence>
     <xsd:element name="Value" >
       <xsd:simpleType>
         <xsd:restriction base="xsd:float"> <!-- for element content -->
           <xsd:minInclusive value="50.0" />
           <xsd:maxInclusive value="110.0" />
         </xsd:restriction>
       </xsd:simpleType>
     </xsd:element>
     <xsd:element name="Recorded" type="xsd:dateTime" />
   </xsd:sequence>
     <xsd:attribute name="scale" use="required">
       <xsd:simpleType>
         <xsd:restriction base="xsd:string"> <!-- for attribute -->
           <xsd:enumeration value="C" />
           <xsd:enumeration value="F" />
           <xsd:enumeration value="K" />
         </xsd:restriction>
       </xsd:simpleType>
     </xsd:attribute>
 </xsd:complexType>
```

Since `TemperatureType6` and `TemperatureType6A` are logically equivalent, they validate the same instances.

Adding Elements to a User-Defined Type

We learned how to constrain the element content of a user-defined type by restriction, using the existing type as the base. How do we *add elements* to a user-defined type by extension? Assuming we have already defined TemperatureType6, how can we use it as the base type to define a new type that adds a Person element with Last and First children as a child of a temperature element? We want an instance of the form:

```
<Temperature9 scale="F">
  <Value>98.6</Value>
  <Recorded>2001-11-22T15:07:00</Recorded>
  <Person>
    <Last>Regnad</Last>
    <First>Kcin</First>
  </Person>
</Temperature9>
```

Since we're adding elements, we again need xsd:complexType and xsd:complexContent. We then include xsd:extension to specify the existing base type, TemperatureType6 in this case. Even though we're adding only one direct child of Temperature9, we need to use the xsd:sequence compositor with Person as its only direct child. Person is defined in terms of an anonymous complex type that consists of a sequence of two elements, Last and First.

```
<!-- Case 9: Extension of Case 6 by adding element Person w/children -->
<xsd:element name="Temperature9" type="TemperatureType9" />

<xsd:complexType name="TemperatureType9">
  <xsd:complexContent>
    <xsd:extension base="TemperatureType6"> <!-- note -->
      <xsd:sequence>
        <xsd:element name="Person" >
          <xsd:complexType>
            <xsd:sequence>
              <xsd:element name="Last" type="xsd:string" />
              <xsd:element name="First" type="xsd:string" />
            </xsd:sequence>
          </xsd:complexType>
        </xsd:element>
      </xsd:sequence>
    </xsd:extension>
  </xsd:complexContent>
</xsd:complexType>
```

Extension of Complex Types with Complex Content

Derivation by *extension* of a complex type means you *add elements or attributes (or both)* to the base type to describe your new type. Consider the complex CDType shown in Listing 6-9, which is based on the CD element and its children from Listing 6-4. Suppose we wanted to add two elements to the original type: ListPrice, a floating point value, and Format, whose content is constrained to be one of an enumerated set of strings. To derive a subclass (derived type) called CDTypeExtended by extension, we need to create a complex type with complex content because we are adding elements. The child of `xsd:complexContent` is `xsd:extension` with `base` attribute set to `"CDType"` in this case. The declaration of `ListPrice` is straightforward since it involves a built-in type. However, the `Format` declaration requires simple type *restriction*, as we've previously seen, because we are limiting the content choices to a subset of `xsd:string`, in this case by `xsd:enumeration` facets. In other words, the extension of one type can include a restriction of another type in the definition of the valid values of one of its element children. An extension can also add attributes to an element present in the base type. In Listing 6-9, we've added the `version` attribute to the `CDTypeExtended` type. As usual, the `xsd:attribute` declaration appears *after* the added element content, but *within* the `xsd:extension` definition.

Listing 6-9 Extending a Complex Type by Adding Elements (cd-ext.xsd)

```
<?xml version="1.0" encoding="UTF-8"?>
<xsd:schema xmlns:xsd="http://www.w3.org/2001/XMLSchema">
<!-- CD portion of Collection.dtd -->

  <xsd:element     name="CD"     type="CDType" />
  <xsd:element     name="CDext"  type="CDTypeExtended" />

  <xsd:complexType name="CDType">
    <xsd:sequence>
        <xsd:element name="Title" type="xsd:string"/>
        <xsd:element name="Artist" type="xsd:string"/>
        <xsd:element ref="Chart"/>
        <xsd:element name="Type" type="xsd:string"/>
        <xsd:element ref="Label" maxOccurs="unbounded"/>
        <xsd:element name="AlbumReleased" type="xsd:string"/>
        <xsd:element ref="Remastered"
                     minOccurs="0" maxOccurs="unbounded"/>
    </xsd:sequence>
  </xsd:complexType>

  <xsd:element name="Chart">
    <xsd:complexType>
      <xsd:sequence>
        <xsd:element ref="Peak" maxOccurs="unbounded"/>
      </xsd:sequence>
    </xsd:complexType>
  </xsd:element>

  <xsd:element name="Peak">
    <xsd:complexType>
      <xsd:simpleContent>
        <xsd:extension base="xsd:string">
          <xsd:attribute name="country" default="US" type="xsd:NMTOKEN"/>
          <xsd:attribute name="weeks" use="optional" type="xsd:NMTOKEN"/>
        </xsd:extension>
      </xsd:simpleContent>
    </xsd:complexType>
  </xsd:element>
```

```
    <xsd:element name="Label">
      <xsd:complexType>
        <xsd:simpleContent>
          <xsd:extension base="xsd:string">
            <xsd:attribute name="country" default="US" type="xsd:NMTOKEN"/>
          </xsd:extension>
        </xsd:simpleContent>
      </xsd:complexType>
    </xsd:element>

    <xsd:element name="Remastered">
      <xsd:complexType>
        <xsd:simpleContent>
          <xsd:extension base="xsd:string">
            <xsd:attribute name="format" use="required" type="xsd:string"/>
          </xsd:extension>
        </xsd:simpleContent>
      </xsd:complexType>
    </xsd:element>

  <!-- derivation by extension (additional elements) -->
    <xsd:complexType  name="CDTypeExtended" >
     <xsd:complexContent>
      <xsd:extension  base="CDType" >
        <xsd:sequence>
          <xsd:element name="ListPrice" maxOccurs="1" type="xsd:float" />
          <xsd:element name="Format"  maxOccurs="1" >
            <xsd:simpleType>
              <xsd:restriction base="xsd:string">
                <xsd:enumeration value="one disk"/>
                <xsd:enumeration value="double disk"/>
                <xsd:enumeration value="triple disk"/>
                <xsd:enumeration value="quadruple disk"/>
                <xsd:enumeration value="box set"/>
                <xsd:enumeration value="CD single"/>
              </xsd:restriction>
            </xsd:simpleType>
          </xsd:element>
        </xsd:sequence>
       <xsd:attribute name="version" type="xsd:string" use="required" />
      </xsd:extension>
     </xsd:complexContent>
    </xsd:complexType>

  </xsd:schema>
```

It's important to understand that the content of the new type derived by extension is the *concatenation* of the new elements with the content of the base type. Specifically, extension implies that the added content model appears *after* the inherited content. In this case, that means that the elements `ListPrice` and `Format` follow immediately after the `Remastered` element. Listing 6-10 shows a valid instance based on the new schema, with the two elements and attribute added as a result of extension in bold.

Listing 6-10 Instance of Extended CD Type (cd-ext.xml)

```
<?xml version="1.0"?>
<CDext xmlns:xsi="http://www.w3.org/2001/XMLSchema-instance"
       xsi:noNamespaceSchemaLocation="cd-ext.xsd"
       version="2001b">
  <Title>Band on the Run</Title>
  <Artist>Wings</Artist>
  <Chart>
    <Peak country="US" weeks="4">1</Peak>
  </Chart>
  <Type>Rock</Type>
  <Label country="US">Capitol</Label>
  <Label country="UK">EMI</Label>
  <AlbumReleased>1973</AlbumReleased>
  <Remastered format="gold CD">1993</Remastered>
  <ListPrice>16.97</ListPrice>
  <Format>one disk</Format>
</CDext>
```

Restriction of Complex Types with Complex Content

Derivation of a complex type by **restriction**, on the other hand, involves limiting or constraining the original type to define the derived type. Conceptually, this is similar to restriction of simple types, except that in this case we constrain *element declarations*, rather than the valid values of a simple type.

Restriction of a complex type can be accomplished by using a more restrictive built-in datatype in an element declaration, using facets to constrain the range of values of attributes or elements, or by adjusting `minOccurs` or `maxOccurs`. Suppose we want to define a `CDTypeRestricted` type that is essentially like the original `CDType`, except that it allows only one `Label` and makes the optional `Remastered` element required. Also, rather than allowing any `xsd:string` for the `Type` element, we want to require an `xsd:NMTOKEN`. For `AlbumReleased`, rather than just an `xsd:string`, we want to constrain it to be an `xsd:gYear`.

Again we define a complex type with complex content, but this time we use an `xsd:restriction` element with the `base` attribute set to `"CDType"`. Next we *copy all of the element declarations* from the base type. Then we selectively change the element declarations. We change the value of `maxOccurs` for the `Label` element from `"unbounded"` to `"1"`.

Similarly, for `Remastered`, we replace the optional but unlimited base type definition:

```
<xsd:element ref="Remastered" minOccurs="0" maxOccurs="unbounded"/>
```

with one that restricts the element to exactly one occurrence, making it mandatory and not repeatable:

```
<xsd:element ref="Remastered" minOccurs="1" maxOccurs="1"/>
```

We change the datatypes of the `AlbumReleased` and `Type` elements:

```
<xsd:element name="Type" type="xsd:NMTOKEN"/>
<xsd:element name="AlbumReleased" type="xsd:gYear"/>
```

Listing 6-11 shows `CDTypeRestricted` definition; refer to Listing 6-9 for the base `CDType` definition and related declarations.

Listing 6-11 Complex Type Derivation by Restriction (cd-restrict.xsd)

```
<xsd:element     name="CDrestrict"  type="CDTypeRestricted" />

<!-- See Listing 6-9 for other definitions and declarations. -->

<!-- Datatype changed for AlbumReleased and Type,
     Label maxOccurs reduced, Remastered minOccurs/maxOccurs reduced. -->

  <xsd:complexType  name="CDTypeRestricted" >
   <xsd:complexContent>
    <xsd:restriction  base="CDType" >
      <xsd:sequence>
        <!-- copied from base type -->
        <xsd:element name="Title" type="xsd:string"/>
        <xsd:element name="Artist" type="xsd:string"/>
        <xsd:element ref="Chart"/>
        <!-- modified from base type -->
        <xsd:element name="Type" type="xsd:NMTOKEN"/>
        <xsd:element ref="Label" maxOccurs="1"/>
        <xsd:element name="AlbumReleased" type="xsd:gYear"/>
        <xsd:element ref="Remastered" minOccurs="1" maxOccurs="1"/>
      </xsd:sequence>
    </xsd:restriction>
   </xsd:complexContent>
  </xsd:complexType>
```

In contrast to derivation by extension, when you restrict a complex type it is necessary to *repeat* all of the element declarations from the base type (`CDType`, in this case), except those that are omitted from the subclass. This may seem undesirable to object-oriented developers. What happens if the base type definition is changed later? You might have to alter your derived type definition as well. The best rationale for this seemingly needless duplication is the difficulty in constructing a language for expressing changes to content models; there are many subtleties that our relatively simple examples don't adequately convey.

As you may have gathered, a restricted complex type is very similar to the base type from which it is derived. It differs only in that it accommodates a more limited set of instance cases. This implies that a valid instance of a restricted complex type is also valid when tested against the definition of its base type. Consider the valid instance of the `CDTypeRestricted` in Listing 6-12.

Listing 6-12 Instance of Restricted CD Type (cd-restrict.xml)

```
<?xml version="1.0"?>
<CDrestrict
      xmlns:xsi="http://www.w3.org/2001/XMLSchema-instance"
      xsi:noNamespaceSchemaLocation="cd-restrict.xsd"
      >
  <Title>Band on the Run</Title>
  <Artist>Wings</Artist>
  <Chart>
    <Peak country="US" weeks="4">1</Peak>
  </Chart>
  <Type>Rock2</Type>
  <Label country="US">Capitol</Label>
  <AlbumReleased>1973</AlbumReleased>
  <Remastered format="gold CD">1993</Remastered>
</CDrestrict>
```

Because the restricted complex type `CDTypeRestricted` is really a subset of the values of the base type, `CDType`, we could actually validate this particular instance in Listing 6-12 against the base type schema by changing only the schema location from

```
xsi:noNamespaceSchemaLocation="cd-restrict.xsd"
```

to

```
xsi:noNamespaceSchemaLocation="cd.xsd"
```

Assuming that the schema `cd.xsd` contains the same `CDType` definition shown in Listing 6-9, we'd find that the instance is a valid instance of the base type. It simply contains only one each of the `Label` and `Remastered` elements, even though the base type would also accept multiple occurrences of these elements (or none, in the case of `Remastered`). In addition, the slightly more constrained `Type` element content ("Rock2" of type `xsd:NMTOKEN`) is a valid instance of the `Type` element's `xsd:string` datatype in the base `CDType` definition. Similary, even though we've used a valid `xsd:gYear` for `AlbumReleased`, this is also valid when checked against the less restrictive base type definition that requires an `xsd:string`. Therefore, this instance is valid regardless of whether we validate against the base type (in `cd.xsd`) or the one derived by restriction (`cd-restrict.xsd`).

Empty Elements with and without Attributes

You may think we've exhausted all possible variations of our temperature example, but we've got a few left. Suppose we want to create an empty element without an attribute:

```
<Temperature5A />
```

At first blush, it might seem that defining something so trivial should also be trivial. While the rules we've learned still apply, it's less than obvious how to apply them. Our first thought might be to use xsd:simpleType. However, for an element, this would imply character content, something that an empty element cannot have. So, it must require xsd:complexType. Now, we have to decide between xsd:simpleContent and xsd:complexContent. By the same reasoning, since xsd:simpleContent allows character data, we'll pick xsd:complexContent. Generally, this is used to contain definitions of child elements, but children aren't necessary, so our xsd:restriction element is itself empty (with the default xsd:anyType as base). The result is:

```
<!-- Case 5A: empty element, no attribute, unabbreviated form -->

<xsd:element name="Temperature5A" >
  <xsd:complexType>
    <xsd:complexContent>                          <!-- implied -->
      <xsd:restriction base="xsd:anyType" />      <!-- implied -->
    </xsd:complexContent>                         <!-- implied -->
  </xsd:complexType>
</xsd:element>
```

Fortunately, this verbose definition can be cut in half when we again use the abbreviated form since we can omit xsd:complexContent and xsd:restriction of xsd:anyType, the defaults when applied to an xsd:complexType parent.

```
<!-- Case 5B: empty element, no attribute, abbreviated form  -->

  <xsd:element name="Temperature5B" >
    <xsd:complexType />
  </xsd:element>
```

The next logical step is to consider how we'd define an empty element with an attribute, a definition that would support instances such as:

```
<Temperature5C value="98.6" />
```

The only difference between this and Temperature5A is that the xsd:restriction element is no longer empty; it must contain the attribute definition (which itself may involve a nested xsd:simpleType with another xsd:restriction to further constrain the attribute, but doesn't in this example).

```
<!-- Case 5C: empty element with attribute, unabbreviated -->

<xsd:element name="Temperature5C" >
  <xsd:complexType>
    <xsd:complexContent>                        <!-- implied -->
      <xsd:restriction base="xsd:anyType">      <!-- implied -->
        <xsd:attribute name="value" type="xsd:float" use="required"/>
      </xsd:restriction>                        <!-- implied -->
    </xsd:complexContent>                       <!-- implied -->
  </xsd:complexType>
</xsd:element>
```

This too can be expressed more compactly by omitting the implied elements.

```
<!-- Case 5D: empty element with attribute, abbreviated -->

  <xsd:element name="Temperature5D" >
    <xsd:complexType>
      <xsd:attribute name="value" type="xsd:float" use="required"/>
    </xsd:complexType>
 </xsd:element>
```

It certainly seems like a contradiction of terms to consider an empty element "complex," especially compared to a "simple" type like `TemperatureType1`, which constrained values to a range of floats, but that's the way it is. The definitions and rules stated in the previous section "Simple Types, Complex Types, Simple Content, Complex Content, and Derivation" still apply. We could even add a tenth rule to Table 6-9:

Rule 10: *When defining an empty element, use complexType with complexContent. If there is no attribute, use an empty restriction. Otherwise, nest the attribute inside the restriction element.*

Summary of Type Definition Cases

This long section on datatypes has covered quite a number of scenarios. Table 6-13 summarizes the major cases and serves as a quick reference. Look in the left column for what you want to accomplish, look at the example on the right, and if you need additional explanation, review the textual discussion. The italicized elements without `xsd:` prefixes are instances of the type defined above them.

TABLE 6-13 Summary of Type Definition Cases

Goal	*Type Definition*	*Example (Schema Fragment and Instance)*
No unique type needs—see p. 296	Use one of the 44 built-in types.	`<xsd:element name="Price" type="xsd:float" />` *`<Price>19.97</Price>`*

Constrain element text content (character data) —see p. 301	`simpleType`, `restriction` (or `list` or `union`)	`<xsd:simpleType name="RatingType">`
		`  <xsd:restriction`
		`    base="xsd:positiveInteger">`
		`    <xsd:minInclusive value="1" />`
		`    <xsd:maxInclusive value="5" />`
		`  </xsd:restriction>`
		`</xsd:simpleType>`
		`<Rating>4</Rating>`

continued

TABLE 6-13 Summary of Type Definition Cases (*continued*)

Goal	*Type Definition*	*Example (Schema Fragment and Instance)*
Constrain element text content using the `pattern` facet—see p. 307	`simpleType`, `restriction`	<xsd:simpleType name="PhoneNumberType3" > <xsd:restriction base="xsd:string"> <xsd:pattern value="\(\d{2,3}\)\s\d{3}-\d{4}"/> <xsd:pattern value="\d{4}\s\d{2}\s\d{3}\s\d{2}"/> <xsd:pattern value="\+\d{2}\s\d{3}\s\d{3}\s\d{4}"/> </xsd:restriction> </xsd:simpleType> *<PhoneNumber3>+44 141 555 1212</PhoneNumber3>*
Constrain attribute value—see p. 314	`simpleType`, `restriction`	<xsd:attribute name="sex" default="male"> <xsd:simpleType> <xsd:restriction base="xsd:NMTOKEN"> <xsd:enumeration value="male"/> <xsd:enumeration value="female"/> </xsd:restriction> </xsd:simpleType> </xsd:attribute> *<Owner sex="female" />*
Add an attribute and also constrain element content—see p. 314	`complexType`, `simpleContent`, `restriction` or `extension`	<xsd:element name="TempBasic"> <xsd:complexType> <xsd:simpleContent> <xsd:extension base="xsd:float"> <xsd:attribute name="scale" type="xsd:string" use="required"/> </xsd:extension> </xsd:simpleContent> </xsd:complexType> </xsd:element> *<TempBasic scale="C">18.3</TempBasic>*
Add element children to extend existing type—see p. 321	`complexType`, `complexContent`, `extension`	<xsd:complexType name="WorldAddressType"> <xsd:complexContent> <xsd:extension base="AddressType"> <xsd:sequence> <xsd:element name="Country" type="xsd:string"/> </xsd:sequence> </xsd:extension> </xsd:complexContent> </xsd:complexType> *<WorldAddr>* *<Street>123 Milky Way</Street>* *<City>Columbia</City>* *<State>MD</State>* *<Zip>20777</Zip>* *<Country>US</Country>* *</WorldAddr>*

TABLE 6-13 *(continued)*

Goal	*Type Definition*	*Example (Schema Fragment and Instance)*
Add element children to restrict generic anyType—see p. 319	complexType, complexContent, restriction	<xsd:complexType name="WorldAddressType"> <xsd:complexContent> <xsd:restriction base="xsd:anyType"> <xsd:sequence> <xsd:element name="Country" type="xsd:string"/> </xsd:sequence> </xsd:restriction> </xsd:complexContent> </xsd:complexType>
Empty element with attribute—see p. 327	complexType, complexContent (implied)	<xsd:element name="Image" > <xsd:complexType> <xsd:attribute name="source" type="xsd:anyURI" use="required"/> </xsd:complexType> </xsd:element> *<Image source="flag.gif" />*
Empty element without an attribute—see p. 327	complexType, complexContent (implied)	<xsd:element name="Divider"> <xsd:complexType/> </xsd:element> *<Divider />*

Limiting Derivation

XML Schema provides several mechanisms for controlling the extent to which the type definitions you create can be modified downstream. That is, you may wish to share your schema in general, but at the same time limit the derivation of some datatypes you've defined. In this section, we briefly cover the `final` attribute of `xsd:complexType` and `xsd:simpleType` and the `fixed` attribute that applies to all facets. For more detail, see the XML Schema Primer (*http://www.w3.org/TR/xmlschema-0/#restrictingTypeDerivs*).

Sometimes it is desirable to define a class in a way that no one can extend it or, in other cases, so that no one can restrict it, or possibly so that the class is *final* and cannot be subclassed at all. These outcomes can be controlled in XML Schema by specifying one of three values for the `final` attribute of the `xsd:complexType` and `xsd:simpleType` elements, as shown in Table 6-14. For example,

```
<xsd:complexType name="TemperatureType6" final="restriction">
```

prevents derivation by restriction of the named type, but permits derivation by extension. Alternatively, the `xsd:schema` element has an optional `finalDefault` attribute to control overall subclassing for the entire schema.

In other situations, it may be necessary to limit users of your schema in terms of the degree to which they can override some of the facets you've defined. This

TABLE 6-14 Controlling Subclassing with the `final` Attribute

Value of `final`	*Description*
`restriction`	Class can be extended but cannot be restricted.
`extension`	Class can be restricted but cannot be extended.
`#all`	Class cannot be derived at all, neither by extension nor by restriction.

control is exercised by attaching a `fixed="true"` attribute/value pair to specific facets you don't want altered. For example,

```
<xsd:simpleType name="TemperatureType1">
  <xsd:restriction base="xsd:float">
    <xsd:minInclusive value="50.0"  fixed="true" />
    <xsd:maxInclusive value="110.0" />
  </xsd:restriction>
</xsd:simpleType>
```

This definition ensures that no derived type can change the lower bounds of the range, although the upper bound is not fixed. It also does not prevent a derived type from adding another facet such as `xsd:fractionDigits` to further constrain the type.

More about Content Models and Model Groups

XML Schema supports all the content models discussed in chapter 4. We've learned that an element's content model defines what types of elements, attributes, or character data may appear nested between its start and end tags, as well as which attributes may appear in its start tag. Earlier, we covered the compositors `xsd:sequence`, `xsd:choice`, and `xsd:all`. In this section, we discuss mixed content, groups, attribute groups, and the generic `xsd:any` content model.

Mixed Content Model

A mixed content model is one that permits a combination of children elements and character data. In terms of our temperature example, we might want to allow mixed content such as:

```
<Temperature7 scale="F">
  <Value>98.6</Value>Normal body temperature.
  <Recorded>2001-11-22T15:07:00</Recorded>
</Temperature7>
```

The complex type element `Temperature7` has `Value` and `Recorded` children (just like `TemperatureType6`), but it also permits a string, "Normal body temperature," to be mixed with the subelements. The only change we need to make to the earlier TemperatureType6 definition to allow mixed content is to add the mixed="true" attribute to xsd:complexType.

```
<xsd:complexType name="TemperatureType7"  mixed="true" >
  <xsd:sequence>
    <xsd:element name="Value" >
      <xsd:simpleType>
        <xsd:restriction base="xsd:float"> <!-- for element content -->
          <xsd:minInclusive value="50.0" />
          <xsd:maxInclusive value="110.0" />
        </xsd:restriction>
      </xsd:simpleType>
    </xsd:element>
    <xsd:element name="Recorded" type="xsd:dateTime" />
  </xsd:sequence>
    <xsd:attribute name="scale" use="required">
      <xsd:simpleType>
        <xsd:restriction base="xsd:string"> <!-- for attribute -->
          <xsd:enumeration value="C" />
          <xsd:enumeration value="F" />
          <xsd:enumeration value="K" />
        </xsd:restriction>
      </xsd:simpleType>
    </xsd:attribute>
</xsd:complexType>
```

The attribute mixed further describes the content model of a xsd:complexType or xsd:complexContent. By default, mixed="false", meaning that the element content can consist of either subelements *or* character data, depending on the rest of the definition, but not both. If, however, mixed="true", content may be a mixture of subelements *and* character data.

There is a major difference between the XML DTD notion of a mixed content model and that of XML Schema. You may recall that the disadvantage of the mixed model in a DTD is that the order and number of elements cannot be constrained. With XML Schema, on the other hand, the order and number of child elements is specified in the schema and enforced by a schema processor, meaning that we have full schema validation for a mixed content model, in contrast to partial validation in the case of DTDs.

In the preceding mixed content model example, a schema validator will enforce that a Value element comes before a Recorded element, and there must be exactly one each of these subelements, according to the type definition. However, we could specify more or less by means of minOccurs and maxOccurs, as usual.

Generic xsd:any Content Model

We've noted previously that xsd:anyType is the root of the datatype hierarchy. All simple types and all complex types are derived from this completely generic type. We've also learned that when we're constructing new complex datatypes, the default situation of adding elements involves `xsd:complexContent` with restriction of `xsd:anyType`.

There is also an `xsd:any` *element*, which permits any content without restriction, other than requiring well-formed XML. Both the `xsd:documentation` and `xsd:appInfo` elements have the `xsd:any` content model, so they allow any XML, especially XHTML, as their content; see the section "Annotations" later in this chapter.

One very handy use of `xsd:any` is, in the process of developing a schema, to allow portions of the hierarchy to be unconstrained in terms of which elements must appear, how many times they can be repeated, and so on. The generic type can serve as a placeholder until schema details are fleshed out.

It's also useful in creating test cases. For example, in `temperature.xsd`, which is really a set of alternative type definitions rather than a hierarchical schema, I found `xsd:any` gave me the flexibility to add test cases without worrying about anything other than that each newly added type definition and corresponding instances in `temperature.xml` were valid. Here's what I used for the outermost element of my test schema:

```
<!-- Tester allows any content so we can keep adding tests. -->
<xsd:element name="Tester">
  <xsd:complexType>
    <xsd:sequence minOccurs="0" maxOccurs="unbounded">
      <xsd:any />        <!-- processContents NOT lax -->
    </xsd:sequence>
  </xsd:complexType>
</xsd:element>
```

One caveat: Don't use `processContents="lax"` if you want the individual elements in the generic element to be validated. The definition says any elements can appear in any order and in any number, but each will be validated.

Group Element

Two mechanisms that facilitate reuse in XML Schema are `xsd:group` and `xsd:attributeGroup`. These elements permit you to create sets of elements and attributes (respectively) that are referenced by name, somewhat like internal parameter entities are used in DTDs for a similar purpose. For example, suppose we have the two following global element declarations:

```
<xsd:element name="Recorded" type="xsd:dateTime" />
<xsd:element name="Value" >
  <xsd:simpleType>
     <xsd:restriction base="xsd:float">
       <xsd:minInclusive value="50.0" />
       <xsd:maxInclusive value="110.0" />
     </xsd:restriction>
  </xsd:simpleType>
</xsd:element>
```

We can group the `Recorded` and `Value` elements with `xsd:group`, assign it the name `ValueGroup`, then include whichever compositor our model requires, and finally insert references to the appropriate element declarations.

```
<xsd:group name="ValueGroup" >
  <xsd:sequence>
    <xsd:element ref="Value" />
    <xsd:element ref="Recorded" />
  </xsd:sequence>
</xsd:group>
```

Elsewhere in the schema, we reference the group by name from any point with the `xsd:group` element. For example, the complex type definition of `TemperatureType12A` uses `ValueGroup` in a sequence with a `Person` element following the group.

```
<xsd:element name="Temperature12A" type="TemperatureType12A" />

<xsd:complexType name="TemperatureType12A" >
  <xsd:sequence>
    <xsd:group ref="ValueGroup" />
    <xsd:element name="Person" type="xsd:string" />
  </xsd:sequence>
</xsd:complexType>
```

The resultant type has a sequence of three elements, exactly as if this was the way we had defined it:

```
<xsd:complexType name="TemperatureType12A" >
  <xsd:sequence>
    <xsd:element ref="Value" />
    <xsd:element ref="Recorded" />
    <xsd:element name="Person" type="xsd:string" />
  </xsd:sequence>
</xsd:complexType>
```

A valid instance is:

```
<Temperature12A>
  <Value>98.6</Value>
  <Recorded>2001-11-22T15:07:00</Recorded>
  <Person>Regnad Kcin</Person>
</Temperature12A>
```

Since the group content model is reusable, let's use it in a slightly more complicated model. In the case of `TemperatureType12B`, we have a choice between the `ValueGroup` and a sequence of the elements `ExternalValue` and `ExternalRecorded`. This complex type definition also requires the `scale` attribute for the outermost element.

```
<xsd:element name="Temperature12B" type="TemperatureType12B" />

<xsd:complexType name="TemperatureType12B" >
  <xsd:choice>
    <xsd:group ref="ValueGroup" />
    <xsd:sequence>
      <xsd:element name="ExternalValue"    type="xsd:float" />
      <xsd:element name="ExternalRecorded" type="xsd:dateTime" />
    </xsd:sequence>
  </xsd:choice>
  <xsd:attribute name="scale" use="required">
      <xsd:simpleType>
        <xsd:restriction base="xsd:string">
          <xsd:enumeration value="C" />
          <xsd:enumeration value="F" />
          <xsd:enumeration value="K" />
        </xsd:restriction>
      </xsd:simpleType>
  </xsd:attribute>
</xsd:complexType>
```

Two valid instances of this type are:

```
<Temperature12B scale="K">
  <Value>55.5</Value>
  <Recorded>2001-11-22T15:07:00</Recorded>
</Temperature12B>

<Temperature12B scale="K">
  <ExternalValue>55.5</ExternalValue>
  <ExternalRecorded>2001-11-03T21:17:00</ExternalRecorded>
</Temperature12B>
```

Since the definition specifies a choice between `ValueGroup` and the sequence of the elements `ExternalValue` and `ExternalRecorded`, we cannot have, for example:

```
<Temperature12B scale="K">
  <Value>55.5</Value>
  <ExternalRecorded>2001-11-03T21:17:00</ExternalRecorded>
</Temperature12B>
```

One catch is that a group definition (as opposed to a reference) must be an immediate child of the root `xsd:schema` element. The immediate children (content) of `xsd:group` must be `xsd:choice`, `xsd:sequence`, `xsd:all`, or `xsd:annotation`. In other words, `xsd:group` itself cannot contain attributes (although the elements nested within the compositor children of `xsd:group` can).

Attribute Groups

Just as elements can be grouped with the `xsd:group` element, attributes can be grouped using the `xsd:attributeGroup` element. Such groupings foster reuse much like their DTD counterparts, parameter entities. As you might expect, we refer to an `xsd:attributeGroup` with a `ref` attribute, and since attribute declarations are required to follow element declarations, `xsd:attributeGroup` declarations must appear last in an `xsd:complexType` definition.

We define an attribute group using the `xsd:attributeGroup` element, assign it a name, and then include each attribute declaration (or reference to global attributes, if any). Let's define the `ScaleAttr` attribute group with three attributes, an optional `marginOfError`, a fixed `source`, and our ever-present restricted `scale`.

```
<xsd:attributeGroup name="ScaleAttrs" >
    <xsd:attribute name="marginOfError" use="optional"
                   type="xsd:float" />
    <xsd:attribute name="source"        fixed="Tempomatic Plus" />
    <xsd:attribute name="scale"         use="required">
      <xsd:simpleType>
        <xsd:restriction base="xsd:string">
          <xsd:enumeration value="C" />
          <xsd:enumeration value="F" />
          <xsd:enumeration value="K" />
        </xsd:restriction>
      </xsd:simpleType>
    </xsd:attribute>
</xsd:attributeGroup>
```

When we wish to use it in the schema, we reference it by name from a point in the complex type definition where you'd normally find attributes, that is, after all elements.

```
<xsd:element name="Temperature12C" type="TemperatureType12C" />

<xsd:complexType name="TemperatureType12C" >
  <xsd:sequence>
    <xsd:group ref="ValueGroup" />
    <xsd:element name="Person" type="xsd:string" />
  </xsd:sequence>
  <xsd:attributeGroup ref="ScaleAttrs" />
</xsd:complexType>
```

Notice that this definition also reuses the previous `ValueGroup` definition. A valid instance of `Temperature12C` including the required `scale` attribute and the optional `marginOfError`, but omitting the fixed `source` attribute, and including all three subelements in the correct order follows.

```
<Temperature12C scale="C" marginOfError=".05" >
  <Value>67.4</Value>
  <Recorded>2001-11-22T15:07:00</Recorded>
  <Person>Regnad Kcin</Person>
</Temperature12C>
```

Miscellaneous XML Schema Topics

The topics in this section are unrelated but definitely worth learning about.

Annotations

Annotations are essentially comments in the schema intended either for human consumption or for applications to process. The `xsd:annotation` element may have zero or more `xsd:documentation` children and/or `xsd:appInfo` children. An `xsd:documentation` element is strictly for readers, whereas an `xsd:appInfo` element provides details intended for the application, similar to the role played by processing instructions in DTDs. Both `xsd:documentation` and `xsd:appInfo` may contain *any content* (unrestricted because their content model is `xsd:any`). Both support an optional `source` attribute as an alternative to supplying textual content inline. In addition, `xsd:documentation` has an optional `xml:lang` attribute to specify the documentation language. XHTML can be embedded as the content of `xsd:documentation`. Annotations may appear as a direct child of `xsd:schema` and as children of the major schema elements, such as `xsd:element`, `xsd:attribute`, `xsd:complexType`, `xsd:simpleType`, and any content model element (e.g., `xsd:choice`). For example:

```
<xsd:schema xmlns="http://www.w3.org/1999/XMLSchema">
  <xsd:annotation>
    <xsd:documentation>Collection DTD, Version 2</xsd:documentation>
  </xsd:annotation>
  <xsd:element name="Collection">
    <xsd:annotation>
      <xsd:documentation xml:lang="en"
           source="/docs/collectionDetails.xml" />
    </xsd:annotation>
    <xsd:complexType>
      <xsd:sequence>
        <xsd:annotation>
          <xsd:documentation >Note that a Collection can be
               completely empty.</xsd:documentation>
        </xsd:annotation>
        <xsd:choice minOccurs="0" maxOccurs="unbounded">
          <xsd:element ref="Book"/>
          <xsd:element ref="CD"/>
        </xsd:choice>
        <xsd:element ref="Owner" minOccurs="0"/>
      </xsd:sequence>
      <xsd:attribute name="version" fixed="3" type="xsd:string"/>
    </xsd:complexType>
  </xsd:element>
  <!-- etc. -->
</xsd:schema>
```

As another example, consider the non-normative `XMLSchema.xsd` available from Part 1 of the specification. The (non-normative) definition of the simple type xsd:short appears in the next code block. (From the non-normative XML Schema schema for XML Schemas: Part 1: Structures at *http://www.w3.org/2001/XMLSchema.xsd*). The W3C uses the xsd:documentation element (which must be nested within an xsd:annotation element) to point to the definition of each datatype in Part 2 of the specification, based on the naming scheme mentioned earlier. That is, the value of the source attribute is a URL with a fragment identifier that locates a named anchor within the W3C specification.

```
<xs:simpleType name="short" id="short">
  <xs:annotation>
    <xs:documentation
        source="http://www.w3.org/TR/xmlschema-2/#short"/>
  </xs:annotation>
  <xs:restriction base="xs:int">
    <xs:minInclusive value="-32768" id="short.minInclusive"/>
    <xs:maxInclusive value="32767" id="short.maxInclusive"/>
  </xs:restriction>
</xs:simpleType>
```

Namespaces and XML Schema

There are four primary uses of namespaces in XML Schema:

1. In the schema document itself, as the default namespace of XML Schema elements and attributes themselves, associated with the URI http://www.w3.org/2001/XMLSchema and by convention with the namespace prefix xsd.
2. In the schema document, as the **target namespace** of the schema being defined, denoted by the xsd:schema attribute targetNamespace. Target namespaces in the schema guide the validation of corresponding namespaces in instance documents. (The target namespace also applies to schemas *included*, but not imported, from other files.)
3. In the schema document, to identify the namespace of an *imported* schema whose elements and type definitions will be merged with those in the current schema.
4. In the *instance* document, as the namespace associated with instances, associated with the URI http://www.w3.org/1999/XMLSchema-instance (the hyphen before instance is literal), typically with the prefix xsi.

It is customary (although not required) to declare all relevant namespaces in the start tag of the xsd:schema element (or in the root element defined by your schema, in the case of an instance document). The most basic case omits the target namespace entirely, as we've seen before:

```
<xsd:schema xmlns:xsd="http://www.w3.org/2001/XMLSchema">
```

A small schema using this `xsd:schema` namespace declaration is shown in Listing 6-13 with a corresponding instance in Listing 6-14. (These are files `ns1.xsd` and `ns1.xml` on this book's CD.)

Listing 6-13 Minimal Schema Namespace Declaration

```
<?xml version="1.0"?>
<xsd:schema
   xmlns:xsd="http://www.w3.org/2001/XMLSchema" >

  <xsd:element name="YourRoot" type="xsd:float" />

  <xsd:element name="Tester">
    <xsd:complexType>
      <xsd:sequence>
        <xsd:any />
      </xsd:sequence>
    </xsd:complexType>
  </xsd:element>

</xsd:schema>
```

Listing 6-14 Instance with Minimal Namespace Support

```
<?xml version="1.0"?>
<Tester
      xsi:noNamespaceSchemaLocation="ns1.xsd"
      xmlns:xsi="http://www.w3.org/2001/XMLSchema-instance">

  <YourRoot>12.34</YourRoot>
</Tester>
```

Every element from the XML Schema is prefixed by `xsd:` as a result of this namespace declaration. This identifies `complexType`, for example, as being from the namespace whose URI is `http://www.w3.org/2001/XMLSchema`. Note that the `xsd:` prefix applies to simple built-in types (e.g., `xsd:float`) as well as to elements. However, the prefix is *not* applied to other attributes such as `name`, `minOccurs`, and `use`, because attributes by default aren't part of any namespace. In this example, the elements `Tester` and `YourRoot` are not associated with a particular namespace, even though these are the elements that appear in an instance that uses this mini schema. Recall that the `xsi:noNamespaceSchemaLocation` attribute tells us where to find the schema, given as a relative or absolute URI.

A more explicit variation of this involves additional attributes for `xsd:schema`, as shown in Listing 6-15 (file `ns2.xsd`). In this case, we've provided a namespace URI for the `targetNamespace` attribute, which becomes the namespace for the schema that we're defining:

```
targetNamespace="http://www.YOUR.com"
```

We've also identified the same URI as the default namespace when no prefix is supplied:

```
xmlns="http://www.YOUR.com"
```

Listing 6-15 Schema with Default Namespace and Target Namespace

```
<?xml version="1.0"?>
<xsd:schema
   xmlns:xsd="http://www.w3.org/2001/XMLSchema"
   targetNamespace="http://www.YOUR.com"
   xmlns="http://www.YOUR.com"
   elementFormDefault="qualified" >

  <xsd:element name="YourRoot" type="xsd:float" />

  <xsd:element name="Tester">
    <xsd:complexType>
      <xsd:sequence>
        <xsd:any />
      </xsd:sequence>
    </xsd:complexType>
  </xsd:element>

</xsd:schema>
```

The `elementFormDefault` attribute and the corresponding `attributeFormDefault` attribute (not shown) indicate the so-called *qualification* of local elements and attributes, respectively. The possible values are "unqualified" and "qualified"; the default value for both attributes of these is "unqualified". The value "qualified" simply means that the elements (or attributes) defined in the schema belong to some namespace, given by `targetNamespace`. (It does not necessarily mean that they will be prefixed.) If the value is "unqualified", they are not in any namespace. Some developers feel that the default value is wrong for these attributes, so within `xsd:schema` elements you will often see:

```
elementFormDefault="qualified"
```

Listing 6-16 shows an instance (`ns2.xml`) that uses this schema. This time, we've associated a namespace prefix `abc:` with the namespace URI, which is the same namespace identified as the `targetNamespace` in the schema. Notice a special attribute that we haven't seen before: `xsi:schemaLocation`. The syntax is particularly unusual. The value of `xsi:schemaLocation` is a white space–separated *list of one or more pairs of URIs and schema filenames*, also white space–separated (not separated by a slash!). In this example, there is only one pair:

```
xsi:schemaLocation="http://www.YOUR.com  ns2.xsd"
```

Here `http://www.YOUR.com` is the namespace URI and `ns2.xsd` is the schema URI. Another example with two namespace/schema URI pairs is:

```
xsi:schemaLocation=
   "http://sall.net/ken/ns/addr addressType-Import.xsd
    http://sall.net/ken/ns/zip  zipcode-Import.xsd"
```

(This certainly looks weird because we don't typically have attribute values that are separate tokens and that may have an embedded newline.)

Listing 6-16 Instance with Prefixed Elements

```
<?xml version="1.0"?>
<abc:Tester
      xmlns:xsi="http://www.w3.org/2001/XMLSchema-instance"
      xmlns:abc="http://www.YOUR.com"
      xsi:schemaLocation="http://www.YOUR.com  ns2.xsd"
>

  <abc:YourRoot>12.34</abc:YourRoot>
</abc:Tester>
```

In some cases, it may be preferable to make XML Schema the *default* namespace and then explicitly identify other namespaces. In Listing 6-17, we're still specifying the `targetNamespace` as the one we're creating, but rather than prefix XML Schema elements and types with the usual `xsd:` prefix, we've indicated a prefix for our *own* schema:

```
xmlns:abc="http://www.YOUR.com"
```

This means if we define our own type named `float`, we'll prefix it so the name is `abc:float`. This example brings to light an interesting paradox. Which float types are we referring to in these two lines?

```
<simpleType name="float">
  <restriction base="float">
```

Well, the first one is `abc:float`, the type we're deriving, and the second is what we normally identify as `xsd:float`, since it's the base type that we're constraining. It turns out that we can't use the prefix in the first line because a type name can't contain a prefix when it's being defined. Yet the schema processor can determine which float is which. Of course, I could have made things a bit more clear if I'd used a different name, such as:

```
<element name="YourRoot" type="abc:limitedFloat" />
<simpleType name="limitedFloat">
  <restriction base="float">
```

But that wouldn't have been as interesting, right?

Listing 6-17 Schema with XML Schema as Default Namespace

```
<?xml version="1.0"?>
<schema
   xmlns="http://www.w3.org/2001/XMLSchema"
   targetNamespace="http://www.YOUR.com"
   xmlns:abc="http://www.YOUR.com"
   elementFormDefault="qualified"
>
  <element name="YourRoot" type="abc:float" />
  <simpleType name="float">
    <restriction base="float">
      <minInclusive value="1.0" />
      <maxInclusive value="10.0" />
    </restriction>
  </simpleType>

  <element name="Tester">
    <complexType>
      <sequence>
        <any />
      </sequence>
    </complexType>
  </element>

</schema>
```

Notice in the instance in Listing 6-18 the prefix `ABC:` is used, rather than `abc:`. While a different prefix was a problem in DTDs, it is not with XML Schema. This is good news if you've developed many instances and suddenly find a need to change the namespace prefix in the schema.

Listing 6-18 Instance Corresponding to Qualified Target Namespace Schema

```
<?xml version="1.0"?>
<ABC:Tester
      xmlns:xsi="http://www.w3.org/2001/XMLSchema-instance"
      xmlns:ABC="http://www.YOUR.com"
      xsi:schemaLocation="http://www.YOUR.com  ns3.xsd"
>
  <ABC:YourRoot>2.34</ABC:YourRoot>
</ABC:Tester>
```

Roger Costello's XML Schema Best Practices Web site discusses a number of technical issues, one of which is relevant to this discussion:

> When creating a schema should XMLSchema (i.e., `http://www.w3.org/2001/XMLSchema`) be the default namespace, or should the target Namespace be the default, or should there be no default namespace?[11]

11. See "Default Namespace—targetNamespace or XMLSchema?" from *http://www.xfront.com/BestPracticesHomepage.html*. This work was developed collaboratively by The MITRE Corporation and members of the xml-dev list group.

Costello's article presents various pros and cons, especially relevant if your schema combines multiple languages. The conclusion, however, is that there is no clear winner; this is essentially a matter of preference.

Import and Include

The two special top-level elements, `xsd:import` and `xsd:include`, enable you to incorporate other schemas into yours, thereby assembling a schema from separate pieces. This is comparable to external parameter entities in DTD, which is the way to construct a DTD from any number of smaller files, many of which can be reused.

The difference between these two elements is that `xsd:import` allows access to elements and type definitions from *different* namespaces, whereas `xsd:include` permits access to elements and type definitions from the *same* namespace. (In other words, in the case of `xsd:include`, the target namespace of the included components must be the same as the target namespace of the including schema.)

> **Note:** Both `xsd:import` and `xsd:include` must appear prior to any other element declarations or type definitions in the schema.

Let's consider an example in which we import a zip code schema and use it to define one of three address types. The other two address types will use local definitions for zip codes. The small zip code schema (`zipcode-Import.xsd`) is shown in Listing 6-19. It does nothing more than define a simple type called `Zip9Type` and declare the namespace URI `http://sall.net/ken/ns/`**`zip`**.

Listing 6-19 Zip Code Schema

```
<?xml version="1.0" encoding="UTF-8"?>
<xsd:schema
    xmlns:xsd="http://www.w3.org/2001/XMLSchema"
    xmlns="http://sall.net/ken/ns/zip"
    targetNamespace="http://sall.net/ken/ns/zip"
    elementFormDefault="qualified">

  <xsd:simpleType name="Zip9Type">
    <xsd:restriction base="xsd:string">
      <xsd:pattern value="\d{5}-\d{4}" />
    </xsd:restriction>
  </xsd:simpleType>

</xsd:schema>
```

Listing 6-20 shows how to import the zip code schema using `xsd:import` by supplying both the `namespace` and the `schemaLocation`. Although `AddressType` and `WorldAddressType` both use local definitions for their `Zip` element, `RestrictedAddressType` specifies

```
type="zc:Zip9Type"
```

This maps to the external zip code type. How does this happen? The "`zc:`" prefix is declared in the `xsd:schema` element as

```
xmlns:zc="http://sall.net/ken/ns/zip"
```

This is the same namespace URI established by the `xsd:import` element. So the schema named by `schemaLocation` attribute, `zipcode-Import.xsd`, is accessed and the `Zip9Type` definition is obtained. Note, however, that this zip code namespace is different from both the target namespace and default namespace in Listing 6-20, which is:

```
http://sall.net/ken/ns/addr
```

Listing 6-20 Schema That Imports Zip Code Schema

```
<?xml version="1.0" encoding="UTF-8"?>
<xsd:schema
    xmlns:xsd="http://www.w3.org/2001/XMLSchema"
    xmlns="http://sall.net/ken/ns/addr"
    targetNamespace="http://sall.net/ken/ns/addr"
    xmlns:zc="http://sall.net/ken/ns/zip"
    elementFormDefault="qualified">

<!-- Obtain zipcode types from external file. -->
<xsd:import  namespace="http://sall.net/ken/ns/zip"
             schemaLocation="zipcode-Import.xsd" />

  <xsd:complexType name="AddressType">
    <xsd:sequence>
      <xsd:element ref="Street" maxOccurs="2" />
      <xsd:element ref="City"/>
      <xsd:element ref="State"/>
      <xsd:element ref="Zip"/>
    </xsd:sequence>
  </xsd:complexType>

  <xsd:element name="Address" type="AddressType" />
  <xsd:element name="City" type="xsd:string"/>
  <xsd:element name="State" type="xsd:string"/>
  <xsd:element name="Street" type="xsd:string" />
  <xsd:element name="Zip" type="xsd:positiveInteger"/>

  <xsd:element name="WorldAddress" type="WorldAddressType" />
  <xsd:element name="RestrictedAddress" type="RestrictedAddressType" />
```

```
  <xsd:complexType name="WorldAddressType">
    <xsd:complexContent>
      <xsd:extension base="AddressType">
        <xsd:sequence>
          <xsd:element name="Country" type="xsd:string"/>
        </xsd:sequence>
      </xsd:extension>
    </xsd:complexContent>
  </xsd:complexType>

  <xsd:complexType name="RestrictedAddressType">
    <xsd:complexContent>
      <xsd:restriction base="AddressType">
        <xsd:sequence>
          <xsd:element ref="Street" maxOccurs="2" />
          <xsd:element ref="City"/>
          <xsd:element ref="State"/>
          <!-- note namespace prefix -->
          <xsd:element name="ZipCode" type="zc:Zip9Type"/>
        </xsd:sequence>
      </xsd:restriction>
    </xsd:complexContent>
  </xsd:complexType>

  <xsd:element name="AddressTest">
    <xsd:complexType>
      <xsd:sequence>
        <xsd:any />
      </xsd:sequence>
    </xsd:complexType>
  </xsd:element>

</xsd:schema>
```

Listing 6-21 demonstrates an instance that is valid with respect to the schema that does the importing. This document identifies the `http://sall.net/ken/ns/addr` namespace URI and the schema via `xsi:schemaLocation`. `RestrictedAddress` uses the format for zip code defined by the `Zip9Type`.

Listing 6-21 Instance Based on Schema with Import

```
<?xml version="1.0" ?>
<AddressTest
  xsi:schemaLocation=
     "http://sall.net/ken/ns/addr addressType-Import.xsd"
  xmlns:xsi="http://www.w3.org/2001/XMLSchema-instance">
  <Address>
    <Street>123 Milky Way Dr.</Street>
    <City>Columbia</City>
    <State>MD</State>
    <Zip>20777</Zip>
```

```
  </Address>
  <WorldAddress>
    <Street>123 Milky Way Dr.</Street>
    <City>Columbia</City>
    <State>MD</State>
    <Zip>20777</Zip>
    <Country>US</Country>
  </WorldAddress>
  <RestrictedAddress>
    <Street>123 Milky Way Dr.</Street>
    <City>Columbia</City>
    <State>MD</State>
    <ZipCode>20777-1234</ZipCode>
  </RestrictedAddress>
</AddressTest>
```

Working with XML Schema

The purpose of this section is threefold: first, to highlight more than a dozen software tools, packages, and utilities designed to make working with schema easier; second, to present several ways to migrate from DTDs to XML Schema, and third, to showcase a few tools that are extremely useful for schema design and validation, plus instance generation.

XML Schema Software

The W3C maintains a list of tools with various degrees of support for XML Schema (*http://www.w3.org/XML/Schema.html#Tools*). A similar list of XML Schema software follows; links appear at the end of this chapter and many are also on the W3C page.

- *xsv*—XML Schema Validator; extremely useful tool for validating XML Schemas or instances that reference schemas; Web form or freeware executable; available on this book's CD.
- *xsbrowser*—Creates human readable document model from an XML Schema or DTD; freeware.
- *dtd2xs*—Converts a DTD to an XML Schema; freeware.
- *TurboXML*—Suite of tools for creating or editing XML Schemas, DTDs, and other schema formats, as well as authoring XML document instances based on schema; can convert from one schema to another; commercial product from TIBCO Extensibility; evaluation copy on this book's CD.
- *XML Spy*—Integrated development environment for creating or editing XML Schemas, DTDs, and other schema formats, with built-in XSLT support; can convert from one schema to another; commercial product from Altova; evaluation copy on this book's CD.

- *Xerces Java Parser 1.4.4*—SAX2 and DOM2 parser with beta XML Schema support. Limitations are documented at *http://xml.apache.org/xerces-j/schema.html*. Xerces2 Java Parser 2.X (*http://xml.apache.org/xerces2-j/index.html*) also supports XML Schema. Both are on this book's CD.
- *Microsoft XML Parser 4.0* (also known as *Microsoft XML Core Services*)—XSD validation with SAX or DOM; nonstandard Schema Object Model (SOM) to access schema information in DOM and SAX; freeware.
- *Oracle's XML Schema Validator*—Available in C, C++, and Java
- *Sun's XML Datatypes Library*—Sun's Java technology implementation of XML Schema Part 2 for use in Java applications; freeware.
- *Sun's XML Instance Generator*—Generates valid (and optionally invalid) XML instances from DTD, RELAX Namespace, RELAX Core, TREX, and a subset of W3C XML Schema Part 1; uses Sun's Multi Schema Validator (MSV) for parsing schemas.
- *Sun's RELAX NG Converter*—Converts schemas written in XML DTD, RELAX Core, RELAX namespace, TREX, and W3C XML Schema to their equivalent in RELAX NG.
- *IBM XML Schema Quality Checker*—Diagnoses improper uses of XML Schema; freeware.
- *XMLValidate*—Enterprise-grade solution for validating streaming XML documents or messages against an XML Schema or DTD; SAX-based implementation for run-time validation provides organizations with the core component in developing high bandwidth, XML-based processing; commercial product from TIBCO Extensibility. *Note:* Not to be confused with XMLValidator by Elcel Technology.

In the remainder of this section, we'll look at `xsv`, TurboXML, and XML Spy in more detail. Each of these schema tools is on the book's CD.

Converting DTDs to XML Schema

If your company has invested considerable time in developing DTDs and is considering leveraging the greater power available when using XML Schema, you can rest assured that you don't need to start from scratch. Several tools support importing a DTD and exporting an XML Schema (as well as other schema formats).

As you would expect, regardless of the tool, this conversion process is a straight translation of your DTD to another syntax, namely that of XSD. As we noted in the earlier section "What Have We Gained?" this does not take advantage of the features that make XML Schema superior to DTDs. However, since XML Schema is generally a superset of DTD functionality, you have lost nothing in the conversion process (except entities) and you have an excellent starting point for tapping the potential of XML Schema. This is one major caveat, however—for complicated DTDs, it may be desirable to redesign your model from the ground up in light of the richer expressiveness of XSD, rather than use existing DTDs as a foundation. This does not preclude at least trying the conversion and seeing whether it provides a reasonable basis for further expansion, however. If nothing else, the exercise is useful to illustrate the XML Schema syntax needed to express something with which you are already familiar—your own DTD.

At the time of this writing, the new kid on the block is Sun's RELAX NG Converter, which converts schemas written in XML DTD, RELAX Core, RELAX namespace, TREX, and W3C XML Schema to their equivalent in RELAX NG. If you're working in a Java development environment and you're interested in an alternative to XML Schema called RELAX NG, this freeware is worth considering. For an example of its output, see the section "RELAX NG" later in this chapter.

Converting with TurboXML by TIBCO Extensibility

You may recall we used XML Authority (the schema component of TurboXML by TIBCO Extensibility) in chapter 4 to generate a DTD from an XML instance and vice versa. However, XML Authority (XA) is primarily a schema editor and convertor. At the time of this writing, XA version 2.2 supports DTDs and a the final W3C Recommendation for XSD, as well as several non-W3C schemas: XDR, BizTalk, SOX Version 2, OneSoft, Software AG's Tamino Server, and more. XA also provides export-only support for DCD, DDML, and RELAX. (The list of supported schema is almost certain to change in subsequent releases.)

The method for converting your DTD to an XML Schema is similar to the way we generated an XML instance from a DTD. From the start-up panel, browse to the DTD of your choice, and select `File | Export` and then select the desired schema format as shown in Figure 6-1. Figure 6-2 showsTurboXML in design view.

Converting with XML Spy IDE by Altova

XML Spy Suite by Altova started life several years ago as a modest XML editor; it is now promoted as an XML IDE (integrated development environment) because it supports XML and DTD editing and validation, as well as XSL Transformations, visual design, database integration, and browser plugins. Although it may not support as many schema formats as TurboXML, it handles DTD conversion quite nicely and also imports databases and Microsoft Word documents. To convert a DTD, go to the `DTD/Schema` menu and select `Convert DTD/Schema`, which invokes the dialog shown in Figure 6-3 from which you can select XML Schema, BizTalk, XDR, DCD, or DTD (to convert *to* a DTD). If you're converting to XML Schema, you can decide whether to generate complex structures as elements or complex types and whether to use local or global definitions for elements that are used only once. See Figure 6-4 for XML Spy in design view. Details may change as the result of later releases.

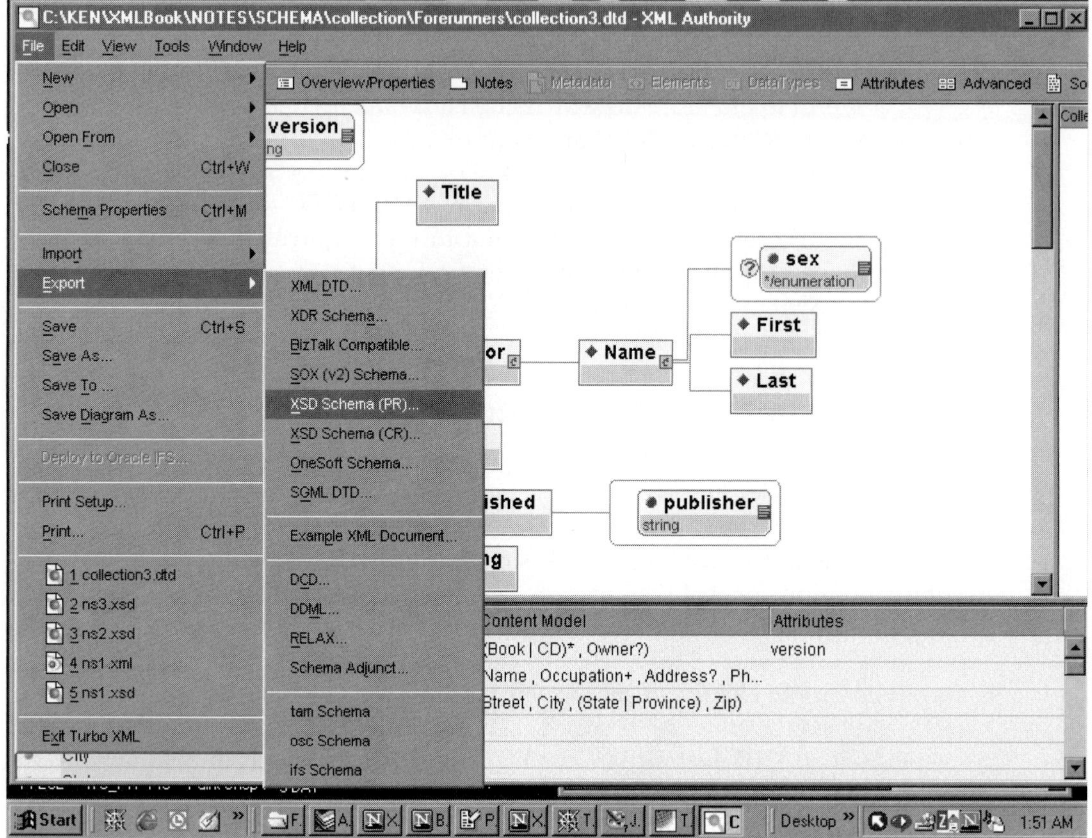

FIGURE 6-1 Converting a DTD to XML Schema using TurboXML

Schema Validation

Validation of schemas is similar to the DTD case, but more complicated from the viewpoint of the schema validator, primarily due to the richness of XSD. You validate an XML Schema to determine whether it is syntactically and structurally correct according to the constraints of the XML Schema specifications. Some of the ways in which an XML Schema can be invalid are:

- It uses elements or attributes other than those defined in the W3C specifications.
- You omit an `xsd:` prefix when you've declared their namespace use.
- It doesn't adhere to the XSD content models (e.g., if an `xsd:element` appears as a direct child of `xsd:complexType`, without an `xsd:sequence`, `xsd:choice`, or `xsd:all` parent).
- In the more trivial case, the XML that comprises your XML Schema is not well-formed.

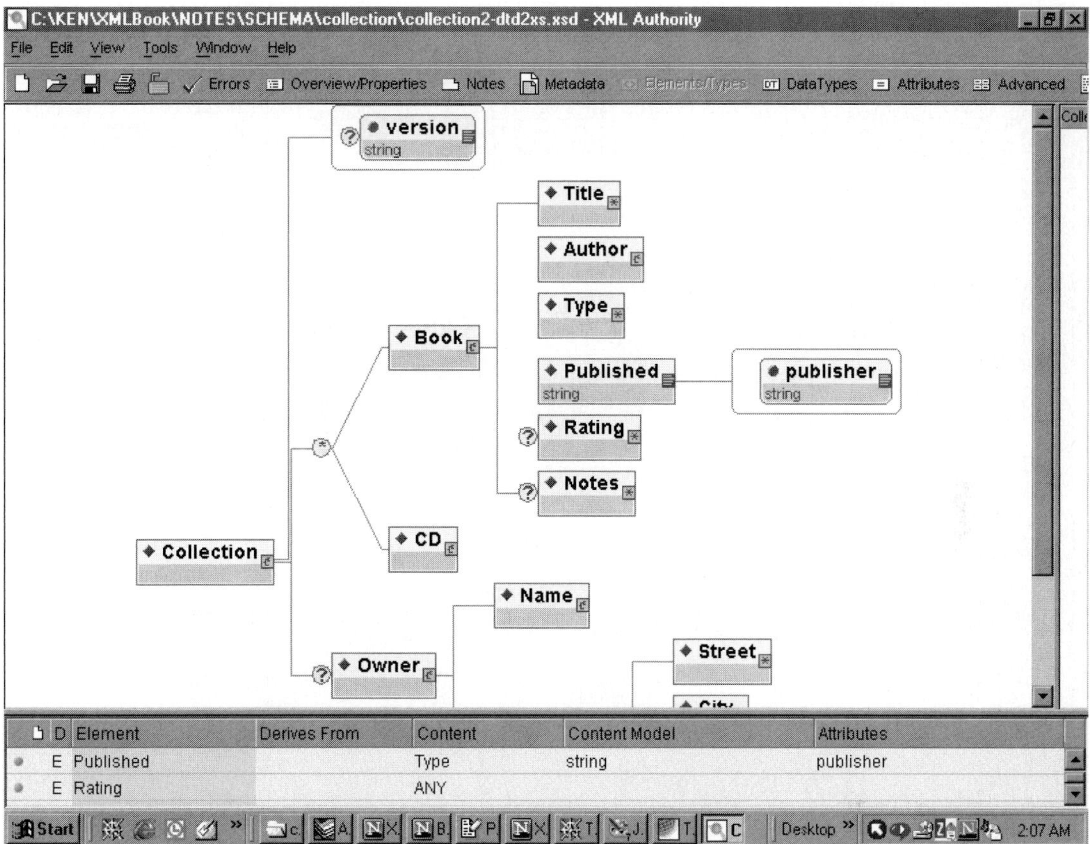

FIGURE 6-2 TurboXML in design view

An XML instance document that references an XML Schema is valid if and only if it is well-formed and its structure matches the constraints imposed by the schema. Similar to instance validation against DTDs, this means it too must use only elements and attributes defined in the schema and must follow the content models as well.

Validation Using XSV by Henry Thompson

Henry Thompson, one of the members of the W3C Schema Working Group, and Richard Tobin have made a utility called `xsv` (XML Schema Validator) available since well before the specifications were finalized. This validator is available both with a Web form interface to validate schema accessible via `http` or using

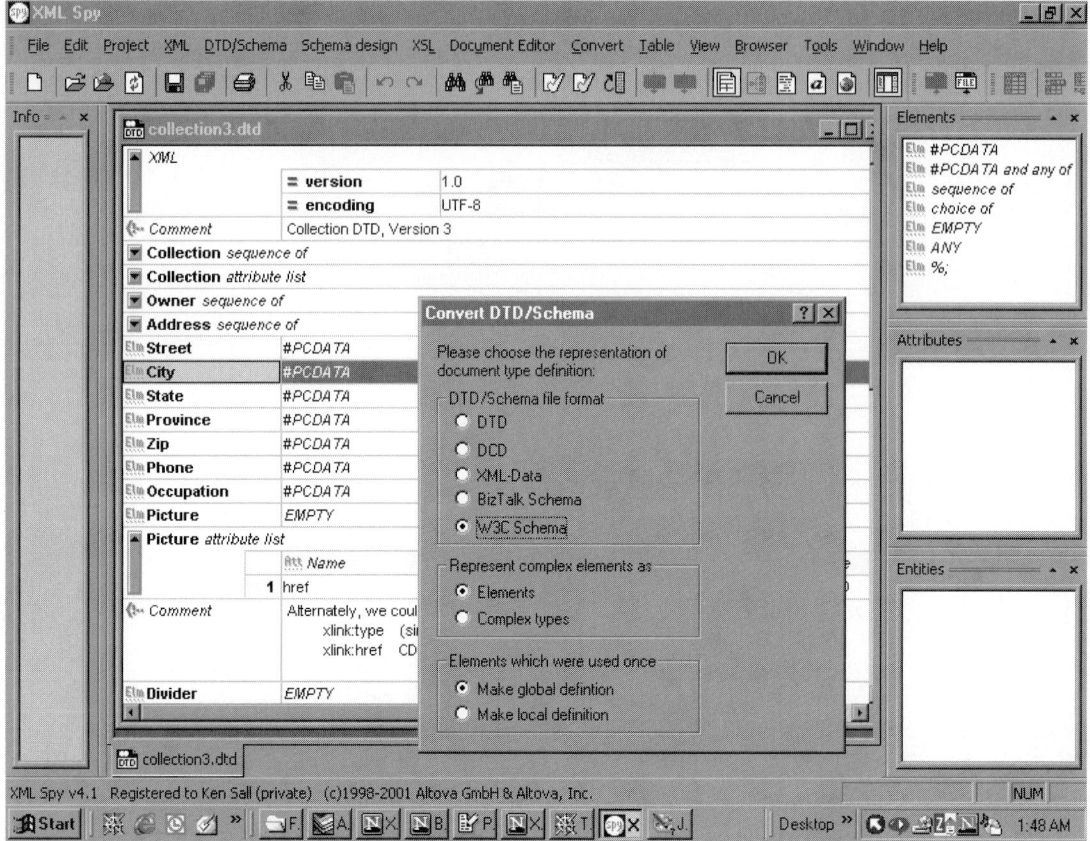

FIGURE 6-3 Converting a DTD to XML Schema with XML Spy

the file upload capability of Web forms (*http://www.w3.org/2001/03/webdata/xsv*). You can also download xsv as a self-extracting Windows executable (*ftp://ftp.cogsci.ed.ac.uk/pub/XSV/*). There is a version on the CD-ROM; however, this software is improved every month or two, so check the FTP site for an update. Although the utility supports many command-line options, the basic usage is:

```
xsv -o outputFile XML_Schema_or_Instance
```

I recommend the `-o` option since the output is voluminous if there is an error. Listing 6-22 shows a successful result in validating `collection3-mods.xsd`. This means that our schema is valid with respect to the rules of XML Schema. Similarly, we could validate an instance that refers to this schema using the same command line.

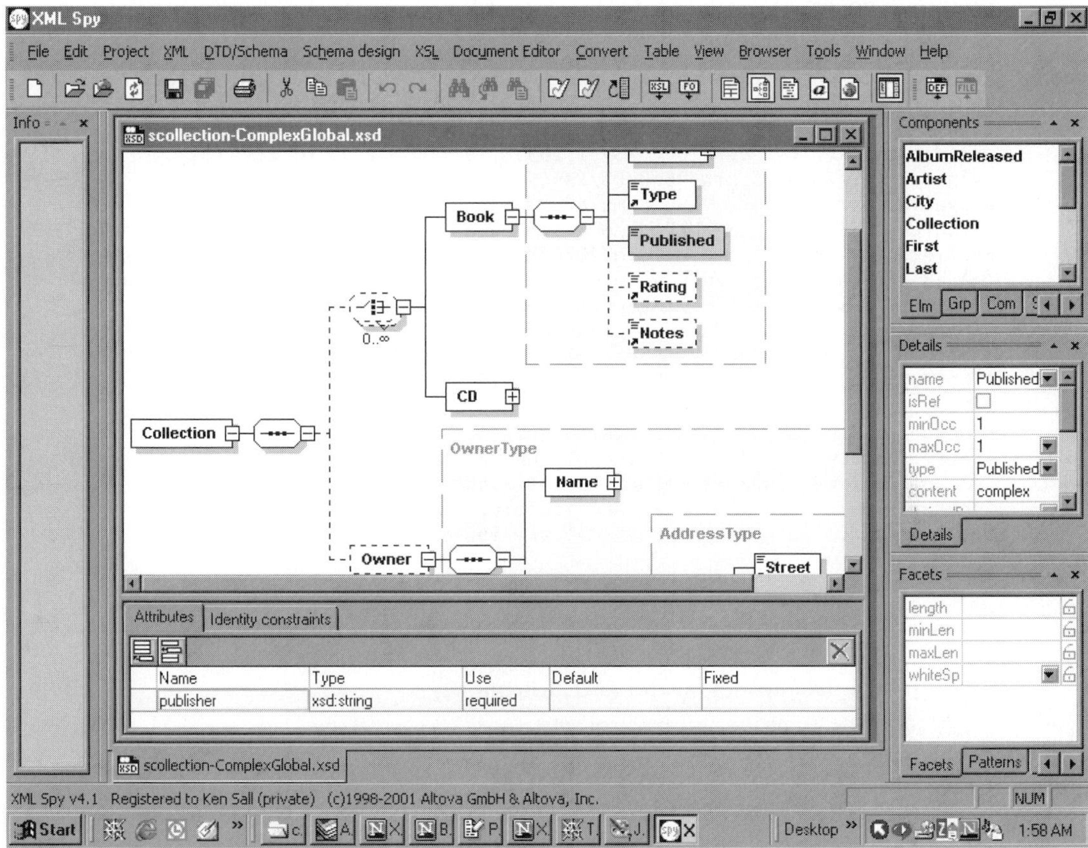

FIGURE 6-4 XML Spy in Schema design view

Listing 6-22 XSV Success Report on Valid Schema

```
<?xml version='1.0'?>
<xsv docElt='{http://www.w3.org/2001/XMLSchema}schema'
instanceAssessed='true' instanceErrors='0' rootType='[Anonymous]'
schemaErrors='0'
target='file:/C:/KEN/XMLBook/NOTES/SCHEMA/collection/collection3-mods.xsd'
validation='strict' version='XSV 1.203.2.19/1.106.2.11 of
2001/11/01 17:07:43' xmlns='http://www.w3.org/2000/05/xsv'/>
```

Listing 6-23 illustrates how `xsv` reports an error, given `address-invalid.xsd` as input (see Listing 6-24). The error output is very verbose; usually only the initial lines are worth studying, so I've truncated the report. This report tells us that on line 7 the element `xsd:element` cannot appear following `xsd:complexType`. It also conveniently lists all elements that *can* be direct children of `xsd:complexType`. As it happens, the problem is that there should be an `xsd:sequence` element between `xsd:complexType` and `xsd:element`.

Listing 6-23 XSV Error Report on Invalid Schema

```
<?xml version='1.0'?>
<xsv docElt='{http://www.w3.org/2001/XMLSchema}schema' instanceAssessed='true'
instanceErrors='8' rootType='[Anonymous]' schemaErrors='0'
target='file:/C:/KEN/XMLBook/NOTES/SCHEMA/address/address-invalid.xsd'
validation='strict' version='XSV 1.203.2.19/1.106.2.11 of 2001/11/01 17:07:43'
xmlns='http://www.w3.org/2000/05/xsv'>
<invalid char='9' code='cvc-complex-type.1.2.4' line='7'
resource='file:/C:/KEN/XMLBook/NOTES/SCHEMA/address/address-invalid.
xsd'>element {http://www.w3.org/2001/XMLSchema}:element not allowed here
(1) in element {http://www.w3.org/2001/XMLSchema}:complexType, expecting
['{http://www.w3.org/2001/XMLSchema}:sequence',
'{http://www.w3.org/2001/XMLSchema}:all',
'{http://www.w3.org/2001/XMLSchema}:anyAttribute',
'{http://www.w3.org/2001/XMLSchema}:simpleContent',
'{http://www.w3.org/2001/XMLSchema}:complexContent',
'{http://www.w3.org/2001/XMLSchema}:group',
'{http://www.w3.org/2001/XMLSchema}:annotation',
'{http://www.w3.org/2001/XMLSchema}:attributeGroup',
'{http://www.w3.org/2001/XMLSchema}:choice',
'{http://www.w3.org/2001/XMLSchema}:attribute']:
<fsm>
<node final='true' id='1'>
<!-- etc -->
```

Listing 6-24 Example of Invalid XML Schema

```
<?xml version="1.0" encoding="UTF-8"?>
<xsd:schema
     xmlns:xsd="http://www.w3.org/2001/XMLSchema">
  <xsd:element name="Address">
    <xsd:complexType>
      <!-- invalid because xsd:sequence is missing -->
        <xsd:element name="Street" type="xsd:string"/>
        <xsd:element name="City" type="xsd:string"/>
        <xsd:element name="State" type="xsd:string"/>
        <xsd:element name="Zip" type="xsd:string"/>
    </xsd:complexType>
  </xsd:element>
</xsd:schema>
```

Validation Using XML Spy

Both TurboXML and XML Spy are also useful in the validation of XML Schema and instances. For the sake of brevity, we'll look only at XML Spy. Figure 6-5 demonstrates how XML Spy reports the same problematic schema shown in Listing 6-24. It correctly detects that `xsd:element` cannot appear at this point in an XML Schema (although it doesn't suggest what *can* appear here).

For an example of validation of an XML instance, see Figure 6-6. The error that XML Spy correctly detects is that the instance uses "May, 1992" as element content

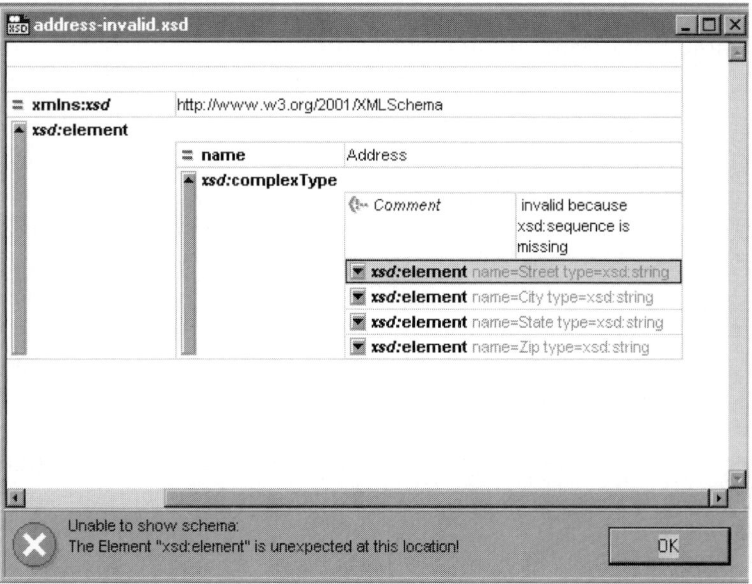

FIGURE 6-5 Schema error reported by XML Spy

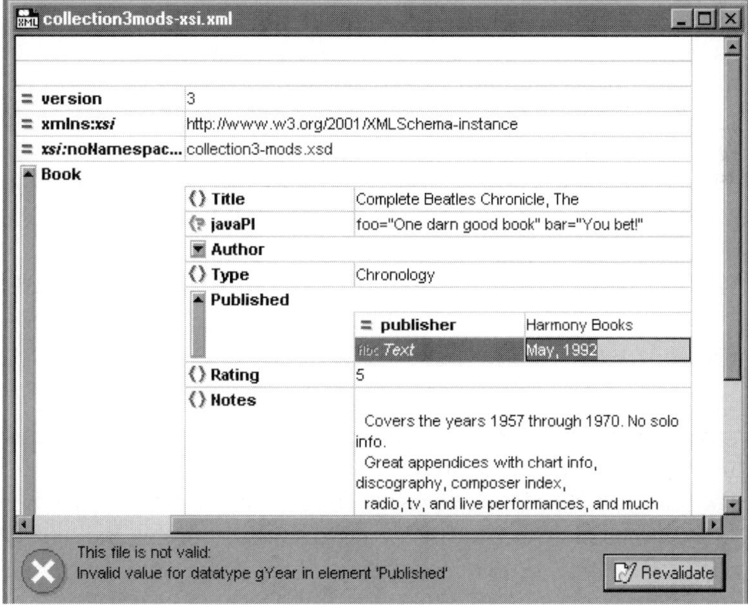

FIGURE 6-6 Instance error detection in XML Spy

for `Published`, which has been defined to use the `xsd:gYear` datatype, which consists of a four-digit year, but no month information.

Schema Repositories and Registries

Certainly before you undertake the task of developing an XML Schema (or DTD), it's worthwhile to do a little research to determine whether existing schema might meet (or nearly meet) your needs. In addition to the substantial savings in development costs, it's usually far preferable to leverage a standard used by multiple organizations than to create a vocabulary that only your application will understand. It's unlikely that an existing schema will match *all* of your requirements, but you now know various ways to extend a schema, so it's not an all-or-nothing proposition.

Before you try a Google search, however, try one of the sites that specialize in schema. There are several major efforts under way to collect and distribute schema. These are primarily DTD and Microsoft XDR schemas at this time, but the number of XML Schema examples is growing quickly. Consider the information in this section to be a snapshot of such efforts from February 2002.

XML.org

The most extensive repositories I know of are the two created and maintained by XML.org (*http://www.xml.org/*), whose parent organization, OASIS (Organization for the Advancement of Structured Information Standards, *http://www.oasis-open.org*), has been a key player in the SGML community for many years. Both OASIS and XML.org are nonprofit organizations with diverse membership and participation from many industries and businesses. XML.org sponsors the creation of comprehensive XML, XSL, and DOM conformance suites, hosts the xml-dev (developers') mailing list, and sponsors the long-running XML Cover Pages, a massive collection of XML news information, standards, and applications. In addition, XML.org provides an open registry and repository for XML DTDs and schemas:

- *Vertical Industries Directory* contains hundreds of DTDs organized in sixty industry-specific categories (Table 6-15)—see *http://www.xml.org/xml/industry_industrysectors.jsp*
- *Search Schemas in XML.org Registry* collects hundreds of XML Schema, XDR schema, and DTDs in roughly twenty-five categories (Table 6-16); you can search by category, type of schema, or keyword—see *http://www.xml.org/xml/registry.jsp*.

The searchable schema repository is still fairly new. The initial categories are shown in Table 6-16.

TABLE 6-15 XML.org's Vertical Industry DTD Categories

Accounting	Education	Publishing/Print
Advertising	Energy/Utilities	Real Estate
Aerospace	Environmental	Religion
Agriculture	Financial Service	Retail
Arts/Entertainment	Food Services	Robotics/AI
Astronomy	Geography	Science
Automotive	Healthcare	Security
Banking	Human Resources	Software
Biology	Industrial Control	Supply Chain
Business Services	Insurance	Telecommunications
Catalogs	Internet/Web	Translation
Chemistry	Legal	Transportation
Computer	Literature	Travel
Construction	Manufacturing	Waste Management
Consulting	Marketing/PR	Weather
Customer Relations	Math/Data	Wholesale
Customs	Mining	XML Technologies
Databases	Multimedia	
E-commerce	News	
EDI	Other Industry	
ERP	Public Service	

TABLE 6-16 XML.org's Schema Repository Search Categories

Arts/Entertainment	E-commerce	News
Astronomy	Education	Real Estate
Automotive	Energy/Utilities	Robotics/AI
Banking	Financial Service	Science
Biology	Food Services	Software
Business Services	Healthcare	Transportation
Catalogs	Human Resources	XML Technologies
Chemistry	Internet/Web	
Construction	Multimedia	

BizTalk

Microsoft's BizTalk.org (*http://www.biztalk.org/*) is a resource site for Enterprise Application Integration (EAI) and business-to-business (B2B) document exchange via XML. The site explains how to use XML messages to integrate software applications and build new solutions, especially by integrating existing data models and application infrastructure, and adapting them for e-commerce. Another major focus of the site is to promote the BizTalk Framework, a set of guidelines for implementing a schema and a set of XML tags used in messaging between applications.

The search interface for Microsoft is located at *http://www.biztalk.org/library/search_objects.asp*. However, since the site requires free registration even to view the schema search categories, they aren't listed here. At the time of this writing, there are approximately 20 categories and nearly 500 documents. Virtually all of these are XDR schema; few of them are XML Schema, although this is likely to change.

Open Applications Group

The Open Applications Group (OAGI, *http://www.openapplications.org/*) is a non-profit consortium focusing on best practices and process-based XML content for e-business and Application Integration. OAGI is building specifications that define the business object interoperability of enterprise business applications. According to its own plans and schedule, each member company develops software that is compliant with the Open Applications Group Integration Specification (OAGIS). To date, they have developed more than 180 DTDs and XDR schemas (sometimes called BODs for *Business Object Documents*) covering, for example, categories such as:

- Order management to accounts receivable
- Purchasing to accounts payable
- Plant data collection/warehouse management
- Manufacturing to purchasing
- Manufacturing to order management
- Invoice matching
- Sales force automation to order management
- Supply chain integration
- Customer service integration
- Engineering change integration
- Maintenance management with maintenance orders

The site includes white papers that describe how to send and receive the OAGI's business message content using Microsoft's BizTalk Framework, RosettaNet's RNIF, and various ebXML specifications.

More Miscellaneous Topics

Before discussing a few alternatives to XML Schema, such as RELAX NG, let's very briefly examine some shortcomings of XML Schema, consider when DTDs might be preferable, and highlight what hasn't been covered in this chapter.

Shortcomings of XML Schema

XML Schema is not the be-all, end-all of schema approaches. Many developers feel that the W3C went a bit too far and created something that is overly complex. It's helpful to keep in mind, though, that the W3C XML Schema Working Group had dozens of participants from different companies, each trying to address particular needs. At one point, there was a possibility of a simpler 1.0 version of the language earlier on. This did not happen, so we're left with a fairly large language, more than many people need. Of course, the counterpoint is that human languages such as English are quite large and few people have to deal with all of the language. Instead, we use the subset of the language that meets our needs. But the richness of XML Schema helps us better appreciate the difficulty for the designers of XML Schema design tools and validators, since they *do* need to be familiar with all of the details.

When to Use DTDs Instead of XML Schema

In "Comparing W3C XML Schemas and Document Type Definitions," an IBM developerWorks article (*http://www-106.ibm.com/developerworks/library/x-matters7.html*) written before the XML Schema specifications became Recommendations, David Mertz summarized several situations in which DTDs are preferable to XML Schema. I've annotated these points with the benefit of hindsight.

- A compact representation of your constraints is needed (still applies).
- Downstream users of your schema need to override or specialize your types (no longer true).
- Your rules are more document-centric than data-centric; that is, they are based mainly on the nesting of elements, rather than on datatype constraints (still applies).
- The tools you use are more supportive of DTDs (still applies, but XML Schema support in tools is improving each month).

XML Schema Topics Not Covered in Detail

The topics in the following list are either not covered or are covered very lightly in this chapter. Interested readers should consult the W3C XML Schema Primer (Part 0). Gluttons for punishment should read the formal XML Schema specifications, Parts 1 and 2. Tutorials, such as the one by Roger Costello, are also an excellent resource. Specialized books on XML Schema provide additional insight, such as *Definitive XML Schema* by Priscilla Walmsley (see "For Further Exploration").

- Multiple documents (including schema using the `xsd:include` element)
- Combining schema with `xsd:import`
- Identity-constraint definitions (`xsd:key`, `xsd:keyref`, `xsd:unique`)
- Notation declarations
- Wildcards
- Particles
- Qualification
- Element *substitution groups* (formerly called equivalence classes)
- Abstract elements and types
- `xsd:field`, `xsd:selector`
- `xsd:anyAttribute`
- `block`, `blockDefault`, `xsi:nil`, and `nillable` attributes
- `xpath` attribute
- Additional namespace details
- Instances that reference DTDs as well as XML Schema

XML Schema Alternatives

Originally, the Last Call Working Draft of XML Schema in late 2000 generated a great deal of controversy due to what some experts believe is its complexity. Simple things should be simple to express in XML Schema, and that is not always the case. Some involved parties were content with the two most fundamental aspects of XSD, the ability to use XML syntax and the wide variety of datatypes (both of which you'll recall date way back to XML-Data). Others felt that the more powerful features such as subclassing, locally scoped namespaces, and substitution groups were needlessly complex; they believed that XML Schema's requirements should be descoped and the underlying model be redesigned. There is little doubt that the task of the Schema Working Group was herculean: to produce a specification that accommodated the needs of all types of data and documents, across all domains and industries, and yet was not painful for developers to implement. Most experts agree that "getting it right" is of the utmost importance in furthering the acceptance and penetration of XML in e-commerce and database communities.

Alternatives to XML Schema have gained popularity because in many ways they are simpler than the W3C specifications. In this section, we briefly cover some of the alternatives: RELAX, TREX, RELAX NG, and Schematron.

RELAX

REgular LAnguage description for XML (RELAX, *http://www.xml.gr.jp/relax/*), an effort supported by the Japanese Standards Association (JSA), is based on hedge automata theory and generated considerable interest as a simpler solution than XML Schema. Compared to DTDs, RELAX permits the use of XML syntax, borrows datatypes from XML Schema Part 2, and supports namespaces. RELAX, much like XML Schema, is a language for describing other XML languages. A *RELAX grammar* is a description of such a language in RELAX syntax. XHTML, for example, could be described using a RELAX grammar. Instance documents can be verified against the grammar.

The RELAX processor receives an XML document and its corresponding RELAX grammar; it reports if the XML document is legitimate against the RELAX grammar. Since it leverages existing XML processor interfaces, there is no need for a specialized RELAX API. RELAX is broken into RELAX Core (sometimes called "classic") and RELAX Namespaces. RELAX Core assumes all elements are in the same namespace, whereas RELAX Namespaces eliminates that assumption and is therefore more complex. RELAX Core itself has two comformance levels:

- *Classic*—Simplest subset to implement because it includes no functionality beyond that provided by DTDs
- *Fully relaxed*—Complete RELAX Core (but single namespace)

Rapid adoption of the classic conformance level was initially anticipated since it provides a solid migration path to XML Schema. The RELAX Core was published in May 2000; it was approved as an ISO/IEC Technical Report one year later (May 2001).

A RELAX grammar is a combination of modules, represented by the `module` element. Content models are expressed with the `elementRule` element, with potential `sequence`, `choice`, `mixed`, and `ref` children. (Other RELAX elements are omitted from this discussion, such as `hedgeRule`, `attPool`, and `attribute`.) For example, our DTD fragment:

```
<!ELEMENT Collection  ( (Book | CD)*, Owner?)>
```

would be expressed as follows in RELAX:

```
<elementRule role="Collection">
  <sequence>
    <choice occurs="*"/>
      <ref label="Book"/>
      <ref label="CD"/>
    </choice>
    <ref label="Owner" occurs="?"/>
  </sequence>
</elementRule>
```

RELAX can be seen as a stepping-stone in the gap between DTDs and XML Schema. XML Authority by Extensibility supports exporting RELAX Core documents. A number of free software tools are available, such as DTD2RELAX, RELAX2DTD, and Relaxer (which generates Java classes that represent the XML

Infoset modeled by RELAX in a way that circumvents much of the DOM tediousness). See the RELAX home page.

TREX

TREX has nothing to do with the Enterprise or Voyager. It stands for Tree Regular Expressions for XML and was the brainchild of James Clark, who has contributed so much to XML specification and parser development. According to the TREX tutorial (*http://www.thaiopensource.com/trex/tutorial.html*):

> A TREX pattern specifies a pattern for the structure and content of an XML document. A TREX pattern thus identifies a class of XML documents consisting of those documents that match the pattern. A TREX pattern is itself an XML document.

TREX supports occurrence indicators, choice, attributes, named patterns, interleaving, strings, modularity, namespaces, name classes, datatyping, and much more (*http://www.thaiopensource.com/trex/*).

Note: TREX has been merged with RELAX to create RELAX NG, which is a much more recent undertaking.

RELAX NG

RELAX NG (Next Generation, again not related to Star Trek ;-) is clearly the XML Schema alternative to monitor. This effort is the work of an OASIS Technical Committee that includes some big names in the field of XML: Fabio Arciniegas, James Clark (Chair), Mike Fitzgerald, KAWAGUCHI Kohsuke, Josh Lubell, MURATA Makoto, Norman Walsh, and David Webber. They have been working since mid 2001 to combine the best ideas of RELAX and TREX, with the active involvement of the authors of both earlier specifications. The charter of the committee nicely summarizes the key benefits of RELAX NG (*http://www.oasis-open.org/committees/relax-ng/*):

> The purpose of this committee is to create a specification for a schema language for XML based on TREX and RELAX. The key features of RELAX NG are that it is simple, [is] easy to learn, uses XML syntax, does not change the information set of an XML document, supports XML namespaces, treats attributes uniformly with elements so far as possible, has unrestricted support for unordered content, has unrestricted support for mixed content, has a solid theoretical basis, and can partner with a separate datatyping language (such W3C XML Schema Datatypes).

The RELAX NG Web site (*http://www.oasis-open.org/committees/relax-ng/*) contains a wealth of information beyond the specification, including tutorials, articles, an ever-growing list of tools that support RELAX NG, and complete examples of complex RELAX NG schema (e.g., a rendering of the XML Schema language as RELAX NG by Jeni Tennison, *http://www.jenitennison.com/schema/xmlschema.rng*).

Listing 6-25 shows an example of converting the collection schema to RELAX NG using an alpha version of Sun's RELAX NG Converter (*http://www.sun.com/software/xml/developers/relaxngconverter/*). The RNG version is roughly twice the number of lines as the XML Schema version for this example. Only the fragment (`collection3-frag.rng`) corresponding to the following DTD declarations appears in the listing. The complete converted file (`collection3dtd.rng`) appears on this book's CD.

```
<!ELEMENT Name  (First, Last)>
<!ATTLIST Name  sex  (male | female )  'male' >
<!ELEMENT First  (#PCDATA)>
```

Listing 6-25 RELAX NG Collection Example Fragment (collection3-frag.rng)

```
<?xml version="1.0"?>
<grammar ns=""
         xmlns="http://relaxng.org/ns/structure/0.9"
         datatypeLibrary="http://www.w3.org/2001/XMLSchema-datatypes">
  <start>
    <choice>
      <ref name="Name"/>
      <ref name="First"/>
      <ref name="Last"/>
      <ref name="Owner"/>
      <ref name="CD"/>
      <ref name="Book"/>
      <!-- etc -->
    </choice>
  </start>

  <define name="Name">
    <choice>
      <notAllowed/>
      <element name="Name">
        <group>
          <optional>
            <attribute name="sex">
              <choice>
                <value type="NMTOKEN">female</value>
                <value type="NMTOKEN">male</value>
              </choice>
            </attribute>
          </optional>
          <ref name="First"/>
        </group>
        <ref name="Last"/>
      </element>
    </choice>
  </define>
```

```
  <define name="First">
    <choice>
      <notAllowed/>
      <element name="First">
        <data type="string"/>
      </element>
    </choice>
  </define>
  <!-- similarly for Last -->
<!-- etc -->
</grammar>
```

Schematron

In contrast to the grammar-based approaches we've seen so far to describe structure validation, Rick Jelliffe's Schematron (*http://www.ascc.net/xml/resource/schematron/*) is fundamentally different in that it is based on pattern matching using the XPath expressions that are also used by XSLT. The Schematron, based on assertions and simple actions, can be used to express constructs that are problematic or impossible in grammar-based schema languages. One aspect that distinguishes the Schematron from other approaches (such as XML Schema and RELAX NG) is that rather than specify content models and datatypes that dictate what is allowed, the Schematron lets you describe what *isn't* allowed. Anything that isn't explicitly prohibited by a Schematron schema is valid, in contrast with other schema approaches.

However, using the Schematron does not preclude using the other schema approaches such as XML Schema, RELAX, and TREX. Roger Costello's Best Practices document, in fact, shows how it is possible to embed Schematron statements within `xsd:appInfo` elements (*http://www.xfront.com/ExtendingSchemas.html*). The Schematron is supported by an error-browser, interface for interactive debuggers, and tutorial, as well as implementations in many languages (XSLT, perl, Python, Java, etc.). The Schematron requires an XSLT processor, however.

Summary

This chapter provides a solid introduction to W3C's XML Schema, as well as an overview of its forerunners and alternatives.

- The XML Schema recommendation addresses many shortcomings of DTDs by providing a large number of datatypes and a mechanism for subclassing, and using XML syntax.
- Forerunners of W3C's XML Schema include XDR (Microsoft et al.), SOX (Commerce One), DCD (IBM et al.), and DDML. Alternatives include RELAX

(Japanese standard), TREX, RELAX NG (OASIS), and Schematron. All of these approaches are generically referred to as "schema," but only the W3C recommendation is called "XML Schema."

- *Definitions* describe types and content models that are relevant mainly to the XML Schema itself. *Declarations* state which elements and attributes may appear in instance documents.
- The datatype hierarchy has the generic `anyType` at its root and divides into `simpleTypes` and `complexTypes`.
- Derivation (subclassing) can be accomplished in any of four ways: by `restriction`, `extension`, `list`, or `union`. The first two are by far the more common.
- There are forty-four built-in datatypes (`ID`, `string`, `integer`, `float`, `dateTime`, etc.), all of which are `simpleTypes`, nearly all of which are derived by `restriction`.
- All user-defined derivations based on restricting the legal values of character content, such as by an integer range or a character pattern, are also `simpleType` definitions.
- Values of a `simpleType` can easily be constrained by using datatype-specific *facets*, such as `maxLength`, `pattern`, `enumeration`, `minInclusive`, and `totalDigits`.
- XML Schema uses perl-like regular expression syntax to describe `pattern` facets.
- Unlike `simpleTypes`, which can contain only character data, `complexTypes` may contain element children and/or attributes.
- Derivation by `extension` involves adding elements or attributes to an existing `complexType` definition.
- The content model of a `complexType` is described as `simpleContent` if only character data may appear.
- A `complexType` is said to have `complexContent` if it contains subelements (and optionally attributes).
- The default case for a `complexType` definition involves `complexContent` and a `restriction` of the generic `anyType`, so the `complexContent` and `restriction` elements may be omitted.
- Element and attribute declarations may be local or global in scope. They are always named.
- Types definitions may be named or anonymous, and are either local or global.
- An empty element is a special case of `complexType` with `complexContent` and an empty `restriction` element.
- The attribute `mixed` further describes the content model of a `complexType`. By default, `mixed="false"`, meaning that the element content can consist of either subelements or character data, but not both. If `mixed="true"`, content may be a

mixture of subelements *and* character data. The XML Schema mixed content model is more expressive than the XML DTD analog.
- A content model may consist of a `sequence` (each element in the given order), a `choice` (one of a set of mutually exclusive elements), or `all` (each element but in any order), or certain nested combinations.
- Model groups may be named for reuse in an XML Schema. Similary, so may groups of attributes, much like internal parameter entities in a DTD. This is accomplished using the `group` and `attributeGroup` elements.
- A schema may be constructed from pieces using the `include` or `import` elements at the beginning of the schema. This serves a purpose similar to external parameter entities in DTDs.
- Repeatability of elements is determined by the attributes `minOccurs` and `maxOccurs`, both of which default to one. Their value may be zero, any positive integer, or even "unbounded". Setting either or both of these to a value other than zero or one gives you much greater flexibility than with DTDs.
- Attribute declarations always appear last in a `complexType` definition.
- By default, attributes are optional. However, you can add `use="required"` to your attribute declaration to make it mandatory or `use="prohibited"` to state the attribute isn't allowed.
- You can also include `fixed="value"` to specify a fixed value for an attribute, or `default="value"` to indicate a default value.
- Derivation can be controlled by the `final` attribute, which can be set to `restriction` (no restriction allowed), `extension` (no extension allowed), or `#all` (no subclassing allowed).
- Derivation can be further limited by specifying `fixed="true"` for individual facets, preventing restriction by facets so fixed.
- The `annotation`, `documentation`, and `appInfo` elements provide better comment and processing instruction capabilities than DTDs, including external references and unconstrained content.
- The Namespace specification is important to validation of XML Schema and instance documents. This involves the attributes `targetNamespace`, `elementFormDefault`, `attributeFormDefault`, `xsi:schemaLocation`, and `xsi:noNamespaceSchemaLocation`, and the typical namespace declarations `xmlns:xsd="http://www.w3.org/2001/XMLSchema"` (in the schema) and `xmlns:xsi="http://www.w3.org/2001/XMLSchema-instance"` (in the instance).
- Common tools for working with XML Schema include xsv, TurboXML, and XML Spy. API libraries also exist from various vendors.
- It's best to search DTD and schema repositories and registries (XML.org, BizTalk, and Open Applications Group) before creating your own schema.

For Further Exploration

Alternatives

RELAX NG (RELAX Next Generaton by OASIS Technical Committee; merges RELAX and TREX)
http://www.oasis-open.org/committees/relax-ng/

RELAX (REgular LAnguage description for XML)
http://www.xml.gr.jp/relax/

Relax, and Take it Easy (Simon St. Laurent)
http://www.xml.com/pub/2000/02/xtech/relax.html

TREX - Tree Regular Expressions for XML
http://www.thaiopensource.com/trex/

DSD - Document Structure Description
http://www.brics.dk/DSD/

Schematron, The (Rick Jelliffe)
http://www.ascc.net/xml/resource/schematron/schematron.html

Schematron Tutorial (Dr. Miloslav Nic)
http://www.zvon.org/HTMLonly/SchematronTutorial/General/contents.html

Articles

XML.com: Understanding W3C Schema Complex Types, Donald Smith [highly recommended]
http://www.xml.com/pub/a/2001/08/22/easyschema.html

XML.com: Schema Type Decision Tree, Donald Smith [extremely useful diagram]
http://www.xml.com/2001/08/22/examples/schematree.pdf

XML.com: W3C XML Schema Made Simple, Kohsuke Kawaguchi [if you read this, also read Donald Smith's counterpoint article above]
http://www.xml.com/pub/a/2001/06/06/schemasimple.html

Uses for Sun's Multi-Schema XML Validator, Kohsuke Kawaguchi [on MSV]
http://dcb.sun.com/practices/devnotebook/xml_msv.jsp

XML.com: Schemas by Example, Leigh Dodds
http://www.xml.com/pub/a/2001/03/28/deviant.html

XML.com: XML 2000 Focuses on XML Schema
http://www.xml.com/pub/a/2000/12/xml2000/schema.html

XML.com: Modeling XML Vocabularies with UML, Dave Carlson [3 parts]
http://www.xml.com/pub/a/2001/08/22/uml.html

XML.com: Using W3C XML Schema [Eric van der Vlist recommended; revised October 2001]
http://www.xml.com/pub/a/2000/11/29/schemas/part1.html

XML.com: XML Schema Datatypes Reference, Rick Jelliffe
http://www.xml.com/pub/a/2000/11/29/schemas/dataref.html

XML.com: XML Schema Structures Reference, Eric van der Vlist [very useful; alphabetical listing of element content models based on the XML Representation Summaries in the specs]
http://www.xml.com/pub/a/2000/11/29/schemas/structuresref.html

XML.com: Describing your Data: DTDs and XML Schemas, Simon St. Laurent
http://xml.com/pub/1999/12/dtd/index.html

Mapping W3C Schemas to Object Schemas to Relational Schemas, Ron Bourret
http://www.rpbourret.com/xml/SchemaMap.htm

IBM: Basics of using XML Schema to define elements
http://www-4.ibm.com/software/developer/library/xml-schema/

IBM: Comparing W3C XML Schemas and Document Type Definitions, David Mertz
http://www-106.ibm.com/developerworks/library/x-matters7.html

XML Schema Specification in Context, Rick Jelliffe [based on early version of XML Schema, but still informative]
http://www.ascc.net/~ricko/XMLSchemaInContext.html

xmlhack: W3C XML Schema still has big problems [based on Proposed Recommendation]
http://xmlhack.com/read.php?item=1097

JavaWorld: Validation with Java and XML Schema, Part 1, Brett McLaughlin
http://www.javaworld.com/jw-09-2000/jw-0908-validation.html

JavaWorld: Validation with Java and XML Schema, Part 2, Brett McLaughlin
http://www.javaworld.com/jw-10-2000/jw-1013-validation2.html

JavaWorld: Validation with Java and XML Schema, Part 3, Brett McLaughlin
http://www.javaworld.com/jw-11-2000/jw-1110-validation3.html

JavaWorld: Validation with Java and XML Schema, Part 4, Brett McLaughlin
http://www.javaworld.com/jw-12-2000/jw-1208-validation4.html

Books

Definitive XML Schema, Priscilla Walmsley [recommended book; by member of the W3C Schema Working Group]
http://vig.prenhall.com/catalog/professional/product/1,4096,0130655678,00.html

Forerunners

SOX—Schema for Object-oriented XML (Version 2.0)
http://www.w3.org/TR/NOTE-SOX

SOX—Schema for Object-oriented XML (Version 1.0)
http://www.w3.org/TR/1998/NOTE-SOX-19980930/

Commerce One: SOX home page
http://www.xcbl.org/sox/sox.html

Commerce One: SOX FAQ
http://www.xcbl.org/sox/faq.html

Commerce One: SOX Tutorial
http://www.xcbl.org/sox/downloads/soxtutorial10r1.pdf

Commerce One: XDK Developer's Guide (includes SOX)
http://www.xcbl.org/xdk/documentation.html

Commerce One: Extending XML Schema for eCommerce, Matt Fuchs
http://wdvl.Internet.com/Authoring/Languages/XML/Conferences/XML2000/fuchs.html

XML Data (Microsoft et al.)
http://www.w3.org/TR/1998/NOTE-XML-data

XML Data: Appendix A: Examples
http://www.w3.org/TR/1998/NOTE-XML-data#AppendixA

XML-Data Reduced (Subset of XML Data)
http://www.ltg.ed.ac.uk/~ht/XMLData-Reduced.htm

DCD—Document Content Description for XML (DCD)
http://www.w3.org/TR/NOTE-dcd

DDML—Document Definition Markup Language (DDML) Specification, Version 1.0
http://www.w3.org/TR/NOTE-ddml

Repositories

XML.org: XML in Vertical Industries [hundreds of DTD-based schema, arranged by categories; very useful]
http://www.xml.org/xml/industry_industrysectors.jsp

XML.org: Search Schemas/DTDs in XML.org Registry
http://www.xml.org/xml/registry.jsp

XML.org XML Standards Report [ZapThink]
http://www.zapthink.com/report.html

XML Acronyms List [ZapThink; besides expanding many acronyms, each links to details]
http://www.zapthink.com/online/acronyms.htm

BizTalk Schema Library Search [requires free login]
http://www.biztalk.org/library/search_objects.asp

Open Application Group (OAGI; roughly 200 business-oriented schema, called Business Object Documents)
http://www.openapplications.org/

Resources

ZVON XML Schema 2001 Reference [updated to match W3C XML Schema Recommendation]
http://www.zvon.org/xxl/xmlSchema2001Reference/Output/index.html

Microsoft's XML Tutorial [SDK 3.0]
http://msdn.microsoft.com/library/default.asp?url=/library/en-us/xmlsdk30/htm/xmtutxmltutorial.asp

WDVL's XML Schema Resources [comprehensive]
http://wdvl.Internet.com/Authoring/Languages/XML/Schema.html

Robin Cover's XML Schema page
http://xml.coverpages.org/schemas.html

xmlhack Schema Category [site-wide search of news articles related to XML Schema and alternatives]
http://xmlhack.com/list.php?cat=32

Xfront.com [great schema material by Roger Costello: tutorial, best practices, ISBN schema, world currency schema, regular expression generator]
http://www.xfront.com/

Best Practices, Roger Costello et al.
http://www.xfront.com/BestPracticesHomepage.html

XML.com: Schema Resource Center
http://www.xml.com/schemas/

SourceForge: Conformance Testing of XML Schema
http://xmlconf.sourceforge.net/?selected=schema

Mapping W3C Schemas to Object Schemas to Relational Schemas, Ron Bourret
http://www.rpbourret.com/xml/SchemaMap.htm

XML and Databases, Ron Bourret [extensive information]
http://www.rpbourret.com/xml/index.htm

Microsoft XML
http://msdn.microsoft.com/xml

Software

XMLSOFTWARE.com: XML schema processors/tools [comprehensive list]
http://www.xmlsoftware.com/T988979103.851/

XSV: XML Schema Validator, Henry S. Thompson [web-access form]
http://www.w3.org/2001/03/webdata/xsv

XSV: XML Schema Validator, Henry S. Thompson [download Windows executable]
ftp://ftp.cogsci.ed.ac.uk/pub/XSV/

XSV: XML Schema Validator, Henry S. Thompson [documentation and status]
http://www.ltg.ed.ac.uk/~ht/xsv-status.html

Sun Multi-Schema XML Validator (MSV) [validates against RELAX NG, RELAX Namespace, RELAX Core, TREX, XML DTDs, and most of XML Schema]
http://www.sun.com/software/xml/developers/multischema/

Apache: Xerces Java Parser
http://xml.apache.org/xerces-j/index.html

Apache: Xerxes 2.x Java Parser [fully conforming XML Schema processor]
http://xml.apache.org/xerces2-j/index.html

Oracle: XML Schema Validator in C, C++, and Java
http://technet.oracle.com/tech/xml/

Microsoft XML Parser 4.0 July 2001
http://msdn.microsoft.com/downloads/default.asp?URL=/code/sample.asp?url=/msdn-files/027/001/677/msdncompositedoc.xml

Turbo XML including XML Authority (TIBCO Extensibility)
http://www.tibco.com/products/extensibility/index.html

XML Spy (Altova)
http://xmlspy.com/

Sun XML Datatypes Library [Sun's Java Technology Implementation of XML Schema Part 2]
http://www.sun.com/software/xml/developers/xsdlib/

Sun XML Instance Generator [generates valid and invalid instances based on several schema formats including XML Schema and RELAX NG]
http://www.sun.com/software/xml/developers/instancegenerator/

Sun RELAX NG Converter [converts XML Schema and others to RELAX NG]
http://www.sun.com/software/xml/developers/relaxngconverter/

XML Schema Quality Checker [IBM]
http://www.alphaworks.ibm.com/tech/xmlsqc

XDRtoXSD [IBM]
http://www.alphaworks.ibm.com/tech/xdrtoxsd

dtd2xs [translates DTD to XML Schema; available as Java class, Web tool and as Java application]
http://puvogel.informatik.med.uni-giessen.de/dtd2xs/

xsbrowser [creates human readable document model from DTD or XML Schema]
http://www.xsbrowser.org/

XML.com: XML Schema Tools Guide
http://www.xml.com/pub/a/2000/12/13/schematools.html

Tutorials

XML Schema Tutorial, Roger L. Costello [excellent and frequently updated!]
http://www.xfront.com/#tutorials

Regular Expressions—XML Schema Style, Daniel Potter
http://www.xfront.org/xml-schema/

Regular Expressions Appendix from W3C Datatypes specification
http://www.w3.org/TR/xmlschema-2/#regexs

Chapter 24: Schema, from Elliott Rusty Harold's *XML Bible, Second Edition*
http://www.ibiblio.org/xml/books/bible2/chapters/ch24.html

Markup Languages: Comparison and Examples [compares XML Schema, RDF, and DAML; for TRELLIS Project]
http://trellis.semanticweb.org/expect/web/semanticweb/comparison.html

W3C Specifications and Information

XML Schema home page
http://www.w3.org/XML/Schema.html

XML Schema Part 0: Primer
http://www.w3.org/TR/xmlschema-0

XML Schema Part 1: Structures (aka XML Schema definition language)
http://www.w3.org/TR/xmlschema-1

XML Schema Part 2: Datatypes
http://www.w3.org/TR/xmlschema-2

XML Schema Part 2: Built-in Datatypes [very useful datatypes hierarchy diagram]
http://www.w3.org/TR/xmlschema-2/#built-in-datatypes

XML Schema Part 2: Constraining Facets
http://www.w3.org/TR/xmlschema-2/#rf-facets

XML Schema Part 0: Appendix B: Simple Types & their Facets [table that indicates which facets apply to each of the built-in datatypes]
http://www.w3.org/TR/xmlschema-0/#SimpleTypeFacets

Schema for Schemas [normative]
http://www.w3.org/TR/xmlschema-1/#normative-schemaSchema

Schema for Schemas [non-normative downloadable version]
http://www.w3.org/2001/XMLSchema.xsd

DTD for Schemas [normative; from XML Schema Part 1]
http://www.w3.org/TR/xmlschema-1/#normative-schemaDTD

DTD for Datatype Definitions [normative; from XML Schema Part 2]
http://www.w3.org/TR/xmlschema-2/#dtd-for-datatypeDefs

XML Schema: Formal Description [of XML types and validity as specified by XML Schema Part 1]
http://www.w3.org/TR/xmlschema-formal/

XML Schema Requirements
http://www.w3.org/TR/NOTE-xml-schema-req

XML Schema Tools
http://www.w3.org/XML/Schema.html#Tools

XML Schema Test Collection [conformance tests]
http://www.w3.org/2001/05/xmlschema-test-collection/

XML Representation Summary: **schema** Element Information Item
http://www.w3.org/TR/xmlschema-1/#declare-schema

XML Representation Summary: **element** Element Information Item
http://www.w3.org/TR/xmlschema-1/#declare-element

XML Representation Summary: **attribute** Element Information Item
http://www.w3.org/TR/xmlschema-1/#declare-attribute

XML Representation Summary: **simpleType** Element Information Item
http://www.w3.org/TR/xmlschema-1/#declare-datatype

XML Representation Summary: **complexType** Element Information Item
http://www.w3.org/TR/xmlschema-1/#declare-type

XML Representation Summary: **simpleContent** (content: restriction, extension)
http://www.w3.org/TR/xmlschema-1/#element-simpleContent

XML Representation Summary: **complexContent** (content: restriction, extension)
http://www.w3.org/TR/xmlschema-1/#element-complexContent

XML Representation Summary: **attributeGroup** Element Information Item
http://www.w3.org/TR/xmlschema-1/#element-attributeGroup

Resource Description Framework (RDF) Schema Specification
http://www.w3.org/TR/rdf-schema

Part II

Parsing and Programming APIs

Chapter 7

Parsing with SAX

In this chapter, we will explore the Simple API for XML (SAX), a grassroots application programming interface used by nearly all contemporary XML parsers. The two chapters that follow this one cover the W3C's Document Object Model (DOM), and related APIs such as JAXP and JDOM. Before diving into SAX, however, we present an overview of XML parsing. Although chapters 7, 8, and 9 have a Java emphasis, readers not familiar with Java should read chapters 7 and 8 (but not 9), concentrating on the concepts rather than the code. Non-Java implementation of SAX and DOM resources are readily available and are referenced in the "For Further Exploration" sections of both chapters. Additionally, the comparsion in the chapter 9 section entitled "SAX vs. DOM vs. JDOM vs. JAXP—Who Wins?" is essential for all readers.

Overview of Parsing and Processing XML

Before we cover SAX, let's discuss several fundamental topics, such as what parsing is, how APIs are important, what different approaches to parsing exist, what is the relationship to XML Information Set, and what parsers are available.

Parsing, Validation, APIs, and Consumers

In chapters 2, 3, and 4, we introduced the concepts of parsing and validation. We learned that at an XML document (instance) at a minimum must be well-formed; if it doesn't adhere to the basic XML syntax rules such as proper nesting of elements, for example, parsing will terminate prematurely. Unlike HTML, there is no code that tries to second guess how the elements are *supposed* to be structured. If the document references a DTD, the parser will first interpret the DTD and build an in-memory model of the expected document structure and the rules it conveys. If a particular XML instance breaks one of the rules (e.g., it's missing a required attribute or using an undefined element), most parsers will signal this as a nonfatal error; parsing may or may not be terminated at that point.

Parsing is the process of splitting a stream of information into its constituent pieces (often called tokens). In the context of XML, *parsing* refers to scanning an XML document (which need not be a physical file—it can be a data stream) in order to split it into its various markup and character data, and more specifically, into elements and their attributes, processing instructions, comments, entities, and so on. XML parsing reveals the structure of the information since the nesting of elements implies a hierarchy. It is possible for an XML document to fail to parse completely if it does not follow the *well-formedness rules* described in the XML 1.0 Recommendation. A successfully parsed XML document may be either well-formed (at a minimum) or valid. **Validation** is the process that a validating parser (optionally) performs by interpreting the DTD or schema, building a model of the constraints it defines, and applying the document instance to the model.

In the XML world, specialized freeware and commercial parsers, some standalone and some embedded in larger applications, read an XML document piece by piece. Just like the parser in a compiler, an XML parser determines what are the tokens of the XML language represented in the document instance. These tokens are the elements, attributes, processing instructions, comments, entities, notations, and so forth that are defined by the XML syntax. Application developers should never need to write their own parsing code; this task is best left to developers who are intimately familiar with all the syntactical details of the XML 1.0 Recommendation and the Namespace Recommendation. In fact, it's useful to think in terms of parsers being producers of XML information items that are then consumed by an application as it goes about its particular processing task.

Different Approaches: SAX and DOM, JDOM, and JAXP

How does the application interact with the parser in order to be delivered the items of interest? One way is by using SAX (the Simple API for XML), and another is by using the DOM. In chapter 9, we'll also discuss other approaches, such as JDOM and JAXP. In a nutshell, the four approaches are:

- *SAX*—First XML API, lightweight, minimal, fast, language independent, maintains no context; data-centric, event-driven model
- *DOM*—From the W3C, memory intensive, complex, very powerful, language independent, context not an issue; document-centric, tree-based model
- *JDOM*—Java-specific, better fit for Java developers; can use with SAX or DOM
- *JAXP*—Layered on top of SAX and DOM to make it easier to swap parsers; Java-specific

We touched on the difference between event-based parsing, typified by SAX, and tree-based parsing used by the DOM, in "Event-Based vs. Tree-Based Parsing" in chapter 3. The event-based approach is data-centric, focused on processing elements and other tokens as they are encountered in the input stream and then forgetting about them. In constrast, the tree-based model is more document-centric since it considers the entire document at once. The W3C's DOM is conceptually a tree view of the hierarchy defined by a specific XML (or HTML) document instance. Once an XML document has been parsed into its corresponding DOM tree, nodes (elements, attributes, etc.) can be accessed to extract or alter information, or to insert or delete nodes and possibly output a modified XML document.

At a very high level, both of these techniques represent some type of abstraction of an XML document that can be used to gain access to elements, attributes, and so on. Think of your application as the consumer of the results of the parse. APIs such as SAX and DOM are the standard and generic interfaces to any XML parser that shelter your application from numerous details that shouldn't concern you in general, such as checking for well-formedness, validating the document against a DTD or XML Schema, propagating namespaces, resolving entity references, and so on. In particular, using these standard APIs means that you can switch from your original parser of choice to the latest, greatest super-charged parser with little or no change to your application, to varying degrees.

As you read the descriptions of the various approaches presented in chapters 7 to 9, it is important to focus on what is special about each, especially in terms of advantages and disadvantages, because the technique you choose to implement for one application will not always be optimal for other applications that have different requirements. At the end of chapter 9, in the section "SAX vs. DOM vs. JDOM vs. JAXP—Who Wins?", we summarize the pros and cons of each approach. (Feel free to read the punchline first, if you prefer.)

Although these chapters emphasize parsing, the reading and breaking of XML input pieces, most APIs also have provisions (either currently or in near future versions) for *writing* XML as well. **Serialization** is the process of outputting the in-memory XML instance either to a file or any output stream.[1] The kind of processing available depends more on the approach, with SAX making it easy to filter XML while DOM and JDOM are more concerned with constructing trees to facilitate navigation, adding, deleting, and changing nodes.

XML Infoset and Its Relation to Parsing

As we saw in chapter 5, the **XML Information Set** specification (called *Infoset* for short) provides an abstract model for describing the logical structure of a well-formed XML 1.0 document. The Infoset model is an abstraction intended to serve as a common reference model for parsing APIs, query languages, editors, browsers, and so on. It is therefore more abstract than XML 1.0 and Namespaces. We learned

1. XML serialization may be implemented as a subclass of Java's Serialization API or by other techniques, but the idea is the same, namely, translating from objects in memory to some persistent form with XML markup. Serialization refers to the sequencing of XML elements, attributes, and other information items into a byte stream that can be written to disk (i.e., an XML document) or sent over a wire (i.e., an XML message). It is a physical representation of the more abstract structure of a particular XML instance.

that the model defines a set of **information items** that are defined by their properties. For example, the *entity information item* is the storage unit for the serialized form of XML. The *element information item* has properties such as `local-name`, `namespace`, and `attributes` (a possibly empty list). An *attribute information item* has an `attribute-type` property in addition to `local-name` and `namespace` properties. Relationships such as `parent` and `child` elements are defined as element properties in Infoset. Altogether the XML Information Set specification defines eleven information items, described in Table 5-2.

In other words, the Infoset represents the key informational chunks of an XML instance without the syntactic details such as angle brackets, quotation marks, and so on. It is precisely this type of abstraction that is of interest when dealing with SAX, the DOM, and other parser-related APIs. For example, we can think of SAX as an API that picks out the various information items of a document and triggers callbacks for each Infoset item for which the application has registered interest. SAX delivers the information items as an ordered stream of events. Applications that use SAX typically do not need to maintain the information items in memory. The DOM, on the other hand, uses the same information items to build an in-memory tree that represents a particular XML instance. The DOM tree consists of generic nodes and objects that can be traversed by starting from the root or by starting at a given node. DOM-based applications need to access the information items in an order different from document order (also called preorder traversal). Examples include XML editors and browsers that permit manipulation of the information items, such as adding, deleting, or changing elements or attributes.

Recommended Java Parsers and Non-Java Support

The number of XML parsers and other tools that include parsing functionality is ever-growing. Table 7-3 on page 394 presents some popular Java SAX parsers. DOM parsers are shown in Table 8-8 (page 448), again with a Java emphasis.

The XMLSoftware.com Parser/Processer list is more comprehensive and is updated regularly (see *http://www.xmlsoftware.com/parsers/*). (If the link times out, try again several hours later.) SAX non-Java language support is described on the SourceForge.net page—*http://www.saxproject.org/?selected=langs*. SAX bindings are available for most popular languages:

- Microsoft's MSXML 3.0 parser defines a COM binding, accessible from C, C++, Visual Basic, etc.
- Apache's Xerces-C defines C and C++ bindings
- GNU Compiler for Java (GCJ) - C++
- SAX in C++
- Perl
- Python

SAX2 is integrated into JDK 1.4 and Python 2.0.

Development of SAX

In the rest of this chapter, we will focus on SAX2, which was finalized in May 2000. However, the origins of SAX date back to the early days of XML (as documented by Megginson at *http://www.saxproject.org/?selected=history1*). A discussion ensued, initiated by Peter Murray-Rust (the creator of the first XML browser, JUMBO) in December 1997 on the xml-dev (XML developers) mailing list about how a common interface to parsers should be written to shield applications from parser nuances. David Megginson collected the suggestions from many contributors and then took the lead in writing the initial SAX specification draft and initial Java implementation, which was circulated in January 1998. After many iterations and contributions, SAX1 (then called simply "SAX") was released to the Internet community in May 1998. As was befitting its community development process, the Java implementation of SAX was given the vendor-neutral package name `org.xml.sax`, the domain name portion of which was denotated by Sun Microsystem's Jon Bosak, one of the fathers of XML.[2]

SAX is such a popular parser interface that implementations have been written for most popular languages: Java, perl, Python, C++, COM, and others. There are also SAX extensions by Apache and Megginson (for details, see *http://www.saxproject.org/?selected=ext*). When Megginson announced his intention to end his role as the maintainer of SAX in late September 2000, possible contenders for taking over the SAX reins included W3C, OASIS, Apache, the IETF, ISO, the Open Group, and xml-dev. However, this distinction ultimately went to SourceForge.net, the world's largest Open Source development Web site, initially in June 2001 and then completely by October 2001. The preferred SAX home page is now *http://www.saxproject.org/* (also *http://sax.sourceforge.net/*). David Brownell is now leading the development efforts of SAX 2.1 and beyond.

In contrast to all of the main topics in this book (except those in chapter 9), SAX has become a de facto standard without ever going through the W3C Recommendation Process discussed in chapter 2. David Megginson even officially abandoned all rights to SAX and placed it in the public domain. So this first XML API has become extremely widespread, supported by nearly all parsers, and is certain to remain very popular because of its flexibility, as well as its public domain status.

SAX: Event Handler Model

SAX is a vendor-neutral, platform-independent, and language-independent API. Its name is quite appropriate: the Simple API for XML (parsers). The main

2. In order to avoid naming conflicts across companies and organizations, by convention Java package names are derived by reversing domain names. For example, packages developed by or for NASA Goddard Space Flight Center (which has the domain name `gsfc.nasa.gov`) would be named `gov.nasa.gsfc.*`.

difference between SAX and other parser-related APIs is that SAX uses an **event handler model**. To those who are familiar with graphical user interface (GUI) programming, this model may seem familiar; but for those unfamiliar with GUI development, it may take a while to get used to the SAX way of thinking. In the GUI world (i.e., Java Swing or AWT, Motif, or GUI classes from the Microsoft Foundation Class [MFC] Library), the application registers *callbacks*, which are functions or methods that are called when a particular event of interest occurs, typically in response to a user action. For example, if the user picks the choice `Print` from a `File` menu, the callback that was registered for this particular `File` menu object is invoked. The underlying GUI model passes the callback certain useful information about the user event, especially the choice that was selected from the menu. The callback handles this event (hence the name "event handler") often by executing other code that depends on the selected choice. Often the event information does not contain everything that the application needs to know to complete the user request. In our example, the name of the file to be printed may not be passed to the event handler. This implies that the application must maintain certain state information, such as the name of the current file that the application is processing. The print method needs to access the remembered filename to perform its function.

The SAX event handler model closely parallels this GUI model. The initialization portions of the application are responsible for defining and registering the event handlers of interest, such as when the parser encounters the beginning of a new element, when it finds the end of the element's content, when it detects a processing instruction, and so forth. Just like in the GUI case, when the element event handler is invoked, it is passed certain context information, such as the name of the element that was encountered, the namespace that pertains to this element (if any), and the attributes of the element (if any). Given that information, the application decides how to respond to a given element.

This model is sometimes called a *streaming model* because the items of interest can be thought of as a stream of events. SAX does not build a hierarchy of the XML document in memory, which is either a strength or a weakness, depending on the needs of your application. This means that, again as in the GUI case, the application is responsible for keeping track of certain state information. For example, when a particular element is detected in the stream, its ancestor elements may be significant to the application.

Consider the XML document, `collection2.xml`, in Listing 7-1 which we'll revisit several times in the next few chapters. The element called `Name` appears as the child of both `Author` (under the `Book` element) and `Owner` elements. If our application is simply told "Here's a `Name` element", we almost certainly will also want to know whether we're being passed an `Author` name or an `Owner` name. However, since events are streaming by, when we encounter `Name`, the event associated with the ancestor is already history. It has passed by our processing window of opportunity, so if we don't keep track of ancestor events, we won't know the context in which the Name event occurred. This is the major disadvantage of SAX for some applications.

On the other hand, SAX is very fast because it does not need to read the entire document before it begins signaling its events to the calling application. In cases where memory is limited and XML documents are potentially large, this can be a significant advantage. SAX makes it possible to process documents that are actually larger than physical memory, making it more likely to be the parsing method of choice for handheld devices, for example.

Since SAX is a simple API, it does not impose large, complex data structures on programmers. It's completely flexible; you are free to design and implement a custom data model specifically tuned for your application, which, although certainly requiring more effort, is more likely to result in a more efficient solution than a completely generic data structure (i.e., the DOM) can provide.

SAX is excellent for the processing of streaming XML, especially when connecting event pipelines between processes. One process, a producer, pipes possibly filtered XML data to a consumer, which may then become a producer for the next pipe of the pipeline. DTD support in SAX (SAX2, that is) surpasses that of many APIs. Furthermore, SAX events map well to the XML Information Set.

Listing 7-1 XML Instance of CD and Book Collection (collection2.xml)

```
<?xml version="1.0"?>
<!DOCTYPE Collection SYSTEM "collection2.dtd">
<!-- A Collection consists of Book and CD elements in no particular order. -->
<Collection   version="2">
  <Book>
    <Title>Complete Beatles Chronicle, The</Title>
    <Author>
      <Name>
        <First>Mark</First>
        <Last>Lewisohn</Last>
      </Name>
     </Author>
    <Type>Chronology</Type>
    <Published publisher="Harmony Books">1992</Published>
    <Rating>5 stars</Rating>
    <Notes>
  Covers the years 1957 through 1970. No solo info.
  Great appendices with chart info, discography, composer index,
  radio, tv, and live performances, and much more.
  </Notes>
  </Book>
  <CD>
    <Title>Band on the Run</Title>
    <Artist>McCartney, Paul and Wings</Artist>
    <Chart>
      <Peak weeks="4">1</Peak>
      <Peak country="UK">1</Peak>
      <!-- guess -->
```

```
    </Chart>
    <Type>Rock</Type>
    <Label>Capitol</Label>
    <Label country="UK">EMI</Label>
    <AlbumReleased>1973</AlbumReleased>
    <Remastered format="gold CD">1993</Remastered>
    <Remastered format="2 disc box set with booklet">1999</Remastered>
  </CD>
  <CD>
    <Title>Venus and Mars</Title>
    <Artist>McCartney, Paul and Wings</Artist>
    <Chart>
      <Peak weeks="1">1</Peak>
      <Peak country="UK">2</Peak>
      <!-- guess -->
    </Chart>
    <Type>Rock</Type>
    <Label>Capitol</Label>
    <Label country="UK">EMI</Label>
    <AlbumReleased>1975</AlbumReleased>
    <Remastered format="gold CD with 3 bonus tracks">1994</Remastered>
  </CD>
  <Book>
    <Title>Many Years From Now</Title>
    <Author>
    <Name>
      <First>Paul</First>
      <Last>McCartney</Last>
    </Name>
    </Author>
    <Type>Autobiographical</Type>
    <Published publisher="Henry Holt and Company">1997</Published>
  <!-- Notice the absence of Notes and Rating elements.
  I haven't read this book yet. This illustrates some optional
  elements that are children of Book element.
  -->
  </Book>
  <Owner>
    <Name sex = "male">
      <First>Ken</First>
      <Last>Sall</Last>
    </Name>
    <Address>
      <Street>123 Milky Way Dr.</Street>
      <City>Columbia</City>
      <State>MD</State>
      <Zip>20794</Zip>
    </Address>
  </Owner>
</Collection>
```

SAX2 Interfaces and Classes

The remainder of this chapter covers details of the Java implementation of SAX2; however, readers without Java background are encouraged to skim the material for the concepts. The interfaces and classes described in Tables 7-1 and 7-2 have names and roles that generally apply to other languages too.

Major Interfaces and Classes

SAX2 contains only two Java packages:

- **`org.xml.sax`** contains all major interfaces such as `ContentHandler`, `Attributes`, `ErrorHandler`, `Locator`, `XMLReader`, `XMLFilter`, `EntityResolver`, and `DTDHandler`.
- **`org.xml.sax.helpers`** contains ancillary interfaces and implementations such as `AttributesImpl`, `DefaultHandler`, `ParserAdaptor`, `XMLFilterImpl`, `XMLReaderFactory`, etc.

The main interfaces defined in these two packages are briefly described in Table 7-1 on the next page; the table does not list every interface, however. Javadoc for these packages can be found at *http://www.saxproject.org/apidoc/overview-summary.html*. Additional extensions and other SAX-related software (e.g., `SAX2-ext`, `XMLWriter`, `RDF Filter`) have been collected on Megginson's page—*http://www.megginson.com/Software/index.html*.

For a considerably more detailed presentation of the SAX2 Java packages and their use, see Elliotte Rusty Harold's *Processing XML with Java*, also published by Addison Wesley. In addition to SAX2, this book covers the DOM, JAXP, and JDOM (see *http://www.ibiblio.org/xml/books/xmljava/*).

Overall SAX Application Sequence

The basic sequence of steps involved in writing a SAX2 application are those that follow:

1. Define Content Handlers (or extend the `DefaultHandler` class) and Error Handlers.
2. Define DTD Handler (for specialized applications only).
3. Add application-specification initialization.

TABLE 7-1 Major SAX2 Interfaces and Classes

Interface or Class	*Description*
`ContentHandler`	*Main interface for most SAX applications*; receives all parser events related to elements and their contents. Events fire in document order, so between a `startElement` and an `endElement` event are events for all child elements and/or character data content, processing instructions, comments, etc. See Table 7-2 for a description of the `ContentHandler` methods that map to the possible events SAX can report.
`Attributes`	Interface that provides three ways to access an element's list of attributes: by attribute index, by namespace plus local name, or by qualified (prefixed) name. Has multiple methods for accessing an attribute value (`getValue`) and its datatype (`getType`). The number of attributes for a given element is reported by the `getLength` method. Order of attributes in this list is not defined and may not match the order in which they appear in the element's start tag.
`ErrorHandler`	Interface that enables applications to provide customized error handling. Parsers use it rather than throwing exceptions directly; this provides the application the final say in error handling. The three `ErrorHandler` methods represent different severity levels: `fatalError` (nonrecoverable), `error` (recoverable), and `warning`.
`Locator`	Interface that provides file, line, and column location information, useful for error reporting (via `getSystemId`, `getLineNumber`, and `getColumnNumber` methods). SAX calls the `setDocumentLocator` method before the `startDocument` method.
`XMLReader`	*Major interface* that provides for registering event handlers (e.g., `setContentHandler`, `setErrorHandler`), setting and getting parser features and properties, and initiating document parsing. Adapters exist to convert a (deprecated) SAX1 `Parser` to a SAX2 `XMLReader`, and vice versa.
`XMLFilter`	Interface that extends (is a subclass of) `XMLReader`. An `XMLFilter` is similar to an `XMLReader`, except that it receives its events from another `XMLReader` (or `XMLFilter`) rather than directly from an XML document or database. Filters can be chained together to selectively process events as they pass to the main application.
`EntityResolver`	Interface that responds to external entities (including the external DTD subset and external parameter entities, if any). Useful for applications that create XML documents on the fly from databases or other specialized input sources. Can be used to look up indirect URI references or to redirect system identifiers to local URIs.
`DTDHandler`	Interface needed only by specialized applications to respond to notation and unparsed entity declarations (the only DTD events required by the XML 1.0 Recommendation). Applications may need to store the information for later reference to attributes of type `NOTATION`, `ENTITY`, or `ENTITIES`. *Typically only needed by XML editors, not for normal document validation, as you might think from the name.*
`DefaultHandler`	*Major convenience base class* that implements `EntityResolver`, `DTDHandler`, `ContentHandler`, and `ErrorHandler` (providing all necessary callbacks). Useful when you only need to customize a portion of these interfaces and wish to leverage as much default behavior as possible. *Note:* Part of the package `org.xml.sax.helpers`.
`XMLReaderFactory`	This class contains static methods for creating an XML reader from an explicit class name, or based on runtime defaults, by means of the `createXMLReader` method. *Note:* Part of the package `org.xml.sax.helpers`.

4. Set Document Locator to provide filename and line number information for event notifications.
5. Instantiate a *specific parser* that supports the SAX2 interface. Consider using the method `createXMLReader` from the `XMLReaderFactory` class to choose a SAX driver dynamically when you invoke Java with the `-Dorg.xml.sax.driver` option. (See "Using SAX with Java" later in this chapter.)
6. Set the Content Handler.
7. Set Error Handlers. If you fail to do this, you won't see validation errors.
8. Set DTD Handler (if applicable).
9. Set Features and/or Properties (if nondefault parser behavior is desired). *This is important for validation and namespace support!*
10. Invoke the parser.
11. Perform application-specific tasks after parse completes.

While these steps are based on a Java example and are somewhat Java-centric, they are conceptually similar in any language that implements the SAX interface.

ContentHandler and Context Tracking

The `ContentHandler` interface is the one most developers need to learn in detail. This interface is concerned with delivering the events to the application related to the document content: the elements, attributes, processing instructions, character data, entities, and so on. The methods shown in Table 7-2 are listed very roughly in the order in which they might be invoked. This table presents the full set of methods.

The `org.xml.sax.helpers` package includes the very useful `DefaultHandler` implementation class for the `ContentHandler` interface. `DefaultHandler` includes a `no-op` (do nothing) method for each possible event. If you're interested in only a few kinds of events (e.g., elements and processing instructions), it may be sufficient to extend the `DefaultHandler` class, overriding only those methods that are of interest to you by defining your own. We'll see an example of this in Listing 7-3 (page 396) in the section "Minimal SAX Example."

On the other hand, if you're really interested in processing most of the possible kinds of events listed in Table 7-2, it may be better to implement your own `ContentHandler`. If you do, however, you must implement *all* methods; those you don't care about still must be defined, but they can be `no-ops`. (If you neglect to include them, the code won't compile.) An example of the `ContentHandler` implementation is shown in Listing 7-5 (pages 398–402).

The method calls between a matching pair of `startElement` and `endElement` calls represent children of the element, parsed character data, or other information

TABLE 7-2 ContentHandler Methods

Method	*Description*
`setDocumentLocator`	Registers information for tracking filename, line number, and column number, useful in error reporting. Called prior to `startDocument` or anything else in the `ContentHandler` interface.
`startDocument`	Receive notification of the beginning of a document.
`startPrefixMapping`	Start scope of a prefix-URI Namespace mapping.
`startElement`	Invoked when the start tag of an element is encountered. The list of attributes specified in the start tag (if any) is available to this method in an argument of type `Attributes`.
`characters`	Triggered when the text character data of an element is seen. Parsers invoke this for each chunk of data. Contiguous character data may be combined in one event or split across events.
`ignorableWhitespace`	Receive notification of ignorable white space in element content. Validating parsers must use this method to notify the application when each chunk of insignificant white space in element content is encountered.
`endElement`	Triggered when the end tag of an element is encountered.
`processingInstruction`	Invoked when a processing instruction is seen.
`skippedEntity`	Receive notification of a skipped entity. Nonvalidating parsers may skip entities defined in an external DTD. Validating parsers may also skip entities, depending on the setting of entity-related features, and if validation is not enabled.
`endPrefixMapping`	End scope of a prefix-URI Namespace mapping.
`endDocument`	Receive notification that the end of the document has been reached.

items such as processing instructions. An XML instance of the Collection example appears in Listing 7-5. Given the XML fragment:

```
<Author>
  <Name>
    <First>Mark</First>
    <Last>Lewisohn</Last>
  </Name>
</Author>
```

events will fire in the following order. (In this case, the attribute value is a default value obtained from the DTD; it is supplied by the parser to the `startElement` method.)

```
startElement: Author
startElement: Name
  attribute: sex = 'male' - type: (male|female)
startElement: First
  characters: [Mark]
```

```
endElement: First
startElement: Last
  characters: [Lewisohn]
endElement: Last
endElement: Name
endElement: Author
```

Attributes can be referenced either by name or position (index) using variations of the `getValue` method on an `Attributes` object. Since attribute order is undefined by XML 1.0 and is therefore unpredictable, the index of a particular attribute is not guaranteed to correspond to its ordinal position in the start tag of the element as it appeared in the original document. For instance, in our previous example, there was no explicit attribute of the `Name` element in the XML document and yet in the `startElement` call for `Name`, we can reference the zeroth attribute, which will be `sex` provided by the DTD. (Well, you know what I mean!) If `Name` had three attributes, with `sex` being first in document order, its index could be zero, one, or two.

As previously mentioned, one of the as-designed limitations of SAX is that maintaining context information is the responsibility of the application that uses SAX. This is a direct result of the streaming nature of events that are triggered as each information item is detected. Most real applications cannot accomplish their processing without some tracking of the nesting order of grandparent, parent, and child elements and usually their attribute values as well. Fortunately, since document order parsing implies a depth-first traversal, it is often sufficient to store only as many elements as the greatest depth of the document. An efficient way to do this is to use a stack (i.e., `java.util.Stack`) to push a copy of the element and its attributes onto the stack in the `startElement` method, reference the copies from subsequent method calls, and then pop them off the stack when the `endElement` method for that particular element is eventually invoked.[3] The `ContentHandler` class is most likely where the stack should be managed.

XMLReader

The `XMLReader` interface is the fundamental interface to the parser. It is the means by which applications register all of their handlers, set and query parser features and properties in the parser, and initiate the parsing process. You obtain a parser object by invoking the `XMLReaderFactory` method from the `org.xml.sax.helpers` package.

3. This stack idea is explained with a code example in David Brownell's book, *SAX2*. The stack concept is also illustrated with an extensive example in a *JavaWorld* article entitled "Mapping XML to Java, Part 2" by Robert Hustead at *http://www.javaworld.com/javaworld/jw-10-2000/jw-1006-sax_p.html*.

In contrast to the `Parser` interface from SAX1 that it replaces, `XMLReader` supports Namespaces and SAX2 features and properties (discussed soon in the section "Features and Properties"). The methods defined in the interface are:

- `parse`—performs the actual reading of XML data from a URI, InputStream, and so on.
- `setContentHandler`
- `setDTDHandler`
- `setEntityResolver`
- `setErrorHandler`
- `setFeature`
- `setProperty`
- `getContentHandler`
- `getDTDHandler`
- `getEntityResolver`
- `getErrorHandler`
- `getFeature`
- `getProperty`

Most of the `set` methods are illustrated in the code example in Listing 7-5, as is the use of `parse`. We also briefly discuss an extension of this interface called `XMLFilter` in the section "SAX Filters."

ErrorHandler: Well-Formedess and Validation

It's very easy to fail to properly set up a SAX application for error reporting because you must follow three steps to get it right:

1. Define `ErrorHandler` methods.
2. Set the `ErrorHandler` via the `XMLReader.setErrorHandler` method.
3. Enable validation via the `SAXParser.setFeature` method (next section) because *most parsers default to nonvalidating* mode.

The `ErrorHandler` interface from the `org.xml.sax` package consists of only three methods, each corresponding to one of the three levels of problems that can occur while parsing:

- `fatalError`—Fatal errors result from a document not following the basic XML syntax rules for *well-formedness*. Parsers should (but do not have to) terminate the parse when a fatal error is encountered.
- `error`—Nonfatal errors are those resulting from an instance that is not valid according to the *constraints defined in the DTD or schema* it references. Whether the parser continues after a nonfatal error is left up to the implementation. Some do not terminate when nonfatal errors are encountered.

- `warning`—Warnings by default cause no action to be taken. The XML instance is well-formed (and possibly valid), but it violates some interoperability guidelines from the XML 1.0 Recommendation.[4] The `warning` method is useful for reporting non-XML problems to the application.

It's important to realize that well-formedness errors are considered fatal, whereas validation errors are not fatal. Applications can determine the actions they wish to take in either case.

SAX defines an `org.xml.sax.SAXException` class, which extends the standard `java.lang.Exception` so you can wrap non-SAX exceptions inside and propagate them to the classes that use SAX. The most common exception subclass is `SAXParseException`, but `SAXNotSupportedException` and `SAXNotRecognizedException` are also defined. `SAXParseException` includes information about location in the XML instance that can be retrieved using methods such as `getMessage`, `getException`, `getLineNumber`, `getColumnNumber`, `getPublicId`, and `getSystemId`. It is precisely this `SAXParseException` object that is passed to the `warning`, `error`, and `fatalError` methods.

For example, the minimal SAX program in Listing 7-3 will not report validation errors, but reports well-formedness errors, even though it calls `setErrorHandler` with a default handler. On the other hand, the application in Listing 7-5 will report both well-formedness and validation errors because it properly enables validation. Also, with the Xerces SAX parser, the minimal application will throw an exception that is propagated to the main program as it aborts on a well-formedness error, whereas the more comprehensive application handles the fatal error as it sees fit.

Features and Properties

SAX2 includes a number of configuration methods defined in the `org.xml.sax.XMLReader` interface that are designed to permit developers to query and set a parser's properties and features. **Properties** are named values, whereas **features** are a special case of properties; they are boolean values that either enable or disable some aspect of the parser (such as validation or namespace recognition). Both properties and features are specified using URI notation similar to namespaces. They are identifiers rather than Web pages. For example:

```
http://xml.org.sax/properties/dom-node
http://xml.org.sax/features/validation
```

4. According to XML 1.0, *interoperability* refers to a "nonbinding recommendation included to increase the chances that XML documents can be processed by the existing installed base of SGML processors" (see *http://www.w3.org/TR/REC-xml#dt-interop*).

The XMLReader interface includes getFeature, setFeature, getProperty, and setProperty methods. You can check the availability of a feature using getFeature(featureURI) and use setFeature(featureURL,value) to toggle the setting. Methods getProperty and setProperty are almost identical, except that the value is usually not boolean. Since all four of these methods can throw SAXNotRecognizedException (if the XMLReader does not recognize the feature) or SAXNotSupportedException (if the XMLReader recognizes the feature, but cannot determine its value at this point), it is best to wrap them in try/catch blocks, as follows:

```
try {
  saxParser.setFeature("http://xml.org/sax/features/validation",
                   true);
} catch (SAXNotRecognizedException e) {
  System.err.println("**** SAXNotRecognizedException: " +
                          "Cannot activate validation: " +
                          e.getMessage());
} catch (SAXNotSupportedException e) {
  System.err.println("**** SAXNotSupportedException: " +
                          "Cannot activate validation: " +
                          e.getMessage());
}
```

The core features and properties are documented at *http://www.saxproject.org/?selected=get-set*. However, parser implementors are encouraged to invent their own features and properties, using names based on URIs under their control. In fact, that is exactly what the Apache team has done (see *http://xml.apache.org/xerces-j/properties.html* and *http://xml.apache.org/xerces-j/features.html*). For example, note the Apache domain name in *some* (but not all) of this partial list of features and properties documented for the Xerces Java parser:

```
http://apache.org/xml/features/validation/schema
http://apache.org/xml/features/validation/schema-full-checking
http://apache.org/xml/features/validation/warn-on-undeclared-elemdef
http://xml.org/sax/features/validation
http://xml.org/sax/features/namespaces
http://apache.org/xml/features/validation/dynamic
http://apache.org/xml/features/nonvalidating/load-external-dtd
http://apache.org/xml/properties/schema/external-schemaLocation
http://apache.org/xml/properties/dom/current-element-node
http://apache.org/xml/properties/dom/document-class-name
http://xml.org/sax/properties/dom-node
```

SAX1 vs. SAX2

If you are familiar with SAX1 or come across software that supports only SAX1 (that is, does not specifically mention SAX2), the SAX1 DocumentHandler interface has been deprecated and replaced by the SAX2 `ContentHandler` interface, which includes Namespace support, among other things. Other deprecated SAX1 interfaces and classes include `Parser` (replaced by `XMLReader`, also with Namespace support), `AttributeList` (replaced by `Attributes`), `HandlerBase` (replaced by `DefaultHandler`), `ParserFactory`, and `AttributeListImpl` (replaced by `AttributesImpl`). See the "Changes from SAX 1.0 to SAX 2.0beta" section on the page *http://www.saxproject.org/?selected=sax2*.

In addition to the replacements just mentioned, SAX2 introduces a number of new interfaces and classes such as `XMLFilter`, `SAXNotSupportedException`, `SAXNotRecognizedException`, plus several from the helpers package: `NamespaceSupport`, `XMLFilterImpl`, `ParserAdapter`, and `XMLReaderAdapter`. Users of SAX1 can use the `ParserAdapter` class to add SAX2 functionality to their SAX1 parser since it implements both the `XMLReader` and `DocumentHandler` interfaces.

Readers not familiar with Java may wish to skip the next section. However, it may be informative to examine the output from several parses beginning with Listing 7-7, which starts on page 406.

Using SAX with Java

Megginson and Brownell outline requirements for using the Java SAX implementation (see the Quickstart help at *http://www.saxproject.org/?selected=quickstart*):

- JDK 1.1 or higher
- SAX2 (`org.xml.sax`) package installed on your Java classpath
- SAX2-compatible parser (e.g., `xerces.jar`) also in your Java classpath
- The fully qualified Java classname of the driver of your selected XML parser

Determining the Parser Driver Classname

The appropriate Java class name is documented by the parser provider. Table 7-3 lists some popular cases. All are validating unless indicated otherwise. (However, most are *nonvalidating* by default, so don't forget to call `setFeature`!) Most of these have SAX2 implementations but check the documentation to be sure. URLs for downloading each parser appear in "For Further Exploration."

Compiling and Running a SAX Application

The batch file `sax2-it.bat` shown in Listing 7-2 is intended for use with Windows 98, Windows 2000, or Windows NT.

TABLE 7-3 Popular SAX Parsers and Their Java Class Names

Parser	*Java Class Name*
Apache's `Xerces` 1.4.3, 1.4.4 and 2.0.0	`org.apache.xerces.parsers.SAXParser`
IBM's `xml4j`, version 3.2.1 (based on Apache Xerces 1.4.2)	`org.apache.xerces.parsers.SAXParser` (formerly named `com.ibm.xml.parser`)
Sun's `JAXP` 1.1	`jaxp.xml.parsers.SAXParser`
Apache's `Crimson` (based on Sun's Project X parser; described as JAXP 1.1 without transform package)	`org.apache.crimson.parser.XmlReaderImpl`
GNU's `Aelfred2` from GNU JAXP project; also includes utilities such as SAX2 DOM parser	`gnu.xml.aelfred2.SAXDriver` (lightweight, *nonvalidating*) or `gnu.xml.aelfred2.XmlReader` (validating)
Microsoft's `MSXML` 3.0 parser (`msxml3.dll`) and `MSXML` 4.0 parser (`msxml4.dll`)	Search for "MSXML parser" on the `msdn.microsoft.com` Web site and follow documentation links; not a Java implementation.
Oracle's XML parser `XDK for Java`	`com.oracle.xml.parser.v2.SAXParser`
Michael Kay's SAXON XSLT processor with modified Aelfred parser	`com.icl.saxon.aelfred.SAXDriver`
James Clark's `xp`	`com.jclark.xml.sax.Driver` (fast, *nonvalidating*)

All batch files shown in this book assume that you've configured your environment according to the instructions that accompany the book's CD-ROM. See Appendix D, Setting Up Your Environment, which describes how to modify and use `xmlsetup.bat`. Among other things, `xmlsetup.bat` defines `%JBIN%`, `%JLIB%`, and `%XERCES%` as `C:\Java\jdk1.3.1\bin`, `C:\Java\jdk1.3.1\lib`, and `C:\XML\Apache\xerces-1_4_3\xerces.jar`, by default. This is easily configurable and is the recommended means to experiment with this book's code examples.

To compile a SAX application, you must include the path to the JAR containing the SAX2 package (`org.xml.sax`), which for Xerces is `xerces.jar`. This can be added to your Java classpath or passed on the command line:

```
%JBIN%\javac -classpath .;%XERCES% YourApplication.java
```

For example:

```
%JBIN%\javac -classpath .;%XERCES% TrySAX2Parser.java
```

In the default environment (re: `xmlsetup.bat`), this maps to:

```
C:\Java\jdk1.3.1\bin\javac -classpath .;C:\XML\Apache\xerces-1_4_3\xerces.jar
TrySAX2Parser.java
```

Listing 7-2 Batch File to Invoke Xerces SAX Parser (sax2-it.bat)

```
REM set PARSER=%XERCES%
set DRIVER=org.apache.xerces.parsers.SAXParser

REM Include your SAX parser in the classpath.
REM      set classpath=.;%JLIB%;%PARSER%

REM compile (or block)
REM %JBIN%\javac -classpath .;%XERCES% %1.java

REM Class and XML input to validate.
REM Save output in file named after input.
REM e.g.  sax2-it TrySAX2Parser collection2.xml
echo on
%JBIN%\java -classpath .;%XERCES% -Dorg.xml.sax.driver=%DRIVER% %1 %2 > %2.txt
```

To run your compiled SAX application, pass the script two parameters on the command line:

```
sax2-it YourApplicationClassName XMLFileToParse
```

For example, to invoke the script on Windows 98 to run the `TrySAX2Parser.java` program (Listing 7-5) with `collection2.xml` as the file to be parsed, type:

```
sax2-it TrySAX2Parser collection2.xml
```

This expands to something like this (depending on your installation locations and Xerces and Java versions in `xmlsetup.bat`):

```
C:\Java\jdk1.3.1\bin\java
-classpath .;C:\XML\Apache\xerces-1_4_3\xerces.jar
-Dorg.xml.sax.driver=org.apache.xerces.parsers.SAXParser
TrySAX2Parser collection2.xml > collection2.xml.txt
```

Note that the name of the parser driver classname must be passed to the Java Virtual Machine, as per the script line fragment:

```
-Dorg.xml.sax.driver=%DRIVER%
```

where `DRIVER` is defined in `sax2-it.bat` as the classname of the Xerces parser shown in Table 7-3:

```
set DRIVER=org.apache.xerces.parsers.SAXParser
```

If you wish to use a different parser, you must change the `DRIVER` definition in `sax2-it.bat` to match the classname of your parser.

Minimal SAX Example

What does the equivalent of the proverbial `"Hello World"` program look like for a SAX2 application? A minimal SAX application that takes advantage of the

DefaultHandler is shown in Listing 7-3. The only event handler defined is one for startElement, which simply prints the name of the element plus any URI, if a namespace applies. This minimal program takes whatever default SAX2 parser is available; that is, it assumes you are passing it the driver classname as described in the previous section.

Listing 7-3 Minimal SAX Application Extending DefaultHandler (MinSAX2Parser.java)

```
import java.io.FileReader;
import org.xml.sax.XMLReader;
import org.xml.sax.Attributes;
import org.xml.sax.InputSource;
import org.xml.sax.helpers.XMLReaderFactory;
import org.xml.sax.helpers.DefaultHandler;

public class MinSAX2Parser extends DefaultHandler
{
 public static void main (String args[])
     throws Exception
 {
     XMLReader xmlreader   = XMLReaderFactory.createXMLReader();
     MinSAX2Parser handler = new MinSAX2Parser();
     xmlreader.setContentHandler(handler);
     xmlreader.setErrorHandler(handler);

     FileReader fr = new FileReader(args[0]);
     xmlreader.parse(new InputSource(fr));
 }

 public MinSAX2Parser ()
 {
     super();
 }

 // Event handlers.
 public void startElement (String uri, String name,
                           String qName, Attributes atts)
 {
     System.out.println("{" + uri + "}" + name);
 }
}
```

Let's compile the program:

```
%JBIN%\javac -classpath .;%XERCES% MinSAX2Parser.java
```

Then run it with collection2.xml (Listing 7-1) as input:

```
sax2-it MinSAX2Parser collection2.xml
```

The results shown in Listing 7-4 (which sax2-it sends to the file collection2.xml.txt, based on the name of the input file) are just a little bit underwhelming.

Listing 7-4 Minimal SAX Application Parse Result

```
{}Collection
{}Book
{}Title
{}Author
{}Name
{}First
{}Last
{}Type
{}Published
{}Rating
{}Notes
{}CD
{}Title
{}Artist
{}Chart
{}Peak
{}Peak
{}Type
{}Label
{}Label
{}AlbumReleased
{}Remastered
{}Remastered
{}CD
{}Title
{}Artist
{}Chart
{}Peak
{}Peak
{}Type
{}Label
{}Label
{}AlbumReleased
{}Remastered
{}Book
{}Title
{}Author
{}Name
{}First
{}Last
{}Type
{}Published
{}Owner
{}Name
{}First
{}Last
{}Address
{}Street
{}City
{}State
{}Zip
```

Since the `DefaultHandler` defines no-ops for every `ContentHandler` method and since we've only overridden the `startElement` method by providing our own, our output consists solely of the names of each element type encountered in document order. The curly brackets indicate the lack of namespaces in the example.

More Robust SAX Example

In Listing 7-5, we show a more complete application, `TrySAX2Parser.java`, that performs all of the steps outlined previously in "Overall SAX Application Sequence" except those related to DTD Handlers. Note that DTD Handler definition and use is only necessary for very specific types of applications like XML editors or user interface design tools.

Despite its name, it has nothing to do with normal document validation that is related to a DTD. In other words, *your application can omit a DTD Handler and validation will still occur if the chosen parser supports validation and the validation property is enabled.*

Listing 7-5 Better SAX2 Application (TrySAX2Parser.java)

```
import java.io.IOException;

import org.xml.sax.XMLReader;
import org.xml.sax.ContentHandler;
import org.xml.sax.Attributes;
import org.xml.sax.ErrorHandler;
import org.xml.sax.SAXException;
import org.xml.sax.SAXParseException;
import org.xml.sax.SAXNotRecognizedException;
import org.xml.sax.SAXNotSupportedException;
import org.xml.sax.Locator;

// For flexibility with parser classname
import org.xml.sax.helpers.XMLReaderFactory;

public class TrySAX2Parser {

    // Replace with your favorite parser classname.
    // See also sax-it.bat and the createXMLReader call below.
    public static String theParseClass =
                         "org.apache.xerces.parsers.SAXParser";

    public void runParser (String url)
    {
        System.out.println("Input file to parse: " + url + "\n");

        // Get instances of our handlers
        ContentHandler contentHandler = new TryContentHandler();
        ErrorHandler   errorHandler   = new TryErrorHandler();

        try {
```

```
        // Instantiate the SAX parser.
        // The zero-arg createXMLReader() method assumes that
        // the parser class name will be passed on the command line.
        // For example:
        //   java -Dorg.xml.sax.driver=
        //         org.apache.xerces.parsers.SAXParser
        //
        // If your Java environment does not support this, use the
        // alternate version of createXMLReader() which passes the
        // class name directly, as shown in the commented out line.
        // This approach requires a recompile if the parser is changed.
        XMLReader saxParser =
            XMLReaderFactory.createXMLReader();
            // XMLReaderFactory.createXMLReader(theParseClass);

        // Register the content handler
        saxParser.setContentHandler(contentHandler);

        // Register the error handler
        saxParser.setErrorHandler(errorHandler);

        // Enable validation
        try {
          saxParser.setFeature("http://xml.org/sax/features/validation",
                          true);
        } catch (SAXNotRecognizedException e) {
          System.err.println("**** SAXNotRecognizedException: " +
                             "Cannot activate validation: " +
                             e.getMessage());
        } catch (SAXNotSupportedException e) {
          System.err.println("**** SAXNotSupportedException: " +
                             "Cannot activate validation: " +
                             e.getMessage());
        }

        // Enable namespace awareness
        try {
          saxParser.setFeature("http://xml.org/sax/features/namespaces",
                          true);
        } catch (SAXNotRecognizedException e) {
          System.err.println("**** SAXNotRecognizedException: " +
                             "Cannot set namespaces: " +
                             e.getMessage());
        } catch (SAXNotSupportedException e) {
          System.err.println("**** SAXNotSupportedException: " +
                             "Cannot set namespaces: " +
                             e.getMessage());
        }

        // Invoke the SAX parser
        saxParser.parse(url);

    } catch (SAXException ex) {
        System.out.println("SAXException during parsing: " +
                           ex.getMessage());
```

```
        } catch (IOException ex) {
            System.out.println("IOException reading file: " +
                                ex.getMessage());
        }
    }

    public static void main(String[] args)
    {
        if (args.length != 1)
        {
            System.out.println("Usage: java TrySAX2Parser XML_filename");
            System.exit(0);
        }

        String uri = args[0];

        TrySAX2Parser trySAX2Parser = new TrySAX2Parser();
        trySAX2Parser.runParser(uri);
    }
}

// Either define ContentHandler or extend DefaultHandler.

class TryContentHandler implements ContentHandler {

    private org.xml.sax.Locator locator;

    public void startDocument()
            throws SAXException
    {
        System.out.println("Begin parse.");
    }

    public void endDocument()
            throws SAXException
    {
        System.out.println("End Parse.");
    }

    public void startElement(String namespaceURI, String localName,
                          String qualifiedName, Attributes attrs)
            throws SAXException
    {
        System.out.print("startElement: " + localName);
        if (!namespaceURI.equals(""))
        {
            System.out.println("\n Namespace = " + namespaceURI +
                                "\n qualifiedName = ["
                                + qualifiedName + "]");
        }
        else
        {
            System.out.println(" - No namespace");
        }
```

```
        for (int i = 0; i < attrs.getLength(); i++)
            System.out.println("  attribute: " +
                               attrs.getLocalName(i) +
                               " = '" + attrs.getValue(i) + "'"
                               + " - type: " + attrs.getType(i) );
    }

    public void endElement(String namespaceURI, String localName,
                           String qualifiedName)
                throws SAXException
    {
        System.out.println("endElement: " + localName + "\n");
    }

    public void characters(char[] ch, int start, int end)
                throws SAXException
    {
        String s = new String(ch, start, end);
        System.out.println("  characters: [" + s + "]");
    }

    public void ignorableWhitespace(char[] ch, int start, int end)
                throws SAXException
    {
        // no-op; could print these chars
    }

    public void processingInstruction(String target, String data)
                throws SAXException
    {
        System.out.println("Processing Instruction: "
                                    + "Target = [" + target + "]"
          + "\n                          Data = [" + data + "]");
    }

    public void startPrefixMapping(String prefix, String uri)
    {
        System.out.println("Begin mapping prefix: " + prefix +
                           "\n Mapped to URI: " + uri);
    }

    public void endPrefixMapping(String prefix)
    {
        System.out.println("End mapping prefix: " + prefix);
    }

    public void setDocumentLocator(Locator _locator )
    {
        // Save notification location info in instance variable.
        // setDocumentLocator is called by SAX2 before startDocument.
        locator = _locator;
    }
```

```
    public void skippedEntity(String name)
                throws SAXException
    {
      // no-op (unlikely to fire, except with non-validating parser
    }
}

class TryErrorHandler implements ErrorHandler  {

    public void fatalError(SAXParseException ex)
                throws SAXException
    {
      System.out.println("Fatal Error ==>\n" +
              " LineNumber: " +  ex.getLineNumber() +
              " at ColumnNumber: " + ex.getColumnNumber() +
              " [approx.]\n" +
              " File: " + ex.getSystemId() + "\n" +
              " Message: " + ex.getMessage());
      throw new SAXException("Fatal Error thrown.");
    }

    public void error(SAXParseException ex)
                throws SAXException
    {
      System.out.println("Error ==>\n" +
              " LineNumber: " +  ex.getLineNumber() +
              " at ColumnNumber: " + ex.getColumnNumber() +
              " [approx.]\n" +
              " File: " + ex.getSystemId() + "\n" +
              " Message: " + ex.getMessage());
      throw new SAXException("Error thrown.");
    }

    public void warning(SAXParseException ex)
                throws SAXException
    {
      System.out.println("Warning ==>\n" +
              " LineNumber: " +  ex.getLineNumber() +
              " at ColumnNumber: " + ex.getColumnNumber() +
              " [approx.]\n" +
              " File: " + ex.getSystemId() + "\n" +
              " Message: " + ex.getMessage());
      throw new SAXException("Warning thrown.");
    }
}
```

In Listing 7-5, the `TryContentHandler` class implements `ContentHandler`, so it must define all eleven methods:

```
public void startDocument
public void endDocument
public void startElement
public void endElement
```

```
public void characters
public void ignorableWhitespace
public void processingInstruction
public void startPrefixMapping
public void endPrefixMapping
public void setDocumentLocator
public void skippedEntity
```

Although some of these are simply no-ops, they all must be defined, as mentioned earlier. The startPrefixMapping and endPrefixMapping methods are triggered when a namespace comes into and goes out of scope, respectively. The characters handler is invoked whenever #PCDATA is encountered, but there's no requirement that the parser fire this method only once for a run of contiguous characters, so you may need to be prepared to buffer the results. The processingInstruction handler is passed the target (the intended application) and the data (parameters, possibly as name/value pairs, but not necessarily).

However, it's the startElement that does the most work in this sample application, as is likely to be the case in many SAX applications. We determine whether the element name contains a namespace URI (which has already been mapped by startPrefixMapping, if there was one) and print it with or without the namespace. Attributes need to be handled in startElement because there is no handler specifically for attributes. Instead, they are passed as a list of type Attributes to startElement. We can iterate over the name/value pairs using the Attributes.getLength method to determine the number of pairs, Attributes.getLocalName to obtain the attribute name without a namespace URI, Attributes.getValue to extract the attribute value (which may come from the DTD if it's a default), and Attributes.getType to determine the datatype of attribute (CDATA, NMTOKEN, enumeration, etc.). If we chose to use a stack to maintain context, it is in startElement that we'd probably push information (element name, attributes, etc.) onto the stack.

The TryErrorHandler class implements ErrorHandler. As previously described in "ErrorHandler: Well-Formedess and Validation," this handler needs to define methods named fatalError, error, and warning. In each case, we print the line number and column where the error was detected, along with the input filename and the message extracted from the SAXParseException that is passed to the handler.

Turning to the TrySAX2Parser class itself, we see the static String theParseClass which is not used. Instead, we've illustrated the greatest flexibility in parser selection by dynamically identifying the class name of the SAX parser by the line:

```
XMLReader saxParser =
            XMLReaderFactory.createXMLReader();
```

This zero-arg method will attempt to get the classname of the SAX parser as a Java property, which you may recall we defined as DRIVER in sax2-it.bat. The advantage of this technique is that we can switch parsers by changing the batch file; no recompile is needed. If we were running the application from the command line or from a servlet, a similar change would be needed. Only the driver classname passed to the JVM needs to change:

```
-Dorg.xml.sax.driver=org.apache.xerces.parsers.SAXParser
```

or whatever the parser is.

A less flexible approach is to hardcode the classname and use the other form of `createXMLReader`, which takes the classname as an argument, as shown in the commented-out portion of the sample SAX application.

Next, we register the `ContentHandler` and `ErrorHandler` we've defined. We then use the `XMLReader.setFeature` method to enable validation and namespace awareness. If we forget to do this, validation errors will never be reported, even though we've defined and registered our `ErrorHandler`. Notice that the strings used to identify the two features

```
http://xml.org/sax/features/validation
http://xml.org/sax/features/namespaces
```

are not parser-dependent since they have `xml.org/sax` in their names. Even though most SAX parsers should have these features, we have try/catch blocks just in case (e.g., if the parser is nonvalidating and/or is not able to process namespaces).

Finally, we invoke the parser by calling `XMLReader.parse` with the name of the file to parse. We could iterate over multiple files from the command line, as long as they are handled sequentially. Since this is an event-driven model, once we invoke the parser, we effectively "sit back and wait to be called" whenever one of the methods in our `ContentHandler` or `ErrorHandler` classes is activated.

Valid Parse Results

So what happens when we run our sample SAX program with valid XML input? Recall our `collection2.xml` example from Listing 7-1. The instance references `collection2.dtd`, shown in Listing 7-6.

Listing 7-6 Collection DTD (collection2.dtd)

```
<?xml encoding="UTF-8"?>
<!--    Collection DTD, Version 2    -->
<!ELEMENT Collection ((Book | CD)*, Owner?)>
<!ATTLIST Collection
    version CDATA "2"
>
<!ELEMENT Owner (Name, Address?)>
<!ELEMENT Address (Street, City, State, Zip)>
<!ELEMENT Street (#PCDATA)>
<!ELEMENT City (#PCDATA)>
<!ELEMENT State (#PCDATA)>
<!ELEMENT Zip (#PCDATA)>
```

```
<!ELEMENT Book (Title, Author, Type, Published, Rating?, Notes?)>
<!ELEMENT Title (#PCDATA)>
<!-- Title defined under CD; applies to Book also. -->
<!-- Name defined under Owner; applies to Book also. -->
<!ELEMENT Author (Name)>
<!ELEMENT Name (First, Last)>
<!ATTLIST Name
    sex (male | female) "male"
>
<!ELEMENT First (#PCDATA)>
<!ELEMENT Last (#PCDATA)>
<!ELEMENT Type (#PCDATA)>
<!ELEMENT Published (#PCDATA)>
<!ATTLIST Published
    publisher CDATA #REQUIRED
>
<!ELEMENT Rating (#PCDATA)>
<!ELEMENT Notes (#PCDATA)>
<!ELEMENT CD (Title, Artist, Chart, Type, Label+, AlbumReleased,
Remastered+)>
<!ELEMENT Artist (#PCDATA)>
<!ELEMENT Chart (Peak+)>
<!--WAS: ATTLIST Label country NMTOKEN #IMPLIED-->
<!ELEMENT Peak (#PCDATA)>
<!ATTLIST Peak
    country NMTOKEN "US"
    weeks NMTOKEN #IMPLIED
>
<!ELEMENT Label (#PCDATA)>
<!ATTLIST Label
    country NMTOKEN "US"
>
<!ELEMENT AlbumReleased (#PCDATA)>
<!ELEMENT Remastered (#PCDATA)>
<!ATTLIST Remastered
    format CDATA #REQUIRED
>
```

Given the input XML document and its corresponding DTD, our program `TrySAX2Parser.java`, produces the output in Listing 7-7. We can see that the start tags for `Collection` and `Book` are processed first (as a result of SAX invoking the `startElement` callback) and then a `Title` element is seen, along with its content (obtained via the `characters` callback), and then the end tag for `Title` is encountered (`endElement`). Next in document order is the `Author` element, which contains a `Name` child, which in turn contains `First` and `Last` elements.

Notice that attributes such as `version` for `Collection` and `sex` for `Name` are available to the `startElement` method (since they are part of the start tag). In this case, `sex` was not specified, but SAX2 reports the value `"male"` because this default value is specified in the DTD based on the attribute definition:

```
<!ATTLIST Name
    sex (male | female) "male">
```

Attribute values and datatypes are available by means of the `getValue` and `getType` methods, respectively. In this example, the datatypes are `CDATA`, `NMTOKEN`, or enumerations. The number of attributes (useful for iteration) is given by the `getLength` method.

As we noted earlier, when the `Name` element is encountered as the child of the `Owner` element (as opposed to being the child of the `Author` element), the `startElement` callback that is invoked with the element `Name` has no idea of its context (`Owner` vs. `Author`). If this contextual information is relevant to your application, you must maintain your own event history or nesting information. This is an inherent limitation of SAX, but not of the DOM, as we'll see in chapter 8.

You are encouraged to trace the output shown in Listing 7-7 and compare it to the input in Listing 7-1 to be sure you understand why events fire in the order indicated by the output, and also to notice that there are no namespace or processing instruction events because they don't exist in `collection2.xml`.

Listing 7-7 SAX2 Output with Valid Input

```
Input file to parse: collection2.xml

Begin parse.
startElement: Collection - No namespace
  attribute: version = '2' - type: CDATA
startElement: Book - No namespace
startElement: Title - No namespace
  characters: [Complete Beatles Chronicle, The]
endElement: Title

startElement: Author - No namespace
startElement: Name - No namespace
  attribute: sex = 'male' - type: (male|female)
startElement: First - No namespace
  characters: [Mark]
endElement: First

startElement: Last - No namespace
  characters: [Lewisohn]
endElement: Last

endElement: Name

endElement: Author

startElement: Type - No namespace
  characters: [Chronology]
endElement: Type

startElement: Published - No namespace
  attribute: publisher = 'Harmony Books' - type: CDATA
  characters: [1992]
endElement: Published
```

```
startElement: Rating - No namespace
  characters: [5 stars]
endElement: Rating

startElement: Notes - No namespace
  characters: [
  Covers the years 1957 through 1970. No solo info.
  Great appendices with chart info, discography, composer index,
  radio, tv, and live performances, and much more.
  ]
endElement: Notes

endElement: Book

startElement: CD - No namespace
startElement: Title - No namespace
  characters: [Band on the Run]
endElement: Title

startElement: Artist - No namespace
  characters: [McCartney, Paul and Wings]
endElement: Artist

startElement: Chart - No namespace
startElement: Peak - No namespace
  attribute: weeks = '4' - type: NMTOKENS
  attribute: country = 'US' - type: NMTOKENS
  characters: [1]
endElement: Peak

startElement: Peak - No namespace
  attribute: country = 'UK' - type: NMTOKENS
  characters: [1]
endElement: Peak

endElement: Chart

startElement: Type - No namespace
  characters: [Rock]
endElement: Type

startElement: Label - No namespace
  attribute: country = 'US' - type: NMTOKENS
  characters: [Capitol]
endElement: Label

startElement: Label - No namespace
  attribute: country = 'UK' - type: NMTOKENS
  characters: [EMI]
endElement: Label

startElement: AlbumReleased - No namespace
  characters: [1973]
endElement: AlbumReleased
```

```
startElement: Remastered - No namespace
  attribute: format = 'gold CD' - type: CDATA
  characters: [1993]
endElement: Remastered

startElement: Remastered - No namespace
  attribute: format = '2 disc box set with booklet' - type: CDATA
  characters: [1999]
endElement: Remastered

endElement: CD

startElement: CD - No namespace
startElement: Title - No namespace
  characters: [Venus and Mars]
endElement: Title

startElement: Artist - No namespace
  characters: [McCartney, Paul and Wings]
endElement: Artist

startElement: Chart - No namespace
startElement: Peak - No namespace
  attribute: weeks = '1' - type: NMTOKENS
  attribute: country = 'US' - type: NMTOKENS
  characters: [1]
endElement: Peak

startElement: Peak - No namespace
  attribute: country = 'UK' - type: NMTOKENS
  characters: [2]
endElement: Peak

endElement: Chart

startElement: Type - No namespace
  characters: [Rock]
endElement: Type

startElement: Label - No namespace
  attribute: country = 'US' - type: NMTOKENS
  characters: [Capitol]
endElement: Label

startElement: Label - No namespace
  attribute: country = 'UK' - type: NMTOKENS
  characters: [EMI]
endElement: Label

startElement: AlbumReleased - No namespace
  characters: [1975]
endElement: AlbumReleased
```

```
startElement: Remastered - No namespace
  attribute: format = 'gold CD with 3 bonus tracks' - type: CDATA
  characters: [1994]
endElement: Remastered

endElement: CD

startElement: Book - No namespace
startElement: Title - No namespace
  characters: [Many Years From Now]
endElement: Title

startElement: Author - No namespace
startElement: Name - No namespace
  attribute: sex = 'male' - type: (male|female)
startElement: First - No namespace
  characters: [Paul]
endElement: First

startElement: Last - No namespace
  characters: [McCartney]
endElement: Last

endElement: Name

endElement: Author

startElement: Type - No namespace
  characters: [Autobiographical]
endElement: Type

startElement: Published - No namespace
  attribute: publisher = 'Henry Holt and Company' - type: CDATA
  characters: [1997]
endElement: Published

endElement: Book

startElement: Owner - No namespace
startElement: Name - No namespace
  attribute: sex = 'male' - type: (male|female)
startElement: First - No namespace
  characters: [Ken]
endElement: First

startElement: Last - No namespace
  characters: [Sall]
endElement: Last

endElement: Name

startElement: Address - No namespace
startElement: Street - No namespace
  characters: [123 Milky Way Dr.]
endElement: Street
```

```
startElement: City - No namespace
  characters: [Columbia]
endElement: City

startElement: State - No namespace
  characters: [MD]
endElement: State

startElement: Zip - No namespace
  characters: [20794]
endElement: Zip

endElement: Address

endElement: Owner

endElement: Collection

End Parse.
```

Error Results

In the previous section, we saw the result of a successful parse. But what happens when the XML instance is either not *well-formed* or is *invalid* according to a particular DTD or schema? How does the SAX interface to parsing handle such errors?

First we'll examine how a parsing error is reported when XML is not well-formed. This book's CD `collection2-bug.xml` file is identical to `collection2.xml` except that the `Last` element ends incorrectly with `<Last>` rather than `</Last>`.

```
<Book>
  <Title>Complete Beatles Chronicle, The</Title>
  <Author>
    <Name>
      <First>Mark</First>
      <Last>Lewisohn<Last>
    </Name>
   </Author>
   <!-- etc. -->
```

The parser output is shown in Listing 7-8.

Listing 7-8 SAX Parse Output When XML Is Not Well-Formed

```
Input file to parse: collection2-bug.xml

Begin parse.
startElement: Collection - No namespace
  attribute: version = '2' - type: CDATA
startElement: Book - No namespace
```

```
startElement: Title - No namespace
  characters: [Complete Beatles Chronicle, The]
endElement: Title

startElement: Author - No namespace
startElement: Name - No namespace
  attribute: sex = 'male' - type: (male|female)
startElement: First - No namespace
  characters: [Mark]
endElement: First

startElement: Last - No namespace
  characters: [Lewisohn]
startElement: Last - No namespace
  characters: [
      ]
Fatal Error ==>
 LineNumber: 11 at ColumnNumber: 13 [approx.]
 File: file:///C:/KEN/XMLBook/NOTES/Ch7-Ex/collection2-bug.xml
 Message: The element type "Last" must be terminated by the matching end-tag
"</Last>".
SAXException during parsing: Fatal Error thrown.
```

This *fatal error* means that the parser that SAX is interfacing to has detected that the second `Last` start tag is not possible until the first `Last` element has been terminated. Even without a DTD, this nesting obviously is not acceptable XML syntax, so the document is not well-formed. SAX invokes the `fatalError` method in our `ErrorHandler` implementation, we print the relevant information, and the parser stops at this point. Note that the error message from the parser is very explicit.

It's worth a brief tangent to point out that there is no standard for SAX error messages. It would be nice if the application could take a certain action based on knowing more than simply whether the error is a well-formedness or a validation problem. Unfortunately, it can't; there are no standard SAX error codes as of this writing. For example, here's the error message from ElCel's XML Validator, given the same input.

```
C:>xmlvalid collection2-bug.xml
collection2-bug.xml [10:29] : Error: element content invalid. Element 'Last' is
not expected here, expecting '</Last>'
collection2-bug.xml [11:13] : Fatal error: end tag '</Name>' does not match
start tag.  Expected '</Last>'
collection2-bug.xml [12:14] : Fatal error: end tag '</Author>' does not match
start tag.  Expected '</Last>'
[etc.]
```

Although both parsers report a similar source of the problem, the messages are different enough to lock us into a particular parser if we were to key off the message strings themselves.

Now let's consider an example of XML data that is well-formed but does not adhere to the DTD it references and is therefore invalid. SAX will report this as well, but with an important difference. Suppose we assign two `Title` elements for one given book (`collection2-invalid-Title.xml`):

```
<Book>
  <Title>Complete Beatles Chronicle, The</Title>
  <Title>Bogus second title</Title>
  <Author>
    <Name>
      <First>Mark</First>
      <Last>Lewisohn</Last>
    </Name>
   </Author>
   <!-- etc. -->
```

The parse result is shown in Listing 7-9. What may seem surprising at first is that the parse does *not* terminate as soon as the second `Title` element is encountered. Instead, the `SAXException` isn't thrown until the parser reaches the end of the model that contains the `Title` element. Since the parent of `Title` in this case is `Book`, the parse terminates when `</Book>` is seen and the children of `Book` haven't matched the model defined in the DTD, namely:

```
<!ELEMENT Book (Title, Author, Type, Published, Rating?, Notes?)>
```

This says there can be only one `Title` and that should be followed immediately by an `Author` element.

Notice that this example, like all those involving errors with DTD constraints, triggers the `error` method since it is nonfatal. It's up to you whether or not your application should continue, depending on whether your code throws an exception.

Listing 7-9 Output with Invalid Input

```
Input file to parse: collection2-invalid-Title.xml

Begin parse.
startElement: Collection - No namespace
  attribute: version = '2' - type: CDATA
startElement: Book - No namespace
startElement: Title - No namespace
  characters: [Complete Beatles Chronicle, The]
endElement: Title

startElement: Title - No namespace
  characters: [Bogus second title]
endElement: Title

startElement: Author - No namespace
startElement: Name - No namespace
  attribute: sex = 'male' - type: (male|female)
```

```
startElement: First - No namespace
  characters: [Mark]
endElement: First

startElement: Last - No namespace
  characters: [Lewisohn]
endElement: Last

endElement: Name

endElement: Author

startElement: Type - No namespace
  characters: [Chronology]
endElement: Type

startElement: Published - No namespace
  attribute: publisher = 'Harmony Books' - type: CDATA
  characters: [1992]
endElement: Published

startElement: Rating - No namespace
  characters: [5 stars]
endElement: Rating

startElement: Notes - No namespace
  characters: [
  Covers the years 1957 through 1970. No solo info.
  Great appendices with chart info, discography, composer index,
  radio, tv, and live performances, and much more.
  ]
endElement: Notes

Error ==>
 LineNumber: 22 at ColumnNumber: 11 [approx.]
 File: file:///C:/KEN/XMLBook/NOTES/Ch7-Ex/collection2-invalid-Title.xml
 Message: The content of element type "Book" must match
"(Title,Author,Type,Published,Rating?,Notes?)".
SAXException during parsing: Error thrown.
```

Similarly, if an element name is misspelled, the parser would assume it encountered an undeclared element. Suppose our XML instance (`collection2-invalid-Types.xml`) contains the line:

```
<Types>Chronology</Types>
```

SAX again reports a nonfatal error since the content is well-formed but doesn't match the DTD:

```
Error ==>
 LineNumber: 14 at ColumnNumber: 12 [approx.]
 File: file:///C:/KEN/XMLBook/NOTES/Ch7-Ex/collection2-invalid-Types.xml
 Message: Element type "Types" must be declared.
SAXException during parsing: Error thrown.
```

More Representative Input

The collection2.xml example does not really cause all of our event handlers to be invoked since it contains no processing instructions, CDATA sections, or entities. Furthermore, the elements are in no declared namespace. What happens if we try a shorter, but more representative example, namely, catalog1.xml from Listing 5-3?

The parse results are more interesting, as shown in Listing 7-10. In this case, we can see that startPrefixMapping is called when the prefix Disc enters scope and endPrefixMapping is invoked when its scope ends. In addition to the local names such as DiscountCatalog, we can access the namespace URI and the qualified name that includes the prefix. We can also see how the processingInstruction handler gets the target and data passed to it separately. For the input lines that contained entity references

```
<Disc:extra>&#169;</Disc:extra>
<Disc:extra>&internalEnt;</Disc:extra>
<Disc:extra>External entity replacement: &externalEnt;</Disc:extra>
```

the parser has substituted the appropriate replacement text:

```
 qualifiedName = [Disc:extra]
  characters: [©]
....
 qualifiedName = [Disc:extra]
  characters: [Internal Entity Replacement Text]
....
 qualifiedName = [Disc:extra]
  characters: [External entity replacement: ]
  characters: [Oh, my!
]
```

(The string Oh, my! with a newline is the contents of the external entity (a file) referenced by &externalEnt;.)

The CDATA section in the input:

```
<Disc:extra>
<![CDATA[
  sale > "500.00" && sale < "2000.00" ? 'munchkin' : 'monkey'
]]>
</Disc:extra>
```

is parsed correctly such that our characters method is passed the literal string, without treating >, &&, or < as special markup characters.

Listing 7-10 SAX Parse Results Given More Thorough XML Instance

```
Input file to parse: catalog1.xml

Begin parse.
Begin mapping prefix: Disc
 Mapped to URI: http://www.HouseOfDiscounts.com/namespaces/Discounts
startElement: DiscountCatalog
 Namespace = http://www.HouseOfDiscounts.com/namespaces/Discounts
 qualifiedName = [Disc:DiscountCatalog]
startElement: category
 Namespace = http://www.HouseOfDiscounts.com/namespaces/Discounts
 qualifiedName = [Disc:category]
  attribute: name = 'Wild Animals' - type: CDATA
startElement: item
 Namespace = http://www.HouseOfDiscounts.com/namespaces/Discounts
 qualifiedName = [Disc:item]
  attribute: name = '      Lion' - type: CDATA
startElement: price
 Namespace = http://www.HouseOfDiscounts.com/namespaces/Discounts
 qualifiedName = [Disc:price]
  attribute: type = 'wholesale' - type: (wholesale|retail)
  attribute: currency = '$US' - type: CDATA
  characters: [999.99]
endElement: price

endElement: item

Processing Instruction: Target = [somePI]
                        Data = [target1="foo"       target2="bar"     ]
startElement: item
 Namespace = http://www.HouseOfDiscounts.com/namespaces/Discounts
 qualifiedName = [Disc:item]
  attribute: name = 'Tiger' - type: CDATA
startElement: price
 Namespace = http://www.HouseOfDiscounts.com/namespaces/Discounts
 qualifiedName = [Disc:price]
  attribute: type = 'wholesale' - type: (wholesale|retail)
  attribute: currency = '$US' - type: CDATA
  characters: [879.99]
endElement: price

startElement: extra
 Namespace = http://www.HouseOfDiscounts.com/namespaces/Discounts
 qualifiedName = [Disc:extra]
  characters: [©]
endElement: extra

startElement: extra
 Namespace = http://www.HouseOfDiscounts.com/namespaces/Discounts
 qualifiedName = [Disc:extra]
  characters: [Internal Entity Replacement Text]
endElement: extra
```

```
startElement: extra
 Namespace = http://www.HouseOfDiscounts.com/namespaces/Discounts
 qualifiedName = [Disc:extra]
endElement: extra

endElement: item

startElement: item
 Namespace = http://www.HouseOfDiscounts.com/namespaces/Discounts
 qualifiedName = [Disc:item]
  attribute: name = 'Bear' - type: CDATA
startElement: price
 Namespace = http://www.HouseOfDiscounts.com/namespaces/Discounts
 qualifiedName = [Disc:price]
  attribute: type = 'wholesale' - type: (wholesale|retail)
  attribute: currency = '$US' - type: CDATA
  characters: [1199.99]
endElement: price

startElement: extra
 Namespace = http://www.HouseOfDiscounts.com/namespaces/Discounts
 qualifiedName = [Disc:extra]
  characters: [External entity replacement: ]
  characters: [Oh, my!
]
endElement: extra

startElement: extra
 Namespace = http://www.HouseOfDiscounts.com/namespaces/Discounts
 qualifiedName = [Disc:extra]
  characters: [
]
  characters: [
   sale > "500.00" && sale < "2000.00" ? 'munchkin' : 'monkey'
]
  characters: [
]
endElement: extra

endElement: item

endElement: category

endElement: DiscountCatalog

End mapping prefix: Disc
End Parse.
```

SAX Filters

SAX2 provides an interface called `org.xml.sax.XMLFilter` and a helper class called `org.xml.sax.helpers.XMLFilterImpl` that are useful for chaining together different processing classes. Each filter can perform a particular task, such as stripping elements from its input that are not of interest for the next filter in the chain. From the perspective of the end application, the entire chain of filters appears as a single SAX application producing events.

The `XMLFilter` interface extends `XMLReader` quite simply: `XMLFilter` is merely an `XMLReader` whose parent is also an `XMLReader`. Each `XMLFilter` reads the events from its parent. From the perspective of the parent `XMLReader`, the `XMLFilter` child is a client to which it passes events.

An implementation of the `XMLFilter` interface usually will also need to implement one or more of the `EntityResolver`, `DTDHandler`, `ContentHandler`, and `ErrorHandler` interfaces. Therefore, the convenience class `XMLFilterImpl` is provided; it implements the `XMLFilter`, `EntityResolver`, `DTDHandler`, `ContentHandler`, and `ErrorHandler` interfaces. A filter derived from `XMLFilterImpl` can override methods as necessary; otherwise, all events are passed through unmodified, so it essentially acts like a null filter.

See *http://www.saxproject.org/?selected=filters* for more details and an example. Also, see Elliotte Rusty Harold's book.

Writing XML Using SAX

David Megginson's `XMLWriter`, a filter that writes an XML document from a SAX event stream, is available from his software page (not SourceForge.net), *http://www.megginson.com/Software/index.html*. The core of this nonstandard SAX software is `com.megginson.sax.XMLWriter` (note the different package name), which extends the standard `org.xml.sax.helpers.XMLFilterImpl`.

`XMLWriter` is a SAX2 filter that serializes events and outputs them to an XML document. In a sense, `XMLWriter` is a generalized streaming XML writing utility. Support for Namespaces and a special class for writing pretty printed, data-oriented XML is provided.

As Megginson writes in the public domain Javadoc that accompanies the `XMLWriter`:

> This class can be used by itself or as part of a SAX event stream: it takes as input a series of SAX2 ContentHandler events and uses the information in those events to write an XML document. Since this class is a filter, it can also pass the events on down a filter chain for further processing (you can use the XMLWriter to take a snapshot of the current state at any point in a filter chain), and it can be used directly as a ContentHandler for a SAX2 XMLReader.

Although this package is nonstandard, it does address the need for serialization.

Summary

The Simple API for XML (SAX), is a lightweight, flexible, language-independent API for parsing XML. Its event-driven model is most applicable when you need to process large files, when you are piping data (possibly filtered) between applications, or interested only in selected elements or element hierarchies within XML data. However, SAX does not maintain context, so programmers often need to add their own data structures. For a complete list of pros and cons, see the section at the end of chapter 9, "SAX vs. DOM vs. JDOM vs. JAXP—Who Wins?"

The current version is SAX2, originally developed by David Megginson, but now maintained by David Brownell on SourceForge.net. Nearly all parsers support SAX2, with language support for Java, Python, perl, C++, C, COM, and more. This chapter primarily addresses the Java interface.

- The two main packages are `org.xml.sax` and `org.xml.sax.helpers`.
- The major interfaces that you typically need are `ContentHandler`, `ErrorHandler`, and `XMLReader`.
- The `ContentHandler` interface defines eleven methods that fire when events of interest (e.g., elements, processing instructions, etc.) are encountered in the input stream.
- You can extend `DefaultHandler` instead of `ContentHandler` if you want default behavior for most kinds of events. Then replace its no-op methods as needed.
- The `ErrorHandler` interface includes three methods that handle fatal errors (well-formedness problems), nonfatal errors (validity constraints), and warnings. Parsing does not necessarily terminate even when a fatal error is encountered.
- `XMLReader` provides a convenient interface to the parser itself, including registering event handlers (e.g., `setContentHandler`, `setErrorHandler`), setting and getting parser features and properties, and initiating document parsing.
- Most validating parsers are nonvalidating by default. You need to call `XMLReader.setFeature("http://xml.org/sax/features/validation", true)` to enable validation.
- Many SAX parsers exist (see Table 7-3).
- If you use the zero-arg version of `XMLReader.createXMLReader`, you can keep specific parser classname dependencies out of your compiled code, so the parser can be changed at runtime, if necessary

For Further Exploration

Articles

SAX Articles on xmlhack
http://xmlhack.com/search.php?q=SAX

Top Ten SAX2 Tips, David Brownell
http://www.xml.com/pub/a/2001/12/05/sax2.html

DOM and SAX Are Dead, Long Live DOM and SAX, Kendall Grant Clark
http://www.xml.com/pub/a/2001/11/14/dom-sax.html

High-Performance XML Parsing With SAX, Kip Hampton [using perl]
http://www.xml.com/pub/a/2001/02/14/perlsax.html

Programming XML in Java, Part 1, Mark Johnson
http://www.javaworld.com/javaworld/jw-03-2000/jw-03-xmlsax_p.html

Programming XML in Java, Part 2, Mark Johnson
http://www.javaworld.com/javaworld/jw-04-2000/jw-0407-advsax_p.html

Mapping XML to Java, Part 1, Robert Hustead
http://www.javaworld.com/javaworld/jw-08-2000/jw-0804-sax_p.html

Mapping XML to Java, Part 2, Robert Hustead
http://www.javaworld.com/javaworld/jw-10-2000/jw-1006-sax_p.html

XML-Deviant: The Benign Dictator of SAX [Megginson's departure from SAX]
http://www.xml.com/pub/2000/10/04/sax/index.html

Books

Processing XML with Java, Elliotte Rusty Harold ([in press], Addison-Wesley)
http://www.ibiblio.org/xml/books/xmljava/

Essential XML: Beyond Markup, Don Box, Aaron Skonnard and John Lam (Addison-Wesley, 2000; ISBN 0-201-70914-7)
http://cseng.aw.com/book/0,3828,0201709147,00.html

SAX2, David Brownell (O'Reilly and Associates, 2002; ISBN 0-596-00237-8)
http://www.oreilly.com/catalog/sax2/

Resources

David Megginson's home page [which links to original SAX home page]
http://www.megginson.com/index.html

Microsoft Visual Basic SAX2 Jumpstart for XML Developers
http://msdn.microsoft.com/xml/articles/Vbsax2jumpstart.asp

Elliotte Rusty Harold's slides from Software Development 2000 East
http://www.ibiblio.org/xml/slides/sd2000east/sax/

SAX

Home Page [since October 2001]
http://www.saxproject.org/

History of SAX
http://www.saxproject.org/?selected=history1

Events vs. Trees [SAX vs. DOM]
http://www.saxproject.org/?selected=event

Features and Properties [validation, namespaces, etc.]
http://www.saxproject.org/?selected=get-set

JavaDoc
http://www.saxproject.org/apidoc/overview-summary.html

Non-Java Language Support
http://www.saxproject.org/?selected=langs

XMLWriter based on SAX2
http://www.megginson.com/Software/

SAX Resource List on xml.com
http://www.xml.com/pub/Guide/SAX

SAX Conformance Testing
http://xmlconf.sourceforge.net/?selected=sax

Software

Apache's Xerces Java (Xerces-J)
http://xml.apache.org/xerces-j/

Apache's Crimson [JAXP 1.1 minus Transform package]
http://xml.apache.org/crimson/

Sun's JAXP
http://java.sun.com/xml/download.html

GNU's Aelfred2 (from GNU JAXP project)
http://www.gnu.org/software/classpathx/jaxp/

Microsoft's MSXML [URL changes too often; sorry]
http://msdn.microsoft.com/

IBM's xml4j [Xerces-J 1.4.2 forms the basis for XML4J 3.2.1]
http://www.alphaWorks.ibm.com/tech/XML4J

Oracle's XML parser XDK for Java
http://otn.oracle.com/tech/xml/content.html

James Clark's xp [fast, non-validating parser]
http://www.jclark.com/xml/xp/index.html

XMLSoftware.com's List of Parsers/Processors [very comprehensive]
http://www.xmlsoftware.com/parsers/

W3C Specifications and Information

XML Information Set
http://www.w3.org/TR/xml-infoset

DOM Home Page
http://www.w3.org/DOM/

Chapter 8

Parsing with the DOM

In this chapter, we'll explore the W3C's Document Object Model, the DOM, which, like SAX in the previous chapter, is an application programming interface available for use with nearly all contemporary XML parsers. The DOM is document-centric and tree-based, which makes it well-suited for applications that must manipulate (interact with) an XML document: to add, change, or delete elements or attributes, to alter the content, to change the style information, and so on. Our discussion will provide insight into which API (SAX or DOM) is best for certain kinds of applications. In the next chapter, we'll cover two related APIs—JAXP, Sun's Java API for XML Processing, and an open-source effort called JDOM, a Java-centric approach to both the DOM and SAX.

Overview of the DOM

In chapter 7, before we covered SAX, we presented an overview of parsing and processing XML. Our nutshell comparison of two approaches, SAX and DOM, was:

- *SAX*—first XML API, lightweight, minimal, fast, language independent, maintains no context; data-centric, event-driven model
- *DOM*—from the W3C, memory intensive, complex, very powerful, language independent, context not an issue; document-centric, tree-based model

If by some chance you skipped the SAX chapter, I strongly encourage you to read it before learning about the DOM so that you'll be in a better position to understand their relative strengths and weaknesses. Many developers make the mistake of learning only one of these approaches, perhaps because they are so different. SAX may seem very foreign if you've never done any serious GUI programming. On the other hand, the DOM may be difficult to learn if you aren't very familiar with object-oriented programming, not to mention that the API is far more involved than is that of SAX.

The DOM and SAX are two completely different approaches to XML parsing and processing. Don't assume that just because the DOM is a W3C Recommendation and SAX is not that DOM is the superior choice in all situations. Similarly, don't conclude that because SAX is a simpler, lightweight API it is better than the DOM. The point here is that *each is excellent for the kinds of applications for which it was designed*. You need to understand both; not just the mechanics, but the pros and cons of each as well. Armed with that knowledge, you'll be in a much better position to know when to create a DOM solution vs. a SAX application.

The W3C DOM Working Group makes this clear in their DOM FAQ in the answer to the question "What is the relationship between the DOM and SAX?" (see *http://www.w3.org/DOM/faq#SAXandDOM*). They talk about provenance, scope, and style being different. I'll address only their style comments here. The major tradeoff is that with the DOM, you have random access to the nodes (XML information items), whereas SAX sacrifices this capability to have a more streamlined API. SAX doesn't incur the significant overhead of the large DOM data structures. The DOM Working Group suggests, however, that if your application requires interaction with the document's nodes (especially to add, delete, or change anything), then the DOM is likely the correct choice. On the other hand, if your application is more of a flow-through of data that doesn't require lots of context (e.g., parsing XML to store in a database), then SAX may be the answer. (Readers interested in database support for XML should see Ronald Bourret's site, *http://www.rpbourret.com/*.) The FAQ also points out that SAX and DOM can often be combined in an application. While this can be tricky, other APIs such as JDOM attempt to make this easier.

Historical Perspective

The Document Object Model (DOM), like XML 1.0 itself, is a formal specification (actually, a set of specifications as separate modules) from the W3C, in contrast to SAX2, which is controlled by no formal organization. DOM Level 2 is the current W3C recommendation and, at the time of this writing, Level 3 is still in Working Draft stages.

The DOM originated from the early JavaScript object model developed by Netscape Communications (now part of AOL). Originally, the development of JavaScript (called LiveScript in its first incarnation) was motivated by the desire to lessen Web server load by giving the browser client the ability to do basic checking of HTML form inputs. Why upload form results for processing if the user entries were invalid? JavaScript therefore needed to know about the structure of the document—to be able to examine and possibly change the values of elements. For example, when the user entered a date in a form, JavaScript could check that the date matched the desired format and was a reasonable date. If it failed the test, the JavaScript code could display an alert box explaining the error, and possibly clear the form input and warp the mouse pointer to the entry area.

Netscape's original model defined objects such as `document`, `window`, and `history`, as well as arrays of objects, such as `images` and `forms`. Since the document object encompassed a hierarchical collection of all the objects contained in a given HTML document, it was possible to reference parts of the document using hierarchical notation. For example, you can set the third image of a page in JavaScript as follows (since the arrays start with index zero):

```
document.images[2].src = "/images/myPhoto.jpg"
```

The DOM, however, is an **object model**[1] of the document as a tree consisting of nodes of various types, such as `Element`, `Attr` (attribute), `Text`, and `Comment` nodes. It represents the *logical* structure of the document. While we will concern ourselves here only with well-formed XML documents, in fact the DOM can be used to address the logical structure of valid HTML documents as well, something that is not true for SAX (unless we are parsing XHTML). Whereas SAX is used for streaming events firing when elements of a static XML document or message are encountered, the DOM is intended for a dynamic situation in which the document structure can be updated under either programmatic or user control.

By means of the DOM application programming interface, elements, attributes, text content, and style information can be *added, modified, or deleted at runtime*, which obviously alters the tree structure. For example, Listing 8-1 is JavaScript DOM code that creates a new `<div align="center">` element that contains an `<h1>XML Family of Specifications</h1>` element and inserts it before the first `<div>` element that was previously part of an XHTML document.

Listing 8-1 JavaScript DOM Code to Create and Insert Element

```
var oldDiv, newDiv, body, heading, headingStr;
// Find first div in document.
oldDiv = document.getElementsByTagName("div").item(0);
body = oldDiv.parentNode;
// Create new div and h1 and set their attributes or content.
newDiv = document.createElement("div");
newDiv.setAttribute("align", "center");
heading = document.createElement("h1");
headingStr = document.createTextNode("XML Family of Specifications");
// Hook new elements to existing elements.
heading.appendChild(headingStr);
newDiv.appendChild(heading);
body.insertBefore(newDiv, oldDiv);
```

Although we speak of documents, the DOM also applies to XML data streams once the entire stream arrives and is read into memory. Any tool that manipulates

1. In this context, an object model is a set of class or interface descriptions, plus their data, member functions (methods), and class-static operations.

XML elements needs to maintain some kind of structured model that represents the document, so prior to the DOM, tools such as early XML editors implemented their own DOM-like models.

Conceptually, the nodes represent objects rather than data structures. The object model describes the document interfaces and objects, their semantics, their behavior and attributes, and how various objects and interfaces are interrelated. This should be differentiated from a *data model,* in which the data is the focus. In the object-oriented DOM, the objects encapsulate both the data and the methods for accessing the data.

The SAX interfaces tend to be Java-centric, although Python and perl implementations exist. The DOM, on the other hand, describes its interfaces using Interface Definition Language (IDL), the generic language component of CORBA from the Object Management Group (OMG). These language-independent DOM interfaces define the means by which applications access and manipulate the information items that we discussed in the preceding SAX chapter, as well as defining analogous interfaces to HTML elements and attributes. Unlike SAX, the DOM treats information items as actual objects, which makes it a better fit in general for object-oriented programming.

The DOM defines **language bindings**[2] for both Java and ECMAScript,[3] the emerging standard scripting language based on JavaScript (Netscape) and JScript (Microsoft). The language-neutral IDL definitions and the language-specific bindings for Java and ECMAScript appear in the appendices of each module of the DOM Level 2 specifications, as well as in the appendix of the older DOM Level 1 Recommendation.[4]

Tree vs. Event Model

We learned that SAX is an event-based model, and the DOM is a tree based-model. Whereas SAX is primarily focused on the parsing process, the DOM is centered on the document structure itself (it's not called the Document Object Model by accident). The DOM is chiefly for *dynamically accessing and updating the content, struc-*

2. Language bindings are the language-specific implementations (e.g., concrete Java classes) that provide the functionality that the IDL interfaces describe.

3. Actually, ECMAScript is a pure programming language. Although it defines objects such as `array`, `string`, `number`, `function`, `date`, and so on to make it Web friendly, ECMAScript does not have built-in knowledge of a document, unlike JavaScript. Like Java and XML itself, ECMAScript supports Unicode characters.

4. For example, the IDL, Java, and ECMAScript bindings for the Core portion of DOM Level 2 are defined in *http://www.w3.org/TR/DOM-Level-2-Core/idl-definitions.html*, *java-binding.html*, and *ecma-script-binding.html*, respectively. If you're interested in bindings for *other languages*, such as C, C++, and Python, see *http://www.w3.org/DOM/Bindings*. Apache Xerces also has perl support for DOM (and SAX).

ture, and style of documents, whereas SAX is essentially for streaming, static access. This fundamental difference between the two parsing APIs has a profound implication on when each should be used.

SAX is most useful when you are ripping through a large XML document or message in order to extract certain pieces of information, such as when you are filtering the content. The DOM, on the other hand, is best suited for an application that operates repeatedly on the contents of the XML instance, such as when a user needs to interact with elements perhaps to expand and contract nodes of the tree, add nodes, or update the values associated with the nodes. If this sounds a bit like the inner workings of an XML editor, it certainly could be! Another example of DOM use is when a set of nodes and their children that match particular criteria is selected and some operation is performed on the node set, such as sending them to another application or applying a different style to them (e.g., changing tabular data to a bar graph).

We will compare and contrast the DOM and SAX in terms of advantages and disadvantages in more detail in the section entitled "SAX vs. DOM vs. JDOM vs. JAXP—Who Wins?" in chapter 9.

Generic Interfaces: Good or Bad?

Although it certainly is useful to have generic interfaces that are language-independent, there is a price to pay for this generalization. First of all, interfaces that attempt to be language neutral cannot take advantage of the special features of a given language. This is especially true when you examine the Java bindings and discover methods that would be unnecessary or perhaps more efficient if they were designed with Java's features in mind and did not need to match the same interface for languages like ECMAScript. Some experts have argued that the design of the DOM is clearly suboptimal from a Java developer's viewpoint, and for that matter, from the perspective of any object-oriented developer. One major effort to construct a more Java-friendly object model is JDOM. See "JDOM: a Java-centric Parsing Approach" in chapter 9. However, the requirement for a truly generic API makes it nearly impossible for the DOM Working Group to have fine-tuned the API to any particular language.

Another wrinkle is that although the interfaces may be parser independent, the way in which these interfaces are implemented (and, to a lesser degree, the *extent* to which they are implemented) is very much parser dependent, meaning that it is not so easy to swap in a different DOM parser as it was with SAX without changing code. Specific classes provided by vendors (e.g., of parsers) implement the interfaces. A given class can implement multiple DOM levels. Vendors are free to add proprietary interfaces as well. This DOM parser swapping may not be a significant shortcoming, however, if you have selected a DOM parser that you intend to use for the entire life cycle of your application. Also, additional APIs such as JAXP (chapter 9) have recently helped to minimize vendor-dependent DOM interfaces.

The W3C DOM efforts are completely focused on defining *interfaces*, not implementations. This focus results in many derived requirements that have impacted the design of the DOM. Its generic nature has contributed to its complexity, which is why simplification efforts such as JDOM may be worth your attention if you are a Java developer. However, simplifications do not address all possible application needs, so an understanding of the W3C DOM is still necessary.

DHTML Comparison

Many Web developers have heard the term Dynamic HTML (DHTML), so it is important to understand that the DOM is a direct outgrowth and superset of DHTML, which was the initial attempt to make document objects accessible via both Java and JavaScript in comparable ways. The W3C does not care much for the term *Dynamic HTML* so you will find no specification that describes DHTML on its Web site. According to the W3C's DOM FAQ:

> Dynamic HTML (DHTML) is a term used by some vendors to describe the combination of HTML, style sheets and scripts that allows documents to be animated. The scripting interfaces provided in DHTML have a significant overlap with the DOM, particularly with the HTML module. Compatibility with DHTML was a motivating factor in the development of the DOM. The DOM, however, is more than DHTML. It is a platform- and language-neutral interface that will allow programs and scripts to dynamically access and update the content, structure and style of documents, both HTML and XML.[5]

Relevant Specifications and Key Resources

Table 8-1 lists the *key starting points* for learning about the DOM that supplement the material in this chapter. As usual, a much more comprehensive list of links appears in "For Further Exploration." Note that the W3C has gone to great lengths to provide information about the DOM. No other XML specification has its own FAQ written by a Working Group or its own Technical Reports page, to my knowledge. Use the W3C resources, Luke!

The material in the section that starts on the next page is applicable to all language bindings for the Document Object Model (with the exception of references to Java package names).

5. What is the difference between DHTML and the DOM? For details see *http://www.w3.org/DOM/faq#DHTML-DOM*.

TABLE 8-1 DOM Specifications and Key Resources

W3C Page Title	*URL*
DOM Home Page: the master index that links to the others below plus more (bookmark this!)	*http://www.w3.org/DOM/*
DOM Activity Statement: concepts described simply; explains the 3 levels with architecure diagrams for each; covers current status	*http://www.w3.org/DOM/Activity*
DOM FAQ: contains lots of great answers, not just for beginners	*http://www.w3.org/DOM/faq*
DOM Technical Reports: one-stop shopping for all of the DOM specifications (all modules) for each of the 3 levels, regardless of maturity; includes links to DOM Requirements (for all levels) and other specifications that have their own DOM (e.g., MathML, SVG, and SMIL)	*http://www.w3.org/DOM/DOMTR*
DOM Technical Materials: zip file of all DOM Level 2 Recommendations, plus generated Java documentation and JAR	*http://www.w3.org/DOM/DOMTM*

DOM Levels

At the time of this writing, there are three levels (or four, depending on where you initialize your counter) of the DOM described by various W3C specifications, with differing degrees of formal acceptance. Therefore, when you select your XML software, especially your XML parser and XSLT processor, it is important to discover which DOM levels your vendor supports and to what degree in order to determine whether the functionality meets the needs of your application.

DOM Level 2 is the currently accepted and most widely implemented level. Therefore, the examples and descriptions in this chapter are based on DOM Level 2. Table 8-2 provides an overview of the different levels and indicates their status. See Tables 8-3 and 8-4 for detailed descriptions of the modules that comprise DOM Levels 2 and 3, respectively.

In Levels 2 and 3, not all modules must be implemented for the parser (or other DOM-based tool) to be considered DOM compliant. Furthermore, vendors are free to implement proprietary extensions and convenience methods, as long as they also implement the required interfaces. As previously mentioned, links to all DOM specifications appear on the DOM Technical Reports page, *http://www.w3.org/DOM/DOMTR*. Current status is available from the DOM Activity Statement, *http://www.w3.org/DOM/Activity*.

TABLE 8-2 Overview of the DOM Levels and Their Status

DOM Level	*W3C Status*	*Description*
"DOM Level 0"	Informal term	Although no formal specification exists, this level refers to HTML document functionality found in Netscape Navigator 3.0 and Microsoft Internet Explorer 3.0. Some attributes or methods have been included in the higher, formal DOM levels for reasons of backward compatibility with this informal level, which can be thought of as the early "HTML DOM."
DOM Level 1	Single W3C Recommendation (October 1998); second edition Working Draft (September 2000)	DOM1 defines core interfaces for both HTML and XML documents. The focus is document navigation and manipulation. DOM1 is ignorant of XML namespaces. *Note*: There is a Second Edition version of the DOM1 specification that incorporates changes indicated by the first-edition errata list. At the time of this writing, the Second Edition is not a Recommendation, however.
DOM Level 2	Multiple Recommendations published as separate modules (November 2000)	DOM2 extends DOM1 by including a CSS stylesheet object model and functionality for dynamically manipulating style information. DOM2 also includes document traversal mechanisms, defines an event model (for document mutation events as well as user-initiated events), and provides support for XML Namespaces (which didn't exist when DOM1 was accepted). As of this writing, there are five completely approved modules in DOM2: • Level 2 Core • Level 2 Views • Level 2 Events • Level 2 Style • Level 2 Traversal and Range Specification At the time of this writing, the status of a sixth module, *Level 2 HTML*, was in flux. It will probably be a completed Recommendation by the time you read this.
DOM Level 3	Several Working Drafts (dated January and February 2002)	DOM3 focuses on reading and writing of documents, access to DTD and XML Schema content models (e.g, getting the datatype of an element or attribute), key events and event groups, and functions to query a DOM tree using XPath. As of this writing, there are four modules under development: • Level 3 Core • Level 3 Abstract Schemas and Load and Save • Level 3 Events • Level 3 XPath They are likely to be completed Recommendations by the time you read this. Another module, *Level 3 Views and Formatting*, was removed from Level 3 development in late 2001. In addition, Level 3 improves support for XML Namespaces, XML Infoset, and XML Base, explores mixed vocabularies in one document, and an Embedded DOM.

DOM Level 2 Specifications

The DOM Level 2 specification, which had previously existed as a single document, was divided into six separately published modules in September 2000. These modules, which became W3C Recommendations in November 2000, are described in Table 8-3. The Java package names closely follow the names of the specifications, but are not exactly one-to-one with the modules:

- `org.w3c.dom` (corresponds to Core)
- `org.w3c.dom.views`
- `org.w3c.dom.events`
- `org.w3c.dom.html`
- `org.w3c.dom.stylesheets`
- `org.w3c.dom.css`
- `org.w3c.dom.traversal`
- `org.w3c.dom.ranges`

Note that most of these modules apply more to HTML than to XML, with the exception of Traversal and Range. The Core specification is fundamental to both HTML and XML.

TABLE 8-3 DOM Level 2 Modules

DOM2 Specification	*Description*
Core	Building on the core API specified in DOM Level 1, the DOM Level 2 Core defines a set of fundamental interfaces to create and manipulate the structure and contents of a document, some of which are XML specific. This specification explains what the DOM is and how it was developed. It includes a useful glossary.
Views	A document may have multiple views that might be dependent on the device on which the document is displayed, style information, or the point in time in which the document is accessed. The DOM 2 Views specification describes the interfaces `AbstractView` (the base interface from which all views are derived) and `DocumentView` (which may have a default view). A view is associated with a target document.
Events	The DOM2 Event Model describes event registration, event flow in a tree structure, and tracking of contextual information. Event bubbling (propagation upward through its ancestors), event capture, event cancellation, and event listener registration are defined. Document change events, as well as user-initiated events, are modeled. Event classes include `UIEvent` (e.g., `DOMFocusIn` and `DOMActivate`), `MouseEvent`, (e.g., `click`, `mousemove`, and `mouseout`) and `MutationEvent` (notification of changes to document structure, including `DOMNodeInserted`, `DOMNodeRemoved`, `DOMSubtreeModified`, and `DOMAttrModified`). Typical HTML JavaScript events (e.g., `load`, `blur`, `select`, `change`, and `submit`) are defined.

continued

TABLE 8-3 DOM Level 2 Modules (*continued*)

DOM2 Specification	*Description*
Style	The DOM Level 2 Style specification refers both to the generic notion of Style Sheets and CSS (Cascading Style Sheets) in particular. It describes how Style Sheets are associated with a document via links and style attributes, as well as how various media type are identified as targets. Both HTML and XML are addressed. This specification defines a mechanism to programmatically access and modify the style and presentation control provided by CSS Level 2 (primarily). Interfaces include `StyleSheet`, `StyleSheetList`, `MediaList`, `CSSStyleSheet`, `CSSStyleRule`, `CSSStyleDeclaration`, and `CSS2Properties`.
Traversal and Range	This is really two mini specifications, both related to navigation. The *Traversal* portion describes interfaces such as `NodeIterator` (nodes as an ordered list, so you can move forward and backward within this list), `NodeFilter`, `TreeWalker` (move to the parent of a node, to one of its children, or to a sibling), and `DocumentTraversal`. The specification states: "In general, `TreeWalkers` are better for tasks in which the structure of the document around selected nodes will be manipulated, while `NodeIterators` are better for tasks that focus on the content of each selected node."[a] The *Range* portion explains how to address a contiguous range of content which effectively selects all of the content between a pair of boundary points. The Range operations are essentially convenience methods that can contribute to optimized common editing patterns. Extracting, deleting, inserting, and cloning content are some of the topics covered. The `Range` interface is fairly involved with more than 20 methods.
HTML	Building on both DOM Level 1 and the DOM Level 2 Core, the DOM Level 2 HTML specification describes a set of specific interfaces to manipulate the structure and contents of an HTML document. Although the DOM is generic, this specification provides for functionality inherent in HTML 4.0. Every HTML 4.0 element is addressed, such as `HTMLBodyElement`, `HTMLFormElement`, and `HTMLImageElement` corresponding to `<body>`, `<form>`, and `<img>` tags.

a. See *http://www.w3.org/TR/2000/REC-DOM-Level-2-Traversal-Range-20001113/traversal.html#Traversal-overview.*

DOM Level 3 Specifications

As of this writing, the DOM Level 3 specifications are still Working Drafts (from late 2001) which, you will recall from chapter 2, are considered *works in progress.* The modules that exist at this time are described in Table 8-4, but it is likely that there will be other modules by the time you read this.

Since they are works in progress, the module names, descriptions, interface names, and Java package names may have changed, so please check the DOM Technical Reports page, *http://www.w3.org/DOM/DOMTR.*

TABLE 8-4 DOM Level 3 Modules

DOM3 Specification	*Description*
Core	This module builds on DOM Level 2 Core to define a platform- and language-neutral interface that allows programs and scripts to dynamically access and update the content, structure, and style of documents.
Abstract Schema and Load and Save	This specification defines two interrelated areas of functionality. The *Abstract Schema* (AS) portion addresses DTDs and XML Schemas, operations on these XML content models (including dynamic modification), and how content model information could be applied to XML documents in both the document-editing and AS-editing worlds. The AS portion also describes additional tests for well-formedness, especially when Namespaces are involved. Abstract Schema interfaces include `ASModel`, `ASObject`, `ASDataType`, `ASElementDeclaration`, `ASContentModel`, `ASAttributeDeclaration`, `ASEntityDeclaration`, `DocumentAS`, `DocumentEditAS`, `NodeEditAS`, `ElementEditAS`, `CharacterDataEditAS`, and more. The *Load and Save* (LS) portion defines an API for loading (parsing) XML instances into a DOM representation and for saving (serializing) a DOM representation as an XML document. The loading model is influenced by Sun's JAXP (Java API for XML Parsing) and by SAX2. The main Load and Save interfaces related to Abstract Schema are `ASDOMBuilder` and `DOMASWriter`. Others include `DOMBuilder`, `DOMWriter`, `DOMInputSource`, `LSLoadEvent`, `LSProgressEvent`, `DOMEntityResolver`, `DOMBuilderFilter`, and `DOMFormatter`.
Events	DOM Level 3 Events expands on the functionality of DOM Level 2 Events by defining new interfaces that are complementary to the earlier interfaces as well as by adding new event sets. Since DOM Level 2, `EventGroup`, `CustomEvent`, and `TextEvent` (virtual keyboard events) interfaces were added. Event capture, event bubbling, and various event listener registration techniques enable events to be handled either locally at the `EventTarget` level or centrally from an `EventTarget` higher in the document tree. This module also describes event cancellation methods.
XPath	This module attempts to resolve differences between the DOM and XPath 1.0 models, so that XPath expressions could be used to locate nodes automatically and declaratively.[a] XPath interfaces include `XPathException`, `XPathEvaluator`, `XPathExpression`, `XPathNSResolver`, `XPathResult`, `XPathNamespace`, and possibly more.

a. XPath is an effective declarative syntax used by XForms, XPointer, XSL, and XQuery, among others. Chapter 11 discusses XPath in connection with XSLT.

Again, the Java package names closely follow the names of the specifications, but are not exactly one-to-one with the modules:

- `org.w3c.dom` (Core)
- `org.w3c.dom.events` (user events and document mutation events)
- `org.w3c.dom.as` (Abstract Schema)
- `org.w3c.dom.ls` (Load and Save)
- `org.w3c.dom.xpath` (XPath queries)

Note that although the Core and Events modules have the same package names as their Level 2 counterparts, they are a superset in terms of functionality. The Abstract Schema and Load and Save specification (once called the Content Model and Load and Save specification) resulted in new packages specifically for XML.

Although no longer part of DOM Level 3, the *Views and Formatting Working Draft* proposes two ways to give a DOM application access to the computed layout and presentation of a `View` (the root of a presentation, owned and maintained by a `Document`, which formats the contents of a document into a particular type of presentation). The two approaches are a Generic View, useful for existing and future target devices (media types), and a media-specific Visual View, which is an easier API to use but is not as flexible. It isn't certain that both approaches are needed, nor whether one is better than the other at this point. The feature strings are `ViewsAndFormatting` and `VisualViewsAndFormatting`, respectively. The W3C states:

> This specification is a very early version of the Views and Formatting API. This document is not guarantee[d] to be part of the DOM Level 3 specification since the Working Group is waiting for more experience and experimentation before going further.[6]

Testing for Feature Support

Due to the different DOM levels and likely partial vendor support for any given level, you might wonder what would happen if you write a DOM application that depends on a particular module that your parser vendor hasn't implemented. It certainly would be desirable to be able to detect a missing feature dynamically and fail gracefully, or better yet, fall back to another approach if some functionality is missing and another option exists. Fortunately, that is precisely why there is a `hasFeature` method of the `DOMImplementation` interface. Each **feature** maps to a module and is identified by a specific string, typically the name of the module as shown in Table 8-5. To check whether the DOM implementation you're using supports Traversal (for example), and assuming we're using the Xerces DOM implementation, the necessary feature test follows:

```
import org.apache.xerces.dom.DOMImplementationImpl;  // for hasFeature
....
DOMImplementationImpl domImpl = new DOMImplementationImpl();
if (domImpl.hasFeature("Traversal", "2.0"))
// safe to use traversal, else use fallback plan
```

where "`Traversal`" is the case-insensitive string associated with the Traversal feature, and "`2.0`" indicates DOM Level 2.

6. For more details, see *http://www.w3.org/TR/2000/WD-DOM-Level-3-Views-20001115/*.

TABLE 8-5 DOM Level 2 Feature Strings

Module	*Feature String (case-insensitive)*	*Dependencies Implied*
XML	`XML`	none
HTML	`HTML`	none
Views	`Views`	XML or HTML
StyleSheets	`StyleSheets`	StyleSheets and XML or HTML
CSS Level 1	`CSS`	StyleSheets, Views, and XML or HTML
CSS Level 2	`CSS2`	CSS, StyleSheets, Views, and XML or HTML
Events	`Events`	XML or HTML
`UIEvent` interface	`UIEvents`	Views, Events, and XML or HTML
`MouseEvents` interface	`MouseEvents`	UIEvents, Views, Events, and XML or HTML
`MutationEvent` interface	`MutationEvents`	Events and XML or HTML
HTML Events	`HTMLEvents`	Events and HTML
Traversal	`Traversal`	XML or HTML
Range	`Range`	XML or HTML

Note that this test involves the Apache-specific implementation of the generic `DOMImplementation` interface. The reason for this is that the DOM specification leaves it up to each parser vendor to determine how to instantiate an object that implements the `DOMImplementation` interface. Therefore, your vendor's method may differ from the `DOMImplementationImpl` first shown.

DOM Level 2 also distinguishes between *fundamental* interfaces and *extended* interfaces but the meaning may surprise you. **Fundamental interfaces** must be implemented by all DOM implementations because they address the basic *HTML* document. **Extended interfaces**, on the other hand, are those that are *XML-specific* and have no relevance for an HTML document. Therefore, the "XML" feature string can be used to test availability of any of the extended interfaces in DOM Level 2, which include `CDATASection`, `Entity`, `DocumentType`, `Notation`, `EntityReference`, and `ProcessingInstruction`.

Similarly, DOM Level 3 defines additional feature strings, such as `"AS-EDIT"` for the Abstract Schema-editing interfaces and `"AS-DOC"` for the document-editing interfaces in Abstract Schema.

Collection DTD and Instance Revisited

For the purposes of this chapter, we will revisit our CD and book collection example, but we are going to make a few minor changes to the `collection2.dtd`. This version, so cleverly named (you guessed it) `collection3.dtd`, adds two entity definitions and changes the version attribute of the Collection element. Entities are added so that we can later exercise DOM code that checks for entity nodes. The complete DTD is shown in Listing 8-2 with the differences in boldface.

Listing 8-2 Collection DTD with Entity Declarations (collection3.dtd)

```
<?xml encoding='UTF-8' ?>
<!--     Collection DTD, Version 3-->
<!ENTITY fab4 "Beatles">
<!ENTITY beat "The Beatles">
<!ELEMENT Collection  ( (Book | CD )* , Owner? )>
<!ATTLIST Collection  version CDATA  '3' >
<!ELEMENT Owner  (Name , Address? )>
<!ELEMENT Address  (Street , City , State , Zip )>
<!ELEMENT Street  (#PCDATA )>
<!ELEMENT City  (#PCDATA )>
<!ELEMENT State  (#PCDATA )>
<!ELEMENT Zip  (#PCDATA )>
<!ELEMENT Book  (Title , Author , Type , Published , Rating? , Notes? )>
<!ELEMENT Title  (#PCDATA )>
<!-- Title defined under CD; applies to Book also. -->
<!-- Name defined under Owner; applies to Book also. -->
<!ELEMENT Author  (Name )>
<!ELEMENT Name  (First , Last )>
<!ATTLIST Name  sex  (male | female )  'male' >
<!ELEMENT First  (#PCDATA )>
<!ELEMENT Last  (#PCDATA )>
<!ELEMENT Type  (#PCDATA )>
<!ELEMENT Published  (#PCDATA )>
<!ATTLIST Published  publisher CDATA  #REQUIRED >
<!ELEMENT Rating  (#PCDATA )>
<!ELEMENT Notes  (#PCDATA )>
<!ELEMENT CD (Title , Artist , Chart , Type , Label+ , AlbumReleased , Remastered* )>
<!ELEMENT Artist  (#PCDATA )>
<!ELEMENT Chart  (Peak+ )>
<!ELEMENT Peak  (#PCDATA )>
<!ATTLIST Peak  country NMTOKEN  'US'
                weeks   NMTOKEN  #IMPLIED >
<!ELEMENT Label  (#PCDATA )>
<!ATTLIST Label  country NMTOKEN  'US' >
<!ELEMENT AlbumReleased  (#PCDATA )>
<!ELEMENT Remastered  (#PCDATA )>
<!ATTLIST Remastered  format CDATA  #REQUIRED >
```

Listing 8-3 shows collection3-frag.xml, an XML instance of the class of documents represented by this DTD, which is the focus of our attention in this chapter. Rather than have multiple Book and CD elements, this instance contains only one Book element. Of more interest to us in dealing with the DOM is the variety of node types that the example illustrates. The main differences from collection2.xml are emphasized by boldface.

Although the XML sample in Listing 8-3 is completely valid with respect to the DTD, it certainly is more than a little contrived. We're just trying for a wider variety

Listing 8-3 Collection XML Instance (collection3-frag.xml)

```
<?xml version="1.0"?>
<?xml-stylesheet type="text/css"
href="http://www.w3.org/StyleSheets/Core/Modernist"?>
<!DOCTYPE Collection SYSTEM "collection3.dtd">
<!-- Collection consists of Book and CD elements in no particular order. -->
<?javaPI sortOrder="alphabetical" selectElements="Book" ?>
<Collection version="3">
  <Book>
    <Title>Complete &fab4; Chronicle, The</Title>
    <Author>
      <Name>
        <First>Mark</First>
        <Last>Lewisohn</Last>
      </Name>
    </Author>
    <Type>Chronology</Type>
    <Published publisher="Harmony Books">1992</Published>
    <Notes>We could display a Beatles photos using SVG like so:
      <![CDATA[
       <svg width="20cm" height="20cm"  viewBox="0 0 500 500" >
         <image x="50" y="50"  width="333" height="267"
           xlink:href="http://mcbeatle.de/beatles/beatles3.jpg"/>
       </svg>
      ]]>
    </Notes>
  </Book>
<!-- Other CD and Book elements omitted. -->
</Collection>
```

of node types. It contains two processing instructions, namely the information items that refer to a specific `xml-stylesheet` that the W3C has defined and a fictitious processing instruction target called `javaPI`. The referenced `xml-stylesheet` does exist and would actually influence the visual display of our document if we used regular HTML elements such as `H1` and `P`, but we don't, so the stylesheet has no effect. (Chapter 10 explains the use of CSS stylesheets with XML.) The `javaPI` reference is something that an application processing a much longer version of this document might need to know to sort multiple entries (books, for example). We've included an entity reference (`&fab4;`) within the `Title` element just to show that it will be detected and processed specially by the DOM. We've also inserted a `CDATA` section as part of the text content of the `Notes` element just to see what the DOM will do with it.[7] In the section entitled "Adding, Changing, and Removing DOM Nodes," we'll see what's involved in adding a `CD` element and all of its children to this document using the DOM.

7. Interestingly enough, the excerpt is valid SVG (Scalable Vector Graphics) markup. If you have installed an SVG Viewer plugin such as the one by Adobe (*http://www.adobe.com/svg/main.html*), and you place this SVG fragment into a separate file and display it in your browser, you'll see a Beatles photo automatically scaled. Try `collection3-frag.svg` on the book's CD-ROM!

At the time of this writing, DOM Level 2 is the highest level of the DOM that has reached Recommendation status. For this reason, and since most parsers are now supporting DOM Level 2, the remainder of this chapter focuses on DOM Level 2.

DOM Nodes and How the DOM Works

In this section, we focus on the `Node` interface, which is the core of the DOM. We'll examine the various node types and see how an XML document maps to a DOM tree.

Node Interface

The DOM interacts only indirectly with the physical document. An XML parser reads the document and converts it into some convenient internal data structure. The DOM then operates on that structure. In the DOM, an XML document is represented as a single tree, consisting of a number of **nodes** of various types. Some of the nodes may contain either optional or required children nodes; these are *internal nodes*. Some nodes are *terminal (leaf) nodes* because they cannot contain children.

The `Node` interface is the fundamental datatype of the entire DOM. All nodes have properties (known as *attributes* in IDL terminology, but not to be confused with attributes of XML elements) such as `nodeName`, `nodeValue`, and `nodeType` that are accessible without downcasting to the specific derived type. Since the `Node` interface is generic and must accommodate every kind of information item from the XML Infoset, sometimes accessing a node's properties results in a null value. For example, elements and entities have a null `nodeValue`, but attributes have a meaningful `nodeValue`. Furthermore, some types of nodes such as elements may have children and others such as comments may not.

The twelve node types defined in DOM Level 2 Core are shown in Table 8-6 along with their possible children, the name of the node, and the value of the node (if any). The examples in the `nodeName` and `nodeValue` columns refer to the code fragment in Listing 8-3. Certain node types have fixed names beginning with `#`, such as `#document`, `#text`, and `#comment`, which are the literal names returned via the `getNodeName` method of the `Node` interface for all nodes of type `Document`, `Text`, and `Comment`, respectively. We'll soon see exactly how to gain access to this information in our code example in "Handling Additional DOM Processing Requirements."

One less than obvious point is that although attributes are described by the `Attr` node type, *attributes aren't actually stored in the DOM tree.* They are, however,

TABLE 8-6 DOM Node Types, Names, Values, and Children

nodeType	*nodeName*	*nodeValue*	*Possible Children*
`Document`	`#document`	null	`Element` (one), `PI` (zero or more), `Cmt` (zero or more), `DocumentType` (zero or one)
`DocumentFragment`	`#document-fragment`	null	`Element`, `PI`, `Cmt`, `Text`, `CS`, `ER`
`DocumentType`	name of `DOCTYPE` (e.g. `Collection`)	null	None
`EntityReference`	name of entity referenced (e.g., `fab4`)	null	`Element`, `PI`, `Cmt`, `Text`, `CS`, `ER`
`Element`	name of element (e.g., `Book`)	null	`Element`, `PI`, `Cmt`, `Text`, `CS`, `ER`
`Attr`	name of attribute (e.g., `version`)	Value of attribute (e.g., "3")	`Text`, `ER`
`ProcessingInstruction`	PI target (e.g., `javaPI`)	Entire tag content minus the target (e.g., `sortOrder= "alphabetical" selectElements= "Book"`	None
`Comment`	`#comment`	String value of comment minus delimitors	None
`Text`	`#text`	String value of the text	None
`CDATASection`	`#cdata-section`	String value of the `CDATA` section	None
`Entity`	name of entity (e.g., `fab4`)	null	`Element`, `PI`, `Cmt`, `Text`, `CS`, `ER`
`Notation`	Name of notation	null	None

Key: `Cmt = Comment`
`CS = CDATASection`
`ER = EntityReference`
`PI = ProcessingInstruction`

associated with the particular element that includes them in its start tag. Therefore, we'll see that when we traverse the tree, we typically need to access the attributes (if any) when we encounter the associated element. (This was also true for SAX with the `startElement` method.)

One very special node type is the `Document` node (described by the `Document` interface), which is the unique root of the entire document tree and therefore contains the document type declaration, top-level processing instructions, top-level comments, and all child elements. This `Document` node contains exactly one very special element child, called confusingly enough the *document element*, but also known as the *root* `Element` node (and described by the `Element` interface). The node type of the document element is `Element`, not `Document`. In other words, the item called the document element is the same as any other element, except that it has the distinction of not having a parent element and being the ancestor of all other elements.

It is this special root `Element` node that is named by the `DOCTYPE` declaration or by the outermost element of the XML document if there is no DTD. By the way, this is the same distinction we encountered in our discussion of the XML Information Set between the Document Information Item and its `[document element]` property, which was a special case of the Element Information Item that identifies the unique document element, which is the root of all elements in the document. See Table 5-2, "Information Items and Selected Properties."

Understanding the distinction between the `Document` node and the document element (an `Element` node) is important to properly access parts of the DOM. Consider `collection3-frag.xml` in Listing 8-3. For that example, each of the following five information items is a direct child of the `Document` node. These five nodes are of the node types `ProcessingInstruction`, `DocumentType`, `Comment`, another `ProcessingInstruction`, and `Element` (which happens to be the document element), in that order.

```
<?xml-stylesheet type="text/css"
href="http://www.w3.org/StyleSheets/Core/Modernist"?>
<!DOCTYPE Collection SYSTEM "collection3.dtd">
<!-- Collection consists of Book and CD elements in no particular order. -->
<?javaPI sortOrder="alphabetical" selectElements="Book" ?>
<Collection version="3">
```

The actual root `Element` node is the one named by the `DOCTYPE` line: the `Collection` element, which as far as the *element* hierarchy is concerned, is the root, or the document element. `Collection` is the outermost element and it contains all children elements such as `Book` elements and `CD` elements (not shown).

If you noticed, I skipped the XML declaration (`<?xml version="1.0"?>`) because the DOM doesn't consider this a node. As we learned, although it looks like a processing instruction, it isn't considered to be one.

NodeList and NamedNodeMap

In addition to the `Node` interface, the specification defines `NodeList` and `NamedNodeMap` interfaces, which represent ordered lists of `Node` children, and unordered sets of nodes referenced by their `name` attribute, respectively. `NamedNodeMap` is often used to access the attributes of an element, as we'll see in the code example. A key benefit of these two interfaces is that they are *live*. If the application has obtained a NodeList or NamedNodeMap, then any changes to the document structure such as adding or deleting nodes and updating values, are immediately and automatically reflected in these list-oriented interfaces. This implies that it's probably not a good idea to copy the data from these interfaces into your own data structures.

Node IDL Definition

All DOM interfaces are defined in terms of IDL definitions, the most fundamental of which is the Node interface, reproduced from the DOM Level 2 Core specification in Listing 8-4 in its entirety.[8] The twelve named constants that you can check against for node types (e.g., ENTITY_NODE) are revealed in the IDL.

In IDL definitions, the term *attribute* is essentially a property, or in Java terms, it's class data that is gettable and settable (if not marked readonly). For instance, the lines:

```
readonly attribute DOMString        nodeName;
         attribute DOMString        nodeValue;
```

tell us that the property nodeName is *not* settable, whereas nodeValue is; both are gettable, however. (We'll see Java methods in Listing 8-5.) The IDL includes other properties such as childNodes and nextSibling which may or may not be meaningful based on the value of nodeType, as mentioned earlier.

The signatures of methods that are defined for the interface are important parts of the IDL definition. For example, the method signature:

```
Node   insertBefore(in Node newChild,
                    in Node refChild)
```

defines a method named insertBefore that takes a new node as its first argument and the reference node, before which the new node is to be inserted. The method returns an object of type Node; we can't tell if the node returned is the new node, the old node, or some other node, however. (In case the suspense is killing you, it returns the node being inserted, according to the JavaDocs.)

Note that the interface definition makes clear via comments which portions have been introduced in DOM Level 2 or modified since DOM Level 1. (The DOM Level 3 interfaces track changes similarly.) We can see, for example, that properties

8. The IDL definition of the Node and other interfaces can be found at *http://www.w3.org/TR/2000-Rec-DOM-Level-2-Core-20001113/idl-definitions.html*. The DOM Level 3 IDL definitions are at *http://www.w3.org/TR/DOM-Level-3-Core/idl-definitions.html*. In addition to Core module interfaces, each individual module has its own IDL definition. For example, the DOM Level 2 Traversal and Range IDL definition is *http://www.w3.org/TR/2000/REC-DOM-Level-2-Traversal-Range-20001113/idl-definitions.html*. Each IDL definition is reachable from the module's specification.

added to the DOM Level 2 Node interface include `isSupported`, `namespaceURI`, `prefix`, and `localName`.

Listing 8-4 IDL Definition of Node Interface

```
interface Node {

  // NodeType
  const unsigned short      ELEMENT_NODE                   = 1;
  const unsigned short      ATTRIBUTE_NODE                 = 2;
  const unsigned short      TEXT_NODE                      = 3;
  const unsigned short      CDATA_SECTION_NODE             = 4;
  const unsigned short      ENTITY_REFERENCE_NODE          = 5;
  const unsigned short      ENTITY_NODE                    = 6;
  const unsigned short      PROCESSING_INSTRUCTION_NODE    = 7;
  const unsigned short      COMMENT_NODE                   = 8;
  const unsigned short      DOCUMENT_NODE                  = 9;
  const unsigned short      DOCUMENT_TYPE_NODE             = 10;
  const unsigned short      DOCUMENT_FRAGMENT_NODE         = 11;
  const unsigned short      NOTATION_NODE                  = 12;

  readonly attribute DOMString        nodeName;
           attribute DOMString        nodeValue;
           // raises(DOMException) on setting
           // raises(DOMException) on retrieval

  readonly attribute unsigned short   nodeType;
  readonly attribute Node             parentNode;
  readonly attribute NodeList         childNodes;
  readonly attribute Node             firstChild;
  readonly attribute Node             lastChild;
  readonly attribute Node             previousSibling;
  readonly attribute Node             nextSibling;
  readonly attribute NamedNodeMap     attributes;

  // Modified in DOM Level 2:
  readonly attribute Document         ownerDocument;
  Node                 insertBefore(in Node newChild,
                                    in Node refChild)
                                          raises(DOMException);
  Node                 replaceChild(in Node newChild,
                                    in Node oldChild)
                                          raises(DOMException);
  Node                 removeChild(in Node oldChild)
                                          raises(DOMException);
  Node                 appendChild(in Node newChild)
                                          raises(DOMException);
  boolean              hasChildNodes();
  Node                 cloneNode(in boolean deep);

  // Modified in DOM Level 2:
  void                 normalize();
```

```
  // Introduced in DOM Level 2:
  boolean            isSupported(in DOMString feature,
                                 in DOMString version);
  // Introduced in DOM Level 2:
  readonly attribute DOMString       namespaceURI;
  // Introduced in DOM Level 2:
           attribute DOMString       prefix;
                                     // raises(DOMException) on setting

  // Introduced in DOM Level 2:
  readonly attribute DOMString       localName;
  // Introduced in DOM Level 2:
  boolean            hasAttributes();
};
```

Node Java Binding

The Java binding for the `Node` interface (in Listing 8-5) closely parallels the IDL definition, as you might expect.[9] For example, the Java binding for the `insertBefore` method is:

```
  public Node insertBefore(Node newChild,
                           Node refChild)
                           throws DOMException;
```

In typical Java fashion, the bindings define `get` methods such as `getNodeType`, `getNodeValue`, `getNodeName`, `getChildNodes`, `getNextSibling`, `getNamespaceURI`, and so on. The only `set` method is `setNodeValue`, which corresponds to the fact that the IDL for the `Node` interface showed that only the `nodeValue` property was not readonly.

Listing 8-5 Java Binding for Node Interface

```
package org.w3c.dom;

public interface Node {
  // NodeType
  public static final short ELEMENT_NODE                = 1;
  public static final short ATTRIBUTE_NODE              = 2;
  public static final short TEXT_NODE                   = 3;
  public static final short CDATA_SECTION_NODE          = 4;
  public static final short ENTITY_REFERENCE_NODE       = 5;
```

9. The Java bindings for DOM Level 2 `Node` and other interfaces can be found at *http://www.w3.org/TR/DOM-Level-2-Core/java-binding.html*. The DOM Level 3 Java bindings are at *http://www.w3.org/TR/DOM-Level-3-Core/java-binding.html*. In addition to Core module interfaces, each module has its own Java binding. For example, the DOM Level 2 Traversal and Range Java binding is *http://www.w3.org/TR/2000/REC-DOM-Level-2-Traversal-Range-20001113/java-binding.html*. Each Java binding is reachable from the module's specification.

```
public static final short ENTITY_NODE                 = 6;
public static final short PROCESSING_INSTRUCTION_NODE = 7;
public static final short COMMENT_NODE                = 8;
public static final short DOCUMENT_NODE               = 9;
public static final short DOCUMENT_TYPE_NODE          = 10;
public static final short DOCUMENT_FRAGMENT_NODE      = 11;
public static final short NOTATION_NODE               = 12;

public String getNodeName();

public String getNodeValue()
                              throws DOMException;
public void setNodeValue(String nodeValue)
                              throws DOMException;

public short getNodeType();

public Node getParentNode();

public NodeList getChildNodes();

public Node getFirstChild();

public Node getLastChild();

public Node getPreviousSibling();

public Node getNextSibling();

public NamedNodeMap getAttributes();

public Document getOwnerDocument();

public Node insertBefore(Node newChild,
                         Node refChild)
                         throws DOMException;

public Node replaceChild(Node newChild,
                         Node oldChild)
                         throws DOMException;

public Node removeChild(Node oldChild)
                        throws DOMException;

public Node appendChild(Node newChild)
                        throws DOMException;

public boolean hasChildNodes();

public Node cloneNode(boolean deep);

public void normalize();

public boolean isSupported(String feature,
                           String version);
```

```
  public String getNamespaceURI();

  public String getPrefix();
  public void setPrefix(String prefix)
                             throws DOMException;

  public String getLocalName();

  public boolean hasAttributes();

}
```

Overview of DOM Interfaces and Their Methods

Up to this point, discussion of DOM interfaces has been limited to the `Node` interface. In this section, we'll explore the other DOM Level 2 interfaces in the `org.w3c.dom` package at a high level. The other DOM2 packages (`org.w3c.dom.css`, `org.w3c.dom.events`, `org.w3c.dom.ranges`, `org.w3c.dom.stylesheets`, `org.w3c.dom.traversal`, and `org.w3c.dom.views`) are not covered at all here, although the Traversal module is illustrated in the code example later in the chapter.

Core DOM Level 2 Interfaces and Methods

Table 8-7 lists all the major DOM Level 2 Core interfaces and the corresponding methods that have been defined for each interface. The intent is to give you a

TABLE 8-7 Core DOM Level 2 Interfaces and Methods

DOM2 Core Interfaces	*DOM2 Core Methods*[a]
`Node`[b]	`appendChild`, `cloneNode`, `getAttributes`, `getChildNodes`, `getFirstChild`, `getLastChild`, `getNextSibling`, `getNodeName`, `getNodeType`, `getNodeValue`, `getOwnerDocument`, `getParentNode`, `getPreviousSibling`, `hasChildNodes`, `insertBefore`, `removeChild`, `replaceChild`, `setNodeValue`; *DOM2 adds* `normalize`,[c] `isSupported`, `getNamespaceURI`, `getPrefix`, `setPrefix`, `getLocalName`, `hasAttributes`
`Document`	`getDoctype`, `getImplementation`, `getDocumentElement`, `getElementById`, `getElementsByTagName`, `createElement`, `createAttribute`, `createTextNode`, `createCDATASection`, `createComment`, `createDocumentFragment`, `createEntityReference`, `createProcessingInstruction`; *DOM2 adds* `importNode`, `createElementNS`, `createAttributeNS`, `getElementsByTagNameNS`

continued

TABLE 8-7 Core DOM Level 2 Interfaces and Methods (*continued*)

DOM2 Core Interfaces	*DOM2 Core Methods*[a]
DocumentFragment	[only inherited methods]
DocumentType	getEntities, getNotations; *DOM2 adds* getInternalSubset, getPublicId, getSystemId
EntityReference	[only inherited methods]
Element	getAttribute, getAttributeNode, getElementsByTagName, getTagName, removeAttribute, removeAttributeNode, setAttribute, setAttributeNode; *DOM2 adds* getAttributeNS, getAttributeNodeNS, removeAttributeNS, setAttributeNS, setAttributeNodeNS, getElementsByTagNameNS, hasAttributes, hasAttributesNS
Attr	getName, getValue, getSpecified, setValue; *DOM2 adds* getOwnerElement
ProcessingInstruction	getTarget, getData, setData
CharacterData[d]	appendData, deleteData, getData, getLength, insertData, replaceData, setData, substringData
Comment	[only inherited methods from CharacterData]
Text	splitText [plus inherited methods from CharacterData]
CDATASection	[only inherited methods from Text]
Entity	getNotationName, getPublicId, getSystemId
Notation	getPublicId, getSystemId
DOMImplementation	hasFeature; *DOM2 adds* createDocument, createDocumentType
NamedNodeMap	getLength, getNamedItem, item, removeNamedItem, setNamedItem; *DOM2 adds* getNamedItemNS, setNamedItemNS, removeNamedItemNS
NodeList	getLength, item
DOMException[e]	[only inherited methods, but the field code indicates the type of error that the DOM implementation is reporting]

a. Methods that end in NS are DOM2 namespace-aware versions of their DOM1 counterparts.

b. All NodeTypes inherit these methods, although some are meaningless for certain NodeTypes.

c. In DOM1, normalize was an Element method, but in DOM2 it moved up to the Node interface.

d. The indentation reflects subinterfaces of CharacterData. The Text and Comment interfaces inherit from CharacterData and CDATASection inherits from Text.

e. DOMException inherits methods from java.lang.Throwable.

feeling for the kind of functionality that each interface encapsulates. It also highlights what methods DOM Level 2 adds beyond the functionality provided in DOM Level 1. Note that some parsers may not yet support all DOM Level 2 methods, although most do.

For a considerably more detailed presentation of the DOM2 Java packages (as well as some DOM3) and their use, see Elliotte Rusty Harold's *Processing XML with Java*, also to be published by Addison-Wesley—see *http://www.ibiblio.org/xml/books/xmljava/.*

Document Interface

The `Document` interface, like the `Node` interface, is very special in the DOM world; it is the root of the entire document tree (which includes the root document element and more). Therefore, the `Document` interface includes factory methods in the Java bindings to create all other node types. For example, nodes of type `Element`, `Attr`, `Text`, `Comments` are created using methods called `createElement`, `createAttribute`, `createText`, and `createComment`, all of which are defined in the `Document` interface, or more precisely in its implementation class, `DocumentImpl`. Each node has a `getOwnerDocument` method which points back to the `Document` with which the node is associated.

In Apache's Xerces DOM implementation, the `DocumentImpl` class implements the DOM Level 2 `DocumentTraversal` interface, which contains factory methods needed to create `NodeIterators` and `TreeWalkers`. When these objects are created, references to the associated document are added.

Using the DOM

Table 8-8 lists some popular DOM parser Java implementations. All are validating unless indicated otherwise. (However, most are *nonvalidating* by default, so don't forget to call `setFeature`!) Most of these have DOM Level 2 implementations but check the documentation to be sure. URLs for downloading each parser appear in "For Further Exploration."

Compiling and Running a DOM Application

The batch file `dom2-it.bat` shown in Listing 8-6 is intended for use with Windows 98, Windows 2000, or Windows NT.

TABLE 8-8 Popular DOM Parsers and Their Java Class Names

Parser	*DOM Java Class Name*
Apache's `Xerces` 1.4.3, 1.4.4 and 2.0.0	`org.apache.xerces.parsers.DOMParser`
IBM's `xml4j`, version 3.2.1 (based on Apache Xerces 1.4.2)	`org.apache.xerces.parsers.DOMParser`
Sun Microsystems' `JAXP` 1.1	`javax.xml.parsers.DocumentBuilder` `javax.xml.parsers.DocumentBuilderFactory`
Apache's `Crimson` (based on Sun's Project X parser; described as JAXP 1.1 without transform package)	`javax.xml.parsers.DocumentBuilder` `javax.xml.parsers.DocumentBuilderFactory`
GNU's `Aelfred2` from GNU JAXP project; also includes utilities such as SAX2 DOM parser	`gnu.xml.aelfred2.SAXDriver` (lightweight, *non-validating*) or `gnu.xml.aelfred2.XmlReader` (validating); you can also set: `javax.xml.parsers.DocumentBuilderFactory = gnu.xml.dom.JAXPFactory`
Microsoft's `MSXML` 3.0 parser (`msxml3.dll`) and `MSXML` 4.0 parser (`msxml4.dll`)	Search for "MSXML parser" on the `msdn.microsoft.com` Web site and follow documentation links; also `Microsoft.XMLDOM`; not a Java implementation
Oracle's XML parser `XDK for Java`	`com.oracle.xml.parser.v2.DOMParser`

All batch files shown in this book assume that you've configured your environment according to the instructions that accompany the book's CD-ROM. See Appendix D, Setting Up Your Environment, which describes how to modify and use `xmlsetup.bat`. Among other things, `xmlsetup.bat` defines `%JBIN%`, `%JLIB%`, and `%XERCES%` as `C:\Java\jdk1.3.1\bin`, `C:\Java\jdk1.3.1\lib`, and `C:\XML\Apache\xerces-1_4_3\xerces.jar`, by default. This is easily configurable and is the recommended means to experiment with this book's code examples.

To compile a DOM application, you must include the path to the JAR that contains the DOM Level 2 implementation packages (implementations of `org.w3c.dom` and `org.w3c.dom.*`), which for Xerces are part of `xerces.jar`. This can be added to your Java classpath or passed on the command line:

```
%JBIN%\javac -classpath .;%XERCES% YourApplication.java
```

For example:

```
%JBIN%\javac -classpath .;%XERCES% TryDOM2Parser.java
```

which in the default environment (re: `xmlsetup.bat`) maps to:

```
C:\Java\jdk1.3.1\bin\javac -classpath .;C:\XML\Apache\xerces-1_4_3\xerces.jar
TryDOM2Parser.java
```

Listing 8-6 Batch File to Invoke Xerces DOM Parser (dom2-it.bat)

```
@echo off
REM set PARSER=%XERCES%

REM Include your SAX parser in the classpath.
REM set classpath=.;%JLIB%;%PARSER%

REM Compile program
REM %JBIN%\javac -classpath .;%XERCES% %1.java

rem Run program
@echo on
 %JBIN%\java -classpath .;%XERCES%  %1  %2 > %2.txt
```

Overview of Apache Xerces Packages

To better appreciate the complexity and power of modern XML parsers, it's worthwhile to examine the Java package organization of a popular parser, such as Xerces by Apache. We've selected Apache both because it is closely following the W3C specifications and because its Javadoc documentation helps clarify the code organization. Note which packages are related to overall framework, which packages support the DOM, which packages support SAX, and which are devoted to value-added features. At the time of this writing, Apache Xerces 1.4.4 contained the packages shown in Table 8-9 (see *http://xml.apache.org/xerces-j/index.html* and *http://xml.apache.org/xerces-j/api.html*). (Approximately eleven packages were added between versions 1.2.1 and 1.4.4, so this list will probably have expanded by the time you read this.)

TABLE 8-9 Apache Xerces Packages (Version 1.4.4)

Package	*Description*
`org.apache.html.dom`	HTML portion of the DOM with classes named `HTMLhhhhElementImpl` where `hhhh` is an HTML 4.0 element.
`org.apache.wml`	Wireless Markup Language support (WML elements) patterned after DOM Level 1.
`org.apache.wml.dom`	Wireless Markup Language support with implementations that are subclasses of their HTML counterparts.
`org.apache.xerces.dom`	Implementations for all W3C node type interfaces and other W3C modules besides Core (except Style), such as `AttrImpl`, `ElementImpl`, `NodeImpl`, `DOMImplementation-Impl`, `RangeImpl`, `TreeWalkerImpl`, etc.
`org.apache.xerces.dom.events`	Implementations of the generic DOM Level 2 `Event` interfaces.

continued

TABLE 8-9 Apache Xerces Packages (Version 1.4.4) (*continued*)

Package	*Description*
`org.apache.xerces.domx`	`XGrammarWriter` method to print the document grammar either as XML Schema or DTD.
`org.apache.xerces.framework`	Contains `XMLParser` class (the base class of all standard parsers), `XMLDTDScanner`, `XMLDocumentScanner`, `XMLErrorReporter`, `XMLDocumentHandler`, and other fundamentals.
`org.apache.xerces.jaxp`	Plugability mechanism to use SAX and DOM parsers; implementation specific classes for JAXP: `javax.xml.parsers.SAXParser`, `javax.xml.parsers.SAXParserFactory`, `javax.xml.parsers.DocumentBuilderImpl`, and `javax.xml.parsers.DocumentBuilderFactoryImpl`
`org.apache.xerces.msg`	Contains error and warning messages for Schema validator, datatype validator, Xerces parser, etc.
`org.apache.xerces.parsers`	`DOMParser` produces a W3C DOM tree; `SAXParser` implements the SAX1 and SAX2 APIs
`org.apache.xerces.readers`	Miscellaneous reader support, such as `XMLEntityHandler` interface and `XMLCatalogReader`, `DefaultEntityHandler`, `StreamingCharReader`, and `MIME2Java` classes.
`org.apache.xerces.utils`	Contains many miscellaneous utility classes such as `StringHasher`, `Hash2intTable`, and `ImplementationMessages`.
`org.apache.xerces.utils.regex`	Regular expression matching engine using Nondeterministic Finite Automaton (NFA), different from POSIX and perl5 regular expressions. Option to conform to XML Schema regular expressions.
`org.apache.xerces.validators.common`	Validation base classes and utilities, such as `XMLValidator` (all-in-one validator used by the parser), `Grammar`, `XMLContentModel`, `AllContentModel`, `MixedContentModel`, `SimpleContentModel`, `DFAContentModel`, `CMNode`, and `GrammarResolverImpl`.
`org.apache.xerces.validators.datatype`	Contains `DatatypeValidator` interface, `AnySimpleType`, `AbstractNumericValidator`, and many validator classes for W3C Schema datatypes (`DecimalDatatypeValidator`, `FloatDatatypeValidator`, `DateTimeDatatypeValidator`, `IDREFDatatypeValidator`, etc.)
`org.apache.xerces.validators.dtd`	Class `DTDGrammar` extends the common `Grammar` class and implements `XMLDTDScanner.EventHandler`; has methods such as `addUnparsedEntityDecl`, `getElementDeclIsExternal` and `startReadingFromExternalSubset`.

TABLE 8-9 *(continued)*

Package	*Description*
org.apache.xerces.validators.schema	Contains classes specific to schema, but not necessarily XML Schema, such as SchemaMessageProvider, TraverseSchema, and SchemaGrammar (which extends the common Grammar class). Also has XUtil class with many useful methods such as getChildText and getLastChildElement.
org.apache.xerces.validators.schema.identity	Includes IdentityConstraint (base class of Schema identity constraint), Field (Schema identity constraint field), Selector (Schema identity constraint selector), and XPath (a "bare minimum" XPath parser).
org.apache.xml.serialize	Includes DOMSerializer and Serializer (DOM and SAX), XMLSerializer, XHTMLSerializer, and HTMLSerializer.
org.w3c.dom	W3C DOM Level 2 Core interfaces (Element, Attr, Text, Node, etc.), implemented in the package org.apache.xerces.dom.
org.w3c.dom.events	W3C interfaces for Event, EventListener, MutationEvent, etc., from the DOM Level 2 Events specification, implemented in the package org.apache.xerces.dom.events.
org.w3c.dom.html	W3C abstract interfaces for HTML elements, implemented in the package org.apache.html.dom.
org.w3c.dom.ranges	W3C DOM Level 2 Range interfaces, implemented in the package org.apache.xerces.dom
org.w3c.dom.traversal	W3C DOM Level 2 Traversal interfaces (TreeWalker, NodeIterator, NodeFilter, etc.), implemented in the package org.apache.xerces.dom.
org.xml.sax	Supports both SAX1 (HandlerBase, DocumentHandler, Parser) and SAX2 (ContentHandler, XMLReader).
org.xml.sax.ext	Includes SAX2 extension handler for DTD declaration events and lexical events.
org.xml.sax.helpers	Contains important SAX2 convenience classes such as DefaultHandler, XMLReaderFactory, XMLReaderAdapter, ParserAdapter, XMLFilterImpl, etc.

This is not the complete set of packages shown in Table 8-3, primarily because the HTML-centric ones have been omitted from the Apache implementation (hey, this is an XML parser, after all). For example, the Style and Views module are not supported. Some packages are named org.w3c.dom.* (interfaces only) and some are org.sax.* (SAX implementations), but most are named org.apache.xerces.*. DOM parser implementations are free to incorporate functionality beyond what the DOM specifications require; in the `org.apache.xerces.*` packages you'll find the many value-added features of Xerces (and similary in other vendors' implementations). The `org.apache.xerces.validators.*` package provides for both DTD and XML Schema validation. Note also that JAXP support is incorporated into Xerces in the `org.apache.xerces.jaxp` package.

When you're evaluating the parsers listed in Table 8-8 to determine which is best for your needs, the JavaDoc can be as useful in determining the true capabilities of each parser. As the Xerces overview shows, this parser provides a considerable amount of functionality. However, if you need SQL-like support, perhaps the Oracle parser is worth investigating, or perhaps Xerces 2.x.

Minimal DOM Application

Well, we're finally ready to tackle a DOM application in Java! The previous sections have covered concepts and a high-level view of the API that we will need, at least in terms of Java bindings. As we did with SAX, we'll start with a trivial program (Listing 8-7) that creates a `DOMParser` object and invokes the `DOMParser.parse` method.

Unlike SAX, though, we next call `DOMParser.getDocument` to get the `Document` object and then call our application-specific `traverseTree` method to do some processing. It's not until `traverseTree` that our application has any real control because we're working with a tree-based, not an event-driven, model. Our processing begins with the tree traversal, in which we simply check for node type by calling `getNodeType` to see if the current node is an element. If it is, we use `getNodeName` to print its name; if it's any type other than element, we still call `getNodeName` but for nonelements we'll expect to get the fixed names such as `#document` and `#text` that we saw in Table 8-6. As is true normally with traversals, ours is recursive.

First we see if the element has children by calling `Node.getChildNodes`, which returns a `NodeList`. We use `NodeList.getLength` to determine the number of children, and we iterate over the children. For each child found, we call `traverseTree`, which processes the new (child) node, examines its children, recurses if necessary, and so on. We are visiting the nodes in depth-first (preorder) traversal, which is also what we've called *document order* before.

Listing 8-7 Minimal DOM Application to Print Element Names (MinDOM2Parser.java)

```
import org.w3c.dom.Document;
import org.w3c.dom.Node;
import org.w3c.dom.Element;
import org.w3c.dom.NodeList;
import org.apache.xerces.parsers.DOMParser;
```

```
import org.xml.sax.SAXException;
import java.io.IOException;

// Minimal DOM Application
public class MinDOM2Parser
{
    public MinDOM2Parser (String xmlFile)
    {
        //  Create a Xerces DOM Parser.
        DOMParser parser = new DOMParser();

        //  Parse document and then traverse DOM tree.
        try {
            parser.parse (xmlFile);
            Document document = parser.getDocument();
            traverseTree (document);
        } catch (SAXException e) {
            System.err.println (e);
        } catch (IOException e) {
            System.err.println (e);
        }
    }

    //  Traversal method just prints names of elements.
    private void traverseTree (Node node)
    {
        int type = node.getNodeType();
        if (type == Node.ELEMENT_NODE)
            System.out.println (node.getNodeName());
        else
            System.out.println ("skipping non-element node: " +
                                node.getNodeName());
        NodeList children = node.getChildNodes();
        if (children != null)
        {
            for (int i = 0; i < children.getLength(); i++)
                traverseTree (children.item(i));
        }
    }

    public static void main (String[] args)
    {
        MinDOM2Parser MinDOM2Parser = new MinDOM2Parser (args[0]);
    }
}
```

Listing 8-8 shows the result on running this application with `collection3-frag.xml` from Listing 8-3 as input. For nonelement nodes, we get the fixed names with # or we get `xml-stylesheet` for the `ProcessingInstruction` node, `Collection` for the `DocumentType` node (which later appears as the name of the document element, `Collection`), `javaPI` for the other `ProcessingInstruction` node, and `fab4` for an `EntityReference` node.

Listing 8-8 Output from MinDOM2Parser with Valid Input

```
skipping non-element node: #document
skipping non-element node: xml-stylesheet
skipping non-element node: Collection
skipping non-element node: #comment
skipping non-element node: javaPI
Collection
skipping non-element node: #text
Book
skipping non-element node: #text
Title
skipping non-element node: #text
skipping non-element node: fab4
skipping non-element node: #text
skipping non-element node: #text
skipping non-element node: #text
Author
skipping non-element node: #text
Name
skipping non-element node: #text
First
skipping non-element node: #text
skipping non-element node: #text
Last
skipping non-element node: #text
skipping non-element node: #text
skipping non-element node: #text
skipping non-element node: #text
Type
skipping non-element node: #text
skipping non-element node: #text
Published
skipping non-element node: #text
skipping non-element node: #text
Notes
skipping non-element node: #text
skipping non-element node: #cdata-section
skipping non-element node: #text
skipping non-element node: #text
skipping non-element node: #text
skipping non-element node: #comment
skipping non-element node: #text
```

Handling Additional DOM Processing Requirements

However, the minimal program that is shown in Listing 8-7 is lacking in several important respects:

1. We need to be able to handle well-formedness and validation errors.
2. For node types other than elements, we need to process type-specific properties.
3. For element nodes, we usually want to process their attributes.

4. We might want to process only certain *kinds* of nodes, such as element and text nodes.
5. Alternatively, it might be necessary to process only those element nodes with certain *names*.
6. We need the ability to add nodes, delete nodes, and change the content of nodes.
7. After making modifications to the DOM tree in memory, we have to be able to write the modified tree to a file.

For most of the remainder of this chapter, we explore each of these new requirements in a much longer code example, called `TryDOM2Parser.java` with a few variants. The complete code listing appears in Listing 8-22 (pages 476–486), but we'll cover each major section separately to address individual requirements. If you'd like a roadmap of where we're headed, here's how the numbered requirements just listed map to methods in the code:

1. class `TrySAXErrorHandler` (`fatalError`, `error`, and `warning` methods)
2. `dumpNode`
3. `dumpNode` also
4. `dom2TraversalFilter`
5. `dom2TraversalFilter` and `CustomFilter`
6. `addCDElement`
7. `serializeDOM`

Error Handling

Error Handling in the DOM borrows heavily from the Simple API of XML. In addition to `DOMExceptions`, DOM parsers can generate `SAXExceptions`. In fact, the same three steps that are necessary for error reporting with SAX apply to the DOM as well (at least with Apache Xerces, at any rate).

1. Define `ErrorHandler` methods as per the `org.xml.sax.ErrorHandler` interface. You must implement the methods `fatalError`, `error`, and `warning`, as discussed in "ErrorHandler: Well-Formedess and Validation" in chapter 7.
2. Set the `ErrorHandler` via the `org.xml.sax.XMLReader.setErrorHandler` method.
3. Enable validation via `DOMParser.setFeature` method because *most parsers default to nonvalidating* mode. See "Features and Properties" in chapter 7.

We need to import SAX packages and the Java `IOException` package:

```
import org.xml.sax.ErrorHandler;
import org.xml.sax.SAXException;
import org.xml.sax.SAXParseException;
import org.xml.sax.SAXNotRecognizedException;
import org.xml.sax.SAXNotSupportedException;
import java.io.IOException;
```

The general idea is similar to the SAX case, as shown in Listing 8-9. This code fragment illustrates another optional feature, `http://apache.org/xml/features/continue-after-fatal-error`, which is set to false in this case. The implementation of the `TrySAXErrorHandler` appears in the complete code (see Listing 8-22); it's the same implementation we used for SAX.

Listing 8-9 Error Handling in DOM Applications

```
    DOMParser parser = new DOMParser();

    // Note that many of the features used below are Apache-specific.
    try {
          // Enable DTD validation
          parser.setFeature(
           "http://xml.org/sax/features/validation",
           true);

          // Terminate on first fatal error.
          parser.setFeature(
           "http://apache.org/xml/features/continue-after-fatal-error",
           false);

          //  Register Error Handler
          ErrorHandler   errorHandler   = new TrySAXErrorHandler();
          parser.setErrorHandler (errorHandler);

          // Perform the parse.
          parser.parse(xmlFile);

        Document document = parser.getDocument();

        // Do application-specific processing.
        dom2Traversal (document);

        } catch (SAXException se) {
          se.printStackTrace();
        } catch (IOException ioe) {
          ioe.printStackTrace();
        } catch (DOMException de) {
          de.printStackTrace();
        }
  }
```

Checking for Feature Availability

The `TryDOM2Parser.java` application takes one of two approaches to traversing the DOM tree, depending on the result of a runtime check of available features. This check is performed by using the `DOMImplementationImpl.hasFeature` method, covered in the earlier section "Testing for Feature Support."

```
if (domImpl.hasFeature("Traversal", "2.0"))
   {
   // implementation supports DOM2 traversal
   dom2Traversal (document);
   }
 else // Use DOM Level 1 fallback.
   {
   // implementation doesn't support DOM2 traversal
   depthFirstTraversal (document);
   }
```

To perform the actual traversal looping, the application-specific `dom2Traversal` method uses the DOM Level 2 method called `NodeIterator.createNodeIterator`, while `depthFirstTraversal` (also defined by the application) uses DOM Level 1 techniques such as `Node.getChildNodes` and explicit recursion. In our sample application, both paths call a `dumpNode` method, discussed next.

Accessing Node Type–Specific Properties

We've seen the simplistic processing of nodes of type `Element`, but what about the other eleven node types? The application-specific `dumpNode` method taps some of the properties (*attributes*, in IDL terminology) that are dependent on particular node types. In addition to calling `getNodeName`, `getNodeType`, and `getNodeValue`, this method switches based on node type and uses the type constants to identify alternative actions, as shown in Listing 8-10.

For example, with `Element` nodes, we can access attributes (see the later section, "Accessing Attributes"). With `ProcessingInstruction` nodes, we can call `getTarget` and `getData`. For the `Document` node, we can invoke `getDocumentElement` to determine the root of all elements. When processing the `DocumentType` node, we can access the `PublicID`, the `SystemID`, and any entities defined in the DTD. In all cases, the properties and methods specific to a particular node type are described in the interface documentation for that node type.

In the next section, we examine the output of this `dumpNode` method with our test XML document.

Listing 8-10 Node Type Case Statement

```
short type = curNode.getNodeType();
switch (type)
{
  case (Node.ELEMENT_NODE):
  {
    NamedNodeMap attrs = curNode.getAttributes();
    for (int i = 0; i < attrs.getLength(); i++)
    {
      Attr attr = (Attr)attrs.item(i);
      System.out.print ("attrName = [" +
                         attr.getNodeName() + "]");
```

```
        System.out.println (" , nodeType = " + typeToName(attr) );
        System.out.print ("attrValue = [" +
                          attr.getNodeValue() + "]");
        System.out.println (" , specified = [" +
                          attr.getSpecified() + "]");
      }
      break;
    }

    case (Node.DOCUMENT_NODE):
    {
      // The Document Element is the root of the element hierarchy.
      Document doc = (Document)curNode;
      Element root = (Element)doc.getDocumentElement();
      System.out.println("Found DocumentElement (aka root): ["
                     + root.getNodeName() + "]");
      break;
    }

    case (Node.DOCUMENT_TYPE_NODE):
    {
      DocumentType dtd  = (DocumentType)curNode;
      System.out.println("Found DocumentType named: [" +
                     dtd.getName() + "]");
      if (dtd.getPublicId() != null)
        System.out.println("PublicId = [" + dtd.getPublicId() + "]");

      if (dtd.getSystemId() != null)
        System.out.println("SystemId = [" + dtd.getSystemId() + "]");

      if (dtd.getEntities() != null)
      {
        NamedNodeMap ents = dtd.getEntities();
        System.out.println("-- There are [" + ents.getLength() +
                       "] Entities in the DTD. --");
        for (int i = 0; i < ents.getLength(); i++)
        {
          Entity ent = (Entity)ents.item(i);
          System.out.print ("entityName = [" +
                          ent.getNodeName() + "]");
          System.out.println (" , entsValue = [" +
                          ent.getNodeValue() + "]");
        }
      } // getEntities
      // Could do something similar with getNotations.

      break;
    } // DOCUMENT_TYPE_NODE

    case (Node.TEXT_NODE):
    case (Node.CDATA_SECTION_NODE):
    {
      // Nothing special to do; already printed the text value.
      break;
    }
```

```
      case (Node.PROCESSING_INSTRUCTION_NODE):
      {
        ProcessingInstruction pi = (ProcessingInstruction)curNode;
        System.out.println("PI target = [" + pi.getTarget() +
                           "] , data = [" + pi.getData() + "]");
        break;
      }

      default:
        break;

    } // switch
```

DOM2 Output with Valid Input

The result of running `TryDOM2Parser.java` with `collection3-frag.xml` as input appears in Listing 8-11. All node names appear in angle brackets (< >) regardless of whether they are element nodes or not. Node values, attribute values, and attribute names appear in square brackets (`[ ]`). Node types that are actually numeric constants are mapped to strings for printing purposes by a nonstandard, custom method called `typeToName`. Some node values span multiple lines such as for `CDATASection` node type or contain what look like multiple name/value pairs, as in the `ProcessingInstruction` node types.

As an exercise, I recommend that you review the input from Listing 8-3 and study the results in Listing 8-11 to be sure that you understand what kind of information is available from the various node types, as well as why the nodes are processed in the order indicated by the output.

Listing 8-11 DOM2 Output Resulting from Traversal of collection3-frag.xml

```
+++This implementation supports DOM2 traversal.
nodeName = <#document> , nodeType = DOCUMENT_NODE
Found Document node (above root)
Found DocumentElement (aka root): [Collection]

nodeName = <xml-stylesheet> , nodeType = PROCESSING_INSTRUCTION_NODE
nodeValue = [type="text/css" href="http://www.w3.org/StyleSheets/Core/
Modernist"]
PI target = [xml-stylesheet] , data = [type="text/css" href="http://
www.w3.org/StyleSheets/Core/Modernist"]

nodeName = <Collection> , nodeType = DOCUMENT_TYPE_NODE
Found DocumentType named: [Collection]
SystemId = [collection3.dtd]
-- There are [2] Entities in the DTD. --
entityName = [beat] , entsValue = [null]
entityName = [fab4] , entsValue = [null]

nodeName = <#comment> , nodeType = COMMENT_NODE
nodeValue = [ Collection consists of Book and CD elements in no particular
order. ]
```

```
nodeName = <javaPI> , nodeType = PROCESSING_INSTRUCTION_NODE
nodeValue = [sortOrder="alphabetical" selectElements="Book" ]
PI target = [javaPI] , data = [sortOrder="alphabetical" selectElements="Book" ]

nodeName = <Collection> , nodeType = ELEMENT_NODE
attrName = [version] , nodeType = ATTRIBUTE_NODE
attrValue = [3] , specified = [true]

nodeName = <Book> , nodeType = ELEMENT_NODE

nodeName = <Title> , nodeType = ELEMENT_NODE

nodeName = <#text> , nodeType = TEXT_NODE
nodeValue = [Complete ]

nodeName = <fab4> , nodeType = ENTITY_REFERENCE_NODE

nodeName = <#text> , nodeType = TEXT_NODE
nodeValue = [Beatles]

nodeName = <#text> , nodeType = TEXT_NODE
nodeValue = [ Chronicle, The]

nodeName = <Author> , nodeType = ELEMENT_NODE

nodeName = <Name> , nodeType = ELEMENT_NODE
attrName = [sex] , nodeType = ATTRIBUTE_NODE
attrValue = [male] , specified = [false]

nodeName = <First> , nodeType = ELEMENT_NODE

nodeName = <#text> , nodeType = TEXT_NODE
nodeValue = [Mark]

nodeName = <Last> , nodeType = ELEMENT_NODE

nodeName = <#text> , nodeType = TEXT_NODE
nodeValue = [Lewisohn]

nodeName = <Type> , nodeType = ELEMENT_NODE

nodeName = <#text> , nodeType = TEXT_NODE
nodeValue = [Chronology]

nodeName = <Published> , nodeType = ELEMENT_NODE
attrName = [publisher] , nodeType = ATTRIBUTE_NODE
attrValue = [Harmony Books] , specified = [true]

nodeName = <#text> , nodeType = TEXT_NODE
nodeValue = [1992]

nodeName = <Notes> , nodeType = ELEMENT_NODE

nodeName = <#text> , nodeType = TEXT_NODE
nodeValue = [We could display a Beatles photos using SVG like so:
      ]
```

```
nodeName = <#cdata-section> , nodeType = CDATA_SECTION_NODE
nodeValue = [
       <svg width="20cm" height="20cm"  viewBox="0 0 500 500" >
         <image x="50" y="50"  width="333" height="267"
           xlink:href="http://mcbeatle.de/beatles/beatles3.jpg"/>
       </svg>
      ]

nodeName = <#text> , nodeType = TEXT_NODE
nodeValue = [
    ]

nodeName = <#comment> , nodeType = COMMENT_NODE
nodeValue = [ Other CD and Book elements omitted. ]
```

Examples of Well-Formedness and Validation Error Handling

Now that we've seen the results with valid input, what happens when there are errors? How does a DOM parser handle malformed or invalid XML? Usually the DOM parser uses SAX for this purpose. Let's assume we've implemented the three-step error handling setup described earlier. First, let's see what happens when our input has an improper `Last` element, a situation that makes our example no longer well-formed XML, which is a fatal error.

```
<Book>
  <Title>Complete &fab4; Chronicle, The</Title>
  <Author>
    <Name>
      <First>Mark</First>
      <Last>Lewisohn<Last>
    </Name>
  </Author>
  <Type>Chronology</Type>
  <Published publisher="Harmony Books">1992</Published>
</Book>
```

With the Apache DOM implementation in Xerces, this results in a `SAXException` and the parsing is terminated at that point since it is a fatal (well-formedness) error:

```
C:\> java -classpath .;%XERCES% TryDOM2Parser collection3-bad-Last.xml
Fatal Error ==>
 LineNumber: 19 at ColumnNumber: 13 [approx.]
 File: file:///C:/KEN/XMLBook/NOTES/Ch8-Ex/collection3-bad-Last.xml
 Message: The element type "Last" must be terminated by the matching end-tag
"</Last>".
org.xml.sax.SAXException: Fatal Error thrown.
        at TrySAXErrorHandler.fatalError(TryDOM2Parser.java:521)
        at org.apache.xerces.framework.XMLParser.reportError
(XMLParser.java:1225)
        at org.apache.xerces.framework.XMLDocumentScanner.reportFatalXMLError
(XMLDocumentScanner.java:579)
[etc.]
```

What happens if we have a misspelled element name?

```
    <Typed>Chronology</Type>
    <Published publisher="Harmony Books">1992</Published>
  </Book>
```

This also results in a `SAXException`, although it is just an error, not a fatal error, since referencing an undeclared element is a validation error:

```
C:\> java -classpath .;%XERCES% TryDOM2Parser collection3-bad-Type.xml
Error ==>
 LineNumber: 21 at ColumnNumber: 12 [approx.]
 File: file:///C:/KEN/XMLBook/NOTES/Ch8-Ex/collection3-bad-Type.xml
 Message: Element type "Typed" must be declared.
org.xml.sax.SAXException: Error thrown.
        at TrySAXErrorHandler.error(TryDOM2Parser.java:532)
        at org.apache.xerces.framework.XMLParser.reportError
(XMLParser.java:1232)
```

We can also expect meaningful diagnostics when the XML instance does not adhere to the rules of the DTD. In the file `collection3-bad-Titles.xml`, the invalid fragment contains two `Title` elements:

```
  <Book>
    <Title>Complete &fab4; Chronicle, The</Title>
    <Title>BOGUS Second Title</Title>
    <Author>
      <Name>
        <First>Mark</First>
        <Last>Lewisohn</Last>
      </Name>
    </Author>
    <!-- etc. -->
  </Book>
```

The diagnostic reflects that our instance doesn't match the `Book` content model, although it doesn't tell us explicitly that the second occurrence of `Title` is the problem:

```
C:\> java -classpath .;%XERCES% TryDOM2Parser collection3-bad-Titles.xml
Error ==>
 LineNumber: 20 at ColumnNumber: 11 [approx.]
 File: file:///C:/KEN/XMLBook/NOTES/Ch8-Ex/collection3-bad-Titles.xml
 Message: The content of element type "Book" must match
"(Title,Author,Type,Published,Rating?,Notes?)".
org.xml.sax.SAXException: Error thrown.
```

Yet another validation error occurs when a required attribute is omitted. Suppose our instance contained:

```
    <Type>Chronology</Type>
    <Published>1992</Published>
```

Since the DTD has the attribute list declaration

```
<!ATTLIST Published  publisher CDATA  #REQUIRED >
```

we can expect this to generate a nonfatal error:

```
C:\> java -classpath .;%XERCES% TryDOM2Parser collection3-bad-no-Pub.xml
Error ==>
 LineNumber: 16 at ColumnNumber: 16 [approx.]
 File: file:///C:/KEN/XMLBook/NOTES/Ch8-Ex/collection3-bad-no-Pub.xml
 Message: Attribute "publisher" is required and must be specified for element
type "Published".
org.xml.sax.SAXException: Error thrown.
```

Accessing Attributes

We have a requirement to process attributes. As noted earlier, attributes are a node type but they aren't stored directly in the DOM tree. To access them, when you are processing a node of type `Element`, you need to use the `getAttributes` method defined in the `Node` interface, surprisingly enough. (It would certainly seem that `getAttributes` should have been defined in the `Element` interface instead since it only applies to element nodes, but I believe the W3C was looking toward the future when some new node type might also have attributes.)

As you can see from Listing 8-12, `Node.getAttributes` returns a `NamedNodeMap`. We can use `NamedNodeMap.getLength` to determine how many attributes the current element has and then use `NamedNodeMap.item` method to iterate over them. Each item of the `NamedNodeMap` is an `Attr` object. We can use `Attr.getNodeName` and `Attr.getNodeValue` to obtain the name of the attribute and its value. The `Attr.getSpecified` method tells us if the value of the attribute came from the instance; a value of true means it was specified in the XML document, false means it was supplied by the DTD as a default value. (If the attribute is *optional* and doesn't appear in the instance, then it won't be in the DOM. And of course, if the attribute is required and missing from the instance, the document is invalid.)

Listing 8-12 Processing Attributes as a NamedNodeMap

```
case (Node.ELEMENT_NODE):
{
  // Any attributes? If so, they will be
  // returned as NamedNodeMap which is "live".
  // Note the attributes don't occur as nodes in traversal,
  // so they must be handled as we encounter the element that
  // contains them.
  NamedNodeMap attrs = curNode.getAttributes();
  for (int i = 0; i < attrs.getLength(); i++)
  {
    Attr attr = (Attr)attrs.item(i);
    System.out.print ("attrName = [" +
                      attr.getNodeName() + "]");
```

```
            System.out.println (" , nodeType = " + typeToName(attr) );
            System.out.print ("attrValue = [" +
                              attr.getNodeValue() + "]");
            System.out.println (" , specified = [" +
                              attr.getSpecified() + "]");
          }
          break;
```

For example, when we're processing the `Name` element in our sample document

```
<Name>
  <First>Mark</First>
  <Last>Lewisohn</Last>
</Name>
```

using `TryDOM2Parser.java`, we access its attribute called `sex`, which is supplied by the DOM parser to the DOM model (obtained from the DTD), we get results that include the default value for the attribute:

```
nodeName = <Name> , nodeType = ELEMENT_NODE
attrName = [sex] , nodeType = ATTRIBUTE_NODE
attrValue = [male] , specified = [false]
```

Filtering Nodes of Interest

You may recall that one of the useful aspects of SAX is the ability to use the API as a filter to extract elements of interest, perhaps to create an altered XML document to pass to another application, or possibly just to extract the content that certain nodes contain. As of DOM Level 2, it is possible to achieve similar results using traversal with filtering. We can filter nodes either by specifying the type of nodes or by providing a custom filter that performs whatever acceptance test we wish.

Let's consider the case of filtering by node type first.The `createNodeIterator` method of the `DocumentTraversal` interface is quite handy in this regard:

```
NodeIterator createNodeIterator(Node root,
                                int whatToShow,
                                NodeFilter filter,
                                boolean entityReferenceExpansion)
```

The argument called `root` is the starting point of the iteration, with the iterator actually positioned just before this node initially, so you need to use the `nextNode` method to advance it. The all-important `whatToShow` flag tells the iterator which node types are of interest; the values are `NodeFilter` constants (from the `NodeFilter` interface), which can be combined using an "or" operator. For example:

```
NodeFilter.SHOW_ELEMENT | NodeFilter.SHOW_TEXT
```

means that only `Element` and `Text` nodes will be allowed to pass through the filter.

The second kind of filtering involves providing a custom filter. The third parameter to `createNodeIterator` is an optional `NodeFilter`. If a custom method is provided, it must implement the `acceptNode` method and return either `NodeFilter.FILTER_ACCEPT`, `NodeFilter.FILTER_REJECT`, or `NodeFilter.FILTER_SKIP`, depending on the result of applying some application-specific test of the node passed as a parameter to the method.

For example, in Listing 8-13 we've defined a custom `NodeFilter` that accepts only nodes named `First` and `Last`. (We did not bother with the redundant check that the node is of type `Element`, but we could have.) The last argument to `creatNodeIterator`, `entityReferenceExpansion`, simply controls whether entity reference nodes are expanded or not.

The code example in Listing 8-14 shows how we could use both the ORing of `NodeFilter` constants and the custom filter to control selective processing of nodes. In the application-specific code, if `dom2TraversalFilter` is called with a value of 1 for the `which` flag, the filter will permit only `Element` and `Text` nodes; if the `which` flag is any other number, the custom filter (`NodeFilter`) will permit only nodes named `First` and `Last`.

Listing 8-13 Custom NodeFilter Class Called for Each Node

```
class CustomFilter implements NodeFilter
{
  public short acceptNode(Node n)
  {
    // DEBUG:
    // System.out.println ("nodeName = <" + n.getNodeName() + ">");
    if ( n.getNodeName().equals("First") ||
         n.getNodeName().equals("Last") )
      return NodeFilter.FILTER_ACCEPT;
    else
      return NodeFilter.FILTER_SKIP;
  }
}
```

Listing 8-14 DOM Level 2 Traversal with Filters

```
public static void dom2TraversalFilter (Document doc, int which)
{
  NodeIterator iter;
  if (which == 1)
  {
    // Process only Element and Text nodes, as specified by
    // flags passed to createNodeIterator().
    // Due to the way our dumpNodes() is written, Attributes will
    // also be processed.
    iter = ((DocumentTraversal)doc).createNodeIterator(doc,
            (NodeFilter.SHOW_ELEMENT | NodeFilter.SHOW_TEXT),
            null, true);
```

```
    }
    else
    {
      // Defer filtering to the CustomFilter class.
      iter = ((DocumentTraversal)doc).createNodeIterator(doc,
                NodeFilter.SHOW_ALL,
                new CustomFilter(), true);
    }

    Node node = iter.nextNode() ;
    for ( ; node != null; node = iter.nextNode() )
    {
      dumpNode(node);
    }
  }
```

Adding, Changing, and Removing DOM Nodes

One of the most compelling reasons for using DOM instead of SAX is the ability to *dynamically* add elements and attributes (or other node types, for that matter), update text content or attribute values, modify entire hierarchies of elements, or delete nodes at will. Methods, such as `insertBefore`, `appendChild`, `removeChild`, `replaceChild`, and so on, are useful in this regard, as are `getChildNodes`, `getFirstChild`, `getLastChild`, `getNextSibling`, `getNodeValue`, `setNodeValue`, and `setAttribute`, all of which are defined in the `Node` interface. To create *new* nodes, however, we need the various `create*` methods (e.g., `createElement`, `createTextNode`, `createAttribute`, `createProcessingInstruction`, etc.) defined as part of the `Document` interface.

Suppose we need to add the `CD` element hierarchy shown in Listing 8-15 to either `collection3-frag.xml` (containing only one `Book` element) or the earlier `collection2.xml` instance (with two `Book` and two `CD` elements, and an `Owner` element). Assume the `Collection` document is already in memory. We need to create a `CD` element, then create a number of child nodes, some containing attributes, and attach them to the `CD` element in a particular sequence, and then append the new `CD` element to the end of the `Collection`, before the `</Collection>` end tag.

Listing 8-15 CD Element to Be Added to the DOM

```
<CD>
  <Title>Beatles 1</Title>
  <Artist>Beatles</Artist>
  <Chart>
    <Peak>1</Peak>
  </Chart>
  <Type>Rock</Type>
  <Label country="US">Capitol</Label>
  <AlbumReleased>November 14, 2000</AlbumReleased>
</CD>
```

The procedure for making these runtime changes to the element hierarchy is illustrated in Listing 8-16. If this seems like a lot of code just to add a handful of XML elements, then you may prefer the JDOM solution presented in the next chapter. The comments in the code sample are mostly self-explanatory. However, it is worth noting that when creating an `Attr` node type, we have the option of the simple technique, which requires calling only `setAttribute` and passing it the name of the attribute to create and its value, or using the more general technique of calling `creatAttribute` (a `Document` method), `setNodeValue` (an `Attr` method), and finally `setAttributeNode` (an `Element` method). The simple technique should suffice when attribute values are merely strings, but if entities or other markup can appear within an attribute value, the multistep approach is necessary.

Listing 8-16 Adding an Element and Its Children

```
public static Node addCDElement (Document doc)
{
  Element cd, title, artist, chart, peak, type, label, albumReleased;
  Text    titleText, artistText, peakText, typeText, labelText,
          albumReleasedText;
  Attr    labelAttr;

  // Create the CD element and its first child, Title, and
  // set the Title's value. Add Title as child of CD.
  cd = doc.createElement("CD");
  title = doc.createElement("Title");
  titleText = doc.createTextNode("Beatles 1");
  title.appendChild(titleText);
  cd.appendChild(title);

  artist = doc.createElement("Artist");
  artistText = doc.createTextNode("Beatles");
  artist.appendChild(artistText);
  cd.appendChild(artist);

  // Similarly with other CD children.
  // Peak also has an optional attribute "country", but
  // we will let this assume the default value from the DTD.
  chart = doc.createElement("Chart");
  peak = doc.createElement("Peak");
  peakText = doc.createTextNode("1");
  peak.appendChild(peakText);
  chart.appendChild(peak);
  cd.appendChild(chart);

  type = doc.createElement("Type");
  typeText = doc.createTextNode("Rock");
  type.appendChild(typeText);
  cd.appendChild(type);

  // Label has an attribute named "country". We want:
  //     <Label country="US" >Capitol</Label>
  // Note that setAttributeNode is more general than
```

```
    // setAttribute, but requires more steps.
    label = doc.createElement("Label");
    // Create and initialize the attribute and then attach
    // to an Element. This is the generic approach.
    labelAttr = doc.createAttribute("country");
    labelAttr.setNodeValue("US");
    label.setAttributeNode(labelAttr);
    // An alternative to the above 3 lines is this one-liner:
    // label.setAttribute("country", "US");
    labelText = doc.createTextNode("Capitol");
    label.appendChild(labelText);
    cd.appendChild(label);

    albumReleased = doc.createElement("AlbumReleased");
    albumReleasedText = doc.createTextNode("November 14, 2000");
    albumReleased.appendChild(albumReleasedText);
    cd.appendChild(albumReleased);

    // Find the end of the Collection child list for appending
    // our new element.
    Node last = doc.getLastChild();
    System.out.println("^^^^^^^^^^^^^^^^^^^^^^^^^^^^^^^^^^^^^^^^^^^^^^^");
    System.out.println("^^^ Last child before appending <CD> = " +
                       last.getNodeName() );
    // Finally we're ready to add CD to the end of the Collection.
    Node newbie = last.appendChild(cd);
    return newbie;  // or cd, since both are identical
  }
```

To test this dynamic modification of a DOM tree, compile and run the CD-ROM example `Try2DOM2Parser.java` with either `collection2.xml` or `collection3-frag.xml` as input. An alternative version of this application, `Try3DOM2Parser.java`, performs several additional changes to the input: it adds an attribute `newAttr` to a `CD` element, changes the character data content of the `Title` child, and removes the `Owner` element. Use `collection2.xml` to test this application.

Although we were able to change the DOM tree in memory and write the new version out (explained in the next section), there is one problem that might not have been obvious. *There is nothing to guarantee that the modified document is still valid.* Validation occurs during parsing, whereas operations on the DOM tree can occur only after parsing has completed. Updating the tree does not trigger a revalidation process. In fact, if you run either `Try2DOMParser.java` or `Try2DOMParser.java` with `collection2.xml` as input, the results will be well-formed but not valid. This instance refers to `collection2.dtd`, which defines the `CD` content model as:

```
<!ELEMENT CD
    (Title, Artist, Chart, Type, Label+, AlbumReleased, Remastered+ )>
```

whereas `collection3.dtd` (referenced by `collection3-frag.xml`) has a slightly more flexible declaration:

```
<!ELEMENT CD
    (Title, Artist, Chart, Type, Label+, AlbumReleased, Remastered* )>
```

The CD hierarchy we added (Listing 8-15) does not contain a Remastered element, so it is invalid according to the first content model above. Even if we change collection2.xml to use collection3.dtd, the Try3DOMParser.java adds an attribute to the CD element that doesn't match the attribute-list declaration in either DTD, which means that application always produces invalid results.

Serializing DOM Trees

Serialization refers to writing the in-memory DOM representation of a particular XML instance to an output stream (e.g., for storage as a disk file). Unfortunately, as of this writing, the DOM Level 2 Recommendation does not specify a standard way to serialize or persist an HTML or XML document.[10] As a result, parser vendors have developed their own proprietary serialization techniques. For example, Apache's Xerces parser 1.4.x includes the package org.apache.xml.serialize with methods such as DOMSerializer and Serializer (DOM and SAX), XMLSerializer, XHTMLSerializer, and HTMLSerializer. Apache also provides an OutputFormat class to control appearance (indentation, word wrap, DTD, etc.). The general approach using the XMLSerializer.serialize method of Apache Xerces is illustrated in Listing 8-17, which serializes our sample document after the CD element was added, as described in Listing 8-16.

Listing 8-17 Serialization Method Using Xerces (nonstandard)

```
public static void serializeDOM (Document doc)
{
  try {
      // OutputFormat for XML, specify the encoding, and indicate
      // that indenting is desired. Write to standard output.
      OutputFormat format = new OutputFormat("XML", "UTF-8", true);
      // setPreserveSpace influences our pretty printing.
      // Better off without it.
      // format.setPreserveSpace(true);
      XMLSerializer serializer = new XMLSerializer(System.out, format);

      // If we serialize starting from the Document node rather than the
      // root Document Element, we get everything including the DOCTYPE,
      // ProcessingInstruction and Comment nodes at the beginning.
      serializer.serialize(doc);
      }
  catch (IOException e) {
      System.err.println(e);
    }
}
```

10. However, serialization is one of the requirements for the Load and Save module of the DOM Level 3 Abstract Schema and Load and Save Specification, which may have become a Recommendation by the time you read this and may even be implemented by major parser vendors.

As the comments indicate, we must start the serialization with the `Document` node rather than its child, the `DocumentElement` node (the root node named `Collection`). If not, we'd be missing lines 2 through 5 from the output shown in Listing 8-18 which involves non-element nodes that are siblings of the `Collection` root element. Serializing any node of the DOM results in all of the nodes below it in the document tree being serialized.

We have elected to take the serializer's default behavior with regard to handling white space by not calling `setPreserveSpace`. The result is that the `Book` element from the original document and its children have less than desirable indentation and spacing, whereas the added `CD` element and its children (shown in boldface) are printed as we would expect, more or less.

Listing 8-18 Serialization Result without Calling setPreserveSpace

```
<?xml version="1.0" encoding="UTF-8"?>
<!DOCTYPE Collection SYSTEM "collection3.dtd">
<?xml-stylesheet type="text/css"
href="http://www.w3.org/StyleSheets/Core/Modernist"?>
<!-- Collection consists of Book and CD elements in no particular order. -->
<?javaPI sortOrder="alphabetical" selectElements="Book" ?>
<Collection version="3">
        <Book>     <Title>Complete Beatles Chronicle, The</Title>
            <Author>       <Name>         <First>Mark</First>
                <Last>Lewisohn</Last>       </Name>     </Author>
        <Type>Chronology</Type>     <Published
        publisher="Harmony Books">1992</Published>        <Notes>We could
display a Beatles photo using SVG like so:
            <![CDATA[
       <svg width="20cm" height="20cm"  viewBox="0 0 500 500" >
         <image x="50" y="50"  width="333" height="267"
           xlink:href="http://mcbeatle.de/beatles/beatles3.jpg"/>
       </svg>
      ]]>     </Notes> </Book> <!-- Other
        CD and Book elements omitted. --> <CD>
        <Title>Beatles 1</Title>
        <Artist>Beatles</Artist>
        <Chart>
            <Peak>1</Peak>
        </Chart>
        <Type>Rock</Type>
        <Label country="US">Capitol</Label>
        <AlbumReleased>November 14, 2000</AlbumReleased>
    </CD>
</Collection>
```

Compare this result to Listing 8-19 in which we have called `setPreserveSpace(true)`. This time we get essentially the opposite result. The `Book` element and its descendants are printed correctly (more or less) whereas the added `CD` element hierarchy is not; the latter is printed as one very long line (which we were forced to wrap for readability in the text, however). At first, it would appear that this difference is a bug in the Apache serialization implementation.

Listing 8-19 Serialization Result with setPreserveSpace(true)

```
<?xml version="1.0" encoding="UTF-8"?>
<!DOCTYPE Collection SYSTEM "collection3.dtd">
<?xml-stylesheet type="text/css"
href="http://www.w3.org/StyleSheets/Core/Modernist"?>
<!-- Collection consists of Book and CD elements in no particular order. -->
<?javaPI sortOrder="alphabetical" selectElements="Book" ?>
<Collection
            version="3">
  <Book>
    <Title>Complete Beatles Chronicle, The</Title>
    <Author>
      <Name>
        <First>Mark</First>
        <Last>Lewisohn</Last>
      </Name>
    </Author>
    <Type>Chronology</Type>
    <Published
        publisher="Harmony Books">1992</Published>
    <Notes>We could display a Beatles photos using SVG like so:
       <![CDATA[
       <svg width="20cm" height="20cm"  viewBox="0 0 500 500" >
         <image x="50" y="50"  width="333" height="267"
           xlink:href="http://mcbeatle.de/beatles/beatles3.jpg"/>
       </svg>
      ]]>     </Notes>
  </Book>
<!-- Other
        CD and Book elements omitted.
            -->
<CD><Title>Beatles 1</Title><Artist>Beatles</Artist><Chart><Peak>1</Peak></
Chart><Type>Rock</Type><Label country="US">Capitol</Label>
<AlbumReleased>November 14, 2000</AlbumReleased></CD></Collection>
```

Upon further experimentation, however, Apache Xerces allows us to set a related feature that influences the appearance of the serialization, namely the `include-ignorable-whitespace` feature.

```
// Omit extra whitespace from tree.
// Without setting this to false, the DOM tree will contain
// numerous Text nodes that consist of only whitespace
// corresponding to every indentation and newline.
parser.setFeature(
 "http://apache.org/xml/features/dom/include-ignorable-whitespace",
 false);
```

Not only does disabling the `include-ignorable-whitespace` feature improve the readability of our serialized output, as shown in Listing 8-20, it also reduces the number of extraneous `Text` nodes that consist only of white space. This is by far the best solution with Xerces in terms of human factors. Of course, with XML readability is not always of primary importance, so consider what type of serialization makes the most sense for your application.

Listing 8-20 Serialization Result with include-ignorable-whitespace Feature Disabled

```
<?xml version="1.0" encoding="UTF-8"?>
<!DOCTYPE Collection SYSTEM "collection3.dtd">
<?xml-stylesheet type="text/css"
href="http://www.w3.org/StyleSheets/Core/Modernist"?>
<!-- Collection consists of Book and CD elements in no particular order. -->
<?javaPI sortOrder="alphabetical" selectElements="Book" ?>
<Collection version="3">
    <Book>
        <Title>Complete Beatles Chronicle, The</Title>
        <Author>
            <Name>
                <First>Mark</First>
                <Last>Lewisohn</Last>
            </Name>
        </Author>
        <Type>Chronology</Type>
        <Published publisher="Harmony Books">1992</Published>
        <Notes>We could display a Beatles photo using SVG like so:
            <![CDATA[
       <svg width="20cm" height="20cm"  viewBox="0 0 500 500" >
         <image x="50" y="50"  width="333" height="267"
           xlink:href="http://mcbeatle.de/beatles/beatles3.jpg"/>
       </svg>
      ]]>     </Notes>
    </Book><!-- Other CD and Book elements omitted. --><CD>
        <Title>Beatles 1</Title>
        <Artist>Beatles</Artist>
        <Chart>
            <Peak>1</Peak>
        </Chart>
        <Type>Rock</Type>
        <Label country="US">Capitol</Label>
        <AlbumReleased>November 14, 2000</AlbumReleased>
    </CD>
</Collection>
```

Finally, we noted earlier in this chapter that the forthcoming Load and Save specification from DOM Level 3 will address the serialization problem by providing a standard interface.

Script Access to the DOM

All of the examples in this chapter have emphasized the Java bindings to the DOM. However, since the API is language independent, you can use ECMAScript or JavaScript with the DOM, provided your browser supports the DOM functionality you choose to use.

We saw a brief example of ECMAScript in XHTML in Listing 8-1. As another example, Listing 8-21 illustrates that the ECMAScript code for `addCDElement` is essentially identical to the Java version we saw in Listing 8-16.

Listing 8-21 ECMAScript Version of addCDElement

```
cd = doc.createElement("CD");
title = doc.createElement("Title");
titleText = doc.createTextNode("Beatles 1");
title.appendChild(titleText);
cd.appendChild(title);

artist = doc.createElement("Artist");
artistText = doc.createTextNode("Beatles");
artist.appendChild(artistText);
cd.appendChild(artist);

chart = doc.createElement("Chart");
peak = doc.createElement("Peak");
peakText = doc.createTextNode("1");
peak.appendChild(peakText);
chart.appendChild(peak);
cd.appendChild(chart);

type = doc.createElement("Type");
typeText = doc.createTextNode("Rock");
type.appendChild(typeText);
cd.appendChild(type);

label = doc.createElement("Label");
label.setAttributeNode("country", "US");
labelText = doc.createTextNode("Capitol");
label.appendChild(labelText);
cd.appendChild(label);

albumReleased = doc.createElement("AlbumReleased");
albumReleasedText = doc.createTextNode("November 14, 2000");
albumReleased.appendChild(albumReleasedText);
cd.appendChild(albumReleased);

last = doc.getLastChild();
newbie = last.appendChild(cd);
```

Microsoft's DOM

This book does not focus on Microsoft-specific technology; there are many books that do serve that purpose. Readers interested in understanding Microsoft's various flavors of Object Models that involve VBScript, Visual Basic, and/or ASP can refer to:

- *XML—The Microsoft Way*, Peter Aitken (Addison-Wesley, 2002)
- DOM Tutorial from W3Schools, *http://www.w3schools.com/dom/*
- TopXML's Microsoft DOM Objects, *http://www.topxml.com/xml/articles/dom_xml_prog/Contents.asp*
- Microsoft's main XML page, *http://msdn.microsoft.com/xml*

- ASP Technology and the XML DOM, *http://msdn.microsoft.com/xml/articles/xml092099.asp*
- A Beginner's Guide to the XML DOM, *http://msdn.microsoft.com/xml/articles/beginner.asp*

For example, this VBScript code fragment uses the `CreateObject` method to create an instance of the `Parser` object (e.g., in Internet Explorer):

```
Set XMLDoc = CreateObject( "Microsoft.XMLDOM" )
```

The corresponding JavaScript line is:

```
var xmlDoc = new ActiveXObject( "Microsoft.XMLDOM")
```

The early Microsoft XML 2.5 SDK is based on DOM Level 1 and it contains scriptable objects such as `DOMDocument`, `XMLDOMNode`, `XMLDOMNodeList`, and `XMLDOMElement`. For developers using C, C++, or Microsoft Visual Basic, DOM objects are exposed as the COM interfaces `IXMLDOMDocument`, `IXMLDOMNode`, `IXMLDOMNodeList`, `IXMLDOMElement`, and so on.

XML 3.0 SDK, which became available as a production (nonbeta) release in late November 2000, supports SAX2 but not DOM Level 2. In September 2001, Microsoft renamed its parser technology Microsoft XML Core Services 4.0—see these:

- What's New in the Microsoft XML Parser Version 3.0 Release, *http://msdn.microsoft.com/xml/general/xmlparser.asp*
- What's New in the September 2001 Microsoft XML Core Services (MSXML) 4.0 RTM, *http://msdn.microsoft.com/library/default.asp?url=/library/en-us/dnmsxml/html/whatsnew40rtm.asp*

DOM-Related Markup Languages

Although not officially part of the W3C DOM Activity, several DOM implementations are part of other W3C specifications:

- DOM for MathML 2.0—generic API for Mathematical Markup Language 2.0 documents
- DOM for SMIL Animation—generic API for Synchronized Multimedia Integration Language animation
- DOM for SVG 1.0—generic API for Scalable Vector Graphics 1.0 documents

DOM for MathML 2.0

The Mathematical Markup Language 2.0 Recommendation, *http://www.w3.org/TR/MathML2/chapter8.html*, describes the `DOMImplementation::hasFeature` method with the test string "`org.w3c.dom.mathml`".

A new chapter describes the Document Object Model for MathML, an extension to the DOM Level 2 Core API:

> This document extends the Core API of the DOM Level 2 to describe objects and methods specific to MathML elements in documents. The functionality needed to manipulate basic hierarchical document structures, elements, and attributes will be found in the core document; functionality that depends on the specific elements defined in MathML will be found in this document.

The actual DOM specification appears in Appendix D of the Document Object Model for MathML—*http://www.w3.org/TR/MathML2/appendixd.html*. The goals of the MathML-specific DOM API are

- to specialize and add functionality that relates specifically to MathML elements and
- to provide convenience mechanisms, where appropriate, for common and frequent operations on MathML elements.

DOM for SMIL Animation

The Synchronized Multimedia Integration Language Animation working draft describes its DOM support in the section *http://www.w3.org/TR/smil-animation/#DOMSupport*:

> Any XML-based language that integrates SMIL Animation will inherit the basic interfaces defined in DOM [DOM-Level2] (although not all languages may require a DOM implementation). SMIL Animation specifies the interaction of animation and DOM. SMIL Animation also defines constraints upon the basic DOM interfaces, and specific DOM interfaces to support SMIL Animation.

DOM for SVG 1.0

The Scalable Vector Graphics 1.0 Recommendation also has support for the DOM Level 2, as described in Appendix B: SVG's Document Object Model—*http://www.w3.org/TR/SVG/svgdom.html*. The SVG DOM:

- Requires complete support for the DOM2 core
- Is modeled after and maintains consistency with the DOM HTML (where appropriate)
- Requires complete support for the DOM2 views
- Requires support for relevant aspects of the DOM2 event model
- Treats DOM2 traversal and range features as optional features
- Requires complete support for the DOM2 style sheets and relevant aspects of the DOM CSS (for applications that support CSS).

In addition, each section of the SVG Recommendation contains a DOM Interface subsection. For example, the Basic Shapes section (*http://www.w3.org/TR/SVG/shapes.html#DOMInterfaces*) defines interfaces called `SVGRectElement`, `SVGCircleElement`, `SVGEllipseElement`, `SVGLineElement`, `SVGAnimatedPoints`, `SVGPolylineElement`, and `SVGPolygonElement`.

Complete DOM Code Example

Listing 8-22 shows the complete DOM Level 2 application, `TryDOM2Parser.java`, that addresses all of the requirements listed in the earlier section "Handling Additional DOM Processing Requirements." The CD-ROM contains alternative versions, which exercise different code paths (see `Try2DOM2Parser.java` and `Try3DOM2Parser.java`).

Listing 8-22 Complete DOM2 Application Addressing Many Requirements (TryDOM2Parser.java)

```
// Demo application using DOM Level 2 and the Apache xerces parser.

// import org.w3c.dom.*;          // only if we are lazy
import org.w3c.dom.Document;
import org.w3c.dom.DocumentType;
import org.w3c.dom.ProcessingInstruction;
import org.w3c.dom.Element;
import org.w3c.dom.Attr;
import org.w3c.dom.Text;
import org.w3c.dom.Node;
import org.w3c.dom.NodeList;
import org.w3c.dom.NamedNodeMap;
import org.w3c.dom.Entity;
import org.w3c.dom.CDATASection;
import org.w3c.dom.DOMException;

import org.w3c.dom.traversal.*;   // DOM Level 2 only

// Vendor specifics for DOM.
import org.apache.xerces.parsers.DOMParser;
import org.apache.xerces.dom.DOMImplementationImpl;
import org.apache.xml.serialize.*;

// Note the need for SAX error handling.
import org.xml.sax.ErrorHandler;
import org.xml.sax.SAXException;
import org.xml.sax.SAXParseException;
import org.xml.sax.SAXNotRecognizedException;
import org.xml.sax.SAXNotSupportedException;
import java.io.IOException;

public class TryDOM2Parser
{
```

```
public static void tryParse (String xmlFile)
{
  DOMParser parser = new DOMParser();

  // Note that many of the features used below are Apache-specific.
  try {
        // Enable DTD validation
        parser.setFeature(
         "http://xml.org/sax/features/validation",
         true);

        // Terminate on first fatal error.
        parser.setFeature(
         "http://apache.org/xml/features/continue-after-fatal-error",
         false);

        // Omit extra whitespace from tree.
        // Without setting this to false, the DOM tree will contain
        // numerous Text nodes that consist of only whitespace
        // corresponding to every indentation and newline.
        parser.setFeature(
         "http://apache.org/xml/features/dom/include-ignorable-whitespace",
         false);

        //  Register Error Handler
        ErrorHandler   errorHandler   = new TrySAXErrorHandler();
        parser.setErrorHandler (errorHandler);

        // Perform the parse.
        parser.parse(xmlFile);

      Document document = parser.getDocument();

      // Special case for Document node and Document Element,
      // but we choose to handle them in dumpNode;
      // therefore, dumpDocumentNode is not called.
      // Element root = dumpDocumentNode (document);

      // Apache-specific way of implementing DOMImplementation.
      // Note that we only need to instantiate
      // because we want to use the hasFeature() method.
      // Normally this class would be used to create new DOM
      // documents, using createDocument(), for example.
      DOMImplementationImpl domImpl = new DOMImplementationImpl();

      // Checking for the availability of a feature.
      if (domImpl.hasFeature("Traversal", "2.0"))
        {
        System.out.println(
          "+++This implementation supports DOM2 traversal.");
        // Uncomment the desired traversal test.
        // 1 = filter permits only Elements and Text nodes,
        // 2 = custom filter permits only nodes named First and Last.
        // Calling  dom2Traversal processes all nodes (no filtering).
        // dom2TraversalFilter (document, 1);
```

```
            dom2Traversal (document);

            // Application-specific test:
            // Add a CD element and all of its children to the end of
            // the tree. Then we traverse again from the top to see if
            // it is there and properly initialized. (Refer to DTD.)
            // Uncomment to test.
            // Node newNode = addCDElement (document);
            // dom2Traversal (document);

            // Next we write out the newly modified tree.
            // Serialization is not standard in DOM2 but should be in DOM3.
            // Uncomment to test.
            // serializeDOM (document);
            }
          else // Use DOM Level 1 fallback.
            {
            System.out.println(
              "+++This implementation doesn't support DOM2 traversal.");
            depthFirstTraversal (document);
            // or try:
            // depthFirstTraversal2 (document);
            }

        } catch (SAXException se) {
          se.printStackTrace();
        } catch (IOException ioe) {
          ioe.printStackTrace();
        } catch (DOMException de) {
          de.printStackTrace();
        }
}

// Method dom2Traversal is only available if the
// parser supports the DOM Level 2 Traversal feature.
// createNodeIterator() optionally permits filtering of nodes.
// See dom2TraversalFilter() below.
public static void dom2Traversal (Document doc)
{
  NodeIterator iter =
          ((DocumentTraversal)doc).createNodeIterator(
            doc, NodeFilter.SHOW_ALL, null, true);

  Node node = iter.nextNode() ;
  for ( ; node != null; node = iter.nextNode() )
  {
    dumpNode(node);
  }
}

// Test DOM2 traversal using a filter.
// The "which" flag is used to test 2 different filtering techniques.
public static void dom2TraversalFilter (Document doc, int which)
{
```

```
    NodeIterator iter;
    if (which == 1)
    {
      // Process only Element and Text nodes, as specified by
      // flags passed to createNodeIterator().
      // Due to the way our dumpNodes() is written, Attributes will
      // also be processed.
      iter = ((DocumentTraversal)doc).createNodeIterator(doc,
               (NodeFilter.SHOW_ELEMENT | NodeFilter.SHOW_TEXT),
               null, true);
    }
    else
    {
      // Defer filtering to the CustomFilter class.
      iter = ((DocumentTraversal)doc).createNodeIterator(doc,
               NodeFilter.SHOW_ALL,
               new CustomFilter(), true);
    }

    Node node = iter.nextNode() ;
    for ( ; node != null; node = iter.nextNode() )
    {
      dumpNode(node);
    }
  }

  // A different approach, for DOM Level 1 and above.
  public static void depthFirstTraversal (Node curNode)
  {
    dumpNode(curNode);
    NodeList kids = curNode.getChildNodes();
    int len = (kids != null) ? kids.getLength() : 0;

    System.out.println("<" + curNode.getNodeName() +
         "> has " + len + " kids.");

    for (int i = 0; i < len; i++)
      {
      depthFirstTraversal(kids.item(i));  // recurse
      }
  }

  // And yet another from DOM Level 1 and beyond.
  public static void depthFirstTraversal2 (Node curNode)
  {
    Node child;

    dumpNode(curNode);
    for (child = curNode.getFirstChild();
         child != null; child = child.getNextSibling() )
      {
      depthFirstTraversal2(child);  // recurse
      }
  }
```

```
// The main work horse of this application which processes
// each node according to its type. Note the operations
// that are common across all node types and which are unique.

public static void dumpNode (Node curNode)
{
  // Common processing.
  System.out.print ("nodeName = <" + curNode.getNodeName() + ">");
  System.out.println (" , nodeType = " + typeToName(curNode) );
  // Could skip printing all pure whitespace values but we don't.
  if (curNode.getNodeValue() != null)
    System.out.println ("nodeValue = [" +
                         curNode.getNodeValue() + "]");

  short type = curNode.getNodeType();
  switch (type)
  {
    case (Node.ELEMENT_NODE):
    {
      // Any attributes? If so, they will be
      // returned as NamedNodeMap which is "live".
      // Note the attributes don't occur as nodes in traversal,
      // so they must be handled as we encounter the element that
      // contains them.
      NamedNodeMap attrs = curNode.getAttributes();
      for (int i = 0; i < attrs.getLength(); i++)
      {
        Attr attr = (Attr)attrs.item(i);
        System.out.print ("attrName = [" +
                           attr.getNodeName() + "]");
        System.out.println (" , nodeType = " + typeToName(attr) );
        System.out.print ("attrValue = [" +
                           attr.getNodeValue() + "]");
        System.out.println (" , specified = [" +
                           attr.getSpecified() + "]");
      }
      break;
    }

    case (Node.DOCUMENT_NODE):
    {
      System.out.println("Found Document node (above root)");

      // The Document Element is the root of the element hierarchy.
      Document doc = (Document)curNode;
      Element root = (Element)doc.getDocumentElement();
      System.out.println("Found DocumentElement (aka root): ["
                  + root.getNodeName() + "]");
      // We could examine the root element now, but we'll see
      // it soon enough as we loop through the elements.
      // dumpNode(root);
      break;
    }
```

```
    case (Node.DOCUMENT_TYPE_NODE):
    {
      DocumentType dtd  = (DocumentType)curNode;
      System.out.println("Found DocumentType named: [" +
                    dtd.getName() + "]");
      if (dtd.getPublicId() != null)
        System.out.println("PublicId = [" + dtd.getPublicId() + "]");

      if (dtd.getSystemId() != null)
        System.out.println("SystemId = [" + dtd.getSystemId() + "]");

      if (dtd.getEntities() != null)
      {
        NamedNodeMap ents = dtd.getEntities();
        System.out.println("-- There are [" + ents.getLength() +
                          "] Entities in the DTD. --");
        for (int i = 0; i < ents.getLength(); i++)
        {
          Entity ent = (Entity)ents.item(i);
          System.out.print ("entityName = [" +
                          ent.getNodeName() + "]");
          System.out.println (" , entsValue = [" +
                          ent.getNodeValue() + "]");
        }
      } // getEntities
      // Could do something similar with getNotations.

      break;
    } // DOCUMENT_TYPE_NODE

    case (Node.TEXT_NODE):
    case (Node.CDATA_SECTION_NODE):
    {
      // Nothing special to do; already printed the text value.
      break;
    }

    case (Node.PROCESSING_INSTRUCTION_NODE):
    {
      ProcessingInstruction pi = (ProcessingInstruction)curNode;
      System.out.println("PI target = [" + pi.getTarget() +
                        "] , data = [" + pi.getData() + "]");
      break;
    }

    default:
      break;

  } // switch

  System.out.println();
}
```

```
// Special handling of the Document and DocumentType node types.
// This method is not currently invoked but could be.
// Instead we have something similar defined within dumpNode().
public static Element dumpDocumentNode (Document document)
{
  System.out.println("Found Document node (above root)");
  dumpNode(document);

  // The Document Element is the root of the element hierarchy.
  Element root = (Element)document.getDocumentElement();

  System.out.println("Found DocumentElement (aka root): ["
                     + root.getNodeName() + "]");
  dumpNode(root);

  DocumentType dtd  = (DocumentType)document.getDoctype();

  System.out.println("Found DocumentType named: [" +
                   dtd.getName() + "]");
  if (dtd.getPublicId() != null)
    System.out.println("PublicId = [" + dtd.getPublicId() + "]");

  if (dtd.getSystemId() != null)
    System.out.println("SystemId = [" + dtd.getSystemId() + "]");

  if (dtd.getEntities() != null)
    {
      NamedNodeMap ents = dtd.getEntities();
      System.out.println("-- There are [" + ents.getLength() +
                         "] Entities.");
      for (int i = 0; i < ents.getLength(); i++)
      {
        Entity ent = (Entity)ents.item(i);
        System.out.print ("entityName = [" +
                          ent.getNodeName() + "]");
        System.out.println (" , entsValue = [" +
                          ent.getNodeValue() + "]");
      }
    } // getEntities
  // Could do something similar with getNotations.

  dumpNode(dtd);
  return(root);
}

// Application specific example:
// We're adding a CD element to the end of the Collection.
// This involves creating lots of child nodes and attaching them
// in the hierarchy defined by the DTD.
public static Node addCDElement (Document doc)
{
  Element cd, title, artist, chart, peak, type, label, albumReleased;
  Text    titleText, artistText, peakText, typeText, labelText,
          albumReleasedText;
  Attr    labelAttr;
```

```
// Create the CD element and its first child, Title, and
// set the Title's value. Add Title as child of CD.
cd = doc.createElement("CD");
title = doc.createElement("Title");
titleText = doc.createTextNode("Beatles 1");
title.appendChild(titleText);
cd.appendChild(title);

artist = doc.createElement("Artist");
artistText = doc.createTextNode("Beatles");
artist.appendChild(artistText);
cd.appendChild(artist);

// Similarly with other CD children.
// Peak also has an optional attribute "country", but
// we will let this assume the default value from the DTD.
chart = doc.createElement("Chart");
peak = doc.createElement("Peak");
peakText = doc.createTextNode("1");
peak.appendChild(peakText);
chart.appendChild(peak);
cd.appendChild(chart);

type = doc.createElement("Type");
typeText = doc.createTextNode("Rock");
type.appendChild(typeText);
cd.appendChild(type);

// Label has an attribute named "country". We want:
//     <Label country="US" >Capitol</Label>
// Note that setAttributeNode is more general than
// setAttribute, but requires more steps.
label = doc.createElement("Label");
// Create and initialize the attribute and then attach
// to an Element. This is the generic approach.
labelAttr = doc.createAttribute("country");
labelAttr.setNodeValue("US");
label.setAttributeNode(labelAttr);
// An alternative to the above 3 lines is this one-liner:
// label.setAttribute("country", "US");
labelText = doc.createTextNode("Capitol");
label.appendChild(labelText);
cd.appendChild(label);

albumReleased = doc.createElement("AlbumReleased");
albumReleasedText = doc.createTextNode("November 14, 2000");
albumReleased.appendChild(albumReleasedText);
cd.appendChild(albumReleased);

// Find the end of the Collection child list for appending
// our new element.
Node last = doc.getLastChild();
System.out.println("^^^^^^^^^^^^^^^^^^^^^^^^^^^^^^^^^^^^^^^^^^^^^");
System.out.println("^^^ Last child before appending <CD> = " +
                   last.getNodeName() );
```

```
    // Finally we're ready to add CD to the end of the Collection.
    Node newbie = last.appendChild(cd);
    return newbie;  // or cd, since both are identical
  }

  // Serialization is not standard in DOM Level 2. However, this
  // method should apply to most applications using Apache xerces.
  public static void serializeDOM (Document doc)
  {
    System.out.println("^^^^^^^^^^^^^^^^^^^^^^^^^^^^^^^^^^^^^^^^^^^");
    try {
        // OutputFormat for XML, specify the encoding, and indicate
        // that indenting is desired.
        OutputFormat format = new OutputFormat("XML", "UTF-8", true);
        // setPreserveSpace influences our pretty printing.
        // Better off without it.
        // format.setPreserveSpace(true);
        XMLSerializer serializer = new XMLSerializer(System.out, format);

        // If we serialize starting from the Document node rather than the
        // root Document Element, we get everything including the DOCTYPE,
        // ProcessingInstruction and Comment nodes at the beginning.
        serializer.serialize(doc);
        }
    catch (IOException e) {
        System.err.println(e);
      }
  }

  // Just a convenient mapping of node types from numeric to string value.
  public static String typeToName (Node node)
  {
    short type = node.getNodeType();
    switch(type)
    {
      case (Node.ATTRIBUTE_NODE):
        return "ATTRIBUTE_NODE";
      case (Node.CDATA_SECTION_NODE):
        return "CDATA_SECTION_NODE";
      case (Node.COMMENT_NODE):
        return "COMMENT_NODE";
      case (Node.DOCUMENT_FRAGMENT_NODE):
        return "DOCUMENT_FRAGMENT_NODE";
      case (Node.DOCUMENT_NODE):
        return "DOCUMENT_NODE";
      case (Node.DOCUMENT_TYPE_NODE):
        return "DOCUMENT_TYPE_NODE";
      case (Node.ELEMENT_NODE):
        return "ELEMENT_NODE";
      case (Node.ENTITY_NODE):
        return "ENTITY_NODE";
      case (Node.ENTITY_REFERENCE_NODE):
        return "ENTITY_REFERENCE_NODE";
      case (Node.NOTATION_NODE):
        return "NOTATION_NODE";
```

```
      case (Node.PROCESSING_INSTRUCTION_NODE):
        return "PROCESSING_INSTRUCTION_NODE";
      case (Node.TEXT_NODE):
        return "TEXT_NODE";
      default:
         return ("Unknown type: " + type); // shouldn't happen
    }
  }

  public static void main (String args[]) {

    if (args.length > 0) {
      String filename = args[0];
      try {
          tryParse(filename);
          } catch (Exception e) {
            e.printStackTrace(System.err);
          }
      }
    else
      {
         System.out.println ("Error: TryDOM2Parser requires an XML filename.");
      }
  } // main
}

// DOM Level 2 supports filtering of nodes during traversal.
class CustomFilter implements NodeFilter
{
  public short acceptNode(Node n)
  {
    // DEBUG:
    // System.out.println ("nodeName = <" + n.getNodeName() + ">");
    if ( n.getNodeName().equals("First") ||
         n.getNodeName().equals("Last") )
      return NodeFilter.FILTER_ACCEPT;
    else
      return NodeFilter.FILTER_SKIP;
  }
}

class TrySAXErrorHandler implements ErrorHandler  {

    public void fatalError(SAXParseException ex)
                throws SAXException
    {
      System.out.println("Fatal Error ==>\n" +
                " LineNumber: " +  ex.getLineNumber() +
                " at ColumnNumber: " + ex.getColumnNumber() + " [approx.]\n" +
                " File: " + ex.getSystemId() + "\n" +
                " Message: " + ex.getMessage());
      throw new SAXException("Fatal Error thrown.");
    }
```

```
    public void error(SAXParseException ex)
                throws SAXException
    {
      System.out.println("Error ==>\n" +
                 " LineNumber: " +  ex.getLineNumber() +
                 " at ColumnNumber: " + ex.getColumnNumber() + " [approx.]\n" +
                 " File: " + ex.getSystemId() + "\n" +
                 " Message: " + ex.getMessage());
      throw new SAXException("Error thrown.");
    }

    public void warning(SAXParseException ex)
                throws SAXException
    {
      System.out.println("Warning ==>\n" +
                 " LineNumber: " +  ex.getLineNumber() +
                 " at ColumnNumber: " + ex.getColumnNumber() + " [approx.]\n" +
                 " File: " + ex.getSystemId() + "\n" +
                 " Message: " + ex.getMessage());
      throw new SAXException("Warning thrown.");
    }
}
```

Summary

The Document Object Model (DOM) is another language-independent API for parsing XML. The DOM is a tree-based API, in contrast to SAX which uses an event-driven model. Although the DOM is often criticized as being too complex, very memory intensive, and requiring that the entire document reside in memory before any application processing can occur, it has many advantages:

- The DOM is useful to dynamically modify, add, or remove content, elements, attributes, or style, so it is well-suited for XML editors or other applications that need to manipulate the document.
- It provides a highly structured and complete model of any XML (or HTML) document.
- The DOM is useful when you need persistent structures. You don't need to maintain context information on your own as you do with SAX.
- You can navigate nodes, looking for specific information or hierarchy of nodes.
- It is a more natural fit for relational databases.

See "SAX vs. DOM vs. JDOM vs. JAXP—Who Wins?" in chapter 9 for a complete list of pros and cons.

The current fully approved W3C Recommendation is DOM Level 2. Nearly all parsers support DOM2, with language support primarily for Java and ECMA-Script, although bindings to C, C++, and Python also exist. This chapter primarily addresses the Java interface.

- We described the three DOM levels completed or under development by the W3C.
- DOM Levels 2 and 3 are divided into modules, each with its own specification (e.g., the DOM Level 2 Traversal and Range specification and the DOM Level 3 Abstract Schemas and Load and Save specification).
- The W3C DOM specifications describe the model in terms of language-independent IDL interfaces and then presents Java and ECMAScript bindings in appendices. It is these bindings that parser vendors use at the starting point for their implementations; they are free to implement value-added features as well.
- Levels 2 and 3 each have a Core module that details numerous fundamental interfaces.
- The Level 2 functionality is a superset of Level 1, and Level 3 similarly builds on Level 2's base.
- The `Node` interface is the key DOM interface. Twelve types of nodes are defined: `Document`, `DocumentFragment`, `DocumentType`, `EntityReference`, `Element`, `Attr`, `ProcessingInstruction`, `Comment`, `Text`, `CDATASection`, `Entity`, and `Notation`. An overview of the key methods for each node type interface is presented.
- For Java developers, this chapter illustrates how to write a minimal DOM application and how to compile and run it using the Apache Xerces DOM parser. (A table of other parsers is also included.) The Xerces DOM-related packages are also presented in summary form.
- The way to check for desired parser features and properties at runtime is covered.
- We discussed tree traversal, which is fundamental to processing the nodes of a DOM tree.
- We provided examples of valid, not well-formed, and invalid XML instances to illustrate how DOM parsers report problems by means of SAX exceptions.
- The handling of a number of other additional processing requirements is illustrated: enabling well-formedness and validation error checking, accessing node type–specific properties, processing attributes of elements, selectively processing certain types of nodes, selectively processing element nodes with certain names, dynamically adding, deleting, and modifying the content of elements and attributes, and writing a modified DOM tree to an output stream.
- An example of script access to the DOM was shown to be virtually identical to the Java case.
- Pointers to Microsoft-specific DOM interfaces are provided.

For Further Exploration

Articles

DOM Articles on xmlhack
http://xmlhack.com/search.php?q=DOM

DOM and SAX Are Dead, Long Live DOM and SAX, Kendall Grant Clark
http://www.xml.com/pub/a/2001/11/14/dom-sax.html

Lowering the bar of the DOM API, Bruce Martin
http://www-4.ibm.com/software/developer/library/jguru-dom/index.html

Programming XML in Java, Part 3, Mark Johnson
http://www.javaworld.com/javaworld/jw-07-2000/jw-0707-xmldom_p.html

Sun's Adelard is a robust alternative to SAX and DOM
http://www.javaworld.com/javaworld/javaone00/j1-00-adelard.html

Books

Processing XML with Java, Elliotte Rusty Harold
http://www.ibiblio.org/xml/books/xmljava/

Essential XML: Beyond Markup, Don Box, Aaron Skonnard and John Lam
http://cseng.aw.com/book/0,3828,0201709147,00.html

Resources

DOM—Robin Cover's page [extensive links]
http://xml.coverpages.org/dom.html

Open Directory pages [great collection of links to DOM software]
http://dmoz.org/Computers/Programming/Internet/W3C_DOM/

DOM Conformance Testing
http://xmlconf.sourceforge.net/?selected=dom

DOM Resource Guide on XML.com
http://xml.com/pub/rg/DOM

DOM Software list on XML.com
http://xml.com/pub/rg/DOM_Software

Elliotte Rusty Harold's slides from Software Development 2000 East
http://www.ibiblio.org/xml/slides/sd2000east/dom/

Microsoft XML DOM Tutorial, W3Schools
http://www.w3schools.com/dom/default.asp

ZVON MathML Reference
http://zvon.org/xxl/MathML/Output/index.html

CORBA IDL [used in DOM specification]
http://www.omg.org/

JavaScript
http://developer.netscape.com/tech/javascript/resources.html

ECMAScript Specification
http://www.ecma.ch/ecma1/STAND/ECMA-262.HTM

Dynamic HTML (DHTML)
http://wdvl.Internet.com/Authoring/DHTML/

Dynamic HTML
http://developer.netscape.com/tech/dynhtml/resources.html

TopXML's Microsoft DOM Objects
http://www.topxml.com/xml/articles/dom_xml_prog/Contents.asp

Microsoft's main XML page
http://msdn.microsoft.com/xml

ASP Technology and the XML DOM
http://msdn.microsoft.com/xml/articles/xml092099.asp

A Beginner's Guide to the XML DOM
http://msdn.microsoft.com/xml/articles/beginner.asp

What's New in the Microsoft XML Parser Version 3.0 Release
http://msdn.microsoft.com/xml/general/xmlparser.asp

What's New in the September 2001 Microsoft XML Core Services (MSXML) 4.0 RTM
http://msdn.microsoft.com/library/default.asp?url=/library/en-us/dnmsxml/html/whatsnew40rtm.asp

Software

4DOM for Python
http://Fourthought.com/4Suite/4DOM

dom4j: the flexible XML framework for Java
http://dom4j.org/

CenterPoint/XML: C++ SAX2 and DOM1 Implementation
http://www.cpointc.com/XML/

Docuverse DOM SDK [formerly called SAXDOM]
http://www.docuverse.com/domsdk/index.html

XML Authority and XML Instance
http://www.extensibility.com/tibco/solutions/

XML Spy
http://www.xmlspy.com/

Apache's Xerces Java Parser 2.x
http://apache.org/xerces2-j/

Apache's Xerces Java (Xerces-J) Parser 1.x
http://xml.apache.org/xerces-j/

Apache's Crimson [JAXP 1.1 minus Transform package]
http://xml.apache.org/crimson/

Sun's JAXP
http://java.sun.com/xml/jaxp/

GNU's Aelfred2 [from GNU JAXP project]
http://www.gnu.org/software/classpathx/jaxp/

Microsoft's MSXML [exact URL changes too often]
http://msdn.microsoft.com/XML

IBM's xml4j [Xerces-J 1.4.2 forms the basis for XML4J 3.2.1]
http://www.alphaWorks.ibm.com/tech/XML4J

Oracle's XML parser XDK for Java
http://otn.oracle.com/tech/xml/content.html

XMLSoftware.com's List of Parsers/Processors [very comprehensive]
http://www.xmlsoftware.com/parsers/

Which Parser Should I Use?
http://www.xml.com/pub/2000/08/23/whichparser/index.html

WDVL's XML Software Guide: XML Parsers
http://wdvl.internet.com/Software/XML/parsers.html

W3C Specifications and Information

DOM home page
http://www.w3.org/DOM/

DOM Activity Statement [includes architecture diagrams for all levels]
http://www.w3.org/DOM/Activity.html

Document Object Model (DOM) Requirements [for Levels 1, 2, and 3]
http://www.w3.org/TR/DOM-Requirements/

DOM FAQ
http://www.w3.org/DOM/faq.html

DOM Glossary [from DOM Level 2]
http://www.w3.org/TR/DOM-Level-2-Core/glossary.html

Document Object Model (DOM) Technical Reports [includes links to all levels, all modules]
http://www.w3.org/DOM/DOMTR

Document Object Model (DOM) Technical Materials [includes JavaDocs]
http://www.w3.org/DOM/DOMTM

Document Object Model (DOM) Conformance Test Suites [W3C and NIST]
http://www.w3.org/DOM/Test/

DOM Level 1 Recommendation (1998)
http://www.w3.org/TR/DOM-Level-1/

DOM Level 1, Second Edition (Working Draft, September 2000)
http://www.w3.org/TR/2000/WD-DOM-Level-1-20000929/

DOM Level 2 Recommendation [same as Core Recommendation]
http://www.w3.org/TR/DOM-Level-2/

DOM Level 2 Core Recommendation (November 2000)
http://www.w3.org/TR/DOM-Level-2-Core/

DOM Level 2 Views Recommendation
http://www.w3.org/TR/DOM-Level-2-Views/

DOM Level 2 Events Recommendation
http://www.w3.org/TR/DOM-Level-2-Events/

DOM Level 2 Style Recommendation
http://www.w3.org/TR/DOM-Level-2-Style/

DOM Level 2 Traversal and Range Recommendation
http://www.w3.org/TR/DOM-Level-2-Traversal-Range/

DOM Level 2 HTML Specification [status in flux]
http://www.w3.org/TR/DOM-Level-2-HTML/

DOM Level 3 Glossary
http://www.w3.org/TR/DOM-Level-3-Core/glossary.html

DOM Level 3 Core Specification
http://www.w3.org/TR/DOM-Level-3-Core/

DOM Level 3 Abstract Schemas and Load and Save Specification
http://www.w3.org/TR/DOM-Level-3-ASLS/

DOM Level 3 Events Specification
http://www.w3.org/TR/DOM-Level-3-Events/

DOM Level 3 XPath Specification
http://www.w3.org/TR/DOM-Level-3-XPath/

DOM Level 3 Views and Formatting Specification [*Note:* no longer part of DOM Level 3]
http://www.w3.org/TR/DOM-Level-3-Views/

DOM Package org.w3c.dom from JAXP Javadocs
http://java.sun.com/xml/docs/api/org/w3c/dom/package-summary.html

What is the relationship between the DOM and SAX? [from DOM FAQ; solid description of when to use each]
http://www.w3.org/DOM/faq#SAXandDOM

What is the difference between DHTML and the DOM? [DOM is essentially a superset of DHTML]
http://www.w3.org/DOM/faq#DHTML-DOM

Document Object Model (DOM) Bindings [non-W3C bindings to C, C++, Python, etc.]
http://www.w3.org/DOM/Bindings

SMIL Animation DOM
http://www.w3.org/TR/smil-animation/#DOMSupport

SVG: Document Object Model for Scalable Vector Graphics
http://www.w3.org/TR/SVG/svgdom.html

MathML: Document Object Model for MathML: Introduction
http://www.w3.org/TR/MathML2/chapter8.html

MathML: Document Object Model for MathML: Specification
http://www.w3.org/TR/MathML2/appendixd.html

Chapter 9

Processing with JDOM and JAXP

We complete our coverage of parser APIs with JAXP, Sun's Java API for XML Processing, and an open-source effort called JDOM, a Java-centric approach to both SAX and DOM parsing. Along the way, we mention several other XML API efforts by Sun, including Java API for XML Messaging (JAXM) and Java Architecture for XML Binding (JAXB). At the end of the chapter, we summarize the pros and cons of SAX, DOM, JAXP, and JDOM. A table of major Java APIs is included.

Overview of Java XML APIs

The number of Java application programming interfaces (APIs) devoted to XML is quite large and constantly growing. Table 9-1 presents a snapshot of the major APIs (excluding SAX and DOM Java parser implementations). URLs for each of these APIs appear in the "For Further Exploration" section. Although this chapter is mainly devoted to discussions of JDOM and JAXP, passing references are made to some other APIs. If you are a Java developer interested in XML, this table and the corresponding links should prove quite handy.

Sun Microsystems's Java Technology & XML page (*http://java.sun.com/xml/index.html*) contains links to home pages for JAXP, JAXB, JAXM, JAXR, and JAX-RPC, and undoubtedly others by the time you read this. The **Java Specification Requests (JSR)** page (*http://jcp.org/jsr/all/index.jsp*) tracks Java development efforts undergoing the Java Community Process (JCP). While the majority of the JSRs have nothing to do with XML, JAXP, JAXB, JAXM, JAXR, and JAX-RPC are all XML-related JSRs. Other XML-related JSRs at the time of this writing include:

- JSR 104: XML Trust Service APIs
- JSR 105: XML Digital Signature APIs
- JSR 106: XML Digital Encryption APIs

Note: Readers not interested in Java APIs for XML should skip this chapter, with the exception of the pros and cons summary (see pages 531–533).

TABLE 9-1 Major Java XML APIs

API Name	*Description*
JAXP	*Java API for XML Processing* (JSR 63); supports DOM Level 2 and SAX2 parser pluggability; includes an XSLT framework based on TrAX (Transformation API for XML); common interface to SAX, DOM, and XSLT APIs, regardless of vendor; enables applications to parse and transform XML documents independent of parser or processor implementation, so swapping a different one doesn't require recompiling.
JAXB	*Java Architecture for XML Binding* (JSR 31); maps XML elements to classes; two-way mapping between XML documents and Java technology-based objects along with a schema compiler tool; compiles schemas (currently DTDs only) into generated Java classes; compiled classes handle parsing and validation often faster than SAX and DOM and may require less memory.
JAXM	*Java APIs for XML Messaging* (JSR 67); for sending *asynchronous* messages; standard mechanism for exchange (packaging and transporting) of XML business documents such as invoices, purchase orders, and order confirmations using Simple Object Access Protocol (SOAP) 1.1 with Attachments messaging; related to ebXML Transport Working Group; supports messaging Profiles (e.g., W3C's XMLP layered on JAXM).
JAXR	*Java API for XML Registries* (JSR 93); for publishing services in an external registry and for lookup of services; abstraction API to access business registries based on JAXM; an XML registry provides infrastructure for building, deploying, and discovering Web services; bindings to ebXML Registry and the UDDI Registry; compare to older JNDI API also from JavaSoft.
JAX-RPC	*Java API for XML-based RPC* (JSR 101); for sending *synchronous* messages; transport-independent API for standard XML-based RPC protocols; for sending SOAP method calls to remote parties and receiving results via the Internet.
Long-Term JavaBeans Persistence	*Long-Term JavaBeans Persistence* (JSR 57); serialization of XML; convert graphs of JavaBeans architecture to and from version resilient file formats (typically XML documents).
JDOM	Not really an acronym; despite the name, JDOM is not just for DOM since it supports SAX also; creates a tree of objects from an XML structure; Java-centric representation of an XML document for easy and efficient reading, manipulation, and writing; targeted for inclusion in J2EE and J2SE (JSR 102).
dom4j	Open-source library for working with XML, XPath, and XSLT using the Java Collections Framework; full support for DOM, SAX, and JAXP; object-oriented alternative to DOM that implements features not yet available in JDOM.
EXML	*ElectricXML;* Java toolkit for parsing and manipulating XML documents; claims to be 5 to 10 times faster than JDOM and Xerces; does not support validation via DTDs; from The Mind Electric.
SAXPath	*Simple API for XPath;* analogous to SAX; provides a simple event-based callback interface for XPath. (XPath is covered in chapter 11.)
Jaxen	*Java XPath Engine;* Jaxen is a universal object model walker, capable of evaluating XPath expressions for DOM, dom4j, EXML, and JDOM.

- JSR 112: J2EE Connector Architecture 2.0
- JSR 156: XML Transactioning API for Java (JAXTX)
- JSR 157: ebXML CPP/A APIs for Java

In addition, the *Java XML Pack*, which first appeared in November 2001, is discussed in "Sun's XML APIs: The Java XML Pack" section later in this chapter.

In chapters 7 and 8, we learned about SAX and DOM, two *language-independent* approaches to parsing and processing XML. Although more than half of each of those chapters was devoted to an overview of Java bindings and Java examples for SAX and DOM, each is implemented in several languages, so each API is useful to non-Java developers, as well. For example, we saw that creating new DOM nodes was similar in both Java and JavaScript.

That is not true of either JDOM or JAXP, both of which are strictly for use by Java programmers since they are *completely language dependent*. No attempt will ever be made to produce non-Java bindings for JDOM and JAXP because it would make no sense. As you read about these Java-centric APIs, think about why they might be advantageous to you as a Java developer. (If you aren't a Java developer, I'd recommend you skip to "SAX vs. DOM vs. JDOM vs. JAXP—Who Wins?" now.)

The code examples and API coverage of JDOM and JAXP in this chapter are based on previous versions (1.0 Beta 5 and 1.1 Early Access Release 2, respectively). Details have definitely changed, especially concerning JDOM. Although this chapter is still useful as a conceptual overview, Java developers interested in more current and in-depth coverage of these APIs should purchase Elliotte Rusty Harold's *Processing XML with Java*, also published by Addison-Wesley—see *http://www.ibiblio.org/xml/books/xmljava/*. (Table 9-1 and the links in "For Further Exploration" do reflect current information at the time of this writing, however.)

JDOM: A Java-centric Parsing Approach

JDOM is a Java-centric approach to reading, manipulating, and writing XML documents by Brett McLaughlin (author of the book *Java and XML*) and Jason Hunter (author of *Java Servlet Programming*). Although JDOM integrates well with the DOM *and SAX*, despite the name similarity, it isn't built on the DOM. Instead, JDOM is an Open Source project consisting of a lightweight, simple API optimized for Java, directly in contrast to the DOM philosophy of a language-independent generic API.

How JDOM Differs from the DOM

Unlike the DOM, JDOM most definitely does take advantage of Java 2 language-specific features, including method overloading, reflection, weak references, and the Java 2 `Collection` interfaces. By design, JDOM hides the complexities of XML from the Java developer. For example, suppose we want to create an `Artist` element with the text content "Beatles" to our `Collection` example (see "Adding, Changing, and Removing DOM Nodes" in chapter 8). We wish to add:

```
<Artist>Beatles</Artist>
```

As we saw earlier, to add elements with text using the DOM, we had to do this:

```
Element artist = doc.createElement("Artist");
Text artistText = doc.createTextNode("Beatles");
artist.appendChild(artistText);
```

With JDOM, the solution simply becomes:

```
Element artist = new Element("Artist");
artist.setText("Beatles");
```

Both APIs model this XML element:

At first you might not be too overwhelmed by saving just one line of code (even if it is a 33 percent reduction); the point is that the JDOM approach is a much more natural one for Java programmers because it doesn't require detailed knowledge of the DOM. In the DOM case, a programmer would need to know that adding an `Element` node that contains textual content requires the creation of a `Text` node to contain that content, and then attaching it to the `Element`.

In contrast, the JDOM approach more closely models what we see: an element that contains text. So we create an object of the `Element` class and invoke its `setText` method, which only does something meaningful if the element's content model in the DTD specifies `#PCDATA`. A JDOM `Element` object also has methods, such as `addContent`, `clone` (a deep hierarchy clone), `getAttribute`, `getAttributeValue`, `getChildren`, `getText`, `getName`, `getNamespace`, `getParent`, `getSerializedForm`, `removeAttribute`, `removeChild`, `setAttributes`, and `setChildren`, and the familiar `toString`. As is typical in object-oriented languages, many of these methods are overloaded (i.e., methods with the same name but different argument signatures). That is just not possible with the DOM because languages such as JavaScript don't permit overloading; the W3C DOM must target the lowest common denominator of modern languages.

Interoperability with both DOM and SAX parsers is another major goal of JDOM. Objects can be read with any DOM or SAX parser via adaptors, converted to JDOM objects, processed internally as JDOM objects, and then converted from JDOM back to DOM or SAX, if necessary, for sending to a non-JDOM application.

Whereas the DOM places a heavy load on memory due to the creation of countless objects for every element and potentially every character of a document, JDOM seeks to provide a lightweight solution. Although JDOM can be used to represent a large document, it is not necessary to have the entire structure in memory at any given time.The JDOM designers believe they have achieved better than the 80/20 rule by providing more than 80 percent of the DOM and SAX functionality with less than 20 percent of the difficulty. In other words, you can do most of the processing in JDOM with considerably less effort, but when your application requires functionality not available in JDOM, you can always drop down to the SAX or DOM level.

The DOM is a Web standard controlled by W3C membership. JDOM, however, has the freedom to progress at its own pace and in line with its own priorities. That being said, the JDOM designers continually integrate changes in relevant XML specifications, such as DOM Level 2 (and eventually Level 3), SAX2, and XML Schema. Plans for the near future call for support for XPath, XLink, XPointer, XSLT (native rather than via Xalan), and **TrAX (Transformation API for XML**, *http://xml.apache.org/xalan-j/trax.html*, an Apache effort for Xalan version 2—Apache's second-generation XSLT processor) at the time of this writing. In February 2001, JDOM became JSR 102 (Java Specification Request), the Java community's method of extending Java capabilities. According to McLaughlin and Hunter, JDOM could eventually be included in JAXP 1.2 or 2.0 and possibly the JDK itself in time. There has been some talk of OASIS support as well. To find out more about the goals and current status of JDOM, see:

- *http://jdom.org/*—home page; documentation, tutorials, downloads, and more
- *http://jcp.org/jsr/detail/102.jsp*— JSR 102

JDOM Packages

JDOM Beta 5 consists of four packages[1] as described in Table 9-2. For details, refer to the JavaDocs at *http://jdom.org/docs/apidocs/index.html.* A typical usage pattern is to read in an XML instance using either `SAXBuilder` or `DOMBuilder`, convert it to an in-memory JDOM `Document` object, manipulate it in some way, and use `XMLOutputter` to serialize the result. The `SAXBuilder` class (recommended for its speed) uses a SAX parser to construct the JDOM `Document`. Both `SAXBuilder` and `DOMBuilder` accept optional arguments to enable or disable validation.

Using JDOM

Until recently the latest version of JDOM was called Beta 5 (prior to a formal 1.0 release). To use JDOM you needed to download the source code from the CVS repository (*http://cvs.jdom.org/*) and build it from scratch using the `build.bat` (or `build.sh` for UNIX). The result of a successful build is deposited in the `build`

1. JDOM Beta 7 (July 2001) has a fifth package, `org.jdom.transform`, which supports TrAX XSLT transformations.

TABLE 9-2 JDOM Packages

Package	*Description*
`org.dom`	Represents an XML document and the major XML Infoset information items as *classes*: `Attribute`, `CDATA`, `Comment`, `DocType`, `Document`, `Element`, `EntityRef`, `Namespace`, `ProcessingInstruction`, `Text`, and `Verifier`. *Note*: This is distinctly different from the W3C DOM model, which defines a generic `Node` interface. In JDOM, each Infoset item is represented by a unique class rather than a subclass.
`org.jdom.adapters`	Consists of classes for connecting JDOM to DOM implementations: `AbstractDOMAdapter`, `OracleV1DOMAdapter`, `OracleV2DOMAdapter`, `ProjectXDOMAdapter`, `XercesDOMAdapter`, `XML4JDOMAdapter`, and `CrimsonDOMAdapter`.
`org.jdom.input`	Contains classes for reading from existing XML documents: `SAXBuilder`, `DOMBuilder`, plus several contributed classes.
`org.jdom.output`	Contains classes for outputting XML in various forms: `SAXOutputter`, `DOMOutputter`, `XMLOutputter`, plus contributed classes.

folder as `jdom.jar`. Examples and discussion of JDOM features and API are based on this September 2000 JDOM Beta 5 release. Details are likely to change.[2]

The Windows batch file for compiling and running a JDOM application, `jdom-it.bat`, is shown in Listing 9-1.

The JDOM batch file differs from those presented in the SAX and DOM chapters in that it is not based on using `xmlsetup.bat`, and it uses a much earlier version of Xerces (1.2.1). You'll need to modify this .bat file for your environment.

Listing 9-1 Batch File for JDOM Compiling and Running

```
set JBIN=C:\JAVA\jdk1.3\bin
set JLIB=C:\JAVA\jdk1.3\lib

set XERCES=C:\XML\APACHE\xerces-1_2_1
set PARSER=%XERCES%\xerces.jar
set JDOM=C:\XML\JDOM-current\jdom\build\jdom.jar

rem Include your parser in the classpath.
set classpath=.;%JLIB%;%JDOM%;%PARSER%

rem Compile program
%JBIN%\javac %1.java

rem Run program
%JBIN%\java %1 %2 %3 > jdom.txt
```

2. Developers no longer have to build JDOM; download the current version from *http://jdom.org/dist/binary/*. This includes `collections.jar`, `crimson.jar`, `jaxp.jar`, `xalan.jar`, `xerces.jar`, and `ant.jar` (building).

For example, to compile and run the example shown in Listing 9-2 with the file `collection3-frag.xml` as input, the command line is:

```
C:\> jdom-it.bat TryJDOM SAX collection3-frag.xml
```

The meaning of the `SAX` argument is explained in the next section.

Reading and Writing with JDOM

In this section, we introduce a sample JDOM application called `TryJDOM.java`, similar to `TryDOMParser.java` in Listing 8-22, that performs three tasks:

1. Read an XML document (using either `SAXBuilder` or `DOMBuilder`) and convert it into a JDOM `Document` object
2. Add a `CD` element and all its necessary children to the end of the `Document`
3. Serialize the expanded document using `XMLOutputter`

The program expects two arguments: the first argument is either `SAX` or `DOM` to indicate whether `SAXBuilder` or `DOMBuilder` should be used, and the second is the filename to read using the builder. According to JDOM documentation, `SAXBuilder` is preferred unless you have a real need to manipulate a DOM tree. Since we're using Xerces as our parser, we've initialized the `DOM_ADAPTER_CLASS` to `org.jdom.adapters.XercesDOMAdapter`, but you can adjust this to match your parser. We call either application-specific method `readSAXDocument` and `readDOMDocument` as appropriate; both return a `Document` object that has a `getRootElement` method.

Note that one of the additional advantages of JDOM is that it gives us the ability to switch not only between SAX parsers or DOM parsers at runtime, but it also lets us *switch between SAX and DOM* completely. In other words, if the parser supports both SAX and DOM, we can conditionally switch between calling `SAXBuilder` or `DOMBuilder` to create our JDOM `Document` object.

The method `addCDElement` illustrates the intuitive nature of adding nodes to a JDOM `Document`. Note the `Element` constructor and the methods `setText`, `addContent`, and `setAttribute`. Compare this method to the `addCDElement` method in our DOM example in the section "Adding, Changing, and Removing DOM Nodes" in chapter 8. The JDOM version requires twenty-seven non-commented lines of code, whereas the DOM version requires forty lines. For most Java developers, the terseness and straightforwardness of the JDOM approach is preferable.

Listing 9-2 JDOM Reading, Adding Elements, and Writing (TryJDOM.java)

```
import java.io.File;
import java.io.IOException;
import java.util.List;      // for processing children
import java.util.Iterator;  // for processing children
```

```
import org.jdom.Document;
import org.jdom.Element;
import org.jdom.input.SAXBuilder;     // reading
import org.jdom.input.DOMBuilder;     // reading (alternative)
import org.jdom.adapters.DOMAdapter; // reading (alternative)
import org.jdom.output.XMLOutputter; // writing
import org.jdom.JDOMException;

public class TryJDOM {

  // Can replace this with others such as OracleV1DOMAdapter,
  // OracleV2DOMAdapter, ProjectXDOMAdapter, or XML4JDOMAdapter.
  // Only needed if using DOMBuilder.
  private static final String DOM_ADAPTER_CLASS =
        "org.jdom.adapters.XercesDOMAdapter";

  public static void main(String[] args) {

    if (args.length < 2) {
      System.out.println("Error: TryJDOM requires:");
      System.out.println("arg1: 'SAX' or 'DOM' (for the Builder)");
      System.out.println("arg2: XML filename for reading.");
      System.exit(-1);
    }
    String whichBuilder = args[0];
    String filename = args[1];

    Document doc = (Document)null;
    Element root = (Element)null;

    try {
        // Use either readSAXDocument or readDOMDocument.
        // The SAX version is more efficient since it is based on
        // the faster SAXBuilder class.
        if (whichBuilder.equalsIgnoreCase("SAX"))
          {
          System.out.println("Using SAXBuilder...");
          doc = readSAXDocument(filename);
          }
        else if (whichBuilder.equalsIgnoreCase("DOM"))
          {
          System.out.println("Using DOMBuilder...");
          doc = readDOMDocument(filename);
          }
        else
          {
          System.out.println("Error: arg1 '" + whichBuilder + "' must be "
                             + "either 'SAX' or 'DOM' (for the Builder)");
          System.exit(-1);
          }

        root = doc.getRootElement();
        System.out.println("Root element = " + root.getName() );

        // JDOM's getSerializedForm is not yet implemented.
        // String serial = doc.getSerializedForm();
```

```
    } catch (JDOMException e) {
        if (e.getRootCause() != null) {
        e.getRootCause().printStackTrace();
        } else {
          e.printStackTrace();
        }
    } catch (Exception e) {
        e.printStackTrace();
    }

    // Create the CD hierarchy and attach it to in-memory DOM.
    Element cd = addCDElement(root);
    root.addContent(cd);

    // Serialize the document that is in memory.
    // XMLOutputter has various signatures. This one says
    // indent 2 spaces and add newlines. Output looks better
    // than when the no-arg XMLOutputter method is used.
    XMLOutputter outputter = new XMLOutputter("  ", true);
    // XMLOutputter outputter = new XMLOutputter();
    try {
      outputter.output(doc, System.out);
    }
    catch (Exception e) {
      System.err.println(e);
    }

    System.out.println("+++ Printing direct children of <CD> element:");
    printChildren(cd);
  }

public static Document readDOMDocument(String filename)
       throws IOException, JDOMException
  {
    DOMAdapter domAdapter;
    Class parserClass;

    try {
        parserClass = Class.forName(DOM_ADAPTER_CLASS);
        domAdapter = (DOMAdapter)parserClass.newInstance();
    } catch (ClassNotFoundException e) {
        throw new JDOMException("Parser class " + DOM_ADAPTER_CLASS +
                                " not found");
    } catch (Exception e) {
        throw new JDOMException("Parser class " + DOM_ADAPTER_CLASS +
                                " other error");
    }

    DOMBuilder builder = new DOMBuilder(true);  // validate
    org.w3c.dom.Document w3cdoc = domAdapter.getDocument(filename, true);
    Document doc = builder.build(w3cdoc);

    return (doc);
  }
```

```
public static Document readSAXDocument(String filename)
       throws IOException, JDOMException
  {
  Document doc = null;

    try {
      SAXBuilder builder = new SAXBuilder(true);  // validate
      doc = builder.build(new File(filename));
    } catch (Exception e) {
       throw new JDOMException("SAXBuilder failed");
    }

    return (doc);
  }

public static Element addCDElement(Element root)
  {
    Element cd, title, artist, chart, peak, type, label, albumReleased;
    // No need for Text or Attr nodes.

    // If we only wanted to do writing (not appending to the input file),
    // we would need these next two lines.
    //    Element root  = new Element("Collection");
    //    Document doc  = new Document(root);

    // Create CD element and its children.
    cd            = new Element("CD");
    title         = new Element("Title");
    artist        = new Element("Artist");
    chart         = new Element("Chart");
    peak          = new Element("Peak");
    type          = new Element("Type");
    label         = new Element("Label");
    albumReleased = new Element("AlbumReleased");

    // Add Label's country attribute.
    label.addAttribute("country", "US");

    // Initialize text content.
    title.setText("Beatles 1");
    artist.setText("Beatles");
    peak.setText("1");
    type.setText("Rock");
    label.setText("Capitol");
    albumReleased.setText("November 14, 2000");

    // Attach elements to the hierarchy.
    cd.addContent(title);
    cd.addContent(artist);
    cd.addContent(chart);
    chart.addContent(peak);
    cd.addContent(type);
    cd.addContent(label);
    cd.addContent(albumReleased);
```

```
    return(cd);
  }

// JDOM takes advantage of Java 2 features such as Lists and Maps.
// Here we use Iterator to cycle through the members of a List.
public static void printChildren(Element element)
  {
  // Get a List of direct children as Elements
  List kids = element.getChildren();
  Iterator iter = kids.iterator();
  while (iter.hasNext()) {
    Object o = iter.next();
    System.out.println("Next kid: " +
      ((Element)o).getName());
    }
  }

} // end class
```

Note the difference between the `readSAXDocument` and `readDOMDocument` methods. In the former, we invoke the builder and then directly create the JDOM `Document` object.

```
SAXBuilder builder = new SAXBuilder(true);  // validate
Document doc = builder.build(new File(filename));
```

In the case of `readDOMDocument`, however, we need to create an *intermediate* W3C DOM `Document` using the previously mentioned `org.jdom.adapters.XercesDOMAdapter`. It is this W3C DOM object, not the `File` object, that is passed to the build method of `DOMBuilder`.

```
DOMBuilder builder = new DOMBuilder(true);  // validate
org.w3c.dom.Document w3cdoc = domAdapter.getDocument(filename, true);
Document doc = builder.build(w3cdoc);
```

We've emphasized that JDOM takes advantage of Java language features since it is a Java-centric rather than language-independent API. Another example of this is the use of Java 2 features such as `Lists`, a subinterface of the `Collection` interface from the `java.util` package (i.e., in JDK 1.2.x and higher). As you can see from the `printChildren` method in Listing 9-2, the `Element.getChildren` method returns a `List`. We can cycle through the `List` members using an `Iterator`.[3] Aside from the fact that we aren't bothering to check whether `getChildren` has returned null (if there are no children elements), we note that this method needs to be recursive to print what might be a deep hierarchy. This is left as an exercise to the reader.

3. The parallel with the DOM was `curNode.getChildNodes()`, which returns a `Nodelist` and doesn't support Java's `Iterator`.

JDOM Output with Valid Input

`TryJDOM.java` reads an XML instance, creates a JDOM `Document` object, adds a `CD` hierarchy, prints all nodes in the expanded tree, and then uses a Java `Iterator` to print the immediate children of the added `CD` element.

Let's run `TryJDOM.java` using `SAXBuilder` with `collection3-frag.xml` (Listing 8-3) as input:

```
C:\> jdom-it.bat TryJDOM SAX collection3-frag.xml
```

The output is shown in Listing 9-3.

Listing 9-3 JDOM Output with Valid Input Using SAXBuilder

```
Using SAXBuilder...
Root element = Collection
<?xml version="1.0" encoding="UTF-8"?>
<!DOCTYPE Collection SYSTEM "collection3.dtd">
<?xml-stylesheet type="text/css"
href="http://www.w3.org/StyleSheets/Core/Modernist"?>
<!-- Collection consists of Book and CD elements in no particular order. -->
<?javaPI sortOrder="alphabetical" selectElements="Book" ?>
<Collection version="3">
 <Book>
  <Title>
Complete &fab4; Chronicle, The  </Title>
  <Author>
   <Name sex="male">
    <First>Mark</First>
    <Last>Lewisohn</Last>
   </Name>
  </Author>
  <Type>Chronology</Type>
  <Published publisher="Harmony Books">1992</Published>
  <Notes>
We could display a Beatles photo using SVG like so:
         <![CDATA[
       <svg width="20cm" height="20cm"  viewBox="0 0 500 500" >
         <image x="50" y="50"  width="333" height="267"
           xlink:href="http://mcbeatle.de/beatles/beatles3.jpg"/>
       </svg>
      ]]>

      </Notes>
 </Book>
 <!-- Other CD and Book elements omitted. -->
 <CD>
  <Title>Beatles 1</Title>
  <Artist>Beatles</Artist>
  <Chart>
   <Peak>1</Peak>
  </Chart>
  <Type>Rock</Type>
```

```
  <Label country="US">Capitol</Label>
  <AlbumReleased>November 14, 2000</AlbumReleased>
 </CD>
</Collection>
+++ Printing direct children of <CD> element:
Next kid: Title
Next kid: Artist
Next kid: Chart
Next kid: Type
Next kid: Label
Next kid: AlbumReleased
```

There are several variations of the XMLOutputter method; our choice greatly influences output readability. The output in Listing 9-3 was generated using the XMLOutputter method that takes an indent string (two spaces, in our case) and a boolean indicating whether to generate newlines (if true):

```
XMLOutputter outputter = new XMLOutputter("  ", true);
```

If instead we use the no-arg version, the result is shown in Listing 9-4, where the line that begins <?xml ...?> through <![CDATA[is one long line, as is the line that begins with </Notes>.

Listing 9-4 JDOM Output with Different XMLOutputter Method

```
Using SAXBuilder...
Root element = Collection
<?xml version="1.0" encoding="UTF-8"?><!DOCTYPE Collection SYSTEM
"collection3.dtd"><?xml-stylesheet type="text/css" href="http://www.w3.org/
StyleSheets/Core/Modernist"?><!-- Collection consists of Book and CD elements
in no particular order. --><?javaPI sortOrder="alphabetical"
selectElements="Book" ?><Collection version="3"><Book><Title>Complete &fab4;
Chronicle, The</Title><Author><Name sex="male"><First>Mark</
First><Last>Lewisohn</Last></Name></Author><Type>Chronology</Type><Published
publisher="Harmony Books">1992</Published><Notes>We could display a Beatles
photos using SVG like so:
      <![CDATA[
       <svg width="20cm" height="20cm"  viewBox="0 0 500 500" >
         <image x="50" y="50"  width="333" height="267"
           xlink:href="http://mcbeatle.de/beatles/beatles3.jpg"/>
       </svg>
      ]]>
    </Notes></Book><!-- Other CD and Book elements omitted. --
><CD><Title>Beatles 1</Title><Artist>Beatles</Artist><Chart><Peak>1</
Peak></Chart><Type>Rock</Type><Label
country="US">Capitol</Label><AlbumReleased>November 14, 2000</
AlbumReleased></CD></Collection>
```

If we use DOMBuilder rather than SAXBuilder, the output results are slightly different in both cases, but not better. In fact, with JDOM Beta 5, the output in Listing 9-3 is the best case, achieved using `SAXBuilder` and the version of `XMLOutputter` with the indent and newlines arguments. As noted previously, this output formatting makes no difference to subsequent processing steps. A multimegabyte XML instance could be all on one line, for all parsers care. These serialization niceties are purely for us mere humans who sometimes like to look at what we give our computers to munch on.

Examples of Well-Formedness and Validation Error Handling

How does a JDOM application handle errors? If we use the same invalid `collection3-bad-Titles.xml` file as input as in the section "Examples of Well-Formedness and Validation Error Handling" in chapter 8, the SAX error is simply a general failure message:

```
C:\> java TryJDOM collection3-bad-Titles.xml
org.jdom.JDOMException: SAXBuilder failed
        at TryJDOM.readSAXDocument(TryJDOM.java:105)  # etc.
```

The error diagnostic is considerably more specific when we use the `DOMBuilder` and the `XercesDOMAdapter`:

```
C:\> java TryJDOM collection3-bad-Titles.xml
java.io.IOException: Error on line 20 of XML document: The content of element
type "Book" must match "(Title,Author,Type,Published,Rating?,Notes?)".
        at org.jdom.adapters.XercesDOMAdapter.getDocument(
XercesDOMAdapter.java:138)
        at org.jdom.adapters.AbstractDOMAdapter.getDocument(
AbstractDOMAdapter.java:92) # etc.
```

Similarly, with `DOMBuilder` and `collection3-bad-Last.xml` (which is not well-formed XML), we get another clear error message:

```
C:\> java TryJDOM collection3-bad-Last.xml > jdom.txt
java.io.IOException: Error on line 19 of XML document: The element type "Last"
must be terminated by the matching end-tag "</Last>".
        at org.jdom.adapters.XercesDOMAdapter.getDocument(
XercesDOMAdapter.java:138)
        at org.jdom.adapters.AbstractDOMAdapter.getDocument(
AbstractDOMAdapter.java:92) # etc.
```

We obtain similar error messages as we saw with SAX and DOM (since ultimately the messages originate from either SAX or DOM). But perhaps more important, we did not have to go through the three-part error-handling setup that was necessary for SAX and DOM: defining an `ErrorHandler`, setting the `ErrorHandler`, and using `setFeature` to enable validation. Presumably, JDOM does this for us by default. We only need to prepare to catch `JDOMException` and Java's generic `Exception`.

JDOM Summary

JDOM makes it considerably easier for Java developers to access and process the information items of an XML document without having to worry about either the DOM complexity or implementing context tracking for SAX. Much like JAXP (which it predated), JDOM does not *implement* parsing; it merely *interfaces* to parsers. However, it can use any SAX or DOM parser and these choices are switchable at runtime.

It is designed for easy and efficient reading, manipulation, and writing of XML documents. JDOM takes advantage of rich Java language features such as method overloading. Support for DOM Level 2, SAX 2.0, XML Schema, JAXP, and TrAX make JDOM an attractive alternative for a Java-centric development environment.

JDOM has garnered enough interest among Java developers to support an active mailing list and to become a JSR for possible inclusion in Sun's Java XML offerings in the near future. However, it does not claim to address the needs of every XML application. Therefore, dropping down to the raw SAX or DOM level can be expected for some applications.

To learn a great deal more about JDOM, see the Documentation area of the JDOM site—*http://jdom.org/downloads/docs.html*. Readers interested in JDOM may also find *dom4j* and *ElectricXML* to their liking (see "For Further Exploration" for URLs).

Sun's XML APIs: The Java XML Pack

Table 9-1 summarizes the key Java XML APIs, the majority of which are from Sun Microsystems. At the XML 2000 Conference in Washington, DC, in December 2000, Sun Microsystems announced early access releases of both the *Java API for XML Parsing (JAXP)* and the *Java API for XML Messaging (JAXM)*. Simultaneously, a third specification, the *Java Architecture for XML Binding (JAXB)*, formerly called Project Adelard, was nearing completion through the Java Community Process (JCP) program. JAXP, JAXM, and JAXB were targeted for release in the Java 2 Platform, Enterprise Edition (J2EE) and Java 2 Platform, Standard Edition (J2SE). Sun indicated that these three APIs were fundamental to providing truly versatile XML support in Java. JAXP is the subject of most of the rest of this chapter because it relates directly to XML parsing, so more about that shortly.

JAXM enables the packaging, routing, and transport of both XML and non-XML business messages via HTTP, SMTP, FTP, and possibly other protocols. Among its other potential uses, JAXM is positioned to facilitate e-business. JAXM is used for the messaging framework of ebXML, the emerging global standard for simple and robust trade facilitation, under joint development by the Organization for the Advancement of Structured Information Standards (OASIS) and the United Nations Centre for Trade Facilitation and Electronic Business (UN/CEFACT).

The purpose of **JAXB** is to bind XML documents to Java objects. The central idea is that a compiler can interpret DTD (and eventually XML Schema) descriptions to generate Java classes that implement the schema. Error and validation will be handled without developers having to write special code. Since the error handling is built in to the generated class, this can result in better performance and reduced memory requirements than a generic SAX or DOM parser.

Approximately one year after its announcement in November 2001 Sun Microsystems began bundling its more mature Java XML offerings into a download called the **Java XML Pack**, updated quarterly. According to Sun (see *http://java.sun.com/xml/javaxmlpack.html*):

> Java XML Pack brings together several of the key industry standards for XML—such as SAX, DOM, XSLT, SOAP, UDDI, ebXML, and WSDL—into one convenient download, thereby giving developers the technologies needed to get started with Web applications and services. Bundling the Java XML technologies together into a Java XML Pack ensures Java developers of a quick and easy development cycle for integration of XML functionality and standards support into their applications.

The initial Java XML Pack Fall 01 contained:

- Java API for XML Processing (JAXP) reference implementation version 1.1.3, which supports the XML processing standards SAX, DOM, and XSLT
- Java API for XML Messaging (JAXM) reference implementation version 1.0, which supports Simple Object Access Protocal (SOAP) 1.1 with attachments messaging

Since JAXP addresses XML *document* processing needs and JAXM handles XML *data format and messaging*, the combination of the two APIs can be used to develop simple Web services[4] such as sending, receiving, and processing catalog data.

Eventually, Java XML Pack will contain a wide variety of Java XML APIs:

- Java API for XML Processing (JAXP)
- Java API for XML Messaging (JAXM)
- Java Architecture for XML Binding (JAXB)
- Java API for XML-based RPC (JAX-RPC)
- Java API for XML Registries (JAXR)

JAX-RPC and JAXR appeared in the spring 2002 version of the Java XML Pack.

The key Web pages for tracking Sun Microsystems's XML APIs are:

- Sun's main XML technology page—*http://java.sun.com/xml/*
- Status of the various efforts from Sun is reflected on their download page—*http://java.sun.com/xml/download.html*

4. A **Web service** is a basic building block for communication over the Internet using the standard SOAP protocol. Web services are described using Web Services Description Language (WSDL).

- Documentation including API overviews, FAQs, tutorials, and specifications—*http://java.sun.com/xml/docs.html*
- Java XML Pack—*http://java.sun.com/xml/javaxmlpack.html*

Our focus for the rest of the chapter is on JAXP, the most mature and widespread of these APIs.

JAXP: Sun's Java API for XML Processing

The **Java API for XML Processing (JAXP)**[5] provides a standardized set of Java Platform APIs for performing fundamental XML processing, including SAX and DOM parsing, as well as XSLT manipulation (XSLT, Extensible Stylesheet Language Transformations, is the subject of chapter 11). JAXP is an abstraction for reading, manipulating, and generating XML documents. In other words, JAXP provides a pluggability layer that enables applications to interact with any compliant XML parser and XSLT processor without code changes and therefore without recompiling. Developers indicate a different choice of parser or processor by changing Java system properties. Therefore, JAXP doesn't really provide any functionality beyond SAX, DOM, and XSLT, but its beauty is in simplifying the task of changing one's tools by sheltering the application for the differences among parsers and among processors. Whereas DOM, SAX, and JDOM all provide methods to actually parse XML, JAXP is focused on easy access to the results of the parse in a portable way. JAXP is useless without an underlying parser. This makes JAXP categorically different from SAX and DOM. Although JAXP and JDOM are similar in that they both provide the ability to connect to any parser, JDOM provides additional XML processing classes that are quite useful, as we've seen.

The JAXP 1.0 version was initially criticized because it was based on an old SAX standard, rather than on the May 2000 SAX2 version. Similarly, JAXP 1.0 supported only DOM Level 1 and was therefore not namespace aware. The final version of JAXP 1.0 was called 1.0.1 and was released in April 2000. In this chapter, our focus is on JAXP 1.1, the reference implementation for the proposed specification at the time of this writing. The first early access release of JAXP 1.1 became available in October 2000, followed by a second early access release in December 2000. At the time of this writing, the final reference implementation of JAXP 1.1 is not available.[6] Our discussion is therefore based upon specifications

5. The acronym JAXP originally meant Java API for XML *Parsing* (JAXP 1.0), but was changed to Java API for XML *Processing* with JAXP 1.1 since XSLT is also supported. Unfortunately, the old name persists in some documentation.

6. *Update*: JAXP 1.1 was finalized in February 2001. JAXP *Reference Implementations* with three-digit version numbers such as 1.1.1 and 1.1.3 surfaced late in 2001. See the JAXP FAQ for clarification about versioning: *http://java.sun.com/xml/jaxp/faq.html*. For example, JAXP Reference Implementation version 1.1.1 implements the JAXP 1.1 specification.

dated October, November, and December 2000, especially the JAXP 1.1 Early Access Release 2. For the most current information about JAXP, see the JSR 63 page or the JAXP home page—*http://jcp.org/jsr/detail/063.jsp* and *http://java.sun.com/xml/jaxp/index.html.*

JAXP 1.1 Components and Packages

JAXP 1.1 Early Access 2 release includes three JAR files: `jaxp.jar`, `crimson.jar`, and `xalan.jar`. However, the actual API described by the JAXP specification is contained entirely within `jaxp.jar`.[7] The other two JARs provide Apache-specific parser and XSLT processor implementations, as shown in Table 9-3.

By default, the XML parser for the reference implementation uses a parser code-named Crimson (contained in `crimson.jar`), which was derived from Sun's Java Project X parser. Apache's Xalan is the default XSLT processor. However, recall that the pluggable architecture of JAXP provides developers the option to switch to different parsers and processors without recompiling code. The `jaxp.jar` is comprised of five packages, one of which is for SAX and DOM parsing, with the others for XSLT transformations, as shown in Table 9-4.[8]

TABLE 9-3 JAXP 1.1 JAR Files

JAR File	*Description*
`jaxp.jar`	The formal JAXP packages shown in Table 9-4.
`crimson.jar`	Apache-specific XML parsing packages, such as `org.apache.crimson.parser`, and `org.apache.crimson.tree` (donated by Sun), plus SAX and DOM implementations in the `org.xml.sax` and `org.w3c.dom` packages. *Not really part of the JAXP specification.*
`xalan.jar`	Apache-specific XSLT processor and XPath packages, `org.apache.xalan` and `org.apache.xpath`. Classes are from the Apache XSLT processor, Xalan-Java 2, which includes TrAX (Transformation API for XML). *Not really part of the JAXP specification.*

7. *Update*: The final release of JAXP 1.1 also contained `jaxp.jar`. However, in the Java XML Pack Fall 01 Release that contains JAXP 1.1.3, `jaxp.jar` has been replaced by adding class files to `crimson.jar`, namely, the `org.apache.crimson.jaxp` package.

8. *Update*: The final JAXP 1.1 release also documents `org.w3c.dom`, `org.xml.sax`, `org.xml.sax.ext`, and `org.xml.sax.helpers`. JAXP 1.1.3 in Java XML Pack adds to these `org.w3c.dom.css`, `org.w3c.dom.events`, `org.w3c.dom.ranges`, `org.w3c.dom.stylesheet`, `org.w3c.dom.traversal`, and `org.w3c.dom.views`.

TABLE 9-4 JAXP 1.1 Packages

Package	*Description*
`javax.xml.parsers`	Provides classes for SAX2 and DOM2 processing of XML documents. Contains only six classes: two for SAX (`SAXParser` and `SAXParserFactory`), two for DOM (`DocumentBuilder` and `DocumentBuilderFactory`), and two for parser configuration problems (`ParserConfigurationException` and `FactoryConfigurationError`).
`javax.xml.transform`	Defines generic TrAX classes and interfaces for processing XSLT transformation instructions and performing a transformation from source to result. Classes and interfaces include `Transformer`, `TransformerFactory`, `ErrorListener`, `URIResolver`, `Source`, `Result`, and `SourceLocator`.
`javax.xml.transform.dom`	Implements DOM-specific XSLT transformation classes, such as `DOMSource`, `DOMLocator` and `DOMResult`.
`javax.xml.transform.sax`	Implements SAX2-specific XSLT transformation classes, such as `SAXSource`, `SAXTransformerFactory`, and `SAXResult`.
`javax.xml.transform.stream`	Implements stream-specific XSLT transformation classes, such as `StreamSource` and `StreamResult`.

Specifications Supported by JAXP

Implementations of the JAXP 1.1 specification are required to conform to the following specifications (all from the W3C except SAX):

- XML 1.0, Second Edition
- XML Namespaces
- SAX 2
- SAX 2 Extensions
- DOM Level 2 Core API
- XSLT 1.0 including an XSLT framework based on TrAX (Transformation API for XML)

Using JAXP 1.1

We'll use a batch file to specify everything we need to use JAXP with the default Apache Crimson parser and Xalan Java 2 XSLT processor, both included with the JAXP distribution (see Listing 9-5). We'll call this batch file (you guessed it) `jaxp-it.bat` and the sample application is `TryJAXP.java`.

The JAXP batch file differs from those presented in the SAX and DOM chapters in that it is not based on using `xmlsetup.bat`. Notice the special classpath setup required. If you use a later version of JAXP, the JAR list may be different. You'll need to modify this .bat file for your environment.

Listing 9-5 Batch File for JAXP Compiling and Running

```
@echo off

REM Adjust for your locations.
set JBIN=C:\JAVA\jdk1.3\bin
set JLIB=C:\JAVA\jdk1.3\lib
set JAXP=C:\XML\JAXP\jaxp-1.lea2

REM These 3 JARS need to be in your classpath.
set JAXP_JARS=%JAXP%\jaxp.jar;%JAXP%\crimson.jar;%JAXP%\xalan.jar

REM Include parser and processor in your classpath.
set classpath=.;%JLIB%;%JAXP_JARS%

REM Compile program
%JBIN%\javac TryJAXP.java

REM Run program
REM Example input: collection3-frag.xml
@echo on
%JBIN%\java TryJAXP %1  > jaxp-out.txt
@echo off
```

For example, to compile and run the example shown in the section "JAXP Code Example" with the input file `collection3-frag.xml`, use the command line:

```
C:\> jaxp-it.bat collection3-frag.xml
```

Enabling Validation

In a JAXP application (in contrast to JDOM), validation errors will only be returned to the application if two conditions are met:

1. Validation must be enabled using the `setValidating` methods of `javax.xml.parsers.DocumentBuilderFactory` or `javax.xml.parsers.SAXParserFactory` (for DOM or SAX, respectively).
2. The application must provide an `ErrorHandler` using the `setErrorHandler` methods of `javax.xml.parsers.DocumentBuilder` or `org.xml.sax.XMLReader`.

The code example in Listing 9-6, which starts on page 514, illustrates validation enabling.

Using SAX with JAXP

There are essentially five steps to using SAX with JAXP.

1. Create a `SAXParserFactory` instance.
2. Set one or more configuration options.
3. Use the factory to create a `SAXParser` that satisfies the configuration constraints.
4. Before parsing, set an `ErrorHandler` using the `setErrorHandler` method of `org.xml.sax.XMLReader`.
5. Perform the parse.

Note that after step 2, you can save the `SAXParserFactory` instance and reuse it to create multiple `SAXParser` instances, provided that they all can use the same configuration options.

Using DOM with JAXP

In the JAXP world, the primary difference between dealing with DOM and SAX is to use `DocumentBuilderFactory` and `DocumentBuilder` instead of `SAXParser-Factory` and `SAXParser`, respectively. Therefore, the five steps for DOM use are as follows:

1. Create a **`DocumentBuilderFactory`** instance.
2. Set one or more configuration options.
3. Use the factory to create a **`DocumentBuilder`** that satisfies the configuration constraints.
4. Before parsing, set an `ErrorHandler` using the `setErrorHandler` method of **`javax.xml.parsers.DocumentBuilder`**.
5. Perform the parse.

Java System Properties for JAXP

To override the default XML parser and/or XSLT processor, set the relevant Java system properties:

- `javax.xml.parsers.SAXParserFactory` (default value for this property is: `org.apache.xerces.jaxp.SAXParserFactoryImpl`)
- `javax.xml.parsers.DocumentBuilderFactory` (default value: `org.apache.xerces.jaxp.DocumentBuilderFactoryImpl`)
- `javax.xml.transform.TransformerFactory` (default value: `org.apache.xalan.processor.TransformerFactoryImpl`)

For example, the following command line overrides the default SAX parser by indicating a fictitious JAXP implementation (not the one from Sun) from the equally fictitious `xmlRUs.com`.

```
java -Djavax.xml.parsers.SAXParserFactory=com.xmlRUs.jaxp.SAXParserFactoryImpl
myParserApp
```

JAXP Code Example

The code example in Listing 9-6 illustrates using JAXP to access a DOM parser. You've seen much of this code already in our other DOM examples. The JAXP particulars are isolated to the `main` method and the private class `MyErrorHandler`. In `main`, we call `DocumentBuilderFactory.newInstance` to obtain a `DocumentBuilderFactory`, which is then used to create a `DocumentBuilder` via the method `newDocumentBuilder`. These calls could result in a `FactoryConfigurationError` or `ParserConfigurationException`, so we catch these exceptions. Next we configure the DOM parser to be validating and establish an `ErrorHandler` by the lines:

```
docBuilderFactory.setValidating(true);
docBuilder.setErrorHandler(new MyErrorHandler(System.err));
```

The `MyErrorHandler` method is borrowed from the `DOMEcho.java` example that accompanied the JAXP 1.1 Early Access 2 release. It handles warning, error, and fatal `SAXParseExceptions`. We actually perform the DOM parsing by invoking the `parse` method of `DocumentBuilder`, which could generate a `SAXException` if the XML isn't well-formed or valid.

If instead we choose to use a SAX parser, we could enable validation via `SAXParserFactory.setValidating`, or we could use the `getProperty` and `setProperty` methods in `SAXParser`, or the `getFeature` and `setFeature` methods in `SAXParserFactory`. For example, we could enable XML Schema validation as follows:

```
saxParserFactory.setFeature
        ("http://apache.org/xml/features/validation/", true);
```

Listing 9-6 JAXP DOM Reading, Adding Elements, and Writing (TryJAXP.java)

```
/*
 * The Apache Software License, Version 1.1
 *
 *
 * Copyright (c) 2000 The Apache Software Foundation.  All rights
 * reserved.
 *
 * Redistribution and use in source and binary forms, with or without
 * modification, are permitted provided that the following conditions
 * are met:
 *
```

```
 * 1. Redistributions of source code must retain the above copyright
 *    notice, this list of conditions and the following disclaimer.
 *
 * 2. Redistributions in binary form must reproduce the above copyright
 *    notice, this list of conditions and the following disclaimer in
 *    the documentation and/or other materials provided with the
 *    distribution.
 *
 * 3. The end-user documentation included with the redistribution,
 *    if any, must include the following acknowledgment:
 *       "This product includes software developed by the
 *        Apache Software Foundation (http://www.apache.org/)."
 *    Alternately, this acknowledgment may appear in the software itself,
 *    if and wherever such third-party acknowledgments normally appear.
 *
 * 4. The names "Crimson" and "Apache Software Foundation" must
 *    not be used to endorse or promote products derived from this
 *    software without prior written permission. For written
 *    permission, please contact apache@apache.org.
 *
 * 5. Products derived from this software may not be called "Apache",
 *    nor may "Apache" appear in their name, without prior written
 *    permission of the Apache Software Foundation.
 *
 * THIS SOFTWARE IS PROVIDED "AS IS" AND ANY EXPRESSED OR IMPLIED
 * WARRANTIES, INCLUDING, BUT NOT LIMITED TO, THE IMPLIED WARRANTIES
 * OF MERCHANTABILITY AND FITNESS FOR A PARTICULAR PURPOSE ARE
 * DISCLAIMED.  IN NO EVENT SHALL THE APACHE SOFTWARE FOUNDATION OR
 * ITS CONTRIBUTORS BE LIABLE FOR ANY DIRECT, INDIRECT, INCIDENTAL,
 * SPECIAL, EXEMPLARY, OR CONSEQUENTIAL DAMAGES (INCLUDING, BUT NOT
 * LIMITED TO, PROCUREMENT OF SUBSTITUTE GOODS OR SERVICES; LOSS OF
 * USE, DATA, OR PROFITS; OR BUSINESS INTERRUPTION) HOWEVER CAUSED AND
 * ON ANY THEORY OF LIABILITY, WHETHER IN CONTRACT, STRICT LIABILITY,
 * OR TORT (INCLUDING NEGLIGENCE OR OTHERWISE) ARISING IN ANY WAY OUT
 * OF THE USE OF THIS SOFTWARE, EVEN IF ADVISED OF THE POSSIBILITY OF
 * SUCH DAMAGE.
 * ====================================================================
 *
 * This software consists of voluntary contributions made by many
 * individuals on behalf of the Apache Software Foundation and was
 * originally based on software copyright (c) 1999, Sun Microsystems, Inc.,
 * http://www.sun.com.  For more information on the Apache Software
 * Foundation, please see <http://www.apache.org/>.
 */

/*
 * The above copyright notice is included because the MyErrorHandler
 * method is borrowed from the Apache $JAXP\examples\DOMEcho.java
 * example that accompanied JAXP 1.1 Early Access 2.
 * The rest of the example is similar to our own TryDOM2Parser.java.
 * -- Ken Sall.
 */
```

```
import java.io.File;
import java.io.IOException;
import java.io.PrintStream; // for ErrorHandler

import javax.xml.parsers.DocumentBuilderFactory;
import javax.xml.parsers.DocumentBuilder;
import javax.xml.parsers.FactoryConfigurationError;
import javax.xml.parsers.ParserConfigurationException;

// NOTE: Crimson XmlDocument is Sun-specific, not part of the JAXP API.
import org.apache.crimson.tree.XmlDocument;

import org.w3c.dom.Document;
import org.w3c.dom.DocumentType;
import org.w3c.dom.ProcessingInstruction;
import org.w3c.dom.Element;
import org.w3c.dom.Attr;
import org.w3c.dom.Text;
import org.w3c.dom.Node;
import org.w3c.dom.NodeList;
import org.w3c.dom.NamedNodeMap;
import org.w3c.dom.Entity;
import org.w3c.dom.CDATASection;
import org.w3c.dom.DOMException;

// SAX error handling
import org.xml.sax.SAXException;
import org.xml.sax.SAXParseException;
import org.xml.sax.ErrorHandler;

public class TryJAXP
{
  // Parse an XML document (file).
  public static void main (String argv [])
  {
    if (argv.length != 1)
        {
        System.err.println ("Usage: cmd filename");
        System.exit (1);
        }

    // Create the DocumentBuilderFactory and use it to obtain the
DocumentBuilder.
    // Then configure the parser and perform the parse.
    DocumentBuilderFactory docBuilderFactory = null;
    DocumentBuilder docBuilder = null;
    Document doc = null;
        try {
            docBuilderFactory = DocumentBuilderFactory.newInstance();
            docBuilder = docBuilderFactory.newDocumentBuilder();

            // Configure the DOM factory to validate.
            System.out.println ("Before: default validation: " +
               docBuilderFactory.isValidating() );
```

```
            // Enable validation.
            docBuilderFactory.setValidating(true);
            System.out.println ("After: setting validation: " +
               docBuilderFactory.isValidating() );
            // Must also setErrorHandler for validation to work.
            docBuilder.setErrorHandler(new MyErrorHandler(System.err));

            // Perform the actual parsing.
            try {
                doc = docBuilder.parse (new File (argv [0]));
            } catch (SAXException se) {
                System.err.println(se.getMessage());
                System.exit(1);
            } catch (IOException ioe) {
                System.err.println(ioe);
                System.exit(1);
            }

        } catch (FactoryConfigurationError fce) {
            System.err.println(fce);
            System.exit(1);
        } catch (ParserConfigurationException pce) {
            System.err.println(pce);
            System.exit(1);
        }

        // Normalize text to combine consecutive white space.
        doc.getDocumentElement().normalize();

        System.out.println ("Root element of the doc is " +
                    doc.getDocumentElement().getNodeName());

        // Add a CD element with all of its children.
        Node newNode = addCDElement (doc);

        // We assume only DOM Level 1 features for traversal.
        depthFirstTraversal (doc);

        // Serialization is not part of the JAXP standard. This shortcoming
        // will be addressed by either the DOM Level 3 spec or JSR 057.
        System.out.println("^^^^^^^^^^^^^^^^^^^^^^^^^^^^^^^^^^^^^^^^^^^^^^^^^");
        XmlDocument xdoc = (XmlDocument) doc;
        try {
            xdoc.write (System.out);
        } catch (IOException ioe) {
            System.err.println(ioe);
            System.exit(1);
        }

    System.exit (0);
  } // main
```

```
// A different approach, for DOM Level 1 and above.
public static void depthFirstTraversal (Node curNode)
{
  dumpNode(curNode);
  NodeList kids = curNode.getChildNodes();
  int len = (kids != null) ? kids.getLength() : 0;

  System.out.println("<" + curNode.getNodeName() +
  "> has " + len + " kids.");

  for (int i = 0; i < len; i++)
    {
    depthFirstTraversal(kids.item(i));  // recurse
    }
}

// The main work horse of this application which processes
// each node according to its type. Note the operations
// that are common across all node types and which are unique.

public static void dumpNode (Node curNode)
{
  // Common processing.
  System.out.print ("nodeName = <" + curNode.getNodeName() + ">");
  System.out.println (" , nodeType = " + typeToName(curNode) );
  // Could skip printing all pure whitespace values but we don't.
  if (curNode.getNodeValue() != null)
    System.out.println ("nodeValue = [" +
             curNode.getNodeValue() + "]");

  short type = curNode.getNodeType();
  switch (type)
  {
    case (Node.ELEMENT_NODE):
    {
  // Any attributes? If so, they will be
  // returned as NamedNodeMap which is "live".
  // Note the attributes don't occur as nodes in traversal,
  // so they must be handled as we encounter the element that
  // contains them.
  NamedNodeMap attrs = curNode.getAttributes();
  for (int i = 0; i < attrs.getLength(); i++)
  {
    Attr attr = (Attr)attrs.item(i);
    System.out.print ("attrName = [" +
              attr.getNodeName() + "]");
    System.out.println (" , nodeType = " + typeToName(attr) );
    System.out.print ("attrValue = [" +
              attr.getNodeValue() + "]");
    System.out.println (" , specified = [" +
              attr.getSpecified() + "]");
  }
  break;
    }
```

```
case (Node.DOCUMENT_NODE):
{
  System.out.println("Found Document node (above root)");

  // The Document Element is the root of the element hierarchy.
  Document doc = (Document)curNode;
  Element root = (Element)doc.getDocumentElement();
  System.out.println("Found DocumentElement (aka root): ["
      + root.getNodeName() + "]");
  // We could examine the root element now, but we'll see
  // it soon enough as we loop through the elements.
  // dumpNode(root);
  break;
}

case (Node.DOCUMENT_TYPE_NODE):
{
  DocumentType dtd  = (DocumentType)curNode;
  System.out.println("Found DocumentType named: [" +
        dtd.getName() + "]");
  if (dtd.getPublicId() != null)
    System.out.println("PublicId = [" + dtd.getPublicId() + "]");

  if (dtd.getSystemId() != null)
    System.out.println("SystemId = [" + dtd.getSystemId() + "]");

  if (dtd.getEntities() != null)
  {
    NamedNodeMap ents = dtd.getEntities();
    System.out.println("-- There are [" + ents.getLength() +
         "] Entities in the DTD. --");
    for (int i = 0; i < ents.getLength(); i++)
    {
      Entity ent = (Entity)ents.item(i);
      System.out.print ("entityName = [" +
           ent.getNodeName() + "]");
      System.out.println (" , entsValue = [" +
           ent.getNodeValue() + "]");
    }
  } // getEntities
  // Could do something similar with getNotations.

  break;
} // DOCUMENT_TYPE_NODE

case (Node.TEXT_NODE):
case (Node.CDATA_SECTION_NODE):
{
  // Nothing special to do; already printed the text value.
  break;
}

case (Node.PROCESSING_INSTRUCTION_NODE):
{
```

```
                ProcessingInstruction pi = (ProcessingInstruction)curNode;
                System.out.println("PI target = [" + pi.getTarget() +
                        "] , data = [" + pi.getData() + "]");
                break;
            }

            default:
                break;

        } // switch

        System.out.println();
    }

  // Just a convenient mapping of node types from numeric to string value.
    public static String typeToName (Node node)
    {
        short type = node.getNodeType();
        switch(type)
        {
            case (Node.ATTRIBUTE_NODE):
                return "ATTRIBUTE_NODE";
            case (Node.CDATA_SECTION_NODE):
                return "CDATA_SECTION_NODE";
            case (Node.COMMENT_NODE):
                return "COMMENT_NODE";
            case (Node.DOCUMENT_FRAGMENT_NODE):
                return "DOCUMENT_FRAGMENT_NODE";
            case (Node.DOCUMENT_NODE):
                return "DOCUMENT_NODE";
            case (Node.DOCUMENT_TYPE_NODE):
                return "DOCUMENT_TYPE_NODE";
            case (Node.ELEMENT_NODE):
                return "ELEMENT_NODE";
            case (Node.ENTITY_NODE):
                return "ENTITY_NODE";
            case (Node.ENTITY_REFERENCE_NODE):
                return "ENTITY_REFERENCE_NODE";
            case (Node.NOTATION_NODE):
                return "NOTATION_NODE";
            case (Node.PROCESSING_INSTRUCTION_NODE):
                return "PROCESSING_INSTRUCTION_NODE";
            case (Node.TEXT_NODE):
                return "TEXT_NODE";
            default:
                return ("Unknown type: " + type); // shouldn't happen
        }
    }

    // Application specific example:
    // We're adding a CD element to the end of the Collection.
    // This involves creating lots of child nodes and attaching them
    // in the hierarchy defined by the DTD.
    public static Node addCDElement (Document doc)
    {
```

```
Element cd, title, artist, chart, peak, type, label, albumReleased;
Text    titleText, artistText, peakText, typeText, labelText,
        albumReleasedText;
Attr    labelAttr;

// Create the CD element and its first child, Title, and
// set the Title's value. Add Title as child of CD.
cd = doc.createElement("CD");
title = doc.createElement("Title");
titleText = doc.createTextNode("Beatles 1");
title.appendChild(titleText);
cd.appendChild(title);

artist = doc.createElement("Artist");
artistText = doc.createTextNode("Beatles");
artist.appendChild(artistText);
cd.appendChild(artist);

// Similarly with other CD children.
// Peak also has an optional attribute "country", but
// we will let this assume the default value from the DTD.
chart = doc.createElement("Chart");
peak = doc.createElement("Peak");
peakText = doc.createTextNode("1");
peak.appendChild(peakText);
chart.appendChild(peak);
cd.appendChild(chart);

type = doc.createElement("Type");
typeText = doc.createTextNode("Rock");
type.appendChild(typeText);
cd.appendChild(type);

// Label has an attribute named "country". We want:
//     <Label country="US" >Capitol</Label>
// Note that setAttributeNode is more general than
// setAttribute, but requires more steps.
label = doc.createElement("Label");
// Create and initialize the attribute and then attach
// to an Element. This is the generic approach.
labelAttr = doc.createAttribute("country");
labelAttr.setNodeValue("US");
label.setAttributeNode(labelAttr);
// An alternative to the above 3 lines is this one-liner:
// label.setAttribute("country", "US");
labelText = doc.createTextNode("Capitol");
label.appendChild(labelText);
cd.appendChild(label);

albumReleased = doc.createElement("AlbumReleased");
albumReleasedText = doc.createTextNode("November 14, 2000");
albumReleased.appendChild(albumReleasedText);
cd.appendChild(albumReleased);
```

```
        // Find the end of the Collection child list for appending
        // our new element.
        Node last = doc.getLastChild();
        System.out.println("^^^ Last child before appending <CD> = " +
                   last.getNodeName() );
        // Finally we're ready to add CD to the end of the Collection.
        Node newbie = last.appendChild(cd);
        return newbie;  // or cd, since both are identical
    }


    // Error handler to report errors and warnings
    private static class MyErrorHandler implements ErrorHandler {
        /** Error handler output goes here */
        private PrintStream out;

        MyErrorHandler(PrintStream out) {
            this.out = out;
        }

        /**
         * Returns a string describing parse exception details
         */
        private String getParseExceptionInfo(SAXParseException spe) {
            String systemId = spe.getSystemId();
            if (systemId == null) {
                systemId = "null";
            }
            String info = "URI=" + systemId +
                " Line=" + spe.getLineNumber() +
                ": " + spe.getMessage();
            return info;
        }

        // The following methods are standard SAX ErrorHandler methods.
        // See SAX documentation for more info.

        public void warning(SAXParseException spe) throws SAXException {
            out.println("Warning: " + getParseExceptionInfo(spe));
        }

        public void error(SAXParseException spe) throws SAXException {
            String message = "Error: " + getParseExceptionInfo(spe);
            throw new SAXException(message);
        }

        public void fatalError(SAXParseException spe) throws SAXException {
            String message = "Fatal Error: " + getParseExceptionInfo(spe);
            throw new SAXException(message);
        }
    }

} // class
```

It is very important to realize that using the `org.apache.crimson.tree.XmlDocument` class for serialization in this example is not desirable in the context of JAXP. Using methods from this parser-specific class pretty much negates the parser independence we gained by using JAXP in the first place. This would lock us into using the Crimson parser, or at the very least, it would force us to replace the `import` statement and the use of `XmlDocument` with the analogous serialization approach in whatever other parser we later desire to use. Sometime in 2002, it is expected that either DOM Level 3 Abstract Schemas and Load and Save module or JSR 057 (Long-Term Persistence of JavaBeans; see *http://www.w3.org/TR/DOM-Level-3-ASLS* and *http://jcp.org/jsr/detail/057.jsp*) will provide a standard way to serialize XML.

TrAX Overview and Basic Example

Transformations of XML data are crucial to the usefulness of XML technology as a whole. Although chapter 11 focuses on transformations by means of XSLT stylesheets, transformations by other methods, such as Java, perl, or proprietary solutions, is common. Inputs and outputs may come in many forms: from a URL, SAX events, a DOM tree, a stream of XML data, or application-specific formats. Just as it's useful to maintain parser independence, it is also highly desirable to have a mechanism for XML transformations that abstracts as much as possible, and can be specialized for particular types of transformations with certain kinds of inputs and outputs. For example, parsing (transforming a stream of data into a tree) and serialization (transforming a tree into a stream) can both be viewed as specialized transformations.

Apache's **TrAX (Transformation API for XML)**—see *http://xml.apache.org/xalan-j/trax.html*—was developed for XSLT processor-neutral XML document transformations, an extremely useful thing when you consider the wide divergence among XSLT processor vendors in terms of optional features and extensions. Experts Scott Boag (Apache Xalan) and Michael Kay (SAXON XSLT processor) developed TrAX, with the help of others. In fact, one of the many goals of TrAX is to model transformation instructions independent of XSLT processor.

To use TrAX, a sequence of steps similar to the SAX and DOM cases must be followed:

1. Create a `TransformerFactory` instance.
2. Optionally set one or more *properties* for the actual XSLT processor using the `setAttribute` method (don't confuse these with XML attributes).
3. Use the factory to create a `Transformer` that satisfies the attribute constraints.

4. Before transforming, set an `ErrorListener` using the `setErrorListener` method of `TransformerFactory`.
5. Specify the XSLT source stylesheet (or alternative source of transformation instructions).
6. Perform the transformation by indicating the input XML source and the result target.

The `ErrorListener` interface is conceptually quite similar to the SAX `ErrorHandler` with `warning`, `error`, and `fatalError` methods. However, the concepts of *source* and *result* are different from anything in SAX or DOM. The `jaxap.xml.transform.Source` interface provides a way to locate input that need not be a physical file. Several implementations are included in JAXP:

- `jaxap.xml.transform.dom.DOMSource` (e.g., a in-memory DOM `Node`)
- `jaxap.xml.transform.sax.SAXSource` (e.g., a SAX `XMLReader` or `InputSource`)
- `jaxap.xml.transform.stream.StreamSource` (e.g., either `System.in`, a `String`, or a `Reader`)

The `jaxap.xml.transform.Result` interface indicates the intended target destination of the transformation, whether it be a file, a DOM object, or a SAX object. JAXP has several implementations that parallel the `Source` versions:

- `jaxap.xml.transform.dom.DOMResult` (e.g., a DOM `Node`)
- `jaxap.xml.transform.sax.SAXResult` (e.g., a SAX `ContentHandler`)
- `jaxap.xml.transform.stream.StreamResult` (e.g., `System.out` or a `Writer`)

At the time of this writing, JAXP 1.1 does not include an example of the use of TrAX excepting code snippets in the API documentation.[9] However, Xalan 2 from Apache includes an example by Scott Boag that is well worth studying; see `samples\trax\Examples.java` which can be downloaded from *http://xml.apache.org/xalan-j/index.html.*

For our purposes, we use a greatly simplified version that illustrates only one of the dozen or so scenarios in the original. We'll use a slightly modified version of our previous `Collection` example, this time called `collection4-frag.xml` (see Listing 9-7), which differs from the `collection3-frag.xml` version mainly because it does not reference a DTD and the `javaPI` Processing Instruction and `xml-stylesheet` lines have been removed, as has the entity `&fab4;`.

9. *Update*: The final JAXP 1.1 release and Java XML Pack Fall 01 both contain Boag's TraX example in the `examples\trax` folder.

Listing 9-7 XML Instance for Transformation (collection4-frag.xml)

```
<?xml version="1.0" standalone="yes" ?>
<!-- Collection consists of Book and CD elements in no particular order. -->
<Collection version="3">
  <Book>
    <Title>Complete Beatles Chronicle, The</Title>
    <Author>
      <Name>
        <First>Mark</First>
        <Last>Lewisohn</Last>
      </Name>
    </Author>
    <Type>Chronology</Type>
    <Published publisher="Harmony Books">1992</Published>
    <Notes>We could display a Beatles photo using SVG like so:
      <![CDATA[
       <svg width="20cm" height="20cm"  viewBox="0 0 500 500" >
         <image x="50" y="50"  width="333" height="267"
           xlink:href="http://mcbeatle.de/beatles/beatles3.jpg"/>
       </svg>
      ]]>
    </Notes>
  </Book>
<!-- Other CD and Book elements omitted. -->
</Collection>
```

We'll use a simple XSLT stylesheet, `tryTrAX.xsl`, shown in Listing 9-8, that depends upon the element hierarchy of the XML instance of Listing 9-7. Don't be concerned with the XSLT syntax; XSLT is the subject of chapter 11. For now, all you need to know is that this stylesheet is intended to transform the `Author` element by extracting the text content of its grandchildren, `First` and `Last`, which are children of the `Name` element. Although XSLT can generate XML, we've chosen to generate HTML, which explains the presence of HTML elements intermixed with those of the XSLT language.

Listing 9-8 XSLT Stylesheet Used by TrAX to Transform Instance (tryTrAX.xsl)

```
<?xml version='1.0'?>
<xsl:stylesheet
      xmlns:xsl='http://www.w3.org/1999/XSL/Transform' version='1.0'>
  <xsl:output method="html"/>
  <xsl:strip-space elements="*" />

  <xsl:template match="/">
   <html>
     <head>
       <title>TrAX Test</title>
     </head>
     <body>
      <xsl:apply-templates select="//Author" />
```

```
    </body>
  </html>
 </xsl:template>

 <xsl:template match="Author">
   <h1><xsl:value-of select="Name/First"/><xsl:text> </xsl:text>
   <xsl:value-of select="Name/Last"/></h1>
 </xsl:template>

</xsl:stylesheet>
```

Listing 9-9 shows the TrAX Java code. A batch file to help us compile and run the code is presented in Listing 9-10. The result of the transformation is shown in Listing 9-11. To apply this stylesheet to our XML file, we *could* use Xalan at the command-line level (or via a process invoked by a server), but for the purposes of this chapter, we'll use JAXP and TrAX, which in turn use Xerces and Xalan for XML parsing and XSLT processing, respectively. Our code example borrows heavily from Scott Boag's example.

Listing 9-9 JAXP TrAX Example Using XSLT (simpleTrAX.java)

```
// Based on samples\trax\Examples.java from Apache Xalan-j
// by Scott Boag (scott_boag@lotus.com)

/*
 * The Apache Software License, Version 1.1
 *
 *
 * Copyright (c) 1999 The Apache Software Foundation.  All rights
 * reserved.
 *
 * Redistribution and use in source and binary forms, with or without
 * modification, are permitted provided that the following conditions
 * are met:
 *
 * 1. Redistributions of source code must retain the above copyright
 *    notice, this list of conditions and the following disclaimer.
 *
 * 2. Redistributions in binary form must reproduce the above copyright
 *    notice, this list of conditions and the following disclaimer in
 *    the documentation and/or other materials provided with the
 *    distribution.
 *
 * 3. The end-user documentation included with the redistribution,
 *    if any, must include the following acknowledgment:
 *       "This product includes software developed by the
 *        Apache Software Foundation (http://www.apache.org/)."
 *    Alternately, this acknowledgment may appear in the software itself,
 *    if and wherever such third-party acknowledgments normally appear.
 *
```

```
 * 4. The names "Xalan" and "Apache Software Foundation" must
 *    not be used to endorse or promote products derived from this
 *    software without prior written permission. For written
 *    permission, please contact apache@apache.org.
 *
 * 5. Products derived from this software may not be called "Apache",
 *    nor may "Apache" appear in their name, without prior written
 *    permission of the Apache Software Foundation.
 *
 * THIS SOFTWARE IS PROVIDED "AS IS" AND ANY EXPRESSED OR IMPLIED
 * WARRANTIES, INCLUDING, BUT NOT LIMITED TO, THE IMPLIED WARRANTIES
 * OF MERCHANTABILITY AND FITNESS FOR A PARTICULAR PURPOSE ARE
 * DISCLAIMED.  IN NO EVENT SHALL THE APACHE SOFTWARE FOUNDATION OR
 * ITS CONTRIBUTORS BE LIABLE FOR ANY DIRECT, INDIRECT, INCIDENTAL,
 * SPECIAL, EXEMPLARY, OR CONSEQUENTIAL DAMAGES (INCLUDING, BUT NOT
 * LIMITED TO, PROCUREMENT OF SUBSTITUTE GOODS OR SERVICES; LOSS OF
 * USE, DATA, OR PROFITS; OR BUSINESS INTERRUPTION) HOWEVER CAUSED AND
 * ON ANY THEORY OF LIABILITY, WHETHER IN CONTRACT, STRICT LIABILITY,
 * OR TORT (INCLUDING NEGLIGENCE OR OTHERWISE) ARISING IN ANY WAY OUT
 * OF THE USE OF THIS SOFTWARE, EVEN IF ADVISED OF THE POSSIBILITY OF
 * SUCH DAMAGE.
 * ====================================================================
 *
 * This software consists of voluntary contributions made by many
 * individuals on behalf of the Apache Software Foundation and was
 * originally based on software copyright (c) 1999, Lotus
 * Development Corporation., http://www.lotus.com.  For more
 * information on the Apache Software Foundation, please see
 * <http://www.apache.org/>.
 */

// Needed JAXP classes
import javax.xml.parsers.ParserConfigurationException;
import javax.xml.transform.*;
import javax.xml.transform.stream.*;

// Needed java classes
import java.io.FileInputStream;
import java.io.IOException;
import java.io.FileNotFoundException;

// Needed SAX classes
import org.xml.sax.SAXException;

public class simpleTrAX
{
  public static void main(String argv[]) throws
         TransformerException, TransformerConfigurationException,
         IOException, SAXException,
         ParserConfigurationException, FileNotFoundException
  {
    System.out.println("\n\n==== exampleSimple ====");
    try {
        exampleSimple1("collection4-frag.xml", "tryTrAX.xsl");
```

```
    } catch( Exception ex ) {
        handleException(ex);
    }

    System.out.println("\n==== done! ====");
  }

  /**
   * Show the simplest possible transformation from system id
   * to output stream.
   */
  public static void exampleSimple1(String sourceID, String xslID)
    throws TransformerException, TransformerConfigurationException
  {
    // Create a transform factory instance.
    TransformerFactory tfactory = TransformerFactory.newInstance();

    // Create a transformer for the stylesheet.
    Transformer transformer
      = tfactory.newTransformer(new StreamSource(xslID));

    // Transform the source XML to System.out.
    transformer.transform( new StreamSource(sourceID),
                           new StreamResult(System.out));
  }

  private static void  handleException( Exception ex ) {
    System.out.println("EXCEPTION: " );
    ex.printStackTrace();

    if( ex instanceof TransformerConfigurationException ) {
      System.out.println();
      System.out.println("Internal exception: " );
      Throwable ex1=((TransformerConfigurationException)ex).getException();
      ex1.printStackTrace();

       if( ex1 instanceof SAXException ) {
          Exception ex2=((SAXException)ex1).getException();
          System.out.println("Internal sub-exception: " );
          ex2.printStackTrace();
      }
    }
  } // handleException

}
```

In contrast to the earlier JAXP example, for TrAX, we need to import portions of the `javax.xml.transform` package.

```
import javax.xml.parsers.ParserConfigurationException;
import javax.xml.transform.*;
import javax.xml.transform.stream.*;
```

We also need to indicate our XML source, a file in this case, as well as the source of transformation instructions, an XSLT stylesheet, in this case:

```
exampleSimple1("collection4-frag.xml", "tryTrAX.xsl");
```

The `exampleSimple1` method creates a `transformer` that knows specifically how to deal with streams (the XSLT stylesheet, in our case):

```
    TransformerFactory tfactory = TransformerFactory.newInstance();
    Transformer transformer
      = tfactory.newTransformer(new StreamSource(xslID));
```

Finally, we invoke the `transformer` on a particular input file in order to produce a `StreamResult` sent to standard output:

```
    transformer.transform( new StreamSource(sourceID),
                           new StreamResult(System.out));
```

Notice that this example uses `StreamSource` for XML instance and XSLT stylesheet and `StreamResult` for the output of the transformations. Boag's original example illustrates many more permutations of input, transformation instructions, and output.

To compile and run the Java code, we need a different batch file, which we'll call `trax-it.bat`. This is similar to `jaxp-it.bat` shown in Listing 9-5, except that it uses `xalan.jar` packaged in the Xalan 2.0 D5 release and `xerces.jar` in place of `crimson.jar`. In other words, from the JAXP 1.1 release, we'll use only the pure JAXP API found in `jaxp.jar`.

The TrAX batch file differs from those presented in the SAX and DOM chapters in that it is not based on using `xmlsetup.bat`. Notice the special classpath setup required. If you use a later version of JAXP or of Xalan, the JAR list may be different. You'll need to modify this .bat file for your environment.

Listing 9-10 Batch File for JAXP TrAX Compiling and Running (trax-it.bat)

```
@echo off

REM Adjust for your locations.
set JBIN=C:\JAVA\jdk1.3\bin
set JLIB=C:\JAVA\jdk1.3\lib
set JAXP=C:\XML\JAXP\jaxp-1.1ea2
set XALAN=C:\XML\APACHE\xalan-j_2_0_D05

REM Note Xalan specifics, such as xerces.jar instead of crimson.jar.
set XALAN_JARS=%XALAN%\bin\xerces.jar;%XALAN%\bin\xalan.jar
set TRAX_EX=%XALAN%\samples\trax
set JAXP_JARS=%JAXP%\jaxp.jar
```

```
REM Include parser and processor in your classpath.
set classpath=.;%JLIB%;%JAXP_JARS%;%XALAN_JARS%

REM Compile program
%JBIN%\javac simpleTrAX.java

REM Run program
@echo on
%JBIN%\java simpleTrAX
@echo off
```

We compile and run the `simpleTrAX.java` example simply by the name of the batch file:

```
C:> trax-it
```

The result, shown in Lisitng 9-11, is an HTML page that contains the name `Mark Lewisohn`, extracted from `collection4-frag.xml` by applying the stylesheet `tryTrAX.xsl` invoked by the transformer in `simpleTrAX.java`. This output may not seem impressive, considering all of the pieces we had to show. However, we have the framework in place for performing other transformations with different XML instances and XSLT stylesheets as sources. We can also can see how this could be extended to other kinds of `StreamSource` and `StreamResult` objects. Notice that we did not need a server to invoke the XSLT processor; this job is handled by TrAX. Furthermore, since the Java code does not specify which XSLT processor to use (even though the batch file does), we're on our way to a better transformation abstraction.

Listing 9-11 Transformation Output

```
==== exampleSimple ====
<html>
<head>
<META http-equiv="Content-Type" content="text/html; charset=UTF-8">
<title>TrAX Test</title>
</head>
<body>
<h1>Mark Lewisohn</h1>
</body>
</html>

==== done! ====
```

JAXP Summary

The Java API for Processing (JAXP, JSR 63) is primarily an abstraction layer for SAX, DOM, and XSLT access that promotes parser and processor independence. JAXP is most useful in rapidly changing development or deployment environments in which you anticipate the need to change XML parsers or XSLT processors. JAXP is part of Sun's Java XML Pack and is likely to become part of J2SE and J2EE. However, it is only an abstraction layer; it requires DOM and/or SAX parser and provides little beyond parser and processor independence.

SAX vs. DOM vs. JDOM vs. JAXP—Who Wins?

In the last three chapters, we covered SAX, DOM, JDOM, and JAXP. Which parsing methodology is best? The answer is: It depends on your needs. Perhaps a better question is, *under which circumstances is one approach better than another?* In Table 9-5, we attempt to answer this question by listing the pros and the cons for each of the four parsing and processing technologies. Comparing them will help you select the best solution for your application. However, it's best to be familiar with each approach and not automatically select the one with which you become most familiar. Each has its own merits.

TABLE 9-5 The Pros and Cons of SAX, DOM, JDOM, and JAXP

Technologies	*Advantages*	*Disadvantages*
SAX	• Lightweight and fast, so well-suited for extracting select information chunks from a very large document (or stream), such as searching for elements or processing large database files • Well-suited as a filter in a chain of processes (e.g., producer/consumer pipelines) • Useful for applications that need to perform flow-through parsing for storage in a database • Event handler approach, with events firing in sequential document order • Entire document never needs to be in memory, so well-suited for devices with limited memory • Can accommodate documents larger than physical memory • Flexible API; does not impose any particular data structures • Useful if you intend to build your own application-specific object model (and don't need the DOM view of your documents)	• Usually inappropriate for applications in which entire document needs to be in memory at one time • Callback does not often provide the entire context you might need, so developer must create a structure to hold context information (e.g., a Java stack) • Requires more application-specific data structures • No child or sibling callbacks, so you often need to process an entire subhierarchy at one time • Not useful for modifying the original document or for writing XML (although writer extensions are available) • No random access; no lookahead or behind (parsing order is fixed)

continued

TABLE 9-5 The Pros and Cons of SAX, DOM, JDOM, and JAXP (*continued*)

	Advantages	*Disadvantages*
SAX (*cont.*)	• Implemented in many major languages: Java, Python, perl, C++, COM, and others (but not JavaScript) • Many SAX parsers exist, so applications can switch parsers with little change (e.g., by specifying a different parser class name) • Nearly all XML parser vendors support SAX both because it is in the public domain and because it is much simpler to implement than is the DOM • Very good DTD access and support (SAX2) • Will be integrated into JDK 1.4	
DOM	• Language independent, that is, at least in theory • Bindings for Java and ECMAScript are available from W3C; bindings for C, C++, perl, and Python are available from other sources • Useful to dynamically update, add, or remove content, elements, attributes, or style • Well-suited for XML editor or other applications that need to manipulate the entire document at once • Provides a highly structured and complete model of any XML (or HTML) document • Useful when you need persistent structures • Can navigate nodes, looking for specific information or hierarchy of nodes • More natural fit for relational databases	• Requires entire document to be read before anything can be accessed, so not well-suited for large documents or devices with limited memory • Heavyweight and slow • Sequence of steps to read the document and change elements is not intuitive • Complex model and not extremely object oriented • Many modules defined in lots of separate W3C specifications • Model is so generic that it is not efficient for many cases • Language independence means the DOM reinvents many features that are built in to Java, so Java developers may find it counterintuitive • Often need to copy information from DOM nodes into application-specific structures, which also hinders efficiency • Two-pass processing is likely: first pass to build the DOM, second pass to traverse it for application specifics • Access to DTD is limited but most implementations have extensions for this • At the time of writing, no standard DOM module for serializing XML exists, although DOM Level 3 Abstract Schema and Load and Save specification will address this need, and most parser vendors have implemented their own (non-standard) writer interfaces

TABLE 9-5 *(continued)*

	Advantages	*Disadvantages*
JDOM	• For Java developers, JDOM is much more intuitive, object-oriented, and Java-centric (takes advantage of Java language features such as method overloading and Collections) • Fewer lines of code needed for most tasks • Less need for developer to know the details of DOM or SAX (most of the time) • Facilitates XML parser and XSLT processor independence • Designed for easy and efficient reading, manipulation, and writing of XML documents • `XMLOutputter` class provides parser-independent serialization solution • Can be much faster than DOM or SAX for some tasks • Supports DOM Level 2, SAX 2.0, XML Schema, JAXP, and TrAX • XPath support in progress (from Jaxen.org) • Targeted for Java 2 Platform Standard Edition (J2SE) and Java 2 Platform Enterprise Edition (J2EE)	• Useless for non-Java developers • Only an abstraction layer; requires DOM and/or SAX parser • Not yet a Java standard, although likely to be wrapped into JAXP eventually (JSR 102) • Doesn't handle all situations, so developers may need to drop down to SAX or DOM level anyway (e.g., traversal is easier with the DOM directly) • May not adequately address other XML technology because the JDOM model makes some simplifying assumptions
JAXP[a]	• Primarily an abstraction layer for SAX, DOM, and XSLT access • Facilitates XML parser and XSLT processor independence • Useful in a rapidly changing development or deployment environment in which you anticipate the need to change XML parsers or XSLT processors • Supports DOM Level 2, SAX 2.0, XML Schema, and TrAX • Part of Sun's Java XML Pack; likely to become part of J2SE and J2EE; see JSR 63	• Useless for non-Java developers • Only an abstraction layer; requires DOM and/or SAX parser (only includes 6 classes that aren't part of DOM or SAX) • Provides nothing beyond parser and processor independence • Not yet a Java standard

a. Some of you may wonder if it even makes sense to include JAXP in this comparison since it is primarily an abstraction layer for SAX, DOM, and XSLT access.

XSLT and XPath, the subject of chapter 11, can also be a viable alternative to parsing, especially in cases where sophisticated processing is necessary and performance is not a major criterion.

For Further Exploration

Articles

XML in Java: Document models, Part 1: Performance, Dennis M. Sosnoski [compares DOM, JDOM, dom4j, ElectricXML, and XML Pull Parser]
http://www-106.ibm.com/developerworks/xml/library/x-injava/index.html

xmlhack Search for JDOM
http://xmlhack.com/search.php?q=JDOM

Introduction to JDOM, Part 1, Shari Jones
http://www.sys-con.com/xml/article.cfm?id=221

Introduction to JDOM, Part 2, Shari Jones
http://www.sys-con.com/xml/source.cfm?id=242

Simplify XML programming with JDOM, Wes Biggs and Harry Evans [includes links to other JDOM articles]
http://www-106.ibm.com/developerworks/java/library/j-jdom/

xmlhack Search for JAXP
http://xmlhack.com/search.php?q=JAXP

All about JAXP, JAXP 1.0, Brett McLaughlin
http://www-106.ibm.com/developerworks/library/x-jaxp/

JAXP Revisited, JAXP 1.1, Brett McLaughlin
http://www-106.ibm.com/developerworks/library/x-jaxp1.html

When less is more: a compact toolkit for parsing and manipulating XML, Graham Glass [ElectricXML article]
http://www-106.ibm.com/developerworks/xml/library/x-elexml/index.html

Books

Processing XML with Java, Elliotte Rusty Harold
http://www.ibiblio.org/xml/books/xmljava/

Java and XML, Second Edition, Brett McLaughlin
http://www.oreilly.com/catalog/javaxml2/

Resources

Sun's Java Technology and XML home page [key site; links to separate home pages for all released Sun XML APIs: JAXP, JAXB, JAXM, JAXR, JAX-RPC]
http://java.sun.com/xml/index.html

All JSRs (Java Specification Requests) [search for "XML"]
http://jcp.org/jsr/all/index.jsp

All XML Java Specification Requests
http://jcp.org/jsr/tech/xml.jsp

JSR-102: JDOM 1.0 [submitted as JSR-000102]
http://jcp.org/jsr/detail/102.jsp

JSR-063: Java API for XML Processing (JAXP 1.1)
http://jcp.org/jsr/detail/063.jsp

JSR-005: XML Parsing Specification (JAXP 1.0)
http://jcp.org/jsr/detail/005.jsp

JSR-067: Java API for XML Messaging (JAXM)
http://jcp.org/jsr/detail/067.jsp

JSR-093: Java APIs for XML Registries (JAXR)
http://jcp.org/jsr/detail/093.jsp

JSR-101: Java APIs for XML-based RPC (JAX-RPC)
http://jcp.org/jsr/detail/101.jsp

JSR-173: Streaming API for XML (S+AX)
http://jcp.org/jsr/detail/173.jsp

JSR-031: XML Data Binding Specification (JAXB) [formerly Project Adelard]
http://jcp.org/jsr/detail/031.jsp

JSR-057: Long Term JavaBeans Persistence [serialization to XML]
http://jcp.org/jsr/detail/057.jsp

Robin Cover's JAXP page
http://xml.coverpages.org/jaxp.html

Sun's Announcement of JAXP, JAMX, and JAXB
http://java.sun.com/pr/2000/12/pr001204-01.html/

Sun's Java Software Platforms for XML [diagram]
http://java.sun.com/xml/xmljavaapi.html

Apache: Transformation API for XML (TrAX)
http://xml.apache.org/xalan-j/trax.html

Apache: Xalan 2 Basic Usage Patterns (TrAX, DOM, SAX)
http://xml.apache.org/xalan-j/usagepatterns.html

dom4j—XML framework for Java [API for XML, XPath and XSLT using Java Collections Framework with full support for DOM SAX and JAXP]
http://dom4j.org/

ElectricXML [another Java API alternative; DTD-less]
http://www.themindelectric.com/products/xml/xml.html

SAXPath: Simple API for XPath
http://saxpath.org/

Jaxen: Java XPath Engine
http://jaxen.org/

ebXML home page
http://www.ebxml.org/

CenterPoint/XML: C++ SAX2 and DOM1 Implementation
http://www.cpointc.com/XML/

Sun's Adelard is a robust alternative to SAX and DOM
http://www.javaworld.com/javaworld/javaone00/j1-00-adelard.html

JDOM: JDOM home page, Jason Hunter and Brett McLaughlin
http://jdom.org/

JDOM: JDOM Documentation [including articles, presentations and tutorials; major starting point]
http://jdom.org/downloads/docs.html

JDOM: JDOM API Documentation
http://www.jdom.org/docs/apidocs/index.html

JAXP: Java API for XML Processing Home Page
http://java.sun.com/xml/jaxp/index.html

JAXP: Java API for XML Parsing 1.1.1 JavaDocs
http://java.sun.com/xml/jaxp/dist/1.1/docs/api/

JAXP: JAXP FAQ (unofficial but extremely valuable and up-to-date)
http://www.apache.org/~edwingo/jaxp-faq.html

Software

Java XML Pack [bundles JAXP, JAXM, JAXR, JAX-RPC, and eventually JAXB in a single download]
http://java.sun.com/xml/downloads/javaxmlpack.html

Java Web Services Developer Pack (WSDP) [Java XML Pack plus Web Services tools]
http://java.sun.com/webservices/webservicespack.html

Tutorials

Overview of the APIs, Eric Armstrong [great intro to JAXP, JAXB, JAXM, JAX-RPC, JDOM; part of JAXP Tutorial]
http://java.sun.com/xml/jaxp/dist/1.1/docs/tutorial/overview/3_apis.html

Working with XML: The Java API for Xml Processing (JAXP) Tutorial, Eric Armstrong [online version, updated regularly]
http://java.sun.com/xml/jaxp/dist/1.1/docs/tutorial/index.html

Working with XML: The Java API for Xml Processing (JAXP) Tutorial, Eric Armstrong [PDF version]
http://java.sun.com/xml/jaxp-1.1/docs/tutorial/xmltutorial-1_1.pdf

Part III

Transforming and Displaying XML

Chapter 10

Styling XML Using CSS2

In this chapter, first we'll learn the basics of Cascading Style Sheets, Level 2, a powerful mechanism for separating presentation from content, and how it is used to style HTML. Then we'll see how to apply the CSS2 Recommendation to rendering XML in a fairly simple way, within certain functional limitations. In the next chapter, we'll see a much more powerful technology called Extensible Stylesheet Language Transformations (XSLT), which is considerably more complicated than CSS. But don't skip this chapter! Sometimes the simple approach of CSS2 is all that you need.

What Is CSS?

Cascading Style Sheets, Level 2 (CSS2—*http://www.w3.org/TR/REC-CSS2/*) became a W3C Recommendation in May 1998. It was a significant improvement over the also impressive Cascading Style Sheets, Level 1 (CSS1) Recommendation from December 1996 (subsequently revised in January 1999). Both specs facilitate the separation of presentation (appearance) from structure (content), which immediately suggests a good fit with XML. Fourth-generation browsers generally support only CSS1, but Netscape 6 and IE 5.5 (to a lesser degree) support CSS2. Prior to Netscape 4.0 and IE 4.0, browser support for CSS was too limited to be useful. The differences between CSS1 and CSS2 are described in Appendix B of the Cascading Style Sheets, Level 2 Specification, 12 May 1998 (see *http://www.w3.org/TR/REC-CSS2/changes.html*).

The abstract of the CSS2 Recommendation clearly states the purpose of CSS2 and how it extends CSS1 capabilities:

> CSS2 is a style sheet language that allows authors and users to attach style (e.g., fonts, spacing, and aural cues) to structured documents (e.g., HTML documents and XML applications). By separating the presentation style of documents from the content of documents, CSS2 simplifies Web authoring and site maintenance. CSS2 builds on CSS1 . . . and, with very few exceptions, all valid CSS1 style sheets are

> valid CSS2 style sheets. CSS2 supports media-specific style sheets so that authors may tailor the presentation of their documents to visual browsers, aural devices, printers, braille devices, handheld devices, etc.

CSS permits Web developers to control various presentational properties, such as:

- Font family, size, color, variant, decoration, style, and weight
- Line and text spacing, line height
- Margins, padding, borders, and text indentation
- Background colors and images (much better than in HTML: transparent, repeat, scroll, etc.)
- Link rendering
- Includes at least nine different unit types:
  - *Absolute* units: `mm`, `cm`, `in`, `pt` (72 points = 1 in.), `pc` (1 pica = 12 pts) vs.
  - *Relative* to specific font: `px` (pixels, relative to the screen resolution), `em` (1 em = point size of a given font), `ex` (the "x"-height); also percentage.

But this list is just the tip of the presentation iceberg!

Complete lists of CSS properties can be found in WebReview's Style Sheet Reference Guide by Eric Myer and in Zvon's CSS2 Reference and Tutorial (*http://www.webreview.com/style/index.shtml* and *http://zvon.org/xxl/CSS2Reference/Output/index.html*).

There are many benefits to using CSS. Although some pertain primarily to HTML, many apply to XML as well:

- *Better control:* More precise control of all aspects of presentation using terms and concepts from the desktop publishing industry.
- *Simplification:* Content writer doesn't have to be as concerned with presentation details.
- *Centralized design/site maintenance:* Designers can define the look of an entire site in one file (or small hierarchy of files).
- *Faster downloads:* Style sheets are cached, so your house style is downloaded only once. Since style info is not directly embedded, in contrast to using many instances of the `<font>` tag (which is deprecated in HTML 4.0), HTML documents can be shorter.
- *Flexibility:* Individual author can partially or completely override a site's style.
- *Resolution independence:* Designers can use relative measurements for layout.
- *Media-specific rendering:* Designers can define different style sheets for various media types (screen, printing, projectors, aural browsers, etc.).
- *Better printing:* Authors are not completely at the mercy of how a given browser decides to print your pages.

- *Reader control:* Users can still influence presentation of documents using CSS, such as requesting larger fonts.
- *Compatibility:* Old browsers ignore style information.
- *Accessibility:* People with disabilities (especially vision impairments) have better access to your pages, such as by having their own style sheet that applies larger font sizes.

CSS Basics: Declarations, Selectors, and Use with HTML

In this section, we present the basics of CSS syntax with examples based on HTML elements. This foundation is necessary before we can discuss how to apply this technology to XML documents.

Rules, Declarations, Selectors, Properties, and Values

A CSS **rule** (or rule set) consists of a selector followed by a declaration block, delimited by curly brackets ({}). A **selector** is generally based on element names; Table 10-1 in the section "CSS2 Selectors" shows many variations of selectors. A **declaration block** is composed of zero or more declarations, separated by semicolons. Each **declaration** is a colon-separated pair of **property** and **value.** If a value contains multiple words, they are usually space separated, except for lists of font families. The general CSS rule syntax is shown in Figure 10-1.

Listing 10-1 shows a complete style sheet with a number of rules for HTML elements. For example, the first rule

```
body {
      font-size: 12pt;
      font-family: "Times New Roman", serif;
      border: thick double silver;
      padding: 10px;
    }
```

uses the selector body (which corresponds to the HTML element <body>) and has a declaration block consisting of four declarations, one each for the properties font-size, font-family, border, and padding. The value of the font-size property is 12pt (12 points). In most cases, white space is insignificant in CSS. A notable exception is that there must not be a space between the value (12) and its unit of

```
selector  { property: value; property: value; ...}
             |- declaration-| |- declaration-|
           |---------- declaration block ----------|
|-------------------- Rule ----------------------|
```

FIGURE 10-1 Anatomy of a CSS Rule

measure (pt). The font-family declaration contains two values for this property: the first is a multiword value, so it must be quoted; the second is a generic family name that will be used if the the specific font, Times New Roman, is not available. The border declaration shown is actually an abbreviation for three declarations, which define three properties:

```
border-width: thick;
border-style: double;
border-color: silver;
```

The padding declaration defines a 10-pixel buffer inside the page.

Rules for specific elements override the rule for body. In this case, elements h1, h2, p, pre, and a each have a custom style defined. (More about the a element and the .myClass rule shortly.) Therefore the default font size of 12 becomes 24 for h1, 18 for h2, and 14 for pre.

Listing 10-1 CSS Level 2 Style Sheet with HTML Elements (tester.css)

```
body {
      font-size: 12pt;
      font-family: "Times New Roman", serif;
      border: thick double silver;
      padding: 10px;
     }
h1   {
      font-size: 24pt;
      font-family: Arial, sans-serif;
      font-weight: bold;
      text-align: center;
      color: #9966cc;
      background-color: white;
     }
h2   {
      font-size: 18pt;
      font-family: Verdana, sans-serif;
      font-weight: bold;
      font-style: italic;
      text-indent: 32pt; margin-top: 10pt;
      background: yellow; color: navy;
      border: thin solid red;
      border-width: 3px;
     }
p    {
      font-size: 12pt;
      font-family: "Comic sans MS", fantasy;
      text-indent: 0.5in;
     }
pre  {
      font-size: 14pt;
      font-family: "New Century", monospace;
      font-weight: normal;
     }
```

```
/* Colon in the selector denotes pseudo-classes.
   Netscape 4 doesn't support hover.
 */
a             {text-decoration: none;}
a:link        {color: red; background-color: #cccccc; font-size: 150%; }
a:visited     {color: blue; background-color: white; font-size: 75%;}
a:active      {color: teal; background-color: black; }
a:hover       {color: white; background-color: black; }

/* Define class myClass for use with HTML class attribute. */
.myClass    {
             color: White;
             background-color:  Fuchsia;
             font-family: Courier, monospace;
             border: solid black;
             border-width : medium;
             margin: 10%;
            }
```

We can make several observations about using CSS, some of which can be concluded from the example, and some that are useful tips:

- More than one declaration can appear on a line.
- A semicolon separates each declaration, regardless of whether they appear on one line or multiple lines.
- Colors can be specified in `#RRGGBB` notation (e.g., `#9966cc`) or as one of a small set of sixteen case-insensitive color words. The sixteen color names are taken from the Windows VGA palette: aqua, black, blue, fuchsia, gray, green, lime, maroon, navy, olive, purple, red, silver, teal, white, and yellow.
- Whenever you use a `color` property, you should also declare a `background-color` property.
- Whenever you specify a particular font via the `font-family` property, you should also indicate one of five fallback generic font families: `monospace` (e.g., `Courier`), `serif` (e.g., `Times`), `sans-serif` (e.g., `Arial`), `cursive`, or `fantasy` (e.g., Comic Sans Ms).
- Don't forget braces, colon, or semicolon. *A single error causes the entire style rule to be silently ignored.* (This is completely unlike error reporting with XML parsing.) I find it useful to make small changes one at a time.
- The last semicolon in a declaration list is optional, but I recommend it so you can add more declarations later without changing it.
- Use C style `/* comment characters */` to block out any portion of a style sheet (rule, declaration, value, etc.).
- To define rules for several related elements (e.g., `h1`, `h2`, `h3`), first define what they all have in common and then define how they differ, (e.g., `h1, h2, h3 {font-family: cursive;} h2 {color: red;}`)

- Less is more, so don't overspecify. Use lots of rules for `body` and only a few for other elements (in general).
- It's useful to have a small, separate style sheet that can be linked in place of your more complex style sheet to isolate changes.
- Avoid quotes in style definitions except in multiword font names:
  `h3 { font-family: Geneva, Arial, "New Century", sans-serif; }`
- When specifying units (point size, inches, etc.), do not use a period after the abbreviation and do not insert a space between the number and the unit:
  `h4 { font-size: 12pt ; text-indent: 1.3cm ; }`
- Read about Inheritance and Cascading Order in the CSS2 specification (*http://www.w3.org/TR/REC-CSS2/cascade.html*).

The `a` anchor element has a so-called *pseudo-class*, which permits us to define different styles for different link states. In Listing 10-1, in all cases of the anchor element, we drop the underline from the link (because of the declaration):

```
a {text-decoration: none}
```

Then we define three color combinations for the normal (`a:link`), previously visited (`a:visited`), and activated (`a:active`) link states. We also declare a style that applies when the mouse pointer hovers over the link (`a:hover`), which works fine in Netscape 6.x and IE 4.x and above, but not for older browser versions.

The declaration for the selector named `".myClass"` needs some explanation. This is clearly not the name of an HTML element. It's an *arbitrary* class name that we can associate with any HTML element by using the `class` attribute that is available for every element in HTML, like this:

```
<anyElement class="myClass">some content</anyElement>
```

Use of the `class` attribute causes the style defined for the class named (`myClass`) to be applied to the content of whichever element contains the `class` attribute. In other words, the text "some content" would appear in white with a fuchsia background, monospace font, and so on.

It's important to note that within the CSS rule, the name must be preceded by a period to signify that a class name will follow, but inside the HTML start tag, you must use the class name *without* a period.

Margin, border, and padding properties are easier to understand if we see a graphic representation of the CSS Box Model (*http://www.w3.org/TR/REC-CSS2/box.html*), shown in Figure 10-2. Border, margin, and padding widths are specified in units (pixels, inches, etc.). Border and content are visible; margin and padding

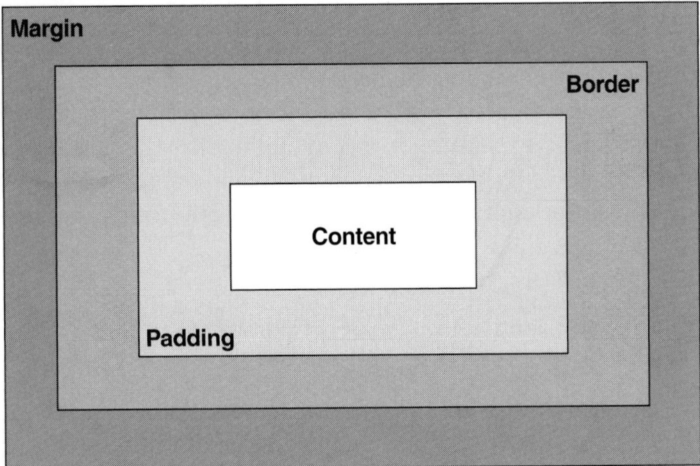

FIGURE 10-2 CSS box model

are not. Therefore border has other properties such as `border-color` and `border-style`, as we've already seen.

Inheritance and Cascading

Inheritance and Cascading are important concepts to CSS. **Inheritance** means that elements tend to inherit property values set by parent elements (those that contain them) unless children explicitly override these values.

- Child elements inherit rules defined for their parents (e.g., `em` inherits from `h2`, `b` inherits from `p`, etc.), if the child has no overriding rule defined.
- Most elements inherit from `body`, so if you want to leverage inheritance considerably, make your `body` rule elaborate.
- Specific rules always override general rules (e.g., `h1.someClass` beats `h1`).
- Order of (unrelated) rules does not matter. However, when multiple rules apply to the same element, later rules win. Therefore, general rules are usually placed before specific rules.
- Rules for more specific contextual selectors override less specific ones.
- Rules embedded in the document (generally) override rules from a linked style sheet. (See the next two sections.)
- Inline elements inherit from the block elements that contain them. Inline elements include `a`, `b`, `em`, `i`, `img`, `span`, and `strong`. Most other elements are block elements, such as `body`, `p`, `div`, `h1`, `h2`, `ul`, and `table`.

So what does "cascading" mean in the term CSS? It refers to the cascading of style sheets from different sources—the browser's defaults, the author's page, and potentially the user—that may influence the document's presentation. Rules are defined to resolve conflicts. **Cascading** refers to the merging of more than one style sheet (from the Web site, the specific Web page, the user, and the browser) to yield one style definition for any element in a given context.

The general rule is: *Author wins over user, and user wins over browser.* However, the `!important` (exclamation point followed by `important`) symbol can be appended to a rule to insist on its use. This is intended to be used primarily by the user, not the author. For example, someone with poor vision might define this style sheet rule:

```
BODY {
     font: 24pt bold sans-serif; !important
     }
```

which will override page author font styles. (How a user establishes a personal style sheet is browser dependent.) One algorithm for resolving conflicts is:

1. Find all rules that apply.
2. Sort the rules by explicit weight.
3. Sort by origin (designer, user).
4. Sort by specificity.
5. Sort by order specified in the document (later rules win).

For a much more detailed treatment of inheritance, cascading, and all CSS2 concepts, refer to *Cascading Style Sheets, Designing for the Web, Second Edition* (Lie and Bos, 1999—*http://cseng.aw.com/book/0,3828,0201596253,00.html*. An excellent overview of CSS Level 2 excerpted from this book is online: *http://www.w3.org/Style/LieBos2e/enter/*. Sample chapters from the first edition (based on CSS Level 1) are online: *http://www.awlonline.com/cseng/titles/0-201-41998-X/liebos/*.

Embedded CSS Style Sheet in HTML

CSS style sheets can be either directly inserted in HTML pages or referenced by means of a link to an external style sheet.

If you want to directly include the style sheet in an HTML document, it must be embedded in the `<head>` element. All rules must be enclosed in a `<style>` element with the attribute `type` set to `"text/css"` as shown in Listing 10-2. Optional comment delimiters surround the rules to protect them from being rendered by very old browsers; in reality, these delimiters aren't necessary for fourth-generation browsers and above. If you use the comment to hide the style sheet, you must not add words such as `"hiding"` and `"end hiding"`. I recommend against using the comment delimiters, unless you anticipate users with *very* old browsers.

Listing 10-2 Embedded CSS Using <style> Element

```
<head>
<title>Testing CSS</title>
<style type="text/css">
<!--
p      {font-size: 24pt; font-family: "Courier", monospace;
        text-indent: 124pt; color: red}

div    {text-indent: 0em; margin-left: 6em; margin-right: 6em;
        border: solid thin black; padding: 5px;}

UL UL {  /* nested list */
        list-style-type: circle;
       }
-->
</style>
</head>
```

External CSS Style Sheet

Alternatively, a style sheet may reside in an external file, in which case there should be no HTML markup, just the CSS rules with no heading as shown in Listing 10-3. This is exactly what appeared as the content of the `<style>` element in the previous example. In general, this is far preferable to embedding the style sheet directly in HTML because it makes it possible for multiple documents to share style information, something that is highly desirable if you're defining style for an entire Web site, or even a small collection of pages.

Listing 10-3 External Style Sheet as a Separate File

```
p      {font-size: 24pt; font-family: "Courier", monospace;
        text-indent: 124pt; color: red}

div    {text-indent: 0em; margin-left: 6em; margin-right: 6em;
        border: solid thin black; padding: 5px;}
       }

UL UL {  /* nested list */
        list-style-type: circle;
       }
```

In fact, linking to external style sheets does not prevent you from directly adding style to the `<head>` element. If you use both methods, definitions in the directly embedded style sheet that have the same selector as those in the referenced style sheet will override the linked definitions. This gives you the ability to define a house style and then specialize it for sections of your site.

Associating External CSS with HTML

How do you reference an external style sheet? The CSS Recommendation describes the use of the `<link>` element to associate style sheets with an HTML document (*http://www.w3.org/TR/REC-CSS2/intro.html#q1*). Set the `type` attribute to `"text/css"` and set the `href` attribute to the relative path to the external CSS file. The `rel` attribute should always be set to `"stylesheet"` when using CSS. For example, suppose the complete style sheet from Listing 10-1 is named `tester.css` and we want to reference it from an HTML file named `tester.html`. In the HTML document, within the <head> element, we add a `<link>` element that references the style sheet:

```
<link rel="stylesheet" type="text/css" href="tester.css">
```

Similarly, if the style sheet is located in another directory, set the value of the `href` to a relative location:

```
<link rel="stylesheet" type="text/css" href="../styles/tester.css">
```

Listing 10-4 shows a simple HTML document (`tester.html`) that associates an external style sheet (`tester.css`). Both files are on the CD-ROM. Figure 10-3 illustrates how this page is rendered by Netscape 6; it looks very similar in Internet Explorer 5.5 and Opera 5.x.

Listing 10-4 HTML Referencing an External Style Sheet (tester.html)

```
<html>
  <head>
    <title>CSS Level 2 Tester</title>
    <link rel="stylesheet" type="text/css"
          href="tester.css" >
    <!--
    <link rel="stylesheet" type="text/css"
          href="http://www.w3.org/StyleSheets/Core/Ultramarine" >
    -->
    <!--
         See http://www.w3.org/StyleSheets/Core/ for W3C Core Styles:
         Chocolate, Midnight, Modernist, Oldstyle,
         Steely, Swiss, Traditional, and Ultramarine
    -->
  </head>
  <body>

  <h1>Heading One</h1>

  This text should simply default to the boring body style
  except for the part that is in
  <span class="myClass">myClass style</span>.
  Here's a link to the <a href="http://www.w3.org">W3C</a> and another
  link to a <a href="http://foobar.org">place that you've never visited</a>.

  <p>This is a paragraph in Comic sans MS or fantasy.</p>

  <h2>Heading Two</h2>
```

```
  <pre>This     text     is     preformatted.</pre>

  <h3>Heading Three with List</h3>

  <ul>
    <li>one</li>
    <li>two</li>
    <li style="font-family: monospace; font-weight:bold">in-line style</li>
    <li><b>bold</b></li>
    <li><i>italics</i></li>
  </ul>

  </body>
</html>
```

There are a few things worth noting in this example. We can see graphically from Figure 10-3 how the content of the element containing the `class` attribute in the line:

```
<span class="myClass">myClass style</span>.
```

is rendered according to the `.myClass` style declaration:

```
.myClass    {
             color: White;
             background-color:  Fuchsia;
             font-family: Courier, monospace;
             border: solid black;
             border-width : medium;
             margin: 10%;
            }
```

The <span> element is very useful for applying style to content that might not otherwise be enclosed in markup. In other words, it is often used with either the `class` or `style` attribute, discussed next.

In addition to the `class` attribute, HTML 4 defines another attribute called `style` that can be applied to any element. For example, the line:

```
<li style="font-family: monospace; font-weight:bold">in-line style</li>
```

defines a one-shot, localized style just for this particular `<li>` element. Notice that the value of the in-line `style` attribute is exactly like a style sheet declaration block without the brackets. Although the use of the `style` attribute doesn't leverage the reusability benefits that style sheets provide, it can be useful when you need a special style that you don't intend to reuse.

Finally, note the hand cursor pointing to the string "W3C". The style of this link is determined by the lines:

```
a              {text-decoration: none;}
a:hover        {color: white; background-color: black; }
```

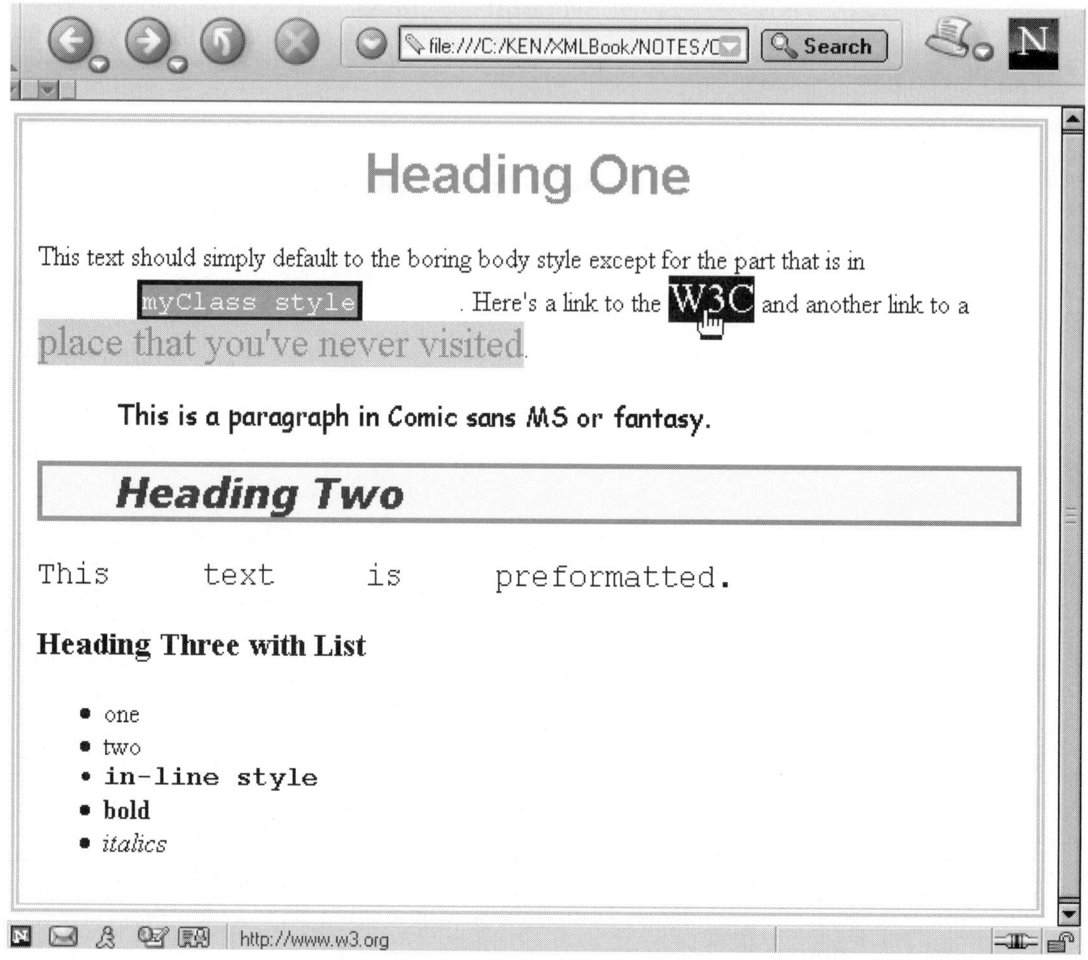

FIGURE 10-3 Display of HTML with custom style sheet in Netscape 6

since this represents the state of hovering over the link. If you compare this look to that of the other link text, "place that you've never visited", it's different because the second link has the default link state appearance, defined by the lines:

```
a            {text-decoration: none;}
a:link       {color: red; background-color: #cccccc; font-size: 150%; }
```

You can also specify a style sheet by means of a complete URL. To illustrate, let's try one of the eight so-called *W3C Core Styles* made available by the W3C. To test them online without editing anything, visit *http://www.w3.org/StyleSheets/Core/*. We can also try them with our example. Each style sheet has the basename *http://www.w3.org/StyleSheets/Core/* followed by the name of the desired style sheet: `Chocolate`, `Midnight`, `Modernist`, `Oldstyle`, `Steely`, `Swiss`, `Traditional`, and `Ultramarine`. For example, to reference the Ultramarine Core Style from `tester.html`, we simply change the `<link>` element to:

```
<link rel="stylesheet" type="text/css"
      href="http://www.w3.org/StyleSheets/Core/Ultramarine" >
```

The result of applying this W3C Core Style is shown in Figure 10-4. The difference in appearance between Figures 10-3 and 10-4 demonstrates how changing only one line in the HTML document (i.e., the `<link>` element) can dramatically change the appearance of the page. (The results are even more dramatic in color, so

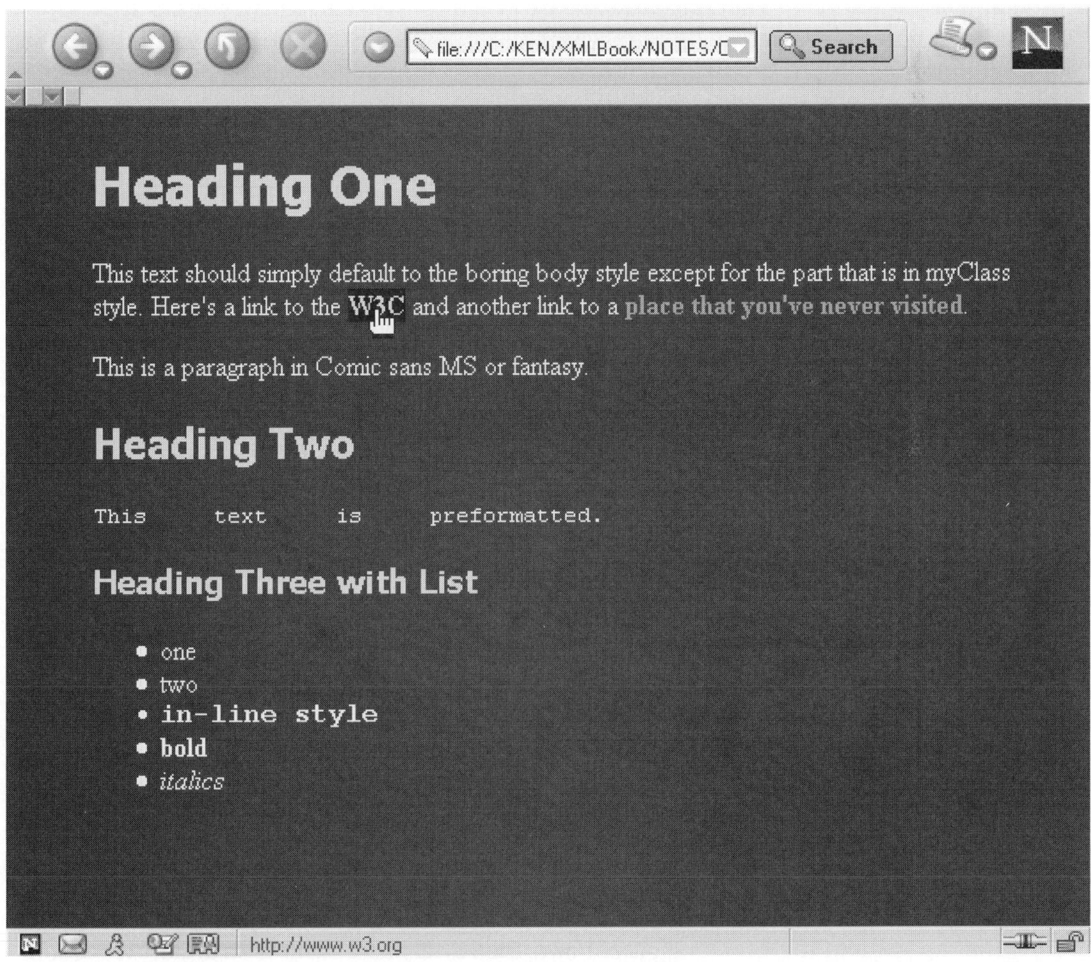

FIGURE 10-4 Display of same HTML with W3C Core Style Ultramarine

try it yourself.) It's not difficult to imagine that if you have a number of pages that link to a particular style sheet, you can alter the appearance of all of them simply by changing the *contents* of the style sheet to which they all link. This is precisely what makes CSS so powerful—the ability to alter the look of an entire Web site by modifying a single file.

CSS2 Selectors

Our example taps only a few of the possibile selectors you can use to declare a style. Table 10-1 presents the full gamut of choices; it is based on the Selectors table from the W3C CSS2 Recommendation, Section 5, Selectors (see *http://www.w3.org/TR/REC-CSS2/selector.html*; see also *http://www.webreview.com/style/css2/charts/selectors.shtml*). As you can see from the examples column, there are quite a few variations of element patterns from which you can draw. Rather than cover these now, we'll see a few different cases in the XML examples later in the chapter.

Netscape 6 vs. Internet Explorer 5.5

Throughout this chapter, we show examples that were captured as displayed in Netscape 6. After a year and a half of experimental releases called Mozilla Milestones, Netscape released Netscape 6 on November 15, 2000 (*http://home.netscape.com/browsers/6/index.html*). According to the datasheet that accompanied the release, Netscape 6 has "[u]nsurpassed support for HTML 4, CSS, XML, RDF and the DOM" (*http://home.netscape.com/browsers/6/datasheet/index.html*). A more neutral source of praise appears on the W3C's CSS home page (*http://www.w3.org/Style/CSS/*), which called Netscape "one of the best CSS implementations to date" upon its release.

At the time of this writing, Internet Explorer 5.5 does a reasonable job displaying the same examples, but the CSS2 implementation is not complete. It's likely that IE 6.0 addresses many of the shortcomings.

Style Sheet or Stylesheet?

The term "style sheet" is written as two words in the CSS2 Recommendation but as the single word "stylesheet" in the XSLT and XSL Recommendations (chapters 11 and 12). I find this terribly confusing. For example, we have the "Cascading Style Sheets, Level 2 (CSS2) Specification" and "Extensible Stylesheet Language (XSL) Version 1.0." The same distinction appears internally in these recommendations and others that are related.

In an attempt to be consistent with the W3C terminology, however, in this chapter when talking about CSS, I've used the term *style sheet* (except for the string that appears in the `<link>` element and the XML processing instruction we'll soon

TABLE 10-1 CSS2 Selectors

Selector Name	*Example Pattern*	*Description*
Grouping	`E, F, G`	Shorthand for separate declarations for elements `E`, `F`, and `G`. *Not really a selector, but relevant.*
Universal selector	`*`	Matches any element.
Type selectors	`E`	Matches any `E` element (i.e., an element of type `E`).
Descendant selectors	`E F`	Matches any `F` element that is a descendant of an `E` element.
Child selectors	`E > F`	Matches any `F` element that is a child of an element `E`.
First-child pseudo-class	`E:first-child`	Matches element `E` when `E` is the first child of its parent.
Link pseudo-classes	`E:link` `E:visited`	Matches element `E` if `E` is the source anchor of a hyperlink of which the target is not yet visited (pseudo-class `:link`) or already visited (`:visited`).

Dynamic pseudo-classes	`E:active`
	`E:hover`
	`E:focus`
		Matches `E` during certain user actions.

`:lang()` pseudo-class	`E:lang(foo)`	Matches element of type `E` if it is in (human) language `foo` (the document language specifies how language is determined).
Adjacent selectors	`E + F`	Matches any `F` element immediately preceded by an element `E`.
Attribute selectors	`E[foo]`	Matches any `E` element with the `foo` attribute set (whatever the value).
Attribute selectors (value matching)	`E[foo="warning"]`	Matches any `E` element whose `foo` attribute value is exactly equal to `"warning"`.
Attribute selectors (list of values)	`E[foo~="warning"]`	Matches any `E` element whose `foo` attribute value is a list of space-separated values, one of which is exactly equal to `"warning"`.
Attribute selectors (lang)	`E[lang|="en"]`	Matches any `E` element whose `lang` attribute has a hyphen-separated list of values beginning (from the left) with `"en"`.
Class selectors	`DIV.warning`	HTML and XHTML only. The same as `DIV[class~="warning"]`.
ID selectors	`E#myid`	Matches any `E` element ID equal to `myid`.

see). In the XSL and XSLT chapters, the single word *stylesheet* is used. These two terms are completely the same.

Using CSS with XML

Now that we've gained a reasonable understanding of CSS syntax and its use in the HTML world, we're finally ready to see what we need to do to make it apply to XML documents. The good news is that there are only a few differences:

- How to reference a style sheet
- How to attach rules to arbitrary elements
- How to use the `display` property to control line breaks

Associating CSS with XML

In June 1999, at the urging of browser vendors, W3C issued a recommendation called Associating Style Sheets with XML Documents (*http://www.w3.org/TR/xml-stylesheet/*). This brief recommendation describes the use of the `xml-stylesheet` processing instruction, again with the `type` attribute set to "`text/css`" and the `href` attribute pointing to the CSS file, an external style sheet.

```
<?xml-stylesheet type="text/css" href="../styles/slides.css"?>
```

It's also possible to reference multiple style sheets from a single XML document, as shown in the W3C document entitled How to Add Style to XML (*http://www.w3.org/Style/styling-XML*), which is an update to the section of the CSS2 spec called A Brief CSS2 Tutorial for XML (*http://www.w3.org/TR/CSS2/intro.html#q2*) (which was written before the Associating Style Sheets with XML Documents Recommendation).

```
<?xml-stylesheet href="common.css" type="text/css"?>
<?xml-stylesheet href="modern.css" title="Modern" media="screen"
  type="text/css"?>
<?xml-stylesheet href="classic.css" alternate="yes"
  title="Classic" media="screen, print" type="text/css"?>
```

In addition to covering the use of a processing instruction to reference external style sheets, the updated document discusses other options, such as embedding style sheets using the `id` attribute, inline style sheets via the `style` attribute, and using the `class` attribute.

Element Names and the Display Property

The first of the two other details you need to know to use CSS with XML is that you must use your own element names for the selectors in each rule. This makes sense because in any given XML vocabulary there are no HTML elements to use as selectors (except, as we'll soon see, when we reference elements from the XHTML namespace). All the CSS selector variations shown in Table 10-1 apply except ones involving classnames, since `class` is an attribute in XHTML, but not in XML. Since XML is case-sensitive, it's important to use the exact element names in your style sheet.

The other essential point is much less obvious than the first, but it also makes sense. Since XML treats white space as significant by default, we need to specify exactly which elements should be followed by newlines and which should not. This is accomplished by using the `display` property, set to either `block` when you want a newline or `inline` when you don't. For example, the following rules state that a `CD` element will be followed by a newline, whereas the `Remastered` element will be displayed inline, so multiple occurrences of `Remastered` elements will appear on the same line:

```
CD          {display:block; color: blue; text-indent: 4em;}
Remastered  {display:inline; font-style:italic; margin-left: 4em;}
```

Rendering Example of XML with CSS

How can we use CSS to render our XML document? Let's first experiment with a very crude style sheet. In Listing 10-5, we revisit our running example of the CD and book collection, this time showing a more developed instance containing three `Book` elements and three `CD` elements. Note that the file `collection5-0.xml` includes an `xml-stylesheet` processing instruction that associates a very basic style sheet named `collection5-0.css`, shown in Listing 10-6, with this particular XML document. The same style sheet could be referenced from any number of XML instances, or individual XML documents could override this style sheet by specifying their own.

Note the XHTML namespace that has been added to the document root element, `Collection`:

```
xmlns:xhtml="http://www.w3.org/1999/xhtml"
```

This enables any child element to (optionally) reference the XHTML 1.0 namespace (via the `xhtml` prefix), as in:

```
<xhtml:h1>Ken's Collection</xhtml:h1>
```

which specifies a large heading. The example also takes advantage of the XHTML anchor element to identify hypertext links for each `Book` or `CD` element, such as:

```
<xhtml:a href="http://www.amazon.com/exec/obidos/ASIN/0600600335/o/
qid=979102681/sr=8-1/ref=aps_sr_b_1_1/103-4097284-9855030">
Complete Beatles Chronicle, The</xhtml:a>
```

Listing 10-5 XML Instance with CSS Style Sheet Reference (collection5-0.xml)

```
<?xml version="1.0" standalone="no"?>
<!DOCTYPE Collection SYSTEM "collection5.dtd">

<?xml-stylesheet type="text/css" href="collection5-0.css"?>

<!-- Collection consists of Book and CD elements in no particular order. -->
<Collection version="2" xmlns:xhtml="http://www.w3.org/1999/xhtml" >
  <xhtml:h1>Ken's Collection</xhtml:h1>
  <Book>
    <Title>
      <xhtml:a href="http://www.amazon.com/exec/obidos/ASIN/0600600335/o/
qid=979102681/sr=8-1/ref=aps_sr_b_1_1/103-4097284-9855030">
Complete Beatles Chronicle, The</xhtml:a>
    </Title>
    <Author>
      <Name>
        <First>Mark</First>
        <Last>Lewisohn</Last>
      </Name>
    </Author>
    <Type>Chronology</Type>
    <Published publisher="Harmony Books">1992</Published>
    <Rating>5 stars</Rating>
    <Notes>
  Covers the years 1957 through 1970. No solo info.
  Great appendices with chart info, discography, composer index,
  radio, tv, and live performances, and much more.
  Second Edition: May 2000 with George Martin as co-author.
  </Notes>
  </Book>
  <CD>
    <Title>
      <xhtml:a href="http://cdnow.com/cgi-bin/mserver/SID=1838724509/page-
name=/RP/CDN/FIND/album.xhtml/artistid=MCCARTNEY*PAUL+&amp;+WINGS/
itemid=644593">
Band on the Run</xhtml:a>
    </Title>
    <Artist>McCartney, Paul and Wings</Artist>
    <Chart>
      <Peak weeks="4">1</Peak>
      <Peak country="UK">1</Peak>
      <!-- guess -->
    </Chart>
    <Type>Rock</Type>
    <Label>Capitol</Label>
    <Label country="UK">EMI</Label>
    <AlbumReleased>1973</AlbumReleased>
    <Remastered format="gold CD">1993</Remastered>
    <Remastered format="2 disc box set with booklet">1999</Remastered>
  </CD>
  <CD>
    <Title>
      <xhtml:a href="http://cdnow.com/cgi-bin/mserver/SID=1838724509/page-
name=/RP/CDN/FIND/album.xhtml/artistid=MCCARTNEY*PAUL/itemid=292677">
Venus and Mars</xhtml:a>
```

```
    </Title>
    <Artist>McCartney, Paul and Wings</Artist>
    <Chart>
      <Peak weeks="1">1</Peak>
      <Peak country="UK">2</Peak>
      <!-- guess -->
    </Chart>
    <Type>Rock</Type>
    <Label>Capitol</Label>
    <Label country="UK">EMI</Label>
    <AlbumReleased>1975</AlbumReleased>
    <Remastered format="gold CD with 3 bonus tracks">1994</Remastered>
  </CD>
  <Book>
    <Title>
      <xhtml:a href="http://www.amazon.com/exec/obidos/ASIN/0805052496/
qid=979103138/sr=1-1/ref=sc_b_1/103-4097284-9855030">
Many Years From Now</xhtml:a>
    </Title>
    <Author>
      <Name>
        <First>Paul</First>
        <Last>McCartney</Last>
      </Name>
    </Author>
    <Type>Autobiographical</Type>
    <Published publisher="Henry Holt and Company">1997</Published>
    <Rating>4 stars</Rating>
    <Notes>654 pages; Reprint edition (October 1998)</Notes>
    <!-- Notice the absence of Rating element.
  I haven't read this book yet. This illustrates some optional
  elements that are children of Book element.
  -->
  </Book>
  <Book>
    <Title><xhtml:a href="http://www.amazon.com/exec/obidos/ASIN/
0811826848/ref=sim_books/107-8617847-9226138">
The Beatles Anthology</xhtml:a></Title>
    <Author>
      <Name>
        <First>Paul</First>
        <Last>McCartney</Last>
      </Name>
    </Author>
    <Author>
      <Name>
        <First>George</First>
        <Last>Harrison</Last>
      </Name>
    </Author>
    <Author>
      <Name>
        <First>Ringo</First>
        <Last>Starr</Last>
      </Name>
    </Author>
```

```
    <Author>
      <Name>
        <First>John</First>
        <Last>Lennon</Last>
      </Name>
    </Author>
    <Type>Autobiographical</Type>
    <Published publisher="Chronicle Books">2000</Published>
    <Rating>5 stars</Rating>
    <Notes>368 pages of the Beatles in their own words and pictures!
    A must-have for true Beatles fans.</Notes>
  </Book>
  <CD>
    <Title><xhtml:a href="http://www.cdnow.com/cgi-bin/mserver/pagename=/
RP/CDN/FIND/album.html/ddcn=SD-7777+29325+2/">
Beatles 1</xhtml:a></Title>
    <Artist>Beatles</Artist>
    <Chart>
      <Peak weeks="6" country="US">1</Peak>
    </Chart>
    <Type>Rock</Type>
    <Label country="US">Capitol</Label>
    <AlbumReleased>November 14, 2000</AlbumReleased>
  </CD>
  <Owner>
    <Name sex="male">
      <First>Ken</First>
      <Last>Sall</Last>
    </Name>
    <Address>
      <Street>123 Milky Way Dr.</Street>
      <City>Columbia</City>
      <State>MD</State>
      <Zip>20794</Zip>
    </Address>
  </Owner>
</Collection>
```

In the crude style sheet shown in Listing 10-6, we've specified the overall appearance of the document element, `Collection`. Then we specify rules for the `CD` and `Book` elements, as well as for all of their children (denoted by the asterisk; refer to Table 10-1 for selector syntax).

Listing 10-6 Very Basic Style Sheet for XML (collection5-0.css)

```
Collection  {display:block; font-size: 12pt;
             background-color: #EEEEA1}
/* Unblock for more obvious difference between CDs and Books.
CD          {display:block; margin-left: 4em; margin-right: 4em;
             border: solid thin black;}
*/
CD *        {display:block; color: blue; text-indent: 4em;}
Book *      {display:block; color: black; text-indent: 4em;}
```

The style sheet reference in the XML instance, which associates the CSS file with the XML document, is:

```
<?xml-stylesheet type="text/css" href="collection5-0.css"?>
```

When we display `collection5-0.xml` in Netscape 6, the results shown in Figures 10-5 and 10-6, although hardly worthy of a Super Duper Web Design award, do clearly illustrate that a very small amount of CSS can go a long way toward rendering XML. (Nearly identical results can be seen with Internet Explorer 5.5 and Opera 5.2.) By stating that all elements should use `display:block`, we immediately see output that is readable, although not necessarily too meaningful. (For example, we can't tell what the various years represent without referring to the document source or perhaps the DTD.) We can also easily distinguish `CD` and `Book` elements because they are colored differently. However, we can do much better than this, as we'll see in the next two sections.

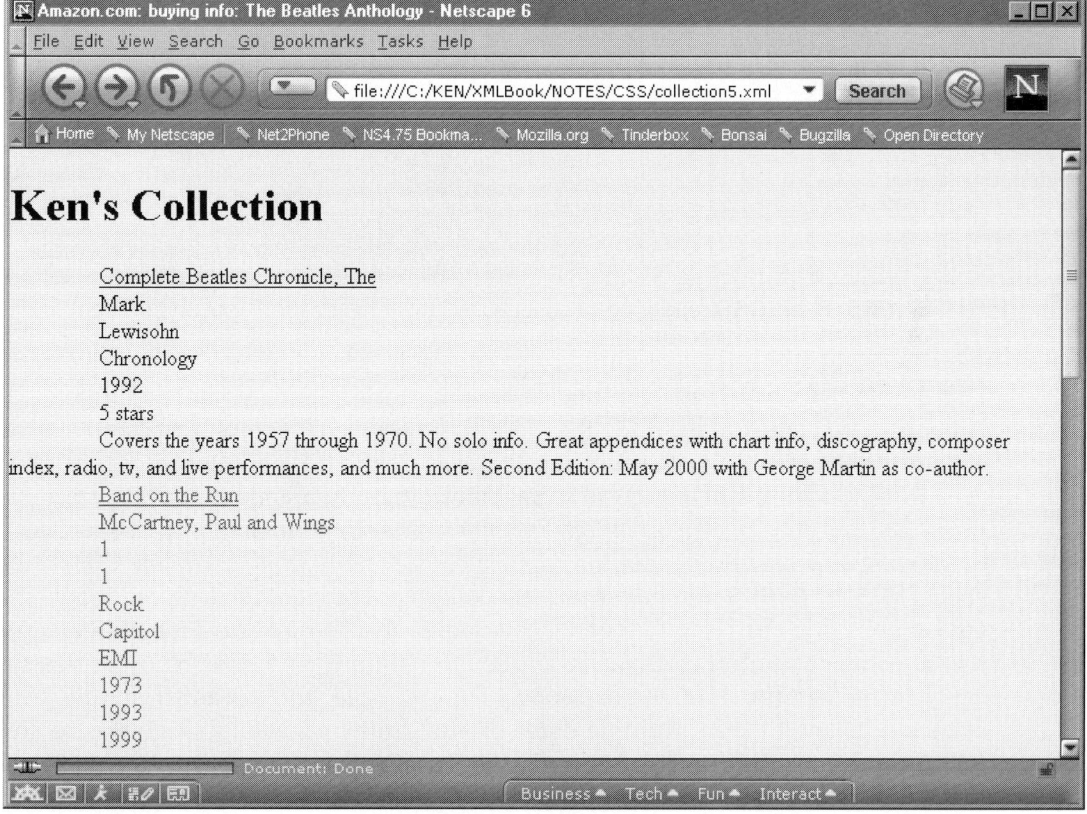

FIGURE 10-5 Basic CSS rendering of collection5-0.xml in Netscape 6 (first screen)

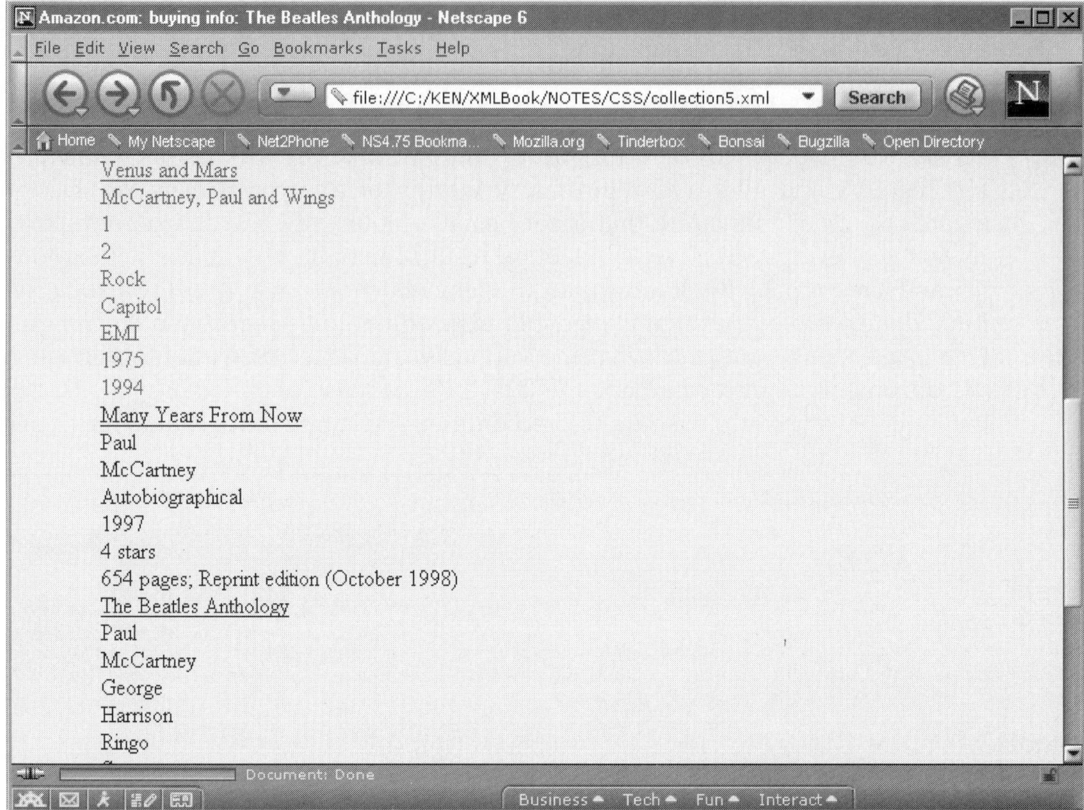

FIGURE 10-6 Basic CSS rendering of collection5.xml in Netscape 6 (second screen)

Improved CSS Style Sheet for XML

A better approach is to examine the elements of our `collection5.dtd` and decide element by element what kind of rendering is desired. We'll alter our style sheet accordingly, taking advantage of CSS inheritance. Remember: *General rules are placed first and overridden where necessary with more specific rules.*

Listing 10-7 shows `collection5.css`, a considerably more complete CSS2 style sheet, which we'll reference from the file `collection5.xml`. Note how the `Collection` rule defines a few general defaults, the `CD` rule adds some details for the `CD` element itself, the `CD *` rule applies to children, and specific overrides for `Remastered`, `Artist`, and `Title` follow. For example, the `Remastered` rule uses `display:inline` to keep multiple dates on the same line, even though the default for `CD` children is `display:block`. A similar set of rules is defined for the `Book` element and its children. The rule:

```
First, Last {display:inline; color:red; font-weight:bold;}
```

indicates that the same style should be used for the elements `First` and `Last` which will appear on the same line. However, the rule

```
Author Last {display:inline; font-style:italic;}
```

partially overrides or refines the declaration for `Last` name descendants of `Author` (but not of `Owner`) so that last names of authors are italicized as well as boldfaced.

A particularly useful CSS2 feature is **attribute selectors**, as illustrated by the rule

```
Published[publisher="Harmony Books"] {color: red; background-color: white;}
```

This rule specifies that when the value of the `publisher` attribute of the `Published` element is exactly equal to the string `"Harmony Books"`, render the content of the `Published` element as red text with a white background. This style will *not* be applied, however, to `Published` elements that have a different value for the `publisher` attribute. This is the closest to conditional processing that CSS2 provides; it's a big improvement over CSS1. Refer to Table 10-1 for other variations in attribute selector syntax.

The rules for `h1`, `a:link`, `a:visited`, `a:active`, and `a:hover` apply to the XHTML namespace. Note that we do not use the `"xhtml:"` namespace prefix in the CSS file, even though we must use the prefix in the XML document. We can also intermix XHTML elements in the context of our own language-specific elements. Consider these rules which state that anchors nested in `Title` elements should have a different appearance from other anchors in other elements (although none of the latter appear in `collection5.xml`).

```
Title  a:link      {color:green;}
Title  a:visited   {color:red;}
Title  a:active    {color:#FF00FF;}
Title  a:hover     {color:lime;}
```

Listing 10-7 Improved Style Sheet (collection5.css)

```
/* Default font size, background color, etc. */
Collection  {display:block; font-size: 12pt;
             background-color: #EEEEA1}

CD          {display:block; margin-left: 4em; margin-right: 4em;
             border: solid thin black;}

/* For all children of CD... */
CD *        {display:block; color: blue; text-indent: 4em;}

/* ... except where overridden. */
/* Note use of inline to keep multiple Remastered dates on the same line. */
Remastered  {display:inline; font-style:italic; margin-left: 4em;}
```

```
Artist       {text-align:center; color: black; font-weight:bold; }

Title        {display:block; color: black; font-weight:bold;
              font-style:italic; text-align:center;}

Book         {display:block; margin-left: 4em; margin-right: 4em;
              border: solid thin blue;}

/* For all children of Book... */
Book *       {display:block; color: black; text-indent: 4em;}

/* ... except where overridden. */
/* Center Name children with First and Last on same line (via inline). */
Name         {text-align:center;}
First, Last {display:inline; color:red; font-weight:bold;}

/* Make element Last look a little different from First. */
Author Last {display:inline; font-style:italic;}

/* Handle special case for "publisher" attribute value. */
Published[publisher="Harmony Books"] {color: red; background-color: white;}

Notes        {text-indent: 0em; margin-left: 6em; margin-right: 6em;
              border: solid thin black; padding: 5px;}

Owner        {display: block; text-indent: 6em; margin-top: 1em;
              font-size: 14pt; font-family: "Comic sans ms";
              background-color: white;}

/* Rest are elements from XHTML namespace. */
h1           {color:maroon; text-align:center;}

/* Default link colors */
a:link       {color:red;}
a:visited    {color:#FF00FF;}
a:active     {color:green;}
a:hover      {color:lime;}

/* Override default link colors for links that are children of Title. */
Title  a:link      {color:green;}
Title  a:visited   {color:red;}
Title  a:active    {color:#FF00FF;}
Title  a:hover     {color:lime;}
```

Figures 10-7, 10-8, and 10-9 show the result of applying `collection5.css` to `collection5.xml`, as viewed in Netscape 6. It should be fairly obvious that by increasing the specificity of our CSS rules, we are able to achieve much finer control over the appearance of XML data.

But it is probably equally obvious that something important is missing. After all, without viewing the XML source (or the DTD), it's still not at all clear what the various numbers and dates represent. Displaying element content on separate lines

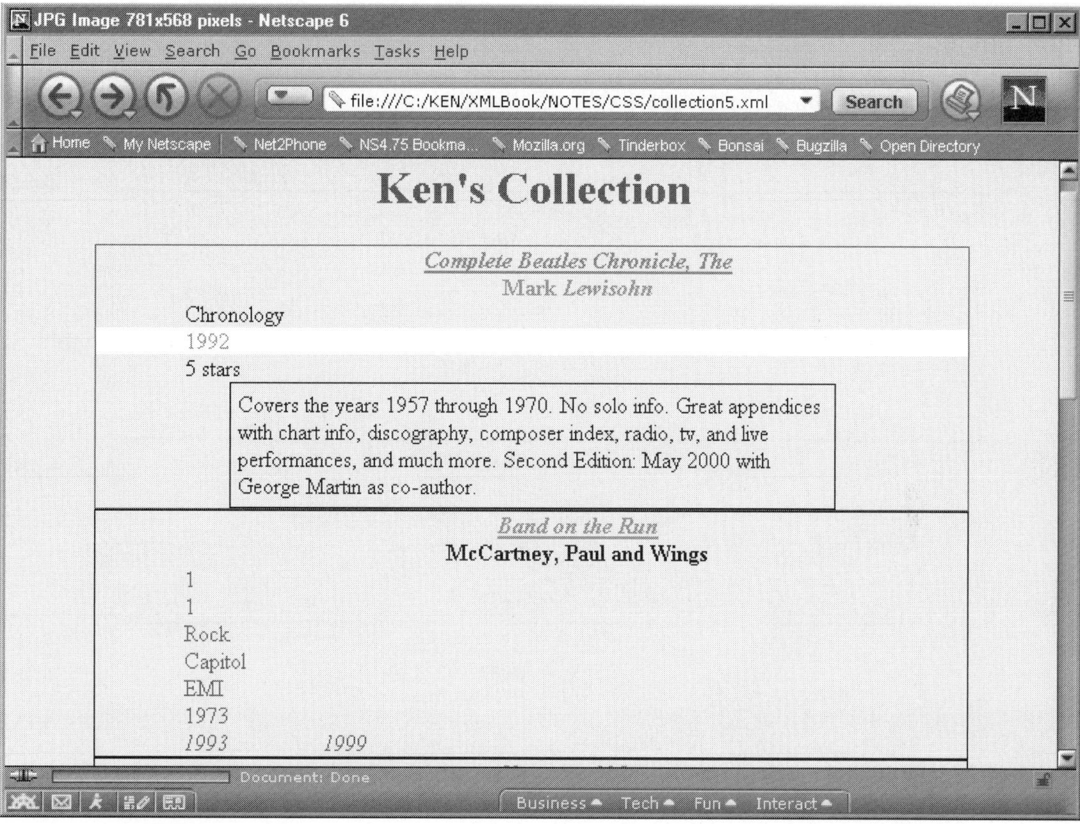

FIGURE 10-7 Improved rendering of collection5.xml in Netscape 6 (first screen)

is helpful, but what we really need is the ability to *label* our XML data, as we'll see in the next section.

Although the example doesn't illustrate this, you can achieve selective filtering of XML data by not specifying *any* rules for elements that you wish to exclude from rendering and carefully assuring that selector inheritance does not result in such unwanted elements inheriting a style. You can explicitly prevent element visibility by means of the `display:none` declaration.

Robust CSS Style Sheet with Generated Text

We can do even better in our display of XML data if we use the CSS2 feature called **generated text** (*http://www.w3.org/TR/CSS2/generate.html*). With CSS2, you can add text content before and/or after your data, produce automatic counters and numbering, and generate markers and lists. In this section, we'll explore the addition of text content that effectively labels our output so that it is much more reader

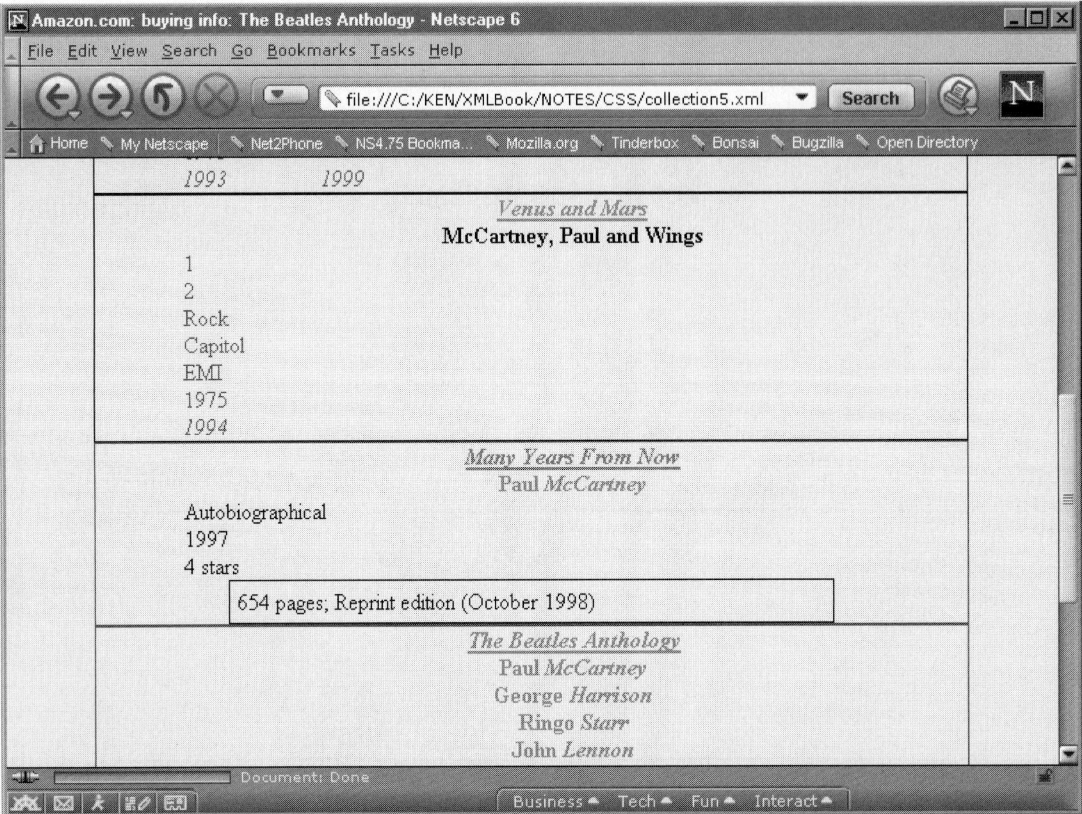

FIGURE 10-8 Improved rendering of collection5.xml in Netscape 6 (second screen)

friendly. This is accomplished by adding rules for the `:before` and `:after` pseudo-elements, which will be inserted before and after the actual content of the XML element. The text to be inserted is specified via the CSS2 `content` property. For example, to insert the label `"Remastered: "` before the year represented by the `Remastered` element, we add this rule with a pseudo-element selector:

```
Remastered:before     {content: "Remastered: "; }
```

With the markup

```
<Remastered>1993</Remastered>
```

the result of this new rule is:

```
Remastered: 1993
```

Of course, the label string does not have to be the same as the element name. Much more sophisticated labeling can be accomplished using attribute selectors

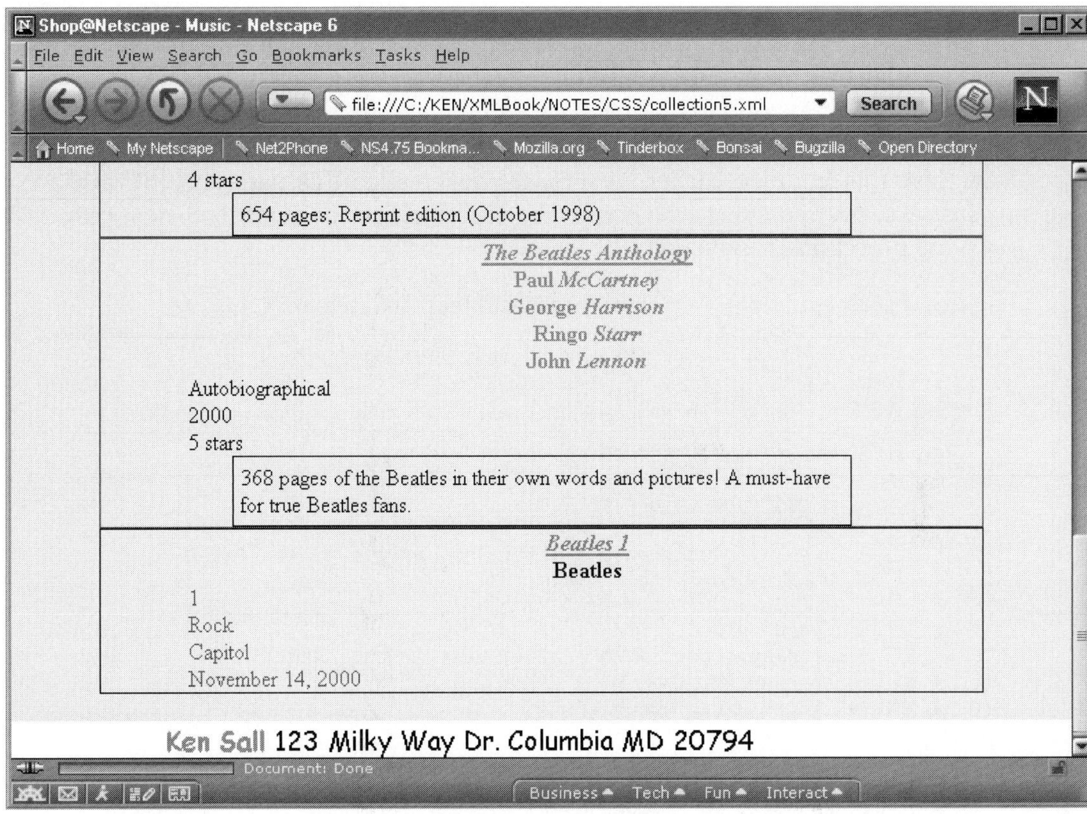

FIGURE 10-9 Improved rendering of collection5.xml in Netscape 6 (third screen)

and the handy `attr` function, which returns the string value of the attribute passed to the function. Consider the rules:

```
Peak[country]:before  {content: "#";}
Peak[country]:after   {content: " in the " attr(country);}
Peak[weeks]:after     {content: " in the US, for " attr(weeks) " weeks";}
```

and the XML data

```
<Peak weeks="4">1</Peak>
<Peak country="UK">1</Peak>
<Peak weeks="6" country="US">1</Peak>
```

When we apply the CSS rules to the data, the result is the output:

```
#1 in the US, for 4 weeks
#1 in the UK
#1 in the US, for 6 weeks
```

Note that the value of the `content` property can be either a single string (as in the `:before` rule above) or a series of space-separated strings (as in the `:after` rules). Multiple strings are concatenated.

The complete, updated style sheet that takes full advantage of generated text using `:before` and `:after` pseudo-elements is shown in Listing 10-8. To distinguish this from the earlier version, we have called this variation `collection5-gen-text.css` and associated it with the XML instance `collection5-gen-text.xml` via the processing instruction:

```
<?xml-stylesheet type="text/css" href="collection5-gen-text.css"?>
```

Listing 10-8 CSS2 Style Sheet with Generated Text (collection5-gen-text.css).

```
/* Default font size, background color, etc. */
Collection  {display:block; font-size: 12pt;
             background-color: #EEEEA1}

CD          {display:block; margin-left: 4em; margin-right: 4em;
             border: solid thin black;}

/* For all children of CD... */
CD *        {display:block; color: blue; text-indent: 4em;}

/* ... except where overridden. */

/*
   Note extensive use of ":before" and ":after" pseudo-elements and the
   "content" property to produce user friendly labels.
   The CSS2 function "attr(foo)" returns as a string the value of attribute
   "foo" for the subject of the selector. Note also that content can be
   concatenated by a series of space-separated strings.
*/

AlbumReleased:before  {content: "Initial Release: "; }

/* Peak:before           {content: "#";} */
Peak[country]:before  {content: "#";}
Peak[country]:after   {content: " in the " attr(country);}
Peak[weeks]:after     {content: " in the US, for " attr(weeks) " weeks";}

Label[country]:after  {content: " (in the " attr(country) ")";}

/* Note use of inline to keep multiple Remastered dates on the same line. */
Remastered            {display:inline; margin-left: 4em;}
Remastered:before     {content: "Remastered: "; }

Artist      {text-align:center; color: black; font-weight:bold; }

Title       {display:block; color: black; font-weight:bold;
             font-style:italic; text-align:center;}
```

```
Book        {display:block; margin-left: 4em; margin-right: 4em;
             border: solid thin blue;}

/* For all children of Book... */
Book *      {display:block; color: black; text-indent: 4em;}

/* ... except where overridden. */
/* Center Name children with First and Last on same line (via inline). */
Name        {text-align:center;}
First, Last {display:inline; color:red; font-weight:bold;}

/* Make element Last look a little different from element First. */
Author Last {display:inline; font-style:italic;}

/* Handle special case for "publisher" attribute value. */
Published:before             {content: "Copyright ";}
Published[publisher]:after {content: " by " attr(publisher);}
Published[publisher="Harmony Books"]
     {color: red; background-color: white;}
Published[publisher="Harmony Books"]:after
     {content: " by Harmony Books, a division of Crown Publishers Inc.";}

Type:before     {content: "Type: "; font-weight:bold;}
CD Type:before  {content: "Type: "; font-weight:bold; color:purple;}

Rating:after    {content: " [Reviewer: K.Sall]";}

Notes:before    {content: "Notes: "; display:block; font-style:italic;}
Notes           {text-indent: 0em; margin-left: 6em; margin-right: 6em;
                 border: solid thin black; padding: 5px;}

Owner           {display: block; text-indent: 6em; margin-top: 3em;
                 font-size: 14pt; font-family: "Comic sans ms";
                 background-color: white;}
Owner > Name    {display: block; }
Owner > Address {display: block; text-align:center; }
Owner:before    {content: "Collection Owner: "; font-family: "courier";}


/* Rest are elements from the XHTML namespace. */
h1          {color:maroon; text-align:center;}

/* Default link colors */
a:link      {color:red;}
a:visited   {color:#FF00FF;}
a:active    {color:green;}
a:hover     {color:lime;}

/* Override default link colors for links that are children of Title. */
Title  a:link      {color:green;}
Title  a:visited   {color:red;}
Title  a:active    {color:#FF00FF;}
Title  a:hover     {color:cyan;}
```

A few words are in order for the rather complicated rules pertaining to the `Published` element:

```
Published:before            {content: "Copyright ";}
Published[publisher]:after {content: " by " attr(publisher);}
Published[publisher="Harmony Books"]
     {color: red; background-color: white;}
Published[publisher="Harmony Books"]:after
     {content: " by Harmony Books, a division of Crown Publishers Inc.";}
```

These rules state that all `Published` elements will have a `"Copyright "` label preceding the year of publication and, by default, the value of the `publisher` attribute (if not null) will be displayed after the year. For example, the XML data:

```
<Published publisher="Chronicle Books">2000</Published>
```

will result in the output:

```
Copyright 2000 by Chronicle Books
```

The rules further state that if the value of the `publisher` attribute is `"Harmony Books"`, in addition to the red font and white background, there will be a special-case string displayed. In other words, for the XML fragment:

```
<Published publisher="Harmony Books">1992</Published>
```

the output will be:

```
Copyright 1992 by Harmony Books, a division of Crown Publishers Inc.
```

Note that the more specific rules appear after the general ones.

One other difference from the previous style sheet is the way the `Owner` element is handled.

```
Owner           {display: block; text-indent: 6em; margin-top: 3em;
                 font-size: 14pt; font-family: "Comic sans ms";
                 background-color: white;}
Owner > Name    {display: block; }
Owner > Address {display: block; text-align:center; }
Owner:before    {content: "Collection Owner: "; font-family: "courier";}
```

The selector `Owner > Name` indicates specific handling for `Name` elements that are the immediate children of `Owner` elements, so that the name (consisting of both `First` and `Last` elements which inherit the rule) appears on a separate line from the label assigned by the `Owner:before` rule. The `Owner > Name` selector distinguishes this case from that of `Name` elements that are the immediate children of `Author`. You can prove to yourself that this rule is needed by commenting out this rule and reloading the XML instance; you'll see that the name is concatenated with the label `"Collection Owner: "`.

The screenshots of the result of applying the revised style sheet, `collection5-gen-text.css`, to our running example appear in Figures 10-10, 10-11, and 10-12. Hopefully, you'll agree that we have achieved a much more satisfactory and useful display of our XML data by taking full advantage of CSS2 features such as generated text to label our output.

Readers interested in a *real* challenge can try to develop a style sheet that displays the data in a much more visually pleasing format, such as in tabular form. Although not discussed in this chapter, CSS2 provides many other values for the `display` property that would be helpful in this exercise, such as `table`, `inline-table`, `table-row-group`, `table-column`, `table-column-group`, `table-header-group`, `table-footer-group`, `table-row`, `table-cell`, and `table-caption`. See the explanation of the CSS2 Table model, at *http://www.w3.org/TR/REC-CSS2/tables.html*.

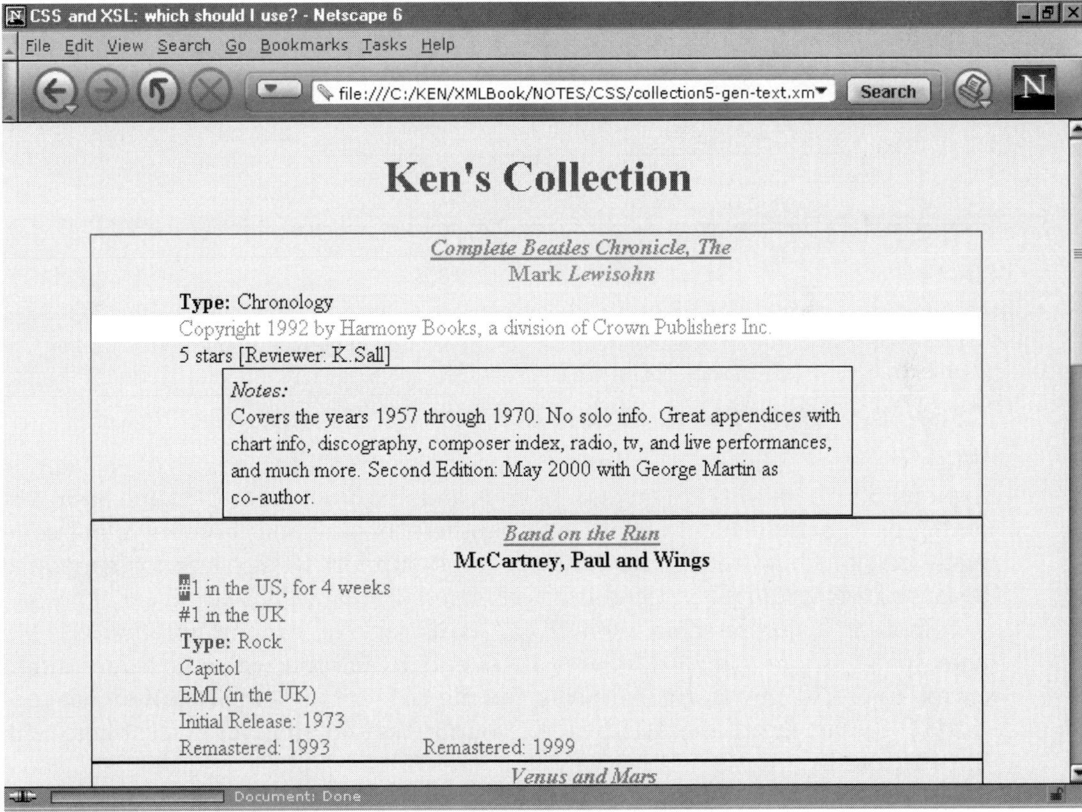

FIGURE 10-10 Rendering of XML with CSS2 generated text in Netscape 6 (first screen)

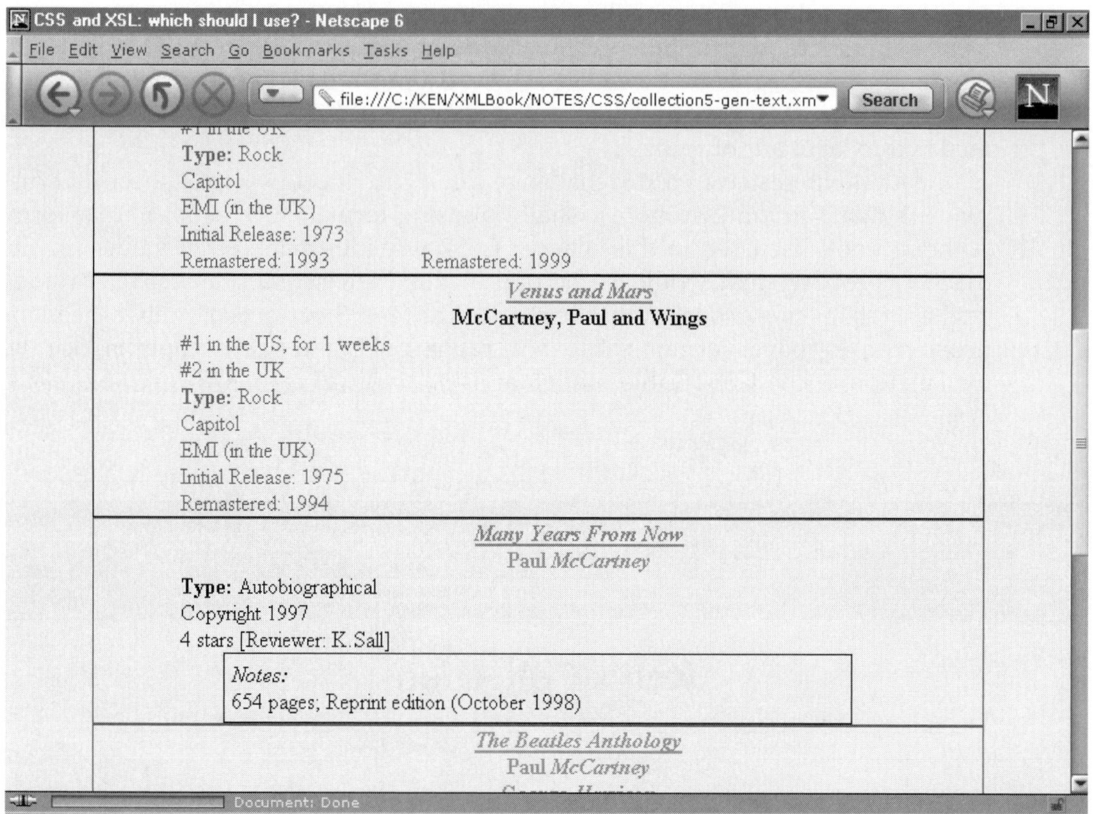

FIGURE 10-11 Rendering of XML with CSS2 generated text in Netscape 6 (second screen)

CSS with Internet Explorer 5.5

When we view either `collection5.xml` or `collection5-gen-text.xml` in Internet Explorer 5.5, the results are mixed. As you can tell from Figure 10-13, the basic rendering of element content is generally handled correctly, but borders aren't complete and, much more significant, there is no support whatsoever for generated text, as of this writing. I expect this has changed dramatically with IE 6.0.

Another major problem with IE 5.5 is its lack of support for the XHTML namespace. If you compare Figures 10-13 and 10-14, you will note a few differences. Figure 10-13 was created using the file `collection5-html.xml`, which uses the HTML namespace that IE 5.5 *does* recognize, as shown in an excerpt here with the `html` prefix:

```
<Collection version="2"
            xmlns:html="http://www.w3.org/TR/REC-html40">
  <html:h1>Ken's Collection</html:h1>
```

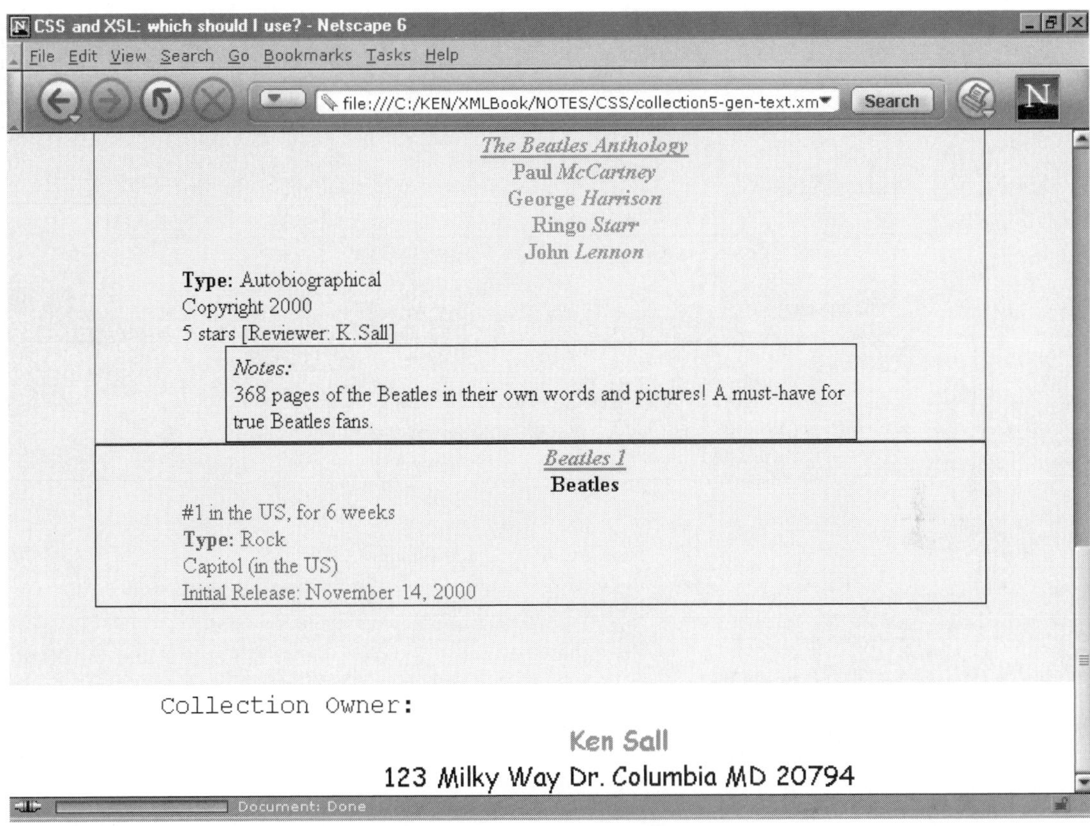

FIGURE 10-12 Rendering of XML with CSS2 generated text in Netscape 6 (third screen)

```
  <Book>
    <Title>
      <html:a href="http://www.amazon.com/exec/obidos/ASIN/0600600335/o/
qid=979102681/sr=8-1/ref=aps_sr_b_1_1/103-4097284-9855030">
Complete Beatles Chronicle, The</html:a>
```

However, IE 5.5 completely ignores the XHTML namespace, so it fails to render the <xhtml:h1> and <xhtml:a> elements in `collection5.xml` correctly (excerpt follows), as you can see in Figure 10-14. In fact, the anchor elements are not even treated as links.

```
<Collection version="2"
            xmlns:xhtml="http://www.w3.org/1999/xhtml" >
  <xhtml:h1>Ken's Collection</xhtml:h1>
  <Book>
    <Title>
      <xhtml:a href="http://www.amazon.com/exec/obidos/ASIN/0600600335/o/
qid=979102681/sr=8-1/ref=aps_sr_b_1_1/103-4097284-9855030">
Complete Beatles Chronicle, The</xhtml:a>
```

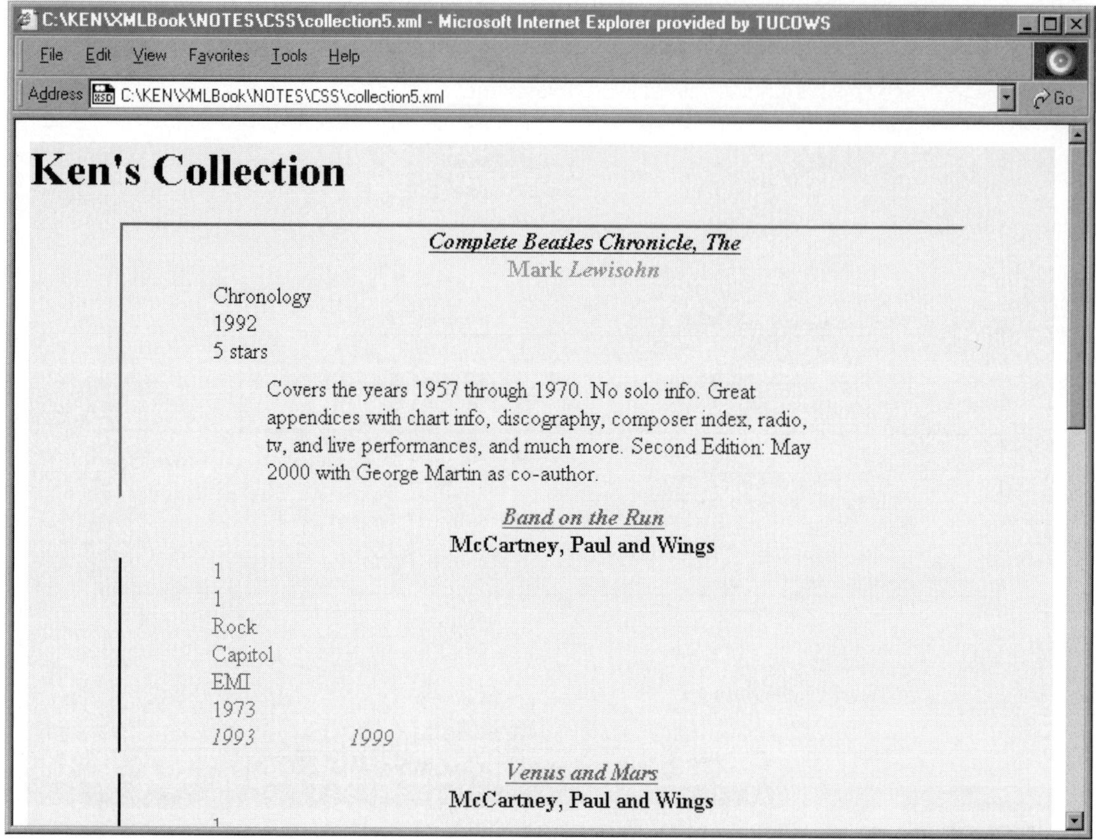

FIGURE 10-13 collection5.xml with HTML Namespace displayed in IE 5.5 (first screen)

Limitations of Using CSS for XML

CSS Level 2 is very appealing for XML rendering because of its relative simplicity. However, simple solutions do not always offer maximal flexibility. Therefore, the W3C advises developers to "[u]se CSS when you can, use XSL when you must." (See *http://www.w3.org/Style/CSS-vs-XSL* which also contains an informative diagram of several rendering paths.) If you can accomplish what you need to with CSS, chances are good that the development and maintenance costs will be lower. If, however, you need to transform the data represented by the XML document, then XSL is necessary. For example, if you need to sort elements or output them in a completely different order than in the original document, XSLT is required. If you need precise and complex page layout, XSLFO is usually necessary. But there will be much more about this in chapters 11 and 12.

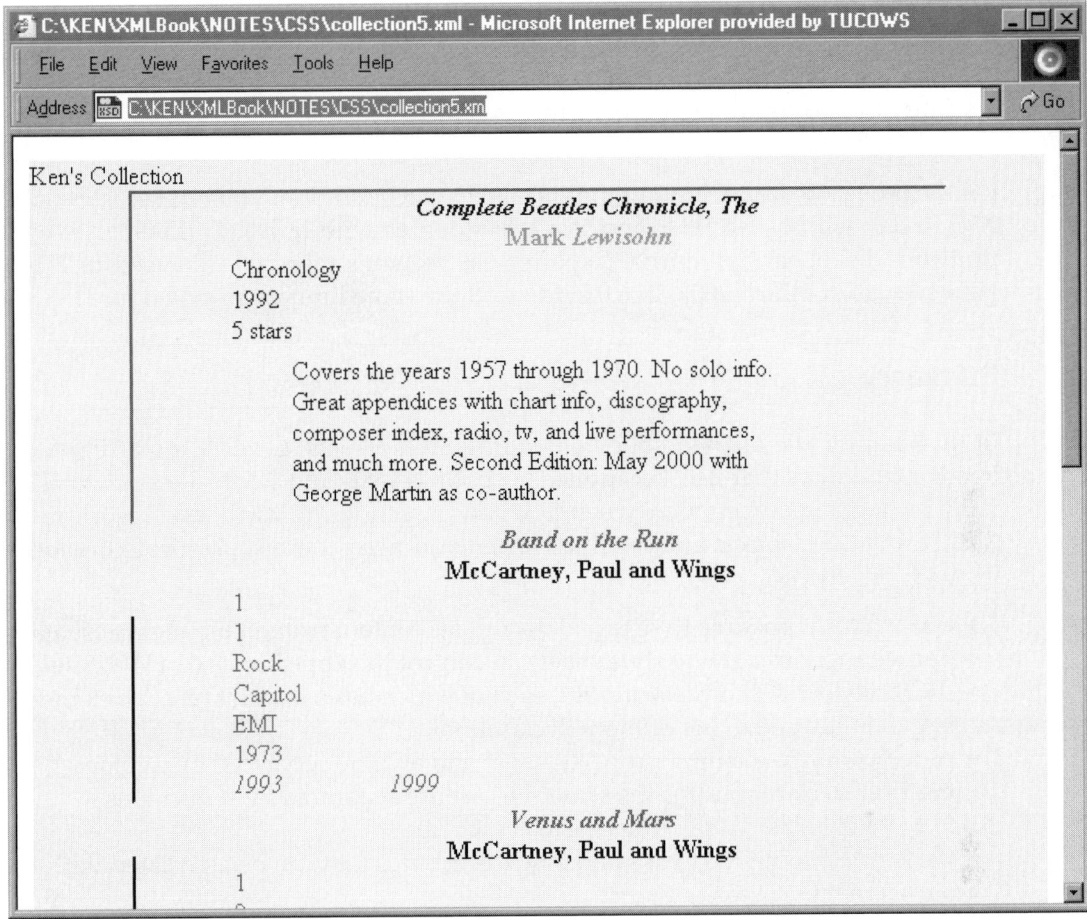

FIGURE 10-14 collection5.xml with XHTML Namespace displayed in IE 5.5 (first screen)

The main limitations of using CSS2 for XML are:

- Since CSS is a client-side rendering process, you are totally dependent on the browser's support of CSS, which in early 2002 is still somewhat inconsistent across vendors and platforms. (See the Browser Compatibility Charts at *http://www.webreview.com/browsers/index.shtml*.) This support is essentially nonexistent for browsers prior to Netscape 4.0 and Internet Explorer 4.0, which can be a consideration if you can't control the browser used by your user base.
- You can assign styles only to elements, not to attributes. Attributes are ignored in CSS1. However, in CSS2, elements can be processed selectively based on attribute presence or attribute value, as we've seen.
- You can process each input element only once.

- You can't transform the order of elements; you are limited to document order.
- You can't add elements to output, although you can add generated text for labels or numbers for headings.
- You can't do conditional processing, except with attributes, as we saw with the `publisher` attribute.

On the plus side, in addition to the simplicity consideration, you *can* use CSS with XML today with Netscape 6, and to a lesser degree with IE 5.5. This disparity will probably disappear as Internet Explorer 6.0 becomes more widely used in 2002. However, as of March 2002, IE 6.0 evidenced the same limitations noted for IE 5.5.

Summary

In this chapter, we learned about Cascading Style Sheets, Level 2, a mature W3C Recommendation that can be applied to both HTML and XML documents. The W3C recommends using CSS when you can for rendering XML, and resorting to XSL Formatting Objects and/or XSLT when you need more sophisticated rendering and/or processing.

- CSS makes it possible to separate document content from manner of presentation; changes in a single style sheet can control the appearance of a Web site.
- A CSS style sheet consists of rules, each of which has a selector (e.g., an element name) followed by one or more declarations.
- A declaration contains a property name and a value separated by a colon; multiple declarations for the same selector are separated by semicolons (e.g., `font-size: 12pt; font-weight: bold`).
- We learned about the `class` and `style` attributes that can be associated with any element.
- *Inheritance* means that elements tend to inherit property values set by parent elements unless children explicitly override these values. Specific rules always prevail over general rules.
- *Cascading* is the merging of more than one style sheet (from the Web site, the specific Web page, the user, and the browser) to yield one style definition for any particular element in a given context. The general rule is: *Author wins over user, and user wins over browser.*
- A style sheet can be embedded directly in HTML using the `<style>` element.
- For maximal reusability benefits, however, referencing an external style sheet using the `<link>` element is far preferable.
- In XML, an external style sheet is associated with an XML document using the `xml-stylesheet` processing instruction, which is very similar to using the `<link>` element. The syntax is `<?xml-stylesheet type="text/css" href="filename.css"?>`.

- When using CSS2 with XML, you use the element and attribute names from your own vocabulary as the selectors.
- To control newline formatting and tabular layout, use the `display` property set to `inline`, `block`, or any of the table values.
- In XML (as in HTML), we can leverage the inheritance of the CSS properties by careful formulation of our selectors.
- In CSS2 (but not CSS1), we can refer to attributes by selector syntax such as `Element[attr]` or `Element[attr="value"]`. This provides some degree of conditional processing.
- CSS2 adds the ability to generate text for labels or numbering. For example, the pseudo-properties `:before` and `:after` can be added to any element name to mandate that the specified text appears before or after the content of the element.
- XHTML and our own vocabulary can be mixed; some subtle browser differences may be a problem, however.
- Finally, we covered limitations of using CSS for display of XML.

For Further Exploration

Articles

xmlhack CSS Category
http://xmlhack.com/list.php?cat=23

XML.com: Cross-Browser XML, Simon St. Laurent (November 2000)
http://www.simonstl.com/articles/xbrowse/index.html

XML.com: Browser XML Display Support Chart [with links to NS 6, IE 5 and Opera 4 articles]
http://www.xml.com/pub/a/2000/05/03/browserchart/index.html

XML.com: On Display: XML Web Pages with Mozilla, Simon St. Laurent (March 2000)
http://www.xml.com/pub/a/2000/03/29/tutorial/index.html

IBM: Improve your XSLT coding five ways [Tip 1 concerns CSS]
http://www-106.ibm.com/developerworks/library/x-xslt5.html

Books

Cascading Style Sheets, Designing for the Web, Second Edition, Håkon Wium Lie and Bert Bos (1999, Addison-Wesley, ISBN 0-201-59625-3) [covers CSS Level 2]
http://cseng.aw.com/book/0,3828,0201596253,00.html

Cascading Style Sheets, Designing for the Web, Håkon Wium Lie and Bert Bos (1997, Addison-Wesley) [online sample chapters for CSS Level 1]
http://www.awlonline.com/cseng/titles/0-201-41998-X/liebos/

Cascading Style Sheets, Designing for the Web, Chapter 2 online [great overview]
http://www.w3.org/Style/LieBos2e/enter/

Resources

Document Style Semantics and Specification Language (DSSSL) [James Clark's links]
http://www.jclark.com/dsssl/

CSS Pointers Group [collection of CSS resources]
http://css.nu/index.html

Zvon: CSS2 Reference with Examples
http://zvon.org/xxl/CSS2Reference/Output/index.html

Zvon: CSS1 Reference
http://www.zvon.org/xxl/css1Reference/Output/index.html

WebReview: Style Sheet Reference Guide, Eric Myer
http://www.webreview.com/style/index.shtml

WebReview: Browser Compatibility Charts, Eric Myer
http://www.webreview.com/browsers/index.shtml

WebReview: CSS2 Selectors Support Chart, Eric Myer
http://www.webreview.com/style/css2/charts/selectors.shtml

WDVL: Cascading Style Sheets [tutorials, resources, and articles]
http://wdvl.Internet.com/Authoring/Style/Sheets/

Software

Netscape 6.x Release
http://home.netscape.com/browsers/6/index.html

TopStyle Pro [excellent CSS editor by creator of HomeSite]
http://www.bradsoft.com/topstyle/

Tutorials

Zvon: CSS2 Tutorial for XML
http://zvon.org/xxl/CSS2Tutorial/General/htmlIntro.html

Introduction to Style Sheets [tutorial by Alan Richmond]
http://wdvl.Internet.com/Authoring/Style/Sheets/Tutorial.html

W3C Specifications and Information

Web Style Sheets [CSS, XSL, etc.]
http://www.w3.org/Style/

Cascading Style Sheets (CSS home page)
http://www.w3.org/Style/CSS/

Style Sheets Activity Statement
http://www.w3.org/Style/Activity

Cascading Style Sheets, Level 2 (CSS2) Specification [May 1998 Recommendation]
http://www.w3.org/TR/REC-CSS2

Cascading Style Sheets Level 1 (CSS1) Specification (December 1996 Recommendation, revised January 1999)
http://www.w3.org/TR/REC-CSS1

CSS2 Appendix B. Changes from CSS1
http://www.w3.org/TR/REC-CSS2/changes.html

CSS2 Selectors
http://www.w3.org/TR/REC-CSS2/selector.html

Associating Style Sheets with XML documents Version 1.0 (June 1999 Recommendation)
http://www.w3.org/TR/xml-stylesheet/

Assigning property values, Cascading, and Inheritance [from CSS2 Recommendation]
http://www.w3.org/TR/REC-CSS2/cascade.html

Generated content, automatic numbering, and lists [from CSS2 Recommendation]
http://www.w3.org/TR/CSS2/generate.html

How to Add Style to XML
http://www.w3.org/Style/styling-XML

Which Should I Use? CSS or XML?
http://www.w3.org/Style/CSS-vs-XSL

Using XSL and CSS Together
http://www.w3.org/TR/NOTE-XSL-and-CSS

CSS3 introduction (Roadmap)
http://www.w3.org/TR/css3-roadmap

CSS3 module: W3C selectors
http://www.w3.org/TR/css3-selectors/

CSS Current Work
http://www.w3.org/Style/CSS/current-work

Simple API for CSS (SAC)—Java, C, and perl Implementations
http://www.w3.org/Style/CSS/SAC/

Simple API for CSS (SAC)
http://www.w3.org/TR/SAC/

CSS Validation Service
http://jigsaw.w3.org/css-validator/

Core Styles [predefined style sheets named Chocolate, Midnight, Modernist, Oldstyle, Steely, Swiss, Traditional, and Ultramarine]
http://www.w3.org/StyleSheets/Core/

Chapter 11

Transforming XML with XSLT and XPath

In this lengthy chapter, you will gain a reasonable understanding of XSL Transformations (XSLT), which is part of the larger Extensible Stylesheet Language (XSL) specification from the W3C. XSLT is a powerful template-driven XML vocabulary used to transform, process, filter, sort, and otherwise manipulate XML input to produce any of several kinds of output. We'll also cover the XML Path Language (XPath), which is used primarily to select or locate individual nodes or sets of nodes in the tree, and secondarily to perform string manipulations, numerical calculations, and boolean tests. Since entire books have been devoted to XSLT and XPath, our coverage, although extensive, necessarily focuses on concepts rather than on providing every detail. We'll point out what topics we're skipping and include references to more detailed treatments of this material. Readers who desire more in-depth coverage should make use of the extensive "For Further Exploration" section. Readers interested in more basic ways to render XML should refer to chapter 10 on styling XML with CSS2.

Overview of XSLT and XPath

This section introduces the key concepts of XSLT and XPath (as well as a little about XSLFO). Some of these points will become more clear as you read later parts of this long chapter. Forward references are unfortunately unavoidable. Cross references are provided for forward references, should you wish to follow them at that point. I recommend that you read Chapter 10 on CSS before this chapter to understand how a simpler approach than XSLT/XPath/XSL might be sufficient for some of your XML applications.

What Is XSL? XSLFO? XSLT? XPath?

The **Extensible Stylesheet Language, XSL**, is essentially a two-part W3C specification for defining stylesheets that describe how to render XML for different target devices (browsers, print media, handhelds, etc.). The main XSL specification, more than 400 pages, describes a particular XML vocabulary for specifying formatting semantics, with elements such as `fo:simple-page-master`, `fo:table-column`, `fo:footnote`, `fo:block`, and `fo:region-body`, as well as CSS-inspired attributes such as `font-size`, `font-family`, `text-align`, and `margin-width`. XSL is a far more sophisticated styling language than CSS; it draws on both CSS and a pre-XML styling standard called the Document Style Semantics and Specification Language (DSSSL) from the SGML community. The formatting portion of the specification is usually called **XSLFO** for **XSL Formatting Objects**. This is sometimes abbreviated as *XSL-FO*, with a hyphen, or *XSL FO*, with a space. XSLFO is the subject of chapter 12, contributed by G. Ken Holman.

Chapter 11, on the other hand, is concerned primarily with the other part of the XSL specification, **XSL Transformations (XSLT)**, a language for expressing transformations of XML into other flavors of XML (such as another XML vocabulary possibly mixed with XSLFO), or into HTML, text, or other formats. The main XSL spec refers to XSLT as the "Tree Construction" portion (Section 2.1), although XSLT is presented in a completely separate document (approximately 90 pages long).[1] XSLT describes how an input document is transformed into another XML document that may or may not use the formatting vocabulary of XSLFO.

According to the W3C's XSL home page, XSL is a language for expressing stylesheets consisting of *three* parts:

1. A language for transforming XML documents: *XSLT*
2. An XML vocabulary for specifying formatting semantics: *XSL Formatting Objects*
3. A syntax for addressing parts of a document: *XPath*, a syntax that is also significant to XLink, XPointer, and the emerging XML Query Language.

An XSL stylesheet actually represents a class of XML documents. It describes how an instance of the class is transformed into an XML document that happens to use some formatting vocabulary. In other words, a stylesheet tells a processor how to convert logical structures (the source XML document represented as a tree) into a presentational structure (the result tree). Note that an XSLT stylesheet is itself an XML document since both XSL Formatting Objects and XSL Transformations use XML syntax. This implies that an XSLT stylesheet must be well-formed and valid.

1. The URLs for XSL, XSLT, XPath, and related specifications and the key pages are listed in Table 11-1.

It is important to understand that the transformation part of XSL can be used independently of the formatting semantics. Common transformations include converting one XML vocabulary to another, changing the order of elements, and selectively processing elements, as well as converting XML to HTML. Furthermore, XML to XML transformations are the heart of many B2B e-commerce applications, EDI transactions, and the transferring of data between heterogeneous databases.

For example, suppose we have an original invoice in the format shown in Listing 11-1 and need to transform it into the format in Listing 11-2. Do these files really represent the same (simplified) business data? After all, the source format has fewer lines than the target; most of the element names are different; attributes are used in the source but not in the target; and the shipping info and item information are in the opposite order. Can we map the data from the source to the target? Yes, we can do this using XSLT. In this case, presentation is not even a consideration since our goal is strictly to map elements and attributes from the source to elements in the target.

Although this is a gross simplification, the EDI community has been doing precisely this kind of mapping on a much more sophisticated level for decades with costly mapper software. Now we are able to do it in XSLT using free processors. For an XML-EDI approach, see *http://xedi.org/* (XEDI from XML Solutions) and *http://www.vcml.net/* (Value Chain Markup Language from Vitria Technology).

Listing 11-1 Source Invoice Format (source.xml)

```
<Invoice custid="123">
  <ShipTo>
    <Name>Nick Danger</Name>
    <Address>
      <Street>101 The Old Same Place</Street>
      <CityAndState>San Jose, CA</CityAndState>
    </Address>
  </ShipTo>
  <Items count="2">
    <Item id="abc">
      <Description>brown paper bag</Description>
      <Price>.02</Price>
    </Item>
    <Item id="xyz">
      <Description>pickle</Description>
      <Price>.55</Price>
    </Item>
  </Items>
</Invoice>
```

Listing 11-2 Target Invoice Format (target.xml)

```
<Inv.Statement>
  <Goods>
    <ItemDetail>
      <ProductNumber>abc</ProductNumber>
      <Price>.02</Price>
      <Note>brown paper bag</Note>
    </ItemDetail>
    <ItemDetail>
      <ProductNumber>xyz</ProductNumber>
      <Price>.55</Price>
      <Note>pickle</Note>
    </ItemDetail>
    <ItemCount>2</ItemCount>
  </Goods>
  <Customer>123</Customer>
  <Shipping>
    <Address>
      <Street>101 The Old Same Place</Street>
      <City>San Jose</City>
      <State>CA</State>
    </Address>
    <Last.Name>Danger</Last.Name>
    <First.Name>Nick</First.Name>
  </Shipping>
</Inv.Statement>
```

In fact, in 1999 and much of 2000, most so-called XSL implementations supported only the transformation part; they did not address the formatting objects at all! On the other hand, the W3C XSLT specification emphasizes the fact that XSLT is not intended to serve as a general-purpose transformation language. Instead, it is targeted for and optimized for those kinds of transformations that XSL requires.

The second major topic of chapter 11 is **XPath**, which is essentially a thirty-four-page spin-off of the XSL Working Group's efforts. XPath is a UNIX path-like, non-XML syntax for addressing portions of an XML document. *XPath is meant to provide common functionality for several members of the XML family:* XSLT, XML Schema (chapter 6, for identity constraints), XPointer (chapter 14), and XQuery. Unlike XSLT, XSLFO, and for that matter everything we've covered so far except CSS and DTDs, XPath is *not* an XML language itself.[2] It's a compact non-XML syntax used to indicate or select portions of an XML document, such as a group of elements, an

2. In early March 2001, on the xml-dev mailing list a discussion ensued, initiated by Charles Reitzel who suggested giving XPath the "SAX treatment" in order to develop a common API for XPath, SAXPath (Simple API for XPath), that could be used across specs. See *http://lists.xml.org/archives/xml-dev/200103/msg00178.html* and the XML.com article Toward an XPath API by Leigh Dodds, at *http://www.xml.com/pub/a/2001/03/07/xpathapi.html*. In summer 2001, SAXPath beta releases appeared from *http://saxpath.org/*.

individual element, an element with a specific attribute, an element with a particular parent, and so on.

In XPath parlance, the information items of the XML Infoset are called **nodes**. XPath expressions are used to specify nodes by name, by node type, by absolute or relative position within the document structure (hierarchy), by the strings elements contain, and much more. In XSLT, XPath is used to match nodes for further processing and to select (extract) values of nodes. In XPointer, the role of XPath is to indicate an element or range of elements that an XLink specifies. XML Schema uses XPath to define constraints. XQuery syntax is similar to, but not identical, to XPath.[3]

XSLT Processing Model

XSLT is a recursive, template-driven, side-effect free, declarative language rather than a more traditional procedural or sequential program like C or perl. That is, rather than define a step-by-step description of how to convert XML to another form, in XSLT you define blueprints that describe what you'd like the output to look like when certain input elements are encountered.

A stylesheet contains one or more **templates** (rules), each of which is a sample output fragment along with XSLT **instructions** (elements defined in the XSLT language) that inform the XSLT processor how to produce the details of the output. You define a template for each significant element, or group of related elements, of your input with the `<xsl:template>` top-level element. Each template consists of a **match pattern** and a possibly null body, the content of the `<xsl:template>` element.[4] Generally speaking, the template for a given element processes that element and then invokes templates for its children elements, if any, via the `<xsl:apply-templates>` instruction. Children templates handle their own elements and call templates for their children, if any, and so on, in a recursive manner.

This kind of depth-first processing parallels document order, so as we recurse, eventually the most deeply nested elements will be processed completely, then their parents, then their grandparents, and so on, until all descendants of the root element are processed. Recursive processing requires knowing the context of where you (or more precisely, the processor) are at any given point in time. **Context** includes the current node (usually an element, but possibly an attribute or

3. XQuery syntax resembles what is called XPath *abbreviated syntax*, corresponding to child, descendant, and attribute axes. In fact, it is the intention of the W3C that eventually both XML Query and XPath 2.0 will share a common data model. Both must use the Infoset as a base model, especially the Post Schema Validation Infoset (PSVI), the infoset that results after schema validation.

4. This body is confusingly called a "template" in the XSLT 1.0 Recommendation. Therefore, I refer to the children of an `<xsl:template>` element as its **content** or **body**.

namespace), its number in the current context (e.g., the third element named `<bar>` that is a child of `<foo>`, or the fifth element named `<foo>` containing an attribute named `kind`), and the list of variables and namespaces that are presently in scope.

All XSLT processors (Xalan, SAXON, XT, etc.) perform the same series of tasks:

1. The input XML document is parsed, producing an internal representation called the **source tree**. Even if the document refers to a DTD or XML Schema, the stylesheet processor (and therefore the XSLT developer) does not have access to that information, unless the processor vendor provides an extension.
2. The XSLT stylesheet is parsed, producing another internal representation called the **stylesheet tree**.
3. The processor locates the template rule that corresponds to the root node (denoted /).
4. It instantiates the contents (body) of the rule.
5. Elements in a template are either (a) *instructions* from the XSLT namespace to be executed by the processor, such as `<xsl:copy>` or `<xsl:for-each>`, or (b) *content* to be copied verbatim to the **result tree**, such as text nodes or elements from another namespace like HTML. These are called **literal result elements** since they are copied unaltered.
6. The processing of elements is generally in document order, except when you direct the processor otherwise by your use of `<xsl:apply-templates>` and `<xsl:call-template>`, so you can refer to the *nth* occurrence of an element or refer to a particular child of a particular parent, for example.

Figure 11-1 illustrates how the XSLT processor works at a high level.[5] The inputs are one or more XML documents and one or more XSLT stylesheets. The processor applies the stylesheet to the source document after creating the internal source and stylesheet trees, builds the result tree template by template, and the output is *either* altered XML (filtered, sorted, or otherwise transformed, possibly streamed to another process), or serialized as XML, as HTML, as XHTML, or as plain text (e.g., an EDI message, Comma Separated Values, Java code, or just unformatted text). In this chapter we consider only a single pair of input files and a single output, but there's much work being done by the W3C to allow more complicated combinations including multiple outputs from a single source document using the `<xsl:document>` element (in the future XSLT 2.0, or now using nonstandard extensions to XSLT 1.0).

5. A much more detailed description of the internals of one particular XSLT processor is given by Michael Kay in his article, Saxon: The Anatomy of an XSLT processor, *http://www-106.ibm.com/developerworks/library/x-xslt2/*

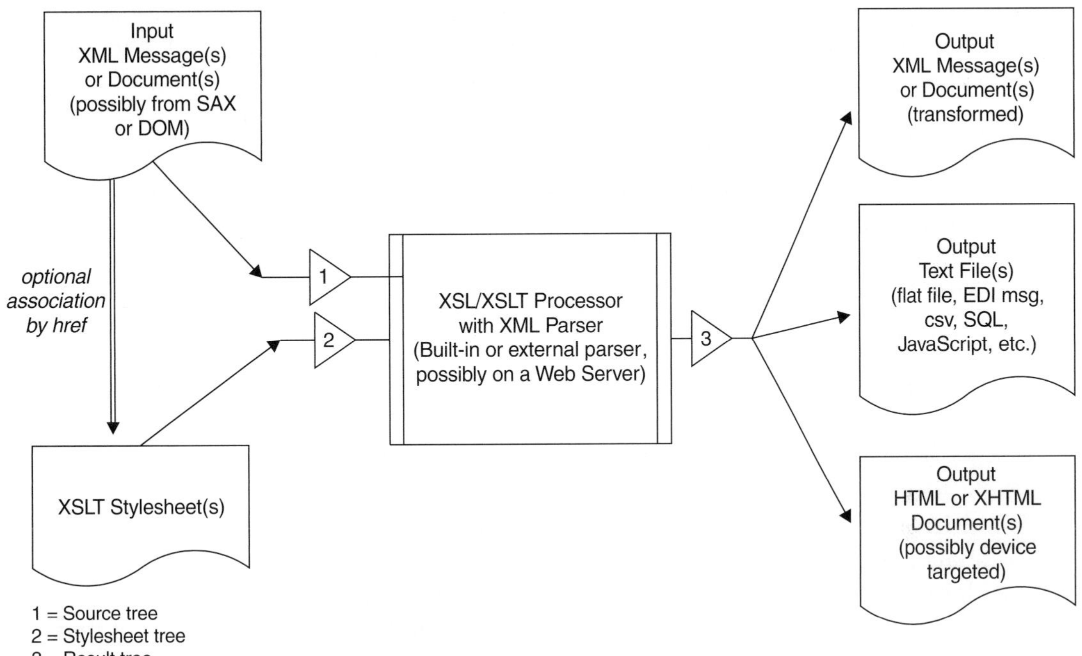

FIGURE 11-1 XSLT processor inputs and outputs

XSLT has several built-in default template rules that have lower precedence than any templates that you define. The defaults come into play only if you don't define a template for a particular information item. Default behavior varies for nodes of different types. For example, the default for elements is to recursively process their children, whereas the default for text nodes is to copy their content (but not their name) to output. All XSLT processors apply specific templates before general ones, so you can easily override the built-in templates by defining your own. If you want to filter out particular nodes, you can even define templates that tell the processor to do nothing when it encounters those nodes.

A single XSLT stylesheet can be applied to multiple instances of a document type, or even to instances of different document types. For example, we could write a stylesheet that simply displays the names of elements and their attributes, and also the attribute values. This stylesheet would work with any input XML document. On the other hand, we could also write multiple stylesheets for processing a single document or class of documents. That is, we could have one stylesheet that processes all elements and attributes, another stylesheet that processes a subset of the elements, and another that sorts elements that have a particular attribute.

In the section "Hello XSLT Example", we consider a basic example, but for now, I'll just whet your appetite with a sneak peek at the example. Try to guess its purpose, even without seeing the input XML document.

```
<?xml version="1.0"?>
<xsl:stylesheet
     xmlns:xsl="http://www.w3.org/1999/XSL/Transform"
     version="1.0">
<xsl:output method="html" />
<xsl:template match="/">
  <b><xsl:value-of select="hi"/></b>
</xsl:template>
</xsl:stylesheet>
```

Later in this chapter, we'll learn about variables and parameters, as well as modes that you can define to alter processing, plus many more XSLT instructions and top-level elements, and functions.

An XSLT processor's view of a stylesheet is a collection or tree of nodes, each of which represents either an XSLT instruction (i.e., an element from the XSLT language) or a literal result element (i.e., an element from HTML, another XML vocabulary, or plain text to be copied unaltered). When writing a stylesheet, you must take into account not only the desired output format, but also the *order* of that output since there is no provision for modifying parts of the result tree once they have been generated. Serialization of the nodes of the result tree is controlled by the output method, which is text, HTML, or XML, perhaps as XSL formatting objects interpreted for a target device, or in rare cases, in a processor-dependent syntax.

As mentioned earlier, built-in default template rules are triggered when no explicit rule is provided by the stylesheet author. Such defaults exist for all node types: root, elements, attributes, text, comments, processing instructions, and namespaces. Often, however, the built-in templates send information to the result tree that is not desired. In those cases, you can override the default template by providing an explicit template that contains an empty body.

XSLT is said to be an example of *side-effect free* programming. This means that the *evaluation of an XPath expression is not permitted to alter the value of a variable or do anything that would not be reproducible the next time the same expression is encountered in the same context.* Furthermore, the XSLT and XPath specifications do not mandate an order of expression evaluation. This is necessary to support parallelism so template rules can be executed in parallel without interdependencies. The good news is that in a side-effects free language, you can't inadvertently modify the value of a global variable, which might impact another function (template) that references that variable. But the bad news is you can't change the value of *any* variable once it is set. The result is that XSLT often requires recursive solutions for problems that, in using procedural languages that permit side effects, you could have used global or static variables to keep track of state.

Historical Perspective

The convoluted development of the XSLT and XPath recommendations is a microcosm of the W3C XML efforts. Their history is interesting and important to understand in case you encounter older software or documentation.

In the early 1990s, Document Style Semantics and Specification Language (DSSSL, ISO/IEC 10179:1996) was created to transform and format SGML, much like XSLT and XSL would eventually be used to transform and format XML. Then in May 1996, when the W3C chartered what was initially called "SGML for the Web" (and eventually became XML), the plans called for only three specifications: XML (syntax), XLink (linking), and XSL (stylesheet language) to parallel the ISO/IEC standards SGML, HyTime (and TEI), and DSSSL, respectively.

A half year before XML 1.0 became a W3C Recommendation, in August 1997, "A Proposal for XSL" was submitted to the W3C by authors from Microsoft Corporation, Inso Corporation, ArborText, University of Edinburgh, and James Clark. At that time, XSL stood for "Extensible *Style* Language." This influential W3C Note eventually gave birth to XSL, XSLT, and XPath.

Microsoft released a technology preview that supported XML and a very early draft of XSL in January 1998. However, it wasn't until May 1998 that the XSL Requirements Summary was published with Norm Walsh (at that time working for ArborText, but later with Sun Microsystems) as editor. Shortly thereafter, in August 1998, the first XSL Working Draft appeared, with the acronym expanded to "Extensible *Stylesheet* Language." In December 1998 a second XSL Working Draft was published; this draft became the basis for Microsoft's support for XSL in IE 5.0, released in March 1999.

Unfortunately, in their push to introduce the new XSL technology early, Microsoft inadvertently created considerable confusion with its MSXML parser, a component first installed with the earlier version of IE 5.x. The "XSL" that IE 5.x supported was actually "XSLT," but a much earlier version (the December 1998 Working Draft) than what the W3C eventually approved in November 1999. To further complicate matters, the IE 5.x version of XSLT required a namespace different from the W3C version: `http://www.w3.org/TR/WD-xsl` (as compared with `http://www.w3.org/1999/XSL/Transform`). This confusion persisted until summer of 2000.

Caution: Remember that any examples on the Microsoft site or in books that refer to the old namespace `http://www.w3.org/TR/WD-xsl` might be obsolete. Although they may resemble the XSLT 1.0 Recommendation elements, such examples will often not work without changes in a non-Microsoft server or non-IE 5.x environment. At a minimum, you'll need to correct the namespace URI.

Shortly after the release of IE 5.0, the third draft of XSL was published in April 1999. This draft marked a major change when the XSL Transformations portion was moved into a separate document. The main XSL spec is sometimes called XSL Formatting Objects, as noted earlier. Several months later, in July 1999, XML Path Language also became a separate document, extracted from the XSLT Working Draft. As discussed earlier, promoting XPath to a full-fledged specification was recognition that the syntax it defined had relevance to other specifications such as XPointer, XML Schema, and what eventually became XQuery, as well as to XSLT itself. Roughly four months after XPath emerged, Extensible Stylesheet Language—Transformations (XSLT) Version 1.0 and XML Path Language (XPath) Version 1.0 both became Recommendations in November 1999.

In March 2000, Microsoft released a beta version of the Microsoft XML Parser Technology Preview Release version 3 (MSXML3 beta) which, in addition to parsing, supported both the outdated December 1998 XSL Working Draft *and* the XSLT 1.0 Recommendation, based on which namespace is specified via the `xml-stylesheet` processing instruction. In July 2000, Microsoft released Internet Explorer 5.5 with improved XML, XSLT, CSS, and DOM support. This included an updated version of MSXML3, which improved support for the November 1999 XSLT 1.0 Recommendation. The final version of MSXML Parser 3.0 (non-beta) was released by Microsoft in October 2000 with server-safe HTTP access, complete implementation of XSLT, XPath, and changes to their Simple API for XML (SAX2) implementation.

In August 2000, the first version of XSLT 1.1 requirements were published. In November 2000, Extensible Stylesheet Language (XSL), which describes a framework for using XSLT to create formatting objects (FO), finally reached Candidate Recommendation status (after seven working drafts), awaiting XSL processor implementations such as FOP from Apache or XEP from RenderX to achieve full acceptance in 2001. Nearly a year later, XSL 1.0 became a W3C Recommendation in October 2001.

In December 2000, the first Working Draft of XSLT Version 1.1 was published. Shortly thereafter, in February 2001, the first set of requirements for XSLT Version 2.0 were issued. Requirements for XPath 2.0 appeared at the same time. However, in April 2001, Sharon Adler, chair of the XSL Working Group, announced at a conference that development of XSLT 1.1 was cancelled as they moved forward with XSLT 2.0 and XPath 2.0, expected some time in 2002. Meanwhile, the XML Query Data Model Working Draft of February 2001 was renamed XQuery 1.0 and XPath 2.0 Data Model in the June 2001 Working Draft. Initial Working Drafts of both XSLT 2.0 and XPath 2.0 appeared in December 2001.

This chapter is based almost exclusively on XSLT 1.0 and XPath 1.0. For extensions and pointers to expected changes in 2.0, see the section entitled "Beyond XSLT 1.0: XSLT 2.0, XPath 2.0, EXSLT, and XSLTSL" later in this chapter.

Relevant Specifications

Quite a number of W3C specifications are related to XSLT and XPath, as shown in Table 11-1. All can be found on the key W3C Technical Reports and Publications page, *http://www.w3.org/TR/*. The table also lists several key URLs that are excellent sources of tracking the W3C plans in these areas.

TABLE 11-1 XSLT, XPath, XSL, and Related Specifications

W3C Specification	*URL* (trailing slash required where indicated)
Associating Stylesheets with XML Documents (W3C Recommendation: June 29, 1999)	*http://www.w3.org/TR/xml-stylesheet/*
XSL Transformations (XSLT) Version 1.0 (W3C Recommendation: November 16, 1999)	*http://www.w3.org/TR/xslt*
XML Path Language (XPath) Version 1.0 (W3C Recommendation: November 16, 1999)	*http://www.w3.org/TR/xpath*
Extensible Stylesheet Language (XSL) Version 1.0 (W3C Candidate Recommendation: November 21, 2000)	*http://www.w3.org/TR/xsl/*
XSL Transformations Requirements Version 1.1 (defunct)	*http://www.w3.org/TR/xslt11req*
XSLT 1.1 Working Draft (defunct)	*http://www.w3.org/TR/xslt11*
Working Drafts	
XSLT Requirements 2.0	*http://www.w3.org/TR/xslt20req*
XSL Transformations (XSLT) Version 2.0	*http://www.w3.org/TR/xslt20/*
XPath Requirements 2.0	*http://www.w3.org/TR/xpath20req*
XML Path Language (XPath) 2.0	*http://www.w3.org/TR/xpath20/*
XQuery 1.0 and XPath 2.0 Data Model	*http://www.w3.org/TR/query-datamodel/*
XQuery 1.0: An XML Query Language	*http://www.w3.org/TR/xquery/*
XQuery 1.0 and XPath 2.0 Functions and Operators	*http://www.w3.org/TR/xquery-operators/*
Related W3C Activity and Working Group Home Pages	
XSL Home Page (worth bookmarking)	*http://www.w3.org/Style/XSL/*
W3C Style Home Page (XSL, CSS, DSSSL, etc.)	*http://www.w3.org/Style*
W3C Style Activity Statement (status, direction)	*http://www.w3.org/Style/Activity*
XSL Working Group (W3C Members Only)	*http://www.w3.org/Style/XSL/Group/*
XSL Working Group Charter (public page; lists order of deliverables, relationship to other Working Groups, etc.)	*http://www.w3.org/Style/2000/xsl-charter.html*
XML Query Home Page	*http://www.w3.org/XML/Query*

Using XSLT

Next we turn to a high-level view of the uses of XSLT on servers, present capabilities and advantages, and conclude with a list of popular XSLT processors.

Server-Side Transformations

Even though XSLT and XPath have been W3C Recommendations since November 1999, at the time of this writing, browser support for client-side XSLT is lacking. Therefore, the vast majority of developers using XSLT are doing so in the context of Web servers. One class of applications calls an XSLT processor (in some server-dependent way) to perform the transformation and often delivers generated HTML to the client browser. Of course, if the XML data being processed is static, it is not necessary for the server to run the XSLT processor at page request time. Instead, it is more typical to have some batchlike process invoke the processor during some downtime, or perhaps only when the XML data changes, or when there is a sitewide style change. Some sites with a significant user base with XML-capable browsers offload much of the server processing by sending XML data to client browsers along with stylesheets that will be processed by the browser.

But XSLT is not only about generating HTML from XML data and delivering the result to browsers. XSLT is equally useful (some might argue *more* useful) in *transforming one kind of XML into another XML vocabulary*, and not just into XSLFO (another XML vocabulary), for which XSLT was originally invented. XSLT can be used to filter XML data, pulling out just those elements of interest to a downstream process, or perhaps sorting the XML data by criteria depending on the application.

Apache Cocoon is a freeware XML/XSL/DOM publishing framework useful in server-side processing (*http://xml.apache.org/cocoon/index.html*). In addition, many commercial products, such as TIBCO Extensibility's XMLTransform, Infoteria's Asteria Platform, and eXcelon Corporation's Stylus Studio, provide these capabilities and more.

XSLT and XSLFO Software Lists

In addition to these server-side transformation products, XSLT processors are listed in Table 11-2. Major sites that list XSLT and XSLFO software include:

- *http://www.xmlsoftware.com/*
- *http://xslt.com/*
- *http://xml.coverpages.org/xslSoftware.html*

You'll also find a long list of XSLT (and XSLFO) software in the "For Further Exploration" section.

Functional Capabilities of XSLT

Some of the many powerful capabilities of XSLT that we'll see by example in this chapter are:

- *Filtering* XML elements from the input document using match patterns
- *Sorting* input based on element names or attribute values
- *Transposing* the order of elements
- *Creating* new elements and attributes
- Incorporating *fixed text* in output
- Repeating text content extracted from the input for *multiple purposes* in the output (e.g., headings and table of contents)
- *Computing new content* based on existing content in the source document
- *Conditional processing* based on values in the XML source
- *Looping* through a set of nodes
- *Copying subtrees* of source documents to output
- Processing elements in multiple ways (passes) based on different template *modes*
- Accessing XPath and XSLT *functions* for string manipulation, basic math operations, and node processing
- *Reusing code* by defining named templates and attribute sets

Advantages of XSL/XSLT Compared to CSS

At the end of chapter 10, we listed a number of limitations of using CSS with XML. Although CSS is still a viable alternative if your processing needs aren't very involved, XSLT affords you much greater flexibility.

- Your application does not have to be restricted to a browser since transformations can be made on the server side and sent between applications.
- You can process elements, attributes, and content selectively based on any combination (e.g., extract the first hyphen-separated part of the content of the fifth element named `Book` that has an attribute named `type` with the value "paperback").
- You can add elements and content to the output that did not appear in the source.
- You can sort or filter input data.
- You can do conditional processing.
- You can invoke numerous built-in functions or add your own user-defined functions, including escaping to languages like Java and JavaScript for sophisticated processing.
- You can achieve complicated, desktop publishing page layouts and styles when XSLT is combined with XSLFO.

Choosing and Using XSLT Processors

There are many good XSLT processors, some freeware and some commercial, and the list is growing constantly (see *http://www.xmlsoftware.com/xslt/* and *http://xslt.com/xslt_tools.htm*). In general, XSLT processors accept as input an XML instance and an XSLT stylesheet, and optionally an output file (which could be XML, HTML, plain text, etc.). Let's refer to these three files as %1 for the XML input, %2 for the XSLT stylesheet, and %3 for the output, regardless of its file type. In Table 11-2, the DOS syntax %CAPS% denotes the installation directory. For example, %XALAN% and %SAXON% refer to locations that have been set either in your environment or in a .bat file, such as:

```
set XALAN=C:\XML\APACHE\xalan-j_2_2_D14\bin
```

or

```
set SAXON=C:\XML\saxon-65
```

For those less familiar with Java, the "jre -cp" lines are calls to the Java Runtime Environment with explicit CLASSPATH settings for locating the Java ARchive (JAR) files that comprise the XSLT processor and possibly a separate XML parser. (The alternative is to set the CLASSPATH environment variable and invoke java directly.) Note that although the command lines are similar across processors, there are differences in the order of the file parameters. The table also

TABLE 11-2 Selected XSLT Processors

Processor	*Vendor*	*Command Line and Download and Documentation URL*

Xalan	Apache	`jre -cp "%XALAN%xalan.jar;%XERCES%xerces.jar"`
		`org.apache.xalan.xslt.Process -in %1 -xsl %2 -out %3`
		See *http://xml.apache.org/xalan-j/index.html*

SAXON	Michael Kay	`saxon -o %3 %1 %2`
		`jre -cp "%SAXON%saxon.jar" com.icl.saxon.StyleSheet -o %3 %1 %2`
		See *http://saxon.sourceforge.net/*

XT	James Clark and 4xt.org	`jre -cp "%JCLARK%xt.jar;%JCLARK%sax.jar;%JCLARK%xp.jar"`
		`com.jclark.xsl.sax.Driver %1 %2 %3`
		See *http://jclark.com/xml/xt.html* and *http://4xt.org/*

Oracle XML Developer's Kit (XDK)	Oracle	`jre -nojit -cp "%ORACLE%xmlparserv2.jar"`
		`oracle.xml.parser.v2.oraxsl %1 %2 %3`
		See *http://technet.oracle.com/tech/xml/xdk_java.html*

iXSLT	Infoteria	`ixslt -a -i:%1 -o:%3 %2` See *http://www.infoteria.com/en/contents/product/ixslt/ index.html*

includes the home page URLs for each processor. In the section "Hello XSLT Example," we'll introduce `xalan-it.bat` to simplify Xalan Java use. If you decide to use a different XSLT processor, you could adapt the .bat file using the command-line information shown in Table 11-2.

When considering which XSLT processor to use, it's a good idea to read what the vendor says about conformance, since at the time of this writing, XSLT 1.0 is the standard, with 1.1 (now defunct) and 2.0 in various stages of planning. For example, the conformance notes that accompany SAXON 6.5 (*http://saxon.sourceforge.net/saxon6.5/conformance.html*) state:

> SAXON is 100 percent conformant to the mandatory requirements of these standards. SAXON also implements certain facilities defined in the draft XSLT 1.1 specification, but these are only available when the stylesheet specifies version="1.1", or when the relevant construct is within a literal result element that specifies xsl:version="1.1". Note that the W3C XSL Working Group has announced that XSLT 1.1 will not be taken beyond working draft status, so there is no guarantee that these features are stable.

It's also useful to consider which extension functions and extension elements, if any, the processor implements. Again using SAXON as an example, SAXON provides additional attributes for the `<xsl:output>` and `<xsl:document>` elements (*http://saxon.sourceforge.net/saxon6.5/extensions.html*).

Of course, processor performance and completeness of specification implementation are both of primary importance. See

- OASIS XSLT/XPath Conformance Technical Subcommittee, *http://www.oasis-open.org/committees/xslt/*
- NIST XSL Testing (XSLFO, XSLT, XPath), *http://xw2k.sdct.itl.nist.gov/xml/page5.html*
- XML.com article, "XSLT Processor Benchmarks," *http://www.xml.com/pub/a/2001/03/28/xsltmark/index.html*
- XSLTMark, *http://www.datapower.com/XSLTMark/*
- XSLBench, *http://www.tfi-technology.com/xml/xslbench.html*

Running the Xalan XSLT Processor

The batch file `xalan-it.bat` shown in Listing 11-3 is intended for running the Apache Xalan XSLT processor with Windows 98, Windows 2000, or Windows NT. If you use one of the other processors listed in Table 11-2, it shouldn't be difficult to modify the batch file based on the information in the table. If you wish to try Saxon, a similar batch file called `saxon-it.bat` is also provided.

All batch files shown in the book assume that you've configured your environment according to this book's CD-ROM instructions. See Appendix D, "Setting Up Your Environment," which describes how to modify and use `xmlsetup.bat`. Among other things, `xmlsetup.bat` defines `%JBIN%`, `%XALAN_HOME%`, and `%XALAN_JARS%` as `C:\Java\jdk1.3.1\bin`, `C:\XML\Apache\ xalan-j_2_2_D14`, and `%XALAN_HOME%\bin\xalan.jar;%XALAN_HOME%\bin\ xml-apis.jar; %XALAN_HOME%\bin\xerces.jar`, by default. This is easily configurable and is the recommended means to experiment with this book's code examples.

To run the Xalan Java XSLT processor, pass the script three parameters on the command line:

```
C:> xalan-it XML_file_to_process XSLT_file_to_run Output_file
```

For example, to invoke the script on Windows 98 to apply the stylesheet `hello.xsl` (Listing 11-4) to transform the input file `hello.xml` into the output `hello.html`, type:

```
C:> xalan-it hello.xml hello.xsl hello.html
```

which expands to something like this (depending on your installation locations and Xalan and Java versions in `xmlsetup.bat`):

```
C:> java -classpath C:\XML\Apache\xalan-j_2_2_D14\bin\xalan.jar;
C:\XML\Apache\xalan-j_2_2_D14\bin\xml-apis.jar;
C:\XML\Apache\xalan-j_2_2_D14\bin\xerces.jar org.apache.xalan.xslt.Process
-IN hello.xml -XSL hello.xsl -OUT hello.html
```

Listing 11-3 Batch File for Running Apache Xalan-Java XSLT Processor (xalan-it.bat)

```
@REM   Using Apache's Xalan-Java XSLT Processor
@echo off


REM Xalan includes its own version of Xerces parser.
REM This file assumes %XALAN_JARS% has been defined in xmlsetup as:
REM  set XALAN_JARS=%XALAN_HOME%\bin\xalan.jar;
%XALAN_HOME%\bin\xml-apis.jar;%XALAN_HOME%\bin\xerces.jar
REM Could set Java classpath.
REM    set classpath=%JLIB%;%XALAN_JARS%
REM    set XSLT_CLASS=org.apache.xalan.xslt.Process
REM Run xalan.
REM   %JBIN%\java -classpath %JLIB%;%XALAN_JARS% org.apache.xalan.xslt.Process
-IN %1 -XSL %2 -OUT %3


@echo on
  %JBIN%\java -classpath %XALAN_JARS% org.apache.xalan.xslt.Process -IN %1
-XSL %2 -OUT %3
@echo off
```

Hello XSLT Example

We're finally ready to consider a simple XSLT example! We'll start with an exceedingly simple XML input document, `hello.xml`, consisting of only one element, `<hi>`, and the XML declaration.

```
<?xml version="1.0"?>
<hi>Hello, XSLT!</hi>
```

Our first task is to write an XSLT stylesheet consisting of a single template that extracts the content from the `<hi>` element and surrounds it with the HTML `<b>` element (to render the content bold). Since XSLT is an XML dialect, we begin our stylesheet, shown in Listing 11-4, with an XML declaration. Then we use the `<xsl:stylesheet>` element to enclose all XSLT instructions and data of our stylesheet; it is always the outermost element of an XSLT stylesheet. Next, we inform the processor that our desired output method is "html" (note the lowercase). If we did not specify this, the processor would produce XML (including an XML declaration) because *XML is the default XSLT output method*.

For our modest purposes, a sole template specifies a match pattern of `"/"`, which matches what the XPath model refers to as the **root node** of our source tree, which is analogous to the *document node* of the DOM model and should not be confused with the *document element*, which is `<hi>` in this example.

The content (or body) of our template uses the `<xsl:value-of>` instruction to extract the value of the selected node, `<hi>`. In terms of XPath, `<xsl:value-of>` is evaluated in the context of the root node, so the full implied XPath expression to reach the selected node is `"/hi"`, which we determine by concatenating the root node with the selected node. (If the element `<hi>` weren't the document element and instead had a parent named `<doc>`, then the path would be `/doc/hi`.)

Listing 11-4 Basic XSLT Stylesheet, hello.xsl (Used with hello.xml)

```
<?xml version="1.0"?>
<xsl:stylesheet
     xmlns:xsl="http://www.w3.org/1999/XSL/Transform"
     version="1.0">
<xsl:output method="html" />
<xsl:template match="/">
  <b><xsl:value-of select="hi"/></b>
</xsl:template>
</xsl:stylesheet>
```

There are many XSLT processors available as we saw in Table 11-2. In this chapter we use Apache Xalan-Java 2.x. We use the batch file `xalan-it.bat`, shown in Listing 11-4, passing it our input XML and XSLT files and the desired output HTML file:

```
C:> xalan-it.bat hello.xml hello.xsl hello.html
```

Our wonderfully exciting result is written to the output file `hello.html`, which contains the single line

```
<b>Hello, XSLT!</b>
```

Of course, this is not a completely valid HTML page since it's missing a DOCTYPE declaration, as well as <html>, <head>, and <body> elements, but all browsers will display it just fine. We'll see how to produce a more comprehensive HTML document in later examples.

We can achieve the identical result if the match expression is explicitly "/hi", the full path to the <hi> element, and the `select` attribute is merely ".", which is **abbreviated syntax** (shorthand) for the current node. The alternative stylesheet is shown in Listing 11-5.

Listing 11-5 Alternative Stylesheet, hello-alt.xsl, Produces the Same Result

```
<?xml version="1.0"?>
<xsl:stylesheet
     xmlns:xsl="http://www.w3.org/1999/XSL/Transform"
     version="1.0">
<xsl:output method="html" />
<xsl:template match="/hi">     <!-- equivalent XPath expression -->
  <b><xsl:value-of select="."/></b>
</xsl:template>
</xsl:stylesheet>
```

If we alter the output formatting by changing the <b> to <i> in the stylesheet `hello-italics.xsl`, as shown in Listing 11-6, the resultant HTML is as you would expect:

```
<i>Hello, XSLT!</i>
```

The visual presentation of both the bold and italics version of the generated HTML files is demonstrated in IE 5.5 in Figure 11-2.

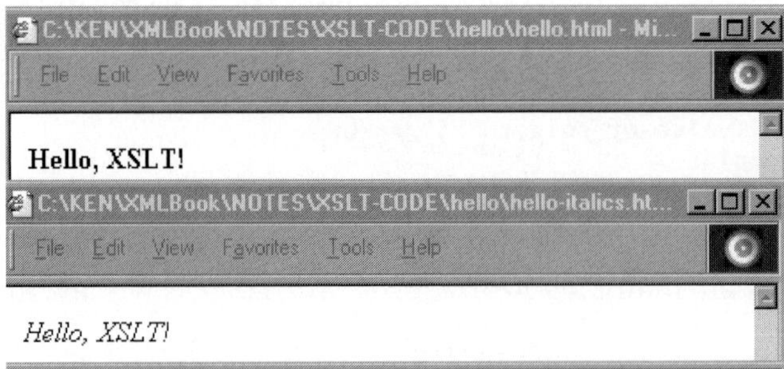

FIGURE 11-2 Hello, XSLT as HTML displayed (bold and italics)

Listing 11-6 Alternative Stylesheet, hello-italics.xsl, Produces Different Result

```
<?xml version="1.0"?>
<xsl:stylesheet
     xmlns:xsl="http://www.w3.org/1999/XSL/Transform"
     version="1.0">
<xsl:output method="html" />
<xsl:template match="/">
  <i><xsl:value-of select="hi"/></i>
</xsl:template>
</xsl:stylesheet>
```

Later in this chapter, we'll revisit this example when we consider other output methods (XML and text) and when we see how to associate an XSLT stylesheet with an XML document.

XSLT Concepts and Examples

In this long section and the next, we'll cover in more depth the concepts already introduced and we'll explore additional details about XSLT and XPath. Because these two specifications are interrelated (or at least XSLT is dependent on XPath for `match` and `select` attributes), some forward references are unavoidable. Table 11-3 is a roadmap of concepts we'll cover with each example in this lengthy chapter.

TABLE 11-3 Code Examples Roadmap

XSLT Filename[a]	*Instructions and Concepts Introduced*
`hello.xsl` `hello-italics.xsl`	`<xsl:stylesheet>`, `<xsl:template>`, `<xsl:value-of>`, basic HTML output
`c6-empty.xsl`	minimal stylesheet, which exercises all built-in defaults
`c6-filter.xsl`	filtering elements of interest via the `match` and `select` attributes, complete HTML output, `<xsl:text>`, `<xsl:template>`, `<xsl:apply-templates>`, `<xsl:value-of>`
`c6-if.xsl`	conditional test using `<xsl:if>`, defining constants with `<xsl:variable>`, `position()` and `last()` functions
`c6-var.xsl`	setting the value of a variable with the `select` attribute of `<xsl:variable>`
`c6-choose.xsl`	multiple decision via `<xsl:choose>`, `<xsl:when>`, and `<xsl:otherwise>`, `name()` function,
`c6-table.xsl`	generating an HTML table with some CSS style support
`c6-attributes.xsl`	selecting and comparing values of attributes, `contains()` function
`c6-attr-set.xsl`	generating an HTML table with `<xsl:attribute-set>` and `<xsl:use-attribute-sets>`

continued

TABLE 11-3 Code Examples Roadmap *(continued)*

XSLT Filename[a]	*Instructions and Concepts Introduced*
c6-copy.xsl	XML output; copying selected nodes but producing only a document fragment
c6-copy-of.xsl	XML output; copying selected nodes producing well-formed output that has slightly different elements from the source document using <xsl:element> and <xsl:attribute>
c6-identity.xsl	XML output; copying via the identity transform
c6-for-each.xsl	sort alphabetically using <xsl:for-each> and <xsl:sort>, numbering nodes in document order via <xsl:number>
c6-sort*.xsl	sort alphabetically using <xsl:apply-templates> and <xsl:sort>, numbering nodes via position() function; several variations
c6-escape.xsl	demonstrates disable-output-escaping attribute of <xsl:text> for displaying character entities
hello.xsl variations	tests variations of <xsl:output> methods (XML and text)
c6-param.xsl	illustrates named templates which can accept parameters and can have default values; <xsl:param>, <xsl:call-template>, <xsl:with-param>, <xsl:template name=....>
c6-loopControl.xsl	shows how to control the number of iterations of a loop by taking advantage of recursion
c6-param-cmdline.xsl	demonstrates passing values from the command line to a stylesheet and overriding default values of <xsl:param> elements
c6-param-return.xsl	shows how to return a value from a named template, much like a function call in more traditional computer languages
c6-identity2.xsl	illustrates the use of *attribute value templates* to determine element and attribute names at runtime
try-import-string.xsl	shows how to import another stylesheet using <xsl:import> and how to reference XSLT named templates from another namespace by setting the extension-element-prefixes attribute of the <xsl:stylesheet> element
c6-axes.xsl	demonstrates all 13 axes (with respect to the context node) defined in the XPath model, such as child, descendant, parent, following-sibling, etc.
c6-nodes.xsl	exercises the XPath node() function, uses count() to determine if a node is a leaf (has no children), uses the comment(), processing-instruction(), and text() functions, uses normalize-space() to display value of the root node
c6-xpath.xsl	illustrates a variety of XPath expressions with and without predicates, including comparing text content and attribute values to known values, moving up and down the tree's path, and processing the same data differently depending on the mode attribute of <xsl:template>
c6-strings.xsl	illustrates most XPath string functions such as string(), string-length(), normalize-space(), substring-before(), substring-after(), translate(), concat(), starts-with(), contains(), and substring().

TABLE 11-3 *(continued)*

XSLT Filename[a]	*Instructions and Concepts Introduced*
`c6-math.xsl`	exercises various XPath math functions such as `format-number()`, `sum()`, `floor()`, `ceiling()`, `round()`, range checking a value, boolean and relational operators, addition and division
`c6-xslt-func.xsl`	`extension-element-prefixes` and namespaces for `<xsl:stylesheet>`; testing for extension elements and extension functions via `element-available()` and `function-available()` functions; conditional setting of variable; using the `system-property()` function to conditionally execute instructions depending on which XSLT processor is running; using the `document()` function to return nodes from a document other than the original source document; using the `format-number()` function; using `<xsl:key>` and the related `key()` function; using the `generate-id()` function
`cs1.xsl`, `cs2.xsl`, `cs3.xsl`, `cs4.xsl`, `case-study.xsl`	a case study; several phases of a solution to a problem that involves filtering a section from an XML document to produce a list of links and link titles, possibly sorted, with CSS style information

a. Listed here in the order in which they are presented in this chapter.

Roughly the first half of this chapter is based on learning by example. Readers who are uncomfortable with this approach and prefer a more formal description of the XSLT elements and XPath concepts and functions can skip ahead to the section "XPath Concepts and Examples" plus the tables presented in "XPath Functions," in "XSLT Elements and Instructions," and in "XSLT Functions." However, I recommend reading this chapter in the order in which I've written it. (Hey, is that called document order, too?)

Example XML Document: collection6.xml

We revisit our CD-ROM and book collection example with the variation named `collection6.xml` shown in Listing 11-7. Unless stated otherwise, this file is the default XML input for all examples in this chapter.

Listing 11-7 XML Document to Be Transformed (collection6.xml)

```
<?xml version="1.0" standalone="yes"?>

<Collection version="2" xmlns:xhtml="http://www.w3.org/1999/xhtml"
xmlns:html="http://www.w3.org/TR/REC-html40">
  <Book>
    <Title>Complete Beatles Chronicle, The</Title>
    <Author>
      <Name>
        <First>Mark</First>
        <Last>Lewisohn</Last>
      </Name>
```

```
      </Author>
      <Type>Chronology</Type>
      <Published publisher="Harmony Books">1992</Published>
      <Rating>5 stars</Rating>
      <Notes>
    Covers the years 1957 through 1970. No solo info.
    Great appendices with chart info, discography, composer index,
    radio, tv, and live performances, and much more.
    Second Edition: May 2000 with George Martin as co-author.
      </Notes>
      <ListPrice>24.95</ListPrice>
    </Book>
    <CD>
      <Title>Band on the Run</Title>
      <Artist>McCartney, Paul and Wings</Artist>
      <Chart>
        <Peak weeks="4">1</Peak>
        <Peak country="UK">1</Peak>
        <!-- guess -->
      </Chart>
      <Type>Rock</Type>
      <Label>Capitol</Label>
      <Label country="UK">EMI</Label>
      <AlbumReleased>1973</AlbumReleased>
      <Remastered format="gold CD">1993</Remastered>
      <Remastered format="2 disc box set with booklet">1999</Remastered>
      <ListPrice>16.97</ListPrice>
    </CD>
    <CD>
      <Title>Venus and Mars</Title>
      <Artist>McCartney, Paul and Wings</Artist>
      <Chart>
        <Peak weeks="1">1</Peak>
        <Peak country="UK">2</Peak>
        <!-- guess -->
      </Chart>
      <Type>Rock</Type>
      <Label>Capitol</Label>
      <Label country="UK">EMI</Label>
      <AlbumReleased>1975</AlbumReleased>
      <Remastered format="gold CD with 3 bonus tracks">1994</Remastered>
      <ListPrice>16.97</ListPrice>
    </CD>


  <?bogus-pi attr1="foo" attr2="foobar" ?>

    <Book>
      <Title>Many Years From Now</Title>
      <Author>
        <Name>
          <First>Paul</First>
          <Last>McCartney</Last>
        </Name>
```

```
    </Author>
    <Type>Autobiographical</Type>
    <Published publisher="Henry Holt and Company">1997</Published>
    <Rating>4 stars</Rating>
    <Notes>654 pages; Reprint edition (October 1998)</Notes>
    <ListPrice>27.50</ListPrice>
    <!-- Notice the absence of Rating element.
  I haven't read this book yet. This illustrates some optional
  elements that are children of Book element.
  -->
  </Book>
  <Book>
    <Title>Beatles Anthology, The</Title>
    <Author>
      <Name>
        <First>Paul</First>
        <Last>McCartney</Last>
      </Name>
    </Author>
    <Author>
      <Name>
        <First>George</First>
        <Last>Harrison</Last>
      </Name>
    </Author>
    <Author>
      <Name>
        <First>Ringo</First>
        <Last>Starr</Last>
      </Name>
    </Author>
    <Author>
      <Name>
        <First>John</First>
        <Last>Lennon</Last>
      </Name>
    </Author>
    <Type>Autobiographical</Type>
    <Published publisher="Chronicle Books">2000</Published>
    <Rating>5 stars</Rating>
    <Notes>368 pages of the Beatles in their own words and pictures!
    A must-have for true Beatles fans.</Notes>
    <ListPrice>60.00</ListPrice>
  </Book>
  <CD>
    <Title>Beatles 1</Title>
    <Artist>Beatles</Artist>
    <Chart>
      <Peak weeks="10" country="US">1</Peak>
    </Chart>
    <Type>Rock</Type>
    <Label country="US">Capitol</Label>
    <AlbumReleased>November 14, 2000</AlbumReleased>
    <ListPrice>18.97</ListPrice>
```

```
    </CD>
    <Owner>
      <Name sex="male">
        <First>Ken</First>
        <Last>Sall</Last>
      </Name>
      <Address>
        <Street>123 Milky Way Dr.</Street>
        <City>Columbia</City>
        <State>MD</State>
        <Zip>20794</Zip>
      </Address>
    </Owner>
</Collection>
```

Sometimes it's instructive to view an XML document in a tree form that reveals the node types. A freeware stylesheet utility called ASCII XML Tree Viewer (`ascii-tree.xsl`) displays the node structure of an XML document as plain text 'ASCII art' using the model explained in Section 5 of the XPath recommendation. The stylesheet is written by Jeni Tennison and Mike J. Brown. (See *http://skew.org/xml/stylesheets/treeview/ascii/* and *http://skew.org/xml/stylesheets/treeview/html/*. A related utility is `showtree.xsl` by Crane Softwrights, *http://www.cranesoftwrights.com/resources/showtree/*.) A fancier version that uses CSS combined with XSLT, called Tree Viewer (`tree-view.xsl`), is also freely available; you can customize the appearance by altering the CSS. I'd recommend using Netscape 6 or IE 5.5 or above to view the fancy version.

We've shown the partial output of the ASCII version in Listing 11-8. Note the nodes labeled root, element, attribute, text (character data), processing instruction, and comment. Not shown is an example of a namespace node. The seven node types are discussed in detail in "NodeTypes, NodeValues, and NodeTests."

Listing 11-8 Partial Output from ascii-treeview.xsl

```
root
  |___element 'Collection'
        |  \___attribute 'version' = '2'
        |___text '\n  '
        |___element 'Book'
        |     |___text '\n    '
        |     |___element 'Title'
        |     |     |___text 'Complete Beatles Chronicle, The'
        |     |___text '\n    '
        |     |___element 'Author'
        |     |     |___text '\n      '
        |     |     |___element 'Name'
        |     |     |     |___text '\n        '
        |     |     |     |___element 'First'
```

```
|       |       |       |       |___text 'Mark'
|       |       |       |___text '\n          '
|       |       |       |___element 'Last'
|       |       |       |       |___text 'Lewisohn'
|       |       |       |___text '\n        '
|       |       |___text '\n      '
|       |___text '\n    '
|       |___element 'Type'
|       |       |___text 'Chronology'
|       |___text '\n    '
|       |___element 'Published'
|       |       |  \___attribute 'publisher' = 'Harmony Books'
|       |       |___text '1992'
|       |___text '\n    '
|       |___element 'Rating'
|       |       |___text '5 stars'
|       |___text '\n    '
|       |___element 'Notes'
|       |       |___text '\n  Covers the years 1957 through 1970. No solo
info.\n  Great appendices with chart info, discography, composer index,\n
radio, tv, and live performances, and much more.\n  Second Edition: May 2000
with George Martin as co-author.\n    '
|       |___text '\n    '
|       |___element 'ListPrice'
|       |       |___text '24.95'
|       |___text '\n  '
|___text '\n  '
|___element 'CD'
|       |___text '\n    '
|       |___element 'Title'
|       |       |___text 'Band on the Run'
|       |___text '\n    '
|       |___element 'Artist'
|       |       |___text 'McCartney, Paul and Wings'
|       |___text '\n    '
|       |___element 'Chart'
|       |       |___text '\n      '
|       |       |___element 'Peak'
|       |       |       |  \___attribute 'weeks' = '4'
|       |       |       |___text '1'
|       |       |___text '\n      '
|       |       |___element 'Peak'
|       |       |       |  \___attribute 'country' = 'UK'
|       |       |       |___text '1'
|       |       |___text '\n      '
|       |       |___comment ' guess '
|       |       |___text '\n    '
|       |___text '\n    '
|       |___element 'Type'
|       |       |___text 'Rock'
|       |___text '\n    '
|       |___element 'Label'
|       |       |___text 'Capitol'
```

```
|       |___text '\n     '
|       |___element 'Label'
|       |      | \___attribute 'country' = 'UK'
|       |      |___text 'EMI'
|       |___text '\n     '
|       |___element 'AlbumReleased'
|       |      |___text '1973'
|       |___text '\n     '
|       |___element 'Remastered'
|       |      | \___attribute 'format' = 'gold CD'
|       |      |___text '1993'
|       |___text '\n     '
|       |___element 'Remastered'
|       |      | \___attribute 'format'='2 disc box set with booklet'
|       |      |___text '1999'
|       |___text '\n     '
|       |___element 'ListPrice'
|       |      |___text '16.97'
|       |___text '\n   '
|___text '\n  '
|___element 'CD'
                  [....stuff deleted....]
|___text '\n\n'
|___processing instruction target='bogus-pi'
                instruction='attr1="foo" attr2="foobar" '
|___text '\n\n  '
|___element 'Book'
etc.
```

Central Concepts

In this section, we'll examine another simple example, but in a bit more detail than the previous one, illustrating more key concepts. (Dave Pawson's XSLT Terminology is a handy list of XSLT definitions—see *http://www.dpawson.co.uk/xsl/vocab.html*.)

Filtering Example

Our first substantial stylesheet, `c6-filter.xsl`, shown in Listing 11-9, is useful for emphasizing several of the main concepts of XSLT. The input document is `collection6.xml` (Listing 11-7). This stylesheet examines only the `CD` and `Book` elements from the source document and, for each, extracts the value (text content) of the `Title` element. To process this example, we again use our batch file to run Xalan:

```
C:> xalan-it collection6.xml c6-filter.xsl c6-filter.html
```

Listing 11-9 Filtering by Template Matching: c6-filter.xsl

```
<?xml version="1.0"?>
<xsl:stylesheet   version="1.0"
  xmlns:xsl="http://www.w3.org/1999/XSL/Transform">
<xsl:output method="html"/>

<xsl:template match="/">
   <html>
     <head>
       <title>XSLT: Filtering Titles</title>
     </head>
     <body>
       <h1>XSLT: Filtering Titles</h1>
       <xsl:apply-templates select="Collection/CD | //Book"/>
       <!-- In this example,  Collection/CD = //CD and
            Collection/Book = //Book.
       -->
     </body>
   </html>
</xsl:template>

<xsl:template match="CD">
   <br /><xsl:text>CD title: </xsl:text>
   <i><xsl:value-of select="Title" /></i>
</xsl:template>

<xsl:template match="Book">
   <br /><xsl:text>Book title: </xsl:text>
   <i><xsl:value-of select="Title" /></i>
</xsl:template>
</xsl:stylesheet>
```

Details of this example are discussed in the next few subsections.

Templates and Match and Select Patterns

The stylesheet consists of the required <xsl:stylesheet>, plus <xsl:output> to specify HTML instead of the default XML, and three <xsl:template> elements. Recall that a template is a rule that indicates which elements are of concern and what to do when they are encountered. Any element that is a direct child of <xsl:stylesheet> is a **top-level element**, such as <xsl:output> and <xsl:template>. (Variables, processing instructions, comments, and a small subset of the XSLT language can be top-level elements.)

The first template is associated with the root node, indicated by the line:

```
<xsl:template match="/">
```

Since there is always exactly one root, it makes sense to perform any setup we need for HTML output here. This time we've generated a more complete HTML document with <html>, <head>, and <body> elements (although no DOCTYPE). Next, we're ready to process children of the root. We can automatically ignore everything except CD and Book elements by calling <xsl:apply-templates> and setting the select attribute to the "or" ("|") of these two elements, which selects nodes named CD *and* nodes named Book.

```
<xsl:apply-templates select="Collection/CD | //Book"/>
```

I deliberately specified the path to the two elements differently to illustrate their equivalence in this example (but not in the general case). Remember that "/" is the *root node*, not the document element, so to reference CD relative to "/", we could use either of these two XPath expressions:

```
Collection/CD
```

or

```
//CD
```

since CD elements are always the direct children of Collection. On the other hand, the latter XPath expression involving the double slash "//" is actually more general, since it refers to CD elements *at any level* (that is, any CD descendants of the document element, Collection, regardless of the number of intermediate levels). If our example were characterized by the (impractical) structure

```
<Collection>
  <CD/>
  <Book/>
  <BoxSet>
    <CD/>
    <CD/>
  </BoxSet>
</Collection>
```

the expression //CD would select all three CD elements, regardless of their depth, whereas the expression Collection/CD would match only the CD that is the immediate child of Collection.

Source Trees, Result Trees, and Literal Result Elements

The **source tree** is the in-memory representation of the XML source document, created as the XSLT processor finishes parsing. The processor also builds a tree for the input XSLT stylesheet. However, it is the **result tree** that you create as stylesheet author when you specify the content that is generated based on element and attribute patterns that occur in the source tree.

A **literal result element** is any element that is neither an XSLT instruction nor an element from any other extension namespace declared in the stylesheet. In our example, all elements from the HTML namespace are literal result elements. When we use XSLT to transform one type of XML to another type of XML, the target XML elements are also literal result elements. In any event, such elements are used to create content in the result tree, whether the content is HTML or XML elements.

Current Node and Context Node

Normally current node and context node refer to the same thing—the node that is currently being processed by the processor. When we cover abbreviated syntax later, we'll see that "." refers to the *current* node at any point during expression evaluation. However, within an XPath **predicate** (the optional part of an XPath expression in square brackets), the two may differ. While the **context node** does not vary during expression evaluation, the **current node** may change depending on the evaluation within the predicate.

The ordered set of nodes that results from triggering a template is called the **current node list**. This list changes whenever a `match` or `select` attribute is encountered. By default, the nodes of the current node list are in document order, although this can be altered using the `<xsl:sort>` instruction, described later. For example, when the template matches all `CD` and `Book` children, the set of all such elements is the current node list. As these elements are encountered in document order, each becomes the current node in turn. Indexing into the current node list begins at one, not zero like some languages. Therefore, `/Collection/CD[2]` refers to the second `CD` element.

In our example, the current node list when the root template calls `<xsl:apply-templates>` contains, in order:

1. `Book[1]`: Complete Beatles Chronicle, The
2. `CD[1]`: Band on the Run
3. `CD[2]`: Venus and Mars
4. `Book[2]`: Many Years From Now
5. `Book[3]`: Beatles Anthology, The
6. `CD[3]`: Beatles 1

Since the first node in the list is `Book[1]`, the book template is invoked next, with `Book[1]` as the current (and context) node.

```
<xsl:template match="Book">
   <br /><xsl:text>Book title: </xsl:text>
   <i><xsl:value-of select="Title" /></i>
</xsl:template>
```

The body (or contents) of the template is executed, sending the literal result element `<br />` to the result tree, followed by the string "Book title:", which is the result of the line

```
<br /><xsl:text>Book title: </xsl:text>
```

The `<xsl:text>` instruction produces a text node in the result tree. Unfortunately, its content is limited to `#PCDATA`. You can include literal text and not a whole lot else. In particular, you can't nest literal result elements such as HTML tags inside `<xsl:text>`. Therefore, if you want the text to be bold (or any other style), the `<b>` and `</b>` tags must enclose `<xsl:text>` and `</xsl:text>`, rather than the reverse.

The "Book title:" string is followed by a literal `<i>` and `</i>` pair. The instruction `<xsl:value-of>` is discussed in the next section, but the short story is that the contents of the `Title` element is extracted and, in this case, italicized.

Having reached the end of the book template, the next node in the current node list, `CD[1]`, now becomes the current node. This triggers the CD template, which is almost identical to the one we just saw (and therefore begs for code reuse, which we'll see eventually, I promise).

```
<xsl:template match="CD">
   <br /><xsl:text>CD title: </xsl:text>
   <i><xsl:value-of select="Title" /></i>
</xsl:template>
```

The order of triggering the templates is determined by the order of the elements in the current node list, which is itself determined by document order (unless sorting is specified). The order of the *templates* in the stylesheet does *not* determine processing order.

Processing continues in turn with `CD[2]`, then `Book[2]`, then `Book[3]`, and finally `CD[3]`. Since the original root template selected only `CD` and `Book` elements, processing returns to the line following the `<xsl:apply-templates>` and we simply output the two end tags to terminate the HTML document.

```
    </body>
  </html>
```

Let's return to `<xsl:text>` for a moment. This XSLT instruction is for wrapping literal character data. The wrapping may affect which white space characters are stripped but it does not otherwise affect how the characters are handled by the XSLT processor. In other words, you can omit `<xsl:text>` in cases where the wrapping doesn't matter. For example, this pair of instructions (intermixed with literal result elements from HTML):

```
<br /><xsl:text>Book title: </xsl:text>
<i><xsl:value-of select="Title" /></i>
```

results in this HTML:

```
<br>Book title: <i>Complete Beatles Chronicle, The</i>
```

A version without <xsl:text>

```
<br />Book title:
<i><xsl:value-of select="Title" /></i>
```

results in:

```
<br>Book title:
   <i>Complete Beatles Chronicle, The</i>
```

with the italicized title on a separate line of the output file. Since HTML ignores white space, this makes absolutely no difference in how the page is displayed (try the file c6-filter-no-text.xsl). It alters the appearance of only the HTML source. However, when our target output format is XML, rather than HTML, the white space considerations might be significant, depending on the application.

Value of a Node or Expression

I glossed over one very important detail in the previous section, namely, what happens when the instruction

```
<xsl:value-of select="Title" />
```

is encountered? The <xsl:value-of> element determines the string value of an XPath expression and sends the result to the result tree. This instruction is the way to extract the value of an element, an attribute, an expression, or a variable to create a text node in the result tree. Exactly *how* the value is determined depends on the node type, as we'll see in Table 11-9, "Values of Different Node Types" on page 708.

In our example, we are selecting the value of the Title element. Regardless of whether the current node is a CD or Book element, there is a Title child. Therefore, when we take into account the context of this instruction, the complete XPath is either[6]

```
/Collection/CD/Title
```

or

```
/Collection/Book/Title
```

In either case, we simply extract the text of the Title element. Since each <xsl:value-of> is nested in a pair of <i> and </i> tags, every title is italicized.

6. Technically, at any given moment, we're processing a specific node, so the expressions are effectively /Collection/CD[n]/Title and /Collection/Book[n]/Title, where n is the position of that particular node with respect to others of the same name.

Now that we've covered how the processing takes place, let's look at the resultant HTML and how it appears in a browser.

HTML Result of Filtering

Listings 11-10 and 11-11 show the HTML generated by Xalan-Java and SAXON, respectively. The serialization on the printed page or the view in a text editor differ, but both will be rendered exactly the same by Netscape and Internet Explorer. Therefore, only the version generated by Xalan is illustrated in Figure 11-3.

Listing 11-10 HTML Generated from c6-filter.xsl Using Xalan

```
<html>
<head>
<META http-equiv="Content-Type" content="text/html; charset=UTF-8">
<title>XSLT: Filtering Titles</title>
</head>
<body>
<h1>XSLT: Filtering Titles</h1>
<br>Book title: <i>Complete Beatles Chronicle, The</i>
<br>CD title: <i>Band on the Run</i>
<br>CD title: <i>Venus and Mars</i>
<br>Book title: <i>Many Years From Now</i>
<br>Book title: <i>Beatles Anthology, The</i>
<br>CD title: <i>Beatles 1</i>
</body>
</html>
```

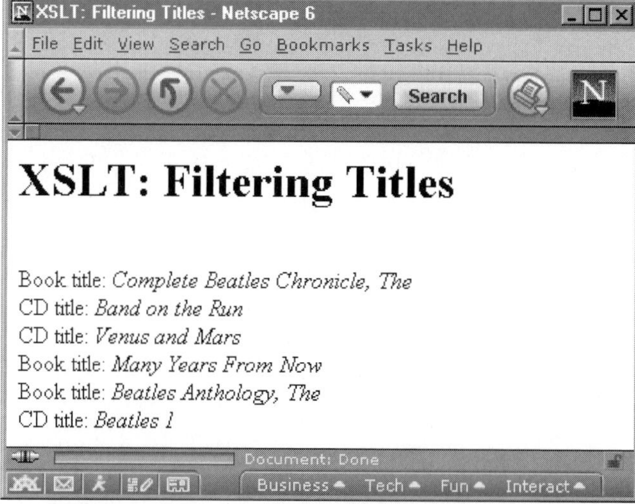

FIGURE 11-3 HTML result of filtering example in Netscape 6

Listing 11-11 SAXON Version of HTML Result of c6-filter.xsl

```
<html>
   <head>
      <meta http-equiv="Content-Type" content="text/html; charset=utf-8">
      <title>XSLT: Filtering Titles</title>
   </head>
   <body>
      <h1>XSLT: Filtering Titles</h1><br>Book title: <i>Complete Beatles
Chronicle, The</i><br>CD title: <i>Band on the Run</i><br>CD title:
<i>Venus and Mars</i><br>Book title: <i>Many Years From Now</i><br>Book
title: <i>Beatles Anthology, The</i><br>CD title: <i>Beatles 1</i></body>
</html>
```

About the HTML Output

By default, both Xalan and SAXON generate UTF-8 content encoding for HTML, as identified by the <meta> element.

```
<META http-equiv="Content-Type" content="text/html; charset=UTF-8">
```

This isn't a problem in normal browsing or in most text editors, but it can be undesirable if you're still using Netscape 4.x and you pick View Source from the Netscape menu while browsing the HTML. Every other character will be unreadable. (This will not happen if you're using Netscape 6.x or IE 5.x.) However, if your <xsl:output> element requests ISO-8859-1 encoding, like this:

```
<xsl:output method="html" indent="yes"  encoding="ISO-8859-1" />
```

then you'll get a <meta> tag that Netscape 4.x will be happier about in View Source mode.

```
<META http-equiv="Content-Type" content="text/html; charset=ISO-8859-1">
```

Default Built-in Template Rules and Node Tests

All XSLT processors are required to supply specific default behavior for each of the seven node types in the XPath model. As you can see from Table 11-5, the built-in rules are the same for root and element nodes, the same for text and attribute nodes, and essentially the same for the three other node types. The match syntax requires a little explanation. Each wildcard or **node test** in Table 11-4 is evaluated in the current context, so the extent of "any" and "all" depends on the context. (Node tests are covered in more detail when we discuss location steps in "XPath Concepts and Examples.")

Did you notice that the template rule for comments and PIs (Table 11-5) is a no-op? It's an empty template rule (no body), so it *does nothing* but ensure that these nodes do not send anything to the result tree by default.

TABLE 11-4 XPath Node Tests

Node Test	*Description*
/	Slash matches only the *root* node (not document element), as previously discussed.
*	Asterisk matches any *element* node, but not attribute, text, comment, or processing instruction nodes; this is an XPath wildcard.
@*	At-asterisk matches any *attribute* node; this is another XPath wildcard.
.	Dot matches the current node, so `<xsl:value-of select="."/>` extracts the value of the current node, regardless of its type, as per Table 11-9 on page 708.
`text()`	XPath node test that selects all text nodes.
`comment()`	XPath node test that selects all comment nodes.
`processing-instruction()`	XPath node test that selects all processing instruction nodes; if invoked with a parameter, only PIs with that particular target are selected.
`node()`	Although not used by the XSLT default rules, this XPath wildcard matches all kinds of nodes: element, attribute, text, comment, processing instruction, and namespace nodes.[a]

a. Actually, this depends on context. Often `node()` is short for the unabbreviated XPath expression `child::node()`, which applies only to nodes that can be children of something else, which would eliminate attribute and namespace nodes.

TABLE 11-5 Default (Built-in) Template Rules

Node Type	*Default Result*	*Built-in Template*

root
element
	Ensures that all element children are processed by invoking their templates (unless overridden)	`<xsl:template match="/|*">`
		`  <xsl:apply-templates/>`
		`</xsl:template>`

attribute
text
	Copies text value (attribute value or text content) to result tree	`<xsl:template match="@*|text()">`
		`  <xsl:value-of select="."/>`
		`</xsl:template>`

comment processing instruction	No output at all for comments or PIs by default; this is a do-nothing template	`<xsl:template match="comment()|` `processing-instruction()" />`
namespace	No output at all	can't be expressed in XSLT; built-in to processors at the source code level; no XPath `namespace()` function

Now that you know about built-in template rules, what do you think would happen if we replaced the root template rule in Listing 11-9 with this template?

```
<xsl:template match="/">
   <html>
     <head>
       <title>XSLT: Filtering Titles</title>
     </head>
     <body>
       <h1>XSLT: Filtering Titles</h1>
       <xsl:apply-templates />
     </body>
   </html>
</xsl:template>
```

The only difference is that we have replaced the instruction

```
<xsl:apply-templates select="Collection/CD | //Book"/>
```

with the more general instruction

```
<xsl:apply-templates />
```

Since we haven't indicated any special elements of interest, the processor will happily chug away on the six `CD` and `Book` elements as before, but then it will encounter the `<Owner>` element, for which no template is defined. Therefore, the default template for elements is applied recursively for `<Owner>` and all of its children, resulting in the extraction of all the content. If you look at Figure 11-4, you'll

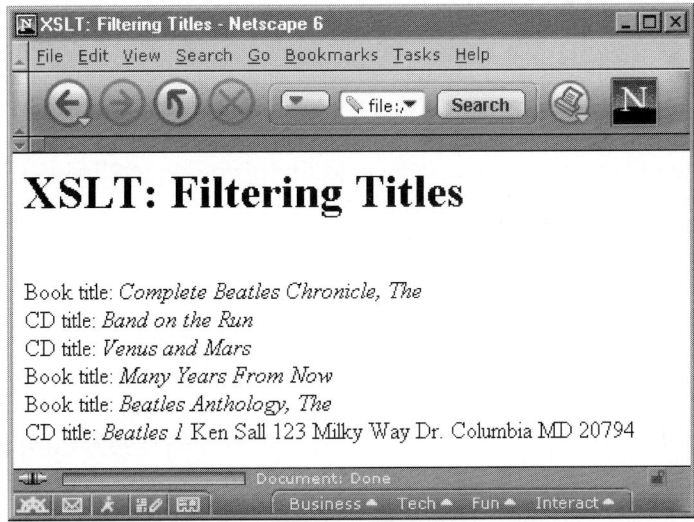

FIGURE 11-4 Buggy HTML result of filtering example in Netscape 6

notice the text of the `<Owner>` element appears without special formatting and without a newline immediately after the last title. I've shown it here as underlined for clarity.

```
CD title: Beatles 1 Ken Sall 123 Milky Way Dr. Columbia MD 20794
```

The point is that by knowing the default rules, we understand that unless we do something to prevent it, all element and attribute content will be sent to the result tree. This is why we specified which elements we wanted to process in the original `<xsl:apply-templates>` case.

The <xsl:stylesheet> Element

The `<xsl:stylesheet>` element (which surrounds all other XSLT instructions and data) identifies the XSLT namespace (see the next section) and the version of XSLT. As of this writing, the value of the `version` attribute must be "1.0" but that will change very shortly as the spec is updated, allowing version "2.0" eventually. Just as with other XML vocabularies, attribute values can appear within either single or double quotes.

```
<xsl:stylesheet
     xmlns:xsl="http://www.w3.org/1999/XSL/Transform"
     version="1.0">
```

Namespaces for XSLT, XPath, and XSLFO

XSLT and XSLFO each have their own namespace. However, XPath does not require a namespace because it is not an XML vocabulary, even though it is used by several XML languages.

- The XSLT namespace is **`http://www.w3.org/1999/XSL/Transform`**. By far, the most common namespace prefix you'll encounter is `xsl:` but some developers use `xslt:` or `transform:` instead. In this book, we'll always use the prevalent `xsl:` prefix, although `transform:` would have been a more clear convention. As noted earlier, avoid the Microsoft namespace `http://www.w3.org/TR/WD-xsl` unless you are working in an exclusively pre-IE 5.5 environment. If you wish, you can make this the default namespace (`xmlns="http://www.w3.org/1999/XSL/Transform"`) and drop the `xsl:` prefix for all instructions, provided you declare namespaces for *other* languages in your stylesheet, including HTML.
- The XSLFO namespace is **`http://www.w3.org/1999/XSL/Format`**. The most common namespace prefix is `fo:` but others are possible. It's probably a poor idea to use `xsl:` since that's what it typically used for XSLT, even though XSLFO is the main portion of the XSL specification. Confusing, isn't it?

The W3C points out that the year 1999 in these namespaces has nothing to do with the version of the specification itself; it merely indicates the year in which W3C *allocated* the namespace.

Caution: If you omit or mistype the namespace URI from the `<xsl:stylesheet>` element, or if you omit the version number, you'll get strange error messages from most XSLT processors and you certainly won't get the output you desire. Note that the URIs do not end in slash, nor do they end in a filename. The correct format for the start tag is:

```
<xsl:stylesheet
    xmlns:xsl="http://www.w3.org/1999/XSL/Transform"
    version="1.0">
```

If the stylesheet uses XSLFO, then the `<xsl:stylesheet>` element should be:

```
<xsl:stylesheet
    xmlns:xsl="http://www.w3.org/1999/XSL/Transform"
    xmlns:fo="http://www.w3.org/1999/XSL/Format"
    version="1.0">
```

Stylesheet Structure

The general structure for a stylesheet is shown in Listing 11-12. You provide a template for the root and one or more templates to handle elements.

Listing 11-12 General Stylesheet Structure (c6-template.xsl)

```
<?xml version="1.0"?>
<xsl:stylesheet
  xmlns:xsl="http://www.w3.org/1999/XSL/Transform"
  version="1.0">

<!-- Other top level elements, if needed, such as:
<xsl:output method="html"/>
<xsl:variable name="label">Some String</xsl:variable>
etc.
-->

  <!-- One or more templates -->
  <xsl:template match="/">
    <!-- XSLT Instructions and/or Literal Result Elements -->
    <xsl:apply-templates/>
  </xsl:template>

  <xsl:template match="*">
      <xsl:apply-templates/>
  </xsl:template>
</xsl:stylesheet>
```

Since the default rule for both the root node and element nodes is to call `<xsl:apply-templates>`, this is equivalent to the completely empty stylesheet, `c6-empty.xsl`:

```
<?xml version="1.0"?>
<xsl:stylesheet
  xmlns:xsl="http://www.w3.org/1999/XSL/Transform"
  version="1.0">
</xsl:stylesheet>
```

In both cases, regardless of the XML input document, these stylesheets will simply dump the text content of all elements, if any. They will not display attribute values, however, since applying templates for elements does not automatically process their attributes.

Implicit vs. Explicit Stylesheets and Push vs. Pull

In his excellent book, *Practical Transformation Using XSLT and XPath*, G. Ken Holman (of Crane Softwrights, Ltd. and a contributor of chapter 12 in this book) makes the distinction between implicit vs. explicit stylesheets (*http://www.CraneSoftwrights.com/training/*). Holman characterizes *implicit* stylesheets as those with just one template for the root element, such as XHTML with embedded XSLT elements. *Explicit* stylesheets, on the other hand, have a root template to handle the head element and then call `<xsl:apply-templates>` to handle the children.

Holman also distinguishes between two different ways to use stylesheets. *Push* is data driven, using `<xsl:template>` and `<xsl:apply-templates>` to push the source tree through stylesheet rules. *Pull* is stylesheet driven, using instructions such as `<xsl:for-each>` and `<xsl:value-of>` to pull data from the source tree. In either case, `match` or `select` patterns trigger the application of template rules to particular elements from the source tree.

Pull is often better when the order of elements within the document being processed is known ahead of time, such as when the document refers to a DTD or schema of which the stylesheet author is aware, or perhaps even has control. Pull can be accomplished using an implicit stylesheet which is an XSL file with HTML literal result elements intermixed with XSLT instructions that together effectively define a template for the entire result tree.

Push is more likely to be appropriate when the exact document structure is less well known. In such cases, the intention might be to create a more generic stylesheet that can accommodate multiple source documents that share some structural aspects in common. For example, if you are processing XML instances that represent journal articles, you might want to extract all of the abstracts (enclosed within `<Abstract>` elements), regardless of the rest of the structure of the document.

In practice, however, its highly likely that some combination of push and pull will be used in a given stylesheet.

Conditionals and Variables

In this section, we discuss XSLT conditionals which are similar to their use in other languages. However, we'll also cover variables which are handled in a manner that may surprise you.

Our next example, c6-if.xsl (Listing 11-13), introduces the <xsl:if> instruction for conditional statements and <xsl:variable> for so-called variables, as well as several XPath functions, name(), position(), and last().

Listing 11-13 Conditional Test (c6-if.xml)

```
<?xml version="1.0"?>
<xsl:stylesheet   version="1.0"
  xmlns:xsl="http://www.w3.org/1999/XSL/Transform">
<xsl:output method="html"/>

<xsl:variable name="label">XSLT: If Test</xsl:variable>

<xsl:template match="/">
   <html>
     <head>
       <title><xsl:value-of select="$label" /></title>
     </head>
     <body>
       <h1><xsl:value-of select="$label" /></h1>
       <xsl:apply-templates select="//CD | //Book"/>
     </body>
   </html>
</xsl:template>

<xsl:template match="CD | Book">
   <br />
   <xsl:if test="name() = 'CD'">
     <xsl:text>CD title: </xsl:text>
   </xsl:if>

   <xsl:if test="name() = 'Book'">
     <xsl:text>Book title: </xsl:text>
   </xsl:if>

   <i><xsl:value-of select="Title" /></i>

   <xsl:if test="position() = last()">
     <xsl:text> {Last Entry}</xsl:text>
   </xsl:if>
</xsl:template>
</xsl:stylesheet>
```

As before, our root template selects only CD and Book elements, but this time they share a single template (in contrast to one each in the filtering example in Listing 11-9). We use <xsl:if> to test which element is the current node. If it is a CD element, we output an appropriate string; if it is a Book, we output a different string. In either case, we extract the value of the Title element. The fragment

```
<xsl:template match="CD | Book">
   <br />
   <xsl:if test="name() = 'CD'">
     <xsl:text>CD title: </xsl:text>
   </xsl:if>
```

uses a match value of CD | Book to apply to both cases. The <xsl:if> element has a test attribute, the value of which represents the condition to be evaluated. If the expression evaluates to true, the body of the <xsl:if> instruction is executed; otherwise it is skipped. In this expression, the XPath name() function returns the name of the current node, which in this example is compared to the string "CD". A similar test is included for Book elements. Since we're in a template that only matches those two elements, the two <xsl:if> instructions represent the only possibilities.

Another conditional is used to check whether we're looking at the last element by comparing the ordinal number of the current node we're processing, returned by position(), to the value of last(), which returns the size of the current node list (the combined set of all CD and Book elements). In other words, we're testing whether the current node is the last node. This comparison is only true for the CD with the title "Beatles 1", after which the string " {Last Entry}" is appended in the result tree.

```
   <xsl:if test="position() = last()">
     <xsl:text> {Last Entry}</xsl:text>
   </xsl:if>
```

The result of applying this stylesheet to our running example document is shown in Figure 11-5.

Near the beginning of the stylesheet, as a top-level element, we added the definition of an XSLT variable:

```
<xsl:variable name="label">XSLT: If Test</xsl:variable>
```

which establishes a variable named label and sets its value to the string "XSLT: If Test". Later, we reference the variable by adding a dollar sign in front of the variable's name:

```
   <title><xsl:value-of select="$label" /></title>
```

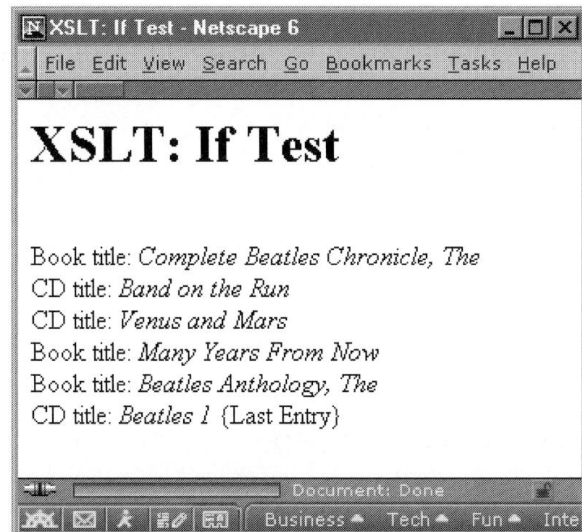

FIGURE 11-5 Display of results created by use of XSLT conditionals

which sets the HTML `<title>` element (not in any way related to the `Title` element from our source document) to the value of the `$label` variable by means of the `select` attribute. There are three not-so-obvious aspects of this variable definition:

1. A **variable** in XSLT is much more like a *constant* in most programming languages because *once its value is set, it cannot be changed*. This always seems odd to programmers and is the source for much initial confusion. The reason for this is discussed in detail in books on XSLT by authors such as Khun Yee Fung, Michael Kay, and G. Ken Holman, listed in "For Further Exploration." The general idea is that XSLT is a declarative, side-effect free language. Templates can be called in any order any number of times, so variables must not change value in different calls. Kay, for example, discusses ways to use recursion to circumvent what at first seems like a real limitation of XSLT, but, in fact, is an as-designed aspect.
2. The scope of the variable depends on where the `<xsl:variable>` element appears. In this example, it is a **top-level element**, that is, it is a direct child of `<xsl:stylesheet>`, at the same level as `<xsl:output>` and `<xsl:template>`. Its scope is therefore the entire stylesheet. However, if we placed the variable definition in a template, its scope would be limited to that template. *The scope of a variable is limited to the element within which it is nested.* That is, a variable of local scope applies only to elements that "follow" the variable definition. (We'll learn later that in XPath axis terminology, this means the `following-siblings` axis and their `descendants`.)

3. This constraint can actually be exploited within a loop to declare a new instance of the same-named variable that is initialized to the result of the body of the variable. (We'll see an example of this when we discuss named templates, Listing 11-38 on page 675.)
4. A variable reference can be used wherever an XPath expression value is required (e.g., as all or part of the value of `match` and `select` attributes), but a variable *cannot* be used for other XSLT language constructs, such as node types, names, and axes.

Note that we also reused the variable `label` for the <h1> element (as well as for `<title>`).

```
<h1><xsl:value-of select="$label" /></h1>
```

This further illustrates how a variable is like a constant used to represent a repeated string. Of course, that is not the only use of variables, nor the only way to initialize their value, as we'll see in later examples, such as `c6-xslt-func.xsl`.

More about Setting Variables

Variables can have either content or a `select` attribute but not both. Therefore, variables are initialized either by

- Evaluating the simple or complex content (body) of the nonempty `<xsl:variable>` element
- Evaluating the value of the optional `select` attribute of an empty `<xsl:variable>` element

We've already seen the simple case of the first kind of initialization. However, a more sophisticated example that involves complex content appears in `c6-xslt-func.xsl`, which is shown in its entirety in Listing 11-49, "XSLT Functions Code Example (c6-xslt-func.xsl)" on page 751. For now, consider just this fragment:

```
<xsl:variable name="processor">
 <xsl:choose>
   <xsl:when
    test="contains(system-property('xsl:vendor'), 'SAXON')" >SAXON
   </xsl:when>
   <xsl:when
    test="contains(system-property('xsl:vendor'), 'Apache')" >Xalan
   </xsl:when>
   <xsl:otherwise>Unknown</xsl:otherwise>
 </xsl:choose>
</xsl:variable>
```

I'll explain the `<xsl:choose>` element and its children in the next section, but for now consider that the value of `<xsl:variable>` is whatever result tree fragment that its content (child elements) produces. In other words, the result of evaluating the `<xsl:choose>` instruction becomes the value of the `$processor` variable. This is a very powerful way to initialize variables—surrounding any set of instructions that produce output with `<xsl:variable>`. Note that in this particular form, the `<xsl:variable>` instruction does *not* use the `select` attribute.

An example of the second type of variable initialization that uses the optional `select` attribute is:

```
<xsl:variable name="ex2"
     select="concat('Another ', 'Variable ', 'Example')" />
```

The XPath `concat()` function does exactly what you'd expect; it concatenates its arguments to form a long string, so after this instruction is executed, the value of `$ex2` variable is the string "Another Variable Example", which is the result of evaluating the value of the `select` attribute. Perhaps a bit more interesting case is the variable `$Booksubtotal` in `c6-math.xsl`, shown in full in Listing 11-48, "XPath Numeric Functions Code Example on page 734:

```
<xsl:variable name="Booksubtotal" select="sum(//Book/ListPrice)" />
```

This extracts the value of all the `ListPrice` elements that are immediate children of every `Book` element in the document, adds them up, and initializes the variable `$Booksubtotal` to that number. Notice that in contrast to the case with the nested `<xsl:choose>` element, the second kind of initialization involves an empty element. The value of the variable is completely determined by the evaluation of the `select` attribute.

Although the two forms are logically equivalent, there are subtle syntax differences. *The nonempty form (without the* `select` *attribute) is generally safer when assigning string values to a variable directly* (instead of by a function like `concat`, which returns a string). We'll see an example of this in "Reuse: Named Templates and Passing Parameters." The nonempty form without the `select` attribute also produces a *result tree fragment*, which leads to a limitation discussed in the later section "Data Types."

In all cases, however, remember that the *scope* of a variable is limited to the element within which it is nested. Therefore, variables that need to be referenced from within multiple templates are defined as top-level elements before any templates.

The name of a variable may contain a namespace prefix, just like any other element.

```
<xsl:stylesheet version="1.0"
    xmlns:xsl="http://www.w3.org/1999/XSL/Transform"
    xmlns:str="http://xsltsl.org/string"
    extension-element-prefixes="str">
<!-- etc -->
<xsl:variable name="str:lower" select="'abcdefghijklmnopqrstuvwxyz'"/>
```

Multiple Decisions

Besides the <xsl:if> instruction, XSLT provides <xsl:choose> for more complicated choices, analogous to multiple decision statements (multiway branches) in other programming languages. Each branch of <xsl:choose> is an <xsl:when> instruction with a `test` attribute. The final branch is an optional <xsl:otherwise> element to handle the default case. Consider the example `c6-choose.xsl` in Listing 11-14.

Listing 11-14 Multiple Decision Branching (c6-choose.xsl)

```
<?xml version="1.0"?>
<xsl:stylesheet   version="1.0"
  xmlns:xsl="http://www.w3.org/1999/XSL/Transform">
<xsl:output method="html"/>

<xsl:variable name="label">XSLT: Choose/When Test</xsl:variable>

<xsl:template match="/">
   <html>
     <head>
       <title><xsl:value-of select="$label" /></title>
     </head>
     <body>
       <h1><xsl:value-of select="$label" /></h1>
       <xsl:apply-templates />
     </body>
   </html>
</xsl:template>

<xsl:template match="CD | Book | Owner">
   <br />
   <xsl:choose>
     <xsl:when test="local-name() = 'CD'">
       <xsl:text>CD: </xsl:text>
       <i><xsl:value-of select="Title" /></i>
     </xsl:when>

     <xsl:when test="local-name() = 'Book'">
       <xsl:text>Book: </xsl:text>
       <i><xsl:value-of select="Title" /></i>
     </xsl:when>
```

```
      <xsl:otherwise>
        <xsl:text>{Skipping Owner} </xsl:text>
        <i><xsl:value-of select="Name" /></i>
      </xsl:otherwise>
    </xsl:choose>

</xsl:template>
</xsl:stylesheet>
```

This time our second template matches three elements: CD, Book, and Owner. We use <xsl:choose> to deal with each of the three elements. The element <xsl:when> behaves like <xsl:if> in that the evaluation of its test attribute determines whether that branch is executed. The <xsl:otherwise> element handles the unspecified cases, which can only be Owner since that's the only element from the current node list that has no specific <xsl:when> test.

You probably noticed that we switched from the name() function to local-name(). Actually, given our source document, collection6.xml, which doesn't have much in the way of namespaces, the two XPath functions produce the same result. However, in the general case in which an element name might have a namespace prefix, local-name() returns the portion to the right of the colon, whereas name() returns the complete name including the namespace prefix, sometimes called the **qualified name**, of the context node. When no namespace is associated with an element name, the two functions return the same value.

Consider what will be sent to the result tree based on the instruction:

```
<i><xsl:value-of select="Name" /></i>
```

If you recall our collection6.xml source, the Name element really contains nested elements, First and Last:

```
  <Owner>
    <Name sex="male">
      <First>Ken</First>
      <Last>Sall</Last>
    </Name>
    <!-- etc. -->
```

We know that the value of an element node that contains character data is simply the text. But the content model of Name consists of two children (also element nodes), each of which contains character data as its content. The value of the Name element node is the normalized value of its children nodes, First and Last, so the string "Ken Sall" is output, as shown in Figure 11-6. What then would you guess would be the result of this instruction?

```
<xsl:value-of select="/Collection" />
```

Try it!

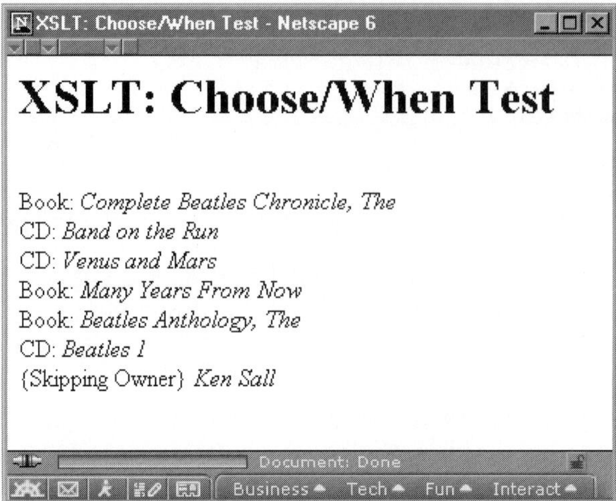

FIGURE 11-6 Display of choose example result (c6-choose.html)

Generating an HTML Table

A common task is to generate an HTML table from XML source using XSLT. Listing 11-15 illustrates a simple case (the file `c6-table.xsl`). The HTML output of this stylesheet and how the result looks in Netscape 6 appear in Listing 11-16 and Figure 11-7, respectively.

This time we've added the attribute setting `indent="yes"` to `<xsl:output>` to explicitly request indentation for our generated HTML. In the template for the root node, we set up the HTML `<table>` element as well as the headings (`<th>`) for the columns. The `<xsl:apply-templates>` instruction selects only `CD` and `Book` elements. After the `<table>` is closed, we again call `<xsl:apply-templates>`, but this time for only the `Owner` element, so it will appear outside the table.

Listing 11-15 Generating an HTML Table (c6-table.xsl)

```
<?xml version="1.0"?>
<xsl:stylesheet   version="1.0"
  xmlns:xsl="http://www.w3.org/1999/XSL/Transform">
<xsl:output method="html" indent="yes" />


<xsl:variable name="label">XSLT: Table</xsl:variable>


<xsl:template match="/">
   <html>
     <head>
       <title><xsl:value-of select="$label" /></title>
```

```
      </head>
      <body>
        <h1><xsl:value-of select="$label" /></h1>


        <table cellpadding="5" border="1" >
          <tr>
          <th> </th>
          <th>Title</th>
          <th>Author or Artist</th>
          <th>Type</th>
          <th>Published <br/>or Released</th>
          </tr>
          <xsl:apply-templates select="//CD|//Book" />
        </table>
        <xsl:apply-templates select="//Owner" />
      </body>
    </html>
</xsl:template>


<xsl:template match="Book">
   <tr bgcolor="#cccccc" style="font-weight: bold;">
   <td><xsl:text>Book</xsl:text></td>
   <td><i><xsl:value-of select="Title" /></i></td>
   <td><xsl:value-of select="Author/Name/Last" /><xsl:text>, </xsl:text>
       <xsl:value-of select="Author/Name/First" /></td>
   <td><xsl:value-of select="Type" /></td>
   <td><xsl:value-of select="Published" /></td>
   </tr>
</xsl:template>


<xsl:template match="CD">
   <tr bgcolor="#eeddcc" style="font-weight: bold;">
   <td><xsl:text>CD</xsl:text></td>
   <td><i><xsl:value-of select="Title" /></i></td>
   <td><xsl:value-of select="Artist" /></td>
   <td><xsl:value-of select="Type" /></td>
   <td><xsl:value-of select="AlbumReleased" /></td>
   </tr>
</xsl:template>


<xsl:template match="Owner">
   <p> </p>
     <h2>
     <xsl:value-of select="Name/First" />
     <xsl:text> </xsl:text>
     <xsl:value-of select="Name/Last" />
     <xsl:text>'s Collection</xsl:text>
     </h2>
     <xsl:value-of select="Address/Street" />
     <br />
     <xsl:value-of select="Address/City" />
```

```
        <xsl:text>, </xsl:text>
        <xsl:value-of select="Address/State" />
        <xsl:text> </xsl:text>
        <xsl:value-of select="Address/Zip" />
    </xsl:template>

</xsl:stylesheet>
```

It's worth noting that we have to go to a bit of trouble to generate a nonbreaking space, written in HTML as the ` ` entity. This character entity is not defined in XML (and therefore not in XSLT), so we can't use it directly. We can, however, use its Unicode equivalent, which is ` `. I've used this to make sure the empty upper left corner of the table has all four borders. In our stylesheet, I've written

```
<th> </th>
```

which in the output HTML becomes

```
<th> </th>
```

The templates for `CD` and `Book` elements are similar in structure but not in the details. Each template is responsible for a single row of output (`<tr>`). We've picked a different color for each kind of row. To populate each cell (`<td>`) of the row, we extract the value of the `Title` and `Type` elements the same way in both cases since both elements are immediate children of both the `CD` and `Book` elements. To obtain the author's name, we specify:

```
<td><xsl:value-of select="Author/Name/Last" /><xsl:text>, </xsl:text>
    <xsl:value-of select="Author/Name/First" /></td>
```

But as we saw earlier, if we didn't care to swap the order of the `First` and `Last` elements, we could have simply written

```
<td><xsl:value-of select="Author/Name" /></td>
```

To extract the artist's name of a `CD` for the corresponding column, we just need to select the `Artist` child. The template for the `Owner` element shows how to assemble the address information in the conventional format in the United States.

Listing 11-16 Indented HTML Generated by Saxon Using c6-table.xsl

```
<html>
   <head>
      <meta http-equiv="Content-Type" content="text/html; charset=utf-8">
      <title>XSLT: Table</title>
   </head>
   <body>
      <h1>XSLT: Table</h1>
      <table cellpadding="5" border="1">
```

```
        <tr>
          <th> </th>
          <th>Title</th>
          <th>Author or Artist</th>
          <th>Type</th>
          <th>Published <br>or Released
          </th>
        </tr>
        <tr bgcolor="#cccccc" style="font-weight: bold;">
          <td>Book</td>
          <td><i>Complete Beatles Chronicle, The</i></td>
          <td>Lewisohn, Mark</td>
          <td>Chronology</td>
          <td>1992</td>
        </tr>
        <tr bgcolor="#eeddcc" style="font-weight: bold;">
          <td>CD</td>
          <td><i>Band on the Run</i></td>
          <td>McCartney, Paul and Wings</td>
          <td>Rock</td>
          <td>1973</td>
        </tr>
        <tr bgcolor="#eeddcc" style="font-weight: bold;">
          <td>CD</td>
          <td><i>Venus and Mars</i></td>
          <td>McCartney, Paul and Wings</td>
          <td>Rock</td>
          <td>1975</td>
        </tr>
        <tr bgcolor="#cccccc" style="font-weight: bold;">
          <td>Book</td>
          <td><i>Many Years From Now</i></td>
          <td>McCartney, Paul</td>
          <td>Autobiographical</td>
          <td>1997</td>
        </tr>
        <tr bgcolor="#cccccc" style="font-weight: bold;">
          <td>Book</td>
          <td><i>Beatles Anthology, The</i></td>
          <td>McCartney, Paul</td>
          <td>Autobiographical</td>
          <td>2000</td>
        </tr>
        <tr bgcolor="#eeddcc" style="font-weight: bold;">
          <td>CD</td>
          <td><i>Beatles 1</i></td>
          <td>Beatles</td>
          <td>Rock</td>
          <td>November 14, 2000</td>
        </tr>
      </table>
      <p></p>
      <h2>Ken Sall's Collection</h2>123 Milky Way Dr.<br>Columbia, MD 20794
   </body>
</html>
```

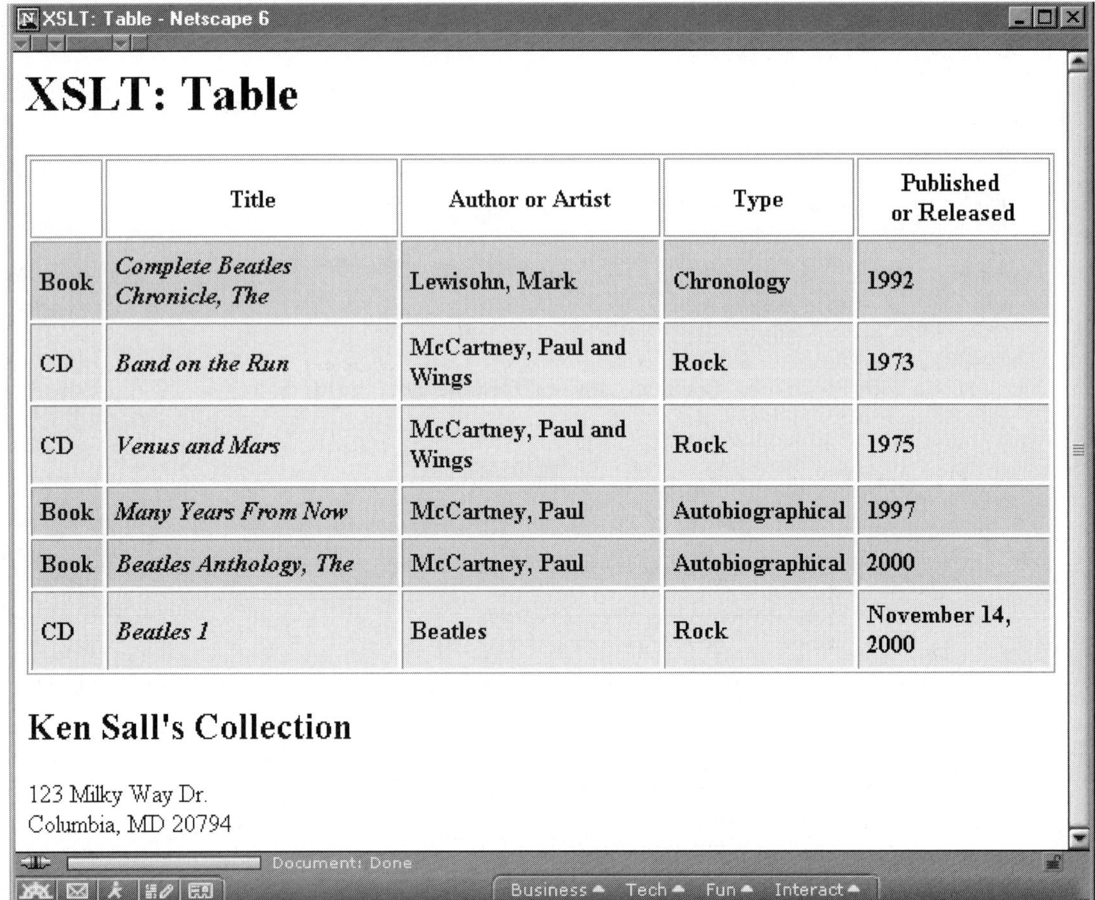

XSLT: Table - Netscape 6

XSLT: Table

	Title	Author or Artist	Type	Published or Released
Book	*Complete Beatles Chronicle, The*	Lewisohn, Mark	Chronology	1992
CD	*Band on the Run*	McCartney, Paul and Wings	Rock	1973
CD	*Venus and Mars*	McCartney, Paul and Wings	Rock	1975
Book	*Many Years From Now*	McCartney, Paul	Autobiographical	1997
Book	*Beatles Anthology, The*	McCartney, Paul	Autobiographical	2000
CD	*Beatles 1*	Beatles	Rock	November 14, 2000

Ken Sall's Collection

123 Milky Way Dr.
Columbia, MD 20794

Document: Done

Business Tech Fun Interact

FIGURE 11-7 Display of table generated from XML

Accessing Attributes

So far I haven't said much about processing attributes. Attributes are a strange kind of animal in the XPath language. Get ready for this one: Although elements are parents of attributes, *attributes are not designated as children of their parents. Attributes, like namespace nodes, have parent element nodes, but they aren't considered to be children of these elements.* This seemingly contradictory state of affairs is different from the case with all other node types (elements, text, comments, processing instructions), which have the normal reciprocal parent-child relationship, with the exception that the root node has no parent.

In the discussion of built-in templates earlier in the chapter, we saw that `@*` (at-asterisk wildcard) denotes all attributes. The `@` (at) symbol by itself is the *abbreviated* XPath syntax for a single attribute node. Therefore, if the context node is an element, a given attribute can be referenced by @ followed by the name of the attribute. So for any arbitrary element elt that is the parent of an attribute attr, we can extract the attribute's value like so:

```
<xsl:template match="elt">
   <xsl:value-of select="@attr" />
</xsl:template>
```

An alternative expression for the attribute using *unabbreviated* syntax involves what is called the attribute **axis**, specified by the literal word attribute followed by a :: (double colons) separator followed by the node() function we encountered earlier:

```
<xsl:template match="elt">
   <xsl:value-of select="attribute::node()" />
</xsl:template>
```

Another alternative is to supply the name of the attribute after the double colons. So, in a template that processes our Peak element, we can extract the value of the weeks attribute like this:

```
<xsl:template match="CD/Chart/Peak">
   <xsl:value-of select="attribute::weeks" />
</xsl:template>
```

Listing 11-17 (c6-attributes.xsl) is an example of attribute processing and Figure 11-8 on page 631 shows the HTML that results. Rather than processing elements in document order, I've chosen to process all CD element and then all Book elements this time. This is accomplished by issuing separate calls to <xsl:apply-templates>.

```
<xsl:apply-templates select="/Collection/CD" />
<xsl:apply-templates select="/Collection/Book" />
```

Note that in this case I've used explicit full path notation: root node, then document element, then CD or Book element.

Listing 11-17 Accessing Attributes (c6-attributes.xsl)

```
<?xml version="1.0"?>
<xsl:stylesheet   version="1.0"
  xmlns:xsl="http://www.w3.org/1999/XSL/Transform">
<xsl:output method="html"/>

<xsl:variable name="label">XSLT: Attributes</xsl:variable>

<xsl:template match="/">
   <html>
     <head>
       <title><xsl:value-of select="$label" /></title>
     </head>
```

```
      <body>
        <h1><xsl:value-of select="$label" /></h1>
        <xsl:apply-templates select="/Collection/CD" />
        <xsl:apply-templates select="/Collection/Book" />
      </body>
    </html>
</xsl:template>

<xsl:template match="//CD/Remastered" >
    <p />
      <i><xsl:value-of select="../Title" /></i>
      <br /><xsl:text>format attribute: </xsl:text>
      <i><xsl:value-of select="./@format" /></i>
      <!-- Next yields same value since only one attribute possible.
      <br /><xsl:value-of select="attribute::node()" />
      -->
      <br /><xsl:value-of select="name()" />
      <xsl:text> = </xsl:text>
      <xsl:value-of select="." />

      <xsl:if test="@format[contains(., 'gold CD')]">
        <b><xsl:text> ++++++ Found 'gold CD'</xsl:text></b>
      </xsl:if>
</xsl:template>

<xsl:template match="//CD/Chart/Peak" >
    <p />
      <i><xsl:value-of select="../../Title" /></i>
      <br /><xsl:value-of select="count(@*)" />
      <xsl:text> Peak attributes: </xsl:text>
      <xsl:for-each select="@*" >
      <!-- Next yields same result regardless of # of attributes.
      <xsl:for-each select="attribute::node()" >
      -->
        <br /><xsl:value-of select="name()" />
        <xsl:text> = </xsl:text>
        <xsl:value-of select="." />
      </xsl:for-each>
</xsl:template>

<xsl:template match="//Book" >
    <p />
      <i><xsl:value-of select="Title" /></i>
      <br /><xsl:text>publisher attribute: </xsl:text>
      <i><xsl:value-of select="Published/@publisher" /></i>
      <br /><xsl:text>Published = </xsl:text>
      <xsl:value-of select="Published" />

      <xsl:if test="./Published/@publisher[.='Chronicle Books']">
        <b><xsl:text> ++++++ Found 'Chronicle Books'</xsl:text></b>
      </xsl:if>
</xsl:template>

<xsl:template match="text()">
</xsl:template>

</xsl:stylesheet>
```

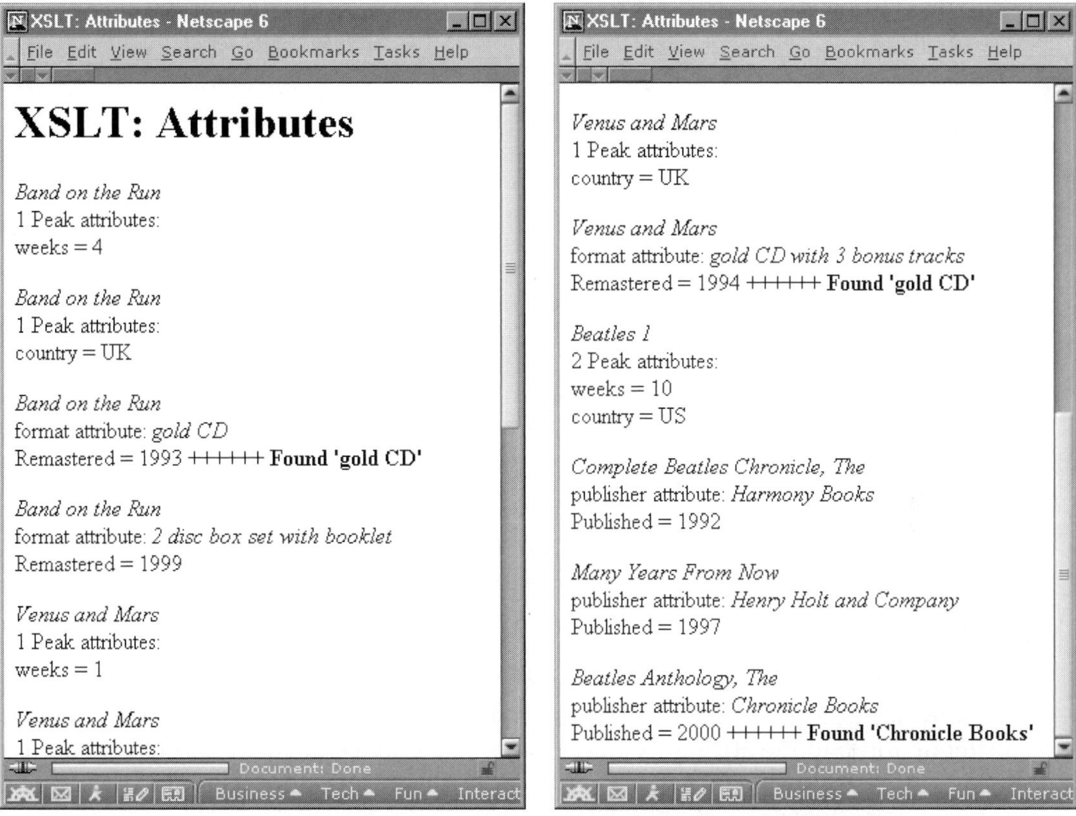

FIGURE 11-8 Display of attributes example (c6-attributes.html)

Since most of the elements in our XML source (`collection6.xml`) don't contain attributes, I've written templates for only three cases:

- `//CD/Remastered`, which has a `format` attribute
- `//CD/Chart/Peak`, which has two optional attributes, `weeks` and `country`
- `//Book`, whose `Published` child element has a `publisher` attribute

Let's examine the first case, the template beginning:

```
<xsl:template match="//CD/Remastered" >
```

When the current node is `//CD/Remastered`, we must use a relative path (`../`) to reference `Title`, since it is a sibling (i.e., at the same level in the element hierarchy) of the `Remastered` element.

```
<i><xsl:value-of select="../Title" /></i>
```

Since `format` is an attribute of `Remastered`, we can use either `@format` or `./@format`.

```
<i><xsl:value-of select="./@format" /></i>
```

We extract the value of the `Remastered` element itself by selecting the current node.

```
<xsl:value-of select="." />
```

To determine if an attribute value contains a particular substring, we use an XPath predicate (an expression within square brackets) with an XPath string function called `contains()`. This test says "if the current node has a `format` attribute whose value contains the string "gold CD", then execute the conditional part."

```
<xsl:if test="@format[contains(., 'gold CD')]">
  <b><xsl:text> ++++++ Found 'gold CD'</xsl:text></b>
</xsl:if>
```

The template for `//CD/Chart/Peak` also has some interesting details. When `Peak` is the context node, we have to move up two levels and down one to obtain the title since `Title` is a sibling of `Chart` (a direct child of `CD`).

```
<i><xsl:value-of select="../../Title" /></i>
```

Since `@*` represents all of the attributes of the current node, `count(@*)` tells us how many attributes there are for the current node. We can then use `<xsl:for-each>` to iterate through the attributes, one by one. The only `CD` element that has more than one attribute for `Peak` is the one entitled "Beatles 1" and our stylesheet reports both `weeks` and `country` correctly.

```
<br /><xsl:value-of select="count(@*)" />
<xsl:text> Peak attributes: </xsl:text>
<xsl:for-each select="@*" >
  <br /><xsl:value-of select="name()" />
  <xsl:text> = </xsl:text>
  <xsl:value-of select="." />
</xsl:for-each>
```

We'll discuss the `<xsl:for-each>` instruction in the later section "Iterating and Sorting." For now, just note that this iterates over all the attributes of `Peak`. For each attribute, we use the `name()` function to obtain the name of the attribute (`weeks` or `country`); this is the same function we used previously to extract the name of elements. Then we select the value of the current node, which at this point is an attribute, so we get the value of the attribute. For example, for the CD "Beatles 1", the preceding fragment results in:

```
2 Peak attributes:
weeks = 10
country = US
```

When the template that matches `//Book` is executed, access to the `publisher` attribute of the `Published` element is relative to `Book`.

```
<i><xsl:value-of select="Published/@publisher" /></i>
```

We extract the text content of the `Published` element by selecting it as a child of the current node, which is still the `Book` element.

```
<xsl:value-of select="Published" />
```

Suppose we want to test for a particular value of a specific attribute. Let's say, we want conditional instructions if the value of the publisher attribute is exactly the string 'Chronicle Books'. The test we need is:

```
<xsl:if test="./Published/@publisher[.='Chronicle Books']">
```

To compare the value of the `publisher` attribute to a known target string, we use another predicate with "`.`" (dot) representing the value of the current attribute node. The = (equals) operator is used for a direct comparison. Note that our comparison string must be an *exact* match, including leading and trailing white space, if any. This differs from the `contains()` function we saw earlier that checks for a substring.

In early chapters, we learned that although element order is well defined (in terms of document order), *attributes are considered to be unordered*. That means if you're processing an element that has more than one attribute, and if you need to process each attribute in a particular order, you must make that order explicit by means of calls to `<xsl:apply-templates>` for each attribute. Suppose we wanted to process an element with four attributes named `first`, `second`, `third`, and `fourth`, and we needed to process them in that order. Our template would need to be explicit about the order:

```
<xsl:template match="Element-with-multiple-attributes">
  <xsl:apply-templates select="@first" />
  <xsl:apply-templates select="@second" />
  <xsl:apply-templates select="@third" />
  <xsl:apply-templates select="@fourth" />
</xsl:template>
```

rather than the more concise but imprecise template, which would result in processing all attributes but in an unpredictable order.

```
<xsl:template match="Element-with-multiple-attributes/@*">
  <xsl:apply-templates select="." />
</xsl:template>
```

If you try the imprecise version and your XSLT processor just happens to process the attributes in order, don't be fooled. If you switch to a different processor, the results could be very different.

We've seen that we can easily match *specific attributes* such as the `format` attribute of the `Remastered` element, as shown in this attribute-specific template that unconditionally displays the value of the `format` attribute, and a special message if the value is exactly equal to the string "gold CD".

```
<xsl:template match="//CD/Remastered/@format" >
   <h5>format: <xsl:value-of select="."/></h5>
   <xsl:if test=". = 'gold CD'">
     <h5>Found exactly a "gold CD" format.</h5>
   </xsl:if>
</xsl:template>
```

Attribute Sets for Reuse

Sometimes it's useful to define a group of related attributes when you plan to associate them with more than one element. This is often the case when you work with XLink, the topic of chapter 13. XLink defines a number of attributes that identify link resources, how links are actuated, and what happens when a link is encountered. Examples of XLink attributes include `xlink:type`, `xlink:href`, `xlink:actuate`, and `xlink:show`. When you devise an XML vocabulary that takes advantage of XLink, it's necessary to specify these attributes along with their possible values and usual default values for every element that is any type of link. Of course, this could become tedious, not to mention error-prone, if it were not for reuse. There are ways of expressing reuse in DTDs and XML Schema that simplify this effort so that changes need be made in only one place.

The analogous attribute reuse concept in XSLT in the `<xsl:attribute-set>` instruction, together with the `<xsl:attribute>` element and the *attribute* `xsl:use-attribute-sets`. The `<xsl:attribute-set>` instruction is used to *define* a named set of related attributes; it must be a top-level XSLT element so the set can be referenced by name from any point in the stylesheet after it is defined. The `<xsl:attribute>` instruction *adds* an attribute to an element in the result tree. While it is typically used in conjunction with `<xsl:element>` as we'll see soon in the section "XML to XML: Shallow Copies," its use in this context is to add attributes to the attribute set. Therefore, `<xsl:attribute>` elements form the body of the `<xsl:attribute-set>` parent. Consider the example in Listing 11-18 in which attribute sets are used to define the appearance of an HTML table.

Listing 11-18 Attribute Sets Example (c6-attr-set.xsl)

```
<?xml version="1.0"?>
<xsl:stylesheet   version="1.0"
  xmlns:xsl="http://www.w3.org/1999/XSL/Transform">
<xsl:output method="html"/>

<xsl:variable name="label">XSLT: Attribute Sets for Re-use</xsl:variable>

<!-- The table in this example does not display correctly in Netscape 4.x -->
```

```
<xsl:attribute-set name="table-style" >
  <xsl:attribute name="align">center</xsl:attribute>
  <xsl:attribute name="width">75%</xsl:attribute>
  <xsl:attribute name="cellpadding">10</xsl:attribute>
  <xsl:attribute name="border">2</xsl:attribute>
</xsl:attribute-set>

<xsl:attribute-set name="row-style" >
  <xsl:attribute name="bgcolor">#bbbccc</xsl:attribute>
  <xsl:attribute name="bordercolor">#ff0000</xsl:attribute>
  <xsl:attribute name="style">font-family:Helvetica; font-weight:bold;</
xsl:attribute>
</xsl:attribute-set>

<xsl:attribute-set name="CD-title-style" >
  <xsl:attribute name="bgcolor">#dddeee</xsl:attribute>
  <xsl:attribute name="style">font-family:Verdana; font-weight:bold; font-
style:italic; text-align:center;</xsl:attribute>
</xsl:attribute-set>

<xsl:template match="/">
   <html>
     <head>
       <title><xsl:value-of select="$label" /></title>
     </head>
     <body>
       <h1><xsl:value-of select="$label" /></h1>

       <!-- Note: XSL as an attribute of HTML table -->
       <table border="2"    xsl:use-attribute-sets="table-style" >
         <xsl:apply-templates select="//CD | //Book"/>
       </table>
     </body>
   </html>
</xsl:template>

<xsl:template match="CD">
   <tr     xsl:use-attribute-sets="row-style" >
   <td>
   <xsl:text>CD</xsl:text>
   </td>
   <td     xsl:use-attribute-sets="CD-title-style" >
   <xsl:value-of select="Title" />
   </td>
   </tr>
</xsl:template>

<xsl:template match="Book">
   <tr     xsl:use-attribute-sets="row-style" >
   <td>
   <xsl:text>Book</xsl:text>
   </td>
   <td> <!-- no special style -->
   <xsl:value-of select="Title" />
   </td>
   </tr>
</xsl:template>

</xsl:stylesheet>
```

Three attribute sets are defined in this example, named `table-style`, `row-style`, and `CD-title-style`. Let's examine the one named `row-style`, which consists of three attributes, named `bgcolor`, `bordercolor`, and `style` (the CSS attribute), each of which is defined by its element content.

```
<xsl:attribute-set name="row-style" >
  <xsl:attribute name="bgcolor">#bbbccc</xsl:attribute>
  <xsl:attribute name="bordercolor">#ff0000</xsl:attribute>
  <xsl:attribute name="style">font-family:Helvetica; font-
weight:bold;</xsl:attribute>
</xsl:attribute-set>
```

Each attribute in the set is defined by means of the `<xsl:attribute>` instruction, setting the `name` attribute to the intended name of the attribute in the result tree. The content of `<xsl:attribute>` is the value of the attribute you are defining. For example, the first attribute above appears in the result tree as:

```
<someElementName bgcolor="#bbbccc" .... />
```

To use this attribute set, reference it by name with the special `xsl:use-attribute-sets` as the *attribute* of either an HTML element (in this case) or another XML (but non-XSLT) element. This is one of the rare instances in which you'll need to use the `xsl:` namespace prefix for an attribute name. For example, in the template for the `CD` element, we reference two attribute sets, one for the row itself and the other for the title of the CD.

```
<xsl:template match="CD">
   <tr      xsl:use-attribute-sets="row-style" >
   <td>
   <xsl:text>CD</xsl:text>
   </td>
   <td      xsl:use-attribute-sets="CD-title-style" >
   <xsl:value-of select="Title" />
   </td>
   </tr>
</xsl:template>
```

It's helpful to look at an excerpt from the HTML output that results (`c6-attr-sets.html`). The following fragment defines the beginning of the table and the first book and CD rows.

```
<table align="center" width="75%" cellpadding="10" border="2">
<tr bgcolor="#bbbccc" bordercolor="#ff0000"
    style="font-family:Helvetica; font-weight:bold;">
<td>Book</td><td>Complete Beatles Chronicle, The</td>
</tr>
<tr bgcolor="#bbbccc" bordercolor="#ff0000"
    style="font-family:Helvetica; font-weight:bold;">
<td>CD</td><td bgcolor="#dddeee"
   style="font-family:Verdana; font-weight:bold; font-style:italic; text-
align:center;">Band on the Run</td>
</td>
```

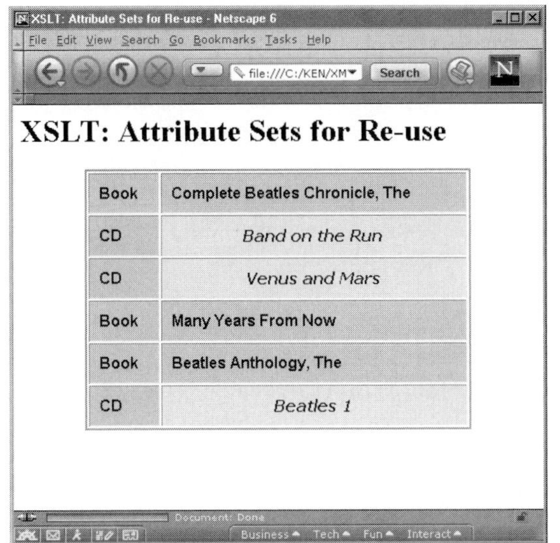

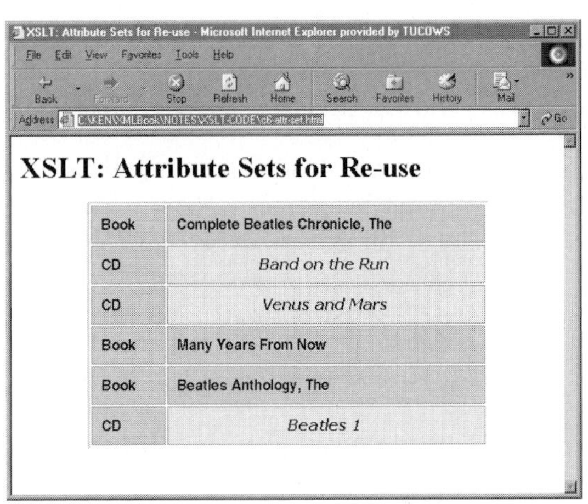

FIGURE 11-9 Display of attribute sets example in Netscape 6.2 and IE 5.5

Note that the `row-style` attribute set is applied to the <tr> element and the `CD-title-style` attribute set is added to the second <td> element in the row, as we intended.

At the time of this writing, there is a difference in the way that Netscape 6.2 and Internet Explorer 5.5 display the border color in the HTML generated by this example, as shown in Figure 11-9. Try the file `CG-attr-sets.html` yourself.

XML to XML: Shallow Copies

In this section and the next, we'll shift gears a bit and consider XML to XML transformations using XSLT; no HTML will be involved. We'll see three examples:

- `c6-copy.xsl`, copying selected nodes to the result tree
- `c6-identity.xsl`, implementing the identity transformation
- `c6-copy-of.xsl`, copying selected nodes and creating new elements and attributes in the result tree

The first example, shown in Listing 11-19, differs in two significant ways from all previous examples. First, no output method is specified, so the default is implicitly XML. Second, because we are transforming XML to XML, the root node template does not need to generate any HTML setup. Assume our task is to filter our source document and just select three particular items from the collection. The root template of c6-copy.xsl simply selects two CDs and one book from the full collection6.xml.

```
<xsl:apply-templates
     select="//CD[1] | Collection/CD[3] | Collection/Book[last()]"/>
```

Specifically, we're selecting the first and third CD elements and the last (third, in this case) Book element. Again, I've used the //CD and Collection/CD XPath expressions interchangeably simply to highlight their equivalence in this instance (although not in general).

The first nonroot template uses the powerful match expression

```
match="*|@*|comment()|processing-instruction()|text()"
```

This matches all element, attribute, comment, PI, and text nodes. This would be equivalent to simply using the node() node test (plus @* for attributes), as explained earlier in "Default Built-in Template Rules and Node Tests." The <xsl:copy> instruction performs a *shallow* copy, which includes the current node and its namespaces; however, it *does not copy the element's children or attributes.* Therefore, rather than the much simpler

```
<xsl:copy>
  <xsl:apply-templates/>
</xsl:copy>
```

we must specify a select attribute that will ensure we process attributes as well.

```
<xsl:copy>
  <xsl:apply-templates
  select="*| @*| comment()| text()| processing-instruction()"/>
</xsl:copy>
```

Listing 11-19 Using <xsl:copy> to Selectively Duplicate Nodes (c6-copy.xsl)

```
<?xml version="1.0"?>
<xsl:stylesheet xmlns:xsl="http://www.w3.org/1999/XSL/Transform"
                version="1.0">
  <!-- Note no output method specified, so defaults to XML. -->
  <!-- xsl:output method="xml" indent="yes" /> -->

  <xsl:template match="/">
    <xsl:apply-templates
         select="//CD[1] | Collection/CD[3] | Collection/Book[last()]"/>
  </xsl:template>

  <xsl:template
       match="*|@*|comment()|processing-instruction()|text()">
    <xsl:copy>
```

```
      <!-- Copy elements, attributes, content, comments, PIs, etc. -->
      <!-- match="node()|@*" would yield the same result. -->
      <xsl:apply-templates select="*| @*| comment()| text()|
                                   processing-instruction()"/>
    </xsl:copy>
  </xsl:template>

  <xsl:template match="CD[3]">
    <xsl:copy>
      <xsl:value-of select="AlbumReleased" />
    </xsl:copy>
  </xsl:template>

</xsl:stylesheet>
```

This will take care of CD[1] and Book[last()]. However, there is a separate template provided for CD[3], which overrides the general processing. Instead, this CD element will be a shallow copy with only the value of the AlbumReleased child copied to the result tree. The XML fragment that results, shown in Listing 11-20, does indeed include CD[1] and Book[last()] and their descendants. For CD[3] we also get exactly what we asked for, namely, an unusual CD element whose content consists of only the date the album was released.

```
<CD xmlns:xhtml="http://www.w3.org/1999/xhtml"
xmlns:html="http://www.w3.org/TR/REC-html40">November 14, 2000</CD>
```

Three points are worth noting. XML output can be atypical since this CD element is certainly not like the others defined in the source document (and would be invalid if a DTD were referenced). Also, the entire result tree does not yield a well-formed XML document because there is no single document element (i.e., Collection) that contains all other elements.

The third point illustrated by this example is that using <xsl:copy> is useful to selectively process certain elements in an application-specific manner and, at the same time, permit other elements to pass through unaltered, perhaps to another process downstream. This is essentially the main reason for using <xsl:copy>—to change part but not all of a source document in an XML to XML transformation.

Listing 11-20 XML Fragment Resulting from <xsl:copy>

```
<?xml version="1.0" encoding="UTF-8"?>
<CD xmlns:xhtml="http://www.w3.org/1999/xhtml"
xmlns:html="http://www.w3.org/TR/REC-html40">
    <Title>Band on the Run</Title>
    <Artist>McCartney, Paul and Wings</Artist>
    <Chart>
      <Peak weeks="4">1</Peak>
      <Peak country="UK">1</Peak>
      <!-- guess -->
```

```
    </Chart>
    <Type>Rock</Type>
    <Label>Capitol</Label>
    <Label country="UK">EMI</Label>
    <AlbumReleased>1973</AlbumReleased>
    <Remastered format="gold CD">1993</Remastered>
    <Remastered format="2 disc box set with booklet">1999</Remastered>
    <ListPrice>16.97</ListPrice>
  </CD><Book xmlns:xhtml="http://www.w3.org/1999/xhtml"
xmlns:html="http://www.w3.org/TR/REC-html40">
    <Title>Beatles Anthology, The</Title>
    <Author>
      <Name>
        <First>Paul</First>
        <Last>McCartney</Last>
      </Name>
    </Author>
    <Author>
      <Name>
        <First>George</First>
        <Last>Harrison</Last>
      </Name>
    </Author>
    <Author>
      <Name>
        <First>Ringo</First>
        <Last>Starr</Last>
      </Name>
    </Author>
    <Author>
      <Name>
        <First>John</First>
        <Last>Lennon</Last>
      </Name>
    </Author>
    <Type>Autobiographical</Type>
    <Published publisher="Chronicle Books">2000</Published>
    <Rating>5 stars</Rating>
    <Notes>368 pages of the Beatles in their own words and pictures!
    A must-have for true Beatles fans.</Notes>
    <ListPrice>60.00</ListPrice>
  </Book><CD xmlns:xhtml="http://www.w3.org/1999/xhtml"
xmlns:html="http://www.w3.org/TR/REC-html40">November 14, 2000</CD>
```

Just for kicks, let's try the *identity transform* that simply copies all of its nodes from the source document to the result tree. This actually can be written quite succinctly in XSLT, as shown in Listing 11-21. There is no explicit template for the root node, so the default template rule, which says process all children, is applied. The example, `c6-identity.xsl`, specifies `"@*|node()"` to capture all nodes, including attributes, PIs, and comments. Given any source document, this stylesheet copies the input to the result tree. The result is identical to the original except for white space handling.

Listing 11-21 Identity Transform Using <xsl:copy> (c6-identity.xsl)

```
<xsl:stylesheet
  xmlns:xsl="http://www.w3.org/1999/XSL/Transform"
  version="1.0">
<xsl:template match="@*|node()">
  <xsl:copy>
    <xsl:apply-templates select="@*|node()"/>
  </xsl:copy>
</xsl:template>
</xsl:stylesheet>
```

XML to XML: Deep Copies and Creating Elements

Next, we'll cover `<xsl:copy-of>`, which performs a *deep* copy of a result tree fragment or a node-set that automatically includes all descendants and attributes. In contrast to `<xsl:copy>`, this is most useful to copy a subtree *unaltered* to the result tree, especially if you need to copy the same node-set more than once.

In Listing 11-22, we use `<xsl:copy-of>` to copy all `CD` elements (and all descendants) and processing instructions to the result tree. These nodes are wrapped inside a completely new kind of element called `CD.Collection` that has three attributes: `owner`, `sex`, and `state`. (Recall that in our original XML, `Owner` and `State` are elements and `sex` is an attribute of `Name`.) The only children of `CD.Collection` are `CD` elements and PIs.

This time, we've explicitly indicated our output method should be indented XML. We initialize a variable called `Owner` to the node represented by the single `/Collection/Owner` element. Note that we can use `$Owner` to refer to this path in `select` attributes.

Generation of the new element is accomplished using `<xsl:element>` with `<xsl:attribute>` instructions as its content. The `name` attribute of `<xsl:element>` is set to the name of the element that is to appear in the result tree, just as the `name` attribute of each `<xsl:attribute>` instruction is set to the desired name of the attribute in the result.

```
<xsl:element name="CD.Collection" >
  <xsl:attribute name="owner" >
   <xsl:value-of select="normalize-space($Owner/Name)" />
  </xsl:attribute>
```

The `/Collection/Owner/Name` element has both `First` and `Last` children, so to trim extraneous white space[7] before we use it to set the `owner` attribute of `CD.Collection`, we use the `normalize-space` XPath function and combine the content of both children by referencing their parent using the `$Owner` variable. To

7. As in XML, the white space characters are `#x20`, `#x9`, `#xD`, or `#xA` (space, tab, carriage return, and newline).

set the sex and state attributes, we use other XPath expressions that involve descendants of $Owner. Note that @sex is necessary for extracting the value of sex because it's an attribute in the original XML.

```
<xsl:attribute name="sex" >
 <xsl:value-of select="$Owner/Name/@sex" />
</xsl:attribute>
<xsl:attribute name="state" >
 <xsl:value-of select="$Owner/Address/State" />
</xsl:attribute>
```

Listing 11-22 Deep Copy Using <xsl:copy-of> Instruction (c6-copy-of.xsl)

```
<?xml version="1.0"?>
<xsl:stylesheet xmlns:xsl="http://www.w3.org/1999/XSL/Transform"
                version="1.0">
  <xsl:output method="xml" indent="yes" />

  <xsl:variable name="Owner" select="/Collection/Owner" />

  <xsl:template match="/">
    <!-- Create a new document element for the output XML. -->
    <!-- Add attributes extracted from Owner element. -->
    <xsl:element name="CD.Collection" >
      <xsl:attribute name="owner" >
       <!-- Need to normal-space since Name has 2 children. -->
       <xsl:value-of select="normalize-space($Owner/Name)" />
      </xsl:attribute>
      <xsl:attribute name="sex" >
       <xsl:value-of select="$Owner/Name/@sex" />
      </xsl:attribute>
      <xsl:attribute name="state" >
       <xsl:value-of select="$Owner/Address/State" />
      </xsl:attribute>

      <!-- Handle children of the document element. -->
      <xsl:apply-templates  select="/Collection"/>

    </xsl:element>
  </xsl:template>

  <xsl:template match="*">
    <!-- Copy only CD elements and PIs (comments omitted). -->
    <xsl:copy-of select="CD | processing-instruction()" />
    <!-- Or, could deep copy everything under the document element.
    <xsl:copy-of select="node()" />
    -->
  </xsl:template>

</xsl:stylesheet>
```

Then for the content of the `CD.Collection` element (as opposed to the content of `<xsl:element>` used to define `CD.Collection`), we process all children of the source document's `Collection` element.

```
<xsl:apply-templates  select="/Collection"/>
```

The only template besides the one for the root node matches all elements (`match="*"`). By using `<xsl:copy-of>` rather than `<xsl:copy>`, a deep copy is performed, which includes all descendants of the context node, including all attributes of each element, comments, and so on. However, for this example, we've selected only `CD` elements and PIs, so `Book` elements and the `Owner` element (from which we've already extracted what we needed) are excluded from the result tree.

The XML result of our transformation is shown in Listing 11-23. In contrast to the example in the previous section, this result is well-formed because the `CD.Collection` element is the (new) document element, complete with the three attributes we obtained from the `Owner` element.

```
<CD.Collection owner="Ken Sall" sex="male" state="MD">
```

`CD.Collection` has three immediate children, namely, the three `CD` elements from the source document. The comments and PI from `collection6.xml` have been captured. Note that the namespace information from the `Collection` element in the source document is included for each `CD` element in the result document.

Listing 11-23 XML Result of Using <xsl:copy-of>, <xsl:element>, and <xsl:attribute>

```
<?xml version="1.0" encoding="UTF-8"?>
<CD.Collection owner="Ken Sall" sex="male" state="MD">
<CD xmlns:xhtml="http://www.w3.org/1999/xhtml"
xmlns:html="http://www.w3.org/TR/REC-html40">
    <Title>Band on the Run</Title>
    <Artist>McCartney, Paul and Wings</Artist>
    <Chart>
      <Peak weeks="4">1</Peak>
      <Peak country="UK">1</Peak>
      <!-- guess -->
    </Chart>
    <Type>Rock</Type>
    <Label>Capitol</Label>
    <Label country="UK">EMI</Label>
    <AlbumReleased>1973</AlbumReleased>
    <Remastered format="gold CD">1993</Remastered>
    <Remastered format="2 disc box set with booklet">1999</Remastered>
    <ListPrice>16.97</ListPrice>
  </CD>
<CD xmlns:xhtml="http://www.w3.org/1999/xhtml"
xmlns:html="http://www.w3.org/TR/REC-html40">
    <Title>Venus and Mars</Title>
    <Artist>McCartney, Paul and Wings</Artist>
```

```
    <Chart>
      <Peak weeks="1">1</Peak>
      <Peak country="UK">2</Peak>
      <!-- guess -->
    </Chart>
    <Type>Rock</Type>
    <Label>Capitol</Label>
    <Label country="UK">EMI</Label>
    <AlbumReleased>1975</AlbumReleased>
    <Remastered format="gold CD with 3 bonus tracks">1994</Remastered>
    <ListPrice>16.97</ListPrice>
  </CD>
<?bogus-pi attr1="foo" attr2="foobar" ?>
<CD xmlns:xhtml="http://www.w3.org/1999/xhtml"
xmlns:html="http://www.w3.org/TR/REC-html40">
    <Title>Beatles 1</Title>
    <Artist>Beatles</Artist>
    <Chart>
      <Peak weeks="10" country="US">1</Peak>
    </Chart>
    <Type>Rock</Type>
    <Label country="US">Capitol</Label>
    <AlbumReleased>November 14, 2000</AlbumReleased>
    <ListPrice>18.97</ListPrice>
  </CD>
</CD.Collection>
```

Although <xsl:copy-of> and <xsl:copy> aren't required in every XML to XML transformation situation, they are certainly useful for copying fragments from the source to the result tree. We've also seen that to create new elements that differ in structure from those in the source document, it's necessary to use <xsl:element> and often <xsl:attribute>. You can also use <xsl:attribute-set> when groups of attributes are to be repeated in the output.

More XML to XML Transformations

You can accomplish XML to XML transformations without <xsl:copy-of> and <xsl:copy>, as we'll see next. Suppose we want to transform our source XML (`collection6.xml`) to result XML (`c6-xml.xml`) that uses different book element names, handles attributes differently, and is a flat hierarchy. In other words, we have specific mapping needs similar to the invoice mapping situation mentioned in Listings 11-1 and 11-2. Listing 11-24 shows the XML result we wish to achieve. The element `Book.List` is similar to `CD.Collection` in the previous section in that it is the document element and it has attributes `seller`, `city`, and `state` that get their values from the `Owner` element in the original XML file.

Listing 11-24 Desired XML Result (c6-xml.xml)

```
<?xml version="1.0" encoding="utf-8"?>
<Book.List seller="Ken Sall" city="Columbia" state="MD">
   <Book.Title kind="Chronology" price="24.95">Complete Beatles Chronicle,
The</Book.Title>
   <Book.Author>Lewisohn, Mark</Book.Author>
   <Book.Publisher publicationYear="1992">Harmony Books</Book.Publisher>
   <Book.Chronology/>
   <Book.Title kind="Autobiographical" price="27.50">Many Years From
Now</Book.Title>
   <Book.Author>McCartney, Paul</Book.Author>
   <Book.Publisher publicationYear="1997">Henry Holt and
Company</Book.Publisher>
   <Book.Autobiographical/>
   <Book.Title kind="Autobiographical" price="60.00">Beatles Anthology,
The</Book.Title>
   <Book.Author>McCartney, Paul</Book.Author>
   <Book.Publisher publicationYear="2000">Chronicle Books</Book.Publisher>
   <Book.Autobiographical/>
</Book.List>
```

For each book, we'll extract the title, type, price, author, and publication information, but we'll keep all of this information at the same level, as immediate children of `Book.List`. See Listing 11-25 for the XSLT stylesheet.

`Book/Author/Name` is mapped to `Book.Author` by extracting the contents of children elements and rearranging them in the order `Last,First`. Notice that we can use the target `Book.Author` element name without using the `<xsl:element>` instruction, which is really required only when we're dynamically computing the element name (as we'll see shortly).

```
<Book.Author>
  <xsl:value-of select="Author/Name/Last" />, <xsl:value-of
                select="Author/Name/First" />
</Book.Author>
```

We'll map `Book/Title` to a `Book.Title` element, `Book/Type` to a `kind` attribute, and `Book/ListPrice` to a `price` attribute. The `<xsl:attribute>` instruction is again used to create an attribute that will appear within the start tag of `Book.Title`. The content of this instruction becomes the value of the attribute (e.g., `kind="Chronology"`).

```
<Book.Title>
   <xsl:attribute name="kind" >
     <xsl:value-of select="Type" />
   </xsl:attribute>
   <xsl:attribute name="price" >
     <xsl:value-of select="ListPrice" />
   </xsl:attribute>
  <xsl:value-of select="Title" />
</Book.Title>
```

For the publication information, we'll reverse the element and attribute relationship, so that source lines like

```
<Published publisher="foo">year</Published>
```

become result lines like

```
<Book.Publisher publicationYear="year">foo</Book.Publisher>
```

We choose to implement this in a separate template. Although we're using `<xsl:element>` here, we could instead use just the literal result element `<Book.Publisher>`. Either way, when we encounter the `Published` element in the source (which represents the year of publication), we start our `Book.Publisher` element. Using `<xsl:attribute>`, we add the attribute `publicationYear`, setting the attribute value to `"."`, which in the current content is the value of the input `Published` node. Next, we extract the value of the source element's `publisher` attribute by means of `<xsl:value-of select="@publisher"/>` to use as the content of the `Book.Publisher` element.

```
<xsl:template match="Published">
  <xsl:element name="Book.Publisher">
    <xsl:attribute name="publicationYear" >
      <xsl:value-of select="." />
    </xsl:attribute>
    <xsl:value-of select="@publisher"/>
  </xsl:element>
</xsl:template>
```

It's necessary to do things in this order when creating an element with attributes: First start the element, then create and set all of its attributes, and finally set the content (if any) of the element itself.

There's one other new trick in this example, which shows a case where `<xsl:element>` really is needed:

```
<xsl:element name="Book.{Type}" />
```

This instruction says, "Create a new element (which happens to be an empty element) and *dynamically determine its name* by computing the value of the `Type` element, and concatenate that with the `"Book."` string. The result is the literal result elements (for the books in order):

```
<Book.Chronology/>
<Book.Autobiographical/>
<Book.Autobiographical/>
```

The curly brackets denote what is called an *attribute value template,* explained more in the section "Attribute Value Templates."

Listing 11-25 XML to XML Transformation (c6-xml.xsl)

```
<?xml version="1.0"?>
<xsl:stylesheet xmlns:xsl="http://www.w3.org/1999/XSL/Transform"
                version="1.0">
  <xsl:output method="xml" indent="yes" />

  <xsl:variable name="Owner" select="/Collection/Owner" />

  <xsl:template match="/">
    <!-- Create a new document element for the output XML. -->
    <!-- Add attributes extracted from Owner element. -->
    <xsl:element name="Book.List" >
      <xsl:attribute name="seller" >
       <!-- Need to normal-space since Name has 2 children. -->
       <xsl:value-of select="normalize-space($Owner/Name)" />
      </xsl:attribute>
      <xsl:attribute name="city" >
       <xsl:value-of select="$Owner/Address/City" />
      </xsl:attribute>
      <xsl:attribute name="state" >
       <xsl:value-of select="$Owner/Address/State" />
      </xsl:attribute>
      <!-- Handle children of the document element. -->
      <xsl:apply-templates  select="/Collection/Book"/>
    </xsl:element>
  </xsl:template>

  <!-- Transform book hierarchy into flat hierarchy with a
       elements Type and ListPrice from original mapped to
       attributes kind and price. Concatenate Last,First name.
  -->
  <xsl:template match="Book">
   <Book.Title>
      <xsl:attribute name="kind" >
        <xsl:value-of select="Type" />
      </xsl:attribute>
      <xsl:attribute name="price" >
        <xsl:value-of select="ListPrice" />
      </xsl:attribute>
     <xsl:value-of select="Title" />
   </Book.Title>
   <Book.Author>
     <xsl:value-of select="Author/Name/Last" />, <xsl:value-of
select="Author/Name/First" />
   </Book.Author>
   <xsl:apply-templates  select="Published"/>

   <!-- Dynamic element naming via attribute value template. -->
   <xsl:element name="Book.{Type}" />

  </xsl:template>
```

```
<!-- Turn element with attribute inside out, changing:
     <Published publisher="foo">year</Published>
     into:
     <Publisher publicationYear="year">foo</Publisher>
-->
<xsl:template match="Published">
  <xsl:element name="Book.Publisher">
    <xsl:attribute name="publicationYear" >
      <xsl:value-of select="." />
    </xsl:attribute>
    <xsl:value-of select="@publisher"/>
  </xsl:element>
</xsl:template>

</xsl:stylesheet>
```

Reader Challenge: Invoice XML to XML Transformation

You now have learned everything you need to know to transform the invoice source in Listing 11-1 to the desired result shown in Listing 11-2. Well, actually you'll also need two or three of the string functions that we haven't yet discussed (see Table 11-14, "String XPath Functions," on page 727). This is an excellent time to stop reading and write the stylesheet that performs the transformation. It will cement the concepts we've covered so far. The answer is somewhere on the CD-ROM. I'm not telling where.

Iterating and Sorting

Now let's return to XML to HTML transformations and learn more XSLT instructions. In this section, we'll see two ways to sort elements from our source document so that they appear in a different order in the result document.

Recall that `CD` and `Book` elements are intermixed in no particular order in `collection6.xml`. For our first sorting example, we'll first sort all `CD` elements in alphabetical order by their titles and then do the same for `Book` elements. The desired result is shown in Figure 11-10.

The stylesheet solution, `c6-for-each.xsl` (Listing 11-26), involves looping through elements using the `<xsl:for-each>` instruction to control the iteration by means of the nodes specified by its `select` attribute. The default iteration order of the nodes is document order. However, if `<xsl:for-each>` contains one or more `<xsl:sort>` children instructions *prior to other instructions*, the nodes will be sorted *before* the iteration begins. In either case, the body of the `<xsl:for-each>` element is applied to each node in its turn.

The `<xsl:sort>` instruction can be the child of either an `<xsl:for-each>` or `<xsl:apply-templates>` instruction, but nothing else. This instruction is an empty element; it has no element children (that is, no content). Multiple sort keys can be achieved by including multiple `<xsl:sort>` elements, the first of which represents the primary sort key, the second of which is the secondary sort key, and so on. The optional `select` attribute defines the key by which to sort. If no `select` attribute is given, the value of the current node (`.`) is implied. An optional `data-type` attribute should only be set to the value `number` when numeric content is being sorted; the default value is `text`, however. The default `order`, another optional attribute, is "ascending" (i.e., a-z).

For this example, I've chosen to sort the `CD` and `Book` elements separately. The first `<xsl:for-each>` iterates over all `CD` elements, after first sorting them in ascending alphabetical order by title. For each `CD`, the `name()` function is used to print the name of the element (`CD`), followed by a number, followed by the value of the `Title` child of the next `CD` in alphabetical order by title. (The same sequence of instructions is given for the `Book` elements.)

```
<xsl:for-each select="//CD">
  <xsl:sort order="ascending" />
  <br />
  <xsl:value-of select="name()" />
  <xsl:text> </xsl:text><xsl:number /><xsl:text>: </xsl:text>
  <i><xsl:value-of select="Title" /></i>
</xsl:for-each>
```

The `<xsl:number>` instruction is new to us. It's used to insert a formatted number into the result tree. If no `value` attribute is specified, then the `<xsl:number>` element inserts a number based on the document order of the current node (influenced by other attributes). Other attributes can be combined to make this a very flexible, multipurposed instruction (see Table 11-18, "XSLT Instructions" on page 744 for details).

Listing 11-26 Iteration Using <xsl:for-each> and <xsl:sort> Instructions (c6-for-each.xsl)

```
<?xml version="1.0"?>
<xsl:stylesheet   version="1.0"
  xmlns:xsl="http://www.w3.org/1999/XSL/Transform">
<xsl:output method="html"/>

<xsl:variable name="label">XSLT: For-Each</xsl:variable>

<xsl:template match="/">
   <html>
     <head>
       <title><xsl:value-of select="$label" /></title>
     </head>
     <body>
       <h1><xsl:value-of select="$label" /></h1>
       <xsl:apply-templates />
     </body>
   </html>
</xsl:template>

<xsl:template match="*"> <!-- note -->
```

```
    <h2>CDs in Ascending Order</h2>
    <xsl:for-each select="//CD">
      <xsl:sort order="ascending" />
      <br />
      <xsl:value-of select="name()" />
      <xsl:text> </xsl:text><xsl:number /><xsl:text>: </xsl:text>
      <i><xsl:value-of select="Title" /></i>
    </xsl:for-each>

    <h2>Books in Ascending Order</h2>
    <xsl:for-each select="//Book">
      <xsl:sort order="ascending" />
      <br />
      <xsl:value-of select="name()" />
      <xsl:text> </xsl:text><xsl:number /><xsl:text>: </xsl:text>
      <i><xsl:value-of select="Title" /></i>
    </xsl:for-each>

</xsl:template>
</xsl:stylesheet>
```

The output of `c6-for-each.xsl` is shown in Figure 11-10. The three `CD` elements are in alphabetical order, as are the three `Book` elements. The numbers resulting from `<xsl:number>` are not in their sort order, but rather their *document order* number among elements of the same name. For example, looking at the `CD` elements, the

FIGURE 11-10 Display of alphabetical sort

generated numbers are 1, 3, and 2, indicating that the first element in document order is also the first in the alphabetical sort, the third in document order is the second in sort order, and the second in document order is the last in sort order. If any two titles had been identical, then in the absence of a secondary sort key (illustrated shortly), document order is used to break ties.

What might not be very obvious is why the value of the `Title` was used for the sort order. After all, the value of `CD` or `Book` nodes is more than just the `Title`. This is a fortunate coincidence of the structure of the `CD` element in the source document. `Title` is the first child of `CD` (in document order) so it is used as the sort key. Expressions involving node-sets return only the first node in certain contexts.

If we wanted to sort both `CD` and `Book` elements together, regardless of element type, we would simply discard one of the `<xsl:for-each>` templates and extend the node-set to include both, like this:

```
<xsl:for-each select="//CD | //Book" >
```

We would expect the numbering to be the same since `<xsl:number>` applies to the specific element name. Our output would look like this:

```
CD 1: Band on the Run
CD 3: Beatles 1
Book 3: Beatles Anthology, The
Book 1: Complete Beatles Chronicle, The
Book 2: Many Years From Now
CD 2: Venus and Mars
```

To prove that the position of the `Title` child is significant, I tried an altered version of the source called `collection6-Title-2nd.xml` with the following structure, in which `Title` became the second direct child of either `CD` or `Book`, moving `Artist` or `Author` to the first position, respectively.

```
<Book>
  <Author>
    <Name>
      <First></First>
      <Last></Last>
    </Name>
  </Author>
  <Title></Title>
  <!-- etc. -->
<CD>
  <Artist></Artist>
  <Title></Title>
  <!-- etc. -->
```

I then modified the stylesheet by combining the iteration over both elements, and by outputting the last name of the author or the artist after the title, just to be sure the position in the stylesheet wasn't the issue.

```
<xsl:for-each select="//CD | //Book">
  <xsl:sort order="ascending" />
  <br />
  <xsl:value-of select="name()" />
  <xsl:text> </xsl:text><xsl:number /><xsl:text>: </xsl:text>
  <i><xsl:value-of select="Title" /></i><xsl:text> by </xsl:text>
  <b><xsl:value-of select="Author/Name/Last | Artist" /></b>
</xsl:for-each>
```

The result of applying `c6-for-each2.xsl` to `collection6-Title-2nd.xml` shows that now the artist or author name, not the title, is used for sorting.

```
CD 3: Beatles 1 by Beatles
Book 1: Complete Beatles Chronicle, The by Lewisohn
CD 1: Band on the Run by McCartney, Paul and Wings
CD 2: Venus and Mars by McCartney, Paul and Wings
Book 3: Beatles Anthology, The by McCartney
Book 2: Many Years From Now by McCartney
```

Notice that the output order is different, as is the numbering, which now reflects that `CD[3]` is first alpabetically by artist, `Book[1]` is second (but first among `Book` elements) by the author's last name, `CD[1]` is third, and so on.

Our second sorting example also involves `<xsl:sort>`, except this time it's used in conjunction with `<xsl:apply-templates>` instead of `<xsl:for-each>`. For variety, we'll first sort `CD` elements in ascending order, then `Book` elements in descending order, then both elements together in ascending order. The stylesheet, `c6-sort.xsl`, is shown in Listing 11-27.

Listing 11-27 Using <xsl:sort> with <xsl:apply-templates>

```
<?xml version="1.0"?>
<xsl:stylesheet   version="1.0"
  xmlns:xsl="http://www.w3.org/1999/XSL/Transform">
<xsl:output method="html"/>

<xsl:variable name="label">XSLT: Sort</xsl:variable>

<xsl:template match="/">
  <html>
    <head>
      <title><xsl:value-of select="$label" /></title>
    </head>
    <body>
      <h2><xsl:value-of select="$label" /></h2>

      <h3>CDs in Ascending Order</h3>
      <xsl:apply-templates select="//CD" >
        <xsl:sort order="ascending" select="." />
      </xsl:apply-templates>
```

```
        <h3>Books in Descending Order</h3>
        <xsl:apply-templates select="//Book" >
          <xsl:sort order="descending" select="." />
        </xsl:apply-templates>

        <h3>CDs and Books (mixed) in Ascending Order</h3>
        <!--  This expression also matches everything except Owner.
        <xsl:apply-templates
             select="/Collection/*[not(name() = 'Owner')]" >
        -->
        <xsl:apply-templates select="//CD | //Book" >
          <xsl:sort order="ascending" select="." />
        </xsl:apply-templates>

      </body>
    </html>
</xsl:template>

<xsl:template match="CD | Book">
   <xsl:value-of select="position()" /><xsl:text>.) </xsl:text>
   <i><xsl:value-of select="Title" /></i><br />
</xsl:template>

</xsl:stylesheet>
```

This time I've specified the `select` attribute, but it again selects the value of the current node as the sort key.

```
<xsl:apply-templates select="//CD" >
  <xsl:sort order="ascending" select="." />
</xsl:apply-templates>
```

All previous examples of `<xsl:apply-templates>` have used the empty element form. However, in this case, `<xsl:apply-templates>` has content, namely, the `<xsl:sort>` instruction, so *the elements will first be sorted and then the matching template will be invoked.* The same is done for `Book` elements except that `order="descending"` is specified.

The template that matches either `CD` or `Book` calls the XPath `position()` function, which returns the ordinal position of the node in the node-set context. Since the nodes have been sorted before the template is called, the order is their *sort order*, not document order as it was in the earlier example. This is an important difference between the `<xsl:number>` instruction used earlier and the `position()` function. A third call to `<xsl:apply-templates>` operates on both `CD` and `Book` together, so the elements are merged in the sorted node-set before the template is applied. The result is shown in Figure 11-11.

What would you expect to happen if we applied this stylesheet to the altered source document, `collect6-Title-2nd.xml`? First, we'll make a slight change just

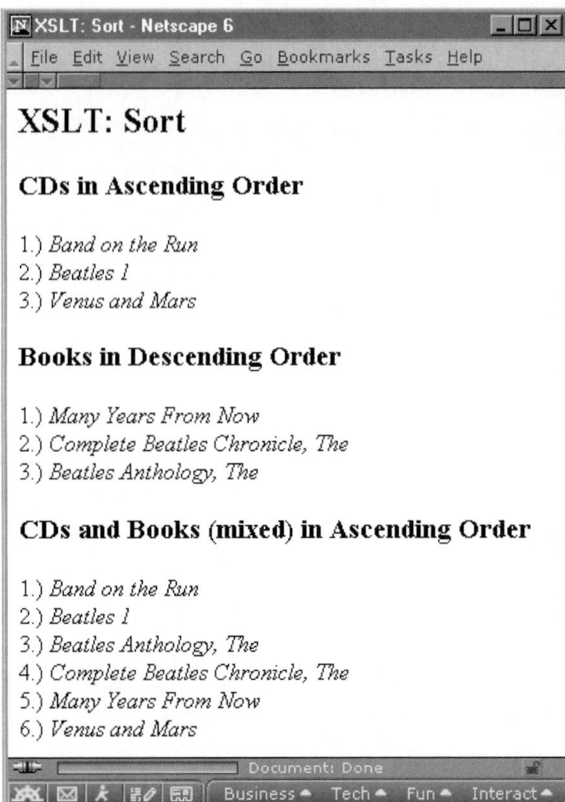

FIGURE 11-11 Display of sorted output using c6-sort.xsl and collection6.xml

so we can better verify the results. Let's replace the template with one that also displays the name of the artist or author (`c6-sort2.xsl`).

```
<xsl:template match="CD | Book">
   <xsl:value-of select="position()" /><xsl:text>.) </xsl:text>
   <i><xsl:value-of select="Title" /></i>
   <xsl:text> by </xsl:text>
   <b><xsl:value-of select="Author/Name/Last | Artist" /></b>
   <br />
</xsl:template>
```

For the answer, see Figure 11-12. The output this time is the same sort order by artist and author that we saw earlier when we supplied the alternative source document. The only real difference is that the `position()` function yields numbers in sorted order, as was the case in Figure 11-11.

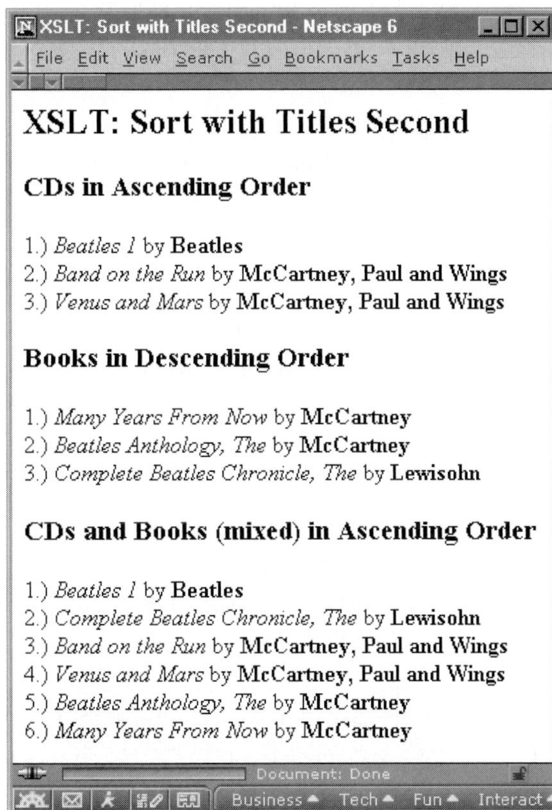

FIGURE 11-12 Sort results with different source (collection6-Titles-2nd.xml)

Primary and Secondary Sort Keys

Suppose we want to specify *more than one* sort key. What if we don't want to be bothered by the order of child elements in our source? Suppose we want to first sort by title (the primary key) and then by artist or author (the secondary key). Suppose further that in the same stylesheet, we'd like to then switch to artist or author as the primary key and use the item's list price as the secondary key. We certainly don't want to have to change our source document structure just to accommodate these new requirements. Instead, we need a more flexible stylesheet like `c6-sort3.xsl`, shown in Listing 11-28.

Multiple sort keys are specified by using the `<xsl:sort>` instruction more than once within the body of `<xsl:apply-templates>` (or `<xsl:for-each>`, for that matter), prior to other instructions. In this case, it's necessary to be specific about the `select` attribute because that will be the sort key. For example, to indicate `Title` as the primary sort key and `Artist` as the secondary key, we provide two `<xsl:sort>` instructions in this order:

```
<xsl:apply-templates select="//CD" >
  <xsl:sort order="ascending" select="Title" />
  <xsl:sort order="ascending" select="Artist" />
</xsl:apply-templates>
```

This means elements will first be sorted by their titles. If two titles are identical, the artist name will be used to determine which is first and which is second. Although identical titles aren't possible with our data, the point is that when we use these keys even with our altered data, `collection6-Titles-2nd.xml`, our results will be sorted by the `Title` element (even though it is the second child of `CD`, after `Artist` or `Author`). A similar pair of keys is used for the `Book` element, although the sort is descending. Verify to yourself from Figure 11-3 that the `CD` sort is alphabetical by title and the `Book` sort is in reverse alphabetical order by title (see page 610).

To further illustrate the flexibility of multiple keys (Listing 11-28), the third `<xsl:apply-templates>` body of `c6-sort3.xsl` switches to `Artist` and `Author` as the primary sort key and `ListPrice` as the secondary key.

```
<xsl:apply-templates select="//CD | //Book" >
  <xsl:sort order="ascending" select="Artist | Author/Name/Last" />
  <xsl:sort order="ascending" select="ListPrice"
            data-type="number" />
</xsl:apply-templates>
```

Note that this time I've added the `data-type="number"` attribute/value pair to be sure `ListPrice` content is compared numerically. When the `Author` key value "McCartney" is identical for the two books, "Many Years From Now" and "Beatles Anthology, The", the `ListPrice` secondary sort key determines that the book with the lower price is output first (see Figure 11-13 on page 658). I made another change in `collection6-Titles-2nd.xml` that emphasizes the secondary key. The `ListPrice` for the "Venus and Mars" disk was changed from $16.97 to $15.98, not because it's on sale, but just so the price can be a tie breaker when the `Artist` key, "McCartney, Paul and Wings", is the same value as that which is associated with the "Band on the Run" disk. In this last case, we're clearly overriding document order with the secondary key since "Venus and Mars" is `CD[2]` while "Band on the Run" is `CD[1]`. If I had not changed the `ListPrice`, these 2 `CD` elements would have identical values for both of the sort keys, in which case they would have been processed in document order (with respect to each other).

Listing 11-28 Stylesheet with Primary and Secondary Sort Keys (c6-sort3.xsl)

```
<?xml version="1.0"?>
<xsl:stylesheet   version="1.0"
  xmlns:xsl="http://www.w3.org/1999/XSL/Transform">
<xsl:output method="html"/>

<xsl:variable name="label">XSLT: Sort with Primary and Secondary
Keys</xsl:variable>

<xsl:template match="/">
   <html>
     <head>
       <title><xsl:value-of select="$label" /></title>
     </head>
     <body>
       <h2><xsl:value-of select="$label" /></h2>

       <!-- Primary sort key=Title, secondary=Artist or Author -->
       <h3>CDs Ascending, 1st=Title, 2nd=Artist</h3>
       <xsl:apply-templates select="//CD" >
         <xsl:sort order="ascending" select="Title" />
         <xsl:sort order="ascending" select="Artist" />
       </xsl:apply-templates>

       <h3>Books Descending, 1st=Title, 2nd=Author</h3>
       <xsl:apply-templates select="//Book" >
         <xsl:sort order="descending" select="Title" />
         <xsl:sort order="descending" select="Author/Name/Last" />
       </xsl:apply-templates>

       <!-- Primary sort key=Artist or Author, secondary=ListPrice -->
       <h3>Mixed Ascending, 1st=Artist or Author, 2nd=ListPrice</h3>
       <xsl:apply-templates select="//CD | //Book" >
         <xsl:sort order="ascending" select="Artist | Author/Name/Last" />
         <xsl:sort order="ascending" select="ListPrice"
          data-type="number" />
       </xsl:apply-templates>

     </body>
   </html>
</xsl:template>

<xsl:template match="CD | Book">
   <xsl:value-of select="position()" /><xsl:text>.) </xsl:text>
   <i><xsl:value-of select="Title" /></i>
   <xsl:text> by </xsl:text>
   <b><xsl:value-of select="Author/Name/Last | Artist" /></b>
   <xsl:text> at $</xsl:text>
   <xsl:value-of select="ListPrice" />
   <br />
</xsl:template>

</xsl:stylesheet>
```

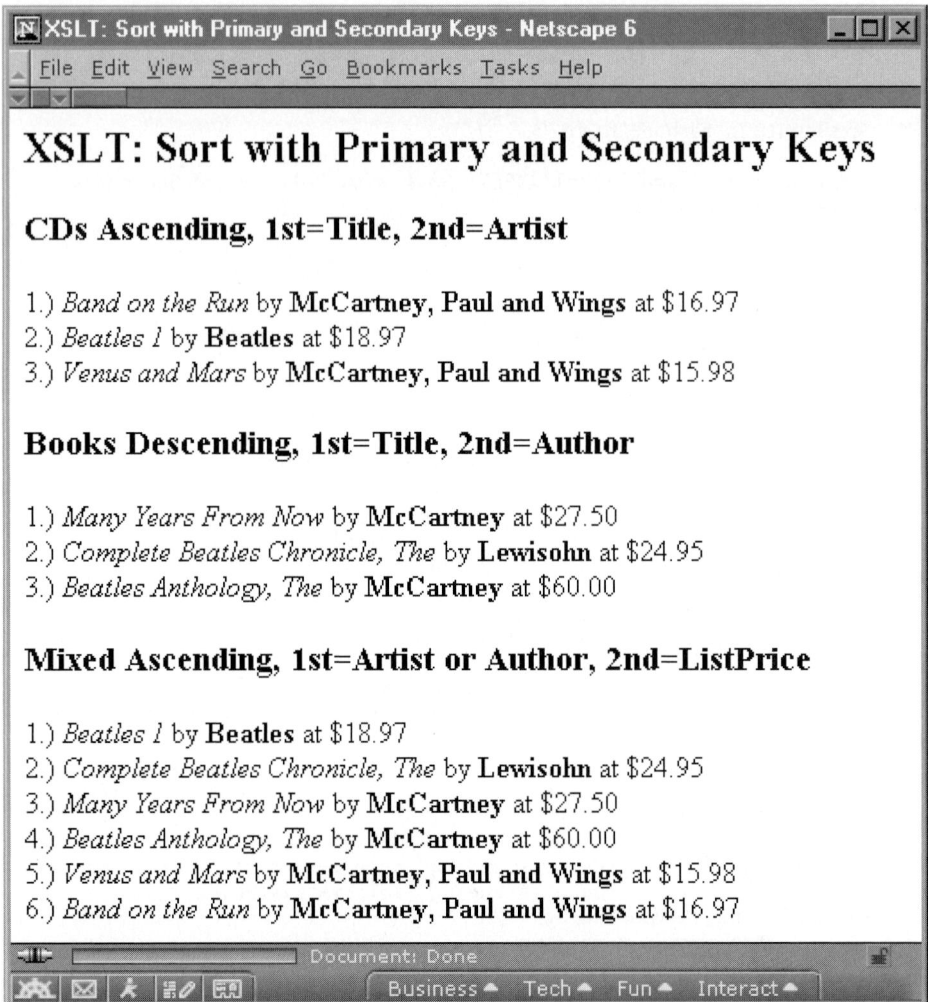

FIGURE 11-13 Sort results with primary and secondary keys (c6-sort3.xsl)

Associating XSL with XML: Processing Instruction or Element

In "Using CSS With XML," we learned about associating a CSS stylesheet with XML by means of the `xml-stylesheet` *processing instruction*, which, by the way, should not be confused with the `<xsl:stylesheet>` element of XSLT. The same processing instruction can be used with XSLT stylesheets, although at the time of this writing, browser support is inconsistent because to support this PI, the browser would need to include an XSLT processing module (just as browsers process CSS natively).

To use the PI with XSLT, set the `type` attribute to `"text/xsl"` and set the `href` attribute to point to the relative path to the XSLT file (in this case, in the same directory), an external stylesheet:

```
<?xml-stylesheet type="text/xsl" href="hello-italics.xsl"?>
```

In Figure 11-14, we revisit the Hello XSLT example with a slight variation called `hello-pi.xml`, which references the stylesheet `hello-italics.xsl` by means of the `xml-stylesheet` PI (windows 1 and 2 in the figure). As the figure illustrates, when

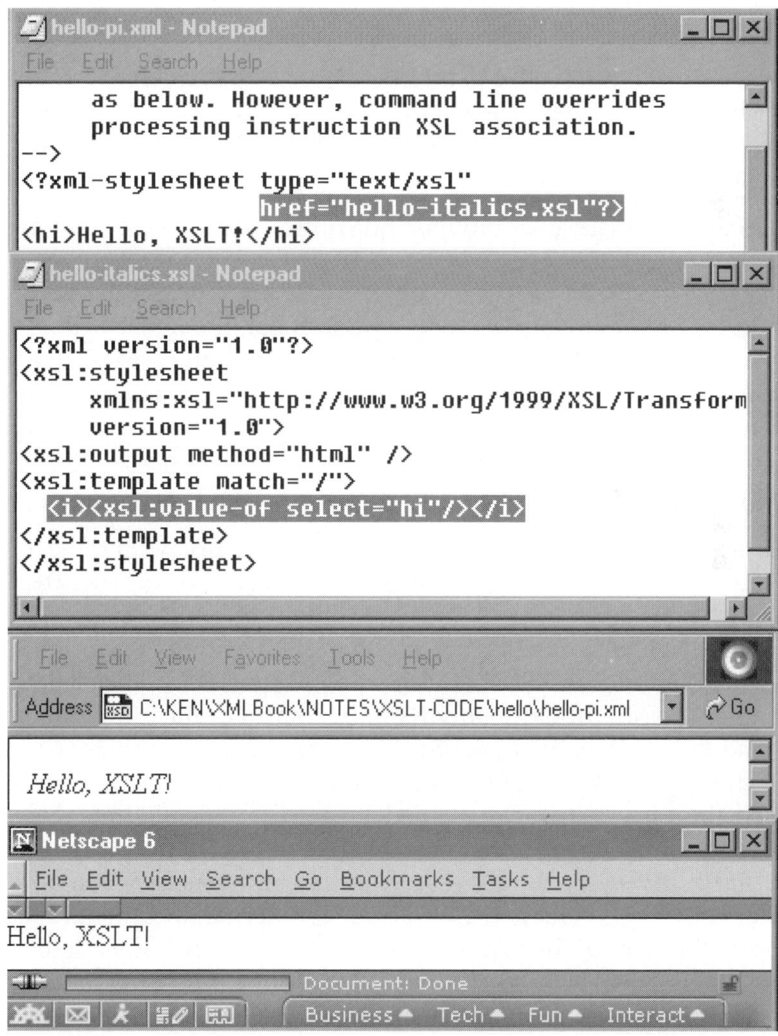

FIGURE 11-14 Associating an XSLT Stylesheet with XML documents

hello-pi.xml is viewed in Internet Explorer 5.5, the correct stylesheet is accessed and applied to the XML document by the browser as a client-side transformation (window 3). Netscape 6.01 silently ignores the PI and simply does its default rendering of XML; that is, it displays the content of all nodes, which in this case is simply the content of the <hi> element (window 4). Fortunately, Netscape 6.2 displays this properly (not shown). Notice that no formatting is applied in the Netscape case, neither the italics that hello-italics.xml would have supplied nor the bold that we saw much earlier when we transformed the original hello.xml externally with hello.xsl.

At the time of this writing, xml-stylesheet processing instruction support can be summarized as follows:

- *Supported:* Netscape 6.2, Internet Explorer 6.0, Internet Explorer 5.5 (depending on your version of MSXML).
- *Not supported:* Netscape 4.75, Netscape 6.01, Internet Explorer 5.1, Opera 6.0, and W3C's Amaya 5.2.

Perhaps a less than obvious but quite useful rule is that even when an xml-stylesheet PI does appear in an XML document, *command-line processing will override the associated stylesheet.* For example, if we apply our original hello.xsl stylesheet to hello-pi.xml, using xalan-it.bat, the result will be the same as it was as when we used hello.xml without a PI. In both cases, the string "Hello, XSLT" would appear in bold font, not italics. This override is useful for server-side transformations.

Special Characters: Disabling Output Escaping

Earlier we learned that <xsl:text> is used to display literal text (#PCDATA), including the preservation and control of white space. The <xsl:text> instruction cannot contain markup characters, so it can contain no child elements.

Next we'll discuss a little problem. How do you deal with special character (general) entities in XSLT? As we saw in "Special Character Entities Revisited," in chapter 4, XML provides only a small handful of the numerous predefined entities found in HTML, namely, &, <, >, ', and " (for &, <, >, ', and "), and that's it. What if we need to send the entity for the copyright symbol or perhaps the Greek character named beta to our result tree? How we handle this depends on whether we're generating XML or HTML output.

If we're dealing with XML output, we must include a definition for each character entity we intend to use as part of an internal document type subset. So, for the copyright symbol (hex A9 or decimal 169) and the Greek letters alpha, beta, and gamma (decimal 945–947), include a document type declaration after the XML declaration in the output document. Any special character other than the five predefined character entities must be explicitly declared or the parser/processor will generate an error.

```
<!DOCTYPE SomeDocumentElement [
  <!ENTITY ourCopyright "&#xA9;">
  <!ENTITY alpha "&#945;">
  <!ENTITY beta  "&#946;">
  <!ENTITY gamma "&#947;">
]>
```

References to the characters in the body of the XML document are written in the usual manner, with the entity name surrounded by ampersand and semicolon.

```
<SomeElement-with-PCDATA-content>
alpha is: &alpha; beta is: &beta; gamma is: &gamma;
This tibdit is Copyright &ourCopyright; NoOneInParticular.
</SomeElement-with-PCDATA-content>
```

You can use hexidecimal character references starting with the &#x, followed by the hex code for the Unicode character, and terminating with a semicolon. The copyright symbol has the hex value A9, so one possible character reference is ©. Alternatively, this entity can be expressed as decimal 169, in which case we omit the x, so the reference is ©.

Normally, characters such as < and & in the source are converted to entity references, < and & in the serialization process. This is called **output escaping**. When it encounters special characters, the XSLT processor is free to choose from among several forms that are equivalent according to the XML Recommendation. For example, the < symbol can be output as <, <, or the more verbose <!CDATA[[<]]> sequence. (Recall the discussion of Canonical XML in chapter 5.) Sometimes it's necessary to override this replacement behavior and instead output the literal characters < and &. The <xsl:text> instruction has an optional disable-output-escaping attribute which, if set to "yes", causes the literal characters to be output (rather than being escaped). The disabling of escaping is necessary when you're generating text in which the literal characters must be seen, when generating JavaScript or other code that treats < and & as operators, or when you want to create your entity references for convenience (text substitution, for example).

If our result tree is HTML, we can take advantage of the character entities that are already defined, but not as easily as we would in HTML directly. The HTML 4.01 Recommendation includes a table of character entity references for ISO 8859-1 characters, known as HTMLlat1, which ranges from nbsp (which can also be written as the hex value) to yuml (ÿ) (see *http://www.w3.org/TR/html401/sgml/entities.html*). For symbols, mathematical symbols, and Greek letters, HTML defines a set called HTMLsymbol (e.g., alpha is α), and for markup-significant and internationalization characters, the set is called HTMLspecial (e.g., circ [circumflex] is ˆ). See Appendix C for the entity tables.

Listing 11-29 illustrates the use of <xsl:text> with the disable-output-escaping set to "no", "yes", or omitted to try the default (which is "no"). I've defined character entities, but I could have simply used the decimal values or their hex equivalents directly. The lines labeled "(internally defined symbols)" refer to the symbolic names such as α and the lines labeled "(numeric)" indicate the direct use of the numeric value (α) in the stylesheet.

Listing 11-29 Text with Disabling Output Escaping (c6-escape.xsl)

```
<?xml version="1.0"?>
<!DOCTYPE xsl:stylesheet  [
<!ENTITY copy  "&#169;">
<!ENTITY nbsp  " "> <!-- or   -->
<!ENTITY alpha "&#945;">
<!ENTITY beta  "&#946;">
<!ENTITY gamma "&#947;">
<!ENTITY circ  "&#710;">
]>
<xsl:stylesheet   version="1.0"
  xmlns:xsl="http://www.w3.org/1999/XSL/Transform">
<xsl:output method="html" indent="yes"/>

<xsl:variable name="label">XSLT: Disable Output Escaping</xsl:variable>

<xsl:template match="/">
   <html>
     <head>
       <title><xsl:value-of select="$label" /></title>
     </head>
     <body>
       <h1><xsl:value-of select="$label" /></h1>
       <h3>View HTML Source for Differences</h3>
       <xsl:apply-templates select="//Book"/>
     </body>
   </html>
</xsl:template>

<xsl:template match="Book[3]">
   <p><xsl:text>Book title: </xsl:text>
   <i><xsl:value-of select="Title" /></i>

   <br />  <!-- correct since default is NOT to disable escaping -->
   default: <xsl:text disable-output-escaping="yes"> &amp;nbsp; &amp;nbsp;
&amp;nbsp; &amp;nbsp;</xsl:text>
   Copyright <xsl:text>&copy;</xsl:text>
   <xsl:value-of select="Published" />

   <br />  <!-- correct -->
   disable=no:<xsl:text disable-output-escaping="yes">&amp;nbsp;</xsl:text>
   Copyright <xsl:text disable-output-escaping="no">&copy;</xsl:text>
   <xsl:value-of select="Published" />

   <br />  <!-- correct, except not for XML output -->
   disable=yes:
```

```
    Copyright <xsl:text disable-output-escaping="yes">&copy;</xsl:text>
    <xsl:value-of select="Published" />
    </p>

    Copyright as hex (xA9): <xsl:text>&#xA9; and as decimal (169):
&#169;</xsl:text>
    <br />
    disable=no (numeric):
    <xsl:text disable-output-escaping="no"> &#945; &#946; &#947; &#169;
&#710;</xsl:text>
    <br />
    disable=yes (numeric):
    <xsl:text disable-output-escaping="yes"> &#945; &#946; &#947; &#169;
&#710;</xsl:text>
    <br />
    disable=no (internally defined symbols):
    <xsl:text disable-output-escaping="no"> &alpha; &beta; &gamma; &copy;
&circ;</xsl:text>
    <br />
    disable=yes (internally defined symbols):
    <xsl:text disable-output-escaping="yes"> &alpha; &beta; &gamma; &copy;
&circ;</xsl:text>
    <br />
    disable=no:
    <xsl:text disable-output-escaping="no">3 nbsp:[   ] &lt;
&gt; &amp; &quot; &apos;</xsl:text>
    <br />
    disable=yes:
    <xsl:text disable-output-escaping="yes">3 nbsp:[   ] &lt;
&gt; &amp; &quot; &apos;</xsl:text>
    <br />

</xsl:template>

<xsl:template match="*">
</xsl:template>

</xsl:stylesheet>
```

The results as displayed by Netscape 4.79 and Netscape 6.2 are shown in Figure 11-15. Somewhat surprisingly, they are not identical and, to my way of thinking, the older version does more what I would have expected. Netscape 6.2 seems to render the entities no matter how I specify them and regardless of the setting of `disable-output-escaping`, whereas the older browser honors the "no" setting by rendering only the symbolic name, except for the five predefined XML entities and also (curiously) for the copyright entity. While the Netscape 6.2 output appears to produce identical rendering for all combinations, if you view the HTML source, shown as Netscape 6.2 displays it in Figure 11-16, you'll note the source reflects differences, but the browser chooses to ignore them.

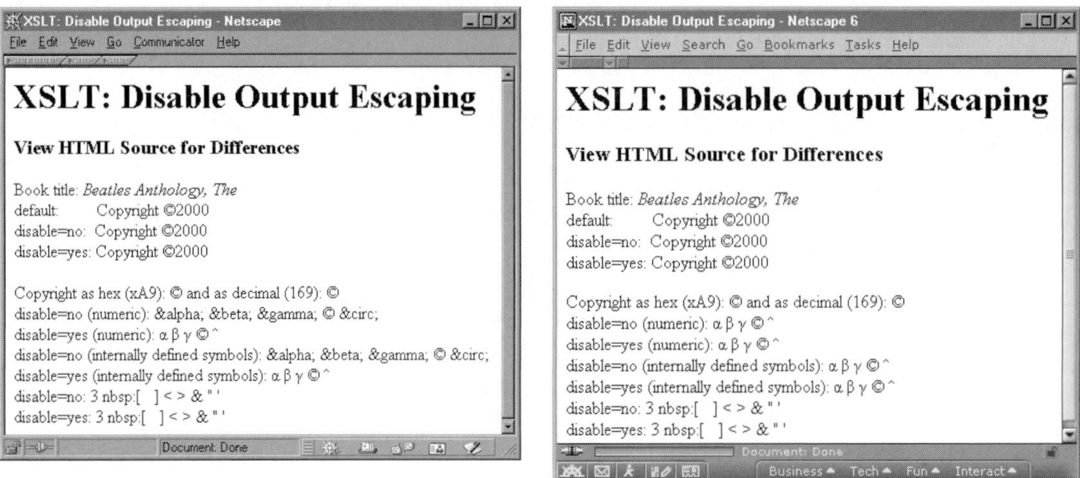

FIGURE 11-15 Display of disabling output escaping in Netscape 4.79 and 6.2

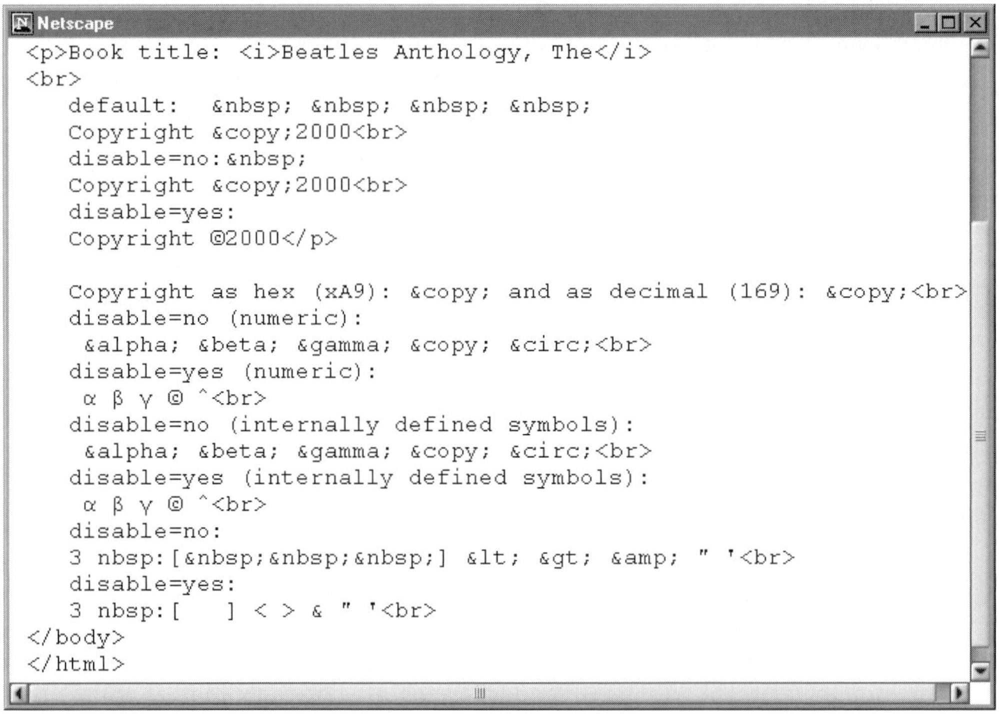

```
Netscape
<p>Book title: <i>Beatles Anthology, The</i>
<br>
   default:         
   Copyright &copy;2000<br>
   disable=no: 
   Copyright &copy;2000<br>
   disable=yes:
   Copyright ©2000</p>

   Copyright as hex (xA9): &copy; and as decimal (169): &copy;<br>
   disable=no (numeric):
    &alpha; &beta; &gamma; &copy; &circ;<br>
   disable=yes (numeric):
    α β γ © ^<br>
   disable=no (internally defined symbols):
    &alpha; &beta; &gamma; &copy; &circ;<br>
   disable=yes (internally defined symbols):
    α β γ © ^<br>
   disable=no:
   3 nbsp:[   ] &lt; &gt; &amp; " '<br>
   disable=yes:
   3 nbsp:[   ] < > & " '<br>
</body>
</html>
```

FIGURE 11-16 HTML Source with special characters (c6-escape.html)

Output Methods Revisited: XML, HTML, Text

In this section, we'll explore several simple variations of the `<xsl:output>` instruction for the `hello.xml` example we considered in the sections "Hello XSLT Example" and "Associating XSL with XML: Processing Instruction or Element."

To produce XML output, the only change needed to `hello.xsl` (from Listing 11-4) is to specify "xml" as the output method, as shown in Listing 11-30.

Listing 11-30 Default XML Output Method (hello-xml-default.xsl)

```
<?xml version="1.0"?>
<xsl:stylesheet xmlns:xsl="http://www.w3.org/1999/XSL/Transform"
                version="1.0">

<xsl:output method="xml" />

<xsl:template match="/">
  <b><xsl:value-of select="hi"/></b>
</xsl:template>

</xsl:stylesheet>
```

This will send XML containing the default XML declaration to the result tree:

```
<?xml version="1.0" encoding="UTF-8"?>
<b>Hello, XSLT!</b>
```

Identical XML results if we explicitly request that the XML declaration not be excluded by changing the `<xsl:output>` instruction to

```
<xsl:output method="xml" omit-xml-declaration="no"/>
```

As you would expect, if we change this to `omit-xml-declaration="yes"`, the resultant XML is simply the single element without an XML declaration

```
<b>Hello, XSLT!</b>
```

If we want text output, we simply adjust the `<xsl:output>` instruction accordingly

```
<xsl:output method="text" />
```

which results in a string with no markup characters

```
Hello, XSLT!
```

Let's change our input document to something just a little bit more interesting (but perhaps not much more[8]), as per Listing 11-31 with the corresponding stylesheet in Listing 11-32.

8. I originally wanted to use the Beatles "Hello Goodbye" for this example but decided against it for copyright reasons. You might try the XSLT stylesheets in this section with a modified input document that marks up the Beatles' lyrics.

Listing 11-31 Hello Goodbye Input XML Document (hello-goodbye.xml)

```
<?xml version="1.0"?>
<hello-goodbye>
  <hi>Hello</hi>
  <bye>Goodbye</bye>
  <hi>Hello, Hello</hi>
  <hi>Hi</hi>
  <bye>Say Goodbye</bye>
  <bye>Bye</bye>
</hello-goodbye>
```

Listing 11-32 Hello Goodbye Stylesheet for HTML Output (hello-goodbye-html.xsl)

```
<?xml version="1.0"?>
<xsl:stylesheet xmlns:xsl="http://www.w3.org/1999/XSL/Transform"
                version="1.0">

<xsl:output method="html" />

<xsl:template match="/">  <!-- or /hello-goodbye -->
  <html>
    <head>
      <title>Hello Goodbye</title>
    </head>
    <body>
      <h1 align="center">Hello Goodbye</h1>
      <xsl:apply-templates />
    </body>
  </html>
</xsl:template>

<xsl:template match="hi">
  <p><b><xsl:value-of select="."/></b></p>
</xsl:template>

<xsl:template match="bye">
  <p><i><xsl:value-of select="."/></i></p>
</xsl:template>

</xsl:stylesheet>
```

This stylesheet, which generates HTML output, consists of three basic templates, one for the root which matches the document element, `hello-goodbye`, one for `hi` elements, and one for `bye` elements.

The HTML that results from applying `hello-goodbye-html.xsl` to `hello-goodbye.xml` is shown in Listing 11-33. The `hi` elements from the input document become bold and the `bye` elements become italicized.

Listing 11-33 HTML Output Result from Applying hello-goodbye-html.xsl

```
<html>
<head>
<META http-equiv="Content-Type" content="text/html; charset=UTF-8">
<title>Hello Goodbye</title>
</head>
<body>
<h1 align="center">Hello Goodbye</h1>

<p>
<b>Hello</b>
</p>

<p>
<i>Goodbye</i>
</p>

<p>
<b>Hello, Hello</b>
</p>

<p>
<b>Hi</b>
</p>

<p>
<i>Say Goodbye</i>
</p>

<p>
<i>Bye</i>
</p>

</body>
</html>
```

If we change just the `<xsl:output>` instruction to "xml", the resultant XML is shown in Listing 11-34. Once again the XML output is different from the HTML case despite identical input and only a single instruction difference in the stylesheets. The HTML output includes a `META` tag that identifies the document as HTML, whereas the XML result has an XML declaration.

The white space format of the two documents also differs; the XML output receives the default indentation. Of course, the XML version includes elements that *look* like HTML tags, but since there is no DTD specified or namespace referenced, their structure is undefined; these elements certainly will not be interpreted as HTML, however.

Listing 11-34 XML Output Resulting from Applying hello-goodbye-xml.xsl

```
<?xml version="1.0" encoding="UTF-8"?>
<html><head><title>Hello Goodbye</title></head><body><h1 align="center">Hello
Goodbye</h1>
  <p><b>Hello</b></p>
  <p><i>Goodbye</i></p>
  <p><b>Hello, Hello</b></p>
  <p><b>Hi</b></p>
  <p><i>Say Goodbye</i></p>
  <p><i>Bye</i></p>
</body></html>
```

Reuse: Named Templates and Passing Parameters

Just in case you dozed off in the last section or two, now is the time to perk right up. In this section, we'll cover the extremely useful concept of named templates.

In XSLT, the equivalent of a user-defined subroutine or function is a **named template**, which is defined using the familiar `<xsl:template>` element. However, in this case, there is a required `name` attribute that indicates the name (handle) by which the template is called. The body of the template is similar to those we've already seen except for three aspects:

1. Parameters (arguments) passed to the named template are defined with the optional `<xsl:param>` element which, if present, must appear *before other instructions* within the template body. A parameter may have a default value; if so, that value is defined in the named template via `<xsl:param>` in the same way that values are initialized for the `<xsl:variable>` element (see "More about Setting Variables" earlier in this chapter). In fact, in XSLT parameters are identical to variables with one key difference: *you can override the default value of a parameter at runtime.*
2. Optionally, the output of the template can be assigned to a variable in the caller, making the named template more like a function in most computer languages.
3. Since a named template is invoked by its `name` attribute, the `match` attribute is seldom used, although it is permitted.

Named templates facilitate reuse since they can be invoked by name at any point from the top level or from within other templates. Any variables associated with a named template may have different values bound to them at each invocation since each call represents a new local scope.

Defining and Invoking a Named Template

Listing 11-35 shows a named template in the stylesheet `c6-param.xsl.` This example is a restructuring of our first sorting styleseheet, `c6-for-each.xsl` (see Listing 11-26). Our goal is to first sort `CD` elements and then `Book` elements, both in ascending order, except this time the sorting via the `<xsl:for-each>` and `<xsl:sort>` instructions is defined in one place—a named template.

The named template definition

```
<xsl:template name="Sorter">
   <xsl:param name="item"     select="'Default CD'" />
   <xsl:param name="itemPath" select="//CD" />
   <!-- other instructions -->
</xsl:template>
```

establishes a template named "Sorter" with two parameters, `item` (a string) and `itemPath` (a node expression). The default value for the `item` parameter is the string "Default CD"; the default `itemPath` is the XPath expression `//CD`.

To assign a single- or multiple-word string such as "CD" or "Default CD" to a parameter (or for that matter, a variable) using the `select` attribute, the string *must* be surrounded by single quotes within double quotes (or vice versa). Otherwise, the processor will think it's an element name or node expression. Alternatively, you can use the nonempty form of `<xsl:param>` or `<xsl:variable>` to assign a string value by means of element content.

To invoke the named template, use the `<xsl:call-template>` instruction with the `name` attribute set to match the name of the desired named template. (You cannot set the `name` attribute to a variable, however.) If you want to pass parameters to the template, such as to override any default `<xsl:param>` definitions within the named template, use the `<xsl:with-param>` instruction within the body of `<xsl:call-template>` as the first instructions. The format of `<xsl:with-param>` is identical to that of the corresponding `<xsl:param>`. The two elements are associated by their required `name` attributes. If no parameters are needed, then simply specify `<xsl:call-template>` as an empty element. For example,

```
<xsl:call-template name="Sorter" >
  <xsl:with-param name="item">Book</xsl:with-param>
  <xsl:with-param name="itemPath" select="//Book" />
</xsl:call-template>
```

This call invokes the "Sorter" named template, passing it the string "Book" to override the default for the `item` parameter and the path `//Book` as the `itemPath` parameter. Although this fragment uses the nonempty form of `<xsl:with-param>` to pass the string "Book" (as opposed to the element `Book`), we could have used the equivalent empty form with the embedded single quotes.

```
<xsl:with-param name="item"     select="'Book'" />
```

Listing 11-35 includes three calls to the named template. The first `<xsl:call-template>` processes the `CD` elements, and the second handles `Book` elements. The third call again processes CDs merely to illustrate what happens when no <xsl:with-param> instructions are given. Notice that in the last case the empty form of <xsl:call-template> is used and that the defaults defined in the named template body are indeed honored. The HTML output resulting from these calls is shown in Figure 11-17.

Listing 11-35 Passing Parameters to Named Templates (c6-param.xsl)

```
<?xml version="1.0"?>
<xsl:stylesheet   version="1.0"
  xmlns:xsl="http://www.w3.org/1999/XSL/Transform">
<xsl:output method="html"/>

<xsl:variable name="label">XSLT: Param, Named Template, Call
Template</xsl:variable>

<!-- Global param -->
<xsl:param name="SortTitle">s in Ascending Order</xsl:param>
<!-- Would also work as a global variable. -->
<xsl:variable name="NotUsed_SortTitle">s in Ascending Order</xsl:variable>

<xsl:template match="/">
   <html>
     <head>
       <title><xsl:value-of select="$label" /></title>
     </head>
     <body>
       <h2><xsl:value-of select="$label" /></h2>
       <!--
           Note single quotes for var "item" so element name 'CD' is
           treated as a string. If not, there is no value-of output.
           In the second call to the Sorter template, we illustrate
           an alternative way of setting the string value for 'Book'.
       -->
       <xsl:call-template name="Sorter" >
         <xsl:with-param name="item"     select="'CD'" />
         <xsl:with-param name="itemPath" select="//CD" />
       </xsl:call-template>

       <xsl:call-template name="Sorter" >
         <xsl:with-param name="item">Book</xsl:with-param>
         <xsl:with-param name="itemPath" select="//Book" />
       </xsl:call-template>

       <!-- Bogus call (no params) to test template defaults. -->
       <xsl:call-template name="Sorter" />

     </body>
   </html>
</xsl:template>

<!--
     This is a named template. Specifying default values for the
     params using the select attribute is optional.
-->
```

```
<xsl:template name="Sorter">
   <xsl:param name="item"     select="'Default CD'" />
   <xsl:param name="itemPath" select="//CD" />

   <h3><xsl:value-of select="$item" />
       <xsl:value-of select="$SortTitle" /></h3>

   <xsl:for-each select="$itemPath" >
     <xsl:sort order="ascending" />
     <br />
     <xsl:value-of select="name()" />
     <xsl:text> </xsl:text><xsl:number /><xsl:text>: </xsl:text>
     <i><xsl:value-of select="Title" /></i>
   </xsl:for-each>

</xsl:template>

</xsl:stylesheet>
```

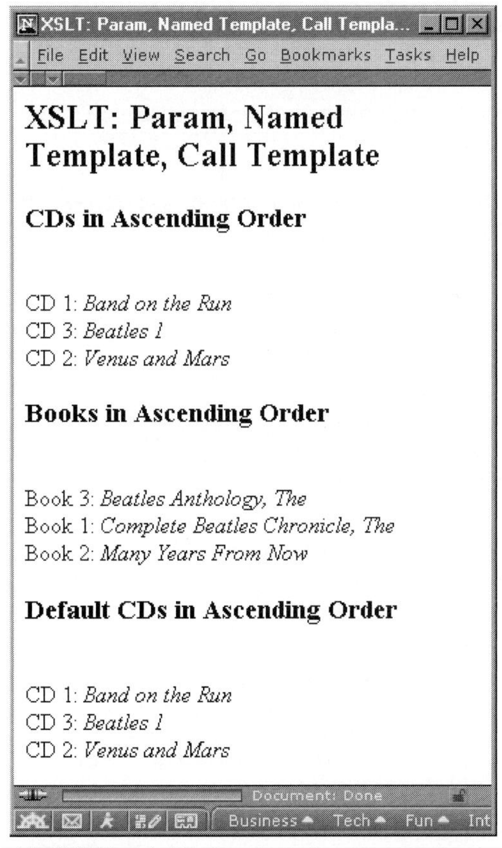

FIGURE 11-17 Display of parameter and named template example (c6-param.html)

Loop Control

If you find yourself limited by the basic looping capabilities of XSLT, consider a recursive solution in which `<xsl:call-template>` calls a named template that contains itself. For example, suppose you need to loop exactly five times (or perhaps until some other condition is met). The stylesheet in Listing 11-36 will do the trick, producing these terribly thrilling results:

```
5
4
3
2
1
```

In this case, the named template called "recursive" defines a parameter called `loopControl` with a default value of 10. To achieve the result of five iterations, however, we invoke the template and override the default:

```
<xsl:call-template name="recursive">
  <xsl:with-param name="loopControl" select="5" />
</xsl:call-template>
```

Listing 11-36 Loop Control via Recursion (c6-loopControl.xsl)

```
<?xml version="1.0"?>
<xsl:stylesheet
  xmlns:xsl="http://www.w3.org/1999/XSL/Transform"
  version="1.0">

<xsl:output method="html"/>

  <xsl:template match="/">
<!-- Take default of 10 iterations.
    <xsl:call-template name="recursive" />
-->
    <xsl:call-template name="recursive">
      <xsl:with-param name="loopControl" select="5" />
    </xsl:call-template>
  </xsl:template>

  <xsl:template name="recursive">
    <!-- Can override loopControl value on initial call to template. -->
    <xsl:param name="loopControl" select="10" />
    <xsl:if test="$loopControl"> <!-- continue if non-zero -->
      <!-- Do something useful here. -->
      <xsl:value-of select="$loopControl" /><br />
      <!-- Recurse but decrement loop control variable first. -->
      <xsl:call-template name="recursive">
        <xsl:with-param name="loopControl" select="$loopControl - 1"/>
      </xsl:call-template>
    </xsl:if>
  </xsl:template>

</xsl:stylesheet>
```

Although not related to the topic of named templates, the `<xsl:with-param>` instruction can also be used to pass parameter values to *matched* templates. For example,

```
<xsl:template match="//Book" >
  <xsl:with-param name="heading" select="'Book Title:'" />
</xsl:template>
```

will pass the string "Book Title:" as the value for the parameter `heading` to *any (unnamed) template* that matches the XPath pattern `//Book`.

Passing Parameters from the Runtime Environment

Fortunately, `<xsl:param>` isn't limited to named templates. It can also be used as a top-level element, in which case its scope is global, visible to the entire stylesheet. This enables stylesheet developers to pass parameter values to the stylesheet from the runtime environment, especially to override default global values. The way each XSLT processor supports this depends on the vendor, but most processors support some kind of command-line parameter passing. For example, Apache Xalan supports a `-PARAM` command-line option, which takes the name of a parameter followed by its value:

```
-PARAM paramName paramValue
```

Saxon uses a different syntax with only the name and value (no option switch):

```
paramName=paramValue
```

Let's add the following `trackNum` and `title` parameters to a file called `c6-param-cmdline.xsl` (see Listing 11-37):

```
<xsl:param name="trackNum" select="2" />
<xsl:param name="title" select="'Even Better Than the Real Thing'" />
```

We'll also create a variation of our batch file called `xalan-PARAM.bat` that adds arguments for these two parameters:

```
set XSLT_CLASS=org.apache.xalan.xslt.Process
java %XSLT_CLASS% -IN %1 -XSL %2 -OUT %3
    -PARAM trackNum '%4' -PARAM title '%5'
```

Suppose we want to override the default `trackNum` value of 2 and set it to 1, and override the `title` default of U2's "Even Better Than the Real Thing" with the value "Beautiful Day". For this example, the source XML is irrelevant, except that one must be provided. We issue the command:

```
C:> xalan-PARAM.bat collection7.xml c6-param-cmdline.xsl
c6-param-cmdline.html 1 "Beautiful Day"
```

which is equivalent to the complete command line:

```
C:> java org.apache.xalan.xslt.Process
-IN collection7.xml -XSL c6-param-cmdline.xsl -OUT c6-param-cmdline.html
-PARAM trackNum '1' -PARAM title '"Beautiful Day"'
```

If you're using Saxon, a comparable command line is

```
C:> java com.icl.saxon.StyleSheet
-o c6-param-cmdline2.html collection7.xml c6-param-cmdline.xsl
trackNum=1 title="Beautiful Day"
```

Regardless of which of these two XSLT processors we use, the result proves that the default values have been overriden by what we passed on the command line:

```
Parameter $trackNum has been set to: '1'
Parameter $title has been set to: 'Beautiful Day'
```

Listing 11-37 Stylesheet with Global Parameters to Override from Command Line (c6-param-cmdline.xsl)

```
<?xml version="1.0"?>
<xsl:stylesheet   version="1.0"
  xmlns:xsl="http://www.w3.org/1999/XSL/Transform">
<xsl:output method="html"/>

<xsl:variable name="label">XSLT: Passing Parameters on the Command
Line</xsl:variable>

<!-- Global parameters -->
<xsl:param name="trackNum" select="2" />
<xsl:param name="title" select="'Even Better Than the Real Thing'" />

<xsl:template match="/">
   <html>
     <head>
       <title><xsl:value-of select="$label" /></title>
     </head>
     <body>
       <h2><xsl:value-of select="$label" /></h2>
       <xsl:text>Parameter $trackNum has been set to: </xsl:text>
       <xsl:value-of select="$trackNum" />
       <br />
       <xsl:text>Parameter $title has been set to: </xsl:text>
       <xsl:value-of select="$title" />
     </body>
   </html>
</xsl:template>

</xsl:stylesheet>
```

Returning a Value from a Named Template

Yet another use of named templates is to achieve functionality similar to that of a function in other programming languages. To accomplish this, we simply wrap the call to the named template within an `<xsl:variable>` instruction, as shown in `c6-param-return.xsl` (Listing 11-38).

Listing 11-38 Named Template Returning a Value (c6-param-return.xsl)

```
<?xml version="1.0"?>
<xsl:stylesheet   version="1.0"
  xmlns:xsl="http://www.w3.org/1999/XSL/Transform">
<xsl:output method="html" indent="yes"/>

<xsl:variable name="label">XSLT: Named Template Returning a
Value</xsl:variable>

<xsl:template match="/">
   <html>
     <head>
       <title><xsl:value-of select="$label" /></title>
     </head>
     <body>
       <h2><xsl:value-of select="$label" /></h2>
       <xsl:apply-templates select="//CD | //Book" />
     </body>
   </html>
</xsl:template>

<xsl:template match="CD | Book">
    <i><xsl:value-of select="Title" /></i>
    <!-- Variable $newPrice receives output of CalcDiscount template. -->
    <xsl:variable name="newPrice">
      <xsl:call-template name="CalcDiscount" >
        <xsl:with-param  name="price"  select="ListPrice" />
      </xsl:call-template>
    </xsl:variable>
    <!-- Check value upon return -->
    <xsl:text> is: $</xsl:text><xsl:value-of select="$newPrice"/>
    <br />
</xsl:template>

<!--
     This named template computes a discount if the passed price meets
     a minimum value. Both the minimum and discount can also be passed in,
     but aren't in the above call.
-->

<xsl:template name="CalcDiscount">
   <xsl:param name="price">0.0</xsl:param>
   <xsl:param name="min">21.99</xsl:param>
   <xsl:param name="percent">0.75</xsl:param>
   <xsl:param name="discountRate">
     <xsl:value-of select="100 * (1.0 - $percent)" />
   </xsl:param>
```

```
    <xsl:choose>
      <xsl:when test="$price &gt;= $min">
        <!-- Apply the discount. -->
        <xsl:value-of select="format-number($price * $percent, '#.00')" />
        <xsl:text> (after </xsl:text>
        <xsl:value-of select="$discountRate" />
        <xsl:text>% discount)</xsl:text>
      </xsl:when>
      <xsl:otherwise>
        <!-- No discount, so return original price. -->
        <xsl:value-of select="$price" />
      </xsl:otherwise>
    </xsl:choose>
  </xsl:template>

</xsl:stylesheet>
```

In this example, the variable $newPrice receives the output of the named template CalcDiscount, which is passed a $price parameter set to the value of the ListPrice element. (The element name to string to number conversions are transparent to us, thankfully.)

```
<xsl:variable name="newPrice">
  <xsl:call-template name="CalcDiscount" >
    <xsl:with-param  name="price"  select="ListPrice" />
  </xsl:call-template>
</xsl:variable>
```

The CalcDiscount named template has four parameters, each with a default value that we can override with the <xsl:with-param> instruction:

```
<xsl:param name="price">0.0</xsl:param>
<xsl:param name="min">21.99</xsl:param>
<xsl:param name="percent">0.75</xsl:param>
<xsl:param name="discountRate">
  <xsl:value-of select="100 * (1.0 - $percent)" />
</xsl:param>
```

Notice that the discountRate parameter is initialized by a computation that will evaluate to either 25 percent if the default for the percent parameter is used, or some other number if percent is overridden in the call.

The named template compares the passed $price to a minimum value. If the price is greater than or equal to the minimum, a discount rate is applied and the new price is output, in this case with an indication that the discount has been applied (don't we always like to know when there is a savings?). The calculation:

```
<xsl:value-of select="format-number($price * $percent, '#.00')" />
```

multiplies the passed $price by the rate (which is expressed as 1.0 minus the discount percentage). Since this may result in more decimal places than we want, the handy `format-number()` XSLT function is used to truncate the result to two decimal places (`'#.00'`).

If the price is below the minimum, only the original price is output. In either case, the `$newPrice` variable in the calling template is set to the output of `CalcDiscount`. So, if we use `collection6.xml` as the input and apply `c6-param-return.xsl`, which specifies a minimum of $21.99 and a rate of 0.75 (a 25% discount), we find that three of the items are discounted:

```
Complete Beatles Chronicle, The is: $18.71 (after 25% discount)
Band on the Run is: $16.97
Venus and Mars is: $16.97
Many Years From Now is: $20.62 (after 25% discount)
Beatles Anthology, The is: $45.00 (after 25% discount)
Beatles 1 is: $18.97
```

Attribute Value Templates

Sometimes you do not know until runtime the value of an attribute because the value is variable. An **attribute value template** is an expression surrounded by curly braces, `{}`, that denotes the variable portion of the value being assigned to an attribute. It may optionally be combined with fixed portions that are not contained within braces. The value of the variable inside the curly braces is substituted, the braces are discarded, the string is combined with the fixed part, if any, and the result becomes the final value of the attribute. For example, if the variable `$imgdir` has the value "/docroot/images" and the variable `$basename` has the value "shuttle", then the attribute value template in the literal result element

```
<img src="{$imgdir}/{$basename}.jpg">
```

evaluates to

```
<img src="/docroot/images/shuttle.jpg">
```

Notice that the dollar sign must appear *inside* the curly braces.

Any literal result element (such as an HTML element) may use attribute value templates, but only certain attributes of particular XSLT elements support them. The only XSLT elements that support attribute value templates to any degree are:

- `<xsl:attribute>`, `name` attribute only
- `<xsl:element>`, `name` attribute only
- `<xsl:number>`, `format`, `lang`, `grouping-separator`, `grouping-size`, and `letter-value` attributes
- `<xsl:processing-instruction>`, `name` attribute only
- `<xsl:sort>`, `order`, `lang`, `data-type`, and `case-order` attributes
- Potentially, extension elements, as per the processor vendor's documentation

Attribute value templates are often useful to determine a value for an attribute that cannot be determined until runtime. Consider a variation on the identity transformation we discussed in Listing 11-21. The version in Listing 11-39 matches only elements and attributes (plus text nodes based on built-in templates), so it effectively strips comments, processing instructions, and namespaces from the source document. Notice the use of curly braces around the `name(.)` function.

Listing 11-39 Identity Variant to Copy Elements, Attributes, and Text (c6-identity2.xsl)

```
<?xml version="1.0"?>
<xsl:stylesheet
    xmlns:xsl="http://www.w3.org/1999/XSL/Transform"
    version="1.0">

<xsl:output method="xml"/>

<xsl:template match="*">
  <xsl:element name="{name(.)}">
    <xsl:for-each select="@*">
      <xsl:attribute name="{name(.)}">
        <xsl:value-of select="."/>
      </xsl:attribute>
    </xsl:for-each>
    <xsl:apply-templates/>
  </xsl:element>
</xsl:template>

</xsl:stylesheet>
```

Another use of curly braces is to surround an XPath expression when extracting the value of an XML element used as an attribute value. For example, in our table creation example, Listing 11-15, if our data contained a pair of hex color values as child elements (named `Color`) of the first `CD` and first `Book` element, we could use braces to extract the color value and assign it to an attribute in a literal result element to generate the row. So, instead of

```
<tr bgcolor="#cccccc" style="font-weight: bold;">
<tr bgcolor="#eeddcc" style="font-weight: bold;">
```

we would write

```
<tr bgcolor="{//Book[1]/Color}" style="font-weight: bold;">
<tr bgcolor="{//CD[1]/Color}" style="font-weight: bold;">
```

We'll see later in this chapter that this abbreviated syntax is effectively identical to the unabbreviated form, so these lines also could be written

```
<tr bgcolor="{/descendant::Book[1]/child::Color}"
    style="font-weight: bold;">
<tr bgcolor="{/descendant::CD[1]/child::Color}"
    style="font-weight: bold;">
```

Regardless of which syntax you choose, this {XPath-expression} notation for assigning values to an attribute is functionally equivalent to using <xsl:value-of select="XPath-expression"/> in other (nonattribute) contexts.

Reuse: Including and Importing

Two instructions, <xsl:include> and <xsl:import>, are provided to facilitate modularization and reuse of stylesheets. Each has a single required attribute, href, which specifies the path to the included or imported stylesheet. Both result in the calling stylesheet having access to the templates defined in the included or imported stylesheet. The major difference between the two instructions is the precedence of the added templates. With <xsl:include>, *the result is a straight text substitution* just like with the #include preprocessor instruction in the C language. The included instructions (everything between the <xsl:stylesheet> begin and end tag of the included stylesheet) are inserted exactly as if they had been directly typed within the calling (including) stylesheet. Therefore, the included templates have exactly the same precedence as any other templates in the original stylesheet.

In the case of <xsl:import>, however, the *imported templates have a lower precedence* than any with the same match pattern in the calling (importing) stylesheet. This allows the caller to benefit from any imported templates that handle cases not specified in the calling stylesheet but, at the same time, to override any imports simply by defining a template in the calling stylesheet that matches the same pattern. The <xsl:import> instruction is a top-level element so it must appear as a child of <xsl:stylesheet> and it *must appear before all other top-level elements*, in contrast to <xsl:include>, also a top-level element, which can occur either before or after other top-level elements.

Listing 11-40 shows a simple example, try-import-string.xsl, which uses <xsl:import> to benefit from a template defined in another stylesheet called string.xsl, which is part of XSLTSL, the XSLT Standard Library from SourceForge (by Steve Ball et al, *http://sourceforge.net/projects/xsltsl/*). The top-level <xsl:import> instruction references a local copy of string.xsl and declares the "str:" namespace prefix[9] within the <xsl:stylesheet> instruction. This namespace is used when invoking two named templates, <str:capitalise> and <str:subst>. For both examples, a global parameter is initialized as follows:

```
<xsl:param name="strToConvert">BEATles anthOLogy</xsl:param>
```

9. Of course, if you are just sharing templates within your own project, rather than interfacing to an external library with its own namespaces as I've done here, you might not need a namespace.

The first external (imported) template, <str:capitalise> not shown here, expects a single parameter called text, representing the string that is to be capitalized. I've invoked the template by passing the previously initialized parameter $strToConvert:

```
<xsl:call-template name="str:capitalise">
  <xsl:with-param name="text" select="$strToConvert"/>
```

The call to the second named template, <str:subst>, requires three parameters: text, the original string, replace, the sequence of characters to replace, and with, the characters to be substituted. Note that the strings may be of different length.

```
<xsl:call-template name="str:subst">
  <xsl:with-param name="text" select="$strToConvert" />
  <xsl:with-param name="replace">BEATles</xsl:with-param>
  <xsl:with-param name="with">Fab Four</xsl:with-param>
```

We might be tempted to set the replace parameter with the select attribute, like so:

```
  <xsl:with-param name="replace" select="BEATles"/>
```

However, this will silently fail because select assumes we're referencing a *node* named "BEATles", rather than a *string*. As mentioned earlier in this chapter, in order to force the string interpetation, you have to add an inner pair of single quotes.

```
  <xsl:with-param name="replace" select="'BEATles'"/>
```

Given the initial input of "BEATles anthOLogy" as $strToConvert, the output from try-import-string.xsl is simply these two lines:

```
Beatles Anthology
Fab Four anthOLogy
```

As expected, in the first case, the book title has been capitalized, regardless of the initial mixed capitalization. In the second, the first part of the unaltered title is replaced with the string "Fab Four" and the other part remains unchanged.

Listing 11-40 Calling an Imported Template (try-import-string.xsl)

```
<?xml version="1.0"?>
<xsl:stylesheet version="1.0"
     xmlns:xsl="http://www.w3.org/1999/XSL/Transform"
     xmlns:str="http://xsltsl.org/string"
     extension-element-prefixes="str">
<!--
     Imported stylesheet from the XSLT Standard Library,
     http://sourceforge.net/projects/xsltsl/
```

```
     This example will fail if the imported stylesheet
     hasn't been downloaded into the same directory as
     the current stylesheet; otherwise, adjust 'href' below.
-->
<xsl:import href="string.xsl" />

<xsl:output method="text" />

<xsl:param name="strToConvert">BEATles anthOLogy</xsl:param>

  <xsl:template match="/">
    <xsl:call-template name="str:capitalise">
      <xsl:with-param name="text" select="$strToConvert"/>
    </xsl:call-template>

    <xsl:text>&#xd;&#xa;</xsl:text> <!-- Newline in DOS -->

    <xsl:call-template name="str:subst">
      <xsl:with-param name="text" select="$strToConvert" />
      <xsl:with-param name="replace">BEATles</xsl:with-param>
      <xsl:with-param name="with">Fab Four</xsl:with-param>
    </xsl:call-template>

  </xsl:template>
</xsl:stylesheet>
```

I glossed over the <xsl:stylesheet> instruction that uses something we've seen only briefly—the declaration of another namespace whose prefix, `str` in this case, is declared using the `extension-element-prefixes` attribute.

```
     xmlns:str="http://xsltsl.sourceforge.net/string"
     extension-element-prefixes="str">
```

This informs the processor that we've extended the XSLT instruction set. The <xsl:import> statement results in the actual definition of the various extension elements, such as <str:capitalise> and <str:subst>. We'll see this extension mechanism in the context of extension elements and extension functions later in this chapter.

Khun Yee Fung discusses the topic of modularization extensively in his recommended XSLT book, *XSLT: Working with XML and HTML* by Addison-Wesley. See also Bob DuCharme's article, "Combining Stylesheets with Include and Import," at *http://www.xml.com/pub/a/2000/11/01/xslt/index.html.*

XPath Concepts and Examples

It's time to shift our focus from XSLT to XPath. In this section, we'll cover details related to XPath, which we've been using throughout this chapter in every XSLT example. Now we'll formalize and expand some of the concepts that so far we've learned mostly by example.

The XPath Model

As we've seen, XPath is used primarily to select or locate individual nodes or sets of nodes in the source tree, and secondarily to perform string manipulations, numerical calculations, and boolean tests. Although XPath is a separate and full-fledged W3C Recommendation, it is intended to be used as a component of other specifications, such as XSLT, XLink, XPointer, XML Schema, and XML Query Language.

XPath operates on an XML document as a conceptual tree consisting of seven node types: root, element, attribute, text, namespace, processing instruction, and comment, described in detail in Table 11-8, "XPath Node Types" later in the chapter. We've learned about **document order** but we haven't explained that this ordering relates to the appearance of the *first character* of the (possibly expanded) XML representation of the node. The root node is always first in document order. Order of elements is determined by the location of their *start tags* within the document. Attribute nodes and namespace nodes of an element are considered to occur *before* the children of that element. Namespace nodes are defined to occur before attribute nodes in document ordering. However, as previously emphasized, the order of the set of attributes or namespaces for a given element is *undefined* by the specification and is therefore implementation dependent; it's best to think of attributes and namespaces as unordered. Sometimes, it's useful to traverse the document tree in **reverse document order**, for example, to first visit the context node, then its immediate parent, then its grandparent, and so on up to the root.

In chapter 3, we learned the terms *parent*, *child*, *ancestor*, and *descendant* in the context of XML. Some points are worth repeating:

- An element is a *child* of exactly one *parent*, which is the element that contains it.
- A parent may have more than one child.
- Immediate children and also children of a child are called *descendants* of the parent. (The *descendants* of a node are the children of the node plus all of the descendants of the children of the node, and so on.)
- An element is an *ancestor* of all its descendants.
- The root is the ancestor of all elements.
- Every element is a descendant of the root.
- Every element has exactly one parent except the root, which has no parent.
- Parent nodes can only be element nodes or the root node.
- The root node and element nodes have an ordered list of child nodes, in document order. (The list is empty if the node has no children.)
- An element can have element, text, processing instruction, or comment nodes as children.

Consider the following XML fragment:

```
<Something>
  <OneThing>leads to</OneThing>
  <Another /> <!-- empty element -->
  <?myJavaApp width="73" height="120" ?>
</Something>
```

The Something element has four children: the elements OneThing and Another, the comment, and a processing instruction. Each of these children has one parent, namely, the Something element. The OneThing element has only one child, which is a text node with the content "leads to". The Another element is empty, so by definition, it has no children. Comments and PIs are always childless as well.

The pathlike syntax specifies which nodes are of interest at any point in time and therefore helps control the processing. For example, consider the two simple templates

```
<xsl:template match="/Collection" >
  <xsl:apply-templates />
</xsl:template>
```

and

```
<xsl:template match="CD[3]" >
  <xsl:value-of select="Title" />
  <xsl:apply-templates />
</xsl:template>
```

In the first template, the path is relative to the root node ("/") and specifies the element Collection, which must be the document element since that's the only element that can be the immediate child element of the root (although nonelement nodes such as processing instructions and comments can also appear immediately under the root node).

In the second template, the path CD[3] is a relative path since it does not begin with a slash. Assuming the second template is in the same stylesheet as the first and that these are the only two templates, the implied fullpath to this element is /Collection/CD[3]. In this case, the title of this element will always be displayed before CD[3] is otherwise processed by the <xsl:apply-templates> instruction to handle its children. This may or may not be true also for other elements since they aren't shown in this fragment.

We've already seen far more complicated uses of XPath expressions in earlier examples. The XPath language is characterized by the following aspects, discussed in the remainder of this section:

- Location paths and steps
- Abbreviated vs. unabbreviated syntax
- Axes (13 different ones)

- Node types (7 types)
- Node tests (7, one for each node type)
- Datatypes (4 or 5 types)
- Predicates
- Expressions
- Operators
- Functions (at least 27)

Location Paths and Steps

Location paths and location steps are fundamental concepts of the XPath language. A **location path** is a string that is not actually XML syntax; it more closely resembles a UNIX-like filename path. Each location path consists of one or more **location steps**, each of which contains an *axis*, a *node test*, and zero or more *predicates*. From the XSLT perspective, the purpose of a location path is to express which nodes are being matched or selected by the XSLT instruction that references the path.

As a location path is evaluated, each location step causes a temporary change in the current node list. Every node test and every predicate changes the list. Since evaluation proceeds from left to right, the rightmost result determines the final evaluation. (Some XSLT processors optimize the interpretation of an entire location path by considering the rightmost nodes first.)

The general syntax of a single location step follows; the double colon and square brackets are literal.

```
axis::node-test[predicate]*
```

The **axis** specifies the tree relationship between the nodes selected by the location step and the context node. It is often the least constraining part of the location step because it could select a large number of nodes. (The thirteen XPath axes are described in Table 11-6.) The **node test** specifies the node type or the expanded name of the nodes selected by the location step. (Node concepts are covered in "Node Types, Node Values, and Node Tests.") The **predicate** is an arbitrary XPath expression that further refines the set of nodes selected by the location step. Notice that the axis name and node test are separated by a double colon, followed by zero or more predicates, each within square brackets. For example, this is a single location step

```
child::CD[last()]
```

which tells the processor to select the last `CD` child of whatever element is the context node at the moment (which in our running example is the `Collection` element). In this example, the axis is the so-called `child` axis, which selects all of the immediate children of the context node (e.g., 3 `CD` elements, 3 `Book` elements, the

Owner element, and the bogus-pi processing instruction, if Collection is the context and collection6.xml is the instance). The node test "CD" selects all of the children with the element name CD (decreasing the children from 8 to 3), and the predicate consists of an XPath function, last(), which returns the ordinal number of the last node of the node-set, that is, the size of (or, number of nodes in) the current node list. The entire location step evaluates to the third CD element.

As we'll see in more detail shortly, this location step can also be expressed in **abbreviated syntax** as simply

```
CD[last()]
```

which tells the processor exactly the same thing because the child:: axis portion is the *default axis*, so it can be omitted without ambiguity. In abbreviated syntax, the axis and the node test are combined. All possible abbreviations are shown in Table 11-7 on page 696.

An example with multiple predicates is

```
Item[@type="produce"][4]
```

which selects the fourth Item element that has a type attribute ("@") with the value "produce".

When a location path contains multiple steps, each step is separated by a slash ("/") as in a UNIX pathname, so the general location path syntax is really:

```
axis::node-test[predicate]*/axis::node-test[predicate]*/...
```

Evaluation of location path is step by step, left to right. Each step potentially alters the node-set in some manner; it typically narrows the set of nodes that the complete path selects. The node list resulting from one step becomes the current node list for the next step to the right, with each step potentially eliminating nodes from the previous step, or increasing/decreasing the number of nodes in the list. The overall result of an XPath expression is the result of the evaluation of the last location step.

Several examples of multiple-step location paths follow. The two-step location path shown next selects the first Label child of the second CD element (which must be a child of the context node)

```
CD[2]/Label[1]
```

Next is a *four*-step location path that selects the Last name of the fourth Author of the third Book. Based on collection6.xml, the value of the selected node is "Lennon".

```
Book[3]/Author[4]/Name/Last
```

Next is a *two*-step location path; the second step contains two predicates, the second of which also contains a location path, `Name/Last`. The expression selects the fourth `Author` of the third `Book`, but only if the `Last` name is "Lennon". However, if we use `<xsl:value-of select="." />` in the template matching this expression, the value of the selected node is "John Lennon", not just "Lennon". Why? Because the first two steps, `Book[3]/Author[4]`, select a specific `Author` node, the value of which is the concatenation of the text of all its children (`Name`, `Last`, and `First`), which is "John Lennon". The predicate `[Name/Last = 'Lennon']` is a boolean test. If the `Last` child of the `Name` element has the value "Lennon", the test is true and the `Author[4]` node is selected. If the test evaluates to false, this `Author[4]` node will not be selected. In the case of the running example, it is selected.

```
Book[3]/Author[4][Name/Last = 'Lennon']
```

The two-step example that follows uses the unabbreviated `descendant` axis. It selects those `Peak` children that *have* a `country` attribute, *regardless of the attribute value*. `Peak` must be a child, grandchild, great grandchild, and so on, of the context node, assumed to be `CD` here, but `Chart` would also apply since the hierarchy is `CD/Chart/Peak`.

```
descendant::Peak[@country]
```

Notice that the square-bracketed notation means something entirely different from `"/@"` below, which refers to the *value* of the `country` attribute of a `Peak` element that is a descendant of the context node:

```
descendant::Peak/@country
```

However, neither of these expressions can be used for a `match` attribute of `<xsl:template>` because *only child and attribute axes* are allowed for a `match` value. They can be used, however, for a `select` attribute, as the following template illustrates.

```
<xsl:template match="CD[2] | CD[3]" >
   <br /><i><xsl:value-of select="Title" /></i>
   <xsl:text>,  Peak/@country: </xsl:text>
   <i><xsl:value-of select="descendant::Peak/@country" /></i>
   <xsl:text>,  Peak[@country]: </xsl:text>
   <i><xsl:value-of select="descendant::Peak[@country]" /></i>
</xsl:template>
```

Given `collection6.xml` as input, the template result is:

```
Venus and Mars, Peak/@country: UK, Peak[@country]: 2
Beatles 1, Peak/@country: US, Peak[@country]: 1
```

Next, we have a location path consisting of two location steps, the second of which has two predicates.

```
Book[position()=last()]/Author[4][@age='40']
```

This expression tells the processor to select the last `Book` element's fourth `Author` child, but only those instances where the attribute named `age` has the value "40". In our running example, the `Author` element has no `age` attribute at all, so this expression will select the null set (nothing), but it does not generate an error.

Location paths come in two flavors, **relative location paths**, which are with respect to the context node, and **absolute location paths**, which begin with a / and are therefore with respect to the root node, not the context node. For example,

```
CD[2]/Label[1]
/Collection/CD[2]/Label[1]
```

represent a relative location path and an absolute location path, respectively. If the context node is the `/Collection` element, the two yield the same node. However, if `/Collection/Book[1]` is the context node, the relative path yields *no* nodes (since `CD` cannot be a child of `Book`), but the absolute path still yields exactly what it did when `/Collection` was the context node because absolute paths ignore the context node.

Many more examples of location paths can be found in Table 11-11, "Examples of XPath Expressions and XSLT Patterns" (pages 719–722). In the next several sections, we'll cover axes, node tests, node types, node values, data types, XPath expressions, and XSLT patterns in considerably greater detail. However, first it's time for another code example.

The stylesheet shown in Listing 11-41 `c6-xpath.xsl` (pages 689–692), illustrates a number of location paths, XPath expressions with and without predicates, single- and multiple-step paths, and so on. This example also introduces the XSLT concept of **modes**, which permits *processing the same patterns with different templates.* The root template includes different `<xsl:apply-templates>` instructions, first for the default (unnamed) mode and then for the mode named `"pass2"`. The XPath expressions are identical, although the order of processing the `CD` vs. `Book` elements is switched between the two modes.

```
<xsl:apply-templates select="//CD" />
<xsl:apply-templates select="//Book" />
<xsl:apply-templates select="//Owner" />
```

versus

```
<xsl:apply-templates select="//Book"    mode="pass2" />
<xsl:apply-templates select="//CD"      mode="pass2" />
<xsl:apply-templates select="//Owner"   mode="pass2" />
```

The first three calls with no mode attribute match the following templates with the indicated results:

- match="Book[position() = 1]" matches the first Book element = Book[1]
- match="Book[position() = last()]" matches the last Book element = Book[3]
- match="Book[2]" matches the second Book element
- match="CD[position() > 2]" matches any CD element with an index greater than[10] CD[2], which in this example is only CD[3]
- match="CD[not(Title/text() = 'Beatles 1')]" matches any CD element whose Title is not "Beatles 1", which in this example matches two CDs, CD[1] and CD[2].

Since each of these templates contains a <xsl:value-of select="Title"/> instruction, the title(s) of the matched books or CDs are sent to the result tree.

The template for the Owner element uses several multistep location paths to extract the different pieces, all relative to the Owner element, such as the owner's first name with a two-step path:

```
<xsl:value-of select="Name/First" />
```

and his street, using a different two-step path involving Address and Street (context node is still Owner):

```
<xsl:value-of select="Address/Street" />
```

The result of applying all of these templates is shown in Figure 11-18 on page 693.

The second triplet of <xsl:apply-templates> instructions specifies mode="pass2", so a template matches only if it also contains that mode attribute *in addition to* the usual match criteria. Consider this two-step location path with a predicate (within square brackets):

```
match="Book/Published[@publisher = 'Harmony Books']"
```

This will match Book elements with Published children that have a publisher attribute with the value "Harmony Books". In order to access the Title when the context node is the Published element, we need to "go up" to the Book parent node (..) and then "down" to the Title child, which is a sibling of the Published node; this is a relative path:

```
select="../Title"
```

10. You may recall that the entities > and < are needed in place of the traditional < and > when they are used as values of attributes so that they are not interpreted as markup.

The second template with mode="pass2" has a single-step path with a predicate that checks for books published in 1993 or later.

```
match="Book[Published &gt;= 1993]"
```

In this case, since the context node is Book, we can extract the title, publication year, and name of the publisher by three simple paths, the third of which references the publisher attribute of the Published element (its parent).

```
select="./Title"
select="./Published"
select="./Published/@publisher"
```

Actually, the "./" portion of these paths is superfluous but it emphasizes that Title and Published are immediate children of the Book context node.

In the third template, we're looking for CDs whose title is not "Beatles 1", which gives us two matches.

```
match="CD/Title[. != 'Beatles 1']"
```

The fourth template looks for Chart elements anywhere in the document ("//"), if they have Peak element children whose weeks attribute has the value 5 or more.

```
match="//Chart/Peak[@weeks &gt;= 5]"
```

Since the above expression selects Peak nodes, the context node within this template is Peak, so to reference the Title element, we have to go up *two* levels to the grandparent and down to the Title using this three-step location path:

```
select="../../Title"
```

If you're wondering why there is no output from pass2 that references the Owner item, it's because I've trapped it with an empty template for generic text nodes that have no specific match defined:

```
<xsl:template match="text()"    mode="pass2" >
</xsl:template>
```

Listing 11-41 XPath Expressions, Location Steps, and Modes (c6-xpath.xsl)

```
<?xml version="1.0"?>
<xsl:stylesheet   version="1.0"
  xmlns:xsl="http://www.w3.org/1999/XSL/Transform">
<xsl:output method="html"/>
```

```
<xsl:variable name="label">XSLT: XPath Expressions and Predicates (also
Modes)</xsl:variable>

<xsl:template match="/">
   <html>
     <head>
       <title><xsl:value-of select="$label" /></title>
     </head>
     <body>
       <h2><xsl:value-of select="$label" /></h2>
       <!--
            Here we are processing all nodes in the default mode,
            and then again in "pass2" mode, but in a different order.
            Consider why there is no output for Owner in pass2.
       -->
       <h2 align="center">Pass 1</h2>
       <xsl:apply-templates select="//CD" />
       <xsl:apply-templates select="//Book" />
       <xsl:apply-templates select="//Owner" />

       <h2 align="center">Pass 2</h2>
       <xsl:apply-templates select="//Book"    mode="pass2" />
       <xsl:apply-templates select="//CD"      mode="pass2" />
       <xsl:apply-templates select="//Owner"   mode="pass2" />
     </body>
   </html>
</xsl:template>
                        <!-- pass1 -->

<xsl:template match="Book[position() = 1]">
   <br /><xsl:text>First Book: </xsl:text>
   <i><xsl:value-of select="Title" /></i>
</xsl:template>

<xsl:template match="Book[position() = last()]">
   <br /><xsl:text>Last Book: </xsl:text>
   <i><xsl:value-of select="Title" /></i>
</xsl:template>

<xsl:template match="Book[2]">
   <br /><xsl:text>Second Book: </xsl:text>
   <i><xsl:value-of select="Title" /></i>
</xsl:template>

<xsl:template match="CD[position() &gt; 2]">
   <br /><xsl:text>CD is greater than 2: </xsl:text>
   <i><xsl:value-of select="Title" /></i>
</xsl:template>

<xsl:template match="CD[not(Title/text() = 'Beatles 1')]">
   <br /><xsl:text>CD title is not "Beatles 1": </xsl:text>
   <i><xsl:value-of select="Title" /></i>
</xsl:template>
```

```
<xsl:template match="Owner">
   <p align="center">
     <xsl:value-of select="Name/First" />
     <xsl:text> </xsl:text>
     <xsl:value-of select="Name/Last" />
     <xsl:text>'s Collection; </xsl:text>
     <xsl:value-of select="Address/Street" />
     <xsl:text>; </xsl:text>
     <xsl:value-of select="Address/City" />
     <xsl:text>, </xsl:text>
     <xsl:value-of select="Address/State" />
     <xsl:text> </xsl:text>
     <xsl:value-of select="Address/Zip" />
   </p>
</xsl:template>
                        <!-- pass2 -->

<!-- COMMENT OUT FROM HERE....
-->

<xsl:template match="Book/Published[@publisher = 'Harmony Books']"
              mode="pass2" >
   <br /><xsl:text>Harmony Books is publisher of book with title:</xsl:text>
   <i><xsl:value-of select="../Title" /></i>
   <xsl:text> ++ date: </xsl:text>
   <i><xsl:value-of select="." /></i>
</xsl:template>

<xsl:template match="Book[Published &gt;= 1993]"    mode="pass2" >
   <br /><xsl:text>Book published >= 1993: </xsl:text>
   <i><xsl:value-of select="./Title" /></i>
   <xsl:text> ++ date: </xsl:text>
   <i><xsl:value-of select="./Published" /></i>
   <xsl:text> ++ publisher: </xsl:text>
   <i><xsl:value-of select="./Published/@publisher" /></i>
</xsl:template>

<xsl:template match="CD/Title[. != 'Beatles 1']"   mode="pass2" >
   <br /><xsl:text>CD title is not "Beatles 1": </xsl:text>
   <i><xsl:value-of select="." /></i>
</xsl:template>

<xsl:template match="//Chart/Peak[@weeks &gt;= 5]"   mode="pass2" >
   <br /><xsl:text>CD with Peek weeks >= 5: </xsl:text>
   <i><xsl:value-of select="../../Title" /></i>
</xsl:template>

<!-- ....TO HERE
-->

<xsl:template match="text()"    mode="pass2" >
</xsl:template>
```

```
<!--  BEGIN COMMENT

      The next few templates work, but are mutually exclusive with the
      pass 2 templates above.

<xsl:template match="Book[3]/Author[4]/Name/Last"
              mode="pass2" >
   <br /><xsl:text> Book 3: </xsl:text>
   <i><xsl:value-of select="." /></i>
</xsl:template>

<xsl:template match="Book[3]/Author[4][Name/Last = 'Lennon']"
              mode="pass2" >
   <br /><xsl:text> Book 3: </xsl:text>
   <i><xsl:value-of select="." /></i>
</xsl:template>

<xsl:template match="Book[3]/Author[2][Name/Last = 'Harrison']"
              mode="pass2" >
   <br /><xsl:text> Book 3: </xsl:text>
   <i><xsl:value-of select="." /></i>
</xsl:template>

<xsl:template match="CD[2] | CD[3]"
              mode="pass2" >
   <br /><i><xsl:value-of select="Title" /></i>
   <xsl:text>,  Peak/@country: </xsl:text>
   <i><xsl:value-of select="descendant::Peak/@country" /></i>
   <xsl:text>,  Peak[@country]: </xsl:text>
   <i><xsl:value-of select="descendant::Peak[@country]" /></i>
</xsl:template>

<xsl:template match="Book[position()=last()]/Author[4][@age='40']"
              mode="pass2" >
   <br /><xsl:text> Got Age, Book 3: </xsl:text>
   <i><xsl:value-of select="." /></i>
</xsl:template>

END COMMENT -->

</xsl:stylesheet>
```

Notice that a number of alternative templates for Pass 2 are commented out. If you uncomment them *and* comment out the early Pass 2 templates, you'll see very different results, or you can just try the alternative version, `c6-xpath-pass2.xsl`. As a challenge, revise the stylesheet so that the commented-out templates become another pass, Pass 3, and arrange for all three passes to display results (so no templates are commented out and all are executed).

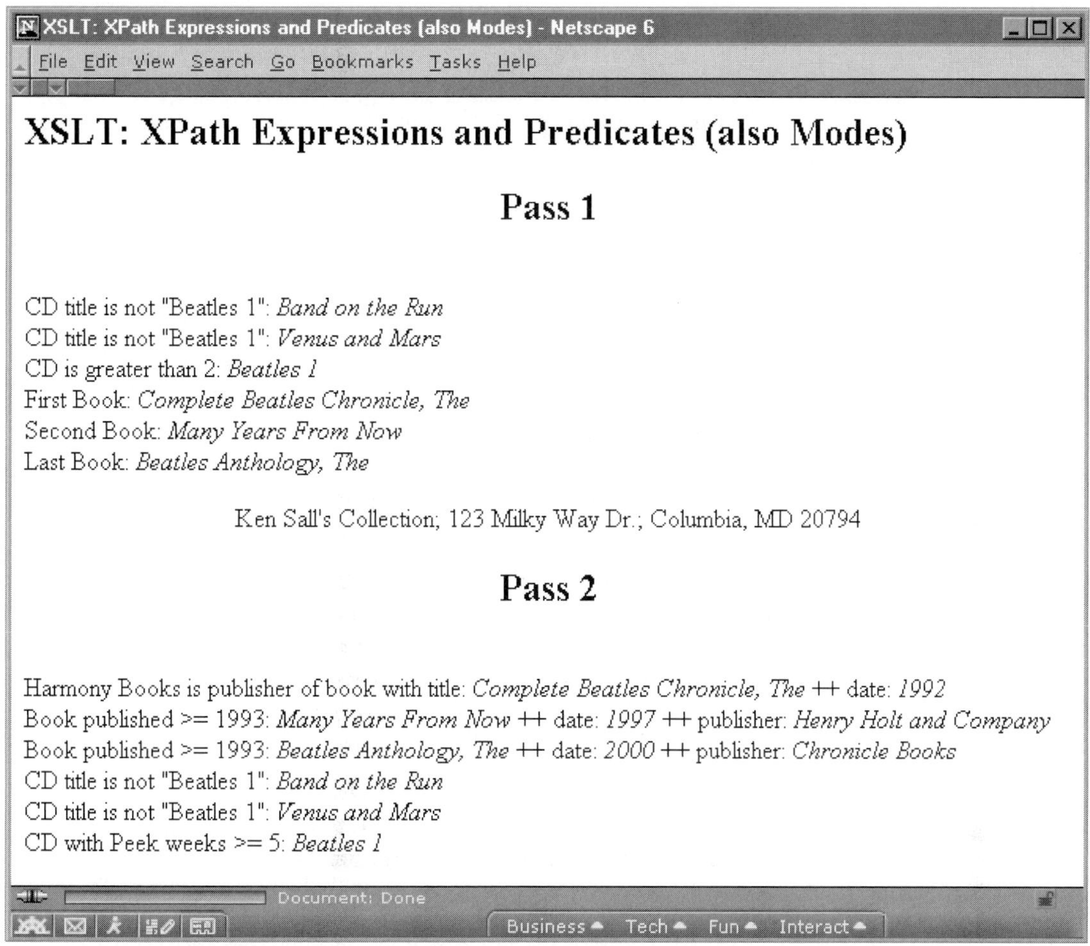

FIGURE 11-18 Display of XPath expression results with two modes

XPath Axes

The XPath specification defines thirteen *axes,* described in Table 11-6, each of which selects a potentially large set of nodes, called a *node list*, relative to the location of the context node[11] in the document tree. Five of these axes partition a document into disjoint (nonoverlapping) subsets: `ancestor`, `descendant`, `following`, `preceding`, and `self`. Together these five axes contain all the nodes in the document

11. Remember that the **context node** refers to the source tree node currently being processed because it is one of the nodes (or perhaps the only node) matched by the `match` attribute of `<xsl:template>`, or selected by the `select` attribute of `<xsl:for-each>` or `<xsl:apply-templates>`.

TABLE 11-6 The 13 Axes Defined by XPath

Axis	*Description*
`child`	Selects the immediate children of the context node, which must be an element or the root (since only they have children), in document order. This does *not* include attribute or namespace nodes since they are not considered to be children of an element. (For any node type other than elements or the root, the `child` axis is empty.) The `child` axis is the *default axis* so it can be omitted in an abbreviation location path. For example, the unabbreviated location path `child::Book/child::Title` can be abbreviated as simply `Book/Title`. Both mean the `Title` child of the `Book` child of the context node.
`descendant`	Selects the children, grandchildren, great grandchildren, and so on of the context node, in document order, again excluding attribute and namespace nodes. Effectively, this selects all element, text, processing instruction, and comment children between the context node's start and end tags. *Limitation:* Cannot be abbreviated, but see `descendant-or-self`, which can.
`descendant-or-self`	Selects the descendants (as per the `descendant` axis description) or the context node itself. The abbreviation "`//`" represents this axis. For example, `/Collection/CD//*` means all descendants of the `CD` element including itself.
`parent`	Selects the root node or element that is the immediate ancestor of the context node, that is, the node that contains the context node. The abbreviation "`..`" represents the parent axis. The root node has no parent, but all other node types have a parent, even attributes (whose parent is the element whose start tag contains them). The parent of comment and processing instruction nodes is the element (or root) that contains them. *Limitation:* Cannot be used as the value of an XSLT `match` attribute.
`ancestor`	Selects the parent of the context node, the grandparent, the great grandparent, and so on, always including the root node (which itself has no ancestors). For this axis, nodes are in *reverse document order*, with the first node being the immediate parent and the last being the root node. For example, `ancestor::*[1]` refers to the first ancestor (i.e., the parent = ".."), `ancestor::*[2]` refers to the second ancestor (i.e., the grandparent), etc. *Limitation:* Cannot be abbreviated.
`ancestor-or-self`	Selects all nodes of the `ancestor` axis as well as the context node itself. Therefore, in reverse document order, the first node in this axis is always the context node and the last is always the root. *Limitation:* Cannot be abbreviated.
`following`	Selects all nodes at any depth that follow the context node in document order, *excluding any descendants* and excluding attribute nodes and namespace nodes. In other words, this axis selects the nodes whose *start tag appears after the end tag* of the context node. Such nodes may or may not be siblings of the context node. Potentially expensive operation. *Limitation:* Cannot be abbreviated.

TABLE 11-6 *(continued)*

Axis	*Description*
`following-sibling`	*Sibling* refers to nodes that have the *same parent* as the context node, so this axis selects nodes that come after the context node in document order and have the same parent. This is a subset of the `following` axis. (If the context node is an attribute or namespace, this axis is empty since such node types have no siblings.) *Limitation:* Cannot be abbreviated.
`preceding`	Selects all nodes at any depth that precede the context node in *reverse document order, excluding any ancestors* and excluding attribute nodes and namespace nodes. In other words, this axis selects the nodes whose *end tag appears before the start tag of the context node.* Such nodes may or may not be siblings of the context node. Potentially expensive operation. *Limitation:* Cannot be abbreviated.
`preceding-sibling`	Selects nodes that come before the context node and have the same parent in reverse document order. This is a subset of the `preceding` axis. (If the context node is an attribute or namespace, this axis is empty since these node types have no siblings.) *Limitation:* Cannot be abbreviated.
`attribute`	Selects all of the attributes, if any, of the context node if that node is an element; selects the null set for any other node type. (This excludes any `xmlns` attributes associated with namespaces.) The abbreviation "`@`" represents the attribute axis. *Limitation:* The order of attributes is not defined and may or may not be in document order. If you need to process the attributes in a particular order, your stylesheet must be explicit about the ordering by referencing attributes by name.
`namespace`	Selects all namespaces that are presently in scope for the context node, including those that are explicitly declared for the element using `xmlns` plus namespaces declared for ancestors (provided they aren't hidden by later namespace declarations). If the context node is anything other than an element, this axis is empty. *Limitation:* As with attributes, the order of the namespace nodes along this axis is undefined.
`self`	Selects the single node that is the context node. The abbreviation "`.`" represents the self axis.

(except for `attribute` and `namespace` nodes). However, the full set of thirteen axes do form overlapping sets. For example, the `ancestor-or-self` axis is the union of all nodes selected by the `ancestor` axis and the `self` axis, the nodes in the set selected by the `following-sibling` axis is a subset of the nodes selected by the `following` axis, and so on.

One confusing aspect of XPath axis terminology is that names like `ancestor` and `descendant` sound like they refer to a single node when in fact they refer to *all* of the ancestors and descendants of the context node. In fact, of the thirteen axes, only `self` and `parent` truly refer to a single node. Therefore, an axis always refers to a set of nodes (which usually has more than one member). The node test and optional predicate portions of a location step select a *subset* of the nodes that the axis has preselected.

Another possible source of confusion is the asymmetry of the parent/child relationship of elements and attributes. Remember that *attributes have a parent which is always an element.* The parent is that element whose start tag includes the attribute's name and value. However, *attributes are not considered to be children* of the element that is their parent. Attributes apparently (no pun intended) want to acknowledge their parentage, but elements have too many other children to worry about, so they don't want to be responsible for attributes too.

With regard to document order, the majority of the axes are called *forward axes* because their nodes are visited in (forward) document order. For example, when `CD[2]` is the context node and we request the `descendant` axis via the instruction

```
<xsl:for-each select="descendant::*" >
```

the order of the nodes is `Title`, `Artist`, `Chart`, `Peak`, `Peak`, `Type`, `Label`, `Label`, `AlbumReleased`, `Remastered`, and finally `ListPrice`, as we'll see in Figure 11-19 on page 698.

However, four of the axes—`ancestor`, `ancestor-or-self`, `preceding`, and `preceding-sibling`—are called *reverse axes* because they select nodes that occur *before* the context node, so these axes return nodes in *reverse document order.* For example, if the context node is the `Peak` element and we select using the `ancestor` axis, the nodes visited in reverse order are `Chart`, `CD[2]`, and `Collection`. When parentheses are used for grouping, however, forward document order is always the result, regardless of the axes involved.

As can be inferred from Table 11-6, most of the XPath axes cannot be abbreviated. In fact, the only axes that *can* be abbreviated are shown in Table 11-7.

Listing 11-42 (pages 702–705) shows a stylesheet, `c6-axes.xsl`, which selects all thirteen axes with `CD[2]`, the second `CD` element in `collection6.xml`, as the context node. The HTML results are shown in Figures 11-19 (see page 698) and 11-20 (see pages 700–701). There is a considerable amount of repetition in this stylesheet.

TABLE 11-7 Abbreviations for Axes

Unabbreviated Form	*Abbreviation*
`child::`	(abbreviated as the null string; this is the default axis)
`descendant-or-self::node()`	`//`
`parent::node()`	`..`
`attribute::`	`@`
`self::node()`	`.`

Interested readers might try to reduce the length by writing a named template or two that could be passed the axis plus any needed details.

Readers interested only in the formal presentation of XPath concepts may skip this example and continue reading with "Node Types, Node Values, and Node Tests."

CD[2] is the one with the title "Venus and Mars". As you can see from Figure 11-19, the context node's only ancestor is the Collection element itself, whereas the ancestor-or-self axis also selects the context node. Since the CD element itself does not have attributes, to test the attribute axis, we can examine the attributes of all *descendants* of the context node using the instruction

```
<xsl:for-each select="//CD[2]/descendant::node()/@*" >
```

This could have been written even more cryptically as

```
<xsl:for-each select=".//@*" >
```

In either case, this says to the XSLT processor, "For all the descendants of the context node, CD[2], iterate over any attributes you find." Since each attribute has a parent, we can determine the name of the element associated with a given attribute by the instruction

```
<xsl:value-of select="name(parent::node())" />
```

which could be abbreviated (for those who like to conserve electrons) as

```
<xsl:value-of select="name(..)" />
```

In this instance, element Peak has two optional attributes and Label and Remastered each have one.

When we select the child axis, we find that the context node has nine immediate children, from Title through ListPrice. Notice that Peak is not included (nor are attributes considered children of the parent element that contains them) because it is a child of Chart, not of CD. The nine children are numbered 1 to 9 in document order as the result of the instruction

```
<xsl:number count="*" />
```

Compare the descendant axis to that of the child axis. The only difference is that the two Peak children of Chart are selected by the descendant axis. Note also that <xsl:number> assigns separate numbering to the Peak elements (1 and 2), which

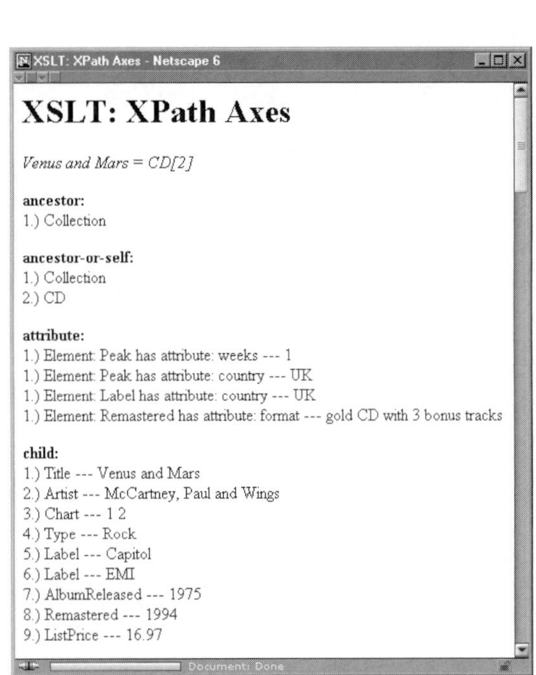

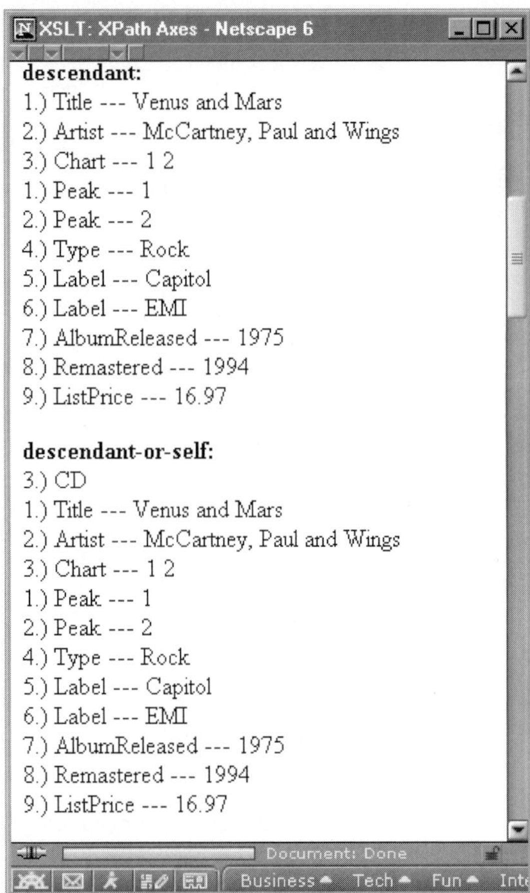

FIGURE 11-19 Tracing XPath axes for selected context node (screens 1 and 2)

reflects their being children of `Chart`. If instead we wanted to number all descendants regardless of level, we would use the instruction

```
<xsl:number level="any" from="//CD[2]" count="*" />
```

Now, turning to Figure 11-20 (pages 700–701), the `following` axis is shown in the first two windows. The `following` axis selects all the nodes whose start tag begins after the end tag of `CD[2]`, including the processing instruction, `Book[2]` (with the title "Many Years From Now"), `Book[3]` ("Beatles Anthology, The"), `CD[3]` ("Beatles 1"), and `Owner` plus all of their descendants. The numbering of these nodes is a bit confusing, but we could modify the `<xsl:number>` instruction to number multiple levels in a hierarchical fashion, like an outline.

```
<xsl:number format="1" level="multiple" count="*" />
```

The numbering for the nodes selected by the `following` axis would then look like this:

```
following:
1.) bogus-pi --- attr1="foo" attr2="foobar"
1.4.) Book
1.4.1.) Title --- Many Years From Now
1.4.2.) Author
1.4.2.1.) Name --- Paul McCartney
1.4.2.1.1.) First --- Paul
1.4.2.1.2.) Last --- McCartney
1.4.3.) Type --- Autobiographical
1.4.4.) Published --- 1997
1.4.5.) Rating --- 4 stars
1.4.6.) Notes --- 654 pages; Reprint edition (October 1998)
1.4.7.) ListPrice --- 27.50
1.5.) Book
1.5.1.) Title --- Beatles Anthology, The
1.5.2.) Author
1.5.2.1.) Name --- Paul McCartney
1.5.2.1.1.) First --- Paul
1.5.2.1.2.) Last --- McCartney
1.5.3.) Author
1.5.3.1.) Name --- George Harrison
[etc.]
1.5.10.) ListPrice --- 60.00
1.6.) CD
1.6.1.) Title --- Beatles 1
1.6.2.) Artist --- Beatles
1.6.3.) Chart --- 1
1.6.3.1.) Peak --- 1
1.6.4.) Type --- Rock
1.6.5.) Label --- Capitol
1.6.6.) AlbumReleased --- November 14, 2000
1.6.7.) ListPrice --- 18.97
1.7.) Owner
[etc.]
```

We can see from the next to last section in Figure 11-20 that the `following-sibling` axis selects a subset of the nodes selected by the more general `following` axis. It selects only the processing instruction, `Book[2]`, `Book[3]`, `CD[3]`, and `Owner`, but *none* of their descendants since siblings are those nodes that share the same parent, `Collection` in this case. Similarly, the `preceding` and `preceding-sibling` axes select those elements whose end tag appears before the start tag of `CD[2]`, with `preceding` including all descendants and `preceding-sibling` selecting only `Book[1]` and `CD[1]` because they have the same parent as `CD[2]`.

The `parent` axis includes only the `Collection` element as we would expect and the `self` axis pertains only to the context node, `CD[2]`. For the `namespace` axis, I haven't asked specifically for the namespaces associated with the document

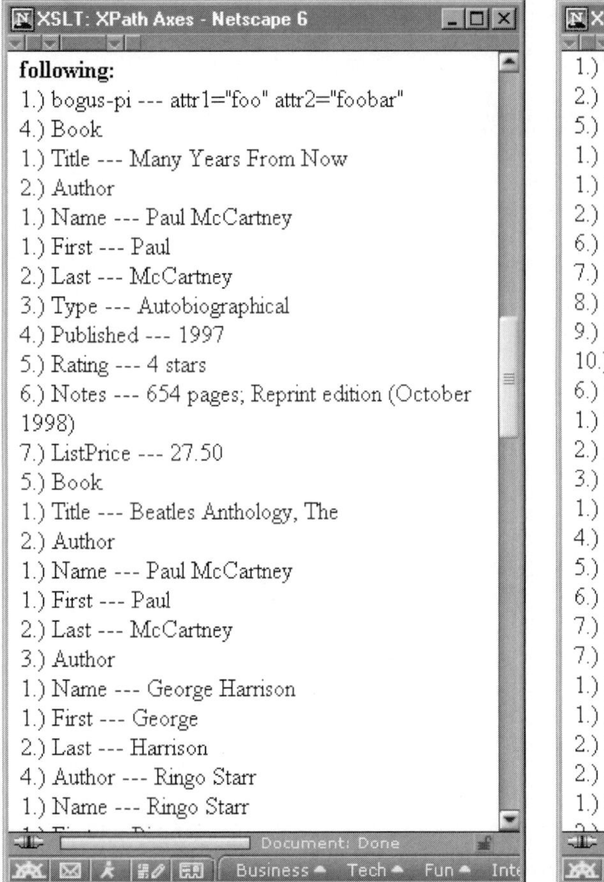

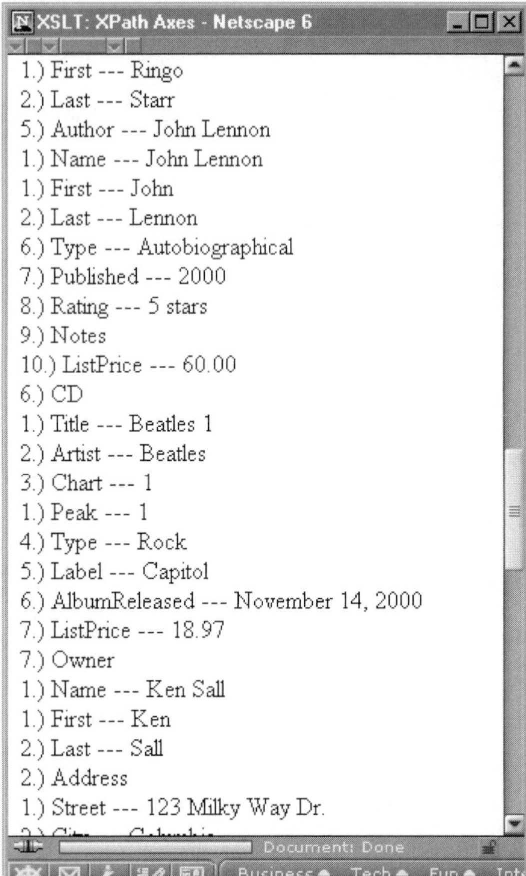

FIGURE 11-20 Tracing XPath axes for selected context node (screens 3 through 6)

element, `Collection`, as it might appear from the figure. As with the other axes, the selection is based on the context node

```
<xsl:for-each select="namespace::node()" >
```

which is equivalent in this case to

```
<xsl:for-each select="/Collection/CD[2]/namespace::node()" >
```

since namespaces apply to all descendants of the element that declares them (`Collection`, in this case) unless overriden by a new namespace scope.

If you were wondering about the presence of the repeated `string-length` test

```
<xsl:if test="string-length(current()) &lt; $maxLength" >
```

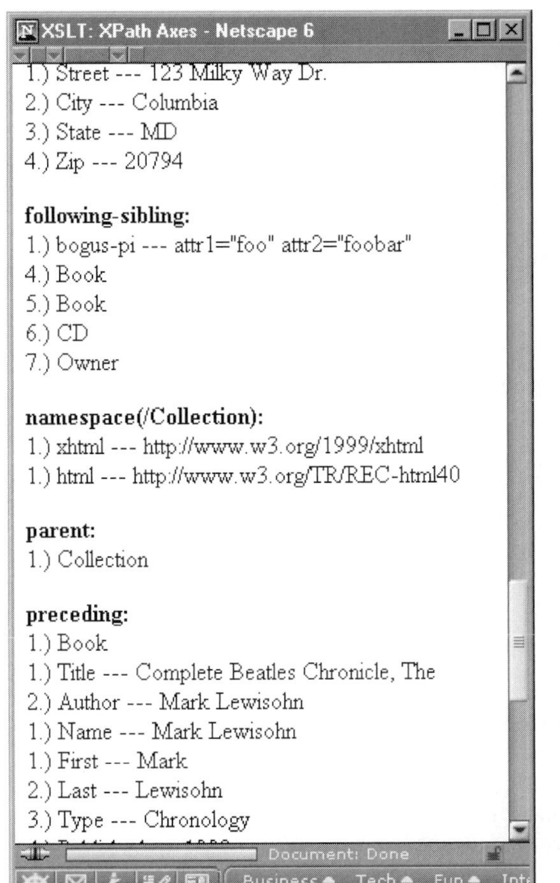

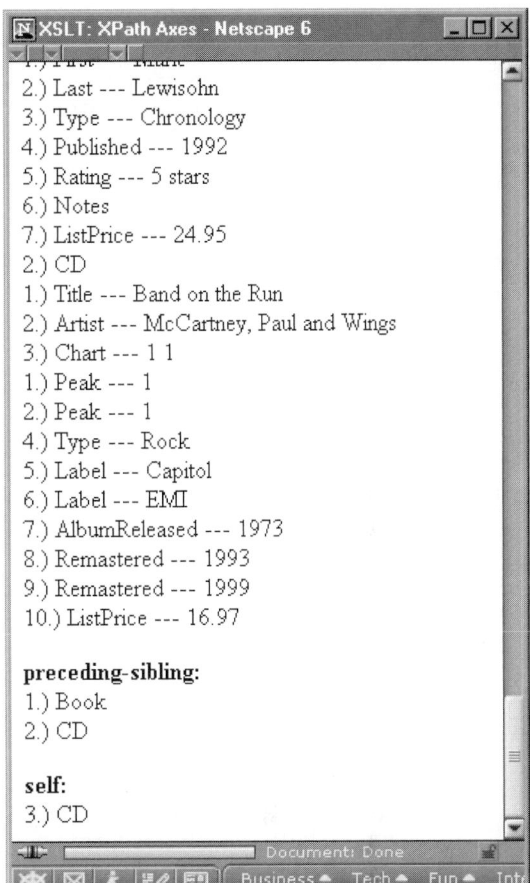

FIGURE 11-20 *(continued)*

it's included merely to prevent voluminous output, omitting anything with more than 50 characters, such as not displaying the value of nodes like `CD[2]` itself, which we know would be the value of all text nodes it contains.

Another shortcut used in this example involves skipping all nodes that have no name, which includes all text and comment nodes. (Namespace nodes are also nameless, but we processed them by their specific axis.) Skipping nameless nodes is accomplished by the test

```
<xsl:if test="name() != ''">
```

which could also be written as simply

```
<xsl:if test="name()">
```

Listing 11-42 Examining the Thirteen Axes (c6-axes.xsl)

```
<?xml version="1.0"?>
<xsl:stylesheet   version="1.0"
  xmlns:xsl="http://www.w3.org/1999/XSL/Transform">
<xsl:output method="html"/>

<xsl:variable name="label">XSLT: XPath Axes</xsl:variable>

<!-- Used to prevent dumping the entire node as a string. -->
<xsl:variable name="maxLength" select="50" />

<xsl:template match="/">
   <html>
     <head>
       <title><xsl:value-of select="$label" /></title>
     </head>
     <body>
       <h1><xsl:value-of select="$label" /></h1>
       <xsl:apply-templates select="//CD | //Book"/>
     </body>
   </html>
</xsl:template>

<!-- This clearly would have been more concise as a named template. -->

<xsl:template match="CD[2]">
   <p />
   <i><xsl:value-of select="Title" /></i>
   <i><xsl:text> = CD[2] </xsl:text></i>

   <p /><b><xsl:text>ancestor: </xsl:text></b>
   <xsl:for-each select="ancestor::node()" >
     <!-- Null test needed to weed out document root. -->
     <xsl:if test="name() != ''">
       <br /><xsl:number /><xsl:text>.) </xsl:text>
       <xsl:value-of select="name()" />
       <xsl:if test="string-length(current()) &lt; $maxLength" >
         <xsl:text> --- </xsl:text>
         <xsl:value-of select="." />
       </xsl:if>
     </xsl:if>
   </xsl:for-each>

   <p /><b><xsl:text>ancestor-or-self: </xsl:text></b>
   <xsl:for-each select="ancestor-or-self::node()" >
     <xsl:if test="name() != ''">
       <br /><xsl:number /><xsl:text>.) </xsl:text>
       <xsl:value-of select="name()" />
       <xsl:if test="string-length(current()) &lt; $maxLength" >
         <xsl:text> --- </xsl:text>
         <xsl:value-of select="." />
       </xsl:if>
     </xsl:if>
   </xsl:for-each>
```

```
<!--
    For the attribute case, we do things a little differently to
    poke inside CD[2] and find any children that have any attribute
    and then to obtain the name of such children and the name and
    value of their attributes.
-->
<p /><b><xsl:text>attribute: </xsl:text></b>
<xsl:for-each select="//CD[2]/descendant::node()/@*" >
  <!--
     We could use "//CD[2]/*/attribute::node()"  but that
     restricts our depth to one level.
  -->
  <xsl:if test="name() != ''">
    <br /><xsl:number /><xsl:text>.) </xsl:text>
    <xsl:text>Element: </xsl:text>
    <xsl:value-of select="name(parent::node())" />
    <xsl:text> has attribute: </xsl:text>
    <xsl:value-of select="name()" />
    <xsl:if test="string-length(current()) &lt; $maxLength" >
      <xsl:text> --- </xsl:text>
      <xsl:value-of select="." />
    </xsl:if>
  </xsl:if>
</xsl:for-each>

<p /><b><xsl:text>child: </xsl:text></b>
<xsl:for-each select="child::node()" >
  <xsl:if test="name() != ''">
    <br /><xsl:number count="*" /><xsl:text>.) </xsl:text>
    <xsl:value-of select="name()" />
    <xsl:if test="string-length(current()) &lt; $maxLength" >
      <xsl:text> --- </xsl:text>
      <xsl:value-of select="." />
    </xsl:if>
  </xsl:if>
</xsl:for-each>

<p /><b><xsl:text>descendant: </xsl:text></b>
<xsl:for-each select="descendant::node()" >
  <xsl:if test="name() != ''">
    <br /><xsl:number count="*" /><xsl:text>.) </xsl:text>
    <xsl:value-of select="name()" />
    <xsl:if test="string-length(current()) &lt; $maxLength" >
      <xsl:text> --- </xsl:text>
      <xsl:value-of select="." />
    </xsl:if>
  </xsl:if>
</xsl:for-each>

<p /><b><xsl:text>descendant-or-self: </xsl:text></b>
<xsl:for-each select="descendant-or-self::node()" >
  <xsl:if test="name() != ''">
    <br /><xsl:number count="*" /><xsl:text>.) </xsl:text>
    <xsl:value-of select="name()" />
    <xsl:if test="string-length(current()) &lt; $maxLength" >
```

```
      <xsl:text> --- </xsl:text>
      <xsl:value-of select="." />
    </xsl:if>
  </xsl:if>
</xsl:for-each>

<p /><b><xsl:text>following: </xsl:text></b>
<xsl:for-each select="following::node()" >
  <xsl:if test="name() != ''">
    <br /><xsl:number count="*" /><xsl:text>.) </xsl:text>
    <xsl:value-of select="name()" />
    <xsl:if test="string-length(current()) &lt; $maxLength" >
      <xsl:text> --- </xsl:text>
      <xsl:value-of select="." />
    </xsl:if>
  </xsl:if>
</xsl:for-each>

<p /><b><xsl:text>following-sibling: </xsl:text></b>
<xsl:for-each select="following-sibling::node()" >
  <xsl:if test="name() != ''">
    <br /><xsl:number count="*" /><xsl:text>.) </xsl:text>
    <xsl:value-of select="name()" />
    <xsl:if test="string-length(current()) &lt; $maxLength" >
      <xsl:text> --- </xsl:text>
      <xsl:value-of select="." />
    </xsl:if>
  </xsl:if>
</xsl:for-each>

<p /><b><xsl:text>namespace(/Collection): </xsl:text></b>
<xsl:for-each select="namespace::node()" >
  <xsl:if test="name() != ''">
    <br /><xsl:number count="*" /><xsl:text>.) </xsl:text>
    <xsl:value-of select="name()" />
    <xsl:if test="string-length(current()) &lt; $maxLength" >
      <xsl:text> --- </xsl:text>
      <xsl:value-of select="." />
    </xsl:if>
  </xsl:if>
</xsl:for-each>

<p /><b><xsl:text>parent: </xsl:text></b>
<xsl:for-each select="parent::node()" >
  <xsl:if test="name() != ''">
    <br /><xsl:number count="*" /><xsl:text>.) </xsl:text>
    <xsl:value-of select="name()" />
    <xsl:if test="string-length(current()) &lt; $maxLength" >
      <xsl:text> --- </xsl:text>
      <xsl:value-of select="." />
    </xsl:if>
  </xsl:if>
</xsl:for-each>
```

```
    <p /><b><xsl:text>preceding: </xsl:text></b>
    <xsl:for-each select="preceding::node()" >
      <xsl:if test="name() != ''">
        <br /><xsl:number count="*" /><xsl:text>.) </xsl:text>
        <xsl:value-of select="name()" />
        <xsl:if test="string-length(current()) &lt; $maxLength" >
          <xsl:text> --- </xsl:text>
          <xsl:value-of select="." />
        </xsl:if>
      </xsl:if>
    </xsl:for-each>

    <p /><b><xsl:text>preceding-sibling: </xsl:text></b>
    <xsl:for-each select="preceding-sibling::node()" >
      <xsl:if test="name() != ''">
        <br /><xsl:number count="*" /><xsl:text>.) </xsl:text>
        <xsl:value-of select="name()" />
        <xsl:if test="string-length(current()) &lt; $maxLength" >
          <xsl:text> --- </xsl:text>
          <xsl:value-of select="." />
        </xsl:if>
      </xsl:if>
    </xsl:for-each>

    <p /><b><xsl:text>self: </xsl:text></b>
    <xsl:for-each select="self::node()" >
      <xsl:if test="name() != ''">
        <br /><xsl:number count="*" /><xsl:text>.) </xsl:text>
        <xsl:value-of select="name()" />
        <xsl:if test="string-length(current()) &lt; $maxLength" >
          <xsl:text> --- </xsl:text>
          <xsl:value-of select="." />
        </xsl:if>
      </xsl:if>
    </xsl:for-each>
  </xsl:template>

  <xsl:template match="*">
  </xsl:template>

  </xsl:stylesheet>
```

Node Types, Node Values, and Node Tests

This section covers node types, node values, and node tests in more detail.

Node Types

The nodes in the XPath data model are very closely related to the *information items* described by the XML Information Set. (In particular, see Table 5-2.) There are seven node types in the XPath model as described in Table 11-8. The *value* of each of the node types is explained in Table 11-9 with reference to Listing 11-43.

TABLE 11-8 XPath Node Types

Node Type	*Description*
root	The root is the unique node that contains all other nodes in the XPath/XSLT model of an XML document. This root plays a role similar to that of the *document node* in the DOM, but different from the *document element* of an XML instance. The root node contains one child node for each comment and processing instruction that appears outside of (i.e., before or after) the document element, and one for the document element itself. However, the root node does not model either the XML declaraction or the document type declaration, which means that a stylesheet has no access to this information (except perhaps by means of an extension function). The root node has no name.
element	Each element node has a name, an optional namespace URI, a parent, an optional list of children (each of which may be of type element, text, processing instruction, or comment). A list of attributes and a list of namespaces within the current scope are also associated with an element, but they are not children of the element.
attribute	An attribute node has a name, a namespace URI, a parent node (the element that contains it within its start tag), and a value. *Paradoxically, even though an attribute always has a parent element, XPath does not consider attributes to be children of the associated element!* (In other words, you can always refer to the parent element of an attribute by means of the parent axis or its abbreviated form, but you cannot access an element's attributes using the child axis; instead use the special "@" symbol.) If the document references a DTD that defines a default value for an attribute and the attribute is not explicitly present in the XML document, the XPath model will include an attribute node with the default value for each instance of the element.
text	A text node has a parent element but it cannot have children. Adjacent text nodes are merged (normalized) so the PCDATA is the largest possible contiguous sequence of text characters. A text node has no name.
processing instruction	A processing instruction node represents whatever appears between <? and ?>. A PI node has a *target* by which it is identified, optional data, a parent, but no children. Its parent may be either the element that contains it or the root node. The name of the PI is the target and the value is the data, if any.
comment	A comment node represents whatever appears between <-- and -->. It has a parent, which is either the element that contains it or the root node. A comment node has no name.
namespace	A namespace node is copied to each element or attribute for which it is in scope, so each element node has one namespace node for each namespace declaration within its scope. As with attribute nodes, there is a paradox in that a namespace node has a parent, but it is not considered a child of its parent.

Node Values

For each type of node, there is a way to determine its string value. In the case of certain node types such as text nodes, the string contained with the start and end tags is the obvious value. For other node types such as element and root nodes, however, the value can be determined only by first obtaining the value of its descendants (recursively). To concretely illustrate the value of each node type, refer to the brief XML document `collection8.xml` shown in Listing 11-43 in conjunction with the explanations in Table 11-9.

Listing 11-43 XML Instance collection8.xml

```
<?xml version="1.0" standalone="yes"?>
<Collection version="2" xmlns:xhtml="http://www.w3.org/1999/xhtml"
xmlns:html="http://www.w3.org/TR/REC-html40">
<!-- Reminder: Get Spizer's "Beatles Records on Vee-Jay" (1998) and "Beatles
on Apple Records" (2002). -->
  <Book>
    <Title>The Beatles' Story on Capitol Records: Part Two: the Albums</Title>
    <?appSpecificPI crossRefType="Book"
    crossRefTitle="The Beatles' Story on Capitol Records: Part One" ?>
    <Author>
      <Name>
        <First>Bruce</First>
        <Last>Spizer</Last>
      </Name>
    </Author>
    <Type>Discography</Type>
    <Published publisher="498 Productions, L.L.C.">2000</Published>
    <Notes>Fascinating 250-page account of the covers, track selections, and
variations of their U.S. 14+ record albums. Part One covers the U.S. singles.
    </Notes>
    <ListPrice>50.00</ListPrice>
  </Book>
  <Owner>
    <Name sex="male">
      <First>Ken</First>
      <Last>Sall</Last>
    </Name>
    <Address>
      <Street>123 Milky Way Dr.</Street>
      <City>Columbia</City>
      <State>MD</State>
      <Zip>20794</Zip>
    </Address>
  </Owner>
</Collection>
```

TABLE 11-9 Values of Different Node Types

Node Type	*What* `<xsl:value-of>` *Sends to the Result Tree*
root	The value of the root node is the value of the *document* element (recursively determined by obtaining the value of all the elements it contains). For the XML instance in Listing 11-43, the value[a] of the root is the same as the value of the `Collection` element: "The Beatles' Story on Capitol Records: Part Two: the Albums Bruce Spizer Discography 2000 Fascinating 250-page account of the covers, track selections, and variations of their U.S. records. Part One covers the U.S. singles. 50.00 Ken Sall 123 Milky Way Dr. Columbia MD 20794"
element	The value of an element is the value of any children and/or character data, if any. The text content of the element is after start and end tags are removed and entity references are resolved. For the XML instance in Listing 11-43, the value of the `Published` element is "2000". The value of the `Name` element is the text content of its two element children (`First` and `Last`), which is "Bruce Spizer", if we normalize space, which converts the newline between the two children to a single space.
attribute	The normalized value of the attribute (extraneous white space is stripped from the beginning and end) is sent to the result tree. For example, the value of the `publisher` attribute of the `Published` element is: "498 Productions, L.L.C."
text	Text content of the node is sent to the result tree. The value of the text node child of the `Published` node is "2000".
processing instruction	Data portion of the PI, specifically excluding the PI target and delimiters (<? and ?>) is sent to the result tree. For example, the value of the processing instruction whose target is `appSpecificPI` is the complete string with interior double quotes and apostrophe: `crossRefType="Book" crossRefTitle="The Beatles' Story on Capitol Records: Part One"`
comment	Comment text, excluding the delimiters (`<!--` and `-->`) is sent to the result tree. For example, the value of the comment is the complete string with interior double quotes and apostrophe: `Reminder: Get Spizer's "Beatles Records on Vee-Jay" (1998) and "Beatles on Apple Records" (2002).`
namespace	Namespace URI, which is typically a URL beginning with `http` (or possibly `urn`). The value of the XHTML namespace whose prefix is "xhtml" is `http://www.w3.org/1999/xhtml`

a. Normalized, that is, with extraneous space removed.

The stylesheet I used with `collection8.xml`, called `c8-node-values.xsl`, is shown in Listing 11-44. I've chosen text output just for variety.

Listing 11-44 Stylesheet Illustrating Node Values (c8-node-values.xsl)

```
<?xml version="1.0"?>
<xsl:stylesheet
  xmlns:xsl="http://www.w3.org/1999/XSL/Transform"
  version="1.0">
<xsl:output method="text" indent="yes" />

<xsl:template match="/">
  <xsl:text>...Value of root= </xsl:text>
  <xsl:value-of select="." />
  <xsl:apply-templates />
</xsl:template>

<xsl:template match="Collection">
  <xsl:text>
...Value of /Collection= </xsl:text>
  <xsl:value-of select="." />
  <xsl:apply-templates select="Book"/>
  <xsl:apply-templates select="comment()"/>
  <xsl:apply-templates select="processing-instruction()"/>
</xsl:template>


<xsl:template match="//comment()">
  <xsl:text>
...Value of comment= </xsl:text>
  <xsl:value-of select="." />
</xsl:template>

<xsl:template match="//processing-instruction()">
  <xsl:text>
...Value of processing-instruction(appSpecificPI) = </xsl:text>
  <xsl:value-of select="." />
<!--  <xsl:value-of select="processing-instruction(appSpecificPI)" /> -->
</xsl:template>


<xsl:template match="Book">

  <xsl:text>
... select="child::*"  results:
</xsl:text>
  <xsl:for-each select="child::*" >
  <!-- same as   <xsl:for-each select="*" > -->

   <xsl:value-of select="position()" />
    <xsl:text>. name = {</xsl:text>
    <xsl:value-of select="name()" />
    <xsl:text>}, value = [</xsl:text>
```

```
    <xsl:value-of select="normalize-space(.)" />
    <!-- <xsl:value-of select="." /> -->
    <xsl:text>]
</xsl:text>
  </xsl:for-each>

    <xsl:text>
... select="child::node()"  results:
</xsl:text>
  <xsl:for-each select="child::node()" >

   <xsl:value-of select="position()" />
    <xsl:text>. name = {</xsl:text>
    <xsl:value-of select="name()" />
    <xsl:text>}, value = [</xsl:text>
    <xsl:value-of select="." />
    <xsl:text>]
</xsl:text>
  </xsl:for-each>

  <xsl:apply-templates />
</xsl:template>

<xsl:template match="Book/Published">
  <xsl:text>
...Value of /Collection/Book/Published= </xsl:text>
  <xsl:value-of select="." />
  <xsl:text>
...Value of /Collection/Book/Published/@publisher= </xsl:text>
  <xsl:value-of select="@publisher" />
</xsl:template>

<xsl:template match="text()">
</xsl:template>

</xsl:stylesheet>
```

We'll discuss these results (shown in Listing 11-45) in the next section as we talk about node tests.

Node Tests

We first encountered node tests in the section "Default Built-in Template Rules and Node Tests." Node tests select a *subset* of the nodes that the current axis preselects. Each location step must contain a node test that is separated from the axis by a double colon (`::`). The seven kinds of node tests are shown in Table 11-10.

Node tests evaluate to either true or false. If the test evaluates to false, the node is not selected, thereby reducing the set of nodes initially selected by the axis. For example, the node test `child::*` selects all *element* children of the context node, and the node test `attribute::*` selects all attributes of the context node. Since the

TABLE 11-10 Node Tests

Node Test	*Description*
*	The asterisk test matches any *element* node, but not text, comment, or processing instruction nodes; this is an XPath wildcard. For example, `child::*` is true for all *element* children of the context node and `attribute::*` is true for all attributes within the context node's start tag. The combination at-asterisk (`@*`) matches any *attribute* node; this is another XPath wildcard.
XMLName	If the *XMLName* is an element, this test matches all elements with this name; if it is an attribute name, it matches only attributes.
`text()`	This test selects all text nodes, collapsing adjacent text nodes into one, whenever possible (such as when white-space-only nodes are involved).
`comment()`	This test selects all comment nodes.
`processing-instruction()`	This test selects all processing instruction nodes; if invoked with a parameter, only PIs with that target are selected. For example, `processing-instruction(appSpecificPI)` selects the PI with the target `appSpecificPI`.
`node()`	This XPath wildcard matches all kinds of nodes: element, attribute, text, comment, processing instruction, and namespace nodes. Actually, this depends on the context in which the test is applied. Often `node()` is short for the unabbreviated XPath expression `child::node()`, which applies only to nodes that can be children of something else, which excludes attribute and namespace nodes.
*NamespacePrefix:**	This matches all elements (or attributes) with the same namespace mapped to the same prefix.

`child` and `attribute` axis can be abbreviated, these node tests are more commonly written as simply "*" to select all elements and "@*" to select all attributes.

The node test `text()` is true for any text node, so it selects all text nodes. For example, `child::text()` selects the text node children of the context node. Similarly, the `comment()` node test is true for any comment node, while the node test `processing-instruction()` is true for any processing instruction. The node test `node()` is true for any type of node.

We can clearly see the difference between `child::*` and `child::node()` by examining the results of applying the stylesheet from Listing 11-44, which tapped node values. The complete results are on your CD-ROM in the file `c8-node-values.txt`. Listing 11-45 includes the portion related to the `<xsl:for-each>` instructions that iterate first over `child::*` and then iterate over `child::node()`. In both cases, the context node was `/Collection/Book`, which contains a processing instruction in addition to the usual element children.

Listing 11-45 Partial Node Value Results (c8-node-values.txt)

```
... select="child::*"  results:
1. name = {Title}, value = [The Beatles' Story on Capitol Records: Part Two:
the Albums]
2. name = {Author}, value = [Bruce Spizer]
3. name = {Type}, value = [Discography]
4. name = {Published}, value = [2000]
5. name = {Notes}, value = [Fascinating 250-page account of the covers,
track selections, and variations of their U.S. 14+ record albums. Part One
covers the U.S. singles.]
6. name = {ListPrice}, value = [50.00]

... select="child::node()"  results:
1. name = {}, value = [
    ]
2. name = {Title}, value = [The Beatles' Story on Capitol Records: Part Two:
the Albums]
3. name = {}, value = [
    ]
4. name = {appSpecificPI}, value = [crossRefType="Book"
    crossRefTitle="The Beatles' Story on Capitol Records: Part One" ]
5. name = {}, value = [
    ]
6. name = {Author}, value = [

        Bruce
        Spizer

    ]
7. name = {}, value = [
    ]
8. name = {Type}, value = [Discography]
9. name = {}, value = [
    ]
10. name = {Published}, value = [2000]
11. name = {}, value = [
    ]
12. name = {Notes}, value = [Fascinating 250-page account of the covers,
track selections, and variations of their U.S. 14+ record albums. Part One
covers the U.S. singles.
    ]
13. name = {}, value = [
    ]
14. name = {ListPrice}, value = [50.00]
15. name = {}, value = [
  ]
```

From the results, we see that `child::*` selects *only the 6 children of the* `Book` *element that are elements:* `Title`, `Author`, `Type`, `Published`, `Notes`, and `ListPrice`. Although `Author` has a `Name` child, and `Name` has `First` and `Last` children, they are not immediate children of `Book`, so the node test `child::*` (or simply `*`) does not select them. However, since the content of an element is the concatenation of the content of its children, when we apply `<xsl:value-of select="normalize-space(.)" />` to Author, we get "Bruce Spizer," the content of the First and Last grandchildren of Author. (Actually, we used the normalize-space() function just so we wouldn't get the two name components on separate lines.)

In contrast, the child::node() axis and node test selects *all 15 nodes that are children of* Book. This includes the same 6 element children as above, plus 8 nameless text nodes containing newlines, plus 1 processing instruction whose name is the PI target (appSpecificPI) and whose value is

```
crossRefType="Book" crossRefTitle="The Beatles' Story on Capitol Records:
Part One"
```

Where do the text nodes come from? They are the newlines that follow all elements so that the XML is easy for mere humans to read. If the XML instance is presented without newlines in this human-unfriendly manner (assume this is one long line without wrapping), it poses no problem for an XML parser.

```
<Book><Title>The Beatles' Story on Capitol
Records: Part Two: the Albums</Title><?appSpecificPI
crossRefType="Book" crossRefTitle="The Beatles' Story on Capitol
Records: Part One" ?><Author><Name><First>Bruce</First>
<Last>Spizer</Last></Name></Author><Type>Discography</Type><Published
publisher="498 Productions, L.L.C.">2000</Published><Notes>Fascinating
250-page account of the covers, track selections, and
variations of their U.S. 14+ record albums. Part One covers the U.S.
singles.</Notes><ListPrice>50.00</ListPrice></Book>
```

Then the 8 text nodes would no longer be present, in which case the only extra child that child::node() would select over child::* would be the processing instruction (in this example).

A more generic stylesheet for processing by node type, c6-nodes.xsl, in illustrated in Listing 11-46, which also shows one method for determining whether or not the current node is a **terminal (leaf) node**—that is, a node that has no children. Unlike the previous example, this stylesheet has no a priori knowledge of the XML instance it is designed to process.

Listing 11-46 Generic Node Processing Stylesheet (c6-nodes.xsl)

```
<?xml version="1.0"?>
<xsl:stylesheet   version="1.0"
  xmlns:xsl="http://www.w3.org/1999/XSL/Transform">
<xsl:output method="html"/>

<xsl:variable name="label">XSLT: XPath Nodes</xsl:variable>

<xsl:template match="/">
   <html>
     <head>
       <title><xsl:value-of select="$label" /></title>
```

```
      </head>
      <body>
        <h1><xsl:value-of select="$label" /></h1>
        <!-- Root node is above the document element (Collection). -->
        <xsl:text>Root Node: (no name) </xsl:text>
        <br /><i><xsl:value-of select="normalize-space(.)" /></i>
        <!--
             In contrast to "*" which only matches element nodes,
             "node()" matches elements, attributes, text, comments,
             PIs, and namespaces nodes. "@*" matches only attributes.
        -->
        <xsl:apply-templates  select="node()" />
        <!--  select="*|@*|comment()|processing-instruction()|text()" />
        -->
      </body>
    </html>
  </xsl:template>

  <!-- * matches only elements -->
  <xsl:template match="*">
     <br /><xsl:text>Element: </xsl:text>
     <i><xsl:value-of select="name()" /></i>
     <xsl:text>  + Child nodes: </xsl:text>
     <i><xsl:value-of select="count(./*)" /></i>
     <!-- If # children is 0, element must be terminal node. -->
     <xsl:if test="count(./*) = 0" >
       <xsl:text>  +++ Leaf node</xsl:text>
     </xsl:if>
     <!-- Handle attributes and then element children. -->
     <xsl:apply-templates select="@*" />
     <xsl:apply-templates />
  </xsl:template>

  <!-- @* matches only attributes -->
  <xsl:template match="@*">
     <br /><xsl:text>Attribute: </xsl:text>
     <i><xsl:value-of select="name()" /></i>
     <xsl:text>  - Value: </xsl:text>
     <b><xsl:value-of select="." /></b>
  </xsl:template>

  <xsl:template match="text()">
    <!-- Skipping whitespace only nodes, plus a little more. -->
    <xsl:if test="string-length(normalize-space(.)) &gt; 1" >
     <br /><xsl:text>text: {</xsl:text>
     <xsl:value-of  select="normalize-space(.)" />
     <xsl:text>}</xsl:text>
    </xsl:if>
  </xsl:template>

  <xsl:template match="comment()">
     <p /><xsl:text>comment: </xsl:text>
     <b><i><xsl:value-of select="." /></i></b>
  </xsl:template>
```

```
<xsl:template match="processing-instruction()">
   <p /><xsl:text>processing-instruction: name: </xsl:text>
   <i><xsl:value-of select="name()" /></i>
   <xsl:text>  --- data: </xsl:text>
   <b><i><xsl:value-of select="." /></i></b>
</xsl:template>

</xsl:stylesheet>
```

Let's apply this stylesheet to our running example, `collection6.xml`. Initially we process the root node and display its value, which is actually the value of its document element child, `Collection`, but first we strip leading and trailing space everywhere, using the XPath `normalize-space()` function. To handle children, we call:

```
<xsl:apply-templates  select="node()" />
```

This is equivalent to calling the more explicit instruction

```
<xsl:apply-templates
     select="*|@*|comment()|processing-instruction()|text()" />
```

to ensure that all node types except namespace nodes will be processed.

We determine whether a particular element is a **terminal (leaf) node** by using the `count()` function to check whether it has children. If the context node has zero children, it is a terminal node by definition, so the test is simply

```
<xsl:if test="count(./*) = 0" >
```

We can process *all attributes* of a node with the call:

```
<xsl:apply-templates select="@*" />
```

The XPath `name()` function returns the name of any node type that has a name. Elements, attributes and processing instructions all have names, but *the root, text nodes, comment nodes, and namespace nodes do not have names.*

Text nodes between elements, as we've seen, consist of white space characters only, such as tabs and newlines. We can filter out white-space-only nodes by the test

```
<xsl:if test="string-length(normalize-space(.)) &gt; 1" >
```

However, this also skips text nodes consisting of a single non-whitespace character too. An alternative is to use the top-level instruction

```
<xsl:strip-space elements="*" />
```

The results of applying this stylesheet to our running example are shown in Figure 11-21.

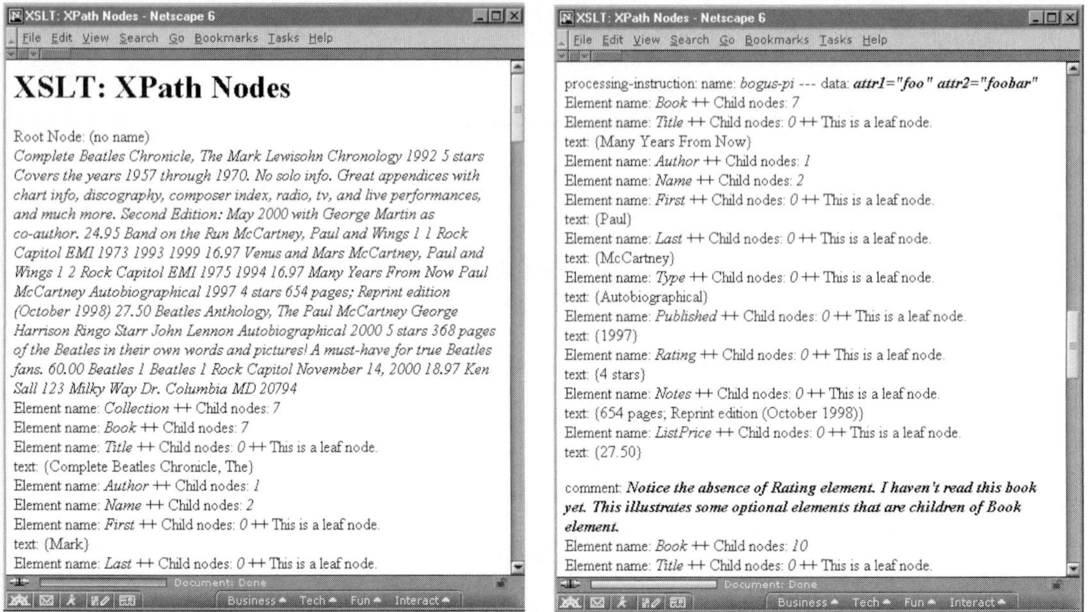

FIGURE 11-21 Display of node tests and leaf node check (c6-nodes.html)

Data Types

XPath itself defines four data types and XSLT adds one more called *result tree fragments*. When an XPath expression is evaluated, the result must be one of these five types.

- *Boolean*—true or false
- *Number*—identical to a Java double (64-bit floating point, IEEE 754-compliant); huge range; positive or negative, with special values `Inf` and `-Inf` (infinity) and `NaN` (not a number).
- *String*—a sequence of Unicode characters, delimited by either single or double quotes
- *Node-set*—a collection of nodes resulting from a location path, usually in document order, except as we've seen when the axis is `ancestor`, `ancestor-or-self`, `preceding`, or `preceding-sibling`, in which case they are in reverse document order.
- *Result tree fragments*—not defined in XPath spec; the term is defined in Section 11.1 of XSLT 1.0 Recommendation. A **result tree fragment**, sometimes abbreviated RTF, is a branch of nodes from the result tree that result from instantiating a template (either `<xsl:template>` or the body of an `<xsl:variable>` or `<xsl:param>` instruction that has no `select` attribute). An RTF may be copied to output with `<xsl:copy-of>`, or converted to a string and used as such in an expression.

RTFs are handled like node-sets but are limited to string kinds of operations. The XSLT 1.0 Recommendation (*http://www.w3.org/TR/xslt#section-Result-Tree-Fragments*) states:

> An operation is permitted on a result tree fragment only if that operation would be permitted on a string (the operation on the string may involve first converting the string to a number or boolean). In particular, it is not permitted to use the /, //, and [] operators on result tree fragments. When a permitted operation is performed on a result tree fragment, it is performed exactly as it would be on the equivalent node-set.

What is less than obvious here is that *the way you define a variable impacts whether it is an RTF and therefore how it can later be used in expressions.* In the previous section "More About Setting Variables," we saw that a variable can be defined with or without the `select` attribute:

```
<xsl:variable name="specialCase">17</xsl:variable>
```

or

```
<xsl:variable name="specialCase" select="17" />
```

The main difference between these two approaches is that the first case (initializing by means of content without a `select` attribute) produces a result tree fragment, whereas the second case produces a string that can automatically be converted to a number (in this example). *A variable created in the RTF manner cannot be directly used as a predicate of an expression.* If you need to use the variable as a predicate (e.g., to index an element), then use the empty form with the `select` attribute to define the variable. An alternative is to force a numeric conversion of the RTF in the predicate itself with the `number()`function:

```
<xsl:value-of select="CD[number($specialCase)]" />
```

XPath Expressions vs. XSLT Patterns

XML Path Language is defined by the specification located at *http://www.w3.org/TR/xpath*. As discussed earlier in this chapter, XPath syntax is used by several W3C specifications, such as XSLT, XPointer, XML Schema, and XQuery. Although XPath expressions (or more precisely, XSLT match patterns) may seem similar to queries, they are really more like CSS selectors. In CSS, a selector is essentially an element pattern that causes an associated rule to be applied when the selector is encountered. In XPath there is an association between an expression and some particular action or instruction that depends on the specification that is leveraging XPath syntax. XSLT, for example, defines templates that contain instructions. The XSLT match patterns are associated with particular templates.

Whereas the XPath Recommendation describes expressions that are evaluated to yield an object of type node-set, boolean, number, or string, the XSLT Recommendation defines a special subset of XPath expressions called *patterns* that always return a node-set (an ordered list of nodes). Therefore, all patterns are XPath expressions, but only those XPath expressions that return a node-set constitute a valid pattern.[12] Formally in XSLT, a **pattern** is a set of location path patterns separated by a vertical bar ("|") to indicate alternatives. A node matches a pattern with one or more | separated alternatives if it matches any of the alternatives. A **location path pattern** is a location path whose steps consist of *only child or attribute axes*. Each location path pattern is evaluated from *right to left*. A node matches only if it satisfies the rightmost step and then the previous steps to the left, in turn.

Although patterns cannot use the descendant-or-self axis, they may use the // or / operators. This might at first seem limiting, but other expressions can be used if they are contained within a square-bracketed predicate, such as [last()] and [position() > 4]. If the steps of a path are separated by //, then any ancestor is a suitable match. If they are separated by a /, then only the immediate parent is an acceptable match.

As we've seen, patterns are used primarily to choose among several template rules based on the value of the match attribute in an <xsl:template> instruction, or to select the type of nodes to be processed via the select attribute of <xsl:apply-templates>. Patterns also occur as the value of the match attribute of the <xsl:key> element, as well as the value of the from and count attributes for <xsl:number>. In all cases, *the purpose of a pattern is to define the selection criterion*, the condition that when evaluated indicates whether a particular node is selected. In addition, values can be computed based on expressions. Norman Walsh and Paul Grosso emphasize two points about XPath expressions:

> Pattern matching occurs in a context; XPath expressions and XSLT elements can change the current context and consequently the nodes which match. XPath is inclusive or greedy, it addresses all matching elements. You must use predicates to refine the set of nodes selected.[13]

Table 11-11 provides a substantial number of examples of abbreviated and unabbreviated XPath expressions and XSLT patterns. *Readers are encouraged to study each example carefully and refer to this table for ideas as you develop your XSLT stylesheets.* The majority of these expressions and patterns appear in the code examples on the CD-ROM. Those that don't can be tested by adding them to one of the provided examples (e.g., c6-xpath.xsl, c8-node-values.xsl, etc.).

12. The term *pattern* does not appear in XPath because it is defined in XSLT, which uses XPath.

13. *XSL Concepts and Practical Use* by Norman Walsh and Paul Grosso, *http://www.nwalsh.com/docs/tutorials/xsl/*.

TABLE 11-11 Examples of XPath Expressions and XSLT Patterns

Expression or Pattern	*Description*
Miscellaneous Expressions and Patterns	
`/`	Selects the root node. The / character at the beginning of any location path means that the path is absolute, i.e., starting at the root node of the document.
`//`	Shorthand for `/descendant-or-self::node()/`.
`/kid`	Selects the immediate child element of the root called `kid`, a top-level element.
`/child::node()`	Selects *all direct children* of the root, including the document element and any processing instructions and comments that appear before or after the document element.
`.`	Selects the context node. Shorthand for `self::node()` [where `self::` indicates an axis].
`..`	Selects the parent element of the context node, which must be either an element or the root node. Shorthand for `parent::node()`.
`../Title`	Selects the `Title` element that is a sibling of the context node (i.e., the `Title` child of the parent of the context node). Shorthand for `parent::node()/child::Title`.
`name(..)`	Returns the name of the element that is the parent of the current node (which may be an element or attribute). The `name()` function is defined only for element, attribute, and processing instruction nodes.
`name(..) = 'someParent'`	Tests whether the name of the parent of the current node is specifically equal to the string "someParent".
`parent::someParent`	Tests whether the name of the parent of the current node is specifically "someParent". (This form works when multiple namespaces are involved.)
`ancestor::*`	Selects all ancestors of the context node.
`//ns:*`	Selects all nodes in the current document with the namespace prefix `ns`. Note the single colon; this is how the processor knows the reference is to a namespace.
`@xlink:href[contains ('.w3.org')]`	Selects `xlink:href` attributes that contain the substring ".w3.org".
`//comment()`	Selects all comments in the current document, regardless of which element contains them.
`<xsl:if test="./Published/@publisher[.='Chronicle Books']">`	Evaluates to true if the value of the `publisher` attribute of the `Published` element child of the context node is the exact string "Chronicle Books".
`<xsl:when test="$price >= $min">`	Evaluates to true if the values of the variable `$price` is greater than or equal to the value of the variable `$min`.

continued

TABLE 11-11 Examples of XPath Expressions and XSLT Patterns (*continued*)

Expression or Pattern	*Description*
Expressions and Patterns Involving Elements	
`*`	Selects all element children of the context node, regardless of name. Shorthand for `child::*`.
`elt`	Selects the children named `elt` of the context node. Shorthand for `./child::elt` or simply `child::elt`.
`not(elt)`	Returns true if the context node has no child named `elt`.
`elt/kid`	Selects the grandchildren named `kid` of the context node, if the parent's name is `elt`. Shorthand for `child::elt/child::kid`.
`*/kid`	Selects all grandchildren named `kid` of the context node, regardless of parent's name.
`elt[3]`	Selects the third child named `elt` of the context node. Note that the index is one relative (i.e., starts with 1), unlike arrays in many computer languages that start with zero.
`./elt[position() = 3]`	Same as `elt[3]`.
`//elt[1]`	Selects *any* element named `elt` in the document that is the first `elt` child of its parent. Shorthand for `/descendant-or-self::node()/elt[1]`.
`(//elt)[1]`	With parentheses to indicate grouping, this selects *only* the *first* instance of the `elt` element in the document. Shorthand for `/descendant::elt[1]`.
`elt[kid]`	Selects all `elt` children of the context node *with one or more children* named `kid`. Note that this differs from `elt/kid`, which selects the `kid` children of `elt`.
`elt[kid="sval"]`	Selects all `elt` children of the context node with one or more children named `kid` having the string value "sval". Remember that the string value of an element is the concatenated string value of all its descendants.
`elt[last()]`	Selects the last child named `elt` of the context node.
`//elt`	Selects all `elt` descendants of the *document root* (all elements named `elt` in the same document as the context node). Shortcut for `descendant-or-self::node()` axis.
`.//elt`	Selects all `elt` descendants of the *context node*. Shorthand for `self::node()/descendant-or-self::node()/child::elt`.
`//elt/kid`	Selects all `kid` elements in the same document as the context node that have a parent named `elt`. Note that `kid` may be a grandchild, great grandchild, etc. of the context node.
`//*[starts-with(name(), 'Beatles')]`	Selects all elements in the document whose element name begins with the string "Beatles".

TABLE 11-11 *(continued)*

Expression or Pattern	*Description*
//*[string-length (name()), < 9)]	Selects all elements in the document whose name has fewer than 9 characters. Note that we need to escape the less than symbol (<) since the expression will be used within quotes as an attribute value of match, select, test, etc.
text()	Selects all text node children of the context node.
//text()	Selects all text nodes in the entire document, including those that are element content.
/Collection/Book[3]/ Author[2]	Selects the second Author from the third Book of the Collection document element.
*[position() < last()]	Selects all child nodes of the context node except the last one.
[last()]	Selects the last node. This and the above pattern are useful in outputting a delimited list (e.g., to get the correct placement of commas).
count(*) <= 5	True if the context node has 5 or fewer children.
Book[not(Published = preceding-sibling::Book/ Published)]	Selects all Book elements with unique years of publication (assumed to be the content of the Published element) with respect to the current Book child of the context node.
Book[not(Author/Last = preceding-sibling::Author/ Last)]	Selects the first Book element by each author based on last names (assuming all last names are unique).
sum(//CD/ListPrice) + sum(//Book/ListPrice)	Returns the numeric sum of all ListPrice elements that are children of either CD or Book parents.
sum(//ListPrice) div count(//ListPrice)	Returns the numeric average of all ListPrice elements.
ancestor//elt	Selects the descendants named elt of the child named ancestor (which is a child of the context node).
xhtml:h2	Selects elements with the local name h2 that have the xhtml namespace prefix (implicitly or explicitly defined).
Expressions and Patterns Involving Attributes	
@attr	Selects the attribute named attr of the context node. Shorthand for ./attribute::attr.
elt/@foo	Selects the foo attribute of all elt children of the context node. Compare this to elt/foo, which selects the foo *children* of the elt children.
elt[@foo]	Selects *only* those elt children of the context node that have a foo attribute.
elt[@*]	Selects all elt children having *any* attribute.
elt[not(@*)]	Selects all elt children that have *no* attributes.
@*	Selects all attributes of the context node.

continued

TABLE 11-11 Examples of XPath Expressions and XSLT Patterns (*continued*)

Expression or Pattern	*Description*
Expressions and Patterns Involving Attributes (*continued*)	
count(@*)	Returns the number of attributes of the context node.
../@attr	Selects the attribute named attr of the parent of the context node.
@attr[. = "val"]	Selects the attribute named attr if its value is "val".
elt[@attr="val"]	Selects all elt children of the context node with an attribute named attr having the value "val".
elt[normalize-space(@attr="val")]	Similiar to the previous example, except first strip all leading and trailing white space, and then test for the value "val".
elt[@attr="val"][4]	Selects the fourth elt child of the context node with an attribute named attr having the value "val".
elt[4][@attr="val"]	Selects the fourth elt child of the context node if that child has an attribute named attr having the value "val".
//*[@attr]	Selects all elements in the document that contain an attr attribute.
@attr1 = @attr2	Tests whether attr1 and attr2 both have exactly the same string value.
elt[@attr1 and @attr2]	Selects all elt children of the context node that have both attr1 and attr2 attributes.
elt[@attr1 = "val1" and @attr2]/@attr3	Selects attributes named attr3 of all elements named elt containing an attr1 with the value "val1" and also containing an attr2 attribute.
not(@attr) or @attr=""	Returns true if the context node does not have an attr attribute or if it has the attribute, but its value is the null string.
@attr != $var	Returns true if the value of attr differs from the value in variable $var; returns false if there is no attribute attr. If $var represents a node-set (e.g., result tree fragment), this is true if *any node* has a value different from the value of attr.
$var//*/@attr	Selects attribute attr of all elements that are descendants of a node that is a member of the node-set represented by the variable $var.
not(//@attr > 98.6)	True if every occurrence of the attribute attr is less than or equal to 98.6.

Assume each example is with respect to some unspecified context node reference ("./") unless the example begins with a slash ("/"). In the table, the names elt and kid represent generic element names, attr is a generic attribute name, val is a generic attribute value, and $var is a generic variable name.

Expressions involving node-sets are true only if the expression results in a non-empty list of nodes (e.g., CD/Remastered[@format] is true only for those CDs whose Remastered child has a format attribute). Numeric value expressions are true only for the node(s) with ordinal position based on the expression (e.g.,

CD[last()] is true only for the last CD in a node-set). Boolean expressions are true only if the entire expression evaluates to true (e.g., CD[position() = 5] is true only for the fifth CD in a node-set).

XPath Operators

Operators are discussed in several sections in the XPath Recommendation, especially sections 3.3 to 3.5. The operands fit into three categories: node-sets, booleans, and numbers, as shown in Table 11-12.

TABLE 11-12 XPath Operators

<table>
<tr><th>Operand Type</th><th>Operator</th><th>Description</th></tr>
<tr><td>Node-sets</td><td>[predicate expr]</td><td>Expression can be function calls, literals, variable references, numbers, etc.; can be combined with or and and operators</td></tr>
<tr><td></td><td>/</td><td>/ separates steps of a location path</td></tr>
<tr><td></td><td>//</td><td>// is the abbreviation for /descendant-or-self::node()/</td></tr>
<tr><td></td><td>|</td><td>| results in the union of nodes with no duplicates in document order (e.g., select="CD | Book" selects CD and Book elements)</td></tr>
<tr><td>Booleans</td><td>and, or</td><td>Normal boolean meaning: and is true if and only if both operands are true; or is true if either operand is true.</td></tr>
<tr><td></td><td>=, !=, <, <=, >, >=</td><td>The interpretation of equality and inequality operators depends on the type of their operands. For numbers, these operators have the normal mathematical meaning. For node-sets, however, two node-sets are equal if any nodes between them are equal. That is, the comparison returns true if and only if there is a node in the first node-set and a node in the second node-set such that the result of performing the comparison on the string values of the two nodes is true.
Note: If the variable $nodes represents a node-set, then $nodes = "val" does not mean the same as not($nodes != "val"). The former is true if and only if some node in the node-set $nodes has the string value "val". The latter is true if and only if all nodes in $nodes have the string value "val".
Limitation: Because angle brackets are special characters in XML, it is necessary to replace them with entities when used in attributes values, such as for match and select. So, use < for <, <= for <=, > for >, and >= for >=. For example: <xsl:if test="$var < 7"></td></tr>
<tr><td>Numbers</td><td>+, -</td><td>Addition and subtraction.
Limitation: Since XML names permit a hyphen, you must surround the minus sign with spaces.</td></tr>
<tr><td></td><td>*, div, mod</td><td>Multiply, divide, and modulo (remainder of division; the % operator in Java and JavaScript)</td></tr>
</table>

In the absence of parentheses, which are used to group expressions, operator precedence from *highest to lowest* is as follows. Within a row, the operators are of equal precedence. Without parentheses, expressions are evaluated left to right (i.e., they are left associative).

```
[]              # highest
/, //
|
*, div, mod
+, -
<, <=, >, >=
=
and
or             # lowest
```

XPath Functions

The XPath specification defines 27 functions (in Sections 4.1 through 4.4), which can be divided into four functional categories:

- *Node-set functions* operate on node-sets (lists of nodes that share a characteristic). See Table 11-13 (pages 725–726).
- *String functions* operate on or create strings. See Table 11-14 on page 726.
- *Boolean functions* return either true or false. See Table 11-15 on page 733.
- *Numeric functions* return a number, which in XPath is a 64-bit, double precision number, like the Java `double`. See Table 11-16 on page 734.

Optional arguments are denoted by a question mark ("?"). In most cases, if an optional argument is not supplied to an XPath (or, for that matter, XSLT) function, the implied argument is the context node. For example, given the template

```
<xsl:template match="Book">
  <xsl:text>
name() = </xsl:text><xsl:value-of select="name()" />
  <xsl:text>
name(child::*[4]) = </xsl:text><xsl:value-of select="name(child::*[4])" />
  <xsl:text>
```

the result is

```
name() = Book
name(child::*[4]) = Published
```

because in the first case, we get `Book`, the name of the context node, whereas in the second case, we're asking explicitly for the name of the fourth child node of the context node.

Node-Set Functions in XPath

Node-set functions (described in section 4.1 of the XPath spec) operate on node-sets—lists of nodes that share a characteristic. See the code example in Listing 11-14 (pages 622–623).

TABLE 11-13 Node-Set XPath Functions

Return Type	*Function Name (arguments)*	*Description*
number	**last()**	Returns the context size, which equals the ordinal value of the last element of the current context. In other words, if the context involves three nodes, last() will return the number 3, the size of the current node list. For example, the expression select= "//CD[last()]" will result in the node-set representing the third CD if there are 3 such elements in the document.
number	**position()**	Returns the ordinal number of the current node in the current context. For example, the expression select= "//CD[position() = 2]" results in the second CD node. One common use of position() is to handle alternate rows of data differently via <xsl:if test="position() mod 2 = 0"> . Another common example is <xsl:if test = "not(position()=last())"> to determine whether we are processing the last node in a node-set.
number	**count**(node-set)	Returns the number of nodes in the argument node-set. One possible use of this function is as the divisor in an expression computing an average value, using the sum() function to compute the numerator, as illustrated in Listing 11-48 on page 734.
node-set	**id**(object)	Returns the node-set in which all members have the specified ID (i.e., all elements with the given ID value for an attribute). This ID may be based on an attribute declared in the associated DTD or XML Schema to be of type ID. When the argument to id() is of type node-set, then the result is the union of the result of applying id() to the string value of each of the nodes in the node-set. When the argument is any other type, it is first converted to a string consisting of one or more tokens, each of which is then treated as an ID, resulting in a node-set matching any of these IDs. See also the generate-id() XSLT function.
string	**local-name**(node-set?)	Returns the local name of the (optional) argument node, which is the element name without an XML namespace prefix. If no argument is supplied, the function returns the local name of the context node. If the argument is of type node-set, then the local name of the *first* element in document order is returned. For example, if we have the element <foo:MyElt xmlns:foo="http://sample.com/bar"/>, the local name is MyElt although the full name is foo:MyElt. See also the name() function.

continued

TABLE 11-13 Node-Set XPath Functions (*continued*)

Return Type	*Function Name (arguments)*	*Description*
`string`	**`namespace-uri`**`(node-set?)`	Returns the namespace URI of the expanded name of the argument node, which is the element name without an XML namespace prefix. If no argument is supplied, the function returns the namespace URI of the context node. If the argument is of type `node-set`, then the namespace URI of the *first* element in document order is returned. (An empty string is returned if the first node has no expanded name or the namespace is null.) For example, if we have the element `<foo:MyElt xmlns:foo="http://sample.com/bar"/>`, the namespace URI is `"http://sample.com/bar"`.
`string`	**`name`**`(node-set?)`	Returns the fully qualified (expanded) name of the argument node, which is the local name plus the namespace prefix, if any. If the argument is of type `node-set`, then the name of the *first* element in document order is returned. (An empty string is returned if the first node has no expanded name.) For example, if we have the element `<foo:MyElt xmlns:foo="http://sample.com/bar"/>`, the name is `foo:MyElt`, although the the local name is simply `MyElt`. See also the `local-name()` function.

TABLE 11-14 String XPath Functions

Return Type	*Function Name (arguments)*	*Description*
`string`	**`string`**`(object?)`	Returns a string representation of the argument, which can be any type of object. The details of the type-dependent conversion are described in section 4.2 of the XPath Recommendation as follows: A node-set is converted to a string by returning the string value of the first node in document order. The boolean false value is converted to the string “false”. The boolean true value is converted to the string “true”. The numbers NaN (not a number), positive zero, negative zero, positive infinity, negative infinity are converted to the strings “NaN”, “0”, “0”, “Infinity” and “–Infinity”, respectively. Integers are represented in decimal form as a Number with no decimal point and no leading zeros, preceded by a minus sign (–) if the number is negative. Any other number is represented in decimal form as a Number including a decimal point with at least one digit before the decimal point and at least one digit after the decimal point, preceded by a minus sign (–) if the number is negative; there must be no leading zeros before the decimal point apart possibly

TABLE 11-14 *(continued)*

Return Type	*Function Name (arguments)*	*Description*
		from the one required digit immediately before the decimal point; beyond the one required digit after the decimal point there must be as many, but only as many, more digits as are needed to uniquely distinguish the number from all other IEEE 754 numeric values. Any other type of object is converted to a string in a way that is dependent on that type. *Note*: The `string()` function operates only on the *first node* of a node-set; subsequent nodes are ignored.
`string`	**`concat`**`(string1, string2, string3*)`	Returns the concatenation of all its argument strings, in order. There must be at least two arguments, but there is no upper limit. For example, `concat("George","Harrison")` results in "GeorgeHarrison". If you need white space in the result, it must be part of the string arguments.
`boolean`	**`starts-with`** `(string1, string2)`	Returns true if and only if the string `string1` starts with the string `string2`.
`boolean`	**`contains`**`(string1, string2)`	Returns true if and only if `string1` contains `string2` (i.e., `string2` is a proper or improper substring of `string1`).
`string`	**`substring-before`** `(string1, string2)`	Returns the substring of `string1` that precedes the *first* occurrence of `string2` within `string1`, or the empty string if `string2` is not a substring of `string1`. For example, `substring-before ("http://samples.com", "://samples")` is `"http"`.
`string`	**`substring-after`** `(string1, string2)`	Returns the substring of `string1` that follows the first occurrence of `string2` within `string1`, or the empty string if `string2` is not a substring of `string1`. For example, `substring-after ("http://samples.com", "://samples")` is `".com"`.
`string`	**`substring`** `(string, startPosition, length?)`	Returns the substring of the argument string starting at the (one-relative) position `startPosition` with `length` specified by the third argument, if any. For example, `substring ("McCartney", 3,4)` returns `"Cart"`. Note that in contrast to popular languages like Java and ECMAScript, the *first character is position 1*, not 0. If the `length` argument is omitted, the returned substring continues to the end of the original string. For example, `substring ("McCartney", 3)` returns `"Cartney"`.
`number`	**`string-length`** `(string?)`	Returns the length (i.e., number of characters) of the argument string. If no argument is provided, the function returns the length of the context node (after it is implicitly converted into a string). For example, `string-length ("Harrison")` is 8.

continued

TABLE 11-14 String XPath Functions (*continued*)

Return Type	*Function Name (arguments)*	*Description*
`string`	**`normalize-space`** `(string?)`	Returns the specified string after stripping leading and trailing white space, and reducing interior sequences of multiple white space characters with a single space. Also all tabs and carriage returns are converted to single spaces. As in XML, the white space characters are `#x20`, `#x9`, `#xD` or `#xA` (space, tab, carriage return, and newline). If the argument is omitted, the default is to convert the context node to a string. For example, `normalize-space (" George  Harrison  ")` returns the string `"George Harrison"` with only one space, even though the original string contains leading, trailing, and multiple interior space between the first and last name.
`string`	**`translate`** `(string1, string2, string3)`	Returns `string1` with occurrences of characters in `string2` replaced by the character at the corresponding position in `string3`. For example, `translate ("John", "nohjq", "NarXQ")` produces `"JarN"`. If there are more characters in `string2` than in `string3`, any unmatched characters are removed from `string1`. For example, `translate ("Harrison", "Hranosi", "hRAN")` results in `"hARRN"`. In this case, the characters 'o', 's', and 'i' have no positional matches in `string3`, so they are dropped from `string1`.

String Functions in XPath

String functions (described in section 4.2 of the XPath spec) operate on or create strings. Most of the string functions are demonstrated in the code example in Listing 11-47, with results displayed in Figure 11-22 on page 732.

Listing 11-47 XPath String Functions Code Example (c6-strings.xsl)

```
<?xml version="1.0"?>
<xsl:stylesheet   version="1.0"
  xmlns:xsl="http://www.w3.org/1999/XSL/Transform">
<xsl:output method="html"/>

<xsl:variable name="label">XSLT: String Functions</xsl:variable>

<xsl:template match="/">
   <html>
     <head>
       <title><xsl:value-of select="$label" /></title>
     </head>
     <body>
       <h2><xsl:value-of select="$label" /></h2>
       <xsl:apply-templates select="//CD | //Book" />
```

```
        <p /><xsl:text>String length of first CD's title: </xsl:text>
        <xsl:value-of select="string-length(/Collection/CD[1]/Title)" />
        <xsl:text> ++ </xsl:text>
        <i><xsl:value-of select="/Collection/CD[1]/Title" /></i>

        <p /><xsl:text>String value of first CD: </xsl:text>
        <xsl:value-of select="string(/Collection/CD[1])" />

        <p /><xsl:text>String value with normalize-space (View Source): </
xsl:text>
        <xsl:value-of select="normalize-space(/Collection/CD[1])" />
      </body>
    </html>
</xsl:template>

<xsl:template match="Book[position() = 1]">
   <p /><xsl:text>First Book: </xsl:text>

   <!-- Store the title in a variable. -->
   <xsl:variable name="title" select="Title/text()"/>
   <i><xsl:value-of select="$title" /></i>

   <br /><xsl:text>substring-before "Beatles": </xsl:text>
   <i><xsl:value-of select="substring-before($title, 'Beatles')"/></i>

   <br /><xsl:text>substring-after "Beatles": </xsl:text>
   <i><xsl:value-of select="substring-after($title, 'Beatles')"/></i>

   <br /><xsl:text>translate "Beatles" to uppercase: </xsl:text>
   <i><xsl:value-of select="translate('Beatles', 'eatles', 'EATLES')"/></i>

   <br /><xsl:text>concat of 'The' and rest of title: </xsl:text>
   <xsl:variable name="titlePart" select="substring-before($title, ',')"/>
   <xsl:variable name="titleExtra" select="substring-after($title, ',')"/>
   <i><xsl:value-of select="concat($titleExtra, ' ', $titlePart)"/></i>
</xsl:template>

<xsl:template match="CD">
   <p />

   <!-- Store the title in a variable. Name is same but different scope. -->
   <xsl:variable name="title" select="Title/text()"/>
   <i><xsl:value-of select="$title" /></i>

   <xsl:if test="starts-with($title, 'Beatles')">
     <br /><xsl:text>Above title starts-with "Beatles".</xsl:text>
   </xsl:if>

   <xsl:if test="substring($title, 6, 6) = 'on the'">
     <br /><xsl:text>Substring from position 6 with length 6 is "on the".</
xsl:text>
   </xsl:if>
```

```
    <xsl:if test="contains($title, 'Mar')">
      <br /><xsl:text>Above title contains the string "Mar".</xsl:text>
    </xsl:if>
</xsl:template>

<xsl:template match="text()">
  <!-- Discard other text content. -->
</xsl:template>

</xsl:stylesheet>
```

In the root template, the call to

```
string-length(/Collection/CD[1]/Title)
```

results in the number 15, the number of characters (including interior white space) in the title "Band on the Run". The call to

```
string(/Collection/CD[1])
```

results in the concatenation of all the text nodes of `CD[1]`. The function call

```
normalize-space(/Collection/CD[1])
```

collapses space, although from the screenshot in Figure 11-22 on page 732, the difference between this and the call to `string()` is not apparent. However, if we look at the HTML that is generated, the `string()` call actually generates

```
    Band on the Run
    McCartney, Paul and Wings

      1
      1


    Rock
    Capitol
    EMI
    1973
    1993
    1999
    16.97
```

But `normalize-space()` produces just one line of text (wrapped around here for readability):

```
Band on the Run McCartney, Paul and Wings 1 1 Rock Capitol EMI 1973 1993
1999 16.97
```

All interior runs of white space (including spaces, tabs, and newlines) are collapsed into single spaces. Of course, in HTML these two variations display exactly the same. However, in applications where extraneous white space is undesirable, `normalize-space()` can be handy.

The second template matches `Book[1]` because of the `<xsl:template match="Book[position() = 1]">` instruction. This template sets `$title` to the string "Complete Beatles Chronicle, The". Subsequent string functions extract various portions of the title. Specifically,

```
substring-before($title, 'Beatles')
```

produces "Complete " (with the trailing space) and

```
substring-after($title, 'Beatles')
```

results in the string " Chronicle, The" (with a leading space). To convert the string "Beatles" to uppercase, we use `translate()`:

```
translate('Beatles', 'eatles', 'EATLES')
```

Changing the title from a trailing "The" to a leading "The" is a simple matter because we can split the title into the parts before and after the comma using `substring-before()` and `substring-after()` and then swap them using `concat()`.

```
<xsl:variable name="titlePart" select="substring-before($title, ',')"/>
<xsl:variable name="titleExtra" select="substring-after($title, ',')"/>
<i><xsl:value-of select="concat($titleExtra, ' ', $titlePart)"/></i>
```

The third template matches all three of the CDs. However, a different `<xsl:if>` instruction applies to each `CD` element because each test condition based on a string function matches a different title. Each of the three times this template is invoked, a new local variable named `$title` is instantiated and initialized to the value of the current `CD` element's `Title` child, which is why the variable is declared locally, within the scope of this template, rather than as a top-level variable.

The first test matches "Beatles 1", the title of `CD[3]`, because it starts with the string "Beatles":

```
<xsl:if test="starts-with($title, 'Beatles')">
```

The second test matches "Band on the Run", the title of `CD[1]`, which contains the substring "on the" starting from character position 6 with length 6 (including the interior space).

```
<xsl:if test="substring($title, 6, 6) = 'on the'">
```

The final test matches `CD[2]` because the title "Venus and Mars" contains the substring "Mar":

```
<xsl:if test="contains($title, 'Mar')">
```

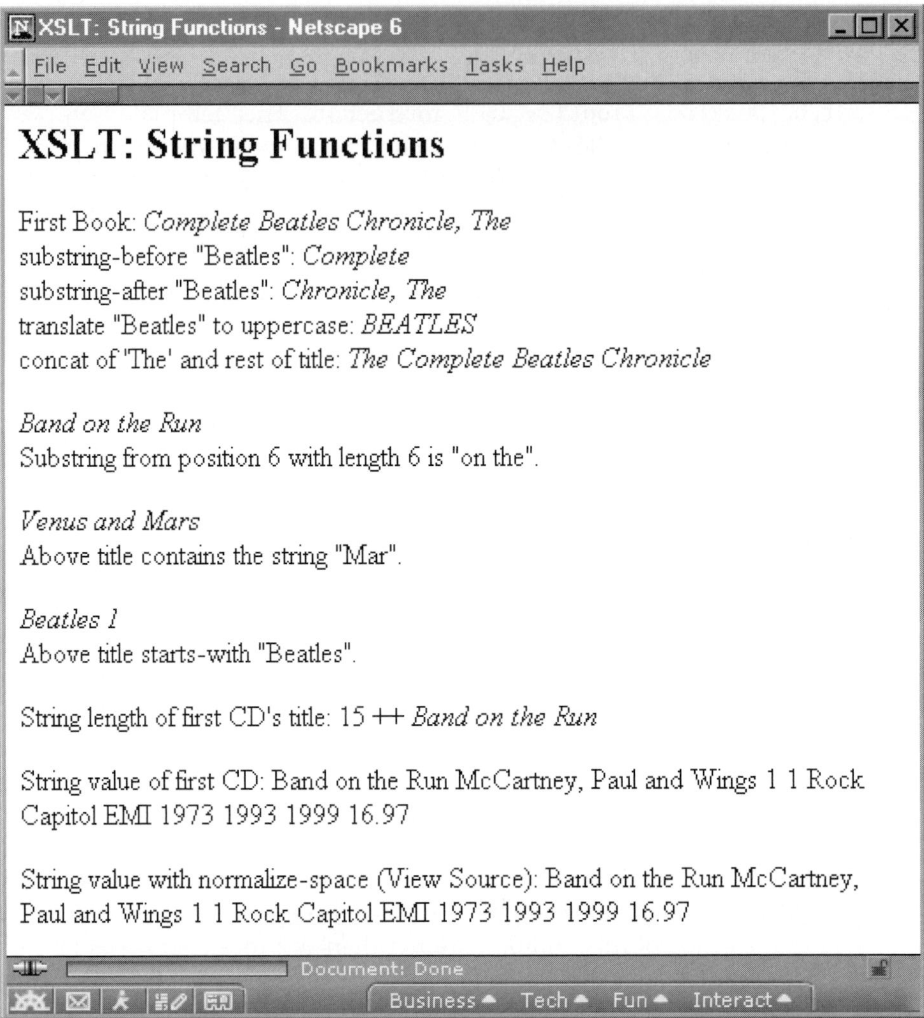

FIGURE 11-22 Output from the XPaths string functions (c6-strings.html)

Boolean Functions in XPath

Boolean functions (described in XPath Section 4.3) return either true or false, as shown in Table 11-15. We've seen two examples of the `not()` function. In `c6-sort.xsl` (see Listing 11-27, pages 652–653), the function was used to find the immediate children of `Collection` other than `Owner` (i.e., those with the name `CD` or `Book`)

```
select="/Collection/*[not(name() = 'Owner')]"
```

TABLE 11-15 Boolean XPath Functions

Return Type	*Function Name (arguments)*	*Description*
`boolean`	**`boolean`**`(object)`	Returns the boolean representation of the argument object. A number is true if and only if it is neither positive or negative, zero nor NaN. (In other words, zero is false, but positive or negative integers are true.) A node-set is true if and only if it is nonempty, but a string is true if and only if its length is nonzero. An object of any other type is converted to a boolean in a way that is dependent on that type. For example, `boolean(*)`, `boolean(5)`, `boolean(0)`, `boolean(-3)`, `boolean (1.25)` yields true, true, false, true, and true, respectively.
`boolean`	**`not`**`(boolean)`	Returns the negation of the boolean expression that is the argument. For example, `not(name(//CD) = name(//Book))` is always true.
`boolean`	**`true`**`()`	Returns true. Note that `<xsl:value-of select="number(true())" />` results in the number 1.
`boolean`	**`false`**`()`	Returns false. Note that `<xsl:value-of select="number(false())" />` results in the number 0.
`boolean`	**`lang`**`(string)`	Returns true if the language of the context node matches the specified language abbreviation string ("us", "gb", "de", "fr", etc.). The language of the context node is determined by the value of the `xml:lang` attribute on the context node, or, if the context node has no `xml:lang` attribute, by the value of the `xml:lang` attribute on the nearest ancestor of the context node that has an `xml:lang` attribute. If there is no such attribute, then `lang()` returns false.

Actually in that example, I opted instead for the expression

```
select="//CD | //Book"
```

Both are equivalent in the context of `collection6.xml`.

In the stylesheet `c6-xpath.xsl` (see Listing 11-41), `not()` was used to match all CDs whose title was not "Beatles 1":

```
match="CD[not(Title/text() = 'Beatles 1')]">
```

Numeric Functions in XPath

Numeric functions (described in XPath section 4.4) return a number, which in XPath is a 64-bit, double precision number, like the Java `double`. These functions are described in Table 11-16 and illustrated in Listing 11-48. The `c6-math.xsl` stylesheet in Listing 11-48 and the corresponding HTML output in Figure 11-23 on page 737 illustrate the numeric functions from Table 11-16.

TABLE 11-16 Numeric XPath Functions

Return Type	*Function Name (arguments)*	*Description*
number	**number**(object?)	Returns a numeric representation of the argument, or, if no argument is supplied, of the context node. A string that represents an IEEE 754 number is stripped of leading and trailing space and then rounded according to the IEEE 754 *round-to-nearest* rule. If the string can't be expressed as a number, the value `NaN` (not a number) is returned. A boolean true is converted to the number 1; a boolean false is converted to 0. A node-set is first converted to a string as if by calling the `string()`; the result is then converted to a number. A non-standard type of object is converted to a number in a type-dependent manner. Note that `<xsl:value-of select= "number('Beatles')" />` results in `NaN` (not a number) since the argument string is not a number.
number	**sum**(node-set)	Returns the sum of the numeric representations of all of the nodes in the argument node-set. For example, `<xsl:value-of select="sum(//ListPrice)" />` results in total of all `ListPrice` nodes in the document.
number	**floor**(number)	Returns the largest integer that is less than or equal to the number. For example, `<xsl:value-of select= "floor(98.6)" />` results in the number 98.
number	**ceiling**(number)	Returns the smallest integer that is greater than or equal to the number. For example, `<xsl:value-of select= "ceiling(98.6)" />` results in the number 99.
number	**round**(number)	Returns the integer that is "closest" to the argument number. If there are two such numbers, then the one that is closest to positive infinity is returned, meaning *we round upwards*. For example, `<xsl:value-of select="round(24.5)" />` results in the number 25 and `<xsl:value-of select= "round(–4.5)" />` results in –4.

Listing 11-48 XPath Numeric Functions Code Example (c6-math.xsl)

```
<?xml version="1.0"?>
<xsl:stylesheet   version="1.0"
  xmlns:xsl="http://www.w3.org/1999/XSL/Transform">
<xsl:output method="html"/>

<xsl:variable name="label">XSLT: Math Functions; Boolean and Relational
Operators</xsl:variable>

<xsl:template match="/">
   <html>
     <head>
       <title><xsl:value-of select="$label" /></title>
```

```
      </head>
      <body>
        <h2><xsl:value-of select="$label" /></h2>
        <xsl:apply-templates />
        <p>
        <!-- We expect the sum of the CD prices and the sum of the Book
             prices to be the same as the sum of all ListPrices items,
             regardless of their parent element.
        -->
        <xsl:text>Grand Total: $</xsl:text>
        <xsl:value-of select="sum(//CD/ListPrice) + sum(//Book/ListPrice)" />
        <xsl:text> should equal </xsl:text>
        <!-- Note the use of format-number to control precision. -->
        <xsl:value-of select="format-number(sum(//ListPrice), '$#.00')" />
        <br /><xsl:text> Unformatted: </xsl:text>
        <xsl:value-of select="sum(//ListPrice)" />
        </p>
      </body>
    </html>
</xsl:template>

<xsl:template match="*"> <!-- note -->

    <h2 align="center">CD Prices</h2>
    <xsl:for-each select="//CD">
      <br />
      <xsl:text>CD </xsl:text><xsl:number /><xsl:text>.)  </xsl:text>
      <xsl:text>$</xsl:text>
      <xsl:value-of select="ListPrice" />
      <xsl:text> - </xsl:text>
      <i><xsl:value-of select="Title" /></i>
      <xsl:text> --- floor: </xsl:text><xsl:value-of
select="floor(ListPrice)" />
      <xsl:text>, ceiling: </xsl:text><xsl:value-of
select="ceiling(ListPrice)" />
      <xsl:text>, round: </xsl:text><xsl:value-of select="round(ListPrice)" />
      <xsl:if test="(ListPrice &gt; 16) and (ListPrice &lt; 18)">
        <xsl:text>  --- Price is between $16 and $18. </xsl:text>
      </xsl:if>
    </xsl:for-each>

    <xsl:variable name="CDsubtotal" select="sum(//CD/ListPrice)" />
    <xsl:variable name="numCDs"  select="count(//CD)" />
    <br />
    <xsl:text>$</xsl:text><xsl:value-of select="$CDsubtotal" />
    <xsl:text> - Total for all </xsl:text>
    <xsl:value-of select="$numCDs" /><xsl:text> CDs</xsl:text>
    <br /><xsl:text>Average price: </xsl:text>
    <xsl:value-of select="format-number($CDsubtotal div $numCDs, '$#.00')" />

    <h2 align="center">Book Prices</h2>
    <xsl:for-each select="//Book">
      <br />
      <xsl:text>Book </xsl:text><xsl:number /><xsl:text>.)  </xsl:text>
      <xsl:text>$</xsl:text>
```

```
    <xsl:value-of select="ListPrice" />
    <xsl:text> - </xsl:text>
    <i><xsl:value-of select="Title" /></i>
    <xsl:text> --- floor: </xsl:text><xsl:value-of
select="floor(ListPrice)" />
    <xsl:text>, ceiling: </xsl:text><xsl:value-of
select="ceiling(ListPrice)" />
    <xsl:text>, round: </xsl:text><xsl:value-of
select="round(ListPrice)" />
    <xsl:if test="(ListPrice &gt; 25) and (ListPrice &lt;= 50)">
      <xsl:text>  --- Price is between $25 and $50 (inclusive). </xsl:text>
    </xsl:if>
  </xsl:for-each>

  <xsl:variable name="Booksubtotal" select="sum(//Book/ListPrice)" />
  <xsl:variable name="numBooks"  select="count(//Book)" />
  <br />
  <xsl:text>$</xsl:text><xsl:value-of select="$Booksubtotal" />
  <xsl:text> - Total for all </xsl:text>
  <xsl:value-of select="$numBooks" /><xsl:text> Books</xsl:text>
  <br /><xsl:text>Average price: </xsl:text>
  <xsl:value-of
select="format-number($Booksubtotal div $numBooks, '$#.00')" />

</xsl:template>
</xsl:stylesheet>
```

After outputting the <head> start and end tags and the <body> start tag, the template that matches the root calls `<xsl:apply-templates>` for all nodes. (When it returns, we do some totaling, which we'll come back to in a minute.) In the second template, which matches all elements, we use `<xsl:for-each>` to loop through all `CD` elements. For each `CD`, we output its ordinal number (document order) via `<xsl:number>`, followed by its price and title (`ListPrice` and `Title` children of the `CD` context node). We then invoke the math functions `floor()`, `ceiling()`, and `round()`, passing each the `ListPrice` node, the string content of which is implicitly converted into a number first. The result of each of these calls is an integer either less than or greater than the price. Next we see if the price is within a certain range by the instruction:

```
<xsl:if test="(ListPrice &gt; 16) and (ListPrice &lt; 18)">
```

This checks whether 16 < `ListPrice` < 18, which is true for the first two `CD` elements only. Notice that the normal rules of XML syntax dictate that an attribute (`test`, in this case) may not contain markup, so the more natural > and < symbols must be replaced by their corresponding character entities, `>` and `<`, respectively.

After processing each CD, we use the `sum()` function to compute the total of all CD prices at any level in the document and save it in a variable, `$CDsubtotal`:

```
<xsl:variable name="CDsubtotal" select="sum(//CD/ListPrice)" />
```

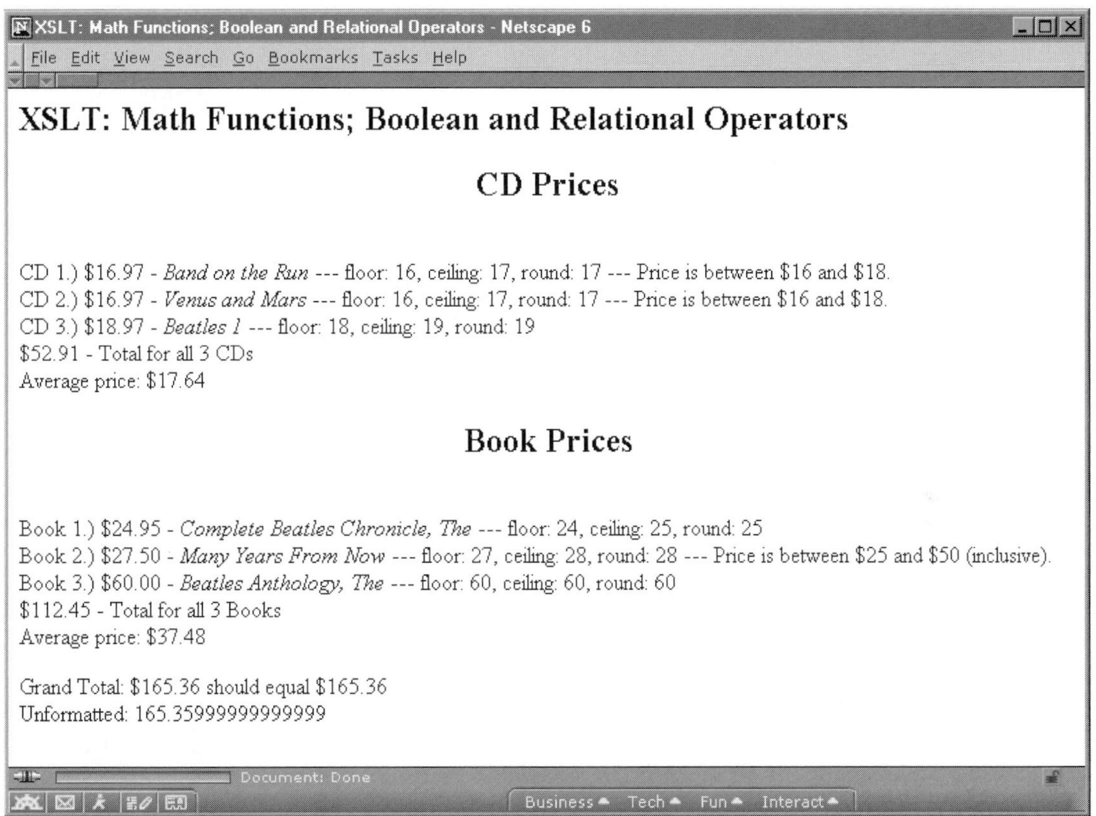

FIGURE 11-23 Output from the XPath Numeric Functions (c6-math.html)

We use `count()` to record the number of CDs encountered, also saved in a variable, `$numCDs`. To calculate the average price of a CD, we apply the `div` operator to our two variables:

```
<xsl:value-of select="format-number($CDsubtotal div $numCDs, '$#.00')" />
```

The `format-number()` function guarantees that we display a dollar sign and exactly two places to the right of the decimal point. Finally, we repeat the iteration, totaling, and averaging steps for all `Book` elements in the file, except the range check is for prices between $25 and $50 (inclusive) which applies only to the second book.

After we complete the second template, the processor returns to the line following the `<xsl:apply-templates>` instruction in the first template. Since the only two elements that have `ListPrice` children are `CD` and `Book`, we expect the two lines:

```
<xsl:value-of select="sum(//CD/ListPrice) + sum(//Book/ListPrice)" />
```

and

```
<xsl:value-of select="sum(//ListPrice)" />
```

to compute the same value, and they do (at least when we use the `format-number()` function).

XSLT Elements and Instructions

All elements of the XSLT language fall into three broad categories:

- *Root level elements* consist of only `<xsl:stylesheet>` and the equivalent `<xsl:transform>` element.
- *Top-level elements* are elements that may appear as direct children of `<xsl:stylesheet>` or `<xsl:transform>`, such as `<xsl:import>`, `<xsl:variable>`, `<xsl:param>`, and `<xsl:template>`.
- *Instructions* elements usually do not (and in most cases, *cannot*) appear at the top level, such as `<xsl:text>`, `<xsl:value-of>`, `<xsl:when>`, and `<xsl:sort>`.

In addition, some XSLT processors define their own extension elements, which may be either top-level elements or instructions. See Listing 11-49 (pages 751–755) for a code example that checks for extension elements, among other things.

XSLT describes two kinds of extensions: *extension elements* and *extension functions*. An **extension element** (called *extension instruction* in the XSLT 2.0 Working Draft) is an element in a namespace, other than the XSLT namespace, identified as an extension namespace. In contrast, an **extension function** is a function available for use within an XPath expression, but is neither a core function defined in the XPath specification nor an additional function defined in the XSLT specification (nor a stylesheet function defined using the new `xsl:function` declaration, in the XSLT 2.0 Working Draft).

In Table 11-17, "Root and Top-Level XSLT Elements" (pages 740–743) and Table 11-18, "XSLT Instructions" (pages 744–748), the following conventions are used to denote valid attribute values:

- ?, +, and * wildcards with the usual XML DTD meaning of zero or one, one or more, or zero or more, respectively
- `"val1" | "val2"` an enumerated list of permissible values for the attribute
- `string` and `char` a text string and a single Unicode character, respectively
- `<!-- Content: template -->` as the content of an element, this merely means which kinds of child elements the current element is permitted to have
- `qname` an XML Name (element, attribute, etc.) either with or without a namespace prefix
- `nmtoken`, `token` XML Names

- `ncname` noncolon name, meaning an XML Name except no colon permitted
- `expression` any XPath expression
- `boolean-expression` an XPath expression that returns true or false
- `number-expression` an XPath expression that returns a number
- `string-expression` an XPath expression that returns a string
- `node-set-expression` an XPath expression that returns a node-set
- `uri-reference` a string that represents a URI, which usually is a URL although it may not point to an existing document
- Empty elements (those which cannot have children content) are denoted with the usual `<emptyElement />` XML syntax.
- Elements that may or must have content are shown with matching begin and end tags, such as `<xsl:template>{content}</xsl:template>`.

Refer to the *XSLT* Recommendation, Appendix B. Element Syntax Summary (*http://www.w3.org/TR/xslt#element-syntax-summary*), Norm Walsh's XSLT Elements Index (*http://www.nwalsh.com/docs/tutorials/xsl/xsl/foil84.html*), or the Zvon XSLT Reference (*http://www.zvon.org/xxl/XSLTreference/Output/index.html*) for more detailed information, especially the meaning of each attribute shown in the left columns of Tables 11-17 and 11-18.

Root and Top-Level Elements

Root elements are the outermost elements of the stylesheet that contains all other XSLT instructions, either as direct children or descendants. **Top-level elements** are immediate children of `<xsl:stylesheet>` (or `<xsl:transform>`). These elements tend to be more global in scope than instruction elements. Some top-level elements can appear *only* as direct children of `<xsl:stylesheet>` (e.g., `<xsl:import>`); others may appear *either* as direct children or as descendants—children of `<xsl:template>` or other other elements that permit children XSLT elements, such as `<xsl:if>` or `<xsl:choose>`. In the left column of the tables, the `"Content:"` comment clarifies which elements may appear between the start and end tags of the element being described. For example, the description

```
<xsl:stylesheet
  xmlns:xsl ="http://www.w3.org/1999/XSL/Transform"
  id = id
  extension-element-prefixes = tokens
  exclude-result-prefixes = tokens
  version = number >
  <!-- Content: (xsl:import*, top-level-elements) -->
</xsl:stylesheet>
```

means that `<xsl:stylesheet>` permits zero or more `<xsl:import>` instructions followed by any other top-level elements. This tells you that if you use `<xsl:import>`, it must precede other instructions. Only top-level elements may be direct children of `<xsl:stylesheet>`.

Elements shown with the /> notation are, of course, empty elements and therefore, by definition, are not permitted to contain content. Such XSLT instructions are completely defined by their attributes. An example of an empty XSLT instruction is

```
<xsl:output
  method = "xml" | "html" | "text" | qname-but-not-ncname
  version = nmtoken
  encoding = string
  omit-xml-declaration = "yes" | "no"
  standalone = "yes" | "no"
  doctype-public = string
  doctype-system = string
  cdata-section-elements = qnames
  indent = "yes" | "no"
  media-type = string />
```

The term "template" used in content descriptions such as

```
<xsl:param
  name = qname
  select = expression >
  <!-- Content: template -->
</xsl:param>
```

is a bit confusing, but that is what the XSLT Recommendation uses. It definitely does not mean `<xsl:template>`. Think of it as an unrestricted sequence of other XSLT instructions or literal result elements that can be nested in the start and end tags of the element being described (`<xsl:param>` in this case). In other words, in this context "template" refers to the body (content) of the element that contains it.

TABLE 11-17 Root and Top-Level XSLT Elements

Root or Top-Level Element	*Description*
<xsl:stylesheet xmlns:xsl = "http://www.w3.org/1999/XSL/Transform" id = id extension-element-prefixes = tokens exclude-result-prefixes = tokens version = number > <!-- Content: (xsl:import*, top-level-elements) --> **</xsl:stylesheet>**	Root element; outermost element of an XSLT stylesheet which contains all other elements. This root element is illustrated in the section "The <xsl:stylesheet> Element." It's very important to specify the namespace and version correctly.
<xsl:transform> **</xsl:transform>**	Root element; a synonym for xsl:stylesheet with exactly the same attributes and namespace.

TABLE 11-17 *(continued)*

Root or Top-Level Element	*Description*
<xsl:attribute-set name = qname use-attribute-sets = qnames > <!-- Content: xsl:attribute* --> **</xsl:attribute-set>**	Defines a named, reusable set of attributes. Attribute sets are referenced by adding a use-attribute-sets attribute to literal result elements, xsl:element, xsl:copy or xsl:attribute-set. The value of the use-attribute-sets attribute is a white-space-separated list of one or more named attribute sets. For a code example, see Listing 11-18 (pages 634–635).
<xsl:decimal-format name = qname decimal-separator = char grouping-separator = char infinity = string minus-sign = char NaN = string percent = char per-mille = char zero-digit = char digit = char pattern-separator = char />	Declares a decimal-format, which controls the interpretation of either the default or specifically named format pattern used by the format-number function. The attributes of this empty element other than name, such as decimal-separator and grouping-separator, give precise control over numerics for different cultures.
<xsl:import href = uri-reference />	Permits referencing other stylesheets, similar to xsl:include, except imported templates have a *lower import precedence* than templates that appear in the importing document, or documents it includes. *This optional element must precede all other top-level element children* of an xsl:stylesheet element, including any xsl:include element children. For a code example, see Listing 11-40 (pages 680–681).
<xsl:include href = uri-reference />	Permits referencing other stylesheets, similar to a text include in other computer languages. Children of the xsl:stylesheet element in the included document replace the xsl:include element in the including document. The import precedence is exactly as if the included templates had originally appeared in the including document. See the section "Reuse: Including and Importing."
<xsl:key name = qname match = pattern use = expression />	Defines a key that can be referenced later using the function key (name, value) which returns a node-set. This is similar to the XML ID and IDREF concept, but more flexible. The name attribute specifies the key's name. The match attribute is a pattern; an xsl:key element gives information about the keys of any node that matches the pattern specified in the match attribute. The use attribute is an expression specifying the key's values; the expression is evaluated once for each node that matches the pattern. For example, given the key assignment <xsl:key name=" AuthorKey" match="Book" use="Author/Name/Last" />, the following instruction will iterate over all books by Paul McCartney: <xsl:for-each select="key('AuthorKey', 'McCartney')" >. For a code example, see Listing 11-49 (pages 751–755).

continued

TABLE 11-17 Root and Top-Level XSLT Elements (*continued*)

Root or Top-Level Element	*Description*
<xsl:namespace-alias stylesheet-prefix = prefix | "#default" result-prefix = prefix | "#default" />	Allows a stylesheet to define one namespace prefix as an alias for another in the result tree. This is particulary useful if you are transforming documents from one version to another version of the same language.
<xsl:output method = "xml" | "html" | "text" | qname-but-not-ncname version = nmtoken encoding = string omit-xml-declaration = "yes" | "no" standalone = "yes" | "no" doctype-public = string doctype-system = string cdata-section-elements = qnames indent = "yes" | "no" media-type = string />	This empty element allows stylesheet authors to indicate how the result tree should be output. The method attribute controls whether serialization should be "xml", "html", "text" (lowercase strings), or an application-specific format. Other attributes control the XML declaration and CDATA sections. If an XSLT processor outputs the result tree, it should do so as specified by the xsl:output element; however, it is not required to do so. All the xsl:output elements occurring in a single stylesheet (plus any that are included or imported) are merged into a single effective xsl:output element. *Note*: When "html" is specified as the output method, various HTML elements are treated as empty elements: area, basefont, br, col, frame, hr, img, input, isindex, link, meta, and system (in either lowercase or uppercase). See the section "Output Methods Revisited: XML, HTML, Text."
<xsl:param name = qname select = expression > <!-- Content: template --> **</xsl:param>**	Defines a named parameter which is later referenced either via xsl:with-param or with a dollar sign. May appear as a top-level element (in which case it has global scope) or as the *first* child of an xsl:template (local scope). Behaves similarly to xsl:variable except that its *initial value may be overridden* either by a value in the environment (e.g., passed on the command line to the processor) or by the calling template. The parameter may optionally specify a default value by either the select attribute or the content of the xsl:param element itself. This default value applies when the calling template (via xsl:call-template or xsl:apply-templates) does not supply a parameter value by means of xsl:with-param. Similar to a subroutine variable in other languages. See also xsl:with-param. For code examples, see Listings 11-35, 11-37, and 11-38.
<xsl:preserve-space elements = NameTests />	Used to specify the list of elements for which extraneous white space is to be retained. The attribute elements is a list of white-space-separated NameTests, which are element names, or an * wildcard, possibly qualified by a namespace prefix. By default, all elements preserve white space. However, when the reciprocal xsl:strip-space element is used, xsl:preserve-space may be useful to partially negate its effect. See xsl:strip-space.

TABLE 11-17 *(continued)*

Root or Top-Level Element	*Description*
<xsl:strip-space elements = NameTests />	This element is the opposite of xsl:preserve-space since it specifies the list of source tree elements for which extraneous input white space is to be discarded. As in XML, the white space characters are #x20, #x9, #xD, and #xA (space, tab, carriage return, and new line). Initially, the set of white-space-preserving element names contains all element names. If an element name matches a NameTest in an xsl:strip-space element, then it is removed from the set of white-space-preserving element names. If an element name matches a NameTest in an xsl:preserve-space element, then it is added to the set of white-space-preserving element names.
<xsl:template match = pattern name = qname priority = number mode = qname> <!-- Content: (xsl:param*, template) --> </xsl:template>	Each template generates a result tree fragment (a portion of the result of the transformation). Templates are invoked either indirectly by the processor or explicitly via calls from other templates. Either a match pattern or a name attribute must be supplied. The match pattern indicates the nodes or nodes to which the template is to be applied; it may *not* contain a reference to a variable. The name attribute is a handle by which the template can be programatically invoked via the xsl:call-template or xsl:apply-templates instruction. In either case, the content of the template element determines the actions taken when the template is invoked. An optional mode attribute further controls under what circumstances the template is applied. An optional priority attribute plays a role in *conflict resolution* when multiple templates match a given pattern. Template rules can be grouped into modes, can include parameters (via xsl:param), and can be named for later reference via the name attribute. This element is sometimes considered an instruction although it may only appear as a direct child of xsl:stylesheet. See the sections "Templates and Match and Select Patterns" and "Reuse: Named Templates and Passing Parameters."
<xsl:variable name = qname select = expression> <!-- Content: template --> </xsl:variable>	Defines a named storage location that is initialized at runtime either by means of the select attribute or the content of the element. If it is initialized via select, it is an object of any of the types that can be returned by expressions. If initialized via content, the value is either a string or the result of a series of instructions that are children of xsl:variable (i.e., the output of these instructions). When this element is used as a top-level element, the variable has *global scope*. This element is sometimes considered an instruction since it can appear as a child of elements other than xsl:stylesheet, in which case the variable has *local scope*. See the section "Conditionals and Variables."

XSLT Instructions

XSLT elements that are *not immediate children* of the root `<xsl:stylesheet>` element are sometimes called **XSLT instructions**, but the main point of distinction is that an XSLT processor will generate an error if you attempt to use a non-top-level element such as `<xsl:sort>` at the top level (i.e., as a direct child of `<xsl:stylesheet>`). Similarly, if you use a top-level element such as `<xsl:template>` at any level other than top level, the processor will flag this as an error too. Additional restrictions concerning the relative positioning of XSLT elements also apply, such as when present, `<xsl:sort>` must be the first child of `<xsl:apply-templates>` or `<xsl:for-each>`. Such restrictions are indicated in the "`Content:`" comments on the left and/or in the descriptions on the right of Table 11-8.

TABLE 11-18 XSLT Instructions

Instruction Element	*Description*
`<xsl:apply-imports />`	This empty element with no attributes directs the processor to process the context node with the "next matching" pattern from an imported stylesheet. A template rule that is being used to override a template rule in an imported stylesheet can use the `xsl:apply-imports` element to invoke the overridden template rule. This is useful when the intent is to extend (modify) the action of the imported template rule.

`<xsl:apply-templates`
`select = node-set-expression`
`mode = qname>`
`<!-- Content: (xsl:sort | xsl:with-param)* -->`
`</xsl:apply-templates>`
	This instruction indicates when additional templates should be invoked to construct other portions of the result tree. Without a `select` attribute, the `xsl:apply-templates` instruction processes *all children* of the current node, including (unstripped) text nodes. Processing the children entails finding matching templates for each child of the current node. This can become recursive if the children also call `xsl:apply-templates` to process their children. (If stripping of white space nodes has not been enabled for an element, then all white space in the content of the element will be processed as text.) Rather than processing all children, a `select` attribute can be specified to process only those nodes selected by an expression. The value of the `select` attribute is an expression that must evaluate to a node-set. The resultant nodes are processed in document order, unless a child `xsl:sort` element is the first child element contained within the `xsl:apply-templates` instruction. An optional `mode` attribute can also be supplied. Optionally `xsl:apply-templates` may contain `xsl:with-param` children to pass parameters to the template. Note that `xsl:sort` and `xsl:with-param` are the *only possible children* of `xsl:apply-templates`. See also `xsl:call-template` and `xsl:sort`. See the section "XSLT Processing Model." For a code example involving the `mode` attribute, see Listing 11-41 (pages 689–692).

TABLE 11-18 *(continued)*

Instruction Element	*Description*
`<xsl:attribute name = { qname } namespace = {uri-ref} > <!-- Content: template --> </xsl:attribute>`	The purpose of the `xsl:attribute` element is to enable dynamically or conditionally adding attributes to the result tree. Instantiating an `xsl:attribute` element adds an attribute node to the containing result tree element node, which *may either be a literal result element or one created with* `xsl:element`. This element has a required `name` attribute, which becomes the name of the attribute in the output, and an optional `namespace` attribute. The value of the attribute is determined by the content of the `xsl:attribute` element. For a code example, see Listing 11-18 (pages 634–635).
`<xsl:call-template name = qname> <!-- Content: xsl:with-param* --> </xsl:call-template>`	The `xsl:call-template` element is used to explicitly invoke another template by name. This call is typically from another template and often includes parameters passed via `xsl:with-param`. In contrast to `xsl:apply-templates`, `xsl:call-template` does not change the current node or the current node list. For a code example, see Listing 11-35 (pages 670–671).
`<xsl:choose> <!-- Content: (xsl:when+, xsl:otherwise?) --> </xsl:choose>`	This element and its children are analogous to a multiple decision statement in other computer languages. The `xsl:choose` element encloses multiple alternatives, each represented by an `xsl:when` element followed by an optional `xsl:otherwise` element. The content of the *first* `xsl:when` element whose expression evaluates to true is inserted into the result tree. If no `xsl:when` expression evaluates to true and if the optional `xsl:otherwise` instruction is present, then the content of `xsl:otherwise` element is delivered to the result tree by default. For a code example, see Listing 11-14 (pages 622–623).
`<xsl:comment> <!-- Content: template --> </xsl:comment>`	This instruction simply inserts an XML comment into the result tree with `<!-- .... -->` syntax. The content of the `xsl:comment` element is a template for the string value of the resultant comment node.
`<xsl:copy use-attribute-sets = qnames > <!-- Content: template --> </xsl:copy>`	The `xsl:copy` instruction provides an easy way to copy the current node. It is often used with the XML output method but is not limited to XML to XML transformations. The content of the `xsl:copy` element is copied directly into the result tree. This is a *shallow copy*: namespace nodes of the current node are automatically copied, but attributes and children of the node are not automatically copied. However, attributes can be copied if the `xsl:copy` contains a child `xsl:apply-templates` with `select="@*"`. To achieve a deep copy, include a child `xsl:apply-templates` with `select="node()|@*"`. See also `xsl:copy-of`. For a code example, see Listing 11-19 (pages 638–639).

continued

TABLE 11-18 XSLT Instructions (*continued*)

Instruction Element	*Description*
`<xsl:copy-of` `  select = expression />`	In contrast to `xsl:copy`, the `xsl:copy-of` instruction provides a *deep copy* capability. Whereas `xsl:copy` uses content to describe what to copy, `xsl:copy-of` uses its required `select` attribute which contains an expression. When the result of evaluating the expression is a result tree fragment, the complete fragment is copied to the result tree (without converting it to a string as `xsl:value-of` does). When the result is a node-set, all the nodes in the set are copied in document order into the result tree. Unlike `xsl:copy`, copying an element node copies the attribute nodes, namespace nodes and children of the element node as well as the element node itself. If the expression evaluates to neither a result tree fragment nor a node-set, this instruction behaves like `xsl:value-of`. For a code example, see Listing 11-22 (page 642).

`<xsl:element`
`  name = { qname }`
`  namespace = { uri-reference }`
`  use-attribute-sets = qnames>`
`  <!-- Content: template -->`
`</xsl:element>`
	This instruction is used to create an element with a dynamically computed name. The content of the `xsl:element` element is a template for the attributes and children of the created element. The `name` attribute is interpreted as an *attribute value template* (i.e., `name="{$someVariable}"`). It is an error if the string that results from instantiating the attribute value template is not a `QName` (qualified name, which has a local part and an optional prefix and colon). See the section "Attribute Value Templates." For code examples, see Listings 11-22 and 11-25.

`<xsl:fallback>`
`  <!-- Content: template -->`
`</xsl:fallback>`
	The `xsl:fallback` generally occurs only as a child of an *extension element*. This element is evaluated only if the extension element cannot be interpreted.

`<xsl:for-each`
`  select = node-set-expression>`
`  <!-- Content: (xsl:sort*,`
`template) -->`
`</xsl:for-each>`
	This instruction permits iteration of elements that match the `node-set-expression` given by the required `select` attribute. For each node selected by evaluating the `node-set-expression`, the effect is to execute the inner template, with the current node being the next node in the node-set. Although the default iteration order is *document order*, if `xsl:for-each` contains one or more `xsl:sort` children, the selected nodes are sorted *before* the iteration begins. If present, the `xsl:sort` instructions must appear before any others in the body of the `xsl:for-each`. In any event, the `xsl:for-each` content template is applied to each node as it is iterated. See `xsl:sort`. For a code example, see Listing 11-26 (pages 649–650).

`<xsl:if`
`  test = boolean-expression>`
`  <!-- Content: template -->`
`</xsl:if>`
	This element provides a basic, single branch conditional. If the `test` expression returns a true value, the content of the `xsl:if` element is evaluated and inserted into the result tree. See also `xsl:choose`. For code examples, see Listings 11-13 (page 617) and 11-47 (pages 728–730).

TABLE 11-18 *(continued)*

Instruction Element	*Description*
`<xsl:message terminate = "yes" | "no"> <!-- Content: template --> </xsl:message>`	The `xsl:message` instruction sends a message to the invoker of the stylesheet in a way that is dependent on the XSLT processor. Exactly how (and whether) the processor responds to the message depends on the environment as well as what messages the processor understands. For example, if run from the command line, the messages could be sent to `stdout` or `stderr`, but if run from a server-side environment, the messages might be directed to a logfile or simply ignored. If the `terminate` attribute is "yes", the processor is supposed to stop processing after generating the message. This instruction is often used as a debugging aid when developing stylesheets and sometimes in production systems to detect unexpected error situations.
`<xsl:number level = "single" | "multiple" | "any" count = pattern from = pattern value = number-expression format = { string } lang = { nmtoken } letter-value = { "alphabetic" | "traditional" } grouping-separator = { char } grouping-size = { number } />`	The `xsl:number` instruction is used to insert a formatted number into the result tree. The number to be inserted may be specified by the `value` attribute, which must contain an expression that evaluates to a number. The expression is evaluated and the resulting object is converted to a number as if by a call to the XPath `number()` function. If no `value` attribute is specified, then the `xsl:number` element inserts a number based on the position of the current node in the source tree (potentially influenced by the `count`, `level`, and `from` attributes). Various attributes can be combined to make this a very flexible, multipurposed instruction. The value of the `format` attribute can be "1", "A", "a", "I", or "i", resulting in sequences of integer, uppercase letters, lowercase letters, Roman numerals, or lowercase Roman numerals, respectively. The format value "01" causes the sequence "01", "02", "03", ... "09", "10", etc. to be generated. The instruction `xsl:number` is often used to number nodes in the source tree, to indicate the position of the node with respect to siblings of the same element name. However, when `xsl:number` includes a `value` attribute, numbering is with respect to the current node list. See also the XSLT `format-number()` function. For code examples, see Listings 11-42 and 11-48.
`<xsl:otherwise> <!-- Content: template --> </xsl:otherwise>`	This defines the (optional) default case in `xsl:choose` instructions. If none of the `xsl:when` alternatives evaluate to true, the content of `xsl:otherwise` element is delivered to the result tree by default. For a code example, see Listing 11-14.
`<xsl:processing-instruction name = { ncname }> <!-- Content: template --> </xsl:processing-instruction>`	This instruction inserts an XML processing instruction into the result tree. The `name` attribute becomes the target of the PI and the content becomes the PI data. For example: `<xsl:processing-instruction name="MyPI">foobar newbar="17.5"</xsl:processing-instruction>` results in the PI `<?MyPI foobar newbar="17.5"?>`.

continued

TABLE 11-18 XSLT Instructions (*continued*)

Instruction Element	*Description*
<xsl:sort select = string-expression lang = { nmtoken } data-type = { "text" | "number" |qname-but-not-ncname} order = { "ascending" | "descending" } case-order = { "upper-first" | "lower-first" } />	The xsl:sort instruction is used to override the default document order traversal. It may appear as the *first* child of either xsl:for-each or xsl:apply-templates, but nowhere else. Multiple sort keys can be achieved by including multiple xsl:sort elements, the first of which represents the primary sort key, the second of which is the secondary sort key, and so on. The select attribute defines the key by which to sort. The data-type attribute should only be "number" when numeric content is being sorted; the default is "text". The default order is "ascending". For code examples, see Listings 11-26 and 11-27.
<xsl:text disable-output-escaping = "yes" | "no"> <!-- Content: #PCDATA --> **</xsl:text>**	The xsl:text instruction is used to wrap literal text (parsed character data). This wrapping may change what white space characters are stripped but does not otherwise affect the XSLT processor's handling of characters. The content of this instruction can only be non-markup text; it cannot have element children, meaning that even HTML elements like <b> and <i> must appear *outside* xsl:text. By default, disable-output-escaping is "no". Change this attribute to "yes" if you need to output special characters (character entities) in HTML such as the copyright symbol: Copyright <xsl:text disable-output- escaping="yes">©</xsl:text> However, with XML output, setting disable-output-escaping to "yes" can result in documents that aren't well-formed. See the section "Central Concepts."
<xsl:value-of select = string-expression disable-output-escaping = "yes" | "no" />	The xsl:value-of instruction is the way to extract the value of an element, an attribute, an expression, or a variable to create a text node in the result tree. The required select attribute is an XPath expression that is converted to a string. Most of the examples in this chapter use xsl:value-of. See the section "Value of a Node or Expression." See Table 11-9 (page 708) for values of various node types.
<xsl:when test = boolean-expression> <!-- Content: template --> **</xsl:when>**	The xsl:when element represents the nondefault branches of the xsl:choose instruction. If the test expression evaluates to true, the contents of the xsl:when element are delivered to the result tree. For a code example, see Listing 11-14.
<xsl:with-param name = qname select = expression> <!-- Content: template --> **</xsl:with-param>**	The xsl:with-param instruction passes a parameter value to a template that contains an xsl:param element with the matching name attribute (required). Use the required select attribute to set the value of the parameter. The xsl:with-param element may be contained in an xsl:call-template or xsl:apply-templates instruction, but nowhere else. See also xsl:param. For code examples, see Listings 11-35, 11-37, and 11-38.

XSLT Functions

Sections 12 and 15 of the XSLT Recommendation add nine functions to those already defined in XPath. These so-called XSLT functions are described in Table 11-19 and in the code example and screenshots following the table.

Examples of XSLT Functions

Nearly all of these XSLT functions plus the `<xsl:key>` element are illustrated in the stylesheet in Listing 11-49. The file `c6-xslt-func.xsl` has a more detailed `<xsl:stylesheet>` element than any we've encountered so far. I've declared namespaces for both Xalan and Saxon processors, as well as provided a space-separated list of `extension-element-prefixes`, namely "xalan" and "saxon". In fact, we'll try this stylesheet with both Xalan and Saxon to compare the results, which we would expect to differ for reasons that will soon become apparent. The result of applying this stylesheet to `collection6.xml` (and, indirectly, `collection7.xml`) is shown in Figures 11-24 (page 758), 11-25 (page 759), and 11-26 (page 761).

TABLE 11-19 XSLT Functions

Return Type	*Function Name (arguments)*	*Description*
`node-set`	**`current`**`()`	Returns a node-set consisting of the *current* node, which is usually the same as the *context* node (abbreviated as `"."`), except in certain cases when the function is called as part of an XPath predicate. In other words, `current()` always yields the node that was originally the current node at the *beginning* of the evaluation of an expression (since the notion of the current node may change during expression evaluation). This may be different from the abbreviated syntax `"."` which refers to the current node *at any point* during evaluation. For example, in a template processing `Foo` elements, `select="elt[. = current()/@bar]"` selects child elements named `elt` whose value equals the value of the currently processing `Foo` element's `bar` attribute. The document filename is indicated by the `object` parameter. See Listing 11-42.
`node-set`	**`document`**`(object, node-set?)`	Permits access to nodes of *other* documents. Returns a node-set consisting of the referenced document's root node. See Listing 11-49 for a code example.
`boolean`	**`element-available`**`(string)`	Used to check whether a specific XSLT element is known to the processor. This is generally useful only if you want to check for *extension elements*. See Listing 11-49 for a code example.

continued

TABLE 11-19 XSLT Functions (*continued*)

Return Type	*Function Name (arguments)*	*Description*
string	**format-number**(number, formatString, decimalFormat?)	Permits nondefault display of numbers according to the formatString attribute and the optional decimalFormat attribute. The function converts its number argument to a string using the format pattern string specified by the formatString argument and the decimalFormat named by the third argument, or the default decimal format, if there is no third argument. The formatString pattern is in the syntax specified by the JDK 1.1 DecimalFormat class. For example, format-number(0.1748,'#.#%') results in 17.5% and format-number(0.1748, '#.##') results in 0.17. See also the <xsl:decimal-format> element. See Listings 11-48 and 11-49 for code examples.
boolean	**function-available**(string)	Used to check whether a specific XSLT function is known to the processor. This is generally useful only if you want to check for *extension functions*. See Listing 11-49 for a code example.
string	**generate-id**(node-set)	Primarily used to generate attributes of type ID and IDREF in an XML document, or <a name> and <a href> elements in HTML documents. Returns a string (that adheres to the XML Name conventions) that uniquely identifies the specified node, or the first node in document order if a node-set is provided. If no argument is provided, the context node is used. The resultant id will consist entirely of alphanumeric characters with an alphabetic first character. An implementation is free to generate an identifier in any convenient way provided that it always generates the *same identifier for the same node* and *different identifiers for different nodes*. An implementation is under no obligation to generate the same ids *each time* a document is transformed (but most do). Two XSLT processors are likely to generate *different* ids for the same node. However, the id will be unique across all nodes in the current document. Therefore, this function can be used to test whether two nodes are the same: <xsl:if test="generate-id($nodeA) = generate-id($nodeB)">. See also the id() function and the key() function. See Listing 11-49 for a code example.

TABLE 11-19 *(continued)*

Return Type	*Function Name (arguments)*	*Description*
`node-set`	**`key`**`(keyname, value)`	Returns a node-set consisting of nodes that match the name `keyname` *and* have the value given by the `value` attribute. To assign key names and values to nodes, see the `xsl:key` top-level element in Table 11-17. For example, given the key assignment `<xsl:key name="AuthorKey" match="Book" use="Author/Name/Last" />`, the following instruction will iterate over all books by Paul McCartney: `<xsl:for-each select="key('AuthorKey', 'McCartney')" >`. See Listing 11-49 for a code example.
`object`	**`system-property`**`(string)`	Returns the value of one of a vendor-specific set of properties. The basic properties that all processors are required to support are `xsl:version`, `xsl:vendor`, and `xsl:vendor-url`. See Listing 11-49 for a code example.
`string`	**`unparsed-entity-uri`**`(string)`	Returns the (relative or absolute) URI of the specified unparsed entity (given by the `string` argument) declared in the DTD associated with the current document, if there is one.

Listing 11-49 XSLT Functions Code Example (c6-xslt-func.xsl)

```
<?xml version="1.0"?>
<xsl:stylesheet   version="1.0"
  xmlns:xsl="http://www.w3.org/1999/XSL/Transform"
  xmlns:xalan="http://xml.apache.org/xalan"
  xmlns:saxon="http://icl.com/saxon"
  extension-element-prefixes="xalan saxon"
>
<!--   Older Saxon namespace was:
       xmlns:saxon="http://com.icl.saxon.functions.Extensions"
-->

<xsl:output method="html" indent="yes" encoding="ISO-8859-1" />

<xsl:variable name="label">XSLT: XSLT Functions and Key</xsl:variable>

<xsl:key name="TitleKey" match="CD | Book" use="Title" />
<xsl:key name="PriceKey" match="CD | Book" use="ListPrice" />
<xsl:key name="AuthorKey" match="Book" use="Author/Name/Last" />

<xsl:template match="/">
   <html>
     <head>
       <title><xsl:value-of select="$label" /></title>
```

```
</head>
<body>
  <!-- Note conditional setting of variable. -->
  <xsl:variable name="processor">
    <xsl:choose>
      <xsl:when
       test="contains(system-property('xsl:vendor'), 'SAXON')" >
           SAXON</xsl:when>
      <xsl:when
       test="contains(system-property('xsl:vendor'), 'Apache')" >
           Xalan</xsl:when>
      <xsl:otherwise>Unknown</xsl:otherwise>
    </xsl:choose>
  </xsl:variable>

  <h2><xsl:value-of select="$label" /></h2>
    <!--
         This example defines other namespaces for referencing
         extension functions. See the xsl:stylesheet element.
    -->
    <h3>function-available: <xsl:value-of select="$processor" /></h3>

    <xsl:text>xsl:function-available('element-available') = </xsl:text>
    <xsl:value-of select="function-available('element-available')" />
    <br />
    <xsl:text>xalan:difference = </xsl:text>
    <xsl:value-of select="function-available('xalan:difference')" />
    <br />

    <xsl:choose>
      <xsl:when test="$processor='SAXON'">
        <xsl:text>saxon:foobar = </xsl:text>
        <xsl:value-of select="function-available('saxon:foobar')" />
      </xsl:when>
      <xsl:when test="$processor='Xalan'">
        <xsl:text>xalan:foobar = </xsl:text>
        <xsl:value-of select="function-available('xalan:foobar')" />
      </xsl:when>
      <xsl:otherwise>
        <xsl:text>foobar = </xsl:text>
        <xsl:value-of select="function-available('foobar')" />
      </xsl:otherwise>
    </xsl:choose>
    <br />

    <xsl:text>saxon:difference = </xsl:text>
    <xsl:value-of select="function-available('saxon:difference')" />
    <br />
    <xsl:text>saxon:forAll = </xsl:text>
    <xsl:value-of select="function-available('saxon:forAll')" />
    <br />

    <h3>element-available: <xsl:value-of select="$processor" /></h3>
```

```
<xsl:text>xsl:text = </xsl:text>
<xsl:value-of select="element-available('xsl:text')" />
<br />
<xsl:text>xsl:foobar = </xsl:text>
<xsl:value-of select="element-available('xsl:foobar')" />
<br />
<xsl:text>xsl:message = </xsl:text>
<xsl:value-of select="element-available('xsl:message')" />
<br />

<xsl:text>xalan:difference = </xsl:text>
<xsl:value-of select="element-available('xalan:difference')" />
<br />

<xsl:choose>
  <xsl:when test="$processor='SAXON'">
    <xsl:text>saxon:foobar = </xsl:text>
    <xsl:value-of select="element-available('saxon:foobar')" />
  </xsl:when>
  <xsl:when test="$processor='Xalan'">
    <xsl:text>xalan:foobar = </xsl:text>
    <xsl:value-of select="element-available('xalan:foobar')" />
  </xsl:when>
  <xsl:otherwise>
    <xsl:text>foobar = </xsl:text>
    <xsl:value-of select="element-available('foobar')" />
  </xsl:otherwise>
</xsl:choose>
<br />

<xsl:text>saxon:preview = </xsl:text>
<xsl:value-of select="element-available('saxon:preview')" />
<br />
<xsl:text>saxon:script = </xsl:text>
<xsl:value-of select="element-available('saxon:script')" />

<h3>system-property</h3>

<xsl:text>xsl:version = </xsl:text>
<xsl:value-of select="system-property('xsl:version')" />
<br />
<xsl:text>xsl:vendor = </xsl:text>
<xsl:value-of select="system-property('xsl:vendor')" />
<br />
<xsl:text>xsl:vendor-url = </xsl:text>
<xsl:value-of select="system-property('xsl:vendor-url')" />

<h3>document</h3>

<xsl:text>document('collection7.xml')/Collection/CD[1]/Title =
</xsl:text>
<i><xsl:value-of
    select="document('collection7.xml')/Collection/CD[1]/Title" /></i>
<br />
```

```
<xsl:variable name="doc" select="document('collection7.xml')" />

<xsl:text>$doc/Collection/Book[1]/Title = </xsl:text>
<i><xsl:value-of select="$doc/Collection/Book[1]/Title" /></i>
<br />
<xsl:text>document('collection7.xml')/Collection/CD[2] = </xsl:text>
<xsl:value-of select="document('collection7.xml')/Collection/CD[2]" />
<br />

<h3>format-number</h3>

<xsl:text>ListPrice of </xsl:text>
<i><xsl:value-of select="$doc//CD[1]/Title" /></i>
<xsl:text> is $</xsl:text>
<xsl:value-of select="$doc//CD[1]/ListPrice" />
<br />
<xsl:text>ListPrice of </xsl:text>
<i><xsl:value-of select="$doc//Book[1]/Title" /></i>
<xsl:text> is $</xsl:text>
<xsl:value-of select="$doc//Book[1]/ListPrice" />
<br />
<xsl:text>Combined price using format-number(sum($doc//ListPrice),
    '$#.00') = </xsl:text>
<xsl:value-of select="format-number(sum($doc//ListPrice), '$#.00')" />

<h3>key</h3>
<!--
     If we know only one match is possible, we could save the
     node in a variable for subsequent processing.
-->
<xsl:variable name="FoundPrice" select="key('PriceKey', '24.95')" />
<xsl:text>Found key('PriceKey', '24.95') with Title = </xsl:text>
<i><xsl:value-of select="$FoundPrice/Title" /></i>
<br />
<!--
     Although it doesn't apply in the first case, we could iterate
     over all of the instances that match a particular key,
     for example, if multiple books had the same author.
-->
<xsl:for-each select="key('TitleKey', 'Venus and Mars')" >
  <xsl:text>Found key('TitleKey', 'Venus and Mars') with ListPrice
      = $</xsl:text>
  <xsl:value-of select="./ListPrice" />
</xsl:for-each>
<br />
<xsl:for-each select="key('AuthorKey', 'McCartney')" >
  <xsl:text>Found key('AuthorKey', 'McCartney') with Title =
       </xsl:text>
  <i><xsl:value-of select="./Title" /></i>
  <br />
</xsl:for-each>

<h3>generate-id</h3>

<b>pass 1: Book and CD Nodes</b><br />
```

```
        <xsl:for-each select="//Book | //CD" >
          <i><xsl:value-of select="./Title" /></i>
          <xsl:text>, id = </xsl:text>
          <xsl:value-of select="generate-id()" />
          <br />
        </xsl:for-each>

        <b>pass 2: Title Nodes</b><br />
        <xsl:for-each select="//CD/Title | //Book/Title" >
          <i><xsl:value-of select="." /></i>
          <xsl:text>, id = </xsl:text>
          <xsl:value-of select="generate-id()" />
          <br />
        </xsl:for-each>

        <b>pass 3: Revisit Book and CD Nodes</b><br />
        <xsl:for-each select="//Book | //CD" >
          <i><xsl:value-of select="./Title" /></i>
          <xsl:text>, id = </xsl:text>
          <xsl:value-of select="generate-id()" />
          <br />
        </xsl:for-each>

    </body>
  </html>
</xsl:template>

</xsl:stylesheet>
```

The key() function and the associated <xsl:key> instruction provide a handy lookup capability more powerful than the basic XML ID and IDREF attributes because keys can associate one or more nodes with a given key. To demonstrate the key() function, the stylesheet contains three <xsl:key> top-level elements:

```
<xsl:key name="TitleKey" match="CD | Book" use="Title" />
<xsl:key name="PriceKey" match="CD | Book" use="ListPrice" />
<xsl:key name="AuthorKey" match="Book" use="Author/Name/Last" />
```

This defines three keys; in each instance, the use attribute is interpreted with respect to the context node(s) selected by the match attribute, effectively concatenating the two paths. The first of these keys is a TitleKey based on the string value of the nodes //CD/Title and //Book/Title (i.e., the titles of all CDs and books). The second <xsl:key> instruction defines a PriceKey based on //CD/ListPrice and //Book/ListPrice, and the third defines an AuthorKey based only on books and set to the author's last name, as given by the XPath expression //Book/Author/Name/Last. Much later in the code, the key() function is used to select nodes matching specific keys, for example:

```
<xsl:variable name="FoundPrice" select="key('PriceKey', '24.95')" /> ....
```

This sets the variable $FoundPrice to the *node* that has the ListPrice of 24.95, which, as we can see from Figure 11-25 on page 759, is the book whose Title is *Complete Beatles Chronicle, The*. Key references can also be iterated, such as with the <xsl:for-each> instruction:

```
<xsl:for-each select="key('TitleKey', 'Venus and Mars')" > ....
<xsl:for-each select="key('AuthorKey', 'McCartney')" > ....
```

The first of these iterates through all nodes whose Title is *Venus and Mars*. Since there is only one such node, this loop has only one iteration. In the second case, however, there are two books for which Paul McCartney is the author, *Many Years From Now* and *Beatles Anthology, The,* although he is actually *one* of four authors of the latter title. (This works because he's listed as the first author of that title.)

Next, the code example illustrates the setting of a variable named $processor based on a runtime check on which XSLT processor is being run.

```
<xsl:variable name="processor">
 <xsl:choose>
   <xsl:when
    test="contains(system-property('xsl:vendor'),'SAXON')">SAXON</xsl:when>
   <xsl:when
    test="contains(system-property('xsl:vendor'),'Apache')">Xalan</xsl:when>
   <xsl:otherwise>Unknown</xsl:otherwise>
 </xsl:choose>
</xsl:variable>
```

The current XSLT processor is determined by checking for a substring of the string returned by the function call:

```
system-property('xsl:vendor')
```

The contains() function checks for a substring since the actual string here is "SAXON 6.5 from Michael Kay". Since contains() is case-sensitive, our code checks for "SAXON" rather than "Saxon". The variable $processor is therefore set to either "SAXON" or "Xalan" depending on the value of the xsl:vendor property. If you use a different XSLT processor, add another <xsl:when> branch for that processor's xsl:vendor property. Since the variable is defined as a top-level element, it is in scope for the remainder of the stylesheet. This code illustrates how to set a variable to the result of evaluating the content of an inner instruction (<xsl:choose> in this case).

Turning our attention to the XSLT function called function-available(), we see how we can test for standard XSLT functions like element-available(), but it is more useful when checking for **extension functions**, such as xalan:difference() supported by Xalan and saxon:difference() supported by Saxon. Note the necessary namespace prefix before the name of the extension function. Figure 11-24 shows the results for Xalan (on the left) and Saxon (on the right). Results are as you would expect, with standard functions like `element-available()` in both cases, but processor-specific functions are available only for a given processor.

Similarly, the function `element-available()` is useful in determining whether an **extension element** is implemented by a particular processor. The function informs us that `<xsl:text>` and `<xsl:message>` are valid XSLT elements, and `<xsl:foobar>` is not. Note that although `xalan:difference()` is a valid extension *function* supported by Xalan, it is not a valid extension *element*. The stylesheet also tests for the `<saxon:preview>` element, a valid extension element from Saxon. Since we're running the Xalan processor, it does not know about elements from the Saxon namespace.[14]

Figure 11-25 shows the result of using the function `system-property()` to check for the three standard properties, `xsl:version`, `xsl:vendor`, and `xsl:vendor-url`. The screenshot was taken with earlier versions of both Xalan and Saxon. At the time of this writing, the results using Xalan 2.2. D14 (a developers' release) and Saxon 6.5 are slightly different:

```
xsl:version = 1
xsl:vendor = Apache Software Foundation
xsl:vendor-url = http://xml.apache.org/xalan-j

xsl:version = 1
xsl:vendor = SAXON 6.5 from Michael Kay
xsl:vendor-url = http://saxon.sf.net/
```

Note that Apache does not include a version number in its `xsl:vendor` string, but Saxon does. The `xsl:vendor-url` property has changed for both processors. The point here is that if you intend to take conditional action based on this information, you should be very careful about the substrings your code examines.

In addition to the output of the `key()` function discussed earlier, Figure 11-25 also shows results of trying two other XSLT functions, `document()` and `format-number()`. The `document()` function is useful to process a document other than the one originally passed to the XSLT processor. It returns the *root* node (rather than the document element) of the document named as an argument. For this example, I supplied `collection7.xml` shown in Listing 11-50 on page 760. This `Collection` instance consists of only one `CD` and one `Book` element. As the output indicates, we can directly use the root node returned by `document()` in an XPath expression to, for example, obtain the title of the first `CD` element. Note that this first CD, *Double Fantasy*, does not appear in the hierarchy of our original command-line input docu-

14. Actually, the Saxon results of *false* for `saxon:preview` and `saxon:script` are surprising to this author since these are two of the many extension elements defined by Saxon. See *http://saxon.sourceforge.net/saxon6.5/extensions.html.*

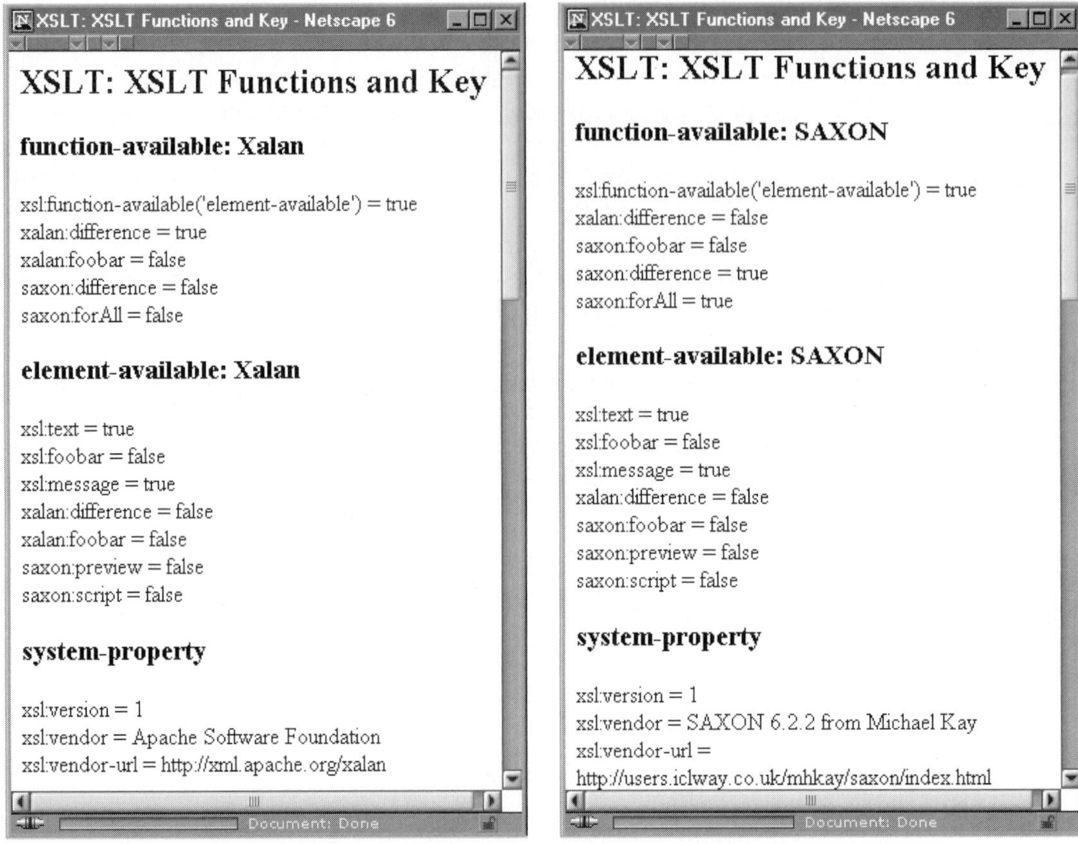

FIGURE 11-24 Output from XSLT functions: Xalan vs. SAXON

ment, `collection6.xml`, proving that the processor did indeed access the file named in the function call. Alternatively, we can use `<xsl:variable>` to save the node as a variable so it can be used later in an XPath expression, as we did to extract the title of `Book[1]`. When we try to take the value of the second `CD` element, there is no output because `collection7.xml` does not contain two CDs.

```
document('collection7.xml')/Collection/CD[1]/Title = Double Fantasy
$doc/Collection/Book[1]/Title = Beatles: After The Break-Up, The
document('collection7.xml')/Collection/CD[2] =
```

Note that after calling the `document()` function, the root of the original input file, `collection6.xml`, is no longer accessible. In cases where you anticipate a need to make such a reference, it's necessary to save the root in a variable prior to invoking `document()`:

```
<xsl:variable name="origRoot" select="/" />
```

The `format-number()` function is necessary sometimes when the double precision numbers used in XSLT don't display the way you'd like. In our example, we use an XPath expression that ultimately returns a number representing all `ListPrice` children of the `$doc` node, previously saved in the variable `$doc` from the call to `document('collection7.xml')`. The `sum()` function adds the prices and then `format-number()` applies the format pattern string '$#.00' to indicate that the result should start with a dollar sign and contain two decimal places.

```
Combined price using format-number(sum($doc//ListPrice), '$#.00') = $52.92
```

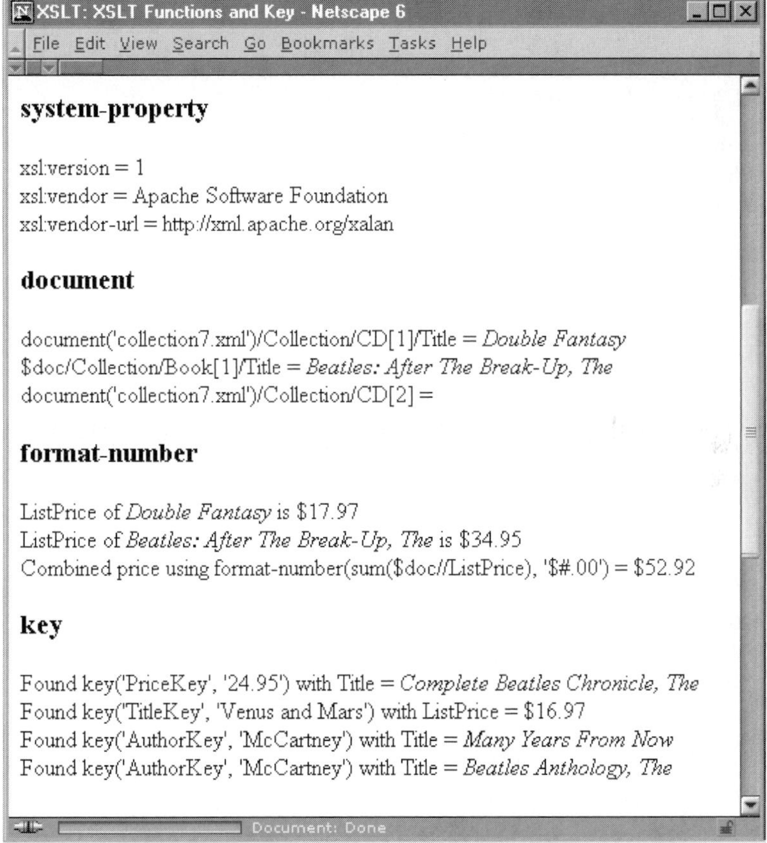

FIGURE 11-25 Output from XSLT functions: document, format-number and key

Listing 11-50 Instance Accessed via document() Function (collection7.xml)

```
<?xml version="1.0" standalone="yes"?>
<Collection version="2" xmlns:xhtml="http://www.w3.org/1999/xhtml"
xmlns:html="http://www.w3.org/TR/REC-html40">
  <CD>
    <Title>Double Fantasy</Title>
    <Artist>Lennon, John and Ono, Yoko</Artist>
    <Chart>
      <Peak weeks="8">1</Peak>
      <Peak country="UK">1</Peak><!-- guess -->
    </Chart>
    <Type>Rock</Type>
    <Label>Capitol</Label>
    <Label country="UK">EMI</Label>
    <AlbumReleased>1980</AlbumReleased>
    <Remastered format="3 bonus tracks and photos">October 10, 2000
        </Remastered>
    <Notes>Released 2 days before Lennon was murdered.
1981 Grammy for Album of the Year.</Notes>
    <ListPrice>17.97</ListPrice>
  </CD>
  <Book>
    <Title>Beatles: After The Break-Up, The</Title>
    <Author>
      <Name>
        <First>Keith</First>
        <Last>Badman</Last>
      </Name>
    </Author>
    <Type>Chronology</Type>
    <Published publisher="Omnibus Press">1999</Published>
    <Notes>631 pp. Covers the years 1970 through 1999 and a brief mention
of 2000. Day-by-day diary format. Extensive coverage of Lennon's murder on
December 8, 1980.
    </Notes>
    <ListPrice>34.95</ListPrice>
  </Book>
  <Owner>
    <Name sex="male">
      <First>Ken</First>
      <Last>Sall</Last>
    </Name>
    <Address>
      <Street>123 Milky Way Dr.</Street>
      <City>Columbia</City>
      <State>MD</State>
      <Zip>20794</Zip>
    </Address>
  </Owner>
</Collection>
```

Our last experiment with XSLT functions demonstrated in the earlier Listing 11-49 involves the `generate-id()` function. We call `generate-id()` three times in our code example: first in pass 1, it is used to create ids for each `Book` or `CD` element, and then in pass 2 for each `Title` element. As you can tell from Figure 11-26, which shows Xalan results on the left and Saxon on the right, each id is unique. However,

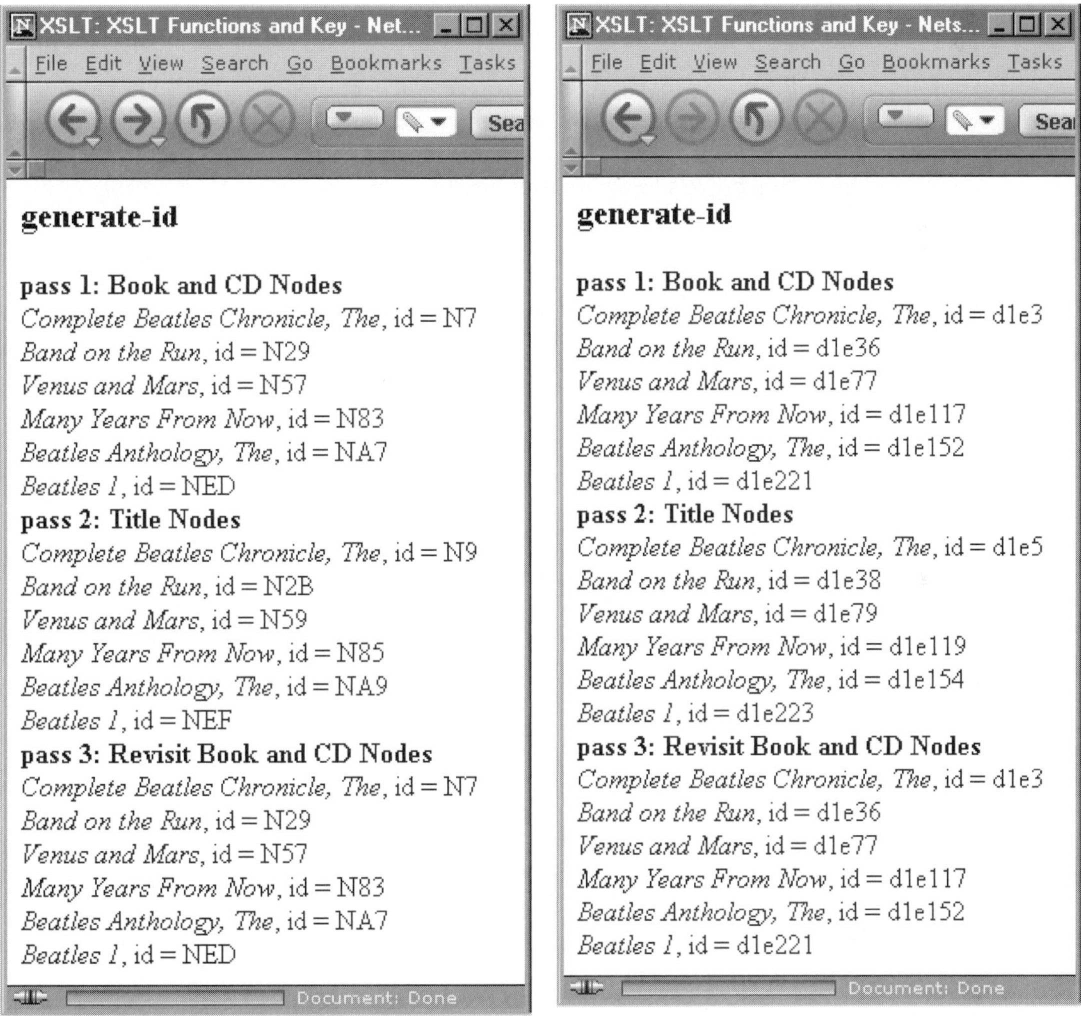

FIGURE 11-26 Output from XSLT generate-id function: Xalan vs. Saxon (generate-id)

when we again call `generate-id()` in pass 3 for all `Book` and `CD` elements, we obtain the same ids as in pass 1. Several conclusions can be drawn:

- Each node (at all levels in the hierarchy) can be identified by a unique id.
- The same id is always generated for a given node by a particular processor, for one execution of the processor. The specification says that these ids may vary in different runs, but this does not happen with Xalan or Saxon. (However, with Xalan 1.x, nodes were of the form N83, but with Xalan 2.x they are of the form N10083.)
- Ids generated by two processors for the same node need not be at all similar.

This concludes our formal presentation of XSLT and XPath. In the next section, we apply many of the concepts learned in this chapter (as well as CSS concepts from chapter 10) to solve a real-world problem, namely how to generate HTML link pages from this book's "For Further Exploration" sections.

Case Study: Generating Link Pages from This Book's "For Further Exploration" Sections

Problem Statement and Goals

When I began writing this book, I wanted the huge number of XML links that I had amassed to become an integral part of the project. In addition to the typical references to specific Web pages in the body of the text, I planned to include a "For Further Exploration" section at the end of each chapter for readers who craved more details and possibly more current information. Of course, I realized the printed pages of links wouldn't be nearly as useful as a Web site that contained all the links from the book, arranged by chapter and perhaps eventually by other sorts. I also wanted the printed pages to contain the links. At the same time, I wanted a reasonable case study that exercised material I had presented about XSLT, XPath, and CSS that would serve as an exercise for readers who wished to test what they had learned.

This book was written using Adobe FrameMaker 5.5.6 which, among many other great features, has the ability to save a chapter as XML with a corresponding CSS stylesheet to display it. I examined the structure FrameMaker created and decided the exercise would be to write a stylesheet that extracts the link titles and URLs and produces a link list for each chapter. The specific requirements for the stylesheet in this exercise (case study) are:

- Handle imperfect XML input, not well structured (as we'll discuss in the next section)
- Filter out only the "For Further Exploration" section regardless of what else appears in the chapter

- For each link title and URL in the section, create an HTML list item, `<li>` and link, <a>
- Accept command-line specification of the chapter number and the chapter title (default values for each should be supplied by the stylesheet to make it clear when nothing was provided on the command line)
- Accept command-line option for either sorting the links by their title or leaving them in document order (defaulting to unsorted)
- Use attribute value templates to specify HTML `style` attributes for parts of the output page, such as for the page header (which uses chapter number and chapter title) and footer (which uses other variables that represent the name of the book, the author, the publisher, etc.)
- Count the number of footnotes in each chapter (just for grins)

The desired result for chapter 9 for the unsorted links case is shown in Figure 11-27. The samples on the CD-ROM are `book-ch9-less-sorted.html` and `book-ch9-less-unsorted.html`.

Examining the Generated XML Structure

The XML structure generated by FrameMaker 5.5.6 is not particularly hierarchical. FrameMaker essentially converts each format style into an element, which is fine, but most elements so generated aren't containers. For example, the "For Further Exploration" section is an `HC` (heading level C) FrameMaker paragraph format, but it doesn't necessarily include all of the things *in* that section, such as the links and link titles, corresponding to the formats I created called `Link-URL` and `Link-Title`. That is, you might *expect* something like

```
<HC>
 <Title>For Further Exploration</Title>
 <Links>
   <Link>
     <Link-Title>One Great Site</Link-Title>
     <Link-URL>http://one-place.com</Link-URL>
   </Link>
   <Link>
     <Link-Title>Another Great Site</Link-Title>
     <Link-URL>http://another-place.com</Link-URL>
   </Link>
   <!-- etc. -->
 </Links>
</HC>
```

But FrameMaker 5.5.6 actually generates something like the structure shown in Figure 11-28 (page 766). I've actually made three modifications to suit our purposes here.

1. The association with the CSS stylesheet via a processing instruction has been commented out so that the XML can be displayed in IE 5.5 using IE's default stylesheet, allowing us to see the hierarchy more easily.

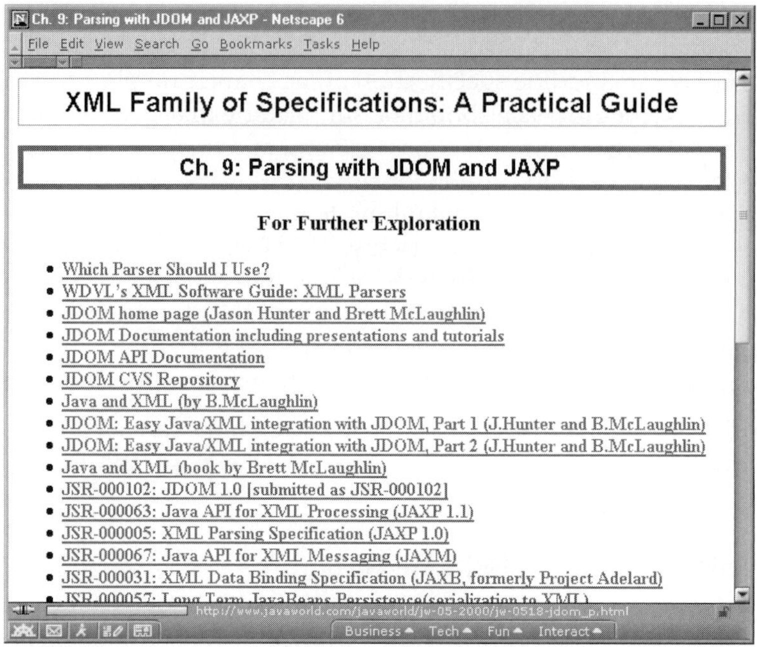

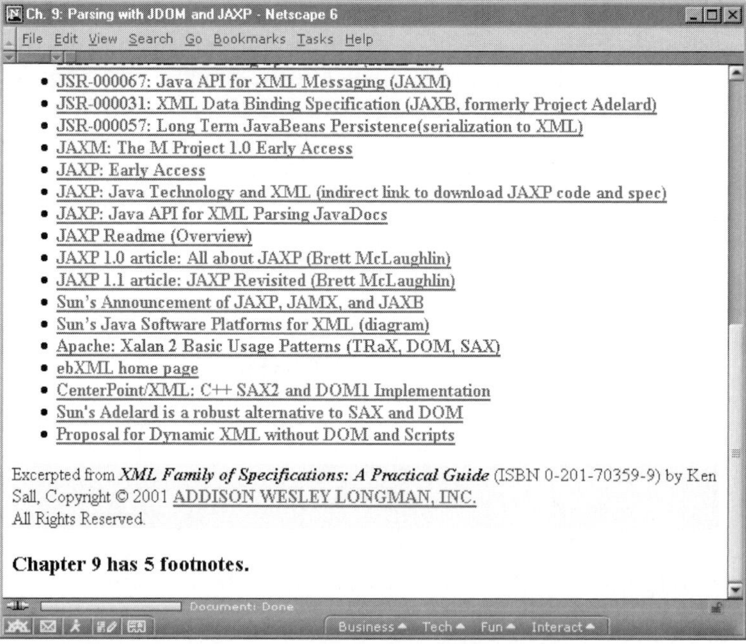

FIGURE 11-27 Desired HTML result for case study

2. The </HC> end tag for the section we're interested in has been moved from the end of the section heading to just after the last link, thereby containing the link URLs and link titles within the <HC> element.
3. For screenshot and simplification purposes, I've deleted <DIV> elements that contained <IMAGE> XLink elements just to put a line above each footnote when the CSS stylesheet is used.

Only modification 2 is actually necessary to make the link generation more straightforward. Perhaps some variation of `following-sibling::Link-Title` would render even this change unnecessary.

My point is not to criticize Adobe. Version 5.5.6 of FrameMaker appeared when XML was a relatively new technology and the output approach was certainly a valiant early attempt. Late in the writing of this book, FrameMaker 6.0 appeared with much better XML support using bundled third-party software, Quadralay WebWorks Publisher Standard Edition (*http://www.adobe.com/products/framemaker/keyfeature7.html*).

Although this new version would have permitted me to map the 50+ formats as XML elements in a manner that would have more closely modeled the structure of each chapter, various reasons precluded switching to FrameMaker 6.0 mid-stream. So I decided to stick with this relatively flat XML hierarchy, reasoning that this case is not unlike some cases you will encounter in the real world as you deal with legacy data. You might not have much control over the original XML structure you need to process because it might be generated from pre–XML-aware systems. You might also not find it reasonable to reformat the XML into a different structure although XSLT can be used precisely for this purpose—converting one type of XML hierarchy into another.

Figure 11-28 shows a portion of the file `Ch10-CSS-CDver.xml`, our input for the case study, which was generated by Framemaker and then minimally edited in the ways just mentioned.[15] Notice that each <FOOTNOTE> element is nested inside the parent <FOOTNOTES> element. Nested in each are <FTN>, <A>, and <C1> elements. There are numerous <A> elements that are irrelevant to our task. In fact, most elements need to be ignored, with the exception of <HC>, <Link-Title>, <Link-URL>, <FOOTNOTES>, and <FOOTNOTE>.

If you wish to attempt to write your own stylesheet to meet the goals enumerated earlier, then stop reading this chapter, locate the relevant files on the CD-ROM, develop your own solution, and when done, return to this point and compare your code to what I used to create the Web pages. One big hint in

15. Chapter 10 section headings and links changed as I revised the book. The input file for this case study reflects the earlier version of the chapter. Also, my editors integrated many of my footnotes into the body of the text.

C:\KEN\XMLBook\NOTES\XSLT-CODE\Case-Study\Ch10-CSS-CDver.xml - Microsoft Internet Explorer provid...

File Edit View Favorites Tools Help

```
<?xml version="1.0" encoding="UTF-8" ?>
<!-- <?xml:stylesheet href="Ch10-CSS-orig.css" type="text/css" charset="UTF-8"?>
  -->
- <XML>
    <TITLE />
  - <HA>
      <A ID="pgfId-1015709" />
    </HA>
  - <HB>
      <A ID="pgfId-1002361" />
      Styling XML Using CSS2
    </HB>
  - <HB>
      <A ID="pgfId-1032813" />
    </HB>
  - <BXT>
      <A ID="pgfId-1032820" />
    - <HC>
        <A ID="pgfId-1032912" />
        What is CSS?
      </HC>
    - <Body>
        <A ID="pgfId-1035723" />
        Cascading Style Sheets, Level 2 (CSS2) became a W3C Recommendation in
        May 1998. It was a significant improvement over the also impressive
        Cascading Style Sheets, Level 1 (CSS1) Recommendation from December
        1996 (subsequently revised in January 1999). Both specs facilitate the
        separation of presentation (appearance) from structure (content), which
```

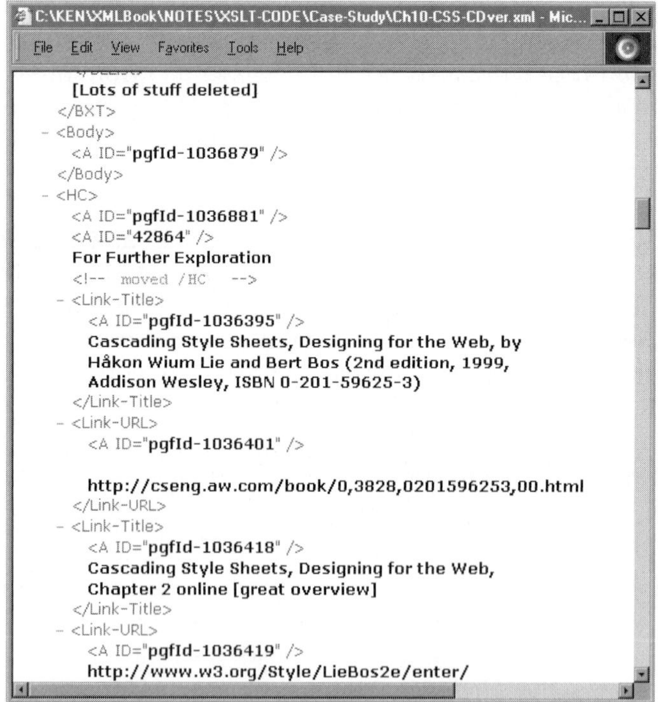

C:\KEN\XMLBook\NOTES\XSLT-CODE\Case-Study\Ch10-CSS-CDver.xml - Mic...

File Edit View Favorites Tools Help

```
      [Lots of stuff deleted]
    </BXT>
  - <Body>
      <A ID="pgfId-1036879" />
    </Body>
  - <HC>
      <A ID="pgfId-1036881" />
      <A ID="42864" />
      For Further Exploration
      <!--  moved /HC   -->
    - <Link-Title>
        <A ID="pgfId-1036395" />
        Cascading Style Sheets, Designing for the Web, by
        Håkon Wium Lie and Bert Bos (2nd edition, 1999,
        Addison Wesley, ISBN 0-201-59625-3)
      </Link-Title>
    - <Link-URL>
        <A ID="pgfId-1036401" />

        http://cseng.aw.com/book/0,3828,0201596253,00.html
      </Link-URL>
    - <Link-Title>
        <A ID="pgfId-1036418" />
        Cascading Style Sheets, Designing for the Web,
        Chapter 2 online [great overview]
      </Link-Title>
    - <Link-URL>
        <A ID="pgfId-1036419" />
        http://www.w3.org/Style/LieBos2e/enter/
```

FIGURE 11-28 Sample of FrameMaker-generated XML

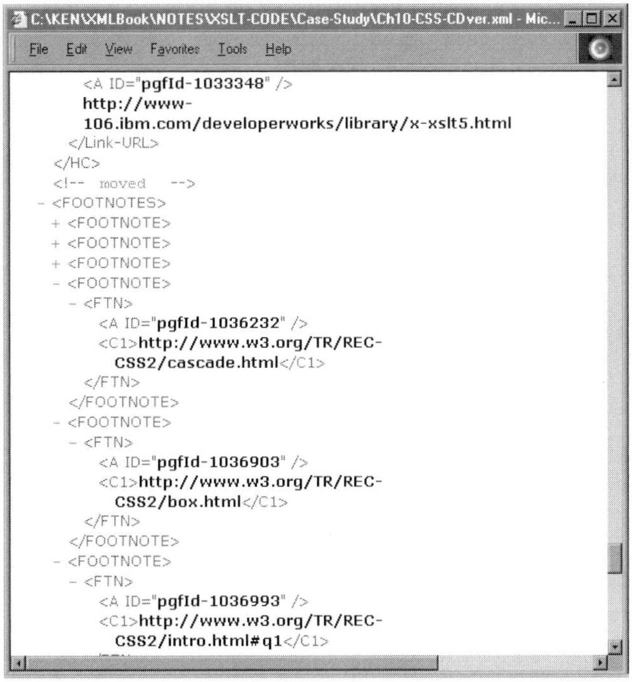

```
C:\KEN\XMLBook\NOTES\XSLT-CODE\Case-Study\Ch10-CSS-CDver.xml - Mic...
File  Edit  View  Favorites  Tools  Help
      <A ID="pgfId-1033348" />
      http://www-
      106.ibm.com/developerworks/library/x-xslt5.html
    </Link-URL>
  </HC>
  <!-- moved -->
- <FOOTNOTES>
  + <FOOTNOTE>
  + <FOOTNOTE>
  + <FOOTNOTE>
  - <FOOTNOTE>
    - <FTN>
        <A ID="pgfId-1036232" />
        <C1>http://www.w3.org/TR/REC-
          CSS2/cascade.html</C1>
      </FTN>
    </FOOTNOTE>
  - <FOOTNOTE>
    - <FTN>
        <A ID="pgfId-1036903" />
        <C1>http://www.w3.org/TR/REC-
          CSS2/box.html</C1>
      </FTN>
    </FOOTNOTE>
  - <FOOTNOTE>
    - <FTN>
        <A ID="pgfId-1036993" />
        <C1>http://www.w3.org/TR/REC-
          CSS2/intro.html#q1</C1>
```

FIGURE 11-28 *(continued)*

developing your solution is that you will need to use the top-level `<xsl:strip-space>` instruction due to the vast number of extraneous white-space-only nodes in the generated XML.

Another approach you might take is to just read one subsection at a time until you think you have all you need to arrive at the rest of the solution.

Basic Structure and Pitfalls

Over the next several pages, we'll examine my solution in stages. In most kinds of programming, it's easier to use a top-down approach, starting with a general solution and then filling in the details. Listing 11-51 shows the overall structure of the stylesheet (cs1.xsl) I developed to extract the links. The HTML `<head>` element will eventually receive the variables and parameters that will be declared as top-level elements. The `<body>` will receive the result of applying templates for `<XML>`, the document element of FrameMaker-generated output.

Listing 11-51 Basic Structure of Case Study Solution (cs1.xsl)

```
<?xml version='1.0'?>
<xsl:stylesheet version="1.0"
                xmlns:xsl="http://www.w3.org/1999/XSL/Transform">
<xsl:output method="html"/>

<!-- This makes a huge difference with our particular input. -->
<xsl:strip-space elements="*" />

<!-- TBD variables, parameters, and style -->

<xsl:template match="/">
   <html>
     <head>
       <title>
       Chapter number and title will go here.
       </title>
     </head>
     <body>
       <xsl:apply-templates select="XML"/>
     </body>
   </html>
</xsl:template>

<xsl:template match="FOOTNOTES">
  <h3>Chapter has
<xsl:value-of select="count(FOOTNOTE)"/> footnotes.</h3>
</xsl:template>

<!-- TBD template to handle HC = "For Further Exploration" -->
<xsl:template match="HC">
  <xsl:value-of select="."/><br/>
</xsl:template>

<xsl:template match="text()">
</xsl:template>

</xsl:stylesheet>
```

This initial version has three templates. The first template counts the number of footnotes. Since the <FOOTNOTES> element contains all <FOOTNOTE> children elements, we can simply use the `count()` function. The template that matches `text()` is included to discard a great deal of text content that is not needed in this example (but certainly was needed by my publisher and hopefully by my readers!). The second template, which is for the <HC> heading, is just a stub for now. It merely sends the content of the <HC> element to the result tree, which for all headings except the one we're interested in is just the section heading. For the "For Further Exploration" section, however, since I edited the generated XML and moved the </HC> end tag to follow the last <Link-URL>, the <HC> element contains the link titles and

URLs as children. So if we apply the stylesheet shown in Listing 11-51 to the XML generated from chapter 10:

```
C:> xalan-it Ch10-CSS-CDver.xml cs1.xsl cs1.html
```

the result is something like this:

```
What is CSS?
For Further Exploration Cascading Style Sheets, Designing for the Web, by
Hakon Wium Lie and Bert Bos (2nd edition, 1999, Addison Wesley, ISBN 0-201-
59625-3)http://cseng.aw.com/book/0,3828,0201596253,00.htmlCascading Style
Sheets, Designing for the Web, Chapter 2 online [great overview]http://
www.w3.org/Style/LieBos2e/enter/ Document Style Semantics and Specification
Language (DSSSL)
[etc.]
WDVL: Introduction to Style Sheets [tutorial by Alan
Richmond] http://wdvl.Internet.com/Authoring/Style/Sheets/Tutorial.html
IBM: Improve your XSLT coding five ways
[Tip #1 concerns CSS] http://www-106.ibm.com/developerworks/library/x-
xslt5.html

Chapter has 16 footnotes.
```

The first two lines contain the titles of the two <HC> sections in the original version of chapter 10, "What is CSS?" and "For Further Exploration". Then, with no line breaks, we see the link titles and link URLs, not because we're explicitly extracting them, but just because they are part of the content of the second <HC> element since I moved the end </HC> to follow the last link. We don't see the content of the first section (other than its title) because we didn't change the FrameMaker generated <HC> structure:

```
<HC>
<A ID="pgfId-1032912"></A>
What is CSS?</HC>
```

Extracting the Links

Now we need to tackle the template for the <HC> element. We want to process only the single instance of the <HC> element whose text content contains the string "For Further Exploration", that is, the section with that particular heading, so we use a predicate to select a subset of the <HC> nodes. We add a few placeholders for headings. Then we set up an unordered list (<ul>) whose contents will be supplied by processing all <Link-Title> elements. Initially, we'll try a very basic <Link-Title> template that just selects the text content, which is the title of the link. Although I've used `select="//Link-Title"`, the two slashes aren't necessary in this case since each <Link-Title> is a child of the <HC> element and appears in no other contexts. Note that the template for <Link-Title> produces <li> tags.

```
<xsl:template match="HC[contains(text(),'For Further Exploration')]">
  <h1 align="center">bookTitle</h1>
  <h2 align="center">chapNum and chapTitle</h2>
  <h3 align="center">For Further Exploration</h3>

  <ul style="font-weight: bold;">
      <xsl:apply-templates select="//Link-Title" />
  </ul>
</xsl:template>

<xsl:template match="Link-Title">
 <li><xsl:value-of select="." /></li>
</xsl:template>
```

Even though there is an <A ID=...> element nested in each input <Link-URL>, the <xsl:value-of> instruction ignores empty elements; it does not contribute to the content that is selected. If we run this revision, we'll see all of the link titles, which proves we've got the right set of elements.

```
C:> xalan-it Ch10-CSS-CDver.xml cs20.xsl cs20.html
```

Next, however, we need to replace the <li> portion with something considerably more sophisticated. Each list item needs to be created as an HTML <a> anchor with an href attribute set to the value of the <Link-URL> that follows the <Link-Title>. We need <xsl:element> to send the <a> element to the result tree and <xsl:attribute> to create the href, setting the value of the attribute using the <xsl:value-of> instruction. Since the <Link-Title> and <Link-URL> elements occur in pairs, always in that order, there are several (in this case) equivalent XPath expressions we could use:

```
following::Link-URL
following::Link-URL[1]
following-sibling::Link-URL
following-sibling::Link-URL[1]
```

I've chosen to use the last expression, which tells the processor to select the first (and in this case, only) <Link-URL> element that is a sibling of the current node (the <Link-Title> being processed) and follows it in document order. (You might think that expressions such as ../Link-URL would work, but they don't. The axis specification is necessary.)

```
<li>
  <xsl:element name="a" >
    <xsl:attribute name="href">
      <xsl:value-of select="normalize-space(following::Link-URL[1])" />
    </xsl:attribute>
    <xsl:value-of select="." />
  </xsl:element>
</li>
```

Due to the irrelevant `<A ID=...>` element nested in each `<Link-URL>`, it's necessary to use the `normalize-space()` function to remove unwanted white space characters like "%0D%OA" before "http" which confuses browsers into thinking the URL contains the `file://` protocol (local URL).

If we apply this stylesheet:

```
C:> xalan-it Ch10-CSS-CDver.xml cs2.xsl cs2.html
```

our output file `cs2.html` has the required link titles and link URLs appropriately paired; each list item is a link to the page identified by the title.

Adding Chapter Information

The next step is to add the ability to pass chapter titles and chapter numbers on the command line (or however your XSLT processor supports obtaining information from the environment). To accomplish this, I've added to the third version of the stylesheet, `cs3.xsl`, several `<xsl:variable>` and `<xsl:param>` instructions at the top level. The parameters we'll pass on the command line are called `$chapNum` and `$chapTitle`. In terms of constants, besides the book title, you'll note that ISBN, author, and publisher information have been added as variables (constants).

```
<!-- Constants -->
<xsl:variable name="bookTitle">XML Family of Specifications: A Practical
Guide</xsl:variable>
<xsl:variable name="isbn">0-201-70359-9</xsl:variable>
<xsl:variable name="author">Ken Sall</xsl:variable>
<xsl:variable name="publisher">ADDISON WESLEY LONGMAN, INC.</xsl:variable>

<!-- Default values; override by command line param passing. -->
<xsl:param name="chapNum" >0000</xsl:param>
<xsl:param name="chapTitle" >Unspecified Chapter Title</xsl:param>
```

Next, where appropriate, references to these variables and parameters are added.

```
<xsl:template match="/">
   <html>
     <head>
       <title>
       Ch. <xsl:value-of select="$chapNum"/>: <xsl:value-of
select="$chapTitle"/>
       </title>
     </head>
     <body>
       <xsl:apply-templates select="XML"/>
     </body>
   </html>
</xsl:template>
```

```
<xsl:template match="FOOTNOTES">
  <h3>Chapter <xsl:value-of select="$chapNum"/> has
<xsl:value-of select="count(FOOTNOTE)"/> footnotes.</h3>
</xsl:template>

<xsl:template match="HC[contains(text(),'For Further Exploration') and
                    not(contains(text(),'Case Study')) ]">

  <h1 align="center"><xsl:value-of select="$bookTitle"/></h1>
  <h2 align="center">Ch. <xsl:value-of select="$chapNum"/>:
      <xsl:value-of select="$chapTitle"/></h2>
  <h3 align="center">For Further Exploration</h3>
```

If we apply `cs3.xsl` to `Ch10-CSS-CDver.xml` without supplying parameters on the command line, the default values for `$chapNum` and `$chapTitle` are incorporated, with this result:

```
              XML Family of Specifications: A Practical Guide

                    Ch. 0000: Unspecified Chapter Title

                           For Further Exploration

Cascading Style Sheets, Designing for the Web, by Håkon Wium Lie and Bert
Bos (2nd edition, 1999, Addison Wesley, ISBN 0-201-59625-3)
                                  [etc.]
Chapter 0000 has 16 footnotes.
```

To supply the parameter overrides, we modify our `.bat` file, calling it `xalan-cs.bat`, and hardcode the parameters and their values:

```
%JBIN%\java -classpath %XALAN_JARS% org.apache.xalan.xslt.Process
-IN %1 -XSL %2 -OUT %3
-PARAM chapNum "10" -PARAM chapTitle "Displaying XML with CSS"
```

Then, to apply the new stylesheet with the parameter overrides, our command becomes:

```
C:> xalan-cs Ch10-CSS-CDver.xml cs3.xsl cs3.html
```

Alternatively, a command line such as the following will do the trick if you're using Xalan:

```
C:> java org.apache.xalan.xslt.Process
-IN Ch10-CSS-CDver.xml -XSL cs3.xsl -OUT cs3.html
-PARAM chapNum "10" -PARAM chapTitle "Displaying XML with CSS"
```

Saxon users should invoke a command line similar to this:

```
C:> java com.icl.saxon.StyleSheet
-o cs3-saxon.html Ch10-CSS-CDver.xml  cs3.xsl
chapNum=10 chapTitle="Displaying XML with CSS"
```

In any case, this results in the expected substitution of the information passed to the execution environment.

```
            XML Family of Specifications: A Practical Guide

                    Ch. 10: Displaying XML with CSS
                                [etc.]
Chapter 10 has 16 footnotes.
```

Sorting the Links

Our next task is to provide a way to indicate whether to sort the links alphabetically by title, with the default being to leave them in document order (unsorted). This can be accomplished by adding a `$sortLinks` `<xsl:param>`, as well as adding a conditional test using `<xsl:when>` (or two separate tests using `<xsl:if>`) to the `<ul>` step.

```
<!-- Controls sorting of link titles -->
<xsl:param name="sortLinks" >no</xsl:param>
```

If `$sortLinks` equals the string "yes", we add an `<xsl:sort>` instruction to the content of the `<xsl:apply-templates>` instruction that handles `<Link-Title>` elements, which first sorts them alphabetically by title and *then* applies the template. On the other hand, if `$sortLinks` is "no", we simply use the empty form of `<xsl:apply-templates>` so that they'll be processed in document order. Note the difference between the non-empty and empty forms of `<xsl:apply-templates>`.

```
<!-- Create bulleted list of link titles and links, possibly sorted. -->
<ul style="font-weight: bold;">
 <xsl:choose>
  <xsl:when test="$sortLinks = 'yes'"> <!-- do sort -->
    <xsl:apply-templates select="//Link-Title">
      <xsl:sort data-type="text" order="ascending" select="." />
    </xsl:apply-templates> <!-- sort & process all Link-Title children -->
  </xsl:when>
  <xsl:when test="$sortLinks = 'no'"> <!-- don't  sort -->
    <xsl:apply-templates select="//Link-Title" /> <!-- process kids -->
  </xsl:when>
 </xsl:choose>
</ul>
```

We'll call this new version of the stylesheet `cs4.xsl`, our command line and `xalan-cs.bat` need to be updated to specify a value for `$sortLinks` (or accept the default of "no"), so for Xalan we have:

```
C:> java org.apache.xalan.xslt.Process
-IN Ch10-CSS-CDver.xml -XSL cs4.xsl -OUT cs4.html
-PARAM sortLinks "yes" -PARAM chapNum "10" -PARAM chapTitle "Displaying XML
with CSS"
```

and for Saxon:

```
C> java com.icl.saxon.StyleSheet
-o cs4-saxon.html Ch10-CSS-CDver.xml  cs4.xsl
sortLinks="yes" chapNum=10 chapTitle="Displaying XML with CSS"
```

Figure 11-29 shows the sorted results when this stylesheet is applied using Saxon.

Adding Style

Well, we've nearly completed this exercise! The only goal that remains from those enumerated in "Problem Statement and Goals" at the beginning of this case study is to use attribute value templates to set the HTML `style` attribute to display a few of our constants using CSS. To accomplish this, I've defined two more XSLT variables, `$bookTitleStyle` and `$chapTitleStyle`, each initialized to a similar (but not

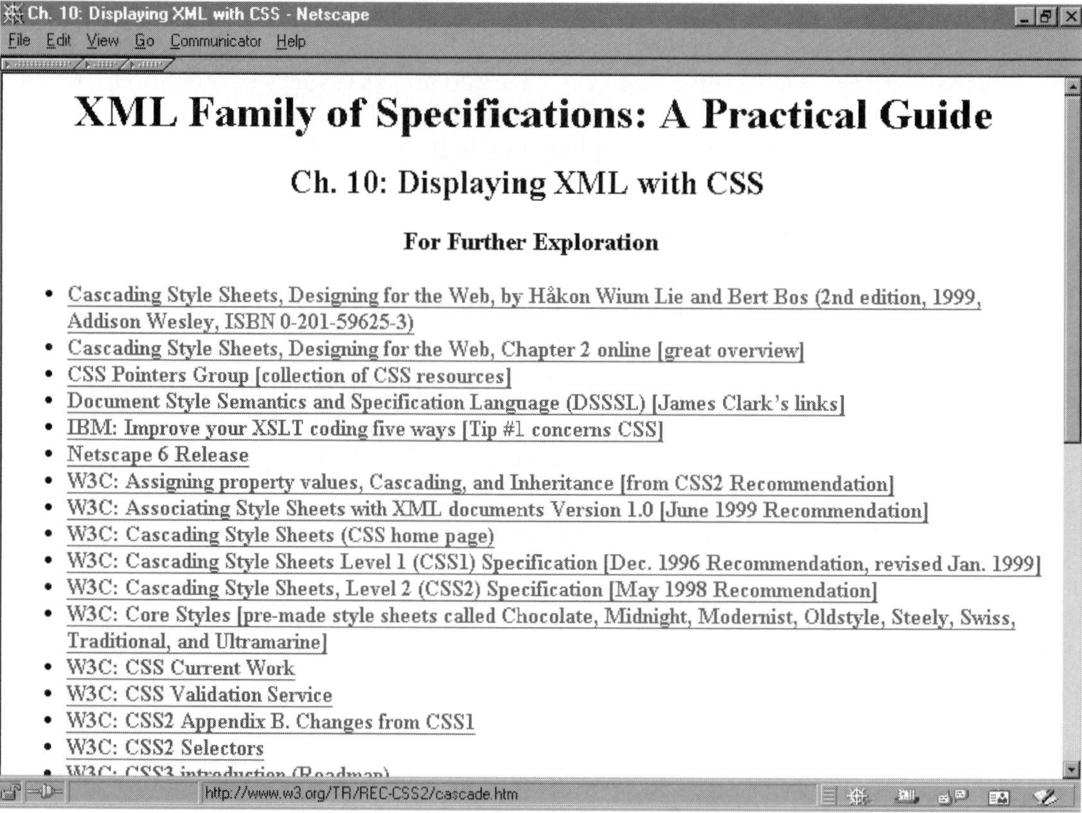

FIGURE 11-29 Sorted link titles using stylesheet cs4.xsl and Saxon

identical) list of CSS declaration blocks. As you'll recall, CSS declarations are `property:value` pairs that can appear either within an HTML `<style>` start tag (with an element-related selector) or as the value of the `style` attribute, which is supported by most HTML 4.0 elements as well as in a separate CSS stylesheet. We'll use the `style` attribute form. We initialize the `$bookTitleStyle` variable with one set of `property:value` pairs as its content, and initialize `$chapTitleStyle` with a slightly different CSS declaration block.

```
<xsl:variable name="bookTitleStyle">padding: 5px; border: thin solid red;
font-size: 150%; font-family: Helvetica, sans-serif; font-weight: bold;</
xsl:variable>
<xsl:variable name="chapTitleStyle">padding: 2px; border: thick solid blue;
font-size: 125%; font-family: Helvetica, sans-serif; font-weight: bold;</
xsl:variable>
```

Later in the stylesheet, we use the curly bracket notation for attribute value templates to substitute the value of the variables as the value of the `style` attribute associated with the <h1> and <h2> elements, or wherever else they are needed.

```
<h1 align="center"
    style="{$bookTitleStyle}"><xsl:value-of select="$bookTitle"/></h1>
<h2 align="center"
    style="{$chapTitleStyle}">Ch. <xsl:value-of select="$chapNum"/>:
    <xsl:value-of select="$chapTitle"/></h2>
```

Of course, we could directly assign a value to the `style` attribute, as shown for the <p> element below. Another point to mention is that we need to use `disable-output-escaping="no"` for the copyright entity, `©`.

```
<!-- Footer is constant for all chapters. -->
<p style="background-color: #ffff00;">
Excerpted from <i><b><xsl:value-of select="$bookTitle"/></b></i>
(ISBN <xsl:value-of select="$isbn"/>)
by <xsl:value-of select="$author"/>,
Copyright <xsl:text disable-output-escaping="no">&#169;</xsl:text> 2002
<!--
    Above works for HTML, but not for XHTML or XML output, we'd need:
    &amp;copy; with  disable-output-escaping="yes"
-->
<b><a href="http://www.awl.com/"><xsl:value-of select="$publisher"/>
</a></b><br/>
All Rights Reserved.
</p>
```

Final Solution

The complete solution for the case study is shown in Listing 11-52. The only significant difference from the fragments discussed in previous sections is that the <HC> template has a second predicate, which is necessary only for the current chapter you're reading. Since the current section's heading for the case study also includes the words "For Further Exploration," but is not the section containing the links, the second predicate excludes it from consideration.

```
<xsl:template match="HC[contains(text(),'For Further Exploration') and
                        not(contains(text(),'Case Study')) ]">
```

Listing 11-52 Complete Solution for Case Study (case-study.xsl)

```
<?xml version='1.0'?>
<!--
      XSLT stylesheet to extract only the link titles and URLs from
      the "For Further Exploration" section of a chapter and generate
      an HTML list of links, sorted by link title. Input is XML as
      output from FrameMaker 5.5.6.

      NOTE: This version is about twice as long and complicated as
      necessary to do the task, mainly to add some frills that
      illustrate useful XSLT functionality.
-->
<xsl:stylesheet version="1.0"
                xmlns:xsl="http://www.w3.org/1999/XSL/Transform">
<xsl:output method="html"/>

<!--
     Alternatively, could generate XHTML output instead:
<xsl:stylesheet version="1.0"
                xmlns:xsl="http://www.w3.org/1999/XSL/Transform"
                xmlns="http://www.w3.org/TR/xhtml1/strict">
<xsl:output method="xml" indent="yes" encoding="iso-8859-1"/>
-->

<!-- This makes a huge difference with our particular input. -->
<xsl:strip-space elements="*" />

<!-- Constants -->
<xsl:variable name="bookTitle">XML Family of Specifications: A Practical
Guide</xsl:variable>
<xsl:variable name="isbn">0-201-70359-9</xsl:variable>
<xsl:variable name="author">Ken Sall</xsl:variable>
<xsl:variable name="publisher">ADDISON WESLEY LONGMAN, INC.</xsl:variable>
<xsl:variable name="bookTitleStyle">padding: 5px; border: thin solid red;
font-size: 150%; font-family: Helvetica, sans-serif; font-weight: bold;</
xsl:variable>
<xsl:variable name="chapTitleStyle">padding: 2px; border: thick solid blue;
font-size: 125%; font-family: Helvetica, sans-serif; font-weight: bold;</
xsl:variable>

<!-- Default values; override by command line param passing. -->
<xsl:param name="chapNum" >0000</xsl:param>
<xsl:param name="chapTitle" >Unspecified Chapter Title</xsl:param>
<!-- Controls sorting of link titles -->
<xsl:param name="sortLinks" >no</xsl:param>
```

```
<!-- end top level elements -->

<xsl:template match="/">
   <html>
   <!-- or xhtml xmlns="http://www.w3.org/1999/xhtml"
xml:lang="en" lang="en" -->
     <head>
       <title>
       Ch. <xsl:value-of select="$chapNum"/>: <xsl:value-of
select="$chapTitle"/>
       </title>
     </head>
     <body>
       <xsl:apply-templates select="XML"/>
       <!-- FrameMaker DOCTYPE (root element) -->
     </body>
   </html>
</xsl:template>

<xsl:template match="FOOTNOTES">
  <h3>Chapter <xsl:value-of select="$chapNum"/> has
<xsl:value-of select="count(FOOTNOTE)"/> footnotes.</h3>
</xsl:template>

<!-- Display all HC headings; not required by the case study.
<xsl:template match="HC">
  <h3>HC =    <xsl:value-of select="$chapNum"/>
<xsl:number format=".1.1" /><xsl:value-of select="."/></h3>
</xsl:template>
-->

<!--
     Start the URL list with the beginning of the
     'For Further Exploration' section.

             KLUDGE:
Unfortunately, the XML exporting of FrameMaker 5.5.6 is limited. It
doesn't maintain the hierarchy that all Link-Title and Link-URL elements
are children of the 'For Further Exploration' <HC> element or better yet, a
<DIV> element that contains <HC> and Link-Title and Link-URL elements.
Therefore, to begin/end the <ul> list properly and to be able to sort the
URLs by Link-Title, it is necessary to manually edit the XML output and
move the end </HC> tag to just after the last link, like so:
          <Link-Title>
          <A ID="pgfId-1034661"></A>
          Whatever Title</Link-Title>
          <Link-URL>
          <A ID="pgfId-1034082"></A>
          http://whatever</Link-URL>
          </HC>
          <FOOTNOTES>
    It would seem that some variation of "following-sibling" would
    make this manual edit unnessary, such as this line in the <ul>:
      <xsl:apply-templates select="following-sibling::Link-Title" />
-->
```

```
<xsl:template match="HC[contains(text(),'For Further Exploration') and
                     not(contains(text(),'Case Study')) ]">
  <!--
       Second predicate is only needed because the XSLT chapter's case study
       contains the words 'For Further Exploration' in its heading!
  -->

  <h1 align="center"
      style="{$bookTitleStyle}"><xsl:value-of select="$bookTitle"/></h1>
  <h2 align="center"
      style="{$chapTitleStyle}">Ch. <xsl:value-of select="$chapNum"/>:
      <xsl:value-of select="$chapTitle"/></h2>
  <h3 align="center">For Further Exploration</h3>

  <!-- Create bulleted list of link titles and links, possibly sorted. -->
  <ul style="font-weight: bold;">
   <xsl:choose>
    <xsl:when test="$sortLinks = 'yes'"> <!-- do sort -->
      <xsl:apply-templates select="//Link-Title">
        <xsl:sort data-type="text" order="ascending" select="." />
      </xsl:apply-templates> <!-- sort & process all Link-Title children -->
    </xsl:when>
    <xsl:when test="$sortLinks = 'no'"> <!-- don't  sort -->
      <xsl:apply-templates select="//Link-Title" /> <!-- process kids -->
    </xsl:when>
   </xsl:choose>
  </ul>

  <!-- Footer is constant for all chapters. -->
  <p style="background-color: #ffff00;">
  Excerpted from <i><b><xsl:value-of select="$bookTitle"/></b></i>
  (ISBN <xsl:value-of select="$isbn"/>)
  by <xsl:value-of select="$author"/>,
  Copyright <xsl:text disable-output-escaping="no">&#169;</xsl:text> 2002
  <!--
      Above works for HTML, but not for XHTML or XML output, we'd need:
      &amp;copy; with  disable-output-escaping="yes"
  -->
  <b><a href="http://www.awl.com/"><xsl:value-of
select="$publisher"/></a></b><br/>
  All Rights Reserved.
  </p>
</xsl:template> <!-- For Further Exploration Section -->

<!--
     Link-Title template assumes there is a DIV element following
     Link-Title which contains the Link-URL associated with the current
     title. This is a bit strange since it would be more natural to have
     the DIV contain both the Link-Title and Link-URL, but that's not what
     is generated since the first Link-Title is in a different DIV.
     We use normalize-space() to get rid of the extra white space due to
     the unnecessary <A> elements FrameMaker generates, such as:
         <Link-URL>
         <A ID="pgfId-1034082"></A>
         http://whatever</Link-URL>
```

```
     Without normalize-space() we'd get characters like "%0D%OA" before
     "http", which confuses browsers into thinking the URL is
     file:// [local].

         KLUDGE:
     Some chapters have an extra <DIV> level, so may need this line instead:
     <xsl:value-of select="normalize-space(following::DIV/Link-URL)" />
-->
<xsl:template match="Link-Title">
 <li>
   <xsl:element name="a" >
     <xsl:attribute name="href">
       <!-- Pick the first Link-URL that follows this Link-Title. -->
       <xsl:value-of
select="normalize-space(following-sibling::Link-URL[1])" />
     </xsl:attribute>
     <xsl:value-of select="." /><!-- link text -->
   </xsl:element>
 </li>
</xsl:template>

<!--
Ignore all styles other than link info. Override default element rule. It is
certainly inconvenient and prone to error to have to explicitly list every
element we want to skip, so we instead override text default.
     <xsl:template
match="BL1|BL|BLList|BX|BXT|Body|C1|CAPTION|CDT|CDT1|CELL|CP1|CP|CPX|Code|E
1|E2|Emphasis|EX|FC|FN|FOOTNOTE|FOOTNOTES|FTN|Glossary-
Term|HA|HB|HC|HD|HE|NL|NL1|NLList|Quota-
tion|ROW|TABLE|TB1|TB|TBX|TCH|TH|TITLE|TN|" >
     </xsl:template>
-->
<xsl:template match="text()">
  <!-- Swallow all text content since we only care about Link-Title -->
</xsl:template>

</xsl:stylesheet>
```

Additional XSLT Topics

Microsoft XSL: Old and in the Way

Before closing this long chapter on XSLT, I feel compelled to say a few words about MSXML XSL.

If you turn way, way back to Listing 2-4 where we sorted `Employee` elements by their `Last` name children, the equivalent version using the outdated XSL imple-

Caution: Some XSLT code examples found on the Web and in older books are based on an old XSL implementation in Internet Explorer 5, based on the December 1998 Working Draft of XSLT, rather than the version that was eventually approved by the W3C in November 1999. Stylesheets based on this IE 5.x version of XSLT can be identified by the namespace `http://www.w3.org/TR/WD-xsl`, in contrast to the W3C-approved namespace, `http://www.w3.org/1999/XSL/Transform`. These examples will work *only* in IE 5.x, in contrast to all the others presented in this XSLT chapter. For details about Microsoft XSLT, see the Unofficial MSXML XSLT FAQ at *http://www.netcrucible.com/xslt/msxml-faq.htm*. Microsoft also has detailed information, but the URLs change too often to be listed here.

mented in Internet Explorer 5 appears in Listing 11-53. The major differences are shown in bold.

One way to use this Microsoft-specific stylesheet is to create an HTML document that uses JavaScript to access the Microsoft DOM, XMLDOM. Another

Listing 11-53 IE5.x XSL Stylesheet (obsolete)

```
<?xml version="1.0"?>
<xsl:stylesheet xmlns:xsl="uri:xsl">
  <xsl:template match="/">
    <html>
      <body>
        <table border="2" bgcolor="white" cellpadding="4" cellspacing="2" >
          <tr>
            <th>Last</th>
            <th>First</th>
            <th>Email</th>
            <th>Cell Phone</th>
          </tr>
          <xsl:for-each select="Employees/Employee" order-by="+Name/Last">
          <tr>
            <td><b><xsl:value-of select="Name/Last"/></b></td>
            <td><xsl:value-of select="Name/First"/></td>
            <td><xsl:value-of select="Email"/></td>
            <xsl:choose>
            <xsl:when test="PhoneNumbers/Cell[. != '']">
              <td><xsl:value-of select="PhoneNumbers/Cell" /></td>
            </xsl:when>
            <xsl:otherwise>
              <td align="center">none</td>
            </xsl:otherwise>
            </xsl:choose>
          </tr>
        </xsl:for-each>
      </table>
    </body>
  </html>
 </xsl:template>
</xsl:stylesheet>
```

approach is to replace the `<xsl:stylesheet>` element with an `<?xml-stylesheet ?>` processing instruction within an XML document to automatically apply the stylesheet whenever the XML file is browsed in Internet Explorer 5. Yet another approach is to convert it to a stylesheet that is fully compatible with the XSLT 1.0 Recommendation. See the Unofficial MSXML XSLT FAQ at *http://www.netcrucible.com/xslt/msxml-faq.htm*.

Topics Not Covered in Detail

There is a great deal more to XSLT and XPath than I could cover even in the space of this lengthy chapter. Readers interested in more depth can find several complete XSLT books listed along with the usual detailed references in this chapter's "For Further Exploration" section. Each book listed has its merits; most include numerous code examples that can be downloaded. In particular, the topics that I've intentionally omitted or covered very lightly are as follows:

- Template conflict resolution and priority; see Section 5.5 of the XSLT 1.0 Recommendation, "Conflict Resolution for Template Rules," *http://www.w3.org/TR/xslt#conflict*
- Extension functions and extension elements; see *http://www.dpawson.co.uk/xsl/sect5/index.html*
- Namespace subtleties
- Multiple result trees
- Embedded stylesheets
- Stylesheet management
- Included and imported stylesheets
- External parsed general entities
- Unparsed entity referencing
- `<xsl:key>` and `key()`
- `<xsl:decimal-format>` and `format-number()`
- `<xsl:number>` variations
- White space details other than `normalize()`, such as `<xsl:preserve-space>` and `<xsl:strip-space>`; see *http://www.dpawson.co.uk/xsl/sect2/N8321.html*
- Server-side details
- Microsoft-specific implementations

Beyond XSLT 1.0: XSLT 2.0, XPath 2.0, EXSLT, and XSLTSL

We noted earlier that XSLT is not, and does not purport to be, a general-purpose programming language. For this reason, some XSLT processor vendors have implemented extensions to the language by means of an extension mechanism defined in the XSLT 1.0 specification. You'll also find hooks to JavaScript, Java, and other languages. In fact, early in 2001, there was considerable controversy among XSLT experts concerning the `<xsl:script>` mechanism originally proposed for XSLT version 1.1 which allows scripting in different languages (for example, see *http://www.xml.com/pub/a/2001/02/14/deviant.html*).

Some of the major changes *originally* slated for XSLT 1.1 were:

- Result tree fragments could be replaced by node-sets. This would involve no syntax changes but it would impact interpretation. The result would be to allow subtrees to be treated just like the full tree.
- Stylesheets can generate multiple results, with a more flexible `<xsl:output>` instruction.
- Addition of `<xsl:script>` to support ECMAScript, JavaScript, and Java, as well as data types not found in XPath, would result in portable extension functions as developers switch between different XSLT processors.

However, in April 2001, Sharon Adler, chair of the XSL Working Group, announced that development of XSLT 1.1 was canceled as they move forward with XSLT 2.0 and XPath 2.0, expected sometime in 2002. The standard extension mechanism initially planned for XSLT 1.1 may become part of XSLT 2.0. As of February 2001, the XSLT 2.0 Requirements Working Draft (*http://www.w3.org/TR/xslt20req*) had enumerated the following goals:

- Simplify manipulation of XML Schema-typed content.
- Simplify manipulation of string content.
- Support related XML standards.
- Improve ease of use.
- Improve interoperability.
- Improve i18n [internationalization] support.
- Maintain backward compatibility.
- Enable improved processor efficiency.

Just in time for holiday reading, the initial XSLT 2.0 Working Draft (*http://www.w3.org/TR/xslt20/*, or *http://www.w3.org/TR/2001/WD-xslt20-20011220/*) was released in late December 2001:

> . . . to provide the XSLT user community with a preview of the revised language specification, and to obtain feedback. It is a draft document and may be updated, replaced, or obsoleted by other documents at any time. . . . While prototype implementations are encouraged, users and vendors are advised that this working draft cannot be regarded as a stable specification. . . . XSLT 2.0 is designed to be used together with XPath 2.0, which has been developed by the W3C XSL Working Group in collaboration with the XML Query Working Group. The current specification of XPath 2.0 can be found in [XPath 2.0].

In the section "Changes from XSLT 1.0 (Non-Normative)" of this early Working Draft, the W3C describes changes that fall into several broad categories:

- XSLT 2.0 Backwards Compatibility
- XPath 2.0 Backwards Compatibility
- Compatibility in the Presence of a Schema
- Changes from XSLT 1.0 to XSLT 1.1
- Changes from XSLT 1.1 to XSLT 2.0

Although `<xsl:script>` seems to have disappeared, see the discussion XSLT 2.0 about stylesheet functions and the new `<xsl:function>` instruction. The initial Working Draft includes a "Checklist of Requirements" section too (*http://www.w3.org/TR/xslt20/#section-Checklist-of-Requirements*).

Also in late December 2001, the first Working Draft of XPath 2.0 appeared (see *http://www.w3.org/TR/xpath20/*, or *http://www.w3.org/TR/2001/WD-xpath20-20011220/*). The W3C makes clear the interrelationship between XSLT, XPath, and XQuery in the "Status" section of this draft:

> This document is the result of joint work by the XSL and XML Query Working Groups, which are jointly responsible for XPath 2.0, a language derived from both XPath 1.0 and XQuery. The XPath 2.0 and XQuery 1.0 Working Drafts are generated from a common source. These languages are closely related, sharing much of the same expression syntax and semantics, and much of the text found in the two Working Drafts is identical. The current version of this document is the first publicly released Working Draft containing the results of integrating these languages. This document is a work in progress. It contains many open issues, and should not be considered to be fully stable.

The initial XPath 2.0 Working Draft also contains a "Backwards Compatibility with XPath 1.0 (Non-Normative)" section (*http://www.w3.org/TR/xpath20/#id-backwards-compatibility*).

Developers in need of extensions prior to XSLT 2.0 might want to investigate the grassroots effort called **EXSLT** by Dave Pawson, Jeni Tennison, Chris Bayes, Jim Fuller, and Uche Ogbuji, available from *http://www.exslt.org/*. The EXSLT site home page explains that:

> EXSLT is an open community initiative to standardise and document extensions to XSLT. . . . One aim of EXSLT is to get the implementers of XSLT processors to standardise the functions that they make available, so that your stylesheets can be more portable. If your XSLT processor doesn't support a particular extension, you can always download packages that you can use to provide functions or templates for your stylesheets.

As of this writing, EXSLT modules (each containing many functions) include:

- Dates and Times
- Dynamic
- Common
- Functions
- Math
- Regular Expressions
- Sets
- Strings

Another effort worth looking into is **XSLTSL**, the XSLT Standard Library work by Steve Ball and others from SourceForge, an open source developers group. XSLTSL provides common functions (templates) for XSLT stylesheets. Functions include useful string, node, and date-time processing capabilities. For example, I used the XSLTSL template called `<str:capitalise>` in the `<xsl:import>` code example in Listing 11-40 (pages 680–681). To download the library, see *http://sourceforge.net/projects/xsltsl/*. At the time of this writing, XSLTSL 1.0 contains modules for string, node, date/time, and URI functionality; the named templates include:

- `str:to-upper`—Make string uppercase
- `str:to-lower`—Make string lowercase
- `str:capitalise`—Capitalize string
- `str:substring-before-first`—String extraction
- `str:substring-after-last`—String extraction
- `str:subst`—String substitution
- `str:count-substring`—Count substrings
- `str:substring-after-at`—String extraction
- `str:insert-at`—String insertion
- `str:backward`—String reversal
- `str:character-first`—Find first occurring character in a string
- `str:string-match`—Match a string to a pattern
- `node:xpath`—Return an XPath location path
- `node:type`—Return node type
- `dt:format-date-time`—Return a string with a formatted date/time.
- `dt:calculate-day-of-the-week`—Calculate the day of the week
- `dt:get-day-of-the-week-name`—Get the day of the week's full name
- `dt:get-day-of-the-week-abbreviation`—Get the day of the week's abbreviation
- `dt:get-month-name`—Get the month's full name
- `dt:get-month-abbreviation`—Get the month's abbreviation
- `dt:calculate-julian-day`—Calculate the Julian Day for a specified date

- `dt:format-julian-day`—Return a string with a formatted date for a specified Julian Day
- `dt:calculate-week-number`—Calculates the week number for a specified date
- `uri:is-absolute-uri`—Determines if a URI is absolute or relative
- `uri:get-uri-scheme`—Get the scheme part of a URI
- `uri:get-uri-authority`—Get the authority part of a URI
- `uri:get-uri-path`—Gets the path part of a URI
- `uri:get-uri-query`—Gets the query part of a URI
- `uri:get-uri-fragment`—Gets the fragment part of a URI

Summary

This lengthy chapter provides a solid introduction to XSLT and XPath.

Extensible Stylesheet Language (XSL) is a language for expressing stylesheets consisting of three parts:

- A language for transforming XML documents: XSLT (XSL Transformations)
- An XML vocabulary for specifying formatting semantics: XSLFO (XSL Formatting Objects)
- A syntax for addressing parts of a document: XPath (XML Path Language)

XSLT is a powerful template-driven XML vocabulary used to transform, process, filter, sort, and otherwise manipulate XML input to produce any of several kinds of output. Transformations of XML to alternative XML, to HTML, and to text are supported.

XSLT is a recursive, template-driven, side-effect free, declarative language; you define blueprints that describe what you'd like the output to look like when certain input elements are encountered.

XSLT is not intended to serve as a general-purpose transformation language. However, it can be used by itself to perform many kinds of transformations of data.

XPath is a UNIX pathlike, non-XML syntax used to indicate or select particular portions of an XML document, such as a group of elements, an individual element, an element with a particular attribute, an element with a particular parent, and so on.

XPath is used primarily to select or locate individual nodes or sets of nodes in the tree, and secondarily to perform string manipulations, numerical calculations, and boolean tests.

XPath is also significant to XLink, XPointer, XML Schema, and the emerging XQuery.

The evaluation of an XPath expression is not permitted to alter the value of a variable or do anything that would not be reproducible the next time the same expression is encountered in the same context.

XSLT elements fall into three broad and sometimes overlapping categories:

- *Root level elements* consist of only `xsl:stylesheet` and the equivalent `xsl:transform` element.
- *Top-level elements* may appear as direct children of `xsl:stylesheet` or `xsl:transform`.
- *Instructions* are elements that usually do not (and in most cases, *cannot*) appear at the top level; these elements are used within `xsl:template`.

Top-level and root elements are shown in Table 11-17.

XSLT Instructions are shown in Table 11-18.

Functions used in XSLT stylesheets are defined mostly in the XPath specfication, but some are specific to XSLT.

XPath functions are shown in Tables 11-13 through 11-16.

XSLT functions are shown in Table 11-19.

For Further Exploration

Articles

XML.com: What Is XSLT?
http://www.xml.com/pub/a/2000/08/holman/index.html

XML.com: Getting Started with XSLT and XPath
http://www.xml.com/pub/2000/08/holman/s2_1.html

XML.com: Transforming XML [series]
http://www.xml.com/pub/q/transformingxml

XML.com: What's New in XPath 2.0
http://www.xml.com/pub/a/2002/038/20/xpath.2.html

XML.com: Style Matters [series]
http://www.xml.com/pub/q/stylematters

XML.com: STYLE [all articles]
http://www.xml.com/pub/q/all_style

XML.com: HTML and XSLT
http://www.xml.com/pub/2000/08/30/xsltandhtml/index.html

XML.com; Toward an XPath API, Leigh Dodds
http://www.xml.com/pub/a/2001/03/07/xpathapi.html

XML.com: XSLT Extensions, Bob DuCharme
http://www.xml.com/pub/a/2001/09/05/extensions.html

XML.com: Processing Inclusions with XSLT
http://www.xml.com/pub/a/2000/08/09/xslt/xslt.html

XML.com: Combining Stylesheets with Include and Import, Bob DuCharme
http://www.xml.com/pub/a/2000/11/01/xslt/index.html

JavaWorld: XML Document Processing in Java Using XPath and XSLT
http://www.javaworld.com/jw-09-2000/jw-0908-xpath.html

JavaWorld: Server-side XML-to-HTML Translation
http://www.javaworld.com/javaqa/2000-04/03-qa-0428-xml.html

Saxon: The Anatomy of an XSLT processor, Michael Kay [describes the internal workings of Saxon]
http://www-106.ibm.com/developerworks/library/x-xslt2/

James Clark: XSLT in Perspective
http://www.jclark.com/xml/xslt-talk.htm

Sun: Articles from Sun XML | Developer Connection [all XML]
http://www.sun.com/xml/developers/

Sun: XSLT Compiler—New Directions for XML Transformations
http://www.sun.com/xml/developers/xsltc/article.html

Oracle: Building Oracle XML Applications: Transforming XML with XSLT
http://www.ora.com/catalog/orxmlapp/chapter/ch07.html

XML.com: XSLT Processor Benchmarks
http://www.xml.com/pub/a/2001/03/28/xsltmark/index.html

Java and XML: Web Publishing Framework (Cocoon), Brett McLaughlin
http://www.oreilly.com/catalog/javaxml/chapter/ch09.html

XML.com: XSLT UK 2001 Report
http://www.xml.com/pub/a/2001/04/25/xsltuk.html

(xml-dev thread): We need an XPath API
http://lists.xml.org/archives/xml-dev/200103/msg00178.html

Books

XSLT: Working with XML and HTML, Khun Yee Fung
http://cseng.aw.com/book/0,3828,0201711036,00.html

XSLT Programmer's Reference, Michael Kay
http://www.wrox.com/Books/Book_Details.asp?isbn=1861003129

XSL Companion, Neil Bradley
http://cseng.aw.com/book/0,3828,0201674874,00.html

Practical Transformation Using XSLT and XPath, G. Ken Holman, (Crane Softwrights, Ltd.)
http://www.CraneSoftwrights.com/training/

Practical Formatting Using XSLFO, G. Ken Holman (Crane Softwrights, Ltd.)
http://www.cranesoftwrights.com/training/#pfux

XSLT and XPath on the Edge, Unlimited Edition, Jeni Tennison
http://catalog.hungryminds.com/product.asp?isbn=0764547763

Inside XSLT, Steven Holzner
http://vig.prenhall.com/catalog/academic/product/1,4096,0735711364,00.html

XSLT Quickly, Bob DuCharme
http://www.snee.com/bob/xsltquickly/

XSLT, Doug Tidwell
http://www.oreilly.com/catalog/xslt/

Historical

History of XSL
http://www.w3.org/Style/XSL/OldStuff.html#history

Historical Style Sheet Proposals
http://www.w3.org/Style/History/

DSSSL (Document Style Semantics and Specification Language)
http://www.jclark.com/dsssl/

DSSSL (Robin Cover's page)
http://xml.coverpages.org/dsssl.html

HyTime (Hypermedia/Time-based Structuring Language)—Robin Cover's page
http://xml.coverpages.org/hytime.html

TEI (Text Encoding Initiative)
http://www.tei-c.org/

Resources

Zvon XSLT Reference [XSLT 1.0, includes XPath 1.0]
http://www.zvon.org/xxl/XSLTreference/Output/index.html

XSL FAQ, Dave Pawson
http://www.dpawson.co.uk/xsl/xslfaq.html

XSLT Glossary [from XSLT 2.0 Working Draft; some terms may be new and in flux]
http://www.w3.org/TR/xslt20/#glossary

XSLT Terminology [from Dave Pawson's XSL FAQ]
http://www.dpawson.co.uk/xsl/xslvocab.html

Things XSLT Can't Do [from Dave Pawson's XSL FAQ]
http://www.dpawson.co.uk/xsl/sect2/nono.html

Mulberry Technologies: XSLT and XPath Quick Reference
http://www.mulberrytech.com/quickref/index.html

XSLT Element Index [from Norm Walsh's slides]
http://www.nwalsh.com/docs/tutorials/xsl/xsl/foil84.html

finetuning.com's XSLT FAQ
http://www.finetuning.com/xsltfaq.html

finetuning.com's XPath FAQ
http://www.finetuning.com/xpathfaq.html

VBXML XSLT Reference
http://www.vbxml.com/xsl/XSLTRef.asp

VBXML XPath Reference
http://www.vbxml.com/xsl/XPathRef.asp

xmlhack: XSLT news
http://xmlhack.com/list.php?cat=2

Conformance: OASIS XSLT/XPath Conformance Technical Subcommittee
http://www.oasis-open.org/committees/xslt/

Conformance: NIST XSL Testing (XSLFO, XSLT, XPath)
http://xw2k.sdct.itl.nist.gov/xml/page5.html

WDVL: XSL: Extensible Stylesheet Language
http://wdvl.Internet.com/Authoring/Languages/XSL/

XML.com Style Resource Center
http://www.xml.com/style/

XML Cover Pages: XSL, Robin Cover
http://xml.coverpages.org/xsl.html

Apache: Getting Up to Speed with XSLT
http://xml.apache.org/xalan/overview.html#uptospeed

Mulberry Technologies: XSL-List [developers' forum]
http://www.mulberrytech.com/xsl/xsl-list/

Mike J. Brown's XML and XSL Stuff
http://www.skew.org/xml/

skew.org XML and XSLT resources
http://www.skew.org/xml/

Oliver's XSLT Page
http://www.informatik.hu-berlin.de/~obecker/XSLT/

Jeni's XSLT Pages
http://www.jenitennison.com/xslt/

XSLT Cookbook, Paul Prescod, Editor in Chief [developer-contributed code]
http://aspn.activestate.com/ASPN/Cookbook/XSLT/

XSL DocBook Stylesheets
http://www.nwalsh.com/docbook/xsl/

Microsoft: Unofficial MSXML XSLT FAQ
http://www.netcrucible.com/xslt/msxml-faq.htm

Microsoft: Code Center [look for XML and XSLT, perhaps in Code Examples/ Web Development/XML/XSLT; links change too often]
http://msdn.microsoft.com/code/default.asp

Microsoft: MSDN Library: XML and Web Services: XML Core [link changes too often]
http://msdn.microsoft.com/library/default.asp

Software

W3C: XSL Software
http://www.w3.org/Style/XSL/#software

Robin Cover: XSL Software
http://www.oasis-open.org/cover/xslSoftware.html

XMLSOFTWARE.com: XSLT Engines [processors, etc.]
http://www.xmlsoftware.com/xslt/

XMLSOFTWARE.com: XSLT Editors
http://www.xmlsoftware.com/xsleditors/

XMLSOFTWARE.com: XSLT Utilities
http://www.xmlsoftware.com/xsltutils/

XMLSOFTWARE.com: XSL Formatters
http://www.xmlsoftware.com/xslfo/

XSLT.com: XSL/XSLT Tools
http://www.xslt.com/xslt_tools.htm

Gallery of Stupid XSL and XSLT Tricks
http://www.incrementaldevelopment.com/xsltrick/

Apache: Xalan-Java 2.x (XSLT processor with TRaX)
http://xml.apache.org/xalan-j/index.html

Apache: Xalan-Java 2.x Javadocs
http://xml.apache.org/xalan-j/apidocs/index.html

Apache: Xalan-Java 2.x Basic Usage Patterns
http://xml.apache.org/xalan-j/usagepatterns.html

Apache: Cocoon (XML/XSL/DOM publishing framework)
http://xml.apache.org/cocoon/index.html

Apache: FOP (Formatting Objects to PDF)
http://xml.apache.org/fop/

SAXON, Michael Kay [XSLT processor]
http://saxon.sourceforge.net/

XT, James Clark [XSLT processor]
http://www.jclark.com/xml/xt.html

Jaxen: Java XPath Engine
http://jaxen.org

XPath Visualizer [XPath and XSLT learning aid]
http://www.topxml.com/xpathvisualizer

4XT.org: Site of resources for XT
http://www.4xt.org/

Microsoft: MSXML 3.0 [older XML parser with XSLT processor]
http://msdn.microsoft.com/xml/general/xmlparser.asp

Microsoft: What's New in the October 2001 Microsoft XML Core Services (MSXML) 4.0 Release [newer XML parser with XSLT processor, and more]
http://msdn.microsoft.com/library/default.asp?url=/library/en-us/dnmsxml/html/whatsnew40rtm.asp

Sun: XSLT Compiler [Developer Connection]
http://www.sun.com/xml/developers/xsltc/

Oracle: XML Developer's Kit [XDK: XSLT processor and XML Parser]
http://technet.oracle.com/tech/xml/

Oracle: XSQL Servlet
http://technet.oracle.com/tech/xml/xsql_servlet/

IBM: XSLbyDemo
http://www.alphaworks.ibm.com/tech/xslbydemo

IBM: XSLerator—generate XSLT scripts from mappings defined using a visual interface
http://www.alphaworks.ibm.com/tech/xslerator

Zvon: XSLTracer [useful for seeing how an XSLT processor steps through templates]
http://www.zvon.org/xxl/XSLTracer/Output/introduction.html

DataPower: XSLTMark [XSLT processor performance benchmarking]
http://www.datapower.com/XSLTMark/

jd.xslt [processor with scripting support]
http://www.aztecrider.com/xslt/index.html

Infoteria: iXSLT [processor]
http://www.infoteria.com/products/product_page.jsp?id=/product/product_1.xml

HTML-Kit [free editor with XML and XSLT support via plugins]
http://www.chami.com/html-kit/

XSLTunit, Eric van der Vlist [framework for testing XSLT transformations written in XSLT]
http://xsltunit.org/

Examplotron, Eric van der Vlist [uses XSLT to build XML Schema by example]
http://examplotron.org/

Schematron, Rick Jelliffe [uses XSLT and XPath for tree patterns to define schema]
http://www.ascc.net/xml/resource/schematron/schematron.html

XSLT Test Tool, Joshua Allen
http://www.netcrucible.com/xslt/xslt-tool.htm

U.S. National Institute of Standards and Technology (NIST): Tests for XSLT, XPath, and XSL Formatting Objects
http://xw2k.sdct.itl.nist.gov/xml/page4.html

Netfish Technologies: XSLTVM—XSLT Virtual Machine
http://www.gca.org/papers/xmleurope2000/papers/s35-03.html

EXSLT [Extensions to XSLT]
http://www.exslt.org/

SourceForge: XSLT Standard Library [XSLTSL]
http://sourceforge.net/projects/xsltsl/

NIST: XSLToolbox [tools to help XML applications talk to one another]
http://ats.nist.gov/xsltoolbox/

FiveSight Technologies: XPath Tester [very handy graphical test environment for XPath expressions]
http://www.fivesight.com/downloads/xpathtester.asp

SAXPath [Simple API for XPath]
http://saxpath.org/

ActiveState: Visual XSLT [XSLT IDE plugin for Visual Studio.NET]
http://www.activestate.com/Products/VisualXSLT/index.html

ActiveState: Komodo [Mozilla framework; allows perl, Python, JavaScript scripting]
http://www.activestate.com/Products/Komodo/index.html

XML Cooktop [IDE for XSLT, XPath, XML instances and DTDs]
http://www.xmlcooktop.com/

Pretty XML Tree Viewer, Jeni Tennison and Mike J. Brown
http://skew.org/xml/stylesheets/treeview/html/

ASCII XML Tree Viewer, Jeni Tennison and Mike J. Brown
http://skew.org/xml/stylesheets/treeview/ascii/

SHOWTREE—XSL Tree Display Stylesheet, G. Ken Holman (Crane Softwrights)
http://www.CraneSoftwrights.com/resources/showtree/index.htm

Tutorials

XSL Concepts and Practical Use, Norm Walsh
http://www.nwalsh.com/docs/tutorials/xsl/xsl/frames.html

XSL Transformations slides from SD2000 East, Elliotte Rusty Harold
http://www.ibiblio.org/xml/slides/sd2000east/xslt/

XSL Transformations: Chapter 14 from *XML Bible*, Elliotte Rusty Harold
http://www.ibiblio.org/xml/books/bible/updates/14.html

Examples from Chapter 14 of *The XML Bible*, Elliotte Rusty Harold
http://www.ibiblio.org/xml/books/bible/examples/14/index.html

Zvon XSL Tutorial
http://www.zvon.org/xxl/XSLTutorial/Books/Book1/index.html

Zvon XSL Tutorial All-in-One
http://zvon.vscht.cz/HTMLonly/XSLTutorial/Books/Book1/bookInOne.html

Zvon XPath Tutorial
http://www.zvon.org/xxl/XPathTutorial/General/examples.html

Transforming XML, Bob DuCharme [series of articles]
http://www.xml.com/pub/q/transformingxml

How to Develop Stylesheets for XML to XSL-FO Transformation, Antenna House
http://www.antennahouse.com/axf11sampleEN.htm

Rescuing XSLT from Niche Status: A Gentle Introduction to XSLT through HTML Templates, David Jacobs
http://www.xfront.com/rescuing-xslt.html

Hands-on XSL, Don Day (IBM) [XSL for fun and diversion]
http://www-106.ibm.com/developerworks/library/hands-on-xsl/

XSL Elements, Michael Kay
http://saxon.sourceforge.net/saxon6.5/xsl-elements.html

What Kind of Language Is XSLT?, Michael Kay
http://www-106.ibm.com/developerworks/library/x-xslt/

Objects by Design: XSLT by Example
http://www.objectsbydesign.com/projects/xslt/xslt_by_example.html

w3schools XSL Tutorial
http://www.w3schools.com/xsl/

VBXML: XSLT Tutorial
http://www.vbxml.com/xsl/tutorials/intro/default.asp

Tutorials XSL and CSS Stylesheets, finetuning.com
http://www.finetuning.com/styletutorials.html

Brick's tutorial: XLink, XPointer, and XPath
http://www.brics.dk/~amoeller/XML/linking.html

W3C Specifications and Information

Extensible Stylesheet Language (XSL) Home Page [good starting point; bookmark]
http://www.w3.org/Style/XSL/

W3C Style Home Page [XSL, CSS, and related efforts]
http://www.w3.org/Style

W3C Style Activity Statement
http://www.w3.org/Style/Activity

XSL Working Group (W3C Members Only)
http://www.w3.org/Style/XSL/Group/

XSL Transformations (XSLT) Version 1.0 [W3C Recommendation: November 16, 1999]
http://www.w3.org/TR/xslt

XML Path Language (XPath) Version 1.0 [W3C Recommendation: November 16, 1999]
http://www.w3.org/TR/xpath

Extensible Stylesheet Language (XSL) Version 1.0
http://www.w3.org/TR/xsl/

Associating Stylesheets with XML Documents [W3C Recommendation: June 29, 1999]
http://www.w3.org/TR/xml-stylesheet/

XSL Working Group Charter
http://www.w3.org/Style/2000/xsl-charter.html

XSLT 1.1 Working Draft [defunct; canceled by W3C in April 2001]
http://www.w3.org/TR/xslt11

XSLT Requirements 2.0
http://www.w3.org/TR/xslt20req

XSL Transformations (XSLT) Version 2.0 [Working Draft]
http://www.w3.org/TR/xslt20/

XSLT 2.0: Changes from XSLT 1.0 [Non-normative]
http://www.w3.org/TR/xslt20/#changes

XPath Requirements 2.0
http://www.w3.org/TR/xpath20req

XML Path Language (XPath) 2.0 [Working Draft]
http://www.w3.org/TR/xpath20/

XPath 2.0: Backwards Compatibility with XPath 1.0 [Non-normative]
http://www.w3.org/TR/xpath20/#id-backwards-compatibility

XML Query Home Page [links to XQuery, XQuery 1.0 and XPath 2.0 Functions and Operators, etc.]
http://www.w3.org/XML/Query

Chapter 12

Practical Formatting Using XSLFO

This chapter gives you a solid overview of the capabilities of the vocabulary and semantics of XSLFO. The first section provides the context for XSLFO by relating it to XML, CSS, DSSSL, and especially XSLT. Although the interrelationship of these specifications is presented in chapter 11 of this book, the explanation here gives you another perspective that you'll find very enlightening. A small- and a medium-sized example are introduced that bring home the XML/XSLT/XSLFO relationship. Each of Ken Holman's diagrams is worth the proverbial 1,000 words.

The second section of this chapter introduces the real meat and potatoes of XSLFO. Holman begins by introducing the important distinctions between layout-based and content-based formatting, as well as contrasting formatting and rendering. Next, you'll find a great explanation of the processing model of formatting, followed by aspects of the actual formatting vocabulary (i.e., XSLFO elements, attributes, properties, functions, and so on). The rest of the chapter presents brief overviews of topics that you'll eventually need to explore more in order to actually use XSLFO (e.g., area and page basics, generic body constructs, floats, spacing and stacking).

Introduction

We often take the printed form of information for granted. Yet how many of us are satisfied with the print-screen functionality of a Web browser? How many times have you printed a lengthy Web document and found the paginated result to be as easily navigated as the electronic original? Navigating a paginated document is

Note: We are delighted to have G. Ken Holman of Crane Softwrights Ltd., a noted XSL expert and chair of the OASIS XSLT/XPath Conformance Technical Committee, contribute this, his introduction to Extensible Stylesheet Language Formatting Objects (XSLFO). He was given very little time and we're quite pleased with the result.

very different from navigating a Web page, and browser-based navigation mechanisms understandably will not work on printed output. How would we follow a hyperlink when the visible clickable content hides the underlying hyperlink target address?

When we want to produce a paginated presentation of our XML information, we necessarily must offer a different set of navigation tools to the consumers of our documents. These navigational aids have been honed since bound books have been used: headers, footers, page numbers, and page number citations are some of the characteristics of printed pages we use to find our way around a collection of fixed-sized folios of information.

This collection of fixed-sized folios may, indeed, have different geometries of page sizes and margin widths, but each page once rendered is fixed in its particular geometry. Layout and typesetting controls give us the power to express our information on pages in a visually pleasing and perhaps meaningful set of conventions conveying information in the presentation itself.

Many aspects of layout are, indeed, applicable on electronic displays and Recommendations such as Cascading Style Sheets (CSS) have defined presentation semantics in areas such as font, margin, and color properties. Paginating marked-up information is not something new, in that the Document Style Semantics and Specification Language (DSSSL) is an international standard for use originally with SGML documents, although it also works unchanged with XML documents.

Accepting that HTML and CSS are suitable and sufficient for browser-oriented rendering of information, the W3C set out to define a collection of pagination semantics for print-oriented rendering. These pagination semantics are equally suitable for an electronic display of fixed-size folios of information, such as page-turner browsers and Portable Document Format (PDF) readers.

The Extensible Stylesheet Language (XSL), also known colloquially in our community as the Extensible Stylesheet Language Formatting Objects (XSLFO), combines the heritage of CSS and DSSSL in a well thought out and robust specification of formatting semantics for paginating information.

The Recommendation itself is a rigorous, lengthy, and involved technical specification of the processes and operations engaged by a formatting engine to effect consistent paginated results compared to other formatting engines acting on the same inputs. Well-written for its intended purpose, the document remains out of reach for many people who just want to write stylesheets and print their information.

In its ever-growing collection of training material, Crane Softwrights Ltd., has published *Practical Formatting Using XSLFO* covering every formatting object of XSLFO and their properties, according to the final XSL 1.0 Recommendation of October 15, 2001. The first two chapters of that book have been rewritten in prose and are made available here as an introduction to the technology and its use. This material assumes no prior knowledge of XSLFO and guides the reader through background, context, structure, concepts, introductory terminology, and a short introduction to each of the formatting objects.

Neither the Recommendation itself nor Crane Softwrights training material attempts to teach facets of typography and attractive or appropriate layout style, only the semantics of formatting, the implementation of those semantics, and the nuances of control available to the stylesheet writer and implemented by the stylesheet formatting tool. XSLFO is a very powerful language with which we can create very ugly or very beautiful pages from our XML-based information.

The Context of XSLFO

First, we will review the roles of W3C Recommendations in the XML family and an International Standard in the SGML family, and overview contexts in which XSLFO is used.

Extensible Markup Language

We use Extensible Markup Language (XML) to express information hierarchically in a sequence of characters according to a vocabulary of element types and their attributes. Using various Recommendations and other industry standards, we can formally describe the makeup and constraints of this vocabulary in different ways to validate the content against our desired document model.

Cascading Style Sheets

Initially created for rendering HTML documents in browsers, CSS formatting properties can ornament the document tree described by a sequence of markup following that specific SGML vocabulary. CSS was revised to describe the ornamentation of XML documents so that CSS-aware browsers can render the information in a decorated document tree described by any XML vocabulary. Browsers that recognize these properties can render the contents of the tree according to the semantics of the formatting model governing the property interpretation.

Document Style Semantics and Specification Language

The International Organization for Standardization (ISO) standardized a collection of style semantics in the Document Style Semantics and Specification Language (DSSSL) for formatting paginated information. DSSSL also includes a specification language for the transformation of Standard Generalized Markup Language (SGML) documents of any vocabulary, and implementations have since been modified to support the styling of XML documents of any vocabulary. This introduced the concept of a flow object tree to comprise objects and properties that reflect the internationalized semantics of paginated output.

Extensible Stylesheet Language Family

Two vocabularies specified in separate W3C Recommendations provide for the two distinct styling processes of transforming and rendering XML instances. The Extensible Stylesheet Language Transformations (XSLT) is a templating markup language used to express how a processor creates a transformed result from an instance of XML information. The Extensible Stylesheet Language Formatting Objects is a pagination markup language describing a rendering vocabulary capturing the semantics of formatting information for paginated presentation. Formally named Extensible Stylesheet Language, this Recommendation normatively incorporates the entire XSLT Recommendation by reference; they used to be defined together in a single W3C Draft Recommendation. Although XSLT is designed primarily for the kinds of transformation required for using XSL, it can also be used for arbitrary transformation requirements.

The XML Family of Recommendations

The XML family of specifications comprises several components, which we will discuss one at a time.

Extensible Markup Language

If you wish to read the complete content of the XML Recommendation, it is available at *http://www.w3.org/TR/REC-xml*.

Two Objectives for Information Representation We use XML to capture our information in a markup language defined by a vocabulary of elements and attributes described by a document model. We can presume a vocabulary informally, or we can declare the grammar, or makeup, of the vocabulary formally so that we may verify that our information adheres to our constraints. This vocabulary represents the labels and the granularity of the concepts we have for the expression of our information.

Consider the simple well-formed XML instance `purc.xml` in Listing 12-1. The constructs represent purchasing information only because we recognize the names and assume the names reflect the concepts that we understand. If we misunderstand the names used, yet believe we understand them correctly, we can "process" the information using our assumed semantics without invalidating the information as represented to us.

Listing 12-1 A Well-Formed XML Purchase Order Instance (*Example 1-1*[1])

```
<?xml version="1.0"?>
<purchase>
  <customer db="cust123"/>
  <product db="prod345">
    <amount>23.45</amount>
  </product>
</purchase>
```

In the same way, we can feed this information to any XML-based application and the application can act on the names it has been programmed to recognize, thus interpreting the semantics of the information the only way it knows how. This may not, indeed, be the semantics assumed by the author of the document.

It is a common misconception that our document models somehow describe the semantics of our information, when in fact they describe only the vocabulary with which we identify components of our information. We can use a document model only to validate that the structure and content of a character stream conforms to the constraints described according to the features and limitations of the expression of the model description. XML 1.0 describes the Document Type Definition (DTD) expression of the grammar of an XML vocabulary. Other approaches such as XML Schema, RELAX-NG Schema, and Schematron offer benefits and limitations different from those of a DTD, and are candidates for validating the contents of XML documents.

The semantics of our information are entirely described by the applications we use to process our documents. What a document "means" is precisely what our applications "think" it means, by the processes they employ against our information by following the corresponding labels.

Not Related to Presentation or Rendition When we present documents visually or aurally, we are rendering the content according to the presentation semantics our stylesheets confer on the content. Nothing inherent in XML is related to presentation or rendition; it is entirely up to other standards to define presentation semantics and the syntax with which to engage them.

Translatable Vocabularies XML vocabularies can be translated to the vocabulary of the semantics of an application. If our document structures are composed in the same structure we wish to use for presentation, we can choose to decorate our structures with recognized formatting properties if that is sufficient to the presentation environment. If an alternative structure is needed, either in the same vocabulary or a vocabulary specific to the presentation technology, then we must

1. Figure and listing (example) numbers that appear in italics within parentheses after this chapter's figure and listing numbers refer to their number as they appear on this book's CD-ROM.

rearrange and/or transform documents following our vocabulary into documents following the presentation vocabulary.

In practice, it is far more beneficial in the long run to design your document structures according to your business practices and your plans for creating and maintaining your information. You should not design models according to how you plan to present your information; you might wish to do the presentation in different ways, both currently and in the future. Through transformation you can rearrange any information you create and maintain it into an order you wish to present. It may be difficult to accommodate business practices and information access requirements if you lock your information into a single presentation.

Markup-based rendering agents are programmed to recognize vocabularies geared for the presentation of information. These vocabularies may be only attribute-based, as is true for CSS. Other vocabularies comprise both elements and attributes, as is true for the HTML. When we want our information to be rendered by one of these agents, we must understand the presentation semantics implemented by the rendering agents.

To present our information, we are in effect interpreting the semantics of our vocabularies and choosing to represent an information packaged into the semantics of a rendering device. We must, therefore, transform instances of our vocabularies into instances of the rendering vocabularies in order for the rendering agents to present our information the way we wish. For example, we can transform our XML vocabularies into the combination of the HTML and CSS vocabularies so that we render our XML documents in a wide range of Web browsers that may, or may not, support CSS stylesheets. Browsers that recognize CSS will recognize those presentation semantics, and browsers that do not recognize CSS will use the accepted presentation semantics inferred by convention of the HTML vocabulary.

Namespace-Based Constructs Namespaces can distinguish constructs in information from different vocabularies. Properly identifying constructs in the information is essential to implementing the semantics of our data in our applications. A rigorous method of identifying constructs in XML information is to use namespaces to prefix element types that have lengthy URI reference strings with protocol specifications that are governed by ownership through domain name registration. Such prefixes are effected through associating a namespace prefix with the URI reference string and then using that prefix in the markup of the document to identify element types and attributes.

But, again, these names are merely labels and the use of namespaces provides a more powerful labeling mechanism by employing names that incorporate the essence of ownership through the domain names of URI references. When we model our vocabularies, we must decide if we are going to use simple naming conventions or namespace-based naming conventions, and accommodate the presence of the namespace URI in our applications if necessary.

An application can, therefore, be rigorous in recognizing namespace-based names to which it applies the assumed semantics of the information. Through proper namespace maintenance, this eliminates the risk of improperly recognizing a construct's label; however, it does not prevent an application from making an incorrect assumption of the semantics of the information based on the correct label.

Moreover, an application should be prepared to accommodate namespaces it does not recognize, either through defined processing or perhaps the throwing of an error.

Namespace-Aware Processors XSLFO processors are rigorous in this area. Well-defined semantics, or behaviors, are captured in an XML vocabulary of elements and their attributes that represent, respectively, formatting objects and their properties. Namespaces are important to an XSLFO processor to recognize not only those constructs from the XSLFO vocabulary, but also any extensions to the vocabulary that are specific to a brand of processor.

In addition, the arbitrary uses of rendering vocabularies for foreign objects in the XSLFO stream are allowed through the use of namespaces, and an XSLFO formatting engine can properly forward rendered content in arbitrary namespaces to the rendering processes incorporated in the tool.

As with all applications, the assumption is that the labels reference the semantics as defined by the specification, and it is up to the user to respect that assumption in order to get the desired formatted result. The use of the XSLFO namespace does not magically confer semantics on the elements. Rather, an XSLFO processor assumes that when XSLFO names are used, the user desires application of the semantics defined by the XSLFO Recommendation.

We learn the XSLFO XML vocabulary as a representation of the semantics assumed by an XSLFO processor, and we engage that processor to paginate and render our information accordingly.

Cascading Stylesheets

Historically, the separation of presentation semantics from information content has been around the Web world for a while, but this was originally developed for use in browsers.

Formatting Properties for Web Documents Not accepting the presentation semantics inferred by HTML browsers for information marked up in HTML, the Web community developed a robust and coherent formatting model for electronic presentation of information. The CSS model implements a set of formatting semantics tied to a vocabulary of attribute values that can be attached to hierarchically structured Web documents.

Initially designed for HTML, a subsequent release of CSS describes the application of formatting properties to XML documents. These formatting properties do not involve manipulation of the document trees; they are merely attached to the document tree and interpreted by a CSS-aware user agent that can effect the formatting inferred by the semantics triggered by the properties.

Inherent in the formatting model is the notion that width and length of the presentation canvas are not fixed. The length of the presentation is essentially infinite, in that the browser agent shows a document tree in its entirety regardless of the length of the information in the instance. The technology of the presentation is essentially electronic, in that readers of the information can dynamically change the width of the canvas, thus requiring the user agent to reflow the content within the new dimensions.

Ornamentation of the Document Tree A CSS-aware user agent views our information as the document tree represented by the markup we choose to use. The stylistic information we decorate the tree with as formatting "ornaments" dictates how we want the user agent to render the content.

The formatting model provides for document content to be prefixed and suffixed with supplemental information found in the stylesheet. White space around information can be controlled and we can place our content in overlapping and transparent rectangular regions of the canvas.

Inheritance plays an important role in CSS. The "cascade" is the application of inherited formatting properties when a given construct does not explicitly supply an inheritable value. Inheritance first starts "up" the ancestry of the document tree, looking for an applicable property specification. The cascade then continues looking at external style sheets of lesser priority than internal style sheets, finally accepting the built-in presentation semantics assumed by HTML user agents.

Multiple Media Type Support The CSS formatting model incorporates a number of layout constructs available to flow our information into a given desired presentation. For example, table-oriented constructs are available to present information in a tabular form, even if our information isn't in HTML table markup.

Because accessibility information to all users of the Web is important, CSS introduced aural presentation properties to shape information for the visually impaired. Note that not only people with sight disabilities are visually impaired; that sighted users of the Web may be in situations where they will not be able to use their sight (perhaps mobile applications while browsing for information in the car). Clever use of aural properties will be a boon to the surfing experience.

Compatibility with Legacy Browsers CSS formatting doesn't (*shouldn't*) interfere with legacy browsers that do not support CSS. CSS properties are expressed in HTML documents through reserved attributes and document metadata. Unfortunately, many legacy HTML browsers were not true SGML applications, but rather simple "angle-bracket processors" unaware of the rules of formal markup practice. Hence, arcane methods of capturing stylesheet information are sometimes required to be resilient to legacy browsers that do not properly implement markup. Even still, there are some non-CSS-aware browsers that end up exposing property specifications on the user's canvas instead of properly recognizing their role as supplemental information to be kept off the canvas.

The property sheets can be external to the document itself, and indeed must be so in XML documents that do not use namespaces. Although this is not seen in practice, a browser could choose to render XML documents that are using namespaces by recognizing CSS properties embedded in style attributes from the HTML vocabulary,

A Common Formatting Model A W3C working group is producing a common formatting model for Web documents. Many W3C Recommendations need to specify formatting or display properties at times. Where applicable, designers of new Recommendations are asked to use the CSS semantics and the property names for those semantics. This promotes a widely understood specification of the common requirements for formatting, including properties related to font, spacing, and a number of other useful presentation areas.

Document Style Semantics and Specification Language

Information about DSSSL (ISO/IEC-10179:1996) is available at *http://www.y12.doe.gov/sgml/wg8/dsssl/readme.htm*.

Standardized Page Formatting Semantics DSSSL describes the international standard for pagination semantics: a set of characteristics and their values that are used to flow information on folios (e.g., printed pages). Both simple and complex page geometries can be specified. Users specify the desired intent of the result of the formatting process by using the semantics described in the standard.

DSSSL does not specify the rendering process itself, only the interpretation of the formatting intent into what needs to be rendered.

The semantics have no bias to any particular writing direction. For example, a stylesheet written for the left-to-right writing direction can simultaneously support top-to-bottom or right-to-left writing systems without changes.

Implementation-Defined Formatting Semantics DSSSL offers a framework for implementation-defined sets of formatting semantics; it is extensible to support any set of semantics defined by a processor. Stylesheets can declare the existence of a formatting concept and then engage the use of that concept in the intent for the result.

James Clark, the author of the JADE (see *http://www.jclark.com/jade/jade.htm*) DSSSL engine, specified and implemented a set of formatting semantics that represents markup syntax. Using these semantics, one can effect an instance transformation by "styling" one's input document into output markup. The OpenJade project (see *http://www.netfolder.com/DSSSL/*) continues the development of JADE.

A Programming Language for Transforming Structured Information The DSSSL specification language is a side-effect-free dialect of the Scheme language. This functional programming language is very powerful, and complex algorithms can be implemented succinctly through the tight LISP-like syntax.

Unfortunately, the parentheses in the specification language scared a lot of people away from DSSSL and it never achieved the recognition or acceptance it should have in the industry. As a result of shying away from the specification language, our markup community never learned the style semantics side of this international standard, and DSSSL was often ignored when it should have been an important contribution to a number of efforts.

Custody of ISO/IEC JTC 1/SC 34/WG 2 The International Organization for Standardization (ISO) has many committees for standards work in many aspects of our daily lives. The joint technical committee (JTC) with the International Electrotechnical Commission (IEC) is responsible for information technology. The subcommittee (SC) for document description and processing languages is numbered 34 and the second working group (WG) of this subcommittee is responsible for DSSSL and other formatting issues such as fonts.

The full title of the working group is ISO/IEC JTC 1/SC 34/WG 2. Prior designations for the committee that has worked on DSSSL from its inception include ISO/IEC JTC 1/WG 4 and ISO/IEC JTC 1/SC 18/WG 8.

Styling Structured Information

Styling is the rendering of information into a form suitable for consumption by a target audience. Because the audience can change for a given set of information, we often need to apply different styling for that information to obtain dissimilar renderings to meet the needs of each audience. Perhaps some information needs to be rearranged to make more sense for the reader. Perhaps some information needs to be highlighted differently to bring focus to key content.

It is important when we think about styling information to remember that not one, but two distinct processes are involved. First, we must transform the information from the organization used when it was created into the organization needed for consumption. Second, when rendering we must express the aspects of the appearance of the reorganized information, whatever the target medium.

Consider the flow of information as a streaming process where information is created upstream and processed or consumed downstream. Upstream, in the early stages, we should be expressing the information abstractly, thus preventing any early binding of concrete or final-form concepts. Midstream, or even downstream, we can exploit the information as long as it remains flexible and abstract. Late binding of the information to a final form can be based on the target use of the final product; by delaying this binding until late in the process, we preserve the original information for exploitation for other purposes along the way.

It is a common but misdirected practice to model information based on how you plan to use it downstream. It does not matter if your target is a presentation-oriented structure, for example, or a structure that is appropriate for another markup-based system. Modeling practice should focus on both the business reasons and inherent relationships in the semantics behind the information being described (as such the vocabularies are then content-oriented).

For example, emphasized text is often confused with a particular format in which it is rendered. Where we could model information using a <b> element type for eventual rendering in a bold typeface, we would be better off modeling the information using an <emph> element type. In this way, we capture the reason for marking up the information (that it is emphasized from surrounding information), and we do not lock any of the downstream targets into using a bold typeface for rendering.

Many times the midstream or downstream processes need only rearrange, relabel, or synthesize the information for a target purpose and never apply any semantics of style for rendering purposes. Transformation tasks stand alone in such cases, meeting the processing needs without introducing rendering issues.

One caveat regarding modeling content-oriented information is that there are applications where the content-orientation is, indeed, presentation-oriented. Consider book publishing where the abstract content is based on presentational semantics. This is meaningful because there is no abstraction beyond the appearance or presentation of the content.

Consider the customer information in Listing 12-1 (*Example 1-1*). A Web user agent doesn't know how to render an element named <customer>. The HTML vocabulary used to render the customer information could be as shown in Listing 12-2.

Listing 12-2 HTML Rendering Semantics Markup for Example (*Example 1-2*)

```
<p>From: <i>(Customer Reference) <b>cust123</b></i>
</p>
```

The rendering result is shown in Figure 12-1 (*Figure 1-1*), with the rendering user agent interpreting the markup for italics and boldface presentation semantics. The figure illustrates these two distinct styling steps: *transforming* the instance of the XML vocabulary into a new instance according to a vocabulary of rendering semantics; and *formatting* the instance of the rendering vocabulary in the user agent.

Two W3C Recommendations To meet these two distinct processes in a detached (yet related) fashion, the W3C Working Group responsible for XSL split the original drafts of their work into two separate Recommendations: one for transforming information and the other for paginating information.

FIGURE 12-1 HTML rendering for Listing 12-2 example

The XSLT Recommendation describes a vocabulary recognized by an XSLT processor to transform information from an organization in the source file into a different organization suitable for continued downstream processing.

The XSL Recommendation describes XSLFO, a vocabulary that reflects the semantics of paginating a stream of information into individual pages. The XSLFO Recommendation normatively includes XSLT; historically, both Recommendations were expressed in a single document.

Both XSLT and XSLFO are endorsed by members of WSSSL, an association of researchers and developers passionate about the application of markup technologies in today's information technology infrastructure.

Extensible Stylesheet Language Transformations

We all need to transform structured information when it is not ordered for a purpose other than how it is created. The XSLT 1.0 Recommendation describes a transformation instruction vocabulary of constructs that can be expressed in an XML model of elements and attributes (see *http://www.w3.org/TR/xslt*) .

Transformation by Example We can distinguish XSLT from other techniques for transmuting information by regarding it simply as "transformation by example," differentiating it from many other techniques regarded as "transformation by program logic." This perspective focuses on the distinction that our obligation is not to tell an XSLT processor how to effect the changes we need; rather, we tell an XSLT processor the end result we want, and it is the processor's responsibility to do the dirty work.

The XSLT Recommendation gives us, in effect, a templating language. It is a vocabulary for specifying templates that represent "examples of the result." Based on how we instruct the XSLT processor to access the source of the data being transformed, the processor will build the result incrementally by adding the filled-in templates.

We write our stylesheets, or "transformation specifications," primarily with declarative constructs, although we can employ imperative techniques (also known as procedural techniques) if and when needed. We assert the desired behavior of the XSLT processor based on conditions found in our source. We supply examples of how each component of our result is formulated and indicate the conditions of the source that trigger which component is next added to our result. Alternatively, we can selectively add components to the result on demand.

Many programmers unfairly deride XSLT as not being a good programming language, when in fact it is a templating language and not a programming language. The idea of declaratively supplying templates of the result and the matching conditions of source tree nodes to the templates is a very different paradigm from imperative programming. I find by far the most disparaging and vociferous attacks against XSLT are from programmers unable or awkwardly trying to follow an algorithm-based imperative approach to the problem instead of the assertion-based declarative approach inherent in the language design.

XSLT is not a panacea, and there will be many algorithmic situations (particularly in character-level text manipulation) where XSLT is not the appropriate tool to use. Node tree rearrangement, and in particular mixed content processing, can be handled far more easily declaratively in XSLT than in many imperative approaches. This templating approach is ideal for the rearrangement of information for use with XSL formatting semantics. Critics will continue to declare XSLT a "bad" programming language until they stop using it as the incorrect pigeonhole for certain classes of problems.

XSLT is similar to other transmutation approaches in that we deal with our information as trees of abstract nodes. We don't deal with the raw markup of source data. Unlike these other approaches, however, the primary memory management and information manipulation (node traversal and node creation) is handled by the XSLT processor, not by the stylesheet writer. This is a significant difference between XSLT and a transformation programming language or interface like the Document Object Model (DOM), where the programmer is responsible for handling the low-level manipulation of information constructs.

Our objective as stylesheet writers is to supply the XSLT processor with enough "templates of the result" that the processor can build the result we desire when triggered by information in our source. Our data file becomes a hierarchy of nodes in our source tree. Our templates become a hierarchy of nodes in our stylesheet tree. The processor is doing the work of building the result node tree from nodes in our stylesheet and source trees. We don't have to be programmers manipulating the node trees or serializing the result node tree into our result file. It isn't our responsibility to worry about the angle brackets and ampersands that may be needed in the result markup.

Consider once again the customer information in our example purchase order in Listing 12-1 (*Example 1-1*). An example of the HTML vocabulary supplied to the XSLT processor to produce the markup in Listing 12-2 is shown in Listing 12-3. An example of XSL vocabulary supplied to the XSLT processor to produce the markup in Listing 12-7 on page 812 is shown in Listing 12-4.

Listing 12-3 Sample XSLT Template Rule for the HTML Vocabulary (*Example 1-3*)

```
<xsl:template match="customer">
  <p><xsl:text>From: </xsl:text>
    <i><xsl:text>(Customer Reference) </xsl:text>
      <b><xsl:value-of select="@db"/></b></i></p>
</xsl:template>
```

Listing 12-4 Sample XSLT Template Rule for the XSL Vocabulary (*Example 1-4*)

```
<xsl:template match="customer">
  <fo:block space-before.optimum="20pt" font-size="20pt">
    <xsl:text>From: </xsl:text>
    <fo:inline font-style="italic">
      <xsl:text>(Customer Reference) </xsl:text>
      <fo:inline font-weight="bold">
        <xsl:value-of select="@db"/>
      </fo:inline></fo:inline></fo:block>
</xsl:template>
```

Comparing both examples, our practice as stylesheet writers is not different in any way. The templates are different in that they express different vocabularies for the elements and attributes in the result tree of nodes, but our methodology is not different. Each template is the example of the desired result for the given <customer> element as expressed in each of two presentation vocabularies.

Comparing the style in both examples to imperative programming techniques, one can see the XSLT stylesheet writer is not responsible for low-level node manipulation or markup generation. By declaring the nodes to be used in the result tree, one is describing the construction through the use of examples. These templates represent the information we want in the result tree that the processor must effect in whatever way necessary so that the information in the example is correctly included in the result. The processor takes only what is given as an example and is free to use whatever syntactic constructs it wishes that the downstream processor interpreting the result will use to understand the same information being represented in the template.

XSLT includes constructs that we use to identify and iterate over structures in the source information. The information being transformed can be traversed in any order and as many times as required to produce the desired result. We can visit source information numerous times if the result of transformation requires that information to be present numerous times.

Users of XSLT also don't have the burden of implementing numerous practical algorithms required to present information. XSLT specifies a number of algorithms that are implemented within the processor itself, and we engage these algorithms declaratively. High-level functions such as sorting and counting are available to us on demand. Low-level functions such as memory-management, node manipulation, and garbage collection are all integral to the XSLT processor.

This declarative nature of the stylesheet markup makes XSLT so very much more accessible to nonprogrammers than the imperative nature of procedurally oriented transformation languages. Writing a stylesheet is as simple as using markup to declare the behavior of the XSLT processor, much like HTML is used to declare the behavior of the Web browser to paint information on the screen.

Not all examples of results are fixed monolithic sequences of markup, however, so XSLT includes the ability to conditionally include portions of a template based on testable conditions expressed by the stylesheet writer. Other constructs allow templates to be fragmented and added to the result on demand based on stylesheet logic. Templates can be parameterized to be used in different contexts by being added with different parameter values.

In this way XSLT accommodates the programmer as well as the nonprogrammer in that there is sufficient expressiveness in the declarative constructs so that they can be used in an imperative fashion. XSLT is (in programming theory) "Turing complete," thus any arbitrarily complex algorithm could (theoretically) be implemented using the constructs available. Although there will always be a tradeoff between extending the processor to implement something internally and writing an elaborate stylesheet to implement something portably, there is sufficient expressive power to implement some algorithmic business rules and semantic processing in the XSLT constructs.

In short, straightforward and common requirements can be satisfied in a straightforward fashion, while unconventional requirements can be satisfied to an extent as well, with some programming-styled effort.

Theory aside, the necessarily verbose XSLT syntax dictated by its declarative nature and use of XML markup makes the coding of some complex algorithms a bit awkward. I have implemented some very complex traversals and content generation with successful results, but with code that could be difficult to maintain (my own valiant, if not always satisfactory, documentation practices notwithstanding).

Users of XSLT often need to maintain large transformation specifications, and many need to tap prior accomplishments when writing stylesheets. A number of constructs are included supporting the management, maintenance, and exploitation of existing stylesheets. Organizations can build libraries of stylesheet components for sharing among their colleagues. Stylesheet writers can tweak the results of a transformation by writing shell specifications that include or import stylesheets known to solve problems they are addressing. Stylesheet fragments can be written for particular vocabulary fragments; these fragments can subsequently be used in concert, as part of an organization's strategy for common information description in numerous markup models.

Not for General-Purpose XML Transformations It is important to remember that XSLT is *primarily for transforming XML vocabularies to the XSL formatting vocabulary.* This doesn't preclude use of XSLT for other transformation requirements, but it does influence the design of the language and it does constrain some of the functionality from being truly general purpose.

For this reason, the specification *cannot* claim XSLT is a general-purpose transformation language. However, it is still powerful enough for *all* downstream processing transformation needs within the assumptions of use of the transformation results. XSLT stylesheets are often called XSLT transformation scripts because they can be used in many areas not at all related to stylesheet rendering. Consider an electronic commerce environment where transformation is not used for presentation purposes. In this case, the XSLT processor may transform a source instance, which is based on a particular vocabulary, and deliver the results to a legacy application that expects a different vocabulary as input. In other words, we can use XSLT in a nonrendering situation when it doesn't matter what markup is used to represent the content, when only the parsed result of the markup is material.

Listing 12-5 shows an example of using such a legacy vocabulary for the XSLT processor. The transformation would then produce the result in Listing 12-6 acceptable to the legacy application.

Listing 12-5 Sample XSLT Template Rule for a Legacy Vocabulary (*Example 1-5*)

```
<xsl:template match ="customer">
  <buyer><xsl:value-of select="@db"/></buyer>
</xsl:template>
```

Listing 12-6 Sample Legacy Vocabulary for Customer Information (*Example 1-6*)

```
<buyer>cust123</buyer>
```

XSLT assumes that results of transformation will be processed by a rendering agent or some other application employing an XML processor as the means to access the information in the result. The information being delivered represents the serialized result of working with the information in XML instance and, if supplied, the XML document model definition of information set augmentation, expressed as a tree of nodes. The actual markup in either the source XML instance or the XSLT stylesheet is, therefore, not considered material to the application and therefore need not be preserved during transformation. All that is important is that the downstream application obtain the processed content, not the markup, from the source and stylesheet.

By focusing on this processed result for downstream applications, there is little or no control in an XSLT stylesheet over the actual XML markup constructs found within the input documents, or for the actual XML markup constructs used in the resulting output document. This prevents a stylesheet from being aware of such constructs or controlling the way they are used. Any transformation requirement that includes "original markup syntax preservation" would not be suited for XSLT transformations.

Therefore, in comparison to imperative languages and interfaces that offer the programmer tight control over the markup of the result of transformation, XSLT cannot be considered general purpose because of the lack of control over the markup. Two examples are that when using XSLT one cannot specify the order of attributes in the start tag of the serialized result tree, nor can one specify the technique by which sensitive markup characters in `#PCDATA` content are escaped.

When working with the XSLFO vocabulary, the result of the XSLT transformation is going to be processed by the XML processor inside the XSLFO processor, therefore, the markup of the result is immaterial as long as it is well formed. The transformation process is, indeed, absolutely general purpose when the result is going to be interpreted for pagination.

Extensible Stylesheet Language

XSL (or XSLFO) describes formatting and flow semantics for paginated presentation that can be expressed using an XML vocabulary of elements and attributes (see *http://www.w3.org/TR/xsl*).

Paginated Formatting and Flow Semantics Vocabulary This hierarchical vocabulary captures formatting semantics for rendering textual and graphic information in different media in a paginated form. A rendering agent is responsible for interpreting an instance of the vocabulary for a given medium to reify a final result. In concept and architecture this is no different from using HTML and CSS as a hierarchical vocabulary and formatting properties for rendering a set of information in a Web browser. Such user agents are not pagination-oriented and effectively have an infinite page length and variable page width.

Indeed, the printed paged output from a browser of an HTML page is often less than satisfactory. Paginated information includes navigation tools such as page numbers, page number citations, headers, and footers to give the reader methods of finding information or finding their location in a printed document.

In essence, when doing any kind of presentation, we are transforming our XML documents into a final display form by transforming instances of our XML vocabularies into instances of a particular rendering vocabulary that expresses the formatting semantics of our desired result. Our choice of vocabulary must be able to express the nature of the formatting we want accomplished. We can choose to transform our information into a combination of HTML and CSS for Web browsers and can choose an alternative transformation of XSLFO for paginated display (be that paginated to a screen, to paper, or perhaps even aurally). In this way, XSLFO can be considered a pagination markup language.

Target of Transformation When using the XSLFO vocabulary as the rendering language, the stylesheet writer's objective is to convert an XML instance of some arbitrary XML vocabulary into an instance of the formatting semantics vocabulary. This formatting instance is the information rearranged into an expression of the intent of the paginated result as a collection of layout constructs populated with the content to be laid out on the rendered pages.

This result of transformation cannot contain any user-defined vocabulary constructs (e.g., an "address", "customer identifier", or "purchase order number" construct) because the rendering agent would not know what to do with constructs labeled with these unknown identifiers.

Consider again the two examples: HTML for rendering on a single page infinite length in a Web browser window, and XSLFO for rendering on multiple separated pages on a screen, on paper, or audibly. In both cases, the rendering agents understand only the vocabulary expressing their respective formatting semantics and wouldn't know what to do with alien element types defined by the user.

Just as with HTML, a stylesheet writer using XSLFO for pagination must transform each and every user construct into a rendering construct to direct the rendering agent to produce the desired result. By learning and understanding the semantics behind the constructs of XSLFO, the stylesheet writer can create an instance of the formatting vocabulary (e.g., area geometry, spacing, font metrics, etc.) to express the desired layout of the final result with each piece of information in the result coming from either the source data or the stylesheet itself.

Consider once more the customer information in Listing 12-1. An XSLFO rendering agent doesn't know how to render a marked-up construct named `<customer>`. The XSLFO vocabulary used to render the customer information could be like the example in Listing 12-7.

Listing 12-7 XSLFO Rendering Semantics Markup for Example (*Example 1-7*)

```
<fo:block space-before.optimum="20pt" font-size="20pt">From:
<fo:inline font-style="italic">(Customer Reference)
<fo:inline font-weight="bold">cust123</fo:inline>
</fo:inline>
</fo:block>
```

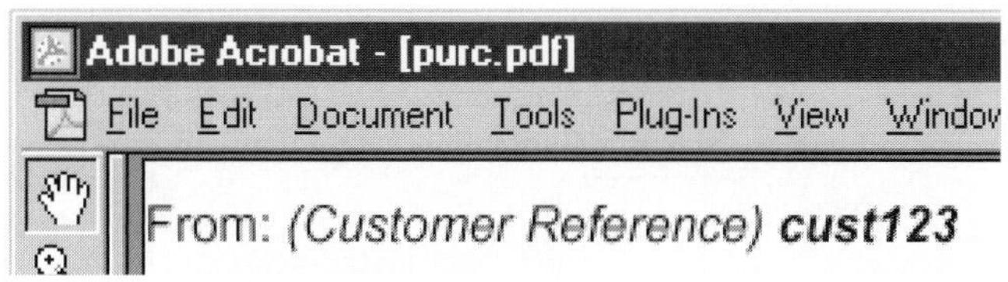

FIGURE 12-2 XSLFO rendering for Listing 12-7 example

The rendering result when using the Portable Document Format (PDF) is shown in Figure 12-2 (*Figure 1-2*), with an intermediate PDF generation step interpreting the XSLFO markup for italics and boldface presentation semantics. The figure again illustrates the two distinctive styling steps: *transforming* the instance of the XML vocabulary into a new instance according to a vocabulary of rendering semantics, and *formatting* the instance of the rendering vocabulary in the user agent.

The formatting semantics of much of the XSLFO vocabulary are device independent, so we can use one set of constructs regardless of the rendering medium. It is the rendering agent's responsibility to interpret these constructs accordingly. In this way, the XSLFO semantics can be interpreted for print, display, aural, or other presentations. There are, indeed, some specialized semantics we can use to influence rendering on particular media, though these are just icing on the cake. Dynamic behaviors can be specified for a highly interactive electronic display that would not function at all, obviously, in the paper form.

Transforming and Rendering XML Information Using XSLFO

When the result tree in an XSLT process is specified to use the XSLFO pagination vocabulary, the normative behavior of an XSLFO processor incorporating an XSLT processor is to interpret the result tree. This interpretation reifies the semantics expressed in the constructs of the result tree to some medium, for example pixels on a screen, dots on paper, and sound through a synthesis device, as shown in Figure 12-3 (*Figure 1-3*).

The stylesheets used in this scenario contain the transformation vocabulary and any custom extensions, as well as the desired result XSLFO formatting vocabulary and any foreign object vocabularies. No other element types from our XML vocabularies are in the result. If there were, rendering processors would not inherently know what to do with an element of type `custnbr` representing a customer number; it is the stylesheet writer's responsibility to transform the information into information recognized by the rendering agent.

There is no obligation for the rendering processor to serialize the result tree created during transformation. The feature of serializing the result tree to XML markup is, however, quite useful as a diagnostic tool. It reveals what we really

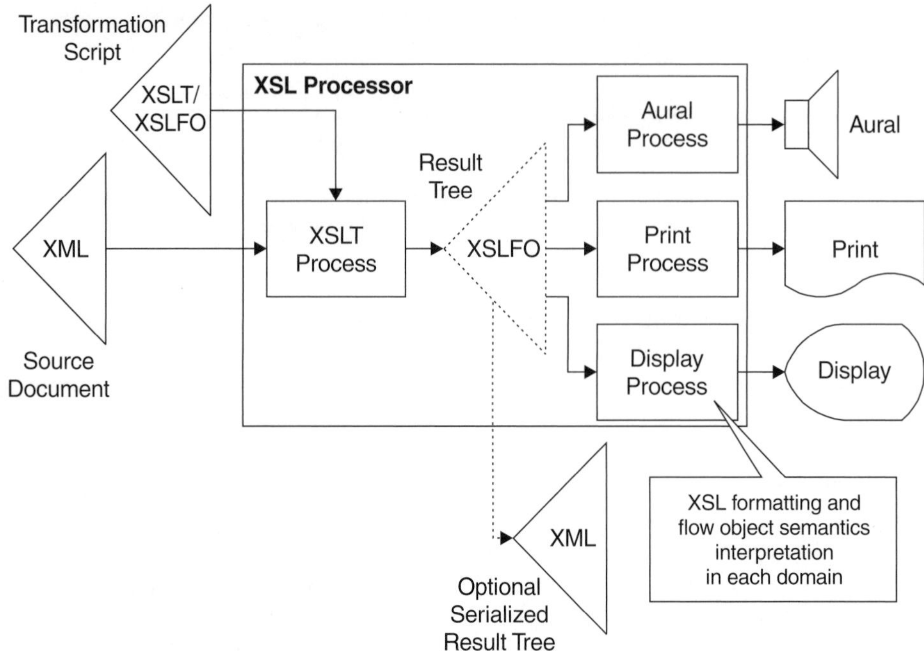

FIGURE 12-3 Transformation from XML to XSL Formatting Semantics

asked to be rendered instead of what we thought we were asking to be rendered when we saw incorrect results. There may also be performance considerations of taking the reified result tree in XML markup and rendering it in other media without incurring the overhead of performing the transformation repeatedly.

Interpreting XSLFO Instances Directly

The XSLFO and foreign object vocabularies can also be used in a standalone XML instance, perhaps as the result of an XSLT transformation using an outboard XSLT processor. The XSLT processor serializes a physical entity from the transformation result tree, and that XML file of XSLFO vocabulary being interpreted by a standalone XSLFO processor, as Figure 12-4 (*Figure 1-4*) shows.

This diagram delineates three distinct phases of the process that are also phases when the XSLT and XSLFO processors are combined into a single application. The transformation phase creates the XSLFO expressing our intent for formatting the source XML. The XSLFO processor first interprets our intent into the information that is to be rendered on the device, then effects the rendering to reify the result.

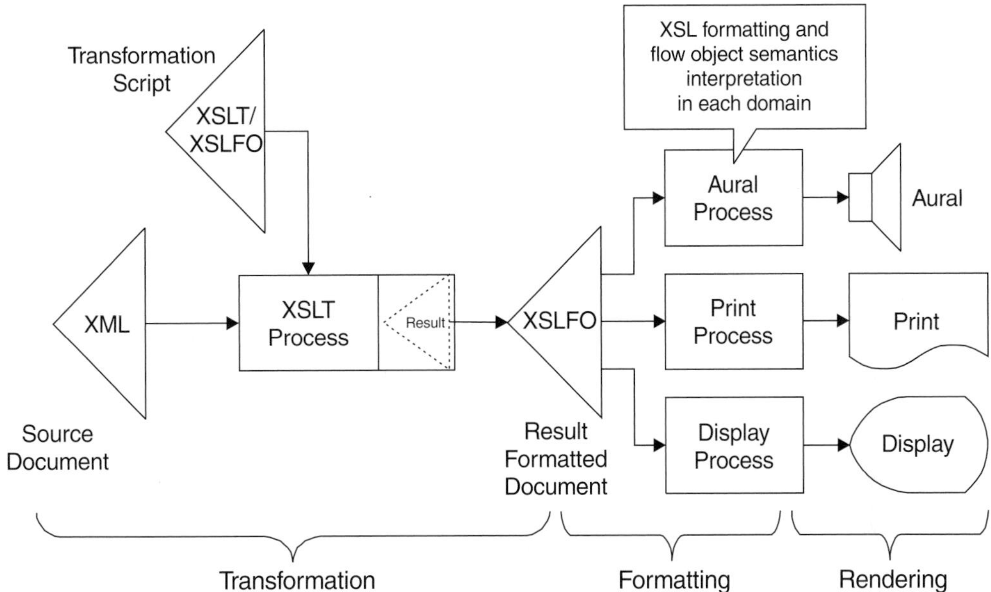

FIGURE 12-4 Creating standalone XML instances of XSL vocabulary

Generating FO Instances

XSLFO need not be generated by XSLT in order to be useful. Consider that when we learned HTML as the rendering vocabulary for a Web user agent, we either coded it by hand or wrote applications that generated the HTML from our information. This information may have come from some source, such as a database.

Learning XSLT, we can express our information in XML and then either transform the XML into HTML to send to the user agent, or send the XML directly to an XSLT process in the user agent.

The typical generation of XSLFO would be from our XML using an XSLT stylesheet, though this need not be the case at all. We may have situations where our applications need to express information in a paginated form, and these applications could generate instances of the XSLFO vocabulary directly to be interpreted for the output medium, as Figure 12-5 (*Figure 1-5*) shows.

We need to remember that XSLFO is just another vocabulary, able to be expressed as an XML instance, requiring an application to interpret our intent for formatting in order to effect the result. This is no different from the use of the HTML vocabulary for a Web browser. The sole requirement is that the namespace of the vocabulary in the instance be `http://www.w3.org/1999/XSL/Format` for the labeled information in the instance to be recognized as expressing the semantics described by the XSLFO Recommendation.

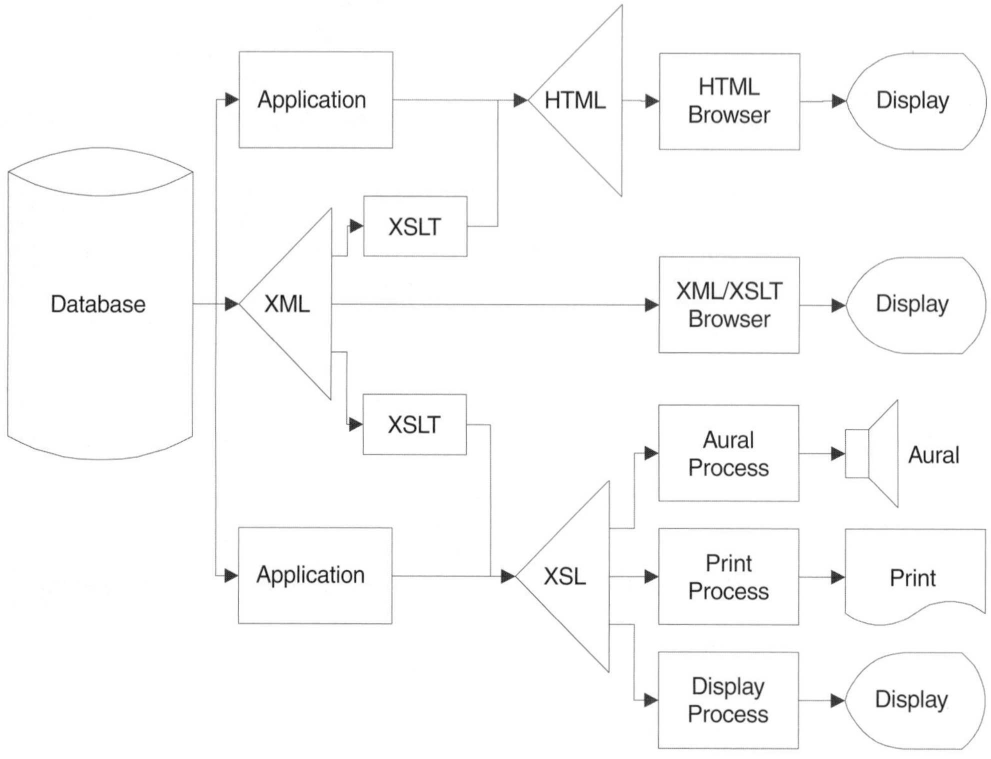

FIGURE 12-5 Generating XML instances of XSL vocabulary

The default namespace may be used for the XSLFO vocabulary, just as is true with any vocabulary. I don't use the popular `fo:` prefix in my stylesheets; it is my habit to use the default namespace and not prefix my XSLFO names in any way. This practice reinforces for me that this is just as simple as HTML, where I don't use namespaces in my stylesheets.

There are processors that interpret standalone XSLFO instances interactively on the screen in a GUI environment. To learn much of the nuances of XSLFO, I often hand-author XSLFO instances experimenting with various objects and properties in elements and attributes, tweaking values repeatedly, and examining the results interactively with the formatting tool. Having hand-authored HTML, using the default namespace for XSLFO is very natural and saves on the amount of typing as well.

Examples

It is important to consider a couple of illustrative examples, both simple and more complex.

Hello World Example

Consider a simple, but complete, XSLFO instance `hellofo.fo` for an A4 page report, as in Listing 12-8. We can see the definition on line 2 of the default namespace being the XSLFO namespace, thus unprefixed element names refer to element types in the XSLFO vocabulary. There are no prefixed element types used by any of the elements, thus the entire content is written in XSLFO.

Listing 12-8 A Simple Example (*Example 1-8*)

```
01  <?xml version="1.0" encoding="UTF-8"?>
02  <root xmlns="http://www.w3.org/1999/XSL/Format"
03        font-size="16pt">
04    <layout-master-set>
05      <simple-page-master
06              margin-right="15mm" margin-left="15mm"
07              margin-bottom="15mm" margin-top="15mm"
08              page-width="210mm" page-height="297mm"
09              master-name="bookpage">
10        <region-body region-name="bookpage-body"
11              margin-bottom="5mm" margin-top="5mm" />
12      </simple-page-master>
13    </layout-master-set>
14    <page-sequence master-reference="bookpage">
15      <title>Hello world example</title>
16      <flow flow-name="bookpage-body">
17        <block>Hello XSLFO!</block>
18      </flow>
19    </page-sequence>
20  </root>
```

The document model for XSLFO dictates the page geometries be summarized in `<layout-master-set>` on lines 4 through 13, followed by the content to be paginated in a sequence of pages in `<page-sequence>` on lines 14 through 19. The instance conforms to this and conveys our formatting intent to the formatter. The formatter needs to know the geometry of the pages being created and the content that belongs on those pages.

Think of the parallel where we learned that the document model for HTML requires the metadata in the `<head>` element and the displayable content in the `<body>` element. Both elements are required in the document model, the first to contain the mandatory title of the page and the second to contain the rendered information. We learned in the vocabulary for HTML, however, that when we create a page we know where the required components belong in the document. The same is true for XSLFO, in that we learn what information is required where, and we express what we need in the constructs the formatter expects.

In this simple example the dimensions of A4 paper are given in a portrait orientation on line 8. Margins are specified on lines 6 and 7 to constrain the main body of the page within the page boundaries. That body region itself, described on lines 10 and 11, has margins to constrain its content, and is named so that it can be referenced from within a sequence of pages.

The sequence of pages in this example refers to the only geometry available and specifies on line 16 that the flow of paginated content is targeted to the body region on each page. The sequence is also titled on line 15, which is used by rendering agents choosing to expose the title outside the canvas for the content.

Consider two conforming XSLFO processors to process the simple `hellofo.fo` example, one interactively through a GUI window interface, and the other producing a final-form representation of the page:

- Antenna House XSL Formatter, an interactive XSLFO rendering tool (*http://www.AntennaHouse.com*)
- Adobe Acrobat, a PDF display tool; PDF was created by RenderX, a batch XSLFO rendering tool (*http://www.RenderX.com*)

Note that the two renderings, shown in Figure 12-6 (*Figure 1-6*), are not identical. If the XSLFO instance is insufficient in describing the entire intent of the for-

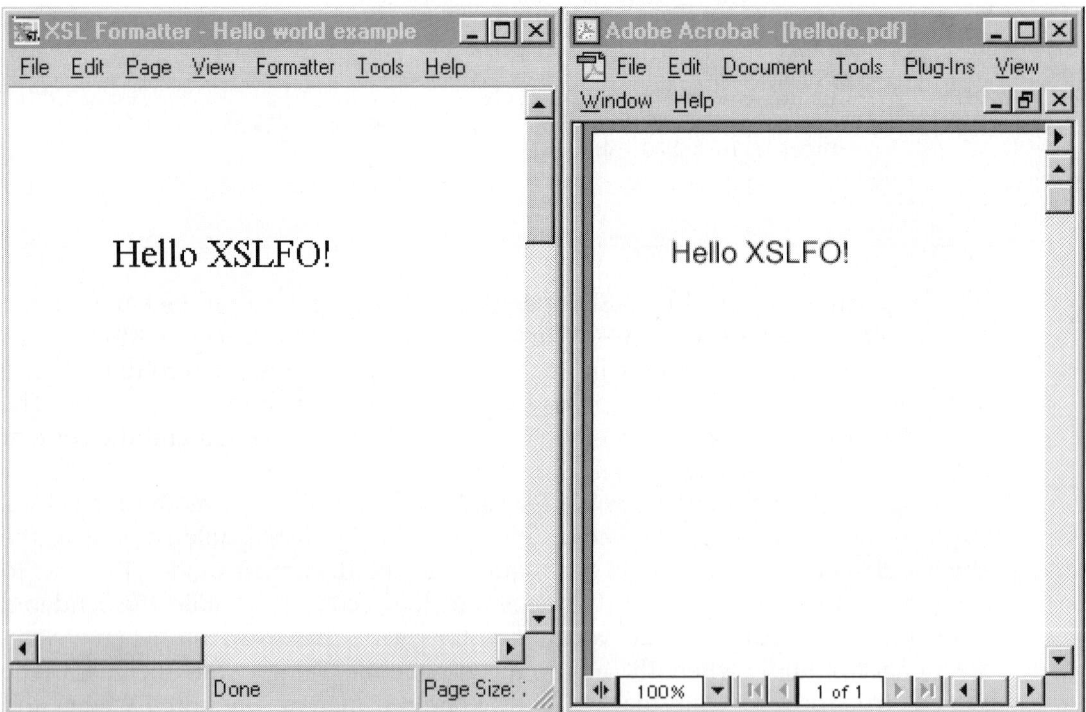

FIGURE 12-6 A simple XSLFO instance example

matting, the rendering may engage certain property values of its own choosing. Page fidelity is not guaranteed if the instance does not express the entire intent of formatting. Even within the expressiveness of the XSLFO semantics, some decisions are still left up to the formatting tool.

This is not different from two Web browsers with different user settings for the displayed font. A simple Web page that does not use CSS style sheets for font settings relies on the browser's tool options for the displayed font choice. The intent of the Web page may be to render "a paragraph", but if two users have different tool option defaults for the font choice, there is no fidelity in the Web page between the two renditions if the formatting intent is absent.

Training Materials Publishing Example

Consider an excerpt of a more complex use of formatting objects to produce a page from an early draft of the instructor-led derivative of this chapter, shown in Listing 12-9. Figure 12-7 (*Figure 1-7*) shows the nesting of the hierarchy of the formatting objects in the example page, and Figure 12-8 (*Figure 1-8*) shows the page rendered in an interactive XSLFO rendering tool.

Listing 12-9 Formatting Objects (Excerpt) for a Page of Handout Material (*Example 1-9*)

```
<flow flow-name="pages-body"><table>
 <table-column column-width="( 210mm - 2 * 15mm ) - 2in"/>
 <table-column column-width="1in"/>
 <table-column column-width="1in"/>
 <table-body><table-row><table-cell><block text-align="start">
     <block font-size="19pt">Training material example</block>
     <block font-size="10pt" space-before.optimum="10pt">Module
1 - The context of XSLFO</block>
     <block font-size="10pt">Lesson 2 - Examples</block></block>
  </table-cell>
  <table-cell><block text-align="end"><external-graphic
   src="url(&quot;..\whitesml.bmp&quot;)"/></block></table-cell>
  <table-cell><block text-align="start"><external-graphic
   src="url(&quot;..\cranesml.bmp&quot;)"/></block></table-cell>
 </table-row></table-body></table>
 <block line-height="3px"><leader leader-pattern="rule"
      leader-length.optimum="100%" rule-thickness="1px"/></block>
 <block space-before.optimum="6pt" font-size="14pt">
This page's material as an instructor-led handout:</block>
 <list-block provisional-distance-between-starts=".43in"
  provisional-label-separation=".1in" space-before.optimum="6pt">
  <list-item relative-align="baseline">
   <list-item-label text-align="end" end-indent="label-end()">
    <block>-</block></list-item-label>
   <list-item-body start-indent="body-start()">
    <block font-size="14pt">excerpts of formatting objects
created through the use of an XSLT stylesheet</block>
   </list-item-body></list-item></list-block>
```

```
29   <block space-before.optimum="12pt div 2" font-family="Courier"
30        linefeed-treatment="preserve" white-space-collapse="false"
31        white-space-treatment="preserve" font-size="12pt"><inline
32   font-size="inherited-property-value(font-size) div 2">01 </inline
33   >&lt;flow flow-name="pages-body"&gt;&lt;table&gt;
34   <inline font-size="inherited-property-value(font-size) div 2"
35   >02 </inline> &lt;table-column column-width...
```

The information above the horizontal rule (line 16) is rendered using a borderless table. Lines 1 through 15 describe the three columns of information: the page title and context, a placebo white box in place of the branding logo for the licensee of the training material, and the Crane registered trademark. The table cell with the page information contains text in different point sizes on lines 6 through 9.

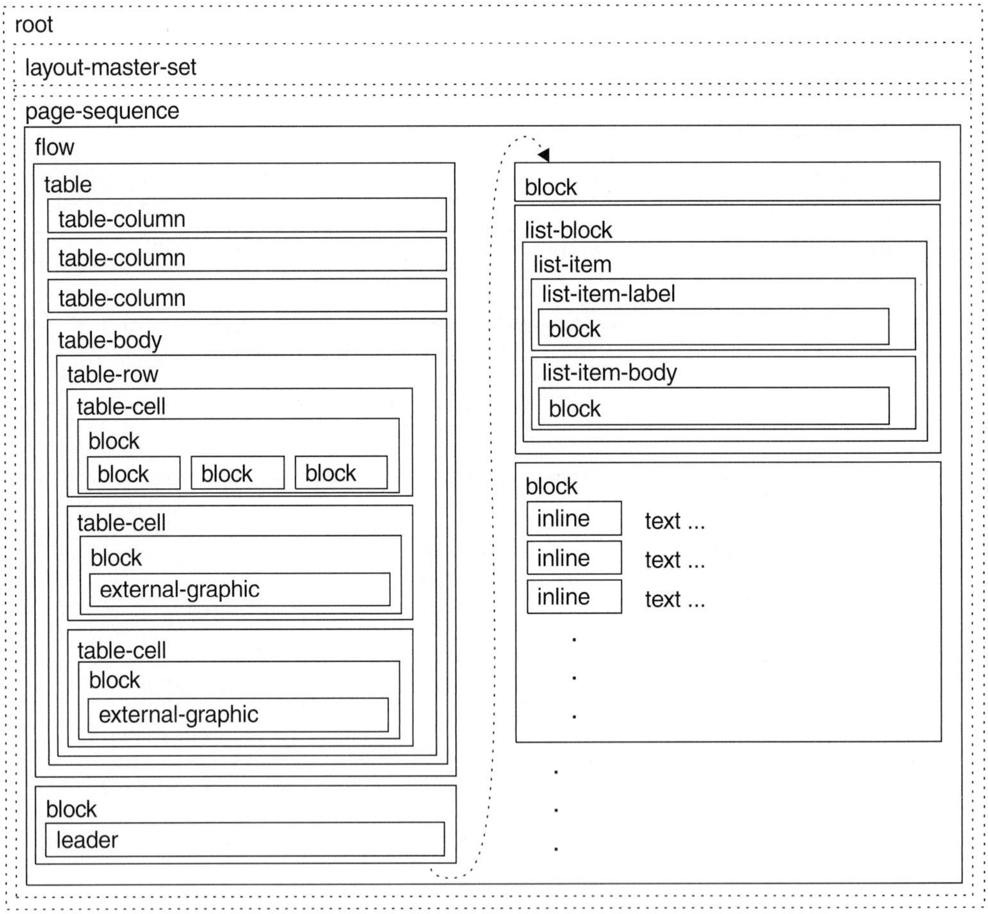

FIGURE 12-7 The nesting of XSLFO constructs in the example

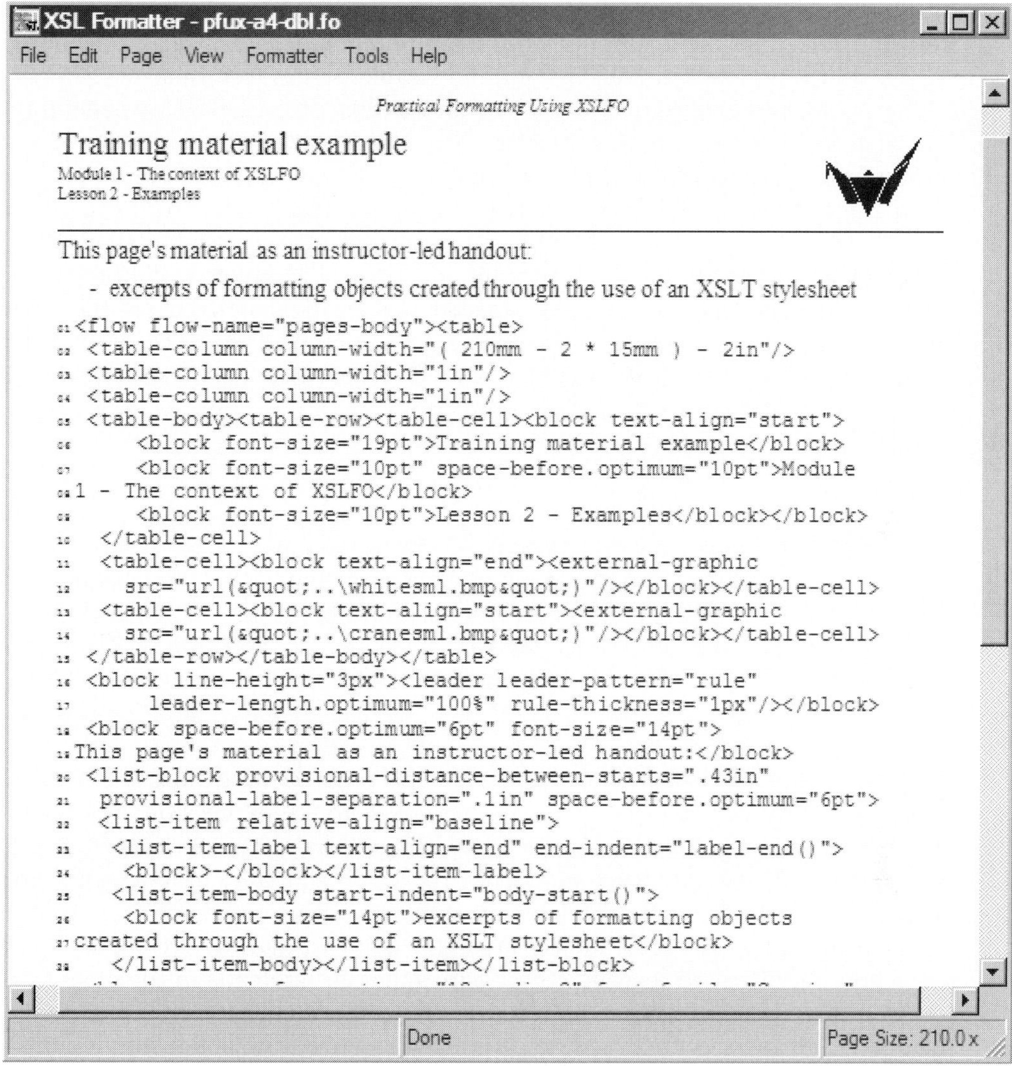

FIGURE 12-8 A page of handouts rendered in XSLFO

Note that attribute value specified on line 2 is an expression, not a hard value. There is an expression language in XSLFO that is a superset of the expression language of XSLT. This can make an XSLT stylesheet easier to write by having it convey property values in a piecemeal fashion in an expression to be evaluated, rather than trying to calculate the resulting value in XSLT.

The horizontal rule below the title information needs to be block-oriented in that it needs to break the flow of information and be separate from the surrounding information. To achieve this effect with the inline-oriented leader construct, note on lines 16 and 17 that the leader is placed inside a block.

The block on lines 18 and 19 lay out a simple paragraph. Lines 20 through 28 lay out a list construct, where the labels and bodies of list items are synchronized and adjacent in the flow of information. This side-by-side effect cannot be achieved with simple paragraphs; it could be achieved to some extent with borderless tables, but the use of the list objects gives fine control over the nuances of list construct's layout.

The list block itself has properties on lines 20 and 21 governing all members of the list, including the provisional distance between the start edges of the list item label and the list item body, and the provisional label separation. These provisional values are very powerful constructs in XSLFO. They allow us to specify contingent behavior for the XSLFO processor to accommodate the varying lengths of the list item labels of the items of the list.

Remember that one of the design goals of XML is "terseness is of minimal importance" (could they have found a terser way of saying that?). Note that the attribute name specifying the first of these provisional property values is 35 characters. Lengthy element and attribute names are not uncommon, and an XSLFO instance always seems to me to be so very verbose to read.

Note on lines 23 and 25 how functions can be used in attribute values. XSLFO defines a library of functions that can be invoked in the expression language. The `label-end()` and `body-start()` functions engage the appropriate use of one of the two provisional list construct properties based on the start indent of the item's label.

Line 29 begins the block that contains the listing of markup. To ensure a verbatim rendering of edited text, line 30 specifies that all linefeeds in the block of content be preserved, and not to collapse the white-space characters. This disengages the default behavior of treating linefeeds as white space and collapsing white space to a single space character, as would be typical for proportional-font paragraphs of prose.

Lines 31 and 32 show an inline sequence of text being formatted differently from the remainder of the text of the block. The desired effect of the line number being half the current font size is specified through the use of the function `"inherited-property-value(font-size)"`, though there are two alternative ways to specify the same relative value: "`50%`" and `".5em"`. Using any of these expressions would produce the same result.

The escaped markup on lines 33 and 35 may look incorrect, but this is an XML serialization of the XSLFO instance. Therefore, sensitive markup characters must be escaped in order to be recognized as text, and not as markup. Since this is a page describing markup, the markup being described needs to be distinguished from the markup of the document itself.

Basic Concepts of XSLFO

Here we review basic aspects of the XSLFO semantics and vocabulary to gain a better understanding of how the technology works and how to use the specification itself.

Layout-Based vs. Content-Based Formatting Two very different approaches to the formatting of information are contrasted. Layout-based formatting respects the constraints of the target medium, where limitations or capacities of the target may constrain the content or appearance of the information on a page. Content-based formatting respects the quantity and identity of the information, whereas much of the target medium is generated to accommodate the information being formatted.

Formatting Is Different from Rendering The distinction between formatting and rendering is overviewed, comparing how to express what you want formatted and expressing how it is to be accomplished on the target device. This contrast is similar to the difference between declarative- and imperative-style programming methods, or the difference between the XSLTs "transformation by example" paradigm and other algorithmic transformation approaches using programming languages.

Formatting Model and Vocabulary Formatting model and vocabulary extends what is currently available for Web presentation. The XSLFO semantics and vocabulary address different requirements than do infinite-length Web user agent windows to meet the needs of imposed arbitrary page boundaries on the presentation of information. These new semantics are inspired by the DSSSL (ISO/IEC 10179), but in practice diverge from DSSSL toward Cascading Style Sheets 2 (CSS2) for compatibility with Web-based processing. The semantics are classified, as follows, based on their relationship to similar CSS properties:

- CSS properties by copy (unchanged CSS2 semantics)
- CSS properties with extended values
- CSS properties "broken apart" to a finer granularity
- XSLFO-specific properties

The XSLFO support of multiple writing directions and a reference orientation are important concepts inherited from DSSSL that are not present in CSS2.

Unambiguous Terminology Different processing model concepts are expressed using unambiguous terminology. The XSLFO specification attempts to be very careful to use precise terminology when what is being referred to has similar concepts that could be confused with other constructs. For example, an XSLFO instance contains elements and their attributes. This is similar to the corresponding formatting object tree with objects and their properties. This is, in turn, similar to the corresponding refined formatting object tree with objects and their area traits. This is, finally, similar to the corresponding area tree with areas and their traits.

XSLFO Objects Related to Basic Issues The XSLFO objects that address functionality in this area are summarized as follows:

- `<root>` *(6.4.2)*,[2] the document element of the XSLFO instance
- `<layout-master-set>` (*6.4.6*), the collection of definitions of page geometries and page selection patterns
- `<page-sequence>` (*6.4.5*), the definition of information for a sequence of pages with common static information
- `<flow>` (*6.4.18*), the content that is flowed to as many pages as required

Basic Concepts

It is important to understand basic concepts of XSLFO formatting semantics to know where it can be most successfully applied, and the processing model to know how a formatter approaches the formatting task.

Layout-Based vs. Content-Based Formatting

Layout-based formatting accommodates the medium being used to present information. The constraints of the medium, or the layout design of the graphic artist, often demands absolute positioning, column location specification, or page number specification. Consider that a magazine may need a particular columnist's article to appear on the right-hand edge of page 7, while the three lead stories must be headlined within the first four pages.

This focus on layout places more emphasis on the appearance and the location of information than on the information itself, dictating the quantity and presentation of the content. Such layout is typically unstructured in both the authoring and the formatting processes, as typified by desktop publishing, journalism, and so forth.

Content-based formatting accommodates the information being presented with the available medium. The constraints of layout are expressed as rules associated with the information that dictate how given information is to be positioned or pre-

2. The italic numbers in parentheses that follow the words in code refer to the section numbers of the XSL Recommendation.

sented. Consider that a single aircraft maintenance manual cannot have each of its 40,000 to 60,000 pages individually formatted.

This focus on information places more emphasis on the content and rules of layout, rather than on the medium, dictating the automatic layout and presentation of constructs found in the information stream. Such layout is typically highly structured in both the authoring and the formatting processes, as typified by technical publications in pharmaceutical, aerospace, automotive, and other industries where either vast amounts of information are presented or the information must be exchanged in a neutral form with other players.

XSLFO is more oriented to content-based formatting than layout-based formatting, though there do exist certain controls for the positioning, cropping, and flowing of information to particular areas of pages in page sequences. XSLFO can express the repetition of page geometries, mechanically accommodating the content as flowed by a transformation of the information into the formatting vocabulary. There is only limited support of the order of specific page sequences, and high-caliber copy-fitting requirements often cannot be met with mechanical unattended transformations.

Note that while XSLFO is not oriented to loose-leaf publishing, that does not prevent it from being used, perhaps by a vendor, to express the content of pages being maintained in a loose-leaf-based environment. A loose-leaf environment supports "change pages" (a.k.a. "A pages") through a database of effective pages and page contents.

XSLFO has no inherent maintenance facilities for past versions of individual pages, and no inherent support of lists of effective pages. Such facilities could be provided outside the scope of individual page presentations. XSLFO is more oriented to the unrestricted flowing of information to as much of the target medium as required to accommodate the content.

Formatting vs. Rendering

When creating XML, we should be designing the structures around our business processes responsible for maintaining the information, instead of the structures used for presentation. An XSLFO instance describes the intent of how that stream of information is to be formatted in the target medium in a paginated fashion. This instance is typically generated by a stylesheet acting on the instance of XML information, rearranging and restructuring the information into the order and presentation desired.

This reordering takes the `#PCDATA` content and attribute content of the instance and repackages it according to our intent based on our understanding of the semantics of the XSLFO vocabulary. We can reify this reordering as an intermediate file of syntax we can use for diagnostic purposes. We could also take the opportunity to store this reordering as an XML instance for "store and forward" strategies where the formatting takes place later or remotely from where the transformation takes place.

Unlike interactive formatting tools such as desktop publishing products and interactive formatting tools, there is no feedback loop from the XSLFO formatter to the stylesheet that creates the XSLFO vocabulary. Therefore, the XSLFO information must be complete with respect to all desired behaviors of the formatter. Any special formatting cases or conditions can be accommodated through contingencies expressed in the XSLFO semantics.

The information arranged in the elements and attributes of our source vocabularies is repackaged into the elements and attributes of the XSLFO formatting vocabulary that express the formatting objects and their properties of the XSLFO semantics. Each formatting object specifies an aspect of layout, appearance and impartation, or the pagination and flow.

The layout semantics express the intent of locating information positioned on the target medium. Areas of content are specified as located and nested within other areas, in a hierarchical tree of rectangles on each page.

The appearance and impartation semantics express the intent of how the information is to be conveyed to the reader. For visual media, this conveyance includes font, size, color, weight, and so forth. For aural synthesis, this conveyance includes voice, volume, azimuth, pitch, and so on.

The pagination and flow semantics express the intent of how the stream of information being presented is to be parceled within the layout areas. The final pagination is the result of accommodating the amount of flow being presented within the areas that have been defined. Each of the formatting objects is expressed in an XSLFO instance as an element. It is not necessary to know all formatting objects to get effective formatted results.

An XSLFO formatter is responsible for interpreting the intent to be rendered, as expressed in the XSLFO semantics corresponding to the elements and attributes in the instance created by the stylesheet. Following the W3C Recommendation, the formatter determines what is to be rendered where by interpreting the interaction of formatting objects. How the formatter does this interpretation is defined in excruciating detail in the W3C Recommendation, which is written more for implementers than for stylesheet writers.

The properties expressed for each object influence, or are included in, the structure of the resulting areas. Some of these properties are targeted for certain media and are ignored by media for which they do not apply.

Processing Model of Formatting

The Recommendation describes the processing model for XSLFO as a series of formal steps in the derivation of the content to be rendered from the instance expressing the intent of formatting, as depicted in Figure 12-9 (*Figure 2-1*). The Recommendation does not cover the creation of the XSLFO instance, nor the detailed

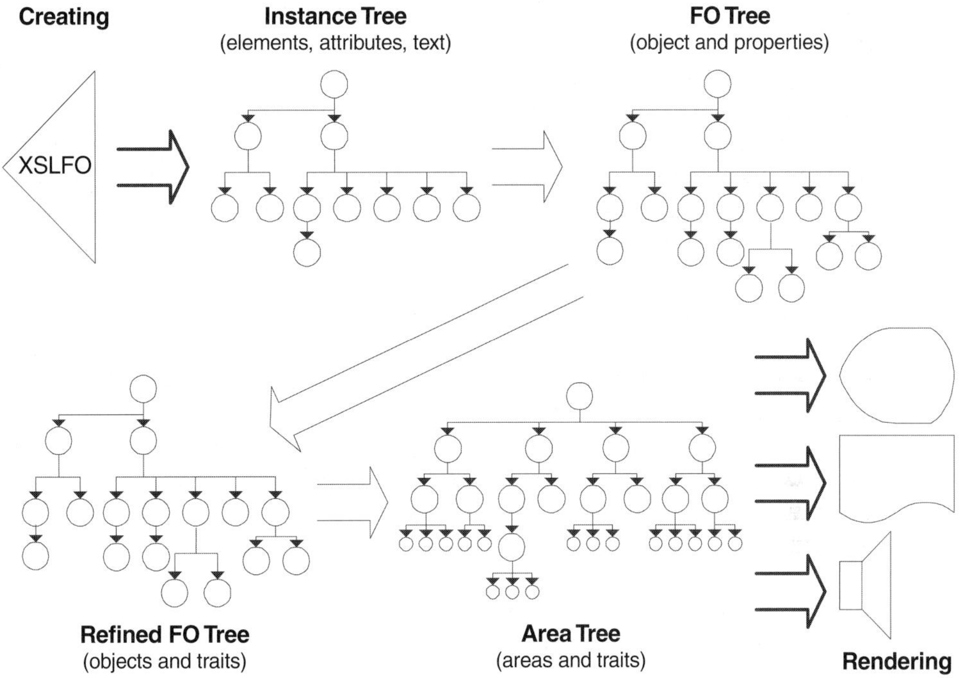

FIGURE 12-9 XSL processing model flow summary

semantics of rendering, but focuses entirely on how to get from the former to the latter.

Although the processing model is described in the Recommendation using constructs and procedural steps following a well-defined sequence, a vendor is not obligated to provide that a particular implementation perform the steps as documented. The only obligation on a formatter is that it produce the rendered result as if it were implemented according to the steps described in the text.

This nuance is important to vendors in that it allows them to implement any algorithm that will produce equivalent results, without constraining the innovation or flexibility to accomplish the results.

One ramification of this flexibility is that the intermediate results described in the processing model cannot be standardized and cannot be required of a particular implementation. Conformance testing would be far simpler if there were a serialization of the abstract result of the interpretation of the formatting intent, without needing to interpret a rendered result as having successfully met the criteria.

First, the instance of elements, attributes, and text becomes a node tree of abstract nodes representing these constructs for processing. It is possible that this node tree is passed directly from the result of transforming some source XML into result XSLFO without instantiating the result as markup characters. However, if the information is presented to a formatter as an instance of markup characters, this must be interpreted into a node tree suitable for the formatter to work with.

This node tree of elements, attributes, and text represents the expression of the intent of what the designer desires in the rendered result. This is called the Instance Tree and includes all of the content, including references to external foreign objects not expressible in XML, that is to appear in the target medium. It is the way the designer expresses the interaction of the documented semantics described in the XSLFO Recommendation.

The Instance Tree is interpreted into the formatting object tree, which is comprised entirely of formatting objects and their properties. This requires the (abstract) breaking of text nodes into sequences of character-formatting objects, and the creation of properties from attributes.

Note that certain white-space-only text nodes of the Instance Tree are irrelevant to the formatting process and do not create text nodes in the formatting object tree. Also removed for later access by the formatter or rendering agent are instream foreign objects (expressions of the result that are expressed in XML but not in the XSLFO vocabulary, for example, a Scalable Vector Graphics, or SVG, fragment), and any objects not from the XSLFO namespace that are used in the `<declarations>` formatting object.

The formatting object tree is interpreted into the refined formatting object tree, which is comprised of objects and traits. Properties can specify two kinds of traits: formatting traits (e.g., size and position) or rendering traits (e.g., style and appearance). Some property specifications are shorthand expressions that encompass a number of trait specifications and their values. Computed property expression values are evaluated and the resulting values assigned to the traits. For example a property value of `2em` when the current font size is `20pt` produces a trait value of `40pt`.

Inheritance plays an important role in trait derivation. Some traits are derived from the closest ancestral corresponding property specification. Some traits that are not inherited by default can have their value inherited by the explicit `inherit` property value.

Once all traits that are applicable to all formatting objects are determined, all traits not applicable to each object are removed. At this point the information is comprised of all objects that are used to create areas and each object has all the traits and only the traits that are applicable to it.

The refined formatting object tree is interpreted into the area tree, which is comprised of areas and traits, according to the semantics of the objects. A given object may create areas at different branches of the area tree. Most objects produce exactly one area, and some objects produce no areas. Each area has a geometric position, z-layer position, content, background, padding, and borders. Areas are nested in the tree within ancestral areas up to the highest (and largest) area, which is the page area.

Page areas are the children of the root node in the area tree. Page areas are ordered by their position in the area tree, but they are not geometrically related in any way.

The rendering agent effects the impartation of the areas in the area tree according to the medium. The Recommendation gives guidelines on the rendering of areas in either visual or aural media. Some missing trait values can be arbitrarily inferred by the rendering agent, such as font or volume. This allowance leads to different renderings by different tools when an XSLFO instance does not express the missing trait values.

The Recommendation is written to direct a formatter implementer in carrying out the requirements of interpreting the formatting intent. Certain traits are boolean values targeted solely to the implementer and reflecting an area's role or order relative to other areas. These traits are not specifiable in the XSLFO instance but are indicated in the Recommendation to make implementation easier.

The rigor of the Recommendation language is necessary to ensure proper interpretation of finely tuned typographical nuances. This makes the Recommendation difficult to read for many people who just want to write stylesheets. Fortunately, simple things can be done simply once you get around the necessary verbosity of the Recommendation.

Vocabulary Structure

The semantics of a formatting object are defined in terms of areas and their traits. The Recommendation describes which areas each object generates (if any), where the areas are placed in the branches of the area tree hierarchy, and the interactions with the areas and specifications from and specifications for other objects.

To trigger the desired semantics, formatting objects and their properties are specified using elements, attributes, and text. This information may be reified in a standalone XML instance being interpreted by a formatter or it may be represented in a node tree passed as the result of a transformation process such as XSLT.

All XSLFO elements input to the processor must be in the namespace with the URI `"http://www.w3.org/1999/XSL/Format"`, and may use the default namespace for this URI.

The "X" in XSLFO does represent "Extensible" and an XSLFO instance may include extension elements and attributes that are recognized by the formatting processor. Any other processor is not obliged to support an extension recognized by a given processor. Extension elements must *not* use the XSLFO URI. Extension attributes *must* have a non-null prefix. Extension constructs must be ignored if not recognized by an XSLFO processor.

The element and attribute names are all specified with letters in lowercase (remember that XML is case-sensitive). A hyphen separates multiple words in a single name and a dot separates names from their compound components. Some abbreviations are used in XSLFO if the name is already used in XML or HTML.

Every property is allowed to be specified on every object in the elements and attributes of the input. This flexibility provides for inheritance in the formatting object tree. Only those traits meaningful to a formatting object are in the refined formatting object tree and are used by the areas created by the object. Some properties not defined to be inheritable by default can be inherited if their values permit this to be explicitly specified.

Every object may have a unique identifier specified using `id=` property. This is used as the target of a reference from other objects. This value is never inherited from other objects and is assigned to the first child area generated by the object. For the reference to work properly, the identifier must be found somewhere in the area tree; if the object doesn't generate any areas, the identifier is lost and the reference is broken.

Extension objects and/or properties are allowed in any other namespace. For example, `xmlns:rx="http://www.renderx.com/XSL/Extensions"` is recognized by the XEP formatter tool for objects and properties implementing semantics defined by the RenderX vendor. Vendors can implement any semantics they wish and have any vocabulary they wish represent a user's intent to engage those extended semantics. There is no obligation on any tool to support any vendor's extension semantics.

This is an important portability issue. A user who engages extension semantics cannot assume these semantics will be available on any other tool than that which implements the semantics. Taking advantage of an extension will most likely lock a user into a particular brand of formatting engine. This may have repercussions on the user's ability to distribute stylesheets to other users who may not be in a position to take advantage of the custom extension.

Direct vs. Constraint Property Specification

Properties influence the behavior of an object in the formatted result. Properties are specified in an XSLFO XML instance or node tree as attributes and become traits in the area tree. Properties can be strategically placed in the hierarchy or specified algorithmically by the stylesheet writer in order to promote maintainability or consistency in the formatted result.

Some properties directly specify a formatting result, such as the `color=` property. The interpretation of a direct property is not influenced by the context of the areas surrounding the area with the property. In this example, the foreground color trait of the area is the given value regardless of where it is used.

Some properties constrain the formatting result based on an interpretation of context in the area tree, such as the `space-before=` property. The interpretation of a constraint property specified identically for two areas may be different based on the context of the generated area (not on the context of the object that generated the area). In this example, the amount of space left before an area is constrained, but if that area is at the top of a reference area (say a page), and the area's conditionality is allowed to discard the space before, then the actual value used is zero because the value of the space before is discarded.

Compound properties have subproperties for fine-grained specification. Often, these originate from the CSS2 specification but they specify too many aspects of formatting in a single specification. XSLFO allows for the subproperties to be individually specified, for example the `space-before.optimum=`, `space-before.minimum=`, `space-before.maximum=`, `space-before.conditionality=`, and `space-before.precedence=` are subproperties of the `space-before=` property.

It is not necessary to know all properties to get effective formatted results.

Property Value Expressions

A property's value can be the evaluation of an expression of either fixed values, such as `space-before="20pt div 2"`, or contextually-sensitive values, such as `space-before="from-parent(font-size) div 2"`.

The expression language is similar to that of XPath 1.0 in that it includes the same operators and the same operands. It also includes length values as operands that are not allowed in XPath 1.0.

Expressions that are influenced by the font size evaluate the font size before evaluating any other components of the expression.

XSLFO defines a core function library useful for property expressions. Some functions give access to property values of the current node, such as `inherited-property-value(`*`property-name`*`)`. This obtains a value that may be specified on the current node or may be inherited from the closest ancestral node that specifies the value. Some functions give access to property values of other nodes, such as `from-parent(`*`property-name`*`)` or `merge-property-values(`*`property-name`*`)`. The former looks for the property value directly from the parent object specification, and the latter looks for the property value directly from the particular sibling object specification corresponding to a given state of the user interface.

There are numerous property datatypes including both simple-valued and compound-valued values.

Shorthand Properties

Shorthand properties specify a number of standalone properties using a single specification. This is different from a compound property; a shorthand property represents a set of standalone properties, whereas a compound property is comprised of a set of subproperties.

Individual properties of a shorthand property are supported severally in that a shorthand property can be used in conjunction with individual properties: those that are specified are more precise than those that are inferred.

Shorthand properties are processed in increasing precision. The precedence order is independent of attribute specification order (remember in XML that attributes are unordered). A more specific attribute name has higher precedence than a less specific attribute name. For example, `border-color=` is more precise than `border=` and `border-bottom-color=` is more precise than `border-color=`. Border named-edge specifications have higher precedence than generic border specifications, even though they have the same specificity, such that `border-bottom=` is more precise than `border-style=`.

A processor is not obliged to support shorthand properties.

Conformance

There are three levels of conformance defined in the Recommendation: complete, extended, and basic. Claiming *complete conformance* requires the implementation to support the entire Recommendation. Claiming *extended conformance* does not require an implementation to support shorthand properties or a very few esoteric positioning- and font-related properties. The remainder of the Recommendation must be fully supported. Claiming *basic conformance* requires a minimum level of visual pagination or aural rendering support. Fallback behaviors are defined for the unsupported extended facilities.

In a given medium, a processor must support all formatting objects and properties specified for the conformance level claimed. The conformance levels are described for two rendering class distinctions: visual media and aural media. A processor can implement fallback processing in media not supported, but conformance qualification does not include fallback processing.

Groupings of Formatting Objects for Flow

There are five groupings of formatting objects that can be use in the flow of information being paginated: block-level, inline-level, neutral, out-of-line, and out-of-line inline-level. Objects of each kind dictate how the areas created by the objects stack next to each other. Areas are added to branches of the area tree and interact with adjacent areas in the area tree. This interaction on the rendered page is the stacking of areas and stacking can be in either the block-progression direction (top-to-bottom of the page in a Western European writing direction) or in the inline-progression direction (left-to-right of the page in a Western European writing direction).

Block-level objects stack next to siblings in the block-progression direction. This has the effect of breaking the flow of information in the block-progression direction, preventing siblings from being "beside" each other in the inline-progression direction. The `<block>` object construct is used frequently for typographical constructs such as for paragraphs, headings, captions, and the contents of table cells.

Inline-level objects stack next to siblings in the inline-progression direction. These objects do not break the flow of information in the block-progression direction. Inline objects specify portions of content to be flowed into the lines of the parent block, where such portions are distinct from their sibling portions, such as bolded or italicized text.

Neutral objects are allowed anywhere and do not impact the stacking of sibling objects, nor interrupt or follow the progression direction of the parent object.

Out-of-line objects generate areas on different branches of the area tree than do sibling objects. As such, the areas of these objects stack out of line to the areas of sibling objects. These do not break the flow of information in any progression direction.

Out-of-line inline-level objects are similar to out-of-line objects in that they generate areas on different branches of the area tree than sibling objects do, but they are restricted to use as inline-level constructs, never as block-level constructs.

Block-Level Objects

Block-level objects are objects represented by the `%block;` parameter entity used in content models:

- `<block>`—the description of canvas content that is distinct from its preceding area content
- `<block-container>`—the specification of a block-level reference area for contained descendant blocks
- `<list-block>`—the parent object of a related set of child pairs of blocks
- `<table-and-caption>`—the parent object of a captioned collection of tabular content
- `<table>`—the parent object of an uncaptioned collection of tabular content

Block-level objects stacked in the block-progression-direction of flow interrupt the block-progression flow of information. Two objects of this type cannot be positioned next to each other in the inline-progression-direction within the same containing object.

Inline-Level Objects

Inline-level objects are represented by the `%inline;` parameter entity used in content models:

- `<basic-link>`—the inline display of the start resource of a unidirectional link to a single endpoint
- `<bidi-override>`—specifies how to override the inherent Unicode text direction for a sequence of characters

- `<character>`—both the abstract formatting object implied by a simple character in an XSLFO instance and the concrete formatting object available to be used in place of a simple character
- `<external-graphic>`—the inline display of graphical or other externally supplied information
- `<inline>`—a description of canvas content that is distinct from its preceding content within a line generated in a block
- `<inline-container>`—the specification of an inline-level reference area for contained descendant blocks
- `<instream-foreign-object>`—the inline display of graphical or other instance-supplied information
- `<leader>`—the inline display of a rule or a sequence of glyphs
- `<multi-toggle>`—the definition of those interaction-sensitive objects within a candidate rendered sequence of formatting objects
- `<page-number>`—an inline-level placeholder replaced with the page number of the current page
- `<page-number-citation>`—an inline-level placeholder replaced with the page number of the first normal area of the cited formatting object

Stacked in the inline-progression-direction of flow, these objects do not interrupt the block-progression flow of information; they reside in the line areas generated by the formatter

Neutral Objects

Neutral objects are typically allowed anywhere that `#PCDATA`, `%inline;`, or `%block;` constructs are allowed:

- `<multi-properties>`—the collection of candidate property sets from which exactly one set influences the properties of a formatting object based on its status or the status of user interaction
- `<multi-switch>`—the collection of candidate formatting object sequences from which exactly one is rendered at any given time based on an interactive condition that is influenced by the operator while being tracked by the formatter
- `<retrieve-marker>`—an inline-level placeholder replaced with the formatting objects of the indicated marker
- `<wrapper>`—a generic container construct for specifying inherited properties for descendant constructs

Note that these individual flow objects may have constraints that prevent their use in particular objects.

Areas returned by the interpretation of these objects are stacked in the progression-direction of the siblings of these objects.

Out-of-Line Objects

Out-of-line objects are typically allowed anywhere #PCDATA, %inline;, or %block; constructs are allowed.

- <float>—content that is to be rendered toward either the before, start, or end edges of a region regardless of where in the region the content is defined; not stacked in the progression-direction of the sibling objects
- areas returned are contained within and governed by ancestral <page-sequence> object

Out-of-Line Inline-Level Objects

These are out-of-line objects that are allowed only inline, that is, anywhere #PCDATA or %inline; constructs are allowed:

- <footnote>—content that is to be rendered toward the after-edge of a region regardless of where in the region the content is defined.

One of two generated areas is stacked in the progression-direction of the sibling inline objects, while the other is contained within and governed by the ancestral <page-sequence> object.

Area and Page Basics

Here we review the area model and how areas interact and act within defined regions of the page.

The area model describes the nature of the areas of content that are created for rendering from the formatting specification. XSLFO 1.0 defines only rectangular areas in the area model, and these areas are arranged in hierarchical order in the area tree. Descendant areas are rendered within ancestral areas. A given formatting object may add areas to multiple branches of the hierarchy.

Different types of areas define the formatter's behavior for the area's content, as depicted in the four rectangles shown in Figure 12-10 (*Figure 3-1*). An area is

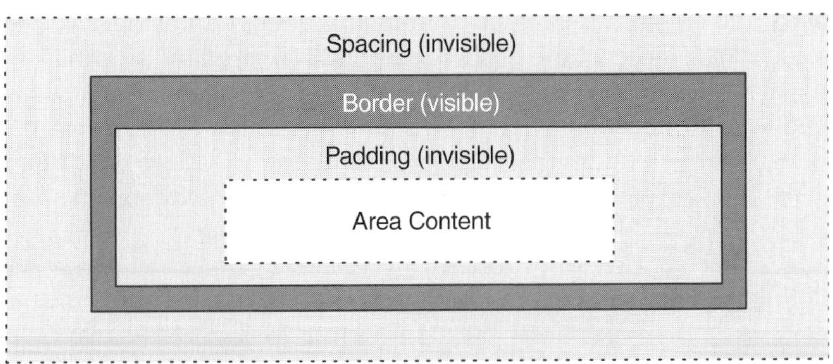

FIGURE 12-10 The rectangles describing an area

spaced between its siblings and within its parent using an invisible spacing specification in the outermost rectangle. A visible border may be specified around content where the thickness of the border is defined by the differences between respective edges of two rectangles. The border is distanced from the area's content by invisible padding.

The two concepts of writing direction and reference orientation govern the visual placement of areas on a page. These values define the block-progression and inline-progression directions for the stacking of descendants of an area. The combinations support natural directions for common writing systems of the world, and the orientation can be overridden to produce special effects in the rendered result. These values also define the before- and after-sides in the block-progression direction and the start- and end-sides in the inline-progression direction.

Most child areas inherit unspecified behaviors from the parent areas. Block and inline content stack in the layout areas as specified by the stacking properties, and it is not usually necessary to specify most behaviors because they are implied from the ancestral areas.

Child "container" objects are used to create areas that override behavior specified by parent areas. Areas created by container objects can alter their behavior to meet specific requirements that differ from the parent areas. For examples, one can specify a different target flow from that being used by the parent; one can specify a block with different overflow behavior than the parent's; one can specify a different writing direction or reference orientation from that of the parent. Both block-level and inline-level containers are available to be used.

Page Geometry

A page in XSLFO is described by the geometry of its size and the various regions and subregions on the page where information is placed by the formatting objects, as shown in Figure 12-11 (*Figure 3-2*).

Every page has a region whose default name is `xsl-region-body`. This is typically (but not necessarily) the region that receives the flow that triggers the pagination and generation of pages. Two conditional subregions are contained within the body region and are placed within the body region only when out-of-line constructs are placed in the body region. If there are any top-floats that belong on the page, the subregion whose fixed name is `xsl-before-float-separator` is rendered between the top-floats and the paginated content. If there are footnotes (bottom-floats) that belong on the page, the subregion whose fixed name is `xsl-footnote-separator` is rendered between the paginated content and the footnotes.

Four available perimeter regions can incur into the body region along its four edges. The writing direction and reference orientation of the page reference area defined by the page geometry determine the before, after, start, and end edges of

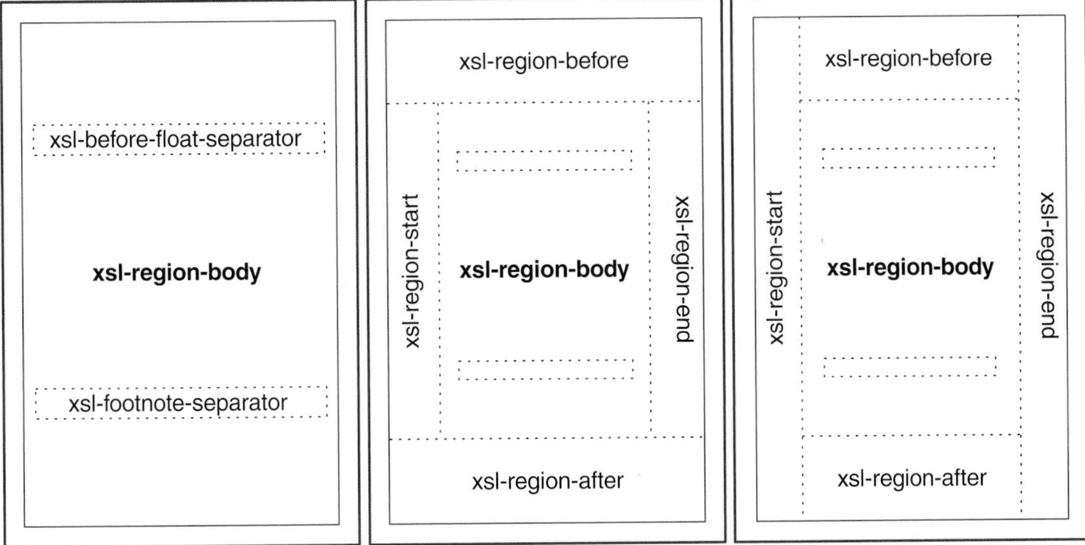

FIGURE 12-11 Regions and subregions of a page

the body for the perimeter regions. Properties can dictate whether the before/after regions or start/end regions occupy the corners of the perimeter. These regions have the default names, respectively, of `xsl-region-before`, `xsl-region-after`, `xsl-region-start`, and `xsl-region-end`.

Regions and subregions are referenced in XSLFO by using their name. Regions can be custom-named, but subregions cannot be custom-named.

The five available page regions in the simple geometry of XSLFO 1.0 are targets for either paginated flow or static content.

The paginated flow triggers as many pages as needed by the amount of the flowed content. When a page's region accepting flow overflows, a new page in the page sequence is triggered to accommodate the continuing flow of content. The flow indicates the name of the target region for the content.

Each page that is triggered by the amount of flow instantiates all regions for the page. The user can define static content for pages, indicating to which region the static content is targeted. Whenever the named region is created, the static content is placed into the region. The static content can have dynamic components populated with the page number and the content of user-defined markers that appear on the page being formatted.

Page regions are parents and ancestors of the formatting objects flowed (for paginated content) or copied (for static content) in the region.

XSLFO Objects Related to Basic Areas and Simple Page Definitions

The XSLFO objects that address functionality in basic areas and simple page definitions are summarized as follows.

Content-Oriented Formatting Objects

- `<wrapper>` (*6.11.2*)—a neutral construct for specifying inherited properties for descendant constructs
- `<block>` (*6.5.2*)—the description of canvas content that is distinct from its preceding area content
- `<initial-property-set>` (*6.6.4*)—an auxiliary construct for specifying properties applied to the first line of the parent
- `<block-container>` (*6.5.3*)—the specification of a block-level reference area for contained descendant blocks
- `<inline>` (*6.6.7*)—a description of canvas content that is distinct from its preceding content within a line generated in a block
- `<inline-container>` (*6.6.8*)—the specification of an inline-level reference area for contained descendant blocks
- `<page-number-citation>` (*6.6.11*)—an inline-level placeholder replaced with the page number of the first normal area of the cited formatting object

Page-Oriented Formatting Objects

- `<simple-page-master>` (*6.4.12*)—the specification of a given page's physical geometry
- `<region-body>` (*6.4.13*)—the definition of the middle area inside any perimeter defined for the page
- `<title>` (*6.4.20*)—a page sequence's ancillary description not rendered on the page canvas

Generic Body Constructs

Many publishing requirements involve common constructs for pairs of synchronized blocks, nontextual information, unidirectional links, and leaders.

A list is a one-dimensional (linear) collection of related and synchronized pairs of blocks. The member pairs of this list may be unordered (as in a bulleted list) or ordered (as in a numbered or sequenced list of some fashion), and are laid out on the page in the block-progression direction as distinct pairs. XSLFO provides a number of objects for the layout of the components of the list, without prejudice to what goes into each of the objects and on the rendered result. A list is a presentation construct in XSLFO, not an information construct. This leaves the user in complete control over what is rendered in the list; the XSLFO objects specify only the layout of the nested components of the list.

Nontextual information is typically a static graphic or photograph of some kind, though an electronic implementation of the presentation of structured information using XSLFO can provide for dynamic components such as windows into spreadsheet-application worksheets. When nontextual information is not expressed in XML syntax, it must be external to the XSLFO instance and is pointed to through properties. When nontextual information is expressed in XML syntax (e.g., SVG vocabulary), it may be either external to the XSLFO instance or embedded in the XSLFO instance.

Unidirectional links can be defined in the XSLFO instance for interactive user agents to render in an electronic format. The user can specify links from areas of the area tree to a target external resource, or from areas of the area tree to a target area in the same area tree. Interactivity engaged by the operator viewing the rendered result can navigate the operator to the target location when the user interface triggers a traversal of the link.

Leaders provide visual guidance or assistance when the eye travels from one side of a page to the opposite side, as used in entries in tables of content. These constructs can be patterned sequences of characters joining information on a single line (e.g., a dot-leader), or drawn straight-ruled marks in the inline-progression direction. Leaders are also useful alone to break up the flow of information with visual barriers

XSLFO Objects Related to Generic Body Constructs

The XSLFO objects that address functionality in these four areas are summarized as follows.

List Objects

- `<list-block>` *(6.8.2)*—the parent object of a related set of child block pairs
- `<list-item>` *(6.8.3)*—a single-item definition of a pair of blocks
- `<list-item-label>` *(6.8.5)*—the block in the pair that is typically on the start-side of each page
- `<list-item-body>` *(6.8.4)*—the block of the pair that is typically on the end-side of each page

Graphic Objects

- `<external-graphic>` *(6.6.5)*—the inline display of graphical or other externally supplied information
- `<instream-foreign-object>` *(6.6.6)*—the inline display of graphical or other instance-supplied information

Link Object

- `<basic-link>` *(6.9.2)*—the inline display of the start resource of a unidirectional link to a single end point

Leader/Rule Object

- `<leader>` *(6.6.9)*—the inline display of a rule or a repeated sequence of glyphs

Tables

Tables present the two-dimensional relationships between two groups of information. The source information needn't be modeled by a table construct, though historical use of structured information tools often forced information designers to model explicit table constructs in their structures. These models insufficiently capture the semantics of the information being related, resulting in a loss of richness and utility in the information source.

Information from any model can be presented in a tabular fashion. XSLT or any other transformation technology can be used to rearrange the source information into the tabular relationships.

A table is a presentation construct in XSLFO, not an information construct. A table is a block-level construct that breaks the flow in the block-progression direction.

Tables in XSLFO have a compound structure with many well-defined behaviors. The caption, heading rows, and footer rows are constructs repeated on all pages where the table's body rows are rendered.

Column properties can be specified once for all cells of rows that are in a given column. Because the linear serialization of a two-dimensional construct necessarily favors one dimension over the other, cells are contained within rows, not columns. A column-oriented construct is necessary to address the second dimension of property assignment. Column-spanning and row-spanning features provide flexible table cell definition.

XSLFO Objects Related to Tables

The XSLFO objects that address functionality in this area are summarized as follows.

- `<table-and-caption>` *(6.7.2)*—the parent object of a captioned collection of tabular content
- `<table-caption>` *(6.7.5)*—the caption of a captioned collection of tabular content
- `<table>` *(6.7.3)*—the parent object of an uncaptioned collection of tabular content

- `<table-column>` (*6.7.4*)—the specification of common columnar properties
- `<table-header>` (*6.7.6*)—the rows of tabular content repeated at the before-edge of every break in body content
- `<table-footer>` (*6.7.7*)—the rows of tabular content repeated at the after-edge of every break in body content
- `<table-body>` (*6.7.8*)—the rows of tabular content flowed as the body content
- `<table-row>` (*6.7.9*)—a row of tabular content
- `<table-cell>` (*6.7.10*)—a column of a row of tabular content

Static Content and Page Geometry Sequencing

Bounded areas (the pages) repeat to accommodate a nonpredetermined amount of information (the flow). This pagination concept differentiates XSLFO semantics from traditional Web browser display semantics, including the inherent HTML display semantics and those of CSS. The pages in the collection need navigational aids repeated on each page. These aids are used by the reader to understand a page's role when not in the context of neighboring pages and include among other things the page number, headers, footers, and information cited on the page.

The page number gives a focus on the specific bounded area of a portion of the information that is being flowed. It is used on the given page for navigation and used on other pages for citations to the given page. These citations might be cross-references or index information.

Headers and footers provide contextual information about a collection of pages in which the given page is found. For example, the chapter title could be repeated in each header of the page. The footer could include a total page count reflecting information about the entire production and not just the page sequence.

Cited information from the page being formatted can be contextual information useful for navigation. This information would not be known about a page by the stylesheet at the time of transformation. The act of pagination dictates the page boundaries, not the generation of the source information. Two examples of information drawn from the flow itself into the static content are "dictionary headers" and subsection citations.

Static content is associated with the name of a region, not with a particular region's position. This is sometimes confusing to the stylesheet writer because the writer must organize the region names on each page geometry and then bind each static content presentation to each region name.

Differences in page geometry are allowed from page to page when more than one page is being rendered in a sequence of pages. These differences can be in the dimensions of the page, the choices of the regions and their names and margins, the presence or selection of headers and/or footers, the column count, and so forth.

One can describe a sequence with recto (odd) and verso (even) page differences to implement features such as alternating headers and footers. Two different static contents are defined with the page number to be rendered on the outside edge of each side of a bound publication. Differences in headers and footers of the geometries alternate the names of the flows for the static content between odd- and even-numbered pages. The page geometry for each of the two kinds of page can have different region names, then the static content for each presentation of the page number can be assigned to each of the two region names.

One can describe a sequence of pages with first, last, and middle page differences, for example, to have no heading on the first page of a chapter sequence.

One can describe a sequence to replace absent content for forced unflowed pages. When forcing a particular number of pages, there may be insufficient flow to fit on the last page of the sequence. This is commonly seen as a "this page intentionally left blank" page.

XSLFO Objects Related to Static Content and Page Geometry Sequencing

The XSLFO objects that address functionality in these two areas are summarized as follows.

Formatting Objects Related to Static Content

- `<region-before>` (*6.4.14*)—the definition of the body region perimeter area whose before-edge is co-incident with the before-edge of the page's content rectangle. In `lr-tb`[3] mode, this is the header at the top of the page.
- `<region-after>` (*6.4.15*)—the definition of the body region perimeter area whose after-edge is coincident with the after-edge of the page's content rectangle. In `lr-tb` mode, this is the footer at the bottom of the page.
- `<region-start>` (*6.4.16*)—the definition of the body region perimeter area whose start-edge is coincident with the start-edge of the page's content rectangle. In `lr-tb` mode, this is the sidebar at the left of the page.
- `<region-end>` (*6.4.17*)—the definition of the body region perimeter area whose end-edge is coincident with the end-edge of the page's content rectangle. In `lr-tb` mode, this is the sidebar at the right of the page.
- `<static-content>` (*6.4.19*)—the definition of content that is primarily unchanged from page to page in a page sequence. Except for page numbers and user-defined markers, the entire sequence is repeated on each page.
- `<page-number>` (*6.6.10*)—an inline-level placeholder replaced with the page number of the current page.

3. The references to the `lr-tb` writing mode refer to the "left-to-right top-to-bottom" style as used in typical Western European writing.

- <retrieve-marker> *(6.11.4)*—an inline-level placeholder replaced with the formatting objects of the indicated marker.
- <marker> *(6.11.3)*—the replacement formatting object content for a marker retrieved in static content.

Formatting Objects Related to Page Geometry Sequencing

- <page-sequence-master> *(6.4.7)*—the definition and name of a particular sequence of using page-masters
- <single-page-master-reference> *(6.4.8)*—the specification of the single use of a page-master within a sequence of page-masters
- <repeatable-page-master-reference> *(6.4.9)*—the specification of the repeated use of a page-master within a sequence of page-masters
- <repeatable-page-master-alternatives> *(6.4.10)*—the collection of possible page-master references from which one is to be used based on status conditions detected by the formatter
- <conditional-page-master-reference> *(6.4.11)*—a page-master choice available to the formatter when selecting from a collection of candidate page-masters

Floats and Footnotes

Floats and footnotes render information supplemental to the information found in the flow, making it easily found by a reader because of a predetermined location on the page. These constructs are defined "in line" of the flow of information being paginated, but are rendered "out-of-line" of the flow of information being paginated. Such information is considered auxiliary enough to not disturb the flow itself for the reader; the reader can choose to examine a float or footnote at leisure without interrupting the flow of reading.

These constructs are dynamically rendered on the page where detected by the formatter in the flow. Floats are rendered to the before, start, or end edges within the body region (not in the perimeter regions). Footnotes are two-part constructs: the footnote citation that is rendered inline in the flow and the footnote body rendered at the after-edge within the body region. An after float is accomplished with a footnote without a footnote citation.

There are many candidate uses of floating constructs. Once can use <float> to float images to the top of a page or to present sidebar portions of content. One can use <footnote> for traditional footnotes, acronym expansions, glossary definitions, or to sink images to the bottom of a page (using an empty inline construct).

There are no endnote layout constructs in XSLFO. An endnote is a two-part footnote-like construct with a citation and a definition, but all endnotes are collected at the end of a section (e.g., chapter) rather than the bottom of the page. To render endnotes, it would be the responsibility of transformation to cite the endnotes inline in the flow of the scope and then collect and render endnotes at the end of the scope. One could then choose to render the citations as part of the flow of the body, or use empty citations to take advantage of the XSLFO footnote construct to sink the collection of endnotes to the bottom of the last page.

Every page's body region has two subregions that are rendered only if necessary. Before-floats and footnotes are stacked in the body region with other block-level constructs, but the reader needs some separation rendered to distinguish content belonging in a float or footnote from the content belonging in the body. The body region is separated into the `before-float-reference-area`, `main-reference-area`, and `footnote-reference-area` portions as these distinct areas, as shown in Figure 12-12 (*Figure 7-1*).

The act of defining these visual separators does not affect their rendering, because they are rendered on a page only if the floated information is being rendered on the page. Static content defines the rendering of a separator. When needed, the static content associated with `xsl-before-float-separator` is rendered at the end of the `before-float-reference-area`. When needed, the static content associated with `xsl-footnote-separator` is rendered at the start of the `footnote-reference-area`.

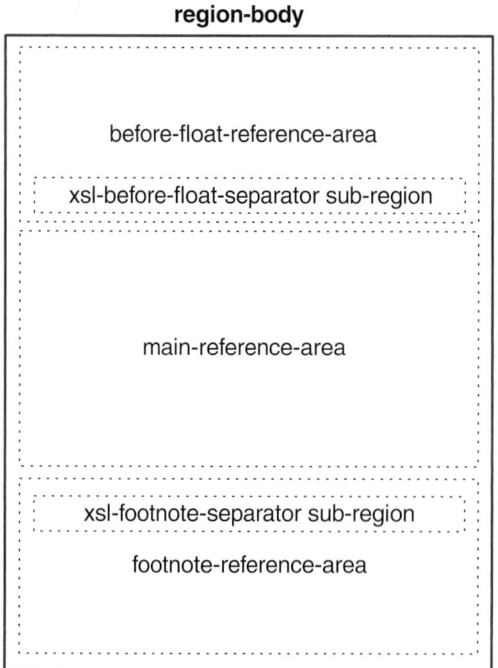

FIGURE 12-12 Conditional areas and subregions

Static content for these subregions should always be defined as a contingency if floats and footnotes are being used, for the chance that a given page may have such a construct. Remember from Figure 12-11 (*Figure 3-2*) the incursion of the perimeter regions into the body: all reference areas shown above are within the body region's margins and not part of the perimeters.

XSLFO Objects Related to Floats and Footnotes

The XSLFO objects that address functionality in these two areas are summarized as follows.

- `<float>` (*6.10.2*)—content to be rendered toward the before, start, or end edges of the body region regardless of where in the region the content is defined
- `<footnote>` (*6.10.3*)—content to be rendered both in the flow and toward the after-edge of the body region regardless of where in the region the content is defined
- `<footnote-body>` (*6.10.4*)—the portion of footnote content rendered toward the after-edge of the body region

Keeps, Breaks, Spacing, and Stacking

An area's stacking rules govern its placement. This happens at the block level in a page in each of the `before-float-reference-area`, `main-reference-area`, and `footnote-reference-area` areas; at the line level inside a block where the lines are generated by the formatter (not the stylesheet); and at the inline level within a line such as characters, rules, graphics, and other inline constructs.

Areas that are stacked are stacked in the pertinent progression direction. Page-level reference areas stack in the `block-progression-direction`. Lines also stack in the `block-progression-direction`. Column and inline areas stack in the `inline-progression-direction`.

For Western European "`lr-tb`" writing mode, with no change to the reference orientation, this is the left-to-right `inline-progression-direction` and top-to-bottom `block-progression-direction`.

The "natural" stacking of areas may produce typographically unpleasant results. The desired breaks, widows, orphans, and keeps can be specified for the precise arrangement of information in reference areas. These settings override the physical arrangement of information implied by the default area properties.

Conditionality and precedence can eliminate areas from being rendered, to prevent the unnecessary use of interblock spacing when pagination renders a block without an adjacent sibling. For example, a block forced to the top of a new page doesn't always need the space defined for between blocks to be rendered.

Formatting special cases can be accommodated easily with simple specifications of intent where the formatter determines the applicability of spaces based on object properties. Not only can the transformation process ascribe such properties easier than determining space behaviors, but it would be impossible for the transformation process to know where the result information will end up in the rendered result and be able to make such a decision.

Numerous properties are available to be used in formatting objects to specify these nuances of layout.

Interactive Objects

XSLFO supports interactive, operator-driven presentation of content. The use of interactive formatting objects enables the operator (i.e., the reader of the document) to select from multiple alternatives prepared by the stylesheet writer, where the interactive object itself reflects previous interaction by its state. This results in dynamically changing presentations, rather than a single static rendering of the information.

XSLFO 1.0 provides two areas where interactivity can influence presentation: reflecting the active state of a linked object using different property values, and selecting and switching between alternate presentations using different subtrees of formatting objects.

Appearance or other impartation differences can distinguish a link that can be but hasn't yet been traversed (future potential for visitation), from a link that would be traversed (active hover), from a link that is about to be traversed (has the focus), from a link that is in the process of being traversed (is activated), from a link that has been traversed (past visitation).

Switching alternative available renderings can be used to implement such interactive presentations as a dynamically expandable and collapsible table of contents.

XSLFO Objects Related to Dynamic Properties and Dynamic Rendering Sequencing

The XSLFO objects that address functionality in these two areas are summarized as follows.

Formatting Objects Related to Dynamic Properties

- `<multi-properties>` (*6.9.6*)—the collection of candidate property sets from which exactly one set influences the properties of a formatting object based on its status or the status of operator interaction

- <multi-property-set> (*6.9.7*)—the set of properties associated with a single possible state of a formatting object or operator interaction

Formatting Objects Related to Dynamic Presentation

- <multi-switch> (*6.9.3*)—the collection of candidate formatting object sequences from which exactly one is rendered at any given time based on an interactive condition that is influenced by the operator while being tracked by the formatter
- <multi-case> (*6.9.4*)—a single formatting object sequence that is a candidate for rendering based on an interactive condition that is influenced by the operator while being tracked by the formatter
- <multi-toggle> (*6.9.5*)—the definition of interaction-sensitive objects within a candidate-rendered sequence of formatting objects

Supplemental Objects

The objects described here are not typically used very often but can provide useful functionality to those with specific formatting requirements in two areas:

- Character-level processing outside the default behaviors
- Constructs of a global nature

Lesser Used XSLFO Objects

The XSLFO objects that address functionality in this area areas are summarized as follows.

- <bidi-override> (*6.6.2*)—specifies how to override the inherent Unicode text direction for a sequence of characters
- <character> (*6.6.3*)—both the abstract formatting object implied by a simple character in an XSLFO instance and the concrete formatting object available to be used in place of a simple character
- <color-profile> (*6.4.4*)—the declaration of a profile of candidate color values from which color specifications can be made by formatting objects
- <declarations> (*6.4.3*)—a global-scope repository of formatting object constructs for an XSLFO instance, which includes the collection of available color profiles and any collections of extended formatting objects supported by an XSLFO processor. It must use a processor-recognized namespace URI other than the XSLFO namespace URI.

For Further Exploration

Articles

Sun: FOP Slide Kit, Paul Sandoz [using FOP and SVG to create slides]
http://www.sun.com/software/xml/developers/fop/

xmlhack.com: XSL-FO Category
http://xmlhack.com/list.php?cat=3

IBM: Transforming XML into PDF, Doug Tidwell [November 2000]
http://www-106.ibm.com/developerworks/education/transforming-xml/xmltopdf/index.html

XML.com: Using XSL Formatting Objects, J. David Eisenberg [January 2001]
http://www.xml.com/pub/a/2001/01/17/xsl-fo/inde.html

XML-Journal: XSL Formatting Objects: Here Today, Huge Tomorrow, Frank Neugebauer [January 2002, highly recommended]
http://www.sys-con.com/xml/article.cfm?id=324

Books

Practical Formatting Using XSLFO, G. Ken Holman [ISBN 1-894049-09-8]
http://www.CraneSoftwrights.com/links/trn-xfs.htm

Historical

Document Style Semantics and Specification Language (DSSSL) [ISO/IEC 10179:199]
http://www.y12.doe.gov/sgml/wg8/dsssl/readme.htm

James Clark's DSSSL Page
http://www.jclark.com/dsssl/

OpenJade
http://www.netfolder.com/DSSSL/

Resources

G. Ken Holman's Home Page
http://www.CraneSoftwrights.com

RenderX: XSL-FO Test Suite
http://www.renderx.com/testcases.html

FO Questions from the XSL FAQ, Dave Pawson
http://www.dpawson.co.uk/xsl/sect3/index.html

ZVON: XSL-FO Reference
http://www.zvon.org/xxl/xslfoReference/Output/index.html

RenderX: Unofficial DTD for XSL Formatting Objects
http://www.renderx.com/Tests/validator/fo.dtd.html

XSL Formatter List at XMLSOFTWARE
http://www.xmlsoftware.com/xslfo/

Software

Apache: FOP [XSL-FO to PDF; see this book's CD-ROM]
http://xml.apache.org/fop/

RenderX: XEP Rendering Engine [XSL-FO to PDF or PS; see this book's CD-ROM]
http://www.renderx.com/FO2PDF.html

Antenna House XSL Formatter
http://www.antennahouse.com/

PassiveTeX
http://www.hcu.ox.ac.uk/TEI/Software/passivetex/

WH2FO: Word HTML 2 Formatting Objects [Word 2000 to XML to XSLFO]
http://wh2fo.sourceforge.net/

FOA: Formatting Objects Authoring [XSL-FO authoring tool]
http://foa.sourceforge.net/

Tutorials

RenderX: XSL-FO Tutorial [highly recommended]
http://www.renderx.com/tutorial.html

XSL-FO: An introduction to XSL Formatting Objects, Dave Pawson [detailed online book]
http://www.dpawson.co.uk/xsl/sect3/bk/index.html

W3C Specifications and Information

Extensible Stylesheet Language (XSL) Version 1.0 [Recommendation, October 2001]
http://www.w3.org/TR/xsl

XSL Home Page [key central resource]
http://www.w3.org/Style/XSL/

Part IV

Related Core XML Specifications

Chapter 13

XLink: XML Linking Language

In this chapter, we'll learn about the XML Linking Language (XLink), an XML-based syntax for describing link relationships between two or more Web-accessible resources. XLinks may be as simple as the hypertext links defined in HTML and XHTML, or far more powerful one-to-many, many-to-many, and multidirectional links, possibly supported by external linkbases. The resources that are located by an XLink need not be XML documents; they can point to HTML, images, and anything that HTML links can. Using XLink, you can even create complex connections between sets of resources for which you do not have write access. XLink's cousin specification, XPointer (the XML Pointer Language), is covered in the next chapter. XPath, a syntax fundamental to XLink and XPointer (as well as XSLT and others) is discussed in chapter 11.

Overview

XML Linking Language (XLink) is positioned to greatly extend hypertext linking capabilities beyond what we can express in HTML.

Why HTML Linking Isn't Sufficient

To appreciate better the importance and flexibility of XLink, it's helpful to first review how linking is accomplished in HTML (see the HTML 4.01 specification section *http://www.w3.org/TR/html401/struct/links.html*). In the HTML 4.01 and XHTML 1.0 worlds, there are only a handful of fixed methods for expressing linking relationships:

1. `<a href="http://www.ex.com/file.html">Replace me.</a>`
2. `<a href="http://www.ex.com/file.html" target="_blank">Display me in a new window.</a>`

3. `<a href="http://www.ex.com/file.html" target="SpecificWindow">Display me in the window called SpecificWindow, creating it if necessary.</a>`
4. `<a href="http://www.ex.com/file.html#section3">Replace me after scrolling to the location named section3.</a>`
5. `<a id="section3" name="section3">Part III</a>`
6. `<img src="http://www.ex.com/pix.jpg" alt="Cool picture" />`
7. `<a href="http://www.ex.com/pixTopic.html"><img src="http://www.ex.com/pix.jpg" alt="Cool picture" /></a>`
8. `<head>...<title>Chapter 13</title><link rel="prev" href="chap12.html"><link rel="next" href="chap14.html">...</head>`

In example 1, we see the most common link behavior, namely, to replace the current page with the target page indicated by the `href` attribute of the <a> (anchor) element. Example 2 shows the use of the `target` attribute to force the display of the linked content in a new window because of the predefined "_blank" value. Example 3 shows a variation of this in which the destination page is displayed in a window with the arbitrary, designated name "SpecificWindow", which will be reused (i.e., its content will be replaced) if it exists; otherwise, the window will be created.

Example 4 illustrates the use of a **fragment identifier** (indicated by a string following the "#" character) appended to the URL, which indicates a named link endpoint within the destination page (which may also be the current page). Browsers will fetch the indicated page and scroll to the designated endpoint. In example 5, the use of the `id` attribute (with or without the similar but deprecated `name` attribute) indicates an anchor that is the destination of other links. The destination of example 4 is the named anchor shown in example 5.[1]

Example 6 shows the typical way that graphics are displayed in HTML/XHTML using the <img> element with the `src` attribute set to the location of the image and the optional but highly recommended `alt` attribute containing a brief description of the graphic. (Many other attributes are omitted because they aren't relevant to this discussion.) When a browser detects the <img> type of link, it fetches the graphic and embeds (inserts) it at the point of the <img> tag. Example 7 shows how to wrap the <img> element inside an <a> element. This makes the embedded image a link that points to the page specified by the anchor; clicking on the image retrieves the destination page.

Example 8 demonstrates the much less common <link> element intended to show relationships among the members of a set of documents. The `rel` attribute is an enumerated list of possible relationships, called *link types*, with values such as

1. The `id` attribute is now preferred by some applications. If both `id` and `name` are present, their value must be the same.

"Next", "Previous", "Index", "Stylesheet", and so on. These link relationships must appear within the <head> element, as shown, whereas the <a> and <img> elements can appear only in the <body> of an HTML or XHTML document. (The full description of these relationships appears in *http://www.w3.org/TR/html401/types.html#type-links*.)

Of course, there are minor variations of these forms, such as adding the `target` or `title` attribute to any <a> element, using relative rather than absolute URLs, and so forth, but this pretty much covers the gamut of HTML linking possibilities.

So, what does this all mean with regard to XML? The most glaring problem is that HTML and XHTML have the *predefined* elements <a>, <img>, and <link> to denote linking relationships. In XML, since we have the complete freedom to name our elements whatever we choose, how is an application (whether it is a browser, a parser, or a specialized utility) supposed to recognize an element that denotes linking? Furthermore, the second limitation of the HTML paradigm when applied to XML is that the link relationships are too constraining. All of the preceding HTML examples represent a very simplistic *unidirectional* linking relationship emanating from the source of the link (e.g., the content of the <a> element) and ending at the single target (e.g., identified by the `href` attribute). When we consider XML applications, it is easy to imagine the need for *multiple* links from one source (e.g., from a movie to all of its actors and actresses) and *multidirectional* links (e.g., between a given actor and all the movies in which he or she appears and between each movie and all its actors). Yet another limitation of HTML linking is that a link can be established only if you at least have write access to the document that contains the source of the link, that is, you can insert an <a>, <img>, or <link> element. In addition, if you want to use a named anchor, you also must either have write access to the destination document, or be lucky enough to discover that the author of the resource you wish to point to was considerate enough to sprinkle liberal helpings of <a id="foo" name="foo"> elements in strategic locations thoroughout the document.

So, how can these rich linking relationships be expressed in XML syntax?

What Is XLink?

The answer to this question is found in the XML Linking Language (XLink). XLink 1.0 is an XML-based syntax that enables content providers and developers to add simple or complex linking behavior and semantics to any XML document, regardless of the vocabulary. In other words, you can extend your XML vocabulary to provide linking just by including a few hooks in your DTD or XML Schema. The essence of XLink is to associate particular *attributes* from the XLink namespace with the elements that you wish to participate in any linking relationship. These attributes, most of which are optional, include those that indicate the kind of link, the behavior that the link provider intends, and semantics that describe the relationship. The XLink namespace is declared in the usual way, for any arbitrary element (especially the document element):

```
<SomeElement xmlns:xlink="http://www.w3.org/1999/xlink" ... />
```

Individuals attributes are then designated with the `xlink:` prefix, such as:

```
<SomeElement xmlns:xlink="http://www.w3.org/1999/XLink"
    xlink:type="simple"
    xlink:href="http://www.ex.com/file.html
    xlink:title="Another file"
    other-Non-XLink-Attributes ... />
```

Actually, `xlink:` is only a convention since the prefix can be anything, but unless you have a compelling reason to do otherwise, following the convention is recommended. Also, since the order of XML attributes is not defined, the order shown here in which all XLink attributes appear together and before other non-XLink attributes is purely for convenience.

The example illustrates the most basic type of XLink, a `simple` link, as designated by the `xlink:type` attribute. The other types of links are `extended`, `locator`, `arc`, `resource`, and `title`, as described in Table 13-1. Although the format above indicates a link that is an empty element (i.e., has no children as content), it is just as acceptable to have a simple link that contains non-XLink children.

XLink attributes are called **global attributes** because they are identified by the XLink namespace (via a namespace prefix) and can appear in the start tags of elements in another namespace. The full set of XLink global attributes is `type`, `href`, `role`, `arcrole`, `title`, `show`, `actuate`, `label`, `from`, and `to`, each of which is referenced with the `xlink:` prefix, as in `xlink:title`. Each attribute is required, optional, or not permitted depending on the type of link, as shown in Table 13-4 on page 874.

However, the process of linking in XML involves more interrelated aspects than does HTML linking, which of course makes it both more flexible and more complex (see Table 13-2.) It includes URIs to locate or identify resources, the XLink that connects the resources by means of an XPath expression, possibly with an appended XPointer reference. In addition, XBase and XInclude may be involved to resolve relative URIs and/or to embed a resource in an XML document, respectively.

Link Types and the xlink:type Attribute

The only *required attribute for every element* that uses XLink is `xlink:type`, which identifies the type of link that this element represents. Link type determines both the kinds of XLink children an element may contain, and which XLink attributes

TABLE 13-1 Types of XLink Elements and Their Allowable Children

xlink:type	*Description*	*Allowed XLink Children*
`simple`	Basic unidirectional link similar to HTML <a> and <`img`> elements; always connects two resources; outbound links only	None[a]
`extended`	May describe multiple links, bidirectional or multidirectional links; can be complicated, including elements that point to remote resources, contain local resources, specify arc traversal rules, and/or specify human-readable titles and machine-readable roles	`arc`, `locator`, `resource`, `title`
`locator`	Identifies a *remote* (*external*[b]) *resource* that is a participant in an extended link	`title`
`arc`	A traversal rule that describes how to traverse a pair of resources, including the direction of traversal and possibly application-specific behavior information; for an extended link, this is the "main event"	`title`
`resource`	Identifies a *local (internal) resource*, a location in the current document that is a participant in an extended link	None
`title`	Descriptive text; useful when the `xlink:title` *attribute* isn't sufficient, such as when additional markup is needed, especially for internationalization; possible child of `extended-`, `locator-`, and `arc-`type elements	None

a. The word *none* does not imply that the link cannot contain child elements that do not involve XLink attributes. It just means that no XLink element children have meaning for this link type. For example, `simple-type` links (i.e., elements with `xlink:type="simple"`) may contain children from your own vocabulary that are not links. Actually, every link type may contain children from other vocabularies (namespaces), something that is difficult to express in DTDs.

b. In this context, the term *external* means external to the link, which may or may not mean the resource is in an external file. Similarly, *internal* means contained in the extended link.

may be associated with the element. This does *not* mean, however, that an element that uses attributes from the XLink namespace is limited to using *only* XLink attributes, nor that it cannot contain other elements that do not have an `xlink:type` attribute (and are therefore children with no other XLink attributes). Table 13-1 presents an overview of link types and their allowed children; each type is described more completely later in this chpater. If an element contains a `xlink:type` of type `foo`, then the specification refers to this as a `foo-type` element. For example, an arbitrary element in our vocabularly that sets `xlink:type="locator"` is called a `locator-type` element.

Terminology and Concepts

Before we introduce a complete example, it's worthwhile to understand many of the terms and concepts in the XLink specification. XLink is primarily concerned with describing the connections between two or more Web-accessible resources. A

resource is any addressable unit of information or service, as defined in RFC 2396 (URIs; *http://www.ietf.org/rfc/rfc2396.txt*):

> A resource can be anything that has identity. Familiar examples include an electronic document, an image, a service (e.g., "today's weather report for Los Angeles"), and a collection of other resources. . . . [A] resource can remain constant even when its content—the entities to which it currently corresponds—changes over time, provided that the conceptual mapping is not changed in the process.

In other words, a resource can be anything you'd normally link to in HTML (other HTML documents, named anchors within HTML documents, images in various formats, etc.), as well as to XML documents in any XML-based vocabulary, plus identified elements or ranges within an XML document (via XPointer). The set of resources that an XLink associates are called the **participants** in the link. In particular, note that resources need not be XML documents, although the XLink elements must themselves *appear* in XML documents.

The specification makes a distinction between an XLink **link**, which is "an explicit relationship between resources or portions of resources," and a **linking element**, which is "an XLink-conforming XML element that asserts the existence of a link." There are six types of links, but only two, `simple` and `extended`, are considered linking elements. The others are children of the `extended` link that further describe the link's characteristics. A **hyperlink** is the specialized kind of XLink that is intended for human presentation, such as the familiar HTML <a> element. However, some of the linking mechanisms described by XLink 1.0 are more targeted for the soon-to-evolve class of applications for which only computers are involved in the processing of the links.

The act of following or using a link is called **traversal**, which always involves exactly two resources (or portions thereof, in the case of a fragment identifier). The source of the traversal is the **starting resource** and the destination is the **ending resource**. An **arc** is the information about "how to traverse a pair of resources, including the direction of traversal and possibly application behavior information as well." A **multidirectional link** is one in which two arcs specify one pair of resources but the starting and ending resources are reversed. The specification emphasizes that simply going back to the starting resource by means of a browser's `Back` button does *not* indicate a multidirectional link.

Support for XLink

At the time of this writing, support for XLink is extremely limited in Web browsers and in other types of applications as well. The list compiled by the W3C is presented later in the section "XLink Implementations." This includes products such as X2X and XTooX. Readers may be interested in downloading the free XLink2HTML by Fabio Arciniegas A (The FAActory; *http://www.thefaactory.com/xlink2html/*). XLink2HTML is a set of XSLT stylesheets for creating HTML representations of XLink elements, especially one-to-many arcs from local resources to locators.

Netscape 6 supports `simple-type` XLinks mainly by recognizing the attribute `xlink:href`. It does not honor the behavioral attributes such as `xlink:show` and `xlink:actuate`, except to replace the current page when the user activates the link, exactly like basic XHTML <a> behavior. (Support may have improved by the time you read this, however.) Bob DuCharme's Simple XLink Demo is a useful browser demo (*http://www.shee.com/xm/xlink/sxlinkdemo.xml*).

It's important to realize that the XLink specification describes *suggested* behavior for various link attributes. Applications are free to ignore these suggestions, or to interpret them in an application-specific manner. For example, a webcrawler engine won't want to wait for user activation to follow a link since its job is to gather as many links as it can find and as quickly as it can.

Relevant Specifications

Table 13-2 lists the specifications that are related to linking in XML. In practice, XLink, XPointer, and XPath are the most significant. The XLink 1.0 specification

TABLE 13-2 XLink and Related Specifications

W3C Specification	*URL (trailing slash required where indicated)*
XML Linking Language (XLink)Version 1.0 Recommendation (June 2001)	*http://www.w3.org/TR/xlink/*
XML XLink Requirements Version 1.0 (W3C Note)	*http://www.w3.org/TR/NOTE-xlink-req/*
XML Linking Language (XLink) Design Principles (W3C Note)	*http://www.w3.org/TR/NOTE-xlink-principles*
XML Pointer Language (XPointer) Version 1.0 *Candidate* Recommendation (September 2001)	*http://www.w3.org/TR/xptr*
XML Path Language (XPath) Version 1.0 Recommendation (November 1999)	*http://www.w3.org/TR/xpath*
XML Inclusions (XInclude) Version 1.0 Candidate Recommendation (February 2002)	*http://www.w3.org/TR/xinclude/*
XML Base Recommendation (June 2001)	*http://www.w3.org/TR/xmlbase*
XLink Markup Name Control (W3C Note)	*http://www.w3.org/TR/xlink-naming*
XML Linking and Style (W3C Note)	*http://www.w3.org/TR/xml-link-style/*
Harvesting RDF Statements from XLinks (W3C Note)	*http://www.w3.org/TR/xlink2rdf/*
Links in HTML Documents	*http://www.w3.org/TR/html401/struct/links.html*
RFC 2396: Uniform Resource Identifiers	*http://www.ietf.org/rfc/rfc2396.txt*
RFC 2732: Format for Literal IPv6 Addresses in URLs	*http://www.ietf.org/rfc/rfc2732.txt*
RFC 3023: XML Media Types	*http://www.ietf.org/rfc/rfc3023.txt*

itself describes how two or more resources are connected, how to traverse the connections, and how these links might behave from both a user and application perspective, although such behavior is stated only in terms of suggestions. The main specifications that are important to XLink are XPath 1.0 and XPointer 1.0. As we learned in the previous chapter, XPath is a syntax used to identify nodes of an XML document. XPointer provides a mechanism for adding an XPath expression to a URI as an appended fragment identifier (more about this later).

The XLink Requirements and XLink Design Principles documents are somewhat old, so it is possible that XLink 1.0 departs from these to some degree. XInclude is useful for embedding external (remote) resources in an XML document. Expect XInclude to become increasingly important in 2002. XML Base is the XML equivalent (the `xml:base` attribute) of the optional HTML 4.01 `<base>` element that may appear in the `<head>` section of a document; relative URIs are interpreted with respect to the base. The RFCs (Requests For Comments from the Internet Engineering Task Force [IETF]) listed in the table describe URIs and URI syntax, plus five new MIME (Multipurpose Internet Mail Extensions) types for exchanging network resources involving XML. URIs are a superset of URLs (Uniform Resource Locators, RFC 1738), which are, of course, the familiar addresses that locate Web pages, ftp sites, newsgroups, and other resources by means of the HTTP protocol.

XLink, XPointer, and XML Base are all the purview of the W3C Linking Working Group, according to the W3C page *http://www.w3.org/XML/Linking*. Their activity statement (*http://www.w3.org/XML/Activity.html#linking-wg*) describes the overall goals:

> The XML Linking Working Group . . . is designing hypertext links for XML. Engineers defining the way that links are to be written in XML have made a distinction for links between objects—"external" links, and "internal" links to locations within XML documents, and both types are receiving detailed treatment by this group. The objective of the XML Linking Working Group is to design advanced, scalable, and maintainable hyperlinking and addressing functionality for XML.

Historical Perspective

Readers not interested in the historical development of XLink can skip this section without serious damage to their psyches.

Early linking concepts were a major part of SGML work called **Hypermedia/Time-based Structuring Language** (**HyTime**, ISO 10744:1997), which dates back to roughly 1992. In the very early days of the Web, HyTime became the linking specification for use with SGML in the documentation world. Of course, HyTime predated XML. Just as SGML is far more complex and flexible than XML, HyTime is similarly a more complicated linking specification than is XLink. HyTime defines location specifier types for all kinds of data, which is relevant to XPointer. HyTime also defines inline, inbound, and third-party link structures (see "Outbound,

Inbound and Third-Party Links" later in this chapter) and some semantic features, including traversal control and presentation of objects, which are a basis for XLink.

In addition to his XML information, Robin Cover's XML Cover Pages are an excellent source for SGML and related pre-XML efforts, such as DSSSL (cf: CSS, XSLT, and XSLFO), HyTime (cf: XLink) and TEI (cf: XPointer). The HyTime section includes links to two introductions that nicely summarize the role and scope of HyTime (*http://xml.coverpages.org/hytime.html*). In 1996 Lloyd Rutledge (*http://xml.coverpages.org/hytimeWhatRutledge.htm*) described HyTime as follows.

> HyTime is an SGML architecture that specifies the generic hypermedia structure of documents. . . . The hypermedia concepts directly represented by HyTime include
>
> - complex locating of document objects
> - relationships (hyperlinks) between document objects
> - numeric, measured associations between document objects
>
> HyTime does not directly specify graphical interfaces, user navigation, user interaction, or the placement of media on timelines and screen displays.

In 1997 W. Eliot Kimber (*http://xml.coverpages.org/hytimeKimber9701.html*) said that HyTime provided two classes of hypertext-related facilities:

> 1. A general model of hyperlinks and syntax for hyperlink representation using SGML elements. This is much more than simple ID/IDREF.
> 2. Facilities for addressing things other than elements with IDs in the local document: cross-document ID refs, references to elements without IDs, references to data characters, references to multiple objects at once.

Although primarily XPointer-related, the **Text Encoding Initiative (TEI)** P3 (Guidelines), first published in nondraft form in 1994, also provides structures for creating links, aggregate objects, and link collections, all of which are relevant to XLink.

In 1996 when the W3C initiated plans for "SGML for the Web," XLink was among the three core languages discussed (along with XML and XSL). In April 1997, Extensible Markup Language, Part 2: Linking, became the first Working Draft of what eventually split into XLink and XPointer in July 1999. By December 1999, both XLink and XPointer became Last Call Working Drafts. XLink became a Candidate Recommendation in July 2000 and a Proposed Recommendation in December 2000. Finally, in June 2001, XLink achieved full Recommendation status. (XPointer is still a Candidate Recommendation, as of this writing.)

Simple Link: Reinventing the Anchor

A `simple-type` link (`xlink:type="simple"`) associates a pair of resources, one *local* and one *remote*, and implicitly defines one arc that describes the traversal from the local resource (e.g., the text that is underlined as internal to the link) to the remote resource (which is external to the link and may or *may not* be a separate document). In other words, a simple-type link usually connects some element in your document to an external page (this is an oversimplification, as we'll see) or fragment of a page. This unidirectional link is very much like the XHTML <a> element; as you read this section, consider the close parallels to the link variations presented earlier in "Why HTML Linking Isn't Sufficient." However, the key benefit of a simple-type link over <a> is that the linking behavior and semantics can be applied to *any element* in your XML vocabulary just by attaching the relevant attributes.

A simple XLink connects an XML element to a remote resource that may be XML, HTML, an image, a soundclip, a movie, or anything else that can be pointed to by a URI. Consider this example:

```
<Beatles-Site xmlns:xlink="http://www.w3.org/1999/xlink"
  xlink:type="simple"
  xlink:href="http://mcbeatle.de/beatles/"
  xlink:title="Harald Gernhardt's Beatles Site"
  xlink:show="replace"
  xlink:actuate="onRequest">Visit Harald Gernhardt's award-winning Beatles
site</Beatles-Site>
```

This simple-type link locates the resource *http://mcbeatle.de/beatles/*, the original home of Harald Gernhardt's Web site (which happens to be an HTML page). The show and actuate attributes suggest the typical HTML link behavior, namely, to replace the current page with the page pointed to when the user activates the link. The text string of the title attribute might be represented as a tooltip. Finally, the content of the <Beatles-Site> element is PCDATA, "Visit Harald Gernhardt's award-winning Beatles site", which might be underlined or color-highlighted as in HTML.

My use of the words *suggest* and *might* in the previous paragraph is quite deliberate. Since the XLink specification merely suggests behavior and presentation, the actual user interface isn't mandated by W3C. Although it's likely that simple-type link behavior will closely parallel the XHTML <a> element, when we discuss extended-type links, it should be clear that user interfaces are likely to be application-dependent, at least until some standard is defined. For example, a W3C Note entitled "XML Linking and Style" describes potential interrelationships between linking and styling across applications (*http://www.w3.org/TR/xml-link-style/*).

Table 13-4 shows that the possible attributes for a simple-type link are type, href, role, arcrole, title, show, and actuate. Of these, only type is required, but in any practical sense, you'll almost always want to specify href and possibly title, show, and actuate as well.

Simple Link Code Example

In our discussion of CSS in chapter 10, we introduced an example that used linking via the XHTML namespace. Let's revisit that example and replace the linking information with XLink attributes attached to elements of our own choosing. More specifically, in the CSS chapter, `collection5.xml` used the `<xhtml:a>` element nested in our `<Title>` element, as shown in boldface in Listing 13-1.

Listing 13-1 Excerpt from XHTML Linking Example (collection5.xml)

```
<?xml version="1.0" standalone="no"?>
<!DOCTYPE Collection SYSTEM "collection5.dtd">

<?xml-stylesheet type="text/css" href="collection5.css"?>

<Collection version="2" xmlns:xhtml="http://www.w3.org/1999/xhtml" >
  <xhtml:h1>Ken's Collection</xhtml:h1>
  <Book>
    <Title>
      <xhtml:a href="http://www.amazon.com/exec/obidos/ASIN/0600600335/o/
qid=979102681/sr=8-1/ref=aps_sr_b_1_1/103-4097284-9855030">
Complete Beatles Chronicle, The</xhtml:a>
    </Title>
    <Author>
      <Name>
        <First>Mark</First>
        <Last>Lewisohn</Last>
      </Name>
    </Author>
    <Type>Chronology</Type>
    <Published publisher="Harmony Books">1992</Published>
    <Rating>5 stars</Rating>
    <Notes>
  Covers the years 1957 through 1970. No solo info.
  Great appendices with chart info, discography, composer index,
  radio, tv, and live performances, and much more.
  Second Edition: May 2000 with George Martin as co-author.
  </Notes>
  </Book>
  <CD>
    <Title>
      <xhtml:a href="http://cdnow.com/cgi-bin/mserver/SID=1838724509/page-
name=/RP/CDN/FIND/album.xhtml/artistid=MCCARTNEY*PAUL+&amp;+WINGS/
itemid=644593">
Band on the Run</xhtml:a>
    </Title>
    <Artist>McCartney, Paul and Wings</Artist>
<!-- etc. -->
```

Listing 13-2 shows the same code fragment with the XLink and XInclude namespaces, which are declared for the document element, `<Collection>`, so their scope is the entire document. (We'll see the DTD later in Listing 13-3 on page 870.)

Each <Book> and <CD> element contains a required <Title> child. In this case, the first <Title> element gains the `xlink:href` *attribute*, which replaces the nested <xhtml:a> *element*. The attribute `xlink:type="simple"` identifies this as a `simple-type` link. This results in the <Title> element playing the dual role that required both <Title> and <xhtml:a> in the earlier CSS version.

```
<Title xlink:type="simple"
       xlink:href="http://www.amazon.com/exec/obidos/ASIN/0600600335/
           ">Complete Beatles Chronicle, The</Title>
```

We've also added a second optional `simple-type` XLink <Picture> element which, in addition to `xlink:type` and `xlink:href` attributes, specifies `xlink:show="embed"` to cause the referenced resource (an image) to be inserted into the document.

```
<Picture xlink:type="simple"
         xlink:show="embed"
         xlink:title="photo of The Complete Beatles Chronicles"
         xlink:href="http://images.amazon.com/images/P/
             0600600335.01.MZZZZZZZ.jpg" />
```

Unfortunately, at the time of this writing, browers don't support this embedding (and not much of XLink), so we won't actually *see* the requested image. However, you can imagine that this <Picture> element corresponds closely to <xhtml:img>. For example, the `xlink:title` attribute can be interpreted as tooltip-like information, much like the `alt` attribute of <xhtml:img>.

The excerpt from `collection9.xml` also shows a <CD> element whose <Title> has been enhanced with XLink attributes exactly the same way as was the <Book> element. No <Picture> element is included for <CD>, but the procedure would be the same.

Listing 13-2 Excerpt Using Simple-Type XLinks (collection9.xml)

```
<?xml version="1.0" standalone="no"?>
<!DOCTYPE Collection SYSTEM "collection9.dtd" >

<?xml-stylesheet type="text/css" href="collection9.css"?>

<Collection version="3"
  xmlns:xlink="http://www.w3.org/1999/xlink"
  xmlns:xi="http://www.w3.org/1999/XML/xinclude" >

  <!-- XInclude not supported by browsers yet. -->
  <xi:include
      href="http://gernhardt.com/beatles/beatles3.jpg" />

  <Book>
    <Title xlink:type="simple"
           xlink:href="http://www.amazon.com/exec/obidos/ASIN/0600600335/
               ">Complete Beatles Chronicle, The</Title>
```

```
    <!-- xlink:show="embed" not supported by browsers yet -->
    <Picture xlink:type="simple"
             xlink:show="embed"
             xlink:title="photo of The Complete Beatles Chronicles"
             xlink:href="http://images.amazon.com/images/P/
                 0600600335.01.MZZZZZZZ.jpg"
    />

    <Author>
      <Name>
        <First>Mark</First>
        <Last>Lewisohn</Last>
      </Name>
    </Author>
    <Type>Chronology</Type>
    <Published publisher="Harmony Books">1992</Published>
    <Rating>5 stars</Rating>
    <Notes>
  Covers the years 1957 through 1970. No solo info.
  Great appendices with chart info, discography, composer index,
  radio, tv, and live performances, and much more.
  Second Edition: May 2000 with George Martin as co-author.
    </Notes>
    <ListPrice>24.95</ListPrice>
  </Book>
  <CD>
    <Title xlink:type="simple"
     xlink:href="http://cdnow.com/cgi-bin/mserver/pagename=/RP/CDN/FIND/
album.html/ArtistID=MCCARTNEY*PAUL+&amp;+WINGS/ITEMID=644593">Band on the
Run</Title>
    <Artist>McCartney, Paul and Wings</Artist>
<!-- etc. -->
```

Although it is not necessary for our understanding of XLink, I've added a line to exercise XInclude (XML Inclusions) even though this W3C Candidate Recommendation is (understandably) not yet supported by Netscape 6. The `<xi:include>` element references an external XML file:

```
  <xi:include  href="plastic-Beatles.xml" />
```

My intention is to *indirectly* embed an image resource, by including a small XML document that contains a `<Picture>` element which, in turn, links to a JPEG image. The contents of `plastic-Beatles.xml` is simply one element that locates the image `http://gernhardt.com/beatles/beatles3.jpg`:

```
<?xml version="1.0" standalone="yes"?>
<Picture xlink:type="simple"
     xlink:show="embed"
     xlink:title="The Plastic Beatles from Harald Gernhardt's Beatles Site"
     xlink:href="http://gernhardt.com/beatles/beatles3.jpg"
/>
```

XInclude can be contrasted to an XLink with `xlink:show="embed"`. Whereas XLink is media-type independent and imposes no particular processing model, XInclude is strictly for merging media-type dependent XML into XML. The included document (e.g., `plastic-Beatles.xml`) becomes part of the information set of the document that contains the `<xi:include>` element (*http://www.w3.org/TR/xinclude/#rel-xlink*).

If we view `collection9.xml` in Netscape 6.2 *without* a stylesheet (i.e., by deleting the `xml-stylesheet` processing instruction, as in `collection9-no-css.xml`), we see from Figure 13-1 that the links are not underlined, but note that the hand

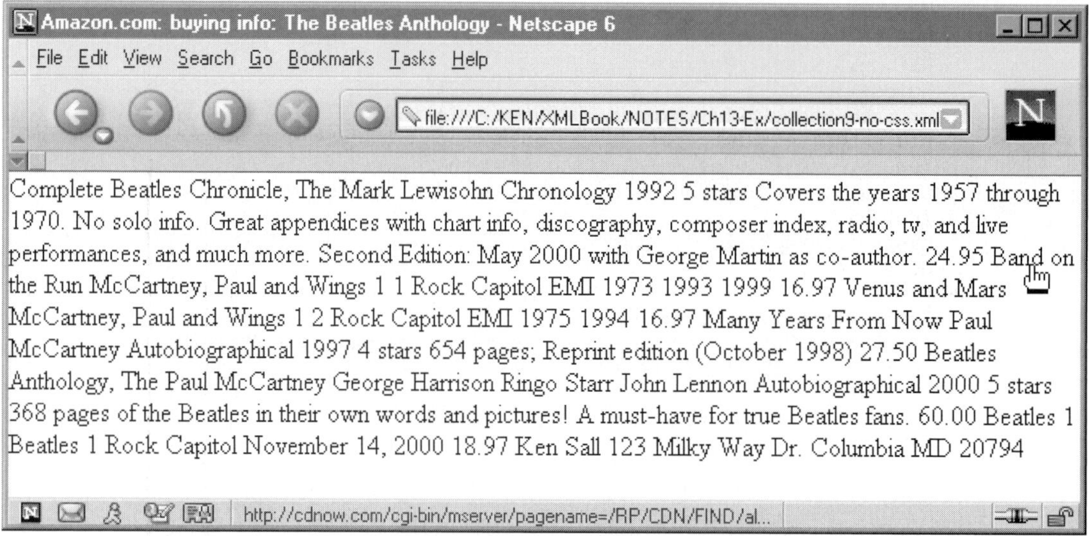

FIGURE 13-1 Raw display of simple-type XLinks without CSS (collection9-no-css.xml)

cursor on the right points to the "Band on the Run" `<Title>` link.[2] Even if the visual cue is a bit different, these `simple-type` XLinks do function as you'd expect; clicking on any of them results in our XML document being replaced by the Amazon or CDNow page that the `xlink:href` points to.

If, however, we make a few small changes to the CSS style sheet, `collection5.css` (refer back to Listing 10-8), we can demonstrate rendering not only the `simple-type` link of the `<Title>` element, but also the `<Picture>` element

2. Actually, an early version of Netscape 6 *did* underline the links but Netscape 6.2 does not. Your mileage may vary.

with its `xlink:show="embed"` attribute. The revised stylesheet, `collection9.css`, differs from the original in only a few lines:

```
ListPrice   {display:block; text-indent: 4em; font-weight:bold; }
Picture     {display:block; border: dashed thin teal; padding: 1em;}
Picture:before {content: "Embedded Image:"}
```

The `ListPrice` line is added merely to display the `<ListPrice>` element that we added to our running example in the XSLT chapter. More significant is the addition of the `Picture` rules, the first of which tells the CSS processor (built in to Netscape) to force a linebreak when `<Picture>` is encountered and enclose the element in a dashed box. The `Picture:before` selector causes the text "Embedded Image:" to be inserted before the content of the element. Figure 13-2 shows the display of

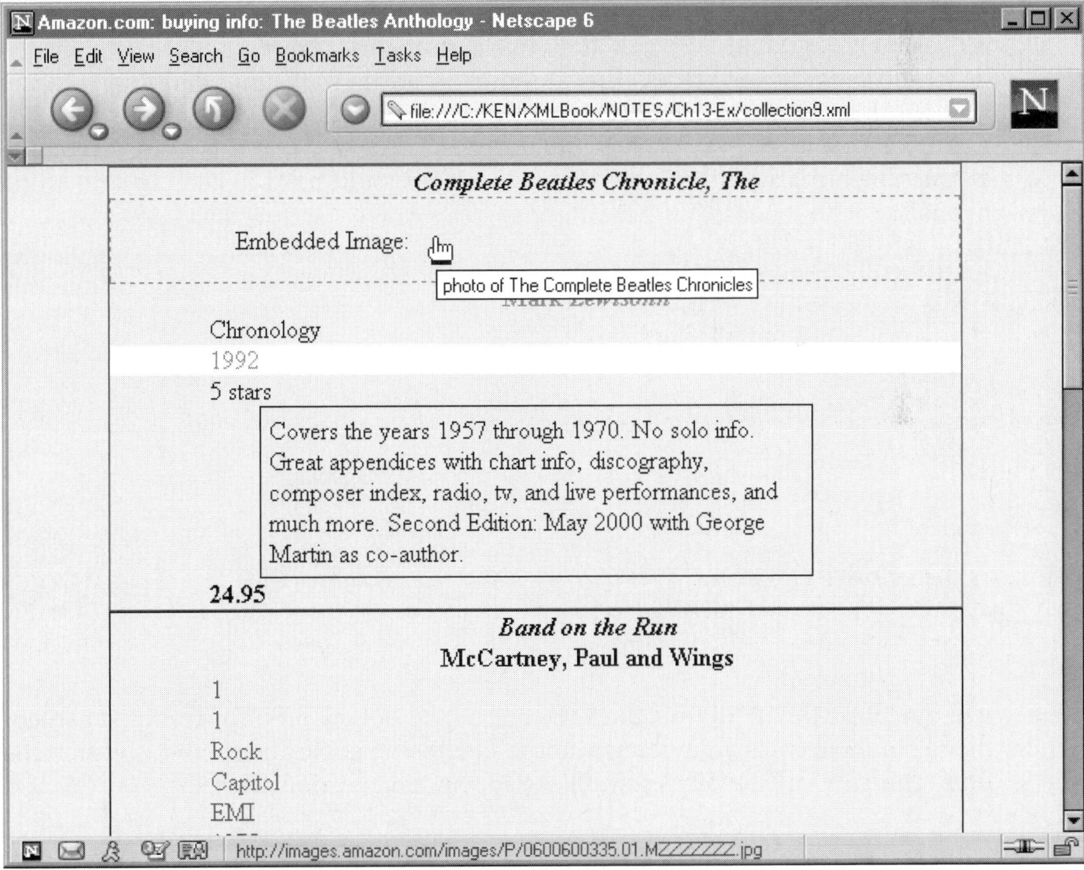

FIGURE 13-2 Display of simple-type XLinks with a CSS style sheet (collection9.css)

collection9.xml via collection9.css, as rendered in Netscape 6. Compare this to Figure 10-6.

A few points are noteworthy. Even though Netscape 6 does not embed the resource linked to by the <Picture> element, it *does* recognize the element, so when we render it using CSS, space is effectively reserved for it. You may have noted the white hand cursor hovering over this link. If you look closely at the browser's status area at the bottom of the window, you'll note that the resource referenced by the xlink:href attribute is reflected in the status area. Similarly, the xlink:href attribute is displayed in the status area when the cursor is over the <Title> element. You can also see the tooltip presentation of the text "photo of The Complete Beatles Chronicles" when the mouse hovers over the (invisible) <Picture> element, indicating that the xlink:title attribute is processed by Netscape 6.2.[3]

Declaring XLinks in DTDs

To benefit from XLink *and* validate your documents, *you must explicitly define all XLink attributes in your DTD*. This amounts to adding attribute definitions to the ATTLIST lines for each element in your vocabulary that uses XLink attributes. For example, for a simple-type element named my-simple-link, if we care to include all possible attributes (see Table 13-4), the DTD would need to contain something like this:

```
<!ELEMENT my-simple-link   ANY >
<!ATTLIST my-simple-link
 xlink:type       (simple)         #FIXED "simple"
 xlink:href       CDATA            #REQUIRED
 xlink:role       CDATA            #IMPLIED
 xlink:arcrole    CDATA            #IMPLIED
 xlink:title      CDATA            #IMPLIED
 xlink:show       (new
                  |replace
                  |embed
                  |other
                  |none)           #IMPLIED
 xlink:actuate    (onLoad
                  |onRequest
                  |other
                  |none)           #IMPLIED>
```

Although this fragment uses the keyword ANY to denote an unconstrained content model, in most cases you would want to be more specific about what children the link element may contain, as we'll see in the next section with the <Title> and

3. Early versions of Netscape 6.x did not display the xlink:title text.

<Picture> elements. Other non-XLink attributes would also need to be reflected, of course.[4]

Validating Simple XLinks with a Modified DTD

The DTD for the original CSS example was called collection5.dtd. To accommodate the XLink attributes and XInclude elements, a revised DTD named collection9.dtd is needed. The differences between the two versions are emphasized by means of bold font in Listing 13-3. First, we need to declare the two relevant namespaces associated with Collection, the document element. These values must be exactly as shown, even though they reflect different years and different capitalization conventions. Of course, in the general case of XLink usage, the XInclude namespace is not necessary.

```
<!ATTLIST Collection
 version      CDATA   "3"
 xmlns:xlink  CDATA   #FIXED  "http://www.w3.org/1999/xlink"
 xmlns:xi     CDATA   #FIXED  "http://www.w3.org/2001/XInclude"
>
```

Let's skip the xi:include element for a moment. We've added an optional Picture element to the list of children of the Book element, and an optional ListPrice for both Book and CD. If present, Picture must follow the Title element. The attribute definition for Title fixes xlink:type to "simple" and makes the xlink:href attribute required. It seems to me that the XLink 1.0 specification is a little unclear about whether xlink:href is required. Table 13-4 on page 874 is based on Section 4.1, "XLink Attribute Usage Patterns," from the XLink specification, which indicates that xlink:href is *optional* for simple-type links but *required* for locator-type links. The optional nature for simple-type links is also expressed in the text of the specification. However, every DTD excerpt defines this attribute as required, even though the DTD fragments are considered nonnormative. In our example, therefore, I've made xlink:href required because these links would not be very meaningful if they didn't point to a resource. No other XLink global attributes are defined for the Title element, so if an XML instance included an xlink:show attribute, for example, this would be invalid, despite the fact that simple-type links in general do support that attribute.

```
<!ELEMENT Title (#PCDATA)>
<!ATTLIST Title
        xlink:type    (simple)     #FIXED   "simple"
        xlink:href    CDATA        #REQUIRED
>
```

4. A DTD that declares all six link types and all attributes appears in the XLink 1.0 Recommendation, in the appendix entitled "Sample DTD (Non-Normative)" at *http://www.w3.org/TR/xlink/#sample-dtd-appx*.

The empty Picture element's attribute list uses more of the possible attributes for a simple-type link because it also specifies xlink:title, xlink:show, and xlink:actuate. Recall that our instance document in Listing 13-2 does not include an xlink:actuate attribute, so the DTD's default value of "onLoad" would be passed to the application from the parser. For both the xlink:show and xlink:actuate attributes, I've omitted the values "other" and "none" from the enumerations, so they would be invalid if used in a document that referenced this DTD.

```
<!ELEMENT Picture EMPTY>
<!ATTLIST Picture
        xlink:type     (simple)     #FIXED    "simple"
        xlink:href     CDATA        #REQUIRED
        xlink:title    CDATA        #IMPLIED
        xlink:show     (new|replace|embed)  "embed"
        xlink:actuate  (onLoad|onRequest)   "onLoad"
>
```

Let's return to XInclude. The relevant DTD portion is

```
<!ELEMENT xi:include EMPTY >
<!ATTLIST xi:include
 xmlns:xi    CDATA        #FIXED       "http://www.w3.org/2001/XInclude"
 href        CDATA        #REQUIRED
 parse       (xml|text)   "xml"
 encoding    CDATA        #IMPLIED
>
```

We've also stipulated that xi:include is an optional, repeatable child of Collection, but it must come before Book and CD elements. The xi:include element itself cannot have children, although the XML document located by its href attribute can of course be arbitrarily complex in terms of its content model. Notice that the attribute name is simply href, not xi:href, because xi:include is a full-fledged element, unlike XLink, which depends on attaching *attributes* from the XLink namespace to elements from different namespaces. I've used default values for parse and encoding because I want the fetched document to be parsed like XML so that the XLinks it contains can also be processed.

Listing 13-3 DTD with Support for Simple-Type XLinks and XInclude (collection9.dtd)

```
<?xml encoding="UTF-8"?>
<!--        Collection DTD, Version 3        -->
<!ELEMENT Collection (xi:include*, (Book | CD)*, Owner?)>
<!ATTLIST Collection
 version      CDATA   "3"
 xmlns:xlink  CDATA   #FIXED  "http://www.w3.org/1999/xlink"
 xmlns:xi     CDATA   #FIXED  "http://www.w3.org/2001/XInclude"
>
```

```
<!ELEMENT xi:include EMPTY >
<!ATTLIST xi:include
 xmlns:xi   CDATA       #FIXED      "http://www.w3.org/2001/XInclude"
 href       CDATA       #REQUIRED
 parse      (xml|text)  "xml"
 encoding   CDATA       #IMPLIED
>
<!ELEMENT Owner (Name, Address?)>
<!ELEMENT Address (Street, City, State, Zip)>
<!ELEMENT Street (#PCDATA)>
<!ELEMENT City (#PCDATA)>
<!ELEMENT State (#PCDATA)>
<!ELEMENT Zip (#PCDATA)>

<!ELEMENT Book (Title, Picture?, Author+, Type, Published, Rating?, Notes?,
ListPrice?)>
<!ELEMENT CD (Title, Artist, Chart, Type, Label+, AlbumReleased, Remastered*,
ListPrice?)>

<!ELEMENT Title (#PCDATA)>
<!ATTLIST Title
        xlink:type    (simple)    #FIXED   "simple"
        xlink:href    CDATA       #REQUIRED
>

<!ELEMENT Picture EMPTY>
<!ATTLIST Picture
        xlink:type    (simple)    #FIXED   "simple"
        xlink:href    CDATA       #REQUIRED
        xlink:title   CDATA       #IMPLIED
        xlink:show    (new|replace|embed)  "embed"
        xlink:actuate (onLoad|onRequest)   "onLoad"
>
<!ELEMENT ListPrice (#PCDATA)>

<!-- Title defined under CD; applies to Book also. -->
<!-- Name defined under Owner; applies to Book also. -->
<!ELEMENT Author (Name)>
<!ELEMENT Name (First, Last)>
<!ATTLIST Name
        sex (male | female) "male"
>
<!ELEMENT First (#PCDATA)>
<!ELEMENT Last (#PCDATA)>
<!ELEMENT Type (#PCDATA)>
<!ELEMENT Published (#PCDATA)>
<!ATTLIST Published
        publisher CDATA #REQUIRED
>
<!ELEMENT Rating (#PCDATA)>
<!ELEMENT Notes (#PCDATA)>
<!ELEMENT Artist (#PCDATA)>
<!ELEMENT Chart (Peak+)>
<!--WAS: ATTLIST Label country NMTOKEN #IMPLIED-->
<!ELEMENT Peak (#PCDATA)>
```

```
<!ATTLIST Peak
        country NMTOKEN "US"
        weeks NMTOKEN #IMPLIED
>
<!ELEMENT Label (#PCDATA)>
<!ATTLIST Label
        country NMTOKEN "US"
>
<!ELEMENT AlbumReleased (#PCDATA)>
<!ELEMENT Remastered (#PCDATA)>
<!ATTLIST Remastered
        format CDATA #REQUIRED
>
```

In developing this example, I found it extremely useful to use a lightweight utility called XML Validator from ElCel Technology (*http://www.elcel.com/*; this company also provides a handy canonical utility). XML Validator, introduced in earlier chapters, can be used to validate against a DTD, including the recognition and processing of namespaces via the `-n` switch:

```
C:> xmlvalid -n collection9.xml
```

This utility generates extremely specific error messages. For example, if my instance used the `xlink:title` attribute for `Picture`, and if I forgot to add it to the DTD, the error message would be:

```
collection9.xml [21:68] : Error: undeclared attribute 'xlink:title' for
element 'Picture'
```

This flags the error on line 21, column 68 of the XML document. Similarly, errors in the DTD itself are also reported. Among the many options, the `-v` flag turns off validation, effectively turning `xmlvalid` into a well-formedness checker. When I'm not working on Java applications using XML, I prefer utilities like XML Validator to Xerces because they are quicker and support many command-line options.

In the next few sections, we'll learn a bit more about which XLink attributes are legal for different link types, what kind of values each attribute must have, and how `xlink:show` and `xlink:actuate` behave in isolation and combination. After that, we'll cover `extended-type` of XLink and its children elements.

XLink Attributes

In this section and the next, we'll take a closer look at the various XLink attributes in terms of their purpose and datatype, which attributes are optional or required for a particular link type, and how `xlink:show` and `xlink:actuate` determine link behavior.

Attributes by Purpose and Datatype

The ten XLink global attributes and corresponding datatypes are listed in Table 13-3. These attribute values are enumerations, URIs, or text. For example, the table shows that the datatype for `xlink:role` and `xlink:arcrole` is a URI that points to a textual description, whereas for `xlink:title`, it is simply `CDATA`, exactly like the `alt` attribute of the HTML <a> element. An `xlink:label` must be a `NMTOKEN`, which you'll recall consists of XML Name characters (but aren't required to have an initial letter) and cannot contain white space.

Most of these attributes are discussed elsewhere in this chapter. However, a few words about the semantic attributes will be helpful here. All three—`xlink:role`, `xlink:arcrole`, and `xlink:title`—are used to describe the *meaning of resources* in the context of a link. Based on Table 13-4, the `role` attribute may be used with `extended-`, `simple-`, `locator-`, and `resource-type` elements, but the `arcrole` attribute may be used only with `arc-` and `simple-type` elements. The `title` attribute may be used for all link types except the `title-type` element. Since DTDs have no URI attribute type, you'll see `CDATA` in declarations for `xlink:role`, and `xlink:arcrole`, but remember they are URIs. In fact, the XLink spec has very few examples of these, but they appear to be similar to the properties we saw with the DOM and SAX, since they look more like handles than actual files. For example:

```
xlink:arcrole="http://www.ex.com/linkprops/singer"
```

TABLE 13-3 XLink Attributes: Purpose and Datatype

Attribute	*Purpose*	*Datatype*
`type`	XLink element type definition	Enumerated list of choices: `simple`, `extended`, `locator`, `arc`, `resource`, `title`
`href`	Locator attribute	URI of *ending* resource (destination)

`role`
`arcrole`
`title`
	Semantic attributes	URI of file containing description for `role` and `arcrole`; small amount of `CDATA` for `title`

`show` `actuate`	Behavioral attributes	Enumerated list of choices: *show:* `new`, `replace`, `embed`, `none`, `other` *actuate:* `onLoad`, `onRequest`, `none`, `other`

`label`
`from`
`to`
	Traversal attributes	`NCName` (XML `Name` minus `":"`, which excludes the use of spaces); this is represented in a DTD as `NMTOKEN` (which doesn't exclude `":"` because it predates namespaces)

Any URI supported by XLink can optionally include an XPointer component at the end. Although XPointer is covered in the next chapter, for now we'll point out a few possible URIs involving XPointers:

```
xlink:href="http://www.ex.com/file.xml#xpointer(id('section2'))"
xlink:role="http://www.ex.com/file.xml#xpointer(//Description[2])"
xlink:href="http://www.ex.com/file.xml#/1/5/4"
```

The first example points to an element whose `id` is "section2" in the document `file.xml`. The second indicates that the role of the link is described in the second element named `Description` that occurs on the page `file.xml`. The final example ignores element names and points to the 4th child of the 5th child of the document element in `file.xml`. As we'll see in the next chapter, XPointers enable us to link to arbitrary locations within a document even when we do not have write access to the target document.

Attributes by Link Type

Table 13-4 lists the same ten attributes vertically and the six XLink element types horizontally. Each cell of the table indicates whether an attribute is required (R), optional (O), or not allowed/meaningless (N) for a given XLink type. For example, the table shows that the `xlink:from` and `xlink:to` attributes apply only to elements where `xlink:type="arc"` and even then, these attributes are optional. It also shows that the `xlink:href` attribute is required when `xlink:type="locator"`, optional when `xlink:type="simple"`, and not allowed for all other types.

TABLE 13-4 Required and Optional Attributes Based on XLink Type

Attribute	`simple`	`extended`	`locator`	`arc`	`resource`	`title`
`type`	R	R	R	R	R	R
`href`	O	N	R	N	N	N
`role`	O	O	O	N	O	N
`arcrole`	O	N	N	O	N	N
`title`	O	O	O	O	O	N
`show`	O	N	N	O	N	N
`actuate`	O	N	N	O	N	N
`label`	N	N	O	N	O	N
`from`	N	N	N	O	N	N
`to`	N	N	N	O	N	N

Source: Based on the "XLink Attribute Usage Patterns" section of the W3C XLink 1.0 specification.

Link Behavior

Link behavior is determined by `xlink:show` and `xlink:actuate`, which we've encountered already. Once again, when the XLink 1.0 Recommendation describes link behavior, such descriptions are merely suggestions that applications are free to interpret as they see fit. Generally these descriptions make the most sense for Web browsers. However, if a nonbrowser application is harvesting links (e.g., a webcrawler), it is easy to imagine that some of the behaviors described would be ignored by such an application. For example, a webcrawler may treat the values "onLoad" and "onRequest" the same for `xlink:actuate` since there is no user to request following the link.

xlink:show Attribute

The `xlink:show` attribute suggests how the ending resource should be *displayed* when the link is traversed. The value of the `xlink:show` attribute must be one of the values "new", "replace", "embed", "other", and "none". The default value is "replace". These values and their meanings are shown in Table 13-5.

TABLE 13-5 xlink:show Attribute Values

`show` *Value*	*Description*
`new`	Load ending resource in a *new window* or frame (or other display context), similar to an XHTML anchor with `target` specified as: `<a href="http://www.ex.com" target="_blank">...</a>`
`replace`	Default value for `xlink:show`. Load ending resource in the *same initial window* or frame (or other display context) from which the link emanated, similar to an XHTML anchor without `target` specified as: `<a href="http://www.ex.com">...</a>`
`embed`	Load ending resource in the position of the *starting* resource (i.e., the link); embedding typically has a different effect than replacing, except for `simple-type` element; similar to the XHTML image element: `<img src="http://www.ex.com/pix.gif" alt="Cool Pix">` *Note:* The presentation of embedded resources is considered to be application dependent.
`other`	Behavior is *unconstrained* by XLink; application should look for *other markup* contained by the link to determine the appropriate presentation behavior.
`none`	Behavior is also *unconstrained* by XLink, and there is no markup to assist the application in determining presentation behavior.

xlink:actuate Attribute

The `xlink:actuate` attribute suggests *when* the traversal is to occur, that is, what triggers traversal from the starting point to the ending point. The value of the `xlink:actuate` attribute must be one of the values "onLoad", "onRequest", "other", and "none". The default value is "onRequest". These values and their meanings are shown in Table 13-6. If we ignore the more application-specific attribute values of "other" and "none" (intended as special-purpose hooks for link application developers), six possible combinations of `xlink:show` and `xlink:actuate` remain. Each of these results in a behavior that is familiar from the HTML/XHTML world, as shown in Table 13-7.

TABLE 13-6 xlink:actuate Attribute Values

`actuate` *Value*	*Description*
`onLoad`	*Automatically* load the resource; traverse to the ending resource immediately upon loading the starting resource; however, if a resource contains multiple arcs with `show="replace"` and `actuate="onLoad"`, application behavior is unconstrained by XLink
`onRequest`	Default value for `xlink:actuate`. Traverse from the starting resource to the ending resource only *when an explicit traversal-related event is triggered* after the starting resource has fully loaded; examples include a user clicking on the starting resource or a countdown timer triggering
`other`	Behavior is *unconstrained* by XLink; application should look for *other markup* contained by the link to determine the appropriate triggering event
`none`	Behavior is also *unconstrained* by XLink, but there is no markup to assist the application in determining when to trigger the traversal

TABLE 13-7 Typical Combinations of xlink:show and xlink:actuate Values

`show`	`actuate`	*Resultant Behavior*
`new`	`onLoad`	*Automatically* display resource in new popup window
`new`	`onRequest`	Open resource in new window when user follows link
`replace`	`onLoad`	*Automatically* redirect to resource pointed to (e.g., URL forwarding)
`replace`	`onRequest`	Similar to the XHTML <a> element; ending resource replaces current page when user activates the link; default case
`embed`	`onLoad`	Similar to the XHTML `<img>` element; ending resource is *automatically* inserted at the point at which the link is defined
`embed`	`onRequest`	Similar to DHTML expand-a-section (show-a-layer) concept

Extended Links: The True Flexibility of XLink

So far, we've concentrated on simple links which, as we've seen, are actually very close to their <a> and <img> forerunners. Apart from giving us the ability to add linking capability to arbitrarily named XML elements (admittedly, a great bonus), simple links still limit us to one-way, source-to-destination links. However, the true power of XLink is the possibilities available when we use extended links (`xlink:type="extended"`). Extended links can describe one-to-many and many-to-many linking relationships among an unlimited number of participating resources of several kinds. Extended links may also be multidirectional or even self-referential. An **extended link** is actually a set of resources plus the connections between them, with arcs that connect pairs of resources based on their labels.

The `extended-type` element may contain any number of the following children elements in any order:

- `locator-type` elements that point to *remote* resources
- `resource-type` elements that describe *local* resources
- `arc-type` elements that dictate traversal rules for all participating resources
- `title-type` elements that provide labels that are human-readable

An extended link can be represented by the following DTD fragment, which echoes the content model just described and also indicates that, aside from the ever-present `type` attribute, the only possible attributes are `role` and `title`, each of which is optional.

```
<!ELEMENT my-extended-link ((locator|arc|title|resource)*)>
<!ATTLIST my-extended-link
 xmlns:xlink     CDATA           #FIXED "http://www.w3.org/1999/xlink"
 xlink:type      (extended)      #FIXED "extended"
 xlink:role      CDATA           #IMPLIED
 xlink:title     CDATA           #IMPLIED>
```

Although not shown in this content model, extended links may also contain non-XLink children elements and other content as well (e.g., PCDATA). In fact, that's also true for all six of the XLink type elements; each can have children elements from other namespaces. Compared to simple links, the extra features available when you use extended links include:

- Connecting any number of local and remote resources
- Specifying an inbound arc from a remote resource to a local resource (instead of merely outbound arcs)
- Associating a title with the arc
- Associating a role or title with the local resource
- Associating a role or title with the extended link itself

Basic Extended Link Example

Let's first consider a fairly basic extended-type link. This link describes a <Beatles-Site> that contains five children: one Name element, which is a resource-type link, two URL elements that are locator-type links, and two Path elements that are arc-type links. We'll formally describe these types in the following sections, but for now, the essence is this: the first arc connects the (local) resource labeled "site" to the remote resource (locator) labeled "home", and the second arc connects the "site" to the remote resource (locator) labeled "USmirror". The extended link therefore describes a unidirectional link because it always originates from "site", but it is also a **multiway** (in this case, *one-to-two*) link because there are two equal destinations, "home" and "USmirror". In other words, we have defined a single extended link that goes from "site" to "home" *and* from "site" to "USmirror".

```
<?xml version="1.0" standalone="yes"?>
<Beatles-Site xmlns:xlink="http://www.w3.org/1999/xlink"
  xlink:type="extended">

  <Name  xlink:type="resource"
    xlink:label="site"
    xlink:title="Harald Gernhardt's Beatles Site" />

  <URL  xlink:type="locator"
    xlink:label="home"
    xlink:href="http://mcbeatle.de/beatles/" />
  <URL  xlink:type="locator"
    xlink:label="USmirror"
    xlink:href="http://gernhardt.com/beatles/" />

  <Path  xlink:type="arc" xlink:from="site" xlink:to="home" />
  <Path  xlink:type="arc" xlink:from="site" xlink:to="USmirror" />
</Beatles-Site>
```

Locator Link Type

We'll now cover each of the four possible children of an extended-type link in turn: locator, resource, arc, and title. A locator-type link (any element with xlink:type="locator") identifies a *remote* resource that participates in an extended link. In this context, remote means that the resource the locator points to is not contained within the extended link parent of the locator. This located resource is usually *external* to the document that contains the extended link, although it can point to a location within the document that contains the extended link, as long as that point is not within the content of the extended link itself. It's helpful to think of locator-type links as providing a level of indirection. An extended-type link contains one or more locator-type links, each of which points to a resource by means of an href attribute.

The `href` attribute is *required* for a `locator-type` link because that is how the ending resource is located (but indirectly, as we'll see). The attributes `role`, `title`, and `label` are optional, but in practice, you'll usually need the `label` to associate an arc with the locator, and the `title` is a good idea since it can provide tooltip-like brief information for certain applications (i.e., browsers). A `locator-type` link may optionally contain any non-XLink content or child elements that are desired.

Resource Link Type

A `resource-type` link (any element with `xlink:type="resource"`) identifies a *local* resource that participates in an extended link. The meaning of "local" here is that the resource is contained *within* the extended link, not in an external document or even another element outside the extended link in the same document. In other words, a `resource-type` link is always a child of an extended link and the resource it describes is local to that parent. This is sometimes called an **inline** link.[5]

Unlike the `locator-type`, no XLink children have any particular meaning for a `resource-type` link. However, it may contain non-XLink children and it may include a `title` *attribute*. The `href` attribute is *not permitted* for a `resource` since it does not point to something external. The attributes `role`, `title`, and `label` are optional.

The link type names `locator` and `resource` are particularly confusing, given that they are both actually resources! Therefore, when you see the term `locator`, think *remote* resource; when you see `resource` as a link type, think *local* resource.

Arc Link Type

An `arc-type` link connects exactly two resources, one being the starting resource or *source*, designated by the arc's `from` attribute, and the other being the ending resource or *destination*, indicated by the arc's `to` attribute. The resources connected by an arc may be either local (`resource-type`) or remote (`locator-type`); that is, a particular connection may be local to remote, remote to local, local to local, or remote to remote.

The value of the `from` and `to` attributes must be of type `NCName`, which means an XML `Name` except that the ":" is not permitted. Since an XML `Name` cannot contain white space, a title-like string is not acceptable. The closest thing to `NCName` in

5. The term *inline* does not appear in the XLink 1.0 Recommendation. It did, however, appear in the earlier XLink Working Draft, *http://www.w3.org/TR/2000/WD-xlink-20000221/*. Similarly, the opposite term, *out-of-line*, appears only in the Working Draft.

DTD types is NMTOKEN, so that's how you see from and to constrained in a DTD. More significant, however, is the fact that these aren't arbitrary values; they *must* match the label attribute of a resource-type link or a locator-type link. It is the labels that the arc references that define the direction and endpoint of the link. In our earlier example, there were two arc-type links defined by our own Path element:

```
<Path  xlink:type="arc" xlink:from="site" xlink:to="home" />
<Path  xlink:type="arc" xlink:from="site" xlink:to="USmirror" />
```

The first arc connects the source, indicated by the from attribute, with the label "site" to the destination, indicated by the to attribute, with the label "home". This connects two resources, the first being a resource-type and the second being a locator-type. Similarly, the second arc connects the resource labeled "site" to the locator whose label is "USmirror". Therefore, the label attribute is key for resource- and locator-type elements; the from and to attributes are crucial for the arc-type element. Collectively, these three attributes (label, from, and to) are called the *traversal attributes* because they govern following a path between starting and ending resources.

Notice that the arc-type link *never directly indicates a URI* since the href attribute is not allowed for this type of link. Instead, the resources whose labels are referenced provide the actual URIs. The major reason for this is reuse. Any number of arcs can refer to the same label (and therefore the same URI), and the same label may be used for multiple resources, as we'll see later.

In addition to the from, to, show, actuate, title, and type attributes, arc-type elements may also have an optional arcrole attribute. As is the case with other semantic attributes, arcrole describes the meaning of the arc's ending resource with respect to its starting resource. The arcrole attribute is similar to a *property* in RDF, with the interpretation that the "starting-resource HAS arcrole ending-resource."

However, the role for a specific ending resource is completely context-dependent, so the same resource can play different roles in different contexts. For example, a particular resource might generally refer to "George Harrison", but depending on the specific arc being described, the arcrole could be "Beatle", "father", "writer", "lead-guitarist", "singer", "person", and so on. It must be understood that there is no automatic way to validate or enforce this role relationship based on XLink.

Some authors have compared the extended links concept to *directed labeled graphs*. In this analogy, the vertices of the graph correspond to resources (locator-type or resource-type), graph labels are represented as URIs (locator-type), and the edges are arcs (arc-type) that connect the resources.

Title Link Type

At first glance, you might wonder why a `title-type` link element is necessary. After all, there is an optional `title` attribute available to every other link type (`simple-`, `extended-`, `locator-`, `resource-`, and `arc-type`). While the `title` attribute is fine for a small amount of text that doesn't contain markup, the `title-type` link element is useful when you need a larger amount of text, especially containing its own markup. A `title-type` link element may contain as many non-XLink children as is desired from another XML vocabulary, such as the XHTML namespace.

Only the `extended-`, `locator-`, and `arc-type` elements may have `title-type` children. These `title-type` elements are especially useful for internationalization and localization, such as when multiple titles need to be defined for different languages. In this regard, the generic `xml:lang` attribute can be effectively added to the element's attribute list:

```
<!ELEMENT my-title-link ANY>
<!ATTLIST my-title-link
  xlink:type   (title)  #FIXED "title"
  xml:lang     CDATA    #IMPLIED>
```

The `xml:lang` attribute is discussed in the section so cleverly entitled "xml:lang" in chapter 5.

Extended Link Code Example

To illustrate the definition of a more elaborate extended link than our earlier example, let's consider how we might represent the relationship between the LP version of *Band on the Run* by Wings (1973) with the five CD versions (1989–1999) available from CDNow.com as of Fall 2001.[6] Our goal is to create a single extended link that contains a resource which represents the original LP, with locators that point to the CDNow page for each CD version, along with arcs that show how to traverse from the LP to each of the five CD configurations.

We'll represent the extended link by an element called `Recording` (`xlink:type="extended"`), the LP by the element `Record` (`xlink:type="resource"`), and each CD format by an element called `CDversion` (`xlink:type="locator"`). Finally, each arc is represented by an element called `Path` (`xlink:type="arc"`). Listing 13-4 shows one version of the desired representation.

6. Beatles completists will note the late 2001 release of the DTS 5.1 version of the album, not incorporated into this example. Readers may find it informative to revise the example code to integrate the newest variant.

Listing 13-4 Extended Link Example, Explicit Version (band-on-the-run.xml)

```
<?xml version="1.0" standalone="no"?>
<!DOCTYPE Recording SYSTEM "recording9.dtd" >

<Recording
   xmlns:xlink="http://www.w3.org/1999/xlink"
   xmlns:xhtml="http://www.w3.org/1999/xhtml"
   xlink:type="extended"
   xlink:title="Various versions of a recording by Wings" >

  <MetaInfo>This is one of the most successful solo Beatles albums.</MetaInfo>

  <Record
     xlink:type="resource"
     xlink:label="LP"
     xlink:title="Original LP release"
     date="1973"><xhtml:h1>Band On The Run</xhtml:h1></Record>

  <CDversion
     xlink:type="locator"
     xlink:href="http://cdnow.com/cgi-bin/mserver/pagename=/RP/CDN/FIND/
album.html/ArtistID=MCCARTNEY*PAUL+&amp;+WINGS/ITEMID=644593"
     xlink:label="double"
     xlink:title="Remastered 2CD set"
     xlink:role="http://sall.net/ksall/book/xlink/record.html"
     date="1999"  tracks="32" />
  <CDversion
     xlink:type="locator"
     xlink:href="http://cdnow.com/cgi-bin/mserver/pagename=/RP/CDN/FIND/
album.html/artistid=MCCARTNEY*PAUL+&amp;+WINGS/itemid=508959"
     xlink:label="dts"
     xlink:title="DTS Surround Sound"
     date="1998"  tracks="10" />
  <CDversion
     xlink:type="locator"
     xlink:href="http://cdnow.com/cgi-bin/mserver/pagename=/RP/CDN/FIND/
album.html/artistid=MCCARTNEY*PAUL+&amp;+WINGS/itemid=292650"
     xlink:label="gold"
     xlink:title="24K Gold Disc"
     date="1993"  tracks="10" />
  <CDversion
     xlink:type="locator"
     xlink:href="http://cdnow.com/cgi-bin/mserver/pagename=/RP/CDN/FIND/
album.html/artistid=MCCARTNEY*PAUL+&amp;+WINGS/ITEMID=429922"
     xlink:label="import"
     xlink:title="Import with bonus tracks"
     date="1993"  tracks="11" />
  <CDversion
     xlink:type="locator"
     xlink:href="http://cdnow.com/cgi-bin/mserver/pagename=/RP/CDN/FIND/
album.html/artistid=MCCARTNEY*PAUL+&amp;+WINGS/itemid=22121"
     xlink:label="original"
     xlink:title="original CD release"
     date="1989"  tracks="10" />
```

```
  <Path
    xlink:type="arc"
    xlink:from="LP"
    xlink:to="double" />
  <Path
    xlink:type="arc"
    xlink:from="LP"
    xlink:to="dts" />
  <Path
    xlink:type="arc"
    xlink:from="LP"
    xlink:to="gold" />
  <Path
    xlink:type="arc"
    xlink:from="LP"
    xlink:to="import" />
  <Path
    xlink:type="arc"
    xlink:from="LP"
    xlink:to="original" />

  <!-- Return link from "double" to "LP". -->
  <Path
    xlink:type="arc"
    xlink:from="double"
    xlink:to="LP"
    xlink:show="new"
    xlink:actuate="onRequest" />

</Recording>
```

As you can see from the code listing, this particular instance of a Recording (extended link) consists of a MetaInfo (non-XLink) element, a single Record element (resource), five CDversion elements (locators), and six Path elements (arcs). The Recording element declares both the XLink and the XHTML namespaces. Since the extended link (the Recording element) contains all other elements in this example, all children can use elements from either namespace, depending of course on the constraints established in collection9.dtd, presented shortly. In fact, the Record element does use the xhtml:h1 XHTML heading element and all elements except MetaInfo use attributes from XLink. MetaInfo is from no particular namespace and is therefore unrelated to either XLink or XHTML; we have no way of knowing how that element will be processed, so we can assume it is application specific.

Both the single resource-type element and the five locator-type elements use the xlink:label and xlink:title attributes. Of these two resources, xlink:label is more significant for link processing; xlink:title is more for human presentation (e.g., tooltips) and perhaps for selecting a choice. It is the xlink:label that the arc-type element references with its xlink:from and xlink:to attributes. More specifically, in Listing 13-4 the Path element defines an arc emanating from the `resource` whose `xlink:label` is named by the `xlink:from` attribute (here set to the string "LP" in all cases) and ending in the `locator` whose `xlink:label` is given by the `xlink:to` attribute. Note that the value of the `xlink:label` attribute for each of the five instances of the `CDversion` element is unique: "double", "dts", "gold", "original", and "import". These are also the values of the `xlink:to` attributes of the `Path` elements, which establishes the connection—an arc connects a resource to a locator, or vice versa.

Notice that a sixth `Path` element represents the only arc whose *ending* point, rather than starting point, is the resource whose `xlink:label` is "LP". This arc has an `xlink:from` value of "double" and `xlink:to` setting of "LP". Notice that the first `Path` element defines an arc in exactly the opposite direction, so this pair of arcs effectively defines a bidirectional link between the "LP" resource and the "double" locator. The six arcs are illustrated in Figure 13-3. Circles represent `locator-type` elements and a diamond indicates the sole `resource-type` element (except for the return link which reverses the meaning). The value of `xlink:label` identifies each participant. This diagram suggests that we've accomplished the goal of connecting the LP to each of the possible CD configurations.

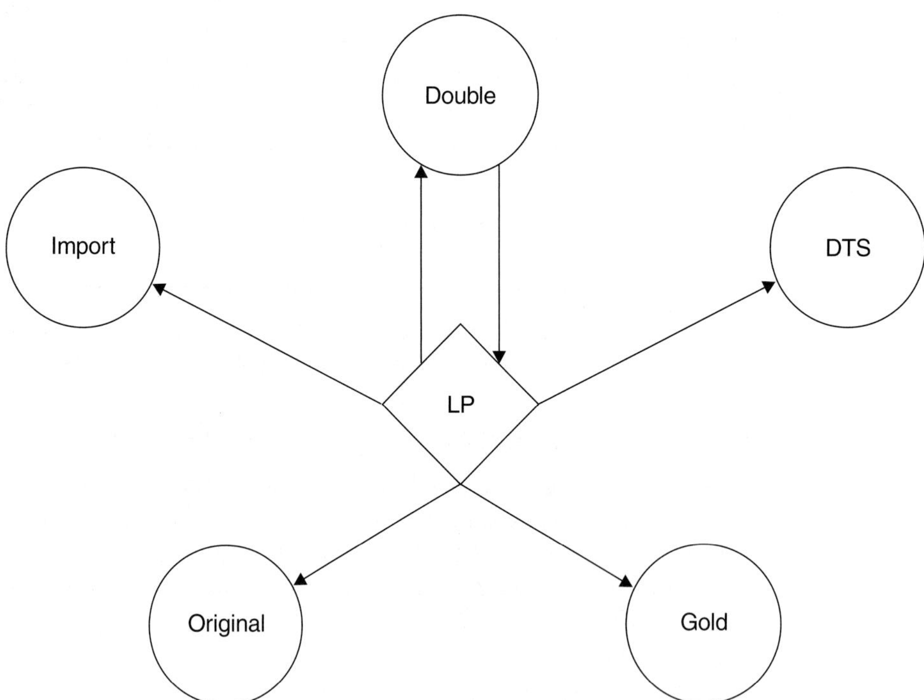

FIGURE 13-3 Graphical view of linking relationship

We can glean several other interesting points from Listing 13-4. First, it includes the attributes `date` and `tracks` that do not use the `xlink:` prefix, so they are from no particular namespace even though they happen to be attached to elements that are XLink elements (i.e., `Record`, a `resource-type` element, and `CDversion`, a `locator-type` element). This is perfectly fine; `date` and `tracks` attributes will be ignored by link processing software but will be available to the rest of the application, perhaps to sort links by date or to find the configuration with the most tracks.

The XLink specification does not mandate a particular user interface for presenting multiple arcs to users. In this example, we've noted that there are five possible paths emanating from the resource labeled "LP". One *possible* interface mentioned by the spec is to present the user with a popup menu or list that contains all potential ending resources. For example, the menu might contain the labels "double", "dts", "gold", "original", and "import", or their corresponding titles, or both.

Another point is that the first `CDversion` element sets the `xlink:role` attribute to an HTML file that presumably tells us something about the purpose of this `locator-type` element. It happens to be the only instance of `xlink:role` in this example (although there could have been one defined for every `locator-type`, `resource-type`, and `extended-type` element). We can only guess that this particular `CDversion` is very special since it's also the one that has the bidirectional link. Perhaps this identifies this particular locator as the preferred format for this album. (This element also has the most recent `date` attribute, so it could mean that it is simply the newest version of *Band on the Run*.) In any event, `xlink:role` is a tip-off to XLink processing software that there is something more to know about this locator, and that fetching the URL should tell the processor what that role is.

The final point is that the sixth `arc-type` element explicitly references two behavioral attributes by setting the `show` and `actuate` attributes:

```
xlink:show="new"
xlink:actuate="onRequest"
```

The DTD in Listing 13-5 defines a default value of "replace" for `xlink:show`, so this arc overrides the default. However, its opposite arc (the first `Path` element from "LP" to "double") inherits only the default behavior. What might this mean? Well, if the user is given a way to select different arcs, such as the popup menu mentioned earlier, going from "LP" to "double" has the same behavior as going from "LP" to any other version, but going from "double" to "LP" results in special handling and something is displayed in a new window, for example.

Let's look at the DTD to see how XHTML is handled. First, the document element, `Recording`, declares the XHTML namespace along with the namespace for XLink. Although that makes it possible to reference XHTML elements, in the one case in which they are used in this example, namely, the `Record` element, it is still necessary to say *where* XHTML may appear in the content model, plus what any XHTML elements we care to use might contain.

```
<!ELEMENT xhtml:h1 (#PCDATA)>
<!ELEMENT Record   (#PCDATA | xhtml:h1)*>
```

You may recall the Record element's content is called a *mixed content model*, indicating that a Record element may contain either character data or text marked up with the xhtml:h1 element. (Listings 13-4 and 13-5 use xhtml: rather than the more conventional html: prefix for XHTML.) A less precise but more flexible approach would be to define the content model as unconstrained:

```
<!ELEMENT Record   ANY>
```

Although this wouldn't help us in terms of validation, it would permit more elaborate content, such as an xhtml:table element to describe our central resource-type element more thoroughly, perhaps with a photo and track samples.

Listing 13-5 DTD Illustrating XLink and Non-XLink Elements and Attributes (recording9.dtd)

```
<!ELEMENT Recording  (MetaInfo?, Record, CDversion*, Path*)>

<!ATTLIST Recording
 xmlns:xlink      CDATA            #FIXED  "http://www.w3.org/1999/xlink"
 xmlns:xhtml      CDATA            #FIXED  "http://www.w3.org/1999/xhtml"
 xlink:type       (extended)       #FIXED   "extended"
 xlink:title      CDATA            #IMPLIED
>

<!ELEMENT MetaInfo    (#PCDATA)>
<!ELEMENT xhtml:h1    (#PCDATA)>

<!ELEMENT Record      (#PCDATA | xhtml:h1)*>
<!-- ELEMENT Record    ANY -->

<!ATTLIST Record
 xlink:type       (resource)       #FIXED    "resource"
 xlink:label      NMTOKEN          #IMPLIED
 xlink:title      CDATA            #IMPLIED
 date             CDATA            #IMPLIED
>

<!ELEMENT CDversion    EMPTY>
<!ATTLIST CDversion
 xlink:type       (locator)        #FIXED    "locator"
 xlink:href       CDATA            #REQUIRED
 xlink:label      NMTOKEN          #IMPLIED
 xlink:title      CDATA            #IMPLIED
 xlink:role       CDATA            #IMPLIED
 date             CDATA            #IMPLIED
 tracks           CDATA            #IMPLIED
>
```

```
<!ELEMENT Path    EMPTY>
<!ATTLIST Path
 xlink:type       (arc)          #FIXED   "arc"
 xlink:from       NMTOKEN        #IMPLIED
 xlink:to         NMTOKEN        #IMPLIED
 xlink:show       (new
                  |replace
                  |embed)                 "replace"
 xlink:actuate    (onLoad
                  |onRequest
                  |other
                  |none)                  "onRequest"
>
```

Now that we have a DTD, we could revisit our XML instance and remove all attributes that are fixed in value (#FIXED), such as the `xlink:type` attribute in all cases and the declaration of the XLink and XHTML namespaces in the `Recording` element. We can also remove the `xlink:actuate="onRequest"` portion of the last `Path` element since that is the default value, according to the DTD. The result is shown in Listing 13-6. Both versions of the instance validate against the same DTD. I prefer the clarity of the version in Listing 13-4, even though it has these redundancies. However, from a maintenance viewpoint, factoring out constant information to the DTD is of course preferable. Another advantage of the version that omits the fixed and default attributes is that the document is about 20 percent shorter than the original. If this were a more complex example with, say, 5,000 arcs and if this is being delivered over a heavily used Web server, reducing the number of bytes without sacrificing informational content would be a real plus.

Listing 13-6 Extended Link Example, Fixed Version (band-on-the-run-fixed.xml)

```
<?xml version="1.0" standalone="no"?>
<!DOCTYPE Recording SYSTEM "recording9.dtd" >

<Recording
   xlink:title="Various versions of a recording by Wings" >

  <MetaInfo>This is one of the most successful solo Beatles albums.</MetaInfo>

  <Record
     xlink:label="LP"
     xlink:title="Original LP release"
     date="1973"><xhtml:h1>Band On The Run</xhtml:h1></Record>

  <CDversion
     xlink:href="http://cdnow.com/cgi-bin/mserver/pagename=/RP/CDN/FIND/
album.html/ArtistID=MCCARTNEY*PAUL+&amp;+WINGS/ITEMID=644593"
     xlink:label="double"
     xlink:title="Remastered 2CD set"
     xlink:role="http://sall.net/ksall/book/xlink/record.html"
     date="1999"  tracks="32" />
```

```
  <CDversion
     xlink:href="http://cdnow.com/cgi-bin/mserver/pagename=/RP/CDN/FIND/
album.html/artistid=MCCARTNEY*PAUL+&amp;+WINGS/itemid=508959"
     xlink:label="dts"
     xlink:title="DTS Surround Sound"
     date="1998"  tracks="10" />
  <CDversion
     xlink:href="http://cdnow.com/cgi-bin/mserver/pagename=/RP/CDN/FIND/
album.html/artistid=MCCARTNEY*PAUL+&amp;+WINGS/itemid=292650"
     xlink:label="gold"
     xlink:title="24K Gold Disc"
     date="1993"  tracks="10" />
  <CDversion
     xlink:href="http://cdnow.com/cgi-bin/mserver/pagename=/RP/CDN/FIND/
album.html/artistid=MCCARTNEY*PAUL+&amp;+WINGS/ITEMID=429922"
     xlink:label="import"
     xlink:title="Import with bonus tracks"
     date="1993"  tracks="11" />
  <CDversion
     xlink:href="http://cdnow.com/cgi-bin/mserver/pagename=/RP/CDN/FIND/
album.html/artistid=MCCARTNEY*PAUL+&amp;+WINGS/itemid=22121"
     xlink:label="original"
     xlink:title="original CD release"
     date="1989"  tracks="10" />

  <Path
     xlink:from="LP"
     xlink:to="double" />
  <Path
     xlink:from="LP"
     xlink:to="dts" />
  <Path
     xlink:from="LP"
     xlink:to="gold" />
  <Path
     xlink:from="LP"
     xlink:to="import" />
  <Path
     xlink:from="LP"
     xlink:to="original" />

  <!-- Return link from "double" to "LP". -->
  <Path
     xlink:from="double"
     xlink:to="LP"
     xlink:show="new" />

</Recording>
```

Another variation we can make to our example illustrates even more flexibility provided by the XLink specification. XLink permits *reusing* the same `xlink:label` value for multiple `locator-type` or `resource-type` elements. This makes it possible for a *single* `arc-type` element to create traversal links to *all* the same-named labels. Therefore, rather than defining five `Path` elements (one for each uniquely named `CDversion` element), we can reduce this to only *one* `Path` that connects the `resource-type` element labeled "LP" to all five `locator-type` elements labeled "CD" with a single `arc-type` element, as shown in Listing 13-7. Unfortunately, if we use this technique, we can no longer create the single reverse link from "double" to "LP" since there is no automatic way to differentiate among the five `locator-type` elements. We could, however, create *five* reverse links just by adding one more `arc-type` element that swaps the `xlink:from` and `xlink:to` values. Alternatively, if we really needed to indicate that the double CD was the default or otherwise special configuration, we could defer this to application code that looked for a particular value of the `xlink:title` attribute, such as `xlink:title="Remastered 2CD set"`, or we could use `xlink:role` for a similar purpose.

Listing 13-7 Extended Link Example, Fewer Arcs (band-on-the-run-arc.xml)

```
<?xml version="1.0" standalone="no"?>
<!DOCTYPE Recording SYSTEM "recording9.dtd" >

<!-- Modification with repeat label value and reduced number of arcs. -->

<Recording
   xmlns:xlink="http://www.w3.org/1999/xlink"
   xmlns:xhtml="http://www.w3.org/1999/xhtml"
   xlink:type="extended"
   xlink:title="Various versions of a recording by Wings" >

  <MetaInfo>This is one of the most successful solo Beatles albums.</MetaInfo>

  <Record
     xlink:type="resource"
     xlink:label="LP"
     xlink:title="Original LP release"
     date="1973"><xhtml:h1>Band On The Run</xhtml:h1></Record>

  <!-- All CDversion elements have label="CD". -->
  <CDversion
     xlink:type="locator"
     xlink:href="http://cdnow.com/cgi-bin/mserver/pagename=/RP/CDN/FIND/
album.html/ArtistID=MCCARTNEY*PAUL+&amp;+WINGS/ITEMID=644593"
     xlink:label="CD"
     xlink:title="Remastered 2CD set"
     xlink:role="http://sall.net/ksall/book/xlink/record.html"
     date="1999"  tracks="32" />
  <CDversion
     xlink:type="locator"
     xlink:href="http://cdnow.com/cgi-bin/mserver/pagename=/RP/CDN/FIND/
album.html/artistid=MCCARTNEY*PAUL+&amp;+WINGS/itemid=508959"
     xlink:label="CD"
     xlink:title="DTS Surround Sound"
     date="1998"  tracks="10" />
```

```
  <CDversion
     xlink:type="locator"
     xlink:href="http://cdnow.com/cgi-bin/mserver/pagename=/RP/CDN/FIND/
album.html/artistid=MCCARTNEY*PAUL+&amp;+WINGS/itemid=292650"
     xlink:label="CD"
     xlink:title="24K Gold Disc"
     date="1993"  tracks="10" />
  <CDversion
     xlink:type="locator"
     xlink:href="http://cdnow.com/cgi-bin/mserver/pagename=/RP/CDN/FIND/
album.html/artistid=MCCARTNEY*PAUL+&amp;+WINGS/ITEMID=429922"
     xlink:label="CD"
     xlink:title="Import with bonus tracks"
     date="1993"  tracks="11" />
  <CDversion
     xlink:type="locator"
     xlink:href="http://cdnow.com/cgi-bin/mserver/pagename=/RP/CDN/FIND/
album.html/artistid=MCCARTNEY*PAUL+&amp;+WINGS/itemid=22121"
     xlink:label="CD"
     xlink:title="original CD release"
     date="1989"  tracks="10" />

  <!-- Arc links locator "LP" to all 5 locators with the label "CD". -->
  <Path
     xlink:type="arc"
     xlink:from="LP"
     xlink:to="CD" />

</Recording>
```

Outbound, Inbound, and Third-Party Links

So far we've classified links in terms of their type (`simple`, `extended`, `locator`, `resource`, `arc`, or `title`). Another way to describe links is in terms of their direction relative to a starting resource. This introduces us to yet more XLink definitions. A **local resource** (`resource-type`) is a link participant that either is itself a linking element or its parent is. A **remote resource** is one that is addressed by a URI, regardless of whether it is contained in the same XML document or even the same linking element. An **outbound arc** points away for the linking element; it has a *local* starting resource and a *remote* ending resource, much like the XHTML <a> element. In contrast, an **inbound arc** goes in the opposite direction—its starting resource is remote and its ending resource is local. If both the starting and ending resources are remote, then the arc is called a **third-party arc**. Typically (although not necessarily) any given extended link contains a uniform kind of arc and can therefore be considered an inbound, outbound, or third-party link. Table 13-8 summarizes the differences.

We've indicated that one of the major benefits of XLink is the ability to connect starting and ending resources for which the link author does not have write access,

TABLE 13-8 Oubound, Inbound, and Third-Party Links

Direction	*From resource*	*To resource*	*Write access*
Outbound	Local (`resource-type`)	Remote (`locator-type`)	Required
Inbound	Remote (`locator-type`)	Local (`resource-type`)	Not required
Third-party	Remote (`locator-type`)	Remote (`locator-type`)	Not required

especially when a resource cannot itself contain XLink elements (e.g., an HTML document). Inbound and third-party arcs provide this flexibility.[7] Discovery and processing of such links is more involved than is the case for outbound links and is touched on later in the section entitled "Linkbases." For the remainder of this section, we'll look at an example of third-party links.

Third-Party Extended Link Example

Let's consider another situation where XLinks are useful. In addition to his wonderful Beatles site, Harald Gernhardt has a "Macca" site called "PLUGGED—the unofficial Paul McCartney homepage," which has an informative Wings Timeline as well as a McCartney/Wings CD Discography (*http://gernhardt.com/macca/wings.html* and *http://gernhardt.com/macca/a/index.html*, respectively.). The latter graphically depicts the order of the CDs by arranging their covers in a grid, and when you click through to a particular CD, you must go back to the discography page to visit the next CD in chronological order. Suppose we wanted to create an extended link that links five CDs in chronological order: *Wings Wild Life*, *Red Rose Speedway*, *Band On The Run*, *Venus And Mars*, and *Wings At The Speed Of Sound*. In addition to forward time order, suppose we'd like to link backward in time. Let's further suppose we wish to connect the first and last CDs to Gernhardt's Wings Timeline page, as well as connect the Wings Timeline to the earliest of the five CDs.

Figure 13-4 is the graphical representation of the extended link we're defining; it may be helpful to look at that diagram before continuing. Listing 13-8 shows an XML document, `wings-timeline.xml`, that depicts an XLink solution using third-party links.

In Listing 13-8, we've defined a single `extended-type` link, the `Timeline` element, that contains one `Band` element (`locator-type`) with the `label` "index" and the URI of Gernhardt's Wings Timeline page, followed by five `Recording` elements (also of `locator-type`), each with a unique `xlink:label` based on the abbreviation

7. The earlier XLink Working Draft, *http://www.w3.org/TR/2000/WD-xlink-20000221/*, contained the term *out-of-line*, which referred to both inbound and third-party links. Out-of-line links do not contain any portion of the resources they connect. They are useful for connecting documents for which you don't have write access, for linking to fragments, and for linking to elements of non-XML content. The term out-of-line does not appear in the XLink 1.0 Recommendation, however.

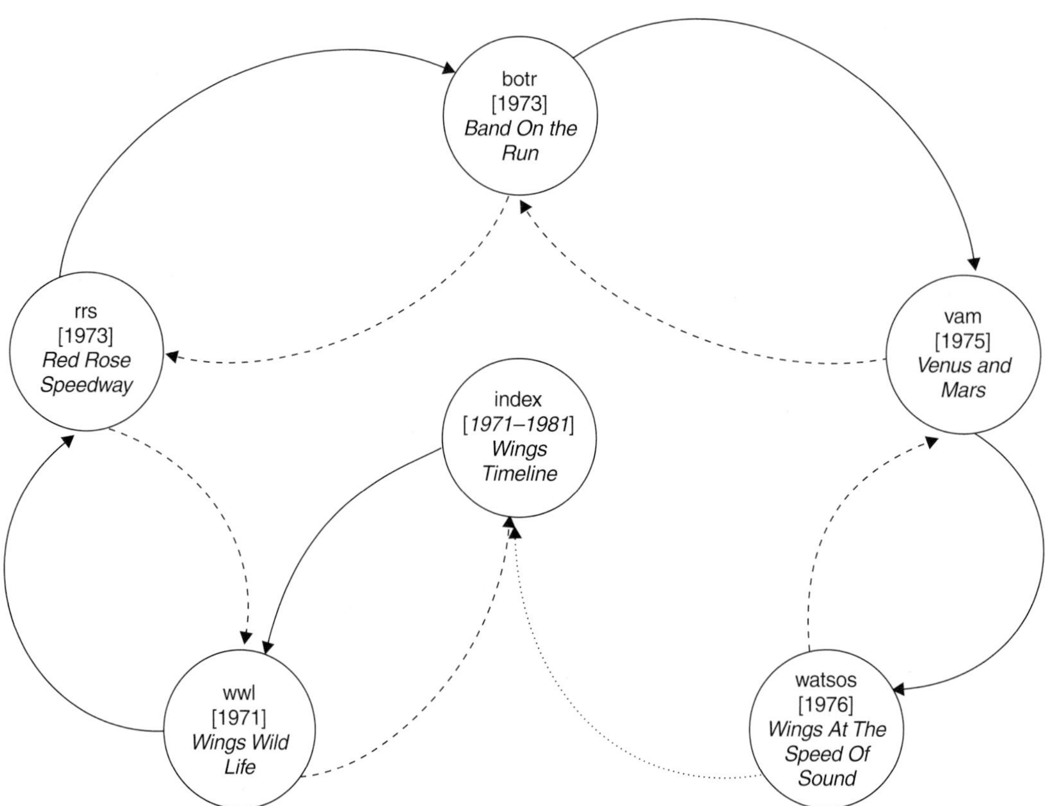

FIGURE 13-4 Graphic representation of third-party extended link

of the CD's title (e.g., "wwl" for *Wings Wild Life*, the earliest album in this example, "watsos" for *Wings At The Speed Of Sound*, the most recent album, "botr" for *Band On The Run*, etc.). Each `Recording` element also contains the URI of the discography page on Gernhardt's site for that particular CD, as well as a non-XLink attribute named `year` that represents the release date of the original album (not the CD version). To make the required connections, we define a total of 11 `arc-type` `Path` elements: four arcs define the forward timeline ("wwl", the earliest, to "rrs" to "botr" to "vam" to "watsos"; based on the `xlink:label` values), four arcs define the reverse timeline ("watsos" . . . "wwl"); a pair of arcs defines the bidirectional link from the "index" page to "wwl" and from "wwl" to "index"; and the final arc describes the connection from "watsos" back to the "index" page.

Note that all the resources in this example are `locator-type`, meaning that all our starting and ending resources are remote. The `Band` and `Recording` elements all point to remote resources that are not under my direct control; I have no write access to Gernhardt's Web site (fortunately for McCartney fans). Yet by defining an extended link consisting of third-party arcs, I can define new linking relationships among his resources, without his knowledge, participation, or permission. (Hope you don't mind, Harald! But please don't terminate my site subscription!)

Listing 13-8 Third-Party Extended Link Example (wings-timeline.xml)

```
<?xml version="1.0" standalone="no"?>
<!DOCTYPE Timeline SYSTEM "timeline9.dtd" >
<Timeline
  xmlns:xlink="http://www.w3.org/1999/xlink"
  xlink:type="extended" >

  <Band   xlink:type="locator"
    xlink:label="index"
    xlink:href="http://gernhardt.com/macca/wings.html">
    Wings Timeline (1971-1981)
  </Band>

  <Recording    xlink:type="locator"
    xlink:label="wwl"
    xlink:href="http://gernhardt.com/macca/a/wwl.html"
    year="1971">Wings Wild Life
  </Recording>
  <Recording    xlink:type="locator"
    xlink:label="rrs"
    xlink:href="http://gernhardt.com/macca/a/rrs.html"
    year="1973">Red Rose Speedway
  </Recording>
  <Recording    xlink:type="locator"
    xlink:label="botr"
    xlink:href="http://gernhardt.com/macca/a/botr.html"
    year="1973">Band On The Run (original LP release)
  </Recording>
  <Recording    xlink:type="locator"
    xlink:label="vam"
    xlink:href="http://gernhardt.com/macca/a/vam.html"
    year="1975">Venus And Mars
  </Recording>
  <Recording    xlink:type="locator"
    xlink:label="watsos"
    xlink:href="http://gernhardt.com/macca/a/watsos.html"
    year="1976">Wings At The Speed Of Sound
  </Recording>

  <!-- forward timeline -->
  <Path  xlink:type="arc" xlink:from="wwl"    xlink:to="rrs" />
  <Path  xlink:type="arc" xlink:from="rrs"    xlink:to="botr" />
  <Path  xlink:type="arc" xlink:from="botr"   xlink:to="vam" />
  <Path  xlink:type="arc" xlink:from="vam"    xlink:to="watsos" />

  <!-- reverse timeline -->
  <Path  xlink:type="arc" xlink:from="watsos" xlink:to="vam" />
  <Path  xlink:type="arc" xlink:from="vam"    xlink:to="botr" />
  <Path  xlink:type="arc" xlink:from="botr"   xlink:to="rrs" />
  <Path  xlink:type="arc" xlink:from="rrs"    xlink:to="wwl" />
```

```
  <!-- connections to/from the index -->
  <Path  xlink:type="arc" xlink:from="index"  xlink:to="wwl" />
  <Path  xlink:type="arc" xlink:from="wwl"    xlink:to="index" />
  <Path  xlink:type="arc" xlink:from="watsos" xlink:to="index" />
</Timeline>
```

Listing 13-9 shows the DTD, `timeline9.dtd`, necessary to validate `wings-timeline.xml`. Notice that we can factor out the common attributes of the `locator`-type elements and define them in an internal parameter entity, `locator-attrs` (see chapter 4). We can then reference entities in the definitions of the attributes for the `Band` and `Recording` elements using the `%locator-attrs;` notation. `Band` needs no additional attributes, but `Recording` adds the non-XLink attribute `year` to the common set.

Listing 13-9 DTD for Third-Party Extended Links (timeline9.dtd)

```
<!ENTITY % locator-attrs
'xlink:type      (locator)       #FIXED   "locator"
 xlink:href      CDATA           #REQUIRED
 xlink:label     NMTOKEN         #IMPLIED'
>

<!ELEMENT Timeline  (Band, Recording*, Path*)>
<!ATTLIST Timeline
 xmlns:xlink     CDATA           #FIXED  "http://www.w3.org/1999/xlink"
 xlink:type      (extended)      #FIXED   "extended"
>

<!ELEMENT Band       (#PCDATA) >
<!ATTLIST Band
 %locator-attrs;
>

<!ELEMENT Recording  (#PCDATA) >
<!ATTLIST Recording
 %locator-attrs;
 year            CDATA           #IMPLIED
>

<!ELEMENT Path   EMPTY>
<!ATTLIST Path
 xlink:type      (arc)           #FIXED   "arc"
 xlink:from      NMTOKEN         #IMPLIED
 xlink:to        NMTOKEN         #IMPLIED
 xlink:show      (new|replace|embed)      "replace"
 xlink:actuate   (onLoad|onRequest)       "onRequest"
>
```

Linkbases

A **linkbase** is a well-formed XML document that contains collections of *inbound* and/or *third-party* links. In other words, a linkbase is one or more extended links stored together, possibly with no other non-XLink elements. In contrast to the simpler outbound case, for inbound and third-party arcs, applications need to be told how to find *both* the starting and ending resources. To inform XLink applications to access a linkbase to uncover these two resources, the extended link must contain an arc with the `arcrole` attribute set to a special (fixed) value, which is essentially a *linkbase locator* (or indicator):

```
xlink:arcrole="http://www.w3.org/1999/xlink/properties/linkbase"
```

When a link that points to a linkbase is detected, traversal involves loading the ending resource (the linkbase) and then extracting but not necessarily traversing the links found within. The starting resource can either be `xlink:type="resource"` or `xlink:type="locator"`, while the ending resource is the linkbase itself. An arc connects from the starting resource to the linkbase locator (via the `xlink:from` and `xlink:to` attributes), perhaps with `xlink:actuate="onLoad"`. See the XLink 1.0 Recommendation for examples and discussion of how an application should process a linkbase (*http://www.w3.org/TR/xlink/#xlg*). A basic example of an extended link that points to a linkbase appears in Listing 13-10.

The linkbase itself is the file `linkbase-ex.xml`, shown in Listing 13-10. The linkbase consists entirely of `extended-type`, `locator-type`, and `arc-type` links. There can be no local links of `resource-type` since the linkbase by definition connects resources that are external to the link, and usually to the file as well.

Readers interested in linkbases may want to read about Topic Maps (*http://www.TopicsMaps.org*).

Listing 13-10 Linkbase Example (linkbase-ex.xml)

```
<baseLink xlink:type="extended" >
  <startResource xlink:type="locator"
        xlink:label="start"
        xlink:href="wings.xml" />
  <linkBase xlink:type="locator"
        xlink:label="myLinkbase"
        xlink:href="wings-timeline.xml" />
  <loadLinks xlink:type="arc"
        xlink:arcrole=
        "http://www.w3.org/1999/xlink/properties/linkbase"
        xlink:from="start" xlink:to="myLinkbase"
        xlink:show="none"
        xlink:actuate="onLoad" />
</baseLink>
```

XML Base Support for Relative URIs

The XML Base Recommendation (*http://www.w3.org/TR/xmlbase/*) describes how the `xml:base` attribute provides a way for relative URIs to be resolved with respect to a common base, much the same as the <base> element in XHTML. For example, Listing 13-11 shows the addition of `xml:base` to the example that is shown in Listing 13-8.

Listing 13-11 Third-Party Extended Link with XML Base (wings-xmlbase.xml)

```
<?xml version="1.0" standalone="no"?>
<!DOCTYPE Timeline SYSTEM "timeline10.dtd" >
<Timeline
  xmlns:xlink="http://www.w3.org/1999/xlink"
  xlink:type="extended"
  xml:base="http://gernhardt.com/macca/" >

  <Band   xlink:type="locator"
    xlink:label="index"
    xlink:href="wings.html">
    Wings Timeline (1971-1981)
  </Band>
  <Recording    xlink:type="locator"
    xlink:label="wwl"
    xlink:href="a/wwl.html"
    year="1971">Wings Wild Life
  </Recording>
  <Recording    xlink:type="locator"
    xlink:label="rrs"
    xlink:href="a/rrs.html"
    year="1973">Red Rose Speedway
  </Recording>
  <Recording    xlink:type="locator"
    xlink:label="botr"
    xlink:href="a/botr.html"
    year="1973">Band On The Run (original LP release)
  </Recording>
  <Recording    xlink:type="locator"
    xlink:label="vam"
    xlink:href="a/vam.html"
    year="1975">Venus And Mars
  </Recording>
  <Recording    xlink:type="locator"
    xlink:label="watsos"
    xlink:href="a/watsos.html"
    year="1976">Wings At The Speed Of Sound
  </Recording>
  <!-- etc. same as before -->
</Timeline>
```

With the addition of the `xml:base` attribute attached to the `Timeline` element, and set to the top of the "UNPLUGGED" Web site, *http://gernhardt.com/macca/*, all `xlink:href` attributes associated with the `Band` and `Recording` elements can now be specified relative to that base. Therefore, the two relative URIs

```
xlink:href="wings.html"
xlink:href="a/wwl.html"
```

will resolve to the absolute URIs

```
xlink:href="http://gernhardt.com/macca/wings.html"
xlink:href="http://gernhardt.com/macca/a/wwl.html"
```

In terms of DTD support, the only changes necessary are to add an `xml:base` attribute to the attribute-list declaration for the `Timeline` element and, optionally, to declare the `xml` namespace.

```
<!ELEMENT Timeline  (Band, Recording*, Path*)>
<!ATTLIST Timeline
 xmlns:xml    CDATA       #FIXED  "http://www.w3.org/XML/1998/namespace"
 xmlns:xlink  CDATA       #FIXED  "http://www.w3.org/1999/xlink"
 xlink:type   (extended) #FIXED   "extended"
 xml:base     CDATA       #REQUIRED
>
```

I said "optionally" because, as we learned in chapter 5, this special `xml` namespace is the *only* namespace that does not need to be explicitly declared. In namespace-aware XML processors, the `xml` prefix is bound to the namespace name `http://www.w3.org/XML/1998/namespace`. In other words, if I delete the `xmlns:xml` line, namespace-aware validating parsers such as XML Validator will not complain about my use of `xml:base`. If I delete the `xmlns:xlink` line, however, the instance will become invalid, with an error message something like "undeclared attribute `'xmlns:xlink'` for element `Timeline`."

The XML Base Recommendation states that the XML Base may not be available to all applications, especially those using earlier XML technology (see *http://www.w3.org/TR/xmlbase/ #introduction*):

> The deployment of XML Base is through normative reference by new specifications, for example XLink and the XML Infoset. Applications and specifications built upon these new technologies will natively support XML Base. The behavior of `xml:base` attributes in applications based on specifications that do not have direct or indirect normative reference to XML Base is undefined.

XLink Implementations

As of this writing, the W3C site lists the following XLink implementations (*http://www.w3.org/XML/2000/09/LinkingImplementations.html* and *http://www.w3.org/XML/Linking*):

- *XLip* (Fujitsu)—free XLink Processor that works with any XML processor or parser that can create DOM and implements a simple interface; limited to Japan
- *X2X* (Empolis)—XML XLink Engine for the creation, management, and manipulation of links. X2X allows linking of documents and information resources without changing the resources that are being linked. X2X removes the requirement to insert link information inside document content.
- *Mozilla* (and Netscape 6)—browser has support for *simple* type of links, except not for `xlink:show="embed"`
- *Amaya* (W3C)—W3C's editor/browser now supports simple links
- *Internet Explorer 6* does not support XLink as of this writing
- *XLink2HTML*—set of XSLT stylesheets for the creation of HTML representations of XLink elements. It is particulary useful to represent one-to-many arcs from local resources to locators. However, other relationships possible in an inline XLink element are implemented.
- *4XLink* (FourThought LLC/Python)
- *xlinkit*—lightweight application service that provides rule-based link generation and checks the consistency of distributed documents andWeb content
- *XTooX*—free XLink processor that turns extended, out-of-line links into inline links. It takes as its input a linkbase (a document that contains only XLinks) and puts the links into the referenced documents.

The W3C site provides links to each of these implementations. See also the XML-Software.com XLink/XPointer tools list at *http://www.xmlsoftware.com/xlink/*. See Bob DuCharme's "XLink: Who Cares?" article for a closer examination of the state of the art as of March 2002 (*http://www.xml.com/pub/a2002/03/13/xlink.html*).

Summary

In this chapter, we mainly discussed XLink, the XML Linking Language, but we also touched on XInclude (XML Inclusions) and XML Base, both of which can be used with XLink.

- XLink supports all of the hypertext capabilities of XHTML/HTML <a> and `<img>` elements with its `simple-type` linking element.
- The true power of XLink is seen in `extended-type` linking elements, which can support one-to-many, many-to-many, and multidirectional links, and even external linkbases.

- Using XLink, you also can create complex connections between sets of resources, even when you do not have write access.
- XLink solves the problem of associating link behavior and semantics with arbitrarily named elements from our own vocabularies.
- This association is in terms of attaching attributes from the XLink namespace to our own elements. Your DTD needs to define the `xmlns:xlink` attribute:

```
xmlns:xlink  CDATA    #FIXED  "http://www.w3.org/1999/xlink"
```

- A *resource* can be anything you'd normally link to in HTML (other HTML documents, named anchors in HTML documents, images in various formats, etc.), as well as to XML documents in any XML-based vocabulary, plus identified elements or ranges within an XML document.
- The act of following or using a link is called *traversal*, which always involves exactly two resources (or portions thereof, in the case of a fragment identifier).
- The source of the traversal is the *starting resource* and the destination is the *ending resource*.
- The six XLink types are `simple`, `extended`, `locator`, `arc`, `resource`, and `title`. You associate a link type with an element by using the attribute `xlink:type="extended"`, for example.
- A `simple-type` link is the basic unidirectional link similar to HTML <a> and <img> elements; always connects two resources.
- An `extended-type` link may describe multiple links, bidirectional or multidirectional links; can include elements that point to remote resources, contain local resources, specify arc traversal rules, and/or specify human-readable titles and machine-readable roles.
- A `locator-type` link identifies a remote (external) resource which is a participant in an extended link.
- An `arc-type` link is a traversal rule that describes how to traverse a pair of resources, including the direction of traversal and possibly application behavior information.
- A `resource-type` link identifies a local (internal) resource, a location in the current document that is a participant in an extended link.
- A `title-type` link provides descriptive text when additional markup is needed, especially for internationalization.
- In addition to the `xlink:type` attribute, other XLink attributes are: `xlink:href`, `xlink:role`, `xlink:arcrole`, `xlink:title`, `xlink:show`, `xlink:actuate`, `xlink:label`, `xlink:from`, and `xlink:to`.
- Other than the `xlink:type` attribute, few attributes are required, but there are several optional attributes for each link type. For example, the `arc-type` link has the optional attributes `arcrole`, `title`, `show`, `actuate`, `from`, and `to`.
- The locator attribute is `href`, which is required for a `locator-type` link and typical for a `simple-type` link.
- The semantic attributes are `role`, `arcrole`, and `title`.

- The behavior attributes are `show` and `actuate`. They control how the linked resource is displayed and what triggers the display.
- Valid values for `xlink:show` are `new`, `replace`, `embed`, `none`, and `other`.
- Valid values for `xlink:actuate` are `onLoad`, `onRequest`, `none`, and `other`.
- The XLink 1.0 Recommendation does not mandate how applications should handle links; it only makes suggestions that will be interpreted differently in different application contexts.
- The traversal attributes are `label`, `from`, and `to`. They control how an extended link is followed.
- An `arc-type` link connects exactly two resources, one being the starting resource or *source*, designated by the arc's `from` attribute, and the other being the ending resource or *destination*, indicated by the arc's `to` attribute.
- The resources that are connected by an arc may be either local (`resource-type`) or remote (`locator-type`); that is, a particular connection may be local to remote, remote to local, local to local, or remote to remote.
- Link direction can be *outbound*—from local resource (resource-type) to remote resource (locator-type); *inbound*—from remote to local; or *third-party*—from remote to remote.
- You can use `xml:base` to establish a base URI against which any relative URIs will be resolved.
- Unfortunately, at the time of this writing, application support for XLink is very limited, especially in Web browsers. A list of XLink-aware applications was presented; few new tools have emerged since XLink was finalized.

For Further Exploration

Articles

XML Linking: State of the Art, Eve Maler [early 2001]
http://www.sun.com/software/xml/developers/xlink/

XML Linking: An Executive Summary, Eve Maler [early 2001]
http://www.sun.com/software/xml/enterprise/xlink.html

XML.com: What Is XLink?, Fabio Arciniegas A. [includes XLink reference]
http://www.xml.com/pub/a/2000/09/xlink/index.html

XML.com: XML Linking Technologies, Eric van der Vlist
http://www.xml.com/pub/a/2000/10/04/linking/index.html

XML.com: XLink: Who Cares?, Bob DuCharme [recommended; reviews current state of the art]
http://www.xml.com/pub/a/2002/03/13/xlink.html

Historical

As We May Think, Vannevar Bush [seminal hypertext article from 1945]
http://www.theatlantic.com/unbound/flashbks/computer/bushf.htm

HyTime
http://xml.coverpages.org/hytime.html

Resources

ZVON: XLink Reference
http://www.zvon.org/xxl/xlink/Output/xlink_refs.html

xmlhack XLink/XPointer News
http://xmlhack.com/list.php?cat=14

XLink, Elliotte Rusty Harold [Chapter 19 from *The XML Bible, Second Edition*]
http://www.ibiblio.org/xml/books/bible2/chapters/ch19.html

WDVL: XLink and XPointer
http://wdvl.Internet.com/Authoring/Languages/XLink/

Simple XLink Demo, Bob DuCharme [try in your favorite browser]
http://www.snee.com/xml/xlink/sxlinkdemo.xml/

XMLSoftware.com: XLink/XPointer Tools
http://www.xmlsoftware.com/xlink/

Tutorials

XLink and XPointer, Elliotte Rusty Harold
http://www.ibiblio.org/xml/slides/xmlonesanjose2001/xlinks/

ZVON: Simple-Type XLink Examples
http://www.zvon.org/xxl/xlink/OutputExamples/xlinksimple_intro.html

ZVON: Extended-Type XLink Examples
http://www.zvon.org/xxl/xlink/xlink_extend/OutputExamples/xlinkextend_intro.html

W3C Specifications and Information

XML Pointer, XML Base and XML Linking [home page for three specifications; also includes links to implementations]
http://www.w3.org/XML/Linking

XML Linking Language (XLink) Version 1.0 [Recommendation]
http://www.w3.org/TR/xlink/

XLink 1.0: Sample DTD (Non-Normative)
http://www.w3.org/TR/xlink/#sample-dtd-appx

XML Pointer Language (XPointer) Version 1.0 [Candidate Recommendation]
http://www.w3.org/TR/xptr

XML Path Language (XPath) Version 1.0 [Recommendation]
http://www.w3.org/TR/xpath

XML Inclusions (XInclude) Version 1.0
http://www.w3.org/TR/xinclude/

XML Base
http://www.w3.org/TR/xmlbase

XML Linking and Style
http://www.w3.org/TR/xml-link-style/

Chapter 14

XPointer: XML Pointer Language

In this chapter, we'll learn about the XML Pointer Language (XPointer), which is used primarily with XLink as a fragment identifier for a URI as a way to reference specific portions of an XML document. XPointers can locate individual XML elements, a set of related elements, a particular point between characters or between children of an element, or a range of XML data between two points. Like XPath upon which it is built, XPointer uses non-XML syntax. XPointer can address nodes and node-sets, as can XPath, but it extends XPath addressing by adding the ability to reference points and ranges. In contrast to XLink, which can be used with non-XML resources, XPointer can be used only with XML documents since it relies on their highly structured hierarchy.

Overview

The XML Pointer Language (XPointer) is a way to reference specific portions of an XML document, similar to using fragment identifiers in HTML, but far more flexible. These portions can be individual XML elements, a set of related elements, a particular point between characters or between children of an element, or a range of XML data between two points. Whereas the use of fragment identifiers in HTML requires either that the author of the target document (or the *ending resource*, in XLink terminology) has provided named anchors (e.g., `<a id="section4" name="section4"/>`) or that the person creating the reference has write access to the target, XPointer does not have these restrictions. Just as with XLink you can connect documents not under your direct control, with XPointer you can address specific parts of an XML document that you do not control.

Note: This chapter is based on the XPointer Candidate Recommendation of September 11, 2001. It is possible that some details may change by the time this becomes a W3C Recommendation, especially as a result of implementation experience reported by vendors and developers. However, the key concepts are likely to be generally stable. See *http://www.w3.org/TR/xptr* for current details, however.

Besides supporting all of the node type forms of referencing we saw with XPath in chapter 11, XPointer extends XPath addressing by adding the concepts of *ranges* and *points* (corresponding to DOM Level 2 ranges and positions). As you read this chapter, imagine how useful XPointer is (or will become) for dynamically including portions of XML data in other documents, or for selecting ranges of XML data in XML processing applications.

More formally, XPointer defines the syntax for specifying a fragment identifier for any URI that points to a resource whose Internet media type is one of the following:

- `text/xml`
- `application/xml`
- `text/xml-external-parsed-entity`
- `application/xml-external-parsed-entity`

Since XPointer relies on the well-formed structure of XML documents, it *cannot be used with HTML documents* (even though XLink can). XPointer can be used with XHTML, however, since XHTML adheres to XML syntax rules.

XPointer provides a context for XPath syntax, much as XSLT does. However, whereas XPath does not address URIs, XPointer does. Another way of looking at this is to say that XPath is a declarative syntax used by XPointer for addressing and by XSLT for pattern matching.

According to the September 2001 XPointer specification, XML Pointer Language Version 1.0, W3C Candidate Recommendation, (*http://www.w3.org/TR/2001/CR-xptr-20010911*):

> XPointer supports addressing into the internal structures of XML documents. It allows for examination of a document's hierarchical structure and choice of its internal parts based on various properties, such as element types, attribute values, character content, and relative position. In particular, it provides for specific reference to elements, character strings, and other parts of XML documents, whether or not they bear an explicit ID attribute.

Regrettably, at the time of this writing, XPointer is not supported by *any* of the major browsers (Netscape, Mozilla, Internet Explorer, Opera, or Amaya). Although you can use the addressing mechanism discussed in this chapter, you cannot test the results in these browsers. See the section "XPointer Implementations" later in this chapter for software that does implement some or all of the XPointer specification.

Relevant Specifications

Table 14-1 lists the W3C documents that are most revelant to a complete understanding of XPointer.

TABLE 14-1 XPointer and Related Specifications

W3C Specification	*URL (trailing slash required where indicated)*
XML Pointer Language (XPointer) Version 1.0 Candidate Recommendation	*http://www.w3.org/TR/xptr*
XML Pointer Requirements Version 1.0 (W3C Note)	*http://www.w3.org/TR/NOTE-xptr-req*
XML Path Language (XPath) Version 1.0 Recommendation	*http://www.w3.org/TR/xpath*
XML Linking Language (XLink)Version 1.0 Recommendation	*http://www.w3.org/TR/xlink/*
Links in HTML Documents	*http://www.w3.org/TR/html401/struct/links.html*
Document Object Model Level 2	*http://www.w3.org/TR/DOM-Level-2*
XML Information Set	*http://www.w3.org/TR/xml-infoset/*
RFC 2396: Uniform Resource Identifiers	*http://www.ietf.org/rfc/rfc2396.txt*

Relationship to XPath

XPointer builds on XPath. *All XPath expressions are valid XPointer expressions*, although the reverse is not true. In addition, XPointer introduces the notion of points and ranges. It generalizes the XPath node to something called a *location*, which is either a node, point, or range. The XPointer extensions to XPath make it possible to address individual characters and ranges as well as nodes, perform string matching, and specify URI references as fragment identifiers. XPointer uses XPath for addressing. (XPath is used by XSLT for pattern matching, by XML Schema for uniqueness and scope descriptions, and by XQuery for selection and iteration.)

You can use XPath functions such as `id()`, as well as eight XPointer functions (`range-to()`, `start-point()`, `origin()`, etc.) to specify an XPointer value. You can also use the XPath axes presented in Table 11-6, "The Thirteen Axes Defined by XPath" (e.g., `child`, `descendant`, `preceding-sibling`, etc.) in constructing an XPointer expression. For examples of XPath expressions, see Table 11-11, "Examples of XPath Expressions and XSLT Patterns." XPath functions begin with Table 11-13, "Node-Set XPath Functions."

As a quick review, recall from "Location Paths and Steps" in chapter 11 that XPath defines location paths that consist of steps separated by a slash (/). Each step consists of an axis, a node-test, and zero or more optional predicates:

```
axis::node-test[predicate]*
```

Some examples of locations paths (most of which use the abbreviated form of the `child` axis) follow.

```
/child::Collection/child::Book[position()=3]/child::Author[position()=2]
/Collection/Book[3]/Author[2]
/Collection/Book/Published/@publisher
//CD[2]/descendant::node()/@*
//Book[position() = 3]
Collection/Book[last()]
//Published[@publisher="Addison Wesley"]
Title/text()
CD[not(Title/text() = 'Beatles 1')]
/elt[@attr1 = "val1" and @attr2]/@attr3
```

All of these XPath expressions can be used as XPointers.

Relationship to XLink

In our previous discussion of XLink, with the exception of one passing reference, all examples intentionally ignored the fact that a URI may contain a fragment identifier. A typical example of a fragment identifier in XHTML is:

```
<a href="http://www.ex.com/file.html#section3">Replace me after scrolling to
the location named section3.</a>
```

This example uses the fragment identifier "#section3" to indicate a link to a named anchor with the `id` (or `name`) attribute set to "section3". In other words, the target (ending resource) of this fragment identifier might be a portion of a document:

```
<a id="section3">Part III</a>
```

Fragment identifiers can be used in XLink, as in this `simple-type` link example that uses an XPointer appended to the URI that is the value of the `xlink:href` attribute.

```
<mySimpleLink
  xmlns:xlink="http://www.w3.org/2000/xlink"
  xlink:type="simple"
  xlink:href="document.xml#xpointer(//someParent/someChild)">
</mySimpleLink>
```

Similarly in the case of extended XLinks, you can add an XPointer to a URI for the `xlink:href` attribute of `locator-type` links. XPointers can also be used for linking within the same document, as we'll see with the `here()` function. Throughout this chapter, most XPointer examples assume an XLink context.

Forms of XPointers

The XPointer specification describes one full form of XPointer addressing and two shorthand forms.

- *Full XPointer*, for example, `#xpointer(//model[@type='707'])` (all instances of the element `model` with an attribute named `type` with a value of "707")

- *Bare-name*, for example, `#section4` (based on an attribute of type `ID` with the value "section4")
- *Child-sequence*, for example, `/1/2/5` (the fifth child of the second child of the document element)

We'll cover each of these in more detail shortly.

Terminology and Concepts

Once again, the XPointer specification introduces a number of concepts that are helpful to define before we dive into the details. Other terms that XPointer borrows come from XPath, DOM Level 2, and XML Information Set.

Point and range are the two location types that XPointer adds to the node types defined by XPath. A **point** is a position within XML data. This idea is analogous to the term *position* in DOM Level 2. A point is actually a zero-length position that usually indicates a particular character in a text node (`PCDATA`). Points are particularly useful for splitting strings such as for applications like XML editors that need to position themselves within selected text, for instance. Points can be positioned before or after start and end tags of elements, but they cannot be *within* the tags since XPointer doesn't operate on the markup characters directly. The **container node** is the node that contains the current point. For example, if a point is pointing to the position between the "e" and the "a" in "Beatles," the container node would be the text node that includes the string "Beatles".

A **range** is a contiguous selection between two points, consisting of the entire XML structure and content between the start point and end points. A range may consist of a span of characters within a text node, or it may cut across element boundaries. It's possible that some nodes will only be *partially* within the range. You can imagine a range also being useful to an XML editor to keep track of the span of text, perhaps including markup, that the document author has selected with his mouse. As we'll see later, a point is selected with the `string-range()` function to select a range, and either `start-point()` or `end-point()` function to select a point from the range. This range concept is also borrowed from DOM Level 2.

A **location** is the generalization of the XPath *node* concept; a location is a node, a point, or a range.[1] Similarly, a **location-set** is the generalization of the XPath *node-set*; it is the ordered list of nodes, points, and/or ranges that results from an XPointer expression. A **singleton** is a location-set consisting of a single location, such as with a point or range XPointer; it is a single, contiguous portion of a document.

1. Recall that there are seven types of XPath nodes: root, element, text, attribute, namespace, comment, and processing instruction. Therefore, in XPointer, with the addition of point and range, there are nine node types, each with its own node test.

A **sub-resource** is that portion of an XML document that an XPointer references, such as an element or text node, or a range of characters; in contrast, a *resource* is the entire XML document that contains the referenced sub-resource. The idea here is that an application that fetches the resource may need to scroll down to the sub-resource to which the XPointer points.

Historical Perspective

Readers not interested in the historical development of XPointer can skip this brief section without missing the point.

As we noted in the XLink chapter, Robin Cover's XML Cover Pages are an excellent source of pre-XML and XML information. His *Text Encoding Initiative (TEI)—XML for TEI Lite* page contains much historical information related to XPointer from the late 1980s and early 1990s (*http://xml.coverpages.org/tei.html*). In particular, pointers and extended pointers are discussed in the "Linking, Segmentation, and Alignment" section of the TEI Guidelines, *Guidelines for Electronic Text Encoding and Interchange* (see *http://www.tei-c.org/Guidelines/SA.htm* and *http://etext.virginia.edu/tei-tocs4.html*). In 1998 C. Michael Sperberg-McQueen (University of Illinois) served as an editor of the TEI Project as well as co-editor of the XML 1.0 Recommendation. The *TEI Extended Pointer* language plays a significant role in the design of XLink and XPointer (for TEI Extended Pointers, see *http://etext.virginia.edu/bin/tei-tocs?div=DIV2&id=SAXR*). HyTime, as discussed in the XLink chapter, defines location specifier types for all types of data. HTML focuses on a particular kind of location specifier, the URL, and its more generic relative, the URI.

Code Example Modification

Before we introduce examples of XPointers, let's update our running CD and book collection example for the XML instance and the corresponding DTD, `collection10.xml` and `collection10.dtd`, shown in Listings 14-1 and 14-2. Please refer to this updated version as we explore XPointer examples later in the chapter.

Listing 14-1 XML Instance for XPointer Examples (collection10.xml)

```
<?xml version="1.0" standalone="no"?>
<!DOCTYPE Collection SYSTEM "collection10.dtd" >

<Collection version="4"
  xmlns:xlink="http://www.w3.org/1999/xlink" >

  <Book>
    <Title keyword="chronicles"
           xlink:type="simple"
           xlink:href="http://www.amazon.com/exec/obidos/ASIN/0600600335/
">Complete Beatles Chronicle, The</Title>
```

```
    <!-- xlink:show="embed" not supported by browsers yet -->
    <Picture xlink:type="simple"
             xlink:show="embed"
             xlink:title="photo of The Complete Beatles Chronicles"
             xlink:href="http://images.amazon.com/images/P/
0600600335.01.MZZZZZZZ.jpg"
    />

    <Author>
      <Name>
        <First>Mark</First>
        <Last>Lewisohn</Last>
      </Name>
    </Author>
    <Type>Chronology</Type>
    <Published publisher="Harmony Books">1992</Published>
    <Rating>5 stars</Rating>
    <Notes>
  Covers the years 1957 through 1970. No solo info.
  Great appendices with chart info, discography, composer index,
  radio, tv, and live performances, and much more.
  Second Edition: May 2000 with George Martin as co-author.
    </Notes>
    <ListPrice>24.95</ListPrice>
  </Book>
  <CD>
    <Title keyword="botr"
           xlink:type="simple"
     xlink:href="http://cdnow.com/cgi-bin/mserver/pagename=/RP/CDN/FIND/
album.html/ArtistID=MCCARTNEY*PAUL+&amp;+WINGS/ITEMID=644593">Band on the
Run</Title>
    <Artist>McCartney, Paul and Wings</Artist>
    <Chart>
      <Peak weeks="4">1</Peak>
      <Peak country="UK">1</Peak>
      <!-- guess -->
    </Chart>
    <Type>Rock</Type>
    <Label>Capitol</Label>
    <Label country="UK">EMI</Label>
    <AlbumReleased>1973</AlbumReleased>
    <Remastered format="gold CD">1993</Remastered>
    <Remastered format="2 disc box set with booklet">1999</Remastered>
    <ListPrice>16.97</ListPrice>
  </CD>
  <CD>
    <Title keyword="vam"
           xlink:type="simple"
     xlink:href="http://cdnow.com/cgi-bin/mserver/pagename=/RP/CDN/FIND/
album.html/ArtistID=MCCARTNEY*PAUL+&amp;+WINGS/ITEMID=429936">Venus and
Mars</Title>
    <Artist>McCartney, Paul and Wings</Artist>
    <Chart>
      <Peak weeks="1">1</Peak>
      <Peak country="UK">2</Peak>
      <!-- guess -->
```

```
    </Chart>
    <Type>Rock</Type>
    <Label>Capitol</Label>
    <Label country="UK">EMI</Label>
    <AlbumReleased>1975</AlbumReleased>
    <Remastered format="gold CD with 3 bonus tracks">1994</Remastered>
    <ListPrice>16.97</ListPrice>
  </CD>

<?bogus-pi attr1="foo" attr2="foobar" ?>

  <Book>
    <Title keyword="years"
           xlink:type="simple"
     xlink:href="http://www.amazon.com/exec/obidos/ASIN/0805052496">Many
Years From Now</Title>
    <Author>
      <Name>
        <First>Paul</First>
        <Last>McCartney</Last>
      </Name>
    </Author>
    <Type>Autobiographical</Type>
    <Published publisher="Henry Holt and Company">1997</Published>
    <Rating>4 stars</Rating>
    <Notes>654 pages; Reprint edition (October 1998)</Notes>
    <ListPrice>27.50</ListPrice>
    <!-- Notice the absence of Rating element.
  I haven't read this book yet. This illustrates some optional
  elements that are children of Book element.
  -->
  </Book>
  <Book>
    <Title keyword="anthologyBook"
           xlink:type="simple"
     xlink:href="http://www.amazon.com/exec/obidos/ASIN/0811826848/">Beatles
Anthology, The</Title>
    <Author>
      <Name>
        <First>Paul</First>
        <Last>McCartney</Last>
      </Name>
    </Author>
    <Author>
      <Name>
        <First>George</First>
        <Last>Harrison</Last>
      </Name>
    </Author>
    <Author>
      <Name>
        <First>Ringo</First>
        <Last>Starr</Last>
      </Name>
    </Author>
```

```
    <Author>
      <Name>
        <First>John</First>
        <Last>Lennon</Last>
      </Name>
    </Author>
    <Type>Autobiographical</Type>
    <Published publisher="Chronicle Books">2000</Published>
    <Rating>5 stars</Rating>
    <Notes>368 pages of the Beatles in their own words and pictures!
    A must-have for true Beatles fans.</Notes>
    <ListPrice>60.00</ListPrice>
  </Book>
  <CD>
    <Title keyword="one"
           xlink:type="simple"
     xlink:href="http://www.cdnow.com/cgi-bin/mserver/pagename=/RP/CDN/
FIND/album.html/ddcn=SD-7777+29325+2/">Beatles 1</Title>
    <Artist>Beatles</Artist>
    <Chart>
      <Peak weeks="10" country="US">1</Peak>
    </Chart>
    <Type>Rock</Type>
    <Label country="US">Capitol</Label>
    <AlbumReleased>November 14, 2000</AlbumReleased>
    <ListPrice>18.97</ListPrice>
  </CD>
  <Owner>
    <Name sex="male">
      <First>Ken</First>
      <Last>Sall</Last>
    </Name>
    <Address>
      <Street>123 Milky Way Dr.</Street>
      <City>Columbia</City>
      <State>MD</State>
      <Zip>20794</Zip>
    </Address>
  </Owner>
</Collection>
```

The main difference between these and the previous versions used in the XLink chapter is the addition of the attribute named keyword for the Title element. This attribute is a handle by which we can refer to either the Title element or the Book or CD element that contains the Title.[2] For example:

```
  <Book>
    <Title keyword="chronicle"
           xlink:type="simple"
```

2. An alternative approach would be to add the keyword attribute to both the Book and CD elements.

```
          xlink:href="http://www.amazon.com/exec/obidos/ASIN/0600600335/
">Complete Beatles Chronicle, The</Title>
   <!-- etc. -->
  </Book>
```

If you refer to the DTD in Listing 14-2, you'll notice we've declared the required keyword attribute to be of type ID. The reason for this will become clear when we discuss the *bare name* form of XPointer. For now, just note that every Title element must have a keyword attribute. You may recall that when an attribute is declared to be of type ID, *every occurrence of that attribute must be unique in the document.* A validating parser such as XML Validator from ElCel Technologies (mentioned in the XLink chapter) will check that there are no repetitions of the value of keyword attribute, and that the attribute is provided for every Title.

```
<!ATTLIST Title
        keyword       ID          #REQUIRED
        xlink:type    (simple)    #FIXED   "simple"
        xlink:href    CDATA       #REQUIRED
>
```

Listing 14-2 DTD for Validation of XML Instance (collection10.dtd)

```
<?xml encoding="UTF-8"?>
<!--       Collection DTD, Version 4        -->
<!ELEMENT Collection (xi:include*, (Book | CD)*, Owner?)>
<!ATTLIST Collection
 version      CDATA    "4"
 xmlns:xlink  CDATA    #FIXED  "http://www.w3.org/1999/xlink"
>

<!ELEMENT xi:include EMPTY >
<!ATTLIST xi:include
 xmlns:xi    CDATA       #FIXED      "http://www.w3.org/2001/XInclude"
 href        CDATA       #REQUIRED
 parse       (xml|text)  "xml"
 encoding    CDATA       #IMPLIED
>

<!ELEMENT Owner (Name, Address?)>
<!ELEMENT Address (Street, City, State, Zip)>
<!ELEMENT Street (#PCDATA)>
<!ELEMENT City (#PCDATA)>
<!ELEMENT State (#PCDATA)>
<!ELEMENT Zip (#PCDATA)>

<!ELEMENT Book (Title, Picture?, Author+, Type, Published, Rating?, Notes?,
ListPrice?)>
<!ELEMENT CD (Title, Artist, Chart, Type, Label+, AlbumReleased, Remastered*,
Notes?, ListPrice?)>
```

```
<!ELEMENT Title (#PCDATA)>
<!ATTLIST Title
        keyword       ID          #REQUIRED
        xlink:type    (simple)    #FIXED   "simple"
        xlink:href    CDATA       #REQUIRED
>

<!ELEMENT Picture EMPTY>
<!ATTLIST Picture
        xlink:type    (simple)    #FIXED   "simple"
        xlink:href    CDATA       #REQUIRED
        xlink:title   CDATA       #IMPLIED
        xlink:show    (new|replace|embed)  "embed"
        xlink:actuate (onLoad|onRequest)   "onLoad"
>
<!ELEMENT ListPrice (#PCDATA)>

<!-- Title defined under CD; applies to Book also. -->
<!-- Name defined under Owner; applies to Book also. -->
<!ELEMENT Author (Name)>
<!ELEMENT Name (First, Last)>
<!ATTLIST Name
        sex (male | female) "male"
>
<!ELEMENT First (#PCDATA)>
<!ELEMENT Last (#PCDATA)>
<!ELEMENT Type (#PCDATA)>
<!ELEMENT Published (#PCDATA)>
<!ATTLIST Published
        publisher CDATA #REQUIRED
>
<!ELEMENT Rating (#PCDATA)>
<!ELEMENT Notes (#PCDATA)>
<!ELEMENT Artist (#PCDATA)>
<!ELEMENT Chart (Peak+)>
<!--WAS: ATTLIST Label country NMTOKEN #IMPLIED-->
<!ELEMENT Peak (#PCDATA)>
<!ATTLIST Peak
        country NMTOKEN "US"
        weeks NMTOKEN #IMPLIED
>
<!ELEMENT Label (#PCDATA)>
<!ATTLIST Label
        country NMTOKEN "US"
>
<!ELEMENT AlbumReleased (#PCDATA)>
<!ELEMENT Remastered (#PCDATA)>
<!ATTLIST Remastered
        format CDATA #REQUIRED
>
```

Forms of XPointers

Full XPointers

In the next three sections, we'll cover full XPointers, bare names, and child sequences.

A full XPointer is not abbreviated and always contains the keyword `xpointer`.[3] It consists of one or more **XPointer parts**, separated by optional white space. Each XPointer part is of the form

```
xpointer(XPointer-expression)
```

and appears at the end of a URI associated with an XML document, separated by a "#" sign. Recall that an XPointer expression is a superset of XPath expressions. For example, the URI

```
collection10.xml#xpointer(/Collection/CD[3]/Title/text())
```

returns the location set of character data of the `Title` element child of the third `CD` child of the `Collection` element. In this URI, we have three parts:

- the resource: filename `collection10.xml`
- an XPointer fragment identifier: `#xpointer(....)`
- an XPointer expression within the parentheses of the XPointer fragment identifier: `/Collection/CD[3]/Title/text()`

If there are multiple XPointer parts, they are evaluated left to right; the first one whose evaluation succeeds becomes the final value of the fragment located by the full XPointer. Consider this example containing two XPointer parts.

```
xpointer(id("section4"))xpointer(//*[@id="section4"])
```

The first XPointer part will succeed if and only if the document contains an element with an attribute of type `ID` (regardless of the name of the attribute) with the value `"section4"`, as supported by a DTD. If these conditions are met, the second part is not evaluated. If there is no such attribute of type `ID`, or if there is no DTD, then the second less precise XPointer part is evaluated. This one attempts to locate *any* element with an attribute named literally `id` with the value `"section4"`, regardless of the type of the attribute.[4]

3. Technically, the word `xpointer` can be replaced by another so-called *scheme*. See *http://www.w3.org/TR/xptr/#schemes* and *http://www.w3.org/TR/xptr/#ns-context*.

4. In other words, in the first XPointer part, `id()` is an XPointer function; in the second XPointer part, `id` is the name of an attribute, as indicated by the "`@`" symbol.

Here are more examples of (mostly single part) full XPointers. They'll be explained in later sections.

```
xpointer(/child::Collection/child::Book[position() = 3]/child::Author
[position() = 2])
xpointer(/Collection/Book[3]/Author[2])
xpointer(/Collection/Book[3]/Author[position() < 4])
xpointer(//Collection/CD[2]) xpointer(//Collection/CD[3])
xpointer(//Artist/text()/start-point()[3])
xpointer(id('chronicle'))
xpointer(descendant::InsertBegin/range-to(following::InsertEnd[1]))
xpointer(id("section4")/range-to(id("section7")))
xpointer(string-range(//Title,'Complete Beatles'))
xpointer(string-range(//Title,'Beatles')[3])
xpointer(start-point(string-range(//CD/Artist,'McCartney'))
xpointer(range(start-point(string-range(//*,'Beatles'))))
xpointer(string-range(//*,"Beatles",1,3)[2])
xpointer(id('chronicle')/following-sibling::Author/range-to(following-
sibling::Published))
```

Some of these should look familiar since we've seen similar XPath expressions before. Others use the various point and range functions that XPointer adds to XPath. We'll cover these a bit later in this chapter. Since XPointers are typically used as the value of an attribute (especially `xlink:href` for simple and extended XLinks), it is necessary to quote the entire URI, so be careful of internal quotes. Single and double quotes are interchangeable, as usual. For example, the XPointer

```
xpointer(id("section4")/range-to(id("section7")))
```

as an attribute value becomes either

```
xlink:href='document.xml#xpointer(id("section4")/range-to(id("section7")))'
```

or

```
xlink:href="document.xml#xpointer(id('section4')/range-to(id('section7')))"
```

Furthermore, it's necessary to escape < and & so the XML will be well-formed. For example,

```
xpointer(/Collection/Book[3]/Author[position() < 4])
```

becomes

```
xlink:href="collection10.xml#xpointer(/Collection/Book[3]/Author[position()
&lt; 4])"
```

Notice that it's entirely possible for an XPointer expression to return a location-set consisting of *multiple* locations. For example the preceding XPointer yields three locations, the `Author` elements that contain the names of Paul, George, and Ringo (refer to Listing 14-1). John is not included because he is `Author[position() = 4]`.

Note that these two XPointers are identical:

```
xpointer(/child::Collection/child::Book[position() = 3]/child::Author
[position() = 2])
xpointer(/Collection/Book[3]/Author[2])
```

because the XPath expression

```
child::anyElementName[position() = n]
```

can be reduced to simply

```
anyElementName[n]
```

The next two sections discuss so-called shortened forms of XPointer, bare names and child sequences.

Bare Names

A **bare name** is a shortened form of XPointer that consists of nothing but the *value* of an attribute of type `ID`. It is intended to represent the most general case of the XHTML fragment identifier, which requires a fixed element name (<a>). Since XML lets you pick element and attribute names, any element could be the one you'd like to identify by a unique id. This form is called a bare name because you don't even use the `xpointer` keyword. For example, to locate the `Title` element containing the text "Complete Beatles Chronicle, The" and the `keyword` attribute (of type `ID`) value "chronicle", we use the bare name pointer that consists solely of the attribute value:

```
chronicle
```

It is simply appended with a # sign to the URI:

```
xlink:href="collection10.xml#chronicle"
```

The bare name shortened form is identical to a full XPointer that uses the XPath `id()` function:

```
xpointer(id("chronicle"))
```

which as an attribute value would be

```
xlink:href="collection10.xml#xpointer(id('chronicle'))"
```

There's a very important assumption underlying the use of bare names. Since they imply the `id()` function, the *attribute associated with the value used as the bare name must be of type* `ID`, which also means there must be a DTD. Without a DTD or XML Schema, you cannot use the bare name form or the `id()` function.

Now you know why we changed the DTD of `collection10.dtd` (Listing 14-2) to add the `keyword` attribute to `Title` and define it to be of type `ID`. The name of the attribute is immaterial. All that is required is that the type of the attribute is `ID` and that the values used are unique throughout the document. The need for the DTD or XML Schema and the uniqueness of the attribute value means that bare name XPointers are most useful if you have control over both the starting and ending resources that are linked. As we noted in a different context in the previous section, you can use a two-part full XPointer to provide a fallback if you know the attribute name and value are correct, but are not sure if the `keyword` attribute is of type `ID`:

```
xpointer(id("chronicle")) xpointer(//*[@keyword="chronicle"])
```

Another limitation of bare names is that you cannot add other location path steps to the expression. For example, if we really wanted the `Book` element that contains the `Title` element with the `keyword` `ID` "chronicle", we'd be forced to use the full XPointer form so we can refer to the parent `Title` element

```
xpointer(../id("chronicle"))
```

In the next section, we'll learn that it's possible to combine a bare name with something called a child sequence.

Child Sequences

We've already seen the abbreviation of the `child` axis in XPath because it is so common to refer to elements based on their well-structured hierarchy in XML. We also noted that these two forms are identical:

```
xpointer(/child::Collection/child::Book[position() = 3]/child::Author
[position() = 2])
xpointer(/Collection/Book[3]/Author[2])
```

A **child sequence** is another shortened form of XPointer that permits even more terse location paths in which each step is merely an integer separated by a slash from the next child in the sequence. Each integer `n` locates the *nth* child element of the previously located element, equivalent to an XPath location step of the form `*[n]`. In other words, the XPointer

```
xpointer(/child::*[position() = 1]/child::*[position() = 3]/child::*[position()
= 2])
```

or its shorter but equivalent full XPointer

```
xpointer(/*[1]/*[3]/*[2])
```

can be written in the shortened child sequence form (without the `xpointer` keyword) as simply

```
/1/3/2
```

All three variations of this XPointer locate the second child of the third child of the *document element* (which is `/1` for all XML documents), which in the case of `collection10.xml` locates

```
<Artist>McCartney, Paul and Wings</Artist>
```

because `/1` locates the `Collection` element, `/3` locates `CD[2]` (because with respect to `Collection`, `Book[1]` is the first child, `CD[1]` is the second child, and `CD[2]` is the third child), and `/2` locates the `Artist` child of the `CD[2]`.

A child sequence is appended to a URI with a # just like the bare name form

```
xlink:href="collection10.xml#/1/3/2"
```

A child sequence may begin with `/1` to denote the first child of the root, which is the document element (`Collection` in our example), or the sequence may begin with a bare name. This second case cannot be illustrated with `collection10.xml` as written because `Title`, the only element with an `ID`-type attribute (required for a bare name), has no children. Suppose instead we defined an `ID`-type attribute called `bookID` for the `Book` element in `collection10.xml` and suppose we had the XML fragment

```
  <Book bookID="b57">
    <Title keyword="years"
           xlink:type="simple"
     xlink:href="http://www.amazon.com/exec/obidos/ASIN/0805052496">Many
Years From Now</Title>
    <Author>
      <Name>
        <First>Paul</First>
        <Last>McCartney</Last>
      </Name>
    </Author>
    <Type>Autobiographical</Type>
    <Published publisher="Henry Holt and Company">1997</Published>
    <Rating>4 stars</Rating>
    <Notes>654 pages; Reprint edition (October 1998)</Notes>
    <ListPrice>27.50</ListPrice>
    <!-- Notice the absence of Rating element.
  I haven't read this book yet. This illustrates some optional
  elements that are children of Book element.
  -->
  </Book>
```

We can now use a combined bare name and child sequence XPointer:

```
b57/2/1/2
```

to locate the second child (`Last`) of the first child (`Name`) of the second child (`Author`) of the `Book` element with an `ID` of `b57`, which is

```
<Last>McCartney</Last>
```

Note that when the two shortened forms are combined, the XPointer *does not begin with a slash* (since bare names do not contain a leading slash), so the URI is simply:

```
xlink:href="collection10.xml#b57/2/1/2"
```

which is equivalent to the full XPointer:

```
xlink:href="collection10.xml#xpointer(id('b57')/*[2]/*[1]/*[2])"
```

Just in case you're wondering if there could be a conflict if the bare name is simply a number, don't worry. An `ID`-type attribute name cannot begin with a digit, which is why I used `b57` rather than `57` for the value.

XPointer Functions

XPath defines about twenty-seven functions (grouped by return values of node sets, string, boolean, and number), as described in chapter 11. XPointer defines eight additional functions, summarized in Table 14-2.[5] The `id()` function is actually defined in the XPath specification and is included as the last row of this table because it is likely you'll need it with XPointer. Nearly all of these functions return a location-set, which is an ordered list of one or more locations (nodes, points, and/or ranges). In the table, the generic term `x` for a location may represent *any XPointer type:* point, range, root, element, text, comment, processing instruction, attribute, or namespace. However, the functions typically operate differently depending on the type categories:

- Points
- Ranges
- Root, elements, text, comments, processing instructions (nodes)
- Attributes, namespaces (special nodes)

5. Earlier versions of the spec contained a ninth function called `unique`, which tested whether an XPointer expression or subexpression locates a singleton (location-set with only one location).

The remainder of this section elaborates on the table and provides examples of each function, except `id()`, which was covered earlier in the sections "Full XPointers" and "Bare Names." Note that each function appears inside of the `xpointer` parentheses. For example:

```
xlink:href="collection10.xml#xpointer(start-point(//Book[3]))"
```

TABLE 14-2 XPointer Functions

Return Type	*Function Name (arguments)*	*Description*
`location-set`	**`start-point`**`(location-set)`	For each location x in the argument location-set, start-point adds a location of type point to the result location-set. That point represents the start point of location `x`.
`location-set`	**`end-point`**`(location-set)`	For each location `x` in the argument location-set, end-point adds a location of type point to the result location-set. That point represents the end point of location `x`.
`location-set`	**`here`**`()`	Enables addressing locations in the same document that contains the XPointer that calls the function. Returns a location-set with one location, which is the node that contains the XPointer being evaluated.
`location-set`	**`origin`**`()`	Enables addressing relative to third-party and inbound links such as defined in XLink. It returns a location-set with a single member, which locates the element from which a user or program initiated traversal of the link. In other words, this is a back link to the point in the source document from which the user came.
`location-set`	**`range`**`(location-set)`	Returns ranges covering the locations in the argument location-set, including markup.
`location-set`	**`range-inside`**`(location-set)`	Returns ranges covering the contents of the locations in the argument location-set, *excluding the outermost markup.*
`location-set`	**`range-to`**`(endPoint-location-set)`	Returns a range from the start point of the context location to the end point of the location found by evaluating the expression argument. Used to specify the *end* of a range. Returns the range location type for selections that are not single XML nodes.
`location-set`	**`string-range`**`(location-set, searchString, index?, length?)`	The string-value of the location is searched for substrings that match the `searchString` argument, and the resulting location-set will contain a range location for each nonoverlapping match, ignoring markup. Returns the range location type for selections that are not single XML nodes.
`node-set`	**`id`**`(object)`	XPath function; selects elements by their unique `ID`, provided the element has an attribute of type `ID` defined in a DTD; the argument is the *value* of an attribute of type `ID`.

start-point() and end-point()

The functions `start-point()` and `end-point()` are used to obtain the set of start and end points of the ranges that cover the locations passed as arguments. Each function returns a set of start/end points representing the start/end point of each of the passed locations, one point for each location. For example

```
start-point(//Book)
```

returns a set of points that locate the beginning of *each* `Book` element (after their start tags), and

```
start-point(//Book[3])
```

returns the point that is the start of the third `Book` element, which is the point immediately *after* the start tag `<Book>` of the book with the title "Beatles Anthology, The."

Similarly, this expression returns the *end* of the third `Book` element, which is the point immediately *before* the *end* tag `</Book>`:

```
end-point(//Book[3])
```

A nonzero index `n` indicates the point immediately *after* the *nth* child node, so this XPointer locates the point immediately *after* the end tag `</Book>` of the Beatles Anthology:

```
xpointer(end-point(range(/Collection/Book[3])))
```

The next example

```
xpointer(start-point(string-range(//*,'Beatles'))
```

returns a location set consisting of three start points denoted "$_x$" before each of the three occurrences of the string "Beatles", given the following XML fragment.

```
<Book>
  <Title keyword="anthologyBook"
        xlink:type="simple"
   xlink:href="http://www.amazon.com/exec/obidos/ASIN/0811826848/">xBeatles
Anthology, The</Title>
  <!-- Author elements not shown -->
  <Type>Autobiographical</Type>
  <Published publisher="Chronicle Books">2000</Published>
  <Rating>5 stars</Rating>
  <Notes>368 pages of the xBeatles in their own words and pictures!
  A must-have for true xBeatles fans.</Notes>
  <ListPrice>60.00</ListPrice>
</Book>
```

here() and origin()

Since the `here()` function returns the single node that *contains* the XPointer, it is useful for referring to locations in the document in which the XPointer appears. This is especially helpful if you need to refer to the parent or sibling of an element in the same document (in contrast to using XPointers that refer to remote resources).

If the XPointer being evaluated appears in a text node, the location returned is the *element* node that contains the text node. Otherwise, the location returned is the node that directly contains the XPointer being evaluated. The following example is from the XPointer 1.0 Candidate Recommendation (XML Pointer Language (XPointer) Version 1.0, W3C Candidate Recommendation, 11 September 2001, *http://www.w3.org/TR/2001/CR-xptr-20010911*). In this case, the `here()` function is contained in an XPointer that is within an *attribute* node. The entire XPointer returns the `Slide` element just preceding the `Slide` element that contains the `xlink:href` attribute node (i.e., that contains its parent `Button` element).

```
<Button
  xlink:type="simple"
  xlink:href="#xpointer(here()/ancestor::Slide[1]/preceding::Slide[1])">
Previous Slide
</Button>
```

The `origin()` function is similar to `here()` in that it refers to the source of a link. However, this function enables addressing relative to *third-party and inbound links,* as we discussed in regard to XLink. It allows XPointers to be used in applications to express relative locations when the links aren't in the source document. The `origin()` function returns a singleton location-set, which points to the element from which the user or program initiated traversal of (i.e., activated) the link. This is essentially a back link that is like the referrer URL that Web servers track (e.g,. from what page did a person come to the server's page), except it is more precise.

range-to()

We noted earlier that a **range** is a contiguous span of XML data between a start and an end point. A range does not necessarily refer to a well-formed XML since it's entirely possible for it to start in the middle of a text node, extend past the end tag of the element that contains the text, include the siblings that follow that element, and perhaps end in the middle of the text of one of these siblings! This is exactly what you might expect if the user of an XML editor could freely select both text and markup, as shown in Figure 14-1.

A range represents *all of the XML markup and content between the start and end points.* The end point of a range is defined by location paths. A **covering range** is a range that completely encompasses a location. The specification describes different covering ranges for each type of location.

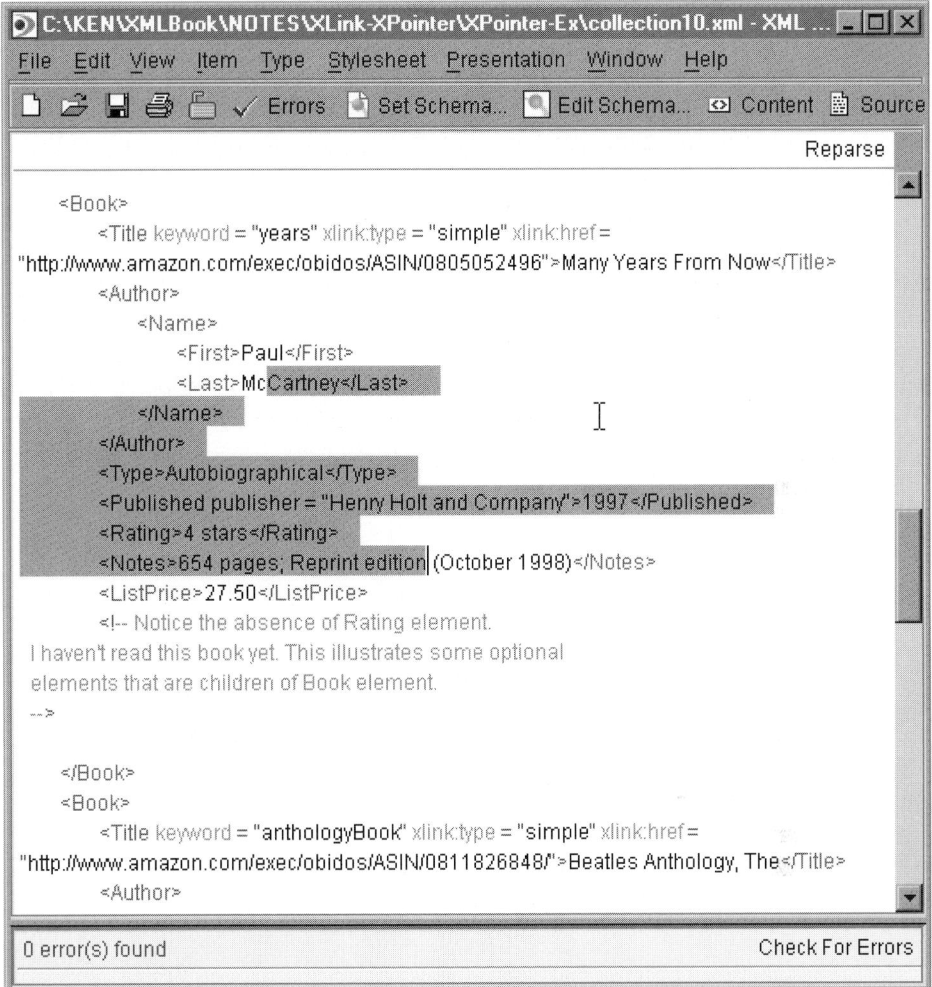

FIGURE 14-1 Arbitrary range of XML data selected in Turbo XML

The general syntax for defining a range involves the `range-to()` function:

```
xpointer(startPointExpr/range-to(endPointExpr))
```

where *`startPointExpr`* and *`endPointExpr`* are any expressions that evaluate to points. Note the slash step separator from XPath syntax that separates the two parts. For example, to express a range that extends from the start of the first `CD` to the end of the second `CD` element, the XPointer is:

```
xpointer(//CD[1]/range-to(//CD[2]))
```

The covering range, shown in Listing 14-3, is the combined `CD[1]` and `CD[2]` elements: all their markup and content, plus anything that happens to appear between them (although nothing does in our running example). In this case, the selected range is *almost* well-formed XML except the two `CD` elements aren't contained in another element; they have no root, so the range isn't well-formed, even though it could have been if our expression selected only one `CD` element (in which case the `CD` element itself would be the root).

Listing 14-3 Covering Range of Two CDs Selected by range-to

```
  <CD>
    <Title keyword="botr"
           xlink:type="simple"
     xlink:href="http://cdnow.com/cgi-bin/mserver/pagename=/RP/CDN/FIND/
album.html/ArtistID=MCCARTNEY*PAUL+&amp;+WINGS/ITEMID=644593">Band on the
Run</Title>
    <Artist>McCartney, Paul and Wings</Artist>
    <Chart>
      <Peak weeks="4">1</Peak>
      <Peak country="UK">1</Peak>
      <!-- guess -->
    </Chart>
    <Type>Rock</Type>
    <Label>Capitol</Label>
    <Label country="UK">EMI</Label>
    <AlbumReleased>1973</AlbumReleased>
    <Remastered format="gold CD">1993</Remastered>
    <Remastered format="2 disc box set with booklet">1999</Remastered>
    <ListPrice>16.97</ListPrice>
  </CD>
  <CD>
    <Title keyword="vam"
           xlink:type="simple"
     xlink:href="http://cdnow.com/cgi-bin/mserver/pagename=/RP/CDN/FIND/
album.html/ArtistID=MCCARTNEY*PAUL+&amp;+WINGS/ITEMID=429936">Venus and
Mars</Title>
    <Artist>McCartney, Paul and Wings</Artist>
    <Chart>
      <Peak weeks="1">1</Peak>
      <Peak country="UK">2</Peak>
      <!-- guess -->
    </Chart>
    <Type>Rock</Type>
    <Label>Capitol</Label>
    <Label country="UK">EMI</Label>
    <AlbumReleased>1975</AlbumReleased>
    <Remastered format="gold CD with 3 bonus tracks">1994</Remastered>
    <ListPrice>16.97</ListPrice>
  </CD>
```

Suppose instead we want to specify a range that begins with the `Title` element whose `keyword` `ID`-type attribute is "botr" and extends to the end of the `Title` element with `keyword` "vam". In other words, we want a continuous span from the `<Title>` start tag of the first `CD` ("Band on the Run") to just after the `</Title>` end tag of the second `CD` ("Venus and Mars"). The following XPointer does the trick.

```
xpointer(id("botr")/range-to(id("vam")))
```

However, the covering range (Listing 14-4) is quite different. This time, no complete `CD` element is selected. We get all of `CD[1]` except the <CD> start tag and we span the start tags of `CD[2]` but only include its first child, the `Title` element. Clearly this is not well-formed XML.

Listing 14-4 Less Complete Covering Range with range-to

```
     <Title keyword="botr"
           xlink:type="simple"
     xlink:href="http://cdnow.com/cgi-bin/mserver/pagename=/RP/CDN/FIND/
album.html/ArtistID=MCCARTNEY*PAUL+&amp;+WINGS/ITEMID=644593">Band on the
Run</Title>
    <Artist>McCartney, Paul and Wings</Artist>
    <Chart>
      <Peak weeks="4">1</Peak>
      <Peak country="UK">1</Peak>
      <!-- guess -->
    </Chart>
    <Type>Rock</Type>
    <Label>Capitol</Label>
    <Label country="UK">EMI</Label>
    <AlbumReleased>1973</AlbumReleased>
    <Remastered format="gold CD">1993</Remastered>
    <Remastered format="2 disc box set with booklet">1999</Remastered>
    <ListPrice>16.97</ListPrice>
  </CD>
  <CD>
    <Title keyword="vam"
           xlink:type="simple"
     xlink:href="http://cdnow.com/cgi-bin/mserver/pagename=/RP/CDN/FIND/
album.html/ArtistID=MCCARTNEY*PAUL+&amp;+WINGS/ITEMID=429936">Venus and
Mars</Title>
```

For our last example of `range-to()`, consider a starting point of `//Owner/Name` and an ending point of the `Last` element:

```
xpointer(//Owner/Name/range-to(Last))
```

which produces this (not well-formed) range of XML markup and content

```
    <Name sex="male">
      <First>Ken</First>
      <Last>Sall</Last>
```

We can shorten the range just a little bit with the XPointer that terminates with the text content of the `Last` name:

```
xpointer(//Owner/Name/range-to(Last/text()))
```

This reduces the range to:

```
<Name sex="male">
  <First>Ken</First>
  <Last>Sall
```

Note that neither of these ranges represents well-formed XML. Of course, we can create ranges that are well-formed, if we wish.

range() and range-inside()

The `range()` and `range-inside()` functions are similar; they essentially take input locations and return ranges. The `range()` function produces the minimal range necessary to cover the argument location. For example,

```
xpointer(range(//Owner/Name/First))
```

produces the range

```
<First>Ken</First>
```

A slightly different XPointer can produce multiple ranges:

```
xpointer(range(//Owner/Name/*))
```

which produces two ranges:

```
<First>Ken</First>
```

and

```
<Last>Sall</Last>
```

The `range-inside()` function also returns ranges corresponding to the passed location paths, but it deals exclusively with the interiors (i.e., the contents) of the location arguments. If the locations are points or ranges, the results are identical to that produced by `range()`. However, if the location argument is an *element*, `range-inside()` returns a range that *excludes* the start and end tags of the element. For example,

```
xpointer(range-inside(//Owner/Name/First))
```

produces the range

```
Ken
```

which is the content of the `First` element without the tags.

string-range()

A primitive level of case-sensitive string matching is possible using `string-range()`. In contrast to the other XPointer functions, `string-range()` operates only on the `PCDATA` of the document, as if all the markup had been removed. White space in a string is matched literally, with no normalization except that provided by XML for attribute values and end of line. This function is most likely to be used with elements, but is suited for attributes, processing instructions, and comments as well. The general syntax for this function differs from the others we've seen because it requires at least two arguments and may have up to four; the last two arguments are optional.

```
string-range(location-set, searchString, index?, length?)
```

For each location in the `location-set` argument, the function returns one range for each nonoverlapping match of the substring `searchString` within the location's string value. If no `index` or `length` argument are provided, the default is that each range starts with the zero-width *character-point* (discussed in the next section) immediately before the first matched character and ends with the point immediately after last character of `searchString`. If supplied, the `index` argument indicates the position of the first character in the resulting range, relative to the start of `searchString`. The `length` argument states the number of characters in the resulting range. Markup characters within the content are ignored and therefore don't enter into the counting. You can also add node tests after `string-range()`, such as to limit the result to one instance of multiple matches.

For example, we can return *all* occurrences of "Beatles" in the document with this XPointer:

```
xpointer(string-range(/, 'Beatles'))
```

We can constrain the search to the content of specific elements by naming them as the first argument. The next XPointer returns ranges only for "Beatles" strings that appear within a `Title` element; however, it could still result in multiple ranges. If used with `collection10.xml`, it will return three ranges of seven characters, one for each match *within* the titles "Complete Beatles Chronicles, The," "Beatles Anthology, The," and "Beatles 1." Note that the function does not return the entire string content of the `Title` elements.

```
xpointer(string-range(//Title, 'Beatles'))
```

The next example returns only the third matching range of "Beatles" within a `Title` element, as the result of adding a node test. This range extends from the character point before the "B" in "Beatles 1" and ends with the character point after the "s".

```
xpointer(string-range(//Title, 'Beatles')[3])
```

As mentioned, `string-range()`supports two optional numeric arguments: the `index` into the string, the position of the first character to be in the returned range, relative to the start of the match, which is index 1, and the `length` of the string to return, which is the number of characters counted from the `index`. The default for `index` is 1 (immediately before the first character of the string) and the default for `length` is the entire length of the `searchString`. Note that the indexing is 1-relative.

For example, the next two XPointers use `index` and `length` arguments to define a collapsed range consisting of only a character-point just before and immediately after each occurrence of "Beatles" in the document, respectively. The zero `length` and the nested call within `start-point()` is what makes these collapsed ranges.

```
xpointer(start-point(string-range(/, 'Beatles', 1, 0)))
xpointer(start-point(string-range(/, 'Beatles', 8, 0)))
```

We can return a range representing the three characters that *follow* "Beatles" with this XPointer:

```
xpointer(string-range(//Title, 'Beatles', 8, 3))
```

We can also combine this string indexing with element indexing. This XPointer returns the substring "eat" from the fourth occurrence of "Beatles" in a `Title` element. The `index` 2 is the point just before the "e" and the `length` of 3 yields "eat".

```
xpointer(string-range(//Title, 'Beatles', 2, 3)[4])
```

Positioning *after* a matched string is possible using `end-point()`. The next example locates a point immediately after the second occurrence of "Beatles" in the document.

```
xpointer(end-point(string-range(/, 'Beatles')[2]))
```

In contrast to the other XPointer functions, *matches may span element boundaries* since `string-range()` operates essentially on the `PCDATA` without markup. For example,

```
xpointer(string-range(//*, 'starsCovers'))
```

matches the boldfaced words in this not well-formed fragment from our running example:

```
<Rating>5 stars</Rating>
    <Notes>
  Covers the years 1957 through 1970. <!-- etc -->
```

A location-set may consist of more than one kind of location. Previous examples have shown only homogenous location-sets. The next XPointer returns a mixed location-set, consisting of a point, a node, and a range, in that order. Note the use of the "or" symbol (|).

```
xpointer(start-point(string-range(//CD/Artist, 'Beatles')[1])
| //Book[2]/Title | string-range(//*, 'Beatles in their own words'))
```

The `string-range()` function can also locate ranges that are contained in other node types, such as attributes, processing instructions, and comments.

Node-Points and Character-Points

A **point** is a position in XML data, defined by a **container node** and a nonnegative integer which identifies the point, called the **index**. The index identifies a location that either precedes an individual character, or precedes or follows a node. The `parent` axis of a point is the container node, and the `self` axis is the point itself. Points can be either node-points or character-points.

Node-Points

If the container node can have child nodes (i.e., an element or root node), then the point is called a **node-point**. The index ranges from zero to the number of child nodes. An index of zero locates the point immediately *before* the child node. An index of `n` points to the location immediately *after* the *nth* child. Consider the following XML fragment. Node-point 0 follows the start tag `<Owner>`. Another node-point follows each end tag. These node-points are numbered in document order.

```
<Owner>
  <Name sex="male">
    <First>Ken</First>
    <Last>Sall</Last>
  </Name>|<----------------- A
  <Address>|<----------------- B
    <Street>123 Milky Way Dr.</Street>
    <City>Columbia</City>
    <State>MD</State>
    <Zip>20794</Zip>
  </Address>
</Owner>
```

We can locate the point marked "**A**" (indicated by an arrow and vertical bar) by the XPointer

```
xpointer(end-point(range(//Owner/Name)))
```

which is equivalent to:

```
xpointer(start-point(range(//Owner/Address)))
```

Similarly, we can point to the spot marked "`B`" by the expression

```
xpointer(start-point(//Address))
```

For our running example in Listing 14-1, we can indicate the point immediately after the second `CD` element with the XPointer:

```
xpointer(end-point(//CD[2]))
```

Note: Node-points use *zero-based* counting. This differs from the one-based counting of `string-range()` and other XPointer and XPath functions.

Character-Points

If the container node *cannot* have child nodes (i.e., text, attribute, comment, and processing instruction nodes), then the point is called a **character-point**. The index ranges from zero to the number of characters in the container node. An index of zero locates the point immediately *before* the first character. An index of `n` points to the location immediately *after* the *nth* character. Consider the following XML fragment, which shows the element node `Artist` containing a text node with the string "Beatles". Character-point 0 follows the start tag `<Artist>` and is immediately before the "B". Another character-point follows each character, with index 1 to 7, in this case. So character-point 1 is after the "B", 2 is after the first "e", 3 is after "a", and so on, with character-point 7 immediately after the "s".

```
<Artist>Beatles</Artist>
```

For example, to point to the position immediately before the "t" in "Beatles", use the character-point XPointer:

```
xpointer(//Artist/text()/start-point()[3])
```

We can point to the very beginning of the *value* of an attribute (but not to the attribute name) using a character-point. Given the `Owner` container element in the previous section, we can point to the string "male" (an attribute value) using this XPointer:

```
xpointer(start-point(//Owner/Name/@sex))
```

The W3C XPointer specification illustrates character- and node-points with a helpful graphic that identifies start and end points for element and text nodes. See the "Document Order" section of the specification, *http://www.w3.org/TR/xptr/#document-order-sec*.

Escaping in XPointers

As mentioned earlier, to use the characters < or & in an XPointer expression, you must escape them using `<` and `&` as we saw with XPath. This is due to their appearance in an attribute value. For example,

```
xlink:href="file.xml#xpointer(//someElement [position() &lt; 5])">
```

If you need to indicate a literal parenthesis within an XPointer expression, escape it using the circumflex ('^') character:

```
xlink:href="file.xml#xpointer(string-range('^(phrase in parentheses^)'))">
```

Of course, to use a literal circumflex in an XPointer expression, you must escape the circumflex (^^).

There are also details about URI escaping of spaces, double quotes, and non-ASCII characters presented in the specification that go beyond the scope of this book. For example,

```
xlink:href="file.xml#xpointer(string-range(//
P,%22a%20little%20hat%20%5E%5E%22))"
```

For details, see *http://www.w3.org/TR/xptr/#uri-escaping*.

XPointer Implementations

As of this writing, XPointer implementations are few and far between. The W3C site—*http://www.w3.org/XML/2000/09/LinkingImplementations.html*—and the XLink/XPointer/XML Base home page (*http://www.w3.org/XML/Linking*) list the following:

- *Amaya*—W3C's browser has partial support
- *X2X*—Empolis offers partial support
- *XLip*—Fujitsu XLink Processor by Fujitsu Laboratories, Ltd., is an implementation of XLink and XPointer
- *libxml*—the Gnome XML library has a beta implementation of XPointer
- *4XPointer*—Python-based XPointer Processor by Fourthought, Inc.

The W3C site provides links to each of these implementations. See also the XMLSoftware.com XLink/XPointer tools list at *http://www.xmlsoftware.com/xlink/*. Be sure to note the date of these implementations. Those earlier than the current version of the XPointer specification are likely to function differently than what has been described in this chapter.

Summary

XPointer, the XML Pointer Language, is used primarily with XLink as a fragment identifier for a URI, as a way to reference specific portions of an XML document.

- XPointers can locate individual XML elements, a set of related elements, a particular point between characters or between children of an element, or a range of XML data between two points.
- Like XPath, on which it is built, XPointer uses non-XML syntax.
- In contrast to XLink, which can be used with non-XML resources, XPointer can be used only with XML documents since it relies on their highly structured hierarchy.
- Besides supporting all XPath node type forms of referencing, XPointer extends XPath addressing by adding the concepts of *ranges* and *points* (corresponding to DOM Level 2 ranges and positions).
- A *point* locates a position immediately preceding or following a character or a node.
- The *container node* is the node that contains the current point.
- A *range* identifies the `PCDATA` between two points, ignoring intervening markup.
- Ranges do not necessarily result in well-formed XML; they can begin or end in the middle of character content or span incomplete element hierarchies.
- A *location* is the generalization of the XPath node concept; a location is a node, a point, or a range.
- A *location-set* is the generalization of the XPath node-set; it is the ordered list of nodes, points, and/or ranges that results from an XPointer expression.
- The general XPointer syntax involves the keyword `xpointer` in a fragment identifier of a URI: `filename#xpointer(XPointer-expression)`.
- The XPointer specification describes one full form of XPointer addressing and two shorthand forms: *full XPointer* (e.g., `#xpointer(//model[@type='707'])`), *bare-name* (e.g., `#section4`), and *child-sequence* (e.g., `#/1/2/5`).
- In addition to the XPath `id()` function, which is very useful with XPointer, the specification defines eight additional functions: `range-to()`, `string-range()`, `range()`, `range-inside()`, `start-point()`, `end-point()`, `here()`, and `origin()`.
- The functions `range-to()` and `string-range()` are particularly powerful.
- At the time of this writing, XPointer is not supported by the major browsers (except partially by Amaya) and implementations are very few.

For Further Exploration

Articles

XML Linking: State of the Art, Eve Maler [early 2001]
http://www.sun.com/software/xml/developers/xlink/

XML Linking: An Executive Summary, Eve Maler [early 2001]
http://www.sun.com/software/xml/enterprise/xlink.html

XML.com: Leigh Dodds: XPointer and the Patent (January 2001) [Controversy surrounding Sun's claim of prior art with 1997 patent]
http://www.xml.com/pub/a/2001/01/17/xpointer.html

XML.com: Leigh Dodds: Towards an XPath API (March 2001)
http://www.xml.com/pub/a/2001/03/07/xpathapi.html

xmlhack: Search for XPointer
http://xmlhack.com/search.php?q=XPointer

Historical

Text Encoding Initiative (TEI)—XML for TEI Lite, Robin Cover
http://xml.coverpages.org/tei.html

Guidelines for Electronic Text Encoding and Interchange
http://www.tei-c.org/Guidelines/index.htm

TEI Guidelines: Linking, Segmentation, and Alignment
http://www.tei-c.org/Guidelines/SA.htm

Resources

ZVON XPointer Reference
http://www.zvon.org/xxl/xpointer/refs/Output/xpointer_refs.html

WDVL: XLink and XPointer
http://wdvl.Internet.com/Authoring/Languages/XLink/

XPointer: Referencing points and ranges inside of documents, Simon St. Laurent
http://www.simonstl.com/articles/xptr/xptr.html

XLinks and XPointers, Elliotte Rusty Harold
http://www.ibiblio.org/xml/slides/xmlonesanjose2001/xlinks/

XLink, XPointer, and XPath, Anders Møller and Michael I. Schwartzbach
http://www.brics.dk/~amoeller/XML/linking/index.html

XMLSoftware.com: XLink/XPointer Tools
http://www.xmlsoftware.com/xlink/

Tutorials

ZVON XPointer Tutorial [Examples]
http://www.zvon.org/xxl/xpointer/tutorial/OutputExamples/xpointer_tut.html

XML Bible, Second Edition, Chapter 20: XPointers, Elliotte Rusty Harold
http://www.ibiblio.org/xml/books/bible2/chapters/ch20.html

W3C Specifications and Information

XML Pointer, XML Base and XML Linking
http://www.w3.org/XML/Linking

XML Pointer Language (XPointer) 1.0
http://www.w3.org/TR/xptr

XML Pointer Requirements Version 1.0
http://www.w3.org/TR/NOTE-xptr-req

XML Path Language (XPath) Version 1.0 Recommendation
http://www.w3.org/TR/xpath

XInclude Version 1.0 [Candidate Recommendation has dependency on XPointer]
http://www.w3.org/TR/xinclude

Fragment Identifiers
http://www.w3.org/Design Issues/Fragment.html

What Does a URI Identify? [TAG Draft, March 2002]
http://www.w3.org/2001/tag/doc/identify.html

Part V

Specialized XML Vocabularies

Chapter 15

XHTML: HTML for the Present and the Future

In this chapter, we'll cover Extensible HTML (XHTML), which is HTML 4 recast in XML syntax. We'll see how XHTML is a much more versatile way of presenting documents, in part because it insists on the rigor of XML, but even more important because it enables us to divide HTML into modules that can be selectively targeted for different purposes. These modules can also be extended to provide additional functionality. For example, vendors of small handheld devices may wish to support only a certain subset of XHTML, so only the modules they require need to be implemented. The W3C has no intention of extending HTML 4; all future hypertext markup efforts will be based on XHTML, which is in itself a small family of specifications, each of which is covered in this chapter. Future efforts will be devoted to markup languages based on the Modularization of XHTML and XHTML 1.1, focusing on structural functionality with stylesheets for presentation.

The XHTML Family

Extensible HyperText Markup Language (XHTML) is the general name of an ever-growing family of W3C specifications based on a reformulation of HTML in XML syntax, and also a partitioning of the language into required and optional modules. Here's the mile-high introduction to the XHTML clan:

- *XHTML 1.0*—HTML 4.01 in XML syntax
- *XHTML Basic*—minimal set of modules especially designed for limited-memory devices such as PDAs
- *Modularization of XHTML*—abstract modules that enable subsetting and extending XHTML.
- *XHTML 1.1* (Module-based XHTML)—forward-looking document type cleanly separated from the deprecated, legacy functionality of HTML 4.

- *Ruby Annotation* (an XHTML Module)—pronunciation and annotation text for Asian languages.
- *XML Events*—a generic approach for integrating event listeners and associated event handlers with DOM Level 2 event interfaces to associate behavior with markup.
- *Modularization of XHTML in XML Schema*—upgrade from DTD modules to XML Schema modules for XHTML Modularization, for all of the benefits of XML Schema over DTDs.
- *XForms*—elaboration of the capabilities of XHTML forms with a clean separation of presentation, logic, and data.
- *XHTML 2.0* (eventually)—building on XHTML 1.1 to fit the latest XML technology and to remove a priori knowledge of HTML 4.01.

Each of these specifications is defined in Table 15-1. XHTML 1.0, XHTML Basic, Modularization of XHTML, and XHTML 1.1 are covered in much more detail in this chapter.

Why Do We Need XHTML?

Way back in chapter 2, in the section called "Fixing the Web," we covered some of the problems with the Web circa 1996 to 1997 that were largely the motivation for the development of XML. Several of these shortcomings are also the motivation behind XHTML. I'll repeat a few of them here but recast them in the context of XHTML as a solution to these particular problems.

HTML standards change too slowly. HTML was defined by a fixed set of elements with little thought for targeting anything but desktop computers initially.[1] In contrast, XHTML provides a way to extend the set of elements that a user agent (browser, mobile phone, PDA, Web TV, etc.) understands. The mechanism for adding elements to a DTD or XML Schema is well defined. Extensibility is precisely what was impossible with HTML and encouraged browser vendors to invent their own (often incompatible) elements in the mid 1990s.

Browser-specific extensions are problematic. XHTML documents must be well-formed and valid with respect to one of several DTDs, as we'll soon see. Vendor-specific elements introduced by Netscape and Microsoft in the Browser Wars of the mid 1990s are essentially obsolete. As a result of modularization, it is possible to extend the language in a way that will discourage any browser vendor from imple-

1. Perhaps that's not entirely fair to Tim Berners-Lee, et al. My understanding is that the original HTML was primarily focused on document structure, but more and more presentational features, such as specific fonts and pixel-oriented measurements, found their way into the language over time.

menting its own elements in a manner inconsistent with this modular extension approach. (Time will tell, but we remain hopeful.) That is not to say that vendors won't implement their own special value-added modules, just that the whole approach to extension will be clearer and more predictable than in the past.

Presentation is fixed for monitors. XHTML defines modules that describe types of functionality, such as Core, Text Extension, Forms, Tables, Images, Imagemaps, Frames, Events, Scripting, and Object Modules. The beauty of this is that vendors of different devices need not support all modules; they need to implement only modules that are essential to the purpose of their devices. If they have no need of imagemaps, frames, or scripting, they simply do not need to implement those modules, which is a key consideration for devices with limited memory such as handhelds.

In May 1999 at WWW8, the Eighth International World Wide Web Conference, John Patrick, IBM Vice President, Internet Technology (who founded the alphaWorks Web site) predicted that by sometime in 2002, PCs will be the *minority* way to access the Web; instead, TV, mobile devices, pagers, and such will be the more common way to surf (see *http://wdvl.internet.com/Internet/Future/patrick.html*). This also has implications for content providers who can either create pages with certain devices in mind (with a clear understanding of which modules these devices do or do not support) or can author one set of pages for full browsers and perhaps just one alternate minimalistic page with only the basic modules as a lowest common denominator for several small devices.

Content changes cause problems. Everything that we learned about XSLT can be applied to XHTML. Unlike HTML documents, well-structured XHTML documents are XML and can be filtered and transformed by XSLT, making sitewide changes less difficult. Especially if the presentational kinds of markup (fonts, colors, and so on) are relegated strictly to CSS style sheets, frequent content changes need not be as problematic, even when the content is targeted for several kinds of devices.

Sloppy HTML causes browser bloat. One of the (arguably) most unfortunate things about HTML was the decision to make browsers remain silent about malformed documents, to quietly ignore missing end tags, improper element nesting, unrecognized elements, and attributes, and many other transgressions. While browser silence was undoubtedly beneficial since it was instrumental in the quick adoption of HTML and the equally quick growth in popularity of the Web as a whole, it also contributed to the false idea that anyone could learn HTML in sixty minutes. Certainly there are millions of pages out there that were written by people who didn't take much more time than that to learn the language. It's a well-established fact that every major browser has a huge proportion of its code (as much as half) devoted to error recovery and workarounds for common HTML blunders. Of course, these "detours" are not necessarily identical across browsers, so some pages "work better" with one browser than another, the use of browser-specific tags aside. This is another way XHTML can be a big win. Since XHTML *is* XML, documents must be well-formed and since they reference a DTD, they must also be valid. This means that the XML parser built in to the browser can (and must) immediately report most kinds of errors to which HTML parsers have turned a blind eye (or silent lips). In the long run, that will mean that XML browsers can be much more compact than today's HTML browsers, yet they will not have to implement additional code to work around poorly structured documents (those that aren't valid against any of the three XHTML 1.0 DTDs).

That is especially good news for developers of limited-memory devices. It is also good news for content developers who can anticipate very predictable parsing of their XHTML in the near future. Any errors in their markup will be known to them before they post their documents on their server and they can be assured that once they ensure the validity of their documents, they will be treated identically by all XML parsers, ignoring CSS differences, that is.

Even more good news is that XHTML can be used today in Netscape 4.x and 6.x, Internet Explorer 5.x and 6.x, Opera 5.x and 6.x, and other major browsers by following several conventions presented in the XHTML 1.0 specification and discussed in detail in this chapter.

Overlap of XHTML Family

I think it's helpful to envision the XHTML family as a series of partially overlapping and partially concentric circles, roughly indicating which spec implements a subset or superset of the elements of another. As shown in Figure 15-1, a so-called **XHTML Host Language** is the smallest subset, consisting of just four core modules: Structure, Text, Hypertext, and Lists. The slightly larger XHTML Basic language is the smallest collection of modules that is presently called an XHTML Host Language. It adds modules for Images, Basic Forms, Basic Tables, and Objects. XHTML 1.0 Strict includes everything that is in XHTML Basic plus elements for more sophisticated forms and tables, client-side imagemaps, and miscellaneous legacy HTML 4.0 features that weren't deprecated. XHTML 1.0 Transitional includes everything in XHTML 1.0 Strict, as well as all the elements and attributes that were deprecated in HTML 4.0, such as `applet`, `center`, `dir`, `font`, `isindex`, `menu`, `bgcolor`, `target`, and many others. XHTML 1.0 Frameset is essentially the same as Transitional, except that it adds frame-related elements and attributes. XHTML 1.1 is basically XHTML 1.0 Strict plus the Ruby Module and a few more elements. The exact constituents of XHTML 2.0 are unknown at this time but it almost certainly will be a superset of XTHML 1.1.

The diagram omits several of the specs listed in Table 15-1 chiefly because they aren't really languages. The most notable omission is Modularization of XHTML, which is the basis of XHTML 1.1. Modules that are not part of XHTML 1.1,

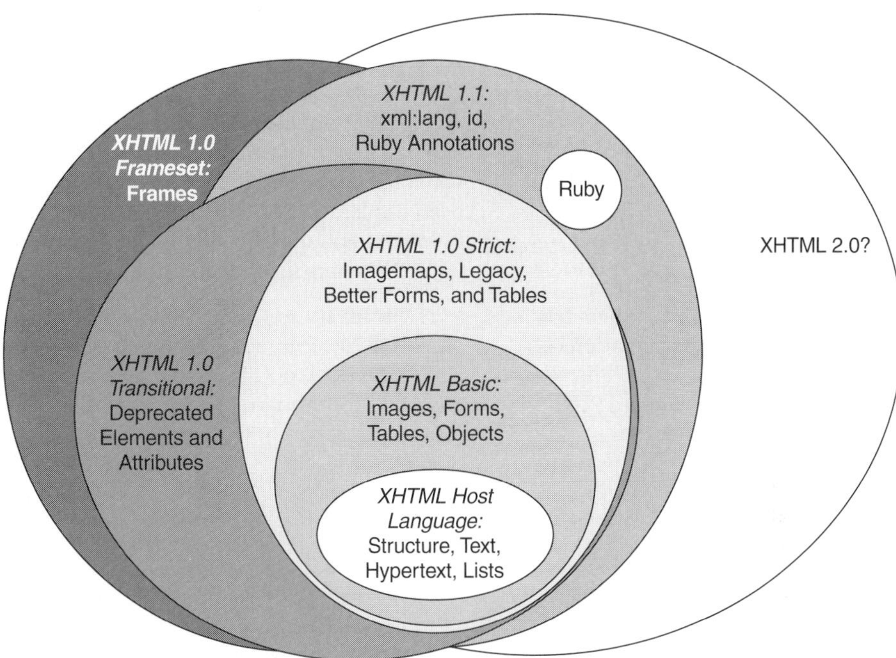

FIGURE 15-1 Overlap of XHTML Family

although they are defined in Modularization of XHTML, include Applet, Frames, Iframes, Target, Basic Forms and Basic Tables, Name Identification, and Legacy Modules (deprecated elements and attributes). It may be useful to think of Modularization of XHTML as a superset of XHTML 1.1 but not necessarily a subset of XHTML 2.0, which will almost certainly not contain the Legacy Module.

Relevant Specifications: The XHTML Family

Within the larger XML family of specifications, XHTML has its own little clan. Table 15-1 lists all the card-carrying members at this time, but more may be added in the near future.

At the time of this writing, HTML 4.01, XHTML 1.0, XHTML Basic, Modularization of XHTML, and XHTML 1.1 are completed W3C Recommendations; XForms 1.0, XML Events, and Modularization of XHTML in XML Schema are still Working Drafts, which means they are works in progress and subject to change. No public version of XHTML 2.0 exists at this time.

TABLE 15-1 XHTML Family of Specifications in Chronological Order

Specification and URL	*Description*
HTML 4.01 Specification (W3C Recommendation, December 1999, a revision of the December 1997 HTML 4.0 Recommendation) *http://www.w3.org/TR/html401/*	Most recent update to HyperText Markup Language. Very likely to be the last version called "HTML" since future versions will be based on XHTML. Most features have been implemented in the major browsers with some unfortunate exceptions (e.g., lack of `id` attribute support for named anchors in Netscape 4.x).
XHTML 1.0: The Extensible HyperText Markup Language: A Reformulation of HTML 4 in XML 1.0 (W3C Recommendation, January 2000; Second Edition, October 2001) *http://www.w3.org/TR/xhtml1/*	XHTML 1.0 is a recasting of HTML 4.01 in XML syntax, based on any of three DTDs that correspond to the three HTML DTDs: Strict, Transitional, and Frameset. The spec describes conformance requirements, how XHTML and HTML differ, and how to use XHTML in today's browsers. It is the earliest basis for a family of document types that subset and extend HTML.
XHTML Basic (W3C Recommendation, December 2000) *http://www.w3.org/TR/xhtml-basic/*	XHTML Basic is a stripped-down version of XHTML 1.1 that is targeted for small devices with limited memory ("thin clients" such as mobile phones, PDAs, pagers, and settop boxes). It defines the minimal set of modules (structure, text, hypertext, and lists) required to be an *XHTML Host Language* document type, and then adds support for images, basic forms, basic tables, and objects. XHTML Basic also provides a simple, common base that can be extended by the addition of other modules. This is crucial for its adoption for use in thin clients; it must be simple enough by omitting unnecessary aspects of XHTML 1.0 or 1.1, yet flexible enough to add custom modules, and rich enough to provide a reasonable content-authoring language. It relies on XHTML module implementations defined in Modularization of XHTML.
Modularization of XHTML (W3C Recommendation, April 2001) *http://www.w3.org/TR/xhtml-modularization/*	This specification describes a modular approach to XHTML which subsets the language into a large number of nonoverlapping "abstract modules," each of which is semantically unique. The abstractions are implemented by DTDs with plans to migrate to XML Schema. Each implementation module describes groups of elements, attributes, and content models based on functionality. XHTML 1.0/HTML 4.01 is decomposed into roughly 40 modules. All of the deprecated elements and attributes of HTML 4.01 have been removed from these modules or relegated to the "legacy" module. Presentational elements are separated from structural elements. The result is well suited for XML since languages that are purely structural can be defined from these modules, leaving presentation to stylesheets.

TABLE 15-1 *(continued)*

Specification and URL	*Description*
Modularization of XHTML *(continued)*	Modularization enables subsetting and extending XHTML for special-purpose devices. Modularizing XHTML helps product designers to specify which elements are supported by a device using standard building blocks. It also helps content providers to deliver content to a large number and wide range of platforms. Modularization paves the way for developers to augment the language with client-specific or document-specific markup. This modularization approach is already in use in MathML, Internationalization, Synchronized Multimedia, the WAP Forum, and OASIS, among others.
XHTML 1.1—Module-based XHTML (W3C Recommendation, May 2001) *http://www.w3.org/TR/xhtml11/*	XHTML 1.1 is essentially a reformulation of XHTML 1.0 Strict using Modularization of XHTML plus a Ruby Module for other character sets. The DTD separates XHTML 1.1 and versions that follow it from the deprecated, legacy functionality of HTML 4.01 (the basis for XHTML 1.0). For example, the `id` attribute replaces `name`, and `xml:lang` replaces `lang`. Since it is built using the modular framework that supports extension, the XHTML 1.1 document type is the basis for future extended XHTML "family" document types.
Ruby Annotation (W3C Recommendation, May 2001) *http://www.w3.org/TR/ruby/*	"Ruby" annotations are short runs of text next to or above regular text, typically used in Japanese and Chinese documents to indicate pronunciation or to provide a short annotation. This specification defines a ruby XHTML module that can, in addition to its usefulness for Asian languages, also be used to mark up acronyms in any language.
XML Events—An Events Syntax for XML (W3C Last Call Working Draft, October 2001) *http://www.w3.org/TR/xml-events/*	This is a work in progress; details may change. XML Events describes an approach for integrating event listeners and associated event handlers with DOM Level 2 event interfaces to associate behavior with markup. The specification defines a `<listener>` element and several global attributes which, as in XLink, can be attached to any element in your vocabulary. The `<listener>` element supports a subset of the DOM's `EventListener` interface by declaring event listeners and registering them with specific nodes in the DOM. Attributes are `event`, `observer`, `target`, `handler`, `phase`, `propagate`, `defaultAction`, and `id`. Design goals include syntactically exposing the DOM event model to an XML document and providing for new event types without requiring modification to the DOM or the DTD.

continued

TABLE 15-1 XHTML Family of Specifications in Chronological Order (*continued*)

Specification and URL	*Description*
XML Events—An Events Syntax for XML (*continued*)	An earlier working draft called "*XHTML* Events—An updated events syntax for *XHTML* and friends" was substantially different.
Modularization of XHTML in XML Schema (W3C Working Draft, December 2001) *http://www.w3.org/TR/xhtml-m12n-schema/*	This is a work in progress. This specification uses XML Schema rather than DTDs to implement the same abstract modules as the earlier Modularization of XHTML Recommendation. As with the DTD implementation, this one includes a set of schema modules that conform to the abstract modules in XHTML plus conventions that describe the interplay of individual modules, and how they can be modified or extended. While this description is subject to potentially substantial change, this approach defines an XML Schema that includes *required* schema modules (divided into *framework* and *core* modules, including datatypes, common attributes, character entities, text, hypertext, lists, ruby, structural, etc.) and about two dozen *optional* schema modules (presentational, link, style, scripting, images, tables, forms, etc.).
XForms 1.0 (W3C Working Draft, December 2001) *http://www.w3.org/TR/xforms/*	The next generation of Web forms based on XML syntax that decouples data, logic (purpose), and presentation. This separation enables the targeting of forms for devices with very different user interfaces, such as handhelds, television, and desktop browsers, plus printers and scanners. XForms consist of the data model (composite datatypes and constraints), the user interface widgets, and XML data transmitted with the form. The datatypes used in XForms are based on XML Schema: Part 2 although in some cases, they differ. Form input is expressed as structured XML instance data. Support for advanced form logic, multipage forms, suspend and resume, and easy integration with other XML vocabularies (especially XHTML and SVG) are some of the goals of XForms. *Note:* XForms is not an acronym and should never be used in the singular form.
XHTML 2.0—No public Working Draft at the time of this writing; can guess that the URL will be *http://www.w3.org/TR/xhtml2*	Superset of XHTML 1.1 altered semantically and syntactically to conform to the requirements of related XML standards such as XML Linking and XML Schema. Expected to have no a priori knowledge of HTML linking, imagemaps, forms, etc.

The best pages for staying current with the rapidly growing XHTML family are these W3C entry points:

- *HyperText Markup Language Home Page*—the original HTML home page of the Web; includes HTML, XHTML, and lots of other useful related links (*http://www.w3.org/MarkUp/*)
- *HTML Working Group Roadmap*—a "work in progress" timeline of future deliverables and milestones already achieved (*http://www.w3.org/MarkUp/xhtml-roadmap/*)
- *XHTML Modularization: An Overview*—gentle and informative three-and-a-half page overview (*http://www.w3.org/MarkUp/modularization*)
- *HyperText Markup Language Activity Statement*—summarizes work of HTML Working Group and XForms Working Group (*http://www.w3.org/MarkUp/Activity*)

Table 15-1 is largely based on material presented on those pages. Another central location for learning about XHTML is a site called XHTML.org at *http://www.xhtml.org/*, which is not affiliated with the W3C.

XHTML 1.0

The first family member we'll visit is also the first one finalized by the W3C way back in January 2000. XHTML 1.0 is a recasting of HTML 4.01 in XML syntax (*http://www.w3.org/TR/xhtml1/*). XHTML 1.0 lets you select from three DTDs that correspond to the three earlier HTML 4.01 DTDs: Strict, Transitional, and Frameset. The spec describes conformance requirements, how XHTML and HTML differ, and how to use XHTML in today's browsers. XHTML 1.0 marked the beginning of the trend to develop document types that subset and extend HTML. It does not, however, contain the *smallest* set of elements, as we'll see, and it is not modular.

Strictly Conforming XHTML Documents

According to the W3C, a conforming XHTML 1.0 document must meet several criteria:

1. It must validate against one of three DTDs:
   - *XHTML 1.0 Strict*—No deprecated elements or attributes allowed; *subset* of XHTML 1.0 Transitional; you are encouraged by W3C to use this DTD whenever possible; somewhat labor-intensive for high-end Web sites to comply with because it disallows many frequently used HTML 4.01 features.
   - *XHTML 1.0 Transitional*—Permits deprecated elements and attributes; it is more likely that most Web sites will use this in the near term.
   - *XHTML 1.0 Frameset*—Same as Transitional except `<body>` is replaced by `<frameset>` and other frame-related elements and attributes are added.

2. The document element must be `<html>` and it must be lowercase.
3. The `<html>` document element must reference the XHTML namespace, which must be exactly this URI: *http://www.w3.org/1999/xhtml*.
4. The document must contain a `DOCTYPE` declaration before the `<html>` document element. The **formal public identifier** (FPI) must reference one of the three DTDs:

```
<!DOCTYPE html
    PUBLIC "-//W3C//DTD XHTML 1.0 Strict//EN"
    "http://www.w3.org/TR/xhtml1/DTD/xhtml1-strict.dtd">
<!DOCTYPE html
    PUBLIC "-//W3C//DTD XHTML 1.0 Transitional//EN"
    "http://www.w3.org/TR/xhtml1/DTD/xhtml1-transitional.dtd">
<!DOCTYPE html
    PUBLIC "-//W3C//DTD XHTML 1.0 Frameset//EN"
    "http://www.w3.org/TR/xhtml1/DTD/xhtml1-frameset.dtd">
```

   To prevent a potential bottleneck as browsers all over the world attempt to validate XHTML documents by accessing the DTDs from the W3C site, you are free to download the DTDs and install them on your Web server, and change the system identifier to match the installation location. For example:

```
<!DOCTYPE html
    PUBLIC "-//W3C//DTD XHTML 1.0 Transitional//EN"
    "DTD/xhtml1-transitional.dtd">
```

More likely, browser vendors will decide to build in all three DTDs so a remote access is never needed. However, it's not clear how they will identify which DTD to use, unless they base that decision on the final portion of the URI (e.g., `xhtml1-strict.dtd`). Browsers would be unlikely to validate extensions, except perhaps their own.

Simple XHTML Example

Listing 15-1 presents an example of a minimal XHTML document (`minimal-xhtml.html`) that validates against W3C's copy of the XHTML 1.0 Strict DTD, `xhtml1-strict.dtd`. It also validates against the XHTML 1.0 Transitional DTD, which is a superset of XHTML 1.0 Strict. We'll learn an easy way to validate a little later in this chapter.

Listing 15-1 Simple XHTML 1.0 Strict Example (minimal-xhtml.html)

```
<?xml version="1.0" encoding="UTF-8"?>
<!DOCTYPE html
    PUBLIC "-//W3C//DTD XHTML 1.0 Strict//EN"
    "http://www.w3.org/TR/xhtml1/DTD/xhtml1-strict.dtd">
<html xmlns="http://www.w3.org/1999/xhtml" xml:lang="en" lang="en">
  <head>
    <title>XHTML 1.0</title>
  </head>
```

```
  <body>
    <h1>Simple XHTML 1.0 Strict Example</h1>
    <p>See the <a href="http://www.w3.org/TR/xhtml1/DTD/xhtml1-
strict.dtd">DTD</a>.</p>
  </body>
</html>
```

Note that the example meets all the criteria for strict conformance.[2] The document element is `<html>`, it references `http://www.w3.org/1999/xhtml`, the XHTML namespace, and it validates against the DTD. (The W3C uses the term "Strictly Conforming XHTML Document," which does not imply that the XHTML 1.0 *Strict* DTD is referenced, although it does happen to do so in this example.)

The document also begins with the optional XML declaration; the W3C recommends that you always include such a declaration. While both the `xml:lang` and `lang` attributes appear in the root element, we'll see that's not true for all members of the XHTML family; most allow *only* `xml:lang`. Both are used to distinguish between country-specific terms (e.g., bathroom vs. loo) and alternative spellings, as well as language-specific prompts. A slightly contrived example follows, which includes both British and US variations of a shopping list. The idea is that an application can selectively display or otherwise process content wrapped in an element that has an `xml:lang` attribute value that matches the user's preferred language. See the section "xml:lang" in chapter 5.

```
<ToDo>
  <ShoppingList xml:lang="en-GB">
    <Item>crisps</Item>
    <Item>bangers</Item>
    <Item>biscuits</Item>
    <Item>maize</Item>
    <Item>tin of mince</Item>
  </ShoppingList>
  <ShoppingList xml:lang="en-US">
    <Item>potato chips</Item>
    <Item>sausages</Item>
    <Item>cookies</Item>
    <Item>corn</Item>
    <Item>can of chopped beef</Item>
  </ShoppingList>
</ToDo>
```

While `minimal-xhtml.html` isn't going to win any Web design awards, it can be displayed in current browsers such Netscape 6.x, Netscape 4.7x, Internet Explorer 6.x, Internet Explorer 5.5, Opera 5.x, and Amaya 4.3.x. Figure 15-2 shows the terribly exciting result in Netscape 6.2.

2. It also is *well-formed*, which we've learned is the minimal requirement for calling the document XML. Well-formedness is one of the differences discussed in detail in the upcoming section "Differences between XHTML 1.0 and HTML 4.01."

FIGURE 15-2 Display of Simple XHTML 1.0 in Netscape 6 (minimal-xhtml.html)

Since the document contains the optional XML declaration, we can simply change the file extension to ".xml" and display `minimal-xhtml.xml` in various browsers again. The results in Netscape 6 are identical to those shown in Figure 15-2. However, Internet Explorer 5.5 uses its own built-in stylesheet to render XML in its typical tree view, as shown in Figure 15-3. Internet Explorer 6.x also displays the file with the ".xml" extension in a tree view, but when the ".html" extension is used, the file is displayed as in the Netscape case (Figure 15-2). Both Netscape 6.x and Internet Explorer 6.x correctly report invalid XHTML. Try `minimal-xhtml-invalid.xml`.

Next we'll see how XHTML and HTML differ in some subtle—and some not so subtle—ways. After that, we'll see a more interesting example as we start with a pretty sloppy (and invalid) HTML document and see how we can convert it to a valid XHTML 1.0 document with relatively little effort, provided that we understand these differences.

Three Flavors of XHTML 1.0 DTDs: Which Should You Use?

Earlier, I mentioned the three DTD choices you have to identify an XHTML 1.0 document type. Each of these is an XML DTD version of a similarly named HTML 4.01

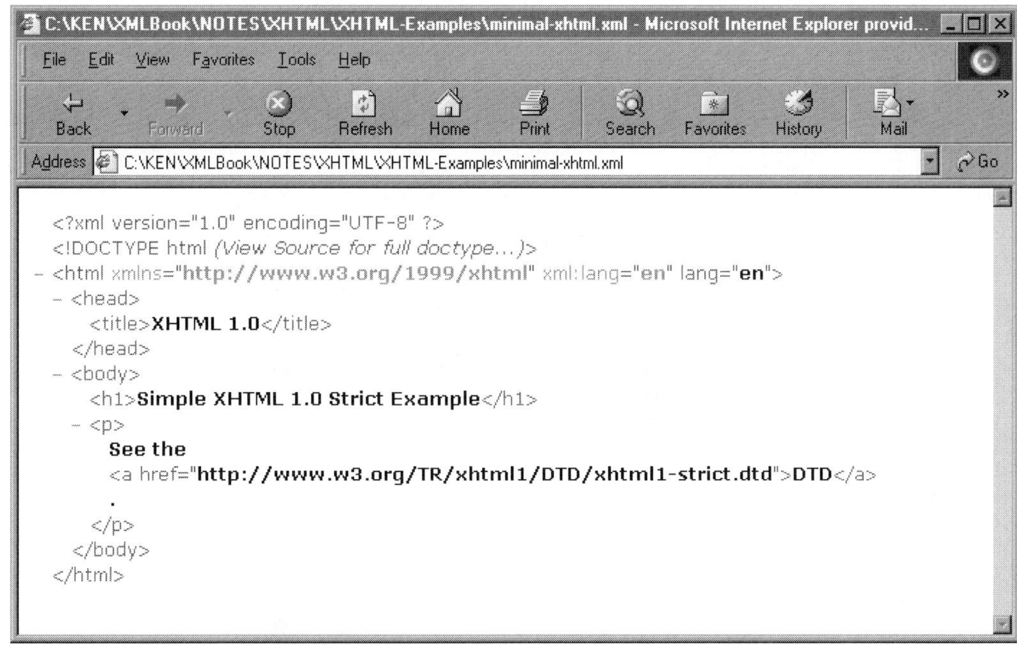

FIGURE 15-3 Display of Simple XHTML 1.0 in IE 5.5 (minimal-xhtml.xml)

DTD (which are SGML DTDs). The exact differences among the three DTDs is not spelled out in the text of the XHTML 1.0 specification. Apparently, developers are supposed to figure out these subtleties by either studying the DTDs or poring over the results of a validator. Therefore, I've used the UNIX `diff` command to compare the Transitional and Strict DTDs to create Table 15-2. The table lists elements and attributes you can use with the Transitional DTD but not with the Strict DTD. The closest reference I've found on the W3C site are the two HTML 4.01 tables of elements and attributes that contain columns marked "deprecated" (see *http://www.w3.org/TR/html401/index/elements.html* and *http://www.w3.org/TR/html401/index/attributes.html*). Essentially, *XHTML 1.0 Strict deletes all elements and attributes that were deprecated in HTML 4.01*, whereas XHTML 1.0 Transitional still permits them. XHTML 1.0 Frameset is the same as Transitional with the addition of all frame-related elements and attributes and the `frameset` element taking the place of `body`. When we study Modularization of XHTML later in this chapter, we'll see that the deprecated elements and attributes that distinguish XHTML 1.0 Transitional and Strict are relegated to something called the Legacy Module in the modularization approach.

Which DTD you use depends entirely upon your immediate needs. If you have lots of Web pages that use many of the elements or attributes shown in Table 15-2, of course it would be extremely tedious and time prohibitive to use XHTML 1.0

TABLE 15-2 Forbidden Elements and Attributes in XHTML 1.0 Strict

Element	*Attributes Deleted*
`applet`, `basefont`, `center`, `dir`, `font`, `isindex`, `menu`, `frame`, `frameset`, `iframe`, `noframes`, `s`, `strike`, `u`	These deprecated elements from HTML 4.01 have been deleted from the XHTML 1.0 Strict DTD. *They simply cannot be used in XHTML 1.0 Strict documents.* Note especially the prohibition about `font` and `center` which should be replaced by CSS stylesheets. CSS properties can also be used in place of the `align` attribute for many elements. In place of `applet`, use `object`, which is more general. If you need `frame`, you cannot use the XHTML 1.0 Strict DTD; use the XHTML 1.0 Frameset.
`a`	`target` (This could be a problem for many sites that create new windows when users click on links.)
`area`	`target`
`base`	`target`
`body`	`bgcolor`, `text`, `link`, `vlink`, `alink`
`br`	`clear`
`caption`	`align`
`div`	`align`
`dl`	`compact`
`form`	`target`
`h1`, `h2`, `h3`, `h4`, `h5`, `h6`	`align`
`hr`	`align`, `noshade`, `size`
`img`	`align`, `border`, `hspace`, `vspace`, `name`
`li`	`type`, `value`
`link`	`target`
`object`	`align`, `border`, `hspace`, `vspace`
`ol`	`compact`, `type`, `start`
`param`	`name` (changed from `#REQUIRED` to `#IMPLIED`)
`pre`	`width`
`script`	`language`
`table`	`align`, `bgcolor`
`td`	`nowrap`, `bgcolor`, `width`, `height`
`th`	`nowrap`, `bgcolor`, `width`, `height`
`ul`	`compact`, `type`

Strict. In that case, using the Transitional DTD makes more sense, unless your site makes heavy use of frames, in which case you'll need XHTML 1.0 Frameset. If your user base consists of people with older browser versions who cannot or will not upgrade, then you are also locked into Transitional (or Frameset). Of course, to be compatible with XML, you'll eventually need to convert your pages to remove deprecated elements and attributes, so keep XHTML 1.0 Strict as a goal in mind.

On the other hand, if you are creating a new site or beginning a new project, it may make sense to seriously consider using the Strict DTD since it eliminates all of the elements and attributes that have been deprecated in HTML 4.0 since the ancient days of December 1997. It's also very clear that these deprecated elements and attributes are being discouraged by the W3C and will not be supported in future W3C languages. In particular, they aren't part of XHTML Basic, so if you want Web pages that will work fine on mobile phones, for example, you need to stop using the forbidden elements and attributes shown in the table.

Differences between XHTML 1.0 and HTML 4.01

Now that we have some idea what the beginning of an XHTML document looks like in terms of the `DOCTYPE` declaration, the document element, and the XHTML namespace, we need to better understand the changes that are necessary for an HTML document to survive the rigorous scrutiny of a validating XML parser. In order for an HTML 4.01 document to be both a well-formed and valid XHTML 1.0 document, you have to make all the changes in this section. (Don't despair; there's a very handy utility called Tidy that makes this easy. We'll cover Tidy in the next section.)

Wherever possible, I've shown how something could appear in HTML and how it must be in XHTML 1.0. The information in this section is based on "Differences with HTML 4" and "Appendix C. HTML Compatibility Guidelines" of the XHTML 1.0 Recommendation see *http://www.w3.org/TR/xhtml1/#diffs* and *http://www.w3.org/TR/xhtml1/#guidelines*.

Well-Formedness

Documents must be well-formed; elements must be properly nested (no overlapping). Browsers are notoriously forgiving about sloppy HTML and go to great lengths to silently fix (or ignore) mistakes such as overlapping. With XHTML, there is no forgiveness since XML that isn't well-formed will not be displayed. That is, if it's not well-formed, it's not XML, and therefore not XHTML.

HTML:
```
<B>Example of <I>improper nesting</B></I> of start and end
tags.
```
XHTML:
```
<B>Example of <I>improper nesting</I></B> of start and end
tags.
```

Lowercase Elements and Attributes

Element and attribute names must always be lowercase. In HTML, you can use uppercase, lowercase, or even mixed case for element names and attributes; start and end tags don't even need to match in case distinction. The enforced convention in XHTML is *lowercase for elements and attributes*; there are no exceptions. (However, DTDs use the same case conventions for keywords such as ELEMENT and ATTLIST that we covered in chapter 4.)

```
HTML:   <A HRef="htt://www.ex.com/index.html">See it now</a>
XHTML:  <a href="htt://www.ex.com/index.html">See it now</a>
```

End Tags

End tags are always required except for empty elements. HTML permits optional end tags[3] such as </P>, </LI>, </BODY>, </DD>, </DT>, </TD>, and </TR>. However, in XHTML, these end tags are *required* since their content models do not specify EMPTY.

```
HTML:   <P>This is a paragraph.
XHTML:  <p>This is a paragraph.</p>
```

Quoted Attribute Values

Attribute values must always be quoted, even if they are numeric. HTML does not require quotation marks surrounding attribute values unless they contain white space. For that reason, many content providers don't quote numeric attribute values or even single word values. In XHTML, all attribute values must be quoted. As usual with XML, either single or double quotes are permitted.

```
HTML:   <IMG src="http://gernhardt.com/beatles/beatles3.jpg"
        border=1 width=333 height=267  alt="Harald Gernhardt's
        Beatles Site">
XHTML:  <img src="http://gernhardt.com/beatles/beatles3.jpg"
        border="1" width="333" height="267"  alt="Harald
        Gernhardt's Beatles Site" />
```

Attribute Minimization

Attribute minimization is not permitted; attribute-value pairs must be explicitly stated. **Attribute minimization** is the SGML and HTML rule that says that boolean attributes may appear in minimized form—the attribute's name appears alone in the element's start tag. The mere presence of the attribute name indicates the "true" value (enabled). For example, in HTML the start tag <OPTION selected="selected"> is often minimized to <OPTION selected>. The list of sometimes minimized attributes

3. For a complete list of HTML 4.01 elements that, among other things, indicates in which cases end tags are optional, see *http://www.w3.org/TR/html401/ index/elements.html*.

is `compact`, `nowrap`, `ismap`, `declare`, `noshade`, `checked`, `disabled`, `readonly`, `multiple`, `selected`, `noresize`, and `defer`. In XHTML, however, this is not permitted since attribute names and values always appear as a pair. Just use the non-minimized form by supplying the attribute name as its value.

```
HTML:   <DL compact>
XHTML:  <dl compact="compact">
```

Empty Elements

Empty elements require a terminating tag, either `<foo />` *or* `<foo></foo>`. When an element is defined to have an `EMPTY` content model, there is no special syntax to denote this in HTML. Empty elements such as `<HR>` simply appear as a normal start tag without a matching end tag. Browsers have hard-coded rules about which HTML elements are empty. However, in XHTML you *must* use either the start/end tag pair with nothing between the tags, or the abbreviated empty element syntax `<foo />`. (Recall that both forms are canonically equivalent.)

```
HTML:   <HR> <IMG src="file.jpg"> <BR>
XHTML:  <hr /> <img src="file.jpg" /> <br />
```

While `<hr/>`, `<br/>`, and such are acceptable empty element syntax in XML, you really should add a space before the slash as shown above. This is essentially a kludge so that pre-XHTML-aware browsers will recognize the empty element. Some browsers may handle either form, but it's safer to include the space. Furthermore, you should use the so-called minimized tag syntax for empty elements (e.g., `<br />`) instead of the alternative syntax `<br></br>` because some browsers will not recognize the latter.

White Space

In elements where the `xml:space` *attribute is set to* `preserve`, *the user agent (e.g., browser) must leave all white space characters intact.* Otherwise, white space surrounding block elements is removed; leading and trailing white space inside a block element is removed; sequence of multiple white space characters are reduced to a single space. For attribute values, user agents map sequences of multiple white spaces (including line breaks) to a single interword space. White space is normalized in XHTML. See "User Agent Conformance" in the XHTML 1.0 Recommendation (*http://www.w3.org/TR/xhtml1/#uaconf*).

```
HTML:   <IMG ... alt="   Visit  PLUGGED - The Unoffical  McCartney
        home page  ">
XHTML:  <img ... alt=" Visit PLUGGED - The Unoffical McCartney home
        page " />
```

script and style Elements

Wrapping the content of the `<script>` *and* `<style>` *elements within a* `CDATA` *section avoids problems with < and & being interpreted as the character entities* `<` *and* `&`. This is a very tough guideline to follow with browsers as of early 2002! It indicates that you should replace JavaScript references that contain < or & such as:

```
<script language="JavaScript" type="text/javascript">
function doIt()
{
    var foo = 3;
    if (foo < 8 )
        alert("Help!");
    else
        alert("I'm Down");
}
</script>
```

with this alternative:

```
<script language="JavaScript" type="text/javascript">
<![CDATA[
function doIt()
{
    var foo = 3;
    if (foo < 8 )
        alert("Help!");
    else
        alert("I'm Down");
}
]]>
</script>
```

The expectation is that using the `CDATA` section should keep XML parsers happy so they won't complain about a well-formedness error when they encounter the < sign, and at the same time the JavaScript code should be honored as a valid function. Results with Netscape 6.2, Netscape 4.79, Internet Explorer 5.5, Opera 6.0, and Amaya 5.3 were disappointing. Unfortunately, of these major browsers, the only one that understands `CDATA` sections in this context is W3C's own Amaya browser (which doesn't support JavaScript). This is because Amaya's XML parser follows the rule that says < is forbidden within `#PCDATA` content (e.g., inside `<script>` or `<style>`) if not escaped by a `CDATA` section. The other browsers complained about a JavaScript syntax error, said the function `doIt()` was not defined, or silently failed when the JavaScript was executed. Therefore, *the best detour for now is to move JavaScript or CSS code into separate files* and then reference them so that special characters aren't parsed as XML. For example, if you remove the `doIt()` function from the XHTML document and place it in a separate file named `foo.js`, you can reduce the <script> tag to a reference to the external script:

```
<script language="JavaScript" type="text/javascript" src="foo.js" />
```

Note that the old HTML trick of hiding JavaScript from old browsers using a comment doesn't particularly help here because XML parsers are free to discard comments. Therefore, the following is *not* recommended for XHTML:

```
<script language="JavaScript" type="text/javascript">
<!-- Hide from ancient browsers
function doIt()
{
    var foo = 3;
    if (foo < 8 )
        alert("Help!");
    else
        alert("I'm Down");
}
// end hiding -->
</script>
```

Similar caveats apply to the use of the <style> element. If your <style> content contains special characters, it is best to use an external stylesheet and include it using the <link> element, as discussed in chapter 10 (CSS).

SGML Exclusions

SGML exclusions (elements that can't be children of given elements) aren't possible to express in XML but they are listed in the XHTML specification. Certain elements are not permitted to contain particular children. For example, the `pre` element cannot contain the `img`, `object`, `big`, `small`, `sub`, or `sup` elements. The complete list of element prohibitions can be found at *http://www.w3.org/TR/xhtml1/#prohibitions*. Except for those concerning the `pre` element, the exclusions are chiefly unlikely situations.

name Attribute

Elements with the `name` *attribute need to use the* `id` *instead (or in addition to* `name`). This is another sticky issue for XHTML that can cause you grief if you aren't careful. As we discussed in the XLink and XPointer chapters, the HTML 4.0 element <a> (anchor) can be used as a fragment identifier for a URI by associating the `name` attribute with destination of the named anchor. However, the `name` attribute isn't sufficient for XML (or XHTML) because a fragment identifier pertains to an attribute of type `ID`. Now, HTML 4.0 added an attribute called `id` to the <a> element (as well as to all others that had a `name` attribute) but some HTML browsers do not yet recognize the `id` attribute.[4] This means that although in HTML 4.0 and XHTML 1.0 you *should* be able to simply say

```
<a id="section4">Part 4</a>
```

instead (at least for the near future) you should *use the redundant form with both attributes* `id` *and* `name` *set to exactly the same value:*

```
<a id="section4" name="section4">Part 4</a>
```

To further complicate the problem, the `name` attribute originally was of type `CDATA`, which is fairly unrestricted. A general XML constraint is that there can only be a single attribute of type `ID` per element. In XHTML 1.0 the `id` attribute is defined to be of type `ID`. The `name` attribute was therefore changed to type `NMTOKEN` to avoid the XML conflict.[5] However, since the `id` attribute of type `ID` is slightly more restrictive and cannot have a value that begins with a digit, for example, it is entirely possible that an existing document may have a `name` attribute with a value that is not compatible for an `id` and will need to be changed. For example,

```
<a id="4thSection" name="4thSection">Part 4</a>
```

is not valid XML. Although "4thSection" is acceptable as a `NMTOKEN`, it isn't valid for type `ID`. Since both `name` and `id` must match, effectively they both must begin with a letter.

This `name` and `id` attribute problem pertains not only to the `a` element, but also to the elements `applet`, `form`, `frame`, `iframe`, `img`, and `map` as well. *XHTML 1.0 documents must use the* `id` *attribute when defining fragment identifiers*, even with elements that traditionally defined a `name` attribute, such as these.

4. Notably Netscape 4.79 and any earlier version. Fortunately, this is fixed in Netscape 6.2. Using only the `id` attribute is also sufficient for IE 5.5, IE 6, Opera 6, and Amaya 5.3 (and probably earlier versions of these browsers). If you've ever used Netscape 4.7x to browse W3C specs (as I have once or twice ;-), you probably noticed that sometimes clicking on items in the table of contents or other internal links does not work and sometimes it does. The failures are always because the document's editors chose to use *only* the `id` attribute for the named anchor destination. The XHTML 1.0 spec uses both `id` and `name` (so the table of contents works in Netscape 4.7x), but XHTML 1.1 and later specs use *only* `id`, as perhaps a not-so-subtle reminder from W3C that the `name` attribute truly is no longer supported for an anchor.

5. Incidentally, don't be confused by the fact that the type of the `name` attribute varies across different elements! For `a`, `object`, and `map`, the type of `name` is `NMTOKEN`. However, for `meta`, `param`, `input`, `select`, `textarea`, and `button`, the type is still `CDATA`. An attribute by any other `name` should smell just as sweet ;-)

Sloppy HTML Example

We've seen a trivial example of a valid XHTML 1.0 Strict document. But what if you know your Web site has hundreds of pages and quite likely a large portion of them consist of HTML that is not exactly up to snuff, possibly not even with HTML 4.01 Transitional? How do you go from malformed HTML to valid XHTML? Let's consider an example that breaks most of the rules that we learned in the last section. I've created this example deliberately to illustrate some of the sloppy HTML that current browsers will silently accept and render as if they were correct. Our original input file is called `bad-ex.html`, shown in Listing 15-2 with line numbers that we'll be referencing. I've used bold font to emphasize the major transgressions, not counting the inconsistent capitalization of tags. The visual display of this poor HTML in any of the major fourth- and fifth-generation browsers is identical; Figure 15-4 shows how it appears in Netscape 6.2.

In particular, from an XHTML perspective, this document has the following problems, more or less in the order listed:

1. Inconsistent indentation (not really a problem, but certainly not pretty)
2. *Very* inconsistent capitalization of element and attribute names (uppercase, lowercase, and mixed case)
3. Use of "<" within the <SCRIPT> element
4. Use of color attributes for the <body> element instead of CSS
5. Use of the deprecated <CENTER> element instead of CSS
6. Empty elements such as <BR> and <HR> not written as <br /> and <hr />
7. Overlapping tags in `<B>Example of <I>improper nesting</B></I>`
8. Failure to quote all attributes values
9. Missing end tags for <P>, <DT>, and <DD>
10. Use of the deprecated <FONT> element instead of CSS
11. Attribute minimization of <HR noshade> and <DL compact>
12. Unescaped use of special characters : &, ', ", <, and >
13. Sequences of multiple interior whitespace in attribute values: `alt="   Visit PLUGGED - The Unoffical   McCartney  home page  ">`

Listing 15-2 Sloppy, Malformed HTML to Be Converted to XHTML (bad-ex.html)

```
1    <HTML>
2    <HEAD>
3        <TITLE>KEN'S BEATLES PAGE</TITLE>
4
5    <SCRIPT language="JavaScript" type="text/javascript" >
6    <!-- Spec says to use CDATA Section but current browsers can't handle
          that. -->
7    function doIt()
8    {
9        var foo = 3;
10       // Just to see if less-than is replaced or wrapped in CDATA section.
```

```
    if (foo < 8 )
        alert("Help!");
    else
        alert("I'm Down");
}
</script>
</hEaD>

<body bgcolor="Silver" text="Black"
link="Blue" alink="White" vlink="Maroon">

<CENTER>
<h2>Ken's Beatles Page</h2>

<A HREF="http://gernhardt.com/beatles/index.html">
<IMG src="http://gernhardt.com/beatles/beatles3.jpg"
 border=1 width=166 height=133
 alt="Harald Gernhardt's Beatles Site"></a>
 <!-- actual size: width=333 height=267 -->
<BR>
<A HREF="#bottom">Jump to Bottom of Page</A><br>
<FONT color="Red">Red Font using &lt;FONT&gt; tag is deprecated.</FONT>
<a href="#" ONCLICK="doIt()">Click for JavaScript.</a>
<P>
<B>Example of <I>improper nesting</B></I> of start and end tags.
This paragraph is missing the &lt;/P&gt; tag.<br>
</CENTER>
<HR noshade>
<!-- Attribute Minimization -->
<DL compact>
  <DT><B>Beatles</b>
  <DD>John, Paul, George & Ringo
  <dt><b>Wings</b>
  <dd>Paul, Linda, Denny & others
</DL>

The minimized &lt;/P&gt; tag that follows this paragraph
should be replaced by the pair &lt;P&gt;&lt;/P&gt;.
<p />

<B>Special Entities: &, ', ", <, ></B>
<DIV align="CENTER">
<!-- alt attribute below had extra leading, trailing, and interior
     whitespace. -->
<a HREF="http://gernhardt.com/macca/index.html"
><IMG SRC="http://gernhardt.com/macca/plugged_prv.gif"
BORDER=0 WIDTH=122 height="35"
alt="    Visit    PLUGGED - The Unoffical    McCartney   home page
    "></a>
<BR><a name="bottom"><i>You are at the Rock Bottom, gang.</i></a>
</DIV>

</bODY>
</Html>
```

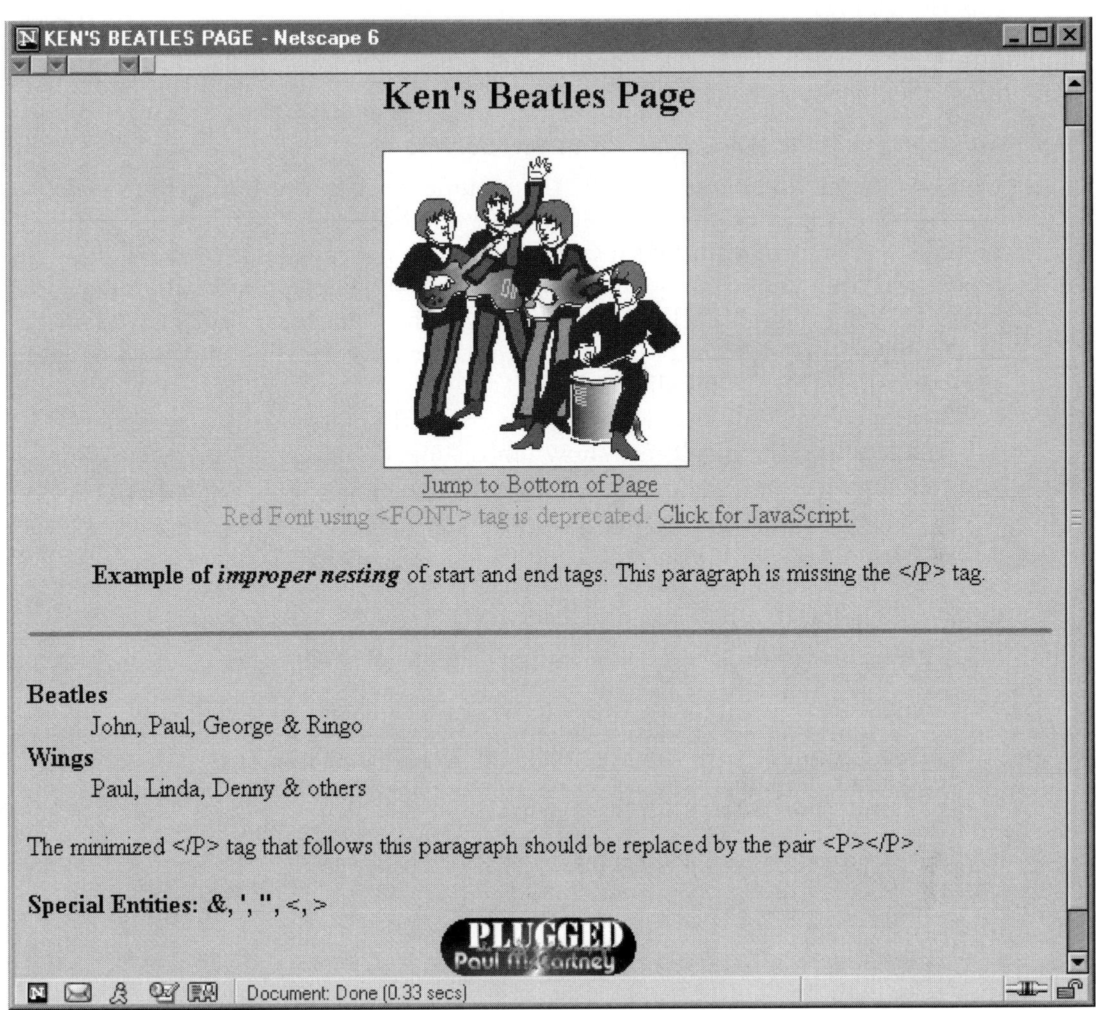

FIGURE 15-4 Sloppy HTML rendered in Netscape 6.2 (bad-ex.html)

Now, although these are all problems with respect to *XHTML*, as far as HTML is concerned, nearly all of them are acceptable according to the HTML 4.01 DTD, with one exception. Can you guess which one?

Validating HTML 4.01 Transitional and Strict

Rather than guess, we'll use an HTML/XHTML validator to tell us. So here's our game plan for the next several sections. First, we'll try a validator or two and see what they report about the HTML validity. Then we'll use a tool called HTML Tidy to convert the sloppy HTML to clean XHTML. Next we'll take HTML Tidy's output and see just how valid the result is compared to the XHTML 1.0 Transitional DTD and then to the Strict DTD. Finally, we'll consider what changes are needed to make the document conform to the Strict DTD.

Validating with the W3C HTML Validation Service

One way to validate your XHTML 1.0 documents is to use the *HTML Validation Service* from the W3C, located at *http://validator.w3.org/*. The W3C validator presents a Web form from which you can validate files available over HTTP or via file upload from your desktop (*http://validator.w3.org/file-upload.html*). It validates both XHTML 1.0 and HTML 4.01 documents against strict, transitional, or frameset DTDs (and earlier versions of HTML as well). The page also has a link to a separate CSS validator, which is equally useful.

First, we'll validate `bad-ex.html`, our original sloppy HTML, against HTML 4.01 Transitional. The results are shown in Listing 15-3. (Apparently, this validator adds a line to the input, perhaps because we have no `DOCTYPE` declaration; the line numbers are one higher than they should be compared to the line-numbered input of Listing 15-2.)

Listing 15-3 HTML 4.01 Transitional Validation Using W3C Validator (bad-ex.html)

```
[W3C] HTML Validation Service Results

Document Checked

   * File: C:\KEN\XMLBook\NOTES\XHTML\XHTML-Examples\bad-ex.html
   * Character encoding: unknown
   * Document type: HTML 4.01 Transitional

Below are the results of attempting to parse this document with an SGML parser.

   * Line 36, column 36:

       <B>Example of <I>improper nesting</B></I> of start and end tags.
                                           ^

     Error: end tag for "I" omitted; possible causes include a missing end
     tag, improper nesting of elements, or use of an element where it is
     not allowed (explanation...)

   * Line 36, column 14:

       <B>Example of <I>improper nesting</B></I> of start and end tags.
                     ^

     Error: start tag was here (explanation...)

   * Line 36, column 40:

       <B>Example of <I>improper nesting</B></I> of start and end tags.
                                               ^
```

```
    Error: end tag for element "I" which is not open; try removing the end
    tag or check for improper nesting of elements (explanation...)

  ---------------------------------------------------------------------

Sorry, this document does not validate as HTML 4.01 Transitional.
```

As you may have guessed, the only *real* error from a transitional HTML perspective is the improper nesting of the <B> and <I> elements from line 36 (line 35 of the original).

However, if we validate against HTML 4.01 *Strict*, the results shown in Listing 15-4 are quite different and much closer to the full set of problems I identified earlier (from an XHTML 1.0 viewpoint). The major problems (besides the nesting error) are the use of deprecated elements and attributes, as well as the repeated use of color and font information without a CSS stylesheet. The validator complains about the `language` attribute of <SCRIPT> on line 6 (line 5 of the original). Most <body> attributes of lines 20 and 21 are rejected. Elements <CENTER> and <FONT> are invalid (lines 23 and 33). So is the `border` attribute for <img> on line 28. The minimized attributes of <HR> and <DL> are flagged on lines 29 and 41. The error from line 48 might be a bit confusing. The suggestion to "try wrapping the text in a more descriptive container" probably means that it should be wrapped in a <P> or <DIV> element (more about that later in the chapter). And finally, the validator isn't happy about the CENTER attribute of the <DIV> tag since alignment is the job of stylesheets.

Listing 15-4 HTML 4.01 Strict Validation Using W3C Validator (bad-ex.html)

```
[W3C] HTML Validation Service Results

Document Checked

   * File: C:\KEN\XMLBook\NOTES\XHTML\XHTML-Examples\bad-ex.html
   * Character encoding: unknown
   * Document type: HTML 4.01 Strict

Below are the results of attempting to parse this document with an SGML parser.

   * Line 6, column 17:

       <SCRIPT language="JavaScript" type="text/javascript" >
                       ^

     Error: there is no attribute "LANGUAGE" for this element (in this HTML
     version) (explanation...)

   * Line 20, column 14:

       <body bgcolor="Silver" text="Black"
                    ^
```

```
    Error: there is no attribute "BGCOLOR" for this element (in this HTML
    version) (explanation...)

  * Line 20, column 28:

      <body bgcolor="Silver" text="Black"
                                     ^

    Error: there is no attribute "TEXT" for this element (in this HTML
    version) (explanation...)

  * Line 21, column 5:

      link="Blue" alink="White" vlink="Maroon">
          ^

    Error: there is no attribute "LINK" for this element (in this HTML
    version) (explanation...)

  * Line 21, column 18:

      link="Blue" alink="White" vlink="Maroon">
                       ^

    Error: there is no attribute "ALINK" for this element (in this HTML
    version) (explanation...)

  * Line 21, column 32:

      link="Blue" alink="White" vlink="Maroon">
                                     ^

    Error: there is no attribute "VLINK" for this element (in this HTML
    version) (explanation...)

  * Line 23, column 7:

      <CENTER>
            ^

    Error: element "CENTER" not defined in this HTML version
    (explanation...)

  * Line 28, column 8:

       border=1 width=166 height=133
              ^

    Error: there is no attribute "BORDER" for this element (in this HTML
    version) (explanation...)

  * Line 33, column 12:

       <FONT color="Red">Red Font using &lt;FONT&gt; tag is deprecated.</
FONT ...
                ^
```

```
     Error: there is no attribute "COLOR" for this element (in this HTML
     version) (explanation...)

   * Line 33, column 17:

       <FONT color="Red">Red Font using &lt;FONT&gt; tag is deprecated.</
FONT ...
                        ^

     Error: element "FONT" not defined in this HTML version
     (explanation...)

   * Line 36, column 36:

       <B>Example of <I>improper nesting</B></I> of start and end tags.
                                           ^

     Error: end tag for "I" omitted; possible causes include a missing end
     tag, improper nesting of elements, or use of an element where it is
     not allowed (explanation...)

   * Line 36, column 14:

       <B>Example of <I>improper nesting</B></I> of start and end tags.
                     ^

     Error: start tag was here (explanation...)

   * Line 36, column 40:

       <B>Example of <I>improper nesting</B></I> of start and end tags.
                                               ^

     Error: end tag for element "I" which is not open; try removing the end
     tag or check for improper nesting of elements (explanation...)

   * Line 39, column 11:

       <HR noshade>
                  ^

     Error: "NOSHADE" is not a member of a group specified for any
     attribute (explanation...)

   * Line 41, column 11:

       <DL compact>
                  ^

     Error: "COMPACT" is not a member of a group specified for any
     attribute (explanation...)

   * Line 48, column 0:
```

```
    The minimized &lt;/P&gt; tag that follows this paragraph
    ^

  Error: text is not allowed here; try wrapping the text in a more
  descriptive container

* Line 53, column 11:

    <DIV align="CENTER">
             ^

  Error: there is no attribute "ALIGN" for this element (in this HTML
  version) (explanation...)

----------------------------------------------------------------------

Sorry, this document does not validate as HTML 4.01 Strict.
```

Validating with ElCel's XML Validator

Before we attempt to correct any of these problems, let's try the handy utility called XML Validator from ElCel Technology that we used earlier with the DOM and XLink. Even though the tool is not intended for use with HTML input, we can still learn something by using it in this context. Since `bad-ex.html` doesn't reference a DTD itself, `xmlvalid` doesn't attempt validation, but it does do a great job of checking for well-formedness, as we can see from Listing 15-5. It reports what would be illegal if this were an XML document, such as the "<" in the JavaScript, the case matching problems throughout, attributes that aren't quoted, missing end tags for <IMG> and <BR> from lines 28 and 37, minimization problems on lines 38 and 40, the direct use of "&" (instead of a character entity) in lines 42 and 44, and so on.

Now we're ready to appreciate the conversion process that Tidy does so—well, tidily.

Listing 15-5 HTML Well-Formedness Checking with ElCel's XML Validator (bad-ex.html)

```
C:> xmlvalid bad-ex.html
bad-ex.html [1:7] : Error: validation not possible without a DTD
bad-ex.html [11:13] : Fatal error: unexpected '< ', expecting element content
or </SCRIPT>
bad-ex.html [16:9] : Fatal error: end tag '</script>' does not match start tag.
Expected '</SCRIPT>'
bad-ex.html [17:7] : Fatal error: end tag '</hEaD>' does not match start tag.
Expected '</HEAD>'
bad-ex.html [27:9] : Fatal error: attribute value must be enclosed by quotes
bad-ex.html [27:17] : Fatal error: attribute value must be enclosed by quotes
bad-ex.html [27:28] : Fatal error: attribute value must be enclosed by quotes
bad-ex.html [28:43] : Fatal error: end tag '</a>' does not match start tag.
Expected '</IMG>'
bad-ex.html [35:37] : Fatal error: end tag '</B>' does not match start tag.
Expected '</I>'
```

```
bad-ex.html [35:41] : Fatal error: end tag '</I>' does not match start tag.
Expected '</B>'
bad-ex.html [37:9] : Fatal error: end tag '</CENTER>' does not match start tag.
Expected '</br>'
bad-ex.html [38:12] : Fatal error: expected '=' after attribute 'noshade'
bad-ex.html [40:12] : Fatal error: expected '=' after attribute 'compact'
bad-ex.html [41:20] : Fatal error: end tag '</b>' does not match start tag.
Expected '</B>'
bad-ex.html [42:27] : Fatal error: entity reference must start with a letter,
'_' or ':'
bad-ex.html [44:27] : Fatal error: entity reference must start with a letter,
'_' or ':'
bad-ex.html [45:5] : Fatal error: end tag '</DL>' does not match start tag.
Expected '</dd>'
bad-ex.html [51:23] : Fatal error: entity reference must start with a letter,
'_' or ':'
bad-ex.html [51:31] : Fatal error: unexpected '<,', expecting element content
or </B>
bad-ex.html [56:8] : Fatal error: attribute value must be enclosed by quotes
bad-ex.html [56:16] : Fatal error: attribute value must be enclosed by quotes
bad-ex.html [57:76] : Fatal error: end tag '</a>' does not match start tag.
Expected '</IMG>'
bad-ex.html [59:6] : Fatal error: end tag '</DIV>' does not match start tag.
Expected '</BR>'
bad-ex.html [61:7] : Fatal error: end tag '</bODY>' does not match start tag.
Expected '</a>'
bad-ex.html [62:7] : Fatal error: end tag '</Html>' does not match start tag.
Expected '</DIV>'
bad-ex.html [63:1] : Fatal error: unexpected end of file, expecting element
content or </dt>
```

HTML Tidy: Converting HTML to XHTML

As we've learned about the many changes that are necessary to convert HTML to XHTML, it would be easy to conclude that the process is far too tedious to do by hand. Even with the best text editor with powerful global substitutions and regular expressions, these changes would still be extremely time consuming. Therefore, the Web community should be eternally grateful to Dave Raggett, an engineer from Hewlett-Packard's UK Laboratories, on assignment to the World Wide Web Consortium.[6] He developed and maintains a small command-line utility called *HTML Tidy* (or sometimes just *Tidy*) that "cleans up" sloppy or malformed HTML and, more important to XML developers, can also convert HTML to XHTML 1.0 with very little fuss. It even supports batch processing.

6. Dave Raggett is the W3C lead for HTML, XForms, Voice Browsers, and Math activities. He is also one of the authors or editors of all HTML specifications since roughly 1993. He is the author of an HTML 4.0 book by Addison-Wesley.

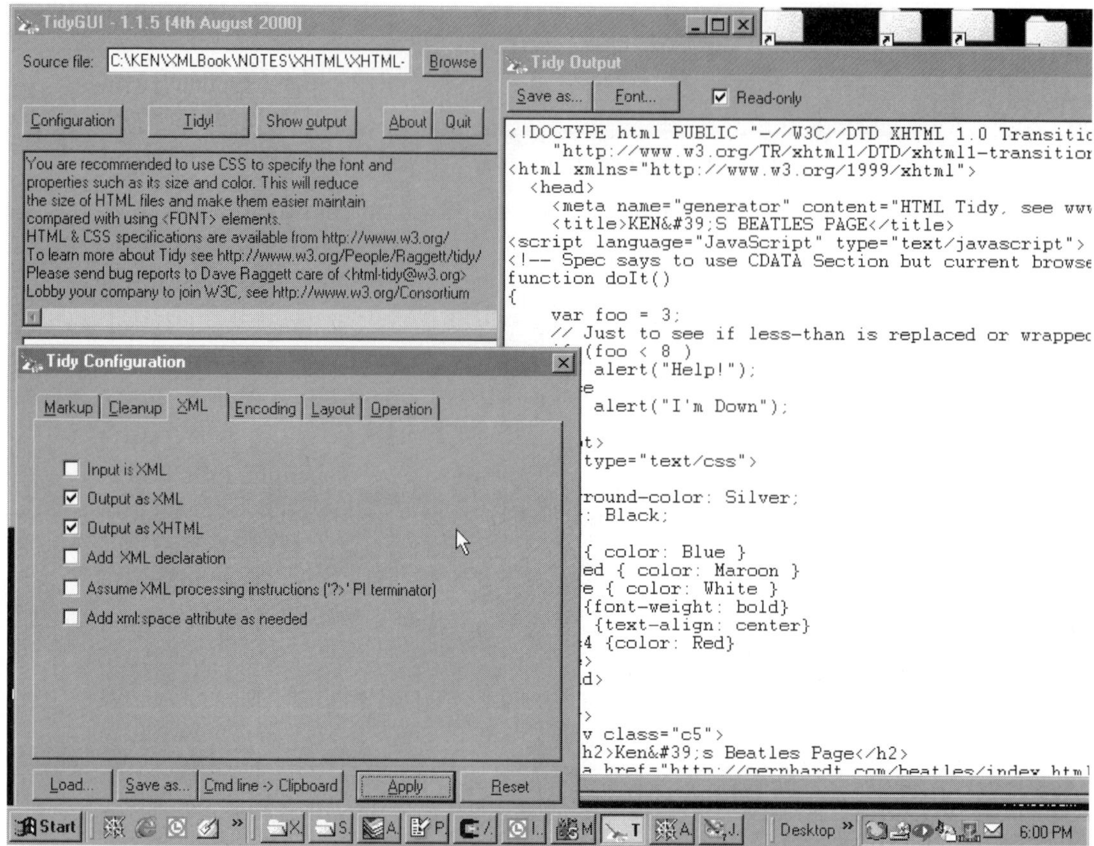

FIGURE 15-5 TidyGUI Front-End

Tidy-Enabled Applications

Raggett's Web page, *http://www.w3.org/People/Raggett/tidy/*, has links to Tidy executables for many platforms, as well as a number of links to HTML editors that have integrated Tidy.[7] For example, on Windows, a small application called TidyGUI (Figure 15-5) which, as its name implies, is a graphical front-end to Tidy. Tidy is integrated into such highly regarded HTML editors as HTML-Kit (Figure 15-6), NoteTab (Figure 15-7, page 968), and Evrsoft's 1st Page 2000 for Windows (Figure 15-8, page 969). There is also a Java port called JTidy, another Source Forge project, so this functionality can be integrated into Java applications, potentially providing a DOM parsing capability (see *http://sourceforge.net/projects/jtidy/*).

7. In September 2001, Tidy became open source and is hosted by SourceForge.net (owned by Open Source Development Network, Inc.) at *http://tidy.sourceforge.net/*.

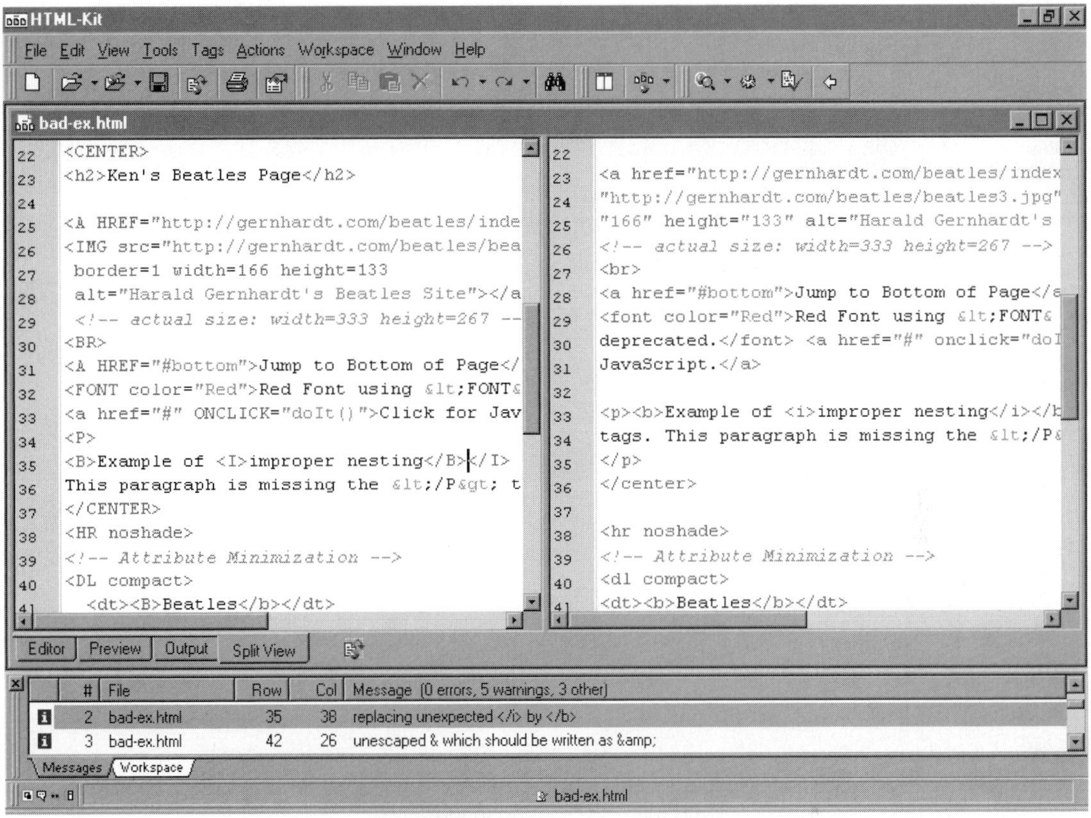

FIGURE 15-6 Tidy in HTML-Kit

Tidy Options and Configuration File

Tidy can be controlled by means of command-line options or by setting options that you use repeatedly in a configuration file.

This section discusses options and results based on the September 2001 version of Tidy from SourceForge.net. At the time of writing, this version has several improvements over the August 2000 version available from Dave Raggett's page on www.w3.org. In particular, it handles the `CDATA` section issue.

Listing 15-6 shows Tidy usage information (`tidy -help`). I've used a bold font to emphasize options that are useful for XHTML, the most important of which is `-asxml` (or `-asxhtml`) to convert from HTML to XML. The `-clean` option removes all color, font, and alignment information from elements and creates CSS styles

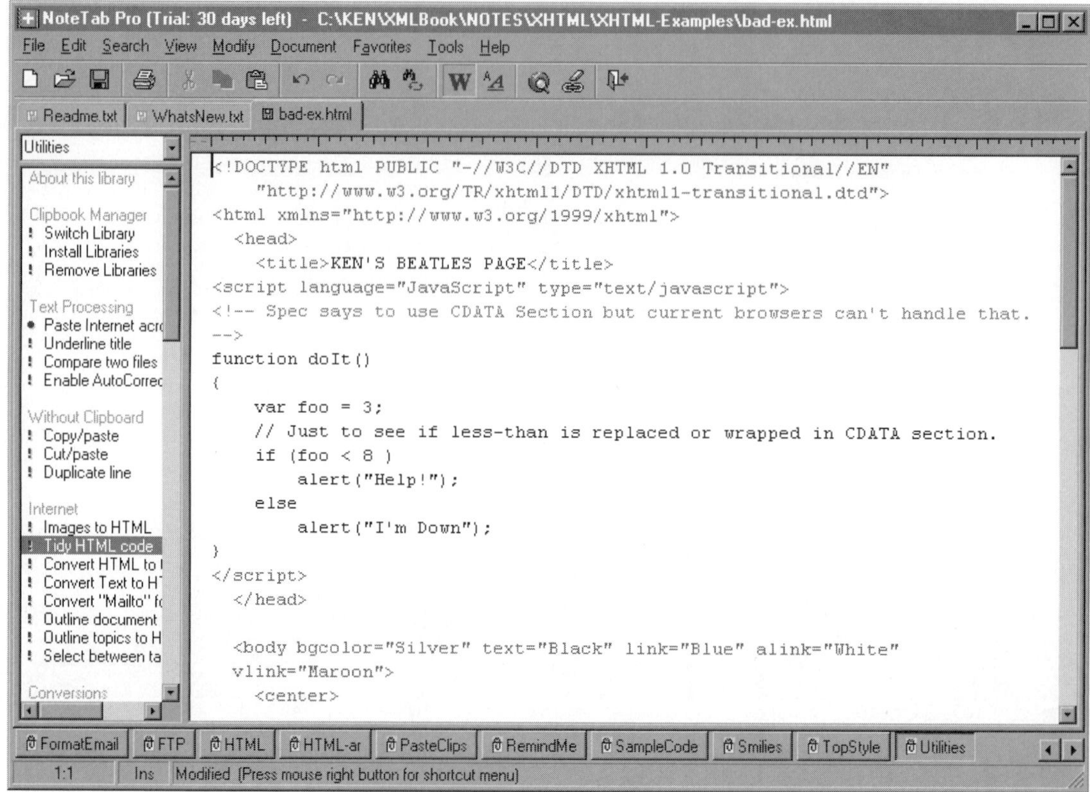

FIGURE 15-7 Tidy in NoteTab

for them. You can potentially avoid problems with entities by using the `-numeric` option. For example, this option should convert the literal string

```
KEN'S
```

into the numeric representation of an entity

```
KEN&#39;S
```

rather than using the entity reference

```
KEN&apos;S
```

but this option appears to be broken in the September 2001 version unless it is set in a configuration file.

At any rate, the command line that I find most useful for XHTML is:

```
C:> tidy -icn -asxhtml input.html > output.html
```

which converts HTML to XHTML 1.0 Transitional. We'll see an example shortly.

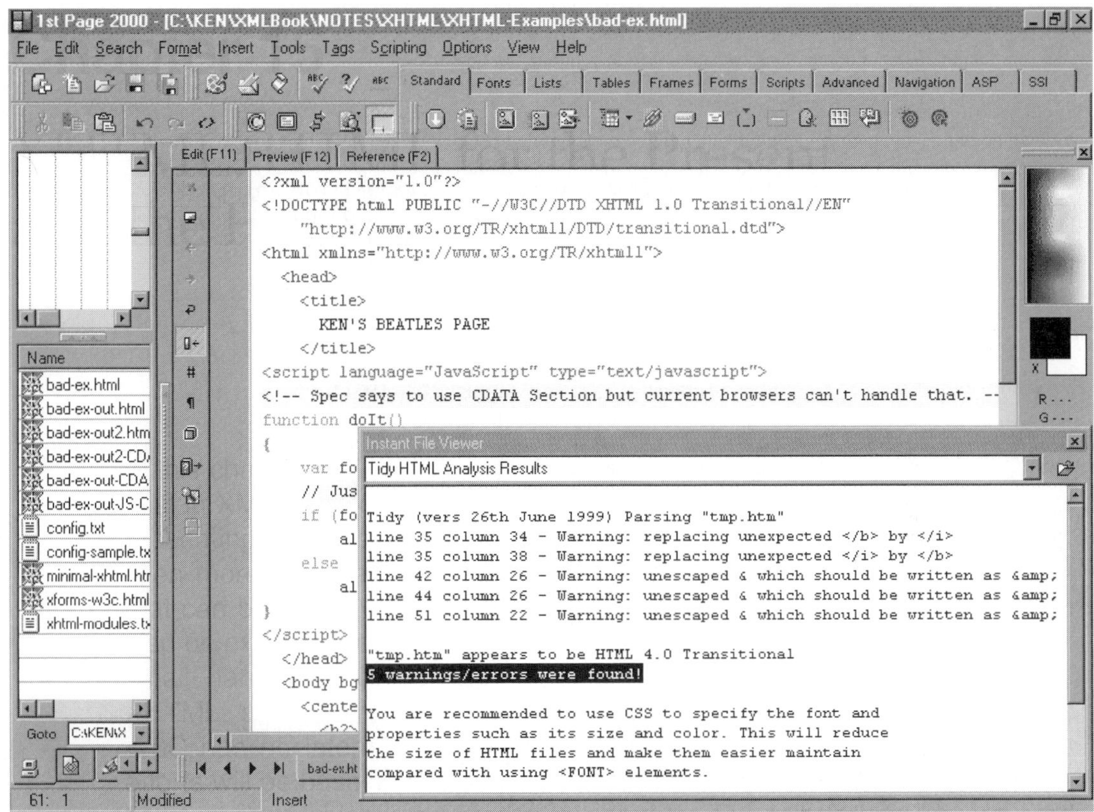

FIGURE 15-8 Tidy in 1st Page

Listing 15-6 Tidy Options (boldface ones useful for XHTML)

```
C:>tidy.exe -help
C:\XML\BIN\TIDY.EXE: file1 file2 ...
Utility to clean up & pretty print HTML files
see http://www.w3.org/People/Raggett/tidy/
options for HTML Tidy for Windows released on 1st September 2001

Processing directives
---------------------
  -indent or -i     indent element content
  -omit   or -o     omit optional end tags
  -wrap 72          wrap text at column 72 (default is 68)
  -upper  or -u     force tags to upper case (default is lower)
  -clean  or -c     replace FONT, NOBR & CENTER tags by CSS
  -bare   or -b     strip out smart quotes and em dashes, etc.
  -numeric or -n    output numeric rather than named entities
  -errors or -e     only show errors
  -quiet or -q      suppress nonessential output
  -xml              use this when input is well formed XML
```

```
  -asxml          to convert HTML to well formed XHTML
  -asxhtml        to convert HTML to well formed XHTML
  -slides         to burst into slides on H2 elements

Character encodings
-------------------
  -raw            leave chars > 128 unchanged upon output
  -ascii          use US-ASCII for output, ISO-8859-1 for input
  -latin1         use ISO-8859-1 for both input and output
  -iso2022        use ISO-2022 for both input and output
  -utf8           use UTF-8 for both input and output
  -mac            use MacRoman for input, US-ASCII for output
  -utf16le        use UTF-16LE for both input and output
  -utf16be        use UTF-16BE for both input and output
  -utf16          use UTF-16 for both input and output
  -win1252        use Windows-1252 for input, US-ASCII for output
  -big5           use Big5 for both input and output
  -shiftjis       use Shift_JIS for both input and output
  -language       set the two-letter language code (for future use)

File manipulation
-----------------
  -config <file>  set options from config file
  -f <file>       write errors to named <file>
  -modify or -m   to modify original files

Miscellaneous
-------------
  -version or -v  show version
  -help   or -h   list command line options
  -help-config    list all configuration file options
  -show-config    list the current configuration settings
You can also use --blah for any config file option blah

Input/Output default to stdin/stdout respectively
Single letter options apart from -f may be combined
as in:  tidy -f errs.txt -imu foo.html
For further info on HTML see http://www.w3.org/MarkUp
```

As an example of Tidy's use with a configuration file, recall the file `bad-ex.html`, the poorly formed HTML document shown in Listing 15-2. For a configuration file named `config.txt` (any name will do), the command line to perform the conversion is:

```
C:> tidy -config config.txt bad-ex.html > bad-config.html
```

Listing 15-7 shows the contents of my `config.txt`. Bold font indicates the more significant options for our purposes. Note that several options are commented out with // so they will assume their default values. The description of the `output-`

xhtml parameter (which serves the same function as the -asxhtml command-line option) from Raggett's Web page is produced here (see also *http://www.w3.org/People/Raggett/tidy/#config*).

> *output-xhtml: bool*
>
> If set to yes, Tidy will generate the pretty printed output writing it as extensible HTML. The default is no. This option causes Tidy to set the doctype and default namespace as appropriate to XHTML. If a doctype or namespace is given, it will be checked for consistency with the content of the document. In the case of an inconsistency, the corrected values will appear in the output. For XHTML, entities can be written as named or numeric entities according to the value of the "numeric-entities" property. The tags and attributes will be output in the case used in the input document, regardless of other options.

Listing 15-7 XHTML Configuration File for Tidy (config.txt)

```
//  config file for HTML tidy
show-warnings: no
quiet: yes
clean: yes

indent: auto
indent-spaces: 2
// wrap: 72
markup: yes

output-xhtml: yes
output-xml: no
input-xml: no

numeric-entities: yes
quote-marks: yes
quote-nbsp: yes
quote-ampersand: no
// break-before-br: no
// uppercase-tags: no
// uppercase-attributes: no
// char-encoding: latin1
```

Converting HTML to XHTML 1.0 Transitional with Tidy

I chose to use the command line to convert our sloppy HTML to XHTML 1.0 Transitional:

```
C:> tidy -icn -asxhtml bad-ex.html > b-icn-asxhtml.html
```

Listing 15-8 shows the line-numbered result of running Tidy. Notice that a DOCTYPE declaration referencing the Transitional DTD and the XHTML namespace was inserted by Tidy. Also note the addition of an internal CSS stylesheet (lines 24–37) to replace the <body>, <FONT>, and <CENTER> elements of the input for color and alignment. All tags are lowercase and all attribute values are now quoted (e.g., line 45), as they must be for XHTML. The improper nesting problem (line 54) is automatically fixed. Empty elements such as `<br />` and `<hr />` have the appropriate minimized element tags. The attribute minimization problems have been fixed (lines 58 and 61). Entities have been replaced with numeric equivalents (lines 64, 68, and 74). Runs of white space have been reduced to single spaces in the `alt` attribute on line 81. Finally, an `id="bottom"` attribute/value pair has been added to the <a> element of line 83 to supplement the deprecated `name` attribute.

Listing 15-8 Tidy Result of Converting Sloppy HTML to Clean XHTML (b-icn-asxhtml.html)

```
1    <!DOCTYPE html PUBLIC "-//W3C//DTD XHTML 1.0 Transitional//EN"
2        "http://www.w3.org/TR/xhtml1/DTD/xhtml1-transitional.dtd">
3
4    <html xmlns="http://www.w3.org/1999/xhtml">
5      <head>
6        <meta name="generator"
7        content="HTML Tidy for Windows (vers 1st September 2001), see
           www.w3.org" />
8
9        <title>KEN'S BEATLES PAGE</title>
10   <script language="JavaScript" type="text/javascript">
11   //<![CDATA[
12   <!-- Spec says to use CDATA Section but current browsers can't handle
          that. -->
13   function doIt()
14   {
15       var foo = 3;
16       // Just to see if less-than is replaced or wrapped in CDATA section.
17       if (foo < 8 )
18           alert("Help!");
19       else
20           alert("I'm Down");
21   }
22   //]]>
23   </script>
24   <style type="text/css">
25   /*<![CDATA[*/
26    body {
27     background-color: silver;
28     color: black;
29    }
30    :link { color: blue }
31    :visited { color: maroon }
32    :active { color: white }
33    dt.c3 {font-weight: bold}
34    div.c2 {text-align: center}
35    span.c1 {color: red}
36   /*]]>*/
37   </style>
```

```
    </head>

    <body>
      <div class="c2">
        <h2>Ken's Beatles Page</h2>
        <a href="http://gernhardt.com/beatles/index.html"><img
        src="http://gernhardt.com/beatles/beatles3.jpg" border="1"
        width="166" height="133"
        alt="Harald Gernhardt's Beatles Site" /></a>
        <!-- actual size: width=333 height=267 -->
        <br />
        <a href="#bottom">Jump to Bottom of Page</a><br />
        <span class="c1">Red Font using &lt;FONT&gt; tag is
        deprecated.</span> <a href="#" onclick="doIt()">Click for
        JavaScript.</a>

        <p><b>Example of <i>improper nesting</i></b> of start and end
        tags. This paragraph is missing the &lt;/P&gt; tag.<br />
        </p>
      </div>
      <hr noshade="noshade" />
      <!-- Attribute Minimization -->

      <dl compact="compact">
        <dt class="c3">Beatles</dt>

        <dd>John, Paul, George &amp; Ringo</dd>

        <dt class="c3">Wings</dt>

        <dd>Paul, Linda, Denny &amp; others</dd>
      </dl>
      The minimized &lt;/P&gt; tag that follows this paragraph should
      be replaced by the pair &lt;P&gt;&lt;/P&gt;.

      <p></p>
      <b>Special Entities: &amp;, ', ", &lt;, &gt;</b>

      <div class="c2">
        <!-- alt attribute below had extra leading, trailing, and interior
             whitespace. -->
        <a href="http://gernhardt.com/macca/index.html"><img
        src="http://gernhardt.com/macca/plugged_prv.gif" border="0"
        width="122" height="35"
        alt=" Visit PLUGGED - The Unoffical McCartney home page " /></
            a><br />

        <a id="bottom" name="bottom"><i>You are at the Rock Bottom,
        gang.</i></a>
      </div>
    </body>
  </html>
```

Tidy also cleans up our little CDATA section problem to protect the JavaScript code. This construct:

```
<script language="JavaScript" type="text/javascript">
//<![CDATA[
            JavaScript code here
//]]>
</script>
```

keeps both HTML browsers and XML parsers happy. The lines shown in bold are ignorable comments as far as JavaScript is concerned, but they delimit a CDATA section that escapes characters such as < and & which would otherwise cause an XML parser to complain. In other words, the page displays fine in the major browsers, there are no JavaScript errors, and the file is valid XML! (But we'll soon see things are not perfect yet.)

The other interesting fix that Tidy implements relates to the font and color information, which it replaces with an embedded CSS stylesheet. This also results in the addition of a CDATA section but the syntax is noticeably different:

```
<style type="text/css">
/*<![CDATA[*/
            CSS style rules here
/*]]>*/
</style>
```

In this case, we note C language comments which are appropriate for a CSS stylesheet. The CSS processing module ignores these lines, but an XML parser is happy because any special characters in the stylesheet will not result in well-formedness errors.

We can quickly verify that the converted file is valid XML:

```
C:> xmlvalid b-icn-asxhtml.html
b-icn-asxhtml.html is valid
```

In fact, XML Validator accesses the DTD given in the document type declaration

```
http://www.w3.org/TR/xhtml1/DTD/xhtml1-transitional.dtd
```

to perform its validation. So, without editing even one line, with the considerable help of HTML Tidy, we've gone from pretty terrible HTML to squeaky clean XHTML 1.0 Transitional!

Validating XHTML 1.0 Transitional and Strict

Now that our sample document is converted to XHTML 1.0, we can try various methods of validating it against both the Transitional and the Strict DTDs. To do so, we'll revisit the W3C Validation Service and ElCel's XML Validator. As in many aspects of XML development, I find it particularly valuable to try two or more tools with the same input because one tool may reveal problems that the other does not. Sometimes comparing the error messages of two tools can point to a solution that was not evident using just one tool.

Detecting XHTML 1.0 Strict Errors with W3C's Validator

When we upload the converted file, `b-icn-asxhtml.html`, for checking via the HTML Validation Service from the W3C, selecting the form choice of "XHTML 1.0 Transitional" (or simply letting the document type default to "specified inline," the document receives a *semi*-clean bill of health, as shown here.

```
Warnings

    * Warning: No Character Encoding detected! To assure correct validation,
processing, and display, it is important that the character encoding is
properly labeled. Further explanations.

Below are the results of checking this document for XML well-formedness and
validity.

No errors found! *

[etc.]
```

Even though the converted file is both well-formed and valid, and although we see the "No errors found!" message, the W3C validator complains about a *lack of character encoding*. We'll fix that in a little while.

First let's see how it stacks up against XHTML 1.0 Strict. To check our converted file against the Strict DTD with the W3C Validation Service, we only need to return to the Upload page, browse to our file again, and use the pulldown menu labeled "Document Type:" to select the "XHTML 1.0 Strict" choice. We don't need to edit our file for this particular check since our objective is to see what needs to be changed in a document that was fine according to the Transitional DTD but is not acceptable with the Strict DTD.

Listing 15-9 indicates that there are still problems such as the `language` attribute of `<SCRIPT>` and all other deprecated elements and attributes, which are obsolete and therefore removed from the Strict DTD. Let's check the file with XML Validator to see if there is a consensus.

Listing 15-9 XHTML 1.0 Strict Validation Errors Using W3C Validator (b-icn-asxhtml.html)

```
Warnings

   * Warning: DOCTYPE Override in effect! Any DOCTYPE Declaration in the....
   * Warning: No Character Encoding detected! To assure correct validation....

Below are the results of checking this document for XML well-formedness and
validity.
```

```
* Line 11, column 17:

    <script language="JavaScript" type="text/javascript">
                     ^
  Error: there is no attribute "language" for this element (in this HTML
  version)

* Line 45, column 61:

          src="http://gernhardt.com/beatles/beatles3.jpg" border="1"
                                                              ^
  Error: there is no attribute "border" for this element (in this HTML
  version)

* Line 59, column 16:

        <hr noshade="noshade" />
                    ^
  Error: there is no attribute "noshade" for this element (in this HTML
  version)

* Line 62, column 16:

        <dl compact="compact">
                    ^
  Error: there is no attribute "compact" for this element (in this HTML
  version)

* Line 71, column 4:

        The minimized &lt;/P&gt; tag that follows this paragraph should
        ^
  Error: text is not allowed here; try wrapping the text in a more
  descriptive container

* Line 75, column 6:

        <b>Special Entities: &amp;, ', ", &lt;, &gt;</b>
          ^
  Error: element "b" not allowed here; possible cause is an inline
  element containing a block-level element
 ------------------------------------------------------------------------

Sorry, this document does not validate as XHTML 1.0 Strict.
```

Detecting XHTML 1.0 Strict Errors with ElCel's XML Validator

At this point, we need to replace the Transitional DTD with the Strict DTD in the `DOCTYPE` declaration so we can run it through a regular XML parser such as XML Validator. We only need to change the initial two lines of the file:

```
<!DOCTYPE html PUBLIC "-//W3C//DTD XHTML 1.0 Strict//EN"
    "http://www.w3.org/TR/xhtml1/DTD/xhtml1-strict.dtd">
```

Let's call the new version `b-icn-asxml-strict.xml` and validate it with the command line:

```
C:> xmlvalid  -c  b-icn-asxml-strict.xml
```

The `-c` option tells XML Validator to add lines of context to the output, which by default are more terse. The results are shown in Listing 15-10; they are similar to what the W3C Validation service reported. The obsolete attributes are reported correctly. Unfortunately, the version of `xmlvalid` I used (0.14.4) seems to report problems with character entities that don't appear to be a problem with W3C's `xhtml-special.ent` file, which is included from the DTD. I've used bold face to emphasize the kinds of errors that differ from our earlier check. We'll discover why shortly.

Listing 15-10 XHTML 1.0 Strict Validation Results Using XML Validator

```
C:> xmlvalid  -c  b-icn-asxml-strict.xml
b-icn-asxml-strict.xml [10:30] : Error: undeclared attribute 'language' for
element 'script'
  Line    10: <script language="JavaScript" type="text/javascript">
  Col     30: -----------------------------^

b-icn-asxml-strict.xml [44:65] : Error: undeclared attribute 'border' for
element 'img'
  Line    44:       src="http://gernhardt.com/beatles/beatles3.jpg" border="1"
  Col     65: ----------------------------------------------------------------^

b-icn-asxml-strict.xml [58:26] : Error: undeclared attribute 'noshade' for
element 'hr'
  Line    58:     <hr noshade="noshade" />
  Col     26: -------------------------^

b-icn-asxml-strict.xml [61:26] : Error: undeclared attribute 'compact' for
element 'dl'
  Line    61:     <dl compact="compact">
  Col     26: -------------------------^

b-icn-asxml-strict.xml [70:19] : Error: unexpected character content within
element 'body'
  Line    70:     The minimized &lt;/P&gt; tag that follows this paragraph should
  Col      19: ------------------^

/TR/xhtml1/DTD/xhtml-special.ent [28:24] : Error: reference to character content
not permitted within element 'body'
  Line    28: &#60;
  Col     24: ----^

b-icn-asxml-strict.xml [70:25] : Error: unexpected character content within
element 'body'
  Line    70:     The minimized &lt;/P&gt; tag that follows this paragraph should
  Col     25: ------------------------^
```

```
/TR/xhtml1/DTD/xhtml-special.ent [29:20] : Error: unexpected character content
within element 'body'
  Line    29: >
  Col     20: ^

b-icn-asxml-strict.xml [71:29] : Error: unexpected character content within
element 'body'
  Line    71:     be replaced by the pair &lt;P&gt;&lt;/P&gt;.
  Col     29: ----------------------------^

/TR/xhtml1/DTD/xhtml-special.ent [28:24] : Error: reference to character content
not permitted within element 'body'
  Line    28: &#60;
  Col     24: ----^

b-icn-asxml-strict.xml [71:34] : Error: unexpected character content within
element 'body'
  Line    71:     be replaced by the pair &lt;P&gt;&lt;/P&gt;.
  Col     34: ---------------------------------^

/TR/xhtml1/DTD/xhtml-special.ent [29:20] : Error: unexpected character content
within element 'body'
  Line    29: >
  Col     20: ^

/TR/xhtml1/DTD/xhtml-special.ent [28:24] : Error: reference to character content
not permitted within element 'body'
  Line    28: &#60;
  Col     24: ----^

b-icn-asxml-strict.xml [71:44] : Error: unexpected character content within
element 'body'
  Line    71:     be replaced by the pair &lt;P&gt;&lt;/P&gt;.
  Col     44: -------------------------------------------^

/TR/xhtml1/DTD/xhtml-special.ent [29:20] : Error: unexpected character content
within element 'body'
  Line    29: >
  Col     20: ^

b-icn-asxml-strict.xml [73:5] : Error: unexpected character content within
element 'body'
  Line    73:     <p></p>
  Col      5: ----^

b-icn-asxml-strict.xml [74:8] : Error: element content invalid. Element 'b' is
not expected here, expecting 'address', 'blockquote', 'del', 'div', 'dl',
'fieldset', 'form', 'h1', 'h2', 'h3', 'h4', 'h5', 'h6', 'hr', 'ins', 'noscript',
'ol', 'p', 'pre', 'script', 'table', 'ul' or '</body>'
  Line    74:     <b>Special Entities: &amp;, ', ", &lt;, &gt;</b>
  Col      8: -------^

b-icn-asxml-strict.xml [79:66] : Error: undeclared attribute 'border' for
element 'img'
  Line    79:       src="http://gernhardt.com/macca/plugged_prv.gif" border="0"
  Col     66: -----------------------------------------------------------------^
```

Fixing Errors

Clearly, if we really want to comply with the Strict DTD, we have some changes to make. The squeaky clean version, `b-icn-asxml-strict-clean.xml`, is presented in Listing 15-11. First of all, we must remove the `language` attribute from line 10. We must leave the CDATA section delimiters (lines 11, 22, 25, and 36) that Tidy added so helpfully. We need to get rid of the `border` attribute from `<img>` on line 44 and line 82, and delete the obsolete attributes, `noshade` and `compact`, from line 58 and line 61.

Listing 15-11 Valid XHTML 1.0 Strict Document (b-icn-asxml-strict-clean.xml)

```
1    <!DOCTYPE html PUBLIC "-//W3C//DTD XHTML 1.0 Strict//EN"
2        "http://www.w3.org/TR/xhtml1/DTD/xhtml1-strict.dtd">
3
4    <html xmlns="http://www.w3.org/1999/xhtml">
5      <head>
6        <meta name="generator"
7        content="HTML Tidy for Windows (vers 1st September 2001), see
            www.w3.org" />
8
9        <title>KEN'S BEATLES PAGE</title>
10   <script  type="text/javascript">
11   //<![CDATA[
12   <!-- Spec says to use CDATA Section but current browsers can't handle
          that. -->
13   function doIt()
14   {
15       var foo = 3;
16       // Just to see if less-than is replaced or wrapped in CDATA section.
17       if (foo < 8 )
18           alert("Help!");
19       else
20           alert("I'm Down");
21   }
22   //]]>
23   </script>
24   <style type="text/css">
25   /*<![CDATA[*/
26    body {
27     background-color: silver;
28     color: black;
29    }
30    :link { color: blue }
31    :visited { color: maroon }
32    :active { color: white }
33    dt.c3 {font-weight: bold}
34    div.c2 {text-align: center}
35    span.c1 {color: red}
36   /*]]>*/
37   </style>
38     </head>
39
```

```
  <body>
    <div class="c2">
      <h2>Ken's Beatles Page</h2>
      <a href="http://gernhardt.com/beatles/index.html"><img
      src="http://gernhardt.com/beatles/beatles3.jpg"
      width="166" height="133"
      alt="Harald Gernhardt's Beatles Site" /></a>
      <!-- actual size: width=333 height=267 -->
      <br />
      <a href="#bottom">Jump to Bottom of Page</a><br />
      <span class="c1">Red Font using &lt;FONT&gt; tag is
      deprecated.</span> <a href="#" onclick="doIt()">Click for
      JavaScript.</a>

      <p><b>Example of <i>improper nesting</i></b> of start and end
      tags. This paragraph is missing the &lt;/P&gt; tag.<br />
      </p>
    </div>
    <hr />
    <!-- Attribute Minimization -->

    <dl>
      <dt class="c3">Beatles</dt>

      <dd>John, Paul, George &amp; Ringo</dd>

      <dt class="c3">Wings</dt>

      <dd>Paul, Linda, Denny &amp; others</dd>
    </dl>

    <div> <!-- KS: added div to match content model of Strict body -->
    The minimized &lt;/P&gt; tag that follows this paragraph should
    be replaced by the pair &lt;P&gt;&lt;/P&gt;.

    <p></p>
    <b>Special Entities: &amp;, ', ", &lt;, &gt;</b>
    </div>

    <div class="c2">
      <!-- alt attribute below had extra leading, trailing, and interior
           whitespace. -->
      <a href="http://gernhardt.com/macca/index.html"><img
      src="http://gernhardt.com/macca/plugged_prv.gif"
      width="122" height="35"
      alt=" Visit PLUGGED - The Unoffical McCartney home page " /></
          a><br />

      <a id="bottom" name="bottom"><i>You are at the Rock Bottom,
      gang.</i></a>
    </div>
  </body>
</html>
```

But what about the other problem we saw related to content models?

- Error: text is not allowed here; try wrapping the text in a more descriptive container.
- Error: element "b" not allowed here; possible cause is an inline element containing a block-level element.
- Error: reference to character content not permitted within element 'body'.
- Error: element content invalid. Element 'b' is not expected here, expecting 'address', 'blockquote', 'del', 'div', 'dl', 'fieldset', 'form', 'h1', 'h2', 'h3', 'h4', 'h5', 'h6', 'hr', 'ins', 'noscript', 'ol', 'p', 'pre', 'script', 'table', 'ul', or '</body>'
- Error: unexpected character content within element 'body'.

It turns out these messages are all related and can be eliminated with one additional HTML element! Upon inspecting the DTD `xhtml1-strict.dtd`, we discover that PCDATA is not allowed in the <body> as a direct child; only block-level elements (those defined by the `%Block;` parameter entity) may be in that position, as shown by this fragment of the DTD:

```
<!ELEMENT body %Block;>
....
<!ENTITY % block
     "p | %heading; | div | %lists; | %blocktext; | fieldset | table">

<!ENTITY % Block "(%block; | form | %misc;)*">

<!-- %Flow; mixes Block and Inline and is used for list items etc. -->
<!ENTITY % Flow "(#PCDATA | %block; | form | %inline; | %misc;)*">
```

This differs from the <body> model found in `xhtml1-transitional.dtd`, which is based on the `%Flow;` parameter entity, defined exactly as above. The conclusion is that PCDATA isn't allowed directly inside <body> in the Strict DTD even though it is in the Transitional DTD. Recall the W3C validator message "try wrapping the text in a more descriptive container"? Well, that's the solution here. We need to wrap the text inside a block-level element such as <p> or `<div>`. I've chosen `<div>` on lines 71 and 77 so that it won't change the appearance (won't add an extra newline) when the file is rendered. It's interesting that fixing the <body> content model also fixed all of the so-called entity problems I mentioned earlier.

Now, when we validate `b-icn-asxml-strict-clean.xml` we get a clean bill of health:

```
C:> xmlvalid -c b-icn-asxml-strict-clean.xml
b-icn-asxml-strict-clean.xml is valid
```

Dealing with Encodings

So now, we'll double-check the result, which we know validates against the XHTML 1.0 Strict DTD, using the W3C HTML Validation Service. There should be no problem, right? Wrong! Remember the "no character encoding" warning message we saw (Listing 15-9) when the Transitional file was uploaded? Figure 15-9 shows this is still a problem.

This is not technically a *validation* problem, however, since character encodings (which you'll recall appear as an optional atttribute within the XML declaration) are *optional* according to the XML Recommendation. But the W3C HTML Validation Service says: "To assure correct validation, processing, and display, it is important that the character encoding is properly labeled."

This message links to a page on internationalization and character sets, `http://www.w3.org/International/O-charset.html`, which states: "It is very important that the character encoding of any XML or (X)HTML document is clearly labeled."

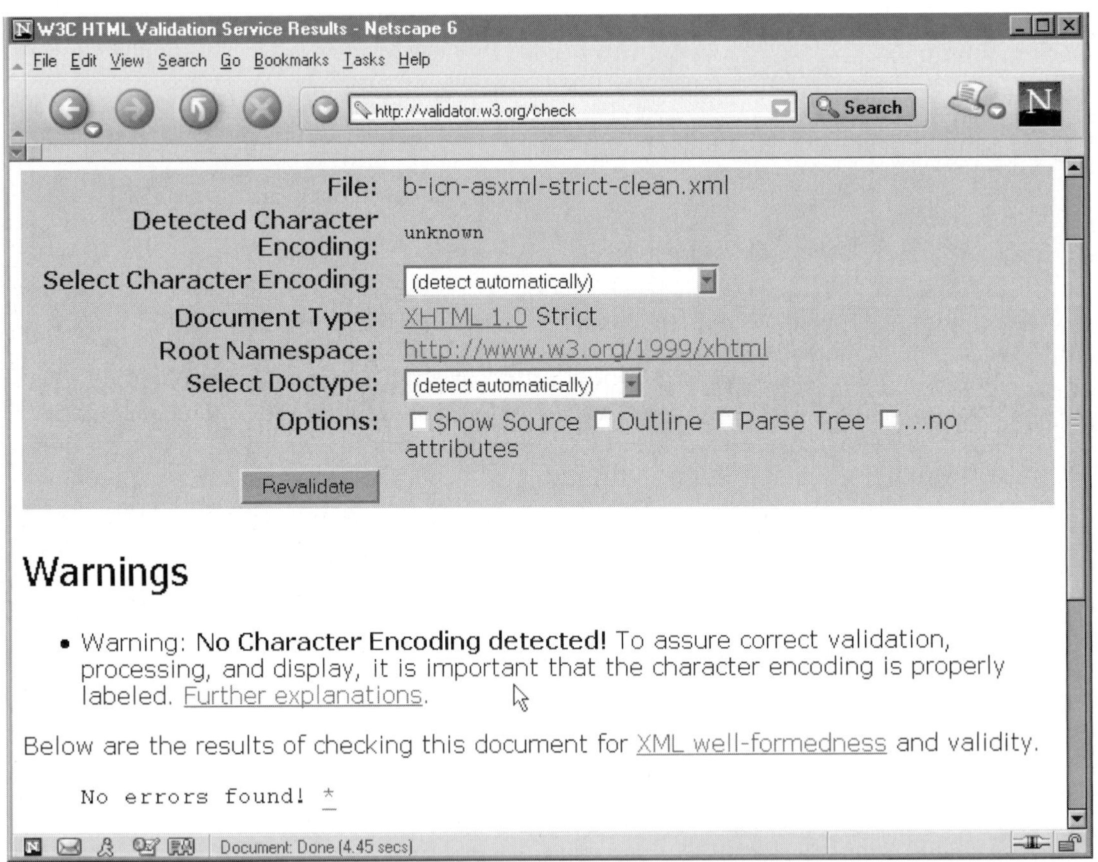

FIGURE 15-9 Encoding warning with valid XHTML 1.0 Strict (b-icn-asxml-strict-clean.xml)

As the W3C explains, there are several simple solutions to this problem, such as to add the optional XML declaration with an encoding attribute. For example, either of these address common Western encoding needs:

```
<?xml version="1.0" encoding="iso-8859-1" ?>
<?xml version="1.0" encoding="UTF-8" ?>
```

For HTML, we can use the `<meta>` tag:

```
<meta http-equiv="Content-Type" content="text/html; charset=utf-8">
```

I added the "iso-8859-1" encoding as the first line of the file `b-icn-asxml-strict-clean-enc.xml`. Finally, we have an XHTML 1.0 Strict document that the W3C HTML Validation Service accepts without qualification, as shown in Figure 15-10.

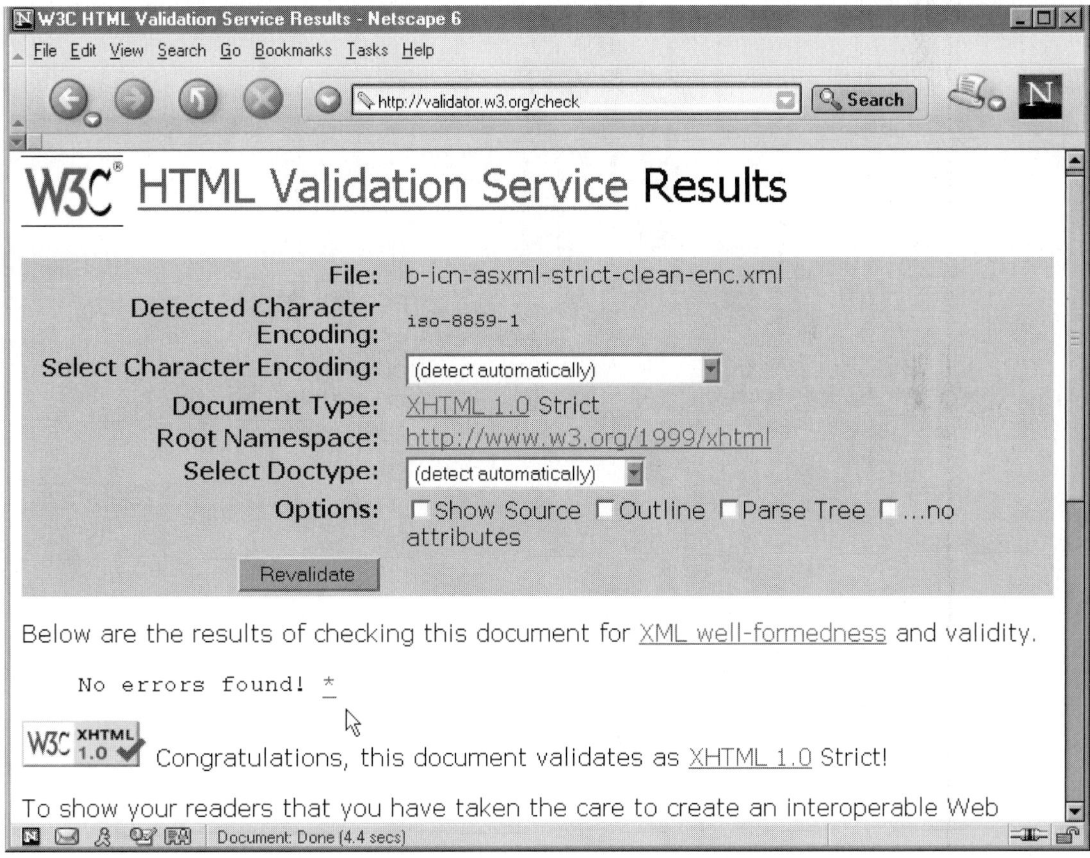

FIGURE 15-10 XHTML 1.0 Strict valid with encoding (b-icn-asxml-strict-clean-enc.xml)

Considerations for Displaying XHTML

As we've seen, you can display XHTML in most browsers if you are careful to follow conventions discussed throughout this chapter, especially the considerations presented in the "Differences between XHTML 1.0 and HTML 4.01" section. Our perfected version, `b-icn-asxml-strict-clean-enc.xml`, is shown in Figure 15-11, displayed in Netscape 6.2. If you compare this to the original `bad-ex.html` displayed in Figure 15-4, you'll see only minor differences.

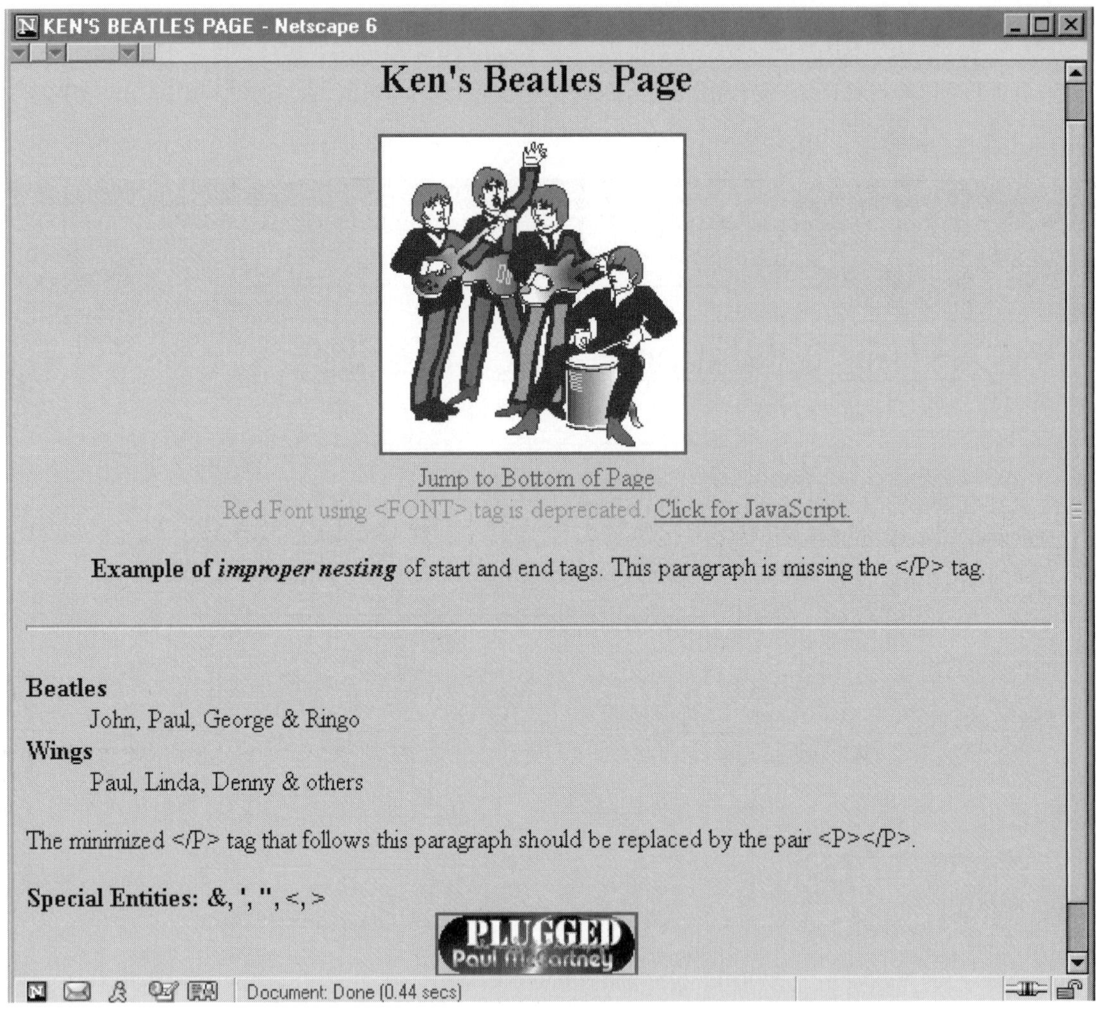

FIGURE 15-11 Display of XHTML 1.0 Strict in Netscape 6.2 (b-icn-asxml-strict-clean-enc.xml)

One consideration is whether to use the `.html` or `.xml` filename extension for XHTML 1.0 documents. At the time of this writing, general browser support for XML is still somewhat limited and definitely different across browsers, so it's probably safer to stick with `.html`. This is especially true if your users still use IE 5.5 or Netscape 4.x. In the absence of any server-side HTTP header information, IE 5.5 insists on using its built-in generic XML stylesheet whenever it encounters a document ending in `.xml`. For example, it applies its expandable tree view to both `b-icn-asxml-strict-clean-enc.xml` (which contains an XML declaration) and `b-icn-asxml-strict-clean.xml` (without an XML declaration). However, if we simply *rename* either file with a `.html` extension without modifying anything inside, IE 5.5 renders it much like Netscape 6.2. As for Netscape 4.7x, XML is not handled at all, but the renamed `.html` versions also display as they do in Netscape 6.2.

If you do use the `.xml` extension, don't forget to consider CDATA section issues. For example, Figure 15-12 shows what happens in Netscape 6.2 when we don't wrap the JavaScript in a CDATA section. The document it's attempting to display is `b-icn-asxml-strict-NO-CDATA.xml`, which is identical to our final XHTML 1.0 Strict solution (Listing 15-11) except that I've deleted the two pairs of CDATA section delimiters. As XML parsers are supposed to behave, Netscape 6.2 refuses to display the page because the "<" symbol causes the document to be not well-formed.

Another consideration is whether to include the XML declaration, `<?xml version="1.0" encoding="UTF-8"?>`. Most recent browsers ignore the declara-

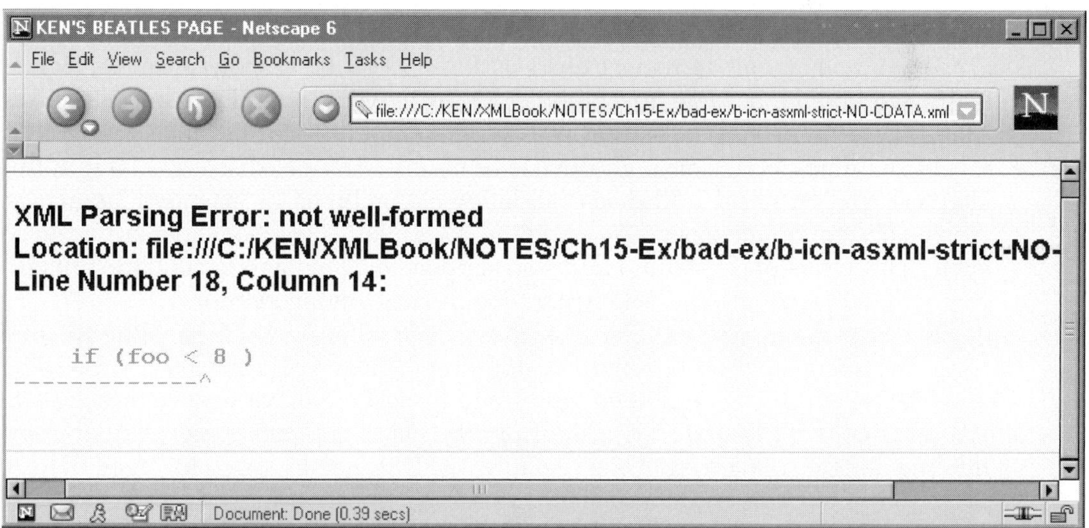

FIGURE 15-12 JavaScript problem with XML in Netscape 6.2

tion because it is an unknown element to them. However, others may render it as literal text. Given that the XHTML specification recommends including the XML declaration, and since we saw how W3C strongly encourages the use of the encoding pseudo-attribute in particular, it is probably best to *include an XML declaration* if you are naming your files `.xml`.

A final possible consideration from a server perspective hinted at on the Roadmap page is what MIME media type should be associated with XHTML. (See *http://www.w3.org/MarkUp/xhtml-roadmap/#media-type* and *http://www.w3.org/MarkUp/* for possible updates on the XHTML media types.) At the time of this writing, an IETF draft proposal suggests `application/xhtml+xml`, but clearly indicates that this was not intended to obsolete the `text/html` MIME type from RFC 2854.

Combining XHTML with Another Vocabulary

In our earlier discussion of XML namespaces, XLink, and XPointer, we've seen how different XML languages can be combined in a single document. Namespaces are used to associate elements and attributes with a particular vocabulary.

Mixing XML vocabularies in a single document is an aspect of XML that is still very immature as of this writing. We hope that browser support will improve and become more standardized in the near future. In other words, if you try the test file in your favorite browser, your mileage may vary.

One advantage of moving from HTML to XHTML is that, since XHTML is XML, we should be able to combine XHTML with other languages, such as MathML, SVG, or languages that we create. While this can be done at the DTD level (combining DTDs through the use of modularization, discussed later in this chapter), that primarily addresses validation of combined or extended languages. An equally important aspect of combining vocabularies is what client applications such as browsers understand. However, support for language combination in current browsers is somewhat lacking and details vary among vendors.

I've used Amaya from the W3C to illustrate combining XHTML, MathML, and SVG. The document, `amaya-xhtml-mathml.html` (Listing 15-12), was created using Amaya 5.0, which is a combined editor and browser. Amaya uses namespaces to indicate the MathML and SVG islands of code (XML fragments) nested within the `html` document element from the (default) XHTML namespace. However, there is no reference to DTDs by default.

Listing 15-12 Combination of XHTML, MathML, and SVG (amaya-xhtml-mathml.html)

```
<?xml version="1.0" encoding="iso-8859-1"?>
<html xmlns="http://www.w3.org/1999/xhtml">
<head>
  <meta http-equiv="Content-Type" content="text/html; charset=iso-8859-1" />
  <title>Mixed XHTML, MathML and SVG</title>
  <meta name="GENERATOR" content="amaya V5.0" />
</head>

<body style="background-color:white">
<h1 style="text-align:center">Mixed XHTML, MathML and SVG</h1>

<p>This is a paragraph.</p>

<h4>List</h4>
<ul>
  <li>one</li>
  <li>two</li>
  <li>three</li>
</ul>

<h4>Switching to MathML</h4>

<p>Expression with under- and overscript, <code>munderover</code>:
<math xmlns="http://www.w3.org/1998/Math/MathML">
  <munderover>
    <mo>&Sum;</mo>
    <mrow>
      <mi>i</mi>
      <mo>=</mo>
      <mn>1</mn>
    </mrow>
    <mi>n</mi>
  </munderover>
</math>
</p>

<h4>Back to XHTML</h4>

<h4>Switching to SVG</h4>
<svg xmlns="http://www.w3.org/2000/svg">
  <rect stroke="black" fill="red" x="40px" y="15px" width="300px"
        height="45px" stroke-width="4"/>
  <circle stroke="black" fill="blue" cx="180px" cy="40px" r="40px"
          stroke-width="2" />
</svg>

<h4>Back to XHTML</h4>
</body>
</html>
```

Figure 15-13 shows this mixed document in Amaya 5.0. Unfortunately, Netscape 6.x and Internet Explorer 5.5 both fail to render either the MathML or SVG sections. For the MathML portion, both browsers display:

```
Expression with under- and overscript, munderover: &Sum; i = 1 n
```

and nothing at all for the SVG portion.

However, there is another approach we can take. We can use the `object` element of XHTML (which replaces `applet`, `embed`, and `bgsound` elements in earlier or proprietary versions of HTML). If we move the entire SVG fragment into a separate

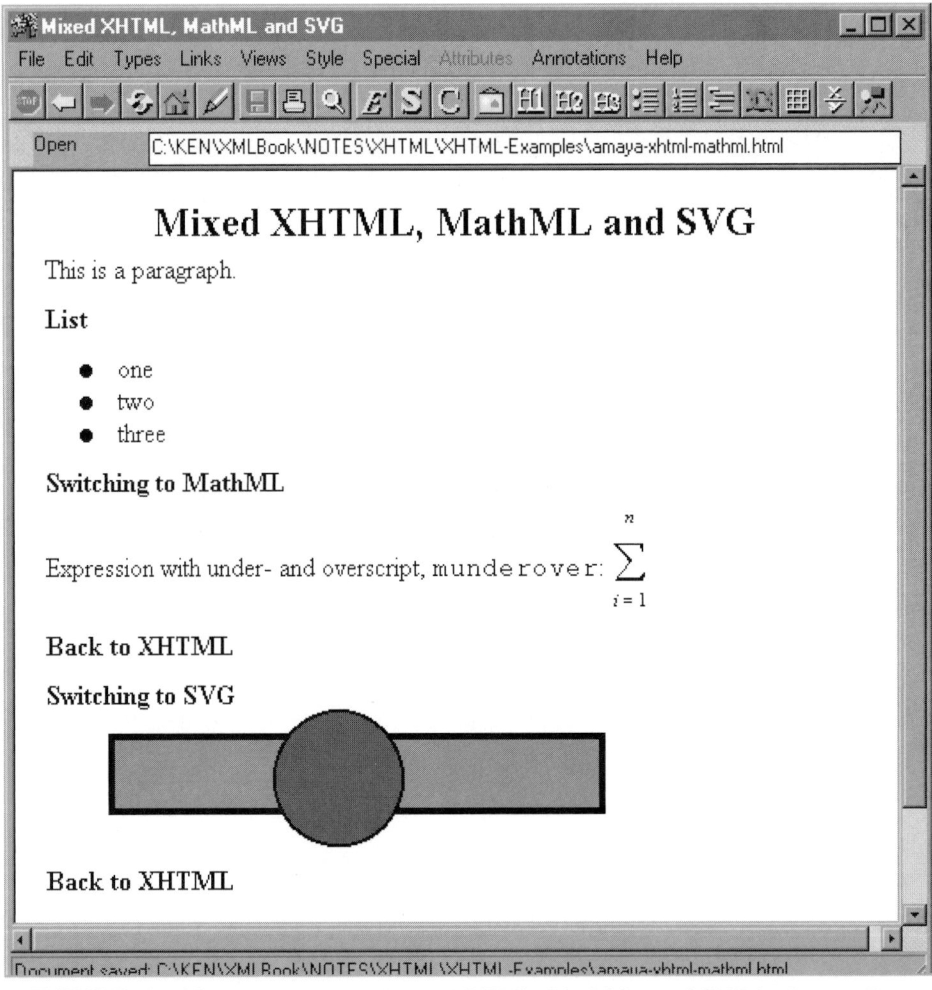

FIGURE 15-13 Displaying combined XHTML, MathML, and SVG in Amaya 5.x

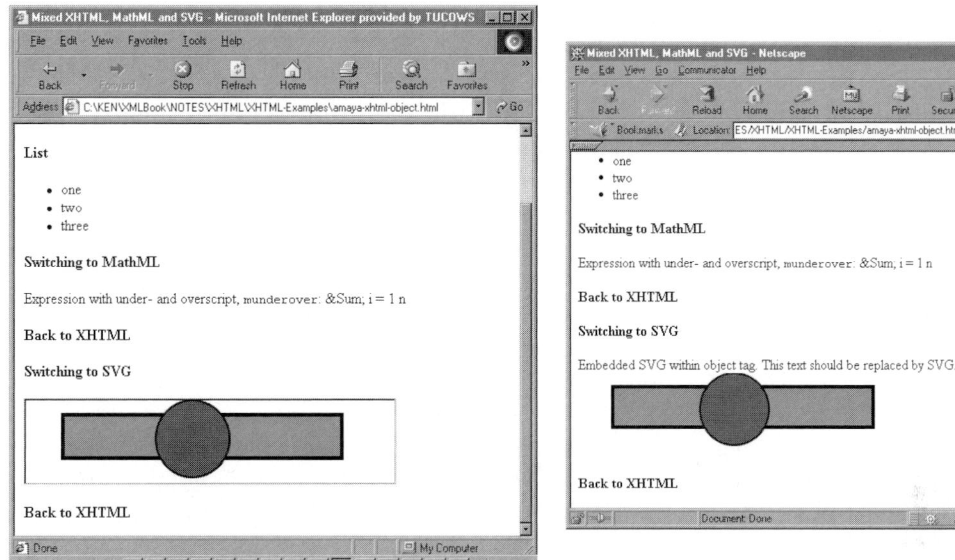

FIGURE 15-14 XHTML with SVG via Object Element in IE 5.5 (*left*) and Netscape 4.7x (*right*)

file named, for example, `simple.svg`, replace the `svg` element with `object`, and specify the MIME content type as `image/svg+xml`, then IE 5.5, Netscape 6.x and Netscape 4.7x *will* render the SVG.[8] It's necessary to include `width` and `height` for a viewport (otherwise, you won't see any of the SVG). The results are shown in Figure 15-14. Netscape 4.7x also displays the character text but IE 5.5 and Netscape 6.x do not. Actually, the text shouldn't be displayed since it's intended as a fallback for browsers that cannot handle the specified content type or do not recognize the `object` element at all.

```
<object data="simple.svg" type="image/svg+xml"
        width="400" height="90" >
        Embedded SVG within object tag.
        This text should be replaced by SVG.
</object>
```

Well, hopefully you enjoyed this little side trip about combining MathML and SVG with XHTML! We now return you to the regularly scheduled discussion of the XHTML family, turning next to the extremely important and forward-thinking modularization effort.

8. It will provided you've installed an SVG plugin, such as Adobe's excellent SVG Viewer, *http://www.adobe.com/svg/main.html*. For Netscape 6.x support, you must use SVG Viewer 3.0 or later. Note that W3C's Amaya does not require a plugin since it has native SVG support.

Modularization of XHTML

The Modularization of XHTML Recommendation (*http://www.w3.org/TR/xhtml-modularization/*) was published in April 2001, about four months after XHTML Basic (which depends on *it*, rather than the reverse!) and one month before XHTML 1.1. This specification describes a modular approach to XHTML that subsets the language into a large number of non-overlapping "abstract modules," each of which is semantically unique. The abstractions are implemented by DTDs with plans to migrate to XML Schema (as discussed in the later section "Modularization of XHTML in XML Schema"). Each implementation module describes groups of elements, attributes, and content models based on functionality. XHTML 1.0/ HTML 4.01 is decomposed into roughly forty modules. All of the deprecated elements and attributes of HTML 4.01 have been either removed from these modules or relegated to the "legacy" module. Presentational elements are separated from structural elements. The result is well-suited for XML since languages that are purely structural can be defined from these modules, leaving presentation (when necesssary) to stylesheets.

Modularization enables subsetting and extending XHTML for special-purpose devices. Modularizing XHTML helps product designers to specify which elements are supported by a device using standard building blocks. It also helps content providers to deliver content to a larger number and wider range of platforms. Modularization paves the way for developers to augment the language with client-specific or document-specific markup. This modularization approach is already in use in MathML, Internationalization, Synchronized Multimedia, as well as by the WAP Forum and OASIS, among others.

W3C's stated high-level design goals for the modularization effort (from *http://www.w3.org/TR/xhtml-modularization/goals.html#s_intro_design*) are:

> [G1] To group semantically related parts of XHTML together.
>
> [G2] Using DTD technology, to support the creation of related languages (subsets, supersets) for specific purposes (small devices, special-purpose devices), while guaranteeing commonality of the overlapping parts.
>
> [G3] To facilitate future development by allowing parts of the language to be replaced by improved modules (for instance, forms) without disturbing the rest of the language.
>
> [G4] To encourage and facilitate the reuse of modules in other languages.

Another key aspect of modularization is the very *deliberate separation of presentation from structure*. Separate presentation modules are defined by this specification in the hopes that CSS or other style mechanisms will be used to assign style to elements, rather than hardcoding style information into the main flow of elements. This formatting model is especially important so that presentation can degrade gracefully if a device doesn't support a particular style mechanism.

Abstract Modules and Implementations

Modularization is the process of composing or decomposing a DTD by dividing its markup declarations into units or groups to support specific goals. Although the logical modules defined by W3C for XHTML do correspond one-to-one with physical entities (files) in which they are stored, that does not need to be the case.

Crucial to the modularization approach is the idea of an **abstract module**, a narrative description of the contents of a module defined in terms of content models, but intended for human consumption, rather than by XML parsers. An abstract module defines a semantically unique group of elements, attributes, and content models. In this context, an XHTML document type is a set of abstract modules. The chief raison d'être for the modularization effort is to provide a framework by which a DTD author can mix elements from multiple abstract modules into what is called a **hybrid document type** containing multiple namespaces, but still permitting full validation.

Although not absolutely required, the W3C encourages the use of abstract modules. Certainly a major benefit of the abstraction is that it leaves implementation issues to the user of the modules who can then, at least potentially, choose a DTD, XML Schema, RELAX-NG, or other schema implementation.

A **module implementation** is a set of elements, attribute-list declarations, and content model declarations, any of which may be empty sets. The abstract modules reference the elements in the implementation module and possibly also elements and attributes in other modules upon which the module depends. Abstract modules can include `PCDATA`. Attributes are of the the familiar types in XML 1.0 (`CDATA`, `NMTOKEN`, `ID`, etc.).

You can optionally draw from several *attribute collections* (attribute sets) that the spec defines:

- `Core`—`class`, `id`, `title` for style, linking, and accessibility, respectively
- `I18N`—`xml:lang` for internationalization ["i18n", get it?] of text
- `Events`—JavaScript events (`onclick`, `onmouseover`, `onkeypress`, etc.) and DOM Level 2 Events eventually
- `Style`—`style` attribute, which can be used with virtually any element
- `Common` = `Core` + `Events` + `I18N` + `Style`

The Modules

The Modularization of XHTML specification includes a DTD folder with more than forty `*.mod` files, each of which is a DTD implementation of an abstract module.[9] These implementations range in size from about 30 to 400 lines. The largest are the

9. You can download all of these DTD modules plus the specification itself via the link *http://www.w3.org/TR/xhtml-modularization/xhtml-modularization.zip*. You'll get more from this chapter if you do so.

Legacy, Table, Form, and Qualified Names modules; among the smallest are those for Inline Style, Presentation, and Block Presentation modules. The entire set of implementation modules is shown in Table 15-3 and the text that follows it. This is a superset of those shown in Table 15-4 on page 1005 for XHTML Basic.

TABLE 15-3 Modules Defined by the Modularization of XHTML

XHTML Module	*Elements (or Attributes)*
Core Modules (= XHTML Host Language)	
(Document) Structure Module `xhtml-struct-1.mod`	`body`, `head`, `html`, `title`
Text Module `xhtml-text-1.mod`	`abbr`, `acronym`, `address`, `blockquote`, `br`, `cite`, `code`, `dfn`, `div`, `em`, `h1`, `h2`, `h3`, `h4`, `h5`, `h6`, `kbd`, `p`, `pre`, `q`, `samp`, `span`, `strong`, `var`
Hypertext Module `xhtml-hypertext-1.mod`	`a`
List Module `xhtml-list-1.mod`	`dl`, `dt`, `dd`, `ol`, `ul`, `li`
Text Extension Modules	
Presentation Module `xhtml-pres-1.mod`	`b`, `big`, `hr`, `i`, `small`, `sub`, `sup`, `tt`
Edit Module `xhtml-edit-1.mod`	`del`, `ins`
Bidirectional Text Module `xhtml-bdo-1.mod`	`bdo`
Forms Modules (note that Basic Forms is a subset of Forms)	
Basic Forms Module *[a] `xhtml-basic-form-1.mod`	`form`, `label`, `input`, `select`, `option`, `textarea`
Forms Module `xhtml-form-1.mod`	`button`, `fieldset`, `form`, `input`, `label`, `legend`, `select`, `optgroup`, `option`, `textarea`
Table Modules (note that Basic Table is a subset of Table)	
Basic Table Module * `xhtml-basic-table-1.mod`	`table`, `caption`, `tr`, `th`, `td`
Table Module `xhtml-table-1.mod`	`caption`, `col`, `colgroup`, `table`, `tbody`, `td`, `tfoot`, `th`, `thead`, `tr`
Applet/Object Modules	
Apple Module [Deprecated; see Object]* `xhtml-applet-1.mod`	`applet`, `param`
Object Module `xhtml-object-1.mod`	`object`, `param`

TABLE 15-3 *(continued)*

XHTML Module	*Elements (or Attributes)*
Miscellaneous Modules	
Ruby Annotation Module xhtml-ruby-1.mod	ruby, rbc, rtc, rb, rt, rp
Image Module xhtml-image-1.mod	img
Client-side Image Map Module xhtml-csismap-1.mod	area, map
Server-side Image Map Module xhtml-ssismap-1.mod	'ismap' attribute for img
Frames Module* xhtml-frames-1.mod	frameset, frame, noframes
Target Module* xhtml-target-1.mod	'target' attribute used for opening windows
Iframes Module* xhtml-iframes-1.mod	iframe (inline frame)
Intrinsic Events Module xhtml-events-1.mod	Events Attributes: onclick, ondblclick, onmousedown, onmouseup, onmouseover, onmousemove, onmouseout, onkeypress, onkeydown, onkeyup, onfocus, onblur, onsubmit, onreset, onselect, onchange, onload, onunload
Metainformation Module xhtml-meta-1.mod	meta
Scripting Module xhtml-script-1.mod	noscript, script
Stylesheet Module xhtml-style-1.mod	style element
Style Attribute Module [Deprecated] xhtml-inlstyle-1.mod	style attribute
Link Module xhtml-link-1.mod	link
Base Module xhtml-base-1.mod	base
Name Identification Module* [Deprecated] xhtml-nameident-1.mod	'name' attribute on form, img, a, map, applet, frame, iframe
Legacy Module* xhtml-legacy-1.mod	Defines elements and attributes that were deprecated in previous versions of HTML and XHTML (e.g., font, basefont, center, s, strike, u, dir, menu, isindex)

a. An asterisk denotes modules that are not part of XHTML 1.1 although they are defined in Modularization of XHTML, namely; Applet, Frames, Iframes, Target, Basic Forms and Basic Tables, Name Identification, and Legacy Modules (deprecated elements and attributes).

The XHTML Catalog Data File (file `xhtml.cat`) in the DTD folder lists the modules in the table plus the following modules and entities that comprise the DTD:

XHTML Character Entities[10]

- `ENTITIES Latin 1 for XHTML: xhtml-lat1.ent`
- `ENTITIES Special for XHTML: xhtml-special.ent`
- `ENTITIES Symbols for XHTML: xhtml-symbol.ent`

XHTML Modular Framework[11]

- `ENTITIES XHTML Modular Framework 1.0: xhtml-framework-1.mod`
- `ELEMENTS XHTML Redeclarations 1.0: xhtml-redecl-1.mod`
- `ELEMENTS XHTML Base Architecture 1.0: xhtml-arch-1.mod`
- `NOTATIONS XHTML Notations 1.0: xhtml-notations-1.mod`
- `ENTITIES XHTML Datatypes 1.0: xhtml-datatypes-1.mod`
- `ENTITIES XHTML Common Attributes 1.0: xhtml-attribs-1.mod`
- `ENTITIES XHTML Qualified Names 1.0: xhtml-qname-1.mod`
- `ENTITIES XHTML Character Entities 1.0: xhtml-charent-1.mod`

XHTML DTD Support Modules[12] (`block`, `inline`, `applet/object param`, etc.)

- `ELEMENTS XHTML Block Phrasal 1.0: xhtml-blkphras-1.mod`
- `ELEMENTS XHTML Block Presentation 1.0: xhtml-blkpres-1.mod`
- `ELEMENTS XHTML Block Structural 1.0: xhtml-blkstruct-1.mod`
- `ELEMENTS XHTML Inline Phrasal 1.0: xhtml-inlphras-1.mod`
- `ELEMENTS XHTML Inline Presentation 1.0: xhtml-inlpres-1.mod`
- `ELEMENTS XHTML Inline Structural 1.0: xhtml-inlstruct-1.mod`
- `ELEMENTS XHTML Param Element 1.0: xhtml-param-1.mod`
- `ELEMENTS XHTML Legacy Redeclarations 1.0: xhtml-legacy-redecl-1.mod`

Anatomy of a Module

Each DTD module is identified by a unique pair of `PUBLIC` and `SYSTEM` identifiers, generally of the form:

```
PUBLIC "-//W3C//ELEMENTS XHTML Something 1.0//EN"
SYSTEM "http://www.w3.org/TR/xhtml-modularization/DTD/xhtml-Something-1.mod"
```

10. See also *http://www.w3.org/TR/xhtml-modularization/dtd_module_defs.html#a_xhtml_character_entities*

11. See also *http://www.w3.org/TR/xhtml-modularization/dtd_module_defs.html#a_xhtml_framework*

12. See also *http://www.w3.org/TR/xhtml-modularization/dtd_module_defs.html#a_dtdsupport*

Element	Attributes	Minimal Content Model
b	Common	(PCDATA | Inline)*
big	Common	(PCDATA | Inline)*
hr	Common	EMPTY
i	Common	(PCDATA | Inline)*
small	Common	(PCDATA | Inline)*
sub	Common	(PCDATA | Inline)*
sup	Common	(PCDATA | Inline)*
tt	Common	(PCDATA | Inline)*

FIGURE 15-15 Presentation Abstract Module from W3C Modularization of XHTML Rec

For example, to specify the Presentation Module, you'd reference:

```
PUBLIC "-//W3C//ELEMENTS XHTML Presentation 1.0//EN"
SYSTEM "http://www.w3.org/TR/xhtml-modularization/DTD/xhtml-pres-1.mod"
```

To get a feel for how the various modules are structured and connected, let's examine the XHTML Presentation module in some detail, in terms of both its abstract model and its DTD implementation.[13] We can see from Table 15-3 that Presentation is a Text Extension module; it is not one of the four core modules necessary for an XHTML Host Language (Structure, Text, Hypertext, and Lists). The abstract module is shown in Figure 15-15.

This abstraction tells us that there are eight elements in the module, all of which have the same attributes (the common set, which is `Core` + `Events` + `I18N` + `Style`, as was described earlier). We can also see that the content model is identical for each element except for the `hr` element, which is an empty element and, therefore, may not contain children or character content. The other seven, however, accept a mixed content model (a mix of character data and elements from an `Inline` group).

The DTD fragment that implements this abstraction is the `xhtml-pres-1.mod` file (Listing 15-13).

13. For the abstraction, see *http://www.w3.org/TR/xhtml-modularization/abstract_modules.html#s_presentationmodule* and for the DTD implementation, see *http://www.w3.org/TR/xhtml-modularization/dtd_module_defs.html#a_module_Presentation*.

Listing 15-13 XHTML Presentation Module

```
<!-- XHTML Presentation Module .............................................. -->
<!-- file: xhtml-pres-1.mod

This is XHTML, a reformulation of HTML as a modular XML application.
Copyright 1998-2001 W3C (MIT, INRIA, Keio), All Rights Reserved.
Revision: $Id: xhtml-pres-1.mod,v 4.0 2001/04/02 22:42:49 altheim Exp $ SMI

     This DTD module is identified by the PUBLIC and SYSTEM identifiers:

       PUBLIC "-//W3C//ELEMENTS XHTML Presentation 1.0//EN"
       SYSTEM "http://www.w3.org/TR/xhtml-modularization/DTD/xhtml-pres-1.mod"

     Revisions:
     (none)
....................................................................... -->

<!-- Presentational Elements

     This module defines elements and their attributes for
     simple presentation-related markup.
-->

<!ENTITY % xhtml-inlpres.module "INCLUDE" >
<![%xhtml-inlpres.module;[
<!ENTITY % xhtml-inlpres.mod
     PUBLIC "-//W3C//ELEMENTS XHTML Inline Presentation 1.0//EN"
            "xhtml-inlpres-1.mod" >
%xhtml-inlpres.mod;]]>

<!ENTITY % xhtml-blkpres.module "INCLUDE" >
<![%xhtml-blkpres.module;[
<!ENTITY % xhtml-blkpres.mod
     PUBLIC "-//W3C//ELEMENTS XHTML Block Presentation 1.0//EN"
            "xhtml-blkpres-1.mod" >
%xhtml-blkpres.mod;]]>

<!-- end of xhtml-pres-1.mod -->
```

This Presentation module is actually composed of two other modules, each residing in a separate file:

- Inline Presentation module in file `xhtml-inlpres-1.mod`
- Block Presentation module in file `xhtml-blkpres-1.mod`

Lines of the form

```
<!ENTITY % something.module "INCLUDE" > . . . . ]]>
```

make use of an SGML `INCLUDE` conditional section mechanism to process everything up to the `]]>` section end marker. We'll soon see how an `IGNORE` definition can override and disable this processing. The suffix `.module` always indicates conditional inclusion in W3C XHTML DTDs, as opposed to the .mod suffix, which identifies the actual module itself, which happens to be implemented as one module per file.

Lines of the form

```
<!ENTITY % xhtml-something.mod
     PUBLIC "-//W3C//ELEMENTS XHTML Something 1.0//EN"
            "xhtml-something-1.mod" >
%xhtml-something.mod;]]>
```

define a parameter entity that represents a module, gives its formal public identifier (FPI) and the relative path to the file that contains the module, and then instantiates the module (the last line above).

The actual elements, attributes, and content model implementations appear in the Inline and Block Presentation modules. For example, the Block Presentation module is reproduced in Listing 15-14.

Listing 15-14 XHTML Block Presentation Module

```
<!-- XHTML Block Presentation Module  .................................... -->
<!-- file: xhtml-blkpres-1.mod

     This is XHTML, a reformulation of HTML as a modular XML application.
     Copyright 1998-2001 W3C (MIT, INRIA, Keio), All Rights Reserved.
     Revision: $Id: xhtml-blkpres-1.mod,v 4.0 2001/04/02 22:42:49 altheim
Exp $ SMI

     This DTD module is identified by the PUBLIC and SYSTEM identifiers:

       PUBLIC "-//W3C//ELEMENTS XHTML Block Presentation 1.0//EN"
       SYSTEM "http://www.w3.org/TR/xhtml-modularization/DTD/xhtml-blkpres-
1.mod"

     Revisions:
     (none)
........................................................................ -->

<!-- Block Presentational Elements

        hr

     This module declares the elements and their attributes used to
     support block-level presentational markup.
-->

<!ENTITY % hr.element  "INCLUDE" >
<![%hr.element;[
<!ENTITY % hr.content  "EMPTY" >
<!ENTITY % hr.qname  "hr" >
<!ELEMENT %hr.qname;  %hr.content; >
<!-- end of hr.element -->]]>
```

```
<!ENTITY % hr.attlist  "INCLUDE" >
<![%hr.attlist;[
<!ATTLIST %hr.qname;
      %Common.attrib;
>
<!-- end of hr.attlist -->]]>

<!-- end of xhtml-blkpres-1.mod -->
```

This implementation module describes only the `hr` element, its content model, and its attributes, in that order, so this is really one of the simplest modules. Unlike the other seven Presentation module elements, `hr` is a block-level element, meaning that a newline follows it. Although most other block-level elements are containers that surround child elements (e.g., `div`, `p`, and `body`), `hr` contains nothing.

Note the extensive use of parameter entities in DTD implementation modules. Most of the naming conventions are reasonably self-evident:

- `hr.element` is the conditional inclusion switch for the `hr` element
- `hr.content` describes the content model (empty, in this case)
- `hr.attlist` controls conditional inclusion of the attribute list

One exception is `hr.qname`, which is the qualified name, in this case, `hr`; this is what we normally call the element name. Qualified names may contain prefixes, in case we're mixing fragments from two DTDs that happen to share the same element name. Therefore, the element declaration

```
<!ELEMENT %hr.qname;  %hr.content; >
```

expands to

```
<!ELEMENT hr  EMPTY >
```

and the compact attribute-list declaration (which appears to be so short)

```
<!ATTLIST %hr.qname;
      %Common.attrib;
```

expands considerably. The `%Common.attrib;` parameter entity is defined in the Common Attributes module (the file `xhtml-attribs-1.mod`) as a combination of several entities in the definition

```
<!ENTITY % Common.attrib
     "%Core.attrib;
      %I18n.attrib;
      %Events.attrib;
      %Common.extra.attrib;"
>
```

This, in turn, defines each of the smaller entities except `%Events.attrib;`, which is defined in the Intrinsic Events module (filename `xhtml-events-1.mod`). We also have to peek into the Datatypes module (`xhtml-datatypes-1.mod`) to unravel all of the parameter entities.[14] Eventually (after several levels of substitution) the `hr` attribute-list declaration expands to

```
<!ATTLIST hr
     xmlns        CDATA         #FIXED    "http://www.w3.org/1999/xhtml"
     id           ID            #IMPLIED
     class        NMTOKENS      #IMPLIED
     title        CDATA         #IMPLIED
     xml:lang     NMTOKEN       #IMPLIED
     dir          (ltr | rtl)   #IMPLIED
     onclick      CDATA         #IMPLIED
     ondblclick   CDATA         #IMPLIED
     onmousedown  CDATA         #IMPLIED
     onmouseup    CDATA         #IMPLIED
     onmouseover  CDATA         #IMPLIED
     onmousemove  CDATA         #IMPLIED
     onmouseout   CDATA         #IMPLIED
     onkeypress   CDATA         #IMPLIED
     onkeydown    CDATA         #IMPLIED
     onkeyup      CDATA         #IMPLIED
>
```

As we can deduce from the earlier abstract module, the Inline Presentation Elements (`xhtml-inlpres-1.mod`) must contain the elements `b`, `big`, `i`, `small`, `sub`, `sup`, and `tt`. Each is defined syntactically and structurally just like `hr`, although of course the content model and attributes are likely to be different. (It turns out though that in this case, the attributes for all of these elements are the same.) For example, here's the `b` element's definition:

```
<!ENTITY % b.element  "INCLUDE" >
<![%b.element;[
<!ENTITY % b.content
     "( #PCDATA | %Inline.mix; )*"
>
<!ENTITY % b.qname  "b" >
<!ELEMENT %b.qname;  %b.content; >
<!-- end of b.element -->]]>

<!ENTITY % b.attlist  "INCLUDE" >
<![%b.attlist;[
<!ATTLIST %b.qname;
      %Common.attrib;
>
<!-- end of b.attlist -->]]>
```

14. Actually, the namespace substitution is more involved than I've suggested since there may be namespaces from other languages to declare. See the entities `%XHTML.xmlns.attrib;`, `%NS.decl.attrib;` and `%XLINK.xmlns.attrib;` in the Qualified Name Module, `xhtml-qname-1.mod`. Also the `dir` attribute is included only if bidirectional text is enabled.

Drivers

A **driver** is typically a relatively short file (usually with the extension `.dtd`) that declares and instantiates the modules of a DTD. This is the glue that binds the many separate modules. The authors of the Modularization spec suggest that a DTD driver should contain no markup declarations that are part of the document model itself. No actual driver accompanies the Modularization of XHTML Recommendation, although drivers *are* provided with XHTML Basic and XHTML 1.1, both of which are built upon this specification. However, illustrative (nonfunctional) drivers are included in the `templates` and `examples` subfolders of the DTD folder.[15]

Listing 15-15 shows an excerpt from `examples\myml-1_0.dtd`. Notice that in addition to including a Framework module, the example driver includes the four required modules to be considered an XHTML Host Language: Text, Hypertext, Lists, and Document Structure. Your custom modules are placed between the Lists and Document Structure modules. Each of the W3C module referenced from this sample DTD driver is named `xhtml11-`*`something`*`-1.mod` because this new `myml` language is based on XHTML 1.1, which is in turn based on Modularization of HTML.

Listing 15-15 Excerpt from Sample DTD Driver (myml-1_0.dtd)

```
<!-- Define the Content Model file for the framework to use -->
<!ENTITY % xhtml-model.mod "MYMODEL">
<!-- stuff deleted -->
<!-- Modular Framework Module  .................................. -->
<!ENTITY % xhtml-framework.module "INCLUDE" >
<![%xhtml-framework.module;[
<!ENTITY % xhtml-framework.mod
     PUBLIC "-//W3C//ENTITIES XHTML 1.1 Modular Framework 1.0//EN"
            "xhtml11-framework-1.mod" >
%xhtml-framework.mod;]]>
<!-- stuff deleted -->

<!-- Text Module (required)  .............................. -->
<!ENTITY % xhtml-text.module "INCLUDE" >
<![%xhtml-text.module;[
<!ENTITY % xhtml-text.mod
     PUBLIC "-//W3C//ELEMENTS XHTML 1.1 Text 1.0//EN"
            "xhtml11-text-1.mod" >
%xhtml-text.mod;]]>

<!-- Hypertext Module (required) ................................ -->
<!ENTITY % xhtml-hypertext.module "INCLUDE" >
<![%xhtml-hypertext.module;[
```

15. You can download the Modularization specification, plus all of the modules, templates, and examples from *http://www.w3.org/TR/xhtml-modularization/xhtml-modularization.zip*. The sample drivers are `DTD\templates\template.dtd` and `DTD\examples\myml-1_0.dtd`.

```
<!ENTITY % xhtml-hypertext.mod
     PUBLIC "-//W3C//ELEMENTS XHTML 1.1 Hypertext 1.0//EN"
            "xhtml11-hypertext-1.mod" >
%xhtml-hypertext.mod;]]>

<!-- Lists Module (required)  .................................. -->
<!ENTITY % xhtml-list.module "INCLUDE" >
<![%xhtml-list.module;[
<!ENTITY % xhtml-list.mod
     PUBLIC "-//W3C//ELEMENTS XHTML 1.1 Lists 1.0//EN"
            "xhtml11-list-1.mod" >
%xhtml-list.mod;]]>

<!-- Your modules can be included here.
     Use the basic form defined above, and be sure to include the public FPI
     definition in your catalog file for each module that you define.
     You may also include W3C-defined modules at this point.
-->

<!-- Document Structure Module (required)  ...................... -->
<!ENTITY % xhtml-struct.module "INCLUDE" >
<![%xhtml-struct.module;[
<!ENTITY % xhtml-struct.mod
     PUBLIC "-//W3C//ELEMENTS XHTML 1.1 Document Structure 1.0//EN"
            "xhtml11-struct-1.mod" >
%xhtml-struct.mod;]]>
```

It should be noted in passing that another sample DTD driver, `template.dtd`, uses different FPI conventions for the four required modules. For example, the Text module is specified:

```
<!ENTITY % xhtml-text.mod
     PUBLIC "-//W3C//ELEMENTS XHTML Basic Text 1.0//EN"
            "http://www.w3.org/TR/xhtml-modularization/DTD/xhtml-text-1.mod" >
%xhtml-text.mod;
```

What this boils down to is that you can reference the actual modules on the W3C site if you wish, or you can download the zip file, place them in a directory of your choosing (i.e., on your Web server, if your DTD is to be Web accessible), and mix in any other modules from other languages you wish to incorporate with XHTML.

Building DTD Modules (Adding Your Own Module)

As we've seen, an XHTML family DTD consists of a large number of DTD fragments, each of which is the implementation of a particular module of related elements. Together these fragments constitute a complete DTD against which documents may be validated. Among other things, the "Building DTD Modules" section of the specification describes all of the important naming conventions that must be followed so that the fragments will mesh properly with existing modules when you either subset or extend XHTML (*http://www.w3.org/TR/xhtml-modularization/dtd_module_rules.html*). We've already seen some of these conventions in the names of parameter entities that ended in `.mix`, `.module`, `.mod`, `.attrib`, `.qname`, `.content`, and so on.

The W3C offers an informative tutorial entitled "XHTML Modules and Markup Languages: How to create XHTML Family modules and markup languages for fun and profit" at *http://www.w3.org/MarkUp/Guide/xhtml-m12n-tutorial/*.

The complete details of this process go beyond the scope of this book, but I will cover the key points and point you to the three key templates. We'll also see an example later in the chapter of how a language called RDDL has used this process effectively. At the top level, there are three major steps, each of which has many steps of its own, namely:

1. Define qualified names, as well as a namespace URI and prefix, for all elements and attributes of your extension.
2. For each abstract module you're creating, develop an implementation module that defines the elements and attributes named in Step 1.
3. Replace the XHTML DTD with a modified driver that instantiates the core modules, plus other XHTML modules you need, plus all new modules you created in Step 2.

The following subsections briefly address each of these steps.

Another section of the spec, "Developing DTDs with defined and extended modules," (*http://www.w3.org/TR/xhtml-modularization/dtd_developing.html*) discusses various scenarios including:

- Adding elements and/or attributes
- Defining a content model
- Creating a new DTD

Defining Qualified Names and Namespaces

The rules for dealing with namespaces are quite involved, but one key recommendation from the W3C worth emphasizing is *not* to specify a namespace prefix for XHTML elements, but to do so for elements from other non-XHTML languages that you're integrating with XHTML. The "Building DTD Modules" section goes into considerable detail about namespace definition, including the Qualified Names submodule, Declaration submodule(s), using the module as a standalone DTD, and various namespace idiosyncrasies.

The W3C provides a template for defining qualified names and a namespace for new elements: *http://www.w3.org/TR/xhtml-modularization/DTD/templates/template-qname-1.mod*. This Qualified Names template contains detailed comments describing the changes that you need to make. Certain case-sensitive naming conventions are important to follow closely:

- `Module` is used for the human-readable markup language name
- `MODULE` is used for a parameter entity name prefix
- `module` is used for the default namespace prefix

Of course, you replace `module` with the case-sensitive module name you're defining. The Qualified Names template is divided into two sections:

- Section A declares parameter entities for namespace-qualified names, namespace declarations, and name prefixing for `Module`.
- Section B declares parameter entities used to provide namespace-qualified names for all `Module` element types. (In other words, every element in your extension module is *named* here, but defined in another file. The beauty of this is that if you decide to change the name of the element, this is the only spot that needs to be updated.)

See the zip file's `examples` folder mentioned earlier, or check the online example at *http://www.w3.org/TR/xhtml-modularization/DTD/examples/myml-qname-1.mod.*

Creating a Module to Define Elements and Attributes

The second step is to create a file that defines the elements you named in the Qualified Names Module, along with their attributes. The relevant template to use is *http://www.w3.org/TR/xhtml-modularization/DTD/templates/template-1.mod*. For example, the template defines a new (non-XHTML) element named `front` with a `%Flow.mix;` content model and the common attributes like so:

```
<!ENTITY % MODULE.front.qname  "front" >
<!ELEMENT %MODULE.front.qname;  ( %Flow.mix; )* >
<!ATTLIST %MODULE.front.qname;
     %MODULE.Common.attrib;
>
```

(Again, you'd replace `MODULE` with the actual module name.) This template also shows how you can reference attributes from different namespaces.

Modifying the DTD Driver

We saw the third step in the earlier section entitled "Drivers." We need to replace the XHTML DTD with a modified driver that instantiates the four core modules, plus any other XHTML modules we need, plus all the new modules we just created in the previous section. Refer to the W3C driver template, *http://*

www.w3.org/TR/xhtml-modularization/DTD/templates/template.dtd. Don't forget that the place to insert the naming and instantiation of the added modules plus any noncore W3C that we need is between the List and Document Structure modules.

Discarding Unwanted Modules

You can omit modules using the `IGNORE` section mechanism, which takes the form:

```
<!ENTITY % what.ever "IGNORE" >
```

For example, the XHTML 1.1 DTD excludes the Legacy module by changing the usual `INCLUDE` to `IGNORE`:

```
<!ENTITY % xhtml-legacy.module "IGNORE" >
<![%xhtml-legacy.module;[
<!ENTITY % xhtml-legacy.mod
  PUBLIC "-//W3C//ELEMENTS XHTML Legacy Markup 1.0//EN"
      "http://www.w3.org/TR/xhtml-modularization/DTD/xhtml-legacy-1.mod">
%xhtml-legacy.mod;]]>
```

Although it may appear as though it is being instantiated with the `%xhtml-legacy.mod;` entity reference, actually everything between the bold brackets is *ignored*. The result is that XHTML 1.1 does not use anything from the Legacy module. That means that the elements `font`, `basefont`, `center`, `s`, `strike`, `u`, `dir`, `menu`, and `isindex` (from Table 15-3 on page 992) are simply unavailable if you use XHTML 1.1.

XHTML Basic

XHTML Basic (*http://www.w3.org/TR/xhtml-basic/*), a W3C Recommendation since December 2000, relies on the XHTML module implementations defined in Modularization of XHTML. XHTML Basic is a stripped-down version of XHTML (and therefore of HTML 4.01) that is targeted for small devices with limited memory ("thin clients" such as mobile phones, PDAs, pagers, and settop boxes).

The modules that XHTML Basic comprises are listed in Table 15-4, along with the elements that are defined in each module. Modules shown in bold (i.e., Structure, Text, Hypertext, and List) are, as we've learned, the four minimum modules required for an **XHTML Host Language**, which is a language that defines its own DTD based on these four core modules and adds others to create a completely new document type. Besides this minimal set of modules required to be an XHTML Host Language document type, XHTML Basic also supports images, basic forms, basic tables, and objects. XHTML Basic also provides a simple, common base that can be extended by the addition of modules. This is crucial for its adoption for use in thin clients; it must be simple enough by omitting unnecessary aspects of XHTML 1.0 or 1.1, yet flexible enough to add custom modules, and rich enough to provide a reasonable content authoring language.

TABLE 15-4 XHTML Basic Modules and Elements

XHTML Basic Module	*Elements*
Structure Module[a] `xhtml-struct-1.mod`	`body`, `head`, `html`, `title`
Text Module `xhtml-text-1.mod`	`abbr`, `acronym`, `address`, `blockquote`, `br`, `cite`, `code`, `dfn`, `div`, `em`, `h1`, `h2`, `h3`, `h4`, `h5`, `h6`, `kbd`, `p`, `pre`, `q`, `samp`, `span`, `strong`, `var`
Hypertext Module `xhtml-hypertext-1.mod`	`a`
List Module `xhtml-list-1.mod`	`dl`, `dt`, `dd`, `ol`, `ul`, `li`
Basic Forms Module `xhtml-basic-form-1.mod`	`form`, `label`, `input`, `select`, `option`, `textarea`
Basic Table Module `xhtml-basic-table-1.mod`	`table`, `caption`, `tr`, `th`, `td`
Object Module `xhtml-object-1.mod`	`object`, `param`
Image Module `xhtml-image-1.mod`	`img`
Metainformation Module `xhtml-meta-1.mod`	`meta`
Link Module `xhtml-link-1.mod`	`link`
Base Module `xhtml-base-1.mod`	`base`

a. **Bold** font indicates core modules required to be considered an XHTML Host Language.

The XHTML Basic Recommendation is targeted for manufacturers of and content providers for so-called **small information appliances** (also known as *thin clients*), devices with limited memory and/or CPU power, exemplified by mobile phones, televisions, PDAs, vending machines, pagers, car navigation systems, mobile game machines, digital book readers, and smart watches.

The functional basis for this subset of XHTML is the common set of features supported by existing subsets and variants of HTML, such as Compact HTML (CHTML, a W3C Note that goes way back to February 1998), the popular Wireless Markup Language (WML), and the W3C's "HTML 4.0 Guidelines for Mobile Access." The most common features were basic text (headings, paragraphs, and lists), hyperlinks, basic forms, basic tables, images, and meta information, so these are the heart of XHTML Basic.

It's very important to realize that although the relatively limited number of elements and attributes in XHTML Basic may *seem* like a loss of functionality compared to HTML 4.01, in fact it is much more attractive to content developers who gain a *single subset* that they can be sure will exist on all devices and also for small-device manufactures who can *exclude complex HTML functionality* (e.g., JavaScript, applets, client-side imagemaps) not needed by their devices.

The specification explains why certain HTML 4.0 features have been omitted from XHTML Basic, mostly due to the limited memory and processing power of small devices:

- Scripting and frames are not supported because it requires precious CPU cycles. Since events are very much device-dependent, event handlers for desktop computers aren't always adequate for small appliances.
- Frames simply aren't realistic for devices with small screens.
- External CSS style sheets are supported and are preferred for specifying presentation information. The `media` attribute can be used to select the appropriate device-dependent style sheets.
- Content developers are cautioned that certain devices have only the most basic fonts. Some devices support only monospace fonts, for example.
- The functionality of the forms and the tables is much more restricted than it is in HTML 4.0. Form features that require a local file system are omitted. In particular, tables cannot be nested, which impacts content developers who use nested tables to achieve page layout. CSS and eventually XSLFO are the alternatives.

As with XHTML 1.0, the document element of an XHTML Basic document must be `<html>` and the default namespace must be the XHTML namespace name, `http://www.w3.org/1999/xhtml`. The `DOCTYPE` declaration must use the Formal Public Identifier shown here (along with the document element).

```
<!DOCTYPE html PUBLIC "-//W3C//DTD XHTML Basic 1.0//EN"
    "http://www.w3.org/TR/xhtml-basic/xhtml-basic10.dtd">
<html xmlns="http://www.w3.org/1999/xhtml" xml:lang="en" >
```

In contrast to XHTML 1.0, however, you must *only* use `xml:lang`, not `lang`, for the language designation. The value of this attribute is only illustrative here; it can be any Language Code.

The driver file for the XHTML Basic document type implementation is *http://www.w3.org/TR/xhtml-basic/xhtml-basic10.dtd*, which is responsible for instantiating each actual module, defined in separate `*.mod` files listed in Table 15-4, such as `xhtml-basic10-model-1.mod`, `xhtml-framework-1.mod`, `xhtml-struct-1.mod`, `xhtml-hypertext-1.mod`, and `xhtml-basic-table-1.mod`.

RDDL: An Extension of XHTML Basic

Now that we have a reasonable understanding of both Modularization of XHTML and XHTML Basic, it's instructive to analyze a real-world example of extending the XHTML Basic language to see exactly what is required to add elements or attributes to those provided by the W3C.

Resource Directory Description Language (RDDL)[16] is a very clever grassroots proposed solution to the problem of what a namespace name should point to: a DTD, an XML Schema, an RDF schema, simply an HTML page, or perhaps nothing at all (as some developers have argued)? A Resource Directory includes a text description of a particular class of resources, as well as resources related to that class, together with a directory of links to these related resources. This description is both human-readable and machine-processible.

RDDL is an extension of XHTML Basic that adds a *single* element, `rddl:resource`, which is defined in terms of a simple XLink, with `xlink:role` indicating the nature of the resource being linked to and `xlink:arcrole` describing the purpose of the link.

RDDL provides its own DTD based on the Modularization of XHTML. The DTD redefines the XHTML `%Flow.mix;` entity to contain `rddl:resource` so it may occur wherever a `p` element can occur (in general). The `rddl:resource` element itself uses the `%Flow.mix;` content model, which boils down to this (after entity substitution):

```
<!ELEMENT rddl:resource (#PCDATA | %Flow.mix;)*>
<!ATTLIST rddl:resource
  id             ID        #IMPLIED
  xml:lang       NMTOKEN   #IMPLIED
  xml:base       CDATA     #IMPLIED
  xmlns:rddl     CDATA     #FIXED    "http://www.rddl.org/"
  xmlns:xlink    CDATA     #FIXED    "http://www.w3.org/1999/xlink"
  xlink:type     (simple)  #FIXED    "simple"
  xlink:arcrole  CDATA     #IMPLIED
  xlink:role     CDATA               "http://www.rddl.org/#resource"
  xlink:href     CDATA     #IMPLIED
  xlink:title    CDATA     #IMPLIED
  xlink:show     CDATA     #FIXED    "none"
  xlink:actuate  CDATA     #FIXED    "none"
>
```

To add the `rddl:resource` element and to accomplish the XHTML Basic `%Flow.mix;` change, RDDL includes a DTD and four modules not found in XHTML

16. See *http://www.rddl.org/*. Authors: Jonathan Borden, The Open Healthcare Group, and Tim Bray, Antarctica Systems, with help from `xml-dev` mailing list. All code in this section is copyright © 2000–2001 Jonathan Borden and Tim Bray. Used with permission.

Basic; it also includes the standard World Wide Web Consortium modules which are unmodified.

- rddl-xhtml.dtd
- rddl-qname-1.mod
- xhtml-rddl-model-1.mod
- rddl-resource-1.mod
- xlink-module-1.mod
- 23 XHTML Basic modules (e.g., xhtml-arch-1.mod, xhtml-blkstruct-1.mod, xhtml-text-1.mod, etc.)

Let's examine each of the RDDL additions.

RDDL DTD

The RDDL DTD is the file rddl-xhtml.dtd, identified by the PUBLIC and SYSTEM identifiers:

```
PUBLIC: "-//XML-DEV//DTD XHTML RDDL 1.0//EN"
SYSTEM: "http://www.rddl.org/rddl-xhtml.dtd"
```

An excerpt follows with the comment <!-- stuff deleted --> indicating where I've omitted something.[17] The RDDL DTD replaces the XHTML Basic 1.0 DTD, *http://www.w3.org/TR/xhtml-basic/xhtml-basic10.dtd*, and is essentially a superset of the W3C DTD. The major differences between the two are indicated by bold font. Besides defining the XLink namespace prefix, the RDDL DTD defines one parameter entity, %xhtml-qname-extra.mod;, that is normally the empty string in XHTML Basic but is set to "rddl-qname-1.mod" here and is necessary to define RDDL-specific qualified names (described in the next section). The entity %xhtml-model.mod; which is normally "xhtml-basic10-model-1.mod" is set to "xhtml-rddl-model-1.mod" instead here. Finally, the additional entity %xlink-module.mod;, which does not appear in XHTML Basic, is set to "xlink-module-1.mod".

```
<!ENTITY % XHTML.version  "-//XML-DEV//DTD XHTML RDDL 1.0//EN" >
<!-- stuff deleted -->
<!ENTITY % XLINK.prefix "xlink">
<!ENTITY % XLINK.prefixed "INCLUDE">
<!ENTITY % XLINK.xmlns "http://www.w3.org/1999/xlink" >
<!-- stuff deleted -->
<?doc type="doctype"
      role="title" {Resource Directory Description Language 1.0 } ?>
<!-- stuff deleted -->
<!-- Bring in the qualified names for the new module -->
<!ENTITY % RDDL.prefixed "INCLUDE">
```

17. The actual files can be obtained in their entirety as a zip file from *http://www.rddl.org/index.html#related.resources*.

```
<!ENTITY % xhtml-qname-extra.mod
     PUBLIC "-//XML-DEV//ENTITIES RDDL QName Module 1.0//EN"
    "rddl-qname-1.mod" >
<!-- stuff deleted -->
<!ENTITY % xhtml-model.mod
     PUBLIC "-//XML-DEV//ENTITIES RDDL Document Model 1.0//EN"
            "xhtml-rddl-model-1.mod" >

<!-- stuff deleted (23 standard XHTML Basic 1.0 modules) -->

<!ENTITY % xlink-module.mod
     PUBLIC "-//XML-DEV//ENTITIES XLink Module 1.0//EN"
            "xlink-module-1.mod" >
%xlink-module.mod;

<!ENTITY % rddl-resource.mod
     PUBLIC "-//XML-DEV//ELEMENTS RDDL Resource 1.0//EN"
            "rddl-resource-1.mod" >
%rddl-resource.mod;
```

RDDL Qualified Names Module

We learned earlier that the purpose of the Qualified Names Module is to establish a namespace and to declare the qualified names of any elements we need, so `rddl-qname-1.mod` contains:

```
<!-- Bring in the datatypes -->
<!ENTITY % RDDL-datatypes.mod
     PUBLIC "-//W3C//ENTITIES XHTML Datatypes 1.0//EN"
            "xhtml-datatypes-1.mod" >
%RDDL-datatypes.mod;

<!-- Declare the actual namespace of this module -->
<!ENTITY % RDDL.xmlns "http://www.rddl.org/" >

<!-- Declare the default prefix for this module -->
<!ENTITY % RDDL.prefix "rddl" >
<!-- stuff deleted -->
<!-- Make sure that the RDDL namespace attributes are included on the XHTML
     attribute set -->
<![%NS.prefixed;[
<!ENTITY % XHTML.xmlns.extra.attrib
     "%RDDL.xmlns.attrib;
     %XLINK.xmlns.attrib;"
 >
]]>
<!ENTITY % XHTML.xmlns.extra.attrib
     "%XLINK.xmlns.attrib;"
>
<!ENTITY % RDDL.resource.qname "%RDDL.pfx;resource">
<!ENTITY % RDDL.bundle.qname "%RDDL.pfx;bundle">
```

The net effect is that the qualified name becomes `rddl:resource`, where `rddl:` is the prefix associated with the namespace name `http://www.rddl.org/`. This prefixing is important because the default XHTML namespace requires no prefix. In other words, in RDDL only one element needs to be prefixed, and that happens by no coincidence to be the only element that RDDL adds to XHTML Basic. (The `rddl:bundle` element is apparently a dangling reference; this is the only reference I could find to that `qname`.)

RDDL 1.0 Document Model Module

We know that the Document Model Module defines the content models that elements may reference in their definitions. The entity `%Flow.mix;` is defined in `xhtml-rddl-model-1.mod` as:

```
<!ENTITY % Flow.mix
     "%Heading.class;
      | %List.class;
      | %Block.class;
      | %Inline.class;
      %Misc.class;"
>
```

which *appears* to be the same as the definition in W3C's `xhtml-basic10-model-1.mod`. However, upon closer examination, `%Block.class;` is based on `%BlkStruct.class;` which RDDL defines as:

```
<!ENTITY % BlkStruct.class "%p.qname; | %div.qname; | %RDDL.resource.qname;" >
```

whereas XHTML Basic defines this as:

```
<!ENTITY % BlkStruct.class "%p.qname; | %div.qname;" >
```

This change essentially establishes that the special element `rddl:resource` can appear wherever the elements `p` and `div` can appear. It is a block-level element.

RDDL Resource Module

The module that actually defines the element `rddl:resource` and its attributes is `rddl-resource-1.mod`.

```
<!ENTITY % RDDL.resource.element  "INCLUDE" >
<![ %RDDL.resource.element; [
<!ENTITY % RDDL.resource.content
     "( #PCDATA | %Flow.mix;)*"
>
<!ENTITY % RDDL.extra.attrib "
     xml:base CDATA #IMPLIED
">

<!ELEMENT %RDDL.resource.qname;  %RDDL.resource.content; >
<!-- end of resource.element -->]]>
```

```
<!ENTITY % RDDL.resource.attlist  "INCLUDE" >
<![%RDDL.resource.attlist;[
<!ATTLIST %RDDL.resource.qname;
    %id.attrib;
    %I18n.attrib;
    %RDDL.xmlns.attrib;
    %RDDL.extra.attrib;
    %xlink.simple.attrib;
    %xlink.namespace.attrib;
>
```

This defines the content model of `rddl:resource` to be a combination of `#PCDATA` and/or anything that is legal within the `%Flow.mix;` entity. The attributes are `id`, any of the internationalization attributes (`xml:lang` and `dir` for bidirectional text), `xml:base`, any of the XLink attributes for a `simple-type` link element, plus the RDDL and XLink namespace attributes.

RDDL XLink Module

The various XLink attributes used by `rddl:resource` are defined in `xlink-module-1.mod` that is excerpted below. Perhaps the most significant of these attributes are `xlink:arcrole`, `xlink:href`, and `xlink:role`. Notice that the default value for `xlink:role` is actually a fragment identifier named `resource` within the RDDL home page, which just so happens to be the section where the element `rddl:resource` is described!

```
<!ENTITY % XLINK.xmlns "http://www.w3.org/1999/xlink">
<!-- stuff deleted -->
<!ENTITY % xlink.simple.attrib '
    %XLINK.pfx;type (simple|arc|locator|resource) #FIXED "simple"
    %XLINK.pfx;arcrole %URI.datatype; #IMPLIED
    %XLINK.pfx;href %URI.datatype; #IMPLIED
    %XLINK.pfx;role %URI.datatype; "%RDDL.xmlns;#resource"
    %XLINK.pfx;title CDATA #IMPLIED
    %XLINK.pfx;show (none) #FIXED "none"
    %XLINK.pfx;actuate (none) #FIXED "none"
    %XLINK.pfx;label CDATA #IMPLIED
    %XLINK.pfx;locator CDATA #IMPLIED
    %XLINK.pfx;resource %URI.datatype; #IMPLIED
'>
```

Sample RDDL Document

The RDDL home page and related resources are themselves written in RDDL! They illustrate how similar RDDL is to XHTML Basic and yet how elegantly RDDL extends the language. Listing 15-16 is a short excerpt from the RDDL home page source that illustrates the essential structure of RDDL. Note in particular:

- The Formal Public Identifier refers to RDDL and its own DTD (*http://www.rddl.org/rddl-xhtml.dtd*), rather than to W3C's XHTML Basic.

- The root `html` element refers to three namespaces: one for XHTML (the default namespace), plus XLink and RDDL namespaces. This makes it easy to use conventional XHTML element names without prefixing, and wherever necessary the `rddl:` and `xlink:` prefixes can be used as well.
- The `rddl:resource` is intended for machine consumption, but it may (should) contain a human-readable portion, as illustrated here by the `div` element nested in the `rddl:resource` element.
- Since the human-readable portion is XHTML, any normal markup applies, including the use of `<div class="resource">` to apply a RDDL-specific style (from the stylesheet `xrd.css`) to make resources stand out from other text.
- Although not shown in the excerpt, the RDDL home page also demonstrates that `rddl:resource` elements may be nested within XHTML container elements as well (e.g., inside the `ul` unordered list element).

The rendering of this modified version of the RDDL home page appears in Figure 15-16. As we might expect, all of the XHTML elements are rendered in the

Listing 15-16 Excerpt from RDDL Home Page

```
<!DOCTYPE html PUBLIC
                "-//XML-DEV//DTD XHTML RDDL 1.0//EN"
                "http://www.rddl.org/rddl-xhtml.dtd">
<html   xmlns="http://www.w3.org/1999/xhtml"
        xmlns:xlink="http://www.w3.org/1999/xlink"
        xmlns:rddl="http://www.rddl.org/"
        xml:lang="en"
        xml:base="http://www.rddl.org/">
<head>
        <title>RDDL Excerpt</title>
        <link href="xrd.css" type="text/css" rel="stylesheet"/>
</head>
<body>
<h1>Resource Directory Description Language: Excerpt</h1>
<!-- Begin Excerpt -->
<div id="role">
<h3>xlink:role</h3>
<p>[...stuff deleted...]</p>

<p>When the related resource is not an XML document but is adequately
distinguished by a MIME type, the value of the
<code>xlink:role</code> attribute may reflect this MIME type with values
formed by the concatenation of the prefix
<code>http://www.isi.edu/in-notes/iana/assignments/media-types/</code> with
a MIME type e.g.
<code>http://www.isi.edu/in-notes/iana/assignments/media-types/text/css</code>.
</p>
<rddl:resource
        xlink:title="RDDL Roles"
        xlink:role="http://www.rddl.org/"
```

```
        xlink:arcrole="http://www.rddl.org/purposes#directory"
        xlink:href="http://www.rddl.org/natures.html"
>
<div class="resource">
        <p>It is anticipated that many related-resource natures will be well
known.
        A list of well-known natures may be found in the RDDL directory
        <a href="http://www.rddl.org/natures.html">http://www.rddl.org/
natures.html</a>.</p>
</div>
</rddl:resource>
<p>If no nature is provided for a related resource, the default value is
<code>http://www.rddl.org/#resource</code>. </p>
</div>
<!-- End Excerpt -->
<p>[...stuff deleted...]</p>
</body>
</html>
```

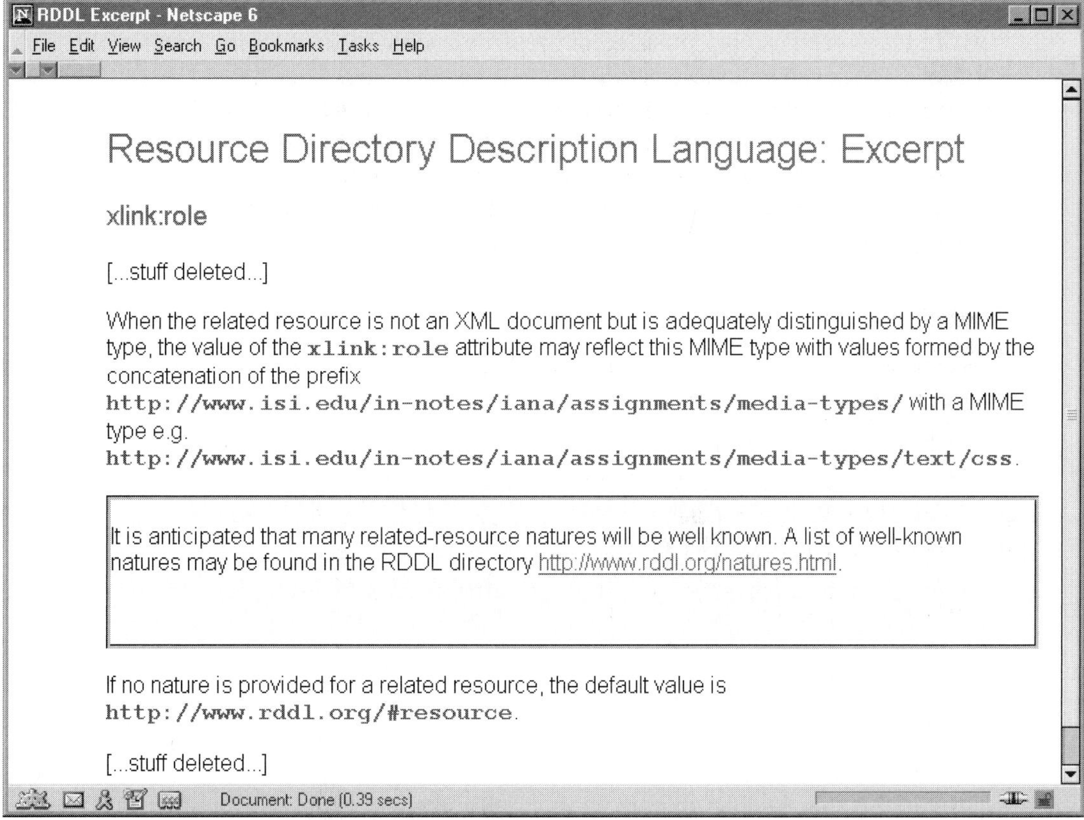

FIGURE 15-16 Excerpt from RDDL home page (rddl-excerpt.html)

Source: From code written by Jonathan Borden and Tim Bray. Used with permission.

usual way, including the application of the stylesheet. Also, as expected, the special RDDL element `rddl:resource` is not itself displayed (except for styling the container), although all its attributes (XLink and others) are available for additional processing from the XML parser.

XHTML 1.1—Module-based XHTML

The XHTML 1.1—Module-based XHTML Recommendation (*http://www.w3.org/TR/xhtml11/*) was published in May 2001. XHTML 1.1 is primarily a reformulation of XHTML 1.0 Strict using XHTML Modules. It may be surprising and somewhat counterintuitive at first to discover that XHTML 1.1 actually includes *fewer* elements than XHTML 1.0, at least when compared to the XHTML 1.0 Transitional or Frameset document types (but not when compared to XHTML 1.0 Strict).[18]

With the advent of the XHTML modules defined in Modularization of XHTML, however, in XHTML 1.1 the W3C has completely and decisively *removed support for deprecated elements and attributes* from the XHTML family. These elements and attributes were largely considered presentational, representing functionality that the W3C believes is handled better via stylesheets or client-specific default behavior. In fact, XHTML 1.1 is essentially the XHTML 1.0 Strict modules, `xml:lang` and `id` attributes, plus the Ruby Module for annotation and pronunciation of Asian languages (especially Japanese and Chinese).[19]

Whereas XHTML 1.0 focused on supporting a relatively painless transition for developers and content providers familiar with HTML 4.01, XHTML 1.1 is a forward-looking effort to cleanly separate structure from presentation, serving as a solid and flexible basis for future markup languages. As Web content becomes targeted for an increasingly diverse group of "small information appliances," the W3C believes it is critical that content can be presented differently on different devices, and that the Web development community has a set of modules they can expect to be fully supported across the gamut of "XHTML family conforming user agents."

The differences between XTHML 1.1 and XHTML 1.0 Strict are:

- For every element, the `lang` attribute has been replaced with `xml:lang`.
- For the `a` and `map` elements, the `name` attribute has been replaced with the `id` attribute. *This means that the* `name` *attribute that was previously deprecated in XHTML 1.0 is now obsolete and invalid in XHTML 1.1.*
- The "ruby" collection of elements has been added.

18. XHTML 1.1 is a *superset* of XHTML 1.0 Strict which is, in turn, a superset of XHTML Basic. However, XHTML 1.0 Transitional and Frameset include popular HTML 4.01 deprecated elements and attributes, which is why they are larger sets than XHTML 1.1 (see Figure 15-1).

19. "Ruby" annotations are short runs of text next to or above regular text, typically used in Japanese and Chinese documents to indicate pronunciation or to provide a short annotation.

XHTML 1.1 Modules and Elements

The set of modules XHTML 1.1 comprises is a proper subset of those described in the Modularization of XHTML specification that is at *http://www.w3.org/TR/xhtml-modularization/abstract_modules.html*. The modules together with the elements they contain are shown in Table 15-5. Once again, bold font indicates the four core modules that constitute the minimal requirements of an XHTML Host Language. Conspicuous by their absence are those modules defined in Modularization of XHTML, but not included in XHTML 1.1: Applet, Frames, Iframes, Target, Basic Forms and Basic Tables, Name Identification (`name` attribute rather than `id`), and Legacy Modules (deprecated elements and attributes). The absence of Basic Forms and Basic Tables is not a problem since the included Forms and Tables modules are supersets of the basic versions. However, the omission of

TABLE 15-5 XHTML 1.1 Modules and Elements

XHTML 1.1 Module	*Elements*
Structure Module	body, head, html, title
Text Module	abbr, acronym, address, blockquote, br, cite, code, dfn, div, em, h1, h2, h3, h4, h5, h6, kbd, p, pre, q, samp, span, strong, var
Hypertext Module	a
List Module	dl, dt, dd, ol, ul, li
Object Module	object, param
Presentation Module	b, big, hr, i, small, sub, sup, tt
Edit Module	del, ins
Bidirectional Text Module	bdo
Forms Module	button, fieldset, form, input, label, legend, select, optgroup, option, textarea
Table Module	caption, col, colgroup, table, tbody, td, tfoot, th, thead, tr
Image Module	img
Client-side Image Map Module	area, map
Server-side Image Map Module	Attribute ismap on img
Intrinsic Events Module	Events attributes
Metainformation Module	meta
Scripting Module	noscript, script
Stylesheet Module	style element
Style Attribute Module [Deprecated]	style attribute
Link Module	link
Base Module	base
Ruby Annotation Module	ruby, rbc, rtc, rb, rt, rp

Applet and Frames may cause some consternation for some Web developers. Actually, the Object module is essentially a superset of Applet, but as for Frames, you're out of luck unless you customize the language to incorporate them yourself. Remember, however, that Frames are not an appropriate metaphor for non-desktop user agents; some argue they aren't an appropriate metaphor at all. (See, for example, Jakob Nielsen's Alertbox for December 1996: *http://www.useit.com/alertbox/9612.html*.)

Conforming XHTML 1.1 Documents and the Driver

The `DOCTYPE` declaration and root element of a conforming XHTML 1.1 document look like this:

```
<?xml version="1.0" encoding="UTF-8"?>
<!DOCTYPE html PUBLIC "-//W3C//DTD XHTML 1.1//EN"
    "http://www.w3.org/TR/xhtml11/DTD/xhtml11.dtd">
<html xmlns="http://www.w3.org/1999/xhtml" xml:lang="en" >
<!-- etc. -->
```

The W3C encourages XHTML content providers to include the optional XML declarations in all their documents. As we've seen, this is especially important for the `encoding` pseudo-attribute. The XML declaration is *required* when the character encoding differs from the default UTF-8 or UTF-16, however.

The driver for the XHTML 1.1 Document Type Definition can be viewed online at *http://www.w3.org/TR/xhtml11/xhtml11_dtd.html* and is downloadable from *http://www.w3.org/TR/xhtml11/DTD/xhtml11.dtd*. The modules referenced by the DTD are those defined in the Modularization of XHTML specification. For example, the DTD cites the FPI for the List Module as:

```
PUBLIC "-//W3C//ELEMENTS XHTML Lists 1.0//EN"
       "http://www.w3.org/TR/xhtml-modularization/DTD/xhtml-list-1.mod" >
```

Recall, however, that the Modularization specification itself does *not* include a DTD (other than samples).

Document Model Module and Customizing XHTML 1.1

There is one exception to my statement that all modules come from the Modularization specification: The parameter entity `%xhtml-model.mod;` is defined in the DTD to point to a file that is unique to XHTML 1.1. Note the relative path with respect to the DTD, in contrast to the path shown in the previous section.

```
<!ENTITY % xhtml-model.mod
     PUBLIC "-//W3C//ENTITIES XHTML 1.1 Document Model 1.0//EN"
            "xhtml11-model-1.mod" >
```

The purpose of this Document Model Module, as discussed under the topic XHTML 1.1 Customizations (*http://www.w3.org/TR/xhtml11/xhtml11_dtd.html#a_xhtml11_customization*) in the spec, is to describe the common element groupings that constitute the content models associated with XHTML 1.1 elements. There are three such predefined content models:

- `%Inline.mix;` = character-level elements (e.g., `<b>`, `<i>`, `<code>`)
- `%Block.mix;` = block-level elements (e.g., `<p>`, `<ul>`, `<div>`)
- `%Flow.mix;` = any block or inline elements

According to the comments in this module, minor extensions to these content models can be made by redeclaring any of three `*.extra;` parameter entities (which, by default are declared as the null string) to contain extension elements:

- `%Inline.extra;` = elements whose parent may be any inline element
- `%Block.extra;` = elements whose parent may be any block element
- `%Misc.extra;` = elements whose parent may be any block or inline element

Use of these parameter entities requires an `OR`-separated list, which must begin with an `OR` ("|") separator (e.g., `"| a | b | c"`).

For example, if you wanted to augment XHTML 1.1 to permit inline MathML and block-level SVG elements, you'd add these lines and reference the MathML and SVG DTDs:

- `<!ENTITY % Inline.extra "| math">`
- `<!ENTITY % Block.extra  "| svg">`

However, it's not quite so simple. You must make sure to instantiate the MathML and SVG DTDs prior to the above entity definitions and defer instantiation of the XHTML 1.1 DTD until after your extension element declarations.

For a detailed tutorial, refer to "XHTML Modules and Markup Languages: How to create XHTML Family modules and markup languages for fun and profit" at *http://www.w3.org/MarkUp/Guide/xhtml-m12n-tutorial/*.

Near Future XHTML

Several XHTML family members are still in their infancy at the time of this writing: XForms, XML Events, Modularization of XHTML in XML Schema, and XHTML 2.0. Here's a glimpse of what the W3C has planned for 2002 and beyond.

At the time of this writing, the specifications discussed in this section are all Working Drafts. The W3C stresses that Working Drafts are works in progress. Therefore, details and possibly even goals described in this section are likely to change. Refer to the HTML Activity page, *http://www.w3.org/Markup/Activity*.

XForms: Next Generation Web Forms

Crude Web forms originated in HTML as early as 1994, grew in capabilities in HTML 2.0 (November 1995), and matured in HTML 3.2 (January 1997). Additional form elements, attributes, and capabilities were added in HTML 4.0 in December 1997, but there have been no significant changes since then. These forms, although an integral part of user input and Web-based e-commerce, are actually very limited chiefly because they do not separate presentation from content and purpose. HTML forms are created from a fixed set of elements that imply a particular visual representation that is often not appropriate for small devices with limited screen real estate.

XForms is the next generation of Web forms based on an XML syntax that decouples data, logic (purpose), and presentation (*http://www.w3.org/TR/xforms/*). This separation enables the targeting of forms for devices with very different user interfaces, such as handheld, television, and desktop browsers, plus printers and scanners. Support for advanced form logic, multipage forms, multiple forms in one page, suspend and resume of data entry, internationalization, and easy integration with other XML vocabularies (especially XHTML and SVG) are some of the goals of the effort. XForms started as a subgroup of the HTML Working Group but now there is a separate XForms Working Group. The XForms home page is *http://www.w3.org/MarkUp/Forms/*. XForms is intended to mesh with the framework of Modularization of HTML, which is why I've included a disucssion in this chapter.

XForms User Interface consists of visual controls that are intended to replace HTML (and XHTML) form controls. These form elements can be embedded in XHTML and other XML document types (e.g., SVG). Form input is expressed as **XML instance data** which, like all XML, has a well-defined structure. A device-independent XML form description, called the **XForms Model**, can connect with either standard or proprietary user interfaces, such as those of the XForms User Interface, XHTML, Wireless Markup Language (WML), SVG, and so on. Among other things, this model describes the structure of instance data, enabling workflow, prefill, and autofill of XForms elements. Another aspect of the model, the **XForms Submit Protocol**, defines how XForms transmit and receive data, including the ability to suspend and resume the completion of a form, something this author has wanted to do on a number of occasions when encountering multipage forms.

Two implementations of XForms are *X-Smiles*, a Java-based XML browser that supports XSLFO, XSLT, SMIL 1.0, and SVG in addition to XForms, and *Mozquito XForms Preview*, a commercial product that reads and writes XML instances without the need for XSL (*http://www.x-smiles.org/ and http://www.mozquito.com/*).

The December 2001 XForms 1.0 Working Draft contains an example of an XHTML document with two small XForms at *http://www.w3.org/TR/xforms/slice2.html#concepts-complete*. It's informative to compare that version to a similar one based only on XHTML, at *http://www.w3.org/TR/xforms/slice2.html#concepts-xhtml*. The benefits of using XForms are summarized in *http://www.w3.org/TR/xforms/slice2.html#concepts-purpose-presentation*.

XML Events: An Events Syntax for XML

The XML Events specification, subtitled "An Events Syntax for XML," appears to be a collaborative effort of the HTML, DOM, XForms, and Synchronized Multimedia (SYMM) working groups, at least on some level, although it is officially an HTML Working Group activity.[20]

The XML Events module defines a mechanism to uniformly integrate event listeners and associated event handlers with DOM Level 2 event interfaces. The goal is to provide an interoperable way to associate behaviors with document-level markup across all XML languages. Design goals include syntactically exposing the DOM event model to an XML document and providing for new event types without requiring modification to the DOM or the DTD.

A major aspect of this effort is the ability to define whether events should be propagated ("bubbled up") to ancestor elements or not. That is, event handlers could be optionally attached to elements so that ancestors could respond to the event either before or after their children. (This is a paradigm that goes way back to Motif and the X Window System and probably to earlier graphical user interfaces as well.)

The DOM provides a way to register event listeners and handlers, as well as a mechanism to pass events and contextual information throughout a tree structure. It also describes how events are captured, bubbled up, and terminated. Events can be handled either at the document node where the event was received, called the *target node,* or at a node higher up in the tree hierarchy. Bubbling the event up encourages centralization of event handling.

The XML Events module uses the XML Namespace identifier `http://www.w3.org/2001/xml-events`. Examples use the namespace prefix `"ev"`. The specification defines a `listener` element and several global attributes which, as in XLink, can be attached to any element in your vocabulary. The `listener` element supports a subset of the DOM's `EventListener` interface by declaring event listeners and registering them with specific nodes in the DOM. Attributes of the `listener` element and their datatypes (subject to change) follow:

- `event (NMTOKEN)`
- `observer (IDREF)`
- `target (IDREF)`
- `handler (URI)`
- `phase ("capture" | "default"*)`
- `propagate ("stop" | "continue"*)`
- `defaultAction ("cancel" | "perform"*)`
- `id (ID)`

20. See *http://www.w3.org/TR/xml-events/*. Earlier versions of the XML Events Working Draft (prior to December 2001) were entitled *The XHTML Events* specification, subtitled "An Updated Events Syntax for XHTML and Friends"; they were substantially different.

Here's an example of a `listener` with a `handler` in an external document:

```
<listener event="activate" observer="someElementIDREF"
          handler="/handlers/events.xml#popup"
          phase="capture" propagate="stop"/>
```

Since the handler is activated during the capture phase, and propagation is stopped, this prevents any child elements of the `someElementIDREF` element from receiving `activate` events. Events can also come from other namespaces, such as SMIL:

```
<listener event="smil:repeatEvent" .... />
```

Experimental support for XML Events is demonstrated in the X-Smiles browser by the Telecommunications Software and Multimedia Laboratory at Helsinki University of Technology (*http://www.x-smiles.org/*). X-Smiles is a Java-based XML browser intended for embedded network devices and for supporting multimedia services, in addition to desktop use. As of this writing X-Smiles provides partial support for XHTML Basic 1.0. The browser also supports quite an impressive list of XML specifications, including XSLT, SMIL 2.0 Basic, XForms, CSS, XSFLO, SVG, XML Events, ECMAScript, and possibly others by the time you read this.

Modularization of XHTML in XML Schema

At the time of this writing, the most recent XHTML effort is a working draft called the Modularization of XHTML in XML Schema (*http://www.w3.org/TR/xhtml-m12n-schema/*). This specification uses XML Schema rather than DTDs to implement the same abstract modules as the earlier Modularization of XHTML Recommendation. Developers will be able to choose whether their implementation of abstract modules should be in terms of DTDs or XML Schema. As with the DTD implementation, this spec includes a set of schema modules that conform to the abstract modules in XHTML, plus it includes conventions that describe the interplay of individual modules, and how they can be modified or extended.

The specification describes a number of convincing motivations for modularizing. Its design goals are essentially those of the earlier DTD-based Modularization of XHTML, aside from the XML Schema advantages. The W3C enumerates some of the key differences between DTDs and XML Schema:

- Common XML features
- Richer data typing
- Full support for XML Namespaces
- Extension mechanisms
- Full support for entities including character entities
- Much less document order dependence

While this description is subject to (possibly substantial) change, the Modularization of XHTML in XML Schema approach defines an XML Schema that includes required **schema modules** (divided into *framework* and *core* modules, including datatypes, common attributes, character entities, text, hypertext, lists, ruby, structural, etc.) and about twenty *optional* schema modules (presentational, link, style, scripting, images, tables, forms, etc.). The required Framework schema modules are:

- Notations
- Datatypes
- XLink
- Events
- Common attributes
- Common content models
- Character entities

The Core required element modules are:

- Structural
- Text
- Hypertext
- Lists
- Ruby

The schema includes twenty optional modules, any of which can be commented out if not needed:

- Edit
- Bdo
- Presentational
- Link
- Meta
- Base
- Scripting
- Style
- Image
- Client-side imagemaps
- Server-side imagemaps
- Param
- Applet
- Object
- Tables
- Forms

- Nameident
- Legacy
- Basic forms
- Basic tables

XHTML 2.0

At the time of this writing, no public working draft of XHTML 2.0 has been posted by the W3C. However, the HTML Working Group Roadmap does make crystal clear the direction in which they are headed (*http://www.w3.org/MarkUp/xhtml-roadmap/*, accessed March 18, 2002). XHTML 2.0 will be a superset of XHTML 1.1, "altered semantically and syntactically to conform to the requirements of related XML standards such as XML Linking and XML Schema," as well as any others that are judged relevant downstream.

Perhaps even more significant is the hope that XHTML 2.0 will be a major step in divorcing XHTML from its HTML ancestry. It is expected that XHTML 2.0 will have no a priori knowledge of HTML linking, imagemaps, forms, and such because it will be a purer XML abstraction, with all presentation information cleanly separated from the data.

Summary

XHTML is the general name given to an ever-growing family of W3C specifications based on a reformulation of HTML in XML syntax, and also a partitioning of the language into required and optional modules. The overlapping and interrelated common goals of all of these W3C XHTML efforts are:

1. Complete separation of document structure from visual presentation, relegating the latter to stylesheets.
2. Division of functionality into discrete DTD (or XML Schema) modules.
3. Clearly defined functional subsets consisting of a collection of modules (e.g., XHTML Host Language consisting of Structure, Text, Lists, and Hypertext modules; XHTML Basic consisting of XHTML Host Language modules plus Images, Basic Forms, Basic Tables, and Objects, etc.).
4. Defining mechanisms that enable small information appliance (thin client; limited memory user agent) vendors to implement only the modules their device needs.
5. Giving content developers a well-defined set of modules that they can count on each alternative user agent supporting to minimize rewriting of content targeted for multiple devices.

This chapter covers a wide variety of topics, all of which are related to XHTML:

- *XHTML 1.0*—HTML 4.01 in XML syntax, with a choice of three DTDs: XHTML 1.0 Transitional (with deprecated elements and attributes), Strict (without deprecations), or Frameset. This specification also describes how XHTML 1.0 differs from HTML 4.01.
- *XHTML Basic* is a minimal set of modules especially designed for limited-memory devices such as PDAs; modules include Structure,Text, Lists, Hypertext, Images, Basic Forms, Basic Tables, and Objects. XHTML Basic also provides a simple, common base that can be extended by the addition of other modules. This is crucial for its adoption for use in thin clients; it must be simple enough by omitting unnecessary aspects of XHTML 1.0 or 1.1, yet flexible enough to add custom modules, and rich enough to provide a reasonable content authoring language.
- *Modularization of XHTML* describes a modular approach to XHTML, which subsets the language into a large number of nonoverlapping "abstract modules," each of which is semantically unique. The abstractions are implemented by DTDs with plans to migrate to XML Schema. Each implementation module describes groups of elements, attributes, and content models based on functionality. XHTML 1.0/HTML 4.01 is decomposed into roughly forty modules. All of the deprecated elements and attributes of HTML 4.01 have been either removed from these modules or relegated to the "legacy" module. Presentational elements are separated from structural elements. The result is well-suited for XML since languages that are purely structural can be defined from these modules, leaving presentation to stylesheets.
- *XHTML 1.1* (Module-based XHTML) is a forward-looking document type cleanly separated from the deprecated, legacy functionality of HTML 4. The DTD separates XHTML 1.1 and versions that follow it from the deprecated, legacy functionality of HTML 4.01 (the basis for XHTML 1.0). Since it is built using the modular framework that supports extension, the XHTML 1.1 document type is the basis for future extended XHTML "family" document types.
- *Ruby Annotation* (an XHTML Module) is a pronunciation and annotation text for Asian languages.
- *XML Event*s describes a generic approach for integrating event listeners and associated event handlers with DOM Level 2 event interfaces to associate behavior with markup.
- *Modularization of XHTML in XML Schema* is an upgrade from DTD modules to XML Schema modules for XHTML Modularization, offering all of the benefits of XML Schema over DTDs. This approach defines an XML Schema that includes required schema modules (divided into framework and core modules, including datatypes, common attributes, character entities, text, hypertext, lists, ruby, and structural), and about two dozen optional schema modules (e.g., presentational, link, style, scripting, images, tables, and forms).

- *XForms* is an elaboration of the capabilities of XHTML forms with a clean separation of presentation, logic, and data.
- *XHTML 2.0* (eventually) will build upon XHTML 1.1 to fit the latest XML technology and to remove a priori knowledge of HTML 4.01.
- We discussed in considerable detail how to use a utility called HTML Tidy to convert HTML to XHTML 1.0, and how to validate the results with the W3C HTML Validation Service and ElCel's XMLValidator.
- We presented an example of RDDL (Resource Directory Description Language) which extends XHTML Basic using the Modularization of XHTML DTD mechanism by adding one element, `rddl:resource`, with XLink capabilities.

For Further Exploration

Articles

xmlhack's XHTML Category
http://xmlhack.com/list.php?cat=16

XML.com: Mix and Match Markup: XHTML Modularization, Rick Jelliffe
http://www.xml.com/pub/a/2001/05/02/xhtmlm12n.html

XHTML: The Clean Code Solution (O'Reilly)
http://www.oreillynet.com/network/2000/04/28/feature/xhtml_only.html

DevX: XHTML: HTML Merges With XML, Kurt Cagle
http://www.devx.com/upload/free/features/webbuilder/2000/wb0300/kc0300/kc0300-1.asp

XHTML in the Real World Part I, Molly E. Holzschlag (June 2001)
http://www.webreview.com/2001/06_08/webauthors/index03.shtml

XHTML in the Real World Part II, Molly E. Holzschlag (June 2001)
http://www.webreview.com/2001/06_15/webauthors/index02.shtml

A List Apart: Validating XML
http://alistapart.zeldman.com/stories/validate/

Books

XHTML-L List of Books [many XHTML books listed here]
http://groups.yahoo.com/group/XHTML-L/links/Books_000957530773/

XHTML Example by Example, Aaron E. Walsh, Dave Raggett (Prentice Hall)
http://www.amazon.com/exec/obidos/ASIN/013040005X/

XHTML: Moving Toward XML, Simon St. Laurent, B. K. DeLong
http://www.amazon.com/exec/obidos/ASIN/0764547097/

Raggett on HTML 4, Second Edition, Dave Raggett, Jenny Lam, Ian Alexander, Michael Kmiec (Addison-Wesley)
http://www.aw.com/catalog/academic/product/1,4096,0201178052,00.html

Resources

ZVON: HTML 1.0 Reference with Examples
http://www.zvon.org/xxl/xhtmlReference/Output/

ZVON: XHTML Basic Reference with Examples
http://zvon.org/xxl/xhtmlBasicReference/Output/index.html

XHTML.ORG—A Source of Information about XHTML
http://www.xhtml.org/

XHTML-L Links [great set of XHTML/HTML references]
http://groups.yahoo.com/group/XHTML-L/links

HTML Writer's Guild: HTML Resources
http://www.hwg.org/resources/?cid=14

WDVL: HTML home page
http://wdvl.com/Authoring/HTML/

Check or Validate XML, Robin Cover
http://xml.coverpages.org/check-xml.html

RFC 3236: The 'application/xhtml+xml' Media Type (January 2002)
http://www.rfc-editor.org/rfc/rfc3236.txt

Historical: W3C's Own View of HTML History
http://www.w3.org/MarkUp/#historical

Tutorials: WDVL: Introduction to XHTML, with eXamples, Alan Richmond [one of the first; still useful]
http://wdvl.Internet.com/Authoring/Languages/XML/XHTML/

Software Lists: XMLSOFTWARE.COM: Conversion Tools
http://www.xmlsoftware.com/convert/

Mailing List: HTML-L [A forum for discussing XHTML issues for both XML and HTML developers]
http://groups.yahoo.com/group/XHTML-L

Software

HTML Tidy, Dave Raggett [converts HTML to XHTML and fixes broken HTML; older home page; see SourceForge page]
http://www.w3.org/People/Raggett/tidy/

HTML Tidy, SourceForge Tidy project home page
http://tidy.sourceforge.net/

XHTML Conversion Using Tidy (O'Reilly) [online form interfaces to Tidy]
http://www.oreillynet.com/network/2000/04/28/feature/

ElCel Technology: XML Validator [free, fast, lightweight utility with many options; can run in batch mode, expands UNIX-like wildcards]
http://www.elcel.com/products/xmlvalid.html

Brown University: XML Validator [file upload or URI]
http://www.stg.brown.edu/service/xmlvalid/

XML well-formedness checker and validator, Richard Tobin [URI only]
http://www.cogsci.ed.ac.uk/%7Erichard/xml-check.html

Infinity Loop: upCast [RTF to XML converter; converts Word documents to XML or XHTML]
http://www.infinity-loop.de/en/products.html

Logictran: Logictran RTF Converter [converts Word and RTF documents to HTML, XHTML, XML, SGML, etc.]
http://www.logictran.com/

Mozquito XForms [sending, receiving, and processing XML form data]
http://www.mozquito.org/

Nokia Mobile Browser Demo [Flash demo of XHTML, CSS, WML, and Forms in Nokia phone]
http://www.nokia.com/xhtmldemo/

X-Smiles [Java-based XML browser for embedded devices]
http://www.x-smiles.org/

W3C Specifications and Information

HTML Home Page [the HTML home page!]
http://www.w3.org/MarkUp/

HTML Working Group Roadmap [goals and plans of the working group for each of its deliverables]
http://www.w3.org/MarkUp/xhtml-roadmap/

HTML Activity Statement [big picture of XHTML and XForms]
http://www.w3.org/MarkUp/Activity

HTML 4.01 Specification (W3C Recommendation, December 1999)
http://www.w3.org/TR/html401/

XHTML 1.0: The Extensible HyperText Markup Language: A Reformulation of HTML 4 in XML 1.0 (W3C Recommendation, January 2000)
http://www.w3.org/TR/xhtml1/

XHTML 1.0: Differences with HTML 4 [tips for migrating from HTML to XHTML 1.0]
http://www.w3.org/TR/xhtml1/#diffs

XHTML 1.0: Appendix C. HTML Compatibility Guidelines [tips for using XHTML in HTML browsers]
http://www.w3.org/TR/xhtml1/#guidelines

XHTML Basic (W3C Recommendation, December 2000)
http://www.w3.org/TR/xhtml-basic/

Modularization of XHTML (W3C Recommendation, April 2001)
http://www.w3.org/TR/xhtml-modularization/

XHTML 1.1—Module-based XHTML (W3C Recommendation, May 2001)
http://www.w3.org/TR/xhtml11/

XHTML Modularization—An Overview (April 2001)
http://www.w3.org/MarkUp/modularization

Tutorial: XHTML Modules and Markup Languages: How to create XHTML Family modules and markup languages for fun and profit, Shane McCarron (September 2001) [highly recommended]
http://www.w3.org/MarkUp/Guide/xhtml-m12n-tutorial/

Ruby Annotation (W3C Recommendation, May 2001)
http://www.w3.org/TR/ruby/

Modularization of XHTML in XML Schema (W3C Working Draft, December 2001)
http://www.w3.org/TR/xhtml-m12n-schema/

XML Events: An Events Syntax for XML (W3C Working Draft, December 2001)
http://www.w3.org/TR/xml-events/

XForms—The Next Generation of Web Forms
http://www.w3.org/MarkUp/Forms/

XForms 1.0 (W3C Working Draft, June 2001)
http://www.w3.org/TR/xforms/

HTML Validation Service [validates XHTML 1.0, HTML 4.01, HTML 3.2, HTML 2.0]
http://validator.w3.org/

Chapter 16

RDF: Resource Description Framework

RDF is a general-purpose language especially designed for representing metadata about Web resources, such as authorship or Web page syndication information, a user's content delivery preferences, or a description of a collection of related resources. It provides a common framework for expressing metadata in a portable and flexible manner, facilitating the preservation of meaning when RDF is used to exchange information between applications.

Overview

In this chapter we cover two specifications that constitute W3C's metadata framework.[1] The Resource Description Framework (RDF) is an application of XML that allows Web-based systems to share "machine-understandable" descriptions of Web resources. RDF has emerged as the cornerstone for most of the so-called Semantic Web efforts. Although there are two separate specifications that define RDF, this chapter reads like a single specification; I have always considered the two specifications more an artifact of workflow and timing than anything else. Therefore the structure here shows the way the RDF specification should have been structured, had there been only one.

Motivation

The World Wide Web has developed primarily as medium of content for *human* consumption. Automating anything on the Web (information retrieval, synthesis of information, etc.) is difficult because human interpretation, in one form or another,

Note: This chapter, contributed by Ora Lassila, is based on the RDF Model and Syntax Specification (W3C Recommendation 1999-02-22) and the RDF Schema Specification (W3C Candidate Recommendation 2000-03-27). At the time of writing, more work is under way in the W3C RDF Core Working Group in order to publish clarifications of the original specifications. Where applicable, anticipated WG changes to the next release of the RDF standard have been indicated.

1. I am grateful to Pat Hayes and Eric Miller for helpful discussions and comments during the preparation of this chapter.

is required to make Web content useful. Offering some relief is the emerging "Semantic Web."[2] In broad terms, it encompasses efforts to create mechanisms that augment content with *formal semantics*, thereby producing content suitable for automated systems to consume. It will allow us to use more automated Web functions (e.g., reasoning, information and service discovery, and autonomous agents), which will ease the human workload. The Semantic Web will also pave the way for true "device independence" and customization of information content for individual users. Information on the Web can then exist in "raw form" and any context-dependent presentation can be rendered on demand (more generally, this represents a departure from the "rendering-oriented" Web). The Semantic Web is not a separate Web but an extension of the current one, in which information, when given this well-defined meaning, better enables computers and people to work in tandem.

The Web is built on relatively simple principles, but its growth has not been without growing pains. Coping with the volume of information on the Web is a real problem, as witnessed by users of Web search engines. Since Web documents are not designed to be understood by machines, the only real form of searching available to us is full-text search. Entering keywords into a search engine and receiving thousands of hits is not necessarily useful: the documents we seek may or may not be among those thousands. Mere words used as search keywords are subject to *cross-disciplinary semantic drift*. Keywords thus perform poorly in situations where a search index covers multiple subject areas, as is the case with the Web.[3]

The Web essentially gives us an infrastructure for "pointing" (i.e., an infrastructure and mechanisms for linkages between documents). This infrastructure is quite general and consequently very powerful, but its problem is that the linking is "indiscriminate"; human interpretation (again) is required to understand what any particular link means. The Semantic Web aspires to change this by associating formal meaning with the linkages. This brings us to its key aspect, something we will refer to as the "ontological approach": Instead of merely introducing new tags (e.g., using XML), the Semantic Web will focus on the *meaning* of the new markup, and on mechanisms that allow us to introduce, coordinate, and *share* the data's formal semantics as well as *reason* (i.e., draw inferences) from the semantic data. In practice, computers will find the meaning of semantic data by following (semantic) hyperlinks to definitions of key terms and rules for reasoning about them logically. This aspect of the resulting infrastructure will enable the development of fully automated services such as highly functional "intelligent" agents.

Tim Berners-Lee, director of the World Wide Web Consortium, once wrote:

> Currently there is not only a large industry in applications to put information from legacy information systems onto the Web, there is also an industry in applications which surf the Web and, programmed with some idea of how the Web pages were

2. Berners-Lee, T., J. Hendler, O. Lassila. 2001. "Semantic Web," *Scientific American* 284(5):34–43.
3. Weibel, S. 1995. "Metadata: The Foundations of Resource Description," *D-Lib Magazine* (July).

automatically generated, retrieve the information and reconvert it into hard, well-defined machine-processable data.[4]

It's clear that as a starting point for the Semantic Web, stronger, more precise means of describing documents are needed. W3C's Resource Description Framework is the piece of the Web architecture designed to do just that, and as such it serves as a cornerstone for current and emerging Semantic Web activities.

History of RDF

The genesis of RDF dates back to 1997: W3C's Metadata Activity was a conscious effort to produce a single metadata framework for all the different applications which needed to use some type of metadata. The design of RDF was influenced by several sources, all of which more or less agreed on the basic principles of metadata representation and transport.[5,6] Key influences came from the Web development community itself, in the form of HTML metadata and the Platform for Internet Content Selection (PICS).[7] Other influences came from the library community, the structured document community (in the form of SGML and, more important, XML), and the knowledge representation community. Framework design contributions also came from object-oriented programming and modeling languages, and databases.

Even earlier, the history of standardized Web metadata mechanisms had begun with the HTML `<META>` and `<LINK>` tags. For example, a `<META>` tag can specify the author of a Web page as follows:

```
<META name="Author" content="Ora Lassila">
```

Although `<META>` is useful, it does have certain shortcomings. What does the name `"Author"` really mean? It could be the name of the person who created the page, or the person who wrote the page contents, or even the Webmaster who maintains the page. The meaning of `"Author"` on one Web page might be different from its meaning on another page. With the advent of document profiles and metadata attribute namespaces (with the HTML 4.0 specification), this shortcoming has been

4. Berners-Lee, T. 1997. "W3C Data Formats," W3C Note, World Wide Web Consortium (*http://www.w3.org/TR/NOTE-rdfarch*).

5. Lassila, O., and R. Swick. 1999. "Resource Description Framework (RDF) Model and Syntax Specification," W3C Recommendation 22 February, World Wide Web Consortium, Cambridge, Mass. (*http://www.w3.org/TR/REC-rdf-syntax/*).

6. Brickley, D., and R. V. Guha. 2000. "Resource Description Framework (RDF) Schema Specification 1.0," W3C Candidate Recommendation 27 March, World Wide Web Consortium, Cambridge, Mass. (*http://www.w3.org/TR/rdf-schema/*).

7. Krauskopf, T., et al. 1996. "PICS Label Distribution Label Syntax and Communication Protocols, Version 1.1," W3C Recommendation, World Wide Web Consortium (*http://www.w3.org/TR/REC-PICS-labels*).

alleviated, but this does not address the issue of attribute values. The structure of these values is not specified; for example, is it "`Ora Lassila`" or "`Lassila, Ora`"?[8]

Another application keenly debated in the standardization community around the time RDF work began was *content rating*. Attempts to balance free speech and protection of minors resulted in PICS, the W3C's content-rating architecture. This is actually a metadata mechanism suited to simple content description, but because attribute values could be chosen only from numeric ranges, it had very limited use as a general metadata architecture. PICS did, however, introduce the notion of machine-interpretable *schemata* for metadata. It also defined various ways in which metadata can be associated with Web resources:

- Embedded in an HTML `<META>` tag in the document head
- Transported in HTTP headers (for direct processing by the requesting client, for example, without having to look "inside" the document); this is also possible with the `<META>` tag by using the attribute "http-equiv" instead of "name"
- Stored in, and retrieved from, a third-party metadata bureau

The following is a typical PICS label providing information about the content of a Web page.

```
(PICS-1.1 "http://www.gcf.org/v2.5"
 by "John Doe"
 labels on "1994.11.05T08:15-0500"
        until "1995.12.31T23:59-0000"
        for "http://w3.org/PICS/Overview.html"
        ratings (suds 0.5 density 0 color/hue 1)
        for "http://w3.org/PICS/Underview.html"
        by "Jane Doe"
        ratings (subject 2 density 1 color/hue 1))
```

Attempts to turn PICS into a general metadata mechanism led the W3C to work on "PICS-NG," RDF's predecessor.[9] The original PICS application of content rating ultimately contributed to the charter of the RDF Model and Syntax Working Group and the requirements specification of RDF.

Others had also worked on proposals for various frameworks for metadata (and more generally machine-interpretable data) for the Web. These proposals included Netscape's Meta Content Framework (MCF) and Microsoft's XML-Data. In the summer of 1997, the authors of the various metadata specifications met at the Massachusetts Institute of Technology and started a joint Web metadata project. Eventually this project got "blessed" by the W3C membership and was chartered as the RDF Model and Syntax Working Group.

8. In HTML, a document profile can be specified with the "profile" attribute of the `<HEAD>` element. A profile can describe the specific meanings of metadata attributes. The "scheme" attribute of the `<META>` element can be used to give hints about the format of the value of the particular metadata attribute.

9. Lassila, O. 1997. "PICS-NG Metadata Model and Label Syntax," W3C Note 1997-05-14, World Wide Web Consortium, Cambridge, Mass. (*http://www.w3.org/TR/NOTE-pics-ng-metadata*).

From the beginning, it was obvious that the creators of RDF had to walk a very fine line between simplicity (and thus the ability to deploy) and the expressive power of the formalism. In some sense, RDF had to be at the same time simple enough for the larger Web community to accept and deploy, and "not too offensive" to the knowledge representation (KR) community to tolerate so that more expressive formalisms could be based on it. The relationship with the KR community was perhaps the more difficult goal, yet it has now been realized with the introduction of the DAML+OIL[10] ontology language.[11]

Model, or "Why Couldn't I Just Use XML?"

What are RDF's major benefits? After all, XML offers structured data that could be used to encode and transport attribute/value pairs. RDF and XML are complementary: RDF defines an object model for metadata, and it only superficially addresses many encoding issues that transportation and file storage require, such as internationalization and character sets. For these issues, RDF relies on XML. But RDF also has several advantages over XML.

One design goal for RDF was to enable metadata authors to specify semantics for data based on XML in a standardized, interoperable manner. RDF also offers features like collection containers and higher-order statements. RDF's main advantage, however, is that it requires metadata authors to designate at least one underlying schema, and that the schemata are sharable and extensible. RDF is based on an object-oriented mindset, and schemata correspond to classes in an object-oriented programming system. Organized in a hierarchy, schemata offer extensibility through subclass refinement. To create a schema slightly different from an existing one only requires that you provide incremental modifications to the base schema. Through schemata sharability, RDF supports the reusability of definitions resulting from the metadata work by individuals and specialized communities.

Due to RDF's incremental extensibility, agents processing metadata will be able to trace the origins of schemata they are unfamiliar with to known schemata. They will be able to perform meaningful actions on metadata they weren't originally designed to process. For example, suppose you were to design an extension to the Dublin Core schema to leverage work done by the library community and also to allow organization-specific document metadata.[12] To do so, you could simply use standard tools designed for plain Dublin Core. Because of the self-describing

10. DAML stands for "DARPA Agent Markup Language," OIL stands for "Ontology Inference Layer." DAML+OIL is the result of collaboration between the US-based DAML work and the European OIL work.

11. van Harmelen, F., P. F. Patel-Schneider, and I. Horrocks (eds.). 2001. "Reference description of the DAML+OIL (March) Ontology Markup Language," DARPA Agent Markup Language draft document (*http://www.daml.org/2001/03/reference.html*).

12. Dublin Core Metadata Initiative. 1999. "Dublin Core Metadata Element Set, Version 1.1: Reference Description" (*http://purl.org/dc/documents/rec-dces-19990702.htm*).

nature of RDF schemata, a well-designed tool would be able to do meaningful processing for the extended properties as well.

RDF's sharability and extensibility also allow a "mix-and-match" use of metadata and metadata schemata. Metadata authors will be able to use multiple inheritance to provide multiple views to their data, leveraging work done by others.[13] Moreover, it's possible to create RDF instance data based on multiple schemata from multiple sources, that is, interleaving different types of metadata. This will lead to exciting possibilities when agents process metadata. For example, a processing agent may know how to process several types of RDF instances individually, but it will later also be able to reason about the combination. Essentially, the combination is more powerful than the sum of its parts.

From an implementation standpoint, RDF offers a clean, simple object model independent of the transport syntax of metadata. It is also important to remember that although the RDF specification defines a serialization syntax for RDF based on XML, RDF itself is not dependent on XML; it could use other syntaxes (e.g., S-expressions or the N3 notation now popular with RDF experimenters).[14]

RDF Specifications

Two separate specifications currently define RDF. The first is the Model and Syntax Specification, which became a W3C Recommendation in February 1999; the second is the Schema Specification, and is currently a W3C Candidate Recommendation (since February 2000). The separation of RDF into two specifications is largely artificial, and mostly reflects workflow issues of the standards process. Some people like to think of RDF Schema as a layer of vocabulary on top of the core RDF model. This separation is not clean, however, because the Model and Syntax specification already defines vocabulary which, strictly speaking, would not have to be part of a minimal core data model. It is therefore easier to think of RDF as just one thing, and consider the separate specifications as chapters of a larger document. This is the approach taken in explaining RDF in the next section. Where applicable, anticipated changes by the W3C RDF Core WG to the next release of the RDF standard have been indicated.

Terminology

RDF is serialized using XML. In order to be comfortable with the syntactic representation you should be comfortable with basic XML. More important from the

13. By *multiple inheritance* we mean, in object-oriented terms, a situation where a class is defined using several superclasses. For example, a "car" might be a subclass of "motor vehicle," but if we also need to consider the financial aspects of owning a car we might want it to be a subclass of, say, "asset."

14. S-expressions are the syntax used by the programming language LISP. For more information on Tim Berners-Lee's N3 notation, see *http://www.w3.org/2000/10/swap/Primer.html*

TABLE 16-1 XML Namespaces Used in This Chapter

Prefix	*URI*	*Description*
`rdf`	`http://www.w3.org/1999/02/22-rdf-syntax-ns#`	The RDF Model and Syntax namespace: some of the basic vocabulary is here.
`rdfs`	`http://www.w3.org/2000/01/rdf-schema#`	The RDF Schema namespace: the rest of the basic vocabulary is defined here.
`dc`	`http://purl.org/dc/elements/1.1/`	As an example, we use the Dublin Core vocabulary (a basic set of metadata elements for cataloging).
`ex`	`http://www.lassila.org/schemata/example/1.0/`	Vocabulary presented as examples belongs to a fictitious namespace identified as `ex`. It has a URI, but for the examples it is not relevant what the URI is.

standpoint of the model are Universal Resource Identifiers (URIs)[15] because they are used to name everything in the model, and the basic mechanics of XML Namespaces,[16] because they are used for a shorthand representation of URIs (namespaces are a handy way of writing down URIs even if you are not dealing with the XML serialization syntax of RDF—see chapter 5). RDF designers anticipated that RDF metadata would typically consist of fragments from many different sources. The probability of name conflicts would thus be high, but the namespace mechanism solves this problem.

In order to give examples of RDF usage, we have certain XML namespaces that are used all the time. They are listed in Table 16-1.

Given that RDF serialization is typically enclosed in an `rdf:RDF` document (or root) element, all subsequent examples are thought of as being inside the following construct:

```
<?xml version="1.0"?>

<rdf:RDF xmlns:rdf="http://www.w3.org/1999/02/22-rdf-syntax-ns#"
         xmlns:rdfs="http://www.w3.org/2000/01/rdf-schema#"
         xmlns:dc="http://purl.org/dc/elements/1.1/"
         xmlns:ex="http://www.lassila.org/schemata/example/1.0/">
```

15. Berners-Lee, T., R. Fielding, and L. Masinter. 1998. "Uniform Resource Identifiers (URI): Generic Syntax," Internet Draft Standard RFC 2396 (August).

16. Bray, T., D. Hollander, and A. Layman. 1999. "Namespaces in XML," W3C Working Draft, World Wide Web Consortium.

(example goes here . . .)

```
</rdf:RDF>
```

I prefer the use of XML internal entities (see chapter 4) for defining the namespaces, so that if you use a prefix *p* for a URI *u*, then the entity &*p*; "expands" to *u*, as follows:

```
<?xml version="1.0"?>

<!DOCTYPE uridef [
  <!ENTITY rdf "http://www.w3.org/1999/02/22-rdf-syntax-ns#">
  <!ENTITY rdfs "http://www.w3.org/2000/01/rdf-schema#">
  <!ENTITY dc "http://purl.org/dc/elements/1.1/">
  <!ENTITY ex "http://www.lassila.org/schemata/example/1.0/">
]>

<rdf:RDF xmlns:rdf="&rdf;"
         xmlns:rdfs="&rdfs;"
         xmlns:dc="&dc;"
         xmlns:ex="&ex;">
```

(example goes here . . .)

```
</rdf:RDF>
```

Later, we will show why the internal entity usage can make it easier to write XML-serialized RDF.

Core Data Model of RDF

At the core of RDF is a model for making statements about objects (we use the term *model* in the same sense as *data model* or *object model*; this is not to be confused with something like *model theory*, described later in this chapter). These objects can be Web resources such as documents and other Web pages, or more generally, they can be anything one can name using a URI, such as an application or a service. In this chapter we describe mainly virtual entities such as documents, but one should remember that RDF has the generality to describe objects from the physical world as well, as long as they have been named appropriately using some URI scheme.

An RDF statement consists of a **subject** (this is the entity the statement is about), a **predicate** (the named attribute of the subject), and an **object** (the value of the named attribute). So, for example, if we say (in natural, human language):

"the author of the RDF M&S Specification is Ora Lassila"

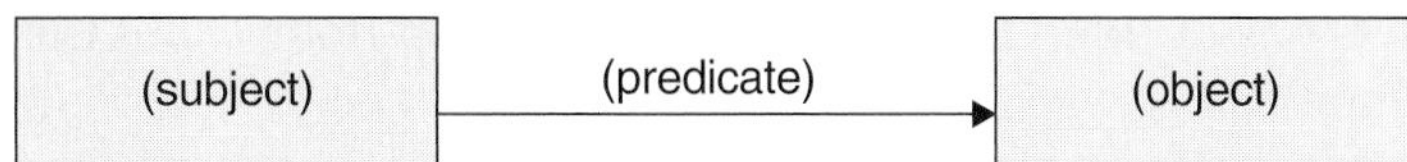

FIGURE 16-1 General pattern of RDF graphs in this chapter

we can identify the constituents of this statement as follows:

"RDF M&S Specification" is the subject

"author" is the predicate

"Ora Lassila" is the object

In RDF, we use a URI to denote the subject; in this case, a natural choice would be the URL of the specification (*http://www.w3.org/TR/REC-rdf-syntax/*). Objects can be other things named by URIs, or they can be string literals. In this case, we might say that `Ora Lassila` is a string literal, but we could choose a URI to represent the person instead (i.e., some applications have used e-mail address URIs for this purpose; whether e-mail addresses are a useful way to identify people is another matter).

If you think of the subjects and objects as nodes in a directed graph, and the predicates as the labels for the directed arcs of the graph, you get a natural and convenient way of thinking about the RDF model. We say that the model is "graph-based," and uses directed, labeled graphs (DLGs). Throughout this chapter we show examples of RDF graphs that look like Figure 16-1.

Another way of thinking about the model would be to make it "node-centric" and consider predicates to be instance variables: this gives us the object-oriented interpretation of the RDF model.

The core RDF data model consists of several types of entities: resources, properties, literals, and statements.

Resources are the nodes of an RDF graph, and thus all things being described by RDF expressions are called resources. A resource may be an entire Web page (e.g., the HTML document *http://www.lassila.org/index.shtml*), a part of a Web page (e.g., a specific HTML or XML element within the document), a whole collection of pages (e.g., an entire Web site), or an object that is not directly accessible via the Web (e.g., a person). Resources are named by URIs (plus optional fragment IDs).

For some nodes of an RDF graph, a URI is not given. These nodes are called "anonymous" and have an important role in the model (the W3C RDF Core

WG has decided to call these "blank" or "b-nodes" but they are still the same thing).

Properties are specific characteristics or relations used to describe a resource. In an RDF graph, the properties are the arcs between the nodes. Each property has a specific meaning, and may define its permitted values, the types of resources it can describe, and its relationship with other properties. The RDF Schema Specification defines how a property can express all this information.

Literals are property values that are not resources but merely text strings. The RDF model does not have an interpretation for literal values.

Statement is a "triple" that consists of a specific resource, a property of that resource, and a value for that property. The three parts of a statement are called, respectively, the *subject*, the *predicate*, and the *object*.

As indicated, it is possible to construct RDF graphs with nodes (resources) for which no URI is given. These nodes are called "blank" or "anonymous." This term can be somewhat misleading because despite the fact that the nodes have not been named, they do not lack identity. Individual anonymous nodes in a graph are separate, and this distinctness is preserved by the RDF serialization syntax.

Since the value of a property can be another resource (which, in turn, can have properties with values, etc.), it is simple to construct arbitrary structures using RDF. We could, for example, use these "structured values" to construct a description of a person: some property (say, `ex:name`) would give a person's name, and another property (say, `ex:email`) would give this person's e-mail address (note that `Ora Lassila` is a literal whereas the e-mail address is given using a URI and is thus a resource from RDF's standpoint) (see Figure 16-2). The structures thus formed can also have cycles, naturally. (Later, it will be demonstrated how the RDF serialization syntax can be used to create such structures.)

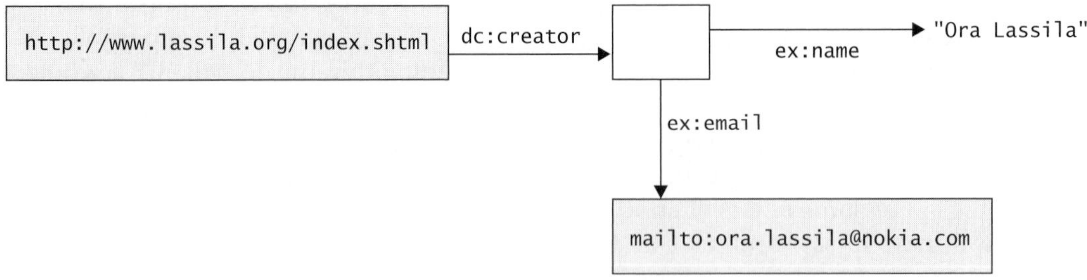

FIGURE 16-2 A property with a structured value

Vocabulary for Ontological Description Using RDF

As mentioned, both the Model and Syntax Specification as well as the Schema Specification introduce some basic vocabulary for constructing models using RDF. Whether a term is introduced by one or the other specification is not important (except, of course, that they come from different namespaces).

Qualified Values: Special Case of Structured Values

As a special case of a structured value, RDF has a property called `rdf:value`. This allows one to "qualify" property values: Often the value of a property has additional contextual information that is considered "part of" that value. Examples of such qualification include naming a unit of measure, a particular restricted vocabulary, or some other annotation. In the RDF model a qualified property value is simply a structured value. The object of the original statement is this structured value and the qualifiers are further properties of this common resource. The principal value being qualified is given as the value of the `rdf:value` property of this common resource. See the example in Figure 16-3.

Classes and Instances

Almost the first thing that one wants to do is to indicate that certain objects (resources, if you will—not to be confused with the "object" in "subject/predicate/object") belong to certain classes (e.g., Person, Document, Organization, etc.). Therefore, the first concrete piece of vocabulary is the relationship between the object itself (we will call it an *instance* to use typical object-oriented terminology) and the class of that object; this relationship, or property, is called `rdf:type`. So, for example, Figure 16-4 shows that a particular resource (a node in a graph) is an instance of a class called `ex:Document`.

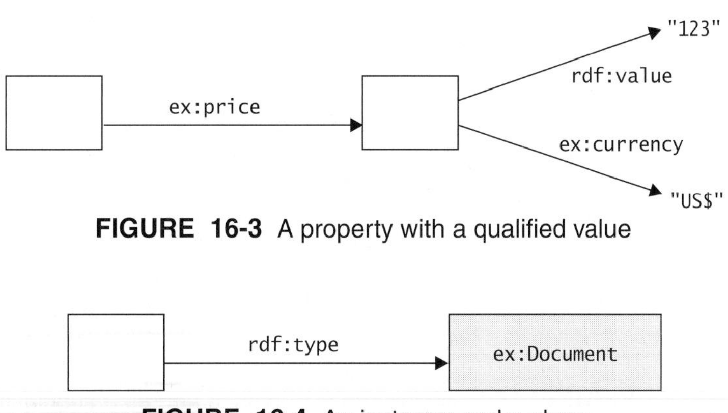

FIGURE 16-3 A property with a qualified value

FIGURE 16-4 An instance and a class

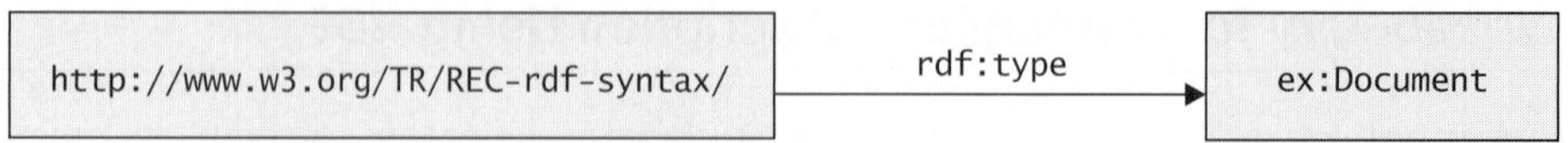

FIGURE 16-5 A document as an instance of a document class

For example, we could say that the RDF Model and Syntax Specification is an instance of the class `ex:Document`, as shown in Figure 16-5.

Implicitly, every class in RDF is a subclass of the class `rdfs:Resource`, and every resource for which a class has not been specified is an instance of this class. To complete the object-oriented type system, all literals, implicitly, are considered to be instances of the class `rdfs:Literal`.

The RDF Schema Specification introduces a way of defining classes and relating these to other classes. The RDF "type system" is object-oriented, and therefore classes can be defined as specializations (or "subclasses") of other classes. For example, a class representing cats might be a subclass of a class representing all feline animals, which in turn might be a subclass of mammals, and so on.
The RDF class system is built by modeling classes using RDF itself. In fact, objects that represent classes are instances of another class, called `rdfs:Class` (in other object-oriented systems, `rdfs:Class` would be called a *metaclass*). To use the earlier introduced class `ex:Document` as an example, its basic definition (as a graph) would look like Figure 16-6.

If we had another class, say `ex:Specification`, which we wanted to be a subclass of `ex:Document`, we would define it as Figure 16-7 shows. Since `ex:Document` is also an instance of `rdfs:Class`, the full graph would look like the one shown in Figure 16-8.

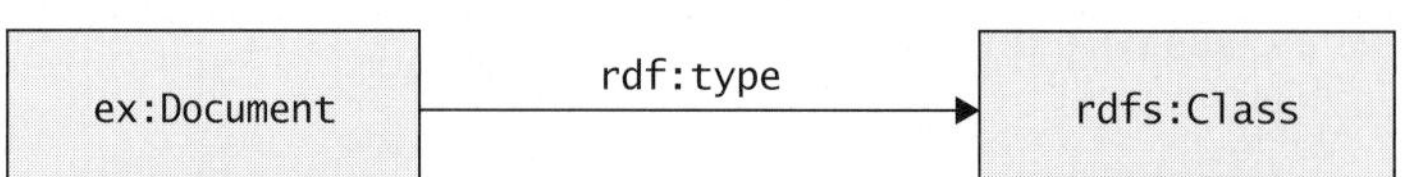

FIGURE 16-6 A class as an instance of a metaclass

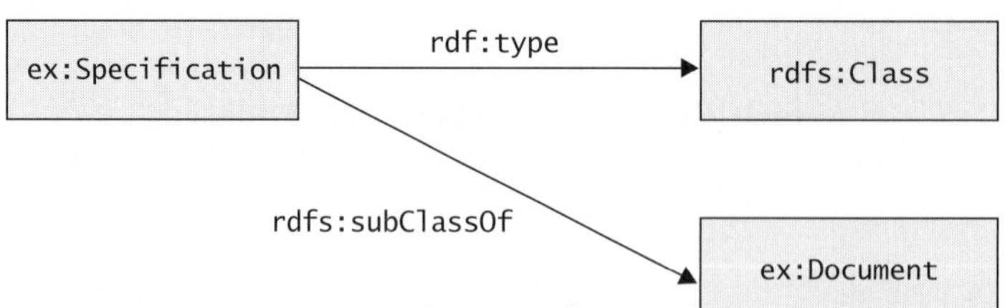

FIGURE 16-7 A class as an instance and as a subclass

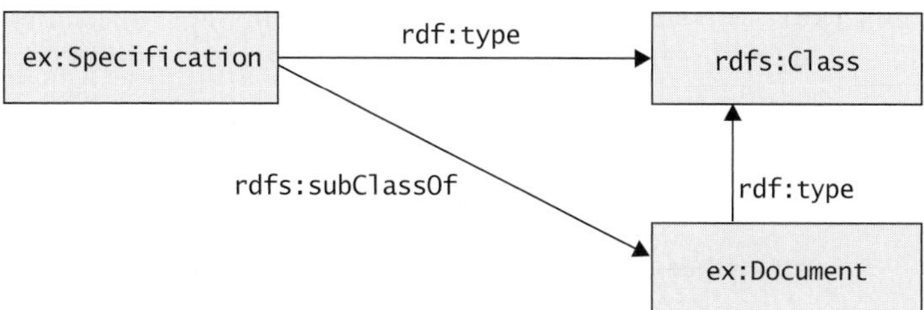

FIGURE 16-8 Completion of Figure 16-7 using Figure 16-6

Since URIs are used only to identify the resources we define, but not to name them for human-readable purposes, the property `rdfs:label` can be used to provide a human-readable name for a class. In the case of `ex:Document` we would probably want to provide the string `Document` as the value of the `rdfs:label` property.

The RDF Schema Specification states that cycles are not allowed in `rdfs:subClassOf` chains.[17] The W3C RDF Core WG has since decided to drop this requirement, making the RDF Schema more in line with DAML+OIL, which uses cycles to infer class equivalence.

Properties, Subproperties, and Property Constraints

The same way we define classes, we can also define properties.[18] The class `rdf:Property` exists for this purpose, and the property `rdfs:label` can be used to provide a human-friendly name. For example, from Dublin Core the property `dc:creator` would be defined as in Figure 16-9.

To take advantage of existing property definitions, new properties can be defined as their subproperties. This allows you, for example, to further refine how

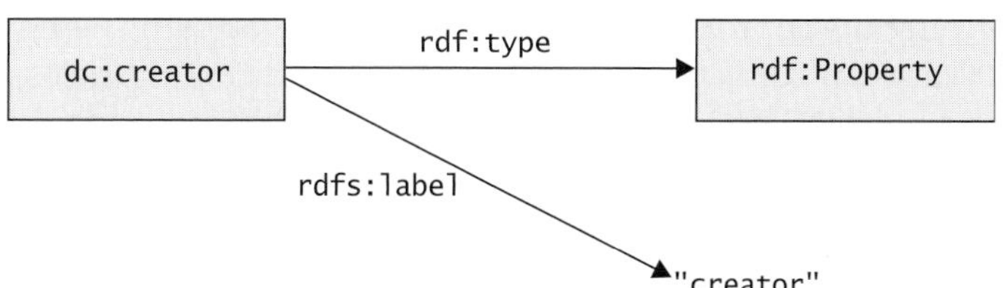

FIGURE 16-9 Giving a property a human-readable name

17. By *cycle* we mean a situation where, for example, A is a subclass of B, B is a subclass of C, and C is a subclass of A.

18. Note that, as a general convention, names of classes are capitalized, but names of properties are not.

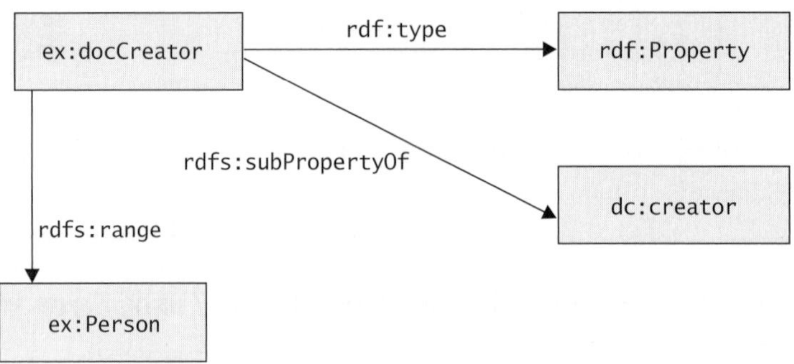

FIGURE 16-10 Specializing a generic property with a range constraint

a property behaves and/or is processed. For example, for our own document management system, we might want to define a special version of the `dc:creator` property that would allow only people as authors (let's imagine that we have a class called `ex:Person` for this purpose). RDF Schema introduces a constraint that can be attached to a property definition, instructing any software processing the definition that values for this property are limited in terms of their type. This constraint is called `rdfs:range`, and its values are classes (instances of `rdfs:Class`). Let's extend our example to demonstrate the new vocabulary, as in Figure 16-10.

Here is a new property, `ex:docCreator`, which is defined as a subproperty of `dc:creator` (using `rdfs:subPropertyOf`). Additionally, we have attached a range constraint to the definition, limiting the values of `ex:docCreator` to instances of the class `ex:Person`.

Another constraint exists, called `rdfs:domain`, which can be used to limit the types of resources a property can be attached to. For example, if we wanted to limit the use of the `ex:docCreator` property to instances of `ex:Document` only, we would add an `rdfs:domain` property (with a value of `ex:Document`) to the definition of `ex:docCreator`.

By defining a subproperty of `dc:creator`, we are still using the Dublin Core metadata. Our own software will be able to do additional processing (e.g., validity checking) on our own metadata; at the same time, any correctly built RDF software intended for processing Dublin Core metadata can also understand our metadata. The caveat here is in the expression "correctly built," obviously. If we take shortcuts in building our software and, for example, ignore `rdfs:subPropertyOf` links, the desired effect will not be achieved.

A collection of class and property definitions in a single document is called a **schema**,[19] and serves as a basic building block of RDF applications (and the entire

19. Conceptually, a schema in RDF serves the same approximate purpose as a schema in XML does.

Semantic Web, for that matter, since it is the sharing of the schemata that principally brings about the power of the vision).

Containers

Frequently it is necessary to refer to a collection of resources; for example, to say that a work was created by more than one person, or to list the students in a course, or the software modules in a package, or a collection of documents available from a Web site. RDF containers are used for such lists of resources or literals. RDF actually defines three types of container objects.

- **Bags**—A bag is an unordered list of resources or literals. Bags are used to declare that property has multiple values and that the ordering of these values has no particular significance. Duplicate values are permitted. Bags are instances of the class `rdf:Bag`.
- **Sequences**—A sequence is an ordered list of resources or literals. Sequence is used to declare that a property has multiple values and that the order of the values is somehow significant. Sequences might be used, for example, to preserve an alphabetical ordering of values. Duplicate values are permitted. Sequences are instances of the class `rdf:Seq`.
- **Alternatives**—This is a list of resources or literals that represent alternatives for the single value of a property. Alternatives might be used to provide alternative language translations for the title of a work, or to provide a list of Internet mirror sites at which a resource might be found. An application using a property whose value is an Alternative container is aware that it can choose any of the items in the list as appropriate. Alternatives are instances of the class `rdf:Alt`.

The definitions of Bag and Sequence explicitly permit duplicate values. The reason that RDF does not define the core concept of a Set (which would be a Bag with no duplicates) is because RDF does not mandate an enforcement mechanism in the event of violations of such constraints.

All three container classes are considered subclasses of the class `rdfs:Container`.[20]

To represent a collection, RDF uses an additional resource that identifies the specific container. This resource must be declared to be an instance of one of the container classes just defined. As with any instance, the `rdf:type` property is used to make this declaration. The membership relation between this container resource and the resources that belong in the collection is defined by a set of properties defined expressly for this purpose. These membership properties are named `rdf:_1`, `rdf:_2`, `rdf:_3`, and so on. They are instances of the class `rdfs:`

20. The `rdfs:Container` class was not defined until the class system was introduced in the RDF Schema specification, hence different namespace from the `rdf:Bag` and such classes.

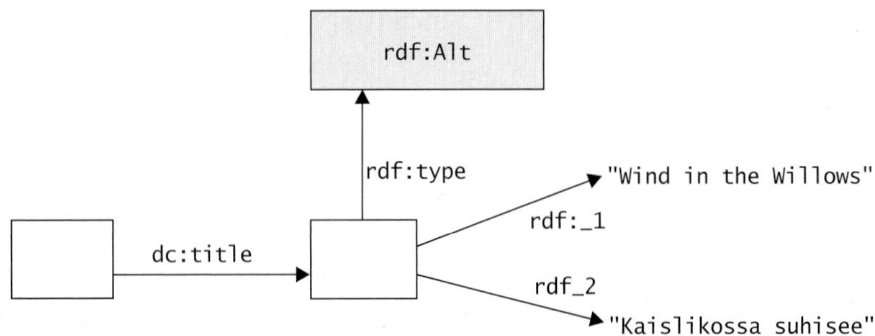

FIGURE 16-11 Using alternatives to give a book two titles

ContainerMembershipProperty which, in turn, is a subclass of rdf:Property. Container resources may have other properties in addition to the membership properties and the rdf:type property. Any such additional statements describe the container itself. The serialization syntax has shorthand notation for making statements about each of the members.

A common use of containers is as the value of a property. When used in this way, the statement still corresponds to a single triple regardless of the number of members in the container; the container resource itself is the object of the statement. Figure 16-11 is an example, a book with two alternative titles. Note that it is up to the application designer to decide how this is different from having two dc:title properties. From the RDF standpoint, they are representationally different, as Figure 16-12 shows.

Miscellaneous Vocabulary

In addition to what has been presented so far, RDF introduces some additional vocabulary. These properties are mainly intended for adding documentation to RDF schemata:

- rdfs:comment is a property that can be used to provide human-readable documentation for a class, property, and so on.
- rdfs:seeAlso is a property that can be used to link a class or property to some other resource (typically a document), which may provide additional information. Understandably, the semantics of this property are rather vague.

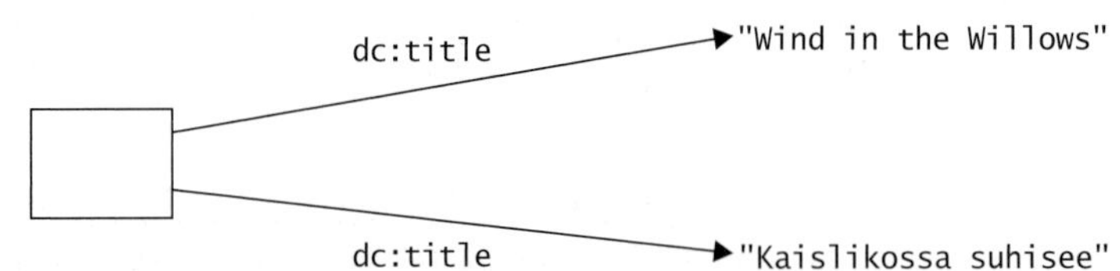

FIGURE 16-12 Using repeated properties to give a book two titles

- `rdfs:isDefinedBy` is a subproperty of `rdfs:seeAlso`; its purpose is to link a class or property to its defining resource (typically a document that contains an RDF schema).

XML Serialization Syntax for RDF

As explained in the previous section, the important thing about RDF is that it is a data model, and thus independent of any serialization syntax. Of course, the reality is that we do need some serialization syntax because people will want to store instances of the RDF model in files, or to communicate these instances from one system to another. XML is the language the designers chose to use in the RDF specification (and this is the reason this chapter is in this book). RDF and XML are complementary: on the one hand, RDF leverages XML, but on the other hand, XML needs RDF for defining what instances of metadata mean, and for allowing agents to agree on a common meaning.

XML is only one syntactic representation for the RDF model; other syntaxes are possible. Some of these other syntaxes were discussed extensively during the development of RDF (including one based on S-expressions, a bit like the PICS syntax). Lately, some unofficial syntaxes have popped up, the most notable being N3 used by many people experimenting with RDF, and N-triples used in communicating test cases (mostly within the W3C RDF Core WG). Debates about the syntax for RDF are likely to go on, both about how XML is used to serialize the graphs as well as whether to use XML at all. Historically, it should be noted that XML was chosen on the basis of its perceived prevalence in Web software, rather than its technical merit.

There are actually two variants of the XML serialization syntax for RDF, and they can be freely mixed. The first one is called *full syntax* and the second *abbreviated syntax*.

Full Syntax

RDF uses what some people have called *striped syntax*: In the syntactic representation, resources and their properties alternate (when proceeding deeper in the nesting of the XML parse tree). The subsequent examples will illustrate this. Our first example is a simple RDF instance, a metadata fragment that describes a Web resource with a given URL and states that "Ora Lassila" is the creator—that is, author in Dublin Core library metadata terms—of this particular resource. In the model, the Web page is a node (a resource) and it has one property, namely `dc:creator`, whose value is the string "Ora Lassila":

```
<rdf:Description rdf:about="http://www.lassila.org/index.shtml">
  <dc:creator>Ora Lassila</dc:creator>
</rdf:Description>
```

As discussed in the model section, property values can be complex objects. In the following example, the `dc:creator` property from the first example now has a value with more structure, an instance with two properties: `ex:name` and `ex:email`:

```
<rdf:Description rdf:about="http://www.lassila.org/index.shtml">
  <dc:creator>
    <rdf:Description>
      <ex:name>Ora Lassila</ex:name>
      <ex:email rdf:resource="mailto:ora.lassila@nokia.com"/>
    </rdf:Description>
  </dc:creator>
</rdf:Description>
```

Two pieces of additional vocabulary are present in these examples: The attribute `rdf:about` designates the URI of the resource being described, and the attribute `rdf:resource` makes references to resources as property values. Here's an example: take the previous example but imagine that the person being used as the value of the `dc:creator` property has a URI (say, using a hypothetical URI scheme "person" it could be `person:US:123-45-6789`) and that the RDF for him resides somewhere else. Then the example would look like this:

```
<rdf:Description rdf:about="http://www.lassila.org/index.shtml">
  <dc:creator rdf:resource="person:US:123-45-6789"/>
</rdf:Description>
```

If you wanted to write the definition of the person resource "inline," it would turn out like this:

```
<rdf:Description rdf:about="http://www.lassila.org/index.shtml">
  <dc:creator>
    <rdf:Description rdf:about="person:US:123-45-6789">
      <ex:name>Ora Lassila</ex:name>
      <ex:email rdf:resource="mailto:ora.lassila@nokia.com"/>
    </rdf:Description>
  </dc:creator>
</rdf:Description>
```

Furthermore, to combine these two approaches, you could take the first form (the one that uses `rdf:resource`) and place the description of the person outside the first description (the one about the document), like this:

```
<rdf:Description rdf:about="http://www.lassila.org/index.shtml">
  <dc:creator rdf:resource="person:US:123-45-6789"/>
</rdf:Description>

<rdf:Description rdf:about="person:US:123-45-6789">
  <ex:name>Ora Lassila</ex:name>
  <ex:email rdf:resource="mailto:ora.lassila@nokia.com"/>
</rdf:Description>
```

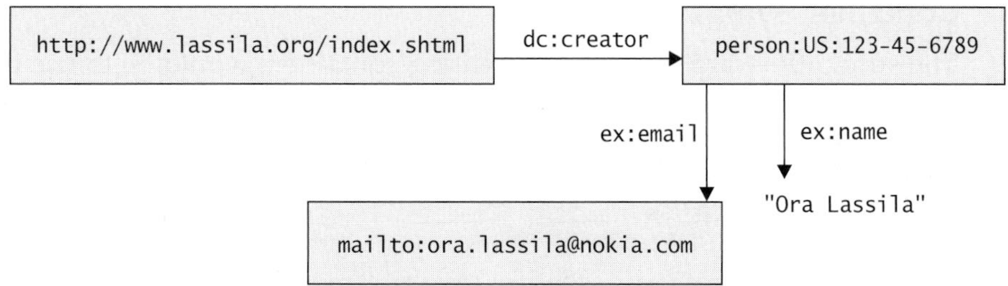

FIGURE 16-13 Multiple syntactic representations can result in the same graph

In all of these cases, the underlying graph would look exactly the same, as it does in Figure 16-13.

Simple rules govern the use of the `rdf:about` and `rdf:resource` attributes. Normally, their value is either a full URI or a relative URI—the relative ones (starting with a # sign) are useful if the resource being described is actually in the same document. If you want to make a reference (in `rdf:about`) to the entire document in which the particular metadata is contained, use an empty string as a value.

One additional attribute needs to be presented here. Let's say you wanted the RDF for the person to have a fragment URI inside the document where all of this RDF resides (for example, to also demonstrate the empty `rdf:about` string convention previously described, let's say that all of this RDF is embedded in the `HEAD` part of the document `http://www.lassila.org/index.shtml`). Using the attribute `rdf:ID` it is possible to establish an identity for the resource, and this in turn will become a fragment URI:

```
<rdf:Description rdf:about="">
  <dc:creator rdf:resource="#ora"/>
</rdf:Description>

<rdf:Description rdf:ID="ora">
  <ex:name>Ora Lassila</ex:name>
  <ex:email rdf:resource="mailto:ora.lassila@nokia.com"/>
</rdf:Description>
```

Notice that the resource whose `rdf:ID` is `ora` can be referred to using a relative URI `#ora`. Since this resource resides in the file `http://www.lassila.org/index.shtml`, its full URI is now `http://www.lassila.org/index.shtml#ora`. The funny thing about `rdf:ID` is that it is actually completely redundant, since the same effect can be achieved by using `rdf:about`, as follows:

```
<rdf:Description rdf:about="#ora">
  <ex:name>Ora Lassila</ex:name>
  <ex:email rdf:resource="mailto:ora.lassila@nokia.com"/>
</rdf:Description>
```

Notice the relative URI with the # sign.

Container Syntax

The straightforward way of representing containers would be to use the serialization syntax directly to map the graph into XML. Given our earlier example of a book with two alternative titles, we would have the following:

```
<rdf:Description>
  <dc:title>
    <rdf:Alt>
      <rdf:_1>Wind in the Willows</rdf:_1>
      <rdf:_2>Kaislikossa suhisee</rdf:_2>
    </rdf:Alt>
  </dc:title>
</rdf:Description>
```

This, however, looks awkward. RDF provides "syntactic sugar," borrowed from HTML lists, to make writing down containers easier:

```
<rdf:Description>
  <dc:title>
    <rdf:Alt>
      <rdf:li>Wind in the Willows</rdf:li>
      <rdf:li>Kaislikossa suhisee</rdf:li>
    </rdf:Alt>
  </dc:title>
</rdf:Description>
```

XML facilities for indicating the language of particular content can be used; they make sense in this example:

```
<rdf:Description>
  <dc:title>
    <rdf:Alt>
      <rdf:li xml:lang="en">Wind in the Willows</rdf:li>
      <rdf:li xml:lang="fi">Kaislikossa suhisee</rdf:li>
    </rdf:Alt>
  </dc:title>
</rdf:Description>
```

Unfortunately there is no correspondence in the RDF graph for the `xml:lang` attributes.

The W3C RDF Core WG has decided to relax the requirement that parsers have special knowledge of container semantics (making it difficult to subclass containers). What this means in practice is that parsers are to produce properties of the form `rdf:_nnn` whenever they encounter the `rdf:li` element, regardless of whether these are in an `rdf:Bag`, `rdf:Seq`, or `rdf:Alt`. The WG also decided that an RDF model may contain partial descriptions of a container, and thus an RDF model is not constrained to have the properties of the form `rdf:_nnn` contiguously starting from `rdf:_1` as dictated by the original specification.

Shorthand notation is provided to allow statements to be made of every member of a container; for example, given a container as follows:

```
<rdf:Bag rdf:ID="RDFDocs">
  <rdf:li rdf:resource="http://www.w3.org/TR/REC-rdf-syntax/"/>
  <rdf:li rdf:resource="http://www.w3.org/TR/rdf-schema/"/>
</rdf:Bag>
```

If we wanted to say that W3C is the publisher of each of these documents, we could write:

```
<rdf:Description rdf:aboutEach="#RDFDocs">
  <dc:publisher>W3C</dc:publisher>
</rdf:Description>
```

This would be the same as saying the following:

```
<rdf:Description rdf:about="http://www.w3.org/TR/REC-rdf-syntax/">
  <dc:publisher>W3C</dc:publisher>
</rdf:Description>

<rdf:Description rdf:about="http://www.w3.org/TR/rdf-schema/">
  <dc:publisher>W3C</dc:publisher>
</rdf:Description>
```

In other words, using `rdf:aboutEach` makes the statements in the description about each member of the target container, instead of about the container as a single object. Along this line, if one wants to make a set of statements about every document defined by a URI pattern, one can use `rdfs:aboutEachPrefix`. For example, saying the following:

```
<rdf:Description rdf:aboutEachPrefix="http://www.w3.org/">
  <dc:publisher>W3C</dc:publisher>
</rdf:Description>
```

would mean that every document on the W3C Web site (more specifically, every document whose URI starts with `http://www.w3.org/`) would have W3C as its publisher. Unfortunately, implementation of this feature is cumbersome, since it might require the enumeration of every document on a Web site, and the specification is unclear as to what happens if documents get added at some point. Therefore, the W3C RDF Core WG decided to remove this feature from the next release of the RDF standard (the actual reason given was "lack of implementation experience," which just means that most, if not all, implementers of RDF parsers left this feature out because it is very hard to implement).

The "distributive" forms of reference (i.e., `rdf:aboutEach` and `rdf:aboutEachPrefix`) would make sense only when used in a description at the "top level" inside the `rdf:RDF` element. The W3C RDF Core WG has therefore decided that rdf:aboutEach attributes are not allowed on an rdf:Description element that is the object of a statement (this was inadvertently omitted from the Model and Syntax Specification).

Abbreviated Syntax

The abbreviated serialization syntax for RDF was invented to allow RDF to be embedded in the HEAD part of HTML documents and have (older) browsers not render it. To do this, all character content had to be avoided. To achieve this goal meant abusing XML somewhat, by turning properties into attributes. For example, instead of writing as follows:

```
<rdf:Description rdf:about="">
  <dc:creator>Ora Lassila</dc:creator>
</rdf:Description>
```

one would write this:

```
<rdf:Description rdf:about="" dc:creator="Ora Lassila"/>
```

XML purists might not like this (because it blurs the distinction between the use of elements and attributes), but it served the purpose for which it was created. It is called the "abbreviated" syntax because as a side effect it tends to make descriptions shorter. It is easy to mechanically convert abbreviated RDF to full RDF.

Parse Types

Sometimes it is necessary to make a property value be "plain" XML (e.g., a larger block of text marked up using XHTML). To do this, we need to make sure that the RDF parser will not try to interpret that markup as serialized RDF. A special attribute, rdf:parseType, can be used for this. Here is an example (taken from the RDF Model and Syntax Specification, with nonessential modifications):

```
<rdf:Description m:xmlns="http://www.w3.org/TR/REC-mathml"
                 rdf:about="http://mycorp.com/papers/NobelPaper1">
  <dc:title rdf:parseType="Literal">
    Ramifications of
    <m:apply>
      <m:power/>
      <m:apply>
        <m:plus/> <m:ci>a</m:ci> <m:ci>b</m:ci>
      </m:apply>
      <m:cn>2</m:cn>
    </m:apply>
    to World Peace
  </dc:title>
</rdf:Description>
```

Using `Literal` as the value of the `rdf:parseType` attribute "escapes" the enclosed markup and prevents interpretation as RDF.

Another use of the `rdf:parseType` attribute is to eliminate seemingly superfluous anonymous `rdf:Description` elements from the (striped) serialization syntax. Think of our earlier example of structured values where we described a person in terms of a name and an e-mail address. The same example could have been written as follows:

```
<rdf:Description rdf:about="http://www.lassila.org/index.shtml">
  <dc:creator rdf:parseType="Resource">
    <ex:name>Ora Lassila</ex:name>
    <ex:email rdf:resource="mailto:ora.lassila@nokia.com"/>
  </dc:creator>
</rdf:Description>
```

Earlier, the `ex:name` and `ex:email` properties were bracketed by an `rdf:Description` element. Since the node this would create in the graph was anonymous (we did not give it a URI), using the `rdf:parseType` with the value `Resource` allowed us to abbreviate the syntactic expression somewhat. The resulting graph is still the same.

Languages built on top of RDF can extend the basic RDF syntax by introducing new values for `rdf:parseType`. An example of this is DAML+OIL, which defines a new container syntax through this mechanism. RDF parsers should signal an error if they encounter an unknown value for this attribute, since it is an indication that some nonstandard form of syntax will follow.

Syntactic Conventions for Schemata

Now that we have described how classes and properties are defined, and how the RDF serialization syntax works, it is time to see what RDF schemata actually look like. Typically, class and property definitions are collected in a document, inside which the definitions can refer to each other using relative (fragment-syntax) URIs. Some people have adopted a convention in which resources are named using `rdf:ID` when first introduced, and using `rdf:about` subsequently, but there is nothing in the specifications that require one to do so.

Here's an example of what the definitions of the earlier `ex:Document` and `ex:Specification` classes and `ex:docCreator` property would look like:

```
<rdfs:Class rdf:ID="Document">
  <rdfs:label>Document</rdfs:label>
</rdfs:Class>

<rdfs:Class rdf:ID="Specification">
  <rdfs:label>Specification</rdfs:label>
  <rdfs:subClassOf rdf:resource="#Document"/>
</rdfs:Class>
```

```
<rdf:Property rdf:ID="docCreator">
  <rdfs:label>docCreator</rdfs:label>
  <rdfs:subPropertyOf rdf:resource="&dc;creator"/>
  <rdfs:domain rdf:resource="#Document"/>
  <rdfs:range rdf:resource="#Person"/>
</rdf:Property>
```

In order to function correctly, this schema really has to reside in what we designated as the URI for the namespace `ex` (specifically, to make the relative URIs correct).[21] If you want to define the schema in such a manner that you could keep it anywhere, yet have all the classes and properties have their correct URIs in the `ex` namespace, you could use `rdf:about` instead of `rdf:ID`, and furthermore use the technique with internal entities described earlier. Here's the revised example (with changed parts in boldface):

```
<rdfs:Class rdf:about="&ex;Document">
  <rdfs:label>Document</rdfs:label>
</rdfs:Class>

<rdfs:Class rdf:about="&ex;Specification">
  <rdfs:label>Specification</rdfs:label>
  <rdfs:subClassOf rdf:resource="&ex;Document"/>
</rdfs:Class>

<rdf:Property rdf:about="&ex;docCreator">
  <rdfs:label>docCreator</rdfs:label>
  <rdfs:subPropertyOf rdf:resource="&dc;creator"/>
  <rdfs:domain rdf:resource="&ex;Document"/>
  <rdfs:range rdf:resource="&ex;Person"/>
</rdf:Property>
```

This is actually my preferred way of writing RDF schemata, because it makes them "location independent" and thus easy to debug before real-life deployment.

Advanced Topics

So far, we have described more or less all of the RDF Model and Syntax and the RDF Schema Specifications, except for a few details that could be designated advanced. It is not only that these features are complicated, but one could also happily use RDF and never have to know what these features are and how they work. They are included here for completeness, and because some people will find them useful (e.g., if you plan on building RDF tools, you may have to study these).

Statements about Statements

In addition to making statements about Web resources, RDF can be used for making statements about other RDF statements; we will refer to these as *higher-order*

21. Note that the definition of the class `ex:Person` has been omitted from this example.

statements. In order to make a statement about another statement, we actually have to build a model of the original statement; this model is a new resource to which we can attach additional properties.

Statements are made about resources. A model of a statement is the resource we need in order to be able to make new statements (higher-order statements) about the modeled statement. For example, let us consider the sentence

> Ora Lassila is the creator of the resource
> `http://www.w3.org/TR/REC-rdf-syntax/`

An RDF processor would regard this sentence (given that it was expressed in proper RDF of course) as a fact. If, instead, we were to write the sentence

> Ken Sall believes that Ora Lassila is the creator of the resource
> `http://www.w3.org/TR/REC-rdf-syntax/`

we have not expressed any facts about the resource `http://www.w3.org/TR/REC-rdf-syntax/`, but we have made a statement involving Ken Sall. In order to express this in RDF, we have to model the original statement as a resource. The RDF Model and Syntax Specification calls this process *reification*, and a model of a statement is called a *reified statement*. For the purposes of our discussion, we can also call these *models of statements*, and the statements made about the models *statements about statements.*

It is important to note that a statement and its corresponding reified version exist independently in an RDF graph, and either may be present without the other. The RDF graph is said to contain the fact given in the statement if and only if the statement is present in the graph, irrespective of whether the corresponding reified statement is present.

To model statements, RDF defines the class `rdf:Statement`, for which the following properties have been defined (all reified statements are instances of this class; that is, they have an `rdf:type` property whose object is `rdf:Statement`):

- `rdf:subject`—The *subject* property identifies the resource being described by the modeled statement; that is, the value of the subject property is the resource about which the original statement was made (in our example, `http://www.w3.org/TR/REC-rdf-syntax/`).
- `rdf:predicate`—The *predicate* property identifies the original property in the modeled statement. The value of the predicate property is a resource representing the specific property in the original statement (in our example, `creator`, but let's pick the predicate from the Dublin Core vocabulary and use `dc:creator`).
- `rdf:object`—The *object* property identifies the property value in the modeled statement. The value of the object property is the object in the original statement (in our example, `Ora Lassila`).

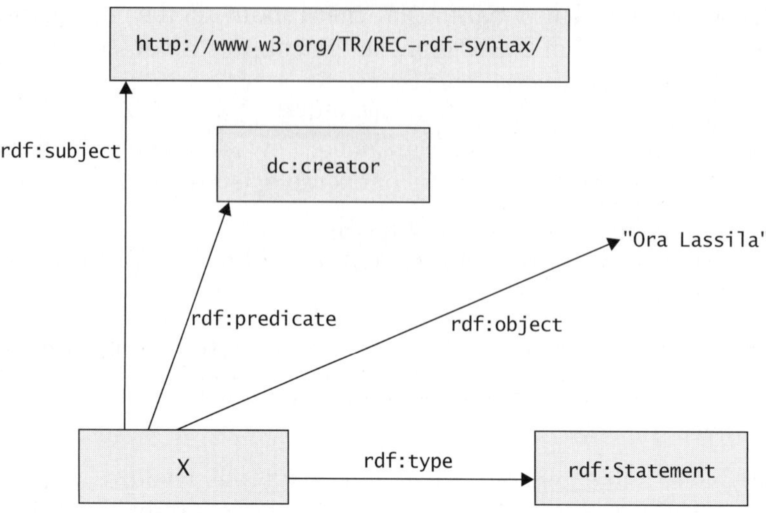

FIGURE 16-14 A reified statement

A new resource with these three properties represents the original statement and can both be used as the object of other statements and have additional statements made about it. The resource with these three properties is not a replacement for the original statement; it is a model of the statement. Figure 16-14 represents the example (the new reified statement is marked `X`).

Given our earlier (natural language) example about Ken Sall believing that Ora Lassila is the creator of the said document, we can now express it as an RDF graph, as shown in Figure 16-15. Other arcs leaving (i.e., properties of) the node X are not shown to keep the size of the graph small. Using full XML serialization syntax for RDF, this could be written as:

```
<rdf:Description>
  <rdf:subject rdf:resource="http://www.w3.org/TR/REC-rdf-syntax/"/>
  <rdf:predicate rdf:resource="&dc;creator"/>
  <rdf:object>Ora Lassila</rdf:object>
  <rdf:type rdf:resource="&rdf;Statement"/>
  <ex:isBelievedBy>Ken Sall</ex:isBelievedBy>
</rdf:Description>
```

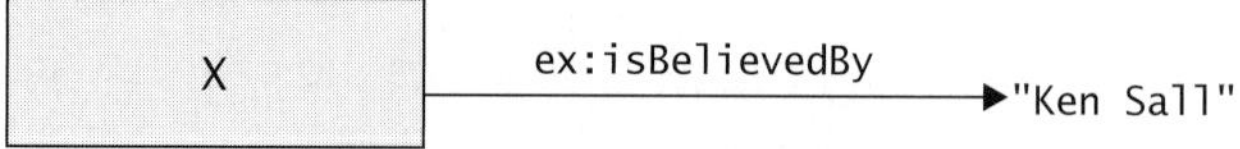

FIGURE 16-15 A statement about another statement (see Figure 16-14)

Using the convenient shorthand for indicating the `rdf:type`, this could be written:

```
<rdf:Statement>
  <rdf:subject rdf:resource="http://www.w3.org/TR/REC-rdf-syntax/"/>
  <rdf:predicate rdf:resource="&dc;creator"/>
  <rdf:object>Ora Lassila</rdf:object>
  <ex:isBelievedBy>Ken Sall</ex:isBelievedBy>
</rdf:Statement>
```

Further, if we wanted to make use of the abbreviated syntax, this could be written as follows:

```
<rdf:Statement rdf:object="Ora Lassila" ex:isBelievedBy="Ken Sall"
  <rdf:subject rdf:resource="http://www.w3.org/TR/REC-rdf-syntax/"/>
  <rdf:predicate rdf:resource="&dc;creator"/>
</rdf:Statement>
```

Reification is also needed to explicitly represent the statement grouping implied by the `rdf:Description` elements of the syntax. The RDF graph model does not have a special construct for descriptions; since descriptions really are collections of statements, a bag container is used to indicate that a set of statements came from the same (syntactic) description. Each statement within an `rdf:Description` is reified and each of the reified statements is a member of the bag representing that `rdf:Description`. As an example, the RDF fragment

```
<rdf:Description rdf:about="http://www.w3.org/TR/REC-rdf-syntax/"
                 rdf:bagID="D_001">
  <dc:creator>Ora Lassila</dc:creator>
  <dc:title>Ora's Home Page</dc:title>
</rdf:Description>
```

results in two reified statements, and a bag with two members (the two reified statements), in addition to the two statements themselves. A new attribute `rdf:bagID` is used. This attribute specifies the resource identifier (the one we would normally use `rdf:ID` for) of the container resource. Please observe that `rdf:bagID` and `rdf:ID` should not be confused: `rdf:ID` specifies the identification of an inline resource whose properties are further detailed in the `rdf:Description`, whereas `rdf:bagID` specifies the identification of the container resource whose members are the reified statements about another resource. An `rdf:Description` may have both an `rdf:ID` attribute and an `rdf:bagID` attribute.

Since attaching an `rdf:bagID` to an `rdf:Description` results in including in the model a bag of the reified statements of the description, we will use this when making statements about statements. For example, if we wanted to say that Ken Sall believes the previous statements, we can simply add to the example:

```
<rdf:Description rdf:aboutEach="#D_001">
  <ex:isBelievedBy>Ken Sall</ex:isBelievedBy>
</rdf:Description>
```

Sometimes one wants to qualify only one, not all, of the statements that are in a description. In this case, one can use an `rdf:ID` attribute on the particular property in question, since it will now name the reified statement. Here is an example:

```
<rdf:Description rdf:about="http://www.lassila.org/">
  <dc:creator rdf:ID="S_001">Ora Lassila</dc:creator>
  <dc:title>Ora's Home Page</dc:title>
</rdf:Description>

<rdf:Description rdf:about="#S_001">
  <ex:isBelievedBy>Ken Sall</ex:isBelievedBy>
</rdf:Description>
```

In this case, we are expressing that Ken believes that Ora is the creator of the particular Web resource, but nothing is said about the statement that talks about the title of the same resource. It should be observed that we have now named a single statement (and will use `rdf:about` to reference it) as opposed to the case with the entire description, where we created a bag of statements (and had to use `rdf:aboutEach` to reference each of the statements).

Introducing Additional Constraints

In the original design of the RDF Schema, a provision was introduced for future language extensions to add new types of constraints (in addition to `rdfs:range` and `rdfs:domain`). The classes `rdfs:ConstraintResource` and `rdfs:ConstraintProperty` are defined for this purpose. They act as a flag for an RDF 1.0 processor to indicate that "all bets are off" when it encounters unknown subclasses of these, since it is likely that these introduce some new processing semantics. Generally, this design was based on the thinking that any properties that you would use with class and property definitions would be either "constraining" or not. This may not be the case; given this, and the lack of implementations that would use this feature, the W3C RDF Core Working Group decided to remove these two classes from the specification.

Model Theory

At the time of this writing, the most significant piece of work from the W3C RDF Core WG is the first draft of the RDF Model Theory.[22] This document provides a

22. Hayes, P. 2001. "RDF Model Theory," W3C Working Draft (25 September), World Wide Web Consortium, Cambridge, Mass. (*http://www.w3.org/TR/2001/WD-rdf-mt-20010925/*).

precise semantic theory for RDF (including RDF Schema), and sharpens the notions of consequence and inference in RDF. In its current form, it does not cover reification, and ignores some aspects of conveying meaning in RDF. It is, however, a serious effort to strengthen the formal logical basis of RDF.

For Further Exploration

Articles

xmlhack.com: RDF (and Topic Maps) Category
http://xmlhack.com/list.php?cat=28

Scientific American: The Semantic Web, Tim Berners-Lee, James Hendler and Ora Lassila (May 2001)
http://www.sciam.com/2001/0501issue/0501berners-lee.html

XML.com: What is RDF?, Tim Bray (January 2001)
http://www.xml.com/pub/a/2001/01/24/rdf.html

XML.com: Berners-Lee and the Semantic Web Vision, Edd Dumbill (December 2000)
http://www.xml.com/pub/a/2000/12/xml2000/timbl.html

Resources

Historical: Meta Content Framework Using XML, R. V. Guha and Tim Bray
http://www.w3.org/TR/NOTE-MCF-XML/

Dave Beckett's Resource Description Framework (RDF) Resource Guide [major RDF resource guide]
http://www.ilrt.bris.ac.uk/discovery/rdf/resources/

RDF Validation Service (W3C form)
http://www.w3.org/RDF/Validator/

Dublin Core Metadata Initiative (DCMI)
http://dublincore.org/

Dublin Core Element Set
http://dublincore.org/documents/dces/

DAML+OIL (DARPA Agent Markup Language; Ontology Inference Layer)
http://www.daml.org/2001/03/daml+oil-index

Reference Description of the DAML+OIL (March 2001) Ontology Markup Language
http://www.daml.org/2001/03/reference.html

DAML Roadmap
http://www.daml.org/roadmap.html

Rich Site Summary (RSS) format, previously known as the RDF Site Summary
http://www.webreference.com/authoring/languages/xml/rss/

RDF Rich Site Summary [Robin Cover's page]
http://xml.coverpages.org/rss.html

W3C Specifications and Information

RDF Model and Syntax Specification (Recommendation, February 1999; edited by Ora Lassila and Ralph Swick)
http://www.w3.org/TR/REC-rdf-syntax/

Resource Description Framework (RDF) Schema Specification 1.0 (Candidate Recommendation, March 2000; edited by Dan Brickley and R. V. Guha)
http://www.w3.org/TR/rdf-schema/

RDF Primer (Working Draft, March 2002)
http://www.w3.org/TR/rdf-primer/

RDF/XML Syntax Specification (Revised) [Working Draft]
http://www.w3.org/TR/rdf-syntax-grammar/

Resource Description Framework (RDF) Home Page
http://www.w3.org/RDF/

Semantic Web Home Page
http://www.w3.org/2001/sw/

RDF Core Working Group
http://www.w3.org/2001/sw/RDFCore/

Frequently Asked Questions about RDF
http://www.w3.org/RDF/FAQ

RDF Model Theory (Working Draft)
http://www.w3.org/TR/rdf-mt/

RDF Test Cases (Working Draft)
http://www.w3.org/TR/rdf-testcases/

Web-Ontology (WebOnt) Working Group
http://www.w3.org/2001/sw/WebOnt/

PICS Label Distribution Label Syntax and Communication Protocols, Version 1.1 (Recommendation, October 1996)
http://www.w3.org/TR/REC-PICS-labels

PICS-NG Metadata Model and Label Syntax (W3C Note)
http://www.w3.org/TR/NOTE-pics-ng-metadata

W3C Data Formats (W3C Note)
http://www.w3.org/TR/NOTE-rdfarch

Appendices

Appendix A

XML Family of Specifications in a Nutshell

Acronym or Name	*Description of Specification*
c14n	*Canonical XML* is that subset of an XML document that defines its logical structure. Two XML documents whose Canonical-XML form is identical are considered logically equivalent for the purposes of many applications. Converting a document to canonical form often results in some information loss, however. *Note:* This acronym is informal.
CSS	*Cascading Style Sheets* predate XML but can be used with XML for simple styling at the element level. Style sheets can be shared across multiple documents. CSS Levels 1, 2, and 3 have been defined, and CSS has its own Object Model. A related specification is BECSS, the Behavior Extensions to CSS.
DOM	*Document Object Model* is conceptually a tree view of the hierarchy defined by a specific XML document instance. The DOM tree is one of the XML parsing models and is usually discussed in contrast to SAX. Once an XML document has been parsed into its corresponding DOM tree, nodes can be accessed to extract or alter information, or to insert or delete nodes and possibly output a modified XML document. According to the W3C, the DOM provides a "platform- and language-neutral interface that allows programs and scripts to dynamically access and update the content, structure, and style of documents." Levels 1 and 2 have been completely defined, and Level 3 is in progress. Level 1 defines core functionality for HTML and XML documents including navigation and manipulation. Level 2 adds namespace support, traversal, an event model, and stylesheet object model. Level 3, according to the DOM activity page, "will address document loading and saving, as well as content models (such as DTDs and schemas) with document validation support. In addition, it will also address. . . , key events and event groups."
m12n	Modularization of XHTML; see XHTML. *Note:* This is an informal acronym.
MathML	*Mathematical Markup Language* is a textual description of math formulae and symbols in XML syntax. MathML 1.0 and 2.0 have been defined. The W3C browser, Amaya, has native support for MathML. Netscape and Internet Explorer can render MathML with the help of plugins such as Design Science MathPlayer or IBM techexplorer.

Note: An asterisk (*) indicates that information is not from a W3C Specification; otherwise, see *http://www.w3.org/TR*.

Acronym or Name	*Description of Specification*
RDDL *	*Resource Directory Description Language* is a clever solution to the problem of what should a namespace point to: a DTD, an XML Schema, an RDF schema, or simply an HTML page? A resource directory includes a textual description of a particular class of resources, as well as resources related to that class, together with a directory of links to these related resources. This description is both human-readable and machine-processible. RDDL is an extension of XHTML Basic that adds the element `rddl:resource`, which is defined in terms of a simple XLink. See *http://www.rddl.org/*.
RDF	*Resource Description Framework* "is a foundation for processing metadata; it provides interoperability between applications that exchange machine-understandable information on the Web. RDF emphasizes facilities to enable automated processing of Web resources." There are two main RDF specs: RDF Schema Specification 1.0 (Candidate Recommendation, March 2000) and the earlier W3C Recommendation, RDF Model and Syntax Specification from Feb. 1999. Three additional specs were first published in Sept. 2001: RDF Test Cases, RDF Model Theory, and Refactoring RDF/XML Syntax. The RDF Schema Specification defines a *schema specification language* that provides "a basic type system for use in RDF models. It defines resources and properties such as `rdfs:Class` and `rdfs:subClassOf` that are used in specifying application-specific schemas." In contrast, the RDF Model and Syntax Specification defines (in XML) the underlying model for representing RDF metadata as well as a syntax for encoding and transporting the metadata with maximal interoperability. The efforts of the RDF CoreWorking Group are part of the W3C SemanticWeb Activity. For a complete list of RDF specifications, see *http://www.w3.org/RDF/#specs*.
RELAX NG *	*REgular LAnguage description for XML, Next Generation* is the work of an OASIS Technical Committee formed to combine TREX (Tree Regular Expressions for XML) and RELAX, each of which takes a simpler approach to schema creation than W3C's XML Schema. See *http://www.oasis-open.org/committees/relax-ng/*.
RSS *	*Rich Site Summary* (aka: RDF Site Summary) is a lightweight vocabulary designed for sharing headlines and other Web content. Developed by My Netscape to feed Netcenter channels, RSS has become a popular means of sharing content among news-oriented sites, such as the BBC, CNET, CNN, O'Reilly, Wired, ZDNet, and many others. See *http://www.oreillynet.com/rss/*.
SAX *	*Simple API for XML* is a non-W3C, grassroots effort to define an event-based application programming interface to XML that is language and parser independent. The SAX interface is supported by virtually every parser. SAX2 is a refinement and expansion of the original SAX API; it is also supported by most parsers at this time. See *http://sax.sourceforge.net/*.
SMIL	*Synchronized Multimedia Integration Language* is used to describe audio and/or video presentations in simple textual markup. Coordination and synchronization is accomplished by using a single timeline for all of the multimedia elements on a page. There are two major versions available, SMIL 1.0 and SMIL 2.0 (formerly called SMIL Boston).

Acronym or Name	*Description of Specification*
SOAP	*Simple Object Access Protocol* provides a basic mechanism for message delivery and response. In that sense, it is a Web service that is flexible and extensible. SOAP allows businesses to access Web Services directly, by using XML messages to invoke method calls on remote objects, and then receiving an XML response. SOAP has four parts: • envelope describing what is in the message, who the intended target is, and whether it is optional or mandatory • optional data encoding rules useful for failure detection • optional RPC convention: rules for forming the Request and Response • optional binding to HTTP (or another network protocol like SMTP) At this time, SOAP 1.2 is under development. See also XMLP.
SOX *	*Schema for Object-Oriented XML* is an early and mature schema effort by Commerce One to provide data types, subclassing (inheritance), and namespaces, features beyond those provided by DTDs. SOX 1.0 appeared in 1998; SOX 2.0 from 1999 was influential in the development of XML Schema. See *http://www.xcbl.org/sox/sox.html*.
SVG	*Scalable Vector Graphics* permits resolution-independent textual descriptions of graphical objects (including complex polygons and line paths), as well as animation, scripting events, spatial translations, filter effects, etc. SVG is tightly integrated with other XML specifications, such as DOM, CSS, XSLT, XLink, and XHTML. Browser plugins based on Java2D provide SVG support. Vector graphics illustrating tools such as Adobe Illustrator, Jasc WebDraw, CorelDraw, and Mayura Draw provide SVG capability.
VoiceXML	*Voice Extensible Markup Language* is a submission from AT&T, IBM, Lucent, and Motorola. W3C's Voice Browser Working Group (*http://www.w3.org/Voice/*) has specified Dialog Markup Language, using VoiceXML as a model. "VoiceXML is designed for creating audio dialogs that feature synthesized speech, digitized audio, recognition of spoken and DTMF key input, recording of spoken input, telephony, and mixed-initiative conversations. Its major goal is to bring the advantages of Web-based development and content delivery to interactive voice response applications"—*http://www.w3.org/TR/voicexml/*. Related specifications include Dialog Markup Language, Speech Recognition Grammar, Stochastic Language Models, Speech Synthesis Markup Language, Natural Language Semantics Markup Language.
WML *	*Wireless Markup Language* is developed and maintained by the WAP Forum, a wireless industry consortium founded by Nokia, Motorola, Phone.com, and Ericsson. Wireless Application Protocol (WAP) is "an open, global standard that empowers mobile users with wireless devices to easily access and interact with information and services instantly." See *http://xml.coverpages.org/wap-wml.html*.
XDR *	*XML Data-Reduced* was a variation on the Microsoft proposal to add data types to XML. This is one of the approaches, previously used by BizTalk.org, that led to the official XML Schema recommendation by the W3C. XDR is not a W3C specification. (XML Data-Reduced files typically have a .xdr extension.) See *http://www.ltg.ed.ac.uk/~ht/XMLData-Reduced.htm*.

Acronym or Name	*Description of Specification*
XForms	XForms 1.0 is the next generation of Web forms based on XML syntax that decouples data, logic (purpose), and presentation. This separation enables the targeting of forms for devices with very different user interfaces, such as handheld, television, and desktop browsers, plus printers and scanners. XForms consists of the data model (composite datatypes and constraints), the user interface widgets, and XML data transmitted with the form. The datatypes used in XForms are based on XML Schema: Part 2, although in some cases they differ. Form input is expressed as structured XML instance data. Support for advanced form logic, multipage forms, suspend and resume, and easy integration with other XML vocabularies (especially XHTML and SVG) are some of the goals of XForms. *Note:* XForms is not an acronym and should never be used in the singular form (XForm).
XHTML	*Extensible HyperText Markup Language* is a term used for a small family of specifications (all described below) that include a reformulation of HTML 4.01 in XML syntax, plus the dividing of HTML into modules that can be implemented separately on different devices. XHTML is clearly the future of HTML; there will never be a version 5 of HTML.
XHTML 1.0	*Extensible HyperText Markup Language 1.0* is a recasting of HTML 4.01 in XML syntax, based on any of three DTDs that correspond to the three HTML 4.01 DTDs: Strict, Transitional, and Frameset. The spec describes conformance requirements, how XHTML and HTML differ, and how to use XHTML in today's browsers. It is the earliest basis for a family of document types that subset and extend HTML.
XHTML Basic	XHTML Basic is a stripped-down version of XHTML targeted for small devices with limited memory ("thin clients" such as mobile phones, PDAs, pagers, and settop boxes). It defines the minimal set of modules required to be an *XHTML Host Language* document type, and adds support for images, forms, basic tables, and objects. XHTML Basic also provides a common base that can be extended by the addition of other modules. It relies on XHTML module implementations defined in Modularization of XHTML.
Modularization of XHTML	This specification describes a modular approach to XHTML which subsets the language into a large number of nonoverlapping "abstract modules," each of which is semantically unique. The abstractions are implemented by DTDs with plans to migrate to XML Schema. Each implementation module describes groups of elements, attributes, and content models based on functionality. Modularization enables subsetting and extending XHTML for special-purpose devices. Modularizing XHTML helps product designers to specify which elements are supported by a device using standard building blocks. It also helps content providers to deliver content to a large number and wide range of platforms. Modularization paves the way for developers to augment the language with client-specific or document-specific markup.
XHTML 1.1	XHTML 1.1 (aka Module-based XHTML) is essentially a reformulation of XHTML 1.0 Strict using Modularization of XHTML plus a Ruby Module for other character sets. The DTD separates XHTML 1.1 and versions that follow it from the deprecated, legacy functionality of HTML 4.01 (the basis for XHTML 1.0). It is built using the modular framework that supports extension, so the XHTML 1.1 document type will be the basis for future extended XHTML "family" document types.

Acronym or Name	*Description of Specification*
Ruby Annotation	"Ruby" annotations are short runs of text next to or above regular text, typically used in Japanese and Chinese documents to indicate pronunciation or to provide a short annotation. This specification defines a ruby XHTML module which also can be used to mark up acronyms in any language.
Modularization of XHTML in XML Schema	This specification uses XML Schema rather than DTDs to implement the same abstract modules as the earlier Modularization of XML. As with the DTD implementation, this one includes a set of schema modules that conform to the abstract modules in XHTML plus conventions that describe the interplay of individual modules and how they can be modified or extended.
XHTML 2.0	XHTML 2.0 will be a superset of XHTML 1.1 altered semantically and syntactically to conform to the requirements of related XML standards such as XML Linking and XML Schema. Expected to have no a priori knowledge of HTML.
XInclude	XML Inclusions "specifies a processing model and syntax for general-purpose inclusion. Inclusion is accomplished by merging a number of XML Infosets into a single composite Infoset." In contrast to the XLink attribute `show="embed"` type of graphical inclusion, XInclude specifies a media-type specific transformation by means of the `xi:include` element. See XLink.
XLink	*XML Linking Language* is an XML-based syntax for describing link relationships between two or more Web-accessible resources. XLinks may be as simple as the hypertext links defined in HTML and XHTML, or far more powerful one-to-many, many-to-many, and multidirectional links, possibly supported by external linkbases. The resources that are located by an XLink need not be XML documents; they can point to HTML, images, and anything that HTML links can. Using XLink, you can even create complex connections between sets of resources for which you do not have write access (see also XPointer, XPath, and XInclude).
XML	*Extensible Markup Language* is a syntax for describing data in a hierarchy that can be easily parsed and validated. XML syntax is the basis for nearly everything discussed in this book. Note that the XML 1.0 Recommendation also describes how XML DTDs are defined. XML DTDs differ in several ways from SGML DTDs used to describe HTML. XML is a metalanguage used to define and build many useful and powerful languages, sometimes called "XML applications" or "XML vocabularies."
XML Base	XML Base defines `xml:base` attributes, which can be used by any XML language, especially XLink, to resolve relative URIs, much like the `<base>` element from HTML.
XML Events	*XML Events—An Events Syntax for XML* is a work in progress; details may change. XML Events (previously known as "XHTML Events") describes an approach for integrating event listeners and associated event handlers with DOM Level 2 event interfaces to associate behavior with markup. Design goals include syntactically exposing the DOM event model to an XML document and providing for new event types without requiring modification to the DOM or the DTD.

Acronym or Name	*Description of Specification*
XML Infoset (or simply Infoset)	*XML Information Set* specification describes an abstract data set containing the information available from a well-formed XML document; the abstraction omits XML syntactical details. The information set consists of two or more information items (document, element, attribute, character, processing instruction, etc.). See XInclude and Canonical XML.
XML Namespaces (or simply Namespaces)	*Namespaces in XML* define a convention based on URI for uniquely qualifying element and attribute names. Namespaces are necessary to prevent name collisions when an XML document combines elements from multiple grammars (e.g., XSL, SVG, RDF, etc.).
XMLP	*XML Protocol* is the name of the emerging effort to define mechanisms for XML-based message passing for application-to-application communication; actively exploring existing mechanisms such as SOAP, XML-RPC, XMI, Jabber, ebXML, WDDX, BizTalk, ICE, P3P, and BXXP.
XML Schema	*XML Schema*, known informally as *XSD (XML Schema Definition language)*, is a way to describe the content and data model of a particular XML vocabulary with strong data typing, subclassing, and constraints expression, far surpassing anything possible with DTDs. The specification is divided into three parts: XML Schema Part 1: Structures (specifies the language constructs) and XML Schema Part 2: Datatypes (describes facilities for defining datatypes or using built-in datatypes), as well as a detailed tutorial-like introduction, XML Schema Part 0: Primer. There is a related document entitled XML Schema: Formal Description.
XML Signature	*XML-Signature Syntax and Processing* is a joint effort of the IETF and the W3C to specify XML syntax and processing rules for creating and representing digital signatures. "XML Signatures provide integrity, message authentication, and/or signer authentication services for data of any type, whether located within the XML that includes the signature or elsewhere."
XPath	*XML Path Language* is a syntax for defining a path within the DOM hierarchy of a document. It addresses the parts of an XML document, such as specific elements and attributes. XPath is intended to be used by both XSLT and XPointer, providing a syntax common to both. XPath is used primarily to select or locate individual nodes or sets of nodes in the tree, and secondarily to perform string manipulations, numerical calculations, and boolean tests.
XPointer	*XML Pointer Language* is used primarily with XLink, as a fragment identifier for a URI, as a way to reference specific portions of an XML document. XPointers can locate individual XML elements, a set of related elements, a particular point between characters or between children of an element, or a range of XML data between two points. Like XPath on which it builds, XPointer uses non-XML syntax. XPointer can address nodes and node sets as can XPath, but is also extends XPath addressing by adding the ability to reference points and ranges. In contrast to XLink, which can be used with non-XML resources, XPointer can only be used with XML documents because it relies on their highly structured hierarchy.

Acronym or Name	*Description of Specification*
XQuery	*XML Query Language* is really the generic name applied to several approaches to SQL-like or XPath-like searches in an XML document. However, the name of the specific query language being developed by W3C is *XQuery*. XQuery is derived from an XML query language called Quilt. The language is described by a series of specifications: XML Query Requirements, XML Query Use Cases, XQuery 1.0 and XPath 2.0 Data Model, XQuery 1.0 Formal Semantics, XQuery 1.0: An XML Query Language, and XML Syntax for XQuery 1.0 (XQueryX). All of these specifications plus many historical query language proposals can be found at *http://www.w3.org/XML/Query*.
XSL	*Extensible Stylesheet Language* is actually a two-part specification, including XSLFO and XSLT. XSL is sometimes used to refer to either of these two parts, but most likely meaning XSLFO. See also XSLT.
XSLFO	*Extensible Stylesheet Language Formatting Objects* is the major portion of the XSL specification that describes sophisticated layout and presentation mechanisms much like those used in the desktop publishing world. This far surpasses what can be accomplished with HTML tables and CSS.
XSLT	*Extensible Stylesheet Language Transformations* is the part (Section 2) of the XSL specification that defines how to transform XML documents into other XML documents or into HTML or text documents. XSLT defines a mechanism for filtering, sorting, or otherwise transforming an XML source tree into a result tree to which style can be applied for presentation, or without styling, can be useful in data exchange between applications. XSLT uses XPath as an expression language.
XTM *	*XML Topic Maps 1.0* is an ISO specification from TopicMaps.org that may eventually be endorsed by W3C. Topic Maps facilitate quick and accurate retrieval of information. They build on the semantics of RDF and the syntax of XLink, and can be used in a variety of ways, one of which is to foster sophisticated navigation within a given site and across a much wider web of "topic space." Topic Maps are XML documents that define topics and state how individual documents relate to these topics. They act as navigation maps across information sets. The same set of documents can be represented by very different Topic Maps. The XTM 1.0 specification provides a grammar for representing the structure of information resources used to define topics, as well as the associations (relationships) between topics. See *http://www.topicmaps.org/*.

Appendix B

E-Commerce Specifications

Organization or Initiative	*Brief Description from Web Site*
ANSI ASC X12/XML and DISA	Major business standards groups. The goal is "to develop uniform standards for inter-industry electronic interchange of business transactions—electronic data interchange (EDI)." Endorsed ebXML (see next page). See *http://www.x12.org/* and *http://www.disa.org/*.
Apache XML Project	While not an e-commerce effort, no list of XML organizations would be complete without the Apache XML Project which, among many other things, has coordinated the development of widely used tools, including Xerces (XML parser), Xalan (XSLT processor), and Cocoon (a Java- and XML-based Web publishing framework). "The goals of the Apache XML Project are to provide commercial-quality standards-based XML solutions that are developed in an open and cooperative fashion, to provide feedback to standards bodies (such as IETF and W3C) from an implementation perspective, and to be a focus for XML-related activities within Apache projects." See *http://xml.apache.org*.
BizTalk.org	Microsoft BizTalk Framework is aimed at application integration and electronic commerce. "It includes a design framework for implementing an XML schema and a set of XML tags used in messages sent between applications." See *http://www.biztalk.org/*; see also OAGI on the next page.
CommerceNet eCo Framework Project	The eCo Framework's main focus "is to demonstrate the value of the integration of three common component-based electronic commerce services. These services are semantic integration of multiple database types with multiple data constructs and data libraries; trusted open registries; and agent-mediated buying." Common framework for Catalog Information Specification. See *http://www.commerce.net/*.
cXML	Ariba's *Commerce XML* for business-to-business (B2B) transactions: "cXML is designed to provide a simple XML-based protocol between entities engaged in Business-to-Business eCommerce transactions over the Internet. Ease of implementation has been a primary focus along with an emphasis on prototype implementations." See also Web Services Description Language (WSDL) on the Ariba Web site. See *http://www.cxml.org/*.

Organization or Initiative	*Brief Description from Web Site*
ebXML	*Electronic Business XML* is a project of UN/CEFACT (United Nations body for Trade Facilitation and Electronic Business) and OASIS (see XML.org on the next page). Goal is "[t]o provide an open XML-based infrastructure enabling the global use of electronic business information in an interoperable, secure, and consistent manner by all parties. . . . A primary objective of ebXML is to lower the barrier of entry to electronic business in order to facilitate trade, particularly with respect to small- and medium-sized enterprises (SMEs) and developing nations." ebXML focus is "cross-industry message exchange processes, guaranteeing interoperability, and reducing redundancy". See *http://www.ebxml.org/*.
ECML	*Electronic Commerce Modeling Language* provides a set of "guidelines for Web merchants that will enable digital wallets from multiple vendors to automate the exchange of information between users and merchants." (A digital wallet is software that allows consumers to store billing, shipping, and payment information; and to use this information to automatically complete a merchant's check-out page.) Participants include American Express, AOL, Brodia, Compaq, CyberCash, Discover, FSTC, MasterCard, IBM, Microsoft, Novell, SETCo, Sun Microsystems, Trintech, and Visa. See *http://www.ecml.org/*.
IDEAlliance	*International Digital Enterprise Alliance* gives "support to working groups engaged in developing industry-specific applications of both vertical and cross-industry open information standard." Efforts include ICE and PRISM, among others. See *http://idealliance.org/*.
Open Applications Group (OAGI)	The OAGI mission is "to define and encourage the adoption of a unifying standard for eBusiness and Application Software interoperability that reduces customer cost and time to deploy solutions." To that end, they have developed roughly 200 Open Applications Group Integration Specification (OAGIS) DTDs and XML Schema covering areas such as order management to accounts receivable, purchasing to accounts payable, plant data collection/warehouse management, manufacturing to purchasing, manufacturing to order management, invoice matching, sales force automation to order management, supply chain integration, customer service integration, engineering change integration, and maintenance management with maintenance orders, among many others. These DTDs have been donated to BizTalk for use as XML Schema (and XML Data-Reduced). For more information, see *http://www.openapplications.org/*.
RosettaNet	RosettaNet concentrates on eBusiness process modeling and analysis, dictionaries, framework, and Partner Interface Processes (PIPs). XML efforts are in terms of Supply Chain Management. See *http://www.rosettanet.org/*.
UBL	In Sept. 2001 an OASIS Technical Committee was formed to create *Universal Business Language* (UBL). UBL will be a synthesis of existing XML business document libraries, starting with Commerce One's xCBL 3.0 and developing the standard UBL library based on industry experience with other XML business libraries and with similar technologies such as Electronic Data Interchange (EDI). See *http://www.oasis-open.org/committees/ubl/*.

Organization or Initiative	*Brief Description from Web Site*
UCC	*Uniform Code Council* states that "[t]he goal of the [XML] program is to execute XML Strategy that will result in implementation of the XML standards for Business-to-Business (B2B) and Business-to-Consumer (B2C) electronic commerce." See *http://www.uc-council.org/*.
UDDI	*Universal Discovery Description and Integration* initiative, according to the UDDI Executive White Paper (Sept. 2000), "creates a global, platform-independent, open framework to enable businesses to (1) discover each other, (2) define how they interact over the Internet, and (3) share information in a global registry that will more rapidly accelerate the global adoption of B2B eCommerce." Based on XML, DNS, HTTP, and SOAP. See *http://www.uddi.org/* and *http://www.uddicentral.com/*.
WSDL	*Web Services Description Language* is the XML vocabulary that describes services and service providers (enabling them to be located using UDDI). See *http://xml.coverpages.org/wsdl.html*.
xCBL	Commerce One's *XML Common Business Library* promotes "cross-industry exchange of business documents such as product descriptions, purchase orders, invoices, and shipping schedules." Another goal is "to make the business documents, forms, and messages that flow between businesses comprehensible to each business no matter what computer system is used." The insightful CBL effort predates the XML 1.0 Recommendation, dating back to 1997. xCBL uses a mature schema specification (*SOX*) which is a forerunner of the W3C's XML Schema standard. See *http://www.xcbl.org/* for details.
XML.org and its parent organization, OASIS	Diverse membership and participation from many industries and businesses. Maintains an extensive DTD/Schema catalog, and repository. "The XML Catalog lists organizations known to be producing industry-specific or cross-industry XML Specifications. The XML Catalog is intended to evolve into the XML.ORG Registry & Repository for XML Schemas, DTDs and specifications." Catalog categories include accounting, advertising, astronomy and space, automotive, banking, communication, computer graphics, content syndication, customer relationship management, directory services, distributed management, economics, education, electronic commerce, electronic data interchange, enterprise resource planning (ERP), financial and capital, forms, healthcare, human resources, industrial automation, intellectual property rights, insurance, legal, music, news, publishing, real estate, retail, science (chemistry, biology, etc.), software, supply chain management (SCM), travel, user interface, voice, Web applications, workflow, among many others. Sponsored creation of comprehensive XML and XSL conformance suites. Took over the xml-dev developer's mailing list in early 2000. Parent organization, Organization for the Advancement of Structured Information Standards (OASIS), has been a key player in the SGML community. "OASIS is a member consortium dedicated to the advancement of structured information standards, such as SGML, XML and CGM." See *http://www.xml.org/* and *http://www.oasis-open.org/*.
XML/EDI Group	Activists since 1997 with large mailing list of interested parties; promotes repository concept; introduced XLink-related BizCodes. See *http://www.geocities.com/WallStreet/Floor/5815/* and *http://www.bizcodes.org/*.

Appendix C

HTML 4.01 Character Entities

This appendix is primarily intended for developers writing DTDs or XML Schema who are in need of special characters. A secondary purpose is to provide another example of processing legacy content, in this case HTML from a W3C specification, and using XSLT (plus some UNIX utilities) to create HTML tables that display each character and its value. The files mentioned are available on the CD-ROM in the `Appendix` folder of the code examples folder.

Figure C-1 shows the three sets of entities defined in HTML 4.01. The output was created using Cygwin UNIX tools for Windows and an XSLT stylesheet. The steps involved were:

- Start with the W3C HTML source document, "Character entity references in HTML 4," taken from *http://www.w3.org/TR/html401/sgml/entities.html*.
- Use UNIX utilities such as `grep`, `cut`, and `paste`, plus a little `vi` magic to create the file `entities.xml` shown in Listing C-1 from the W3C source.
- Run the stylesheet `entities.xsl` (Listing C-2) with `entities.xml` as the source to generate `entities.html` as the output.
- Display the results in Netscape 6, which (like IE 5.5) displays most, but not all, of the symbols.

Listing C-1 Special Characters entities.xml Based on HTML 4.01 Recommendation

```
<?xml version="1.0"?>
<HTML-Entities>
   <HTMLlat1>
      <Ent><Name>nbsp</Name> <Amp>&amp;#160;</Amp> <Value> </Value></Ent>
      <Ent><Name>iexcl</Name> <Amp>&amp;#161;</Amp> <Value>&#161;</Value></Ent>
      <Ent><Name>cent</Name> <Amp>&amp;#162;</Amp> <Value>&#162;</Value></Ent>
<!-- many lines deleted -->
  </HTMLlat1>

   <HTMLsymbol>
      <Ent><Name>fnof</Name> <Amp>&amp;#402;</Amp> <Value>&#402;</Value></Ent>
     <Ent><Name>Alpha</Name> <Amp>&amp;#913;</Amp> <Value>&#913;</Value></Ent>
<!-- many lines deleted -->
   </HTMLsymbol>
```

```
    <HTMLspecial>
        <Ent><Name>quot</Name> <Amp>&amp;#34;</Amp> <Value>&#34;</Value></Ent>
        <Ent><Name>amp</Name> <Amp>&amp;#38;</Amp> <Value>&#38;</Value></Ent>
<!-- many lines deleted -->
        <Ent><Name>euro</Name> <Amp>&amp;#8364;</Amp> <Value>&#8364;</
Value></Ent>
  </HTMLspecial>
</HTML-Entities>
```

Listing C-2 Stylesheet for Displaying Special Characters (entities.xsl)

```
<?xml version="1.0"?>
<xsl:stylesheet   version="1.0"
  xmlns:xsl="http://www.w3.org/1999/XSL/Transform">
<xsl:output method="html" indent="yes" />

<xsl:variable name="label">HTML 4.01 Entities</xsl:variable>

<xsl:template match="/">
   <html>
     <head>
       <title><xsl:value-of select="$label" /></title>
     </head>
     <body>
       <h3><xsl:value-of select="$label" /></h3>
       <table cellpadding="5" border="1" align="left" >
       <xsl:apply-templates select="/HTML-Entities"/>
       </table>
     </body>
   </html>
</xsl:template>

<xsl:template match="HTMLlat1 | HTMLsymbol | HTMLspecial">
   <xsl:choose>
     <xsl:when test="name() = 'HTMLlat1'">
       <tr><th colspan="3">HTMLlat1</th></tr>
     </xsl:when>
     <xsl:when test="name() = 'HTMLsymbol'">
       <tr><th colspan="3">HTMLsymbol</th></tr>
     </xsl:when>
     <xsl:when test="name() = 'HTMLspecial'">
       <tr><th colspan="3">HTMLspecial</th></tr>
     </xsl:when>
   </xsl:choose>

   <xsl:for-each select="Ent">
     <tr>
       <td><xsl:value-of select="Name" /></td>
       <td align="center"><xsl:value-of select="Value" /></td>
       <td><xsl:value-of select="Amp" /></td>
     </tr>
   </xsl:for-each>
</xsl:template>

</xsl:stylesheet>
```

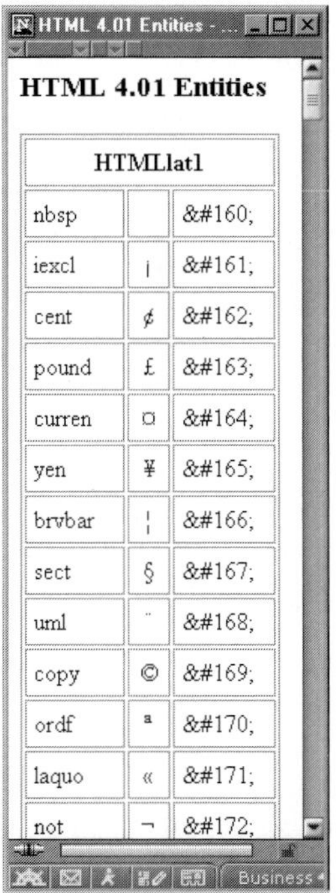

HTML 4.01 Entities

HTMLlat1		
nbsp		
iexcl	¡	¡
cent	¢	¢
pound	£	£
curren	¤	¤
yen	¥	¥
brvbar	¦	¦
sect	§	§
uml	¨	¨
copy	©	©
ordf	ª	ª
laquo	«	«
not	¬	¬

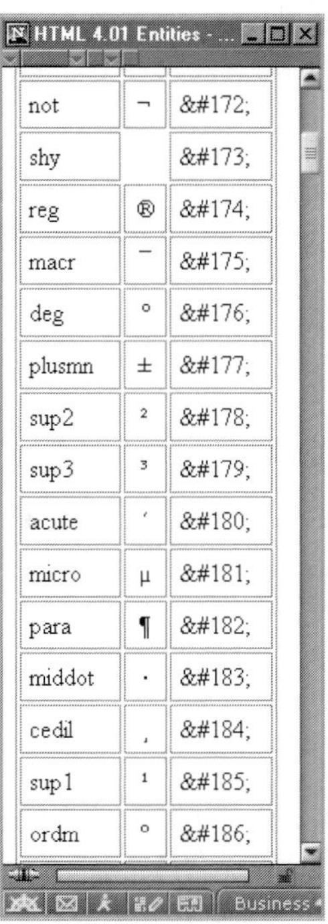

not	¬	¬
shy		
reg	®	®
macr	¯	¯
deg	°	°
plusmn	±	±
sup2	²	²
sup3	³	³
acute	´	´
micro	µ	µ
para	¶	¶
middot	·	·
cedil	¸	¸
sup1	¹	¹
ordm	º	º

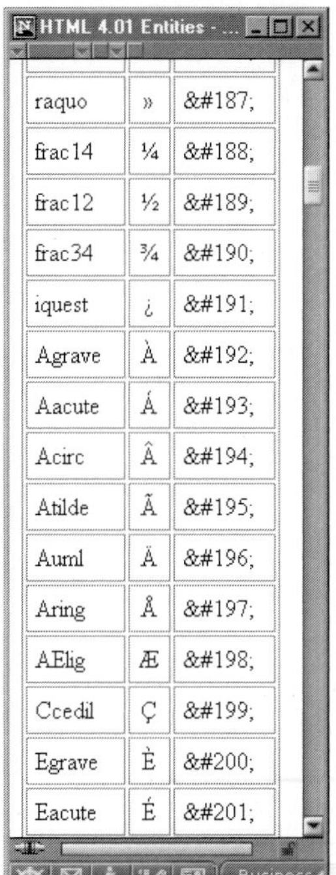

raquo	»	»
frac14	¼	¼
frac12	½	½
frac34	¾	¾
iquest	¿	¿
Agrave	À	À
Aacute	Á	Á
Acirc	Â	Â
Atilde	Ã	Ã
Auml	Ä	Ä
Aring	Å	Å
AElig	Æ	Æ
Ccedil	Ç	Ç
Egrave	È	È
Eacute	É	É

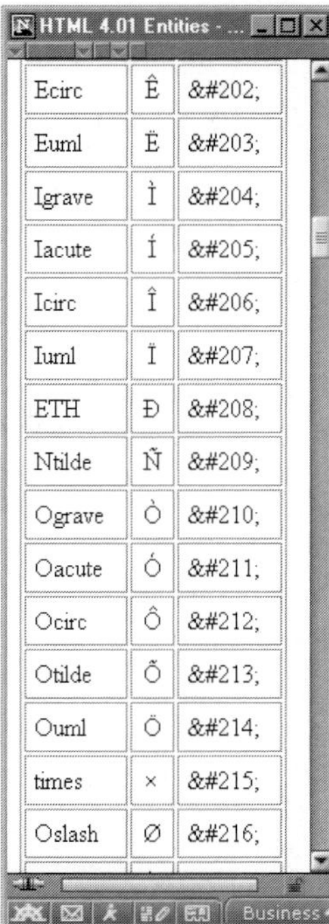

Ecirc	Ê	Ê
Euml	Ë	Ë
Igrave	Ì	Ì
Iacute	Í	Í
Icirc	Î	Î
Iuml	Ï	Ï
ETH	Ð	Ð
Ntilde	Ñ	Ñ
Ograve	Ò	Ò
Oacute	Ó	Ó
Ocirc	Ô	Ô
Otilde	Õ	Õ
Ouml	Ö	Ö
times	×	×
Oslash	Ø	Ø

FIGURE C-1 HTML 4.01 Character Entities

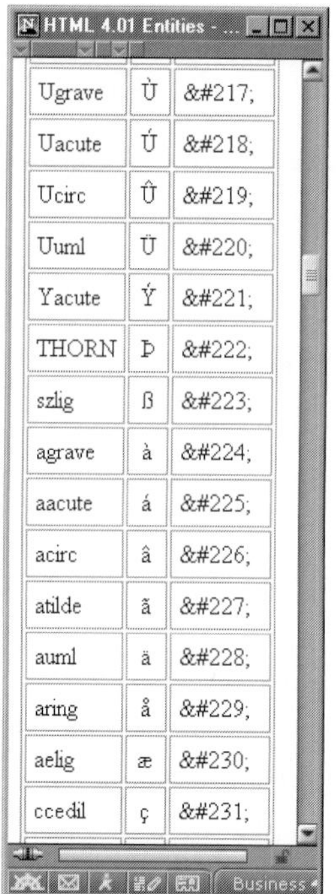

Ugrave	Ù	Ù
Uacute	Ú	Ú
Ucirc	Û	Û
Uuml	Ü	Ü
Yacute	Ý	Ý
THORN	Þ	Þ
szlig	ß	ß
agrave	à	à
aacute	á	á
acirc	â	â
atilde	ã	ã
auml	ä	ä
aring	å	å
aelig	æ	æ
ccedil	ç	ç

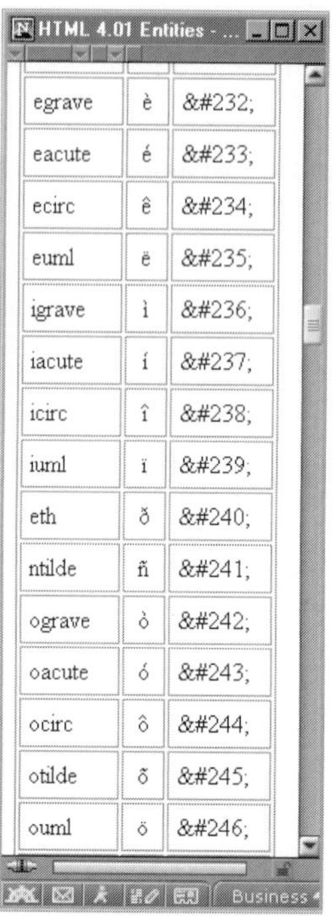

egrave	è	è
eacute	é	é
ecirc	ê	ê
euml	ë	ë
igrave	ì	ì
iacute	í	í
icirc	î	î
iuml	ï	ï
eth	ð	ð
ntilde	ñ	ñ
ograve	ò	ò
oacute	ó	ó
ocirc	ô	ô
otilde	õ	õ
ouml	ö	ö

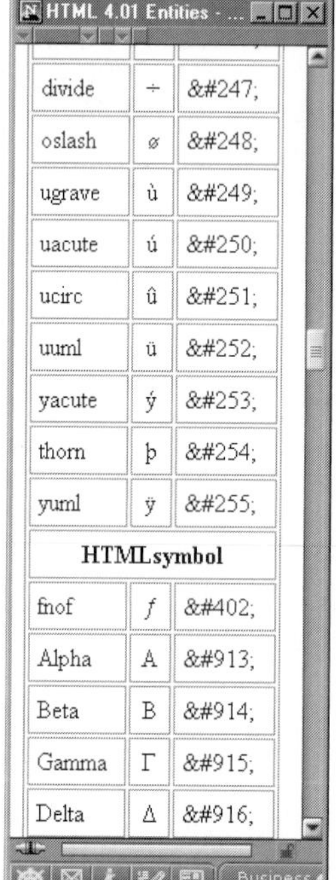

divide	÷	÷
oslash	ø	ø
ugrave	ù	ù
uacute	ú	ú
ucirc	û	û
uuml	ü	ü
yacute	ý	ý
thorn	þ	þ
yuml	ÿ	ÿ
HTMLsymbol		
fnof	ƒ	ƒ
Alpha	Α	Α
Beta	Β	Β
Gamma	Γ	Γ
Delta	Δ	Δ

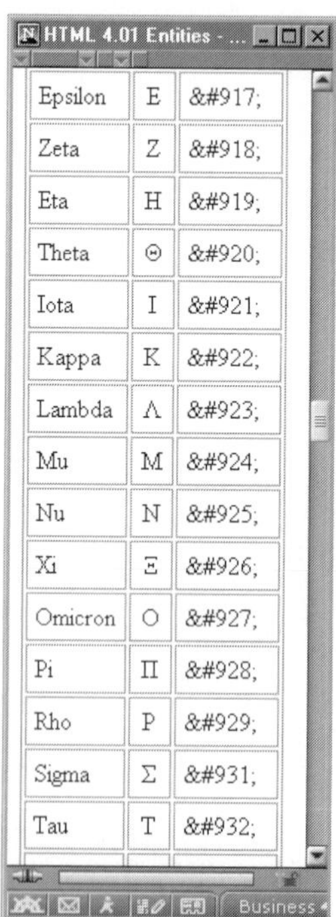

Epsilon	Ε	Ε
Zeta	Ζ	Ζ
Eta	Η	Η
Theta	Θ	Θ
Iota	Ι	Ι
Kappa	Κ	Κ
Lambda	Λ	Λ
Mu	Μ	Μ
Nu	Ν	Ν
Xi	Ξ	Ξ
Omicron	Ο	Ο
Pi	Π	Π
Rho	Ρ	Ρ
Sigma	Σ	Σ
Tau	Τ	Τ

FIGURE C-1 HTML 4.01 Character Entities (*continued*)

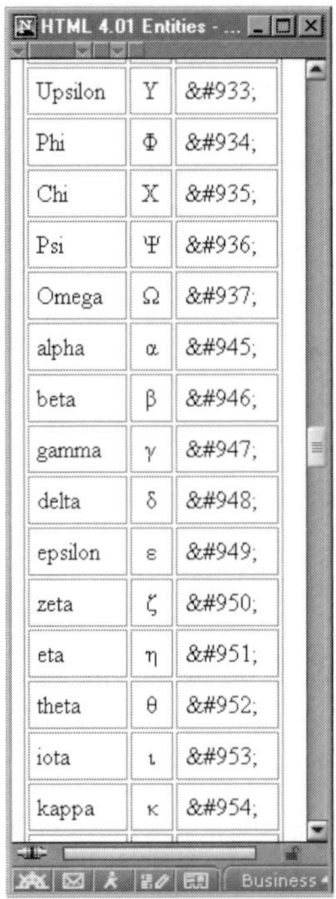

Upsilon	Υ	Υ
Phi	Φ	Φ
Chi	Χ	Χ
Psi	Ψ	Ψ
Omega	Ω	Ω
alpha	α	α
beta	β	β
gamma	γ	γ
delta	δ	δ
epsilon	ε	ε
zeta	ζ	ζ
eta	η	η
theta	θ	θ
iota	ι	ι
kappa	κ	κ

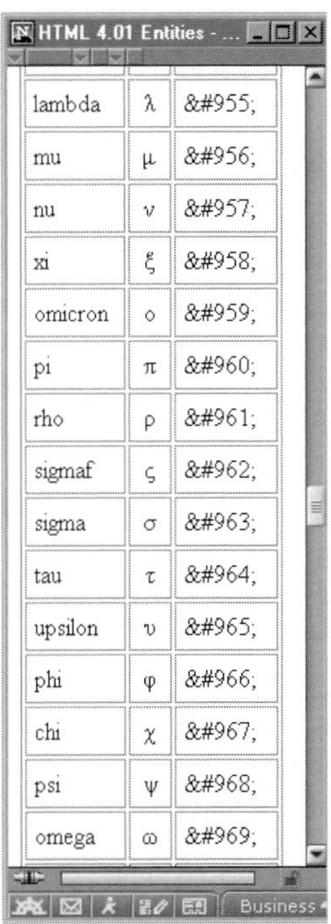

lambda	λ	λ
mu	μ	μ
nu	ν	ν
xi	ξ	ξ
omicron	ο	ο
pi	π	π
rho	ρ	ρ
sigmaf	ς	ς
sigma	σ	σ
tau	τ	τ
upsilon	υ	υ
phi	φ	φ
chi	χ	χ
psi	ψ	ψ
omega	ω	ω

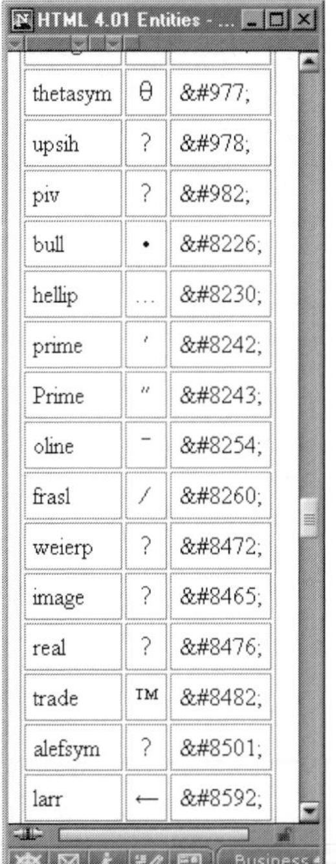

thetasym	Θ	ϑ
upsih	?	ϒ
piv	?	ϖ
bull	•	•
hellip	…	…
prime	′	′
Prime	″	″
oline	‾	‾
frasl	⁄	⁄
weierp	?	℘
image	?	ℑ
real	?	ℜ
trade	™	™
alefsym	?	ℵ
larr	←	←

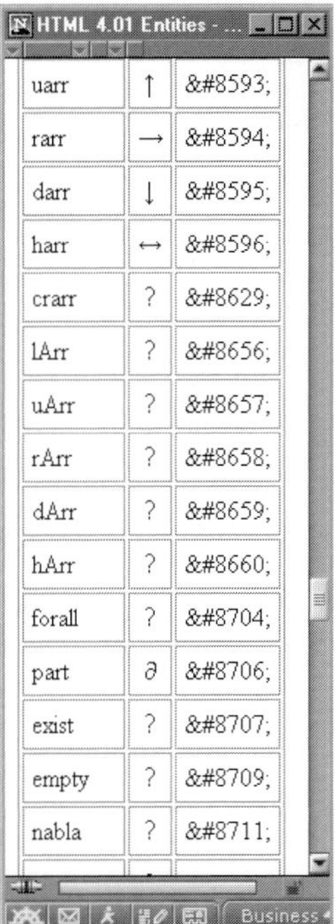

uarr	↑	↑
rarr	→	→
darr	↓	↓
harr	↔	↔
crarr	?	↵
lArr	?	⇐
uArr	?	⇑
rArr	?	⇒
dArr	?	⇓
hArr	?	⇔
forall	?	∀
part	∂	∂
exist	?	∃
empty	?	∅
nabla	?	∇

FIGURE C-1 *(continued)*

isin	?	∈
notin	?	∉
ni	?	∋
prod	∏	∏
sum	∑	∑
minus	−	−
lowast	?	∗
radic	√	√
prop	?	∝
infin	∞	∞
ang	?	∠
and	∘	∧
or	?	∨
cap	∩	∩
cup	?	∪

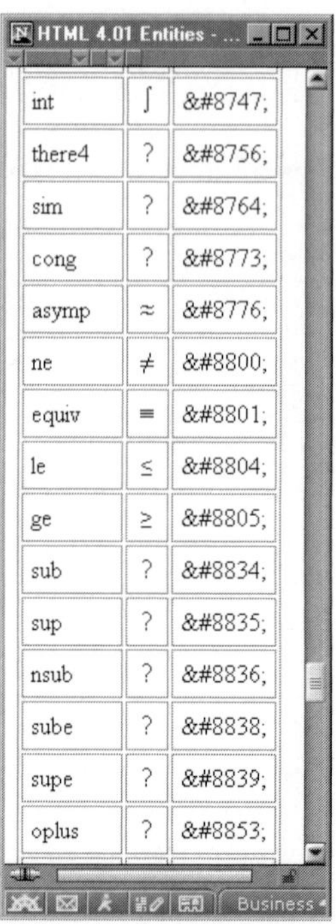

int	∫	∫
there4	?	∴
sim	?	∼
cong	?	≅
asymp	≈	≈
ne	≠	≠
equiv	≡	≡
le	≤	≤
ge	≥	≥
sub	?	⊂
sup	?	⊃
nsub	?	⊄
sube	?	⊆
supe	?	⊇
oplus	?	⊕

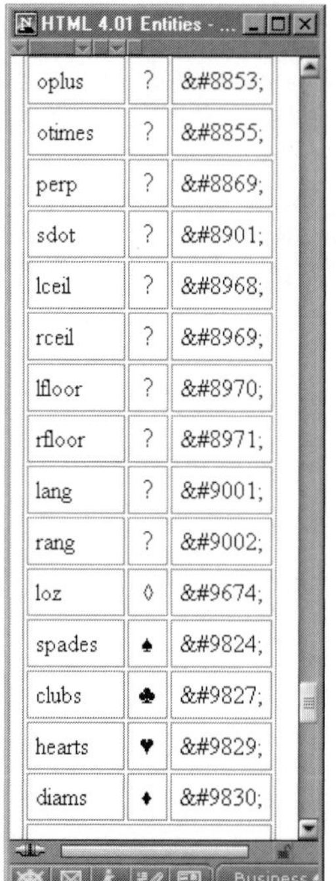

oplus	?	⊕
otimes	?	⊗
perp	?	⊥
sdot	?	⋅
lceil	?	⌈
rceil	?	⌉
lfloor	?	⌊
rfloor	?	⌋
lang	?	〈
rang	?	〉
loz	◊	◊
spades	♠	♠
clubs	♣	♣
hearts	♥	♥
diams	♦	♦

HTMLspecial		
quot	"	"
amp	&	&
lt	<	<
gt	>	>
OElig	Œ	Œ
oelig	œ	œ
Scaron	Š	Š
scaron	š	š
Yuml	Ÿ	Ÿ
circ	ˆ	ˆ
tilde	˜	˜
ensp	?	
emsp		
thinsp	?	

FIGURE C-1 HTML 4.01 Character Entities (*continued*)

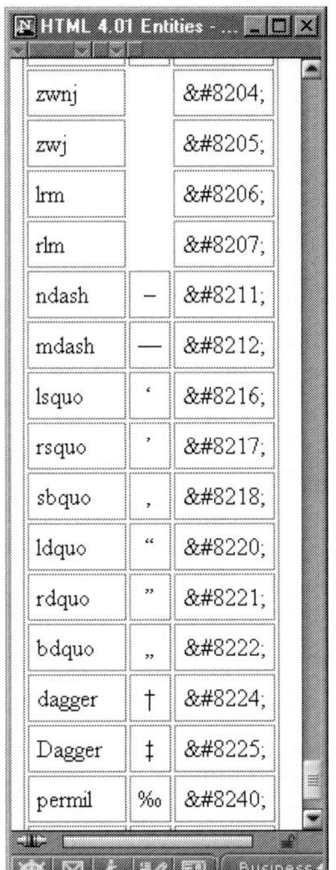

zwnj		‌
zwj		‍
lrm		‎
rlm		‏
ndash	–	–
mdash	—	—
lsquo	‘	‘
rsquo	’	’
sbquo	‚	‚
ldquo	“	“
rdquo	”	”
bdquo	„	„
dagger	†	†
Dagger	‡	‡
permil	‰	‰

lsaquo	‹	‹
rsaquo	›	›
euro	€	€

Appendix D

Setting Up Your XML Environment

Overview of Setup

This appendix explains how to install XML software, utilities, and batch files from the CD-ROM that comes with this book. By making a few changes to one file, `xmlsetup.bat`, you can customize the location of most software to fit your needs. The overall goal is to be able to type `xmlsetup` from a new DOS Window prompt to automatically establish a path that looks *something* like this (Win98 shown):

```
C:\WINDOWS;C:\WINDOWS\COMMAND;C:\JAVA\JDK1.3.1\BIN;
C:\XML\BIN;C:\XML\BATCH;C:\XML\XSV
```

After establishing `%XML_ROOT%` and a few other locations, you'll be placing all *.bat* files in `%XML_ROOT%\batch`, as well as all small utilities such as `xmlvalid` in `%XML_ROOT%\bin`. Freeware software from Apache will be installed under `%APACHE_ROOT%`. Evaluation copies of commercial software can be installed anywhere; they do not need to be installed under `%XML_ROOT%`, although they can be.

Experienced Windows developers familiar with modifying system files to set path and other variables should still read these instructions and adapt them to their own needs. This is also true of JAR file location to an extent, but be careful with Apache JARs of the same name.

Setting up your XML environment, including software installation, involves the following steps:

1. Before you start
2. Create `XML_ROOT` hierarchy
3. Download code examples
4. Download batch files
5. Change Read Only attribute
6. Edit `xmlsetup` and install

7. Install free software
8. Reboot
9. Verify your setup
10. Install commercial software

These steps are described in detail on the CD-ROM file **XML-Environment\index.html**, or by browsing to the top level `index.html` file on the CD, and then clicking on the link entitled "Setting Up Your XML Environment."

Appendix E

What's on the CD-ROM

The CD-ROM that comes with this book includes a dozen of the most popular XML tools, nearly all of the mature XML-related W3C specifications in PDF format, the book's code examples, all of the links from the "For Further Exploration" sections, and much more.

Software

The CD contains both commercial software and freeware, with evaluation copies provided for the former. The files have been prepared for use on all platforms. However, much of the software is only useful when working on the Windows platform, and some software requires Java (see "Setting Up Your XML Environment" on the CD for details).

- XML Spy 4.3 by Altova (evaluation copy; Windows)
- TurboXML 2.3 by TIBCO Extensibility (evaluation copy; Windows and Linux x86 2.2 platforms)
- XMLTransform 1.1.0 by TIBCO Extensibility (evaluation copy; Windows and Linux x86 2.2 platforms)
- XEP Rendering Engine 2.72 by RenderX (evaluation copy; Microsoft JVM and Sun JVM versions)
- Xerces Java 1.4.3 and 1.4.4 from the Apache XML Project
- Xerces2 Java 2.0.1 from the Apache XML Project
- FOP (Formatting Objects Processor) 0.20.3 from the Apache XML Project
- Batik SVG Toolkit 1.1.1 from the Apache XML Project
- Xalan-Java 2.3.1 from the Apache XML Project
- Saxon and Instant Saxon 6.5, 6.5.1, 6.5.2, and 7.0 from SourceForge
- HTML Tidy (April 2002 and April 2000 versions) from SourceForge
- XSV (XML Schema Validator) version XSV14 from the W3C and LTG
- XML Validator and Canonical XML Processor by ElCel Technology (HTML pages)

W3C Specifications in PDF Format

All of the W3C specifications (other than early Working Drafts) that relate to this book's topics are included on the CD in PDF format for convenient offline reading. Links to the current versions of each spec are included although nearly all of these documents are mature W3C Recommendations (designated as "REC" in the list here and on the poster at the back of this book); date of publication is shown in CCYYMMDD format.

- XML 1.0 [Second Edition]—REC: 20001006
- XML 1.0 [First Edition]—REC: 19980210
- Namespaces in XML—REC: 19990114
- XML Information Set—REC: 20011024
- Canonical XML Version 1.0—REC: 20010315
- XML Schema Part 0: Primer—REC: 20010502
- XML Schema Part 1: Structures—REC: 20010502
- XML Schema Part 2: Datatypes—REC: 20010502
- Document Object Model Level 2 Core—REC: 20001113
- Document Object Model Level 2 Views—REC: 20001113
- Document Object Model Level 2 Events—REC: 20001113
- Document Object Model Level 2 Style: REC—20001113
- Document Object Model Level 2 Traversal and Range: REC—20001113
- Document Object Model Level 2 HTML—WD: 20011210
- Cascading Style Sheets, level 2 (CSS2) Specification—REC: 20010502
- XSL Transformations (XSLT), Version 1.0—REC: 19991116
- XML Path Language (XPath), Version 1.0—REC: 19991116
- Extensible Stylesheet Language (XSL), Version 1.0—REC: 20011015
- XML Linking Language (XLink) Version 1.0—REC: 20010627
- XML Inclusions (XInclude) Version 1.0—CR: 20020221
- XML Base—REC: 20010627
- XML Pointer Language (XPointer) Version 1.0—CR: 20010911
- HTML 4.01 Specification—REC: 19991224
- XHTML 1.0: The Extensible HyperText Markup Language: A Reformulation of HTML 4 in XML 1.0—REC: 20000126
- XHTML Basic—REC: 20001219
- Modularization of XHTML—REC: 20010410
- XHTML 1.1–Module-based XHTML—REC: 20010531
- Modularization of XHTML in XML Schema—WD: 20010322

- XML Events—WD: 20011016
- Resource Description Framework (RDF) Model and Syntax Specification—REC: 19990222
- Resource Description Framework (RDF) Schema Specification 1.0—CR: 20000327
- Scalable Vector Graphics (SVG) 1.0 Specification—REC: 20010904

Additional Features

In addition to software and PDF versions of the W3C specifications, this book's CD-ROM contains a wealth of other useful information.

- *Code Examples*—More than 100 examples of XML, DTDs, Namespaces, XML Schema, CSS2, XSLT, DOM2, SAX2, XLink, XPointer, XHTML, and more.
- *Setting Up Your XML Environment*—This document explains how to install XML tools and batch files from the CD-ROM. By making a few changes to one file, `xmlsetup.bat`, you can customize the location of software to fit your needs.
- *For Further Exploration*—Nearly 900 links have been organized by chapter titles. You'll find hundreds of links to XML specifications, books, tutorials, articles, software, resources, reference guides, and more.
- *XML Glossary*—Provided by TIBCO Extensibility; copyright © 1997–2002, TIBCO Software Inc. Used with permission.
- *Practical Formatting Using XSLFO*—G. Ken Holman's contributed chapter in HTML format with links to further details.
- *Big Picture of XML Family of Specifications*—This is an imagemap version of the Big Picture diagram that appears on the inside front cover of the book. The imagemap on the CD-ROM connects you to each specification, or to a collection of information about each of the 70 topics in the diagram. A handy XML acronym list with more than 50 terms is also included.

Index